SOURCEBOOK
ON
PUBLIC LAW

Cavendish
Publishing
Limited

SOURCEBOOK
ON
PUBLIC LAW

Helen Fenwick, BA, LLB
Lecturer in Law
University of Durham
Gavin Phillipson, BA, LLM (Cantab), Solicitor
Lecturer in Law
University of Sussex

Cavendish
Publishing
Limited

First published in Great Britain 1997 by Cavendish Publishing Limited, The Glass House, Wharton Street, London WC1X 9PX
Telephone: 0171-278 8000   Facsimile: 0171-278 8080

Fenwick, Helen
Sourcebook on Public Law
1 Public Law – England
I Titles II Phillipson, Gavin
344.102

ISBN 1 85941 182 7

Printed and bound in Great Britain

For Paul and for Beatriz

PREFACE

This book is intended to make a distinctive contribution to the materials and commentary available to those interested in the field of public law. It is widely recognised that any worthwhile study of this area of law requires perusal of a wide selection of materials lying beyond law's domain; this is partly because large areas of the British constitution are regulated, or at least influenced by conventions, practices, shared understandings, but, furthermore, because of the prevalence of non-legal rules in the constitution, it is clearly necessary to seek the views of those with first hand knowledge or specialist expertise in the contentious areas: civil servants, MPs, government ministers, Ombudsmen, experts in public administration as well as judges, barristers, and academics. In selecting sources, we have tried to choose those which present the clearest insights into the issue concerned, rather than invariably choosing primary sources, regardless of how helpful they are. Because of the wide spread of views and expertise which the book presents, it is hoped that it will find a readership beyond students of the law; anyone concerned with our system of government, public administration, constitutionalism, or the state of liberty in this country will, we hope, find something of interest to them here. At the same time, the book covers all the areas students of public law are required to consider: it is therefore suitable for those studying undergraduate courses in constitutional and administrative law, whilst containing material which would also facilitate study or enquiry at other levels.

Books of this type vary considerably in the amount of authorial input they contain. Some are literally just a collection of various materials, with no commentary by the authors. Others contain almost equal amounts of authorial and source material. We have attempted to steer a middle course between these two extremes. In particular, the topics covered are presented in a strongly structured way, with authorial introductions to the different sections, and a clear ordering of the different issues raised. Additionally, fairly extensive commentary is provided, which not only explains basic issues where this is appropriate, but also provides additional insights and information, and, in places, takes a clear stance in an ongoing debate. Questions designed to provoke a critical and sceptical approach to the existing conventional and legal order are also included. To assist in encouraging such an approach, a variety of critical views are presented. Whilst the predominant ideological thrust of the authorial material is firmly within the tradition which Martin Loughlin has labelled 'liberal normativism', a conscious attempt has been made to give some space to the views of Marxist, realist, and functionalist critics of the more familiar liberal and conservative paradigms.

It is generally acknowledged that public law has a particularly dynamic and fluid nature. This is especially apparent at the present time. One might cite, for example, the recent publication of the Scott and Nolan Reports, moves towards greater openness in government, continuing rapid progression in both the application and principles of judicial review, challenges to key liberties long thought sacrosanct, significant reforms of Parliament promised by the Opposition; most radically of all, suggestions have been made by members of the judiciary (as yet uttered extra-judicially only) that the most basic principle of the British constitution, the sovereignty of Parliament, may itself be ripe for revision on grounds quite separate from the modifications the doctrine has required to take account of Britain's membership of the EU. It is hoped that the book reflects this dynamism: a conscious attempt has been made to use recent or contemporary examples wherever possible, and to use constitutional history only where this is essential for an understanding of the area in question.

Part I examines basic concepts and principles of constitutional theory, and explores the expression or negation of such ideas within the British constitution. It follows a fairly conventional path in terms of classification whilst, it is hoped, including some perspectives not usually encountered in this context. The idea of the Rule of Law is given particular prominence; challenges to traditional notions of parliamentary sovereignty are also explored fairly fully. A separate chapter is devoted to the impact of the European legal order on Parliamentary sovereignty.

Part II traces the rapid growth in the power of the supranational European institutions and legal instruments, including the European Convention on Human Rights. Chapter 1 examines the institutions and legal order of the European Community and Union looking in particular at how the already considerable impact of the European legal order on the British constitution will take new directions with the creation of the European Union which extends the areas of intergovernmental cooperation. Chapter 2 presents a clear exposition of the principles governing implementation of European law in Member States including detailed analysis of the *Francovich* principle. Chapter 3 is devoted to consideration of The European Convention on Human Rights. The chapter considers in particular whether the already considerable influence of the Convention on the law of the contracting states may be consolidated and augmented due to its increasingly close relationship with the European Union.

Part III examines the changing role of Parliament, attempting to site an analysis of Parliament's daily work within a framework which takes account of Parliament's inherent limitations and assigns it realistic roles. The long first chapter on the House of Commons is divided into two main parts. The first considers its legislative role in some detail, using examples of important recent debates on the Scott Report and the Prevention of Terrorism Act 1996. The second part examines the Commons' efforts to scrutinise the Executive, with particular reference to the work of the Select Committees. The House of Lords is dealt with in a separate chapter; detailed consideration is given to proposals for reform. Chapter 3 deals with the issues raised by Parliamentary privileges and standards, which have been almost continually in the public eye during the writing of this book. Two key areas are given particular prominence. Firstly, we examine freedom of speech: the case law in this area and the impact of the Defamation Act 1996 are subjected to particularly critical scrutiny. Secondly, the chapter explores the now highly politicised issue of standards in public life. The Nolan Reports and parliamentary reaction to them are covered in some detail, with extended extracts from the Reports and the relevant debates.

Part IV, on the Executive, commences with a chapter on prerogative powers, in which particular emphasis is placed on judicial control of the prerogative. Chapter 2 examines first the system of cabinet government, aiming not at a detailed factual description, but rather at a normative analysis which evaluates the practice of central government and the convention of collective responsibility in the light of the principles of limited government. After a short analysis of the centralisation of governmental power within the UK which the last 17 years have witnessed, the second part of the chapter looks at the main mechanism for ensuring the accountability of central government: ministerial responsibility. We regard this as one of the key areas of principle in the British constitutional order. A comprehensive analysis of the 'new' doctrine of ministerial responsibility put forward by Sir Robin Butler and apparently accepted by the government is attempted; particular emphasis is placed upon the challenges to old and new theories of responsibility posed by the introduction of the 'Next Steps' Agencies. The extent of the duty not to mislead Parliament is subjected to sustained analysis; here we draw heavily on the findings of the Scott Report and consider the significance of the recent reformulation of the obligation not to mislead Parliament as set out in *Questions of Procedure for Ministers*.

The third chapter in Part IV examines access to government information. In contrast to nearly all modern democracies, the UK has no freedom of information legislation, whilst the government has extensive powers to punish those who make unauthorised disclosures of information. The Major government has, however, recently introduced a voluntary Code allowing the release of a limited amount of information. Chapter 4 considers the changing and yet unchanged face of official secrecy in the UK, placing particular emphasis on recent developments in the doctrine of public interest immunity, including the impact of the Scott Report; the operation of the new Code is also given detailed consideration.

Part V provides an introduction to key areas of administrative law. In Chapter 1, the procedural issues relating to judicial review are subjected to detailed analysis with particular reference to the controversial doctrine of procedural exclusivity. Chapter 2 examines the principles of judicial review. The chapter seeks to explain the basic issues clearly and focus on areas of particular controversy and rapid change, including the duty to give reasons and the doctrine of legitimate expectation. A section is devoted to discussion of the development of judicial review with particular reference to theories of review which stress its potential to afford greater protection for individual rights. Chapter 3 examines the work and evaluates the effectiveness of the parliamentary and local Ombudsmen.

Whilst Britain has always had a respectable human rights record, protection for civil liberties is becoming increasingly uncertain, incoherent and precarious. The last 15 years have seen a creeping erosion of fundamental individual freedoms due to the burgeoning power of the state, and further erosion is threatened. The purpose of Part VI is to examine key aspects of the protection of civil liberties in Britain in the light of Britain's obligations under the European Convention on Human Rights. Protection for liberty under the unwritten constitution and the Bill of Rights debate, police powers, public order and freedom of expression are dealt with in four separate chapters. The topics chosen within these areas and the emphasis placed on them highlight those issues which are of particular significance at the present time, including increases in police powers, erosion of safeguards for suspects and limitation of the freedom to protest. It will be argued that the position of the UK – as almost the only democracy without a Bill of Rights – is coming to seem untenable, and that this is reflected in current judicial activism and in the growing influence of the European Convention on Human Rights.

We would like to thank our partners and family for their support and encouragement during the writing of this book. Kate Nicol of Cavendish has been invariably enthusiastic and shown patience and flexibility during the book's long evolution. We would also like to thank all owners of copyright material who have given their permission to include such material in this book. A word of explanation as to our treatment of footnotes in source material is perhaps in order. Our policy has been to retain those footnotes which gave references (they have been moved into the text and appear in square brackets) whilst deleting the remainder.

The law is stated as at 1 July 1996 but it has been possible to include some later material.

Helen Fenwick
Gavin Phillipson
November 1996

ACKNOWLEDGMENTS

Grateful acknowledgment is made for the following:

Brazier, Rodney (editor) *Constitutional Texts* (1990) reproduced by permission of Oxford University Press

Calvert, H, *Introduction to British Constitutional Law* (Blackstone Press, 1985)

Lord Carrington, *Reflect on Things Past* (Collins, 1985)

Crick, B, *The Reform of Parliament* (2nd edn, Weidenfeld & Nicolson, 1964)

Dworkin, R, *A Bill of Rights for Britain* (Random House UK Ltd, 1990)

Erskine May, *Parliamentary Practice* (20th edn, Butterworths, 1983)

Harlow, C (editor) *Public Law and Politics* (Sweet & Maxwell, 1986)

Griffith, JAG & Ryle, M, *Parliament: Functions, Practice and Procedures* (Sweet & Maxwell, 1989)

Jowell, Jeffrey & Oliver, Dawn (editors), *The Changing Constitution* (3rd edn, 1994) reproduced by permission of Oxford University Press

Marshall, Geoffrey, *Constitutional Conventions* (1984) reproduced by permission of Oxford University Press

Marshall & Moodie, *Some Problems of the Constitution* (5th edn, 1971, Stanley Thornes Publishers Limited)

McAuslan & McEldowney (editors), *Law Legitimacy and the Constitution* (Sweet & Maxwell, 1995)

McEldowney, John F, *Public Law* (Sweet & Maxwell, 1994)

Munro, Colin, *Studies in Constitutional Law* (Butterworths, 1987)

Rawls, John, *A Theory of Justice* (1972) reproduced by permission of Oxford University Press

Schaeur, Frederick, *Playing by the Rules* (1991) reproduced by permission of Oxford University Press

Tushnet, Michael, *Red White and Blue: A Critical Analysis of Constitutional Law* (Harvard University Press, 1988)

Wade, HWR, *Constitutional Fundamentals* (Sweet & Maxwell, 1989)

Waldron, Jeremy, *The Law* (Routledge, 1990)

Zander, Michael, *The Law Making Process* (Butterworths, 1994)

Grateful acknowledgment to Butterworths for extracts from *Legal Studies*; to Sweet & Maxwell for extracts from *Criminal Law Review*; *European Law Review*; *Law Quarterly Review*; and *Public Law*; to Blackwell Publishers for extracts from *Modern Law Review*; to Cambridge University Press for extracts from *Cambridge Law Journal*; to Oxford University Press for extracts from *Oxford Journal of Legal Studies* and *Parliamentary Affairs*; to SLS Legal Publications for extracts from *Northern Ireland Legal Quarterly*; to the Incorporated Council of Law Reporting for England and Wales for permission to reproduce extracts from the Law Reports and Weekly Law Reports. Parliamentary and Crown Copyright material is reproduced with the permission of the Controller of Her Majesty's Stationery Office.

Every effort has been made to trace all the copyright holders but if any have been inadvertently overlooked the publishers will be pleased to make the necessary arrangement at the first opportunity.

CONTENTS

Contents

TABLE OF CASES

TABLE OF STATUTES

PART I
CONSTITUTIONAL FUNDAMENTALS

CHAPTER 1

CONSTITUTIONAL THEORY AND THE BRITISH CONSTITUTION[1]

INTRODUCTION

In Part I, the nature of constitutions in general is considered and the UK constitution is placed in this context. The desirability of a new written constitutional settlement as a means of curbing executive power will also be touched on. The chapters in Part I concentrate on four particular characteristics of the British constitution: the use of constitutional conventions; the Rule of Law; the Separation of Powers; and parliamentary sovereignty.

FUNDAMENTAL IDEAS IN CONSTITUTIONAL THEORY

We might begin by asking what is the basic purpose of a constitution. One influential answer, at least in Western constitutional thought, has been that constitutions are necessary in order to control the power of the state; another strand in that train of thought emphasises the role constitutions play in ensuring that that power derives from a legitimate source. On the one hand it tells us how power may be used, on the other, from whence it should derive. To the first idea may be attributed the notions of the Rule of Law, and the Separation of Powers, whilst the second is clearly related to the notion of democratic legitimacy. It is clear that there can be a tension between these two basic ideas. The following extract portrays that tension at work in history.

Francis Sejersted, 'Democracy and the Rule of Law: Some Historical Experiences of Contradictions in the Striving for Good Government' in J Elster and R Slagstad (eds), *Constitutionalism and Democracy* (1988), pp131–133

The Rule of Law and democracy correspond to the two different concepts of liberty: the negative, which makes liberty dependent on the curbing of authority; and the positive, which makes it dependent on the exercising of authority. These two concepts of liberty are, according to Isaiah Berlin, 'two profoundly divergent and irreconcilable attitudes to the ends of life'. Each of them have, however, 'an

---

1   General reading (additional to that referred to in this chapter): TRS Allan, *Law Liberty and Justice* (1995); Marshall, *Constitutional Theory*; Marshall and Moodie, *Some Problems of the Constitution* (1971); Jennings, *The Law and the Constitution*, 5th edn (1959); essays in McEldowney and McAuslan, *Law, Legitimacy and the Constitution* (1985); Wheare, *Modern Constitutions* (1966); Turpin, *British Government and the Constitution*, 3rd edn (1995); Rune Slagstad, 'Liberal Constitutionalism and its Critics' (and other essays) in Elster and Slagstad (eds), *Democracy and Constitutionalism* (1988); Hart, *The Concept of Law* (1967); Craig, *Public Law and Democracy in the United Kingdom and United States*; Sir John Laws, 'Law and Democracy' (1995), PL 72; Home and Elliot, *Time for a New Constitution* (1988); IPPR, *The Constitution of the United Kingdom* (1991); Beetham, *The Legitimisation of Power* (1991); Friedrich, *Limited Government: a Comparison* (1991); Woolf-Phillips, 'A Long Look at the British Constitution', (1984) 37(4) *Parliamentary Affairs*; SA De Smith, *Constitutional and Administrative Law*, 6th edn (1994); A Bradley and ECS Wade, *Constitutional and Administrative Law*, 11th edn (1993); O Hood Phillips, *Constitutional and Administrative Law*, 7th edn (1987); Hilaire Barnett, *Constitutional and Administrative Law*, (1995).

equal right to be classed among the deepest interests of mankind' (1958, pp51–52). ... Is there really such a contradiction between democracy and the Rule of Law?

Democracy and Rule of Law can be seen as two different means of overcoming the inherent contradiction between state and society. State-building is necessary to society, but also represents a threat. Rule of Law was meant to curb state authority, while democracy was meant to mobilise society in the exercising of state authority. This contradiction between state and society must have been strongly felt in the centuries following the Renaissance. There was a need for peace, order and public security, and it went along with a general distrust of human nature. Man was governed by passions and could not withstand the temptations of power. On the other hand there was a growing belief in the possibility of constructing a state where the power was bound and the passions were kept under control. This was the basis for all the intellectual energy which was put into the constitutionalist philosophy of that time. There were two main trends, the one recommending mixed government which opposed power with power, and the other recommending a Separation of Powers. The fundamental trait the two trends had in common was a purely negative approach to the exercise of power. This rather intense process of ideologisation seems to be important as a driving force behind the 'spontaneous outbreak of constitution-making' in the late 18th and early 19th century in the American states and in Europe. This 'conservative element' is now commonly seen as an important element in the American Revolution. Although the European case is not so clear, it seems as if the general tendency in this time of revolutions was the same, namely to block power rather than to take power. Hannah Arendt has argued that the constitutions were not the *result* of revolutions. 'Their purpose was to stem the tide of revolution' (1963, p143). It is certainly true that constitution-making could have this counter-revolutionary appearance. In the American Revolution it seems, however, to have been weak, and this is also the case in Norway. Constitution-making was not a reaction to a revolutionary situation; if anything, it was a revolution in itself, directed against the power of the king and furthered by the openness of the situation. The point is that constitution-making was directed against the power of the state, no matter who held power – a king or a democratically elected assembly.

Notes

1   Carl Schmidt argued that the attack on state power represented by liberal constitutionalism was aimed at securing two principle ends: firstly, certain guarantees of freedom, ie as R Slagstad puts it,[2] 'freedom from state interference'; secondly, a degree of stability and permanence, achieved by basing the constitution on a written document which is more difficult to amend than normal legislation. It is noteworthy that Schmidt includes in his list of freedoms guaranteed, both negative (civil) liberties and the positive right to 'a minimum of popular participation in the legislative process'.[3] Whilst on the one hand, participation in law-making can protect the participator from the power being exercised, it also gives him the opportunity to wield power, thereby giving him the means both to change

---

2   We follow here Rune Slagstad's exposition of Schmidt's thought, in 'Liberal Constitutionalism and its Critics: Carl Schmidt' in Elster and Slagstad (eds), *Democracy and Constitutionalism* (1988). The quotes in the text are at p104.

3   Quoted *ibid*.

his own life and to impact on the lives of others. It does not therefore seem particularly helpful to analyse the right to legislative participation as a negative 'freedom from' state interference. Sejersted's analysis seems to unpack the values underlying liberal constitutionalism more helpfully.

2   If guarantees of freedom and institutionalised stability are, as Schmidt contends, the two hallmarks of Western liberal constitutional theory, it is worth noting as an initial observation that neither of them can be found in the formal structure of the British constitution.

3   Constitutions, on the above account, are faced with a fairly Herculean role. To be able to carry it out, they evidently need to be seen as both legitimate and authoritative. How can they lay claim to such attributes?

Harry Calvert, *British Constitutional Law* (1985), pp4–5, 7, 8, 9, 14–15

So far as is known, the constitution of Al Capone's gang has never been published. Yet it undoubtedly had one. It probably contained little more than the basic rule or norm that 'what Big Al says, goes' and, in exercise of this 'authority', Big Al no doubt authorised lieutenants to issue instructions and to order that double-crossers be rubbed out. The appearances are that the Papa Doc regime in Haiti and Idi Amin's regime in Uganda functioned in much the same way.

They headed regimes which, for a while, and within the confines of the immediately pressing political environment, functioned effectively. Whether the Al Capone gang and the modern nation-state differ in other respects is something we must now consider.

It is tempting to seek to distinguish between 'proper' constitutions and other regimes of organisation. In much the same way that we all know an elephant when we see one without necessarily being able to proffer a very good definition of it, so also do we not all recognise a 'proper' state, 'properly' constituted when we see it? The Capone gang clearly fails; Papa Doc and Idi Amin were mere ephemeral aberrations. If there is such a distinction, however, wherein does it lie?

Suffice it to say for the present, that if the legality of the source of a constitution were the criterion of its validity, it would be a brave man who would assert that the UK has ever had a valid constitution. The modern constitution dates (with a few minor quibbles) from the revolution of 1688. Prior to that, the history of England at least is one of dubious claims to title to the Crown, conquests, schisms and broken treaties all offering extremely unsure ground on which to base a legal title.

It would be a marvellous thing for the economy of the UK if only legal criteria were the sole relevant criteria. We might, then, be able to continue to exploit valuable colonies on the eastern seaboard of North America. The celebrated United States Declaration of Independence was an act of treason, hardly capable in law of giving birth to the United States of America. Of course, by an act of the prerogative, the Crown 'recognised' the USA in the Treaty of Paris, 1783 a mere few years after the insurrection. From that point onwards, the USA enjoyed a legal existence of sorts under the constitution of the UK although a mere treaty, by itself, could not serve to divest His Majesty's subjects within the realm of their property in North America. It would, however, be a bold man, if not a fool, who sought now to base his title upon the legalities which prevailed before the USA came into being. A more valuable lesson would be that the acquiescence which a constitution requires is likely to be impaired, and its effectiveness likely to be lost if its operation stretches the patience of subjects beyond breaking-point. ...

Lawyers may find it difficult to live with notions of competing constitutionalities or with the idea of legitimacy being a matter of degree. It is, unfortunately for them, a common feature of the real contemporary world.

The Spanish civil war gave birth to similar problems, and, nearer our own time, events in Zimbabwe (formerly Rhodesia) illustrate the difficulties vividly. The unilateral Declaration of independence of the Smith regime in 1965 was, according to the Judicial Committee of the Privy Council, in *Madzimbamuto v Lardner-Burke* [1969] 1 AC 645, illegal and of no effect (although there were those in Rhodesia who, on the strength of an alleged 'convention' of non-interference by Westminster, were inclined to doubt this). For the Rhodesian courts, however, from which appeal was taken, the issues were not as readily resolved. It did, in truth, make little sense, for general purposes, to regard the only legitimate authority in Rhodesia to be its pre-revolutionary governor, holed up ineffectively in Government House proclaiming his loyalty to the Crown. Whilst sensitive to and perhaps even perplexed by the implications of 'legality', the Rhodesian courts nevertheless clearly felt conduced by the realities, which included the eminent desirability that there should be, in some sense, lawful authority to carry on government in Rhodesia, and the brute fact that if anyone was effectively in control in Rhodesia, it was the Smith regime. They therefore tended to find (as does international law) a convenient bolt-hole in the notion of *de facto* authority, which manages to encompass in a single phrase the idea that a government is, at one and the same time, lacking in but clothed with the authority to rule. Even in the Judicial Committee, consciousness of the necessity for some such accommodation was not wholly lacking. ...

So, legality of source will not serve to distinguish between 'proper' and 'improper' constitutions. Such a criterion condemns the constitutions of most of the world's oldest and most stable societies. What clearly is illustrated is that a regime illegal in its origins may nevertheless, in some mysterious way, come to generate its own legality. In international law, this event may be prompted by 'recognition' which, according to some schools of thought, confers legality whilst, according to others, merely declares a legality deriving otherwise. Within the 'state', and after a coup d'état purporting to establish a new constitution but without any initial basis in legality, the courts sometimes come to acknowledge the new 'validity' and consequent legality and offer a variety of reasons for so doing (see, eg, *The State v Dosso* 1958 SC 533, re Pakistan). It will not do, however, to regard such decisions as constituting the legality of the new regime, as opposed merely to accepting it as a pre-existing fact. If we do so, we get into all sorts of logical difficulties – whence comes the authority of the court to constitute? Can it really be the case that a constitution firmly in place nevertheless remains invalid pending the caprice of an application to the courts?

Perhaps the distinction is best sought elsewhere. If we are not to look to the pre-existing legal order for validity, perhaps we should look to another source. It is an established historical fact that the constitutions of many modern states were specifically adopted as constitutions intended and resolved to act as the foundation for the new order. There is a superabundance of such instances. Most of the old Commonwealth countries still have, as their constitutional cases, Acts of the old imperial Parliament – here legality and specific adoption meld. In the case of some newer Commonwealth countries, as in the case of the USA, a new constitution has been promulgated without regard for the pre-existing legal order but in title of some asserted natural right so to do. In some cases, such as that of the Republic of Ireland (formerly the Irish Free State) an old constitution has legitimately spawned a newer one. Even in the case of the UK, it may be possible to conjure such a incident out of the legislation of the revolutionary 'Parliament' of 1688–9 and the later Acts of Union with Scotland and Ireland.

In all cases of specific adoption, it is possible to point to a constitutional instrument of some sort. Whilst this is an extremely common phenomenon, however, it does not seem to be absolutely necessary. A few of the world's acknowledged states boast no such instrument yet it would be hard to deny any constitutional function for them. It is normal to rank the UK amongst them for, in truth, the legislation referred to above hardly amounts to a written constitution as the term is usually understood.

If we go back even further, either in history or in sophistication of social organisation, we reach a point where acts of specific adoption are unknown yet it would be hard to deny any constitutionality to the groups in question. In many primitive societies, as in a few advanced ones, constitutions have simply emerged from custom. A particular way of tackling the business of governing in whatever that may consist, has simply emerged and become accepted as being the correct way. It is first merely the usual way; eventually it becomes the expected way; and finally, by some mysterious process, it becomes the required way. ...

Lawyers tend to yearn for legal criteria, and constitutional lawyers, or at least some of them, would like to be able to say when a constitution is 'in force'. This may be a practical problem where they have had to decide whether or not to regard a new regime as valid. The insuperable problem is, however, that there is no legal system to which one can refer for such questions. *Ex hypothesi*, the legality of a constitution cannot be found within itself. International law purports to offer criteria but they are inapt for the present purpose. Recognition, by which international law purports to confer or endorse constitutional validity, has frequently been withheld for long periods from 'states' undoubtedly functioning under constitutions of one sort or another. Constitutions are simply facts. As facts, we may well make all sorts of intelligent speculations about their origins, functions and prospects. A constitution may simply develop, or be imposed or adopted. It may regulate state activity in a variety of ways. It always stands to be overthrown; how likely this is depends upon how precariously it is in place.

For one interested in studying the function of rules as regulating political behaviour within a state, the only relevant question is: 'Is a given constitution effective in this respect?' Effectiveness and stability are both greatly enhanced by acquiescence – the more the people (who are the potential rebels) are content with the existing regime, the more likely it is to remain in charge. To the extent that acquiescence is lacking, force is necessary. Recognition by other states may make economic and political life somewhat easier for the regime in question but will have only a marginal effect upon its stability. Little more can be said.

Questions

1   On Calvert's account it appears that, in the last resort, constitutional legitimacy is parasitic upon efficacy and acquiescence. Is it therefore the case that, if the Capone gang had eventually become so powerful that it defeated the US Government and its agents and took effective control over the USA, the rules governing the gang would (if Capone had so wished) have become its constitution?

2   Does it follow that if, as in the case of the USA, it is not possible to derive the legitimacy of the constitution from a pre-existing legal system, it is necessary

to fall back immediately upon the criterion of actual effectiveness? Does such a criterion give the citizens of the state concerned any reasons to abide by the provisions of the constitution, other than practical ones?

3 The above questions go to the issue of whether and why a constitution has any claims to legitimacy. The practical relevance of such questions touches us all in everyday life, when we encounter sets of rules; we then tend to characterise the question as one of applicability. For example, the rules of a university are applicable to its students, but lack jurisdiction over members of the public. Frederick Schauer considers the consequences of this mode of thinking to the issue of constitutional legitimacy.

Frederick Schauer, *Playing by the Rules: A Philosophical Examination of Rule-Based Decision-Making in Law and in Life* (1991), pp118–120

Any rule presents the threshold question of its applicability. Does this rule apply to this situation, to me, and to the decision that I must now make? If we look at the rule itself, what looks like an answer will be therefore before us. Rules necessarily specify the scope of their application since the designation of scope is part of the factual predicate of the rule. This designation of scope may not appear on the face of the rule, but if not will be either implicit or incorporated by reference to some other rule within the same array of rules. Thus a 'No dogs allowed' sign on a restaurant is not a universal prohibition of dogs in society, but only of dogs *in* the restaurant, with the 'in the restaurant' clause being implicit in the location of the sign (as well as in our understanding of the jurisdiction of the restaurant's proprietors). Similarly, the rules of law necessary specify the people and places to whom their requirements attach, as when an income tax provision applies only to residents and those earning money within the geographic boundaries of the taxing authority, and not to complete strangers to the jurisdiction. The tax laws of France, where I do not live and do not earn money, do not apply to me.

Designation in the rule – whether explicit, implicit or arising from the operation of some secondary jurisdictional rule – is thus a necessary condition for the applicability of a rule. That such designation is a necessary condition for applicability, however, does not make it a sufficient condition, and at this point figuring out the issue of applicability becomes more treacherous. If the tax laws of France were specifically amended so that they did explicitly purport to extend their requirements to foreign residents who earned no money in France, I would still not (assuming I stayed out of France) take them as reasons for paying taxes to France. ... And consider the effect of altering the sign on the restaurant so that it read, without referring to any other rule, 'No dogs allowed in any restaurant in this city'.

Such examples show that the mere assertion of applicability is insufficient to make it so. But what is missing? Preliminarily we must distinguish applicability from validity, for a rule that by its terms appears applicable may still be an invalid rule and therefore inapplicable. Validity, itself a function of other rules, is thus a necessary condition for applicability. The regulations of the Interstate Commerce Commission are applicable throughout the United States not merely because those regulations say they are, but because an Act of Congress grants national regulatory authority to the Commission. Similarly, that Act of Congress is applicable throughout the United States not because it says so, but because the Constitution of the United States grants national regulatory authority over interstate commerce to Congress.

Rules are therefore ordinarily situated within hierarchical rule systems which establish, among other things, the internal validity of rules within those systems. We have learned from Hart's discussion of rules of recognition [Hart, *The Concept of Law*, pp92–97, 245–7] and from Hans Kelsen's hierarchical analysis of norms [Hans Kelsen, *Pure Theory of Law, passim*] that a rule is valid just in case there is a rule within the rule system making it so. But for a rule to be valid within some rule system does not say anything about the validity of the system itself. The validity of the regulations of the Interstate Commerce Commission pursuant to a chain of validity going back to the constitution of the United States does not establish the validity (and thus the applicability for which it is a necessary condition) of a document called the 'constitution of the United States' in the United States. Why is it that the constitution of the United States regulates the behaviour of Americans in a way that the German basic law does not? And why is the 'constitution of the United States' applicable *to* the United States when a document I might draft tomorrow, looking for all the world like a constitution for the United States, is not? Even if all the internally specific conditions of my newly written constitution's validity and applicability were satisfied, that would not be sufficient for it to supplant the 'constitution of the United States' as the constitution of the United States, and that is because, as elucidated by Kelsen in his discussion of the *grundnorm* and by Hart in describing the ultimate rule of recognition, the validity of a system is not a question of validity at all, but of the social fact that a certain system is treated as the law of some community by that community.

Note

Schauer concludes, like Calvert, that the notion of the applicability of a constitution comes down to the social fact of the obedience of the citizens to the relevant state. But it may then be asked, for what reasons do citizens give their loyalty to a state? In liberal theory, citizens consent to be governed by the (liberal) state because they recognise the justice and fairness of the state's arrangements, which also serves their own rational self interest;[4] indeed the essence of liberal theory lies in the notion that the state can and must command such allegiance without itself espousing any substantive theory about how citizens should lead their lives or what kinds of goals and activities are most worthwhile.[5] It is the fairness of the state in guaranteeing the equal freedom of citizens to pursue their own conceptions of the good which ensures its citizens' loyalty. Theorists on the Left, by contrast, postulate rather more pragmatic reasons for such loyalty.

Rodney Barker, 'Obedience, Legitimacy and the State' in C Harlow (ed), *Public Law and Politics* (1986), pp4–9

Political scientists, in asking how in practice states come to be obeyed, and when their commands are resisted, have distinguished between coerced and willing

4   See generally John Rawls, *A Theory of Justice* (1973). The statement in the text represents of course only the most simplified indication of Rawls' theory. It is from the hypothetical choices of rational, self-interested men (temporarily deprived of the knowledge of their own abilities, position in life and substantive moral convictions) that, in Rawls' theory, the constitution of a just state is framed.

5   This particular aspect of liberal theory has been emphasised most strongly by Ronald Dworkin; see his 'Taking Rights Seriously' in *Taking Rights Seriously* (1977) and 'Liberalism' in *A Matter of Principle* (1985). The liberal state does of course impose on its citizens the requirement that they must not infringe each other's liberties.

obedience, or between coercion and legitimacy. Recent events might seem to suggest that conflict between the state and its subject is a matter of coercion and of resistance to coercion. But although, in the last resort, simple physical coercion is available to maintain the state's power, and is used to maintain that power, in general the state in the UK is obeyed because its legitimacy is accepted. The state's monopoly of legitimate power is precisely that. The power is not that of the stronger arm, but of the arm whose right to strike and to arrest and to imprison in the last instance is accepted. Thus the coercive power of the state is uniquely strengthened and sustained by being regarded as legitimate. And once that legitimacy is destroyed, the state may be able to contain its subjects, but it can scarcely govern them.

But how does it come about that the state is regarded as legitimate, and when it is so regarded, what does this entail for the conduct of the state's subjects? ...

James O'Connor in his book, *The Fiscal Crisis of the State* (1973), argued that the principal way in which the state maintains its own legitimacy or, as he less elaborately puts it at one point, preserves 'loyalty', is by using social services to maintain materially marginal groups in society: the poor, the sick, the old. The state thus provides benefits in order to 'pacify' the poorer parts of the nation, maintaining itself by quietening material discontent. The social services he describes as 'designed chiefly to keep social peace among unemployed workers', and to 'pacify and control the surplus population' [O'Connor, *op cit* p7]. ...

A wider constituency for the state's legitimising work has been suggested by Claus Offe, following the arguments of Jurgan Habermas, and by Barrington Moore Jr [Jurgen Habermas, *Legitimation Crisis* (tr Thomas McCarthy (1976)) Barrington Moore Jr, *Injustice: The Social Bases of Obedience and Revolt* (1978)]. Offe argues that legitimacy is strained when the state fails to meet the demands of its citizens for material well-being. The problem of legitimacy is thus not one of placating materially peripheral groups, but of maintaining mass consensus through both economic growth and some system of at least apparent redistribution of material benefits. The bargain is an economic one and, when either direct personal or indirect social or environmental living standards being to fall, or even to fail to rise, then the implicit contract is placed under stress and willing obedience is threatened [Claus Offe, *Contradictions of the Welfare State* (1984)]. Thus, whilst Offe and Habermas develop their argument on foundations laid by Marx, they do so in a way which gives an explanation of the loyalty of the mass of subjects, and not just of a minority. For Marx himself, the ideological superstructure contributed to the regulation of the broad mass of the state's subjects.

The pluralist account of legitimacy is best represented by SM Lipset and Richard Rose. Writing in 1959, Lipset identified effectiveness and legitimacy as the two pillars on which any system of government rested [SM Lipset, *Political Man* (1959)]. The latter, Lipset argued, was likely to be threatened either when there was a challenge to the status of 'major conservative institutions' or when there were 'major groups' which did not have access to political power. ... When such conflicts are not resolved, the 'moderate state of conflict' which is 'another way of defining a legitimate democracy' is eroded or destroyed [Lipset, *op cit* p83]. On the one hand, therefore, Lipset uses legitimacy not to describe circumstances where loyal obedience exists, but to describe those where it does not. Legitimacy as a term is used when its absence is identified, rather than when its presence is described. It is the normal and unremarked characteristic of liberal pluralist societies, and is, like the weather, only commented upon when it turns nasty. It is easier to describe the absence of legitimacy than its presence. ...

Pluralist theory sees legitimacy as more evident when it is eroded, though Lipset does see political culture as its positive cultivator. Marxist theory sees legitimacy as a deliberate creation, the constitutional aspect of what Gramsci called hegemony. Yet both liberal pluralist theory and Marxist theory see the breakdown of legitimacy as a consequence of the state's failure to meet political and economic expectations, and the creation and maintenance of legitimacy as a result of its success in doing so. To that extent the explanation for legitimacy or willing obedience lies in the social and economic arrangements of society or in the actions, expectations, and condition of its members in so far as with greater or lesser success they are affected by the actions and inactions of the state. For the pluralist this is so because government is seen largely as a reflexive activity, so that even satisfactions and dissatisfactions about essentially political matters are expressed through government, rather than created by it. For the Marxists, it is the economic relations which form the basis for the political and governmental ones. And perhaps in so far as both liberal pluralist and Marxist political scientists examine legitimacy as the positive creation of efficient governmental achievement of social and economic goals, the question is put the wrong way round. For any subject living in the UK, or at least in Great Britain today, the state as an institution commanding and gaining obedience precedes his or her consciousness of its governance over them. At no time are they faced with a decision whether or not in general to obey. They grew up with the state, and before they knew what they did, they obeyed it. Moreover there has been no time over the last 250 years when any deliberate decision has been taken to establish or disestablish a particular form of government or a particular form of state. At least, this has been so for Great Britain, though not for Ireland. If the question is 'under what circumstances is the legitimacy of the state eroded, and in what ways does the state preserve, or attempt to preserve, its own legitimacy?', then the historical starting point is with legitimacy as the normal condition of government. Thus whilst it may indeed be 'sustained', such a term is more appropriate than 'created'. And the nature of that sustenance will perhaps most easily be seen when it is interrupted or withdrawn.

Whilst a conception such as contract can be employed at a theoretical level to explain why citizens might agree to submit to a state which they had consciously established, it is of less use in explaining a situation which has never, for any single subject, or group of subjects in the UK, existed. The state has not been established but has been absorbed as a part of a received social environment. Nonetheless it might be possible to use the notion of contract in a negative way. In other words, although a contract may never have been made, and although subjects may have no articulate conception of such a thing, there will be circumstances where their obedience will be withheld or questioned. These may be seen as circumstances where a contract, dormant but implicit, has been articulated in its breach. When a reason is adduced for not obeying, then the circumstances for obedience are by implication stated also. And in practical terms, an identification of the circumstances which strain the obedience of subjects will suggest in what other circumstances that obedience will be maintained and even strengthened. Legitimacy is principally a matter of habit, but the character of the habit will be most easily viewed when it is broken.

Question

Barker postulates that loyalty is not so much given as an act of conscious choice but bred into us before we know it; it is the withdrawal, rather than the giving of loyalty which is likely to be a matter of choice. Why has Britain been so conspicuously successful historically in retaining this inbred loyalty?

CLASSIFICATIONS OF CONSTITUTIONS

Constitutions can be classified in a number of ways. One distinction often made is between written and unwritten constitutions. Calvert considers the significance of such a distinction below, together with the 'rigid'/'flexible' division.

Harry Calvert, *British Constitutional Law* (1985), pp9–12

'Written' and 'unwritten' constitutions are often considered to be of two radically different kinds, and it is customary, in discussing constitutions in general, to labour the distinction between them. Commonly, as is stated below, they have distinctive features, but the essential difference between them is nevertheless formal rather than substantial. Take, for example, the differences between the constitutions of the UK and the USA.

So much of the constitution of the UK, as is in writing, hardly amounts to a written constitution, for too much is omitted. Consider the question whether our courts may strike down, as invalid, an Act of Parliament, commonly a very important function discharged in, for example, the USA by its Supreme Court. We would search in vain for any formal written statement of the position in this respect so far as the UK's constitution is concerned. Written statement says neither that the courts may, not that they may not, undertake this task. It is left to the courts themselves, as authors of the common law, to declare that they may not, a position progressively arrived at as a result of slow development over centuries.

We would, however, search the written constitution of the USA equally vainly. It has never been denied that the USA functions under a written constitution, yet the fundamentally important power which the Supreme Court exercises to declare invalid laws which transgress the constitution is nowhere written into it. Rather it derives from what the Supreme Court itself has perceived to be the inherent logic of the constitutional structure of the USA – since the constitution of the USA does impose limitations upon legislative power, the Court is confronted by the necessity to choose between enforcing the superior constitutional, or the inferior law and, as a matter of logic, it does the former. The logic is not actually compelling, for a constitution can, and some constitutions do, vest such a function elsewhere, or even state explicitly that the limitations imposed are for guidance only. The function of judicial review on grounds of constitutionality is a later development of the constitution of the USA which has come to be accepted. It is not part of it.

If we were to study a sample of written constitutions in their socio- and politico-historical contexts, we might well conclude that a 'written' constitution is, in many cases, if not all, no more than a frame in a film. It will have historical antecedents, often of a customary sort and may, indeed, amount to no more than the codification of pre-existing constitutional practice. Then the written constitution itself will come to function as the substructure on which the later developments, essentially customary in character, are built. It would be pressing the argument too far to argue that there is no difference between a written and an unwritten constitution, for the statement, in written form, of a constitution will often crystallise the then existing state of affairs and a peculiar sanctity may well come to attach to it, inhibiting later customary development to some extent. The difference remains, nevertheless, one of degree rather than of kind. The dustbins of history are full of constitutional instruments, which were denied change, adaptation and development according to customary processes. They became obsolete, were replaced and discarded.

One common feature of written constitutions may offer us a criterion whereby to distinguish between regimes such as that of Al Capone or Papa Doc and others. Written constitutions are commonly 'rigid' or 'semi-rigid' in terms, ie they are explicitly stated to be unchangeable, or able to be changed only by resort to extraordinary processes of amendment. An amendment may require, for example, to be accepted by popular referendum or by a two-thirds majority in a popular assembly. Although in practice most written constitutions are at least semi-rigid, it is not inherently necessary that they should be so; a written constitution could be, and some are, totally flexible, ie able to be changed by ordinary legislative processes. In this latter case, such a constitution would differ from that of a state such as the UK which is supposed to have an unwritten constitution, only in that at one fleeting moment in history, there would be a constitutional text contained in a single instrument. To say of the constitution of the UK that it is unwritten is, therefore, merely to say that its text is not to be found (and, possibly, never was to be found) in a single document, and that is to say very little of any substantial importance about it. ...

Social change is a part of human history and if an organised society is to survive as such, its constitution must be adaptable and sensitive at least to the great tides of social change. A flexible constitution is, by definition, freely adaptable. Beyond that, however, the danger is of making a virtue of necessity. Because we have a flexible constitution (and perhaps also because in some quarters the myth prevails that there is no mechanism by which we could adopt a rigid constitution if we wanted to), we tend to assume that is a good thing in itself. The danger here is that of mistaking the reasons for the present relatively smooth functioning of the existing constitution. If our flexible constitution is working apparently well, not because of any inherent virtue of its own but merely because at this stage in our history we have no need to rely upon it, we are living in a fool's paradise and are no more secure, in the final analysis, than were the members of Al Capone's gang or the victims of the Tonton Macoute.

Note

As Calvert usefully points out, the distinction between flexible and rigid constitutions is rather more important in practice than between unwritten and written. Indeed, Colin Munro considers any distinction based on writing to be fundamentally flawed.

Colin Munro, *Studies in Constitutional Law* (1987), pp1–3, 4–5

Every state in the world has a constitution in the original sense of the word, by which is meant the body of rules and arrangements concerning the government of the country. In the UK, where the principal institutions of government have developed over hundreds of years, many of these rules are customary in origin. Some of the rules are to be found in legislation, including such famous enactments as Magna Carta and the Bill of Rights, as well as modern statutes like the Representation of the People Act 1983 and the British Nationality Act 1981. Others reside in the judgments of the courts, although Dicey, the greatest of our constitutional lawyers, exaggerated the importance of this element when he characterised our constitution as 'judge-made' [AV Dicey, *Introduction to the Study of the Law of the Constitution* (10th edn), p196]. Some other matters which call for consideration are not legal at all: the government of a country could not be fully described without reference to political facts, practices and obligations.

In the 18th century, another meaning of the word 'constitution' came into fashion. Following their success in the War of Independence, the Americans had chosen to establish a framework for national government in a single document which was called a 'constitution for the United States of America'. Similarly, the revolutionaries in France had drawn up a constitution in 1791 which limited the authority of the king. These were the models which the radical politician Thomas Paine had in mind when he complained that 'no such thing as a constitution exists in England' [*The Rights of Man,* Part 2, Chapter 4]. Later the contrast with the United States and France inspired the French writer de Tocqueville to remark that our constitution was one which did not exist [*Democracy in America,* Vol 1, Part 1, Chapter 6]. De Tocqueville, who was an admirer of the British constitution, was merely drawing attention to the absence of a single document referred to as 'the constitution'.

The term 'constitution' continues to be used in two senses. Of course, if we are speaking of the British constitution, only one meaning is possible. On other occasions, it is generally clear from the context which meaning is intended. Not content with that, however, some writers coined the term 'written constitution' to describe a document such as the United States constitution of 1787. What is worse, countries were then divided by some commentators into those having a written constitution or, lacking that, an unwritten constitution. This was a singularly unhappy distinction. It suggested, wrongly, that in countries such as the UK, constitutional rules were only customary and could not be found in written form in statutes, reported cases and books, perhaps even that they were 'transmitted orally from generation to generation, like the earliest poetry of ancient Greece' [*The Usages of the American Constitution* (1925), p1]. It also suggested, wrongly, that in countries such as the United States, all the rules and arrangements concerning government had been reduced to writing in a single document. In practice, this is never the case. The documents called constitutions are often fairly short, and so many constitutional matters are regulated by ordinary legislation. Over the years, too, the framework in the document becomes overlaid with judicial interpretations and political practices. In other words, the constitution of a country, in the older sense of the word, includes, but is invariably larger than, the constitution in the newer sense.

The true distinction, it may be seen, is simply between states where some of the more important constitutional rules have been put in a document, or, set of associated documents, given special sanctity, and states where the constitution has many sources, none of which enjoys such recognition.

It is easy to understand why, in many countries, the fundamental framework of government has been set out in a document. What was more natural in post-revolutionary Russia in 1917 or newly independent Nigeria in 1960, or Zimbabwe after an independence settlement giving civil equality to the black majority was agreed in 1979? When there is a break with the past, and the institutions of government are altered, a formal embodiment of the new arrangements seems appropriate. The births of new nations and the unions of partners are aptly marked by rites of passage in the form of constitutional documents to which a special significance is attached. If later, in a state which has had such a constitution, it is desired to change some fundamentals, as in Canada in 1982, when a new constitution was adopted which could be amended without recourse to the UK Parliament, then a formal document is likely to be employed, so that the new arrangements may present as much appearance of legitimacy as did the old.

The circumstances which have led to the making of constitutions in other countries have largely been absent in this one. The British have not suffered conquest, or the loss of a major war, or revolution, for several hundred years.

The principal institutions of government in this country – Parliament, the Crown and the courts – have been refashioned, and their relations with each other altered, as a result of social and political changes. But they may all be traced back as far as the 12th century (when Henry II made the Kings' courts important) or the 13th (when in the reign of Edward I the English Parliament acquired something like its present form), times when constitution-making was not in fashion. Consequently, the development of governmental institutions has been evolutionary. As Sir Ivor Jennings put it, 'the British Constitution has not been made but has grown', and, mixing his metaphors: 'The building has been constantly added to, patched, and partially reconstructed, so that it has been renewed from century to century; but it has never been razed to the ground and rebuilt on new foundations.' [*The Law and the Constitution*, 5th edn (1959), p8.]

Munro then considers certain constitutional enactments.

The clauses of Magna Carta were designed to check some particular royal abuses. The Bill of Rights embodied the terms upon which the Crown was offered to William and Mary, which included the establishment of certain parliamentary rights and privileges and further limitations upon the royal powers. The Acts of Union united the countries concerned, and their Parliaments, but left the Scottish courts in being and Scots law separate; they also provided for an established religion in each part of the kingdom, and contained some provisions about trade and taxes. However, none of these enactments dealt systematically with the institutions of government and their relations with each other; in each case much was assumed. Nor has any of them been treated by Parliament as impossible to amend in the ordinary way.

For these reasons, no doubt, such enactments, important as they are in our constitutional history, have not generally been regarded as constitutions. However, it is a matter of interpretation rather than anything else, for the meaning of the term 'constitution' used in this sense is, like many of the terms used in political science, inexact. If we chose to define 'constitution' in a particular way, say that it is a document from which the institutions of government derive their authority, or that it is that part of a country's law which may not be altered or repealed in the ordinary manner, then we should have a certain criterion. But the difficulty in adopting such a criterion is that the variety of terms and characteristics found in documents regarded as constitutions means that no particular feature is universal. By stipulating criteria such as those mentioned, one would be liable to exclude from the category documents which, in their own countries, are regarded as constitutions. ...

In this country the principal rules about government have not been embodied in a single document, except during the Interregnum. One could, however, if one wished, assemble together eight or ten of this country's most important constitutional enactments, and regard them collectively as a constitution (and indeed, for purposes of comparison or exposition, some authors have done so). The result would be distinguishable from other countries' constitutions only by the number and disparateness of the enactments selected, and because of those enactments not being generally regarded as comprising a constitution.

These differences are not very important, and so it would appear that too much importance has been attached to whether a country has a constitution or not. What every schoolboy knows is that this country has no constitution; but what he knows turns out to be a distinction without a difference.

Notes

1   Munro is perhaps being too sweeping when he argues that the 'eight or ten of this country's most important constitutional enactments ... would be distinguishable from other countries' constitutions only by [their] number and their disparateness and because [they are] not generally regarded as compromising a constitution'. Surely they would be wholly silent as to a very wide and important range of matters, mainly involving the central executive. Unlike nearly all other 'constitutions' they would have nothing (or nothing of substance) to say about the Prime Minister, the Cabinet or the Royal Prerogative. They would tell us very little about the actual position of the Head of State (the Queen), and they would not mentioning the single most important rule of the British constitution: the legislative supremacy of Parliament.

2   Munro's argument against using 'written' or 'unwritten' as a mode of classification seems more persuasive. Calvert offers a series of more helpful classifications.

Harry Calvert, *British Constitutional Law* (1985), pp15–17

The variety of forms which a constitution can take is infinite. It is, nevertheless, helpful to consider some of the variables.

(a) Range of powers

A constitution may provide for the assumption of powers of government at any point on a scale extending from anarchy to totalitarianism. We tend to take what we know as 'natural'. Yet little more than two centuries ago the notion that constitution could confer power on a Government to expropriate private property would have been thought extraordinary. Today, different 'human rights' are regarded as sacrosanct in some degree in different constitutions. In some, power over matters of religion is withheld from the secular authorities; in others, the secular state is omnipotent.

(b) Distribution of powers

The powers assumed can be concentrated or deconcentrated in a variety of ways. The simplest model is the total unitary state, all powers being concentrated in a single central authority. Further along the scale, such a single central authority might nevertheless seek to administer via regional or local agencies. Further still, powers might be devolved to regional or local agencies with the reservation to the centre of only a supervisory function.

'Federation' is a term best used to describe those structures where the totality of power is distributed geographically between the centre and the regions, neither exercising a final supervisory jurisdiction over the other. This may come about as result of either centripetal or centrifugal forces. Independent powers may coalesce into a federation; or a unitary state may reconstruct itself on a federal basis. In most modern federations, there is tendency for the centre to dominate. There is some truth, if not the whole truth, in the notion that true federation will work where it is not needed, but will not work where it is needed.

Confederation differs from federation in that the central authority may exercise only such powers as are conferred by the states members and is thus subordinate to them. In a typical confederation, the centre will enjoy only such authority as is unanimously conferred by the Member States.

In addition to the geographical distribution of powers, powers may be distributed functionally, ie there may be more than one 'Government' in the same territory. Historically, this has presented itself in the case of the ongoing Church and State question; occasionally, condominium, or the rule within a particular territory of two or more states, has been resorted to. Less dramatically, it may be decided to vest control over a particular function in a special body not responsible or at least not readily responsible to central Government. In Belgium the geographical and functional distribution of power has been combined in the establishment of the Flemish and Walloon Cultural Councils.

(c) Types of government

There is, again, a great possible variety of forms. One scale is the autocracy-oligarchy-democracy scale. Typical autocrats are monarchs and presidents. A monarchy may hold absolute power, or may be merely a figurehead, or be somewhere in between. The UK has a 'constitutional monarch'; that signifies an absence of absolutism and a largely formal, figurehead role. Cabinet government in the UK is oligarchical but not absolute. Parliament's House of Commons infuses a democratic element, again not absolute.

Presidential systems may parallel this. Some modern states, eg the USA and France, have executive presidents invested with great power. In other cases, eg the Republic of Ireland, the president discharges a role almost identical with that of a constitutional monarch.

The central feature of most purportedly modern democratic states is a popular assembly of some sort. The electorate, term of office and range of powers of an assembly are infinitely variable. There are many different electoral systems and election may be indirect as well as direct. 'One party' democracy is becoming increasingly common and is often a euphemism for oligarchy. A popular assembly may exercise final control over all branches of government. It may, for example, have unfettered legislative power, appoint and control an executive and the judiciary. At the other extreme, its function may be merely nominal and effectively confined to rubber stamping the acts of the executive, or even confined to a right to consultation.

Monarchs, presidents, oligarchies, popular assemblies may all be removable at will, or self-perpetuating, or responsible in some degree in between.

(d) Forms

As has been indicated above, constitutions may be 'written' or 'unwritten'. This largely corresponds to source, 'written' constitutions being the preferred form for acts of specific adoption, 'unwritten' constitutions emerging from custom. A given constitution may be 'rigid' or 'flexible' in any degree. The term 'entrenchment' is commonly used of particular provisions to which rigidity is attached in an otherwise flexible constitution. It is currently a matter for debate in the UK whether or not a Bill of Rights should be 'entrenched' in the constitution and, if so, how.

Notes

1   McEldowney, adopting Professor Wheare's classifications,[6] (similar to those listed by Calvert) finds that 'it is at once apparent that the UK has a unitary, flexible constitution whose powers are fused'.[7] It is, of course the flexibility of the British constitution that is its most remarkable feature. Within the UK

---

6   Wheare, *Modern Constitutions* (1966), pp4–8.

7   John F McEldowney, *Public Law* (1994), p4.

there is no written constitution which has a higher status than the rest of the law. The body of rules relating to the structure, functions and powers of the organs of state, their relationship to one another, and to the private citizen is to be derived from common law, statute and constitutional conventions. Therefore the constitution does not impose express limits on what may be done by ordinary legislation in the way that many constitutions do. The legislative competence of the UK Parliament is formally unlimited. The lack of any supreme constitutional law means that no Parliament may bind its successors or be bound by its predecessors and the courts cannot question the validity of an Act of Parliament. Thus, every aspect of the constitution (with the possible exception of parliamentary sovereignty itself)[8] is subject to change by ordinary act of Parliament. O Hood Phillips stresses that such flexibility cannot be directly attributable to the (largely) unwritten nature of the UK constitution, pointing out by way of example that 'the constitution of Singapore is written but entirely flexible'.[9]

2   This radical subjugation of all other aspects of the constitution, however fundamental, to parliamentary sovereignty has led some commentators to decide that, contrary to Munro's contentions, the UK has no constitution, in any meaningful sense of that word.

F F Ridley, 'There is no British Constitution: A Dangerous Case of the Emperor's Clothes' (1988) 41 *Parliamentary Affairs* 340, 342, 359–60

Having a constitution seems to be a matter of self-respect; no state is properly dressed without one. Every democracy except Britain, New Zealand and (with qualifications) Israel seems to have a written constitution, plainly labelled. Not to be left out of the world of constitutional democracies, British writers define constitution in a way which appears to give us one too, even though there is no document to prove it. The argument is that a constitution need not be embodied in a single document or, indeed, wholly written. We say instead that a country's constitution is a body of rules – some laws, some conventions – which regulate its system of government. Such a definition does not, however, bridge the gap between Britain and the rest of the world by providing us with a substitute for a documentary constitution: it simply shifts the ground, by using the word in an entirely different way.

We see this ambiguity in KC Wheare's now classic book on constitutions. 'The word constitution is commonly used in at least two senses in ordinary discussion of political affairs. First of all, it is used to describe the whole system of government, the collection of rules which establish and regulate it. These rules are partly legal and partly non-legal. When we speak of the British constitution, that is the normal, if not the only possible meaning the word has.'

Everywhere save Britain the constitution is defined as a special category of law. British usage dissolves the distinction between constitutional law and other laws because British courts recognise no such distinction. British political scientists, for their part, dissolve the distinction between law and other rules of behaviour because they are not much interested in law: for them, the constitution is practice ...

---

8   See below, Chapter 4.
9   *Constitutional and Administrative Law*, 7th edn (1987), p7.

Use of the word constitution as the manner in which a policy is organised, the main characteristic of its governmental system is undoubtedly the historic one. By the end of the 18th century, however, the word came to have another meaning. The American War of Independence and the French Revolution marked a turning point after which the new meaning became universal, Britain excepted. It applied to a special form of law embodied as a matter of convenience in a single document. As used elsewhere, it is now a term of law not politics. Constitutions therefore have certain essential characteristics, none of them found in Britain. Without these characteristics, it is impossible to distinguish a constitution from a description of the system of government in a way that is analytically precise. Without them, it is impossible to say that a country has a constitution in the current international sense of the word. More important, lest this be thought a linguistic quibble, without them a system of government lacks the legitimacy a constitution gives and a political system the protection it offers.

The characteristics of a constitution are as follows.

(1) It establishes, or constitutes, the system of government. Thus it is prior to the system of government, not part of it, and its rules can not be derived from that system.

(2) It therefore involves an authority outside and above the order it establishes. This is the notion of the constituent power ('*pouvoir constituant*' – because we do not think along these lines, the English translation sounds strange). In democracies that power is attributed to the people, on whose ratification the legitimacy of a constitution depends and, with it, the legitimacy of the governmental system.

(3) It is a form of law superior to other laws – because (i) it originates in an authority higher than the legislature which makes ordinary law and (ii) the authority of the legislature derives from it and is thus bound by it. The principle of hierarchy of law generally (but not always) leads to the possibility of judicial review of ordinary legislation.

(4) It is entrenched – (i) because its purpose is generally to limit the powers of government, but also (ii) again because of its origins in a higher authority outside the system. It can thus only be changed by special procedures, generally (and certainly for major change) requiring reference back to the constituent power.

Ridley then acknowledges his debt to James Bryce's earlier analysis and considers specific aspects of the British 'constitution'.

The term British constitution is near meaningless ... It is impossible to isolate parts of the system of government to which the label constitutional may authoritatively be attached. There is no test to discriminate between constitutional and less than constitutional elements since labelling has no defined consequence, unlike countries where constitutions are a higher form of law. If used descriptively, as Wheare and others suggest, it is simply a fancy-dress way of saying the British system of government is at best redundant. More dangerous, those who talk of a British constitution may mislead themselves into thinking that there are parts of the system to which a special sanctity attaches. But in that normative sense the term is equally meaningless. When significant parts of the system are reformed, we have no test to tell us whether the outcome is an improper breach of the constitutional order, a proper amendment, or whether the reformed institutions were not part of the 'constitution' at all. I may be told that this is an academic quibble since our democratic politicians know what is of constitutional significance in our way of government, approach such matters differently from other reforms, and are politically if not legally constrained. That, however, is not the case. Our system of government is being changed, with increasing disregard for tradition, the only unwritten rules to which one might appeal as 'constitutional' principles.

There is cause for concern about the muddled way we think about the British 'constitution'; there is even greater cause for concern about the political consequences of its nature. It is sometimes said that our 'constitution' is now under stress as major changes occur far more rapidly than before in its written and unwritten parts. Is this due to changing ideas about how the British system of government should be organised, widely held, or is it simply that the Government of the day is using its power to change the system in the pursuit of its own political goals? Is the constitutional order evolving or is it under attack? We have moved from consensus to conflict in politics: have we moved in that direction, too, as regards our constitutional order, taking that to mean the broad principles underlying the way government is organised and power exercised? Many old principles no longer command universal agreement and there are well-supported demands for new principles. We have had debates on the entrenchment of rights; on federalism or regional devolution as against the unitary state; on the case for consensus rather than majority as a basis for government, on the relative weight of national versus local mandates and the independence of local government; on the duty of civil servants; on electoral reform with all its implications for the operation of government; on who should define the national interest; on open government and official secrecy; on complementing representative democracy by referenda and other forms of participation – and much else. Political disagreement and disagreement on the proper constitutional order are linked. An ideologically-committed Government, determined to implement its policies, will support different constitutional principles from those who want consensus policy-making; those concerned primarily with individual freedom and the rights of the public will support different principles from those who want strong government – and so on. Since opinion is now deeply divided on so many issues, one can probably no longer talk of the constitutional order as if it were a reflection of public opinion.

Notes

1   Two criticisms may be made of Ridley's analysis. Firstly, due to its insistence that any constitution worth the name must be entrenched it excludes constitutions, like those of Singapore, which are fully written (in a constitutional document) but entirely flexible. It may therefore be seen to distance academic analysis too far from political reality (though of course Ridley's whole thesis is that the word 'constitution', having been used politically, is in danger of becoming so vague a term as to be practically meaningless). Secondly, he arguably goes too far in alleging that there are no parts of the British constitutional order to which any special sanctity attaches. It is surely not complacent to assert that if (say) the Government procured the passing of an Act of Parliament which criminalised the publication of any matter critical of Government, it would be universally, and with reason, be regarded as having acted unconstitutionally. A more apt criticism of the present arrangements would be that the normative (conventional) aspects of the constitution would bite only in the most extreme (and therefore unlikely to materialise) cases. In more marginal instances (witness the response to the recent curtailment of the right to

silence)[10] the indeterminacy of the constitutional order prevents such a clear cut verdict.

2   Ridley's argument also rests upon the notion that fundamental attributes of the constitution could all be changed by ordinary Acts of Parliament, which is, after all, the orthodox view. However, recent articles indicate that members of the judiciary, including a very senior member, no longer accept this viewpoint. Lord Woolf has opined[11] that the courts would not apply an act of Parliament which purported to remove the power of judicial review from the courts on the basis that this would represent an intolerable attack upon the Rule of Law, on which the constitution is based. Similarly, Sir John Laws (a judge in the High Court) has argued[12] that the constitution, not Parliament, is supreme, and that the 'higher order law' which the constitution represents would inhibit Parliament from successfully assailing fundamental human rights, democratic institutions and the Rule of Law. He acknowledges that 'constitutional theory has perhaps occupied too modest a place here in Britain', but urges that 'though our constitution is unwritten, it can and must be articulated'.[13]

3   McEldowney, having considered this thesis, notes the solutions offered by Colin Turpin to the various problems identified.

John F McEldowney, *Public Law* (1994), pp21–3

Turpin addresses [*British Government and the Constitution* (1990), pp222–3] much the same question and provides a number of possible solutions. First, the courts provide an important role in maintaining legal rules against the excesses of administrators. This raises a question of how the courts might be said to be themselves accountable and to whom? Still further limitations on the courts' power to interpret legislation are that the courts are ultimately subject to parliamentary sovereignty and their decisions may be reversed by Act of Parliament. Principles of judicial review, exercised by the courts, are restrained by the political decisions of Ministers who are ultimately answerable to Parliament for their decisions. While the courts have been active in developing principles of judicial review, especially in the last decade, they are as de Smith [*Judicial Review of Administrative Action*, 3rd edn, Stevens, 1973, p3] has admitted, 'inevitably sporadic and peripheral'. Not every decision of a public authority is reviewable and the possibility of legal redress through the courts cannot always be available to every aggrieved citizen.

Secondly, the institutions of government may provide their own internal 'checks and balances'. Civil servants and ministers operate within important conventions, principles and understandings. Occasionally these procedures have a legal framework such as the processes and procedures used by government to account for public money. Often the procedures come in the form of minutes, letters, circulars and public statements. Inevitably there are restraints which are never made public but exist beneath the surface – personal promotion, professional standards and ultimately self-advancement all serve to provide

---

10   By virtue of ss34–36, Criminal Justice and Public Order Act 1994. See Part VI, Chapter 4, pp1003–11.

11   See 'Droit Public – English Style' (1995) PL 57.

12   In 'Law and Democracy' (1995) PL 72.

13   Extracts from both these articles appear in Part I, Chapter 4, pp133–5. On the relevance of Britain's membership of the EU to this issue see Part II, Chapter 1, pp198–204.

standards in the machinery of government decision taking.

None of these arrangements, however, will guarantee that government conforms to the acceptable and high standards which should reasonably be expected. Occasionally civil servants and ministers may be subject to scrutiny such as before a select committee or in a parliamentary debate. Even here the ultimate sanction may not be found in resignation or judicial rebuke, but in the day to day political life of the nation. Newspapers and the news media have a contribution to make through investigative journalism in providing information and critical analysis of government activities.

Counterbalancing any likely effect this combination of factors may have, is the secrecy which surrounds government in Britain. It begins with the need for collective Cabinet decision-taking and the anonymity of civil servants. Supported by both the civil and criminal law, Britain's secrecy laws have penetrated deeply inside the very culture of the machinery of government. Commercial confidentiality between government and business or industry in their contractual relationships also provides a reason for secrecy in many government activities.

The third, and final, check on government may be found in the use of elections which ultimately determine the fate of government policies. Political parties, individual politicians and pressure groups all promote the political agenda of the nation. In a constitutional sense political parties look to the electorate for a mandate to govern. Local as well as central government has to account to electoral choices determined by popular support.

The weakness about elections serving as a mainstay of fundamental principles is that the results are not necessarily representative of public opinion. There is a sizeable number, estimated in 1981 at 2.5 million, of eligible electors who are not registered to vote. The turnout at central government elections fluctuates from 70–85% of the electorate. More significantly, the British electoral system does not favour fairness between the number of votes cast at the election in favour of one particular party and the number of seats held in Parliament by that party. The statistical returns of all the general elections since the franchise was reformed in the 19th century show how 'the first past the post system' may distort electoral preferences. For example, at the general election in 1992, the Conservative and Labour parties respectively won 42% and 34% of the votes, each winning 336 and 271 seats. The Liberal Democrats won 18% of the vote but only 20 seats. These results are used to support the claim that the plurality system (as it is known), or two-party system, may discriminate against a third party or minority parties. More importantly, while the present electoral system may favour strong government, ie a Government which holds a majority overall in the House of Commons, this may be at the expense of representative government. To the extent that this is true it may considerably weaken the case for relying on electoral choice as a mainstay of constitutional protection of fundamental principles.

The conclusion which may be drawn from the above analysis is that, while there are many important and disparate elements containing fundamental principles in the working of the UK's constitution, political scientists have been correct to point out to constitutional lawyers, that the Constitution does not fit easily within the ideas of constitutionalism resulting from the experience of modern written constitutions. It may seem surprising that British constitutional lawyers who have written many constitutions throughout the world should be reluctant to adopt a written constitution for Britain.

Question

Is there any unifying thread in the inadequacy of existing accountability mechanisms (as analysed by McEldowney)?

Note

Whilst the unwritten nature of the British constitution may not necessarily be related to the substantive deficiencies discussed above, this characteristic may be blamed for the *uncertainty* of many constitutional doctrines.

P McAuslan and J McEldowney, ' Legitimacy and the Constitution: The Dissonance Between Theory and Practice' in McAuslan and McEldowney (eds), *Law, Legitimacy and the Constitution* (1985), pp12–15

What makes the issue of the legitimacy of our constitutional arrangements so problematic is the general open-endedness of those arrangements; that is, the difficulty of knowing whether a practice or non-practice is or is not constitutional. The example given above of 'packing' the Appellate Committee of the House of Lords with overt political supporters of the ruling party was put forward as a clear example, yet 50 or 60 years ago it would not have been thought particularly remarkable for a Prime Minister to appoint known supporters of his party to the House of Lords or to do likewise with the office of Chief Justice. Judicial appointments in Scotland are still influenced by political considerations and in Northern Ireland by politico-religious ones. Practices, in other words, change over time and may differ in different parts of the UK.

Even where practices may not differ over time, or place, there may be an inconsistency, a lack of knowledge or a long-standing dispute about them, which could make it equally difficult to argue that following or not following a practice was or was not constitutional or legitimate. Probably the best example of this is the use of the Royal Prerogative, and the extent to which the courts may pass judgment on any particular use. Notwithstanding that the Royal Prerogative as a source of power for the Government antedates Acts of Parliament, has been at the root of a civil war and a revolution in England and has been litigated about on countless major occasions in respect of its use both at home and overseas, its scope is still unclear as is the role of the courts in relation thereto. The use by the Prime Minister of powers under the Royal Prerogative to ban trade unions at the Government Communication Headquarters at Cheltenham in 1983 was contested both for its lawfulness – ie whether such powers could be used and if so whether they were used correctly – and also for its legitimacy – ie whether, even if the constitutional power existed, this was a proper and fair use of the power. It can be seen that questions of lawfulness and legitimacy shade into one another here though the answers do not: the lawfulness of the action taken, confirmed by the House of Lords in 1984 [*Council of Civil Service Unions v Minister for the Civil Service* [1984] 3 All ER 935], did not and does not dispose of its legitimacy.

The GCHQ case is valuable for another point. We have pointed out that lawfulness is not to be confused with legitimacy. No more is constitutionality. What the Prime Minister did was not merely lawful; she exercised the constitutional powers of her office in the way in which those powers had always been exercised. That is, the use of the Royal Prerogative as the legal backing for the management of the public service, the principle that a civil servant is a servant of the Crown and holds office at the pleasure of the Crown is one of the best known principles of constitutional law, hallowed by usage and sanctioned by the courts. What is in issue from the perspective of legitimacy is whether the particular use made of that undoubted constitutional power, the manner of its use, and the justification both for the use and manner of use – that considerations of national security required both a banning of trade unions and no consultation with affected officers before the ban was announced – was a fair and reasonable use of power? Did it accord with legitimate expectations of fair and reasonable persons or was it a high-handed exercise of power of a kind more to be expected of an authoritarian Government than one guided by and subscribing to principles of limited government?

In considering the issue of legitimacy in relation to our constitutional arrangements and the exercise of governmental power, what has to be done is to examine a range of practices, decisions, actions (and non-practices, -decisions and -actions), statements and policies which between them can amount to a portrait of power, so that we can form a judgment or an assessment of that power set against the principles of limited government outlined and discussed so far. It is not every failure to comply with law or every constitutional and non-constitutional short cut which adds up to an approach to powers which gives rise to questions of legitimacy. If that were so, there would scarcely be a Government in the last 100 years which could be regarded as legitimate, but it is those uses of power and law which seem to betray or which can only be reasonably explained by a contempt for or at least an impatience with the principles of limited government and a belief that the rightness of the policies to be executed excuse or justify the methods whereby they are executed. If, as we believe to be the case, powers are being so exercised, then the issue of constitutional legitimacy which arises is quite simply: what is the value or use of a constitution based on and designed to ensure the maintenance of a system of limited government if it can, quite lawfully and even constitutionally, be set on one side? Have we not in such circumstances arrived at that 'elective dictatorship' of which Lord Hailsham gave warning in 1977 [The Dimbleby Lecture 1977, expanded in *The Dilemma of Democracy* (London, 1978), especially Chapter 20]:

> It is only now that men and women are beginning to realise that representative institutions are not necessarily guardians of freedom but can themselves become engines of tyranny. They can be manipulated by minorities, taken over by extremists, motivated by the self-interest of organised million [p13]. ...
>
> All the more unfortunate does this become ... when at least one of the parties believes that the prerogative and rights conferred by electoral victory, however narrow, not merely entitle but compel it to impose on the helpless but unorganised majority irreversible changes for which it never consciously voted and to which most of its members are opposed [p21].

Lord Hailsham was writing in the context of the Labour Government of 1974–79 which never had a majority in the House of Commons greater than three and for much of the time was in a minority and reliant on the Liberal and other parties to support it. During that period the Government expanded the scope of the Welfare State, conferred significant legal rights on trade unionists and trade unions, nationalised the shipbuilding and aircraft manufacturing industries and attempted to provide for a measure of devolution of power ... to Scotland and Wales. All these matters were spelt out in manifestos in the two elections of 1974 and, in the case of devolution, there was in those elections, in terms of votes cast, an absolute majority for that in those two countries. Nonetheless it could be argued, and was being so by Lord Hailsham, that a Government elected by a clear minority of the voters, albeit with a majority in the House of Commons would be wrong – ie it would not be legitimate – to attempt to bring about 'irreversible changes' to which the majority of the voters are opposed, and to the extent to which those Labour Governments sought to do that, they were abusing the electoral process and not acting in a legitimate manner.

24

Note

It is important to understand what the authors are arguing at this point. They are *not* saying that they agree with Hailsham's contentions – indeed later in the same essay they note that the changes which he identifies as being 'irreversible' were in fact all reversed by the Thatcher administration (at p16). Rather they are using Hailsham's attack as an illustration of the way in which the indeterminacy of our constitutional arrangements so often leave the legitimacy of Government actions open to question.

THE INFLUENCE OF DICEY

The absence of authoritative codification of the constitution has allowed the role to be taken on, to an extent, by academics. The work of Albert Venn Dicey is generally recognised as one of the key influences on the development of the British constitution and on the way it is perceived.

John F McEldowney, *Public Law* (1994), pp23–5

Recently Paul Craig has assessed Dicey's influence in his book *Public Law and Democracy in the United Kingdom and the United States of America* [OUP, 1990]. Craig makes a number of points about Dicey's influence and importance. First, that Dicey believed in legislative monopoly partly because he assumed that the House of Commons did control the executive with significant and important government power directed through Parliament, which was duly elected. Secondly, that Dicey supported what he articulated as the 'Rule of Law', a term which Craig explains had both a descriptive and a narrative content:

In descriptive terms it was assumed that the regular law predominated, that exercise of broad discretionary power was absent, and that all people were subject to the ordinary law of the realm. Public power resided with Parliament. In normative terms it was assumed that this was indeed a better system than that which existed in France, where special rules and a distinctive regime existed for public law matters [*op cit*, p21].

Thirdly, that in asserting the pre-eminence of ordinary law which he assumed applied to all aspects of government, Dicey rejected for England any coherent or separate body of administrative law which resembled the French *droit administratif*. The courts in Britain were at first reluctant to develop administrative law. They were concerned as to the level of intervention in decision-making which could be justified through judicial review. Craig describes the courts' role in terms of 'non-constitutional review'. This means that the role of the courts is limited by the fact of parliamentary sovereignty. Although Dicey later recanted his objections to *droit administratif* and admitted that English law had developed through the courts, a body of administrative law rules, Dicey's ideas had taken root so firmly that the growth and development of administrative law in Britain has been one of restrained growth until relatively recently when judicial intervention has become more widespread. The hallmark of judicial development has been to reserve a large measure of discretion for the courts in setting the conditions where they might choose to intervene.

Fourthly and finally, Craig notes that Dicey perceptively shifted his views about the constitution. Particular changes such as the increase in the power of Cabinet government, the rise of the party system, the use of referendum to curtail the dangers of democratic government and the growth of administrative discretion, were all recognised by Dicey but they did not cause him to re-think his basic evaluation of the constitution centred in his original text in *Law of the Constitution*. As Craig points out, not only did Dicey's major text remain unaltered, but also constitutional writers who were Dicey's immediate predecessors failed to understand the changing social, political and economic influences which overtook the principles Dicey espoused. This point we will return to when considering the process of elections and the value of democracy and in the influence of Dicey's successors on generations of constitutional lawyers.

The reality of constitutional power, beginning in the latter part of the 19th century in Britain, contains lessons for the concerns of the constitutional lawyer today. Government had expanded its role from its traditional preserve of raising revenue, entering foreign relations and maintaining peace throughout the realm. Legislation, including the redefinition of Parliament's powers in the Parliament Acts of 1911 and 1949, expanded to cover a wide range of social issues such as health, education, local government, factories, railways and, in the 1930s ,malnutrition. This provided a radical transformation in the role of government and the state. The growth of party politics and the strengthening of cabinet decision-making altered the classical principles underlying Dicey's explanation of the constitution, namely that Parliament could control the executive.

Dicey's legacy is that his assumptions, while overtaken by events and of questionable validity, have endured as an explanation of what he perceived as constitutional historical practice. At best, Dicey provides an explanation of the principles which have guided the development of our unwritten constitution – such as the Rule of Law and the sovereignty of Parliament. At worst, Dicey's influence has inhibited the growth of administrative law and restrained constitutional reform in the UK.

Note

McEldowney stresses the dangers that reside in the attempt to transplant Dicey's analysis wholesale from its historical context and apply it to the contemporary constitution. This is a theme given a somewhat different expression by writers on the Left who site Dicey's theory firmly in the context of old fashioned Whiggery's fears, towards the end of the 19th century, at the prospect of truly popular government and the growing influence of the working class; these ideas find expression in the following critical review of Dicey's *Law and Opinion*.

Review of Dicey's *Law and Opinion* (1983) 46 *Modern Law Review* 109

For Dicey, like many others 'lights of liberalism', the reconceptualisation of the law became imperative as their fear of socialism and the breakdown of ordered government increased in the final decades of the 19th century. To 'old Liberals' like Sidgwick, Stephen, Maine, Dicey and Bryce, the Liberal party was trying to buy working class votes with an ambiguous programme of land and social reform which it was feared weakened the defences of property and the power of the propertied classes. As a result, business and landowners united under the Conservative party's banner; the Liberal party lost its crucial middle class support including the 'old Liberal' intellectuals.

Dicey's preoccupation with 'collectivism' and stability has occasionally been acknowledged as an important influence on *Law and Opinion*. However, it also possibly had as material an effect on Dicey's purely legal work, particularly his writings on constitutional law. The conservative sentiments of 'old Liberals' such as Maine, Dicey and Bryce is clearly manifested in their increasing tendency to view the United States as the model constitutional democracy. This aspect of Dicey's thinking helps illuminate the nature and form of his constitutional scholarship. Dicey defined the political problem of the age as '... how to form conservative democracies ... to give to constitutions resting on the will of the people the stability and permanence which has hitherto been found only in monarchical or aristocratic states ... The plain truth is that ... the American republic affords the best example of a conservative democracy; and now that England is becoming democratic, respectable Englishmen are beginning to consider whether the constitution of the United States may not afford means by which ... may be preserved the political conservatism dear and habitual to the governing classes of England' [cited in HA Tulloch, 'Changing Attitudes Towards the United States in the 1880s' (1977) *Historical Journal* 825, at pp834–35]. The basic conservatism underlying Dicey's constitutional writings and his 'Americo-mania' is exemplified in three specific examples. Firstly, in his growing interest in the referendum as a device to mitigate the full impact of parliamentary sovereignty. Secondly, Dicey attributed the stability and conservatism of the United States to its legalistic spirit. In particular, he envied the way in which the Rule of Law, which in Britain grew haphazardly through custom, precedent and convention, was deified in America and enshrined within its fundamental constitution. 'There, law rather than government held the federation together, judges not politicians were the ultimate arbiters, and litigation had replaced legislation.' The prospect of a vast nation ran on the lines of a solicitor's office in Lincoln's Inn must have been very satisfying to Dicey and many of his legal contemporaries [*ibid*, at p837].

Note

Ironically perhaps, liberals today, anxious to see the protection of fundamental rights given greater protection in the constitution, find Dicey's perhaps complacent belief in the effectiveness of such protection under the British constitution rather an irritant. Dicey considered that, as Fenwick sums up his view, the 'absence of a written constitution in the UK is not a weakness but a source of strength ... because the protection of the citizen's liberties are not dependent on vaguely worded constitutional documents but, rather, flow from specific judicial discussions which give the citizen specific remedies for infringement of his or her liberties'.[14] Dicey also placed reliance on the various interpretative presumptions developed by the judges, by means of which they resolved any ambiguities in a statute in favour of the liberty of the subject. Many commentators now believe that the common law is unable to offer a satisfactory level of protection in this area. This debate will be considered in more detail in Part VI, Chapter 1. However, the controversy is of interest here because the ability of a constitution to afford effective protection to fundamental rights is widely seen as a key criterion to be used in its normative assessment. TRS Allan has argued that the easy association of more effective rights protection with Bills of Rights must be challenged.

TRS Allan, 'Constitutional Rights and Common Law' (1991) 11 *Oxford Journal of Legal Studies* 453–55

It is today often argued, and widely assumed, that the common law is inherently

---

14 Fenwick, *Civil Liberties* (1994), p81.

inferior to other, more modern, arrangements for protecting constitutional rights. It has become fashionable to identify modern constitutionalism with enacted or entrenched Bills or Charters of Rights – so much so that a reference in same breath to common law and constitutional rights now sounds strange, almost paradoxical. It seems to be thought that constitutional rights imply a 'written constitution'; neither common law nor ordinary statute can supply sufficient legal or moral authority.

When counsel recently suggested that a statute had introduced a 'constitutional right' – a right to refuse disclosure of sources of published information – the House of Lords was largely unsympathetic [*Secretary of State for Defence v Guardian Newspapers* [1985] AC 339]. For example, Lord Roskill rejected a submission that the relevant section was 'akin to an "entrenched" provision in a written constitution': the statute was clearly vulnerable to ordinary legislative repeal. Moreover, 'the fact that a section affects specific freedoms or confers specific privileges or immunities. whether on individuals or on the media. does not give it a special constitutional status in our law' [*ibid*, 369]. Characteristically, Lord Scarman was more receptive to counsel's argument: 'There being no written constitution, his words will sound strange to some. But they may more accurately prophesy the direction in which English law has to move under the compulsions to which it is now subject than many are yet prepared to accept' [*ibid*, 361]. If, however, it is impermissible to attribute special constitutional status to statutory rights, it may still be insisted that constitutional rights – in one sense of that expression – exist at common law, even if they are not 'entrenched' against ordinary legislative encroachment. It is often asserted that the common law provides a poor foundation for protecting basic civil liberties because its concept of liberty is only residual. Eric Barendt has written of Great Britain that, 'The absence of any constitutional or legislative statement of a freedom of speech means that the liberty is largely residual. In other words, the freedom exists where statute or common law rules do not restrict it' [*Freedom of Speech* (Oxford 1985), p29]. He accepts, however, that freedom of expression is also recognised as a principle of the common law; and it follows that it cannot be *wholly* residual. A legal principle must be applied, where it is relevant, both in the interpretation of statutes and in deciding particular cases at common law. It does not, of course, follow that freedom of speech is adequately protected in English law; but the question is plainly a complex one which justifies further analysis.

Barendt observes that the protection of freedom of speech may be entrusted (as it is in Britain) to a political tradition of government restraint, or to legislative principles which are not enforceable by the courts. 'The case for constitutional guarantees rests on further contentions ... first, that the legislature and government are not to be relied on always to respect the freedom, and second, that the courts in the absence of a constitutional text are unable to give adequate weight to the freedom when it conflicts with other public values and interests' [*ibid* p299]. Although the first contention may be readily accepted, the second needs closer inspection. For it is not always clear how the weight of fundamental principles – or of the basic rights which they enshrine – can be enhanced by positive enactment, even as a 'constitutional text'.

It is, of course, possible to strengthen individual rights against legislative encroachment by permitting the courts to strike down offending statutes; the right to freedom of speech (for example) becomes a 'constitutional right' in that sense. In effect, necessary judgments of the relative weights of individual rights and conflicting public interests are made by judges rather than politicians: if the weight of such rights is thereby enhanced, it is because they are accorded more weight by courts than by legislatures and governments.

It is a controversial question whether there are any common law rights in this sense, and if so, what limits they impose on the legislature. It is not universally accepted that parliamentary sovereignty is wholly unlimited, and many lawyers would reject Dicey's view that physical resistance is the only legitimate response even to the grossest legislative invasion of fundamental liberties [*The Law of the Constitution*, 10th edn (1959), pp78–81]. In *Attorney-General v Times Newspapers*, the House of Lords upheld the award of an injunction restraining the *Sunday Times* from publishing an article concerning the negligence action arising out of the deformities caused by the Thalidomide drug. Lord Diplock held that such public discussion of the merits of the action would amount to contempt of court as likely to inhibit the litigants' exercise of their 'constitutional right to have their legal rights and obligations ascertained and enforced in courts of law' [[1974] AC 273, 310]. Although the statement inevitably suffers from the ambiguity of the expression 'constitutional right', Lord Diplock may fairly be interpreted as acknowledging a fundamental right of access to the courts for the determination of one's legal rights, which even Parliament may not be lawfully empowered wholly to deny. Sir Robin Cooke has reached similar conclusions from reflection on Lord Diplock's speech in *Re Racal Communications* [[1981] AC 374], rejecting the distinction between jurisdictional and non-jurisdictional errors of law on the part of administrative tribunals. He suggests that:

> ... we are on the brink of open recognition of a fundamental rule of our mainly unwritten constitution: namely that determination of questions of law is always the ultimate responsibility of the courts of general jurisdiction. ... Inherent in our system of checks and balances is the practical truth that every Act of Parliament, even one touching the jurisdiction of the courts themselves, is ultimately subject to interpretation by the superior courts of general jurisdiction. ... If these courts were to accept that some Act deprived them of a significant part of that function, they would be acquiescing *pro tanto* in a revolution' ['The Struggle for Simplicity in Administrative Law, *Judicial Review of Administrative Action in the 1980s* (ed M Taggart, 1986) 10].

The existence and competence of independent and impartial courts of law may reasonably be taken to be an integral and inseparable feature of the constitutional arrangements under which Parliament's sovereignty is generally acknowledged.

Notes

1 Whilst Allan may be right to say that, as a matter of constitutional theory, rights may be effectively protected through the development of judicial principles (the New Zealand judiciary appear to be leading the way in this respect),[15] when, later in the article, Allan presents the evidence for the realisation of this theory in English common law, 'a rather ironic pattern emerges'. Allan contents that the case law shows support for civil liberties; he quotes from cases which purportedly demonstrate his contention – and then finds himself apologising for the inadequacies of the Law Lords' approach. Having cited *Wheeler v Leicester City Council* (1985)[16] as an instance of the sturdy defence of free speech, he concedes that Lord Roskill did not use free speech grounds at all while Lord Templeman did, in general terms, but unfortunately 'failed to address the level of principle demanded by the freedoms at issue' [p459]. When he turns to the *Spycatcher* litigation,

---

15 See David Feldman, *Civil Liberties and Human Rights in England and Wales* (1993), pp53–4, esp n 74.

16 [1985] AC 1054; 2 A11 ER 1106, HL.

he is forced to concede from the outset that the speeches are 'disappointing'. Having praised Lord Keith for affirming the general freedom to speak, he then goes on to admit that his lordship failed to injunct only because 'all possible damage to the interests of the Crown had already been done' and that he was 'unwilling to ... base his decision on any considerations of freedom of the press' [p460].[17]

2   A perusal of the law reports can leave the reader with not only a lack of evidence to support Allan's thesis, but also positive evidence against it. Anthony Lester considers two such cases.

Anthony Lester QC, 'Fundamental Rights: the UK Isolated?' (1984) Public Law 46, 49

Let me give two examples of the way in which the absence of a system of positive principles of public law now favours public authorities at the expense of personal freedom. In *Malone's* case [*Malone v Metropolitan Police Commissioner* [1979] Ch 344], Sir Robert Megarry VC decided that, since there is no general right of privacy in English law, the police are as much entitled to tap my telephone as any private person. The police are not private persons. They are public officers, performing public duties, in their official capacity; the State is responsible under the ECHR if they fail to respect the right to privacy. But, because the right to privacy, guaranteed by Article 8 of the Convention, has not been incorporated into the UK law, neither the police nor the Home Secretary have any enforceable public law obligation to respect the privacy of the individual.

The second example is *habeas corpus*. For Dicey [*An Introduction to the Study of the Constitution* (1959), p199], although the Habeas Corpus Acts 'declare no principle and define no rights, they are for practical purposes worth 100 constitutional articles guaranteeing individual liberty'. But in two judgments the European Court of Human Rights has held that he English remedy of *habeas corpus* is too narrow to accord with the right to liberty guaranteed by Article 5 of the Convention, an Article which is regarded elsewhere in Europe as a distinctively Anglo-Saxon guarantee. In the *Irish State* case, the European Court held [*Ireland v the United Kingdom* (1978) 2 EHRR 25, paras 81–84, 200, 220] that, because the judges could not inquire into the reasonableness or fairness of the suspicion held by a person effecting an arrest under the special powers then operative in Northern Ireland or of the decision to exercise the power of the arrest, the remedy of *habeas corpus* was inadequate. If there had not been a valid derogation because of the state of public emergency in Northern Ireland, there would have been a breach of Article 5(4). In *X v the United Kingdom* [(1981) series A no 46, 4 EHRR 188, paras 55–59] the European Court held that a judicial review as limited as that available in the *habeas corpus* procedure was not sufficient for the continuing confinement of a patient in a special secure mental hospital. The vice was that, under English law:

> When the terms of a statute afford the executive a discretion, whether wide or narrow, the review exerciseable by the [English] courts in *habeas corpus* proceedings will bear solely upon the conformity of the exercise of that discretion with the empowering statute.

Pace Dicey, Article 5 of the Convention, guaranteeing liberty in terms of positive principle, is for practical purposes worth 100 Habeas Corpus Acts.

---

17   Fenwick, *Civil Liberties* (1994), pp84–5. See further, Part VI, Chapter 1.

Notes

1   Since Lord Lester wrote this piece, an important decision has leant renewed credibility to the Dicyean thesis. In *Derbyshire v Times Newspapers* (1993)[18] the House of Lords found that the importance the common law attached to freedom of speech was such that defamation could not be available as an action to local (or – *obiter* – central) government (see further Part VI, Chapter 3).

2   Whatever the significance of the decision in *Derbyshire*, it is plain that the Lords were only able to come to it because the law was not settled in this area. Where, however, legislation clearly establishes a framework in which individual rights are accorded very low weight, the judges can do little about it; indeed, where national security is in play, they seem to have little inclination to do so. Ian Leigh considers a representative decision which was concerned with the legality of the detention (pending deportation) of one Cheblak pursuant to regulations made under s18 Immigration Act 1971.

Ian Leigh, 'The Gulf War Deportations and the Courts' (1991) *Public Law* 333–35

The relevant regulations provided that a notice of deportation had to include a statement of the 'reason for the decision' [Immigration Appeals (Notices) Regulations 1984 (SI No 2040)]. Cheblak was served with a notice that he would be deported because his departure from the UK 'would be conducive to the public good for reasons of national security'. It was subsequently claimed that this notice was deficient in failing to provide sufficient details of his alleged wrongdoing. The argument failed because the Court of Appeal found that, within the structure of the Act, 'national security' was a reason amplifying the ground that the deportee's continued presence was not 'conducive to the public good'. In Lord Donaldson's view the applicant was asking not for reasons but rather for 'reasons for reasons', to which there was no statutory entitlement [*ex parte Cheblak* [1991] 2 All ER at 329, citing *ex parte Swati* [1986] 1 WLR 477, 490 (Parker LJ)].

The court went on to reject an argument that the reasons given were insufficient. Lord Donaldson held that the court could not, in the absence of bad faith, go behind an affidavit sworn for the Home Office that to give further details might itself threaten national security. Nolan and Beldam LJJ both asserted the court's independent power of inquiry, under the Habeas Corpus Act 1816, s3, into the sufficiency of the reasons, even in cases to which s15(3) of the 1971 Act applied. However, they too found that national security prevented further inquiry in this case.

The argument over reasons was in the event a somewhat academic one so far as Cheblak was concerned, because he was provided with fuller details of the reasons for the decision under the provision in the Immigration Rules connected with the non-statutory review of his case. However, this was not at the time of his detention in the form of a statutory notice, but by a statement read out in court and a letter. The central passage, which bears also on the attack to the substance of the deportation decision, stated:

> The Iraqi Government has openly threatened to take terrorist action against unspecified Western targets if hostilities break out in the Gulf. In the light of this, your known links with an organisation which we believe could take

---

18   [1993] 1 All ER 1011.

such action in support of the Iraqi regime make your presence in the UK an unacceptable security risk [[1991] 2 A11 ER at 324].

The applicant argued that, in basing the decision to deport upon this reason, the Home Secretary had either failed to take account of all relevant circumstances or had acted irrationally. The applicant contended that he had no terrorist connections and was opposed to terrorism. Not surprisingly these arguments were met squarely at first instance and in the Court of Appeal with judicial protestations of non-justiciability because of national security. Since the court was presented with affidavit evidence of the Secretary of State's assertion of national security, it regarded its supervisory role as restricted, unless it could be shown (and it could not) that the Home Secretary has acted in bad faith. All three judgements are replete with the now customary arguments that national security is for the executive not the courts, coupled with expressions of regret at the possible infringement of civil liberties. For readers of *GCHQ* [*CCSU v Minister for the Civil Service* [1985] AC 384], *Ruddock* [*Secretary for the Home Department, ex p Ruddock* [1987] 2 A11 ER 518] and *Hodges* [*Director of GCHQ, ex p Hodges, The Times*, 26 July 1988], this is familiar terrain. On this occasion Lord Donaldson sugared the pill by referring, first, to the Secretary of State's accountability to Parliament for the decisions to deport and, secondly, to the more satisfactory nature of the advisory panel's proceedings for dealing with the issues which the applicant wished to raise. The courts would act as a long stop to supervise the actions of the panel but, as the *dicta* in *Hosenball* make clear, there would have to be exceptional irregularity before they would be prepared to intervene.

Although it is certainly arguable that political accountability for national security decisions is preferable to judicial supervision, existing constitutional practice seems flattered by Lord Donaldson's claim that the Home Secretary 'is fully accountable to Parliament for his decisions whether or not to deport and, as part of that accountability, for any failure to heed the advice of the non-statutory panel'. 'Full accountability' is likely to amount to little more than the minister's preparedness to suffer the temporary embarrassment of refusing to answer questions on grounds of national security. Accountability for failure to follow the panel's advice is fictitious: since the panel's recommendations are confidential, there is no way of knowing whether or not they are followed in a particular case.

Note

The protection afforded to deportees considered to pose a threat to national security has not improved since Leigh wrote. In the recent case of *Secretary of State for the Home Department, ex p McQuillan*[19] the Divisional Court once again refused to review an exclusion order made by the Home Secretary against a Northern Irish citizen under s5 of the Prevention of Terrorism (Temporary Provisions) Act 1989. The applicant applied for review of the Home Secretary's original decision to exclude him from Great Britain and his subsequent refusal to reconsider that decision in spite of the changed circumstances of the applicant. It was held that, despite evidence adduced by the applicant that (a) he had not at any time been involved in any terrorist activity and (b) Sedley J's finding that there was a 'real and continuing threat to [his] life' and consequential 'inhuman treatment'[20] if he was forced to live in Northern Ireland, the Home Secretary's decision must stand; he could not be required to

---

19 [1995] 4 All ER 400.
20 *Ibid*, at 423.

give any reasons for his decision, and thus the court was unable to assess its rationality, legality or otherwise.

A WRITTEN CONSTITUTION?

May it be concluded that a written constitution, incorporating an entrenched Bill of Rights, is the only viable answer to the deficiencies explored above? Whilst the Conservative party remains resolutely opposed to such a step, a number of writers on the Left are also sceptical. In what follows, John Griffith sketches a critique of such a reform, using as examples the proposals for constitutional reform brought forward by Lords Hailsham and Scarman at the end of the 1970s.

John Griffith, 'The Political Constitution', (1979) 42 *Modern Law Review* 1, 8–18

It is clear that Lord Hailsham is particularly concerned about the legislative powers of governments, particularly minority governments. 'Fundamental and irreversible changes', he says, 'ought only to be imposed, if at all, in the light of an unmistakable national consensus. ... My thesis is that our institutions must be so structurally altered that, so far as regards permanent legislation, the will of the majority will always prevail against that of the party composing the executive for the time being, and that, whoever may form the Government of the day will be compelled to follow procedures and policies compatible with the nature of parliamentary democracy and the rule of freedom under law' [*The Dilemma of Democracy* (1978), pp21–22].

Within the limits of the theme of his book he indicates three types of safeguards. The first is legal and is the setting of limits 'beyond which politicians may not be allowed to go without a special mandate protected by proportional voting and referenda'. The second type would 'so rearrange the balance of forces within the separate organs of the constitution as to make dominance by any one of them impossible'. The third type of safeguard 'involves an examination of existing voting processes and the value, if any, of referenda on particular issues' [p 68].

Lord Hailsham's constitutional package includes a Bill of Rights, a proportionately elected second chamber, a limit by law on the right of Parliament to legislate without restriction, and devolution to Scotland, Wales, Northern Ireland and the English regions in a federal structure. The object of this new constitution would be 'to institutionalise the theory of limited government' [p226]. Lord Hailsham refers with alarm to the position 'when a Government elected by a small minority of voters, and with a slight majority in the House, regards itself as entitled, and, according to its more extreme supporters, bound to carry out every proposal in its election manifesto. This has happened, he says, 'more than once in the past few years and it seems to me that, *at almost any cost*, we must ensure that it cannot happen again' [p129] (emphasis added).

Lord Scarman's prescription is close to Lord Hailsham's. Lord Scarman wants a new constitutional settlement, the basis of which would be entrenched provisions (including a Bill of Rights) and restraints upon administrative and legislative power, protecting it from attack by a bare majority in Parliament; a supreme court charged with the duty of protecting the constitution; an immediate study of the problems of codification, drafting and interpretation in the new context of entrenched provisions and codified law; and the establishment of machinery for handling the problem of the law's development and reform, especially of administrative law [*English Law – The New Dimension*, pp81–82].

The philosophical basis of Lord Hailsham's position, as we have seen, rests on the dangers (as he sees them) of the present way of carrying on. For this he blames the sexual coupling of utilitarianism and legal positivism which produced elective dictatorship. By legal positivism he means the definition of law as nothing but the command of the ruler. At one and the same time he accepts the positivist analysis and yet disapproves of it.

> [The enforcement of law] says Lord Hailsham: rests, of course, upon those possessing political power, and since the possession of political power cannot self-evidently be said to be based on moral right, this has given rise throughout the ages to legal positivism in one of its many forms, the simplest expressed of which is that of Austin, that law is nothing else but the command of the ruler. In a sense all lawyers must be legal positivists. They could not advise their clients if they did not take political authority as a given fact and argue their cases before the established courts without questioning the basis upon which they were established. Political authority in the modern world is almost always based historically upon some forcible acquisition of power, and since it is in the nature of sovereignty to demand a monopoly of force, even the most primitive of sovereigns is faced with the necessity of settling disputes, enforcing the settlements, and imposing results on those who take the law into their own hands [*op cit*, p88].

The central question, says Lord Hailsham, both for jurisprudence and for political theory, is that law and government are about compulsion. And so justification is needed and this is to be found not in utilitarianism but in notions like 'justice and morality, right and wrong, responsibilities, duties and moral rights' [p91].

Griffith then goes on to consider, by way of illustration, the Thalidomide litigation in which the British law of contempt of court was found by the European Court of Human Rights to be unduly restrictive of freedom of expression (see Part VI, Chapter 3).

> To my mind the whole story shows why we should not try to solve our problems by the application of ... a Bill of Rights. If we incorporate the European Convention into our domestic law, questions like those in the Thalidomide case will be left for determination by the legal profession as they embark on the happy and fruitful exercise of interpreting wholly principles and even woollier exceptions. Clearly the House of Lords will take some persuading that restrictions on freedom of expression are not 'necessary' when the conflict with some more positive Rule of Law.
>
> The solution to such problems should not lie with the imprecision of Bills of Rights or the illiberal instincts of judges. The law of contempt of court is highly unsatisfactory. It has been recently examined by a committee whose report [Cmnd 5794] has been commented on in a White Paper [Cmnd 7145]. Arguments continue about that report and the White Paper. And they may result in some hard, blackletter reform of the common law which can be put in a statute in words which will be relatively precise.
>
> If we had a Bill of Rights, such attempts at reform would be fobbed off. And political questions of much day-to-day significance would, even more than at present, be left to decision by the judiciary.
>
> But the objection is more broadly based.
>
> As part of the recent movement to reintroduce natural law concepts into the

theory and practice of politics, 'the law' has been raised from its proper and useful function as a means towards ends (about which it is possible to have differing opinions) to the level of a general concept. On this view, individual rules of law may be good or bad, but 'the law' is undeniably good and must be upheld or chaos will come again. there is more than a suspicion of sleight of hand here. For nobody, except committed anarchists, suggests that 'the law' should be dispensed with.

The ground is then shifted slightly and what become sacred and untouchable is something called the Rule of Law. The Rule of Law is an invaluable concept for those who wish not to change the present set up. A person may be said not to be in favour of the Rule of Law if he is critical of the Queen, the Commissioner of Metropolitan Police, the Speaker of the House of Commons, or Lord Denning. Statutes may be contrary to the Rule of Law (like some, but not all, Indemnity Acts) but the common law, it seems, can never be. Objection to the rules of international law in their application to the UK is wholly excusable on proper occasions. Defiance of regulations and directives emanating from Brussels may often be accounted a positive virtue.

If the Rule of Law means that there should be proper and adequate machinery for dealing with criminal offences and for ensuring that public authorities do not exceed their legal powers, and for insisting that official penalties may not be inflicted save on those who have broken the law, then only an outlaw could dispute its desirability. But when it is extended to mean more than that, it is a fantasy invented by Liberals of the old school in the late 19th century and patented by the Tories to throw a protective sanctity around certain legal and political institutions and principles which they wish to preserve at any cost. Then it is become a new metaphysic, seeming to resolve the doubts of the faithful with an old dogma.

The proposals for a written constitution, for a Bill of Rights, for a House of Lords with greater powers to restrain governmental legislation, for regional assemblies, for a supreme court to monitor all these proposals, are attempts to write laws so as to prevent Her Majesty's Government from exercising powers which hitherto that Government has exercised.

The fundamental political objection is this: that law is not and cannot be a substitute for politics. This is a hard truth, perhaps an unpleasant truth. For centuries political philosophers have sought that society in which government is by laws and not by men. It is an unattainable ideal. Written constitutions do not achieve it. Nor do Bills of Rights or any other devices. They merely pass political decisions out of the hands of politicians and into the hands of judges or other persons. To require a supreme court to make certain kinds of political decisions does not make those decisions any less political.

I believe firmly that political decisions should be taken by politicians. In a society like ours this means by people who are removable. It is an obvious corollary of this that the responsibility and accountability of our rules should be real and not fictitious. And of course our existing institutions, especially the House of Commons, need strengthening. And we need to force Governments out of secrecy and into the open. So also the freedom of the Press should be enlarged by the amendment of laws which restrict discussion. Governments are too easily able to act in an authoritarian manner. But the remedies are political. It is not by attempting to restrict the legal powers of government that we shall defeat authoritarianism. It is by insisting on open government.

That is why these present proposals by Lord Hailsham, Lord Scarman and others are not only mistaken but positively dangerous. They seem to indicate a way by which potential tyranny can be defeated by the intervention of the law and the intervention of institutional devices. There is no such way. Only political control, politically exercised, can supply the remedy.

The philosophical objection to the new proposals stems from an unease about a formulation based exclusively on rights. I suspect I shall be misunderstood on this. So I had better begin by saying that my distrust of Governments and of the claims made by those in authority is as profound as any man's and more profound than most.

I begin by rejecting the existence of that abstraction called the state ... the state is yet another metaphysic invention to conceal the reality of political power. Secondly, then, I reject the notion that those who hold political power have any moral right or moral authority to do so, however they came to their positions. They are there and they have power. No more. Thirdly, following from what I have said, the power they exercise is not special. It is no different in kind from the power exercised by other groups in the community like the owners or controllers of large accumulations of capital or the leaders of large trade unions. Fourthly, it is misleading to speak of certain rights of the individual as being fundamental in character and inherent in the person of the whole individual. As an individual I make claims on the authorities who control the society in which I live. If I am strong enough – and I shall have to join with others to be so – my claim may be recognised within certain limits. It may even be given legal status. There is a continuous struggle between the rulers and the ruled about the size and shape of these claims and that is what is meant by Curran's statement, that the condition upon which God hath given liberty to man is eternal vigilance although, as you will have gathered, I am not persuaded that we have a divine donor in this respect.

I referred earlier to the wearisome condition of humanity which results from the intolerable dilemma – which has nevertheless to be tolerated – of our being at the same time individual and social animals. As an individual I may say that I have certain rights – the right to life being the most fundamental. But those who manage the society in which I live will reply: 'put up your claim and we will look at it; don't ring us, we'll ring you'.

In this political, social sense there are no over-riding human rights; no right to freedom, to trial before conviction, to representation before taxation; no right not to be tortured, not to be summarily executed. Instead there are political claims by individuals and by groups.

One danger of arguing from rights is that the real issues can be evaded. What are truly questions of politics and economics are presented as questions of law.

But paradoxically, arguments advanced avowedly for the protection of human rights are often concealed political propaganda. Those for a written constitution, a Bill of Rights, a supreme court and the rest are attempts to resolve political conflicts in our society in a particular way, to minimise change, to maintain (so far as possible) the existing distribution of political and economic power.

So also the appeals to 'national consensus', to 'community morality', to fundamental legal principles, to theories of justice, likewise enable the political and economic conflicts to be, if not ignored, at least relegated to the kind of lower class arguments that take place below stairs.

It seems to me that to call political claims 'inherent rights' is to mythologise and confuse the matter. The struggle is political throughout and moral only in the purely subjective sense that I may think I ought to be granted what I claim. Those in authority may think I ought not to be granted my claim. And there is no logic which says that their view is more based on their self-advancement (rather than, say, the public good) than mine is. ...

Similarly with lawmakers, like ministers and judges. They have regard to the political ends they subserve. Partly politicians being rather less homogeneous a group than judges are likely to make decisions more distinguishable then the decisions judges make. And the political ends which Ministers subserve are not identical with those which judges subserve. But it seems to me that to suggest ministers or judges are seeking abstractions like justice or the conscience of the community or whatever is 'nonsense on stilts'. They are political animals pursuing political ends which are far narrower, more limited and more short term, than those abstractions.

I am therefore much more concerned to create situations in which groups of individuals may make their political claims and seek to persuade Governments to accept them. I therefore want greater opportunities for discussion, more open government, less restriction on debate, weaker Official Secrets Acts, more access to information, stronger pressure from back-benchers, changes in the law of contempt of court.

A further advantage in treating what others call rights as political claims is that their acceptance or rejection will be in the hands of politicians rather than judges, and the advantage of that is not that politicians are more likely to come up with the right answer but that, as I have said, they are so much more vulnerable than judges and can be dismissed or at least made to suffer in their reputation. ...

Questions

1 When Griffith states that 'A person may be said to be not in favour of the Rule of Law if he is critical of the Queen, the Commissioner of Metropolitan Police, the Speaker of the House of Commons or Lord Denning', is he criticising the substance of the doctrine or its misuse? If he is merely complaining that the doctrine is abused (like most theories), is he saying anything of interest?

2 Griffith asks for 'more open government, less restriction on debate, weaker Official Secrets Acts, more access to information'. He also states (in an unquoted section of the article) that he does not see the problem as being 'the sovereignty of Parliament as the legislative institution'. But suppose that, through political campaigning, such reforms were introduced; is it not a 'problem' that any Government which found the reforms inconvenient could almost certainly procure their repeal by Parliament? What is the core of Griffith's arguments against legally guaranteed protection for freedom of information?

Notes

1 Griffith's argument is that questions of rights are political and should be resolved by politicians, who are accountable. The problem with this approach appears to be this: rights are usually rights against Government – eg the right to freedom of information which gives the electorate access to information which may be embarrassing to the Government, or the right to life or liberty of the person which prevents the British Government from using its armed forces to kill known members of the IRA in the absence of an immediate threat by them. Therefore, governments have a vested interest in eroding rights, in order to increase their freedom of action. If there are no legally entrenched rights, then the only sanction to prevent governments

from eroding rights is the fear that this will result in political unpopularity. Unfortunately, at least in the UK, questions of rights are simply not major political issues. For example, the 1992 general election was fought almost entirely on social and economic issues,[21] in particular on taxation, the economy, education and health. At the time of writing, the Government has recently severely curtailed the right to silence[22] without any indication that this has damaged its standing with the general electorate. The political accountability on rights issues which, in Griffith's scheme, both argues against 'legalising' rights and supposedly ensures their protection, is simply not there in practice.

2   Griffith describes both judges and politicians as 'political animals, pursuing political ends'. Whatever the argument about the extent to which judges are affected by their personal political views (and Griffith's thesis, put forward elsewhere,[23] that the judges are strongly influenced by their ingrained conservatism, has been vigorously attacked)[24] Griffith surely fails to make a basic distinction: whilst judges purport to approach a politically contentious legal issue from a standpoint of neutrality, and must therefore at least be seen to be non-biased in their assessment, politicians make a profession out of constant, unremitting bias in favour of the policies of the party to which they owe their allegiance.

3   The debate about whether the UK should now adopt a written constitution goes wider than the Bill of Rights issue, however. In 1976 Lord Hailsham put forward the view, touched on by Griffith above, that the current constitutional arrangements amounted to an elective dictatorship for which the only remedy was a written constitution. This view has since been endorsed many times from the other end of the political spectrum. It arises due to a perception that the House of Commons has become subordinate to the Government which controls it through the party machine. Lord Hailsham wrote that legislation of major importance was passed with wholly inadequate debate and that Parliament was being reduced to little more than a rubber stamp. He also considered that, although absolute power was conferred on Parliament, those powers were concentrated in an executive Government formed out of one party which, due to the electoral system, might not fairly represent the popular will.

4   When the Government in power has a large majority and is putting forward a political programme of a strongly marked tendency which diverges from moderate policies, this problem tends to be exacerbated. Ewing and Gearty, observing government in the 1980s, commented: 'Mrs Thatcher has merely utilised to the full the scope for untrammelled power latent in the UK constitution but obscured by the hesitancies and scruples of previous

---

21   For an analysis of the campaigning in that election see Kavanagh and Jones, 'Voting Behaviour' in Jones (ed), *Politics UK* (1994), pp193 *et seq*.

22   By virtue of the Criminal Justice and Public Order Act (1994); for discussion, see Part VI, Chapter 4.

23   *The Politics of the Judiciary*, 3rd edn (1985).

24   K Minogue, 'The Biases of the Bench' TLS, 6 January 1978, and S Lee, *Judging Judges* (1988).

consensus-based political leaders'.[25] An example which might be given is the use of a three line whip against a Conservative back-bencher's Private Members Bill (Richard Shepherd's Bill in 1988, intended to reform Section Two of the Official Secrets Act 1911) and guillotining of parliamentary debate on the Official Secrets Bill 1989. Government secrecy which cloaks the actions of ministers hampers the Opposition in scrutinising their actions. The corollary of Government secrecy is misinformation: the case of *Ponting* (1985)[26] testified to its extent whilst the Scott Inquiry provided a more thorough dissection of the politics of secrecy.[27] These and other issues are considered by McEldowney below.

John F McEldowney, *Public Law* (1994), pp689–93

Demands for a written constitution have come from the Liberal Democrats ['*We the people ...*' – *Towards a Written Constitution (1990)*], the Institute of Public Policy Research [*The Constitution of the United Kingdom* (1991)] and from Charter 88. Prominent constitutional lawyers have called for a written constitution, most notably Lord Scarman ['Bill of Rights and Law Reform' in Holme and Elliott, *Time for a New Constitution* (1988), pp103–111] and Lord Hailsham, though the latter has been less enthusiastic lately. In recent years an increasing body of intellectual opinion has favoured constitutional reform from political thinkers on both the Left and the Right in politics. However, contemporary writing of the 1980s and 90s is reminiscent of writing in the 1970s and even past diagnosis of the post-war period. Oliver has identified [*Government in the United Kingdom* (1991), pp3–40] a number of factors which may have created pressure for reform and may be summarised as follows.

The post-war consensus over the range of activities carried out by the public sector has come under strain. Polarisation of the two major political parties has contributed to marked differences in attitudes to the public sector. The election of Mrs Thatcher's Government in 1979 and four successive Conservative party election victories thereafter have allowed many fundamental changes to be introduced into the delivery of public services. Privatisation is also relevant in the trend away from state ownership in favour of Public Company Act companies for the delivery of public services. Market forces and the consumer are perceived as satisfactory regulators of public services with the minimum of direct state intervention.

Changes in policy perceptions in the early 1980s about the role of local government have created tensions in the relationship between central and local government. The trend in favour of more centralised power has encouraged stronger central government as preferable to weak local authorities. Centralisation has a number of motives behind it. A desire to change existing institutions and cultures in line with a greater reliance on market enterprise is more readily accommodated with central control. Strong political ideologies in the 1980s facilitated more central control. Popular causes such as privatisations and council house sales to tenants are seen as attainable only from a strong executive government and carry favour with those who see strong government as a virtue of the UK's political system. At the same time, discontent over the

---

25 Ewing and Gearty, *Freedom under Thatcher* (1989), p7.

26 Crim LR 318.

27 For the Scott Report, see Part IV, Chapter 2, pp575–89, 591, 595–6 and Part III, Chapter 1, pp358–60, 363–67, 377–78.

UK's constitutional arrangements argue for reform and some go as far as to include a written constitution.

Supporters of constitutional reform highlight the weaknesses in parliamentary control over the executive as evidenced by the accretion of centralised governmental power. In the aftermath of a period of strong government with large overall majorities, electoral reform is favoured, linked to the need for a fairer balance in the composition of the House of Commons.

There is also criticism on how the Cabinet form of government decision-making operates. This relates to the view that the Cabinet is not able to make longer term strategic plans. The Thatcher inheritance suggested that the Cabinet system had developed into a presidential style of government. However, Mrs Thatcher's resignation suggested to some commentators that Cabinet government had been restored. Currently there is concern that political divisions under a more collective style of government may make the Government appear weak in office but not able to exercise authority. It is argued that the Cabinet system of government needs reform. Oliver noted:

> Neither the Cabinet as a whole nor ministers individually have the support of staff that could enable them to take a strategic view of Government policy, or indeed of the policy in their own departments.

During the life cycle of party politics, the style and perception of government may differ, very often according to the personality of the Prime Minister. However, to some commentators, weaknesses in the institutions of the Government such as the Cabinet system are apparent and suggest that reforms should be introduced.

The ethos of governmental secrecy is also perceived as a major weakness in the system of parliamentary accountability. This is said to limit the amount of information available on the administration of government and allows the Government too much flexibility in deciding on the ground rules which apply to its decisions. The temptation is to see secrecy, as supported by the law, as self-serving the interests of Government in its political objectives rather than serving the interests of Parliament. The quality of Government decision-making is said to suffer from the lack of transparency in Government consultation and discussion. When Government chooses to be more open, such as the recent appointment of seven advisers to the Chancellor of the Exchequer and the Treasury's publication of a *Monthly Monetary Report* together with the Bank of England's *Inflation Report*, such steps are welcomed and said to improve Government decision-making, and increase parliamentary accountability. This in turn may increase Government credibility in the money markets and with financial institutions. Demanding greater openness in government may not necessarily increase Parliament's role in holding the Government to account for its actions.

Centralisation is said to cause pressure on the efficiency and effectiveness of Government because the system of Cabinet decision-making suffers from 'overload.' This phenomenon is not confined to the Government but may be found in the various parliamentary methods of accountability such as select committees, debates on the passage of Bills and the scrutiny of government legislation. The tendency is that back-bench MPs may become overworked and inefficient. It appears impossible for any single MP to undertake a broad oversight of the entire working of government. The technical detail and complexities make this impossible as well as the scale of the enterprise for which individual MPs are lacking in resources. Instead the approach undertaken by many is to concentrate on a few specialist areas in which to develop their own expertise. Doubts about the present institutional resources of Parliament to scrutinise the executive have a long history of reluctance on the part of the Government of the day to accept criticism or make amendments to Bills in response to back-bench concerns.

Notes

1   All the issues raised by McEldowney are discussed individually and in depth later in this book. Thus, the question of the contracting out the use of quangos, together with issues surrounding Cabinet government, are discussed in Part IV, Chapter 2, together with changes in central/local government relations; government secrecy is discussed in Part IV, Chapters 2 and 3. The efficacy of Parliamentary scrutiny of the executive is considered in Part III, Chapter 1.

2   The case for the introduction of some form of devolution is also taken to justify a written constitution. Devolution, as a response to nationalism in Scotland and Wales in the late 1970s, may also be seen as a means to decentralise central government powers. In election manifestos, both in 1987 and in 1992, the Labour Party and the Liberal Party/SDP contained proposals for devolution; in Labour's case for Scotland only.[28] More recently, in its White Paper on Scotland in the Union,[29] the Government has identified administrative tasks which may be reallocated and better organised within a form of administrative devolution in Scotland through the Scottish Office. Reallocation of civil servants, improved administration and management of the Government in Scotland are intended to locate more decision-making at the point of delivery of the various public sector services. Such proposals fall short of legislative devolution and financial power devolved to an elected local assembly. More radical proposals may be found in the IPPR draft constitution. These include assemblies for Scotland, Wales, Northern Ireland and the regions of England. The latter is problematic because of the size, diversity and traditions which need to be recognised in any proposal. These proposals follow the minority report of the Royal Commission on the Constitution which favoured the creation of elected regional authorities to take over responsibilities of central government.

---

28   See the Labour Party, *Meet the Challenge, Make the Change* (1989). Labour is now committed to holding referenda on legislative dissolution for both Scotland and Wales.

29   Cm 2225.

CHAPTER 2

THE NATURE AND ROLE OF CONSTITUTIONAL CONVENTIONS[1]

INTRODUCTION

It is a characteristic of constitutions in general that they contain large areas which are governed by conventions rather than by strict law. Even where a country sets out to develop a written constitution, customary usages tend to evolve around the various rules. This is a particular feature of the UK constitution; many of its important features are regulated by convention alone. For example, there is no common law or statutory rule that there must be a Prime Minister. Similarly, the rule that the Queen will only exercise her very wide statutory and prerogative powers on and in accordance with the advice of ministers is found in convention alone.

In general, conventions are particularly significant because they represent a means of bringing about developments in the constitution without the need for formal repeal or amendment of the law. The distinction between strict law and conventions grew up due to the need to effect a quiet erosion of the prerogative powers of the monarch. Such powers could be by convention vested in the Cabinet thereby avoiding the need for any formal statutory declaration that this had occurred. Conventions thus allow the constitution to evolve and keep up to date with changing circumstances.

THE VARIETY OF CONVENTIONS

Conventions rear their head in a great many areas of the British constitution. Dicey considers a number of the more prominent examples below.

A V Dicey, *An Introduction to the Study of the Law of the Constitution*, 10th edn (1959), pp419–21

... In short, by the side of our written law, there has grown up an unwritten or conventional constitution. When an Englishman speaks of the conduct of a public man being constitutional or unconstitutional, he means something wholly different from what he means by conduct being legal or illegal. A famous vote of the House of Commons, passed on the motion of a great statesman, once declared that the then ministers of the Crown did not possess the confidence of the House of Commons, and that their continuance in office was therefore at variance with the spirit of the constitution. The truth of such a position, according to the traditional principles on which public men have acted for some generations, cannot be disputed; but it would be in vain to seek for any trace of such doctrines in any page of our written law. The proposer of that motion did not mean to charge the existing ministry with any illegal act, with any act which could be made the subject either of a prosecution in a lower court or of impeachment in the High Court of Parliament itself. He did not mean that they,

---

1   General reading (additional to that cited in this chapter): sources referred to in n 1 of Chapter 1 of this Part; also, Johnston, *In Search of the Constitution* (1977), esp Ch 3; Madison, *The Federalist Papers*; Colin Munro, 'Law and Conventions Distinguished' (1975) 91 LQR 218; Mitchell, *Constitutional Law*, 2nd edn (1968); Jennings, *Cabinet Government* (2nd edn), esp Ch 1; Marshall, *Constitutional Conventions* (1984).

ministers of the Crown, appointed during the pleasure of the Crown, committed any breach of the law of which the law could take cognisance, by retaining possession of their offices till such time as the Crown should think good to dismiss them from those offices. What he meant was that the general course of their policy was one which, to a majority of the House of Commons, did not seem to be wise or beneficial to the nation, and that therefore, according to a conventional code as well understood and as effectual as the written law itself, they were bound to resign offices of which the House of Commons no longer held them to be worthy.' [Freeman, *Growth of the English Constitution*, 1st edn,(1872), pp109–110.]

The one exception which can be taken to this picture of our conventional constitution is the contrast drawn in it between the 'written law' and the 'unwritten constitution'; the true opposition, as already pointed out, is between laws properly so called, whether written or unwritten, and understandings or practices which, though commonly observed, are not laws in any true sense of that word at all. But this inaccuracy is hardly more than verbal, and we may gladly accept Mr Freeman's words as a starting-point whence to inquire into the nature or common quality of the maxims which make up our body of constitutional morality.

Examples of constitutional understandings

The following are examples of the precepts to which Mr Freeman refers, and belong to the code by which public life in England is (or is supposed to be) governed. 'A Ministry which is outvoted in the House of Commons is in many cases bound to retire from office.' 'A Cabinet, when outvoted on any vital question, may appeal once to the country by means of a dissolution.' 'If an appeal to the electors goes against the Ministry they are bound to retire from office, and have no right to dissolve Parliament a second time.' 'The Cabinet are responsible to Parliament as a body, for the general conduct of affairs.' 'They are further responsible to an extent, not however very definitely fixed, for the appointments made by any of their number, or to speak in more accurate language, made by the Crown under the advice of any member of the Cabinet.' 'The party who for the time being command a majority in the House of Commons, have (in general) a right to have their leaders placed in office.' 'The most influential of these leaders ought (generally speaking) to be the Premier, or head of the Cabinet.' These are precepts referring to the position and formation of the Cabinet. It is, however, easy to find constitutional maxims dealing with other topics. 'Treaties can be made without the necessity for any Act of Parliament; but the Crown, or in reality the ministry representing the Crown, ought not to make any treaty which will not command the approbation of Parliament.' 'The foreign policy of the country, the proclamation of war, and the making of peace ought to be left in the hands of the Crown, or in truth of the Crown's servants. But in foreign as in domestic affairs, the wish of the two Houses of Parliament or (when they differ) of the House of Commons ought to be followed.' 'The action of any ministry would be highly unconstitutional if it should involve the proclamation of war, or the making of peace, in defiance of the wishes of the House.' 'If there is a difference of opinion between the House of Lords and the House of Commons, the House of Lords ought, at some point, not definitely fixed, to give way ...

Note

It is interesting to note that the last of these conventions has been at least partially codified, by means of the Parliament Acts 1911–49. Nevertheless, that codification has not hindered the continuing influence of more generalised conventions relating to the relationship between Lords and Commons.[2] Geoffrey Marshall considers whether the variety of connections is not in fact more rich than Dicey allowed for.

Geoffrey Marshall, *Constitutional Conventions* (1984), pp3–5

In his *Introduction to the Study of the Law of the Constitution* AV Dicey picked out a number of rules as being constitutional conventions. ... He also mentioned various questions that raise issues of conventional (rather than legal) propriety. What, he asked, are the conventions under which a ministry may dissolve Parliament? May a large number of peers be created for the purpose of overruling the Upper House? On what principle may a Cabinet allow of open questions? These last examples appear to be cases in which it cannot be clearly stated what the conventions are, or cases in which the relevant conventions are conflicting or controversial.

Dicey's discussion implied that the conventions of the constitution relate mainly to the exercise of the Crown's prerogatives and he suggested that their purpose was to ensure that these legal powers, formally in the hands of the Crown, were in practice exercised by ministers in accordance with the principles of responsible and representative government. But though the conventions do provide the framework of cabinet government and political accountability, and often modify rules of law, they spread more widely than Dicey's description suggests. Besides the conventional rules that govern the powers of the Crown there are many other constitutional relationships between governmental persons or institutions that illustrate the existence of rules of a conventional character. Examples are:

- relations between the Cabinet and the Prime Minister
- relations between the Government as a whole and Parliament
- relations between the two Houses of Parliament
- relations between ministers and the Civil Service
- relations between Ministers and the machinery of justice
- relations between the United Kingdom and the member countries of the Commonwealth.

Many of these relationships are in part governed by law and in part by convention, [eg] the relationships of the member countries of the Commonwealth are in a number of fundamental ways regulated by the statute of Westminster, but in other ways rest upon agreements or conventions (some of which are mentioned in the preamble to the Statute).

Amongst the conventions of the Constitution there are some whose formulation is reasonably precise and specific, and others whose formulation is in more general terms. An example of the first kind is the rule that the Queen must assent to Bills that have received the approval of both Houses. An example of the second kind is that the House of Lords should not obstruct the policy of an elected Government with a majority in the House of Commons. Many conventions fall into the second category. This, perhaps, explains why so many questions of constitutional propriety remain unsettled. Might a British Government ever be dismissed by the Crown (comparably with what happened in Australia in 1975)? Is a Prime Minister entitled to dissolve Parliament and hold a general election whenever she wishes? Can a Government continue in office if its major legislation is defeated in the House of Commons? May a minister blame

---

2   See below, Part III, Chapter 2.

his civil servants if mistakes are made in the work of his department? The answers to all these questions are uncertain because, in each case, there is a general rule whose limits have not been fully explored; or possibly there may be two rules which are potentially in conflict.

Note

Examples of the uncertainty of many important conventions may be multiplied. To give just one example, Marshall and Moodie note[3] Ivor Jennings's suggestion that 'in framing social legislation the appropriate department must consult the appropriate "interest" and ask, "what exactly is the rule?" Must every interest be consulted on every piece of social legislation? At what stage must they consulted?'.

ATTEMPTS TO DEFINE CONVENTIONS

Colin Munro has noted that Dicey's methodology in dealing with conventions was not 'to offer a definition'. Instead, 'Conventions were illustrated by examples, and negatively defined by the fact that they were not court-enforced'.[4] He considers the success of this method, and its critics, particularly Sir Ivor Jennings.

Colin Munro, *Studies in Constitutional Law* (1987), pp40–43, 46–7

One technique employed by Jennings was to point to certain kinds of similarity or interaction between laws and conventions. Both sorts of rule rested upon general acquiescence, he suggested, and the major conventions were as firmly fixed and might be stated with almost as much accuracy as principles of common law [*The Law and the Constitution* (5th edn), pp72, 117]. The late Professor JDB Mitchell built up further arguments of this sort:

> Conventions cannot be regarded as less important than rules of law. Often the legal rule is the less important. In relation to subject-matter the two types of rule overlap: in form they are often not clearly distinguishable ... very many conventions are capable of being expressed with the precision of a Rule of Law, or of being incorporated into law. Precedent is as operative in the formation of convention as it is in that of law. It cannot be said that a Rule of Law is necessarily more certain than is a convention. It may therefore be asked whether it is right to distinguish law from convention [*Constitutional Law*, 2nd edn (1968), p34]. ...

These statements appear to be of varying acceptability, but are apt to mislead. For example, there seems to be only a small number of conventions in this country whose existence and precise formulation are generally agreed, so that the statements about precision and certainty are very questionable. Sometimes there seems to be force in the assertion that the convention is more important than the law, but it is hard to see how their relative importance can be measured. In the United States, in the 1930s, the convention that a President should not stand for re-election more than once might have been considered more important than the law, which imposed no restriction. But what would we say in retrospect, knowing that in 1940 Franklin D Roosevelt was elected for a third term, and in 1944 for a fourth?

---

3   *Some Problems of the Constitution*, 5th edn (1971), pp31–2.
4   *Studies in Constitutional Law* (1987), p53.

Besides, the important point is that none of Mitchell's propositions, even if accurate, would entail the conclusion which he went on to derive from them, that any effort to distinguish laws and conventions is bound to fail. This is readily illustrated by applying some of the comparisons to other bodies of rules.

Rules of morality cannot be regarded as less important than rules of law ... in relation to subject-matter the two types of rules overlap ... Very many *religious edicts* are capable of being expressed with the precision of a Rule of Law, or of being incorporated into law. Precedent is as operative in the formation of *etiquette* as it is in that of law. It cannot be said that a Rule of Law is necessarily more certain than is a *rule of cricket*.

These new statements are just as accurate as the others, to put it no higher. We cannot draw from them the conclusion that the laws are *indistinguishable* from rules of morality, religion, etiquette or cricket. In fact, the explanation of why conventions, and all these, reveal some similarities to laws is simple: they are all rules operating in society, and certain similarities, especially of form, are only to be expected.

A ginger ale, however, is not the same as a whisky, merely because each is amber in colour and liquid in form. The critical question is whether laws may be *differentiated* from conventions. Dicey, who was in no doubt that they might be, also suggested a means:

> The rules which make up constitutional law, as the term is used in England, include two sets of principles or maxims of a totally distinct character. The one set of rules are in the strictest sense 'laws', since they are rules which (whether written or unwritten, whether enacted by statute or derived from the mass of custom, tradition or judge-made maxims known as the common law) are enforced by the courts; these rules constitute 'constitutional law' in the proper sense of that term, and may for the sake of distinction be called collectively 'the law of the constitution'.

> The other set of rules consist of conventions, understandings, habits or practices which, though they may regulate the conduct of ... officials, are not in reality laws at all since they are not enforced by the courts. This portion of constitutional law may, for the sake of distinction, be termed the 'conventions of the constitution', or constitutional morality [Dicey, p23].

Laws and enforcement

One challenge to Dicey's test is posed by areas of law where the jurisdiction of the courts is apparently excluded, perhaps by an explicit provision that a duty may not be enforced in court proceedings or by the provision of an administrative channel as the exclusive remedy. Sometimes there are provisions of written constitutions in other countries which are expressed as non-justiciable, or are interpreted as such [eg the Directive Principles of State Policy in the Constitution of India, which Article 37 declares not enforceable by any court].

Take the example that Jennings gives, a statutory duty upon local authorities to provide adequate sewers and disposal works, which was, under a statute, only remediable by means of complaint to the Minister of Housing and Local Government. When proceedings were brought in court, the House of Lords held that Parliament had deprived the courts of jurisdiction in that area, and that the complaint to the ministry was the sole means of redress (*Passmore v Oswaldwistle UDC*). The error that Jennings makes is in using the case as evidence that the law concerned was not court-enforced. The case is the best evidence possible that the law was court-enforced. Certainly a statutory duty was not judicially enforced, but that was precisely because the law said it should not be, and the courts obeyed the law and put it into effect. Other such examples may be explained in the same way. When provisions are unsusceptible to judicial enforcement, the correct analysis is either that no obligation is involved, as with some of the ideological pronouncements found in written constitutions, or is that an imperfect obligation has been created. None of this should surprise us. A legal system does not consist only of obligations for breach of which there is redress ...

These points are related to a larger contrast which may be drawn. Rules of law form parts of a system. Included in the system are rules about the rules: these are provisions about entry to, and exit from, the system, and procedures for the determination and application of the rules. We cannot conceive of a single legal rule, in isolation from a system. However, conventions do not form a system. There is no unifying feature which they possess, and no apparatus of secondary rules. They merely evolve in isolation from each other.

Here, incidentally, lies the answer to Jennings's specious argument that laws and conventions are the same because both 'rest essentially upon general acquiescence' [*op cit*, p117]. That is quite misleading. Conventions rest entirely on acquiescence, but individually. If a supposed convention is not accepted as binding by those to whom it would apply, then there could not be said to be a convention, and this is a test on which each must be separately assessed. Laws do not depend upon acquiescence. Individual laws may be unpopular or widely disobeyed, but it does not meant that they are not laws. No doubt the system as a whole must possess some measure of *de facto* effectiveness for us to recognise it as valid, although it might be stretching language to describe the citizens of any country occupied by enemy forces, or the black majority in the Republic of South Africa, as 'acquiescing' in the laws which govern them. In any event, is it obvious that the comparison is inapt.

Notes

1   Munro appears to provide a neat refutation of Jennings's point that certain areas of law are not court-enforced, by pointing out that when the courts refuse to intervene in such areas, it is the law which tells them not to do so (above). But does this get us very far? When the courts refuse to enforce a convention it is precisely because the law tells them not to. In the light of this, Munro's argument seems to be reduced simply to affirming the axiom that the courts obey the law. But if it is the case that some conventional rules have all the attributes of law, except that they are not enforced by the courts, pointing out that the courts do not enforce all laws either is a fair point, and saying that it is the law which tells them not to enforce certain laws does not seem an adequate answer.

2   The distinction Munro draws as to the role which general acquiescence plays in relation to laws on the one hand and conventions on the other is a useful one. Jeremy Waldron has also considered this point, and draws a more general conclusion about the nature of conventions and the British constitution, after (in an earlier section of his essay) describing the appointment of Harold Macmillan's successor as Prime Minister.

Jeremy Waldron, *The Law* (1990), pp62–7

Constitutional conventions

The term used to describe the sort of customs, practices and understandings that were at stake in the succession to Harold Macmillan is 'conventions'. They are not written rules but 'conventions' of the constitution. Or sometimes we are told helpfully that they are 'conventional' and not 'legal' rules. So what is a 'convention'?

It is important to say first that a convention is just a regularity in political behaviour; it is not just a prediction of what reliably happens. Every year the Prime Minister moves to Chequers from Downing Street for Christmas. We can predict that she will do this, and we would be surprised if she didn't. But surprise is all that would be occasioned by such an 'irregularity'. We wouldn't criticise the Prime Minister for not spending Christmas at Chequers. We don't see it as a principle or norm to judge her by. It is a regularity we have discerned in Prime Ministerial behaviour, not a standard Prime Ministers are supposed to live up to.

Now constitutional conventions are not like that. They are normative. They are used for saying what ought to be done, and, as we saw, they are used as a basis for criticism if someone's behaviour does not live up to them. We use them to judge behaviour not merely to predict it.

But although they are norms, they would never be enforced by a court: you could never get a judge to declare that a convention ought to be followed as a matter of law, and if someone decided to flout a convention the only remedy would be political not legal. (Either those in possession of political power – the people, the other office-holders, the military perhaps in the last resort – would put up with what had happened or they wouldn't. If they did, the convention would in effect have been changed. If they did not, there would be something akin to a revolution.) Most writers have said that since these are norms but not legal norms, the only conclusion possible is that they are moral norms – norms of political morality. AV Dicey, for example, wrote that conventions 'consisting (as they do) of customs, practices, maxims, or precepts which are not enforced or recognised by the courts, make up a body not of laws, but of *constitutional or political ethics*'. And Geoffrey Marshall says that they 'simply spell out the *moral duties, rights, and powers of office-holders*' in relation to the machinery of government'.

But calling them 'moral' or 'ethical' doesn't really help. There are all sorts of different views about 'constitutional or political ethics' and about 'the moral duties, rights, and powers of office-holders'. Pacifists may think that MPs have a moral duty not to authorise expenditure on nuclear weapons. Radical democrats believe that no law should be passed without a referendum. Christian fundamentalists may believe that atheists should not be allowed to hold public office. All these are held by their proponents as moral norms, but I take it none of them would regard their principles as conventions of the constitution. Certainly, we think or we hope that there are moral justifications for the conventions we have. But there is no reason to be confident that they capture the best political morality. It is not their moral justification that makes them conventions of the British constitution. We have got to say something more specific.

Sir Kenneth Wheare once wrote that a convention is 'a rule of behaviour accepted as obligatory by those concerned in the working of the constitution'. That is an interesting definition because it suggests that, in the last resort, these rules have no other basis than the fact that the people involved accept them as standards for their behaviour. They follow them in most cases; they feel guilt or compunction when they don't; they criticise deviations from them by others; and, what's more, everyone knows what is going on when these criticisms are made, for everyone has in mind roughly the same set of standards. They are not merely habits or regularities of behaviour; they enter into people's consciousness and become the subject-matter of reflection and of a sense of obligation. But they are not merely subjective views about morality either. They have a social reality, inasmuch as they capture a way in which people interact, a way in which people make demands on one another, and form attitudes and expectations about a common practice with standards that they are all living up to. They get mentioned in newspapers, in periodicals and in learned treaties. Politicians refer to them when they are evaluating one another's behaviour. They are social facts, not mere abstract principles, because they bind people together into a common form of life.

All this sounds very fragile compared with the robust reality of a statutory law or a written constitution. I have made it sound as though constitutional conventions are rules that pull themselves up by their own boot straps. They are rules because they are accepted as rules by those they bind, and if they weren't accepted by those they bind they wouldn't be rules at all. They have no other validity, no other force, than their common acceptance by the people they govern.

Waldron then goes on to consider the jurisprudential aspect of this question, giving a brief outline of Hart's theory that each system of law is based ultimately upon a supreme rule, which he terms 'The rule of recognition'.[5]

Rules of recognition

In Britain, the rule of recognition says (among other things) that a bill passed (in the appropriate way) by the two Houses of Parliament and assented to by the Queen has the force of law, and prevails over any earlier law or any other rule that conflicts with it. It tells us, in effect, to look at the institutional pedigree of a norm to see if it is a legal rule; look at its date, the process of its enactment and the formalities associated with it, and that is all you need to know about its legal status. Other countries have more complicated rules of recognition; in the United States one has to look not only at how and when the Bill was passed (by both Houses of Congress, and with the President's assent or a fresh majority of two-thirds or more in each house of Congress) but also at its compatibility with the Bill of Rights embodied in the 1787 Constitution. And a full statement of the American rule of recognition would have to include the procedures for amending the constitution as well. Whatever the complexities, Hart's argument is that a legal system needs some such rule of recognition to identify what are to count at any time as its laws.

What gives the rule of recognition its legal force? What makes it the authoritative way of determining what the law is? The question does not really have an answer. It's a bit like asking what makes the US Constitution constitutional. The rule of recognition is just there. It is a social fact about the way people involved in the workings of our society – particularly lawyers, parliamentarians, judges, policemen, and so on – behave, and above all it's a fact about how they think they ought to behave. No doubt, judges and so on have their reasons for thinking they should defer to the edicts of Parliament. Some of them may be democratic reasons; some of them may be reasons of tradition. But their practice of doing so – their practice of deferring to Parliament, their practice of taking this as their standard – is not consecrated by any further authority. Their practice, their readiness to regard themselves as bound by this rule, is what makes our society a legal system; it's the fulcrum or the foundation of the rest. Without some social practice of this kind, there would be no legal system in Britain – that is, no shared sense among officials and people of which rules and commands they should expect to be upheld.

I brought up positivism and Hart's rule of recognition because I wanted to illustrate a general point about the foundations of political life. There is tradition, there is morality, there is affection, there is charisma, there is ideology, there is mystification, there are lies and – ultimately – there are bayonets and bullets. All

---

5   Hart's theory is set out in *The Concept of Law* (1961).

of these are important in the analysis of politics, and all of them – including the last two (think of Northern Ireland) – have a part to play in explaining the stability of our political system. But there is also law and there is political order, regulating authority, succession, and the transfer and exercise of power. Law and political order matter an awful lot to us. But in the end they amount to an interlocking system of rules and practices that depend on nothing more concrete and nothing more secure than the readiness of those involved in political life to regulate and judge their own and others' behaviour by certain standards. Hart's theory of the rule of recognition implies that something no more secure than this lies at the foundation of every legal system. What we have said about constitutional conventions indicates that they fall into this category as well. It is the fragile readiness of those involved in political life to order their conduct by certain implicit standards that forms the basis of whatever claim Britain has to be a constitutional regime.

What is different, then, about the British constitution is not that it rests in the last resort on a set of fragile understandings; that is true of every legal and constitutional system. Rather, the distinguishing fact about Britain is that so much of its constitutional law has that status. In other countries, there is a written charter whose authority rests implicitly on such a presupposition. Americans tacitly presuppose the authority of the delegates at the 1787 convention who began their document with 'We the People of the United States ...' when they accept that document is binding. In Britain, however, the whole thing is a structure of tacit presuppositions from start to finish. There is no great charter whose authority is tacitly presupposed. There are just tacit presuppositions. that is the peculiar feature of our political life.

Notes

1   It should be noted that many jurists do not accept that the law can be identified solely by reference to its source, and that a legal system is thus based ultimately on a Rule of Recognition which identifies that source. The Natural Law school argues that the ascertainment of whether a rule is a law is at bottom a moral exercise,[6] whilst Ronald Dworkin has offered a 'third theory of law', in which interpretation and normative analysis play a key role[7] in the identification of law, which, he argues, may exist before it is declared by any authoritative source.

2   Key to the definition of conventions is the manner in which they are treated by the courts. Whilst at one time some commentators believed that 'the law courts can take no notice' of conventions at all,[8] this notion has now been firmly scotched by the courts themselves. The Court of Appeal delivered an important judgment in a case arising out of the publication of the diaries of a former Cabinet Minister; the convention concerned was that of the collective responsibility of the cabinet.

Attorney General v Jonathan Cape Ltd [1976] QB 752, 764, 770–71

Lord Widgery CJ: '... It has always been assumed by lawyers and, I suspect, by politicians and the Civil Service, that Cabinet proceedings and Cabinet papers

---

6   For the classical exposition see Aquinas, 'Summa Theologica' in P D'Entreves, *Selected Political Writings* (1970).

7   See, eg *Law's Empire* (1987).

8   Keith, *The Government of the British Empire* (1935), p6.

are secret, and cannot be publicly disclosed until they have passed into history. It is quite clear that no court will compel the production of Cabinet papers in the course of discovery in an action, and the Attorney-General contends that not only will the court refuse to compel the production of such matters, but it will go further and positively forbid the disclosure of such papers and proceedings if publication will be contrary to the public interest.

The basis of this contention is the confidential character of these papers and proceedings, derived from the convention of joint Cabinet responsibility whereby any policy decision reached by the Cabinet has to be supported thereafter by all members of the Cabinet whether they approve of it or not, unless they feel compelled to resign. It is contended that Cabinet decisions and papers are confidential for a period to the extent at least that they must not be referred to outside the Cabinet in such a way as to disclose the attitude of individual ministers in the argument which preceded the decision. Thus, there may be no objection to a minister disclosing (or leaking, as it was called) the fact that a Cabinet meeting has taken place, or, indeed, the decision taken, so long as the individual views of ministers are not identified.

There is no doubt that Mr Crossman's manuscripts contain frequent references to individual opinions of Cabinet ministers, and this is not surprising because it was his avowed object to obtain a relaxation of the convention regarding memoirs of ex-ministers. ... There have, as far as I know, been no previous attempts in any court to define the extent to which Cabinet proceedings should be treated as secret or confidential, and it is not surprising that different views on this subject are contained in the evidence before me. ...

It is convenient next to deal with [the] submission, ... that the evidence does not prove the existence of a convention as to collective responsibility, or adequately define a sphere of secrecy. I find overwhelming evidence that the doctrine of joint responsibility is generally understood and practised and equally strong evidence that it is on occasion ignored. The general effect of the evidence is that the doctrine is an established feature of the English form of government, and it follows that some matters leading up to a Cabinet decision may be regarded as confidential. Furthermore, I am persuaded that the nature of the confidence is that spoken for by the Attorney-General, namely, that since the confidence is imposed to enable the efficient conduct of the Queen's business, the confidence is owed to the Queen and cannot be released by the members of Cabinet themselves. I have been told that a resigning minister who wishes to make a personal statement in the House, and to disclose matters which are confidential under the doctrine, obtains the consent of the Queen for this purpose. Such consent is obtained through the Prime Minister.

The Cabinet is at the very centre of national affairs, and must be in possession at all times of information which is secret or confidential. Secrets relating to national security may require to be preserved indefinitely. Secrets relating to new taxation proposals may be of the highest importance until Budget day, but public knowledge thereafter. To leak a Cabinet decision a day or so before it is officially announced is an accepted exercise in public relations, but to identify the ministers who voted one way or another is objectionable because it undermines the doctrine of joint responsibility.

It is evident that there cannot be a single rule governing the publication of such a variety of matters. In these actions we are concerned with the publication of diaries at a time when 11 years have expired since the first recorded events. The Attorney-General must show (a) that such publication would be a breach of confidence; (b) that the public interest requires that the publication be restrained, and (c) that there are no other facts of the public interest contradictory of and more compelling than that relied upon. Moreover, the court, when asked to restrain such a publication, must closely examine the extent to which relief is necessary to ensure that restrictions are not imposed beyond the strict requirement of public need.

Applying those principles to the present case, what do we find? In my judgment, the Attorney–General has made out his claim that the expression of individual opinions by Cabinet ministers in the course of Cabinet discussion are matters of confidence, the publication of which can be restrained by the court when this is clearly necessary in the public interest.

The maintenance of the doctrine of joint responsibility within the Cabinet is in the public interest, and the application of that doctrine might be prejudiced by premature disclosure of the views of individual Ministers. ...

In the present case there is nothing in Mr Crossman's work to suggest that he did not support the doctrine of joint Cabinet responsibility. The question for the court is whether it is shown that publication now might damage the doctrine notwithstanding that much of the action is up to 10 years old and three general elections have been held meanwhile. So far as the Attorney-General relies in his argument on the disclosure of individual ministerial opinions, he has not satisfied me that publication would in any way inhibit free and open discussion in Cabinet hereafter.

Notes

1   The Court of Appeal thus found that the convention in question could support an argument (based on breach of confidence) for legal restraint of publication, though, in the event, the action failed on the ground that, due to the lapse of time, the material had lost its confidential quality. The case is not the only example of conventions being taken into account by the courts. For example, in *Liversidge v Anderson* (1942)[9] and *Carltona Ltd v Commissioner of Works* (1943)[10] the courts supported the refusal to review the grounds on which executive discretionary powers had been exercised on the basis that a minister is responsible to Parliament for the exercise of his power.

2   In 1982, the Supreme Court of Canada had to consider a convention of the utmost importance, namely the understanding that the Senate and House of Commons of Canada would not seek to amend the constitution of Canada in such a way as to affect either the legislative role or the status of the provincial legislatures without first obtaining the consent of all Canada's provinces to such a change. It was argued before the court that the convention, which undoubtedly existed, had 'crystallised' into a (constitutional) law. The court rejected this argument, finding that failure to obtain the necessary consents would not render any subsequent amendment unlawful. It was, however, prepared to say that 'the agreement of the Provinces of Canada, no views being expressed as to its quantification, is constitutionally required' and that acting without such consents 'would be unconstitutional in the conventional sense'.[11] Although the Canadian

---

9   AC 206.

10   2 All ER 560.

11   *Reference re Amendment of the Constitution of Canada* (1982) 125 DLR (3d) 1. An extract from the case appears below at pp57–8.

Government would, strictly speaking, have been free to ignore this judgement, it clearly did not wish to act in a way which the Supreme Court had described as 'unconstitutional' and therefore entered into negotiations with the provinces, eventually obtaining the consent of nine out of 10 of them to its plans.

3   A more systematic attempt to define conventions has been attempted by Sir Ivor Jennings. His analysis is considered by Marshall and Moodie below, and then critiqued by Monro.

Marshall and Moodie, *Some Problems of the Constitution*, 5th edn (1971), pp28–33.

Sir Ivor Jennings's account of conventions [in *The Law and the Constitution* (3rd edn), Ch 3] is more convincing, but it is not entirely free from obscurity. His criteria for deciding whether a particular convention exists are these:

> First, what are the precedents; secondly, did the actors in the precedents believe that they were bound by a rule; and thirdly, is there a reason for the rule? A single precedent with a good reason may be enough to establish the rule. A whole string of precedents without such a reason will be of no avail, unless it is perfectly certain that the persons concerned regarded them as bound by it [*The Law and the Constitution*, p131].

For a convention to exist and operate the actors must obviously be aware of it and, in particular, of its obligatory character (even if in fact they conform to it for reasons other than self-conscious virtue). This awareness of obligation is a necessary characteristic of a convention, but it is a sure guide only if this obligation is felt very generally among those who work the constitution, ie among the authorities. Its absence may be conclusive, but not its presence. In and of itself it is not and cannot be a sufficient test: the actors may be divided in their opinions or they may be mistaken about their obligations ...

4 Precedents

How then are reasons for conventional rules related to precedents? In the English legal system all cases decided in the highest courts of the judicial hierarchy are precedents, in the sense that these decisions are binding upon all other courts in all other similar cases. In this manner, judicial decisions, or precedents, may be said to establish rules of law. Where conventions are concerned, however, it seems that not even a series of similar precedent actions will always suffice to establish a conventional rule – if indeed it ever suffices. A distinction has therefore been drawn by Sir Ivor Jennings between precedents which do, and those which do not, establish a rule, ie between 'normative' and 'simple' precedents [Jennings, *Cabinet Government*, 2nd edn, p7]. But in both legal and ordinary English we tend to use the word 'precedent' to refer to instances which, for some reason other than the fact of occurrence itself, are deemed to be relevant, desirable, or acceptable models for future action. Sir Ivor remarks at one point of the 'agreement to differ' amongst ministers in 1932: 'No harm was done by the precedent of 1932 provided that it is not regarded as a precedent' [*ibid*, 3rd edn, p281]. A 'simple' precedent, in other words, could hardly be distinguished from no precedent at all. ...

The instance of 1924 is an instructive one. It is justifiable to query the opinion that King George V established a new rule (that the Prime Minister should always be a Member of the House of Commons) when he appointed Mr Baldwin instead of Lord Curzon. On the other hand, there now seems to exist a widespread view that a Prime Minister should not belong to a Chamber in which one party has little representation and in which few major debates or decisions occur. For some such reason, the King's action in 1924 may now be referred to as a precedent. But this reason would have existed whether or not there had existed a noble alternative to Mr Baldwin.

5 *Obedience to conventions*

Neither a general feeling of obligation among the authorities, nor precedents, therefore, suffice either to establish a rule or conclusively to demonstrate its existence and precise content.

The first part of the answer is contained in Jennings's suggestion that 'conventions are obeyed because of the political difficulties which follow if they are not' [*ibid*, p129]. To complete the answer one must inquire what sort of political difficulties they are, for it is clear that political difficulties can arise from many actions which involve no breach of a convention. A Government runs into 'political difficulties' whenever it displeases some section of the community, whether it be by raising rents or refusing to issue a stamp commemorating the birth of Robert Burns, but it cannot seriously be claimed that either decision is an any sense 'unconstitutional'. Nevertheless it is by examining the effects of a breach of conventions that the reason for their existence is to be found. If a UK Government had, before 1931, legislated for a 'dominion', or had, since then, introduced legislation affecting the status of the Crown, without obtaining the consent of the countries concerned, it is likely that one or more members of the Commonwealth might have severed their connections with it; or, at least, that Commonwealth ties would have been imperilled. The serious breach in the conventions limiting the power of the House of Lords which occurred in 1909 resulted directly in the passing of the Parliament Act of 1911, just as Roosevelt's re-election for a third and fourth term led to the adoption of the 22nd Amendment to the American Constitution which makes a third term legally impermissible. ... These examples indicate that the conventions describe the way in which certain legal powers must be exercised if the powers are to be tolerated by those affected. The monarch's legal powers to rule, the House of Lords' legal powers to reject a bill passed by the Commons, the legal power of the UK Parliament to pass imperial legislation – all these powers are or were retained only for so long as they are exercised (or not exercised) in accordance with the conventions which have been established. Their potential abolition constitutes the 'political difficulties' which would probably follow upon a breach in the conventions of the constitution.

From this view of the nature of conventions it follows that a crucial question must always be whether or not a particular class of action is likely to destroy respect for the established distribution of authority.

Such an account of the relationship between law and convention bears a resemblance to that put forward by Dicey, but it differs therefrom in an important respect. According to Dicey, a breach in a convention involved the probability of a consequential breach of the law. But the truth is rather that a breach of a convention is likely to induce a change in the law or even in the whole constitutional structure. In this relationship, it may be suggested, is to be found the 'reason' for the conventions, stated in its most general form.

Colin Munro, *Studies in Constitutional Law* (1987), pp54–55

... Jennings ... proceeded to ask the question, 'When is it possible to say that a convention has been established?' His answer was [the three-fold test outlined above] ...

The point is given more emphasis by a section headed 'Mere practice is not enough'. Jennings, by stipulating the conditions for the existence of a convention, as Dicey had not, had implicitly divided the non-legal into two classes, those rules which amounted to conventions, and those which did not.

Sir Kenneth Wheare more explicitly divided the non-legal rules into two relevant classes:

These non-legal rules are given a variety of names, as has been indicated. It appears convenient to adopt two terms, usage and convention. By convention is meant an obligatory rule; by usage, a rule which is no more than the description of a usual practice and which has not yet obtained obligatory force. A usage, after repeated adoption whenever a given set of circumstances recurs, may for a sufficient reason, acquire obligatory force and thus become a convention. But conventions need not have a prior history as usages. A convention may, if a sufficient reason exists, arise from a single precedent. Or again it may result from an agreement between the parties concerned, declared and accepted by them as binding [*The Statute of Westminster and Dominion Status*, 5th edn, (1953), p10].

... Wheare's approach has been effectively criticised by two authors, in a passage which merits careful consideration:

There is ... a difficulty in the common sense distinction which is involved in saying that it is a convention that the monarch should give her assent to any bill duly passed by both Houses of Parliament, but that her agreement to dissolve the House of Commons when requested to do so by the Prime Minister is a matter of usage, in that her consent is not mandatory under all circumstances. Not all authorities would agree that the first of these alone provides an example of an obligatory rule; but if the second may be assumed to be a 'usage', it could not with equal justice be referred to as a 'rule'. A rule must prescribe something if it is to guide action or state obligations, whereas, according to [Wheare's] definition, a usage would only describe actual behaviour. But the reasons why a particular action is not mandatory cannot lie in the fact that any statement about it is [to quote Wheare] 'no more than description'. A description is not a weak kind of prescription [G Marshall and GC Moodie, *Some Problems of the Constitution*, 5th edn, (1971), p26].

There is considerable force in these arguments and their implication is that, while other matters of political facts and behaviour may also be of interest, the non-legal rules relevant to the constitution are best viewed as being of one type, even if their precision and obligatoriness are variable. If that is accepted, then the exercise of stipulating tests for the establishment of a convention seems misconceived.

Note

As the authors note, of obvious relevance to this debate is the reasons which may be given for the obedience of this affected by them to conventions, an issue considered by Marshall below.

G Marshall, *Constitutional Conventions* (1984), pp5–8

In the opening chapter of the *Law of the Constitution* Dicey, in discussing 'the rules that belong to the conventions of the Constitution', remarks that 'some of these maxims are never violated and are universally admitted to be inviolable. Others on the other hand have nothing but a slight amount of custom in their favour and are of disputable validity' [*Law of the Constitution* (10th edn), p26]. Confusingly, he goes on to explain this difference as one that rests upon the distinction between rules that bring their violators into conflict with the law of the land, and rules 'that may be violated without any other consequence than that of exposing the Minister or other person by whom they were broken to blame or unpopularity' [ibid]. This does not chime very easily with the thesis that the reason for obedience to all conventions is that breach of the conventions leads more or less directly to a breach of law. Dicey has often been criticised for holding this view, but it seems clear that he did not hold it in relation to all conventions. Indeed, it seems an explanation confined to a single contingency, namely the possibility that a Government might try to remain in office and raise taxes after losing the confidence of the House of Commons. But Dicey mentions a number of examples in which no illegal consequences would follow a breach of conventional principles. A Government that persuaded the House of Commons to suspend the Habeas Corpus Acts after one reading, or induced the House to alter the rules as to the number of times a Bill should be read would not, he said, come into conflict with the law of the land. Nor indeed would the House of Lords if it rejected a series of Bills passed by the Commons.

Some who have criticised Dicey's supposed explanation for obedience to conventions have suggested alternative reasons. Sir Ivor Jennings argued, for example, that conventions are obeyed 'because of the political difficulties which follow if they are not' [The Law and the Constitution (5th edn), p134]. Others have suggested that they are obeyed not because of the probability of a consequential breach of law, but because disregard of convention is likely to induce a change in the law or in the constitutional structure. But it could be objected that, in the case of many infringements of convention, legal or structural change would be an unlikely outcome. It may be more illuminating first to remember that widespread breach of political (as of linguistic) convention may itself sometimes lead to a change of convention, and secondly that conventions are not always obeyed. So, although we can sensibly ask what the uses or purposes of conventions are, it may be unnecessary to ask why they are obeyed when they are obeyed, since we pick out and identify as conventions precisely those rules that are generally obeyed and generally thought to be obligatory. Those who obey moral or other non-legal rules they believe to be obligatory, characteristically do it because of their belief that they are obligatory, or else from some motive of prudence or expected advantage. Those who disobey them do so because they do not regard them as obligatory, or wish to evade them, or wish to change them. In other words we do not need any special or characteristic explanation for obedience to the rules of governmental morality. Whatever we know about compliance with moral rules generally, will suffice.

Note

If the reason that conventions are obeyed is simply that they are thought obligatory by those affected by them, then it appears that the more important question is, what purposes do conventions serve? Whilst answers to this question have been touched on (Dicey: to avoid a breach of the law; Jennings: to avoid political difficulty) these are too general answers, as they would also serve as plausible explanations for a great deal of human behaviour. Can more specific purposes for conventions be elucidated?

THE ROLE OF CONVENTIONS

Reference re Amendment of the Constitution of Canada (1982) 125 DLR (3d) 1

... The main purpose of constitutional conventions is to ensure that the legal framework of the constitution will be operated in accordance with the prevailing constitutional values or principles of the period. For example, the constitutional value which is the pivot of the conventions stated above and relating to responsible government is the democratic principle: the powers of the state must be exercised in accordance with the wishes of the electorate; and the constitutional value or principle which anchors the conventions regulating the relationship between the members of the Commonwealth is the independence of the former British colonies.

Being based on custom and precedent, constitutional conventions are usually unwritten rules. Some of them, however, may be reduced to writing and expressed in the proceedings and documents of imperial conferences, or in the preamble of statutes such as the Statute of Westminster 1931, or in the proceedings and documents of federal-provincial conferences. They are often referred to and recognised in statements made by members of governments.

Perhaps the main reason why convention rules cannot be enforced by the courts is that they are generally in conflict with the legal rules which they postulate, and the courts are bound to enforce the legal rules. The conflict is not of a type which would entail the commission of any illegality. It results from the fact that legal rules create wide powers, discretions and rights which conventions prescribe should be exercised only in a certain limited manner, if at all.

[An] example will illustrate this point. As a matter of law, the Queen, or the Governor General or the Lieutenant Governor could refuse assent to every Bill passed by both Houses of Parliament or by a legislative assembly as the case may be. But by convention they cannot of their own motion refuse to assent to any such Bill on any ground, for instance, because they disapprove of the policy of the Bill. We have here a conflict between a legal rule which creates a complete discretion and a conventional rule which completely neutralises it. But conventions, like laws, are sometimes violated. And if this particular convention were violated and assent were improperly withheld, the courts would be bound to enforce the law, not the convention. They would refuse to recognise the validity of a vetoed bill. This is what happened in *Gallant v The King* (1949) 2 DLR 425 ... a case in keeping with the classic case of *Stockdale v Hansard* (1839) 9 Ad and E1, 112 ER 1112, where the English Court of Queen's Bench held that only the Queen and both Houses of Parliament could make or unmake laws. The Lieutenant-Governor who had withheld assent in *Gallant* apparently did so towards the end of his term of office. Had it been otherwise, it is not inconceivable that his withholding of assent might have produced a political crisis leading to his removal from office, which shows that if the remedy for a breach of a convention does not lie with the courts, still the breach is not necessarily without a remedy. The remedy lies with some other institutions of Government; furthermore, it is not a formal remedy and it may be administered with less certainty or regularity than it would be by a court.

It should be borne in mind, however, that, while they are not laws, some conventions may be more important than some laws. Their importance depends on that of the value or principle which they are meant to safeguard. Also, they form an integral part of the constitution and of the constitutional system. ...

That is why it is perfectly appropriate to say that to violate a convention is to do something which is unconstitutional, although it entails no direct legal consequence. But the words 'constitutional' and 'unconstitutional' may also be used in a strict legal sense, for instance with respect to a statute which is found *ultra vires* or unconstitutional. The foregoing may perhaps be summarised in an equation: constitutional conventions plus constitutional law equal the total constitution of the country.

Questions

1   Is it not rather a paradoxical state of affairs for any nation that prides itself on upholding the Rule of Law that 'important parts of [its] constitution' which 'may be more important than some laws' may be violated with 'no direct legal consequences'?

2   The court found that the basic purpose of conventions is 'to ensure the legal framework of the Constitution in accordance with the prevailing constitutional values or principles of the period'. No doubt responsiveness to changing views as to what political morality demands is desirable. But take the case of a minister whose department bungles the implementation of a new policy in such a way that there is room for doubt as to whether the policy or its implementation are at fault.[12] The minister claims that the convention of ministerial responsibility has now developed in such a way that it only requires ministerial resignation if it is conclusively shown that policy, rather than its implementation, is to blame. Is it necessary that the person who would suffer through the imposition of a conventional rule upon them must be the person who also decides what that rule is?[13] Can flexibility be achieved without allowing people to be judges in their own cause in this way?

Notes

1   Marshall and Moodie note the prevalence of conventions in all constitutions and link this with what they see as their role.

> ... No general Rule of Law is self-applying, but must be applied according to the terms of additional rules. These additional rules may be concerned with the interpretation of the general rule, or with the exact circumstances in which it should apply, about either of which uncertainty may exist, and the greater the generality the greater will the uncertainty tend to be. Many constitutions include a large number of additional legal rules to clarify the meaning and application of their main provisions, but in a changing word it is rarely possible to eradicate or prevent all doubts on these points by enactment or even by adjudication. The result often is to leave significant degree of discretion to those exercising the rights or wielding the powers legally conferred, defined, or permitted. As Dicey pointed out, it is to regulate the use of such discretionary power that conventions develop [*ibid*, pp426–9].

> The definition of 'conventions' may thus be amplified by saying that their purpose is to define the use of constitutional discretion. To put this in slightly different words, it may be said that conventions are non-legal rules regulating the way in which legal rules shall be applied.[14] ...

2   The above analysis does not really explain why the postulated purpose of conventions demands their outstanding distinguishing feature, namely the fact that they cannot be enforced in court. The judges spend much of their

---

12 The responsibility of Home Secretary Michael Howard for the problems in the Prison Service revealed by the Learmont Report in October 1995 is a case in point.

13 The views of the Prime Minister and other ministers on the content of the convention will also obviously be important. However, since resignation (in the example given in the text) would amount to an admission of responsibility for the errors which have come to light, these other parties also have a clear vested outcome in the decision.

14 Marshall and Moodie, *op cit*, pp24–25.

time making law which 'defines the use ... of discretion' (eg the vast number of cases on the discretion to exclude unfairly obtained evidence under s78 of the Police and Criminal Evidence Act 1984)[15] and in general, working out legal rules to govern the application of statutory provisions. To define conventions as non-legal rules supplementing legal rules is not therefore particularly helpful, since many legal rules often do this too. This definition of the role of conventions thus only distinguishes their role from that of legal rules by reiterating that conventions are not laws, returning us to Dicey's basic distinction.

SHOULD CONVENTIONS BE CODIFIED?

The uncertainty surrounding the content and even the existence of certain conventions has led a number of commentators to question whether conventions should now be set down in an authoritative text.

Marshall and Moodie, *Some Problems of the Constitution*, 5th edn (1971), pp34–36

Dr HV Evatt has argued that the practice of enacting conventions, exemplified in such laws as the Parliament Act and the Statute of Westminster, should be extended into other fields in order to end uncertainty about, for example, the royal power of dissolution [*The King and his Dominion* Governors, p268]. In so far as this would lead to more precise formulation of the rules and the use of the courts to give authoritative decisions about their meaning and application, or to the extent that people are more disposed to obey legal than non-legal rules, the advantages are obvious and important. It is nevertheless argued by some that the disadvantages are of greater significance. Thus the Statute of Westminster was resisted in the House of Lords on the grounds that this country 'never has had a written constitution of any sort or kind, and the consequence has been that it has been possible to adapt, from time to time, the various relationships and authorities between every component part of this state, and without any serious mistake or disaster. ... You should avoid as far as possible putting a definition of what the relationships may be into the unyielding form of an Act of Parliament' [Lord Buckmaster, quoted in Wheare, *The Statute of Westminster and Dominion Status*, pp5–6]. This view is hard to accept. Quite apart from the fact that statutes may be repealed or amended with relative ease by a determined Government, or that what are conventions in one country may exist as laws elsewhere without any disastrous effects, the objection overlooks the fact that new conventions may come to quality any legal rule. British constitutional history would have been very different were statute-law necessarily a source of 'disastrous rigidity' in the constitution.

It would be equally wrong, however, to overestimate what enactment of the conventions would achieve. Let us try to draw up a 'balance sheet' of what it could and could not do.

1   Obedience to the rules would not become any more enforceable than it is now. There would undoubtedly be occasions when the mere clarification of a rule would ensure constitutional behaviour. The courts, moreover, can do much to secure observance of the law by such means as declarations and

---

injunctions. But there are several limits to the effectiveness of judicial, or even legislative, action in the face of determined opposition to the law by a Government or, for that matter, by any powerful social group. The sanctions behind constitutional law, as well as convention, are a compound of the desire to abide by the rules, to be 'constitutional', and of the political penalties of disobedience. Ultimately, revolution or civil war may be necessary to procure obedience, as has been amply demonstrated by the history of American legislation and adjudication upon the rights of Negro population in the south.

2   In the absence of a sufficient body of judicial decisions, even well-established legal principles may (at any given time) be of uncertain formulation and application; the principle of the sovereignty of Parliament itself is a case in point. however, in the event of an important dispute turning upon the interpretation of a legal rule, the machinery exists for an authoritative decision upon its meaning and precise application.

3   Legislation, as we have noted, would not prevent the growth of new conventions, about which uncertainty may exist.

4   It could not prevent dispute about what the rules ought to be. And it is important to realise that it is this type of dispute which underlies many arguments about (apparently) what the rules are. This was obviously the case, for example, in the argument about the royal power to 'veto' legislation which took place in 1913, or the Commons' debates about the extent of parliamentary privilege in 1958. It would be foolish to expect anything else, for convention may be described as the 'battleground' between conflicting political forces and constitutional beliefs in society. But this is true not only of disputes about conventional rules. It applies also to legal argument. To cite American experience again, it is evident that constitutional debates about racial segregation in education, or the powers of the federal government in the social an economic fields, have been more than mere scholarly disputations about the 'real' meaning of the 14th Amendment or the 'inter-state commerce clause', although this is the way in which they may be presented. Primarily, these debates have been attempts to persuade the Supreme Court Justices of what the documentary constitution ought to mean; and the standing of the court at any period will depend, in part, upon whether its interpretations conflict with the wishes and beliefs of the most powerful forces in society at the time. Conversely, it is at least arguable that the high standing of the British courts owes something to the fact that many of the most important constitutional rules are, at present, of a non-legal character. Another important factor is, of course, that the doctrine of parliamentary supremacy saves the British courts from having to give the last word on legal points. However, it is doubtful whether this would prevent the courts from a loss of prestige if they were constantly called upon to decide (even subject to parliamentary 'reversal') a whole series of constitutional controversies.

5   What has just been said suggests that the attempt to enact conventional rules might itself prove extremely difficult. It is likely that the fiercely disputed Parliament Act of 1911 rather than the Statute of Westminster would prove to be typical of the process. Even if agreement could be reached about what the rules are, it is hard to believe that no attempt would be made to formulate the rule with greater precision, in line with particular views as to what it should be. It can be argued, with come conviction, that this is in fact what happened with the Parliament Act and with the American 'third-term' amendment. It is, moreover, most unlikely that in fact any attempt will be made to 'codify'

the conventions until and unless their precise meaning has become a crucial factor in a constitutional crisis – in which case it might not be of very great significance whether the disputed rule was or was not a law, in that further legislation may anyway be needed to settle the dispute.

6   Enactment of the conventions may nevertheless be important, if once successfully achieved. Just as some course of action desired by a section of the community acquires a significant degree of legitimacy and authority simply by virtue of its acceptance as a convention, so a convention may acquire greater legitimacy and authority by its transformation into law. The exact significance of this 'evaluation' will probably vary with different rules.

Notes

1   One of the more cogent arguments against codification is the loss of prestige which the courts might face if forced to adjudicate on controversial issues of convention. However, this point clearly has far more force in relation to some conventions than others. Clearly, areas such as individual and collective ministerial responsibility should not be handed over to the courts for adjudication;[16] for one thing, the latter, and on some occasions the former, are generally in the interest of the Government and will therefore be enforced by it, within flexible limits. Additionally, individual ministerial responsibility is clearly at the heart of the notion of parliamentary accountability, and the stuff of everyday political conflict. Other conventions, however, such as those relating to the powers of the monarch to refuse assent to legislation and to dissolve Parliament, or the obligation of a Government to resign upon being defeated in a general election are in a different category. Firstly, both because the situations would rarely arise at all, and because, if they did, the conventional rules would probably be followed, just as they are now, the fear that the courts would be 'constantly called upon to decide ... constitutional controversies' is groundless. Secondly, these conventions are vital to democracy itself; as indicated above it seems absurd to exclude constitutional fundamentals from the Rule of Law.

2   On the question of the role of the courts, it should also be pointed out that conventions could be codified, but the code made non-justiciable. Some clarification would thus be achieved without risking the prestige of the courts.

3   Codification would resolve the intolerable situation in which the very existence of some conventions has been in doubt. To give a historical example, in 1708 the Royal Assent was withheld from a Bill of which the monarch in question, Queen Anne, disapproved, whereas in 1829 George IV gave consent to a Bill which he disliked. Sometime during those 100 years the convention in question must have come into being. However, it would

---

16   There is no reason, however, why an independent committee (staffed, say, by judges, academics and MPs) should not be given the power to make non-binding findings on whether a particular convention has or has not been breached. Such findings might (by convention!), come to achieve such prestige that a Government would find it impossible (or at least very politically damaging) to ignore them. The establishment of such a committee would of course raise a whole host of questions, such as its jurisdiction, whether it was to follow its previous decisions, etc.

be impossible to pinpoint the stage at which this occurred; if, during that time, the question had arisen as to whether withholding the Royal Consent was unconstitutional, no answer would be available to the monarch in question; in effect it would not be available until after he or she had acted.

4   Some conventions, of course, benefit from their indeterminacy. The doctrine of collective Cabinet responsibility provides an example. Under the doctrine, ministers are collectively responsible to Parliament for their actions in governing the country and therefore should be in accord on any major question. A minister should resign if he or she is in disagreement with the policy of the Cabinet on any such question. Examples of such resignation include Sir Thomas Dugdale's in 1954 due to his disagreement with the Government as to the disposal of an area of land known as Crichel Down (this resignation is not always cited as an example of policy disagreement, but such appears to have been its basis), and Sir Anthony Eden's resignation in 1938 over Chamberlain's policy towards Mussolini. However, there appears to have been some blurring and weakening of the doctrine dating from the mid-1970s. In 1975 the Labour Cabinet was divided on the question of whether the UK should remain in the Common Market. It was agreed that, in the period before the referendum on the question, Cabinet ministers should be able to express a view at variance with the official view of the Government that the UK should remain a member of the Common Market. Some weakening of the convention also appears from the Westland affair which, on the face of it, provides an example of its operation; when Michael Heseltine resigned from the Cabinet in 1986 due to his disagreement with Government policy, he specifically stated that he did not do so as a result of his perception of an obligation arising from the convention. When John Major's administration was considering whether to allow a referendum on a single currency, the option of suspending collective Cabinet responsibility during the referendum campaign was canvassed as a legitimate possibility open to the Prime Minister, the 1975 suspension being cited as a precedent.

5   If the convention of collective responsibility were enshrined in a statute, departure from it as in 1975 might have been less readily undertaken, even if the provisions of the statute were made non-justiciable. In any event it would be difficult, and probably undesirable, to define the convention, as discretion in complying with it may be said to be endemic in it. Political inconvenience would clearly arise, and it might be argued that the democratic process would be endangered if ministers could not at times express their views on exceptionally important issues with some freedom. Therefore, it may be argued that no advantage would be gained by enacting such a statute; such crystallisation of the convention would clearly reduce its value.

6   The only sensible conclusion seems to be that a selective approach towards codification would be a prerequisite for reform.

CHAPTER 3

THE RULE OF LAW AND THE SEPARATION OF POWERS[1]

INTRODUCTION – THE THEORETICAL BASIS OF THE RULE OF LAW

The Rule of Law is a chameleon-like notion.[2] Used by different people it may mean radically different things. As noted in Chapter 1, an influential commentator on the Left, John Griffith, objects to the notion being used to denote anything more substantive than a set of basic restraints on the powers of the state, particularly its ability to penalise it citizens;[3] Griffith complains that, contrary to his prescription, the doctrine is sometimes used in a much wider sense to create loyalty towards the status quo. Professor Raz notes that, in 1959, the International Congress of Jurists came up with a definition of the Rule of Law which effectively made it a shorthand for 'a complete social philosophy', prescribing a full panoply of civil, political, economic and social rights.[4]

However, both of these writers, and indeed the vast majority of commentators dealing with this subject, assume that the notion of the Rule of Law must mean at least that people should be ruled by rules (though even traditionalists have now disclaimed Dicey's notion that the granting of discretionary powers to the executive necessarily infringes the doctrine).[5] But is even this modest assumption justifiable? Frederick Schauer considers that the essence of a system run according to law is the notion that power must be allocated according to law. Whether that power must then be exercised according to a set of pre-ordained rules is another question.

Frederick Schauer, *Playing by the Rules: A Philosophical Examination of Rule-Based Decision-Making in Law and in Life* (1991), pp167–8, 10–11

Is there a connection between rule-based decision-making and decision-making within that institution we conventionally refer to as 'law'? What is the place of rules within a 'legal system'? To many people these questions answer themselves. Law just *is* decisions according to rules, for rules to these people are what distinguish law both from the naked exercise of power and the unedited practice of politics. To support this conclusion, those who equate decision according to law with decision according to rules can point out common

---

1   General reading (additional to that cited in this chapter): sources referred to in n 1 of Chapter 1 of this Part; also *Report of the Committee on Minister's Powers* (Cmnd 4060), K Davis, *Discretionary Justice* (1971); Loughlin, *Public Law and Politics* (1992); Barendt, 'Dicey and Civil Liberties' (1985) PL 596; Craig, 'Dicey: Unitary, Self-correcting Democracy and Public Law' (1990) 106 LQR 105; Hayek, *The Road to Serfdom* (1944); Vile, *Constitutionalism and the Separation of Powers* (1967); De Smith, 'The Separation of Powers in New Dress' (1966) 12 McGill LJ 491; Munro, 'The Separation of Powers: not such a Myth' (1981) PL 19.

2   For the basic principles of the doctrine see, in this chapter, 'Principles deriving from the Rule of Law' below p77 *et seq*. This introduction considers the theoretical background to the doctrine.

3   See Griffith, 'The Political Constitution', (1979) 42 MLR p15; quoted in Chapter 1, pp33–7.

4   J Raz, 'The Rule of Law and its Virtue' (1977) 93 LQR p195; quoted below, at pp78–80.

5   See for example, Heuston, *Essays in Constitutional Law*, 2nd edn (1964), pp41–2; quoted below, at pp83–4.

linguistic usage and the phrase 'the Rule of Law'. What is the Rule of Law, it can be said, if not the rule of rules?

Are we able to make sense out of the idea of a legal system without rules? Can there be law without decision according to rules of sufficient generality such that the power of the state is not deployed, and disputes among citizens not resolved, on something other than strictly an *ad hoc* basis? From one perspective, the answer to this question is 'no', but from another there appears ample room for an idea of law without rules. ...

It is worth emphasising that nothing in the conception of a regulative rule suggests either a neutral affinity to, or exclusive location within, the political state's mechanisms of social control and dispute resolution. Thus the relationship between rules and a 'legal system' is contingent, for decision according to rules is but one among several sorts of decision-making. As a result, although empowering rules create the institutions of dispute resolution and empower certain officials to resolve certain sorts of disputes, disputes could still be resolved largely without reference to mandatory rules imposing substantive constraint on the content of the decisions. Having been empowered to resolve a dispute, the adjudicator would be authorised, as in Weber's description of the *qadi*, to come to a conclusion as open-endedly as appropriate in the circumstances. Similarly, if rule-based decision-making is only one option among several, it need not be central to social control and co-ordination. Rather than rely largely on rules, governments could control and co-ordinate behaviour through the discretionary acts of subordinate governmental officials whose particularised judgement was uncontrolled by rules. (Again, empowering rules would be necessary to establish the authority of those subordinate officials, but the necessity of such rules is consistent with distinguishing systems in which the rules that authorise subordinate officials to act, prescribe nothing further about the substance of those actions from systems in which rules not only create authority, but attempt to guide the substance of the exercise of that authority.)

In creating these stylised alternatives to rule-based dispute resolution and social control, I do not intend to endorse them. Nor even do I want to suggest that such totally rule-sterile systems are socially possible. Yet although these ruleless alternatives are caricatures, the caricatures suggest less extreme and more pervasive manifestations of the fact that much of the mechanism we call the 'legal system' need not operate according to the conception of rules I elaborate in this book. If we assume at the outset that law just *is* a system of rules, especially of mandatory rules, we may assume that legal decision-making is necessarily rule-based. Such an approach, however, will distort the analysis of rules, for rules would then need to be *defined* in conformity with the objectives of a legal system. Instead, however, some of those objectives may be ill-served by rule-bound decision-making. This is hardly implausible, and explains why modern legal systems often avoid the use of mandatory rules. Consider child custody determinations, in which an open-ended 'best interests of the child' standard, rather than any more constraining set of rules, provides guidance for the decision-maker; the system of equity, no less part of the legal system for embodying flexibility and particularly as its method; the traditional sentencing process, in which the range of factors permissibly relevant to the decision is virtually unlimited; and the increasing use of substantially rule-free arbitration, mediation, and conciliation procedures as adjuncts to or substitutes for formal adjudication. These are but a few among many examples of forms of legal decision-making that, only with difficulty, can be characterised as rule-based. Consequently, I want to start with the assumption that rule-governed decision-making is a subset of legal decision-making rather than being congruent with it.

Note

Schauer's distinction between power-allocating and power-exercising rules is useful in that it forces us to realise that a state could dispense altogether with the idea of governing according to substantive rules without acting illegally; eg Parliament could repeal the criminal law in its entirety and substitute for it an Act stating that certain Government appointees were to have exclusive power to punish, as they thought fit, such acts as they thought ought to be punished within specified geographical areas allocated to them. Whilst such an Act would violate many of the fundamental doctrines of the Rule of Law as they are commonly understood to be, such an Act would not be 'illegal', since Parliament would be exercising power allocated to it by law.[6] (It is also worth noting that judicial review of decisions made under the Act would still be possible if, for example, an appointee purported to punish a citizen in respect of an act which was not committed in his or her allocated area.) Thus Schauer's point both helps to clear up some confusion between illegal 'laws' and ones which violate the principles of the Rule of Law, and also make it clear that those principles are not the necessary attributes of any state established under law but rather are contingent, and therefore vulnerable to erosion.

FUNDAMENTAL ATTRIBUTES OF THE RULE OF LAW

The basic notion that no one may exercise power unless that power has been granted to him by law can also be expressed in the notion of Government under the law. Jeremy Waldron explains why this notion has such significant connotations.

Jeremy Waldron, *The Law* (1990), pp31–2

For many of us, the policeman on patrol is the most visible expression of the power of the British state. He represents an organisation that has the ability to overwhelm any of us with physical force if we resist its demands, and he can call on that force any time he wants. Though there is no national police force in Britain, events like the miners' strike of 1984–5 have shown that the police forces will co-operate to whatever extent is necessary to overwhelm those who defy them. Similarly, although the police in Britain are not armed as a matter of course except with truncheons, they do have access to firearms and, as events in Northern Ireland have shown, they can ask political leaders to deploy military force if that is necessary to resist some challenge to their authority. Their potential power, like that of any government official, is enormous, for in the last resort they can call upon all the organised force of the state. And the same is true of other officials as well – from taxation officials to social welfare clerks. They are all the agents of an immensely powerful organisation.

When you put it like that, it is hard to resist the image of one group of people – the organised events of the state – wielding power over another, much larger group of people – the rest of us, relatively powerless in ourselves and abjectly vulnerable to their demands. Some are powerful, some are not. The state is the rule of one group of people by another. And that, of course, is an affront and an indignity to the people who are in the subordinate position, since it leaves us unfree and evidently unequal.

---

6   The hypothetical Act would of course breach numerous provisions of both the European Convention of Human Rights and the International Covenant on Civil and Political Rights.

Ever since Aristotle, political philosophers have tried to mitigate or qualify that image. Politics, they have argued, need not be the arbitrary rule of man over man. Perhaps we can imagine a form of political life in which everyone is a subject and everyone is ruled, not by a person or by any particular group of people, but by a shared set of abstract rules. If I am subject to another person, then I am at the mercy of his whims and passions, his angers and prejudices. But if we are both subject to the law, then the personal factor is taken out of politics. By subjecting everyone to the law, we make ourselves, in a sense, equal again.

Notes

1   Waldron's conclusion, that the Rule of Law renders us, 'in a sense equal again', refers to a notion of *formal* equality; it does not of course imply that the content of individual laws could not promote *substantive* inequality. As Jeffrey Jowell puts it,[7] the concern of formal equality 'is not with the content of the law but with its *enforcement and application* alone. As long as laws are applied equally, that is without irrational bias or distinction, then formal equality is complied with. Formal equality does not however prohibit *unequal* laws. It constrains, say, racially-biased enforcement of the law, but it does not inhibit racially discriminatory laws from being enacted' (original emphasis). We will return to this distinction again below.

2   If Government is under law, then since the courts are empowered to make the authoritative determination of what the law is, this must mean that the Government is in a sense under, and therefore obliged to obey orders of the courts. The normal sanction for failure to obey an order of the court is a finding of contempt of court. Perhaps surprisingly, the question whether Ministers of the Crown were obliged to obey court orders, and risked a finding of contempt if they did not, remained undecided in law until the case of *M* in 1993.

M v Home Office [1992] 2 WLR 73, 80, CA; *In Re M* [1993] 3 WLR 433, 437–8 and 465–6, HL

In 1993, M, a citizen of Zaire, sought political asylum in the UK. His application was refused by the Home Office, and leave to apply for judicial review of the Home Office's decision was also refused. Just before his removal, a fresh application for judicial review, alleging new grounds, was made to Garland J in chambers; the judge indicated that he wished M's removal to be delayed pending consideration of the fresh application and understood counsel for the Home Office to have given an undertaking that this would be done. However, M's removal was not delayed, due to various mistakes and breakdowns in communication. Learning of this, Garland J then made an *ex parte* order requiring the Home Secretary to procure M's return to England. The Home Secretary, having taken legal advice, decided that the judge had no jurisdiction to make a mandatory interim injunction against him, as a Minister of the Crown. Proceedings were then brought against the Home Secretary, alleging that he had been in contempt of court by virtue of his refusal to obey the *ex parte*

---

7   'The Rule of Law Today' in Jowell and Oliver (eds), *The Changing Constitution*, 3rd edn (1994), p76.

order and the failure to comply with the terms of counsel's undertaking. The case was dismissed at first instance, and came to the Court of Appeal.

> **Lord Donaldson of Lymington MR:** ... this is a matter of high constitutional importance. Indeed I would say of the very highest. I agree with him that the day to day relationship between the judiciary and all governments and ministers in modern times has been based upon trust. In a sense the same is true of its relationship with all who resort to the courts for justice in civil disputes. The system would be put under intolerable strain and would be likely to break down if a significant number of citizens treated the courts' orders as mere requests which could be complied with or ignored as they thought appropriate. I share his confidence that, in the foreseeable future, governments and ministers will recognise their obligations to their opponents, to the courts and to justice. Where I have somewhat less confidence is in the suggestion that, were it ever otherwise, there would be a heavy political price to pay. There might well be, but I am not sure that there would be if, in particular circumstances, popular opinion was firmly on the side of the government and against the person who had obtained the order. Yet it is precisely in those circumstances that individual citizens should be able to look to the judiciary for protection under the law. I therefore do indeed think that it would be a black day for the Rule of Law and for the liberty of the subject if the first instance judge has correctly interpreted the law. I have reached the firm conclusion that he was mistaken. ...

The Court of Appeal found the Home Secretary personally to have been in contempt of court. He appealed to the House of Lords.

> **Lord Templeman:** My Lords, Parliament makes the law, the executive carry the law into effect and the judiciary enforce the law. The expression 'the Crown' has two meanings; namely the monarch and the executive. In the 17th century Parliament established its supremacy over the Crown as monarch, over the executive and over the judiciary. Parliamentary supremacy over the Crown as monarch stems from the fact that the monarch must accept the advice of a Prime Minister who is supported by a majority of Parliament. Parliamentary supremacy over the judiciary is only exercisable in statute. The judiciary enforce the law against individuals, against institutions and against the executive. The judges cannot enforce the law against the Crown as monarch because the Crown as monarch can do no wrong but judges enforce the law against the Crown as an executive and against the individuals who from time to time represent the Crown. A litigant complaining of a breach of the law by the executive can sue the Crown as executive bringing his action against the minister who is responsible for the department of state involved, in the present case the Secretary of State for Home Affairs. To enforce the law the courts have power to grant remedies including injunctions against a minister in his official capacity. If the minister has personally broken the law, the litigant can sue the minister, in this case Mr Kenneth Baker, in his personal capacity. For the purpose of enforcing the law against all persons and institutions, including ministers in their official capacity and in their personal capacity, the courts are armed with coercive powers exercisable in proceedings for contempt of court.

> In the present case, counsel for the Secretary of State argued that the judge could not enforce the law by injunction or contempt proceedings against the minister in his official capacity. Counsel also argued that in his personal capacity Mr Kenneth Baker, the Secretary of State for Home Affairs, had not been guilty of contempt.

> My Lords, the argument that there is no power to enforce the law by injunction or contempt proceedings against a minister in his official capacity would, if

upheld, establish the proposition that the executive obey the law as a matter of grace and not as a matter of necessity, a proposition which would reverse the result of the Civil War. For the reasons given by noble and learned friend, Lord Woolf, and on principle, I am satisfied that injunctions and contempt proceedings may be brought against the minister in his official capacity and that in the present case the Home Office for which the Secretary of State was responsible was in contempt. I am also satisfied that Mr Baker was, throughout, acting in his official capacity on advice which he was entitled to accept and under a mistaken view as to the law. In these circumstances I do not consider that Mr Baker personally was guilty of contempt. I would therefore dismiss this appeal substituting the Secretary of State for Home Affairs as being the person against whom the finding of contempt was made.

Lord Woolf: ... The Court of Appeal were of the opinion that a finding of contempt could not be made against the Crown, a government department or a minister of the Crown in his official capacity. Although it is to be expected that it will be rare indeed that the circumstances will exist in which such a finding would be justified, I do not believe there is any impediment to a court making such a finding, when it is appropriate to do so, not against the Crown directly, but against a government department or a minister of the Crown in his official capacity.

Nolan LJ, at p311, [in the Court of Appeal] considered that the fact that proceedings for contempt are 'essentially personal and punitive' meant that it was not open to a court, as a matter of law, to make a finding of contempt against the Home Office or the Home Secretary. While contempt proceedings usually have these characteristics and contempt proceedings against a government department or a minister in an official capacity would not be either personal or punitive (it would clearly not be appropriate to fine or sequest the assets of the Crown or a government department or an officer of the Crown acting in his official capacity), this does not meant that a finding of contempt against a government department or minister would be pointless. The very fact of making such a finding would vindicate the requirements of justice. In addition an order for costs could be made to underline the significance of a contempt. A purpose of the courts' powers to make findings of contempt is to ensure that the orders of the court are obeyed. ...

In cases not involving a government department or a minister the ability to *punish* for contempt may be necessary. However, as is reflected in the restrictions on execution against the Crown, the Crown's relationship with the courts does not depend on coercion and in the exceptional situation when a government department's conduct justifies this, a finding of contempt should suffice. In that exceptional situation, the ability of the court to make a finding of contempt is of great importance. It would demonstrate that a government department has interfered with the administration of justice. It will then be for Parliament to determine what should be the consequences of that finding.

... the object of the exercise is not so much to punish an individual as to vindicate the Rule of Law by a finding of contempt. This can be achieved equally by a declaratory finding of the court as to the contempt against the minister as representing the department.

Notes

1   It should be noted that counsel for the Home Secretary explicitly stated in argument that it was not part of his case to contend that the Crown was above the law, indeed 'he accepted that the Crown has a duty to obey the law as declared by the courts'.

2   As TRS Allan notes,[8] the finding in this decision was of symbolic, rather than practical value, since 'The relationship between the courts and the Crown cannot ... ultimately be a matter of coercion (as the current restrictions on execution against the Crown confirm)'. Nevertheless, its symbolic value should not be understated: to hold, as Simon Brown J did at first instance, that undertakings given by Crown officers were 'no more than unenforceable assurances', and that coercive orders were unavailable against them, would have driven a coach and horses through the notion of equality before the law.

3   As well as promoting the notion of equality, the Rule of Law has perhaps a still more basic purpose: that of acting as a constraint on Government power, a power which, as Waldron remarks, 'has the ability to overwhelm any of us with physical force'.[9] Two questions have been posed from the Left about this aspect of the doctrine. The first is whether the Rule of Law can actually achieve its aim of restraint. The second, more historic concern, is whether it is desirable that Government power should be constrained in this way. These questions will be dealt with in turn.

Can the Rule of Law restrain power?

Michael Tushnet considers this question, using as examples certain well-known decisions of the American Supreme Court.

Michael Tushnet, *Red, White and Blue: A Critical Analysis of Constitutional Law* (1988), pp46–51

The Rule of Law, according to the liberal conception, is meant to protect us against the exercise of arbitrary power. The theory of neutral principles asserts that a requirement of consistency, the core of the ideal of the Rule of Law, places sufficient bounds on judges to reduce the risk of arbitrariness to an acceptable level. The question is whether the concepts of neutrality and consistency can be developed in ways that are adequate for the task. This section examines two candidates for a definition of neutrality. It argues that each fails to provide the kinds of constraints on judges that the liberal tradition requires. The limits they place on judges are either empty or dependent on a sociology of law that undermines the liberal tradition's assumptions about society.

If neutrality is to serve as a meaningful guide, it must be understood not as a standard for the content of principles but rather as a constraint on the process by which principles are selected, justified, and applied. Thus, the possible explications of neutrality focus on the judicial process and the need for 'neutral application'. This focus transfers our attention from the principles themselves to the judges who purpose to use them. ...

What, then, are methodologically neutral principles? The best explication looks to the past. It would impose, as a necessary condition for justification, that a decision be consistent with the relevant precedents. Michael Perry's discussion of the abortion funding cases exemplifies this approach.

In 1973 the Supreme Court held in *Roe v Wade* that state criminal statutes

---

8   (1994) 53 CLJ 1.
9   *op cit*, p31.

restricting the availability of abortions were unconstitutional [410 US 113]. Seven years later the Court upheld legislation that denied public funds for abortion to those otherwise qualified for public assistance in paying for medical care [*Harris v McRae* 448 US 297 (1980)]. Perry contends that the abortion funding decision is 'plainly wrong' because it 'is inconsistent with the narrowest possible coherent reading of *Roe*'. Perry extracts that reading as follows. The Court struck down the statutes in *Roe* because the pregnant woman's interest in terminating the pregnancy is greater than the government's interest in preventing the taking of the life of the foetus. According to Perry, this entails the conclusion that 'no governmental action can be predicated on the view that ... abortion is *per se* morally objectionable' [Perry, 'Why the Supreme Court was Wrong', pp1114, 1120, 1115–16]. Perry's premise is that government is permitted to use a factor as a predicate for restrictive legislation only if that factor is entitled to no constitutional protection.

Perry rejects as 'deeply flawed' and 'fundamentally confused' the position taken by the Court in the funding cases and repeated by Peter Western [Id p1117, Peter Western, ' Correspondence', 33 *Stanford Law Review* 1187, 1188 (1981)]. This position is that *Roe* barred the government from criminalising abortions only because criminal sanctions place an undue burden on the woman's interest in terminating the pregnancy; refusing to fund abortions does not similarly burden that interest. Perry claims that *Roe* is coherent only if it precludes the government from taking any action predicated on the view that abortion is wrong. To allow the government to take such action would force us to the 'rather strange' position that the constitution permits the government 'to establish a legal principle' and simultaneously 'protect(s) a person's interest in disregarding that principle once established' [Perry pp1116–17].

There is nothing strange, however, about the supposed paradox; whether we think the position is strange depends on how we define principles and interest. The applicable general principle might be that government can take all actions predicated on the moral view except insofar as they unduly burden some individual interest.

Alternatively, we might identify an *independent* moral principle for objecting to tax-funded abortions – for example, that governments may be responsive to the views of taxpayers who object, on moral grounds, to the use of their money to pay for abortions. The government would not be taking the view that abortion is wrong, and its actions would therefore not be inconsistent with what Perry describes as the minimum principle of *Roe*.

The argument just made can be generalised. At the moment a decision is announced we cannot identify the principle that it embodies. Each decision can be justified by many principles, and we learn what principle justified case 1 only when a court in case 2 tells us. Behind the court's statement about case 1 lies all the creativity to which the hermeneutic theory of historical understanding directed our attention. When *Roe* was decided we might have thought that it rested on Perry's principle, but the funding cases show us that we were 'wrong' and that *Roe* 'in fact' rested on one of the alternatives just spelled out. The theory of neutral principles thus loses almost all of its constraining force. We have only to compare case 2, which is now decided, with case 1 to see if a principle from case 1 has been neutrally applied in case 2. If the demand is merely that the opinion in case 2 deploy some reading of the earlier case from which the holding in case 2 follows, the openness of the precedents means that the demand can always be satisfied. And if the demand is rather that the holding be derived from the principles actually articulated in the relevant precedents, differences between case 2 and the precedents will inevitably demand a degree of reinterpretation of the old principles. New cases always present issues different from those settled by prior cases. [Indeed, if it did not so depart we ought to wonder why the later case was litigated at all.] Thus, to decide a new case a judge must take some liberties with the old principles if they are to be applied at all. There is, however, no principled way to determine how many liberties can be taken; hence this reading of the theory likewise provides no meaningful constraints.

The central problem here is that, given the difficulty of isolating a single principle for which a particular precedent stands, we lack any criteria for distinguishing between cases that depart from, and those that conform to, the principles of their precedents. In fact, any case can compellingly be placed in either category. Such a universal claim cannot be validated by example. But two examples of cases that simultaneously depart from and conform to their precedents can at least make the claim plausible.

The first is *Griswold v Connecticut*, in which the Court held that a state could not constitutionally prohibit the dissemination of contraceptive information or devices to married people [381 US 479 (1965)]. *Griswold* relied in part on *Pierce v Society of Sisters* [268 US 510 (1925)] and *Meyer v Nebraska* [262 US 390 (1923)]. *Pierce* held unconstitutional a requirement that children attend public rather than private schools; *Meyer* held that state could not prohibit the teaching of foreign languages to young children. In *Griswold* the Court said that these cases relied on a constitutionally protected interest, conveniently labelled 'privacy', that was identical to the interest in the contraceptive case.

In one view *Griswold* tortures these precedents. Both were old-fashioned substantive due process cases, which emphasised interference 'with the calling of modern language teachers ... and with the power of parents to control the education of their own'. In this view the most one can fairly find in *Meyer* and *Pierce* is a principle about freedom of inquiry, rather narrower than a principle of privacy. Yet one can say with equal force that *Griswold* identifies for us the true privacy principle of *Meyer* and *Pierce*, in the way that the abortion funding cases identify the true principle of *Roe v Wade*, but this retrospective approach to neutral principles must recognise the extensive creativity exercised by a judge when he or she imputes to a precedent 'the' principle that justifies both the precedent and the judge's present holding.

The examples illustrate a general point. In a legal system with a relatively extensive body of precedent and well-developed techniques of legal reasoning, it will always be possible to show how today's decision is consistent with the relevant past ones, but, conversely, it will also always be possible to show how today's decision is inconsistent with the precedents. This symmetry, of course, drains 'consistency' of any normative content.

The result of the inquiry into neutral principles theory indicates that, although it is possible to discuss a given decision's consistency with previous precedents, requiring consistency of this kind similarly fails to constrain judges sufficiently and thereby fails to advance the underlying liberal project.

Questions

1   Much of Tushnet's critique appears to be founded on the fact that the US constitution is drafted in broad, general terms and that US judges have claimed to find that certain quite specific rights may be deduced inevitably from its terms. How relevant is his analysis to the British constitution?

2   Later in the same chapter, Tushnet comments, 'Insofar as *Roe* gives us evidence, we can conclude that Justice Blackman is a terrible judge' (p 53). If the interpretative endeavour is essentially a charade, as Tushnet claims, in

what sense can one still say that there are 'good' and 'bad' judges, or judgements? Is such an evaluations made purely by reference to criteria internal to the legal system concerned?

3   If Tushnet is right, are businesspeople and others who pay considerable sums of money to be advised by lawyers on the probable outcome of constitutional cases simply throwing their money away?

Is such restraint desirable?

The Marxist historian E P Thompson has made the claim that, 'The Rule of Law itself, the imposing of effective inhibitions upon power and the defence of the citizen from power's all intrusive claims, seems to me an unqualified human good'.[10] In a critical response, M J Horowitz expresses vigorous disagreement:

> I do not see how a man of the Left can describe the Rule of Law as an 'unqualified human good'. It undoubtedly restrains power, but it also prevents power's benevolent exercise. It creates formal equality – a not inconsiderable virtue – but it *promotes* substantive inequality by creating a consciousness that radically separates law from politics, means from ends, processes from outcomes. By promoting procedural justice it enables the shrewd, the calculating, and the wealthy to manipulate its forms to their own advantage. And it ratifies and legitimates an adversarial, competitive, and atomistic conception of human relations.[11]

Question

What kinds of 'benevolent' exercises of power would be restrained by the prohibition of arbitrary, unchecked, unaccountable power, exercised without warning, and under no ascertainable authority?

Note

Jowell considers that Horowitz is simply confused, conflating the 'Rule of Law with the substance of particular laws'; he adds that 'To claim that unjust laws and their rigorous enforcement demonstrate that the Rule of Law is an instrument of oppression is ... [profoundly] misleading'.[12] However, Waldron, looking back to Engel's analysis, provides a more qualified and subtle refutation of the 'partisan model' of law which, using his terminology, writers like Horowitz represent.

Jeremy Waldron, *The Law* (1990), pp21–4

> Nowadays few on the Left view the state as merely a 'committee' of the bourgeoisie. In its ethos, its personnel, and its social function, the state stands somewhat apart from the interests of business and capital. One of its specific jobs is to maintain some sort of order in the midst of class conflict – to mitigate the struggle as it were, so that production and economic life can proceed. Marx's collaborator, Frederick Engels, is often cited here:
>
> > 'In order that these opposites, classes with conflicting economic interests, shall not consume themselves and society in fruitless struggle, it became

---

10   E P Thompson, *Whigs and Hunters* (1975), p266.

11   Horowitz, 'The Rule of Law: an Unqualified Human Good?' (1977) 86 Yale LJ 591.

12   In Jowell and Oliver, *op cit*, pp72.

necessary to have a power seemingly standing above society that would moderate the conflict and keep it within the bounds of "order".' [*The Origin of the Family, Private Property and the State* (1978), pp205–6]

Although he believed that the state was ultimately a tool of 'the most powerful, economically dominant class', Engels thought it was a tool that would work only if it avoided being comprehensively identified in everyone's mind with the interests of the dominant class. People must have some reason for regarding the state as an independent force (even if that is, in the last analysis, an illusion), otherwise the ruling class gains no advantage from dominating through the state as opposed to dominating through brute economic force. Now, to put it bluntly, in order to be perceived as an independent source of order, the state must, some of the time, ... be an independent source of order. And in its institutions and personnel, it will develop practices and attitudes orientated towards that end.

The point was sometimes made by saying that the state is 'relatively autonomous' from society and determined by economic forces only 'in the last resort'. What this means is that the state has some degree of independence: it can act on its own initiative, though of course it is subject to constraints. Given those constraints, there is some room for the *political* partisan model to operate, and perhaps some room also for a view of the state as neutral. If the state is partly independent of the ruling class, then it makes a difference how that independence is exercised by the people working within it, and we may be interested once again in the party-political provenance of various laws, and in the aspiration of legality and reciprocity in politics.

Much the same can be said about the role of law. Even if its contribution to bourgeois dominance is to mystify the people and make them think in terms of a neutral or transcendent order, it has got to give them *some* reason for thinking in that way. The point has been powerfully stated by the historian EP Thompson in response to the claim made by some 'structuralist' Marxists that law is *simply* a devise for mystifying the masses and masking the reality of class dominance:

> People are not as stupid as some structuralist philosophers suppose them to be. They will not be mystified by the first man who puts on a wig. It is inherent in the especial character of law, as a body of rules and procedures, that it shall apply logical criteria with reference to standards of universality and equity. It is true that certain categories of person may be excluded from this logic (as children or slaves), that other categories may be debarred from access to parts of the logic (as women or, for many forms of 18th century law, those without certain kinds of property). All this, and more, is true. But if too much of this is true, then the consequences are plainly counterproductive. Most men have a strong sense of justice, at least with regard to their own interests. If the law is evidently partial and unjust, then it will mask nothing, legitimate nothing, contribute nothing to any class's hegemony. The essential precondition for the effectiveness of law, in its function is ideology, is that it shall display an independence from gross manipulation, and shall seem to be just. It cannot seem to be so without upholding its own logic and criteria; indeed, on occasion, by actually being just. [*Whigs and Hunters* (1977), pp262–3]

Two points follow. First, it is always possible for members of the ruling class, and certainly the personnel of the state, to become caught up in their own rhetoric. Thompson notes that a ruling ideology cannot usually be dismissed as mere hypocrisy: 'even rules find a need to legitimise their power, to moralise their functions, to feel themselves to be useful and just'. Moreover if their ideology is something as complex as law, 'a discipline that requires years of exacting study to master', many of its practitioners are bound to become to immersed in its logic that they take seriously and in good faith its substance and its reasoning.

The other point is more subtle but even more important. The ideology of the Rule of Law, legality, and so on can help sustain class power only if it is – considered in itself – a morally appealing set of ideas. We may overlay something nasty with something sweet in order to make the nastiness more palatable, but then the something sweet must really *be* sweet, considered in itself, or else it will contribute nothing to the palatability. Law helps to legitimate class power by presenting it to all concerned masked in a form which, if it actually *did* correspond to reality, would be the form of a society that was good and fair and just. The idea of a set of rules that apply the same to everyone, the idea that anyone, whatever her class, may come to an impartial tribunal and ask that justice be done, the idea that force may not be used even by those in authority except in pursuance of a general principle – these ideas may be a misdescription of what actually goes on in modern Britain (or in the England that Thompson was writing about), but they are attractive nevertheless and a society which really did conform to them would be a good society.

If this is true, and if the earlier point is true – that a ruling class must actually submit to the Rule of Law some of the time in order to sustain the general *pretence* of legality – then it seems to follow that law and legality, even if they are instruments of class domination, do also make a positive contribution to society. There is a difference, as Thompson notes, between 'direct unmediated force (arbitrary imprisonment, the employment of troops against the crowd, torture, and all those other conveniences of power with which we are all conversant)' and the Rule of Law, even if both are modes of class domination.

All this points in the direction of an approach to law that may not be cynical to all. If we agree that legality and the Rule of Law are *capable* of modifying class conflict and oppression in desirable ways, then maybe we should think favourably about the concept of a society actually ruled by law, not as a description of our society, but as a social ideal, something to be aimed at. Maybe, as things stand at present, legal rules are used to serve partisan ends. We need to be realistic and clear about what is actually going on. But we also need an ideal or an aspiration for political life – some sense of what it would be for things to be better. For this purpose, even in the midst of its partisan embroilment, the image that law projects is an attractive one.

Note

Waldron thus concludes that we should distinguish between the Rule of Law used as a complacent description of the way in which Western democracies are governed today, in which it may indeed veil political inequality, and the doctrine as an aspiration, as a blueprint for good government. As Halden and Lewis put it: 'The Rule of Law is not the description of a set of working practices espoused by Dicey. It is a belief in the governance of the nation through order, choice and free expression. In the conditions of the late 20th century, in Britain in particular, the Rule of Law is much more of a rallying cry than an institutional reality.'[13]

---

13   I Harden and N Lewis, *The Noble Lie: The British Constitution and the Rule of Law* (1986), p73.

PRINCIPLES DERIVING FROM THE RULE OF LAW

The notion that the executive is not above the law is related to the Diceyan notion that the Rule of Law includes the idea that there should be one law for all, governed and government alike. Jeremy Waldron discusses a practical application of this notion and the principles which may be derived from it, referring to the case of *Pedro v Diss* (1981)[14] in which Pedro was acquitted of assault after physically resisting an unlawful arrest made by police constable Diss.

Jeremy Waldron, *The Law* (1990), pp37–8

Think back for a moment to Ya Ya Pedro and Constable Diss. Diss grabs hold of Pedro, and Pedro punches him in the struggle to free himself. The magistrates say he is guilty of assault. On appeal, the High Court says (in effect): 'No. Unless the arrest is lawful, Pedro is entitled to defend himself against Martin Diss just as if he were any other citizen who tried to grab hold of him. Once they go beyond their specified powers, the police have no special privileges. The ordinary rules of self-defence apply. If it's wrong for me to attack Pedro, it's also wrong for Constable Diss to attack Pedro. The law is the same for everyone.'

This requirement of universality – the idea of 'one law for all' – is a prominent feature of the normative ideal of the Rule of Law. But why is universality a good thing? Why is it desirable that there should be one law for everyone, irrespective of who they are, or their official status?

One obvious application of universality is that we don't, on the whole, allow personalised laws; we don't have laws that make exceptions for particular people. In medieval England, there used to be things called 'Bills of Attainder', announcing that someone in particular (the Earl of Warwick, or the king's brother for example) was thereby banished from the realm and his estates confiscated. The idea of the Rule of Law is that the state should not use personalised mechanisms of that sort.

Moral philosophers link this requirement of universality with morality and with rationality. They say that if you make a moral judgement about someone or something, your judgement can't be based simply on that person or that incident in particular, or if it is, it's arbitrary. It must be based on some feature of the person or action – something *about* what they did, something that might in principle be true of another person or another situation as well. In other words it must be based on something that can be expressed in a universal proposition. For example, if I want say, 'It is all right for Diss to defend himself', I must say that because I think self defence is all right in general in that sort of case, not merely because I want to get at Pedro or say something special about Diss. So I must also be prepared to say that it would be all right for Pedro to defend himself in a similar circumstance. Unless I can point to some clearly relevant difference between the two cases, then I must accept that the same reasoning applies to both.

Another way of putting it is that universalisability expresses an important principle of justice: it means dealing even-handedly with people and treating like cases alike. If I am committed to treating like cases alike, then I ought to be able to state my principles in a universal form. If I cannot – that is, if I can't find a way to eliminate references to particular people from my legislation – that is probably a good indication that I am drawing arbitrary distinctions based on bias or self-interest or something of that sort.

---

14   2 All ER 59.

Notes

1   There are numerous exceptions to the notion of one law applying equally to all. Members of Parliament enjoy complete civil and criminal immunity in respect of words spoken during 'proceedings in Parliament' by virtue of the Bill of Rights 1688, while judges also enjoy various legal privileges. Diplomatic and consular immunities arise under the Diplomatic Privileges Act 1964 and the Consular Relations Act 1968, and these have been left undisturbed by the State Immunity Act 1978 s16.

2   Waldron demonstrates how principles of justice (treating like cases alike) can be deduced from the simple notion of the law being addressed to, and applicable to, everybody. These ideas have found perhaps their most prominent proponents in the writings of Joseph Raz and John Rawls.

3   Raz is concerned to pare down the notion of the Rule of Law to what he sees as its logically necessary content (as we noted in the introduction to this chapter) whilst demonstrating that it yet proscribes a number of important principles about the application of coercive force within a legal system. Raz's exposition is followed by an extract from Rawl's *A Theory of Justice* (1972) in which he develops in detail the principles of justice which can be derived from the Rule of Law.

J Raz, 'The Rule of Law and its Virtue' (1977) 93 *Law Quarterly Review* 195–198

F A Hayek has provided one of the clearest and most powerful formulations of the ideal of the Rule of Law: 'stripped of all technicalities this means that government in all its actions is bound by rules fixed and announced beforehand – rules which make it possible to foresee with fair certainty how the authority will use its coercive powers in given circumstances, and to plan one's individual affairs on the basis of this knowledge' [*The Road to Serfdom* (London 1944), p54]. At the same time the way he draws certain conclusions from this ideal illustrates one of the two main fallacies in the contemporary treatment of the doctrine of the Rule of Law: the assumption of its overriding importance. My purpose is to analyse the ideal of the Rule of Law in the spirit of Hayek's quoted statement of it and to show why some of the conclusions which he drew from it cannot be thus supported. But first we must be put on our guard against the other common fallacy concerning the Rule of Law.

Not uncommonly when a political ideal captures the imagination of large numbers of people its name becomes a slogan used by supporters of ideals which bear little or no relation to the one it originally designated. The fate of 'democracy' not long ago and of 'privacy' today are just two examples of this familiar process. In 1959 the International Congress of Jurists gave official blessing to a similar perversion of the doctrine of the Rule of Law.

> The function of the legislature in a free society under the Rule of Law is to create and maintain the conditions which will uphold the dignity of man as an individual. This dignity requires not only the recognition of his civil and political rights but also the establishment of the social, economic, educational and cultural conditions which are essential to the full development of his personality.

The report goes on to mention or refer to just about every political ideal which has found support in any part of the globe during the post-war years.

If the Rule of Law is the rule of the good law then to explain its nature is to propound a complete social philosophy. But if so, the term lacks any useful function. We have no need to be converted to the Rule of Law just in order to discover that to believe in it is to believe that good should triumph. The Rule of Law is a political ideal which a legal system may lack or may possess to a greater or lesser degree. That much is common ground. It is also to be insisted that the Rule of Law is just one of the virtues which a legal system may possess and by which it is to be judged. It is not to be confused with democracy, justice, equality (before the law or otherwise), human rights of any kind or respect for persons or for the dignity of man. A non-democratic legal system, based on the denial of human rights, on extensive poverty, on racial segregation, sexual inequalities and religious persecution may, in principle, conform to the requirements of the Rule of Law better than any of the legal systems of the more enlightened Western democracies. This does not mean that it will be better than those Western democracies. It will be an immeasurably worse legal system, but it will excel in one respect: in its conformity to the Rule of Law. ...

'The Rule of Law' means literally what it says: the rule of the law. Taken in its broadest sense this means that people should obey the law and be ruled by it. But in political and legal theory it has come to be read in a narrower sense, that the government shall be ruled by the law and subject to it. The ideal of the Rule of Law in this sense is often expressed by the phrase 'government by law and not by men'. No sooner does one use these formulae than their obscurity becomes evident. Surely government must be both by law and by men. It is said that the Rule of Law means that all government action must have foundation in law, must be authorised by law. But is not that a tautology? Actions not authorised by law cannot be the actions of the government as a government. They would be without legal effect and often unlawful.

It is true that we can elaborate a political notion which is different from the legal one: government as the location of real power in the society. It is in this sense that one can say that Britain is governed by The City or by the trade unions. In this sense of government it is not a tautology to say that government should be based on law. If the trade union ruling a country breaks an industrial relations law in order to impose its will on the parliament or if the President or the FBI authorise burglaries and conspire to pervert justice they can be said to violate the Rule of Law. But here the Rule of Law is used in its original sense of obedience to law. Powerful people and people in government just like anybody else should obey the law. This is no doubt correct, and yet does it exhaust the meaning of the Rule of Law? There is more to the Rule of Law than the law and order interpretation allows. It means more even than law and order applied to the government. I shall proceed on the assumption that we are concerned with government in the legal sense and with the conception of the Rule of Law which applies to government and to law and is no mere application of the law and order conception.

The problem is that now we are back with our initial puzzle. If government is, by definition, government authorised by law, the Rule of Law seems to amount to an empty tautology, not a political ideal.

The solution to this riddle is in the difference between the professional and the lay sense of law. For the lawyer anything is the law if it meets the conditions of validity laid down in the system's rules of recognition or in other rules of the system [I am, here, following Hart, *The Concept of Law* (1961), pp97–107]. This includes the constitution, parliamentary legislation, ministerial regulations, policeman's orders, the regulations of limited companies, conditions imposed in trading licences, etc. To the layman the law consists only of a sub-class of these.

To him the law is essentially a set of open, general and relatively stable laws. Government by law and not by men is not a tautology if 'law' means general, open and relatively stable law. In fact the danger of this interpretation is that the Rule of Law might set too strict a requirement, one which no legal system can meet and which embodies very little virtue. It is humanly inconceivable that law can consist only of general rules and it is very undesirable that it should. Just as we need government both by laws and by men, so we need both general and particular laws to carry out the jobs for which we need the law.

The doctrine of the Rule of Law does not deny that every legal system should consist of both general, open and stable rules (the popular conception of law) and particular laws (legal orders), an essential tool in the hands of the executive and the judiciary alike. As we shall see, what the doctrine requires is the subjection of particular laws to general, open and stable ones. It is one of the important principles of the doctrine that *the making of particular laws should be guided by open and relatively stable general rules*.

This principle shows how the slogan of the Rule of Law and not of men can be read as a meaningful political ideal. The principle does not, however, exhaust the meaning of the Rule of Law and does not by itself illuminate the reasons for its alleged importance. Let us, therefore, return to the literal sense of the Rule of Law. It has two aspects: (1) that people should be ruled by the law and obey it; and (2) that the law should be such that people will be able to be guided by it. As was noted above, it is with the second aspect that we are concerned: the law must be capable of being obeyed. A person conforms with the law to the extent that he does not break the law. But he obeys the law only if part of his reason for conforming is his knowledge of the law. Therefore, if the law is to be obeyed *it must be capable of guiding the behaviour of its subjects*. It must be such that they can find out what it is and act on it.

This is the basic intuition from which the doctrine of the Rule of Law derives: the law must be capable of guiding the behaviour of its subjects. It is evident that this conception of the Rule of Law is a formal one. It says nothing about how the law is to be made: by tyrants, democratic majorities or any other way. It says nothing about fundamental rights, about equality or justice. It may even be thought that this version of the doctrine is formal to the extent that it is almost devoid of content. This is far from the truth. Most of the requirements which were associated with the Rule of Law before it came to signify all the virtues of the state can be derived from this one basic idea.

John Rawls, *A Theory of Justice* (1972), pp236–40

Let us begin with the precept that ought implies can. This precept identifies several obvious features of legal systems. First of all, the actions which the rules of law require and forbid should be of a kind which men can reasonably be expected to do and to avoid. Secondly, the notion that ought implies can convey the idea that those who enact laws and give orders do so in good faith. Legislators and judges, and other officials of the system, must believe that the laws can be obeyed; and they are to assume that any orders given can be carried out. Moreover, not only must the authorities act in good faith, but their good faith must be recognised by those subject to their enactments. Laws and commands are accepted as laws and commands only if it is generally believed that they can be obeyed and executed. If this is in question, the actions of authorities presumably have some other purpose than to organise conduct. Finally, this precept expresses the requirement that a legal system should recognise impossibility of performance as a defence, or at least as a mitigating circumstance. In enforcing rules a legal system cannot regard the inability to perform as irrelevant. It would be an intolerable burden on liberty if the liability to penalties was not normally limited to actions within our power to do or not to do.

The Rule of Law also implies the precept that similar cases be treated similarly. Men could not regulate actions by means of rules if this precept were not followed. To be sure, this notion does not take us very far. For we must suppose that the criteria of similarity are given by the legal rules themselves and the principles used to interpret them. Nevertheless, the precept that like decisions be given in like cases significantly limits the discretion of judges and others in authority. The precept forces them to justify the distinctions that they make between persons by reference to the relevant legal rules and principles. In any particular case, if the rules are at all complicated and call for interpretation, it may be easy to justify an arbitrary decision. But as the number of cases increases, plausible justifications for biased judgements become more difficult to construct. The requirement of consistency holds of course for the interpretation of all rules and for justifications at all levels. Eventually reasoned arguments for discriminatory judgements become harder to formulate and the attempt to do so less persuasive.

The precept that there is no offence without a law (*nulla crimien sine lege*), and the requirements it implies, also follow from the idea of a legal system. This precept demands that laws be known and expressly promulgated, that their meaning be clearly defined, that statutes be general both in statement and intent and not be used as a way of harming particular individuals who may be expressly named (Bills of Attainder), that at least the more severe offences be strictly construed, and that penal laws should not be retroactive to the disadvantage of those to whom they apply. These requirements are implicit in the notion of regulating behaviour by public rules. For if, say, statutes are not clear in what they enjoin and forbid, the citizen does not know how he is to behave. Moreover, while there may be occasional Bills of Attainder and retroactive enactments, these cannot be pervasive or characteristic features of the system, else it must have another purpose. A tyrant might change laws without notice, and punish (if that is the right word) his subjects accordingly, because he takes pleasure in seeing how long it takes them to figure out what the new rules are from observing the penalties he inflicts. But these rules would not be a legal system, since they would not serve to organise social behaviour by providing a basis for legitimate expectations.

Finally, there are those precepts defining the notion of natural justice. These are guidelines intended to preserve the integrity of the judicial process. If laws are directives addressed to rational persons for their guidance, courts must be concerned to apply and to enforce these rules in an appropriate way. A conscientious effort must be made to determine whether an infraction has taken place and to impose the correct penalty. Thus a legal system must make provisions for conducting orderly trials and hearings; it must contain rules of evidence that guarantee rational procedures of inquiry. While there are variations in these procedures, the Rule of Law requires some form of due process: that is, a process reasonably designed to ascertain the truth, in ways consistent with the other ends of the legal system, as to whether a violation has taken place and under what circumstances. For example, judges must be independent and impartial, and no man may judge his own case. Trials must be fair and open, but not prejudiced by public clamour. The precepts of natural justice are to insure that the legal order will be impartially and regularly maintained.

Now the connection of the Rule of Law with liberty is clear enough. Liberty, as I have said, is a complex of rights and duties defined by institutions. The various liberties specify things that we may choose to do, if we wish, and in regard to which, when the nature of the liberty makes it appropriate, others have a duty not to interfere. But if the precept of no crime without a law is violated, say by statutes being vague and imprecise, what we are at liberty to do is likewise vague and imprecise. The boundaries of our liberty are uncertain. And to the extent that this is so, liberty is restricted by a reasonable fear of its exercise. The same sort of consequences follow if similar cases are not treated similarly, if the judicial process lacks its essential integrity, if the law does not recognise impossibility of performance as a defence, and so on. The principle of legality has a firm foundation, then, in the agreement of rational persons to establish for themselves the greatest equal liberty. To be confident in the possession and exercise of these freedoms, the citizens of a well-ordered society will normally want the Rule of Law maintained.

Notes

1 Perhaps the most important aspect of the Rule of Law, according to Rawls and Raz, is its freedom-promoting nature: in making known in advance and in a clear way what the restrictions on conduct are, they allow people to plan and thus control their own lives.

2 The principles which Rawls 'extracts' from the doctrine of the Rule of Law may be summed up as follows: laws must not require the impossible; like cases must be treated alike; conduct can only be criminalised by law which is both reasonably ascertainable (and therefore non-retroactive) and of sufficient clarity; cases must be tried fairly (therefore by an independent judiciary) and according to due process. To these principles, Raz[15] adds that the making of particular laws should be governed by more general 'open stable and clear rules', that the courts must be easily accessible, and that they must have review power to ensure adherence to the other principles.

3 It is interesting to try to ascertain whether these principles find expression in the law of the UK, and if so which ones.

THE RULE OF LAW IN THE BRITISH CONSTITUTION

Some examples

Historically, constitutional lawyers in this country have prided themselves on its adherence to the Rule of Law, as upheld by the judges in a number of famous cases. One of these is *Entick v Carrington*,[16] in which agents of the King, acting under a warrant issued by the Secretary of State, broke into the house of Entick, alleged to be the author of seditious writings, and removed certain of his papers. It was found that because the action was justified by no specific legal authority, it was a common trespass, for which the Secretary of State was liable in damages. Lord Camden CJ said: 'By the laws of England, every invasion of private property, be it ever so minute, is a trespass. No man can ever set his foot upon my ground without my licence, but he is liable to an action. ... If he admits the fact, he is bound to shew by way of justification, that some positive law has empowered or excused him.'

---

15 Raz, *op cit*, pp199–201.
16 (1765) 19 St Tr 1029.

Another well-known case is described below by Heuston, who turns to it after considering *Entick*.

RFV Heuston, *Essays in Constitutional Law* (1964), pp36–8

Here is the second case. It is the case of *Wolfe Tone* [(1798) 27 St Tr 614], of which Dicey himself said that 'no more splendid assertion of the supremacy of the law can be found than the protection of Wolfe Tone by the Irish Bench' [*Law of the Constitution*, p294]. Wolfe Tone was an Irishman who held a commission in the French Army and who landed in Ireland in November 1798 with the intention of stirring up rebellion. He was tried and found guilty of high treason by a court-martial sitting in Dublin and sentenced to die at 1pm on the following Monday. On that morning, however, the case was brought before the Court of King's Bench on an affidavit by Tone's father. Counsel for Tone's father was the great John Philpot Curran. Here is an extract from the argument as reported in the *State Trials*.

Mr Curran: I do not pretend to say that Mr Tone is not guilty of the charges of which he was accused – I presume the officers were honourable men – but it is stated in the affidavit as a solemn fact that Mr Tone had no commission under His Majesty, and therefore no court-martial could have cognisance of any crime imputed to him while the Court of King's Bench sat in the capacity of the great criminal court of the land. In times when war was raging, when man was opposed to man in the field, courts-martial might be endured; but every law authority is with me while I stand upon his sacred and immutable principle of the constitution – *that martial law and civil law are incompatible*; and that the former must cease with the existence of the latter. This is not the time for arguing this momentous question. My client must appear in this court. *He is cast for death this day.* He may be ordered for execution while I address you. I call on the court to support the law. I move for a *habeas corpus* to be directed to the provost marshal of the barracks of Dublin and Major Sandys to bring up the body of Mr Tone.

Lord Chief Justice Kilwarden: Have a writ instantly prepared.

Mr Curran: Our client may die while his writ is preparing.

Lord Chief Justice: Mr Sheriff, proceed to the barracks and acquaint the provost marshal that a writ is preparing to suspend Mr Tone's execution; *and see that he be not executed.* [The court awaited, in a state of the utmost agitation, the return of the sheriff.]

Mr Sheriff: My Lord, I have been at the barracks in pursuance of your order. The provost marshal says he must obey Major Sandys. Major Sandys says he must obey Lord Cornwallis.

Mr Curran: Mr Tone's father, my Lord, returns after serving the *habeas corpus*. He says General Craig will not obey it.

Lord Chief Justice: Mr Sheriff, take the body of Tone into your custody. Take the provost marshal and Major Sandys into custody: and show the order of this court to General Craig. [The sheriff returns.]

Mr Sheriff: I have been at the barracks. Mr Tone having cut his throat last night is not in a condition to be removed.

So although the result of this case is a little uncertain, in that a final decision was avoided because of Tone's suicide, we can nevertheless see that Lord Kilwarden and his fellow judges were prepared to do their utmost to see that everyone in the country obeyed the law, whether he was the General Officer Commanding in Ireland, the provost marshal or the Viceroy, and although Wolfe Tone was a man whose ideals they loathed and despised.

Notes

1   Heuston sees in the case the principle of the equal applicability of the law; however, it also embodies the principle that only punishments imposed by lawful authority may be inflicted: since martial law had no jurisdiction over Tone, he could not be made subject to its penalties.

2   In *Phillips v Eyre* (1870) LR 6 QB 1, 23 the strong presumption of the courts that Parliament does not intend to infringe the Rule of Law by penalising people retrospectively was made clear: '... the courts will not ascribe retrospective force to new laws affecting rights unless by express words or necessary implication it appears that such was the intention of the legislature.'

3   Difficulties with ensuring that laws are clear and prospective have arisen in the sphere of EC law, due in part to political unwillingness to implement EC directives. In *Kolpinghuis Nijmegen* (1986)[17] the European Court of Justice held that the obligation on domestic courts to interpret national law to comply with EC law was limited by the general principles of legal certainty and non-retroactivity. However, in *Marleasing SA v La Commercial Internacional de Alimentacion SA* (1990)[18] the ECJ held that, where a domestic court was faced with legislation which ran clearly counter to the terms of a non-directly effective Directive, it should give effect to the Directive regardless of the terms of the national legislation. In *Marleasing* the European Court of Justice seemed to be suggesting that domestic courts should entirely ignore the plain meaning of domestic legislation in order to ensure that no departure from Community law occurred. Although it appears that this principle would not apply to statutes creating criminal liability, it would still mean that private individuals would be uncertain as to their legal obligations.

4   The House of Lords had previously demonstrated some willingness to accept the *Marleasing* principle in *Litster v Forth Dry Docks Ltd* (1989).[19] It had determined that, even where EC law is not directly effective, priority for EC law should be ensured by means of national law. The House of Lords was prepared to construe the domestic legislation contrary to its *prima facie* meaning because it had been introduced expressly to implement the directive in question. This does not go as far as *Marleasing*; nevertheless it is arguable that, if the *Litster* reasoning is taken any further, the Rule of Law will be infringed because unacceptable uncertainty will be imported into UK law.

5   In the criminal sphere, the principle of non-retroactivity has been emphatically reaffirmed by the House of Lords.

Waddington v Miah [1974] 1 WLR 377, 378–380 HL

Lord Reid: My Lords, the respondent was tried in the Crown Court at Grimsby on an indictment which contained two counts. Count 1 stated the offence charged as 'Illegal immigrant, contrary to s24 of the Immigration Act 1971', and

---

17   [1989] 2 CMLR 18.
18   [1990] ECR I–4135.
19   [1989] 1 All ER 1134.

count 2 stated the offence as 'Possession of false passport, contrary to s26 of the Immigration Act 1971'. That Act was passed on 28 October 1971 but the greater part of it, including ss24 and 26, did not come into force until 1 January 1973. But the particulars given under count 1 were that the respondent: 'on a day unknown between the 22nd day of October 1970 and the 29th day of September 1972, being a person who was not patrial within the meaning of the Immigration Act 1971, knowingly entered the UK without leave.'

And the particulars given under count 2 were that the respondent: 'on the 29th day of September 1972, had in his possession for the purposes of the Immigration Act 1971, a passport no. AC386290 which he had reasonable cause to believe to be false.'

Despite objection that the Act is not retrospective, the respondent was convicted. His conviction was quashed by the Court of Appeal [1974] 1 All ER 1110. That court in granting leave to the prosecution to appeal certified the following questions: 'Whether the appellant could be convicted of offences against the Immigration Act 1971 in respect of things done by him before the Act came into force, and in particular offences against ss24(1)(a) and 26(1)(d) of the Act.'

Lord Reid then considered the facts of the case and relevant provisions of the European Convention on Human Rights and the Unilateral Declaration, concluding:

... it is hardly credible that any government department would promote or that Parliament would pass retrospective criminal legislation.

Yet whoever authorised this prosecution must somehow have formed an opinion that Parliament had made ss24 and 26 of the 1971 Act retrospective. That contention was strongly urged in the Crown Court and in the Court of Appeal, but when this case was opened before your lordships, counsel said that he had been unable to find any arguments which he thought he could properly submit to the House. In so doing I think that he acted with complete propriety. But nevertheless he drew our attention to every possible aspect of the matter and in view of the importance of the general principle we spent two days on a full investigation.

In the courts below the prosecution relied chiefly of s34(1) of the 1971 Act but also relied to some extent on s35(3). These provisions are as follows:

34(1) Subject to the following provisions of this section, the enactments mentioned in schedule 6 to this Act are hereby repealed, as from the coming into force of this Act, to the extent mentioned in column 30 of the schedule; and – (a) this Act, as from its coming into force, shall apply in relation to entrants or others arriving in the United Kingdom at whatever date before or after it comes into force; and (b) after this Act comes into force anything done under or for the purposes of the former immigration laws shall have effect, in so far as any corresponding action could be taken under or for the purposes of this Act, as if done by way of action so taken, and in relation to anything so done this Act shall apply accordingly ...

35 ... (3) The provisions of s28(1) and (2) above shall have effect, as from the passing of this Act, in relation to offences under section 1A (unauthorised landing) of the Commonwealth Immigrants Act 1962 as amended by the Commonwealth Immigrants Act 1968, other than offences committed six months or more before the passing of this Act, as those provisions are expressed to have effect in relation to offences to which the extended time limit for prosecutions is to apply under ss24, 25 and 26 above; but where proceedings for an offence under s4A of the Commonwealth Immigrants Act

1962 would have been out of time but for this subsection, s4A(4) (under which, in certain cases, a person not producing a passport duly stamped by an immigration officer is presumed for purposes of that section to have landed in contravention of it, unless the contrary is proved) shall not apply...

I can see nothing retrospective in s34(1). I use retrospective in the sense of authorising people being punished for what they did before the Act came into force. But there is nothing to prevent Parliament from authorising discrimination in the future between various classes of people and one ground of discrimination could be that if certain people have done a certain thing in the past or had a certain ancestry they shall be treated differently in future from those who have not done that thing or had a different ancestry. Whether that is good policy is a matter of opinion. But in my opinion that is what Parliament has done by this Act.

Section 34(1)(a) makes the 1971 Act apply to all 'entrants' and 'entrant' is defined in s33 as 'a person entering or seeking to enter the UK'. His entry need not have been unlawful and it may have taken place a long time ago. Some entrants are given a right of abode here. Some are given indefinite leave to enter and remain here. The position of others is more precarious. I cannot see how s34(1)(a) can be construed as having any reference to what any entrant may have done in this country before the Act came into force. All that it does is to subject to the provisions of the Act for the future anyone who entered in the past.

Section 34(1)(b) refers to 'the former immigration laws' which include the Acts of 1962 and 1968. It applies to anything 'done under or for the purposes of' those laws. So it does not apply to anything done contrary to, or to any offence against, those laws. And it certainly does not support the view that an act done before the 1971 Act came into force can be treated as an offence against that Act.

Section 35(3) requires more explanation. Under former immigration laws there was a time limit for prosecution of six months. Section 28 applied to certain offences against the 1971 Act a time limit of three years. Section 35(3) applies the new time limit to old offences against s4A of the 1962 Act where, but only where, the provisions of s35(3) are satisfied. Those provisions are complicated but the general effect appears to me to be that if prosecution for an old offence had become time-barred before the passing of the 1971 Act the old offence was not revived. So as the Act was passed on 28 October 1971 offences committed before 28 April 1971 remained time-barred. I do not think that s35(3) can be said to have retrospective effect or that it can lend any support to the validity of the present prosecution. We are not concerned with any question whether in the circumstance of this case any charges could have been made of offences against former immigration laws.

This is a very clear case. I do not think it necessary to examine the details of the counts in this indictment.

I would dismiss the appeal. [The other Law Lords agreed.]

Note

It could be said that arbitrary power, although apparently contrary to the Rule of Law, is exercised by ministers in the sense that legislation is often enacted conferring on them a discretion to act as appears appropriate in any particular circumstance. Section 10 of the Broadcasting Act 1990 provides an example of a very widely drafted discretion: the Home Secretary can order the Independent Television Commission to 'refrain from broadcasting any matter or classes of matter'. Once a discretion of this width is granted to a minister, might it be said that he or she can act in a manner which is unregulated by the law? Clearly, in a narrow sense the minister is acting within the law because the discretionary power is lawfully granted. However, such an answer begs the question at issue. To some extent it may be said that the minister is indeed able to exercise arbitrary power in the sense that any specific action has no specific legal authority; the only check on such actions is represented by the availability of judicial review. However, the courts are prepared to invalidate a minister's actions according to the House of Lords in *Padfield v Minister of Agriculture* (1968),[20] where he or she purports to act within a broadly drafted power on the ground that the actions do not promote the policy and objects of the statute conferring the power, the judges determining what that policy is. Although the check thus represented by judicial review on a minister's actions may suggest that the Rule of Law is recognised by the constitution, it might be equally plausible to suggest that such a check springs from the doctrine of Parliamentary sovereignty, in that it is designed to ensure that powers exercised by ministers and other bodies do not rise above those of Parliament itself. The issue of discretionary powers is considered in detail below (in 'The applicability of the Rule of Law to contemporary British Society').

Dicey and the Rule of Law

The most influential, though also one of the most controversial, expositions of the importance of the Rule of Law in the British constitutional scheme has been that put forward by Dicey, considered by Jeffrey Jowell.

Jeffrey Jowell, 'The Rule of Law Today' in Jowell and Oliver (eds), *The Changing Constitution*, 3rd edn (1994), pp58–62

... According to Dicey, the Rule of Law has at least three meanings. The first is a view that individuals ought not to be subjected to wide discretionary powers. He wrote that no one 'is punishable or can be lawfully made to suffer in body or goods except for a distinct breach of law established before the ordinary courts of the land. In this sense the Rule of Law is contrasted with every system of government based on the exercise by persons in authority of wide, arbitrary or discretionary powers of constraint' [*An Introduction to the Study of the Constitution*, 10th edn (1959), p188]. Here Dicey contends that wide official powers are akin to arbitrary powers, to which no one should be forced to submit. He writes that 'wherever there is a discretion there is room for arbitrariness' and so would exclude discretionary powers from what he later calls 'regular law'.

Dicey's second meaning relates to the equality – the 'equal subjection' – of all classes to one law administered by the ordinary courts. He distinguished what he saw as special exemptions for officials in continental countries such as France, where he saw the French *droit administratif* operating a separate form of justice for officials. 'With us', he wrote, 'every official, from the Prime Minister down to a constable or a collector of taxes is under the same responsibility for every act done without legal justification as any other citizen' [*ibid*, p193].

Thirdly, Dicey saw the Rule of Law as expressing the fact that there is here no separate written constitutional code, and that the constitutional law is 'the result

---

20 [1968] AC 997.

of the judicial decisions determining the rights of private persons in particular cases brought before the courts' [*ibid*, p195].

The second and third of Dicey's meanings of the Rule of Law display a concern not to allow the British to go the way of other countries, where a separate system of public law is administered by separate courts dealing with cases between the State and the individual. In 1928 William Robson wrote his celebrated book *Justice and Administrative Law*, in which he roundly criticised Dicey for his misinterpretation of both the English and French systems on that ground. He pointed out that there were in England 'colossal distinctions' [2nd edn (1947), p343] between the rights and duties of private individuals and those of the administrative organs or government even in Dicey's time. Public authorities possessed special rights and special exemptions and immunities, to the extent that the citizen was deprived of a remedy against the State 'in many cases where he most requires it'. [*Ibid*, p345] Robson also convincingly showed how Dicey had misinterpreted French law, where the *droit administratif* was not intended to exempt public officials from the rigour of private law, but to allow experts in public administration to work out the extent of official liability. Robson also noted the extent of Dicey's misrepresentation that disputes between officials and private individuals in Britain were dealt with by the ordinary courts. He pointed to the growth of special tribunals and inquiries that had grown up to decide these disputes outside the courts, and was in no doubt that a 'vast body of administrative law' existed in England [*ibid*]. ...

Despite this onslaught on Dicey's revision of the Rule of Law, its epitaph refused to be written. In the late 1950s ... the Franks Committee revived interest in Diceyan notions by suggesting judicial protections over the multiplying tribunals and inquiries of the growing State. It was in the 1960s, however, that disparate groups once again started arguing in favour of legal values. Some of these groups were themselves committed to a strong governmental role in providing social welfare, but objected to the manner in which public services were carried out. Recipients of supplementary benefit, for example, objected to the fact that benefits were administered by officials in accordance with a secret code (known as the 'A code') and asked instead for publication of a set of welfare 'rights'. They also objected to the wide discretion allowed their case-workers to determine the level of their benefits. The heirs of Jennings and his followers, such as Professor Richard Titmus, opposed this challenge to the free exercise of official discretion and objected strongly to a 'pathology of legalism' developing in this area ['Welfare 'Rights', Law and Discretion' (1971) 42 Polit Q 113].

Notes

1   Heuston, a loyal supporter of Dicey, concedes that his view is no longer applicable in this respect, but attempts to place Dicey's opinion within its historical context.

'It has been said that Dicey erred in saying that the doctrine of the Rule of Law "excludes the existence even of wide discretionary authority on the part of the government". This is certainly not true today. Modern government, as is well known, cannot be carried on at all without a host of wide discretionary powers, which are granted to the executive by the large number of statutes annually passed by Parliament. But it must be remembered, first of all, the kind of man Dicey was, and secondly, the times in which he wrote. First, Dicey was in politics an old-fashioned Whig. He was also a very typical example of the common lawyer who does not seriously believe in the existence of the Statute Book. To the true common lawyer the law is to be found in the law reports and books of authority. There are indeed statutes, but they can always be looked up if the opportunity arises. the judges, as has been well said, have never entered into the spirit of the Benthamite game and have always treated the statute as an interloper upon the rounded majesty of the common law. Secondly, it must be recalled that Dicey's great work was written in the early 1880s, a period when the *laissez faire* state of the Victorians was only just beginning to give way to the welfare state of the modern world. Dicey was an acute, a marvellously acute, judge of public opinion and of the impact upon public opinion of legislative power, but even he hardly foresaw the extent to which statutory powers of government would change the nature of English constitutional law. Today the fundamental problem is that of the control of discretionary powers, and it is indeed a serious criticism of Dicey's doctrine that he suggests that discretionary powers are in some way undesirable or unnecessary.'[21]

2   Heuston notes that Dicey was above all a common law lawyer; as discussed in Chapter 1, he considered the specific guarantees of liberty offered by the common law to be of far more value than generally worded constitutions. In this respect, Dicey was merely finding a different application for the view long held by English jurists that common law was inherently superior to statute, due to its organic and evolutionary nature. Thus in 1612, Sir John Davies, after describing how a 'custome' of the people on being 'continued without interruption time out of mind ... obtaineth the force of a *Law*', goes on to argue: 'And this *Customary Law* is the most perfect and the most excellent, and without comparison the best, to make and preserve a Commonwealth. For the *Written Laws* ... are imposed upon the Subject before any Triall or Probation made, whether the same be fit and agreeable to the nature and disposition of the people, or whether they will be any inconvenience or no ...'.[22] ATH Smith, however, turns this thesis, and the Dicyean conception of the protection of liberty on its head.

ATH Smith, 'Comment; 1' (1985) *Public Law* 608–10.

Whilst constitutional lawyers and jurists talk in terms of Dicyean rhetoric – that 'no man is punishable or can be made lawfully to suffer in body or goods except for a distinct breach of law established in the ordinary legal manner before the ordinary courts of the land, and in this sense the Rule of Law is contrasted with every system of government based on the exercise by persons in authority of wide, arbitrary, or discretionary powers of constraint' [*Introduction to the Study of the Law of the Constitution* (10th edn), p188], the reality within the criminal process is rather different. My thesis is that (1) English criminal law is inherently offensive to the principle of legality – being a common law system, it is in places highly uncertain, and one that is therefore necessarily retrospective in character when the law is judicially developed; (2) that the judges (by whom I mean principally the House of Lords) in administering it are not currently sufficiently concerned with the protection of civil liberties; and (3) that the enactment of a criminal code would provide a fixed and objective starting point for delineating the permissible restrictions on the right to personal freedom, even if it could not solve all the problems of certainty inherent in a government by laws and men.

The Dicyean model was that the judges constituted a bulwark between the citizen and the state in the protection of the citizen's civil liberties. He illustrated

---

21   Heuston, *op cit*, pp41–2.

22   Sir John Davies, Preface to *Irish Reports* (1612), quoted in M Loughin, *op cit*, p44 (all emphasis original).

this by reference to freedoms of the person, speech, and assembly, and argued that the law had been developed by the judges to support and bolster these values. It is commonly supposed by constitutional theorists and jurists that this protective pattern repeats itself throughout the criminal process, and that the Rule of Law infiltrates and permeates the criminal justice system through the application of *nulla poena* principles, with concomitant rules enjoining the strict interpretation of criminal statutes and narrowing where possible the ambit of the criminal law. Criminal lawyers think otherwise. Glanville Williams, for example, observes: '... in criminal cases, the courts are anxious to facilitate the conviction of villains, and they interpret the law wherever possible to secure this' [*Textbook of Criminal Law*, 2nd edn (1983), p5]. There seems to be, then, a gap between rhetoric and practice in the application and moulding of the scope of the substantive criminal law, and one that should be recognised and if possible accommodated by constitutional theorists.

... the aims of the criminal justice system should include provision for the best safeguards of civil liberties as are compatible with maximum social protection, and a starting point for this should be the enactment of a criminal code. Decisions as to the mental element of the law of murder or rape, for example, upon which the liberty of the subject vitally depends, should be treated as legislative ones, and not be left at large for determination by the judiciary as at present. My criticism of the present system of criminal adjudication is arguably less apt now than it was in Dicey's time. Since then the judges have formally foresworn their claim to be able to create new crimes [Knuller (1973) AC 435]. But I find it strange that Dicey did not see that the state of the substantive criminal law, with the discretion that it accorded to the judges themselves, was at odds with the principles he espoused. ...

Notes

1   In *R* (1991)[22a] the House of Lords found that husbands had no immunity from prosecution in respect of the rape of their wives. This finding was probably contrary to the position prior to the ruling and therefore it seemed that the defendant in *R* was being penalised retrospectively. The European Commission on Human Rights has now considered the case under Article 7 of the European Convention on Human Rights and has found no violation on the ground that there were clear indications that marital rape would give rise to criminal liability prior to the House of Lords' decision. This conclusion is arguable; legal advice at the time in question would probably have been to the effect that in the circumstances the immunity would apply. This decision thus arguably represents a departure from the principle of non-retroactivity. The issue of discretionary powers will be discussed in greater detail below.

2   In *Shaw v DPP* (1962),[23] the House of Lords declared that the common law included a doctrine known as conspiracy to corrupt public morals, although no precedents were cited demonstrating that it had ever existed except as a variant of the power exercised by Star Chamber judges to punish offences against conventional morality.

3   Can a more fundamental criticism of Dicey be made? Dicey wrote that the Rule of Law and the doctrine of parliamentary sovereignty were the two

---

22a   4 All ER 481.

23   [1962] AC 220.

fundamental principles upon which the British constitution rests. However, it might appear that the two principles seem to lie uneasily with one another since the Rule of Law operates as a check on executive power – power which may have been legitimised by Parliament and ultimately by the democratic process which in itself appears to lend Parliament its legitimacy. TRS Allan has however suggested that the Rule of Law is not in conflict with Parliamentary supremacy, taking into account the argument that Parliament derives its legitimacy from the democratic process.

TRS Allan, 'Legislative Supremacy and the Rule of Law' (1985) *Cambridge Law Journal* 132, 133, 139–141

The reconciliation between the demands of legislative supremacy and the Rule of Law has perhaps been most revealingly illustrated in the context of procedure. The strongest example of bold statutory interpretation in this field is Coke's notorious dictum in *Dr Bonham's* case (1610) 8 Co Rep 114, 118a. Its force of expression, however, matched the strength of the common law principle that no man should be constituted judge in his own cause. The idea that the Royal College of Physicians should be granted the right to try offences against its own regulations, impose fines and retain half of the moneys resulting for itself was so offensive to ordinary notions of justice that it must be rejected as a mistake, and in that sense contrary to Parliament's true intention. The statute was analogous to contradictory, 'repugnant', laws or laws which required the impossible, and hence 'against common right and reason.' Parliament's ultimate authority remained unquestioned since, says Coke, 'some statutes are made against law and right, which those who made them perceiving, would not put them in execution' [Citing *Thomas Tregor's* case, 8 E3 30 ab]. In our own century the speeches in *Ridge v Baldwin* [1964] AC 40 have demonstrated that a statutory power of dismissal from a public office could not be validly exercised if the principle *audi alteram partem* were not respected. Application of the principles of natural justice is required if the power is analogous to the judicial; but even where purely administrative or executive functions are concerned, an obligation to act fairly may be implied, eg *Pearlberg v Varty* [1972] 2 All ER 6. There is no threat here to parliamentary supremacy, properly interpreted. The common law requirements of justice may be imposed, as in *Ridge v Baldwin,* to supplement a statutory procedure. 'But before this unusual kind of power is exercised it must be clear that the statutory procedure is insufficient to achieve justice and that to require additional steps would not frustrate the apparent purpose of the legislation' [*Wiseman* v *Borneman* [1971] AC 297, 308 (Lord Reid)].

The powers and duties of the judiciary in the face of legislation whose form or content offers scope for abuse and injustice are, therefore, considerable. Properly articulated and developed, the basic constitutional principle of the Rule of Law provides a powerful breakwater, if not an impenetrable dam, against encroachment on important rights and liberties by means of statutory authority. Nor can the scope of the principle be limited to those liberties and interests – chiefly liberty of the person and property interests – which have received the most assiduous judicial attention in the past. The traditional political liberties, especially freedoms of speech and assembly, which constitute important features of modern bills of rights, fall equally naturally within its compass. There is nothing in the residual nature of common law conceptions of freedom and human rights which precludes their restatement and development to meet new demands ...

In one sense, the courts' continuing adherence to any set of political or moral values, and judicial interpretation of statutes in accordance with the spirit of such values, runs counter to parliamentary authority. Obviously, those values may sit uncomfortably with the immediate legislative objectives of a particular political majority in Parliament. To this extent, the Rule of Law represents a limit on the scope of parliamentary authority: the imposition of constraints on the political power of the sovereign body in the interests of minorities or for the protection of individual liberties is the essence of constitutionalism. It was, however, Dicey's failure to develop his second constitutional characteristic in terms of legal principle which has prevented modern theorists from escaping what seems to be the 'irreducible contradiction' in his account. Properly formulated as a constitutional principle, the Rule of Law operates to govern the interpretation of parliamentary intent: it provides the legitimate vehicle for the application of the statutory wording to the particular circumstances of the case in hand. Some such vehicle is demanded by the nature of the legislative process: the intrinsic ambiguity of language and the inherent incompleteness of parliamentary intent alike require some background values or preconceptions to be supplied. It seems obvious that those values and preconceptions should reflect, as fairly as possible, those traditional and liberal principles which the judges perceive as fundamental to the legal order. Moreover, as previously noted, the principle of parliamentary sovereignty accords authority only to the statutory text. As a matter of constitutional law, therefore, the contradiction dissolves. The Rule of Law authorises, and requires, a manner of interpreting the statutory text: it is that text, as interpreted, which constitutes the law.

The incorporation of common law notions of justice and fairness is not therefore properly viewed as a curb on parliamentary intention, but as an integral part of the process of ascertaining that intention. The objection that this reconciliation is only formal – that the political effect may be to curb (albeit within a limited compass) the power of a parliamentary majority to enforce its will – misses the point. That the resolution of potentially conflicting aims and values should (in a particular case of dispute) be ultimately a legal one – for which responsibility resides in the courts – is the basis of constitutionalism.

It cannot, however, be denied that the role of the courts in articulating and applying basic constitutional values places important political authority beyond democratic control. There remains an ineradicable tension between the democratic principle of majority rule and the restraints of constitutionalism. Every democratic society has to decide what reconciliation is appropriate to its own needs and traditions. The principal objection to judicial review of legislation, on the basis of an entrenched Bill of Rights, is that that tension is enhanced. In any conflict between the choice of legislative goals and those values perceived as fundamental by the judges, it is the judges' views which prevail. The efficacy of governmental schemes designed to enhance social or economic justice may necessitate invasions of the fundamental political liberties, as traditionally conceived. Legislation designed to curb incitements to racial hostility or to restrict the sale of pornography, for example, will necessarily impose limits on the individual's freedom of expression. ...

The advantages of reliance on the Rule of Law seem clear ... Once it is understood that the scope and content of a statute are necessarily incomplete and uncertain at the time of enactment, it does not seem contrary to democratic principle to fix that scope and content – for the particular case – by reference to fundamental principles reflecting basic notions of fairness and justice. The Rule of Law, whilst requiring an application of social policy which is sympathetic to fundamental liberties, nevertheless leaves the ultimate reconciliation of conflicting values with Parliament alone. It does not deny the right of the majority to flout judicial conceptions of society's fundamental values – where that intention actually does enjoy majority support and is expressed in unambiguous form. The only claim is that, in the event of uncertainty, the courts will interpret legislation consistently with those fundamental values – as the courts conceive them – for such an interpretation is more likely to reflect both the expectations of the citizen and the actual intentions of most members of the legislative majority which adopted the measure in question. Every democratic society has to decide what reconciliation of popular sovereignty and individual liberty is appropriate to its own needs and traditions. The British approach has long been to impose careful limits on the role of the judiciary. 'Are we to act as regents over what is done by Parliament with the consent of the Queen, lords, and commons? I deny that any such authority exists ... The proceedings here are judicial, not autocratic, which they would be if we could make laws instead of administering them [*Lee v Bude and Torrington Junction Railway Co* (1871) LR 6 CP 576, 582 (Willes J)]. The greatest strength of the Rule of Law, as a vehicle for the articulation and development of individual liberties, is that it requires only the reassertion of the traditional role of the courts. The legitimacy of the judicial role needs no special defence: the historical continuity of the common law conception of the importance of the individual provides its own justification. The triumph of democracy is tempered by the constraints of constitutionalism.

Notes

1   It is not entirely clear what Allen means when he states that the Rule of Law 'does not deny the right of the majority to flout judicial conceptions of society's fundamental values – *where that intention actually does enjoy majority support*' (emphasis added). Is Allen implying that the judges would try to ascertain whether a liberty-destroying measure had genuine popular support before deciding whether to apply it or not?

2   It is interesting to note that Allan states quite clearly that judicial interpretation of statutes (a) is essential and (b) should *not be* 'value-free' but should be based on 'traditional and liberal principles'. This would appear to indicate that the leftist charge that liberal constitutional theory aims to import liberal values under the guise of strict neutrality is partly vindicated. There is no pretence at neutrality, so no deception is being practised. But can the charge of imposition of values be substantiated? Ronald Dworkin, by whose thinking Allan is heavily influenced,[24] would doubtless say[25] with Allan that the interpretative exercise is inescapable; that judges should not simply use their discretion to effectively 'legislate' when confronted by apparent gaps in the law, but rather construe legislation such that (a) it is consistent, so far as possible with existing law in the field and (b) it is given the most morally attractive interpretation possible. Finding the answer to what (b) requires will require the judge to form a general theory identifying the fundamental values of the constitution in which he is working, an exercise which, as Dworkin puts it, will take the judge 'very deep into moral and political theory'.[26] The moral attractiveness of the interpretation in question will be then assessed by reference to this theory. Since Dworkin

---

24   See for example Allan's 'Dicey and Dworkin: the Rule of Law as Integrity' (1988) 8 OJLS 266; 'Constitutional Rights and Common Law' (1991) 11 OJLS 453.

25   See for example, Chs 2–4 of *Taking Rights Seriously* (1977).

26   *op cit*, p67.

considers that the US – and the UK – constitutions are best explained by an underpinning liberalism, he would argue that it is legitimate and indeed necessary for a judge to employ 'liberal values' when interpreting a statute in those constitutions.

The Rule of Law in practice

Jeffrey Jowell develops the theme touched on by Allan above, that in the field of judicial review, the judiciary is both upholding Parliamentary sovereignty (in acting as the guardians of Parliament's purpose) and also applying, in a highly practical way, the principles of the Rule of Law.

Jeffrey Jowell, 'The Rule of Law Today', *op cit*, pp73-75

Beyond Parliamentary legislation the practical application of the Rule of Law is more obvious. It is applied through judicial review of the actions and decisions of all officials performing public functions. It is enforced through our administrative law. In large part, administrative law is the implementation of the constitutional principle of the Rule of Law. There are three principal 'grounds' of judicial review: review for 'illegality', for 'procedural impropriety', and for 'irrationality' (or unreasonableness). The implementation of each of these grounds involves the courts in applying different aspects of the Rule of Law.

Under the ground of illegality the courts act as guardian of Parliament's purpose, and may strike down official decisions which violate that purpose. Even when wide discretionary power is conferred upon an official,the courts are not willing to permit decisions which go outside its 'four corners'. Under the ground of procedural propriety the courts may, even where the statute is silent, supply the 'omission of the legislature' in order to insist that the decision-maker grant a fair hearing to the applicant before depriving him or her of a right, interest or legitimate expectation. (The doctrine of legitimate expectation is itself rooted in the notion of legal certainty; the courts require a decision-maker at least to provide the affected person with a hearing before disappointing him of an expectation reasonably induced. At times the promised benefit itself may be required. In either case certainty triumphs over administrative convenience.)

It is perhaps more difficult to countenance the application of the Rule of Law in the third ground of judicial review, that of irrationality or unreasonableness, because it raises the question whether the principle governs the substance and not merely the procedure of official action.

To what extent does the Rule of Law touch on the substance, as well as the procedure, of official action? We have seen that laws in practice are not always enforced rigorously, but rather selectively, allowing for personal and other mitigating factors (as with the doctor speeding to the scene of an accident in the early hours of the morning). But suppose the police decide to charge only bearded male drivers with traffic offences and leave the clean-shaven and women drivers alone; or to charge only drivers of a particular race! Suppose an education authority chose to dismiss all teachers with red hair! Would these decisions infringe the Rule of Law on the ground of their substance? Courts in this country interfere with this kind of decision on the ground of its being an abuse of discretion, the term used being 'unreasonableness' in the sense set out in the celebrated *Wednesbury* case [*Associated Provincial Picture Houses v Wednesbury Corporation* [1948] 1 KB 223]. Is this judicial interference ultimately justified on the ground that the offending decision was a breach of substantive Rule of Law? If so justified, judges lay themselves open to accusations of improper interference with the substance of administration, about which they are reputed to know very little.

Denials of substantive interference are made on the ground that what the courts are doing when interfering with arbitrary, capricious, or oppressive decisions is ensuring that the official action is faithful to the law's purpose, thus achieving the containment of the administration in accordance with an implied legislative scheme. Even if a minister has power to act 'as he thinks fit', it is assumed that the statute conferring that power requires standards that are rationally related to purpose, and that the charging of only bearded drivers could not be related to the purpose of preventing unsafe driving. In practice, however, the legislation frequently has no clear 'purpose' itself, and to pretend otherwise is to adopt a fiction. Parliament often delegates enforcement to ministers, other authorities, or officials precisely in order to allow them to define and elaborate purpose. Implementation is often a process from the bottom up, rather than from the top down. When the Rule of Law allows judicial interference on grounds of 'unreasonableness', 'irrationality', or 'oppressiveness', it does become a substantive doctrine, one that is less easily accepted than the procedural, particularly in a society without a written constitution. Courts therefore tread warily on substantive Rule of Law and seek to exclude (or disguise) policy considerations from the decision. The 'unreasonableness' doctrine itself carefully avoids judicial second-guessing of the administration on the grounds of mere disagreement, and only permits interference if the official decision verges on the outlandish.

Nevertheless, in certain cases the 'unreasonableness' doctrine does not even attempt to pretend that judicial interference with administrative action is based on lack of fidelity to statutory purpose. Take, for example, the case where a condition attached to a planning permission was held 'unreasonable' because it required the owner to dedicate some of his land to the local authority for a public right of way [*Hall and Co Ltd v Shoreham-by-Sea UDC* [1964] 1 All ER 1]. The condition here is by no means unrelated to the purpose of the planning legislation (the right of way was necessary for good planning), but it violates the owner's legitimate expectation not to be deprived of his property without compensation. Here the Rule of Law as substantive principle justifies judicial intervention. A local authority which withdrew the licence of a rugby football club because some of their members had visited South Africa also fell foul of the principle in the form of the doctrine that there should be no punishment where there was no law (prohibiting contact with South Africa) [*Wheeler v Leicester City Council* [1985] AC 1054 (HL)].

Note

As Jowell remarks, the courts tread warily when the application of judicial review risks importing more substantive values than mere procedural fairness, and fidelity to statutory purpose into the decision-making process. A number of commentators have expressed frustration with the manner in which the *Wednesbury* unreasonableness head of judicial review has largely stood still, due to this judicial caution. For proposals for more substantive development of the law in this area see Jowell and Lester, 'Beyond Wednesbury: Substantive Principles of Administrative Law'[27] and Laws J, 'Is the High Court the Guardian of Fundamental Human Rights?'[28]

---

27 (1987) PL 368.
28 (1993) PL 67.

THE APPLICABILITY OF THE RULE OF LAW TO CONTEMPORARY BRITISH SOCIETY

I Harden and N Lewis, *The Noble Lie: The British Constitution and the Rule of Law* (1986), pp71–72

The development of a centralised state apparatus, with para-state concentrations of power linked to it through clienteles and the new feudalism of corporate power, has occurred, while lip-service continues to be paid to a concept of the Rule of Law which is largely silent about the true anatomy of public power. If the central weakness of Dicey, even at the time he wrote, was a concentration upon formalistic judicial power to the exclusion of the growth of bureaucratic power, how much weaker is the claim of the orthodoxy to continued relevance in a massively altered framework? Britain is little different from other welfare states in terms of the types of issues with which it is confronted, but the problems here are in many ways more acute because reconciling demands and performance takes place in a more restricted arena. It is the informality of the political system, a major advantage in accommodating political change in the 19th century, that now facilitates the extension of executive powers in unforeseen ways, and insulates policy-making from its environment.

In bureaucratic, if not in democratic, terms a centralised rule-based system of law may be acceptable when dealing with routine and repetitive conditions. However, this is hardly appropriate when societies are faced with the formidable elaboration of the agendas of government tending towards 'rationality crises', the severe difficulty of tracing causality in policy terms and the equivalent problems of monitoring outcomes. Where it is important to organise people and systems for carrying out activities which are novel and where future conditions are unstable, it makes far less sense to prescribe from the centre the concrete actions that ought to be taken to accomplish these various tasks. Democratic concerns and the need for learning processes to ensure the efficiency of the policy process lead ineluctably to the view that some form of participatory decision-making is required as a source of knowledge, a vehicle of information and a foundation for consent. The urgent task for constitutional lawyers then becomes to reconstitute the Rule of Law in terms of its institutional expressions, retaining commitment to the underlying principles which espouse non-arbitrariness, the containment of unaccountable discretion and the perhaps newer commitment to a decision-making process which is rational. This latter desideratum is simply another way of expressing the belief that a public learning process is required for the resolution of many problems facing an increasingly complex national and international community and that institutions directed to advancing that process are a necessity. The Rule of Law, as we have argued, is a master ideal and a legitimating sentiment which needs to be constantly related to modern concerns and periodically updated in institutional settings.

Note

The central thrust of the contention is that the immense complexity of the modern state, the desirability of de-centralised decision making, and the growth in sources of (corporate) economic power which can rival those of the state, all mean that a simplistic application of a rather rusty 19th-century conception of the Rule of Law will be both ineffective and inappropriate. Jowell considers both the continuing value of the doctrine and the aspects of it which warrant re-examination in contemporary society.

Jeffrey Jowell, 'The Rule of Law Today', *op cit*, pp62–71

Certainty and the Rule of Law

An official possessed of discretion frequently has a choice about how it should be operated: whether to keep it open-textured, maintaining the option of a variety of responses to a given situation, or to confine it by a rule of standard – a process of legalisation. For example, officials administering welfare benefits could provide them on a case-by-case basis according to their conception of need, or they could announce precise levels of benefit for given situations. Similarly, laws against pollution could be enforced by a variable standard whereby the official must be satisfied that the polluter is achieving the 'best practicable means' of abatement. Alternatively, levels of pollution could be specified in advance, based on the colour of smoke emission, or the precise quantities of sulphur dioxide. A policy of promoting safe driving could, similarly, be legalised by a rule specifying speeds of no more than 30mph on given streets.

Now for Dicey, and particularly for Hewart and Hayek, who mistrusted the grant of virtually any official discretion, the virtue of rule-bound conduct was principally that it allowed affected persons to know the rules before being subjected to them *ex post facto*. As a principle of justice, it was felt that no person should be condemned without a presumed knowledge of the rule alleged to have been breached. This assumes a penal law or criminal regulation of one form or another, and is understandable in that context where the lack of rules would involve risky guesses with serious consequences for non-compliance. It is fairer to a person prosecuted for a tax offence to have been made aware of the precise tax required than for the levels to be determined at the discretion of an official.

This argument, however, has a somewhat different compulsion when dealing not with penalties but with regulation involving the allocation of scarce resources. Should an applicant for a university place be entitled, out of fairness, to know the precise grades required for entrance? Should the applicant for welfare benefits be entitled to know the rules about allocations of winter coats? In cases such as these the argument in favour of rules over discretion is an argument less from certainty than from *accountability*. This argument has two facets, the first being a concern to provide a published standard against which to measure the legality of official action and thus to allow *individual redress* against official action that does not accord with the rule or standard. Thus, an announced level of resources to qualify for welfare assistance ought to allow redress to a person who qualifies but is refused assistance. The second facet of accountability refers to the fact that the actual process of making rules and their publication generates *public assessment* of the fidelity of the rule to legislative purpose. Many statutes confer powers on officials to further the policy of the Act in accordance with wide discretion. The power may be to allocate council housing, or to provide for the needy, or to diminish unacceptable pollution of the air or water. The process of devising a points system for housing allocation, benefits for the needy, and acceptable emission levels of pollution thus forces the official into producing a formal operational definition of purpose.

Legislative purpose is not always clear, and indeed often can only be defined in its implementation. However, the legalisation of policy does not simply allow officials to 'congratulate themselves – and await obedience' [P Selznick, *Law Society and Industrial Justice* (1969), p29]. The process of making rules, as well as the rules themselves, may generate scrutiny and appraisal that make officials subject to assessment on the basis of fidelity to whatever purpose is considered apposite. Once the definition of purpose in the form of rules has been exposed, they are more likely to be held to account than if they were working under a cloak of discretion.

The virtues of rules, as we have seen, include their qualities of legality, certainty, consistency, uniformity, congruence to purpose, and accountability loosely so called, all of which play an important part in the control of official discretion and may be seen as concrete manifestations of the Rule of Law. KC Davis, a leading American administrative lawyer, proposes in his book *Discretionary Justice* (1969) three main methods of controlling discretion. First is the 'confining' of discretion through rules akin to the legalisation we have just been discussing. He suggests that, wherever possible, discretion should be shaved down to the minimum compatible with the task to be performed. He proposes two other means of controlling discretion: its 'structuring' through open procedures, like the exacting federal rule-making procedures with which administrative agencies in the US must comply before issuing their regulations (Britain, incidentally, almost entirely lacks these procedures); and the 'checking' of discretion by means of a second look (not necessarily by the courts – internal administrative checks would suffice). The last two methods will be considered when we discuss procedural fairness, below.

The limits of rules

Looking now a little closer at the arguments above about rules governing administrative action, we should consider whether they are after all wholly beneficial in the way that some constitutional theorists have assumed. Maitland wrote that 'Known general laws, however bad, interfere less with freedom than decisions based on no previously known rule' [*Collected Papers*, vol i (1911), p81]. Hayek, taking a similar line of argument, gives an example: 'it does not matter whether we all drive on the left or the right-hand side of the roads so long as we all do the same. The important thing is that the rule enables us to predict other people's behaviour correctly, and this requires that it should apply in all cases – even if in a particular instance we feel it to be unjust' [*The Road to Serfdom* (1943), p60].

We should start by challenging a central assumption of those in favour of rules, that their principal purpose is to constrain officials straining to escape from their legal shackles in order to indulge in discretion unconfined. Officials are well aware of the benefit of rules to their own efficiency. Rules announce or clarify official policies to affected parties, and thus facilitate obedience. They may also allow routine treatment of cases, thus increasing the speed of decision-making. A zoning system in planning, a list of features of 'substandard' housing, and a list of grades for university admission all allow decisions to be taken more quickly than a system that requires constant reappraisal of each case on its merits. Rules, therefore, reduce the anxiety and conserve the energy needed to reach decisions on a case-by-case basis. The sociologist Max Weber's portrayal of his ideal-type bureaucrat applying rules *sine ira et studio* – without hatred or passion, and hence without affection or enthusiasm [*The Theory of Social and Economic Organisation*, trans A Henderson and T Parsons, (1947), p340] – alludes to the non-affective approach of a legalised framework, to the possibility of insulating the decision-maker from the pressure of constant reconsideration. Despite the fact that rules may promote criticism, they also, in the short run at least, provide a shield behind which officials may hide, pleading consistent and uniform justice in response to criticism that the individual's case is unique.

So here we have the tension: the virtues of rules – their objective, even-handed features – are opposed to other administrative benefits, especially those of flexibility, individual treatment, and responsiveness. The virtue of rules to the administrator (routine treatment) may be a defect to the client with a special case (such as the brilliant applicant for a university place who failed to obtain the required grades because of a family upset or illness just before the examination).

The administrator's shield may be seen as an unjustified protection from the client's sword. Officials themselves may consider that the job itself requires flexibility, or genuinely want to help a particular client, but feel unable to do so: hence the classic bureaucratic response, 'I'd like to help you – but there is this rule'.

Our administrative law itself recognises the limits of rule-governed conduct in terms of individual justice in its development of the principle against the 'fettering' of discretion. Where an official has wide discretion – for example, to provide grants to industry or to impose penalties upon overspending local authorities – a rule will often be introduced both to assist in the articulation of the standard and its even-handed application, and also to announce the standard to affected persons. The courts have not objected to the rule itself, but they have objected to its blanket application without giving a person with something new or special to say about his case the opportunity to put his argument to the decision-maker. The principle against the fettering of discretion acknowledges how rules can militate against good and fair public administration.

[In the area of planning law] ... recent years have seen an abandonment of a rule-bound approach, not only in favour of more flexible 'material considerations', taking in ever-widening factors, but also involving a move away from a generalised approach to planning standards to one bargained on a case-by-case basis. Instead of being granted or refused planning permission in accordance with known rules and standards (however flexible), an applicant might offer in exchange for planning permission a benefit to the community that was not part of the original application. Thus, for example, an applicant for permission to build offices may have been granted that permission, perhaps at a density higher than the norm, on condition that he agree to dedicate part of the site to be used as a public right of way, a community centre, or housing for use by the local authority.

The Rule of Law as procedural fairness

As we have seen, predetermined rules provide one way of controlling official discretion and achieving fairness for persons affected by public regulation. Procedural techniques provide another. I refer to these in connection with the notion contained in the Rule of Law that no person should be condemned unheard, a procedural protection also expressed in terms such as 'due process' or 'natural justice', the essence of which is the participation of affected persons in decisions affecting their rights or interests. This kind of 'structuring' or 'checking' of discretion attempts, like open rules, to promote fidelity to organisational purpose, both by permitting the persons affected to argue their case and, where a reasoned decision is required, giving, through the process of justification, what Fuller has described as 'formal and institutional expression to the influence of reasoned argument in human affairs' ['Collective Bargaining and the Arbitrator' (1963) Wisconsin L Rev 1, p3]. Where the decisions are published, there is the opportunity of public criticism; accountability, in one sense of the term, is thus achieved.

Of course, adjudicated decisions can be exercises in what has been called 'symbolic reassurance' [M Edelman, *The Symbolic Uses of Politics* (1964)]. We have all come across instances where decision-makers go through procedural motions with anodyne justifications, but have really made up their minds in advance. The fact that the forms were followed thus often adds legitimacy to an otherwise questionable decision. Nevertheless, the process itself does encourage 'purposive decisions' [P Nonet, 'The Legitimation of Purposive Decisions' (1980) Calif L Rev 263], as justification must usually be made by reference to a general rule, standard, or principle. Overt reference to arbitrary or particularistic factors (such as the defendant's race or political views) will be difficult to sustain.

British public administration is deeply infused with the notion that adjudicative mechanisms of one form or another are necessary to provide procedural checks on discretion in order to comply with the Rule of Law. Some are provided through appeals – for example, in planning, from local to central government by means of written representations or a public inquiry. In other cases special tribunals exist to permit appeals from the decisions of a variety of officials upon issues as diverse as the registration of a new variety of rose to compensation for the acquisition of land. Some tribunals and inquiries decide not only rights between the individual and the public organisation, but also questions of policy, such as whether a motorway should be built over a stretch of land. Because of their variety, not all tribunals and inquiries are suited to all the procedural protections obtaining in courts of law, where individual rights are in issue, but the trend, at least since the Franks Committee, is towards more judicialisation.

English courts have affirmed the principle of 'natural justice', or a right to a fair hearing, even where the statute conferring the power to decide is silent on the matter.

This kind of procedural protection through adjudication, whether established by statute or the common law, is a concrete Rule of Law. Its content is variable ... As with rules, adjudication is not appropriate in all situations. Where speed and administrative despatch are required, it may be excluded: could one really allow a pavement hearing before a police officer is able to tow away an illegally parked car? In some situations it is felt that an authoritative judgment without the opportunity of challenge is required (the marking of examination scripts may serve as an example here, or admission to a university). Sometimes parties who have to live with each other after the dispute prefer techniques of mediation or conciliation to negotiate an acceptable solution. These forms of resolving disputes differ from adjudication where the final decision is taken by the independent 'judge' and is imposed rather than agreed, a feature not acceptable in all situations and which also partially explains the move to negotiated solutions noted above. Finally, it should be borne in mind that the opportunity for a hearing may not easily be taken: hearings take time, may need expertise, and are often costly (legal aid is generally not provided to parties before administrative tribunals or inquiries).

Mention was made earlier of an increasingly prevalent view that techniques of adjudication should be applied in non-judicial settings. In particular, the central characteristic of participation of affected parties is sought (in urban redevelopment, for example) by those who feel themselves excluded from decisions that shape their environment. They are not willing to rely on parliamentary controls on day-to-day official decisions which are rarely open to national debate. Neighbours thus want to be consulted about an application for planning permission on a local site, and amenity groups want a say in decisions about the abstraction of water. Coal mining unions and even inhabitants of villages want to be consulted about the closure of coal pits.

This argument endorses what Patrick McAuslan has called an ideology of 'public participation' rather than the public interest or private property rights [*The Ideology of Planning Law* (1980)]. If the Rule of Law is concerned to protect an individual from being deprived of his rights without an opportunity to defend himself, the concern is only narrowly stretched to protect group-interests from being overridden without the opportunity to express their views on the matter to be decided. Court decisions have affirmed the principle that local authorities, before embarking on significant spending, must consider the interests of ratepayers (to whom the authority owes a 'fiduciary duty') [*Bromley LBC v GLC* [1983] 1 AC 768]. In so far as this 'fiduciary' principle is a procedural one, it recognises the right of groups (in this case the ratepayers) to some form of consideration before decisions affecting their interests are taken.

THE SEPARATION OF POWERS

Reduced to its bare essentials, the doctrine of the Separation of Powers identifies three main organs of government – Legislature, Executive and Judiciary – and demands first that each should be separate and to an extent independent of each other, and second that each organ should be vested with one main function of Government: thus, as Lord Templeman has put it '... Parliament makes the law, the executive carry the law into effect and the judiciary enforce the law'.[29] It is immediately apparent that the doctrine is associated with that of the Rule of Law, which is strongly concerned with the manner in which the judiciary can keep the executive and (in the UK only to a very limited sense) the legislature within the bounds of their lawful authority. The other substantial concern of the doctrine is the relationship between the legislature and the executive, which is considered in detail in Part 2. Therefore what follows will confine itself to a brief discussion of the theoretical basis for the doctrine and its application in the UK.

The classic formulation of the doctrine is Montesquieu's:

When the legislative and executive powers are united in the same person, or in the same body of magistrates, there can be no liberty ... Again, there is no liberty if the power of judging is not separated from the legislative and executive. If it were joined with the legislative, the life and liberty of the subject would be exposed to arbitrary control; for the judge would then be the legislator. If it were joined to the executive power, the judge might behave with violence and oppression. There would be an end to everything, if the same man, or the same body, whether of the nobles or of the people, were to exercise those three powers, that of enacting laws, that of executing public affairs, and that of trying crimes or individual causes [quoted in R Shackleton 'Montesquieu, Bolingbroke and the Separation of Powers' (1949) 3 FS].

Notes

1 As Munro notes[40], Montesquieu advocated that 'the three agencies of Government should perform their functions *separately*' but did not make it quite clear what form the separation should take, nor whether a 'complete separation of personnel' for the different agencies was required.

2 Apart from doubts as to the applicability of the doctrine to the British constitution (discussed below), considerable doubts have been expressed as to the value and coherence of the doctrine itself. These criticisms are discussed and answered in an important, essay[41] by Eric Barendt. He first of all notes the criticisms of Sir Ivor Jennings, namely that 'there are no

---

29 *In re M* [1993] 3 WLR 433.
40 *Studies in Constitutional Law* (1987), p191.
41 Barendt, 'Separation of Powers and Constitutional Government' (1995) PL 599.

material differences between the three functions, so the separation principle fails to explain why certain functions should be given to one body rather than another'.[42] He also notes Marshall's arguments[43] which are to similar effect; Marshall also notes that, on the US version of the theory, judicial review of legislation is appropriate 'to check the legislative and executive branches, [which] would be an unwarrantable violation of ... the pure theory' and concludes that the doctrine 'may be counted little more than a jumbled portmanteau of arguments for policies that should be supported or rejected on other grounds'.[44] In reply, Barendt first of all argues that Jennings exaggerated the difficulties of distinguishing genuinely different functions of Government.[45] He then goes on to defend the doctrine on more fundamental grounds, and goes on to consider its wider significance.

E Barendt, 'Separation of Powers and Constitutional Government' (1995) *Public Law* 599, 606–7, 608–10, 611–12 and 613

But perhaps a more significant point to make in reply to the critique of Jennings and Marshall is that the Separation of Powers is not in essence concerned with the allocation of functions as such. Its primary purpose, as we saw earlier in this article, is the prevention of the arbitrary government, or tyranny, which may arise from the concentration of power. The allocation of functions between three, or perhaps more, branches of government is only a means to achieve that end. It does not matter, therefore, whether powers are always allocated precisely to the most appropriate institution – although an insensitive allocation would probably produce incompetent government and run counter to Locke's efficiency rationale.

This point is perhaps most clearly appreciated if we consider what has become one of the most complex areas for Separation of Powers analysis: the organisation, and control, of administrative authorities and agencies. These range from bodies which allocate social security and welfare benefits (such as public housing), to regulatory bodies, eg the Independent Television Commission and the Monopolies and Mergers Commission, and finally to supervisory or investigatory officers, such as the Comptroller and Auditor-General and the Parliamentary Commissioner for Administration (PCA). Now it can be asked whether these bodies perform legislative (or rule-making, to use the American term), administrative, or judicial functions. But these are impossible questions to answer. For, in truth many agencies perform at least two, and perhaps all three, functions. This is apparent in the US, where it is common for an independent regulatory agency to engage in rule-making, to formulate and apply policies, and to take individual decisions, often after a formal hearing. Perhaps in the UK the only authorities which consistently discharge all three functions are local authorities, which may make by-laws, formulate planning, highways and housing policies, and decide applications for planning permission which might be characterised as judicial, or at least quasi-judicial, decisions. But certainly

---

42 *Ibid*, p603. Barendt here cites Jennings' *The Law and the Constitution*, 5th edn (1959), App I, 281–2 and 303.

43 *Ibid*, pp603–4. Barendt refers to Marshall's *Constitutional Theory* (1971), Ch V.

44 Marshall, *op cit*, p124; quoted in Barendt at p604.

45 *Ibid*, pp605–6.

many agencies, including Government ministers, exercise a variety of functions, some of which can be characterised as executive and some as judicial.

Does this phenomenon mean that Separation of Powers analysis should be abandoned as hopeless? It would seem so, if the pure theory is adopted, with its rigid insistence that each function of government is discharged by a separate institution. But the answer may be quite different if we see the principle as essentially concerned with the avoidance of concentrations of power. For, then, questions may be asked about the relationship of the agency to the three traditional branches of government. Does Parliament or the Government have sole right to hire and fire members of the authority and its staff? Does the Government have exclusive power to issue directions or guidance to the agency? If the agency takes judicial or quasi-judicial decisions, how far is it subject to review by the ordinary courts? On this approach there would be a violation of the principle if the executive were entitled, without assent of the legislature, to give detailed directions to an agency, and appoint its members, when that agency takes decisions affecting individual rights and judicial review is (virtually) excluded. That would not be because an executive agency carried out judicial functions, but because it was so structured as to create or reinforce a concentration of power in the hands of the Government.

The partial separation theory

The argument in the previous section has shown that the Separation of Powers should not be explained in terms of a strict distribution of *functions* between the three branches of government, but in terms of a network of rules and principles which ensure that power is not concentrated in the hands of one branch. (In practice the danger now is that the executive has too much power, though it is worth remembering that at other times there was more anxiety about self-aggrandisement of the legislature.) That does not mean that the allocation of functions is wholly irrelevant. I will explain in the next section of this article how, in civil liberties cases, courts may properly insist that general rules be made by the legislature and that the executive does not act without legislative authorisation to deprive individuals of their rights. But the importance of a correct definition and allocation of functions should not be exaggerated. Madison for instance was not troubled by these questions, though nobody has argued so cogently for the Separation of Powers principle.

Outside the context of court rulings in civil liberties cases, the principle is most frequently applied in the architecture of the constitution itself. Powers are allocated to different institutions. The legislature is normally divided into two branches, a procedure recommended by Madison on the ground that otherwise it would be too powerful [*Federalist Papers*, no 51]. Each branch is empowered to check the others by exercising a *partial agency or control* over their acts [*Ibid*, no 47]. That is why, for example, in the US constitution the Senate must give its advice and consent to the appointment of ministers, ambassadors and judges, and the President may veto Bills passed by the House of Representatives and the Senate, subject to an override by a two-thirds majority vote in each House. It is not very helpful to ask whether, in the former, instance the Senate is exercising an executive power and whether, in the latter, the President acts as a third branch of the legislature. What is important is that there is a system of checks and balances between institutions which otherwise might exercise excessive power. As Madison put it in *Federalist Paper 51*, the structure of government should be so arranged 'that its several constituent parts may, by their mutual relations, be the means of keeping each other in their proper places'.

Implications of the Separation of Powers

It is worth exploring some of the implications of commitment to the Separation of Powers found in other legal systems before turning to the significance of the principle in the modern UK constitution. For it has been argued that the principle is too ambivalent to be useful. It is also said that it has been compromised by, for example, the need to tolerate extensive executive law-making under the welfare state. Yet there are a number of cases in the US, and more recently France and Germany, where Separation of Powers arguments have been decisive in litigation. In particular (though not exclusively) they have been used to bolster claims that a citizen's fundamental rights have been violated.

This coupling of the two arguments is no accident. For the litigant may be uncertain whether his right will prevail against the substantial public interest which, according to the Government, justifies its infringement. Alternatively, the contours of the right may be uncertain or controversial. It may be relatively easier to deploy an argument that the decision has been taken unconstitutionally by the executive when it was only appropriate for the legislature to act. Moreover, under this argument, judicial review is less susceptible to the charge that it is fundamentally undemocratic. Indeed, when a court requires the legislature to impose clearer standards on the executive or the police, it would be reinforcing democratic values. Individuals and pressure groups enjoy readier access to legislators than they do to ministers, civil servants or police officers, and so may in theory exercise some influence on the drafting of legislation. Equally, the courts should be particularly willing to strike down retrospective criminal legislation, insofar as it interferes with the general liberty of the defendants and also with their rights to a fair trial. In these circumstances, the civil rights argument reinforces the case that the legislature is violating the structural limits on its powers.

Courts are, therefore, right to look with particular suspicion on acts of the executive which affect individuals and which are entirely unauthorised by statute. This is exemplified by a number of US cases, among them the famous Supreme Court decisions in the *Steel Seizure* ... case. ... The Court held President Truman had violated the Separation of Powers when he issued an order directing seizure of all steel mills [*Youngstown Steel and Tube Co v Sawyer* 343 US 579 (1952)]. Put simply, there was neither constitutional nor congressional authority for the order, which at least two members of the majority, Black J and Douglas J, regarded as an attempt on the part of the President to exercise legislative power. Moreover, it trespassed on the mill owners' constitutional property right guaranteed by the Fifth Amendment. ...

In other First Amendment cases the Supreme Court has invalidated legislation conferring wide licensing powers on city officials or police officers. In *Lovell v Griffin* it struck down an ordinance giving a city manager unfettered discretion to ban the public distribution of circulars and pamphlets [303 US 444 (1938)]. Other decisions have applied the same principle in the context of the allocation of permits to use loudspeakers, and to hold public meetings. In all these cases the official was free to formulate for himself the grounds on which he determined the applications. In effect the city ordinance gave him a legislative as well as an executive power. This is clearly undesirable. Without detailed standards to constrain official discretion, it is unlikely that due regard will be paid to the constitutional rights at issue. Moreover, such wide power can be applied selectively, say, to political groups favoured by the official or chief of police, without any opportunity for democratic control.

The second set of circumstances involves political parties and the rights of members of the legislature. Continental European constitutions recognise the distinctive role of political parties and other groups, a matter on which both UK and US constitutions are silent. One of the earliest decisions of the *Conseil constitutionnel* held a rule of the national assembly unconstitutional with regard to Article 4 of the constitution [Decision 59-2 of 17, 18 and 24 June 1959, GD 34]. That guarantees the right to form parties, though '[T]hey must respect the principles of national sovereignty and democracy'. Article 19-3 of a draft assembly regulation would have given it the power to decide whether a party respected these principles and hence should be recognised for parliamentary purposes. The *Conseil* clearly thought it undesirable to leave this sensitive matter to the judgment of the majority party or coalition in the assembly, in effect to the will of the Government. In Germany the Basic Law reserves this assessment for the Constitutional Court. Only it may decide that a political party is unconstitutional because it 'seeks to impair or abolish the free democratic basic order or to endanger the existence' of the country. In principle, it must be right to allocate this decision to the judicial branch, since both legislature and executive have an interest in its outcome, which may run counter to democratic values. ...

The Separation of Powers principle is therefore not simply a formal guide to the organisation of state power. It can be given teeth by constitutional courts to reinforce the protection conferred by the constitution on individual rights, and to prevent one branch of government from accumulating excessive powers. Whatever its theoretical defects may be, case law in other systems shows that it is not as vacuous as its English critics have alleged.

Note

Barendt goes on to find the doctrine to be only patchily embodied in the British constitution, a theme explored in more depth by Colin Munro below.

Colin Munro, *Studies in Constitutional Law* (1987), pp192–6, 209–11

The doctrine of the Separation of Powers was put forward as a *prescription* of what ought to be done for the promotion of certain values, and the question of its validity is a question of political theory. A question of particular interest to British constitutional lawyers is the extent to which as a matter of *description* our constitution exhibits the kind of separation which the doctrine would require.

Two initial observations may be made. The first is that the British constitution, with its long and largely unbroken history, is above all the product of experience and experiment. Its development has been characteristically pragmatic rather than principled, and so it is hardly likely absolutely to conform (or not to conform) to any ideal type. A second and related point is that the outlines of the modern British constitution had already been formed by the late 17th century. Therefore, even if earlier versions of the doctrine may not have been without some effect, Montesquieu's formulation of it in the mid-18th century could only have affected such developments as occurred after that date. ...

What about the 20th century constitution? Writers on the constitution seem to speak almost with one voice in denying that the Separation of Powers is a feature of the constitution. ... WA Robson, whose *Justice and Administrative Law* was first published three years later, likened Montesquieu's doctrine to 'a rickety chariot' and claimed that: '... the division of powers enunciated in this theory, and their allocation to separate branches of the government has at no period of history borne a close relation to the actual grouping of authority under the system of government obtaining in England' [*Justice and Administrative Law*, 3rd edn (1951), p16].

Moreover, he thought, 'when we come to the present day, we find a mingling of functions more extensive than any that has existed since the 16th and early 17th centuries' [*ibid*, p22]. In *Halsbury's Laws of England*, Sir William Holdsworth denied that the doctrine had ever 'to any great extent corresponded with the facts of English government' [2nd edn (1932), Vol 6, p385].

These views seemed still to represent the academic orthodoxy 40 years later. Griffith and Street considered that 'the doctrine is so remote from the facts that it is better to disregard it altogether'. Hood Phillips believed that the negation of the doctrine in most of its meanings was 'generally acknowledged' by students of the British constitution. SA De Smith obviously thought likewise:

> Mention the theory of Separation of Powers to an English constitutional lawyer and he will forthwith put on parade the Lord Chancellor, the Law Lords, the parliamentary executive, delegated legislation and administrative adjudication, and shift the conversation to more significant topics. He tends to regard the theory as a somewhat tiresome talking point, appropriate for political philosophers and inquisitive experts on comparative government, but an irrelevant distraction for the English law student and his teachers. ['The Separation of Powers in New Dress' (1966) 12 McGill LJ 491.]

In his textbook, the verdict was short and sharp: 'No writer of repute would claim that it is a central feature of the modern British constitution' [*Constitutional and Administrative Law*, 5th edn (1985), p31].

However, in recent years some distinguished judges have risked incurring disrepute. In a Privy Council appeal in 1977, Lord Diplock referred to some of the Commonwealth constitutions as having been drafted by persons 'familiar ... with the basic concept of separation of legislative, executive and judicial power as it had been developed in the unwritten constitution of the UK' [*Hinds v R* [1977] AC 195 at 212]. He returned to the theme when the House of Lords, in a case concerning an industrial dispute, felt it necessary to rebuke the Court of Appeal for having strayed beyond its proper constitutional function:

> At a time when more and more cases involve the application of legislation which gives effect to policies that are the subject of bitter public and parliamentary controversy, it cannot be too strongly emphasised that the British constitution, though largely underwritten, is firmly based on the Separation of Powers: Parliament makes the laws, the judiciary interpret them. [*Dupont Steels Ltd v Sirs* [1980] 1 All ER 529 at 541]

Lord Scarman, in his speech in the same case, also remarked that 'the constitution's Separation of Powers, or more accurately functions, must be observed if judicial independence is not to be put at risk' [at 551]. In another case later, an applicant was seeking to determine the prospective validity of a draft Order in Council which had yet to be laid before the Houses of Parliament as required. The Court of Appeal held that there was jurisdiction to entertain such a challenge, although it had to be exercised with great circumspection and due regard to the dangers of encroaching on any functions of Parliament. Sir John Donaldson MR said:

> Although the UK has no written constitution, it is a constitutional convention of the highest importance that the legislature and the judicature are separate and independent of one another, subject to certain ultimate rights of Parliament over the judicature which are immaterial for present purposes. It therefore behoves the courts to be ever sensitive to the paramount need to refrain from trespassing on the province of Parliament.

There is something of a puzzle here, which we shall have to try to unravel. On the one side, there is distinguished judicial support for the view that our constitution is 'firmly based' on the Separation of Powers. On the other, there is the weight of academic judgment these 50 years past, almost wholly to the opposite effect.

Of course, the differences might be explained by differences in usage. As we have already seen, the Separation of Powers doctrine is susceptible to a variety of meanings, and this is apt to bedevil discussions of it. But these difficulties, although real, should not be exaggerated. What Lord Diplock seems to have had in mind is a version of the doctrine which would require that the persons who exercise one kind of governmental function should not also exercise another; and from the evidence which they individually adduce, that is a formulation which, as regards British government, Hood Phillips, De Smith and the others took to be negated. The disagreement seems to be real, and nor merely apparent.

In order to explore this further, we should make a survey of the extent to which, in the constitution of the present day, the legislature, executive and judiciary are separated or mixed. It is necessary to define these terms. In speaking of 'the legislature' we are thinking of Parliament. In speaking of 'the executive' we would include the Sovereign as its nominal head, the Prime Minister and other members of the government, and the Civil Service. 'The judiciary' consists of the judges who preside in courts of law. ...

It is easy enough to portray the Lord Chancellor as a sort of dangerous one man band [he sits in the House of Lords (the Legislature), is a member of the Cabinet (the executive) and is head of the Judiciary – Ed], but a consideration of constitutional practice might be more informative. When some jurors complained to the Lord Chancellor about a judge's conduct of a trial, Lord Hailsham, in his reply to them, observed that he was a member of the Cabinet, and that if he were to comment upon the conduct of controversial trials, 'the distinction, which is vital to the whole system, between the courts and the government would be destroyed' [*The Times*, 1 February 1980].

Many other matters deserve to be put under a similarly searching spotlight. Yes, the Law Lords are members of the legislature and of a court; but no, they do not participate crucially, or even freely, in legislative business. Yes, the Privy Council is an executive body which (through a committee) exercises a judicial function; but its judicial tasks are specialised, and its largely ritual executive functions carried out by different members. Yes, the Houses of Parliament have a penal jurisdiction; but the House of Lords does not seem to use it, and even the House of Commons has not imprisoned anyone for more than a hundred years. In the British constitution, where conventions and practice count for such a lot, it is all the more necessary to see behind the forms.

There are substantial, and not merely trivial, links between the legislature and the executive, because of there being Cabinet government with a parliamentary executive. But this is not to show that the Separation of Powers doctrine has been without effect. True, members of the government may sit in the Commons but only up to a statutorily limited number. True, a large volume of legislation emanates from the executive. But by convention primary legislation is the appropriate embodiment for matters of principle, and over subordinate legislation Parliament retains a number of controls. Thus, even where the doctrine is apparently breached, it has had an important effect in limiting the extent of the breach. The same may be argued with respect to administrative tribunals. The protection of their members from dismissal and the improved rights of appeal conferred in the Tribunals and Inquiries Act 1958 [replaced by Tribunals and Inquiries Act 1971, ss8, 13] were designed to bring them closer to a 'judicial' model. It was doubtful anyway whether their members could be considered part of the executive, so that representing the work of the tribunals as the executive exercising judicial functions was strained, to say the least.

In fact, it is significant that features of modern government such as delegated legislation and adjudication by tribunals should have been perceived as problematic. In the 1920s and 1930s that perception was widespread. In books such as *The New Despotism* (1929) by Lord Hewart of Bury (who was Lord Chief Justice at the time) and *Bureaucracy Triumphant* (1931) by CK Allen, there were dire warnings of the dangers involved in the increasing use of these techniques. It was in response to these concerns that the Committee on Ministers' Powers [Cmnd 4060] was set up in 1929 and the Committee on Administrative Tribunals and Enquiries [Cmnd 218] in 1956. The two reports were reassuring. Delegated legislation and adjudication by tribunals were regarded as necessary and useful features of a developed state, provided that they were accompanied by safeguards to prevent abuse. The thinking behind the reports has been immensely influential in modern public administration and administrative law. What is interesting for our present purpose is the underlying concern and the stress laid on safeguards to allay it. In this there is eloquent testimony to the depth of Separation of Powers ideas in our political consciousness.

When one looks around today, there are plenty of other examples to the same effect. It was early in Lord Denning's judicial career when he was accused by Viscount Simonds of 'a naked usurpation of the legislative function' [*Magor and St Mellons RDC v Newport Corpn* [1952] AC 189 at 191]. But at the end of that career, Lord Denning was still being criticised regularly, by politicians and the media as well as by fellow judges and lawyers, for assuming a role which properly belonged to the legislature. The merits of the criticisms do not concern us here. What is instructive is that they should be made in these terms.

Whenever governments anxious to reduce the prison population try to influence sentencing policy, there are objections raised on constitutional grounds. Even a sensitively phrased circular addressed to magistrates' clerks, which asked for the co-operation of courts in keeping custodial sentences to a minimum, was criticised by Professor Michael Zander as 'an unprecedented example of the executive trying to influence the courts' judicial decision-making' [*The Guardian*, 23 October 1980].

When in the European Communities Act 1972 Parliament provided for Community obligations to be implemented by ministerial legislation, it was careful not to transfer some of its traditional functions, so that subordinate legislation may not be used for the imposition of taxes or for the creation of major criminal offences [See European Communities Act 1972, s2; and Chapter 6].

In a variety of important ways, ideas of the separate of powers have shaped constitutional arrangements and influenced our constitutional thinking, and continue to do so. The separation in the British constitution, although not absolute, ought not to be lightly dismissed.

Notes

1 It is apparent that, as ever, in the British constitution a careful, empirical study of the actual practices, understandings and codes of conduct of the personnel of Government, judiciary and legislature is required to balance the perception yielded by an examination of the formal position.

2 There is clearly a strong tension between the doctrine of the Separation of Powers and the demands of practical and efficient government. This tension is felt particularly keenly in the US, where the doctrine has been strongly

embodied by the institution of a legislature which can often be controlled by a party hostile to the President. In November 1995, opposition by the Republican-controlled Congress to the Budget proposed by President Clinton resulted in a complete impasse in which Congress refused to allow the President access to even temporary sources of funding. This stalemate resulted in the country defaulting on its debt repayments for the first time in its history, and being forced to send home millions of state employees, most state institutions being closed down. In the extract below, Jeremy Waldron considers this perennial tension.

Jeremy Waldron, *The Law* (1990), pp71–73

If anything, the Separation of Powers doctrine runs into the criticism that it works too well – that by giving distinct institutions independent roles in the process of government, it gives each the power to frustrate the purposes of the other, leading sometimes to a deadlock in which recriminations flow back and forth and the political power of the community is simply not exercised at all. This may be music to the ears of those who fear strong government as a threat to individual liberty. But many believe there are other things to be done in society besides protecting individual freedom from the state. The constitutionalist strategy of playing distinct institutions off against one another may be a good way of preventing political oppression, but it is also a good way of ensuring the paralysis of government and the neglect of social policy.

Part of the problem is that the doctrine gives no account of the relation between the formulation of social and economic policy, on the one hand, and its implementation, on the other. The experience of modern government is that social problems are chronic and complex and any possible solutions need to be thought through and formulated by a specialised body of experts under coherent political direction. The solutions may still take a legislative form, but there needs to be reasonably tight co-ordination between those who are responsible for their formulation, those who are responsible for their implementation, and those who are responsible for their authoritative passage into law. On a number of occasions in the past 100 years – and the present debate about the federal budget deficit is one of them – there has been a widespread feeling in the United States that the constitutional Separation of Powers in effect prevents this co-ordination.

Waldron then notes the general non-conformity of the British system of government with the doctrine, and goes on:

It is supposed to be a virtue of an unwritten constitution that it does not bind us to institutional structures that might seem appropriate in one age but inappropriate or outdated in another. We are not bound even to pay lip-service to formulae laid down in 1787 in the way the Americans are. Our unwritten conventions give us flexibility in this regard: we can, if we want, address old problems in new ways. But that advantage is easily lost if it is taken as an excuse for not addressing the problems of power and its accumulation at all, and that has been for too long the experience in Britain. The flexibility of our political institutions – the lack of structural constraint – has worked greatly to the advantage of the executive in its quest for more efficient administration and more centralised control. Indeed, this cherished flexibility is itself somewhat 'inflexible' in the way it resists the introduction of constraints and mechanisms for scrutiny. We do not need to say that this is a sinister process: mostly it has been done with the best will in the world, to better achieve the goals of public policy. But whether the intentions are sinister or not, the fact is that there is something dangerous – for the future – about the shift of power from periphery to centre, from Parliament to the committee that controls it, from a functionally articulated structure to a unitary state. Our lack of a written constitution has allowed that to happen without forcing anything like a public debate about the fundamentals of power and liberty. Once again, we feel the lack most sharply, not for the actual constraint that it might exercise, but for the way it might force us to face up honestly to the principles and concerns of constitutionalism.

CHAPTER 4

PARLIAMENTARY SOVEREIGNTY[1]

Three main issues are covered in this chapter: the nature of parliamentary sovereignty; possible legal limitations on sovereignty; and the question of entrenchment. The next chapter will consider the impact of Community law on the traditional doctrine of parliamentary sovereignty. The main concern will be the extent to which the legislative competence of Parliament has been fettered by the impact of Community law.

THE NATURE OF PARLIAMENTARY SOVEREIGNTY

The basic idea of sovereignty

The notion of 'parliamentary sovereignty' or the 'legislative supremacy of Parliament', as it is sometimes termed, can be seen to have both political and legal aspects. Given that the dominant body in Parliament, the Commons, is democratically elected, the notion can be seen as representing a description of the democratic basis for legislation in the UK. As used by constitutional lawyers, however, it means something much more specific: 'By the legislative supremacy of Parliament is meant that there are no *legal* limitations upon the legislative competence of Parliament'.[2]

As AW Bradley has summed up the doctrine:

> The sovereignty of Parliament describes in formal terms the relationship which exists between the legislature and the courts. As analysed by Dicey, the Queen in Parliament (the legislature) has 'the right to make or unmake any law whatever' and no person or body outside the legislature 'is recognised by the law of England as having a right to override or set aside the legislation of Parliament' [Dicey, *Law of the Constitution*, 10th edn (1959) p40]. In other words, there are no legal limits to the legislative authority of Parliament. When that authority is exercised in the form of an Act of Parliament, no court or other body has power to hold such an Act to be void or invalid or in any respect lacking in legal effect.[3]

Notes

1 It will be seen that two distinct notions emerge from the above quotations. The first is the lack of legal, as opposed to conventional or moral constraints on Parliament. Lord Reid has expressed this idea thus:

> It is often said that it would be unconstitutional for the UK Parliament to do certain things, meaning that the moral, political and other reasons against doing them are so strong that most people would regard it as highly improper if Parliament did these things. But that does not mean that it is beyond the power

---

1 General reading (additional to that cited in this chapter): sources referred to in n 1 of Chapter 1 of this Part; also J Jaconelli, 'Comment' (1985), PL 630; Winterton, 'The British *Grundnorm*: Parliamentary Supremacy Re-examined' (1976) LQR 591; Sir Robin Cooke, 'Fundamentals' (1988) NZLR 158; Lee, (1985) PL 633.

2 Bradley and Wade, *Constitutional and Administrative Law*, 11th edn (1993), p69.

3 'The Sovereignty of Parliament: in Perpetuity?' in Jowell and Oliver (eds), *The Changing Constitution* (1994), p81.

of Parliament to do such things. If Parliament chose to do any of them the courts would not hold the Act of Parliament invalid.[4]

The second is the fact that the doctrine, as currently understood, apparently pays no heed to the make-up of Parliament, or its internal proceedings. Thus, for example, the doctrine is not concerned with whether the Commons is in fact representative of the electorate[5] or whether the balance of power between the Commons and the Lords is politically acceptable.

2   If it is accepted that there are conventional restraints upon Parliament's powers (the legal and political considerations referred to by Lord Reid) then does this mean that the concept of legislative supremacy is parasitic upon the more general distinction between law and convention already considered in chapter 3?

3   There is some dispute as to whether it is necessary and/or desirable to separate wholly the political and legal aspects of the doctrine. Loughlin, writing from a stance critical of the traditional position, concludes that, in Dicey's thought, the political and legal aspects of sovereignty are in fact interdependent:

> I do not consider that Dicey's beliefs on the nature of political authority can be, or should be, divorced from his conception of legal sovereignty. In Bernard Crick's words: 'the legal doctrine of sovereignty was almost consciously confused with the empirical, pseudo-historical doctrine: that political stability, indeed law and order themselves, depended on parliamentary sovereignty.[6]

Loughlin notes that Blackstone, whose analysis predated Dicey's and influenced the latter, drew no strict distinction between the legal and political aspects of the doctrine. By contrast, Munro insists that clarity demands the maintenance of a strict distinction.

Colin Munro, *Studies in Constitutional Law* (1987), pp84–6[7]

In order to prevent misunderstanding, one point needs to be emphasised ... the principle of the sovereignty of Parliament only expresses certain legal rules.

... A careful reading of Dicey suggests that, even if he has inadvertently misled his readers, his own understanding of the point was clear enough. Parliamentary sovereignty was, he said, the dominant characteristic of our political institutions 'from a legal point of view' [Dicey p39]. Later he criticises Austin for blurring the distinction between different uses of the term 'sovereignty', as follows:

> It should, however, be carefully noted that the term sovereignty, as long as it is accurately employed in the sense in which Austin sometimes uses it, is a merely legal conception, and means simply the power of law-making unrestricted by any legal limit [Dicey, p72].

---

4   *Madzimbamuto v Lardner-Burke* [1969] 1 AC 645, 723.

5   It is a truism that the British electoral system, operating on a first-past-the-post basis, disadvantages smaller parties. One of the most striking, recent examples of this was the 1983 general election, in which the SDP-Liberal alliance gained 25% of the total votes cast but only 3.5% of the seats. At the time of writing, the Liberal Democrats advocate a change to proportional representation, the Labour Party is committed to holding a referendum on the subject, whilst the Conservative Party remains opposed to both courses of action.

6   Loughlin, *Public Law and Political Theory* (1992), p148.

7   All references to Dicey in this extract are to his *Law of the Constitution*, 10th edn (1959).

Thus employed, and it is in this sense that constitutional lawyers debate it, the concept of parliamentary sovereignty is only indicative of the legal relationship between the legislature and the courts, nothing less but nothing more.

The use of the term 'sovereignty' to express this relationship is perhaps to be regretted, for the word had a past history of usage in political writings, and besides bears other meanings in constitutional law (where the monarch may be referred to as the Sovereign) and in international law (where sovereignty is an attribute of states). However, Dicey not only did his best to make clear the sense in which he was employing the term, but additionally sought to dispose of one of the most obvious sources of possible confusion:

> The word 'sovereignty' is sometimes employed in a political rather than in a strictly legal sense. That body is 'politically' sovereign or supreme in a state the will of which is ultimately obeyed ... In this sense of the word the electors of Great Britain may be said to be ... the body in which sovereign power is vested. ... But this is a political, not a legal fact ... The political sense of the word 'sovereignty' is, it is true, fully as important as the legal sense or more so. But the two significations ... are essentially different ... [Dicey, pp73–74].

This, it is submitted, is a perfectly clear and sensible distinction. Even if, in more sophisticated times, sociologists or political scientists might dispute that political power is to be so easily located in 'the electors', this does not affect the central point. However, Dicey's clarity has not saved him from being misunderstood. Sir Ivor Jennings said with regard to Dicey's distinction that 'if this is so, legal sovereignty is not sovereignty at all. It is not supreme power' [*The Law and the Constitution*, 5th edn (1959), p149]. But this is a criticism which depends upon the assumption that sovereignty may mean only one thing, which is unfounded. Jennings cited Harold Laski in support, but Laski was hardly an exemplar in this respect, as has been observed:

> Sometimes the target that Laski called 'sovereignty' was the immunity of the Crown: sometimes it seemed to be unjust legislation or unqualified allegiance. Sometimes again it appeared as absolute power and at other times it became the 'Austinian' theory of unlimited legal authority [Geoffrey Marshall, *Constitutional Theory* (1971), p40].

Even an editor of Dicey, ECS Wade, was occasionally subject to confusion, as where he suggested that the sovereignty of Parliament was 'difficult to reconcile with the state of affairs in which governments were dominant within Parliament' [in his introduction to *Law of the Constitution*, 10th edn (1959) pxxi].

The drawing of a distinction between legal and political sovereignty has been criticised, but it seems obvious that if confusion is to be avoided, just such a distinction has to be made. Parliamentary sovereignty, as lawyers use the phrase, is only concerned with the effect to be given by the courts to Acts of Parliament. It is not concerned with the politics of the making of legislation, or with political dominance in the state.

Another feature of discussions of the sovereignty of Parliament since Dicey's time may be traced to the same confusion between legal authority and political realities. If Parliament can do anything, why does it not command that all blue-eyed babies be killed, asked Dicey's contemporary, Leslie Stephen [*The Science of Ethics* (1882)]. 'There are many things ... which Parliament cannot do,' says Jennings, who suggested that 'it never passes any laws which any substantial section of the population violently dislikes' [*ibid*, p148]. However, a *non sequitur* is present in discussions of this sort. Parliamentary sovereignty denotes only the absence of legal limitations, not the absence of *all* limitations or, a more appropriate word, inhibitions on Parliament's actions.

It is perfectly obvious that utterly abhorrent legislation is unlikely to be enacted by the UK Parliament; that governments are influenced by political considerations in deciding what legislation to propose; that international law and international obligations and relations are factors which affect the making of legislation; and that certain conventions are customarily observed by Parliament, so that, to give one example, it does not normally seek to legislate for the Channel Islands in domestic affairs. But these are not legal limitations, and there should be no need to mention them in a discussion of this sort, provided again that it is understood that sovereignty is only a legal conception. Dicey felt compelled to deal with the difficulty, and divided 'actual limitations' into the 'internal limit' (what the sovereign cannot bring himself to do) and the 'external limit' (what the subjects would not tolerate without resistance) [Dicey, pp76–85]. No doubt this is an imperfect analysis, which does not exhaust the different kinds of inhibition to which Parliament is subject, but his heart cannot have been in a task which he rightly perceived as peripheral to the matter in hand.

Note

Even if one accepted in full Munro's contention that the legal/political distinction ought to borne in mind when considering sovereignty, it is also helpful to be aware that the views of contributors to the debate on the legal aspect of sovereignty are likely to be affected by political considerations such as their theory of democracy and its practice at Westminster. AW Bradley brings this point out in a helpful discussion.

AW Bradley, The Sovereignty of Parliament: In Perpetuity? in Jowell and Oliver (eds), *The Changing Constitution* (1994), pp78–81.

'The sovereignty of Parliament' is an evocative phrase. In an important but imprecise way it may be thought to express the democratic ideal — that the Palace of Westminster, and in particular the debating chamber of the House of Commons, should exercise greater public authority than other centres of governmental and political power. Only the House of Commons consists of elected representatives coming from every part of the UK; election thus gives legitimacy to the legislative process and to the whole structure of government. Now, whether Parliament today occupies this central place in the structure of government is an important subject ... But for a constitutional lawyer, the doctrine of the sovereignty or supremacy of Parliament has a much more specific meaning, which provides a formal base to the system by which laws are made and applied.

Since the publication in 1885 of AV Dicey's *The Law of the Constitution*, the sovereignty of Parliament has been accepted as one of the fundamental doctrines of constitutional law in the UK. Despite political and social changes that have occurred since 1885, and despite the attention given to the doctrine by lawyers and political scientists, it retains what seems to be an absolute and immutable character. The doctrine may be seen either as a bulwark of the British constitution or as an obstacle to desirable forms of constitutional development.

... For Dicey, the sovereignty of Parliament was 'an undoubted legal fact' [p68], and a fundamental proposition of constitutional law. However, Dicey's belief in the legislative power of Parliament was directly related to his view of the representative character of the legislature in the 1880s. Thus he wrote:

'... as things now stand, the will of the electorate, and certainly of the electorate in combination with the Lords and the Crown, is sure ultimately to prevail on all subjects to be determined by the British Government. ... *The electors can in the long run always enforce their will*' [p73, emphasis added].

Dicey came close to identifying this expression of the democratic ideal with the identity or sovereignty of the nation itself, whose 'secret source of strength is the absolute omnipotence, the sovereignty of Parliament' [Dicey, 'England's Case against Home Rule' (1886), 168]. This proclamation of faith is today echoed in some British views about the future of Europe; but it is confusing to equate a formal analysis of the sources of law with the essence of national identity. To the extent that the electors in the 1880s had the power to ensure that their will prevailed, this was a 'political, not a legal fact' [Dicey, *Law of the Constitution*, p73].

In reality, the doctrine of legislative sovereignty does not in itself imply any particular degree of democracy in the structure of Parliament. However, if the perceived nature of the political system in the late 19th century was a vital influence on the legal doctrine, any significant change in that system (such as a shift in the balance of power between the executive and the elected House of Commons) requires us to reassess the legal doctrine in the light of the changed political process. One question that arises today is indeed whether the legal doctrine of legislative sovereignty entrusts excessive power to a legislature in which the executive power is the predominant voice — thus effectively vesting such power in the executive. Even if the majority in the Commons accurately represented the wishes of most of the electors (which it does not), should the government be able to use that majority to carry into law all of its favoured proposals?

Wherever effective power may be located within the legislative process, there remains within a democratic legal system that adheres to the 'Rule of Law' a fundamental distinction between the legislative process, which derives its constitutional authority from the elected legislature, and the judicial process, founded upon an independent judiciary. As the President of the New Zealand Court of Appeal, Sir Robin Cooke, has said, the modern common law should be 'built on two complementary and lawfully unalterable principles: the operation of a democratic legislature and the operation of independent courts' ['Fundamentals' (1988) NZLJ 158, 164]. The democratic basis for legislation, regarded as a constitutional fundamental, serves *inter alia* to validate the whole legal system and the role of the courts. Indeed, one's approach to the legal doctrine of legislative sovereignty is likely to be coloured by one's perception of the democratic element in the composition and functioning of the legislature.

Questions

1   Is what Bradley calls the 'constitutional fundamental' of the democratic basis for legislation a notion that would be recognised as part of constitutional law by the courts?

2   Is Bradley's notion that such a 'constitutional fundamental' exists compatible with his statement that 'In reality, the doctrine of legislative sovereignty does not in itself imply any particular degree of democracy in the structure of Parliament itself'?

The historical background

The historical background to the acquisition by Parliament of legislative supremacy represents something of an irony. During the 17th century, in which the relevant events took place, both parliamentarians and common lawyers were united behind a concern to check and control the prerogative powers of the monarch. As Munro observes:

In alliance, [the parliamentarians and the common lawyers] subordinated the powers of the King, and the means of defeating the Crown's attempts to rule by prerogative was the judge's insistence that the limits of prerogative powers, as part of the common law, are determinable by the courts. ... For the common lawyers there was a price to pay, and that was the abandonment of the claim they had sometimes advanced, that Parliament could not legislate in derogation of the principles of the common law. As Lord Reid commented in a case in 1974:

> In earlier times many learned lawyers seem to have believed that an Act of Parliament could be disregarded in so far as it was contrary to the law of God or the law of nature or natural justice, but since the supremacy of Parliament was finally demonstrated by the revolution of 1688 any such idea has become obsolete [*British Railways Board v Pickin* [1974] 1 All ER 609 at 614].[8]

Note

The efforts of the common lawyers to contain the prerogative powers of the King reached their high water mark in *The Case of Proclamations* (1611), described by De Smith as 'perhaps the leading case in English constitutional law'.[9]

The Case of Proclamations (1611) 12 Co Rep 74

The King issued proclamations prohibiting the construction of new homes in London and the production of starch from wheat. When the Commons complained that the prerogative power was abused by such usage, the opinion of Chief Justice Coke was sought:

> ... it was resolved by the two Chief Justices, Chief Baron, and Baron Altham, upon conference betwixt the Lords of the Privy Council and them, that the King by his proclamation cannot create any offence which was not an offence before, for then he may alter the law of the land by his proclamation in a high point; for if he may create an offence where none is, upon that ensues fine and imprisonment: also the law of England is divided into three parts, common law, statute law and custom; but the King's proclamation is none of them: also *malum ant est malum in se, aut prohibitum*, that which is against common law is *malum in se, malum prohibitum* is such an offence as is prohibited by Act of Parliament, and not by proclamation.

> Also, it was resolved, that the King hath no prerogative, but that which the law of the land allows him.

Notes

1 When the Crown alleged that the security of the realm was threatened, however, the courts were more compliant: *see The Case of Ship Money* (1637)[10] and *The Case of Impositions* (1606).[11] Not only was the use of the prerogative to impose emergency taxation upheld in these decisions, but the courts forbore to make any inquiry as to whether the alleged threat to national security justified the measure proposed, holding such a determination to be the exclusive purview of the Crown.

---

8   Munro, *op cit*, p81.
9   De Smith, *op cit*, p75, n 26.
10 *Hampden* (1637) 3 St Tr 371.
11 *Bate's* case (1602) 2 St Tr 371.

2 As Munro remarked, the common lawyers accepted the dominance of statute law as the price for finally achieving decisive control over the Royal Prerogative. In doing so they appeared to relinquish the idea that the common law would not always bow supinely to the force of statute, regardless of its content. This had not always been their attitude.

In *Dr Bonham's case* (1610), it was said that (per Coke LJ) (1610):

> ... when an Act of Parliament is against common right and reason, or repugnant, or impossible to be performed, the common law will control it, and adjudge such Act to be void.[12]

Hobart CJ had said in the same year that,

> ... even an Act of Parliament, made against natural equity, as to make a man judge in his own case is void in itself.[13]

3 The irony of these historical events lies in the fact that the common lawyers abandoned such contentions in order to secure the dominance of Parliament, as a safeguard against the threat to liberty poised by royal (that is, executive) absolutism. However, since the executive now substantially controls Parliament, through the party machine, it is Parliament's unlimited law-making capability which now poses one of the main threats to civil liberties in the UK.[14] Blackstone foresaw this as long ago as 1776, when he remarked that: '... it was a known apophthegm of the great lord treasurer Burleigh, "that England could never be ruined but by a Parliament".'[15] (See Part VI, Chapter 1.)

Traditional doctrine scrutinised

Now that the basic parameters of the doctrine and its historical antecedents have been indicated, the substantive content of the doctrine may be considered more closely. As Bradley indicated above, Dicey's conception of the doctrine has been easily the most influential and has to an extent marked out the parameters of the debate which has gone on ever since.

A V Dicey, *An Introduction to the Study of the Law of the Constitution*, 10th edn (1959), ppxxxiv–v (introduction by ECS Wade)

> The principle of parliamentary sovereignty was repeated by the author in each edition of this book up to 1914, when he emphasised that the truth of the doctrines had never been denied. They were:
>
> (1) Parliament has the right to make or unmake any law whatever.
>
> (2) No person or body is recognised by the law of England as having a right to override or set aside the legislation of Parliament.
>
> (3) The right or power of Parliament extends to every part of the Queen's dominions.

---

12 8 Co Rep 113b, 118a.

13 Hobb 85, 97.

14 The classic exposition of the thesis can be found in Lord Hailsham's 1976 Hamlyn lecture, *Elective Dictatorship*.

15 W Blackstone, *Commentaries on the Laws of England* (1776), Bk 1, pp160–1. Quoted in Loughin, *op cit*, p147.

Despite recent criticism, it is still true today as a proposition of the law of the UK to say that Parliament has the right to make or unmake any law whatever. Nor can any court within the UK set aside the provisions of an Act of Parliament. All that a court of law can do with such an Act is to apply it, ie to interpret the meaning of the enactment. This is enough to satisfy the lawyer, but it must be admitted that the conception is purely a legal one. The examples which the author gives in the text can be multiplied by reference to recent enactments, the Parliament Act 1911, the Government of Ireland Act 1920, the Irish Free State (Agreement) Act 1922, and Declaration of Abdication Act 1936. It is probably also safe to include the Statute of Westminster 1931, and more certainly the Acts giving independent status to other Member States of the Commonwealth, such as the Indian Independence Act 1947.

Notes

1   Whatever the controversies surrounding Dicey's views of sovereignty, one thing is certain. it is no longer true to say that '[No] court within the [UK] [can] set aside ... an Act of Parliament'. This has in fact happened in relation to the provisions of two statutes, the Merchant Shipping Act 1988 and the Employment Protection (Consolidation) Act 1978.[16] The impact of EC law on parliamentary sovereignty is discussed in the next chapter, but this important caveat to the traditional view must be borne in mind during this chapter.

2   Dicey's view is in fact not as monolithic as first appears; Colin Munro 'unpacks' the various strands of the Diceyan conception of sovereignty.

Colin Munro, *Studies in Constitutional Law* (1987), pp82–84

In his search for the guiding principles of the British constitution, Dicey discovered three, and the first of these in importance, 'the very keystone of the law of the constitution' [*Law of the Constitution* (10th edn). p70 (hereafter, Dicey)], was what he called the sovereignty of Parliament. The nature of parliamentary sovereignty, he said, was: 'that Parliament ... has ... the right to make or unmake any law whatever; and further, that no person or body is recognised by the law of England as having a right to override or set aside the legislation of Parliament' [Dicey, pp39–40], 'and these two aspects he called 'the positive side' and 'the negative side' [Dicey, pp40–41].

The negative aspect, more fully expounded, is that 'there is no person or body of persons who can, under the English constitution, make rules which override or derogate from an Act of Parliament, or which (to express the same thing in other words) will be enforced by the courts in contravention of an Act of Parliament' [Dicey, p40]. We may notice that this is no more than a recognition that Acts of Parliament are supreme within the hierarchy of laws and *a fortiori* prevail over any principles or rules which are not laws. Dicey demonstrates the point by reference to the absence of any legislative power able to compete with Parliament [Dicey, pp50–61]: the Crown's authority to legislate had, since the *Case of Proclamations* [(1611) 12 Co Rep 74] been restricted; judge-made law was recognisably subordinate to statute; one of the Houses of Parliament acting alone, even the House of Commons, could not make law, as *Stockdale v Hansard* [(1839) 9 Ad and El 1] showed; the electorate, which chose the members of the

---

16   The cases were, respectively: *Secretary of State for Transport, ex p Factortame* [1990] 2 AC 85; *ex p Factortame (No 2)* [1991] 1 AC 603; and *Secretary of State for Employment, ex p Equal Opportunities Commission* [1994] 2 WLR 409.

Commons, had no other role in the legislative process. All of these points were uncontroversial, for they were already well established.

The positive aspect of sovereignty, however, is made to carry much more weight. 'It means not only that Parliament may legislate upon any topic, but also that any parliamentary enactment must be obeyed by the courts' [Dicey pp87–91 and Ch 2]. In a further reworking, sovereignty is said to involve first, that there is no law which Parliament cannot change, so that even constitutional laws of great importance may be changed in the same manner as other laws; secondly, the absence of any legal distinction between constitutional and other laws; and thirdly, that there exists no person or body, executive, legislative or judicial, which can pronounce void any enactment of Parliament on the ground of its being opposed to the constitution or any other ground.

Dicey's treatment of all these points as attributes of a sovereign legislature, and his referring to the positive and negative 'sides' of sovereignty, imply that we have here a number of corollaries flowing from the same proposition. Such an inference, however, would be wrong. That statute law is superior to other forms of law in the hierarchy does not necessarily entail that Parliament may legislate upon any topic or repeal any law; for example, it would be possible to maintain (and some do) that some parts of the Acts of Union between England and Scotland are unalterable, without doubting that Acts of Parliament prevail over other kinds of law. Again, the absence of a judicial power to hold Acts of Parliament void does not of itself mean that the legislature is unlimited, for in some countries excess of legislative authority may be left as a matter between the legislature and the electors, or may be dealt with by a non-judicial process. Dicey did recognise this last point, but the general impression left by his account is that the different attributes he ascribes to Parliament are all of a piece. This is not so, and it is instructive to unpack Dicey's doctrine. When we do, we see that, while the 'negative side' of sovereignty was uncontroversial, the other propositions advanced by Dicey were more wide-reaching and not so obviously justified.

In purporting to show that Parliament's legislative authority was unlimited, Dicey offered evidence of a different sort [Dicey, pp41–50, 61–80]. He cited the opinions of Coke, Blackstone and De Lolme. He exhibited historical instances of the width of Parliament's powers; it could alter the succession to the throne, as it did in the Act of Settlement; it could prolong its own life, as with the Septennial Act of 1715; it could make legal past illegalities by Acts of Indemnity. He argued that some supposed limitations on Parliament's capacity were not real – the existence of inalienable prerogative powers could no longer be maintained; that doctrines of morality or the rules of international law could prevail against Acts of Parliament found no support in case law. Finally, Dicey denied that earlier Acts had ever limited what a Parliament could do. The language of certain enactments, such as the Acts of Union, suggested an intention to restrict later Parliaments, but their subsequent history demonstrated the futility of the attempts. Therefore, Parliament's authority was not only unlimited, but illimitable, for attempts to bind succeeding Parliaments would be ineffective.

These matters, informative as they are, scarcely compel us to accept Dicey's case. ... Dicey does not really establish that Parliament is unlimited, still less that it is illimitable. But if his propositions are not verifiable, they are falsifiable by appropriate evidence. No evidence to that effect existed at Dicey's time. We may see whether it has been thrown up in the 100 years since.

Notes

1 The actual record of matters which have been affected by legislation is undoubtedly impressive:

Parliament has in fact passed retroactive penal legislation, prolonged its own existence, transformed itself into a new body by the Acts of Union with Scotland and Ireland, repealed and amended provisions of those Acts which were to have permanent effect, altered the procedure for making laws (under the Parliament Acts) and followed the new procedure, and changed the succession to the throne (by the Bill of Rights, the Act of Settlement 1701, and Declaration of Abdication Act 1936).[17]

However, as Professor Calvert has pointed out:

One no more demonstrates [that the powers of the UK Parliament are unlimited] by pointing to a wide range of legislative objects than one demonstrates the contrary by pointing to matters on which Parliament has not, in fact, ever legislated.[18]

2   Clearly, a more systematic approach is required, in which all the main possible limitations on sovereignty are examined in turn. It is to this task that the rest of this chapter is devoted.

POSSIBLE LIMITATIONS ON SOVEREIGNTY

There are a number of ways in which, theoretically, Parliament's legislative omnipotence could be limited. These fall into three main categories: firstly, limitations as to the *form* of the measure passed by Parliament – such limitations would arise if the courts were empowered to make an authoritative determination as to what was to count as a valid Act of Parliament; secondly, limitations based on the *substance* of the Act, eg it's conflict with other legal systems, or with fundamental constitutional principles; thirdly, limitations imposed on sovereignty by Parliament itself. These matters will be examined in turn.

Limitations based on form

An Act of Parliament is an expression of the sovereign will of Parliament; if, however, Parliament is not constituted as Parliament or does not function as Parliament within the meaning of the law it, would seem to follow that it cannot express its sovereign will in the form of an Act of Parliament. However, the courts have declined opportunities to declare an Act a nullity where it has been asserted that something which appears to be an Act of Parliament and which bears the customary words of enactment is not authentic, or was tainted by bad faith or fraud.

Nevertheless, the fact that any Act must bear the customary words of enactment is significant. The courts will not apply the doctrine of sovereignty to motions of the constituent bodies of Parliament that do not constitute actual enactments. Bradley and Wade note that: ... the courts do not attribute legislative supremacy to ... resolution[s] of the House of Commons[19] ... [nor] instrument[s] of subordinate legislation which appear to be issued under the

---

17   De Smith, *op cit*, pp77–8.

18   H Calvert, *Constitutional Law in Northern Ireland* (1968), p14.

19   *Stockdale v Hansard* (1839) 9 A and E 1; *Bowles v Bank of England* [1913] 1 Ch 57.

authority of an Act of Parliament,[20] even though approved by the resolution of each House of Parliament.'[21] '... and will if necessary decide whether or not they have legal effect'. Thus, for example: 'If it should appear that a measure has not been approved by one House, then (unless the Parliament Acts 1911–49 apply) the measure is not an Act'.[22]

Notes

1   Dicey considered that it was partly due to the fact that '... the commands of Parliament can be uttered only through the combined actions of its three constituent parts'[23] which made the doctrine of parliamentary sovereignty compatible with the Rule of Law; Parliament would not in practice wield arbitrary power because, as Keeton puts it, 'it was a combination of diverse elements, linked together by an intricate system of "checks and balances"'.[24] It should be noted that since Dicey wrote, this balance has been tipped markedly in favour of the Commons as a result of the Parliament Acts 1911–14.[25]

2   As already indicated, the courts combine this very limited but important role of distinguishing Acts of Parliament from other emanations of the legislature with a refusal to enquire into the manner and means by which an apparently authentic Act was passed by the constituent parts of Parliament. The rationale for this refusal is partly the fear that such an inquiry, which could for example involve determining whether the House of Commons' own Standing Orders had been complied with, could bring the courts into conflict with Parliament, which would undoubtedly have made its own inquiry on the matter, the finding of which could differ from that made by the courts.

The other reason is Art 9 of the Bill of Rights 1687 which provides that 'Freedom of speech and debates or proceedings in Parliament ought not to be impeached or questioned in any court or place out of Parliament', the most important effect of which is to confer complete civil and criminal immunity upon those speaking during proceedings in Parliament (for full discussion, see Part III, Chapter 3). However, Art 9 has also been construed so as to forbid any 'questioning' in the courts of the procedures used in Parliament to pass legislation: hence the refusal to consider finding an Act of Parliament to be invalid on the grounds of defective procedure, deception of the House etc.

3   In *Edinburgh and Dalkeith Railway Co v Wauchope* (1842)[26] the court was asked to find that the legislation in question, a Private Act, had been improperly passed in that Standing Orders of the House of Commons had not been complied with, and the Act was therefore invalid. Lord Campbell said,

---

20   For example, *Chester v Bateson* [1920] 1 KB 829; Ch 27.
21   *Hoffman-La Roche v Secretary for Trade and Industry* [1975] AC 295.
22   Bradley and Wade, *op cit*, pp70, 82.
23   Dicey, *op cit*, p402.
24   Keeton, *The Passing of Parliament* (1952), p6, quoted in Loughin, *op cit*, p152.
25   See Part III, Chapter 2.
26   8 Cl and F 710.

obiter, that if according to the Parliament roll an Act has passed both Houses of Parliament and had received the Royal Assent, a court cannot enquire into the manner in which it was introduced into Parliament nor into what passed in Parliament during its progress through the various parliamentary stages.

4   This rule, now known as 'the enrolled Bill rule', was relied upon in *Pickin v British Railways Board* (1974).[27] Mr Pickin had sought to challenge a Private Act of 1836 on the basis that Parliament had been misled by fraud. The House of Lords held that he was not entitled to examine proceedings in Parliament to show that the Act had been passed due to fraud. The action therefore failed.

Pickin v British Railways Board [1974] AC 765, 786–8

Lord Reid: ... In my judgment the law is correctly stated by Lord Campbell in *Edinburgh and Dalkeith Railway Co v Wauchope* (1842) 8 Cl and F 710; 1 Bell 252, in which Mr Wauchope claimed certain wayleaves. The matter was dealt with in a Private Act. He appears to have maintained in the Court of Session that the provisions of that Act should not be applied because it had been passed without his having had notice as required by Standing Orders. This contention was abandoned in this House. Lord Brougham and Lord Cottenham said that want of notice was no ground for holding that the Act did not apply. Lord Campbell based his opinion on more general grounds. He said, 1 Bell 252, 278–279:

> My Lords, I think it right to say a word or two before I sit down, upon the point that has been raised with regard to an Act of Parliament being held inoperative by a court of justice because the forms, in respect of an Act of Parliament, have not been complied with. There seems great reason to believe that (*sic*) notion has prevailed to a considerable extent in Scotland, for we have it here brought forward as a substantive ground upon which the Act of the 4th and 5th William the Fourth could not apply: the language being, that the statute of the 4th and 5th William the Fourth being a private Act, and no notice given to the pursuer of the intention to apply for an Act of Parliament, and so on. It would appear that that defence was entered into, and the fact was examined into, and an inquiry, whether notice was given to him personally, or by advertisement in the newspapers, and the Lord Ordinary, in the note which he appends to his interlocutor, gives great weight to this. The Lord Ordinary says 'he is by no means satisfied that due parliamentary notice was given to the pursuer previous to the introduction of this last Act. Undoubtedly no notice was given to him personally, nor did the public notices announce any intention to take away his existing rights. If, as the Lord Ordinary is disposed to think, these defects imply a failure to intimate the real design in view, he would be strongly inclined to hold in conformity with the principles of Donald, November 27, 1832, that rights previously established could not be taken away by a Private Act, of which due notice was not given to the party meant to be injured.' Therefore, my Lord Ordinary seems to have been most distinctly of opinion, that if this Act did receive that construction, it would clearly take away the right to this tonnage from Mr Wauchope, and would have had that effect if notice had been given to him before the Bill was introduced into the House of Commons; but that notice not having been given, it could have no such effect, and therefore the Act is wholly inoperative. I must express some

---

27   AC 765.

surprise that such a notion should have prevailed. It seems to me there is no foundation for it whatever; all that a court of justice can look to is the parliamentary roll; they see that an Act has passed both Houses of Parliament, and that it has received the Royal Assent, and no court of justice can inquire into the manner in which it was introduced into Parliament, what was done previously to its being introduced, or what passed in Parliament during the various stages of its progress through both Houses of Parliament. I therefore trust that no such inquiry will hereafter be entered into in Scotland, and that due effect will be given to every Act of Parliament, both private as well as public, upon the just construction which appears to arise upon it.

No doubt this was *obiter* but, so far as I am aware, no one since 1842 has doubted that it is a correct statement of the constitutional position.

The function of the court is to construe and apply the enactments of Parliament. The court has no concern with the manner in which Parliament or its officers carrying out its Standing Orders perform these functions. Any attempt to prove that they were misled by fraud or otherwise would necessarily involve an inquiry into the manner in which they had performed their functions in dealing with the Bill which became the British Railways Act 1968.

In whatever form the respondent's case is pleaded he must prove not only that the appellants acted fraudulently but also that their fraud caused damage to him by causing the enactment of s18. He could not prove that without an examination of the manner in which the officers of Parliament dealt with the matter. So the court would, or at least might, have to adjudicate upon that.

For a century or more both Parliament and the courts have been careful not to act so as to cause conflict between them. Any such investigations as the respondent seeks could easily lead to such a conflict, and I would only support it if compelled to do so by clear authority. But it appears to me that the whole trend of authority for over a century is clearly against permitting any such investigation.

Notes

1   Lord Reid might also have cited *Lee v Bude & Torrington Junction Railway Co* (1871) LR 6 CP 576, *per* Willes J in support of his finding:

If an Act of Parliament has been obtained improperly, it is for legislature to correct it by repealing it; but so long as it exists in law, the courts are bound to obey it.

2   Lord Reid appears to leave the possibility open that the courts might be prepared to question whether the purported statute before them was in fact an Act of Parliament, indeed this is arguably implicit in his reference to the fact that the courts will 'apply the *enactments* of Parliament' (emphasis added). However, he also states that the courts will not enquire into 'the way in which' Parliament or its officers carry out its Standing Orders. The problem here is that it is the Standing Orders of the two Houses which go much of the way towards defining what 'enactments' of Parliament are; Lord Reid leaves it unclear whether the courts will enquire into whether Standing Orders had been complied with at all.

3   This problem has never been confronted by the courts. In considering it, it is inadequate simply to reiterate that, provided an Act has 'passed' both Houses (and received the Royal Assent), the courts will not enquire into the

proceedings by which it was passed, for this begs the question of what 'passed' means. Orthodoxy tells us that the courts will not in general enquire as to whether Standing Orders have been complied with and reminds us that 'It must surely be for Parliament to lay down the procedures which are to be followed before a Bill can become an Act'.[28] But does this principle apply to all the internal rules of the Commons and to a situation in which they were changed out of recognition or flouted wholesale? Ewing and Bradley note that:

> The rule that a bill must be read three times in each House is not a requirement of the common law but is part of the *lex et consuetudo Parliament'* and could therefore be abolished by either House.[29] Suppose therefore, that the executive procured the passing of resolutions in the Commons to the effect that a Government bill was deemed to have been passed by that House if it was simply read once, but never voted on, and then proceeded to pass legislation by that method (using the Parliament Acts procedure to bypass the Lords if necessary).[30] Clearly, such a change in the Commons' procedure would wholly subvert the democratic basis for legislation and remove at a stroke all but a bare formal function for Parliament as a legislative body. Would the courts, faced with legislation passed by such methods merely solemnly invoke the enrolled bill rule, apply the legislation in question and decline to enquire by what means it had been passed, when such knowledge was a matter of public record and public outcry?

4   De Smith suggests that there are other circumstances in which a court might treat a purported statute as nugatory; a Bill to prolong the life of a Parliament beyond five years might be passed in the Commons but not in the Lords (such a Bill is explicitly excluded from the Parliament Act procedure) and receive the Royal Assent. It would state that it had been passed in accordance with the Parliament Acts; if so a court might treat it as a nullity as 'bad on its face'; its defective nature would be apparent without needing to enquire into proceedings in Parliament.

5   Considerations such as these reveal that the apparent simplicity of the enrolled Bill rule is deceptive. Moreover, the courts have recently displayed that they will at least modify the rule that they will not enquire into the parliamentary history of a statute where common sense demands this, as an aid to interpreting the statute. Commentary by Lord Lester follows the extract from the decision.

Pepper v Hart [1993] 1 All ER 42, 50, 64

Lord Griffiths: ... In summary, I agree that the courts should have recourse to Hansard in the circumstances and to the extent [Lord Browne-Wilkinson] proposes. I agree that the use of *Hansard* as an aid to assist the court to give effect to the true intention of Parliament is not 'questioning' within the meaning of Article 9 of the Bill of Rights. I agree that the House is not inhibited by any Parliamentary privilege in deciding this appeal.

---

28   *Per* Lord Morris, in *Pickin's* case (above).

29   Bradley and Wade, *op cit*, p82.

30   It is, of course, theoretically possible that the Royal Assent would be refused in such a case: see Part I, Chapter 2.

Lord Browne-Wilkinson: My Lords, I have come to the conclusion that, as a matter of law, there are sound reasons for making a limited modification to the existing rule (subject to strict safeguards) unless there are constitutional or practical reasons which outweigh them. In my judgment, subject to the questions of the privileges of the House of Commons, reference to parliamentary material should be permitted as an aid to the construction of legislation which is ambiguous or obscure or the literal meaning of which leads to an absurdity. Even in such cases, references in court to parliamentary material should only be permitted where such material clearly discloses the mischief aimed at or the legislative intention lying behind the ambiguous or obscure words. In the case of statements made in Parliament, as at present advised I cannot foresee that any statement other than the statement of the minister or other promoter of the Bill is likely to meet these criteria.

... my main reason for reaching this conclusion is based on principle. Statute law consists of the words that Parliament has enacted. It is for the courts to construe those words and it is the court's duty in so doing to give effect to the intention of Parliament in using those words. It is an inescapable fact that, despite all the care taken in passing legislation, some statutory provisions when applied to the circumstances under consideration in any specific case are found to be ambiguous. One of the reasons for such ambiguity is that the members of the legislature in enacting the statutory provision may have been told what result those words are intended to achieve. Faced with a given set of words which are capable of conveying that meaning, it is not surprising if the words are accepted as having that meaning. Parliament never intends to enact an ambiguity. Contrast with that the position of the courts. The courts are faced simply with a set of words which are in fact capable of bearing two meanings. The courts are ignorant of the underlying parliamentary purpose. Unless something in other parts of the legislation discloses such purpose, the courts are forced to adopt one of the two possible meanings using highly technical rules of construction. In many, I suspect most, cases references to parliamentary materials will not throw any light on the matter. But in a few cases it may emerge that the very question was considered by Parliament in passing the legislation. Why, in such a case, should the courts blind themselves to a clear indication of what Parliament intended in using those words? The court cannot attach a meaning to words which they cannot bear, but if the words are capable of bearing more than one meaning why should not Parliament's true intention be enforced rather than thwarted?

Lord Lester of Herne Hill QC, *'Pepper v Hart* Revisited' (1992) 15(1) *Statutory Law Review* (1994) 10, 18–20

The main arguments in favour of abolishing the absolute prohibition against any reference to the parliamentary record as an extrinsic aid to statutory interpretation can be summarised in this way:

1. The purpose of using the parliamentary record is to help give better informed effect to the legislative outcome of parliamentary proceedings. It is therefore irrational for the courts to maintain an absolute rule depriving themselves of access to potentially relevant evidence or information for this purpose. Why, in Lord Denning's words, should judges grope about in the dark searching for the meaning of an Act, when they can so easily switch on the light?

2. The history of a statute, including the parliamentary debates, may be relevant to determine the meaning of legislation where a provision is ambiguous or obscure, or where the ordinary meaning is manifestly absurd or unreasonable.

3. The parliamentary record may be of real assistance to the court:

(a) by showing that Parliament has considered and suggested an answer to the issue of interpretation before the court;

(b) by showing the object and purpose of the legislation and the mischief which the Act was designed to remedy;

(c) by explaining the reason for some obscurity or ambiguity in the wording of the legislation; and

(d) by providing direct evidence for the origins, background, and historical context to the legislation.

4. Where a statutory provision has been enacted following an authoritative ministerial statement as to the understanding by the executive of its meaning and effect, such a statement may provide important evidence about the object and purpose of the provision and the intention of Parliament in agreeing to its enactment, and may create reasonable expectations among members of Parliament and those affected by the legislation.

5. The courts do not consider themselves confined exclusively by the text for the purposes of interpreting the statute. There is no basis in principle or logic for them to be willing to have regard to extrinsic aids in White Papers, etc, while rigidly excluding any recourse to parliamentary debates.

6. A purposive approach to interpretation requires the courts to construe legislation in accordance with its purposes. It is therefore illogical to hold that courts are entitled to read a report to determine the mischief sought to be remedied, but must ignore it when considering the statute. The main arguments against any alteration in the rule were summarised by the New Zealand Law Commission as follows:

(1) The text of the statute as enacted is the law; those affected by the statute should be able to rely on the text passed by the House, assented to by the Crown and appearing in the statute book.

(2) Use of the material may involve an improper, even an unconstitutional examination of the proceedings of Parliament.

(3) The parliamentary material may be unreliable and may indeed be created to support a particular interpretation.

(4) The parliamentary material is not likely to help since the issue in dispute may not have been anticipated.

(5) The process may cause delay and increase the cost of litigation.

There is, of course, force in each of these points, but the Law Commission of New Zealand concluded that they do not lead to the conclusion that the material cannot or should not be used in appropriate cases. Of course, the text of a statute is sacred, but where there is real controversy about what it means, so that the statutory language cannot itself be relied upon, courts should not be confined exclusively to the text for the purposes of interpretation.

Judicial use of the parliamentary material does not alter the constitutional relationships between Parliament, the executive, and the judiciary or the nature of the judicial process of statutory interpretation. This is because it does not mean that the courts must become, in Lord Wilberforce's words, 'a reflecting mirror of what some other interpretation agency may do'. It is for the courts to determine whether to consider parliamentary materials and to decide what weight and value to attach to them. It is for the courts to exercise their judgment in determining the relevance of the material and its evidential weight. It is for the courts to ensure that there is no unnecessary recourse to *Hansard* in litigation. Moreover, the records of parliamentary debates is no less accessible than White Papers, etc, and as regards accessibility, this can be facilitated in various practical ways.

Limitations based on substance

Possible limitations here could be based on two grounds: first, that the statute conflicted with laws derived from other legal systems; second, that it contravened fundamental liberties or other constitutional principles. Such limitations could take the form of a refusal to apply the statute in question, the imposition of the requirement of express words on Parliament or the employment of a restrictive interpretation to the statute.

Conflict with other legal systems

If UK law conflicts with international law, or with a provision in a treaty to which the British Government is a signatory, the position seems clear.

In the Scottish case of *Mortensen v Peters* (1906), a direct conflict arose between domestic and international law: Mortensen, a Norwegian fisherman, was charged with illegal fishing in the Moray Firth, contrary to a byelaw passed under s7 of the Herring Fishery (Scotland) Act 1889. The byelaw extended to the whole of the Mory Firth, even though much of the Firth comprised international waters. Mortensen had been fishing in international waters, but inside the banned area and was convicted under the byelaw. He appealed.

Mortensen v Peters 1906 14 SLT 227

The Lord Justice General: In this court we have nothing to do with tne question of whether the legislature has or has not done what foreign powers may consider a usurpation in a question with them. Neither are we a tribunal sitting to decide whether an act of the legislature is *ultra vires* as in contravention of generally acknowledged principles of international law. For us an Act of Parliament, duly passed by Lords and Commons and assented to by the King, is supreme, and we are bound to give effect to its terms. ...

It is said by the appellant ... that international law has firmly fixed that a locus such as this is beyond the limits of territorial sovereignty; and that consequently it is not to be thought that in such a place the legislature could seek to affect any but the King's subjects.

It is a trite observation that there is no such thing as a standard of international law, extraneous to the domestic law of a kingdom, to which appeal may be made. International law, so far as this Court is concerned, is the body of doctrine regarding the international rights and duties of states which has been adopted and made part of the law of Scotland.

Notes

1   Lord Kyllachy in his judgment in the case noted that 'the language of the enactment ... is fairly express ... to the effect of making an unlimited and unqualified prohibition, applying to the whole area specified, and affecting

everybody, whether British subjects or foreigners'.[31] It may be inferred that, if the words of the Act had been less unambiguous, the courts might have attempted an interpretation which either exempted foreign nationals or limited the ambit of the Act to territorial waters, or both. Indeed, it was confirmed in *Treacy v DPP* (1971)[32] that 'It is ... a general rule of construction that, unless there is something which points to a contrary intention, a statute will be taken to apply only to the UK ... clear and express terms [would be needed to go against this rule] (p552).

2   The finding in *Mortensen* was confirmed by the Privy Council in *Croft v Dunphy PC* (1933),[33] in which it was said (*per* Lord MacMillan at p164):

> Legislation of Parliament, even in contravention of generally acknowledged principles of international law, is binding upon, and must be enforced by, the courts of this country.

The point may be regarded as settled (the position is of course wholly different if the conflict is with European Union law – see Part I Chapter 5).

3   The courts apply the same principle even if contravention of the international provision in question would result in the UK breaching its treaty obligations. In *Cheney v Conn* (1968),[34] a taxpayer appealed against an assessment of income tax made under the Finance Act 1964 on the basis that part of the money would be used for the construction of nuclear weapons, contrary (so it was argued) to the Geneva Convention, to which the UK was a party. His appeal was dismissed and Ungoed Thomas J said:

> What the statute itself enacts cannot be unlawful, because what the statute says and provides is itself the law, and the highest form of law that is known to this country.

Question

Did this *dicta* go further than was necessary to decide the case?

Note

Numerous other decisions have confirmed that domestic law overrides conflicting treaty obligations; see eg Re *M and H (Minors)* (1990)[35] and *Secretary of State for the Home Department, ex p Brind and Others* (1991).[36] However, the latter case, amongst others, also confirmed that it is a general principle of statutory interpretation that the courts will strive to construe a statute in such a way as to be consistent with the UK's treaty obligations, where possible.

---

31   *Ibid.*
32   AC 537.
33   AC 156.
34   1 All ER 779.
35   [1988] 3 WLR 485 at 498.
36   1 AC 696.

Limitations based on protection of constitutional principles

At first sight, the notion that the courts could refuse to apply a statute on the basis that it violated fundamental constitutional or moral principles seems both to fly in the face of theory, and to be flatly contradicted by authority. For example, the question of finding a statute to be invalid was rapidly dismissed in *Jordan* (1967).

Jordan (1967) *Criminal Law Review* **483**

The defendant was sentenced to eighteen months' imprisonment for offences under the Race Relations Act 1965. He applied for legal aid to apply for a writ of *habeas corpus* on the ground that the Act was invalid as being a curtailment of free speech.

Held, dismissing the application, that Parliament was supreme and there was no power in the courts to question the validity of an Act of Parliament. The ground of the application was completely unarguable.

Notes

1　Such decisions highlight the apparently stark contrast between the UK and other jurisdictions where judicial review of legislation is a well accepted aspect of the constitution. For example, in the famous US case of *Marbury v Madison*, Chief Justice Marshall said:

The constitution is either a superior paramount law, unchallengeable by ordinary means, or it is on a level with ordinary legislative acts, and, like other acts, is alterable when the legislature shall be pleased to alter it. If the former part of the alternative is true, then a legislative act contrary to the constitution is not law; if the latter part be true, then written constitutions are absurd attempts, on the part of the people, to limit a power in its own nature illimitable [(1803) 1 Cranch 137, 177].

As Bradley sums up the case: [The finding was therefore that] it was for the court where necessary to hold that an Act of Congress was void should it conflict with the terms of the constitution.'[37] Bradley goes on to note that a similar approach is adopted in many other countries where there is a written constitution, including the Republic of Ireland, Canada, Australia, and Germany.

2　However, the contrast may not be as stark as would first appear. Whilst there is no precedent for a refusal to apply a statute on such grounds, and many *dicta* against the notion, the courts are in certain cases prepared to impose on Parliament very strong presumptions that it cannot have intended to violate certain principles. This may lead them to require that Parliament must in some way make its meaning clear beyond doubt.

3　Thus in *Phillips v Eyre* (1870) LR 6 QB 1, 23 it was said:

... the courts will not ascribe retrospective force to new laws affecting rights unless by express words or necessary implication it appears that such was the intention of the legislature.

A similar rule relating to statues intended to have extra-territorial effect has already been noted (above). Furthermore, in the administrative law field, the

---

37　AW Bradley, *op cit*, p81.

courts have shown themselves willing effectively to disregard an apparently clear statutory attempt to oust their power of supervisory review[38] (see further, Part V, Chapter 2).

4   If the courts are prepared to impose requirements on the *manner* in which Parliament expresses itself, in order to protect fundamental constitutional principles, might they be prepared to go further, *in extremis*? Bradley and Wade consider that 'It is not possible, by legal logic alone to demonstrate the [the courts] have utterly lost the power to 'control' an Act of Parliament, or to show that a judge who is confronted with a statue fundamentally repugnant to moral principle (eg a law condemning all of a certain race to be executed) must either apply the statute or resign his office'.[39] TRS Allan discusses this issue below.

TRS Allan, 'The Limits of Parliamentary Sovereignty' (1985) *Public Law* 614, 620–2, 623–4 and 627

The legal doctrine of legislative supremacy articulates the courts' commitment to the current British scheme of parliamentary democracy. It ensures the effective expression of the political will of the electorate through the medium of its parliamentary representatives. If some conception of the nature and dimensions of the relevant political community provides the framework for the operation of the doctrine, equally some conception of democracy must provide its substantive political content. In other words, the courts' continuing adherence to the legal doctrine of sovereignty must entail commitment to some irreducible, minimum concept of the democratic principle. That political commitment will naturally demand respect for the legislative measures adopted by Parliament as the representative assembly, a respect for which the legal doctrine is in almost all likely circumstances a suitable expression. That respect cannot, however, be a limitless one. A parliamentary enactment whose effect would be the destruction of any recognisable form of democracy (for example, a measure purporting to deprive a substantial section of the population of the vote on the grounds of their hostility to Government policies) could not consistently be applied by the courts as law. Judicial obedience to the statute in such (extreme and unlikely) circumstances could not coherently be justified in terms of the doctrine of parliamentary sovereignty since the statute would plainly undermine the fundamental political principle which the doctrine serves to protect. The practice of judicial obedience to statute cannot itself be based on the authority of statute: it can only reflect a judicial choice based on an understanding of what (in contemporary conditions) political morality demands. The limits of that practice of obedience must therefore be constituted by the boundaries of that political morality. An enactment which threatened the essential elements of any plausible conception of democratic government would lie beyond those boundaries. It would forfeit, by the same token, any claim to be recognised as law.

Although, therefore, Dicey's sharp distinction between the application and interpretation of statute suffices for most practical purposes, it ultimately breaks down in the face of changing views of the contours of the political community or of serious threats to the central tenets of liberal democracy. Presumptions of legislative intent, which draw their strength from judicial perceptions of widely

---

38   *Anisminic Ltd v Foreign Compensation Commission* [1969] 2 All ER 147.
39   Bradley and Wade, *op cit*, p75.

held notions of justice and fairness, cannot in normal circumstances override the explicit terms of an Act of Parliament. This is because a commitment to representative government and loyalty to democratic institutions are themselves fundamental constituents of our collective political morality. Judicial notions of justice must generally give way to those expressed by Parliament where they are inconsistent. The legal authority of statute depends in the final analysis, however, on its compatibility with the central core of that shared political morality. If Parliament ceased to be a representative assembly, in any plausible sense of the idea, or if it proceeded to enact legislation undermining the democratic basis of our institutions, political morality might direct judicial resistance rather than obedience. No neat distinction between legal doctrine and political principle can be sustained at this level of adjudication. Questions about the scope and limits of the doctrine of sovereignty are necessarily questions about the proper relations between the courts and Parliament. Such questions cannot be settled by resort to competing formulations of some supposed pre-existing legal rule: it is the scope and content of that rule which is itself in issue. Answers can only be supplied as a matter of political morality and in terms of the values which the judges accept as fundamental to our constitutional order. ...

A residual judicial commitment to preserving the essentials of democracy does not provide the only constraint on parliamentary supremacy. The political morality which underlies the legal order is not exhausted by our attachment to democratic government. It consists also in attitudes about what justice and fairness require in the relations between government and governed, and some of these must be fundamental. If these attitudes authorise a restrictive approach to the interpretation of statutes which, more broadly construed, would threaten fundamental values, they might equally justify rejection of statutes whose infringement of such values was sufficiently grave. If an ambiguous penal provision should, as a matter of principle, be narrowly construed in the interests of liberty and fairness, a criminal statute which lacked all precision – authorising the punishment of whatever conduct officials deemed it expedient to punish – should, on the same principle, be denied any application at all. It would be sufficient for the court to deny its application to the particular circumstances of the case before it: there would in practice be no need to make a declaration of invalidity. The result, however, would be the same: the strength of the principle of interpretation, in effect denying the statute any application at all, would reflect the scale of the affront to the moral and political values we accept as fundamental.

The limits of the principle which requires recognition of foreign penal or confiscatory legislation provide a good illustration. Legislation by a foreign, sovereign state in respect of its own nationals or assets situated within its own territories will normally be accorded recognition in English courts even when it is considered immoral or unjust. Refusal to accord it validity as part of the relevant foreign law would be considered a serious breach of international comity [*Aksionairnoye Obschestro AM Luther v James Sagor and Co* [1921] 3 KB 532]. In *Oppenheimer v Cattermole (Inspector of Taxes)* [1976] AC 249, however, a majority of the House of Lords refused to recognise a Nazi decree of 1941, depriving expatriate German Jews of their citizenship and providing for the confiscation of their property. Respect for the claims of international comity gave way in the face of grave iniquity. The court was confronted with 'legislation which takes away without compensation from a section of the citizen body singled out on racial grounds all their property on which the state passing the legislation can lay its hands and, in addition, deprives them of their citizenship.' In the view of Lord Cross, 'a law of this sort constitutes so grave an infringement of human rights that the courts of this country ought to refuse to recognise it as a law at all' [*ibid*, at p278B-C]. Both the rule according legal validity to Acts of Parliament and the rule requiring the recognition of foreign penal legislation are alike important components, or products, of the political morality which informs judicial decision. Neither rule has absolute force, but is necessarily subject to certain ultimate constraints imposed by that morality.

Almost all modern discussions of sovereignty share the error of seeking to provide a single determinate solution which can be applied, in advance, to every question concerning the limits of the doctrine which may arise in the future. Once the real nature of the ultimate rule of the constitution has been properly ascertained, or its correct formulation authoritatively settled, the limits of sovereignty can be clearly stated as a matter of law. If, however, the scope and authority of the doctrine are embedded in a more fundamental constitutional morality, such attempts to state its limits for all purposes are bound to fail.

In each and every such case, the indeterminacy of the fundamental rule necessitates a thoroughgoing examination of the moral and political imperatives of the situation. The jurist cannot escape his moral responsibilities by seeking shelter in a formal doctrine providing legal neutrality – he is forced by events to set the boundaries of his doctrine.

Questions

1 Allan states that 'The practice of judicial obedience to statute cannot itself be based on the authority of statute: it can only reflect a judicial choice based on an understanding of what ... political morality demands'. Might not such obedience be attributable rather to more mundane matters, such as historical fact, the weight of tradition and the inherent conservatism of the judiciary?[40]

2 A wholesale and transparent attack by any British government on fundamental liberties is highly unlikely. The realistic threat comes from the prospect of a creeping and insidious erosion, in which each individual provision is of a minor nature in itself and characterised by the executive as being in the best interests of the community as a whole.[41] Does this fact render Allan's theory irrelevant, even if true?

Notes

1 To understand Allan's position, an awareness of the jurisprudential theory which underlines it is necessary. In the article quoted, Allan is essentially applying the 'principled' view of law, postulated by the American jurist Ronald Dworkin, to constitutional issues. Dworkin's position was framed in opposition to legal positivism, as expounded by HLA Hart[42] and his followers, which (very roughly speaking) argues that law is recognisable as such by virtue of its source, rather than its substantive content. Dworkin's argument is complex, but in essence argues that the content of the law can only be elucidated by a more comprehensive, interpretive inquiry,

---

40 For the best known analysis of alleged judicial conservative bias, see Griffiths, *The Politics of the Judiciary*, 4th edn (1991).

41 Eg, the curtailment of the right to silence by the Criminal Justice and Public Order Act 1994.

42 *The Concept of Law* (1961) is the fullest length exposition of Hart's position.

necessitating consideration of normative political theory.[43] Dworkin's influence on Allan can be seen in the latter's insistence that fundamental principles of constitutional law rest in turn upon basic axioms of shared political morality.

2   Allan's thesis could strike one as theoretically interesting, but unrealistic as a prediction of how the judiciary would react to abhorrent acts of Parliament. But his view that sovereignty is itself subject to higher order considerations has recently received influential and important judicial support, albeit by judges speaking extra-judicially only. Lord Woolf first of all considers how the courts would and should react if confronted with an Act of Parliament which purported to abolish the system of judicial review.

The Rt Hon Lord Woolf of Barnes, *'Droit Public* – English Style' (1995) *Public Law* 57, 67, 68, 69

But what happens if a party with a large majority in Parliament uses that majority to abolish the courts' entire power of judicial review in express terms? It is administratively expensive, absorbs far too large a proportion of the legal aid fund and results in the judiciary having misconceived notions of grandeur. Do the courts then accept that the legislation means what it says? I am sure this is in practice unthinkable. It will never happen. But if it did, for reasons I will now summarise, my own personal view is that they do not. ...

Our parliamentary democracy is based on the Rule of Law. One of the twin principles upon which the Rule of Law depends is the supremacy of Parliament in its legislative capacity. The other principle is that the courts are the final arbiters as to the interpretation and application of the law. As both Parliament and the courts derive their authority from the Rule of Law so both are subject to it and can not act in manner which involves its repudiation. ...

I see the courts and Parliament as being partners both engaged in a common enterprise involving the upholding of the Rule of Law. It is reflected in the way that frequently the House of Lords in its judicial capacity will stress the desirability of legislation when faced with the new problems that contemporary society can create rather than creating a solution itself.

There are, however, situations where already, in upholding the Rule of Law, the courts have had to take a stand. The example that springs to mind is the *Anisminic case* [1969] [2 AC 147]. In that case even the statement in an Act of Parliament that the Commission's decision 'shall not be called in question in any court of law' did not succeed in excluding the jurisdiction of the court. Since that case Parliament has not again mounted such a challenge to the reviewing power of the High Court. There has been, and I am confident there will continue to be, mutual respect for each other's roles.

---

43 See *Taking Rights Seriously* (1977) for the most accessible explanation of Dworkin's adjudicative theory. His later *Law's Empire* (1986) represents a fuller development of the theory, but also a move towards a more purely interpretative approach to law, which appears also to be parasitic upon a more general and grandiose concept of the purpose of law which is open to objections independent of those applicable to the adjudication theory; in particular it has been argued that Dworkin's analysis leaves out of account the more practical and functional aspects of law (see, eg N Simmonds, 'Imperial Visions and Mundane Practices' (1987) *CLJ* 465). An interesting collection of essays on the Hart–Dworkin debate generally can be found in M Cohen (ed), *Ronald Dworkin and Contemporary Jurisprudence* (1984).

However, if Parliament did the unthinkable, then I would say that the courts would also be required to act in a manner which would be without precedent. Some judges might chose to do so by saying that it was an unrebuttable presumption that Parliament could never intend such a result. I myself would consider there were advantages in making it clear that ultimately there are even limits on the supremacy of Parliament which it is the courts' inalienable responsibility to identify and uphold. They are limits of the most modest dimensions which I believe any democrat would accept. They are no more than are necessary to enable the Rule of Law to be preserved.

Note

Lord Woolf thus issues quite a clear warning that Parliament, being itself bound by the Rule of Law, may not transgress its basic requirements. Sir John Laws (a High Court judge) has approached the same question of possible limitations to parliamentary sovereignty. He considers the issue from a rather broader perspective than Lord Woolf, examining the consequences following from the imperative of protecting fundamental human rights and democracy itself, and also examining the restraints placed upon Parliament by the fact that it is itself constituted by law.

The Hon Sir John Laws, 'Law and Democracy' (1995) *Public Law* 72, 84, 85–6, 87–8, 92

Now it is only by means of compulsory law that effective rights can be accorded, so that the medium of rights is not persuasion, but the power of rule; the very power which, if misused, could be deployed to subvert rights. We therefore arrive at this position: the constitution must guarantee by positive law such rights as that of freedom of expression, since otherwise its credentials as a medium of honest rule are fatally undermined. But this requires for its achievement what I may call a higher-order law: a law which cannot be abrogated as other laws can, by the passage of a statute promoted by a Government with the necessary majority in Parliament. Otherwise the right is not in the keeping of the constitution at all; it is not a guaranteed right; it exists, in point of law at least, only because the Government chooses to let it exist, whereas in truth no such choice should be open to any Government. ...

It is also a condition of democracy's preservation that the power of a democratically elected Government – or Parliament – be not absolute. The institution of free and regular elections, like fundamental individual rights, has to be vindicated by a higher-order law; very obviously, no Government can tamper with it, if it is to avoid the mantle of tyranny; no Government, therefore, must be allowed to do so.

But this is not merely a plea to the merits of the matter, which can hardly be regarded as contentious; the need for higher-order law is dictated by the logic of the very notion of government under law. If we leave on one side a form of society in which a single ruler rules only by the strength of his arm, and where the only law is the ruler's dictat, we can see that any Government holds office by virtue of a framework of rules. The application of the rules determines what person or party is entitled (or, under some imaginable systems, obliged) to become the Government. This is a necessary, not a contingent, truth, since the institution of government is defined by the rules; were it otherwise, we are back to the case we have proposed to set aside. Richard Latham of All Souls said this over 40 years ago:

When the purported sovereign is anyone but a single actual person, the designation of him must include the statement of rules for the ascertainment of his will, and these rules, since their observance is a condition of the validity of his legislation, are rules of law logically prior to him.

... The thrust of this reasoning is that the doctrine of Parliamentary sovereignty cannot be vouched by Parliamentary legislation; a higher-order law confers it, and must of necessity limit it. ...

So the rules which establish and vindicate a Government's power are in a different category from laws which assume the existence of the framework, and are made under it, because they prescribe the framework itself. In states with written constitutions the rules are of course to be found in the text of the constitution, which, typically, will also contain provisions as to how they may be changed. Generally the mechanisms under which the framework may be changed are different from those by which ordinary laws, not part of the framework, may be repealed or amended; and the mechanisms will be stricter than those in place for the alteration of ordinary law.

But in Britain the rules establishing the framework possess, on the face of it, no different character from any other statute law. The requirement of elections at least every five years may in theory be altered by amending legislation almost as readily – though the 'almost' is important – as a provision defining dangerous dogs. The conventions under which Cabinet Government is carried on could in theory be changed with no special rules at all, as could any of the norms by which the Government possesses the authority to govern. The rules by which the power of a Government is conferred are in effect the same as the rules by which the Government may legislate upon other matters after it has gained power.'

Parliament ... possesses what we may indeed call a political sovereignty. It is a sovereignty which cannot be objected to, save at the price of assaulting democracy itself. But it is not a constitutional sovereignty; it does not have the status of what earlier I called a sovereign text, of the kind found in states with written constitutions. Ultimate sovereignty rests, in every civilised constitution, not with those who wield governmental power, but in the conditions under which they are permitted to do so. The constitution, not the Parliament, is in this sense sovereign.

Can Parliament limit its own powers?

According to orthodox theory, the answer is no. Parliament can expressly repeal any Act which it has previously passed, and, by the doctrine of implied repeal, if there is any inconsistency between the provisions of two different statues the later statue is deemed to impliedly repeal any provisions of the earlier statute which are inconsistent with it. No Parliament can protect its enactments from future express or implied repeal. As Munro explains:

It is evident that, if every succeeding Parliament is to enjoy the same degree of legislative authority as its predecessors, then attempts to bind subsequent Parliaments do not succeed. Dicey expressed this by numbering preceding Acts amongst the things which had been alleged to be, but were not, limitations on Parliament's legislative authority. However, another way of presenting the matter would be by saying that 'there is one thing which Parliament cannot do' (ie to pass a law which would bind its successors), or viewing it as a limitation upon or exception to Parliament's sovereignty. This perplexed Dicey, or so at least it is alleged. Again, however, the answer is simple enough when the distinction between law and fact is remembered. To say that Parliament 'cannot' bind its successors is like saying that Parliament cannot require good weather over England or cannot turn a woman into a man: 'cannot' in these contexts

135

means 'is not able effectively to in fact'. But when we say that Parliament 'can' make any law, we mean only that anything enacted by Parliament will be treated as valid by the courts. ... Acts which purport to bind later Parliaments, assuming Dicey was correct in his view, are not invalid, but merely ineffective (like, in varying degrees many other provisions) and, like all other enactments, liable to repeal.[44]

Question

Is Munro's distinction between 'ineffective' and 'invalid' acts a particularly helpful one, given that any invalid act will also obviously be ineffective?

Notes

1   There is a clear distinction between two ways in which future Parliaments could be bound: firstly, they could be bound as to the substance, the content of future enactments; secondly a requirement could be imposed that any legislation on a certain subject must bear a particular form, or will be valid only if passed in a certain manner, eg by a two-thirds majority, or with the approval of some outside body. The decisions normally cited for the proposition that Parliament cannot bind its successors in either way are those in *Vauxhall Estates v Liverpool Corp* [1932] 1 KB 733 and *Ellen Street Estates v Minister of Health* [1934] 1 KB 590, CA, which, as Munro describes them: 'concerned a provision in the Acquisition of Land (Assessment of Compensation) Act 1919 which, in regulating the compensation to be paid when land was compulsorily acquired, said that if land was acquired under the terms of any other stature, then so far as inconsistent with this Act those provisions shall cease to have or shall nor have effect. These words could be read as an attempt to preclude repeal, and since the compensation allowed for under the later Housing Act 1925 was less generous, it was in the interests of the companies involved in the two cases to plead the invalidity of the 1925 Act on that ground.'[45]

Munro notes that the argument was rejected by the courts; in *Vauxhall Estates* it was said (*per* Avory J):

> It must be admitted that such a suggestion as that is inconsistent with the principle of the constitution of this country. Speaking for myself, I should certainly hold, until the contrary were decided, that no Act of Parliament can effectively provide that no future Act shall interfere with its provisions.

In the *Ellen Street Estate* case, it was said (*per* Maugham LJ):

> The legislature cannot, according to our constitution, bind itself as to the form of subsequent legislation and it is impossible for Parliament to enact that in a subsequent statute dealing with the same subject-matter there can be no implied repeal. If in a subsequent Act Parliament chooses to make it plain that the earlier statute is being to some extent repealed, effect must be given to that intention just because it is the will of the legislature [(1934) 1 KB 590 at 597].

2   It should be noted that Avory J is hardly bullish about his view of sovereignty; he states only that he would hold it 'until the contrary were decided'.

---

44   Munro, *op cit*, pp86–7.
45   *Ibid*, p91.

3   Neither case dealt with an attempt by Parliament to impose the requirement that any future legislation on the same subject must bear a particular *form*. Hence Bradley and Wade's comment that 'Maughan LJ went far beyond the actual situation' in stating that such an attempt would fail. They also note that there were only 'very weak grounds for suggesting that in 1919 Parliament had been attempting to bind its successors';[46] the decisions were hardly therefore surprising, in the circumstances. It seems therefore that the traditionally cited authority for the proposition that Parliament cannot itself as to either form or substance is not conclusive. The two possibilities will therefore now be considered in more detail.

Attempts to bind as to substance

The Acts of Union with Scotland (1707) and Ireland (1800) expressed certain aspects of the constitutions of the newly created states to be fixed, variously, 'for ever', for 'all time coming' or as 'established and ascertained for ever'.[47] De Smith considers that:

> It can reasonably be argued that the Acts of Union with Scotland and Ireland were constituent Acts, establishing a new UK Parliament and setting limits to its powers. The case for still regarding the Act of Union with Ireland 1800 in this light has been undermined by a series of basic legislative changes. The case for so regarding the Acts of Union with Scotland 1707 is not so weak. Much water has indeed flowed under the bridges since that time, but the position of the Established Church in Scotland and the Scottish system of judicature, entrenched as fundamental and unalterable in the Articles of Union, remains largely intact. Although the immunity of the surviving fundamental principles of the Union from legislative encroachment by the UK Parliament without Scottish consent is probably to be regarded now as a matter of convention rather than of strict law, one cannot be certain that Scottish courts would take this view.[48]

The theory behind the argument that certain aspects of the Act of Union are not susceptible to repeal by the UK Parliament is simple. The Act was passed not by the UK Parliament but by the English and Scottish Parliaments.[49] By passing the Act, they abolished themselves and created a successor which was constituted from the start as limited by the provisions of the Act which created it.

The problem with this theory is that, as Munro notes, the UK Parliament appears to have felt free to enact, and the courts appear to felt themselves compelled to give effect to, legislation derogating from virtually all the fundamental principles of the Act of Union with Ireland and many of those contained in the Scottish Union Act.[50] However, it appears that the Scottish judiciary, at least, may regard certain aspects of the Act of Union with Scotland as immune from ordinary repeal.

---

46   Bradley and Wade, *op cit*, p77.
47   For a general discussion of these Acts see Munro, *op cit*, pp61–78.
48   De Smith, *op cit*, pp78–9.
49   Respectively, the Union with England Act 1707 and the Union with Scotland Act 1706.
50   *Op cit*, Chapter 4.

MacCormick v Lord Advocate 1953 SC 396

The Lord President (Cooper): ... The principle of the unlimited sovereignty of Parliament is a distinctively English principle which has no counterpart in Scottish constitutional law. ... Considering that the Union legislation extinguished the Parliaments of Scotland and England and replaced them by a new Parliament, I have difficulty in seeing why it should have been supposed that the new Parliament of Great Britain must inherit all the peculiar characteristics of the English Parliament but none of the Scottish Parliament, as if all that happened in 1707 was that Scottish representatives were admitted to the Parliament of England. That is not what was done. Further, the Treaty and the associated legislation, by which the Parliament of Great Britain was brought into being as the successor of the separate Parliaments of Scotland and England, contain some clauses which expressly reserve to the Parliament of Great Britain powers of subsequent modification, and other clauses which either contain no such power or emphatically exclude subsequent alteration by declarations that the provision shall be fundamental and unalterable in all time coming, or declarations of a like effect. I have never been able to understand how it is possible to reconcile with elementary canons of construction the adoption by the English constitutional theorists of the same attitude to these markedly different types of provisions.

The Lord Advocate conceded this point by admitting that the Parliament of Great Britain 'could not' repeal or alter such 'fundamental and essential' conditions. ... I have not found in the Union legislation any provision that the Parliament of Great Britain should be 'absolutely sovereign' in the sense that that Parliament should be free to alter the Treaty at will. ...

Notes

1 The Lord President went on to find the issue non-justiciable.

2 In certain cases, it is clear that Parliament has attempted to divest itself of authority to legislate at all in respect of certain former colonies. Section 2 of the Canada Act provides that 'No Act of the Parliament of the UK passed after the Constitution Act 1982 (Canada) comes into force shall extend to Canada as part of its law'. No one doubts that the Canadian courts would ignore any legislation subsequently passed by the UK Parliament which purported to extend to Canada, but how would the British courts react? In *Manuel v Attorney-General* (1983), a case concerning the issue of whether the Canada Act had itself been properly passed, the following opinion was given (*per* Megarry VC).

Manuel v Attorney-General [1983] Ch 77, 87, 88

I do not think that, as a matter of law, it makes any difference if the Act in question purports to apply outside the UK. I speak not merely of statutes such as the Continental Shelf Act 1964 but also of statutes purporting to apply to other countries. If that other country is a colony, the English courts will apply the Act even if the colony is in a state of revolt against the Crown and direct enforcement of the decision may be impossible: see *Madzimbamuto v Lardner-Burke* [1969] 1 AC 645. It matters not if a convention had grown up that the UK Parliament would not legislate for that colony without the consent of the colony. Such a convention would not limit the powers of Parliament, and if Parliament legislated in breach of the convention, 'the courts could not hold the Act of Parliament invalid': see p723. Similarly if the other country is a foreign state which has never been British, I do not think that any English court would or could declare the Act *ultra vires* and void. No doubt the Act would normally be ignored by the foreign state and would not be enforced by it, but that would not invalidate the Act in this country. Those who infringed it could not claim that it was void if proceedings within the jurisdiction were taken against them. Legal validity is one thing, enforceability is another. Thus a marriage in Nevada may constitute statutory bigamy punishable in England (*Trial of Earl Russell* [1901] AC 446), just as acts in Germany may be punishable here as statutory treason: *Joyce v Director of Public Prosecutions* [1946] AC 347. Parliament in fact legislates only for British subjects in this way; but if it also legislated for others, I do not see how the English courts could hold the statute void, however impossible it was to enforce it, and no matter how strong the diplomatic protests.

I do not think that countries which were once colonies but have since been granted independence are in any different position. Plainly, once statute has granted independence to a country, the repeal of the statute will not make the country dependent once more; what is done is done, and is not undone by revoking the authority to do it. Heligoland did not in 1953 again become British. But if Parliament then passes an Act applying to such a country, I cannot see why that Act should not be in the some position as an Act applying to what has always been a foreign country, namely, an Act which the English courts will recognise and apply but one which the other country will in all probability ignore.

Notes

1   Munro cites this *dicta* with approval, to support his view that if, using Sir Ivor Jenning's example, a law was passed in the UK Parliament making it an offence for Frenchmen to smoke in the streets of Paris, '... English courts, if a guilty Frenchman could be apprehended while visiting Folkestone, would enforce it'.[51] It should be noted however that Megarry VC's remarks were strictly *obiter* and that the Court of Appeal did not take the opportunity to endorse them.

2   Lord Denning, in *Blackburn v Attorney-General* (1971), considers the case of the Acts 'which have granted independence to the dominions and territories overseas'. He asks, 'Can anyone imagine that Parliament could or would reverse those laws and take away their independence? Most clearly not. Freedom once given cannot be taken away. Legal theory must give way to practical politics.'[52] Megarry VC in *Manuel*, however, opined that, '... it is clear from the context that Lord Denning was using the word "could" in the sense of "could effectively"; I cannot read it as meaning "could as a matter of abstract law"'.[53] Is this clear?

3   The case of *Madzimbamuto v Lardner Burke* (1969)[54] concerned the attempt by Parliament to reassert its right to legislate for Southern Rhodesia, after that country, having 'in practice enjoyed self-government and legislative autonomy for many years'[55] unilaterally declared full independence. The Privy Council found that the UK Parliament was, as a matter of law, still

51   Munro, *Studies in Constitutional Law*, (1987), p97.

52   [1971] 1 WLR 137, 140.

53   At p89.

54   [1969] 1 AC 526.

55   Munro, *op cit*, p95.

competent to legislate for Rhodesia. It should be noted however that there had, in that case, been no formal renunciation by Parliament of legislative competence, along the lines of s2 of the Canada Act. This case did not therefore really answer the question whether Parliament can deprive itself of legislative competence; it stated only that the unilateral act of a dependant territory could not do so, a scarcely surprising finding.

Attempts to bind as to the manner and form of future legislation

Evidence from decided cases

Here, we look at the courts' likely response to attempts by one Parliament to provide that any Acts of Parliament dealing with a given subject must have a particular form, eg bear certain words, or be passed in a certain manner, eg with a two-thirds majority or with the consent of some outside body.

For example, s1 of the Northern Ireland Constitution Act 1973 provides that Northern Ireland will not cease to be part of her Majesty's dominions without the consent of the majority of the people of Northern Ireland voting in a poll. How would the courts treat this provision? Some guidance may be gleaned from cases in which the Privy Council or courts in other common law jurisdictions have had to rule on the lawfulness of such provisions. Colin Munro provides a useful discussion.

Colin Munro, *Studies in Constitutional Law*, pp100–102

A case much relied on is *A G for New South Wales v Trethowan* [1932] AC 526, PC, a decision of the Privy Council which concerned the New South Wales legislature. That legislature was subject to s5 of the Colonial Laws Validity Act 1865, which provides:

... every representative legislature shall, in respect to the colony under its jurisdiction, have, and be deemed at all times to have had, full power to make laws respecting the constitution, power and procedure of such legislature; provided that such laws shall have been passed in such manner and form as may from time to time be required by any Act of Parliament, letters patent, order in council, or colonial law for the time being in force in the said colony.

In 1929 the Parliament of New South Wales passed an Act which provided that no Bill for abolishing the upper house of the legislature (the Legislative Council) should be presented for the Royal Assent unless it had been approved at a referendum by a majority of the electors. It was further provided that this requirement of a referendum might not itself be repealed except by the same process. The Government which sponsored the legislation was a right wing one, and its aim was to 'entrench' the position of the upper house, which the Labour party had declared its intention of abolishing. In 1930, however, a new Parliament was elected in which the Labour Party held the majority of seats in the lower house. Two Bills were passed through both Houses, the first purporting to repeal the referendum requirement, and the second purporting to abolish the Legislative Council. Neither Bill was submitted to the electors, and accordingly two members of the threatened Legislative Council sought an injunction to restrain the submission of these Bills for the Royal Assent. The Supreme Court of New South Wales granted the injunction, and appeals to the High Court of Australia and the Judicial Committee of the Privy Council were unsuccessful.

What does this case show? Two views are possible. The first is that there is a general rule that legislation may be enacted only in such manner and form as is laid down by law, and that the UK Parliament is just as subject to that rule as was the New South Wales legislature. However, the opposing view is that the decision has no relevance at all. The Privy Council said that the case depended 'entirely upon a consideration of the meaning and effect of s5 of the Act of 1865' [*ibid* at 539], and it is hard to see how this can tell us anything about the UK Parliament, whose powers are not defined in or derived from any statute. Dicey had had no difficulty in classing the New South Wales legislature as a non-sovereign, law-making body, and the *Trethowan* decision merely emphasises that it was indeed subordinate to a higher law (the 1865 Act passed by the Imperial Parliament) and that its purported legislation could be *ultra vires*.

What the *Trethowan* case shows is merely that some legislatures are limited with respect to the procedure by which they may legislate. But Dicey, who devoted two chapters of his book to non-sovereign legislatures and legislatures in federal countries, would certainly not have denied this. Of course, it is a logical possibility that any particular legislature may be of that sort, but what we wish to know is whether the British Parliament is, and *Trethowan* seems to advance us no further. ...

Other cases are open to the same objection. In *Harris v Minister of the Interior* 1952 (2) AD 428, *sub nom Harris v Donges* (1952) I TLR 1245, the Appellate Division of the Supreme Court of South Africa held that a measure passed by the South African Parliament in 1951 (depriving Cape coloured voters of electoral rights) was not a valid Act, because the matter was subject to an entrenched clause in the constitution, contained in the South Africa Act 1909. The 'manner and form' required for alteration, namely a two-thirds majority of both Houses of Parliament sitting together, had not been complied with. This merely shows that the South African legislature, even if unlimited as to the area of its power, was procedurally subject to a higher law, the Act which established it and was logically and historically prior to it.

In *Bribery Comr v Ranasinghe* [1965] AC 172, [1964] 2 All ER 785, PC, the Privy Council held that the bribery tribunal by which the respondent had been convicted was not lawfully appointed, because it had been set up by an ordinary Act of the Parliament of Ceylon whereas, since it was inconsistent with provisions in the constitution concerning judicial appointments, a special majority was required under the constitution. An argument that the Parliament of Ceylon was sovereign and that the courts must regard official copies of its Acts as conclusive of their validity was rejected. Much has been made of one of the remarks of Lord Pearce, who delivered the opinion:

> The proposition which is not acceptable is that a legislature, once established, has some inherent power derived from the mere fact of its establishment to make a valid law by the resolution of a bare majority which its own constituent instrument has said shall not be a valid law unless made by a different type of majority or by a different legislative process [*ibid* at 198].

Geoffrey Marshall says of this that Lord Pearce 'seemed to imply ... that both non-sovereign and sovereign legislatures may be made subject to procedural rules entrenching parts of the law from simple majority repeal' [*Constitutional Theory* (1971), p55]. However, this perhaps does not take sufficient account of the possibility that the UK Parliament is sovereign precisely because it is not subject to any 'constituent instrument' such as Lord Pearce describes. Earlier in his speech, Lord Pearce had said exactly that: 'In the UK there is no governing instrument which prescribes the law-making powers and the forms which are essential to those powers' [(1965) AC 172 at 195].

The cases cited by the 'manner and form' school do not, in the end, seem very helpful. The powers and forms of law-making by the UK Parliament, as Lord Pearce observed, are not prescribed by any higher law. As to whether Parliament may alter these so as to restrict future Parliaments, the suggestion has not been supported in British cases, and was denied in *Vauxhall Estates Ltd v Liverpool Corpn* [1932] 1 KB 733 and *Ellen St Estates Ltd v Minister of Health* [1934] 1 KB 590. It should, however, be said that the *dicta* in those Housing Act cases hardly settle the question finally with regard to all possible circumstances. It is at best doubtful whether, in that instance, Parliament had intended to prevent repeal, and it was scarcely an issue which would tempt judges to break new ground.

Note

Munro thus leaves open the question as to whether Parliament may alter the present law as to its ability to bind its successors.

Questions

1   In relation to the Northern Ireland Constitution Act 1973, how would the courts react if:

   (a) The UK Parliament passed an Act ceding Northern Ireland to the Republic of Ireland, and the Act did not recite that a majority of Northern Ireland citizens had approved the change in a poll?

   (b) The UK Parliament passed an Act repealing the s1 guarantee without taking a poll?

2   In relation to (b), would it make any difference if s1 had stated that its own provisions could not be repealed without taking a poll?

3   In relating to (a), would it matter whether a poll had actually been held, as long as the Act ceding Northern Ireland stated on its face that it had?

Note

This latter issue was addressed in *Manuel v Attorney-General* (1983).[56] Section 4 of the earlier Statue of Westminster Act 1931 stated that the UK Parliament could henceforth only legislate for, *inter alia*, Canada if the Act in question stated on its fact that the consent of Canada to the legislation had been obtained. The case dealt with the question of whether that consent had been properly obtained. In the Court of Appeal, Slade LJ stated that the Court was 'content to assume in favour of the plaintiffs' that it was 'correct' to state that 'Parliament can effectively tie the hands of its successors, if it passes a statute which provides that any future legislation on a specified subject shall be enacted only with certain specified consents' (at pp104–105). Although he stated that the court was 'not purporting to decide [the issue]' the fact remains that had the Court regarded s4 as simply unenforceable, there would have been no need to decide whether consents had been properly obtained, as none would have been needed at all.

Slade LJ then went on to consider what s4 actually required.

---

56   (1983) Ch 77.

Manuel v Attorney-General (1983) Ch 77, 106, 107

What then are the conditions which s4 imposes? It is significant that, while the preamble to the Statute of 1931 recites that:

'... it is in accord with the established constitutional position that no law hereafter made by the Parliament of the UK shall extend to any of the said dominions as part of the law of that dominion otherwise than at the request and with the consent of that dominion: ...'

Section 4 itself does not provide that no Act of the UK Parliament shall extend to a dominion as part of the law of that dominion unless the dominion has in fact requested and consented to the enactment thereof. The condition that must be satisfied is a quite different one, namely, that it must be 'expressly declared in that Act that that dominion has requested, and consented to, the enactment thereof'. Though Mr Macdonald, as we have said, submitted that s4 requires not only a declaration but a true declaration of a real request and consent, we are unable to read the section in that way. There is no ambiguity in the relevant words and the court would not in our opinion be justified in supplying additional words by a process of implication; it must construe and apply the words as they stand: see *Maxwell on Interpretation of Statutes*, 12th edn (1969), p33 and the cases there cited. If an Act of Parliament contains an express declaration in the precise form required by s4, such declaration is in our opinion conclusive so far as s4 is concerned.

There was, we think, nothing unreasonable or illogical in this simple approach to the matter on the part of the legislature, in reserving to itself the sole function of deciding whether the requisite request and consent have been made and given. The present case itself provides a good illustration of the practical consequences that would have ensued, if s4 had made an actual request and consent on the part of a dominion a condition precedent to the validity of the relevant legislation, in such manner that the courts or anyone else would have had to look behind the relevant declaration in order to ascertain whether a statute of the UK Parliament, expressed to extend to that dominion, was valid. There is obviously room for argument as to the identity of the representatives of the Dominion of Canada appropriate to express the relevant request and consent. Mr Macdonald, while firm in his submission that all legislatures of the provinces of Canada had to join the Federal Parliament in expressing them, seemed less firm in his submission that all the Indian nations had likewise to join. This is a point which might well involve difficult questions of Canadian constitutional law. Moreover, if all the Indian nations did have to join, further questions might arise as to the manner in which the consents of these numerous persons and bodies had to be expressed and as to whether all of them had in fact been given. As we read the wording of s4, it was designed to obviate the need for any further inquiries of this nature, once a statute, containing the requisite declaration, had been duly enacted by the UK Parliament. Parliament, having satisfied itself as to the request and consent, would make the declaration and that would be that.

Mr Macdonald submitted in the alternative that, even if s4 on its proper construction does not itself bear the construction which he attributed to it, nevertheless, in view of the convention referred to in the third paragraph of the preamble, the actual request and consent of the dominion is necessary before a law made by the UK Parliament can extend to that dominion as part of its law. Whether or not an argument on these lines might find favour in the courts of a dominion, it is in our opinion quite unsustainable in the courts of this country. The sole condition precedent which has to be satisfied if a law made by the UK Parliament is to extend to a dominion as part of its law is to be found stated in the body of the Statute of 1931 itself (s4). This court would run counter to all principles of statutory interpretation if it were to purport to vary or supplement the terms of this stated condition precedent by reference to some supposed convention, which, though referred to in the preamble, is not incorporated in the body of the Statute.

Note

At first sight it seems clear from this decision that, where a procedural requirement is imposed a recitation in an Act that it has been complied with will suffice. The courts will not look behind such a statement to the reality. It should be noted, however, that in *Manuel*, there was only a rather complex and politically contentious argument that proper consent had not been obtained before the court, examination of which would, as Slade LJ noted, have raised 'difficult questions of Canadian constitutional law' (p107). It does not necessarily follow that, in the case of the Northern Ireland Constitution Act, the courts would accept a declaration in the Act that a poll had taken place if it was a simple and unequivocal matter of public record that it had not.

Manner and form: the theory

Colin Munro, *Studies in Constitutional Law*, pp97–100

The most sustained attack on Dicey's views has come with the argument that a Parliament may limit its successors as to 'manner and form'.

The challenge was posed by Sir Ivor Jennings, who contrasted two kinds of authority:

If a prince has supreme power, and continues to have supreme power, he can do anything, even to the extent of undoing the things which he had previously done. If he grants a constitution, binding himself not to make laws except with the consent of an elected legislature, he has power immediately afterwards to abolish the legislature without its consent and to continue legislating by his personal decree.

But if the prince has not supreme power, but the rule is that the courts accept as law that which is made in the proper legal form, the result is different. For when the prince enacts that henceforth no rule shall be law unless it is enacted by him with the consent of the legislature, the law has been altered, and the courts will not admit as law any rule which is not made in that form. Consequently a rule subsequently made by the prince alone abolishing the legislature is not law, for the legislature has not consented to it, and the rule has not been enacted according to the manner and form required by the law for the time being [*The Law and the Constitution*, 5th edn (1959), p152].

It is, of course, correct as a matter of theory to say that either of these situations is possible. The question is, to which does the British constitution correspond? Dicey held the sovereignty of the UK Parliament to be of a continuing nature, but did not particularly consider whether any distinction should be drawn between the substance of legislation and the composition or procedures of the legislative body. Jennings says that it is unclear whether our Parliament corresponds to his first prince or his second because there is a dearth of judicial authority, but it is evident that he prefers the proposition that 'the law is that Parliament may make any law in the manner and form provided by the law'. Some other writers were less equivocal in their support for it, and by 1961 Professor Heuston felt able to claim that the 'new view' of sovereignty, as he called it, had made considerable headway [*Essays in Constitutional Law* (1st edn (1961, 2nd edn (1964), Ch 1].

With more support from writers such as Geoffrey Marshall [*Parliamentary Sovereignty and the Commonwealth* (1957); *Constitutional Theory* (1971), Ch 3], JDB Mitchell [*Constitutional Law*, 2nd edn (1968), Ch 4] and SA de Smith [*Constitutional and Administrative Law*, 2nd edn (1973), Ch 4], the view could justifiably be said to be favoured by 'the great majority of modern constitutional lawyers' [George Winterton, 'The British Grundnorm: Parliamentary Supremacy Re-examined' (1976) 92 LQR 591 at 606].

Such a popular view deserves to be examined. In Heuston's formulation, it is this:

(1) Sovereignty is a legal concept: the rules which identify the sovereign and prescribe its composition and functions are logically prior to it.

(2) There is a distinction between rules which govern, on the one hand, (a) the composition, and (b) the procedure, and, on the other hand, (c) the area of power, of a sovereign legislature.

(3) The courts have jurisdiction to question the validity of an alleged Act of Parliament on grounds 2(a) and 2(b), but not on ground 2(c).

(4) This jurisdiction is exercisable either before or after the Royal Assent has been signified – in the former case by way of injunction, in the latter by way of declaratory judgment [*Essays in Constitutional Law*, 2nd edn (1964), pp6–7].

The practical consequences of such a view, if it is correct, are spelt out by Marshall:

> Parliament as at present constituted might conceivably bind the future or circumscribe the freedom of future legislators, not by laying down blanket prohibitions or attempting to enact a fundamental Bill of Rights, but by using their authority to provide different forms and procedures for legislation. A referendum or a joint sitting, for example, might be prescribed before certain things could be done. Or a two-thirds majority. Or a 75% or 80% majority. If it is also provided that any repeal of such provisions should not be by simple majority, the courts may be able to protect the arrangements laid down by declaring in suitable proceedings that any purported repeal by simple majority of a protected provision is *ultra vires* as being not, in the sense required by law, an 'Act of Parliament'. In this finding they would not be in any way derogating from parliamentary sovereignty but protecting Parliament's authority from usurpation by those not entitled for the purpose in hand to exercise it. [*Constitutional Theory* (1971), p42]

Thus, if this is correct, provisions in a Bill of Rights, or any other provisions which it was desired especially to safeguard, might be protected by requirements of special procedures or majorities. They might be 'entrenched', as it is often described.

... It is undeniable that the courts decide what is or is not an Act of Parliament, but as has been said, 'this is not a matter of limiting Parliament, but of identifying its enactments' [O Hood Phillips, *Essays in Constitutional and Administrative Law*, 6th edn (1978), p80]. Once something is identified as an Act of Parliament, the 'enrolled Bill rule' comes into operation, which, as we have seen, means that the courts have no choice but to accept it.

So runs the Diceyan view. But the 'new view', while conceding that Parliament is unlimited with regard to the subject matter of legislation, maintains that it may be limited as to composition and procedure, or, as it is often put, 'manner and form'.

Note

We have been discussing a possible 'rule' or 'law' that Parliament cannot bind itself. What is the source of this law? The answer, interestingly enough, is directly related to the question whether Parliament can change or 'break' this law.

AW Bradley, 'The Sovereignty of Parliament: In Perpetuity?', *op cit*, pp85, 87–89

Even in the United States constitution, no express provision authorises the Supreme Court to hold that legislation by Congress is unconstitutional. This power was declared in *Marbury v Madison* to be implicit in the constitution. No American lawyer would now deny that the court may exercise this power. In the absence of a written constitution for the UK, where is the source of the legal rule that there are no limits on the legislative capacity of Parliament and that the courts may not review the validity of legislation? For reasons of logic, we should not expect to find this rule created by an Act of Parliament. As was said by the jurist Salmond, 'No statute can confer this power upon Parliament, for this would be to assume and act on the very power to be conferred' [*Salmond on Jurisprudence*, 12th edn, ed PJ Fitzgerald (1966), 111]. In fact the UK Parliament has never expressly attempted to confer upon itself legislative omnipotence, although on two occasions (in 1766 concerning the restive American colonies and again in 1965 following the Rhodesian declaration of independence) it made a legislative declaration that it retained full power to legislate for the territories which were then challenging British authority. Nonetheless, for the reason stated by Salmond, it is to the decisions of the courts that we must look to discover propositions about the legislative powers of Parliament.

... The legislative authority of Parliament includes power to make changes in constitutional law, and no special procedure is needed for such legislation. For example, Parliament authorised abdication of the monarch, has reformed the electoral system, has altered the life of Parliament, sought to devolve legislative powers upon Scottish and Welsh assemblies, and authorised the holding of a referendum of Britain's continuing membership of the EEC. Such changes may impinge closely upon the composition of Parliament and on the process by which legislation is enacted. In particular, the Parliament Acts 1911 and 1949 took away the general power of the House of Lords to veto legislation, thus enabling bills in certain circumstances to become law when they have been approved solely by the Commons and the Crown. The precise effect of the Parliament Acts is not easy to determine. Has the sovereign Parliament been redefined, or are measures passed under the Parliament Acts nothing more than delegated legislation?

[Does] the legislative authority of Parliament to make changes in constitutional law, ... include power to legislate about all constitutional fundamentals? Two aspects are particularly difficult. First, it is widely held that a sovereign Parliament is not bound by the Acts of its predecessors, and thus that no Parliament can bind its successors. Second, it is said that an Act of Parliament may change all rules of the common law except the rule whereby the courts recognise as law the Acts of Parliament [HWR Wade, 'The Basis of Legal Sovereignty' (1955) LJ 172 at 186–9].

Nonetheless, since the power of Parliament extends to legislating on constitutional matters, it is plain that legislation may have a considerable effect in determining who the successors of Parliament are; a House of Commons elected by universal suffrage or a House of Lords containing life peers is a very different body from earlier forms of each House.

Closely related to the problem of whether one Parliament can bind its successors is the proposition that the one rule of the common law which Parliament may not change is the rule that courts recognise Acts of Parliament as law. We have already seen that legal authority for the sovereignty of Parliament has to be found in decisions of the courts rather than in legislation. Professor Sir William Wade, in a celebrated exposition of the legal basis of sovereignty, argued thus: 'If no statute can establish the rule that the courts obey Acts of Parliament, similarly no statute can alter or abolish that rule' [Wade, 'Basis of Legal Sovereignty', 187]. ... Professor Wade's argument at this crucial point depends for its logical strength upon the word 'similarly' (consider the argument 'No person can bring his own life into being; similarly, no person can bring his own life to an end'), and it does not take adequate account of the fact that Parliament's legislative power includes power to make constitutional changes. What we must now consider is whether the sovereignty of Parliament can accommodate any alteration in the fundamental rule that the courts recognise as binding upon them every Act of Parliament and have no authority to review the validity of such Acts. Closely related to this is whether there are any circumstances in which the rule that the latest Act of Parliament prevails over earlier inconsistent Acts (the doctrine of implied repeal) could give way to a situation in which the courts might legitimately apply an earlier Act rather than a later inconsistent Act.

Note

Sir Ivor Jennings has argued on this point as follows: the rules governing sovereignty are derived from the common law; Parliament can change the common law in any way; therefore Parliament can change the rules which relate to its own sovereignty.[57] Wade has replied to this argument as follows.

HRW Wade, 'The Basis of Legal Sovereignty' (1955) *Cambridge Law Journal* 186–9

At the heart of the matter lies the question whether the rule of common law which says that the courts will enforce statutes can itself be altered by a statute. Adherents of the traditional theory, who hold that future Parliaments cannot be bound, are here compelled to answer 'no.' For if they answer 'yes,' they must yield to Jennings' reasoning.

But to deny that Parliament can alter this particular Rule of Law is not so daring as it may seem at first sight; for the sacrosanctity of the rule is an inexorable corollary of Parliament's continuing sovereignty. If the one proposition is asserted, the other must be conceded. Nevertheless some further justification is called for, since there must be something peculiar about a rule of common law which can stand against a statute.

The peculiarity lies in this, that the rule enjoining judicial obedience to statutes is one of the fundamental rules upon which the legal system depends ...

Once this truth is grasped, the dilemma is solved. For if no statute can establish the rule that the courts obey Acts of Parliament, similarly no statute can alter or abolish that rule. The rule is above and beyond the reach of statute, as Salmond so well explains, because it is itself the source of the authority of statute. This puts it into a class by itself among rules of common law, and the apparent paradox that it is unalterable by Parliament turns out to be a truism. The rule of judicial obedience is in one sense a rule of common law, but in another sense –

---

57   This formulation of Jenning's argument is given by HRW Wade, *op cit*, p103.

which applies to no other rule of common law – it is the ultimate political fact upon which the whole system of legislation hangs. Legislation owes its authority to the rule: the rule does not owe its authority to legislation. To say that Parliament can change the rule, merely because it can change any other rule, is to put the cart before the horse.

What Salmond calls the 'ultimate legal principle' is therefore a rule which is unique in being unchangeable by Parliament – it is changed by revolution, not by legislation; it lies in the keeping of the courts, and no Act of Parliament can take it from them. This is only another way of saying that it is always for the courts, in the last resort, to say what is a valid Act of Parliament; and that the decision of this question is not determined by any Rule of Law which can be laid down or altered by any authority outside the courts. It is simply a political fact. If this is accepted, there is a fallacy in Jennings' argument that the law requires the courts to obey any rule enacted by the legislature, including a law which alters this law itself. For this law itself is ultimate and unalterable by any legal authority.

Note

Wade's argument appears to blur the legal/political distinction which is at the heart of the traditional doctrine of parliamentary sovereignty. He thereby (paradoxically) seems to be lending support to writers like Allan who argue that, in the end, sovereignty is based not on strict law, but on fundamental principles of political morality which might impose legal limitations on the exercise of legislative supremacy. Indeed, Sir John Laws[58] has deployed part of the quotation from Wade's article appearing above, in support of his argument that 'a higher order law confers [sovereignty on Parliament] and must of necessity limit it'.

---

58 'Law and Democracy' (1995) PL 72 at 86–7.

CHAPTER 5

THE EUROPEAN UNION AND PARLIAMENTARY SOVEREIGNTY

INTRODUCTION[1]

The UK became a member of the European Community with effect from 1 January 1972 by virtue of the Treaty of Accession 1972. Treaties and Community law capable of having direct effect in the UK were given domestic legal effect by the European Communities Act 1972 which, by s2(1), incorporated all existing Community law into UK law. No express declaration of the supremacy of Community law is contained in the Act; the words intended to achieve this are contained in s2(4), which reads as follows: 'any enactment passed or to be passed ... shall be construed and have effect subject to the foregoing provisions of this section ...' The words 'subject to' appear to suggest that the courts must allow Community law to prevail over a subsequent Act of Parliament. 'The foregoing' are those provisions referred to in s2(1) giving the force of law to 'the enforceable Community rights' there defined. Section 3(1) provides that questions as to the meaning or effect of Community law are to be determined 'in accordance with the principles laid down by any relevant decision of the European Court.'

The problem arises in respect of statutes passed after 1 January 1972. Clearly, any Community law will prevail over UK legislation enacted before 1 January 1973. Authority for this can be found in rulings such as those in *Henn* (1981)[2] and *Goldstein* (1982).[3] This is uncontroversial and merely accords with the ordinary operation of the doctrine of parliamentary sovereignty. According to the traditional doctrine of parliamentary sovereignty the later Act should prevail as representing the latest expression of Parliament's will, but the community doctrine of primacy of EC law and s2(4) would require Community law to prevail.

THE POSITION OF THE EUROPEAN COURT OF JUSTICE

The European Court of Justice has made clear its view that Community law should prevail over national law.

---

1 General reading, see: L Collins, *European Community Law in the United Kingdom*, 4th edn (1990); TC Hartley, *The Foundations of European Community Law*, 2nd edn (1988); AJ Mackenzie Stuart, *The European Communities and the Rule of Law* (1977); JA Usher, *European Community Law and National Law: The Irreversible Transfer?* (1981); J Steiner, *EC Law*, 4th edn (1994); S Weatherill and P Beaumont, *EC Law* (1993); S Weatherill, *Cases and Materials on EC Law* (1994); Collins, *European Community Law in the UK*, 4th edn (1990); AW Bradley, 'The Sovereignty of Parliament: In Perpetuity?' in *The Changing Constitution*, Jowell and Oliver (eds), 3rd edn (1994); JP Warner (1977) 93 LQR 349; O Hood Phillips (1979) 95 LQR 167; Mitchell, Kuipers and Gall (1972) 9 CML Rev 134; Jaconelli (1979) 28 ICLQ 65; HWR Wade (1991) 107 LQR 1; Dawn Oliver (1991) 54 MLR 442; N Gravells (1991) PL 180.

2 2 All ER 166.

3 1 WLR 804.

Costa v ENEL Case 6164 [1964] ECR 585, 586, judgment of 15 July 1964, ECJ

By creating a Community of unlimited duration, having its own institutions, its own personality, its own legal capacity and capacity of representation on the international plane, and, more particularly, real powers stemming from a limitation of sovereignty or a transfer of powers from the states to the Community, the Member States have limited their sovereign rights and have thus created a body of law which binds both their nationals and themselves.

The integration into the laws of each Member State of provisions which derive from the Community and, more generally the terms and the spirit of the Treaty, make it impossible for the states, as a corollary, to accord precedence to a unilateral and subsequent measure over a legal system accepted by them on a basis of reciprocity. Such a measure cannot therefore be inconsistent with that legal system. The law stemming from the Treaty, an independent source of law, could not because of its special and original nature, be overridden by domestic legal provisions, however framed, without being deprived of its character as Community law and without the legal basis of the Community itself being called into question.

The transfer by the states from their domestic legal system to the Community legal system of the rights and obligations arising under the Treaty carries with it a permanent limitation of their sovereign rights.

Amministrazione delle Finanze dello Stato v Simmenthal SpA Case 106/77 [1978] ECR 629, 645–6, ECJ

[The Court ruled:] A national court which is called upon, within the limits of its jurisdiction, to apply provisions of Community law is under a duty to give full effect to those provisions, if necessary refusing of its own motion to apply any conflicting provision of national legislation, even if adopted subsequently, and it is not necessary for the court to request or await the prior setting aside of such provisions by legislative or other constitutional means.

Note

The far-reaching finding in *Amministrazione delle Finanze dello Stato v Simmenthal SpA* was to the effect that conflict between provisions of national law and directly applicable Community law must be resolved by rendering the national law inapplicable, and that any national provision or practice withholding from a national court the jurisdiction to apply Community law even temporarily was incompatible with the requirements of Community law.

THE POSITION OF THE UK COURTS

The purposive approach

How have the UK courts approached this conflict? In *Felixstowe Dock and Railway Co v British Transport Docks Board* (1976)[4] Lord Denning MR disposed of a challenge to UK law on the basis that 'once a Bill is passed by Parliament and becomes a statute, that will dispose of all discussion about the Treaty. These

---

4   CMLR 655.

courts will have to abide by the statute without regard to the Treaty at all'. This was the traditional approach; however it then gave way to what has been termed a 'rule of construction' approach to s2(4). In *Garland v British Rail Engineering* (1983)[5] Lord Diplock suggested (without resolving the issue) that, even where the words of the domestic law were incompatible with the Community law in question, they should be construed so as to comply with it. He said that national courts must strive to make domestic law conform to Community law however 'wide a departure from the *prima facie* meaning may be needed to achieve consistency'. However, he added that they should do so only while it appeared that Parliament wished to comply with EC law.

This approach was applied in *Pickstone v Freemans* (1988)[6] in the House of Lords, although not in the Court of Appeal. The Court of Appeal ruled that domestic legislation – the Equal Pay Amendment Regulations made under s2(2) of the European Communities Act – was inconsistent with Art 119 of European Community law. It then treated Art 119 as having more authority than the Amendment and made a ruling consistent with Art 119.

Pickstone v Freemans [1988] 2 All ER 803, 813–5

Mrs Pickstone and other warehouse operatives were paid less than male warehouse checkers, but one man was employed as an operative. The defendants therefore argued that her claim to equal pay was barred due to the wording of s1(2)(c) of the Equal Pay Act 1970 as amended: 'where a woman is employed on work which, not being work to which (a) or (b) applied is ... of equal value ...'. Paragraph (a) did apply because one man was employed doing the same work and therefore it could be argued that a like work claim arose but not an equal value one. The House of Lords considered that allowing this argument to succeed would mean that Parliament had failed once again to implement its obligations under Art 119; and it could not have intended such a failure. In such circumstances any interpretation should take into account the terms in which the 1983 amending regulations were presented to Parliament; in other words, a purposive approach should be adopted. Using this approach the defendants' argument could be rejected.

> **Lord Templeman:** Under Community law, a woman is entitled to equal pay for work of equal value to that of a man in the same employment. Under the ruling of the European Court in *EC Commission v UK* Case 61/81 [1982] ECR 2601, the Equal Pay Act 1970 as amended in 1975 was held to be defective because the Act did not entitle every woman to claim before a competent authority that her work had the same value as their work, but only allowed a claim by a woman who succeeded in persuading her employer to consent to a job evaluation scheme. The 1983 regulations were intended to give full effect to Community law and to the ruling of the European Court which directed the UK Government to introduce legislation entitling any woman to equal pay with any man for work or equal value if the difference in pay is due to the difference in sex and is therefore discriminatory. I am of the opinion that the 1983 regulations, on their true construction, achieve the required result of affording a remedy to any woman who is not in receipt of equal pay for work equal in value to the work of a man in the same employment.

---

5   2 AC 751.
6   3 WLR 265; 2 All ER 803; for comment see (1988) MLR 221; (1988) PL 483.

In *Murphy v Bord Telecom Eireann* Case 157/86 [1988] 1 CMLR 879, 29 women were employed as factory workers engaged in such tasks as dismantling, cleaning, oiling and reassembling telephones and other equipment; they claimed the right to be paid at the same rate as a specified male worker employed in the same factory as a stores labourer engaged in cleaning, collecting and delivering equipment and components and in lending general assistance as required. The European Court in its judgment (at p886, para 9) said that the principle of equal pay for men and women:

'... forbids workers of one sex engaged in work of equal value to that of workers of the opposite sex to be paid a lower wage than the latter on grounds of sex, it *a fortiori* prohibits such a difference in pay where the lower-paid category of workers is engaged in work of higher value.'

I cannot think that in Community law or in British law the result would be any different if, instead of there being 29 women working on telephone maintenance and one male stores labourer, there were 28 women and one man working on telephone maintenance and one male stores labourer.

The draft of the 1983 regulations was not subject to any process of amendment by Parliament. In these circumstances the explanations of the government and the criticisms voiced by members of Parliament in the debates which led to approval of the draft regulations provide some indications of the intentions of Parliament. The debate on the draft regulations in the House of Commons which led to their approval by resolution was initiated by the Under Secretary of State for Employment, who, in the reports of the House of Commons for 20 July 1983 (46 HC Official Report (6th series), col 479), said:

> The Equal Pay Act allows a woman to claim equal pay with a man ... if she is doing the same or broadly similar work, or if her job and his have been rated equal through job evaluation in effort, skill and decision. However, if a woman is doing different work from a comparable man, or if the jobs are not covered by a job evaluation study, the woman has at present no right to make a claim for equal pay. This is the gap, identified by the European Court, which we are closing.

Thus it is clear that the construction which I have placed on the regulations corresponds to the intentions of the Government in introducing the regulations. In the course of the debate in the House of Commons, and in the corresponding debate in the House of Lords, no one suggested that a claim for equal pay for equal work might be defeated under the regulations by an employer who proved that a man who was not the subject of the complaint was employed on the same or on similar work with the complainant. The minister took the view, and Parliament accepted the view, that paragraph (c) will only apply if paragraphs (a) and (b) are first held by the tribunal not to apply in respect of the work of the woman and the work of the man with whom she seeks parity of pay. This is also the only view consistent with Community law.

In *von Colson and Kamann v Land Nordrhein-Westfalen* Case 14/83 [1984] ECR 1891 at 1909 (para 28), 1910–1911 (operative part of the judgment (para 3)) the European Court advised that in dealing with national legislation designed to give effect to a directive:

3.It is for the national court to interpret and apply the legislation adopted for the implementation of the directive in conformity with the requirements of Community law, in so far as it is given discretion to do so under national law.

In *Duke v GEC Reliance Systems Ltd* [1988] 1 All ER 626, [1988] 2 WLR 359 this House declined to distort the construction of an Act of Parliament which was not drafted to give effect to a directive and which was not capable of complying with the directive as subsequently construed by the European Court. In the present case I can see no difficulty in construing the 1983 regulations in a way which gives effect to the declared intention of the Government of the UK responsible for drafting the regulations and is consistent with the objects of the EEC Treaty, the provisions of the equal pay directive and the rulings of the European Court. I would dismiss the appeal.

Notes

1   Thus the House of Lords avoided the controversial approach of finding that EC law would prevail over national law but by a less overtly contentious route achieved the same result. It adopted a purposive interpretation of the domestic legislation which was not in conflict with Art 119. This was done on the basis that Parliament must have intended to fulfil its EC obligations in passing the Amendment regulations once it had been compelled to do so by the European Court of Justice.

2   The House of Lords followed a similar approach to that taken in *Pickstone* in *Litster v Forth Dry Dock Engineering* (1989).

Litster v Forth Dry Dock Co Ltd (1989) 1 All ER 1134, 1152–3

Lord Oliver: The critical question, it seems to me, is whether, even allowing for the greater latitude in construction permissible in the case of legislation introduced to give effect to this country's Community obligations, it is possible to attribute to reg 8(1), when read in conjunction with reg 5, the same result as that attributed to Art 4 in the *Bork* case [1989] IRLR 41. Purely as a matter of language, it clearly is not. Regulation 8(1) does not follow literally the wording of Art 4(1).1t provides only that, if the reason for the dismissal of the employee is the transfer of the business, he has to be treated 'for the purposes of Part V of the 1978 Act' as unfairly dismissed so as to confer on him the remedies provided by ss69–79 of the Act (including, where it is considered appropriate, an order for reinstatement or re-engagement). If this provision fell to be construed by reference to the ordinary rules of construction applicable to a purely domestic statute and without reference to treaty obligations, it would, I think, be quite impermissible to regard it as having the same prohibitory effect as that attributed by the European Court to Art 4 of the Directive. But it has always to be borne in mind that the purpose of the Directive and of the regulations was, and is, to 'safeguard' the rights of employees on a transfer and that there is a mandatory obligation to provide remedies which are effective and not merely symbolic to which the regulations were intended to give effect. The remedies provided by the 1978 Act in the case of an insolvent transferor are largely illusory unless they can be exerted against the transferee as the directive contemplates, and I do not find it conceivable that, in framing regulations intending to give effect to the Directive, the Secretary of State could have envisaged that its purpose should be capable of being avoided by the transparent device to which resort was had in the instant case. *Pickstone v Freemans plc* (1988) 2 All ER 803, (1989) AC 66 has established that the greater flexibility available to the court in applying a purposive construction to legislation designed to give effect to the UK's treaty obligations to the Community enables the court, where necessary, to supply by implication words appropriate to comply with those obligations: see particularly the speech of Lord Templeman ((1988) 2 All ER 803 at 813–814, (1989) AC 66 at 120–121). Having regard to the manifest purpose of the regulations, I do not, for my part, feel inhibited from making such an implication in the instant case. The provision in reg 8(1) that a dismissal by reason of transfer is to be treated as an unfair dismissal, is merely a different way of saying that the transfer is not to 'constitute a ground for dismissal' as contemplated by Art 4 of the Directive and there is no good reason for denying to it the same effect as that attributed to that Article. In effect this involves reading reg 5(3) as if there were inserted after the words 'immediately before the transfer' the words 'or would have been so employed if he had not been unfairly dismissed in the circumstances described in reg 8(1)'. For my part, I would make such an implication which is entirely consistent with the general scheme of the regulations and which is necessary if they are effectively to fulfil the purpose for which they were made of giving effect to the provisions of the directive.

Notes

1   *Litster* was concerned with an indirectly effective Directive. Nevertheless, the approach of the House of Lords suggested that, where legislation had been introduced specifically to implement a Directive, the UK courts must interpret it so as to conform with the Directive, supplying the necessary words by implication, in order to achieve such conformity.

2   It appears from these rulings that primacy of even indirectly effective instruments was assured except in instances where no domestic legislation had been introduced to implement them or where the instrument in question would not bear the interpretation sought to be imposed on it.[7] These decisions provide authority for the proposition that plain words in a statute will be ignored if they would involve departure from the provisions of European Community law.

3   It might appear to follow from the findings in *Pickstone* and *Litster* that Parliament has succeeded in partially 'entrenching' s2(1) of the European Communities Act by means of s2(4) by imposing a requirement of form (express words) on future legislation designed to override Community law. However, the House of Lords in both *Litster* and *Pickstone* justified its disregard of statutory words by the finding that Parliament intended them to bear a meaning compatible with Community obligations.

The primacy of Community law

Dicta of Lord Denning in *Macarthys v Smith* (1981)[8] suggest more clearly that partial 'entrenchment' of s2(1) of the 1972 Act has occurred: ' we are entitled to look to the Treaty ... not only as an aid but as an overriding force. If ... our legislation ... is inconsistent with Community law ... then it is our bounden duty to give priority to Community law'. Further support for Lord Denning's view comes from the *Factortame* litigation which might also support the inference that words in a statute, although expressly requiring a court to do so, could not override Community obligations. *Secretary of State for Transport, ex p Factortame* made a very significant contribution to resolving the question of the primacy of EC law because the UK courts had to confront directly a conflict between EC law and domestic law.

---

7   See further, Part II, Chapter 2.
8   1 All ER 111; [1980] ECR 1275.

Secretary of State for Transport, ex p Factortame (1990) 2 AC 85

Under the Merchant Shipping (Registration of Fishing Vessels) Regulations 1988 made under the Merchant Shipping Act 1988, British fishing vessels were required to re-register on a new register from 1 March 1988. Vessels could qualify for entry on to the new register only if their owners or, in the case of companies, their shareholders, were British citizens or were domiciled in Britain. The applicants were unable to comply with these conditions and consequently could not qualify for entry. The applicants sought a ruling by way of judicial review that the legislation contravened provisions of the EC Treaty by depriving them of Community law rights. These included the prohibition of discrimination on grounds of nationality, the prohibition of restrictions on exports between Member States, the provision for the free movement of workers and the requirement that nationals of Member States are to be treated equally with respect to participation in the capital of companies established in the EC. A ruling on the substantive questions of Community law was requested from the European Court of Justice and pending that ruling, which could not be expected for another two years, the Divisional Court made an order by way of interim relief, setting aside the relevant part of the 1988 regulations and allowing the applicants to continue to operate their vessels as if they were British registered.

This order was set aside by the Court of Appeal. Bingham LJ said, however, that where the law of the Community is clear 'whether as a result of a ruling given on an Art 177 reference or as a result of previous jurisprudence or on a straightforward interpretation of Community instruments, the duty of the national court is to give effect to it in all circumstances ... To that extent a UK statute is not as inviolable as it once was'. In the instant case it had not yet been established that the statute was inconsistent with Community law and in those circumstances it was held that the court had no power to declare a statute void.

The applicants appealed to the House of Lords which upheld the ruling of the Court of Appeal and referred to the European Court of Justice for a preliminary ruling the question whether Community law required that a national court should grant the interim relief sought. Lord Bridge said that if it appeared after the European Court of Justice had ruled on the substantive issue that domestic law was incompatible with the Community provisions in question, Community law would prevail.

Lord Bridge: ... By virtue of s2(4) of the Act of 1972, Part II of the Act of 1988 is to be construed and take effect subject to directly enforceable Community rights and those rights are, by s2(1) of the Act of 1972, to be 'recognised and available in law, and ... enforced, allowed and followed accordingly;' ... This has precisely the same effect as if a section were incorporated in Part II of the Act of 1988 which in terms enacted that the provisions with respect to registration of British fishing vessels were to be without prejudice to the directly enforceable Community rights of nationals of any Member State of the EEC. Thus it is common ground that, in so far as the applicants succeed before the ECJ in obtaining a ruling in support of the Community rights which they claim, these rights will prevail over the restrictions imposed on registration of British fishing vessels by Part II of the Act 1988, and the Divisional Court will, in the final determination of the application for judicial review, be obliged to make appropriate declarations to give effect to these rights.

The European Commission then successfully sought a ruling in the European Court of Justice that the nationality requirement of s14 of the Merchant Shipping Act should be suspended (*Re nationality of fishermen: EC Commission v UK* (1989))[9] pending the delivery of the judgment in the action for a declaration. This decision was given effect in the UK by means of the Merchant Shipping Act 1988 (Amendment) Order 1989. The European Court of Justice then ruled on the question of interim relief relying on *Amministrazione delle Finanze dello Stato v Simmenthal SpA*.[10] Predictably, it found that a national court must set aside national legislative provisions if that were necessary to give interim relief in a case concerning Community rights (*Secretary of State for Transport, ex p Factortame Ltd* (1989)[10a]).

The House of Lords then considered the application for interim relief, and decided to grant it.

Factortame Ltd v Secretary of State (No 2) [1991] 1 AC 603

Lord Bridge of Harwich: My Lords, when this appeal first came before the House in 1989 (see *Factortame Ltd v Secretary of State for Transport* [1989] 2 All ER 692, [1990] 2 AC 85) your Lordships held that, as a matter of English law, the courts had no jurisdiction to grant interim relief in terms which would involve either overturning an English statute in advance of any decision by the Court of Justice of the European Communities that the statute infringed Community law or granting an injunction against the Crown. It then became necessary to seek a preliminary ruling from the Court of Justice as to whether Community law itself invested us with such jurisdiction.

In June 1990 we received the judgment of the Court of Justice replying to the questions we had posed and affirming that we had jurisdiction, in the circumstances postulated, to grant interim relief for the protection of directly enforceable rights under Community law, and that no limitation on our jurisdiction imposed by any rule of national law could stand as the sole obstacle to preclude the grant of such relief. In the light of this judgment we were able to conclude the hearing of the appeal in July and unanimously decided that relief should be granted in terms of the orders which the House then made, indicating that we would give our reasons for the decision later.

Some public comments on the decision of the Court of Justice, affirming the jurisdiction of the courts of Member States to override national legislation, if necessary, to enable interim relief to be granted in protection of rights under Community law, have suggested that this was a novel and dangerous invasion by a Community institution of the sovereignty of the UK Parliament. But such comments are based on a misconception. If the supremacy within the European Community of Community law over the national law of Member States was not always inherent in the EEC Treaty it was certainly well established in the jurisprudence of the Court of Justice long before the UK joined the Community. Thus, whatever limitation of its sovereignty Parliament accepted when it enacted the European Communities Act 1972 was entirely voluntary. Under the terms of the 1972 Act it has always been clear that it was the duty of a UK court, when delivering final judgment, to override any rule of national law found to be in conflict with any directly enforceable rule of Community law. Similarly, when decisions of the Court of Justice have exposed areas of UK statute law which

---

9   Case C–248/89R [1989] 3 CMLR 601; [1991] 3 CMLR 706.

10   [1978] ECR 629.

10a   3 CMLR 1.

failed to implement Council directives, Parliament has always loyally accepted the obligation to make appropriate and prompt amendments. Thus there is nothing in any way novel in according supremacy to rules of Community law in those areas to which they apply and to insist that, in the protection of rights under Community law, national courts must not be inhibited by rules of national law from granting interim relief in appropriate cases is no more than a logical recognition of that supremacy.

Lord Goff of Chieveley: The question which arose for consideration by your Lordships, following the ruling of the Court of Justice, concerned the appropriateness of an order for an interim injunction in a case such as the present, which is concerned with a challenge to the lawfulness of an Act of Parliament as being incompatible with European law. ...

The interim order of the President was made on an application to him by the European Commission. The Commission brought an action under Art 169 of the Treaty for a declaration that, by imposing the nationality requirements enshrined in ss13 and 14 of the 1988 Act, the UK had failed to fulfil its obligations under Arts 7, 52 and 221 of the Treaty. The Commission further applied under Art 186 of the Treaty and Art 83 of the Rules of Procedure for an order requiring the UK to suspend the application of the nationality requirements enshrined in s14(1)(a) and (c) of the Act, read in conjunction with subsections (2) and (7) of the section, as regards the nationals of other Member States and in respect of fishing vessels which, until 31 March 1989, were pursuing a fishing activity under the British flag and under a British fishing licence. Under Art 83(2) of the Rules of Procedure, interim measures such as those requested may not be ordered unless there are circumstances giving rise to urgency and factual and legal grounds establishing a *prima facie* case for the measures applied for.

The President granted the interim order asked for by the Commission ((1989) 3 CMLR 601 at 607–608) ... in agreement with the remainder of your Lordships, I concluded that the appeal should be allowed and interim relief granted in the terms of the order made.

Notes

1 In *Secretary of State for Transport, ex p Factortame Ltd (No 3)* (1991)[11] the European Court of Justice had to consider the substantive issue in this case. It ruled that, while at present competence to determine the conditions governing the nationality of ships was vested in the Member States, such competence must be exercised consistently with Community law. It then determined that Part II of the Merchant Shipping Act 1988 was discriminatory on the grounds of nationality contrary to Art 52 and therefore did not so conform. Thus the ECJ found that Art 52 had been breached due to the national and residence requirements laid down in the Act for registration of owners of fishing vessels. The ruling meant that Community law must be applied in preference to the Merchant Shipping Act 1988, which must be disapplied.[12]

---

11 Case 221/89 [1991] 3 CMLR 589; [1992] QB 680.

12 In further proceedings, claims were made by the applicants for loss suffered due to the breach of EC law by the UK. In *Secretary of State for Transport, ex p Factortame (No 4)* [1996] 2 WLR 506 the ECJ found that the *Francovich* principle of state liability would apply and would mean that reparation should be commensurate with the loss sustained; exemplary damages could be awarded against the state in claims founded on Community law if they could be awarded in similar claims founded on domestic law. See further Part II, Chapter 2, pp263–9.

2   Once the issue as to the question of interim relief was resolved in the House of Lords it appeared that the UK courts had come to accept that, where Community law is certain, it should be applied in preference to domestic law. If Community law is unclear, and applicants who wish to rely on it have a seriously arguable case, domestic law should be disapplied if that is necessary to give interim relief pending a ruling on the issue from the European Court.

3   After the *Factortame* litigation it may be said that the courts clearly have the power to refuse to obey an Act of Parliament if it conflicts with Community law, and Parliament is therefore effectively constrained in its freedom to legislate on any subject. If it does legislate inconsistently with Community law its legislation may be disapplied or an amendment may be forced upon it by the European Commission. If it wishes to avoid this restraint it will have to use express words demonstrating its intention. Since in practice it is highly improbable that such express words would be used, it appears to be impossible for Parliament to depart from the principle of the primacy of Community law unless it decides to withdraw from the Community.

4   In relation to the grant of interim relief against a Minister of the Crown Lord Bridge considered (i) that as a matter of domestic law injunctions could not be granted in judicial review proceedings against a Minister of the Crown, although he accepted (ii) (after the ruling of the ECJ on the matter) that there was an overriding principle of Community law requiring the grant of interim relief to a party whose claim to be entitled to directly effective rights under Community law was seriously arguable. In *M v Home Office* (1994),[13] Lord Woolf disagreed with his finding as regards point (i).

5   In contrast to *dicta* of Lord Denning in *Macarthys v Smith* (1979)[14] to the effect that a domestic court would give regard to express words in a statute requiring it to override Community law, Lord Bingham in *Factortame* did not enter a caveat that effect would have been given to express words used in the Merchant Shipping Act 1988 declaring that its provisions should prevail over those of Community law. He came close to suggesting that effect would not be given to such words in observing 'any rule of domestic law which prevented the court from giving effect to directly enforceable rights established in Community law would be bad'.

6   The impact of the *Factortame* decision on sovereignty is discussed by Szyszcak below. Her comments on the course of the *Factortame* litigation in the domestic courts indicate that the process of achieving compliance with Community law and accepting its primacy was a gradual one which was strongly resisted at a number of stages.[15]

---

13 1 AC 377. For the judgment see Part 1, Chapter 3, pp68–70.

14 (1979) 3 All ER 325.

15 For further discussion of the *Factortame* litigation see: C Turpin, *British Government and the Constitution: Text, Cases and Materials*, 3rd edn (1995), pp308–9; N Gravells (1989) PL 568; N Gravells (1990) PL 568; N Gravells (1991) PL 180; Barav (1989) 26 CML Rev 369; Churchill (1989) 14 EL Rev 470.

Erika Szyszczak, 'Sovereignty: Crisis, Compliance, Confusion, Complacency?' (1990) 15(6) *European Law Review* 480–2

Factortame concerned the compatibility of national legislation with the Common Fisheries Policy and the availability of immediate protection and enforcement of Community rights. Briefly, in order to prevent 'quota hopping', whereby the UK's fishing quotas were drained by ships registered in the UK but owned and operated by non-British companies, the UK introduced the Merchant Shipping Act 1988. This stipulated that, in order to register as British fishing vessels, ships had to be British owned and, in the case of ships owned by companies, 75% of shareholders had to be British citizens, resident and domiciled in the UK. As a result of this Act, 95 fishing vessels registered in the UK, but controlled by Spanish companies, were effectively banned from fishing in British waters. Facing economic ruin the Spanish companies applied to the High Court for judicial review of the measures contained in the Merchant Shipping Act 1988 and for a declaration that the measures relating to nationality and residence requirements should not be applied since they contravened Community law.

The High Court referred the issue of the compatibility of national law with Community law to the European Court [(1989) 2 CMLR 353; Case 221/89, OJ 1989 C211/10]. Following *Secretary of State for the Home Department, ex p Herbage* [1987] 1 QB 872 and *Licensing Authority established under Medicines Act 1968, ex p Smith and Kline (No 2)* [1989] WLR 378, it was accepted that, in proceedings for judicial review, interim relief was now available against the Crown (the Government). Relying upon the ruling of the European Court in *Simmenthal* [Case 106/77], Neill LJ held that:

> ... the High Court now has the duty to take account of, and to give effect to, European Community law and where there is a conflict, to prefer the Community law to national law.

The UK Government appealed against the order on the ground that the High Court had no power to suspend the application of an Act of Parliament or grant an injunction against the Crown.

The Court of Appeal unanimously quashed the order, rebuking the High Court in the process.[16] While the Master of the Rolls, Lord Donaldson, accepted the supremacy of Community law, he could find no authority in either Community law or English law allowing national courts to interfere, even on a temporary basis, with primary or secondary legislation.

The House of Lords therefore made a preliminary reference to the European Court asking, *inter alia*, whether or not Community law empowered or imposed an obligation on a national court to grant interim relief in the situation where a preliminary reference on a point of Community law had been made. The European Court ruled that, where the direct enforceability of the Community rights had been established, there was a duty upon the national courts to grant interim relief pending the final adjudication of the case. This obligation is of the very essence of Community law, and any national provision which impedes the effectiveness of the Community system of rights is incompatible with Community law. Although invited to, the European Court did not issue any guidelines as to when interim relief should be available. Thus the circumstances and the form in which interim relief is granted are left to the discretion of the national courts, subject to the ruling in *Amministrazione delle Finanze dello Stato v*

---

16   (1989) 2 CMLR 353.

SpA San Giorgio [Case 199/82 [1983] ECR 3595], that the conditions must not render the right to interim relief virtually impossible. It may be justifiable to subject the grant of interim relief against primary legislation to more stringent conditions than those applied to secondary legislation and administrative decisions. This may be a matter for the national court to assess alongside other issues such as whether damages may be an appropriate remedy.

Notes

1   The principle accepted by the House of Lords in *Factortame* was reiterated in *Secretary of State for Employment, ex p EOC* (1995).[17] Certain provisions of the Employment Protection (Consolidation) Act 1978 governed the right not to be unfairly dismissed, compensation for unfair dismissal and the right to statutory redundancy pay. These rights did not apply to workers who worked less than the specified number of hours a week. The Equal Opportunities Commission (EOC), a body whose remit is to curb sex discrimination, considered that since the majority of those working for less than the specified number of hours were women, the provisions operated to the disadvantage or women and were therefore discriminatory. The EOC accordingly wrote to the Secretary of State for Employment expressing this view and arguing that since the provisions in question were indirectly discriminatory they were in breach of EC law. The Secretary of State replied by letter that the conditions excluding part-timers from the rights in question were justifiable and therefore not indirectly discriminatory. The EOC applied for judicial review of the Secretary of State's refusal to accept that the UK was in breach of its obligations under EC law. The application was amended to bring in an individual, Mrs Day, who worked part time and had been made redundant by her employers but her claim was found to be a private law claim which could not be advanced against the Secretary of State who was not her employer and was not liable to meet the claim if it was successful. The Secretary of State argued that no decision or justiciable issue susceptible of judicial review existed. However, the House of Lords found that, although the letter itself was not a decision, the provisions themselves could be challenged in judicial review proceedings. Judicial review was found to be available for the purpose of securing a declaration that certain UK primary legislation was incompatible with EC law, following *Secretary of State for Transport, ex p Factortame* (1992).[18] Thus the EOC, but not an individual applicant, was entitled to bring judicial review proceedings in order to secure a declaration that UK law was incompatible with EC law. Declarations were made that the conditions set out in the provisions in question were indeed incompatible with EC law.

2   The final result of the *Factortame* litigation and of the *EOC* case seems to be an unequivocal acceptance of the primacy of Community law by the British courts and the consequent fettering of the legislative competence of the UK Parliament. These decisions represent a departure from the 'rule of construction' approach to s2(4) of the 1972 Act as exemplified in *Pickstone v*

---

17   1 AC 1.
18   QB 680.

Freemans and in *Garland v British Rail Engineering* (1983),[19] which arguably left sovereignty intact in that such an approach was applied only where it was clear that Parliament intended to comply with Community law. Statements made as to the nature of parliamentary sovereignty must now undergo some modification; for example it might now be said 'once an instrument is recognised as an Act of Parliament and is compatible with any enforceable Community law, no English court can refuse to obey it or question its validity' (a modification of a statement made by Sir Robert Megarry in *Manuel v Attorney-General* (1983)).[20] Nevertheless, these decisions are consistent with the probable intention of Parliament as expressed in s2(4) of the European Communities Act 1972; arguably *Factortame* merely brought about full acceptance of the implications of that provision by the judiciary.

3   The change in attitude of the UK judiciary over the last 20 years is very notable. Like the judiciary in the other Member States, the UK judiciary has gradually come to a full realisation of the need to achieve a uniform application of Community law throughout the Member States. However, this has taken some time as can be seen by comparing a case such as *H P Bulmer Ltd v J Bollinger SA* (1974)[21] with *Factortame*. The *Bulmer* case is in this sense similar to a German case: *Internationale Handelsgesellschaft GmbH* (1974).[22]

4   Below, Bradley reviews the impact of the Community legal order taking into account the decisions above relating to sovereignty.

AW Bradley, 'The Sovereignty of Parliament: In Perpetuity?', in Jowell and Oliver (eds) *The Changing Constitution*, 3rd edn (1994), pp91–4, 97–8

Parliamentary sovereignty in the European Union

It is evident that the Community legal order is inconsistent with the traditional doctrine of the sovereignty of Parliament. Thus, Dicey asserted that 'no person or body is recognised by the law of England as having a right to override or set aside the legislation of Parliament' [*Law of the Constitution*, p40]. In fact, UK law now recognises that Community organs have the right to make decisions and issue regulations, which may have the effect of overriding legislation by Parliament. The supremacy or primacy of Community law within the economic or social areas with which it deals cannot stand comfortably alongside a simple version of national legislative supremacy. While the problem takes a special form in the UK, other Member States have experienced comparable difficulties in adjusting their own systems of constitutional law to take account of the requirements of Community law. Yet the European Court of Justice has continued to emphasise that the application of Community law should not be obstructed or delayed by obstacles at national level.

---

19   2 AC 751.
20   Ch 87.
21   Ch 401.
22   2 CMLR 540.

When these provisions [ss2(1), (4) and 3 of the European Communities Act 1972] were debated in Parliament, it was widely agreed that they did not exclude the possibly that the UK Parliament might one day wish to repeal the Act and thus effectively prevent the continued operation of Community law within the UK. In this sense the ultimate sovereignty of Westminster was not affected, as ministers admitted, even though they refused to allow a statement to this effect to be included in the Act. But there was for many years uncertainty about a less extreme situation, should an Act passed after 1972 be found to contain a provision inconsistent with an established rule of Community law. In this situation, we have already seen that the European Court will insist that Community law must prevail. But should the British courts take up the same position (as s3 of the 1972 Act would indicate is their duty), or does the later Act of Parliament override the 1972 Act, including ss2 and 3, to the extent of requiring the conflict to be resolved from a British standpoint?

Since this duty of the UK courts to apply Community law [recognised in *Factortame*] derives from the European Communities Act 1972, it would appear that the Westminster Parliament could by subsequent legislation modify or abrogate that duty only if it expressed a direct intention to do so. That intention was not to be implied in the Merchant Shipping Act 1988 from the fact that its provisions were inconsistent with rights guaranteed by Community law. It would therefore be necessary for express words to be used in a future statute should the Westminster Parliament wish to exercise what might be called its ultimate sovereign right to require British courts to depart from their duty to protect rights which arise under Community law. And it must be uncertain where the duty of the British courts would lie unless that statute also manifested the plainest intention by Parliament to leave the European Union.

There will continue to be cases in which provisions of national law give way before the 'higher law' of the European Community [*Marshall v Southampton Health Authority (No 2)* [1993] 4 All ER 586] so long as the UK remains in membership. Thus the exercise by Parliament of its legislative sovereignty in 1972 has brought about a profound change in the operation of parliamentary sovereignty, one in which a significant area of legislative authority has passed into the control of an indeterminate and intangible political sovereign that can be identified only through the diffuse procedures of the European Union.

Note

See further on the question of the courts' reaction to a statutorily expressed intention of Parliament to override a Community provision: De Smith (1971) 34 MLR 597 at 614. John F McEldowney sums up the change in the doctrine of Parliamentary sovereignty which has occurred as follows.

John F McEldowney, *Public Law* (1994), pp30–3

The European dimension

Sovereignty and the EC

Dicey's analysis of parliamentary sovereignty faces a severe challenge, when the outline of the EC discussed above is considered. His formulation gave Parliament ultimate sovereignty with potentially unlimited power. Even Dicey accepted that, in exercising such powers, Parliament's democratic basis might mean limitations on how future powers were exercised. Nevertheless, Dicey might insist that the theoretical power of Parliament would hold sway. Certain difficulties arise with EC membership. Loughlin sees the challenge of EC membership as having more far reaching effects than the narrow legal issues of sovereignty [*Public Law and Political Theory* (1992) at p196]. Judicial developments notwithstanding, it could be argued that we still face major legal challenges. The courts may have adjusted their conceptual language but this cannot disguise the lack of an intellectual and institutional infrastructure. The UK's membership of the EC is, without a written constitution, dependant on ss2 and 3 of the European Communities Act 1972. Community law in the UK may be said to be derived from this Act. Section 2(4) permits EC law to be given priority to any UK legislation passed prior to 1972 ...

A close reading of s2(4) might suggest that, in those terms, Parliament in 1972 had given authority for priority to be given to EC law after 1972 and that, even where there is conflict with a UK statute, EC law must prevail. Dicey's traditional view is that parliamentary sovereignty does not leave Parliament free to bind its successors. Priority for EC law is not consistent with parliamentary sovereignty because entrenchment of EC law is impossible.

Craig suggests that two possibilities might be adopted by the courts to resolve the problem. One is to modify Dicey's doctrine and accept that EC law has priority as part of the UK's membership conditions. The second possibility is to adopt an interpretation that Parliament is presumed not to intend statutes to override EC law, and therefore it is assumed that statutes passed after 1972 are impliedly consistent with EC law.

Factortame is the clearest indication that EC membership is no longer compatible with Dicey's classical doctrine of Parliamentary sovereignty. The House of Lords has, in effect, abandoned Dicey's view in favour of a construction which indicates a willingness to apply EC law even where it may conflict with national law.

The *Factortame* case also makes clear the compatibility of EC law and international law or customary law. Britain had unsuccessfully relied on the Art 5 provisions of the Geneva Convention to make its case. Thus a Member State of the EC cannot rely upon its rights, even if granted under international treaty law, to justify non-compliance with the rules of the Community [Case C–246/89, *EC Commission v UK (Re Nationality of Fishermen)* [1989] ECR 3125; 1991] 3 CMLR 706].

The EC and future constitutional arrangements in the UK: some conclusions

The UK's membership of the EC applies a whole variety of different laws to the UK. Regulations bind all Member States and take effect without the need for further implementation. Directives are binding on Member States but leave the choice to national authorities as to the form and method. They are not directly applicable but in certain circumstances can be directly applied by the courts. Decisions made by the European Court are directly applicable and binding on those to whom it is addressed. This provides for the strengthening of EC policy over a wide variety of issues of national concern.

The development of Community institutions such as the Council, Commission and Parliament lead after 1992 to a single European market and gradually shifted more power to the European Parliament. There is the possibility of widening European membership to include eastern Europe and parts of the Soviet Union. Some favour adopting a federal states of Europe perspective with the necessary constitutional changes in both European and national institutions. The traditional doctrines of the UK's constitution which help explain our present constitutional arrangements do not necessarily help us to understand the future of our existing institutions.

Notes

1 McEldowney suggests that, even where express words were used in a statute demonstrating Parliament's intention to legislate in conflict with EC law, a UK court might not give them effect. This suggests that entrenchment of s2(1) of the 1972 Act has been brought about on the basis of a requirement of manner rather than form; if a UK statute is to override Community law, s2(4) of the European Communities Act must first be repealed.

2 The argument that the doctrine of express repeal has been unaffected by the primacy of Community law rests on the proposition that the judges, in disapplying statutory provisions, are simply carrying out Parliament's will as expressed in s2(4) of the 1972 Act. This notion becomes harder to sustain in the face of provisions which appear to be intended to infringe Community law, such as the nationality requirements under the 1988 Merchant Shipping Act. Nevertheless, in the face of such provisions, the judges appear to take the view that (i) Parliament in passing such provisions had in mind an interpretation of them which would render them compatible with Community law, and (ii) that Parliament would not have wished the provisions to override Community law once the ECJ had ruled that they were incompatible.

3 If express words were used in a statute, such as 'these provisions are to take effect notwithstanding Art 52 of the Treaty', Parliament would appear to be expressing its intention that such provisions should be applied, regardless of a finding of the ECJ, to the effect that they breach Art 52. In such an instance, judges would therefore be unable to hide behind the notion of fulfilling Parliament's will in disapplying the domestic provisions. If it is assumed that those provisions contained an implied term enacting that the requirements they laid down were to be without prejudice to directly enforceable Community rights, such a term would directly contradict the express notwithstanding clause. Since a term may only be implied into a statute where there is room to do so under its express wording, it would seem that the judges would have to allow the express words to prevail and therefore the requirements in question would override Community rights. Turpin considers that a UK court would be unlikely to refuse to apply a statute employing such express words.[23]

4 While Parliament retains the power to withdraw from the Union, it arguably still retains its ultimate sovereignty. It may be concluded that, where Community law conflicts with domestic law, the traditional doctrine of implied repeal will not be applied but, although the doctrine of Parliamentary sovereignty has been greatly affected, it is arguable that it would revive in its original form if the UK withdrew from the Community.

Questions

1 Has the doctrine of parliamentary sovereignty been fundamentally changed by membership of the Community?

2 How can the judges justify departing from the doctrine of implied repeal in

---

23 Turpin, *British Government and the Constitution* (1995), p310.

relation to domestic provisions which are incompatible with Community law? Could they use the same argument to justify departing from the doctrine of express repeal?

3   There has been a great deal of controversy as to the most effective but politically acceptable method of protecting a Bill of Rights from implied or even express repeal. We have found, above, that the judiciary has been prepared to suspend the doctrine of implied repeal in response to European Union law. Can we assume that such readiness would also be evident in relation to protection of a Bill of Rights?

4   Does the judicial treatment of the European Communities Act 1972 discussed above represent:

(a)   a restriction as to the 'manner and form' of enactments bearing on European Union law; or

(b)   a restriction as to the substance of such enactments?

PART II

EUROPEAN LAW
AND INFLUENCE

CHAPTER 1

THE EUROPEAN UNION: INSTITUTIONS AND LEGAL ORDER

INTRODUCTION[1]

This Chapter considers the constitutional framework of the European Union and European Community, the notion of the European constitution and the possible future of European legal integration. It goes on to examine the changing role of the main Community institutions and their relationships with each other. It ends by considering the role of the principle of subsidiarity.

The European Coal and Steel Community was established by the Treaty of Paris in 1951, which was signed by Belgium, France, Germany, Italy, Luxembourg and the Netherlands with the objective of creating a single market in coal and steel. These six states decided to widen their economic co-operation by extending the notion of the single market beyond coal and steel. To this end they created two new communities, the European Economic Community and the European Atomic Energy Community by two Treaties of Rome signed on 25 March 1957.

The UK became a member of the European Communities in 1973 by signing the Treaty of Rome. At present there are three communities, of which the most significant is the European Community (formerly the European Economic Community). The others are the European Atomic Energy Community and the European Coal and Steel Community. The communities became known as the European Union under the Treaty of European Union signed at Maastricht. The Treaty of Rome, together with the Single European Act 1987 and the Treaty of European Union, creates the constitutional framework of the Union.

The Treaty on European Union was signed at Maastricht on 7 February 1992. However, due to delays in the ratification of the Treaty by some of the Member States, including the UK, the European Union established by the Treaty only came into existence on 1 November 1993. The Treaty was adopted into the UK by the European Communities (Amendment) Act 1993. The Treaty of European Union established the European Union (EU) without displacing the three existing communities, of which, as noted above, the most important is the European Community with its own founding Treaty, amended by the Single European Act 1986, a Treaty signed by all the Member States. The EU is founded on the three communities and has been said to provide an 'umbrella' for them. The European Union has also been compared to a temple supported by three pillars. The main pillar is made up of the three Communities each of which has its own founding Treaty, as amended. The other pillars are the Common Foreign and Security Policy (CFSP) and Co-operation in Justice and Home Affairs (CJHA).

---

1   General reading, see: J Steiner, *EC Law*, 4th edn (1994); N Brown and F Jacobs, *The Court of Justice of the European Communities*, 4th edn (1994); TC Hartley, *The Foundations of European Community Law*, 3rd edn (1994); D Lasok and J Bridge, *Law and Institutions of the European Union*, 6th edn (1994); S Weatherill and P Beaumont, *EC Law* (1993); S Weatherill, *Cases and Materials on EC Law* (1994); C Turpin, *British Government and the Constitution: Text, Cases and Materials*, 3rd edn (1995), pp264–94; H Barnett, *Constitutional and Administrative Law* (1995).

An indication of the long and complex political process which occurred before ratification of the Maastricht Treaty took place in the UK is given below.

Richard Rawlings, 'Legal Politics: The United Kingdom and Ratification of the Treaty on European Union (Part 1)' (1994) *Public Law* 254, 261

In August 1993 the UK became the last but one Member State of the Community to ratify the Treaty on European Union [the Treaty eventually came into force in November 1993, following the failure of the legal challenge before the German Federal Constitutional Court in *Brunner v The European Union Treaty* [1994] 69 CMLR 57]. Famously, the act of ratification followed on a parliamentary struggle more fierce and protracted than any since the Conservatives returned to office in 1979. ...

The peculiar *shape* assumed by the conflict was in large measure dictated by the choice of strategy of Her Majesty's Opposition, and in particular the refusal of the Shadow Cabinet to go against the principle of the legislation. We find a policy of abstaining on second and third readings; the Opposition's favoured forum for dispute was the committee stage of the Bill. On the one hand, pressure could be put upon the Government's legislative programme by reason of the peculiar opportunities for trench warfare offered by a committee of the whole house on a Bill of constitutional importance. On the other hand, the committee provided the Opposition with the opportunity to particularise the dispute in terms of the opt-out. The conflict is in this sense more bounded, which in party political terms clearly helped to present the united face of Opposition [see Baker, Gamble and Ludlum, (1994) 47 *Parliamentary Affairs* 37, pp51–52].

The tactical problem confronted the Opposition with circumventing the Parliamentary majorities in favour of both the opt-out and the Treaty. In the state of the parties, the Government could realistically only be defeated with the aid of right-wing Conservative rebels most antagonistic to Community social policy. The Opposition strategy aimed to present ministers with the limited choice of no opt-out or no Treaty. The enticement to a Conservative rebellion lay in the prospect that ministers, unable to ratify the Treaty, would refuse to renegotiate. But the Opposition strategy was clearly premised on irresistible pressure on the Government from other Member States and pro-European Conservative MPs not to wreck the Treaty.

Note

Eventually, by incorporating the resolution on the protocol on social policy in a vote of confidence, the Government managed to coerce the Conservative rebel MPs into voting for the European Communities Amendment Bill.

THE TREATY OF ROME AND THE TREATY ON EUROPEAN UNION: THE CONSTITUTIONAL FRAMEWORK OF THE UNION AND THE EC

Extracts from the Treaty on European Union and the Treaty of Rome as amended are set out below. These Treaties set up the framework of the Union and the European Community and set out their objectives.[2] Words in square brackets were added to the European Community Treaty, the Treaty of Rome,

---

2   For discussion see Hartley (1993) ICLQ 213; Nugent (1993) JCMS 311.

by the Treaty on European Union (TEU); words in other brackets were added by the Single European Act 1986 (SEA), and in certain instances are shown below in order to indicate the changes that have been made to the original Treaty.

The Treaty of Rome (as amended)

Part one. Principles

Article 1. By this Treaty, the High Contracting Parties establish among themselves a European {Economic} Community.

Article 2. The Community shall have as its task, by establishing a common market and [an economic and monetary union and by implementing the common policies or activities referred to in Articles 3 and 3a] {progressively approximating the economic policies of the Member States}, to promote throughout the Community a harmonious [and balanced] development of economic activities, [sustainable and non-inflationary growth respecting the environment, a high degree of convergence of economic performance, a high level of employment and of social protection, the raising of the standard of living and quality of life, and economic and social cohesion and solidarity among Member States] {a continuous and balanced expansion, an increase in stability, an accelerated raising of the standard of living and closer relations between the States belonging to it.}

Article 3. For the purposes set out in Article 2, the activities of the Community shall include, as provided by this Treaty and in accordance with the timetable set out therein:

(a) the elimination as between Member States, of customs duties and quantitative restrictions on the import and export of goods, and of all other measures having equivalent effect;

(b) [a common commercial policy;] {the establishment of a common customs tariff and of a common commercial policy towards third countries;}

(c) [an internal market characterised by] the abolition, as between Member States, of obstacles to the free movement of [goods], persons, services and capital;

[(d) Measures concerning the entry and movement of persons in the internal market as provided for in Article 100c;]

[(e)] {(d) the adoption of} a common policy in the sphere of agriculture [and fisheries;]

[(f)] {(e) the adoption of} a common policy in the sphere of transport;

[(g)]{(f) the institution of} a system ensuring that competition in the common market is not distorted;

{(g) the application of procedures by which the economic policies of Member States can be co-ordinated and disequilibria in their balances of payments remedied;}

(h) the approximation of the laws of the Member States to the extent required for the {proper} functioning of the common market;

(i) [a policy in the social sphere comprising] {the creation of} a European Social Fund {in order to improve employment opportunities for workers and to contribute to the raising of their standard of living;}

[(j) the strengthening of economic and social cohesion;] {the establishment of a European Investment Bank to facilitate the economic expansion of the Community by opening up fresh resources;]}

[(k) a policy in the sphere of the environment;] {the association of the overseas countries and territories in order to increase trade and to promote jointly economic and social development.}

[(l) the strengthening of the competitiveness of Community industry;

(m) the promotion of research and technological development;

(n) encouragement for the establishment and development of trans-European networks;

(o) a contribution to the attainment of a high level of health protection; a contribution to education and training of quality and to the flowering of the cultures of the Member States; a policy in the sphere of development cooperation; the association of the overseas countries and territories in order to increase trade and promote jointly economic and social development;

(s) a contribution to the strengthening of consumer protection;

(t) measures in the spheres of energy, civil protection and tourism.]

[Article 3a 1. For the purposes set out in Article 2, the activities of the Member States and the Community shall include, as provided in this Treaty and in accordance with the timetable set out therein, the adoption of an economic policy which is based on the close coordination of Member States' economic policies, on the internal market and on the definition of common objectives, and conducted in accordance with the principle of an open market economy with free competition.

2. Concurrently with the foregoing, and as provided in this Treaty and in accordance with the timetable and the procedures set out therein, these activities shall include the irrevocable fixing of exchange rates leading to the introduction of a single currency, the ecu, and the definition and conduct of a single monetary policy and exchange rate policy the primary objective of both of which shall be to maintain price stability and, without prejudice to this objective, to support the general economic policies in the Community, in accordance with the principle of an open market economy with free competition.

3. These activities of the Member States and the Community shall entail compliance with the following guiding principles: stable prices, sound public finances and monetary conditions and a sustainable balance of payments.]

[Article 3b. The Community shall act within the limits of the powers conferred upon it by this Treaty and of the objectives assigned to it therein.

In areas which do not fall within its exclusive competence, the Community shall take action, in accordance with the principle of subsidiarity, only if and in so far as the objectives of the proposed action cannot be sufficiently achieved by the Member States and can therefore, by reason of the scale or effects of the proposed action, be better achieved by the Community.

Any action by the Community shall not go beyond what is necessary to achieve the objectives of this Treaty.]

Article 4 1. The tasks entrusted to the Community shall be carried out by the following institutions:

- an Assembly,
- a Council,
- a Commission,
- a Court of Justice.
- a Court of Auditors]

Each institution shall act within the limits of the powers conferred upon it by this Treaty.

2. The Council and the Commission shall be assisted by an Economic and Social Committee [and a Committee of the Regions] acting in an advisory capacity.

{3. The audit shall be carried out by a Court of Auditors acting within the limits of the powers conferred upon it by this Treaty.}

[Article 4a. A European System of Central Banks (hereinafter referred to as 'ESCB') and a European Central Bank (hereinafter referred to as 'ECB') shall be established in accordance with the procedures laid down in this Treaty; they shall act within the limits of the powers conferred upon them by this Treaty and by the Statute of the ESCB and of the ECB (hereinafter referred to as 'Statute of the ESCB') annexed thereto.]

[Article 4b. A European Investment Bank is hereby established, which shall act within the limits of the powers conferred upon it by this Treaty and the Statute annexed thereto.]

Article 5. Member States shall take all appropriate measures, whether general or particular, to ensure fulfilment of the obligations arising out of this Treaty or resulting from action taken by the institutions of the Community. They shall facilitate the achievement of the Community's tasks.

They shall abstain from any measure which could jeopardise the attainment of the objectives of this Treaty.

{Article 6 1. Member States shall, in close co-operation with the institutions of the Community, co-ordinate their respective economic policies to the extent necessary to attain the objectives of this Treaty.

2. The institutions of the Community shall take care not to prejudice the internal and external financial stability of the Member States.}

Article [6] {7} Within the scope of application of this Treaty, and without prejudice to any special provisions contained therein, any discrimination on the grounds of nationality shall be prohibited.

[The Council acting in accordance with the procedure referred to in Article 189c] {on a proposal from the Commission and in co-operation with the European Parliament} may adopt {by a qualified majority} rules designed to prohibit such discrimination.

Article [7] {8} 1. The common market shall be progressively established during a transitional period of 12 years.

[Part two. Citizenship of the Union]

[Article 8 1. Citizenship of the Union is hereby established.

Every person holding the nationality of a Member State shall be a citizen of the Union.

2. Citizens of the Union shall enjoy the rights conferred by this Treaty and shall be subject to the duties imposed thereby.]

[Article 8a 1. Every citizen of the Union shall have the right to move and reside freely within the territory of the Member States. subject to the limitations and conditions laid down in this Treaty and by the measures adopted to give it effect.

2. The Council may adopt provisions with a view to facilitating the exercise of the rights referred to in paragraph 1; save as otherwise provided in this Treaty the Council shall act unanimously on a proposal from the Commission and after obtaining the assent of the European Parliament.]

[Article 8b. 1 Every citizen of the Union residing in a Member State of which he is not a national shall have the right to vote and to stand as a candidate at municipal elections in the Member State in which he resides, under the same conditions as nationals of that State. This right shall be exercised subject to detailed arrangements to be adopted before 31 December 1994 by the Council, acting unanimously on a proposal from the Commission and after consulting the European Parliament; these arrangements may provide for derogations where warranted by problems specific to a Member State.

2. Without prejudice to Article 138(3) and to the provisions adopted for its implementation, every citizen of the Union residing in a Member State of which he is not a national shall have the right to vote and to stand as a candidate in elections to the European Parliament in the Member State in which he resides, under the same conditions as nationals of that State. This right shall be exercised subject to detailed arrangements to be adopted before 31 December 1993 by the Council, acting unanimously on a proposal from the Commission and after consulting the European Parliament; these arrangements may provide for derogations where warranted by problems specific to a Member State.]

[Article 8c. Every citizen of the Union shall, in the territory of a third country in which the Member State of which he is a national is not represented, be entitled to protection by the diplomatic or consular authorities of any Member State, on the same conditions as the nationals of that State. Before 31 December 1993, Member States shall establish the necessary rules among themselves and start the international negotiations required to secure this protection.]

[Article 8d. Every citizen of the Union shall have the right to petition the European Parliament in accordance with Article 138d.

Every citizen of the Union may apply to the Ombudsman established in accordance with Article 138e.]

[Article 8e. The Commission shall report to the European Parliament, to the Council and to the Economic and Social Committee before 31 December 1993 and then every three years on the application of the provisions of this Part. This report shall take account of the development of the Union. ...

{*Part three. Policy of the Community*}

Chapter 3. Approximation of laws]

Article 100. The Council shall, acting unanimously on a proposal from the Commission [and after consulting the European Parliament and the Economic and Social Committee], issue directives for the approximation of such laws, regulations or administrative provisions of the Member States as directly affect the establishment or functioning of the common market.

{The Assembly and the Economic and Social Committee shall be consulted in the case of directives whose implementation would, in one or more Member States, involve the amendment of legislation.

[For the 1985 Products Liability Directive, see below, p583.]

Article 100a 1. By way of derogation from Article 100 and save where otherwise provided in this Treaty, the following provisions shall apply for the achievement of the objectives set out in Article [7a] {8a}. The Council shall. acting [in accordance with the procedure referred to in Article 189b] {by a qualified majority on a proposal from the Commission in co-operation with the European Parliament} and after consulting the Economic and Social

Committee, adopt the measures for the approximation of the provisions laid down by law, regulation or administrative action in Member States which have as their object the establishing and functioning of the internal market.

2. Paragraph 1 shall not apply to fiscal provisions, to those relating to the free movement of persons nor to those relating to the rights and interests of employed persons.

    The Commission, in its proposals envisaged in paragraph 1 concerning health, safety, environmental protection and consumer protection, will take as a base a high level of protection.

4. If, after the adoption of a harmonisation measure by the Council acting by a qualified majority, a Member State deems it necessary to apply national provisions on grounds of major needs referred to in Article 36, or relating to protection of the environment or the working environment, it shall notify the Commission of these provisions.

    The Commission shall confirm the provisions involved after having verified that they are not a means of arbitrary discrimination or a disguised restriction on trade between Member States.

[Article 100c 1. The Council, acting unanimously on a proposal from the Commission and after consulting the European Parliament, shall determine the third countries whose nationals must be in possession of a visa when crossing the external borders of the Member States.

2. However, in the event of an emergency situation in a third country posing a threat of a sudden inflow of nationals from that country into the Community, the Council, acting by a qualified majority on a recommendation from the Commission, may introduce, for a period not exceeding six months, a visa requirement for nationals from the country in question. The visa requirement established under this paragraph may be extended in accordance with the procedure referred to in paragraph 1.

3. From 1 January 1996, the Council shall act by a qualified majority on the decisions referred to in paragraph 1. The Council shall, before that date, acting by a qualified majority on a proposal from the Commission and after consulting the European Parliament, adopt measures relating to a uniform format for visas.]

Part five. Institutions of the Community

Title 1. Provisions governing the institutions

Chapter 1. The institutions

Section 1. The [European Parliament] {Assembly}

Article 137. The [European Parliament] {Assembly}, which shall consist of representatives of the peoples of the States brought together in the Community, shall exercise the {advisory and supervisory} powers {which are} conferred upon it by this Treaty.

Article 138. [NB Article 138(1) and (2) lapsed on 17 July 1979 in accordance with the Council Decision and Act of 20 September 1976 on Direct Elections. Articles 1 and 2 as amended are as follows.]

Council Decision and Act of 20 September 1976 on Direct Elections

Article 1. The representatives in the Assembly of the peoples of the State brought together in the Community shall be elected by direct universal suffrage.

Article 2. The number of representatives elected in each Member State shall be as follows:

Belgium	25
Denmark	16
Germany	99
Greece	25
Spain	64
France	87
Ireland	15
Italy	87
Luxembourg	6
The Netherlands	31
Portugal	25
United Kingdom	87

[Article 138a. Political parties at European level are important as a factor for integration within the Union. They contribute to forming a European awareness and to expressing the political will of the citizens of the Union.]

[Article 138b. In so far as provided in this Treaty, the European Parliament shall participate in the process leading up to the adoption of Community acts by exercising its powers under the procedures laid down in Articles 189b and 189C and by giving its assent or delivering advisory opinions.

The European Parliament may, acting by a majority of its members, request the Commission to submit any appropriate proposal on matters on which it considers that a Community act is required for the purpose of implementing this Treaty.]

[Article 138c. In the course of its duties, the European Parliament may, at the request of a quarter of its members, set up a temporary Committee of Inquiry to investigate, without prejudice to the powers conferred by this Treaty on other institutions or bodies, alleged contraventions or maladministration by the implementation of Community law, except where the alleged facts are being examined before a court and while the case is still subject to legal proceedings.

The temporary Committee of Inquiry shall cease to exist on the submission of its report.

The detailed provisions governing the exercise of the right of inquiry shall be determined by common accord of the European Parliament, the Council and the Commission.]

[Article 138d. Any citizen of the Union, and any natural or legal person residing or having its registered office in a Member State, shall have the right to address, individually or in association with other citizens or persons, a petition to the European Parliament on a matter which comes within the Community's fields of activity and which affects him, her or it directly.]

[Article 138e. The European Parliament shall appoint an Ombudsman empowered to receive complaints from any citizen of the Union or any natural or legal person residing or having its registered office in a Member State concerning instances of maladministration in the activities of the Community institutions or bodies, with the exception of the Court of Justice and the Court of First Instance acting in their judicial role.

In accordance with his duties, the Ombudsman shall conduct inquiries for which he finds grounds, either on his own initiative or on the basis of complaints submitted to him direct or through a member of the European Parliament, except where the alleged facts are or have been the subject of legal proceedings. Where the Ombudsman establishes an instance of maladministration, he shall refer the matter to the institution concerned, which shall have a period of three months in which to inform him of its views. The Ombudsman shall then forward a report to the European Parliament and the institution concerned. The person lodging the complaint shall be informed of the outcome of such inquiries.

The Ombudsman shall submit an annual report to the European Parliament on the outcome of his inquiries.

Article 139. The Assembly shall hold an annual session. It shall meet, without requiring to be convened, on the second Tuesday in March.

The Assembly may meet in extraordinary session at the request of a majority of its members or at the request of the Council or of the commission.

Article 140. The Assembly shall elect its President and its officers from among its members.

Members of the Commission may attend all meetings and shall, at their request, be held on behalf of the Commission.

The Commission shall reply orally or in writing to questions put to it by the Assembly or by its members.

The Council shall be heard by the Assembly in accordance with the conditions laid down by the Council in its rules of procedure.

Article 141. Save as otherwise provided in this Treaty, the Assembly shall act by an absolute majority of the votes cast.

The rules of procedure shall determine the quorum.

Article 142. The Assembly shall adopt its rules of procedure, acting by a majority of its members.

The proceedings of the Assembly shall be published in the manner laid down in its rules of procedure.

Article 143. The Assembly shall discuss in open session the annual general report submitted to it by the Commission.

Article 144. If a motion of censure on the activities of the Commission is tabled before it, the Assembly shall not vote thereon until at least three days after the motion has been tabled and only by open vote.

If the motion of censure is carried by a two-thirds majority of the votes cast, representing a majority of the members of the Assembly, the members of the Commission shall resign as a body, they shall continue to deal with current business until they are replaced in accordance with Article 158. [In this case, the term of office of the members of the Commission appointed to replace them shall expire on the date on which the term of office of the members of the Commission obliged to resign as a body would have expired.]

Section 2. The Council

Article 145. To ensure that the objectives set out in this Treaty are attained, the Council shall, in accordance with the provisions of this Treaty:

- ensure co-ordination of the general economic policies of the Member States;
- have power to take decisions.
- confer on the Commission, in the acts which the Council adopts, powers for the implementation of the rules which the Council lays down. The Council may impose certain requirements in respect of the exercise of these powers. The Council may also reserve the right, in specific cases,

to exercise directly implementing powers itself. The procedures referred to above must be consonant with principles and rules to be laid down in advance by the Council, acting unanimously on a proposal from the Commission and after obtaining the opinion of the European Parliament.

[Article 146. The Council shall consist of a representative of each Member State at ministerial level, authorised to commit the government of that Member State.

The office of President shall be held in turn by each Member State in the Council for a term of six months, in the following order of Member States:

- for a first cycle of six years: Belgium, Denmark, Germany, Greece; Spain, France, Ireland, Italy, Luxembourg, Netherlands, Portugal, United Kingdom;

- for the following cycle of six years: Denmark, Belgium, Greece, Germany, France, Spain, Italy, Ireland, Netherlands, Luxembourg, United Kingdom, Portugal.]

[Article 147. The Council shall meet when convened by its President on his own initiative or at the request of one of its members or of the Commission.]

Article 148. Save as otherwise provided in this Treaty, the Council shall act by a majority of its members.

2. Where the Council is required to act by a qualified majority, the votes of its members shall be weighted as follows:

Belgium	5
Denmark	3
Germany	10
Greece	5
Spain	8
France	10
Ireland	3
Italy	10
Luxembourg	2
The Netherlands	5
Austria	4
Portugal	5
Finland	3
Sweden	4
United Kingdom	10

For their adoption, acts of the Council shall require at least:

54 votes in favour where this Treaty requires them to be adopted on a proposal from the commission.

54 votes in favour, cast by at least eight members, in other cases.

3. Abstentions by members present in person or represented shall not prevent the adoption by the Council of acts which require unanimity.

{Article 149. 1. Where, in pursuance of this Treaty, the Council acts on a proposal from the Commission, unanimity shall be required for an act constituting an amendment to that proposal.

2. Where, in pursuance of this Treaty, the Council acts in co-operation with the European Parliament, the following procedure shall apply:

(a) The Council, acting by a qualified majority under the conditions of paragraph 1, on a proposal from the Commission and after obtaining the opinion of the European Parliament, shall adopt a common position .

(b) The Council's common position shall be communicated to the European Parliament. The Council and the Commission shall inform the European Parliament fully of the reasons which led the Council to adopt its common position and also of the Commission's position.

If, within three months of such communication, the European Parliament approves this common position or has not taken a decision within that period, the Council shall definitively adopt the act in question in accordance with the common position.

(c) The European Parliament may within the period of three months referred to in point (b), by an absolute majority of its component members, propose amendments to the Council's common position. The European Parliament may also, by the same majority, reject the Council's common position. The result of the proceedings shall be transmitted to the Council and the Commission.

If the European Parliament has rejected the Council's common position, unanimity shall be required for the Council to act on a second reading.

(d) The Commission shall, within a period of one month, re-examine the proposal on the basis of which the Council adopted its common position, by taking into account the amendments proposed by the European Parliament.

The Commission shall forward to the Council, at the same time as its re-examined proposal, the amendments of the European Parliament which it has not accepted, and shall express its opinion on them. The Council may adopt these amendments unanimously.

(e) The Council, acting by a qualified majority, shall adopt the proposal as re-examined by the Commission.

Unanimity shall be required for the Council to amend the proposal as re-examined by the Commission.

(f) In the cases referred to in points (c), (d) and (e), the Council shall be required to act within a period of three months. If no decision is taken within this period, the Commission proposal shall be deemed not to have been adopted. ...}

Article 152. The Council may request the Commission to undertake any studies which the Council considers desirable for the attainment of the common objectives. and to submit to it any appropriate proposals.

Article 153. The Council shall, after receiving an opinion from the Commission, determine the rules governing the committees provided for in this Treaty.

Section 3. The Commission

Article 155. In order to ensure the proper functioning and development of the common market, the Commission shall:

- ensure that the provisions of this Treaty and the measures taken by the institutions pursuant thereto are applied;

- formulate recommendations or deliver opinions on matters dealt with in this Treaty if it expressly so provides or if the Commission considers it necessary;

- have its power of decision and participate in the shaping of measures taken by the Council and by the Assembly in the manner provided for in this Treaty;

- exercise the powers conferred on it by the Council for the implementation of the rules laid down by the latter.

[Article 156. The Commission shall publish annually, not later than one month before the opening of the session of the European Parliament, a general report on the activities of the Community.]

[Article 157. 1. The Commission shall consist of 17 members, who shall be chosen on the grounds of their general competence and whose independence is beyond doubt.

The number of members of the Commission may be altered by the Council, acting unanimously.

Only nationals of Member States may be members of the Commission.

The Commission must include at least one national of each of the Member States, but may not include more than two members having the nationality of the same State.

2.   The members of the Commission shall, in the general interest of the Community, be completely independent in the performance of their duties.

[Article 158 1. The members of the Commission shall be appointed, in accordance with the procedure referred to in paragraph 2, for a period of five years, subject, if need be, to Article 144.

Their term of office shall be renewable.

2.   The governments of the Member States shall nominate by common accord, after consulting the European Parliament, the person they intend to appoint as President of the Commission.

The governments of the Member States shall, in consultation with the nominee for President, nominate the other persons whom they intend to appoint as members of the Commission.

The President and the other members of the Commission thus nominated shall be subject as a body to a vote of approval by the European Parliament. After approval by the European Parliament, the President and the other members of the Commission shall be appointed by common accord of the governments of the Member States.

[Article 161. The Commission may appoint a Vice-President or two Vice-Presidents from among its members.]

[Article 162. 1. The Council and the Commission shall consult each other and shall settle by common accord their methods of cooperation.

2.   The Commission shall adopt its rules of procedure so as to ensure that both it and its departments operate in accordance with the provisions of this Treaty. It shall ensure that these rules are published.]

[Article 163. The Commission shall act by a majority of the number of members provided for in Article 157.

Section 4. The Court of Justice

Article 164. The Court of Justice shall ensure that in the interpretation and application of this Treaty the law is observed.

Article 165. The Court of Justice shall consist of 13 Judges.

The Court of Justice shall sit in plenary session. It may, however, form chambers, each consisting of three or five Judges, either to undertake certain preparatory inquiries or to adjudicate on particular categories of cases in accordance with rules laid down for these purposes.

[The Court of Justice shall sit in plenary session when a Member State or a

Community institution that is a party to the proceedings so requests. [{Whenever the Court of Justice hears cases brought before it by a Member State or by one of the institutions of the Community or, to the extent that the chambers of the Court do not have the requisite jurisdiction under the Rules of Procedure, has to give preliminary rulings on questions submitted to it pursuant to Article 177, it shall sit in plenary session.}

Article 166. The Court of Justice shall be assisted by six Advocates-General.

It shall be the duty of the Advocate-General, acting with complete impartiality and independence, to make, in open court, reasoned submissions on cases brought before the Court of Justice, in order to assist the Court in the performance of the task assigned to it in Article 164.

Should the Court of Justice so request, the Council may, acting unanimously, increase the number of Advocates-General and make the necessary adjustments to the third paragraph of Article 167.

Article 167. The Judges and Advocates-General shall be chosen from persons whose independence is beyond doubt and who possess the qualifications required for appointment to the highest judicial offices in their respective countries or who are juriconsults of recognised competence; they shall be appointed by common accord of the Governments of the Member States for a term of six years.

[Article 168a. 1. A Court of First Instance shall be attached to the Court of Justice with jurisdiction to hear and determine at first instance, subject to a right of appeal to the Court of Justice on points of law only and in accordance with the conditions laid down by the Statute, certain classes of action or proceeding defined in accordance with the conditions laid down in paragraph 2. The Court of First Instance shall not be competent to hear and determine questions referred for a preliminary ruling under Article 177.

2. At the request of the Court of Justice and after consulting the European Parliament and the Commission, the Council, acting unanimously, shall determine the classes of action or proceeding referred to in paragraph I and the composition of the Court of First Instance and shall adopt the necessary adjustments and additional provisions to the Statute of the Court of Justice. Unless the Council decides otherwise, the provisions of this Treaty relating to the Court of Justice, in particular the provisions of the Protocol on the Statute of the Court of Justice, shall apply to the Court of First Instance.

4. The Court of First Instance shall establish its rules of procedure in agreement with the Court of Justice. Those rules shall require the unanimous approval of the Council.]

{Article 168a. At the request of the Court of Justice and after consulting the Commission and the European Parliament, the Council may, acting unanimously, attach to the Court of Justice a court with jurisdiction to hear and determine at first instance, subject to a right of appeal to the Court of Justice on points of law only and in accordance with the conditions laid down by the Statute, certain classes of action or proceeding brought by natural or legal persons. That court shall not be competent to heal and determine actions brought by Member States or by Community Institutions or questions referred for a preliminary ruling under Article 177. ...

Article 169. If the Commission considers that a Member State has failed to fulfil an obligation under this Treaty, it shall deliver a reasoned opinion on the matter after giving the State concerned the opportunity to submit its observations.

If the State concerned does not comply with the opinion within the period laid down by the Commission the latter may bring the matter before the Court of Justice.

Article 170. A Member State which considers that another Member State has failed to fulfil an obligation under this Treaty may bring the matter before the Court of Justice.

Before a Member State brings an action against another Member State for an alleged infringement of an obligation under this Treaty, it shall bring the matter before the Commission.

The Commission shall deliver a reasoned opinion after each of the States concerned has been given the opportunity to submit its own case and its observations on the other party's case both orally and in writing.

If the Commission has not delivered an opinion within three months of the date on which the matter was brought before it, the absence of such opinion shall not prevent the matter from being brought before the Court of Justice.

Article 171 [1.] If the Court of Justice finds that a Member State has failed to fulfil an obligation under this Treaty, the State shall be required to take the necessary measures to comply with the judgment of the Court of Justice.

[2. If the Commission considers that the Member State concerned has not taken such measures it shall, after giving that State the opportunity to submit its observations, issue a reasoned opinion specifying the points on which the Member State concerned has not complied with the judgement of the Court of Justice.

If the Member State concerned fails to take the necessary measures to comply with the Court's judgment within the time-limit laid down by the Commission, the latter may bring the case before the Court of Justice. In so doing it shall specify the amount of the lump sum or penalty payment to be paid by the Member State concerned which it considers appropriate in the circumstances.

If the Court of Justice finds that the Member State concerned has not complied with its judgment it may impose a lump sum or penalty payment on it.

This procedure shall be without prejudice to Article 170.]

Article 172. Regulations [adopted jointly by the European Parliament and the Council, and] {made} by the Council pursuant to the provisions of this Treaty, may give the Court of Justice unlimited jurisdiction in regard to the penalties provided for in such regulations.

Article 173. The Court of Justice shall review the legality of acts [adopted jointly by the European Parliament and the Council, of acts] of the Council, [of] {and} the Commission [, and of the ECB] other than recommendations and opinions [, and of acts of the European Parliament intended to produce legal effects *vis-à-vis* third parties].

It shall for this purpose have jurisdiction in actions brought by a Member State, the Council or the Commission on grounds of lack of competence, infringement of an essential procedural requirement, infringement of this Treaty or of any Rule of Law relating to its application, or misuse of powers.

[The Court shall have jurisdiction under the same conditions in actions brought by the European Parliament and by the ECB for the purpose of protecting their prerogatives.]

Any natural or legal person may, under the same conditions, institute proceedings against a decision addressed to that person or against a decision which, although in the form of a regulation or a decision addressed to another person, is of direct and individual concern to the former.

The proceedings provided for in this Article shall be instituted within two months of the publication of the measure, or of its notification to the plaintiff, or, in the absence thereof, of the day on which it came to the knowledge of the latter, as the case may be.

Article 174. If the action is well founded, the Court of Justice shall declare the act concerned to be void.

In the case of a regulation, however, the Court of Justice shall, if it considers this necessary, state which of the effects of the regulation which it has declared void shall be considered as definitive.

Article 175. Should the [European Parliament,] the Council or the Commission, in infringement of this Treaty, fail to act, the Member States and the other institutions of the Community may bring an action before the Court of Justice to have the infringement established.

The action shall be admissible only if the institution concerned has first been called upon to act. If, within two months of being so called upon, the institution concerned has not defined its position, the action may be brought within a further period of two months.

Any natural or legal person may, under the conditions laid down in the preceding paragraphs, complain to the Court of Justice that an institution of the Community has failed to address to that person any act other than a recommendation or an opinion.

[The Court of Justice shall have jurisdiction, under the same conditions, in actions or proceedings brought by the ECB in the areas falling within the latter's field of competence and in actions or proceedings brought against the latter.]

Article 176. The institution or institutions whose act has been declared void or whose failure to act has been declared contrary to this Treaty shall be required to take the necessary measures to comply with the judgment of the Court of Justice.

This obligation shall not affect any obligation which may result from the application of the second paragraph of Article 215.

[This Article shall also apply to the ECB.]

Article 177. The Court of Justice shall have jurisdiction to give preliminary rulings concerning:

(a) the interpretation of this Treaty;

(b) the validity and interpretation of acts of the institutions of the Community [and of the ECB];

(c) the interpretation of the statutes of bodies established by an act of the Council, where those statutes so provide.

Where such a question is raised before any court or tribunal of a Member State, that court or tribunal may, if it considers that a decision on the question is necessary to enable it to give judgment, request the Court of Justice to give a ruling thereon.

Where any such question is raised in a case pending before a court or tribunal of a Member State, against whose decisions there is no judicial remedy under national law, that court or tribunal shall bring the matter before the Court of Justice.

Article 178. The Court of Justice shall have jurisdiction in disputes relating to the compensation for damage provided for in the second paragraph of Article 215.

Article 179. The Court of Justice shall have jurisdiction in any dispute between the Community and its servants within the limits and under the conditions laid down in the Staff Regulations or the Conditions of Employment.

Article 185. Actions brought before the Court of Justice shall not have suspensory effect. The Court of Justice may, however, if it considers that circumstances so require, order that application of the contested act be suspended.

Article 186. The Court of Justice may in any cases before it prescribe any necessary interim measures.

Article 187. The judgments of the Court of Justice shall be enforceable under the conditions laid down in Article 192.

Article 188. The Statute of the Court of Justice is laid down in a separate Protocol.

The Council may, acting unanimously at the request of the Court of Justice and after consulting the Commission and the European Parliament, amend the provisions of Title III of the Statute.

The Court of Justice shall adopt its rules of procedure. These shall require the unanimous approval of the Council.

[Section 5. The Court of Auditors]

[Article 188a. The Court of Auditors shall carry out the audit.]

[Article 188b. The Court of Auditors shall consist of 12 members.

2.   The members of the Court of Auditors shall be chosen from among persons who belong or have belonged in their respective countries to external audit bodies or who are especially qualified for this office. Their independence must be beyond doubt.

3.   The members of the Court of Auditors shall be appointed for a term of six years by the Council, acting unanimously after consulting the European Parliament.

[Article 188c. 1. The Court of Auditors shall examine the accounts of all revenue and expenditure of the Community. It shall also examine the accounts of all revenue and expenditure of all bodies set up by the Community in so far as the relevant constituent instrument does not preclude such examination

The Court of Auditors shall provide the European Parliament and the Council with a statement of assurance as to the reliability of the accounts and the legality and regularity of the underlying transactions.

Chapter 2. Provisions common to several institutions

Article 189. In order to carry out their task and in accordance with the provisions of this Treaty, [the European Parliament acting jointly with the Council,] the Council and the Commission shall make regulations and issue directives, take decisions, make recommendations or deliver opinions.

A regulation shall have general application. It shall be binding in its entirety and directly applicable in all Member States.

A directive shall be binding, as to the result to be achieved, upon each Member State to which it is addressed, but shall leave to the national authorities the choice of form and methods.

A decision shall be binding in its entirety upon those to whom it is addressed.

Recommendations and opinions shall have no binding force.

[Article 189a 1. Where, in pursuance of this Treaty, the Council acts on a proposal from the Commission, unanimity shall be required for an act constituting an amendment to that proposal, subject to Article 189b(4) and (5).

2.   As long as the Council has not acted, the Commission may alter its proposal at any time during the procedures leading to the adoption of a Community act.]

[Article 189b. 1. Where reference is made in this Treaty to this Article for the adoption of an act, the following procedure shall apply.

2.   The Commission shall submit a proposal to the European Parliament and the Council.

The Council, acting by a qualified majority after obtaining the opinion of the European Parliament, shall adopt a common position. The common position shall be communicated to the European Parliament. The Council shall inform the European Parliament fully of the reasons which led it to adopt its common position. The Commission shall inform the European Parliament fully of its position.

If, within three months of such communication, the European Parliament:

(a)   approves the common position, the Council shall definitively adopt the act in question in accordance with that common position;

(b)   has not taken a decision, the Council shall adopt the act in question in accordance with its common position;

(c)   indicates, by an absolute majority of its component members, that it intends to reject the common position. it shall immediately inform the Council. The Council may convene a meeting of the Conciliation Committee referred to in paragraph 4 to explain further its position. The European Parliament shall thereafter either confirm, by an absolute majority of its component members, its rejection of the common position, in which event the proposed act shall be deemed not to have been adopted, or propose amendments in accordance with sub-paragraph (d) of this paragraph;

(d)   proposes amendments to the common position by an absolute majority of its component members, the amended text shall be forwarded to the Council and to the Commission, which shall deliver an opinion on those amendments.

3.   If, within three months of the matter being referred to it, the Council, acting by a qualified majority, approves all the amendments of the European Parliament, it shall amend its common position accordingly and adopt the act in question; however, the Council shall act unanimously on the amendments on which the Commission has delivered a negative opinion. If the Council does not approve the act in question, the President of the Council, in agreement with the President of the European Parliament, shall forthwith convene a meeting of the Conciliation Committee.

4.   The Conciliation Committee, which shall be composed of the members of the Council or their representatives and an equal number of representatives of the European Parliament, shall have the task of reaching agreement on a joint text, by a qualified majority of the members of the Council or their representatives and by a majority of the representatives of the European Parliament. The Commission shall take part in the Conciliation Committee's proceedings and shall take all the necessary initiatives with a view to

reconciling the positions of the European Parliament and the Council.

5. If, within six weeks of its being convened, the Conciliation Committee approves a joint text, the European Parliament, acting by an absolute majority of the votes cast, and the Council, acting by a qualified majority, shall have a period of six weeks from that approval in which to adopt the act in question in accordance with the joint text. If one of the two institutions fails to approve the proposed act, it shall be deemed not to have been adopted.

6. Where the Conciliation Committee does not approve a joint text, the proposed act shall be deemed not to have been adopted unless the Council, acting by a qualified majority within six weeks of expiry of the period granted to the Conciliation Committee, confirms the common position to which it agreed before the conciliation procedure was initiated, possibly with amendments proposed by the European Parliament. In this case, the act in question shall be finally adopted unless the European Parliament, within six weeks of the date of confirmation by the Council, rejects the text by an absolute majority of its component members, in which case the proposed act shall be deemed not to have been adopted.

7. The periods of three months and six weeks referred to in this Article may be extended by a maximum of one month and two weeks respectively by common accord of the European Parliament and the Council. The period of three months referred to in paragraph 2 shall be automatically extended by two months where paragraph 2(c) applies.

8. The scope of the procedure under this Article may be widened, in accordance with the procedure provided for in Article N(2) of the Treaty on European Union, on the basis of a report to be submitted to the Council by the Commission by 1996 at the latest.]

[Article 189C. Where reference is made in this Treaty to this Article for the adoption of an act, the following procedure shall apply:

(a) The Council, acting by a qualified majority on a proposal from the Commission and after obtaining the opinion of the European Parliament, shall adopt a common position.

(b) The Council's common position shall be communicated to the European Parliament. The Council and the Commission shall inform the European Parliament fully of the reasons which led to the Council to adopt its common position and also of the Commission's position.

If, within three months of such communication, the European Parliament approves this common position or has not taken a decision within that period, the Council shall definitively adopt the act in question in accordance with the common position.

(c) The European Parliament may, within the period of three months referred to in point (b), by an absolute majority of its component members, propose amendments to the Council's common position. The European Parliament may also, by the same majority reject the Council's common position. The result of the proceedings shall be transmitted to the Council and the Commission.

If the European Parliament has rejected the Council's common position, unanimity shall be required for the Council to act on a second reading.

(d) The Commission shall, within a period of one month, re-examine the proposal on the basis of which the Council adopted its common position, by taking into account the amendments proposed by the European Parliament.

The Commission shall forward to the Council, at the same time as its re-examined proposal, the amendments of the European Parliament which it has not accepted, and shall express its opinion on them. The Council may adopt these amendments unanimously

(e) The Council, acting by a qualified majority shall adopt the proposal as re-examined by the Commission.

Unanimity shall be required for the Council to amend the proposal as re-examined by the Commission.

(f) In the cases referred to in points (c), (d) and (e), the Council shall be required to act within a period of three months. If no decision is taken within this period, the Commission proposal shall be deemed not to have been adopted.

(g) The periods referred to in points (b) and (f) may be extended by a maximum of one month by common accord between the Council and the European Parliament.]

Article 190. Regulations, directives and decisions [adopted jointly by the European Parliament and the Council, and such acts adopted by] {of} the Council or the Commission, shall state the reasons on which they are based and shall refer to any proposals or opinions which were required to be obtained pursuant to this Treaty.

Article 191. [1. Regulations, directives and decisions adopted in accordance with the procedure referred to in Article 189b shall be signed by the President of the European Parliament and by the President of the Council and shall be published in the Official Journal of the Community. They shall enter into force on the date specified in them or, in the absence thereof, on the 20th day following that of their publication.

2.] Regulations [of the Council and of the Commission, as well as directives of those institutions which are addressed to all Member States] shall be published in the Official Journal of the Community. They shall enter into force on the date specified in them or, in the absence thereof, on the twentieth day following that of their publication.

[3. Other] directives and decisions shall be notified to those to whom they are addressed and shall take effect upon such notification.

Article 192. Decisions of the Council or of the Commission which impose a pecuniary obligation on persons other than States shall be enforceable.

Enforcement shall be governed by the rules of civil procedure in force in the State in the territory of which it is carried out. The order for its enforcement shall be appended to the decision, without other formality than verification of the authenticity of the decision, by the national authority which the Government of each Member State shall designate for this purpose and shall make known to the Commission and to the Court of Justice.

When these formalities have been completed on application by the party concerned, the latter may proceed to enforcement in accordance with the national law, by bringing the matter directly before the competent authority.

Enforcement may be suspended only by a decision of the Court of Justice. However, the courts of the country concerned shall have jurisdiction over complaints that enforcement is being carried out in an irregular manner.

Chapter 3. The Economic and Social Committee

Article 193. An Economic and Social Committee is hereby established. It shall have advisory status.

The Committee shall consist of representatives of the various categories of economic and social activity, in particular, representatives of producers, farmers, carriers, workers, dealers, craftsmen, professional occupations and representatives of the general public.

Article 194. The number of members of the Committee shall be as follows:

Belgium	12
Denmark	9
Germany	24
Greece	12
Spain	21
France	24
Ireland	9
Italy	24
Luxembourg	6
The Netherlands	12
Austria	12
Portugal	12
Finland	9
Sweden	12
United Kingdom	24

The members of the Committee shall be appointed by the Council, acting unanimously, for four years. Their appointments shall be renewable.

Article 197. The Committee shall include specialised sections for the principal fields covered by this Treaty.

In particular, it shall contain an agricultural section and a transport section, which are the subject of special provisions in the Titles relating to agriculture and transport.

These specialised sections shall operate within the general terms of reference of the Committee. They may not be consulted independently of the Committee.

Sub-committees may also be established within the Committee to prepare, on specific questions or in specific fields, draft opinions to be submitted to the Committee for its consideration.

The rules of procedure shall lay down the methods of composition and the terms of reference of the specialised sections and of the sub-committees.

Article 198. The Committee must be consulted by the Council or by the Commission where this Treaty so provides. The Committee may be consulted by these institutions in all cases in which they consider it appropriate. [It may take the initiative of issuing an opinion in cases in which it considers such action appropriate.]

[Chapter 4. The Committee of the Regions]

[Article 198a. A Committee consisting of representatives of regional and local bodies, hereinafter referred to as the 'Committee of the Regions', is hereby established with advisory status.

The number of members of the Committee of the Regions shall be as follows:

Belgium	12
Denmark	9
Germany	24
Greece	12
Spain	21
France	24
Ireland	9
Italy	24
Luxembourg	6
Netherlands	12
Austria	12
Portugal	12
Finland	9
Sweden	12
United Kingdom	24

The members of the Committee and an equal number of alternate members shall be appointed for four years by the Council acting unanimously on proposals from the respective Member States. Their term of office shall be renewable.

The member of the Committee may not be bound by any mandatory instructions. They shall be completely independent in the performance of their duties, in the general interests of the Community.

Article 198b. The Committee of the Regions shall elect its chairman and officers from among it members for term of two years.

It shall adopt its rules of procedure and shall submit them for approval to the Council acting unanimously.

The Committee shall be convened by its chairman at the request of the Council or of the Commission. It may also meet on its own initiative.

Article 198c. The committee of the Regions shall be consulted by the Council or by the Commission where this Treaty so provides and in all other cases in which one of these two institutions considers it appropriate.

The Council or the Commission shall, if it considers it necessary, set the Committee, for the submission of its opinion, a time-limit which may not be less than one month from the date on which the chairman receives notification to this effect. Upon expiry of the time-limit, the absence of an opinion shall not prevent further action.

Where the Economic and Social Committee is consulted pursuant to Article 198, the Committee of the Regions shall be informed by the Council or the Commission of the request for an opinion. Where it considers that specific regional interests are involved, the Committee of the Regions may issue an opinion on the matter.

It may issue an opinion on its own initiative in cases in which it considers such action appropriate.

The opinion of the Committee, together with a record of the proceedings, shall be forwarded to the Council and to the Commission.

Treaty on European Union

His Majesty the King of the Belgians,
Her Majesty the Queen of Denmark,
The President of the Federal Republic of Germany,
The President of the Hellenic Republic,
His Majesty the King of Spain,
The President of the French Republic,
The President of Ireland,
The President of the Italian Republic,
His Royal Highness the Grand Duke of Luxembourg,
Her Majesty the Queen of the Netherlands,
The President of the Portuguese Republic,
Her Majesty the Queen of the United Kingdom of Great Britain and Northern Ireland,

RESOLVED to mark a new stage in the process of European integration undertaken with the establishment of the European communities,

RECALLING the historic importance of ending of the division of the European Continent and the need to create firm bases for the construction of the future Europe,

CONFIRMING their attachment to the principles of liberty, democracy and respect for human rights and fundamental freedoms and of the Rule of Law,

DESIRING to deepen the solidarity between their peoples while respecting their history, their culture and their traditions,

DESIRING to enhance further the democratic and efficient functioning of the institutions so as to enable them better to carry out, within a single institutional framework, the tasks entrusted to them,

RESOLVED to achieve the strengthening and the convergence of their economies and to establish an economic and monetary union including, in accordance with the provisions of the Treaty, a single and stable currency,

DETERMINED to promote economic and social progress for their peoples, within the context of the accomplishment of the internal market and of reinforced cohesion and environmental protection, and to implement policies ensuring that advances in economic integration are accompanied by parallel progress in other fields,

RESOLVED to establish a citizenship common to nationals of the countries,

RESOLVED to implement a common foreign and security policy including the eventual framing of a common defence policy, which might in time lead to a common defence, thereby reinforcing the European identity and its independence in order to promote peace, security and progress in Europe and in the world,

REAFFIRMING their objectives to facilitate the free movement of persons, while ensuring the safety and security of their peoples, by including provision on justice and home affairs in this Treaty,

RESOLVED to continue the process of creating an ever closer union among the peoples of Europe, in which decisions are taken as closely as possible to the citizen in accordance with the principle of subsidiarity,

IN VIEW of further steps to be taken in order to advance European integration,

HAVE DECIDED to establish a European Union ...

Title I. Common provisions

Article A. By this Treaty, the High Contracting Parties establish among themselves a European Union, hereinafter called 'the Union'.

This Treaty marks a new stage in the process of creating an ever closer union among the people of Europe, in which decisions are taken as closely as possible to the citizen.

The Union shall be founded on the European Communities, supplemented by the policies and forms of cooperation established by the Treaty. Its task shall be to organise, in a manner demonstrating consistency and solidarity, relations between the Member States and between their peoples.

Article B. The Union shall set itself the following objectives:

- to promote economic and social progress which is balanced and sustainable, in particular through the creation of an area without internal frontiers, through the strengthening of economic and social cohesion and through the establishment of economic and monetary union, ultimately including a single currency in accordance with the provisions of this Treaty;

- to assert its identity on the international scene, in particular through the implementation of a common foreign and security policy including the eventual framing of a common defence policy, which might in time lead to a common defence;

- to strengthen the protection of the rights and interests of the nationals of its Member States through the introduction of a citizenship of the Union;

- to develop a close cooperation on justice and home affairs;

- to maintain in full the *'acquis communautaire'* and build on it with a view to considering, through the procedure referred to in Article N(2), to what extent the policies and forms of cooperation introduced by this Treaty may need to be revised with the aim of ensuring the effectiveness of the mechanisms and the institutions of the Community.

The objectives of the Union shall be achieved as provided in this Treaty and in accordance with the conditions and the timetable set out therein while respecting the principle of subsidiarity as defined in Article 3b of the Treaty establishing the European Community.

Article C. The Union shall be served by a single institutional framework which shall ensure the consistency and the continuity of the activities carried out in order to attain its objectives while respecting and building upon the 'acquis communautaire'.

The Union shall in particular ensure the consistency of its external activities as a whole in the context of its external relations, security, economic and development policies. The Council and the Commission shall be responsible for ensuring such consistency. They shall ensure the implementation of these policies, each in accordance with its respective powers.

Article D. The European Council shall provide the Union with the necessary impetus for its development and shall define the general political guidelines thereof.

The European Council shall bring together the Heads of State or of Government of the Member States and the President of the Commission. They shall be assisted by the Ministers for Foreign Affairs of the Member States and by a Member of the Commission. The European Council shall meet at least twice a year, under the chairmanship of the Head of State or of

Government of the Member State which holds the Presidency of the Council.

The European Council shall submit to the European Parliament a report after each of its meetings and a yearly written report on the progress achieved by the Union.

Article E. The European Parliament, the Council, the Commission and the Court of Justice shall exercise their powers under the conditions and for the purposes provided for, on the one hand, by the provisions of the Treaties establishing the European Communities and of the subsequent Treaties and Acts modifying and supplementing them and, on the other hand, by the other provisions of this Treaty.

Article F.

1. The Union shall respect the national identities of its Member States, whose systems of government are founded on the principles of democracy.

2. The Union shall respect fundamental rights, as guaranteed by the European Convention for the Protection of Human Rights and Fundamental Freedoms signed in Rome on 4 November 1950 and as they result from the constitutional traditions common to the Member States, as general principles of Community law.

3. The Union shall provide itself with the means necessary to attain its objectives and carry through its policies.

Title V. Provisions on a common foreign and security policy

Article J. A common foreign and security policy is hereby established which shall be governed by the following provisions.

Article J.1.

1. The union and its Member States shall define and implement a common foreign and security policy, governed by the provisions of the Title and covering all areas of foreign and security policy.

2. The objectives of the common foreign and security policy shall be:

   - to safeguard the common values, fundamental interests and independence of the Union;

   - to strengthen the security of the Union and its Member States in all ways;

   - to preserve peace and strengthen international security, in accordance with the principles of the United Nations Charter as well as the principles of the Helsinki Final Act and the objectives of the Paris Charter;

   - to promote international co-operation;

   - to develop and consolidate democracy and the Rule of Law and respect for human rights and fundamental freedoms.

3. The Union shall pursue these objectives;

   - by establishing systematic co-operation between Member States in the conduct of policy, in accordance with Article J.2;

   - by gradually implementing, in accordance with Article J.3, joint action in the areas in which the Member States have important interests in common.

4. The Member States shall support the Union's external and security policy actively and unreservedly in a spirit of loyalty and mutual solidarity. They

shall refrain from any action which is contrary to the interests of the Union or likely to impair its effectiveness as a cohesive force in international relations. The Council shall ensure that these principles are complied with.

Article J.2.

1. Member States shall inform and consult one another within the Council on any matter of foreign and security policy of general interest in order to ensure that their combined influence is exerted as effectively as possible by means of concerted and convergent action.

2. Whenever it deems it necessary, the Council shall define a common position.

   Member States shall ensure that their national policies conform on the common positions.

3. Member States shall co-ordinate their action in international organisations and at international conferences. They shall uphold the common positions in such fora.

   In international organisations and at international conferences where not all the Member States participate, those which do take part shall uphold the common positions.

Article J.3. The procedure for adopting joint action in matters covered by foreign and security policy shall be the following:

1. The Council shall decide, on the basis of general guidelines from the European Council, that a matter should be the subject of joint action.

   Whenever the Council decides on the principle of joint action, it shall lay down the specific scope, the Union's general and specific objectives in carrying out such action, if necessary its duration, and the means, procedures and conditions for its implementation.

2. The Council shall, when adopting the joint action and at any stage during its development, define those matters on which decisions are to be taken by a qualified majority.

   Where the Council is required to act by a qualified majority pursuant to the preceding sub-paragraph, the votes of its members shall be weighted in accordance with Article 148(2) of the Treaty establishing the European Community, and for their adoption, acts of the Council shall require at least 54 votes in favour, cast by at least eight members.

3. If there is a change in circumstances having a substantial effect on a question subject to joint action, the Council shall review the principles and objectives of that action and take the necessary decisions. As long as the Council has not acted, the joint action shall stand.

4. Joint actions shall commit the Member States in the positions they adopt and in the conduct of their activity.

5. Whenever there is any plan to adopt a national position or take national action pursuant to a joint action, information shall be provided in time to allow, if necessary, for prior consultations within the Council. The obligation to provide prior information shall not apply to measures which are merely a national transposition of Council decisions.

6. In cases of imperative need arising from changes in the situation and failing a Council decision, Member States may take the necessary measures as a matter of urgency having regard to the general objectives of the joint action. The Member State concerned shall inform the Council immediately of any such measures.

7.	Should there be any major difficulties in implementing a joint action, a Member State shall refer them to the Council which shall discuss them and seek appropriate solutions. Such solutions shall not run counter to the objectives of the joint action or impair its effectiveness.

Article J.4.

1.	The common foreign and security policy shall include all questions related to the security of the Union, including the eventual framing of a common defence policy, which might in time lead to a common defence.

2.	The union requests the Western European Union (WEU), which is an integral part of the development of the Union, to elaborate and implement decisions and actions of the Union which have defence implications. The Council shall, in agreement with the institutions of the WEU, adopt the necessary practical arrangements.

3.	Issues having defence implications dealt with under this Article shall not be subject to the procedures set out in Article J.3.

4.	The policy of the Union in accordance with this Article shall not prejudice the specific character of the security and defence policy of certain Member States and shall respect the obligations of certain Member States under the North Atlantic Treaty and be compatible with the common security and defence policy established within that framework.

5.	The provisions of this Article shall not prevent the development of closer co-operation between two or more Member States on a bilateral level, in the framework. of the WEU and the Atlantic Alliance, provided such co-operation does not run counter to or impede that provided for in this Title.

6.	With a view to furthering the objective of this Treaty, and having in view the date of 1998 in the context of Article XII of the Brussels Treaty, the provisions of this Article may be revised as provided for in Article N(2) on the basis of a report to be presented in 1996 by the Council to the European Council, which shall include an evaluation of the progress made and the experience gained until then.

Article J.5.

1.	The Presidency shall represent the Union in matters coming within the common foreign and security policy.

2.	The Presidency shall be responsible for the implementation of common measures; in that capacity it shall in principle express the position of the Union in international organisations and international conferences.

4	Member States which are also members of the United Nations Security Council will concert and keep the other Member States fully informed. Member States which are permanent members of the Security Council will, in the execution of their functions, ensure the defence of the positions and the interests of the union, without prejudice to their responsibilities under the provisions of the United Nations Charter.

Article J.6. The diplomatic and consular missions of the Member States and the Commission Delegations in third countries and international conferences, and their representations to international organisations, shall cooperate in ensuring that the common positions and common measures adopted by the Council are complied with and implemented.

Article J.7. The Presidency shall consult the European Parliament on the main aspects and the basic choices of the common foreign and security policy and shall ensure that the views of the European Parliament are duly taken into consideration. The European Parliament shall be kept regularly informed by the Presidency and the Commission of the development of the Union's foreign and security policy.

The European Parliament may ask questions of the Councils or make recommendations to it. It shall hold an annual debate on progress in implementing the common foreign and security policy.

Article J.8.

1. The European Council shall define the principles of and general guidelines for the common foreign and security policy.

2. The Council shall take the decisions necessary for defining and implementing the common foreign and security policy on the basis of the general guidelines adopted by the European Council. It shall ensure the unity, consistency and effectiveness of action by the Union.

   The Council shall act unanimously, except for procedural questions and in the case referred to in Article J.3(2).

3. Any Member State or the Commission may refer to the Council any question relating to the common foreign policy and may submit proposals to the Council.

4. In cases requiring a rapid decision, the Presidency, of its own motion, or at the request of the Commission or a Member State, shall convene an extraordinary Council meeting within 48 hours or, in an emergency, within a shorter period.

Article J.9. The Commission shall be fully associated with the work carried out in the common foreign and security policy field.

Title VI. Provisions on cooperation in the field of justice and home affairs

Article K. Co-operation in the fields of justice and home affairs shall be governed by the following provisions.

Article K.1. For the purposes of achieving the objectives of the Union in particular the free movement of persons, and without prejudice to the powers of the European Community, Member States shall regard the following areas as matters of common interest:

1. asylum policy;

2. rules governing the crossing by persons of the external borders of the Member States and the exercise of controls thereon;

3. immigration policy and policy regarding nationals of third countries;

   (a) conditions of entry and movement by nationals of third countries on the territory of Member States;

   (b) conditions of residence by nationals of third countries on the territory of Member States, including family reunion and access to employment;

   (c) combating unauthorised immigration, residence and work by nationals of third countries on the territory of Member States;

4. combating drug addiction in so far as this is not covered by 7 to 9;

5. combating fraud on an international scale in so far as this is not covered by 7 to 9;

6. judicial co-operation in civil matters;

7. judicial co-operation in criminal matters;

8. customs co-operation;

9. police co-operation for the purposes of preventing and combating terrorism. unlawful drug trafficking and other serious forms of international crime, including if necessary certain aspects of customs co-operation, in connection with the organisation of a Union-wide system for exchanging information within a European Police Office (Europol).

Article K.2

1. The matters referred to in Article K.1 shall be dealt with in compliance with the European Convention for the Protection of Human Rights and Fundamental Freedoms of 4 November 1950 and the Convention relating to the Status of Refugees of 28 July 1951 and having regard to the protection afforded by Member States to persons persecuted on political grounds.

2. This Title shall not affect the exercise of the responsibilities incumbent upon Member States with regard to the maintenance of law and order and the safeguarding of internal security.

Article K.3

1. In the areas referred to in Article K.1, Member States shall inform and consult one another within the Council with a view to co-ordinating their action. To that end, they shall establish collaboration between the relevant departments of their administration.

2. The Council may:

    ● on the initiative of any Member State or of the Commission, in the areas referred to in Article K.1(1) to (6);

    ● on the initiative of any Member State, in the areas referred to in Article K.1(7) to (9):

        (a) adopt joint position and promote, using the appropriate form and procedures, any cooperation contributing to the pursuit of the objectives of the Union;

        (b) adopt joint action in so far as the objectives of the Union can be attained better by joint action than by the Member State acting individually on account of the scale or effects of the action envisaged; it may decide that measures implementing joint action are to be adopted by a qualified majority;

        (c) without prejudice to Article 220 of the Treaty establishing the European Community, draw up conventions which it shall recommend to the Member States for adoption in accordance with respective constitutional requirements.

    Unless otherwise provided by such conventions, measures implementing them shall be adopted within the Council by a majority of two-thirds of the High Contracting parties.

    Such conventions may stipulate that the Court of Justice shall have jurisdiction to interpret their provisions and to rule on any disputes regarding their application, in accordance with such arrangements as they may lay down.

Article K.4

1. A Co-ordinating Committee shall be set up consisting of senior officials. In addition to its co-ordinating role, it shall be the task of the Committee to:

    ● give opinions for the attention of the Council, either at the Council's request or on its own initiative;

    ● contribute, without prejudice to Article 151 of the Treaty establishing the

European Community, to the preparation of the Council's discussions in the areas referred to in Article K.1 and, in accordance with the conditions laid down in Article 100d of the Treaty establishing the European Community, in the areas referred to in Article 100c of that Treaty.

2. The Commission shall be fully associated with the work in the areas referred to in this Title.

3. The Council shall act unanimously, except on matters of procedure and in cases where Article K.3 expressly provides for other voting rules.

    Where the Council is required to act by a qualified majority, the votes of its members shall be weighted as laid down in Articles 148(2) of the Treaty establishing the European Community, and for their adoption, acts of the Council shall require at least 54 votes, cast by at least eight members.

Article K.5

Within international organisations and at international conferences in which they take part, Member States shall defend the common position adopted under the provisions of this Title.

Article K.6

The Presidency and the Commission shall regularly inform the European Parliament of discussion in the areas covered by this Title.

The Presidency shall consult the European Parliament on the principle aspects of activities in the areas referred to in this Title and shall ensure that the views of the European Parliament are duly taken into consideration.

The European Parliament may ask questions of the Council or make recommendations to it. Each year, it shall hold a debate on the progress made in implementation of the areas referred to in this Title.

Article K.7

The provisions of this Title shall not prevent the establishment or development of closer cooperation between two or more Member States in so far as such cooperation does not conflict with, or impede, that provided for in this Title.

Article K.8

1. The provisions referred to in Articles 137, 138, 139 to 142, 146, 147, 150 to 153, 157 to 163 and 217 of the Treaty establishing the European Community shall apply to the provisions relating to the areas referred to in this Title.

2. Administrative expenditure which the provisions relating to the areas referred to in this Title entail for the institutions shall be charged to the budget of the European communities.

    The Council may also:

    - either decide unanimously that operational expenditure to which the implementation of those provisions gives rise is to be charged to the budget of the European Communities; in that event, the budgetary procedure laid down in the Treaty establishing the European Community shall be applicable;

    - or determine that such expenditure shall be charged to the Member States, where appropriate in accordance with a scale to be decided.

Article K.9

The Council, acting unanimously on the initiative of the Commission or a

Member State, may decide to apply Article 100c of the Treaty establishing the European Community to action in areas referred to in Article K.1(1) to (6), and at the same time determine the relevant voting conditions relating to it. It shall recommend the Member States to adopt the decision in accordance with their respective constitutional requirements.

Title VII. Final provisions

Article L

The provisions of the Treaty establishing the European Community, the Treaty establishing the European Coal and Steel Community and the Treaty establishing the European Atomic Energy Community concerning the powers of the Court of Justice of the European Communities and the exercise of those powers shall apply only to the following provisions of this Treaty:

(a) provisions amending the Treaty establishing the European Economic Community with a view to establishing the European Community, the Treaty establishing the European Coal and Steel Community and the Treaty establishing the European Atomic Energy Community;

(b) the third sub-paragraph of Article K.3(2)(c);

Article M

Subject to the provisions amending the Treaty establishing the European Economic Community with a view to establishing the European Community, the Treaty establishing the European Coal and Steel Community and the Treaty establishing the European Atomic Energy Community, and to these final provisions, nothing in this Treaty shall affect the Treaties establishing the European Communities or the subsequent Treaties and Acts modifying or supplementing them.

Article O. Any European State may apply to become a Member of the Union. It shall address its application to the Council, which shall act unanimously after consulting the Commission and after receiving the assent of the European Parliament, which shall act by an absolute majority of its component members.

The conditions of admission and the adjustments to the Treaties on which the Union is founded which such admission entails shall be the subject of an agreement between the Member States and the applicant State. This agreement shall be submitted for ratification by all the contracting States in accordance with their respective constitutional requirements. ...

Article Q. This Treaty is concluded for an unlimited period.

Article R.

1. This Treaty shall be ratified by the High Contracting Parties in accordance with their respective constitutional requirements. The instruments of ratification shall be deposited with the government of the Italian Republic.

Note

For discussion of the constitutional aspects of the TEU see: U Everling (1992) 29 CML Rev 1053; D Curtin (1993) 30 CML Rev 17; T Hartley (1993) ICLQ 213; Professor I Ward (1996) 16(1) OJLS 161; Professor TC Hartley (1996) 112 LQR 95; W Van Gerven (1996) 2(1) *European Public Law* 81; P Eleftheriadis (1996) 21(1) EL Rev 32. Below, Ian Harden discusses the sense in which the European Union has a constitution and argues that the operation of its constitutional principles is unlikely to lead to something recognisable as a federal European government.

Ian Harden, 'The Constitution of the European Union' (1994) *Public Law* 609–10, 611–19, 620–2

The Treaty on European Union is not explicitly a constitutional document. Many of its provisions were an uneasy compromise between traditional 'federalist' aspirations and opposition to the further erosion of national sovereignty. Some of the assumptions underlying the Treaty's core provisions for economic and monetary union (EMU) have proved mistaken, leading to renewed uncertainty about whether, when and how a single currency will be introduced. However, monetary union less than five years from now represents the baseline against which the Inter-Governmental Conference of 1996 will take place. Whether or not the 1999 date is regarded as legally binding (a matter on which the German Constitutional Court has thrown doubt), a decision must be made to re-affirm, revise or abandon it. This article proceeds on the assumption (not a prediction) that monetary union will take place in something like the form laid out in the Treaty, although possibly with some postponement.

The article puts forward three main propositions:

(i)   the European Union (EU) already has a constitution;

(ii) the emergent principles of that constitution involve a transformation of the relationship between public power and the economy that has typified the 20th century state;

(iii) this transformation means that future development of the EU constitution is unlikely to produce a European executive branch of government analogous to those in Member States, or in existing federal states outside the EU. …

European legal integration

… EC lawyers have also tended to assert that EC law is a separate system. Historically, emphasis on the idea of separateness was a necessary aspect of the development of EC law. In particular, it was essential to the first statement of the principle of supremacy [*Costa v ENEL* (Case 6/64) [1964] ECR 585]. There is continuing justification for a notion of 'separateness', in that some EC law deals with matters internal to the Community institutional system. It was in this context that the European Court of Justice described the Treaty of Rome as 'the basic constitutional charter of the [then] EEC' [Case 294/83 *Parti Ecologiste 'Les Verts' v European Parliament* [1986] ECR 1339 at 1365].

In a more fundamental sense, however, EC law has ceased to be separate from national law as a result of the jurisprudence of the European Court of Justice. The court has, to a large extent, succeeded in depriving states of the possibility of 'selective exit' from Community obligations [JHH Weiler (1991) 100 *Yale Law Review* 8]. It has done this through progressive extension of the rights of individuals under EC law and of the duties of national courts to give effect to those rights, particularly through the principle of 'direct effect'. Where this principle applies, governments are deprived of the power of non-implementation, unless they are prepared to defy their own national courts and judges.

The result of these developments is to harness the everyday practices and belief-system of a powerful professional group, as well as the legitimacy of the courts and of law, to the cause of integration. For the producers and users of concrete legal decisions – judges, lawyers and their clients – national law and Community law are now increasingly an integrated hierarchy of norms, which national courts must apply.

British constitutionalists ought to be particularly alert to the implications of this. There is no single founding document which calls itself the 'constitution of the

EU', any more than there is such a document for the UK. Nonetheless, there are rules and principles governing the legitimate exercise of public power in Britain and the allocation of that power between different public authorities. In this sense, we are accustomed to think that the UK does have 'a constitution', although its adequacy and appropriateness for a modern state are questionable. The question is what rules and principles govern the legitimate exercise of public power in the European Union and how they affect the UK's rules and principles.

The dominant approach to understanding the British constitution remains the conclusions of the 19th century constitutional theorist, Dicey. Dicey's great achievement was to find a way to posit constitutional principles, despite the absence of a founding constitutional document. He did this by offering a normative interpretation of the actions of judges and of other public officials. The interpretation sought to make explicit the 'implicit understandings' which govern those actions. ...

Dicey's interpretation based the constitution on two principles; the Rule of Law and the sovereignty of Parliament. At the time he wrote, those principles provided a plausible way of explaining how the law applied by British courts formed part of a coherent framework of legitimate constitutional authority. They no longer do so. In the *Factortame* case, the House of Lords accepted that EC laws creating individual rights rank higher than subsequently-enacted statutes of the UK Parliament in the hierarchy of legal norms applied by British courts.

The importance of this acceptance was minimised by tracing the validity of EC law in the UK to the European Communities Act 1972, a statute which could legitimately be repealed by the UK Parliament. Is this way of reconciling new realities with old doctrines convincing? I think not. The present constitutional position is that the UK is part of the EU. The existence of legitimate mechanisms for altering existing constitutional arrangements does not mean that the present reality of those arrangements can be ignored.

For Dicey, the fact that Parliament was a sovereign law-maker was not a conceptual necessity, derived from the concept of a constitution as such, but a contingent feature of the British constitution [See N MacCormick, (1993) 56 *Modern Law Review* 1–18]. The present reality of the UK's constitutional relationship with the European Community is that Parliament no longer enjoys legislative omnicompetence. Such competence as it retains, however, is inherent, not delegated from the Union.

To make constitutional sense of what Parliament and courts in Britain now do requires reference to a European constitution governing the legitimate exercise of public power by Community institutions and the relationship between the state and Union levels of government. There can be no doubting that the EU already has a 'constitution' in this sense. That is, there are substantive and procedural requirements governing what Community institutions may and may not do, and a division of competences and powers between different levels of government and different institutions.

What the EU lacks is any explicit statement of the principles that are supposed to underlie existing arrangements and which could provide criteria against which the present situation and proposals for change could be critically evaluated. As set out in the Treaty on European Union, 'subsidiarity' is a recognition of the need for such principles, rather than the statement of a specific principle capable of meeting that need.

If we applied Dicey's method, instead of clinging to his results, we would seek to identify the principles of the existing European constitution. We might not expect to find answers that were wholly convincing, but without making the effort we cannot know. The fact that the effort has not been made is attributable to the (in my view mistaken) assumption that there is an essential link between a 'constitution' and a 'state'.

The constitution, the state and the executive

... The sovereignty of Parliament also evokes the constitutional idea that in every political community there must be a single, indivisible and unlimited authority. In practice the unlimited legislative power of the Crown-in-Parliament is at the disposal of a government which can command a majority in the House of Commons. The assumption that the executive or government is the authentic representative of 'the State' follows naturally, so discouraging any idea that constitutional authority might inhere in different persons or institutions for different purposes.

This assumption is reflected in, and further encouraged by, constitutional emphasis on the unity of the executive, which is expressed in the indivisibility of the Crown and in the collective responsibility of ministers to Parliament. Constitutional theory in Britain (or, more often, a vague and inconsistent set of beliefs about constitutional theory) thus tends to lead to two assumptions:

(a) that government ministers are entitled to exercise power throughout the public sphere. Furthermore, they are required to do so, in order to ensure the accountability of public power. This is because ministerial responsibility to Parliament is the only constitutionally recognised form of accountability of the executive;

(b) that 'political union' means the creation of a European government, with functions and powers similar to those of the executive in a nation-state. It is this second assumption which opponents of a European government find particularly objectionable. I shall argue below that the emerging principles of the European constitution challenge both these assumptions.

The state and the economy

The belief, implicit or explicit, that 'constitution' implies 'state' is reinforced by the link between 'the state' and 'the economy'. ... It is trite wisdom that the construction of Europe has involved undermining one aspect of the Keynesian state; that is, the separateness of national economies. The idea that the creation of a common market had political, as well as economic, implications has always been essential to the whole European project. A common market implies direct restrictions on the instruments of economic policy which States can use – tariffs, quotas, or equivalent measures, etc. As economies became more integrated, it was believed, further supra-national competences and institutions would be seen to be necessary in one policy area after another, as purely national policies ceased to be effective.

However, alongside the integration process and separately from it, there has also been a fundamental re-assessment of what the Keynesian state could be expected to deliver even if there were a 'national economy'. This has occurred partly because supposed economic instruments do not – or no longer – produce their intended beneficial effects, or produce unintended harmful ones. The other factor in the re-assessment has been the re-discovery by economists of an old constitutional truth: that discretionary powers can be abused and that the prevention of such abuse is, in part at least, a matter of institutional and constitutional design.

The economic constitution

The central provisions of the Treaty on European Union are about economic and monetary union (EMU). The institutions and procedures of EMU represent not just a significant step towards further European economic and political integration, but also a constitutional step away from the unconstrained discretionary economic power of the 'Keynesian state'.

The primary objective of monetary and exchange rate policy is to be price stability. Pursuit of other economic objectives is to be without prejudice to this objective [Arts 3a(2); 105(1)]. The central banks of Member States must become independent during the second stage of EMU, which began on 1 January 1994. This obligation crystallises at the beginning of the third stage, even for a state which is unable to adopt the single currency because it does not meet the convergence criteria. The European Central Bank (ECB) is also to be independent. These provisions are really an extension of the constitutional model of the Bundesbank to the other states and to the Union.

The only exception to the requirement of central bank independence is the Bank of England. The UK 'opt-out' Protocol allows the UK to decide not to move to the third stage of monetary union. The Protocol also has the effect of allowing the present status of the bank of England to continue unless and until the UK does move to the third stage. The fact that EMU has two aspects – European integration and constitutionalising of the Keynesian state – is clearly illustrated by the fact that the current British debate about independence of the Bank of England largely brackets off the former issue and focuses on the question of accountability to Parliament. The central difficulty is overcoming the constitutional prejudice that independence from government means absence of accountability. ...

In general, the fiscal aspects of the European constitution apply to the UK as to other states. However, Art 11 of the UK Protocol provides that the UK Government may maintain its 'ways and means' (ie overdraft) facility with the Bank of England, if and so long as the UK does not move to the third stage. The recitals to the Protocol note the practice of the UK Government to fund its borrowing requirement by the sale of debt to the private sector. The Protocol thus provides only a partial and limited exemption from Art 104 of the Treaty and any use of the ways and means facility for monetary financing of government borrowing would be a breach of the Article.

The arrangements for EMU thus have a dual significance. They are about integration, but also about constitutionalising the relationship between public power and the economy. This was recognised by the German Constitutional Court in its judgment concerning the Maastricht Treaty. It described the constitutional independence of the future ECB as a 'modification of the principle of democracy' [p78]. The same could also be said of the provisions of the Treaty concerning excessive deficits and the constitutional position of national central banks in the second stage of EMU.

As constitutional lawyers, the 'modification of the principle of democracy' with which we are most familiar is, of course, judicial review of primary legislation. Its justification is the subject of a huge constitutional literature, to which an interesting recent contribution has been made by the American author Bruce Ackerman. Ackerman proposes a 'dualist' theory of democratic representation, in which a distinction is drawn between the level of political support which needs to be mobilised for 'normal' law-making and that which is needed for 'higher' law-making in the name of 'we the people' [We the People vol 1 (1991)]. It is this distinction which justifies denying plenary law-making powers to the winners of the last election.

The distinction is not based on a theory of individual rights which democratic institutions must always respect. It derives from the claim that, in ordinary circumstances, institutions of government do not represent the sovereign people as a whole, but competing interest groups and factions. By focusing not on the rights of individuals, but on the legitimacy of claims by elected politicians to determine the collective interest, the dualist theory provides a constitutional rationale for various kinds of institutional constraint on public power – the Separation of Powers. checks and balances and federalism – as well as for judicial view of legislation.

This approach is interesting since its logic can be applied to the emerging economic constitution of the European Union. The susceptibility of elected governments to short-term pressures is the main argument for central bank independence and for constraints on government deficits. The institutions and procedures which the Treaty contains can be understood as attempts to avoid foreseeable distortions in representing the public interest on the part of institutions of collective decision-making.

On a 'dualist' interpretation of democracy, this kind of constitutional design can be understood not as a modification, but as an application, of the principle. Naturally, this is completely opposed to the orthodox view of the British constitution in which, as was mentioned above, ministerial responsibility to Parliament is assumed to be the only mechanism for making public power accountable. ...

Constitutional identity

Economic relationships are important, but cannot provide the sole foundation of a constitution. Ensuring the supply of public goods, including redistribution and the correction of market failures, is a fundamental task of public authority. However, states are also the principal guarantors of individual rights of all kinds (civil, political, social, etc) and the principal focus for citizens' participation in public life and for the expression of social solidarity.

This may, and, it is hoped, will, change. As a broader concept, 'subsidiarity' is not just about the relationship between states and the Union, but also about the search for a richer variety of collectivities, political and otherwise, which individuals can use as a meaningful context for their actions. However, at present states remain the most important form of political community. This fact is recognised by the Treaty on European Union, which refers to an ever closer union among 'the peoples of Europe' and to 'relations between the Member States and between their peoples' [Art A]. The latter formulation is neatly ambiguous on the question of whether there is a precise coincidence of states and peoples; perhaps there are more (or fewer) peoples than states. However, it clearly excludes the idea that there is, at present, a European 'people'. ...

The Union level of government: some tentative conclusions and questions

The analysis of the preceding sections has three implications.

(1) Forging a European constitutional identity through a European equivalent of the American 'new deal', in which the power of the federal government *vis-à-vis* that of the states was expanded through new spending, is undesirable and unlikely. There simply is not the willingness amongst citizens of the European Union to pay for additional public goods.

(2) The possibility of large-scale transfer of existing areas of spending and of existing tax bases to the Union should be viewed with scepticism. Public finance involves conflicts between different interests; conflicts over the size of the public sector *vis-à-vis* the private, over spending priorities and over distribution of the burden of taxation. Transferring these conflicts from national budgetary processes to a Union budget would make them more, not

less, difficult to resolve. Persuading tax-payers to pay is likely increasingly to involve a clearer demonstration of the link between the costs and the benefits of public services. This is easier to achieve through spending and taxing decisions which are less, rather than more, centralised. Defence is the only major possible exception. Despite the efficiency arguments in favour of centralising defence expenditure, I assume that only the revival of a major external threat is likely to produce spending on defence by the Union level of government. This is, of course, far from inconceivable.

(3) Part of the business of EMU left unfinished at Maastricht was the question of a Community-level fiscal counterpart to the ECB. If the analysis in (1) and (2) is correct, we should expect the answer to be found primarily in further mechanisms of co-ordination of states' fiscal and budgetary policies. Devising an effective institutional framework for this purpose is one of the most challenging tasks for 1996.

Notes

1   The preambles to both the EC Treaty and the TEU set out a declaration of principles which together can perhaps be summed up as: achieving closer union 'between the peoples of Europe'; ensuring economic and social progress within the Community; and demonstrating attachment to democratic principles and respect for human rights.

2   Attainment of these aims is to be achieved by means of the single market and economic and monetary union. The means of ensuring respect for human rights is not made clear. Thus it can be said that the entire Community legal system is based upon the economic goal of the creation and expansion of the single internal market, by means of market forces.[3] Although Community law is intended to create social benefits in addition to economic benefits, social benefits are conceived of as a by-product of, or adjunct to, economic integration.[4]

3   A significant characteristic of the TEU is its provision for Member States to opt-out of its provisions. The UK has done so in relation to the Social Protocol. The Conservative Government reaffirmed its commitment to the opt-out from the Social Chapter in its 1996 White Paper on the future of the EU, *A Partnership of Nations*, published on 12 March 1996. It has the option of opting out in relation to economic and monetary union.

4   As noted above, the three pillars of the Union consist of (i) the three Communities, (ii) the Common Foreign and Security Policy (CFSP), and (iii) Co-operation in Justice and Home Affairs (CJHA). Under the TEU, the CFSP and CJHA are outside the scope of the other pillar; they are intergovernmental pillars and generally action under these heads must be taken by all 15 Member States. Thus voting in the Council under these heads must generally be unanimous.

---

3   See Treaty of Rome, preamble and Arts 1–3. See also, in a different context, Szyszczak, 'Race Discrimination: the Limits of Market Equality', in Hepple and Szyszczak, *Discrimination: The Limits of Law* (1992), p125.

4   This is exemplified in the case of harmonisation of a minimal level of employment protection provisions in order to create a 'level playing field' of competition for employers in the Single Market. See, eg, Nielsen and Szyszczak, *The Social Dimension of the European Community*, 2nd edn (1993), pp15–18; Hoskyns, 'Women, European Law and Transnational Politics' (1986) 14 Int J Soc Law, 299–315.

5   The TEU contains certain features which may be said to reflect its internal contradictions. On the one hand it contains the possibility of opt-out, and the adoption of the principle of subsidiarity in Art 3(b) and the preamble, together with the exclusion of the jurisdiction of the ECJ from certain areas, particularly foreign and security policy. On the other, it provides for closer union in certain areas, particularly economic and monetary union (due to be completed in 1999) and may represent a stage in a movement towards political union.

6   The 1996 Intergovernmental Conference (IGC) to be held at Turin will review the Maastricht changes and will consider in particular the extension of majority voting in a number of areas including foreign and security policy, the transition to a single currency by 2000 and expansion of the Union from 15 to 27 states.[5]

Questions

1   What messages may have been sent to the policy-making bodies within the community by the process of ratifying the Maastricht Treaty?

2   How far have the Member States given up sovereignty in the areas of foreign and security policy?

3   What contribution did the TEU make to the advancement of political and social integration?

4   In what sense does Harden consider that the EU has a constitution?

5   What distinction does Harden draw between the EU constitution and the British constitution?

COMMUNITY INSTITUTIONS

Introduction

The four main institutions of the Community, the Council, the Parliament, the Commission and the Court of Justice, clearly do not conform in many respects to UK constitutional expectations of such institutions. It might appear that the Council and the Parliament would correspond to the legislature, the Commission to the executive and the Court to the judiciary.

However, the original Parliament (or, as it was under the Treaty of Rome, Assembly) was not intended to act as a legislative body. Since the introduction of direct elections to the Parliament in 1979 it has become increasingly important in a consultative capacity; the Council must consult the Parliament in relation to legislation although it need not follow Parliament's opinion. Under the Single European Act (SEA), Parliament was given a second opportunity to consider draft legislation; if it continues to object to it the Council can still adopt it but has to act unanimously and within three months. The Treaty of European Union (TEU) also introduced a right of co-decision with the Parliament in

---

5   See further on the IGC 'Justus Lipsius' (1995) 20 EL Rev 3, 235–67; P Craig (1996) PL 13.

certain specific areas (Art 189b EC), thereby increasing the influence of the Parliament.[6]

The Council, which is now referred to as the Council of the European Union, consists of representatives of the Member States who are 'authorised to commit the government of that Member State' (Art 146 EC). When the Council is to discuss particularly significant matters of policy, it may consist of the heads of state, and it is then known as the European Council. The Council is the main legislative body; it decides either by unanimous voting, by qualified majority voting or by a simple majority. Under qualified majority voting the influence of the 'big four' states is assured since they carry 10 votes each. Originally it was thought that unanimous voting would be used for all the more sensitive areas of the Treaty, but one of the results of the SEA and TEU has been to increase the scope for qualified majority voting. Thus, its influence on policy-making in Member States may increase although particular national governments may disagree with certain policies. This possibility is likely to sharpen one of the main criticisms of the Council – its lack of democratic legitimacy (see Raworth below). Parliament, which is directly elected, was originally conceived as a body subordinate to the Council. Although it may be said that, after Maastricht, Parliament is moving closer to a position of equality with the Council, it has not achieved it. Thus, these arrangements represent the converse of those in the UK in relation to its bicameral system.

Although the Commission is to some extent an executive body and its officials perform a role similar to that of the UK civil service, it also has some law making powers. The Commission consists at present of 17 members (two from each of the 'big four' states and one from each of the other states). They are supposed to act independently of their own Member State; they are headed by a president chosen from among their number. The Commission has three main functions. It acts as an initiator of Community action, basing itself on the EC Treaty in formulating proposals or acting under the power provided by Art 235. It also seeks to bring to an end any infringements of Community law by Member States, bringing proceedings under Art 169 if this is necessary. It also acts, as noted above, as a form of civil service, implementing decisions of the legislature. Its membership must be approved by Parliament and the members may be removed by the Court for serious misconduct. They cannot be removed by the Council. The whole Commission (but not individual Commissioners) can be removed by a two-thirds majority vote in Parliament. There would of course be nothing to stop the Member States simply re-appointing the same Commissioners.

The Separation of Powers in the European Constitution is much greater than in the UK. For example, the personnel of the Commission, the Council and the Parliament are all completely separate. But within the bodies, the functions are blurred. The Commission fairly clearly performs executive functions – except that its role in initiating policy is very much shared with the Council. But it does have the normal executive role of implementing and administering policy. However, unlike the executive in the UK, it is clearly less important than the

---

6   For discussion of the co-decision procedure see: S Boyron (1996) 45(2) ICLQ 293.

Council, which is the main legislator. Whereas in the UK the formal legislature and the actual legislature (in practice the Cabinet) are different, in Europe, the actual and theoretical legislatures (the Council) are one. But the Council also concludes treaties, and can initiate policy; in that sense it is more like the executive than the legislator.

The changing relationship between the Council, the Parliament and the Commission

The main institutions originally set up by the Treaty of Rome are considered by Munro below. This account gives an indication of the respective roles of the Council, Parliament and Commission as they were originally conceived and provides a useful background against which to set the changes brought about by the SEA and TEU. As the next part of this chapter makes clear, significant development of these institutions has occurred, most notably as regards the powers of the Parliament.

Colin Munro, *Studies in Constitutional Law* (1987), pp113–18

Community institutions – The Council

The Council of the European Communities, often called the Council of Ministers, is the principal decision-making and legislative body. It is the Council which enacts most of the important legislation, adopts the budget, and concludes international agreements on behalf of the Community. It is the body charged under the EEC Treaty with ensuring 'that the objectives set out in this treaty are attained' [EEC Treaty, Art 145].

Meetings of the Council are normally attended by members of the Commission, although they do not have the right to vote. The Council spends much of its time on considering legislative proposals from the Commission. Normally these proposals will have been sent first to the European Parliament for its opinion, and sometimes also to the Community's Economic and Social Committee, a consultative body representing trade unions, employers, consumers and other interest groups. Then the proposals would be studied by a working party, under the supervision of the Committee of Permanent Representatives (Coreper). That body, consisting of the officials who are ambassadors to the Community from its Member States, is responsible, in the words of the Merger Treaty, for 'preparing the work of the Council and for carrying out the tasks assigned to it by the Council' [Merger Treaty, Art 4]. In fact, with its permanent presence on site and its diplomatic skills, Coreper has come to play a distinctive and important role in Community affairs.

There is a subtle balance of power between Council and Commission. The Council appears to have the ascendancy, and, unlike the Commission, is not constitutionally responsible to the European Parliament (or to anyone else, for that matter, although its members may be responsible for their actions in their own countries). However, it is the Commission which has the right of initiative as to legislation, and moreover the Council may only amend a Commission proposal by unanimous vote, and otherwise must accept it, reject it, or return it for reconsideration. The Council's ability to act of its own accord is limited, although it may do so to an extent in the co-ordination of economic policy, and through a provision which empowers it to request appropriate proposals from the Commission for the attainment of the Treaty's objectives [EEC Treaty, Art 152].

The interplay between Commission and Council is often interesting, for the Council, as a forum for the views of national governments, is obviously the least supranational of the institutions. A supranational philosophy may be detected in the Treaties' provisions allowing for majority voting on many decisions. However, a constitutional convention developed to limit majority voting. In 1966, after France had adopted its 'empty chair' policy of boycotting Community institutions for some months, it was agreed in the 'Luxembourg Accords' that unanimity must be sought (and reached, according to the French view) before taking decisions where 'very important interests of one or more partners' were at stake. That this was no more than a convention was shown in 1982 when the UK's opposition to a decision on agricultural prices did not avail against the majority view. Besides, in 1986 the Member States agreed to extend majority voting so as to expedite decision-making [in the Single European Act: cmnd 9758]. But it remains to be seen whether governments will swallow their national interests more easily. ...

The Commission

[The members of the Commission] are appointed 'by common accord of the Governments of the Member States' [Merger Treaty, Art 11], and must be nationals of a Member State, although no more than two must be nationals of the same state. In practice, two Commissioners have been appointed from the larger states (France, Germany, Italy, the UK and Spain) and one from each of the smaller states. The appointees have usually had a background in national politics, and the nominations have been influenced by domestic political considerations. For example, the UK Commissioners have been drawn equally from the Labour party and the Conservative party.

Once appointed, Commissioners may not seek or accept instructions from any Government, and the Member States in turn are bound not to try to influence Commissioners in their work. The requirement that the Commission's members act independently makes it the most genuinely supranational of the political institutions. The Commission represents and expresses the Community's interests, and its impartiality is its greatest asset. Moreover, it decides and acts as a collective body, on the basis of a simple majority vote if required.

The Commission is really the motive force of the Community, with a variety of political and executive functions. First, as we have already seen, it is the initiator of policy, and since the merger of the institutions it is the co-ordinator of the Communities' policies. It has the power, and in some instances the obligation, to propose to the Council measures likely to advance the development of Community aims. The Commission tries to anticipate and meet possible objections from the Council, sometimes successfully, sometimes not. Often the end result, after a process of dialogue, is something of a compromise between the Commission's Community-centred view and the national interests involved. In limited fields, or where powers are delegated to it by the Council, the Commission itself may legislate.

As the guardian of the treaties, the Commission acts to ensure that Community law is obeyed. For this purpose, it has investigative powers, and can impose fines on individuals or companies, notably those who are found to be in breach of competition rules [appeals against these decisions are heard by the Court of Justice]. The Commission deals with requests from Member States to invoke the provisions which allow for temporary waivers or derogations from Community obligations. It also instigates infringement proceedings when Member States seem not to be complying with Community law, at the rate of 200–300 per year. If it remains dissatisfied with the state's response, it can issue a reasoned opinion to that effect, and if necessary it will bring proceedings against the state before the Court of Justice.

The Commission has a number of other executive roles. It is responsible for maintaining relations with international organisations such as the United Nations. It acts sometimes as the agent or delegate of the Council, for example in the negotiation of trade agreements with other countries, and in the management of agricultural markets. In the coal and steel sector, the Commission has especially wide powers of its own, and it also has important powers of decision over the functioning of the common market in matters such as the customs union and the competition rules. It also prepares the draft budgets of the Communities, and administers and implements them after their adoption.

The Parliament

The Parliament was, until 1979, composed of delegates nominated by the Member States' legislatures from amongst their own members. However, Art 138, as later amended, required direct elections under a uniform procedure. In 1976 the Council agreed to institute direct elections, and provided for some aspects of these, including the numbers of seats allocated to each Member State [OJ 1976, L 278/1]. The influence of national interests is evident in the arrangements made, for the numbers do not fully reflect the differences in population. The UK, in common with the other larger states, has 81 seats, whereas Luxembourg has six. But the UK population is more than 150 times that of Luxembourg. In the absence of agreement on some other aspects of the elections, national legislatures were able to make their own arrangements for the 1979 election, and that was still the position in 1984 [for this country, see European Assembly Elections Acts 1978 and 1981]. The procedures adopted here were similar to those for parliamentary elections, and the same first-past-the-post voting system was employed for the British constituencies, while different systems obtained in the other countries.

The functions which the Parliament does have, according to Art 137 of the EEC Treaty, are 'advisory and supervisory'. The advisory aspect is most obviously its role with regard to legislation. In this respect, the Parliament works mainly through its standing committees, which meet during another two weeks of the month. There are committees specialising in all the main areas of Community activity, such as the Transport, Social and Employment, and Agriculture, Fisheries and Food Committees. Often, members of the Parliament are able to influence the content of proposed legislation before it is drafted, either at sessions of the committees, which are attended by members of the Commission too, or in the plenary sessions, at which they are also present. Moreover, there are many provisions in the treaties requiring that the Parliament be consulted on proposed legislation before its adoption by the Council, and a failure to observe this requirement may lead to the annulment of the legislation.

Note

The roles of the Council, the Parliament and the Commission, as described by Munro, are developing due to the changes brought about by the Maastricht Treaty. In particular, the role of the Parliament is becoming more significant. The recent development of these institutions is considered below.

V Bogdanor, 'Britain and the European Community' in Jowell and Oliver (eds), *The Changing Constitution*, 3rd edn (1994), pp7–9

Formally, the European Parliament is primarily a consultative rather than a legislative body which must be consulted on all major issues and has the right to dismiss the Commission by a vote of censure. Under the Single European Act which came into effect in July 1987, the Parliament was given additional powers over the bulk of legislation concerning the single internal market. The Maastricht Treaty increased the powers of the Parliament still further and, under Art 158 of the Treaty of Rome, as amended, Parliament must approve the President and the other members of the Commission.

The European Parliament, however, as well as the Council of Ministers as a legislative body (and even, in some ways, the domestic parliaments of the Continental Member States) are parliaments of an entirely different sort from Westminster, the working of which British legislators find it difficult to understand. For Westminster is dominated by the executive, while the European Parliament is able to carry on a dialogue with other Community institutions — the Commission and the Council of Ministers. Until the Maastricht Treaty, there was a 'democratic deficit' in the Community, since powers had been transferred from the Member States where they were, in theory, under the supervision of parliaments, to a Community whose executive — the Commission and the Council of Ministers — was not, in the same way, under the supervision of the European Parliament. Maastricht helped to resolve this deficit by increasing the powers of the European Parliament, a process which had been begun by the Single European Act. The Maastricht Treaty was, however, perceived as a threat by British policy-makers for whom the only acceptable form in which the Community should be governed was through a confederal Council of Ministers, a Council operating under rules of unanimity and secrecy so as to secure a 'Europe des patries' after the style of the late General de Gaulle.

The House of Commons is fundamentally a debating chamber, dominated by the binary dialogue between Government and Opposition. The standing committee procedure for the scrutiny of legislation is in essence an extension of the process of debate; indeed, it has been suggested that these committees could be more accurately termed 'debating committees'. Parliament is, as Bernard Crick once put it, a continuous election campaign. Its procedures are geared to informing the electorate of issues in dispute between Government and Opposition, and it implies the existence of two disciplined armies in the House of Commons articulating two quite different philosophies. Community legislation, however, is not being promoted by a government, nor attacked by an opposition. Most Community legislation does not fit in to the binary conception of politics dominant at Westminster; it departs from the normal pattern of a series of measures to which the Government is committed and which it has an interest in defending. Community legislation, therefore, is bound to impose a strain upon the House of Commons as it struggles to assimilate an entirely different legislative process into its traditional procedures.

Turning from legislative activity to democratic institutions, it should be noted that the European Parliament, by contrast with Westminster, is, like most Continental legislatures, a multi-party parliament, operating through carefully constructed coalitions. Since the implementation of the Single European Act in 1987, its driving force has been a coalition between the Christian Democrats – the European people's party – and the socialists: in other words, between a party group of the moderate Right and a party group of the moderate Left. It was, for example, this coalition which in the 1989 Parliament secured the election of the Spanish socialist, Enrique Baron Crespo, as President of the Parliament for the first two-and-a-half years, in exchange for an agreement that there would be a Christian Democrat president for the second half. Such coalitional politics are quite unfamiliar to British politicians. In Britain, coalitions occur either in war time – 1915–16, and 1940 – or at a time of economic emergency – 1931 – but they are seen as essentially temporary, as involving a suspension of normal adversarial party politics. On the Continent, by contrast, coalitions, in political systems characterised by multi-party politics and proportional representation, are generally seen as involving a continuation rather than a suspension of party politics. The parties engaged in a governmental coalition, eg the Christian Democrats and Free Democrats in the Federal Republic, continue to argue out their differences, but within government rather than outside it. Such a conception of politics is almost wholly alien to British experience.

The European Parliament, like a number of other Continental legislatures, is horseshoe-shaped rather than rectangular after the manner of Westminster; and, like other Continental legislatures, it is essentially a working legislature, rather than a debating one, devoted primarily to legislative scrutiny rather than to adversarial politics or the general scrutiny of the executive. There is in the European Parliament an absence of confrontation when compared with Westminster. That is partly because there is no party-supported government at Strasbourg seeking to promote its legislation or to secure support for its policies.

As compared to the European Parliament, Westminster is geared to consider legislation only when it reaches a fairly final form, rather than to scrutinise draft legislation. By the time that legislation reaches Parliament, it will generally have been drafted and redrafted many times, following consultation with various interested parties, and the backing and prestige of the Government will normally be behind it. A legislative proposal put forward by the Commission and a subsequent decision taken in principle by the Council of Ministers, on the other hand, although already the subject of consultation with interested parties before formal presentation, is subject to considerable amendment as it goes through the legislative process until the negotiations in the Committee of Permanent Representatives of the Member States prior to the meeting of the Council of Ministers. This method is quite unknown in British constitutional experience.

In contrast to the House of Commons, the European Parliament has strong specialised committees whose function is both legislative and investigatory. In the Commons, standing committees do not begin to scrutinise legislation until after second reading, ie after the principle of the legislation has been agreed. The Commons, unlike the European Parliament, has no committee whose role is that of pre-legislative scrutiny of domestic legislation, nor do its standing committees hear oral evidence or receive written evidence. The European Parliament is thus a legislature of a quite different kind. It is not surprising that the two Parliaments find it difficult to communicate with and understand each other. Their attempt to do so resembles a dialogue between two incompatible computers.

Philip Raworth, 'A Timid Step Forwards: Maastricht Treaty and the Democratisation of the European Community,' (1994) European Law Review 16, 17–28, 30-32

The European Community is conceived within the parliamentary tradition, but, despite the existence of a directly elected legislative chamber since 1979, it has lacked democratic legitimacy at both the executive and legislative level.

Executive power within the Community is exercised partly by the Commission and partly by the Council. The Commission is theoretically under the political control of the directly elected European Parliament [Case 302/87, *Parliament v Commission* [1988] ECR 5637 at p5640], but Parliament's means of enforcing this control have been weak. The Council is completely autonomous; it may answer questions put by members of Parliament (MEPs) but it is not responsible in any way to Parliament [see Parliament's resolution of 17 June 1988 (1988) OJ C187/229, pts 4, 14].

In the Community legislature, the normal relationship between the two houses in a parliamentary democracy is inverted under the pre-Maastricht legislative procedures. Here it is the Council, which is an unelected body composed of ministerial delegates from the Member States, that has the sole power of decision. The directly elected Parliament fulfils a merely consultative role. It has no legislative power at all, which has caused it to be dismissed as 'in no sense a parliamentary body' [D Lasok and J Bridge, *Law and Institutions of the European Communities* (1987), p222].

If the Community only served to regulate relations between the Member States, this democratic deficit would not have become an issue. However, even before Maastricht, the Community was already involved in legislating for many domains of national life and its laws directly affect individuals in the Member States. In effect, Community law is more akin to federal than international law, which calls for an appropriate institutional response. It is not surprising, therefore, that there was general agreement that the extension of the Community's competences by the Maastricht Treaty had to be complemented by progress towards democratic legitimacy.

The solution to democratic legitimacy in the Community must be found, as Parliament has emphasised, at the Community level [resolution of 17 June 1988, pts 9, 19]. This is the standpoint from which Maastricht should be judged.

Reform of the Legislature

Co-decision

The procedure – The main reform introduced by the Maastricht Treaty is the so-called co-decision procedure [Art 189b EC], which follows the same steps in the first round as the co-operation procedure but which strengthens Parliament's position substantially in the second round. Now, Parliament's rejection of the common position ends the legislative process unless the Council can persuade it to change its mind at a meeting of the Conciliation Committee, which consists of 12 Ministers representing the Council (or their representatives) and 12 MEPs. Also, if Parliament amends the common position and the Council does not accept all these amendments or rejects Parliament's text outright, the Conciliation Committee meets to put together a compromise text.

Where the Conciliation Committee agrees upon a joint text, this must be approved by a qualified majority of the Council and by a simple majority of votes cast in Parliament. Once approved by the two institutions, it becomes law. On the other hand, failure by either institution to approve the text ends the legislative process. Where the Conciliation Committee fails to agree on a joint text, the legislative process is similarly brought to an end unless the Council decides to confirm its common position, with or without the inclusion of parliamentary amendments. It will then be up to Parliament to reject this common position anew by an absolute majority of MEPs, failing which it will become law. This option is not open to the Council where the Committee's joint text fails to secure the necessary approvals.

Under co-decision, Parliament and the Council share legislative power, and the final text is enacted by both institutions and bears the signature of the Presidents of the Council and Parliament [Art 191(1) EC]. This emancipation of Parliament has three important consequences for the legislative process.

Parliament gains a control over the legislation process – Under the two pre-Maastricht procedures, Parliament had no certain means of preventing the enactment of legislation. While the Court of Justice has confirmed that Parliament's opinion is a procedural necessity [Case 138/79, *Roquette Frères v Council* [1980] ECR 3333 at pp3360–3361], academic opinion is almost unanimous in interpreting the Court's judgment as indicating that Parliament cannot delay the legislative process indefinitely by refusing to give its opinion.

While it is true that the co-operation procedure gives Parliament the right to reject the Council's common position at its second reading [Art 189c EC], there are several reasons why this does not significantly improve Parliament's control over the legislative process. In the first place, the Council can override any rejection if it acts by unanimity, although it may not be easy for it to find the necessary consensus. In October 1988, when Parliament rejected the common position on the protection of workers exposed to benzene at work, the Council was unable to enact the legislation. However, it is equally difficult for Parliament to muster the absolute majority of its members that is needed to reject a common position. In national parliaments, a simple majority of votes cast is usually sufficient to defeat a legislative proposal. Rejection by Parliament of a common position also ends the legislative process rather than bringing about a meaningful exchange of views with the Council.

Understandably, MEPs are reluctant to engage in such a negative and counter-productive strategy. Parliament has in practice made little use of its right to reject.

Under co-decision, Parliament acquires an absolute right to reject proposed legislation. More importantly, although the rejection still takes place at Parliament's second reading and continues to require an absolute majority of MEPs, it is no longer a last-minute, negative veto but a means of forcing the Council into constructive negotiations in order to secure a text that is acceptable to both institutions. This should make it easier for Parliament to find the necessary majority to oppose the Council and prevent the enactment of legislation of which it disapproves.

Parliament acquires an effective means of input into the final legislation – The co-operation procedure improves Parliament's input into the final legislation by giving it two opportunities to bring forward its views. Although only a few of Parliament's major second-round amendments are taken up by the Council, they must be added to those already accepted from the first reading. Parliament may also wield some additional influence by threatening to reject the common position, but as it is difficult to assemble the necessary majority to undertake this step, the threat may lack credibility. All in all, the co-operation procedure has resulted in only a modest increase in Parliament's input.

Under co-decision, the Council must take Parliament's views seriously as the final text requires the latter's approval before it can become law. Equally important for Parliament's input into the final text is that it now deals directly with the Council during the second round; it is its own advocate and can insist itself on the accommodation of its views. Indeed, the Maastricht Treaty encourages such accommodation, even at the expense of the Commission, by allowing the Council to approve a test emanating from the Conciliation Committee by a qualified majority even where it is opposed by the Commission [Art 189a(1) EC].

No more unilateral changes to a text approved by Parliament – Under co-decision, there is no possibility of unilateral changes by the Council subsequent to Parliament's second reading as the final text requires Parliament's approval. The Council could still make such changes after Parliament's first reading, but these too will eventually have to be approved by Parliament. This need for Parliament's ultimate approval may encourage the Council to follow the former's rules on reconsultation more closely.

Co-decision and the limits of the democratic principle – There is, of course, a limit to the compromises that may be made with the democratic principle without impairing the legitimacy of the Community legislature. At the very least, Parliament as the directly-elected, lower chamber must have an equal say in the legislative process.

But, there's the rub. The Maastricht Treaty does not make Parliament the Council's equal. First and foremost, co-decision is restricted in scope [it is used under Arts 49, 54(2), 56(2), 57(1), 57(2), 100a(1), 100h(1), 126(4), 128(5), 129(4), 129a(2), 129d, 130I(1) and 130s(3) EC] and so, in the majority of matters, the Council remains the sole legislator. The procedure is not used, *inter alia*, for the budget, justice and home affairs or any aspects of EMU. However, it is not clear how significant this limited ambit of co-decision will turn out to be, as the Maastricht Treaty provides for its extension to other matters and for an intergovernmental conference to do this. [Arts 189b(8) EC; N(2) TEU]. Unfortunately, this will not resolve the problem as co-decision is structured in such a way as to favour the Council.

In the first round, the Council is under no time restraints, which means that it can simply refuse to act on the Commission's proposal. Parliament, on the other hand, can probably be by-passed if it does not complete its first reading within a reasonable time and, even if it rejects the Commission's proposal, the Council can still enact a common position by a qualified majority. Parliament would have required the Council to act within six months and to adopt a common position by unanimity where Parliament has rejected the Commission's proposal [suggested Article 188b].

At its second reading, Parliament requires an absolute majority of MEPs to amend or reject the common position and thus bring the conciliation process into operation. Moreover, if it fails to act, this constitutes approval by default of the common position. The Maastricht Treaty ignores Parliament's suggestions [suggested Art 188b] that it be allowed to amend or reject a common position by a simple majority of votes cast and that the Conciliation Committee should meet where it fails to act at all. By contrast, if the Council fails to act on Parliament's text during the second round or cannot muster a qualified majority to approve it as is, the Maastricht Treaty provides for the Conciliation Committee to meet. It is, therefore, much easier for members of the Council to bring a matter to conciliation.

Perhaps the most significant advantage enjoyed by the Council is its ability to confirm its original common position if conciliation fails. Parliament has criticised this provision, arguing that it forces it into a third reading and puts on it the onus of holding up the progress of the Community [resolution of 11 July 1990, (1990) OJ C231/97, pt 32]. It is also conceivable that, by this stage, enough MEPs may decide not to pursue the conflict with the Council that the legislation passes by default.

The superiority that the Council retains under co-decision is unnecessary. The legitimate defence of the Member States' interests in the legislative process is guaranteed by retaining the Council in its present form and making it a co-legislator. There is no need to go further. To do so is to call into question the democratic legitimacy that co-decision seeks to confer on the Community's legislative process. ...

Right of legislative initiative

The Maastricht Treaty gives Parliament the right to request the Commission to submit legislative proposals that Parliament considers necessary for implementing the Treaty [Art 138b EC). However, this new right does not permit

Parliament to make the proposal itself if the Commission does not act within a set time limit, as Parliament had wanted [suggested Art 188a(2)]. Thus, the Commission retains its almost exclusive right to initiate Community legislation. Furthermore, if, as the Commission believes, it is free to withdraw its proposals at any time during the legislative process, maintaining this exclusivity keeps an effective executive veto. However, before criticising the timidity of Maastricht's approach, we should bear in mind that the practice of the executive in a parliamentary system may be very similar to that of the Commission. It often monopolises the initiation of legislation and withdraws proposals at will.

Reform of the Executive

The Council

The Council as executive – In the Community, the Council as well as the Commission exercises executive power. The Council's executive acts are controlled by Parliament to some extent by use of the assent procedure, but this is not sufficient. The democratic principle requires the Council to be politically responsible to Parliament, which it is not. Parliament has neither any influence over its composition nor a means of removing it. The Maastricht Treaty makes no changes here.

A solution is to make the Commission the sole repository of executive power in the Community, as Parliament and the national parliaments advocate [see Parliament's resolution of 12 December 1990]. Unfortunately, this is not realistic. The Community is still an association of sovereign states in which the national identity dominates and the national interest must be accommodated. In sensitive areas, this inevitably means that Community action is only possible by way of intergovernmental decision-making. Thus, Maastricht retains the Council's executive role and even extends it to the new areas of foreign and security policy, economic and monetary union and co-operation in justice and home affairs [Art 103(3), 104c, EC; J 8(2), K 3(2) TEU]. Whatever their preferred solution, Parliament and the Commission appear to accept this situation.

Transfer of executive power to the Commission – Maastricht could, however, have been bolder and restricted the Council's executive role to those areas where decisions have to be made by an intergovernmental body. Elsewhere the Commission would exercise the executive power. Apart from some specific instances enumerated by Parliament [see resolution of 18 April 1991], there are two areas that seem to call for a transfer of power.

The first of these is the conduct of the Community's external commercial and economic relations. Parliament had suggested that the Commission be wholly responsible for administering the common customs tariff and for negotiating and concluding agreements with other countries [suggested Arts 28 and 228].

The second area that should be assigned to the Commission is the enactment of secondary legislation that implements and applies the basic laws of the Community.

The transfer of executive power to the Commission only makes sense, of course, if this institution is itself properly responsible to Parliament. It is to this final topic that we now turn. ...

Responsibility of the Commission to Parliament – Parliament exercises a certain amount of control over the Commission on an ongoing basis by virtue of the latter's obligation to submit an annual general report to Parliament, to respond to questions from MEPs and to take note of Parliament's amendments and resolutions [Arts 143 140 EC]. The democratic principle requires above all, however, that the Commission enjoys the continuing support of Parliament.

Under the new system introduced by Maastricht, the Commission must obtain the initial approval of Parliament before it can be appointed by the Member States. This is not a universal practice in parliamentary states, but it would seem a democratic necessity in the Community. In a nation state, members of the government belong to a homogeneous political class and are chosen as the representatives of prevailing opinion in that class. The situation in the Community is very different.

Perhaps even more important than the right to demonstrate its initial confidence in the executive is the legislature's right to censure the government's subsequent conduct of affairs. The vote of censure has been described as 'one of the essential attributes of a parliamentary system of government'. A successful vote forces the resignation of the government, as in the Community, or precipitates new elections. Parliament disposes of such a mechanism [Art 144 EC], but it has been widely criticised as ineffective. Not all of this criticism is justified.

[the censure mechanism] ... has been dismissed as a 'blunt weapon' because it entails the resignation of the whole Commission. Such criticism is inappropriate as this is the common result of a vote of censure in parliamentary states because of the collegial nature of government.

Parliament's censure mechanism has also been castigated as an unpredictable 'leap in the dark' because the new Commission is appointed by the Member States, who are unlikely to appoint a more pliant replacement. This may change with Maastricht as Parliament must now formally approve the Commission's replacement. However, it is still the Member States who nominate the new Commission. Thus, instead of a replacement from among representatives of the new prevailing opinion in Parliament, which is what happens on a national level, the Commission will again be chosen from outsiders in accordance with prevailing national political opinion. This certainly reduces the effectiveness of Parliament's censure mechanism and with it the Commission's political responsibility to Parliament.

Notes

1   The changes brought about by the TEU have not radically transformed the role of the Council. The Council as a collective entity is still not directly accountable to anyone and there is no convention of resignation (individual members of it may of course be accountable, in varying degrees, to their national representative institutions). This is partly because, out of the European institutions it clearly represents the inter-governmental as opposed to the supranational principle. It is not pretended that decisions are taken solely in the interest of the Community: they are taken not after debate and discussion on mutually agreed agendas reflecting the interests of the Community, but as a result of bargaining, deal making and negotiation based on various national interests. This process remains largely secretive.

2   The Council remains the most powerful of the European institutions. It does, of course, have to engage in consultative legislation in certain areas and, after the TEU, in joint legislation in others. It largely remains to be seen how the joint legislative procedure will work in practice; in relation to the consultation process, Parliament has complained repeatedly that the Council does not explain its reasons for its proposals, or its reasons for initially rejecting Parliament's amendments.

3   The Parliament, since Maastricht, does have a clear legislative role (as is apparent from Munro's account above, it was previously merely a weak consultative body) but it does not have any major role as a scrutiniser of either Commission or Council. Its scrutiny of both bodies is not remotely comparable to British Parliamentary scrutiny of government; in particular, the European Parliament does not have an Opposition as such – since the Council and Commission are not formed from the Parliament, but rather appointed by the Member States. Therefore, there is no organised, disciplined body of members with a vested interest in rooting out corruption, maladministration and failures of policy as the Opposition has in Britain.

4   The problem with giving greater powers to the European Parliament is that, whilst this would reduce the 'democratic deficit' discussed by Raworth, it would also be a step in the direction of the Community as a body made up of the peoples of Europe, whereas those concerned to protect national sovereignty wish to preserve it as a confederation of sovereign states. Thus, the Conservative Government stated in its 1996 White Paper on the future of the EU, *A Partnership of Nations*, Cm 3181 that the European Parliament cannot displace the primacy of the national Parliaments. As long as such primacy is to be retained, then the Governments of the Member States must play the most important role. Greater powers for the European Parliament would undermine national sovereignty, particularly because the Parliament decides measures by ordinary majority voting, whereas certain key decisions in the Council require unanimity. Nevertheless, it would still be possible to ensure, at the least, greater accountability of the Commission to the Parliament, and radically improve its procedures for scrutinising policies put forward by both the Council and Commission.

5   See further on the 'democratic deficit' since the Maastricht process: G de Burca (1996) 59(3) MLR 349 esp, 361–66.

Questions

1   Has Maastricht resolved the 'democratic deficit' of the Community?

2   Is the process of integration still continuing and irreversible?

3   Are there grounds for viewing the TEU as marking a stage on the road towards a European public law?

4   Raworth considers the relationship between Parliament and executive in the European Community, and the change brought about in that relationship by the Maastricht Treaty, arguing that the control exercised by Parliament over the executive is weak in comparison with other Parliamentary systems. He suggests that the weakness of the Parliament may call into question the democratic legitimacy of the EC. However, if, as Oliver and Jowell suggest, the Parliament carries on a 'dialogue' with the Council and Commission, is it useful and desirable to seek to establish greater 'accountability' of either or both of those bodies to the Parliament? Would it tend, counter-productively, to introduce the adversarial into a non-adversarial process?

The role of the European Court of Justice

The Court is the ultimate authority on all matters of Community law. Its role is to ensure 'that in the interpretation and application of this treaty the law is observed' (Art 164). It adopts a teleological or purposive approach to the Treaty since it is a framework treaty and the Court views its role as one of 'gap-filling'. Thus, although the Court plays a role in developing the European constitution which may resemble that of the UK judiciary, it has taken decisions, particularly those relating to the supremacy of the Community law (see Part I, Chapter 5), which the UK judiciary would probably have regarded as lying within the province of Parliament.

The European Court of Justice, as the supreme authority on all matters of Community law, has to deal with matters of constitutional law, social and economic law and administrative law. In order to relieve some of the pressure placed on it, in 1986 the Single European Act provided for the setting up of a new Court of First Instance with a limited jurisdiction.

The work of the European Court of Justice and, in particular, its policy-making role, is considered below.

Colin Munro, *Studies in Constitutional Law* (1987), pp119–121

The Court of Justice

[Judges] are appointed by common accord of the Member States' governments. That formulation is intended to underline the Court's supranational character, as is the difference between the numbers of judges and Member States. But the invariable practice has been to appoint a judge from every Member State, although the treaties do not require this, and the 'extra' judge has been selected from the larger states in rotation.

The advocates-general, now six in number, are appointed to assist the Court. After the parties in proceedings before the Court have completed their submissions, an advocate-general considers the issues impartially and presents the Court with a reasoned submission. His submission is not binding on the Court, and he does not participate in the Court's composition of a judgment; but the Court frequently accepts his conclusions and generally refers to his submissions in its judgment. The office has no British counterpart, but is similar to that of *Commissaire du Gouvernement*, a public interest attorney in the French *Conseil d'Etat*. In other respects, too, the Court's procedures are more like those of Continental courts, and written submissions are more important than oral argument. The Court deliberates in secret, and decides by majority vote if necessary, but delivers a single judgment in open court without dissenting opinions. The full Court hears the most important cases, but many are decided by a chamber of three, four or five judges.

Each of the treaties establishing the Communities uses the same broad terms to define the Court's responsibilities, which are to 'ensure that in the interpretation and application of this treaty the law is observed' [for example, EEC Treaty, Art 164]. In fact, the kinds of proceeding which may come before the Court are quite varied, extending to such matters as the Community's contractual and non-contractual liability, and disputes between the Communities and their staff (which occupy a disproportionate share of the Court's time).

There are three types of proceeding which are especially important. First, there are actions against Member States for failure to fulfil a Community obligation.

Such actions may be brought by the Commission or, provided the matter has been brought before the Commission first, by another Member State. If the state is held by the Court to be in breach of its obligations, then, according to Art 171 of the EEC Treaty, it 'shall be required to take the necessary measures to comply with the judgment of the Court of Justice'. However, the Court has no coercive powers to enforce that. The Court's ruling in 1979, that French regulations which prevented the free importing of British lamb were illegal, was defied by the French government for some months, simply as a tactical manoeuvre [Case 232/78 *EC Commission v France* [1979] ECR 2729, [1980]; I CMLR 418].

Another kind of proceeding is that which is brought against a Community institution in order to review the legality of its act. This corresponds to the jurisdiction of the British courts in controlling the actions of the government and other public authorities, although the grounds of challenge are modelled on those found in French administrative law. Actions of this sort may be brought by a Member State or by a Community institution, or in some circumstances by affected persons. The defendant is normally the Council or the Commission, but in 1981 the Grand Duchy of Luxembourg brought proceedings for the annulment of a resolution of the Parliament concerning its place of sitting, and the application was held admissible, although it failed on the merits [Case 230/81 *Grand Duchy of Luxembourg v Parliament* [1983] ECR 255]. Proceedings may also be brought against a Community institution for its failing to act when a treaty imposes a duty to act.

Aside from its contentious jurisdiction, the Court has an important interpretative jurisdiction. Under Art 177 of the EEC Treaty, it gives preliminary rulings on the interpretation of the treaties and on the validity and interpretation of Community legislation, when a national court refers a question to it because its interpretation or ruling is necessary for the decision in a case. The Court only rules on Community law; the case has to be remitted to the national court for disposal by the application of that law (and national law, if it is relevant) to the facts. But, as to Community law, the national court is bound to follow the Court's preliminary ruling.

Anthony Arnull, 'Judging the New Europe' in Jowell and Oliver (eds), *The Changing Constitution*, 3rd edn (1994), pp13–15

The effect of the Treaty on European Union

The Treaty on European Union betrays a certain ambivalence on the part of the Member States about the role to be played by the Court in the new Europe. Art L, for example, purports to exclude from the Court's jurisdiction new provisions on a common foreign and security policy and on co-operation in the fields of justice and home affairs. These pillars of the Union are to be essentially intergovernmental in nature. Whatever its effect, Art L might be construed as a kind of threat; are the Member States perhaps saying that they consider the Court too unpredictable to be given jurisdiction in these areas? Is there an implication that, unless the Court becomes more circumspect, the Member States might seek to remove other areas from the ambit of its powers?

In addition, the Treaty provides, in Art N2, for an intergovernmental conference to be convened in 1996 to examine some of its provisions. It is likely that the Member States will take the opportunity to carry out a general review of the treaties. That will be the third occasion in 10 years that they have done so. In a Community in which the political institutions are functioning reasonably effectively and the Member States are carrying out regular reviews of the treaties, the need for, and even the legitimacy of, an overtly activist approach by the

Court of Justice may increasingly come to be questioned. It is significant that agreement was reached at Maastricht on two protocols designed to limit the potential effects of controversial decisions of the Court, one on pensions [case C–262/88, *Barber* [1990] ECR 1–1889], the other on abortion [Case C–159/90, *SPUC v Grogan* [1991] 3 CMLR 849]. More frequent intergovernmental conferences will make it easier for the Member States to employ this device again.

By contrast, the Treaty on European Union endorses the Court's case law on fundamental rights [see Art F2] and on the status of the European Parliament in annulment proceedings [Art 173]. It also confers on the Court important new powers. These include the power to impose sanctions on Member States which fail to take the steps necessary to comply with previous rulings of the Courts [Art 171]; the power to review the legality of acts adopted by the European Central Bank [Art 173]; and the power to hear actions brought by the Council of the European Central Bank against national central banks which are alleged not to have complied with the Treaty [Art 180(d)]. Moreover, the Treaty introduces a new type of legislative procedure [Art 189b] alongside the existing procedures. This will inevitably produce a further growth in litigation between the institutions over the correct legal basis of legislation.

The Treaty also envisages greater involvement by the Court in assessing the merits of legislation through the famous principle of subsidiarity, or 'nearness'. According to that principle, in areas where the Community shares competence with the Member States, if may only act where the objectives of the proposed action cannot be sufficiently achieved by the Member States acting alone. It is widely acknowledged that the question whether action needs to be taken at the Community level in order to achieve a particular objective is essentially a political one. Although it is a question that the Court might prove reluctant to confront directly, the inclusion of the principle of subsidiarity in the body of the Treaty seems to demonstrate a willingness on the part of the Member States that it should do so.

Conclusion

On balance, the effect of the Treaty on European Union will therefore be to consolidate the critical position the Court has carved for itself in the institutional framework of the Community. Nonetheless, although the Council's decision to extend the jurisdiction of the Court of First Instance has relieved some of the pressure on the Court, there remain grounds for doubting whether in the long run it will be able fully to assume the responsibilities which are to be cast upon it. The Court's large case load has already led it to modify its attitude towards the preliminary rulings procedure, which has hitherto played a central role in the Community's development. National courts are now required to set out the background to cases which are referred more fully and to explain why a ruling from the Court of Justice is deemed necessary. Otherwise, the Court is likely to refuse to answer the questions submitted to it [see Case C–343/90, *Lourenço Dias v Director da Alfandega do Porto*, judgment of 16 July 1992; Case C–83/91, *Meilicke v ADV/ORGA*, judgment of 16 July 1992]. It is a reflection of the pressures under which the Court is now operating that it is prepared to jeopardise in this way the goodwill of the national courts, which it has worked so hard to build up and which is crucial to the functioning of the preliminary rulings procedure. The Maastricht Treaty can only add to those pressures.

If the Court is to play the role which seems to have been reserved for it in the European Union, it may therefore be necessary to contemplate more radical changes to the Community's judicial architecture [this phrase was coined by

Jacque and Weiler (1990) 27 CML Rev 185] than those which have hitherto been made. These might include a right to appeal directly to the Court of First Instance against decisions taken by national authorities in the application of Community rules on certain matters. Examples are customs classification, agriculture and social security. At present, the Court is effectively required to review many such decisions itself, through the filter of the preliminary rulings procedure. Because of its constitutional importance, that procedure is likely to remain the exclusive preserve of the Court for some time [Art 168a(1)]. A more expensive alternative, but one which would reduce the risk of overloading the Court of First Instance, would be to establish regional courts of first instance, with jurisdiction to hear certain categories of action arising in particular Member States. The Court might also be given the power to refuse to deal with certain cases which, although not manifestly unfounded, seem to the Court unlikely to have a significant impact on the development of Community law.

Perhaps the greatest threat to the Court's place in the institutional structure of the Community therefore comes not from the politicians, but from the sheer number of cases it is called upon to resolve. Those cases are a tribute to the Court's success in fashioning a Community based on the Rule of Law. It would be ironic if that very success contained the seeds of the Court's demise. Member States which are genuinely attached to the Rule of Law will not need to be reminded of the paramount need to avoid that result.

Below, de Burca considers the policy-making role of the ECJ in relation to the particular area of sex equality law and suggests that it does not represent a very 'friendly environment for interest representation'.

G de Burca 'A Community of Interests? Making the Most of European Law', (1992) 55 *Modern Law Review* 346–9

The three celebrated and influential cases which initiated the equality litigation in the ECJ came from Belgium. Defrenne allowed her name to be used in litigation which ultimately involved three appeals to the Court of Justice. The second of these [*Defrenne v Sabena (No 2)* [1976] ECR 455] established the key point for campaigners that Art 119 was 'directly effective' in Member States of the Community insofar as equal pay was concerned. This meant that it could be enforced by individual litigants in national courts, giving a new point of entry into national policy making. The true nature of the Court of Justice as a policy making court was rammed home in these cases when the UK and Ireland, which were not parties to the action, intervened in the action with a socio-economic brief prophesying economic doom if equal pay provisions had to be implemented immediately. Although their objections of principle were swept aside, the Court made a crucial concession to the intervenors by denying retrospectivity to the judgment, an unusual move widely seen by women as induced by pressure from commercial lobbies acting through the Governments of Member States. The decision therefore emphasised to the movement the need for political campaigning in parallel to litigation. It also stressed the importance of Community policies as a vehicle for legal change.

The Court of Justice and interest-representation

If, as has been suggested [J Weiler (1982) 21 J of Common Market Studies 39], the European Court of Justice is developing something of the policy making function possessed by the United States Supreme Court, then it is not, as presently constituted, a particularly friendly environment for interest representation. It remains essentially the constitutional court of a transnational organisation with procedures available primarily to Member States and Community institutions. In layman's language, individuals can institute proceedings only against Community decisions, which, whether addressed to themselves or to a third party, are of 'direct and individual concern' to them. This requirement has been restrictively construed by the Court [see *Plaumann v Commission* [1963] ECR 95: *Fruit and Vegetable Cases* [1962] ECR 171]. The rights of individuals to intervene in a case to present evidence or argument to the Court are similarly restricted, being in general reserved for the Commission or Member States, though there is one favourable precedent in which consumer groups were allowed to intervene in an unfair competition case brought by the Commission against Ford Motors [*Ford of Europe Inc and Ford-Werke AG v Commission* [1984] 1 CMLR 649]. Here, BEUC and the British Consumers' Association were both given permission to intervene because the case had originated in complaints made by them to the Commission. In this way. the groups were able to inform the Court directly of their views on cartels instead of being restricted to oblique representation by the Commission.

This is a crucial precedent. As matters now stand, entry to the European Court of Justice is virtually restricted to Member States, which already hold the political strings, and those who have the Commission's ear. These are not always the big battalions but, given the weight of commercial lobbying power at Brussels, there is a very real danger that they may be. Consider the case of Lord Bethell, an MEP and also chairman of the Freedom of the Skies Campaign, a consumer group which had been fighting to terminate air passenger cartels. The group first tried lobbying the Commission to bring Art 169 infringement proceedings against the major airlines but without success. So Lord Bethell tried to circumvent the standard procedure by an action for judicial review by the Court for failure to take action under Art 169. The Court ruled that Lord Bethell had no standing to sue either as an air passenger or in his capacity as chairman of a consumer organisation [*'Lord Bethell v Commission*, Business and Government in Europe', *European Affairs*, 4 October 1990]. A new window of opportunity for interest-representation is urgently needed and the Court should adapt its procedure so that unofficial voices can more easily and more conveniently be heard.

Notes

1 In *Henn* (1981)[7] Lord Diplock said of the ECJ: 'It seeks to give effect to what it conceives to be the spirit rather than the letter of the treaties; sometimes, indeed, to an English judge, it may seem to the exclusion of the letter'.

2 Steiner, in *EC Law*, 4th edn (1994), observes at p20 that the Court was at its most active in the 1970s and 1980s and that recent decisions show signs of a new conservatism. Arnull suggests above that the Member States demonstrated their nervousness regarding the activism of the Court in the Maastricht Treaty.[8]

3 Recent conservatism of the Court may perhaps be seen in certain decisions on sex discrimination, an area in which until recently it was generally thought to take a dynamic stance.[9] The Court took, it is suggested, a

---

7 AC 850.

8 See also Bradley (1988) 13 EL Rev 379; Ehlermann (1992) 29 CML Rev 213; D Edwards (1995) 20 EL Rev 6, 539.

9 See Ellis, 'The Definition of Discrimination in European Community Sex Equality Law' (1994) 19 EL Rev 563, 567–8.

restrictive stance in Case C-399/92 *Stadt Lengerich v Helmig*[10] and Case C-297/93 *Grau-Hupka v Stadtgemeinde Bremen*.[11] However, a recent and very significant decision in this area does not entirely fit this pattern. In Case 450/93 *Kalanke v Freie Hansestadt Bremen*,[12] the Court found that a German quota system aimed at reducing an imbalance between men and women in sectors of the German public service was unlawful under the Equal Treatment Directive. Thus, it took what might be termed a conservative and yet activist stance.

4   The role of the Advocates-General has been extremely significant in determining the directions taken by the Court since the Court usually accepts their opinions.[13]

5   The 1996 White Paper on the future of the EU, *A Partnership of Nations*, included proposals to place certain curbs on the powers of the ECJ including placing limitations on the retrospective application of its judgments and adopting measures enabling the rapid amendment of EU legislation which has been interpreted in a manner unintended by the Council.

Question

The generally activist stance of the European Court of Justice may be seen as standing in marked contrast to the stance taken by the UK judiciary. How far could the ECJ claim legitimacy for adopting such a stance at the present time?

SUBSIDIARITY

The Maastricht Treaty appears from the discussions above to have increased centralisation of power within the EU. However, centralisation may be countered by use of the principle of subsidiarity.

V Bogdanor, 'Britain and the European Community' in Jowell and Oliver (eds), *The Changing Constitution*, 3rd edn (1994), pp21–27

The Maastricht Treaty undoubtedly centralises power through extending the competences of the Community in areas such as energy and the environment, as well as in its proposals for economic and monetary union. But, at the same time, the Treaty signifies a first attempt to counteract the trend towards creeping centralisation and to seek a new equilibrium capable of balancing power between the Community, Member States and local authorities. This is to be achieved in two ways: first, through the principle of subsidiarity; and second, through the establishment of a new consultative Committee of the Regions.

The principle of subsidiarity is introduced in the preamble to the Maastricht Treaty, and enacted by a newly inserted Art 3b of the Treaty.

---

10   Judgment of 15 December 1994, joined with Cases C-409/92, C-425/92, C-50/93, C-78/93.

11   Preliminary ruling, 13 December 1994; see Fenwick, 'Indirect Discrimination in Equal Pay Claims: Backward Steps in the European Court of Justice?' (1995) 1(3) *European Public Law*, 331–8. See also Fenwick and Hervey 32 CMLR 443–70.

12   Judgment of 17 October 1995; [1995] IRLR 660.

13   See further on their role AA Dashwood (1982) 2 LS 202; Sir G Slynn (1984) 33 ICLQ 409; T Koopmans (1991) PL 53–63.

The principle of subsidiarity was put into the Treaty partly as a result of the concern of the German *Lander* that the development of the Community should not undermine its federal system of government, since it is the Federal Government rather than the *Lander* which is legally responsible for ensuring compliance with Community provisions. But the British Government also pressed for its inclusion for a quite different reason — to reserve powers for the Member States as against the Community; for Britain, the principle of subsidiarity is a substitute for a states' rights clause, on the lines of the 10th amendment to the American Constitution or Art 30 of the German Constitution, a provision conspicuously absent from the Treaty of Rome.

The principle of subsidiarity takes its place in the constitution of the European Community as a principle of judicial interpretation, a guide for the European Court of Justice. It is legally binding upon the institutions of the Community, and imposes a three-fold test upon putative Community legislation. The first is whether there is a legal basis for a Community action. That was, of course, already part of Community law before the Maastricht Treaty, and Art 164 required the Court of Justice to ensure it. The second is whether, even if there is a legal basis, the Community should activate it, or whether instead the objective of the proposal might not be sufficiently achieved by the Member States. Moreover, even if the objective in question cannot be sufficiently achieved by the Member States, the question has to be asked whether the objective can be better achieved by the Community. The third test relates to the intensity rather than the scope of Community legislation, and asks whether the Community is leaving enough discretion to the Member States. Is it, for example, using a regulation that is directly applicable in a situation where a directive that would leave implementation to a Member State would suffice?

The second test applies to 'the areas which do not fall within' the 'exclusive jurisdiction' of the Community. It bears some similarity to Art 72 of the German Constitution providing for the role of the *Lander* in cases of concurrent powers. It does not apply, therefore, to areas such as the common agricultural policy, the common commercial policy and the external tariff, which fall within areas of admitted exclusive Community competence. The second test applies to areas where there is a mixed competence of both the Community and Member States, so that there is a choice between Community action and national action.

The third test, however, in the final paragraph of Art 3b, known as the proportionality test, applies to all Community legislation, whether it lies within a field of exclusive competence or not. According to Douglas Hurd, the Foreign Secretary, the British delegation at Maastricht insisted that the proportionality test be put into a separate third paragraph precisely to emphasise its contrast with the previous provision which applies only to areas where the Community lacks exclusive competence. In fact, however, given the case-law of the European Court of Justice, this third paragraph adds little, if anything, to existing legal rules.

It is at the present time impossible to predict what use the European Court will make of the principle of subsidiarity. It could generate a burgeoning jurisprudence as the commerce clause and the equal protection clause have done in the American constitution; or it could, alternatively, come to have very little juridical significance, as Art 72 of the German Constitution appears to have done. It may be that the European Court will take the view that it has to prove manifest error or abuse of powers to strike down Community legislation on grounds of subsidiarity. Many British lawyers would take this view since they believe that subsidiarity is otherwise too imprecise a term to be properly justiciable. Subsidiarity may well therefore prove to be a constitutional convention of the Community rather than a justiciable principle.

... the principle of subsidiarity may well influence, albeit indirectly, central-local relations. For the principle is likely to operate at the political as well as the legal level. It is likely to prove a political constraint upon Community institutions — upon the Commission when proposing legislation, the European Parliament when proposing amendments, and the Council of Ministers when making decisions. At the Lisbon summit in June 1992, the Member States agreed that all existing Community legislation had to be examined by the end of 1993 so that the Council could decide which items ought to be repealed in accordance with subsidiarity criteria. Proposals for new legislation are now accompanied by a justification from the Commission showing that they are in accordance with the principle of subsidiarity.

Although the principle of subsidiarity will not directly affect central-local relations, it may well give rise to a new mood in which decentralisation is seen as a necessary complement to the transfer of competences to the Community. In such circumstances it is difficult to believe that Britain will or can remain unaffected. For, if the question: 'Has the Community made the case that this competence cannot be carried out at Member State level?' comes to be asked, so also might the question: 'Has the case been made that this competence cannot be carried out at local level?'. If that happens, the principle of subsidiarity will have helped to create a new atmosphere in central-local relations, and one which is far more favourable to local government.

The principle is, moreover, complemented by Arts 198a–c of the Maastricht Treaty, establishing a Committee of the Regions. The establishment of this Committee may be regarded as an institutional means of ensuring that subsidiarity leads to the devolution of powers to sub-national levels of government, as well as from the Community to Member States.

... the setting up of the Committee constitutes a clear institutional recognition on the part of the Community that the construction of European Union requires the contribution of regional and local bodies, as well as that of national governments. Since the regions and localities are responsible for the implementation of some Community legislation, and often have to enforce it, logic requires that they should be given a voice in helping to determine what that legislation should be. The Maastricht Treaty transforms the regional problem from a merely economic one to a political and institutional one. It recognises the role of sub-national bodies, and seeks to organise their participation in the decision-making process of the Community.

John Peterson, 'Subsidiarity: A Definition to Suit Any Vision?' (1994) 47(1) *Parliamentary Affairs* 116–19

In the debate about the future of the European Community, anyone unable to use the principle of 'subsidiarity' to defend their position — whatever it may be — risks being excluded from the debate altogether. Yet, no student of the EC should be deterred from joining in. The debate has gone public. In the late 1980s, national sovereignty was often transferred to the EC without much discussion at the behest of an activist European Commission which reduced political decisions to small, gradual and apparently technical steps. But no longer; the 'new' debate about Europe features low barriers to entry in part because one of several definitions of subsidiarity can be marshalled to support virtually any vision of the EC's future, from a United States of Europe led and dominated by EC institutions to a Gaullist *'Europe des patries'* in which nation-states make all important decisions. Of course, the recent proliferation of interpretations has a downside, too. It has acted to confuse and obfuscate a concept which has the potential to guide clear-sighted, enlightened decisions about the future of European governance.

Subsidiarity has been applauded across a wide political spectrum in Europe as a principle for determining how powers should be divided or shared between different levels of government. It has featured extensively in a debate about the Maastricht Treaty on European Union which has been sterile and even xenophobic, but which may, in the end, help revitalise European democracy. The tendency for otherwise implacable foes to unite behind the banner of subsidiarity has at least allowed humour to seep into the debate. For example, subsidiarity was discussed at the panicky European summit of July 1992 in Lisbon, which followed Denmark's 'no' vote in its first referendum on Maastricht. Afterwards, *The Economist* (4 July 1992) suggested that the first act of 'Maastricht, the musical' had ended with the 12 EC heads of Government singing 'I'm gonna wash that man right out of my hair'; 'The man is [Commission President] Jacques Delors ... The shampoo is a fashionable brand known as subsidiarity. The dramatic irony is that Mr Delors himself invented this shampoo, and is seen singing happily with the leaders'.

Origins and interpretations

The *Oxford English Dictionary* contains only one definition of subsidiarity: 'the quality of being subsidiary; specifically the principle that central authority should have a subsidiary function, performing only those tasks which cannot be performed effectively at a more immediate or local level'.

The OED credits Pope Pius XI (not Jacques Delors) with first developing subsidiarity as a doctrine of Catholic social philosophy. His Encyclical Quadragesimo Anno of 1931 implied that social life in modern states had disintegrated mostly because the state had usurped the functions of small social groups, such as the family. It asserted that 'it is an injustice, a grave evil and a disturbance of the right order for a larger and higher association to arrogate to itself functions which can be performed more efficiently by smaller and lower societies'. Subsidiarity was deemed 'valid for social life in all its organisations'.

By the late 1970s, subsidiarity had become part of the popular lexicography of the European Parliament, where it was frequently cited, particularly by members of Christian democratic parties, as grounds for increasing the EC's powers. This use of subsidiarity is less paradoxical than it first appears for two reasons. First, enthusiasm for European integration is long-standing within continental Christian democratic thought as a means for avoiding war between nation states. Second, the so-called 'government overload' crisis of the 1970s sapped confidence in the ability of nation states to cope adequately with their most urgent problems. The thesis that national policies, especially for the environment and industry, were inadequate entered the mainstream of continental political thought. The need to transfer sovereignty to the Community was justified by subsidiarity because only common policies could match the scale of the problems. By the mid-1980s, subsidiarity began to feature in a range of publications which argued for new Community actions to free the internal market. After meeting with the premiers of the German federal states in 1988, Delors argued that European federalism, featuring increased powers for EC institutions after the implementation of the Single European Act, was wholly compatible with the conservation of national or regional sovereignties and identities. Anxieties shared by leaders of the German states and other sub-national authorities about the possible encroachment of the Community on their powers were soothed by Delors' insistence that subsidiarity could act as a guide for dividing powers between different levels of authority in a federal Europe. Powers would be divided according to which level could wield them most democratically and efficiently in specific areas of policy.

Subsidiarity found its first legal expression in an EC Treaty when it appeared in the Single European Act's article on environmental protection. The EC had been created as an 'economic' community and had traditionally lacked a legal basis for a common environmental policy, despite the transnational nature of air and water pollution, toxic waste disposal, global warming, etc. All Member States recognised the need to remedy this gap in the Community's powers. However, several (particularly Denmark) feared that a common EC policy would act to weaken their strict national environmental standards. Thus, the Act stated that 'the Community shall take action relating to the environment to the extent to which the objectives ... can be attained better at Community level than at the level of individual Member States'.

The Act's environmental policy article remains the clearest application of subsidiarity in EC practice. Yet, even here subsidiarity is more a political than a legal doctrine. Inevitably, a large measure of political judgment is involved whenever decisions are made about whether the EC or its Member States acting on their own can better achieve a certain goal. Ideology also colours such judgments; differing visions of the proper relationship between state and society can lead to radically different views about which level of government should intervene in any given set of circumstances, or even whether government should intervene at all.

Broadly speaking, three competing 'ideologies' of subsidiarity may be identified. First, the Christian democratic version embraces the familiar themes of Catholic social philosophy. Small social groups should be autonomous and sovereign in a pluralist society, yet united in a common morality which stresses duty and harmony. They should be assisted in their activities by a state which neither substitutes for social groups nor is shackled by their demands, but which serves the public good and provides legal order. Christian democrats take a dynamic — as opposed to a centralist view — of politics. They envision state intervention only for limited periods to address specific social needs. However, Christian democrats also view themselves as the natural defenders of the Church and the family, as is revealed in their support for EC restrictions on Sunday working hours.

A second and alternative ideology of subsidiarity is based on the principles of German federalism. It argues for a 'total concept' or clear plan for the political evolution of the EC, which specifically defines the duties and powers of different levels of government in Europe. The German states in particular want to see their substantial powers, which are guaranteed by the German constitution, protected against trespass by EC institutions as European integration proceeds. In contrast to the Christian democratic version of subsidiarity, the German federalist version is more static: it seeks to constitutionalise a division of powers between different levels of government in a federal constitution for Europe. Such orderliness may seem too rigid in view of the need constantly to adapt political structures in accordance with the pace of economic integration in Europe. But it is difficult to argue that the post-war German experiment with federalism has not been largely a successful one.

Third, and finally, a British conservative ideology of subsidiarity emerged in 1991 during the intergovernmental conference on political unity which produced the Maastricht Treaty. It achieved full expression when the Major government held the EC Presidency in late 1992. British Conservatives view subsidiarity as a principle for limiting the EC's powers. They assume a narrow definition which sanctions EC action only when it is necessary to ensure the single market's 'four freedoms': the free movement of goods, people, services and finance across borders. British Conservative ideology refuses to accept the logic of continental versions of subsidiarity which can be — and increasingly have been — to justify decentralising powers to 'subsidiary' or sub-national units of government. The British constitutional settlement makes the UK, with the possible exception of Ireland, by far the most centralised state in the EC. British Conservatives remain reticent about tampering with a system which has given them unshared political power with 42–45% of the national vote in general elections since 1979. They insist on a version of 'territorial government' which resists any constraints — internal or external — on the autonomy of central government. At the level of the EC, subsidiarity means that, in the absence of clear rationale to support EC action to uphold the internal market, national governments should rule. The British Government's line on subsidiarity is by no means a mainstream view in the Community as a whole.

Notes

1   The preamble to the Maastricht Treaty and Art 3b expressly adopt the principle of subsidiarity. Art 3b provides, in essence, that (i) the Community must have legal authority to act and (ii) subsidiarity must operate in areas in which the Community does not have 'exclusive competence' – areas in which the Member States remain competent to act since the Treaty does not lay down a comprehensive requirement to adopt a common policy. If the area is not one of exclusive competence, the question to be asked is whether the objective in question could be better achieved by the Community than the Member State. Obviously, this test leaves an enormous amount of room for interpretation.[14]

2   The third part of the principle of subsidiarity which, as Bogdanor points out above, relates to all areas of Community law, whether in the area of 'exclusive competence' or not, restates the principle of proportionality. It reflects the notion of subsidiarity in the sense that it may allow restriction of the area of Community policy-making, since it means that policy-making in the Member States in Community-related areas should be restricted to what is strictly necessary and appropriate to achieve Community objectives. Thus, in the areas of 'exclusive competence', only one test need be applied to Community law; in the areas of 'non-exclusive competence' two tests need to be applied.

3   Proportionality has been defined by the Court as meaning that the means adopted are an appropriate means of achieving the end in question and necessary to that end (the test from *Johnston*, para 38).[15] In Case C-331/88 *Minister of Agriculture etc and the Secretary of State for Health, ex p Fedesa* the Court found 'when there is a choice between several appropriate measures recourse must be had to the least onerous, and the disadvantages caused must not be disproportionate to the aims pursued'.[16]

---

14   For discussion of the principle see: N Emiliou (1992) 17 EL Rev 383; AG Toth (1992) 29 CML Rev 1079; JP Gonzalez (1995) 20 EL Rev 4.

15   Case 222/84 *Johnston v Chief Constable of the RUC* [1986] ECR 1651.

16   [1990] ECR I-4023, 4063.

4   It is very difficult to predict how the principle of subsidiarity will work in practice. An example may illustrate the difficulties. Imagine that a new equal treatment directive covering race is to be introduced. First, it must be found that the Community has legal authority to act in this area. Assuming that this is the case, it must be asked if this is an area of non-exclusive competence. Since this would seem to be the case, it must secondly be found that measures preventing race discrimination can be dealt with better at Community level. Making such a determination would be likely to be complex and fraught with uncertainty. If it can be done, the measures which might be introduced should be considered. If two measures are available, one of which would have less far-reaching effects than the other but which would still achieve the objective – the promotion of the race equality principle – that one should be chosen. But determining whether certain less far-reaching measures, such as the exclusion of some forms of positive action, would or would not still allow the objective in question to be achieved and would be appropriate to achieving it would entail extensive and very complex investigations. It would also mean adopting a very precise definition of race equality. Moreover, answering the questions raised by the third test – the principle of proportionality - might lead back to and overlap with answering questions raised initially by the second – the issue of dealing with race discrimination better at Community level. All these questions would, it seems, be asked and answered at the Community level. Should they be asked and answered at local level? Assuming that that might not be appropriate in this instance, can circumstances be envisaged in which it would be? In other words, is it conceivable that the principle of subsidiarity might ultimately demand that determinations as to its applicability should be made at local level?

Questions

1   Would you expect the principle of subsidiarity to be used by the ECJ to strike down Community legislation?

2   In political terms what kind of impact might you expect the principle of subsidiarity to have?

3   Applying the principles of subsidiarity and of exclusive competence, is it clear when decision should be taken at local or national level rather than at Community level?

CHAPTER 2

DIRECT AND INDIRECT EFFECTS OF EC LAW IN DOMESTIC LAW; THE *FRANCOVICH* PRINCIPLE

INTRODUCTION[1]

In this chapter, discussion will concentrate on the extent to which individuals can rely on Community law directly before national courts. It will ask which Community instruments can be relied on and against whom. A movement will be traced towards the surer enforcement of EC provisions in national law and towards further protection of individuals under EC provisions. Chapter 5 of Part I considers the difficulties raised when Community instruments conflict with national instruments.

The difficulties surrounding the concept of direct effects in Community law have arisen due to the lack of clear provision for enforcement of Community law in the Treaty of Rome. It might have been expected that anything recognisable as EC law could be relied upon by individuals in national courts since, otherwise, harmonisation of laws between Member States could not occur or would occur patchily and precariously. However, this stance was not adopted probably because it would have seemed too abrupt an erosion of sovereignty to be politically acceptable. Thus complex rules have developed as to direct effects, but it is arguable that by their means the ECJ is now approaching the straightforward position outlined above.

Of course, this whole issue would not have arisen had Member States merely passed legislation fully implementing EC law and within the timetable provided to do so. However, this has not been the case and the ECJ has therefore sought to avoid the position whereby the only recourse for an individual in a Member State denied a remedy under EC law is to await the passing of fully implementing national legislation.

Lord Lester of Herne Hill QC, 'European Human Rights and the British Constitution', in Jowell and Oliver (eds), *The Changing Constitution*, 3rd edn (1994), pp51–2

The direct effect of Community law

Community law comes in different forms. There are provisions of the EC Treaty itself, as well as EC regulations and EC directives, and decisions of the EC institutions. The Community principle of direct effect means that appropriately worded provisions of the Treaty, or of regulations, or directives, may give rise to individual rights which national courts are bound to safeguard, even though there may have been no national implementing legislation, or only incomplete national legislation. The European Court of Justice decides when the principle of direct effect applies, and national courts translate the principle into practical reality in concrete cases. It can be a formidable judicial partnership.

---

1   General reading, see: J Steiner, *EC Law*, 4th edn (1994); S Weatherill and P Beaumont, *EC Law* (1993); S Weatherill, *Cases and Materials on EC Law* (1994); C Turpin, *British Government and the Constitution: Text, Cases and Materials*, 3rd edn (1995), pp281–90; Collins, *European Community Law in the UK*, 4th edn (1990); D Curtin (1990) 15 EL Rev 195; D Curtin (1990) 27 CML Rev 209; C Lewis and S Moore (1993) PL 151; M Plaza (1994) 43 ICLQ 26.

Directives are a particularly influential form of Community legislation in the area of social policy. Both the Court of Justice and British courts have frequently had to wrestle with the problems of the direct effect of directives. It is now well established [*Marshall v Southampton and South West Hampshire Area Health Authority*, Case 152/84 [1986] ECR 723; *Foster v British Gas* [1990] ECR 3313] that appropriately worded directives have direct effect as against the central government and any body which is an emanation of the state. What happens, however, if the state has failed to implement a directive correctly, because the claimant is, for example, seeking a remedy against a private law body, such as a private employer?

In its recent case law, the Court of Justice has become increasingly bold and creative in providing effective remedies for the individual who suffers as a result of the state's failure as legislator. The Court has held (*Marleasing SA v La Commercial International de Alimentacion SA*, Case C–108/89 [1990] ECR 4135] that national courts must apply directives to pre-existing legislation not enacted specifically to implement a Community rule. In the same case it held that national courts must as far as possible interpret national legislation in conformity with directives. Again, it has held (*Emmott v Minister for Social Welfare* [1991] IRLR 387] that, until such time as a directive has been properly transposed into national law, a defaulting Member State may not rely on national time limits as a defence to an individual claim.

Most far reaching of all, the Court has held, in the *Francovich* case (*Francovich and Bonifaci v Italian Republic*, joined Cases C–6/90 and C–9/90, judgment of 19 November 1991; (1992) 21 IRLR 84] that a Member State is obliged to make good the damage suffered by individual as a result of the state's failure to implement a directive correctly, where (i) the result to be achieved by the directive involves attributing rights to individuals; (ii) the subject-matter of these rights can be identified by reference to the provisions of the directive; and (iii) there is a causal link between the infringement of the state's obligation and the damage suffered by the aggrieved individual. In such circumstances there is a Community right to compensation against the state for damage suffered by reason of a failure to implement a directive correctly in domestic law. This is in marked contrast to the unsatisfactory position under British administrative law which enables an individual to obtain damages, not for a public law wrong, but only for a private law wrong such as negligence, breach of statutory duty or misfeasance in public office.

As the impact of these recent and far-reaching decisions of the Court of Justice comes to be understood, British judges will increasingly be called upon to adjudicate as constitutional judges and to fashion new remedies for the citizens of Europe within their jurisdiction. The judicial lions will have to move from their sheltered position beneath the throne of the sovereign Queen in and outside Parliament.

Notes

1   As Lord Lester suggests, there were three stages in the movement towards surer enforcement of EC provisions in national courts. These three stages are discussed in the next three sections below. First, the ECJ identified those EC instruments which would have direct effects in national courts and determined when they would have such effects. Second, the ECJ found that if the directive does not produce direct effects – since it is being invoked against an individual or non-state body – it may produce indirect effects. Third, the ECJ decided that, where an individual has suffered due to the failure of a state to implement a directive properly, the individual may have

a claim against the state in damages. This last, very far-reaching, possibility may leave the doctrine of indirect effects with a very circumscribed role.

2   It was made clear in *Costa v ENEL* Case 6/64 (1964)[2] that Treaty provisions could be directly relied upon in national courts. This was reiterated and clarified in *Amministrazione delle Finanze dello Stato v Simmenthal SpA* (1978):[3] 'Treaty provisions are a direct source of rights and duties for both individuals and the state in the Member States.'

3   This gave rise to the first question: if a provision of Community law arises from a directive or other community instrument rather than a Treaty, will it produce direct effects in national law?

THE POLICY OF THE ECJ: DIRECT EFFECTS AND DIRECTIVES

Van Duyn v Home Office (1975)[4] marked an early stage in the development of the doctrine of direct effect. The ECJ found that Council Directive 64/221 could confer rights upon individuals and that the national courts must protect those rights.

Van Duyn v Home Office Case 41/74 [1974] ECR 1337, ECJ

[11] The UK observes that, since Art 189 of the Treaty distinguishes between the effect ascribed to regulations, directives and decisions, it must therefore be presumed that the Council, in issuing a directive rather than making a regulation, must have intended that the directive should have an effect other than that of a regulation and accordingly that the former should not be directly applicable.

[12] If, however, by virtue of the provisions of Art 189 regulations are directly applicable and, consequently, may by their very nature have direct effects, it does not follow from this that other categories of acts mentioned in that Article can never have similar effects. It would be incompatible with the binding effect attributed to a directive by Art 189 to exclude, in principle, the possibility that the obligation which it imposes may be invoked by those concerned. In particular, when the Community authorities have, by directive, imposed on Member States the obligation to pursue a particular course of conduct, the useful effect of such an act would be weakened if individuals were prevented from relying on it before their national courts and if the latter were prevented from taking it into consideration as an element of Community law. Art 177, which empowers national courts to refer to the Court questions concerning the validity of the interpretation of all acts of the Community institutions, without distinction, implies furthermore that these acts may be invoked by individuals in the national courts. It is necessary to examine, in every case, whether the nature, general scheme and wording of the provisions in question are capable of having direct effects on the relations between Member States and individuals.

[13] By providing that measures taken on grounds of public policy shall be based exclusively on the personal conduct of the individual concerned, Art 3(1) of

---

2   CMLR 425; ECR 585.

3   ECR 629.

4   2 WLR 760.

Directive 64/221 is intended to limit the discretionary power which national laws generally confer on the authorities responsible for the entry and expulsion of foreign nationals. Firstly, the provision lays down an obligation which is not subject to any exception or condition and which, by its very nature, does not require the intervention of any act on the part either of the institutions of the community or of Member States. Secondly, because Member States are thereby obliged, in implementing a clause which derogates from one of the fundamental principles of the Treaty in favour of individuals, not to take account of factors extraneous to personal conduct, legal certainty for the persons concerned requires that they should be able to rely on this obligation even though it has been laid down in a legislative act which has no automatic direct effect in its entirety.

[14] If the meaning and exact scope of the provision raise questions of interpretation, these questions can be resolved by the courts, taking into account also the procedure under Art 177 of the Treaty.

[15] Accordingly, in reply to the second question, Art 3(1) of Council Directive 64/221 of 25 February 1964 confers on individuals rights which are enforceable by them in the courts of a Member State and which the national courts must protect.

Notes

1   In *Publico Ministerio v Ratti* Case 148/78 (1979)[5] the ECJ found that individuals could rely on directives as long as the obligations thereby imposed were 'unconditional and sufficiently precise' (para 23) and the period for their implementation by national legislation must have expired (para 24).

2   These limitations on the principle of the direct effect of directives meant that the ECJ was then confronted with questions as to which provisions of EC law enshrined in directives could be relied upon directly by individuals in national courts, when, and against whom.[6]

Marshall v Southampton and South West Hampshire Area Health Authority (Teaching) Case 152/84 [1986] ECR 723, ECJ

... it is necessary to consider whether Art 5(1) of Directive 76/207 may be relied upon by an individual before national courts and tribunals.

The appellant and the Commission consider that that question must be answered in the affirmative. They contend in particular, with regard to Arts 2(1) and 5(1) of Directive 76/207, that those provisions are sufficiently clear to enable national courts to apply them without legislative intervention by the Member States, at least so far as overt discrimination is concerned.

In support of that view, the appellant points out that directives are capable of conferring rights on individuals which may be relied upon directly before the courts of the Member States; national courts are obliged by virtue of the binding nature of a directive, in conjunction with Art 5 of the EEC Treaty, to give effect to the provisions of directives where possible, in particular when construing or applying relevant provisions of national law (judgment of 10 April 1984 in Case 14/83 *von Colson and Kamann v Land Nordrhein-Westfalen* [1984] ECR 1891). Where

---

5   ECR 1629.

6   See further Steiner (1990) 106 LQR 144.

there is any inconsistency be
cannot be removed by means
national court is obliged to c
inconsistent with the directiv

The Commission is of the
76/207 are sufficiently cl
national court. They m
Discrimination Act 1986
Appeal, has been extend
therefore become ineffec
retirement ages for men

The respondent and the
be answered in the neg
circumstances, have direct en.
may not rely on its failure to perio..
However, they maintain that a directive can nev..
individuals and that it can only have direct effect again..
public authority, and not against a Member State *qua* employer. As
a state is no different from a private employer. It would not therefore be prop
to put persons employed by the state in a better position than those who are
employed by a private employer.

With regard to the legal position of the respondent's employees, the UK states
that they are in the same position as the employees of a private employer.
Although, according to UK constitutional law, the health authorities, created by
the National Health Service Act 1977, as amended by the Health Services Act
1980 and other legislation, are Crown bodies and their employees are Crown
servants, nevertheless the administration of the National Health Service by the
health authorities is regarded as being separate from the Government's central
administration and its employees are not regarded as civil servants.

Finally, both the respondent and the UK take the view that the provisions of
Directive 76/207 are neither unconditional nor sufficiently clear and precise to
give rise to direct effect. The directive provides for a number of possible
exceptions, the details of which are to be laid down by the Member States.
Furthermore, the wording of Art 5 is quite imprecise and requires the adoption
of measures for its implementation.

It is necessary to recall that, according to a long line of decisions of the Court (in
particular its judgment of 19 January 1982 in Case 8/81 *Becker v Finanzamt
Munster-Innenstadt* [1982] ECR 53), wherever the provisions of a directive appear,
as far as their subject matter is concerned, to be unconditional and sufficiently
precise, those provisions may be relied upon by an individual against the state
where that state fails to implement the directive in national law by the end of the
period prescribed or where it fails to implement the directive correctly.

That view is based on the consideration that it would be incompatible with the
binding nature which Art 189 confers on the directive to hold as a matter of
principle that the obligation imposed thereby cannot be relied on by those
concerned. From that the Court deduced that a Member State which has not
adopted the implementing measures required by the directive within the
prescribed period may not plead, as against individuals, its own failure to
perform the obligations which the directive entails.

With regard to the argument that a directive may not be relied upon against an
individual, it must be emphasised that, according to Art 189 of the EEC Treaty,
the binding nature of a directive, which constitutes the basis for the possibility of

ore a national court, exists only in relation to 'each
addressed'. It follows that a directive may not of itself
individual and that a provision of a directive may not be
inst such a person. It must therefore be examined whether,
ndent must be regarded as having acted as an individual.

must be pointed out that, where a person involved in legal
able to rely on a directive as against the state, he may do so
the capacity in which the latter is acting, whether employer or
rity. In either case it is necessary to prevent the state from taking
of its own failure to comply with Community law.

the national court to apply those considerations to the circumstances of
ase; the Court of Appeal has, however, stated in the order for reference that
espondent, Southampton and South West Hampshire Area Health Authority
eaching), is a public authority.

The argument submitted by the UK that the possibility of relying on provisions
of the directive against the respondent *qua* organ of the state would give rise to
an arbitrary and unfair distinction between the rights of state employees and
those of private employees, does not justify any other conclusion. Such a
distinction may easily be avoided if the Member State concerned has correctly
implemented the directive in national law.

Finally, with regard to the question whether the provision contained in Art 5(1)
of Directive 76/207, which implements the principle of equality of treatment set
out in Art 2(1) of the directive, may be considered, as far as its contents are
concerned, to be unconditional and sufficiently precise to be relied upon by an
individual as against the state, it must be stated that the provision, taken by
itself, prohibits any discrimination on grounds of sex with regard to working
conditions, including the conditions governing dismissal, in a general manner
and in unequivocal terms. The provision is therefore sufficiently precise to be
relied on by an individual and to be applied by the national courts.

It is necessary to consider next whether the prohibition of discrimination laid
down by the directive may be regarded as unconditional, in the light of the
exceptions contained therein and of the fact that according to Art 5(2) thereof the
Member States are to take the measures necessary to ensure the application of the
principle of equality of treatment in the context of national law.

With regard, in the first place, to the reservation contained in Art 1(2) of
Directive 76/207 concerning the application of the principle of equality of
treatment in matters of social security, it must be observed that, although the
reservation limits the scope of the directive *ratione materiae*, it does not lay down
any condition on the application of that principle in its field of operation and in
particular in relation to Art 5 of the directive. Similarly, the exceptions to
Directive 76/207 provided for in Art 2 thereof are not relevant to this case.

It follows that Art 5 of Directive 76/207 does not confer on the Member States the
right to limit the application of the principle of equality of treatment in its field of
operation or to subject it to conditions, and that that provision is sufficiently
precise and unconditional to be capable of being relied upon by an individual
before a national court in order to avoid the application of any national provision
which does not conform to Art 5(1).

Consequently, the answer to the second question must be that Art 5(1) of Council
Directive 76/207 of 9 February 1976, which prohibits any discrimination on
grounds of sex with regard to working conditions, including the conditions
governing dismissal, may be relied upon as against a state authority acting in its

capacity as employer, in order to avoid the application of any national provision which does not conform to Art 5(1).

Notes

1   In *Marshall*, the ECJ limited the principle of direct effect to vertical effect. In other words, individuals could rely on a directive against a state body but not against a non-state body.[7] The justification for this is that directives are addressed to states and therefore impose obligations upon states, which states should not be able to escape simply by failing to implement the directive or by inadequate implementation. Thus directives do not have horizontal effect – effects in relation to non-state bodies, private companies or individuals.

2   The decision in *Marshall* threw up questions as to what constitutes a state body; these are particularly pertinent in view of privatisation, contracting out and marketisation. This question was addressed in *Foster v British Gas* (1990).

Foster v British Gas Case C-188/89 [1990] ECR I–3313, ECJ

By virtue of the Gas Act 1972 which governed the BGC [British Gas Corp] at the material time, the BGC was a statutory corporation responsible for developing and maintaining a system of gas supply in Great Britain, and had a monopoly of the supply of gas.

The members of the BGC were appointed by the competent Secretary of State. He also had the power to give the BGC directions of a general character in relation to matters affecting the national interest and instructions concerning its management.

The members of the BGC were obliged to submit to the Secretary of State periodic reports on the exercise of its functions, its management and its programmes. Those reports were then laid before both Houses of Parliament. Under the Gas Act 1972 the BGC also had the right, with the consent of the Secretary of State, to submit proposed legislation to Parliament.

The BGC was required to run a balanced budget over two successive financial years. The Secretary of State could order it to pay certain funds over to him or to allocate funds to specified purposes.

The BGC was privatised under the Gas Act 1986. Privatisation resulted in the establishment of British Gas plc, the respondent in the main proceedings, to which the rights and liabilities of the BGC were transferred with effect from 24 August 1986.

The appellants in the main proceedings were required to retire by the BGC on various dates between 27 December 1985 and 22 July 1986, on attaining the age of 60. These retirements reflected a general policy pursued by the BGC, that of requiring its employees to retire upon reaching the age at which they were entitled to a state pension pursuant to British legislation, that is to say 60 years of age for women and 65 for men.

The appellants in the main proceedings, who wished to continue to work, brought proceedings for damages before the British courts asserting that their retirement by the BGC was contrary to Art 5(1) of Directive 76/207. According to that provision, 'application of the principle of equal treatment with regard to

---

7   See further Stuyck and Wytinck (1991) 1 CMLR 205.

working conditions, including the conditions governing dismissal, means that men and women shall be guaranteed the same conditions without discrimination on grounds of sex.

According to the order of the House of Lords, the parties to the main proceedings are agreed that on the basis of the judgment of the Court in Case 152/84 *Marshall v Southampton and South-West Hampshire Area Health Authority* (1986) ECR 723 the dismissals were contrary to Art 5(1) of Directive 76/207. They are also agreed that those dismissals were not unlawful under the British legislation in force at the material time and that, according to previous judgments of the House of Lords, that legislation cannot be interpreted in a manner consistent with Directive 76/207. The parties are in dispute over the issue whether Art 5(1) of the directive may be relied on against the BGC.

It was in those circumstances that the House of Lords stayed the proceedings and referred the following question to the Court for a preliminary ruling:

> Was the BGC (at the material time) a body of such a type that the appellants are entitled in English courts and tribunals to rely directly upon Council Directive 76/207 of 9 February 1976 on the implementation of the principle of equal treatment for men and women as regards access to employment, vocational training and promotion, and working conditions so as to be entitled to a claim for damages on the ground that the retirement policy of the BGC was contrary to the directive?

The jurisdiction of the court

Before considering the question referred by the House of Lords, it must first be observed as a preliminary point that the UK has submitted that it is not a matter for the Court of Justice but for the national courts to determine, in the context of the national legal system, whether the provisions of a directive may be relied upon against a body such as the BGC.

The question was what effects measures adopted by Community institutions have and, in particular, whether those measures may be relied on against certain categories of persons necessarily involves interpretation of the articles of the Treaty concerning measures adopted by the institutions and the Community measure in issue.

It follows that the Court of Justice has jurisdiction in proceedings for a preliminary ruling to determine the categories of persons against whom the provisions of a directive may be relied on. It is for the national courts, on the other hand, to decide whether a party to proceedings before them falls within one of the categories so defined.

Reliance on the provisions of the directive against a body such as the BGC

As the Court has consistently held (see the judgment in Case 8/81 *Becker v Finanzamt Munster-Innenstadt* (1982) ECR 53, paras 23–25), where the Community authorities have, by means of a directive, placed Member States under a duty to adopt a certain course of action, the effectiveness of such a measure would be diminished if persons were prevented from relying upon it in proceedings before a court, and national courts were prevented from taking it into consideration as an element of Community law. Consequently, a Member State which has not adopted the implementing measures required by the directive within the prescribed period may not plead, as against individuals, its own failure to perform the obligations which the directive entails. Thus, wherever the provisions of a directive appear, as far as their subject matter is concerned, to be unconditional and sufficiently precise, those provisions may, in the absence of implementing measures adopted within the prescribed period, be relied upon as against any national provision which is incompatible with the directive or in so far as the provisions define rights which individuals are able to assert against the state.

The Court further held in its judgment in Case 152/84 *Marshall*, para 49, that where a person is able to rely on a directive as against the state he may do so regardless of the capacity in which the latter is acting, whether as employer or as public authority. In either case it is necessary to prevent the state from taking advantage of its own failure to comply with Community law.

On the basis of those considerations, the Court has held in a series of cases that unconditional and sufficiently precise provisions of a directive could be relied on against organisations or bodies which were subject to the authority or control of the state or had special powers beyond those which result from the normal rules applicable to relations between individuals.

The Court has accordingly held that provisions of a directive could be relied on against tax authorities (the judgments in Case 8/81 *Becker*, cited above, and in Case C-221/88 *ECSC v Acciaierie e Ferriere Busseni (in liquidation)* [1990] ECR I-495), local or regional authorities (judgment in Case 103/88 *Fratelli Costanzo v Comune di Milano* [1989] ECR 1839), constitutionally independent authorities responsible for the maintenance of public order and safety (judgment in Case 222/84 *Johnston v Chief Constable of the Royal Ulster Constabulary* [1986] ECR 1651), and public authorities providing public health services (judgment in Case 152/84 *Marshall*, cited above).

It follows from the foregoing that a body, whatever its legal form, which has been made responsible, pursuant to a measure adopted by the state, for providing a public service under the control of the state, and has for that purpose special powers beyond those which result from the normal rules applicable in relations between individuals, is included in any event among the bodies against which the provisions of a directive capable of having direct effect may be relied upon.

With regard to Art 5(1) of Directive 76/207, it should be observed that in the judgment in Case 152/84 Marshall, cited above, para 52, the Court held that that provision was unconditional and sufficiently precise to be relied on by an individual and to be applied by the national courts.

The answer to the question referred by the House of Lords must therefore be that Art 5(1) of Council Directive 76/207 of 9 February 1976 may be relied upon in a claim for damages against a body, whatever its legal form, which has been made responsible, pursuant to a measure adopted by the state, for providing a public service under the control of the state, and has for that purpose special powers beyond those which result from the normal rules applicable in relations between individuals.

Faccini Dori v Recreb (1994) Case C–91/92 ECR I-3325, ECJ

(Whether the provisions of the directive concerning the right of cancellation may be invoked in proceedings between a consumer and a trader.)

[21] The national court observes that, if the effects of unconditional and sufficiently precise but transposed directives were to be limited to relations between state entities and individuals, this would mean that a legislative measure would operate as such only as between certain legal subjects, whereas, under Italian law as under the laws of all modern states founded on the Rule of Law, the state is subject to the law like any other person. If the directive could be relied on only as against the state, that would be tantamount to a penalty for

failure to adopt legislative measures of transposition as if the relationship were a purely private one.

[22] It need merely be noted here that, as is clear from the judgment in *Marshall*, cited above (paras 48–49), the case law on the possibility of relying on directives against state entities is based on the fact that under Art 189 a directive is binding only in relation to 'each Member State to which it is addressed'. That case law seeks to prevent 'the state from taking advantage of its own failure to comply with Community law'.

[23] It would be unacceptable if a state, when required by the Community legislature to adopt certain rules intended to govern the state's relations – or those of state entities – with individuals and to confer certain rights on individuals, were able to rely on its own failure to discharge its obligations so as to deprive individuals of the benefits of those rights. Thus the Court has recognised that certain provisions of directives on conclusions of public works contracts and of directives on harmonisation of turnover taxes may be relied on against the state (or state entities) (see the judgment in Case 103/88 *Fratelli Costanzo v Comune di Milano* [1989] ECR 1839 and the judgment in Case 8/81 *Becker v Finanzamt Münster-Innenstadt* [1982] ECR 53).

[24] The effect of extending that case law to the sphere of relations between individuals would be to recognise a power in the Community to enact obligations for individuals with immediate effect, whereas it has competence to do so only where it is empowered to adopt regulations.

[25] It follows that, in the absence of measures transposing the directive within the prescribed time-limit, consumers cannot derive from the directive itself a right of cancellation as against traders with whom they have concluded a contract or enforce such a right in a national court.

[26] It must also be borne in mind that, as the Court has consistently held since its judgment in Case 14/83 *Von Colson and Kamann v Land Nordrhein-Westfalen* (1984) ECR 1891, para 26, the Member States' obligation arising from a directive to achieve the result envisaged by the directive and their duty under Art 5 of the Treaty to take all appropriate measures, whether general or particular, is binding on all the authorities of Member States, including, for matters within their jurisdiction, the courts. The judgments of the Court in Case C-106/89 *Marleasing v La Comercial Internacional de Alimentación* [1990] ECR I-4135, para 8, and Case C-334/92 *Wagner Miret v Fondo de Garantía Salarial* [1993] ECR I-6911, para 20, make it clear that, when applying national law, whether adopted before or after the directive, the national court that has to interpret that law must do so, as far as possible, in the light of the wording and the purpose of the directive so as to achieve the result it has in view and thereby comply with the third paragraph of Art 189 of the Treaty.

[27] If the result prescribed by the directive cannot be achieved by way of interpretation, it should also be borne in mind that, in terms of the judgment in joined Cases C-6/90 and C-9/90 *Francovich and Others v Italy* [1991] ECR I-5357, para 39, Community law requires the Member States to make good damage caused to individuals through failure to transpose a directive, provided that three conditions are fulfilled. First, the purpose of the directive must be to grant rights to individuals. Second, it must be possible to identify the content of those rights on the basis of the provisions of the directive. Finally, there must be a causal link between the breach of the state's obligation and the damage suffered.

[28] The directive on contracts negotiated away from business premises is undeniably intended to confer rights on individuals and it is equally certain that the minimum content of those rights can be identified by reference to the provisions of the directive alone (see para 17 above).

[29] Where damage has been suffered and that damage is due to a breach by the state of its obligation, it is for the national court to uphold the right of the aggrieved consumers to obtain reparation in accordance with national law on liability.

[30] So, as regards the second issue raised by the national court, the answer must be that in the absence of measures transposing the directive within the prescribed time limit, consumers cannot derive from the directive itself a right of cancellation as against traders with whom they have concluded a contract or enforce such a right in a national court. However, when applying provision of national law whether adopted before or after the directive, the national court must interpret them as far as possible in the light of the wording and purpose of the directive.

Notes

1   In its ruling in *Foster*, the ECJ adopted a wide definition of 'state body', thereby extending the ambit of the doctrine of vertical direct effect. But, whatever the definition of 'state body', it is clear that private citizens and private companies providing non-public services, and without the 'special powers' referred to, fell outside it. This created an anomaly since a citizen could claim Community rights only if the body claimed against fell within the borders of the definition of a state body, which, as has been found above, was a complex one.[8] The definition appears to create arbitrary distinctions between citizens in terms of their entitlements to such rights.

2   A further anomaly was created by the doctrine of direct effect since the answer to the question whether or not a citizen could claim a Community right would depend on the date on which it was claimed; if it happened to be claimed before the date for implementation of the directive by the state had passed, the claim would fail.

3   In *Faccini Dori* the Court refused to take a position in favour of the horizontal direct effect of directives. Thus, the Court did not appear to attempt to address the anomalies referred to above which were created by *Marshall (No 1)*. However, there is one further possibility. In stating that a state cannot rely on its own failure to implement directives where they govern the relationship between public entities and individuals (para 23 of the judgment in *Faccini Dori*), the Court may have intended to address the anomaly of placing public and private sector employees in different positions as regards their Community rights. It may have intended to do this by 'levelling down'; some directives not intended to govern such a relationship would have no vertical direct effect; those that did govern it would not apply in the private sector in any event. Thus both sets of employees would be in the same position as regards the direct effect of directives and both could rely on *Francovich* when Community rights were denied due to the failure of the state to implement a directive.[9]

---

8   See Curtin (1990) 15 EL Rev 195.

Questions

1 Bearing the points above in mind, do you consider that the ECJ should have allowed directives to have horizontal direct effect – direct effects as between non-state bodies? What are the arguments for and against allowing such effect? (See Steiner *EC Law*, 4th edn (1994), p33.)

2 What argument could be put forward against the suggestion made above as to the possible interpretation to be placed on paragraph 23 of the judgment of the ECJ in *Faccini Dori*?

DIRECTIVES: INDIRECT EFFECTS

The doctrine of vertical effect seemed to create unfairness since it meant *inter alia* that an individual who happened to be employed by a state body might be able to claim a remedy for denial of rights which would not be available to an individual employed by a non-state body. In response to this perception of unfairness, the ECJ developed the doctrine which has been termed the doctrine of indirect effect. It is explained in *Marleasing*, below.

Marleasing SA v La Commercial Internacional de Alimentacion SA Case C-106/89 (1990) ECR I-4135, I-4157–I-4160, ECJ

... Those questions arose in a dispute between Marleasing SA, the plaintiff in the main proceedings, and a number of defendants including La Commercial Internacional de Alimentacion SA (hereinafter referred to as 'La Commercial'). The latter was established in the form of a public limited company by three persons, including Barviesa SA, which contributed its own assets.

It is apparent from the grounds set out in the order for reference that Marleasing's primary claim, based on Arts 1261 and 1275 of the Spanish Civil Code, according to which contracts without cause or whose cause is unlawful have no legal effect, is for a declaration that the founders' contract establishing La Commercial is void on the ground that the establishment of the company lacked cause, was a sham transaction and was carried out in order to defraud the creditors of Barviesa SA, a co-founder of the defendant company. La Commercial contended that the action should be dismissed in its entirety on the ground, in particular, that Art 11 of Directive 68/151, which lists exhaustively the cases in which the nullity of a company may be ordered, does not include lack of cause amongst them.

The national court observed that in accordance with Art 395 of the Act concerning the Conditions of Accession of Spain and the Portuguese Republic to the European Communities (*Official Journal* (1985) L 302, p23) the Kingdom of Spain was under an obligation to bring the directive into effect as from the date of accession, but that that had still not been done at the date of the order for reference. Taking the view, therefore, that the dispute raised a problem concerning the interpretation of Community law, the national court referred the following question to the Court:

Is Art 11 of Council Directive 68/151/EEC of 9 March 1968, which has not been implemented in national law, directly applicable so as to preclude a

---

9 For further discussion of *Faccini Dori* and horizontal direct effect see: W Robinson (1995) 32 CML Rev 2, 629–39; D Kinley (1995) 1 EPL 1, 7983; S Turner (1995) 46 NILQ 2 244–55; N Bernard (1995) 24 ILJ 1, 97–102; S Douglas-Scott (1995) KCLJ 6, 117–20; A Mair and A Grimm (1995) LE 5–6.

declaration of nullity of a public limited company on a ground other than those set out in the said article? ...

With regard to the question whether an individual may rely on the directive against a national law, it should be observed that, as the Court has consistently held, a directive may not of itself impose obligations on an individual and, consequently, a provision of a directive may not be relied upon as such against such a person (judgment in Case 152/84 *Marshall v Southampton and South-West Hampshire Area Health Authority* (1986) ECR 723).

However, it is apparent from the documents before the Court that the national court seeks in substance to ascertain whether a national court hearing a case which falls within the scope of Directive 68/151 is required to interpret its national law in the light of the wording and the purpose of that directive in order to preclude a declaration of nullity of a public limited company on a ground other than those listed in Art 11 of the directive.

In order to reply to that question, it should be observed that, as the Court pointed out in its judgment in Case 14/83 *Von Colson and Kamann v Land Nordrhein-Westfalen* (1984) ECR 1891, para 26, the Member States' obligation arising from a directive to achieve the result envisaged by the directive and their duty under Art 5 of the Treaty to take all appropriate measures, whether general or particular, to ensure the fulfilment of that obligation, is binding on all the authorities of Member States including, for matters within their jurisdiction, the courts. It follows that, in applying national law, whether the provisions in question were adopted before or after the directive, the national court called upon to interpret it is required to do so, as far as possible, in the light of the wording and the purpose of the directive in order to achieve the result pursued by the latter and thereby comply with the third paragraph of Art 189 of the Treaty.

It follows that the requirement that national law must be interpreted in conformity with Art 11 of Directive 68/151 precludes the interpretation of provisions of national law relating to public limited companies in such a manner that the nullity of a public limited company may be ordered on grounds other than those exhaustively listed in Art 11 of the directive in question.

With regard to the interpretation to be given to Art 11 of the directive, in particular Art 11(2)(b), it should be observed that that provision prohibits the laws of the Member States from providing for a judicial declaration of nullity on grounds other than those exhaustively listed in the directive, amongst which is the ground that the objects of the company are unlawful or contrary to public policy.

According to the Commission, the expression 'objects of the company' must be interpreted as referring exclusively to the objects of the company as described in the instrument of incorporation or the articles of association. It follows, in the Commission's view, that a declaration of nullity of a company cannot be made on the basis of the activity actually pursued by it, for instance defrauding the founders' creditors.

That argument must be upheld. As is clear from the preamble to Directive 68/151, its purpose was to limit the cases in which nullity can arise and the retroactive effect of a declaration of nullity in order to ensure 'certainty in the law as regards relations between the company and third parties, and also between members' (sixth recital). Furthermore, the protection of third parties 'must be ensured by provisions which restrict to the greatest possible extent the grounds on which obligations entered into in the name of the company are not valid'. It follows, therefore, that each ground of nullity provided for in Art 11 of the directive must be interpreted strictly. In those circumstances the words 'objects of the company' must be understood as referring to the objects of the company as described in the instrument of incorporation or the articles of association.

The answer to the question submitted must therefore be that a national court hearing a case which falls within the scope of Directive 68/151 is required to interpret its national law in the light of the wording and the purpose of that directive in order to preclude a declaration of nullity of a public limited company on a ground other than those listed in Art 11 of the directive.

Notes

1   Previously in *Kolpinghuis Nijmegen* (1987)[10] the ECJ had suggested a more limited view of the doctrine of indirect effects, holding that the obligation on domestic courts to interpret national law to comply with EC law was limited by the general principles of legal certainty and non-retroactivity. In contrast, in *Marleasing SA v La Commercial Internacional de Alimentacion SA* (1990), the ECJ found that, where a domestic court was faced with legislation which ran directly counter to the terms of a directive, it should give effect to the directive regardless of the terms of the national legislation. This ruling seems to threaten the general principles in question.

2   The decision in *Marleasing* left the individual who wished to rely on EC provisions against a non-state body in a difficult position; he or she could not be sure that the national court would be prepared to find that the national legislation could be interpreted in such a way as to give effect to the EC provision in question. It might be unlikely to do so where the domestic legislative body had impliedly indicated in the legislation that it was not intended to comply with the directive. As discussed below, this has already occurred in the UK. Also, where a directive had not been implemented at all, and the national legislation did not cover the particular question at issue, an individual seeking redress under it against a private body would have no clear argument available since it would be hard to identify the provisions which could be interpreted so as to provide such redress.[11]

3   The complexities and weaknesses inherent in the development of the principles of direct and indirect effects are discussed below by de Burca and Steiner.

G de Burca, 'Giving Effect to European Community Directives' (1992) *Modern Law Review* 215–9

Introduction

... The ECJ developed the doctrine of direct effect at an early stage in its jurisprudence, to ensure that the body of law provided for in the EC Treaties would have effect in the various Member States without the need for national implementing legislation [Case 26/62,*Van Gend en Loos* [1963] 2 CMLR 105]. Art 189 of the EEC Treaty provides that directives shall be binding as to their aim, but that the choice of form and method of their implementation remains with the

---

10   ECR 3969; [1986] 2 CMLR 18.

11   See further Mead (1991) 16 EL Rev 490; Docksey and Fitzpatrick (1991) 20 ILJ 113; E Deards (1996) 2(1) *European Public Law* 81.

Member States. Despite this provision, the ECJ nevertheless decided that directives could be relied upon directly by litigants before national courts in certain situations [Case 41/74, *Van Duyn v Home Office* [1974] ECR 1337, [1975] I CMLR 1]. The Court has declared that directives will not have direct effect where their terms are insufficiently precise or where, although clear and precise, those terms are conditional or leave some discretion to the Member States [*ibid*]. The major limitation on their direct effectiveness, however, is that directives cannot be directly enforced in a 'horizontal' situation, ie in proceedings against a private party rather than against the state [see Case 152/84, *Marshall v Southampton and South West Hampshire Area Health Authority (Teaching)* [1986] ECR 723, [1986] 1 CMLR 680]. The case for their direct enforcement against the state appears to be based on a concept of estoppel whereby the state may not rely as against an individual, upon its own failure to implement a directive properly and on time [see Case 148/78, *Pubblico Ministero v Tullio Ratti* [1979] ECR 1629, [1980] 1 CMLR 96].

This limitation on direct effect remains an awkward problem for the Community, since the effectiveness of its laws and their equal and uniform application in all of the Member States is a prerequisite to the attainment of the objectives which the Community was founded to achieve. The combination of the states' frequent non-implementation of directives, with the fact that directives cannot in themselves be directly enforced against individuals, means that their effectiveness as a legislative form is seriously undermined. In practical terms, many of the Community's important legislative policies, such as that embodied in the Equal Treatment Directive [76/207, OJ no 39, p40] have been hindered or frustrated.

The second problem which has dogged the effectiveness of directives is the fact that, even where a directive is sought to be enforced against the state and has been held to confer a right directly upon an individual, the Member State in question may not have provided a suitable domestic remedy for the enforcement of that right. National courts have frequently had to grapple with the problem of what to do when faced with a directly enforceable Community right for which no national remedy exists [a celebrated example in the UK being the case of *Factortame Ltd v Secretary of State for Transport* [1990] 2 AC 85 and [1991] 1 AC 603].

The ECJ, following on from its elaboration of the doctrine of direct effect, has continued its attempt to ensure the effectiveness of directives by the involvement of domestic courts in their enforcement. In the case of directives which lack direct effect, the Court has developed a principle of interpretation which imposes a very strong obligation on national courts to construe provisions of national law in the light of EC directives [Case 14/83, *Von Colson* [1984] ECR 1891, [1986] 2 CMLR 430]. And, in the case of directives which are directly enforceable, but which do not themselves specify any particular remedy for breach, the ECJ has stressed that there is an obligation upon national courts to provide adequate and effective remedies [*ibid*].

Both problems involve fundamental legal and constitutional issues for the EC as a whole and for the Member States individually. The effectiveness of EC law in advancing the EC's aims and policies depends on the readiness of national courts to give effect to that law. It is therefore important that directives, which the Member States have failed to implement, be enforced by courts throughout those states, and that a comprehensive system of procedures and remedies for the enforcement of rights derived from directives be made available.

The development of the interpretive obligation

In *Von Colson v Land Nordrhein-Westfalen,* the defendant was held by a German court to have breached the Equal Treatment Directive by refusing employment on the grounds of sex, but the remedy provided under national law appeared to be inadequate. On a reference to the ECJ, it was held that, although the directive did not of itself require any specific remedy, nevertheless EC law imposed certain obligations on the domestic courts. The ECJ, in effect, held that Art 5 of the EEC Treaty imposed an obligation on the part of national courts to ensure the effectiveness of EC law, in particular by interpreting national law in the light of the wording and purpose of directives. However, the judgment failed to clarify certain issues, in particular whether this obligation to interpret applied only to domestic legislation which was deliberately designed to implement the relevant directive.

Art 5 of the Treaty is a general provision included amongst the introductory part of the Treaty setting out the fundamental principles on which the European Community is based ('Member States shall take all appropriate measures ... to ensure fulfilment of the obligations arising out of this Treaty or resulting from action taken by the institutions of the Community.']. The strategy of the *Von Colson* rule of interpretation highlights the central role which the ECJ has allocated to the national courts in the enforcement of EC law and in the fulfilment of state obligations. Since the original exposition of the concept of direct effect, the ECJ has continually advanced the effectiveness of EC law by stepping into the breach created while the legislative process was hampered by political difficulties over voting procedures. The ECJ has continued to pursue this strategy, despite the tension between its policy and the domestic constitutional constraints within which national courts must operate [*Internationale Handelsgesellschaft* [1970] CMLR 294, [1972] CMLR 177, [1974] 14 CMLR 540]. Its policy has been particularly significant in ensuring that EC directives which ought to have been properly implemented by the Member States are given effect. Where the Member States legislatures have not fulfilled their Treaty obligation to implement directives on time [see Arts 5 and 189 of the EEC Treaty], the ECJ's response has been to substitute the national courts as performers of this duty instead. The Court's use of Art 5 to extend the national courts role in the implementation of EC law [see eg Case 106/77, *Simmenthal* [1978] ECR 629, [1978] 3 CMLR 263] provides a good illustration of the ECJ's interpretive method, which has come in for criticism from various commentators. However, the precise limits of the interpretive obligation remained unclear after *Von Colson,* in particular the constraints which might be imposed by the clear contrary language of a domestic provision. Subsequent ECJ case law, in expanding on this obligation, has failed to clarify several matters of importance for national courts faced with the task of interpretation.

In *Kolpinghuis Nijmegen* [Case 80/86, [1987] ECR 3969, [1989] 2 CMLR 18], the ECJ reiterated the obligation to interpret national law in the light of the wording and purpose of directives, but introduced a further twist into the tale. The judgment appears to indicate that the obligation arises as soon as the directive has been adopted at Community level, and regardless of whether or not the time limit provided for its implementation by the states has expired. The *Kolpinghuis* ruling specifies that the duty of the national court to interpret provisions of national law in accordance with relevant directives is unaffected by the question of whether or not the time limit for their implementation has expired. If this means that national courts are obliged to construe domestic law in conformity with directives as soon as they are adopted, several questions arise.

One advantage of a time limit for implementation is that it can ensure uniformity in the direct application of EC directives throughout the Member States. This is one reason why directives cannot be directly applied against the states until the expiry of the time limit for their implementation [see Case 148/78, *Pubblico Ministero v Tullio Ratti* [1979] ECR 1629]. The same reasoning is applicable to the obligation to interpret, since greater legislative harmony between the Member States would be achieved by imposing an obligation on national courts to interpret domestic law in conformity with non-implemented or badly implemented directives only after the uniform time limit has expired [disparities, of course, would still exist if, in some Member States, there was no domestic legislation in the relevant field, thus precluding the possibility of interpretation]. *Kolpinghuis* does not clearly resolve the question of how national courts are to interpret domestic law after the adoption of a relevant directive, but before the expiry of the time limit for its implementation. It is not clear whether the ECJ requires national courts to interpret the new legislation in conformity with the directive, or whether it empowers or requires them to respect the states' own 'choice as to form and methods' [see Art 189 of the EEC Treaty]. within the given time period. How national courts ought to approach the interpretation of domestic law in these situations evidently depends considerably on the purpose served by the time limits for implementing directives.

If the use of a directive, rather than a directly applicable Community legal instrument, is viewed as a deliberate policy decision to give Member States the political choice as to how best to adapt a measure to their domestic legal system, then national legislation should not be construed purposively until the time limit has expired and there has not yet been compliance. But this brings to light one of the difficulties inherent in an interpretation principle of this nature. It would become difficult to fulfil even the most minimal Rule of Law requirement, ie that of ensuring that the law is reasonably clear to those who are subject to it and that they have some means of knowing of it. Reasonable consistency in the use of statutory language would be impossible if a measure were to be given two different readings depending on whether or not a particular date had passed. It would be extremely difficult for those potentially affected by a measure to know whether to act according to domestic law as currently interpreted, or in accordance with an EC directive in conformity with which the domestic law would be read. The ECJ is risking creating a very convoluted legal situation in its desire to ensure directives are given effect through domestic law, but without wanting to go so far as to allow individuals to enforce the rights they derive from directives directly against other individuals and non-state bodies.

Its most recent development of the interpretive obligation in the case of *Marleasing* does little to clarify matters. It provides little guidance for national courts faced with conflicting obligations under existing provisions of national law on the one hand, and under the provisions of a non-implemented EC directive on the other.

Josephine Steiner, 'From Direct Effects to *Francovich*: Shifting Means of Enforcement of Community Law' (1993) 18(3) *European Law Review* 3–7

The success of the new legal order of the Community depended from the first on full compliance by all Member States with Community law. Both the EEC Treaty and secondary legislation imposed extensive obligations on Member States to act, or refrain from acting, in order to achieve defined Community goals. Yet provisions made under the Treaty for the enforcement of these obligations was weak (although no doubt all that was politically possible at the time). Whilst the Court of Justice had jurisdiction under Arts 169 EEC ['if the Commission considers that a Member State has failed to fulfil an obligation under this Treaty' it may bring the matter before the Court of Justice] and 170 EEC [a Member State may take another Member State before the Court of Justice if it considers that that state has 'failed to fulfil an obligation under this Treaty'] (and other lesser provisions, eg Art 933) to rule on Member States' failures, and states were obliged under Art 171 to 'take the necessary measures to comply with the Court's judgments,' no sanctions were provided to compel states to fulfil their obligations. This omission posed a real threat to the uniform application of Community law, indeed to the Community's very existence. Without solidarity, the full compliance with Community law by all Member States, the Community would be unlikely to survive. It thus fell to the Court of Justice, whose duty it is to see that 'the law is observed' [Art 164 EEC], to maximise the effective enforcement of Community law by judicial means.

The development of the principles of direct effects [starting with Case 26/62 *Van Gend en Loos* [1963] ECR 1] and supremacy of Community law [starting with Case 6/64, *Costa v ENEL* [1964] ECR 585] represented the Court's first major contribution in this sphere. If Community law was directly effective, it could be invoked by individuals before their national courts to challenge or evade inconsistent national law; the principle of supremacy of Community law ensured its application in priority over domestic law. If the offending national law was not set aside as a result of this process, at least it was inapplicable [Case 106/77, *Simmenthal SpA (No 2)* [1978] ECR 629].

The Court's reasoning, based on inferences drawn from the scheme of the EEC Treaty (states had agreed to the Community institutions; they had agreed to be bound by Community law) and the need to ensure the useful effect *('effet utile')* of Community law, was persuasive, and, despite the delicate and difficult constitutional issues raised, largely successful in winning acceptance from the Courts of Member States [*Frontini* [1974] 3 CMLR 540 (Italian Constitutional Court): *Re Kloppenberg* [1988] 3 CMLR I (German Constitutional Court); *Factortame Ltd v Secretary of State for Transport (No 2)* (House of Lords) [1991] 1 All ER 106].

But these principles were not sufficient to secure the full and effective enforcement of Community law. Community obligations, binding on the state, may not be sufficiently precise and unconditional for direct effects. Even where it is, the principle of direct effects only operates to protect Community rights and secure their enforcement in the individual case, where individuals are aware of their directly effective rights and willing to enforce them. Whilst a ruling in the individual's favour based on a directly effective provision of Community law is binding *erga omnes,* it does not in itself correct shortcomings in national law. As long as the discrepancy between national and Community law exists, the individual is in a state of uncertainty. He is thus unaware of the full extent of his rights, and Community law is only occasionally and haphazardly enforced.

However, the main drawback of the principle of direct effects is its inadequacy as a means of enforcement of directives. Even when they are sufficiently precise and unconditional to be capable of direct effects, they are not directly effective against all parties. The logic of the Court's reasoning on the direct effect of directives, based on the nature of directives [Art 189 EEC] and the estoppel principle [states cannot plead their own wrong in an action based on a directive: see Case 8/81, *Becker* (1982) ECR 53], succeeded in gaining acceptance for the principle of vertical effects, but it was inadequate to provide a satisfactory basis for horizontal effects. The Court was forced to draw the line between vertical and horizontal effects in *Marshall v Southampton AHA.* Apart from the uncertainty as to what might constitute a 'public' body, an 'emanation of the state,' and the anomaly in respect of individuals' rights created by the public/private distinction, this left a serious gap in the direct enforcement of directives.

The Court's attempts to bridge this gap in *Von Colson* and *Kamann v Land Nordrhein-Westfalen* [Case 14/83 [1984] ECR 1891] by a principle of indirect effect, whereby national courts, as agents of the state, are obliged under Art 5 EEC to interpret domestic law to achieve the results required by the directive even when it is not directly effective [because it is being invoked against a 'private' party, not because it is not unconditional and sufficiently precise], were also of limited efficacy as a mean of enforcement of directives. Even as qualified in *Marleasing* [Case C–106/89 [1990] ECR 4135] to the effect that the obligation applied whether the national provisions in question were adopted before or after the directive, it could not guarantee success. Whilst national courts might be prepared to construe domestic law to comply with Community law when the former was ambiguous, and capable of an interpretation in conformity with the directive, or where domestic law had been introduced, either before or after the directive, in order to comply with the directive [eg, *Litster v Forth Dry Dock and Engineering Co Ltd* [1990] 1 AC 546], there were circumstances in which they not unnaturally felt that they had no discretion to give a directive indirect effect. Such might be the case where:

(a) (*quaere*) national law was perhaps compatible with Community law, but there was evidence that domestic law was not intended to have the meaning contended for [eg, *Duke v GEC Reliance Ltd* [1988] AC 618, HL];

(b) national law was clearly incompatible with Community law, and there was no evidence that domestic law was intended to comply with the directive; or

(c) there was no domestic law to 'interpret' in accordance with the directive.

Furthermore, in these types of case it could be argued, with some justice, that it would be unfair, in breach of individuals' legitimate expectations [see *Kolpinhuis Nijmegen* Case 80/86 [1987] ECR 3969], to 'interpret' domestic law to comply with Community law. To do so would be to introduce direct effects by the back door.

With the move towards completion of the internal market by 31 December 1992, to be achieved largely through harmonisation by directive [under Art 100A EEC], the problem of enforcement became acute. States were failing increasingly to implement directives on time. Despite redoubled efforts by the Commission under Art 169, states continued to neglect their duties of implementation and even successful proceedings failed to secure compliance. In 1989, 26 Art 169 proceedings were brought for the second time. If the internal market programme were to succeed, something more had to be done.

For some years the possibility had been canvassed that states might be liable in damages in tort for infringements of Community law. Art 5 in particular had been invoked as providing a legitimate base. As early as 1960 the Court of Justice had suggested, in the context of a claim for restitution [Case 6/60 *Humblet v Belgium* [1960] ECR 559], that the state was liable to make good, for individuals, the unlawful consequences of a breach of Community law. The principle that national courts must provide real and effective protection for individuals' Community rights [introduced in *Von Colson v Land Nordrhein-Westfalen* Case 14/83 [1984] ECR 1891] was fully established. Provided Community law was directly effective it could be invoked to support a claim for any remedy available under national law. But the lack of provision for financial penalties to underpin the specific enforcement provisions of Arts 169 and 170 EEC was a barrier, both legal and psychological, to the introduction of a general principle of liability in damages for Member States' failure to fulfil their Community obligations. On ratification, the Treaty on European Union will amend Art 171 EEC to allow the Court of Justice to impose penalties on Member States which have failed to comply with its judgments under Arts 169 and 170. But it can only do so after a reasoned opinion on that failure from the Commission and on the expiry of a time limit imposed by the Commission for compliance. Thus, if and when the Treaty on European Union comes into effect, there will exist an effective means of enforcement of Community law against Member States. But it will still take time to secure compliance, and it will not provide compensation for individuals who have meanwhile suffered damage as a result of being wrongfully deprived of their community rights. Again it fell to the Court of Justice to bridge the gap. It had the perfect opportunity in *Francovich and Bonifaci*.

Question

1　Why did the ECJ need to develop the doctrine of indirect effect? What are its drawbacks?

FRANCOVICH AND STATE LIABILITY

Francovich v Italy Joined Cases C–6/90 and C–9/90 [1991] ECR I-5357, ECJ

Mr Francovich, a party to the main proceedings in Case C–6/90, had worked for CDN Elettronica SnC in Vicenza but had received only sporadic payments on account of his wages. He therefore brought proceedings before the Pretura di Vicenza, which ordered the defendant to pay approximately LIT 6 million. In attempting to enforce that judgment the bailiff attached to the Tribunale di Vicenza was obliged to submit a negative return. Mr Francovich then claimed to be entitled to obtain from the Italian State the guarantees provided for in Directive 80/987 or, in the alternative, compensation.

In Case C–9/90 Danila Bonifaci and 33 other employees brought proceedings before the Pretura di Bassano del Grappa, stating that they had been employed by Gaia Confezioni Srl, which was declared insolvent on 5 April 1985. When the employment relationships were discontinued, the plaintiffs were owed more than LIT 253 million, which was proved as a debt in the company's insolvency. More than five years after the insolvency they had been paid nothing, and the receiver had told them that even a partial distribution in their favour was entirely improbable. Consequently, the plaintiffs brought proceedings against the Italian Republic in which they claimed that, in view of its obligation to implement Directive 80/987 with effect from 23 October 1983, it should be ordered to pay them their arrears of wages, at least for the last three months, or in the alternative to pay compensation.

It was in those circumstances that the national courts referred the following questions, which are identical in both cases, to the Court for a preliminary ruling:

'(1)　Under the system of Community law in force, is a private individual who has been adversely affected by the failure of a Member State to implement Directive 80/897 — a failure confirmed by a judgment of the Court of Justice — entitled to require the state itself to give effect to those provisions of that directive which are sufficiently precise and unconditional, by directly invoking the Community legislation against the Member State in default so as to obtain the guarantees which that state itself should have provided and in any event to claim reparation of the loss and damage sustained in relation to provisions to which that right does not apply?

(2)　Are the combined provisions of Arts 3 and 4 of Council Directive 80/987 to be interpreted as meaning that where the state has not availed itself of the option of laying down limits under Art 4, the state itself is obliged to pay the claims of employees in accordance with Art 3? ...

The first question submitted by the national courts raises two issues, which should be considered separately. It concerns, first, the direct effect of the provisions of the directive which determine the rights of employees and, secondly, the existence and scope of state liability for damage resulting from breach of its obligations under Community law.

The direct effect of the provisions of the directive which determine the rights of employees

The first part of the first question submitted by the national courts seeks to determine whether the provisions of the directive which determine the rights of employees must be interpreted as meaning that the persons concerned can enforce those rights against the state in the national courts in the absence of implementing measures adopted within the prescribed period.

As the Court has consistently held, a Member State which has not adopted the implementing measures required by a directive within the prescribed period may not, against individuals, plead its own failure to perform the obligations which the directive entails. Thus, wherever the provisions of a directive appear, as far as their subject matter is concerned, to be unconditional and sufficiently precise, those provisions may, in the absence of implementing measures adopted within the prescribed period, be relied upon as against any national provision which is incompatible with the directive or in so far as the provisions of the directive define rights which individuals are able to assert against the state (judgment in Case 8/81 *Becker v Finanzamt Münster-Innenstadt* [1982] ECR 53).

It is therefore necessary to see whether the provisions of Directive 80/987 which determine the rights of employees are unconditional and sufficiently precise. There are three points to be considered: the identity of the persons entitled to the guarantee provided; the content of that guarantee; and the identity of the person liable to provide the guarantee. In that regard, the question arises in particular whether a state can be held liable to provide the guarantee on the ground that it did not take the necessary implementing measures within the prescribed period.

With regard first of all to the identity of the persons entitled to the guarantee, it is to be noted that, according to Art 1(1), the directive applies to employees' claims arising from contracts of employment or employment relationships and existing against employers who are in a state of insolvency within the meaning of Art 2(1), the latter provision defining the circumstances in which an employer must be deemed to be in a state of insolvency. Art 2(2) refers to national law for the definition of the concepts of 'employee' and 'employer'. Finally, Art 1(2) provides that the Member States may, by way of exception and under certain conditions, exclude claims by certain categories of employees listed in the annex to the directive.

Those provisions are sufficiently precise and unconditional to enable the national court to determine whether or not a person should be regarded as a person intended to benefit under the directive. A national court need only verify whether the person concerned is an employed person under national law and whether he is excluded from the scope of the directive in accordance with Art 1(2) and Annex 1 (as to the necessary conditions for such exclusion, see the judgments in Case 22/87 *Commission v Italy*, cited above, paras 18–23, and Case C–53/88 *Commission v Greece* [1990] ECR I–3917, paras 11–26), and then ascertain whether one of the situations of insolvency provided for in Art 2 of the directive exists. ...

Art 3 of the directive thus leaves the Member State a discretion in determining the date from which payment of claims must be ensured. However, as is already implicit in the Court's case law (see the judgments in Case 71/85 *Netherlands v*

FNV [1986] ECR 3855 and Case 286/85 *McDermott and Cotter v Minister for Social Welfare and Attorney General* [1987] ECR 1453, para 15), the right of a state to choose among several possible means of achieving the result required by a directive does not preclude the possibility for individuals of enforcing before the national courts rights whose content can be determined sufficiently precisely on the basis of the provisions of the directive alone.

In this case, the result required by the directive in question is a guarantee that the outstanding claims of employees will be paid in the event of the insolvency of their employer. The fact that Arts 3 and 4(1) and (2) give the Member States some discretion as regards the means of establishing that guarantee and the restriction of its amount do not affect the precise and unconditional nature of the result required. ...

It must therefore be held that the provisions in question are unconditional and sufficiently precise as regards the content of the guarantee. ...

It has been submitted that, since the directive provides for the possibility that the guarantee institutions may be financed entirely by the public authorities, it is unacceptable that a Member State may thwart the effects of the directive by asserting that it could have required other persons to bear part or all of the financial burden resting upon it.

That argument cannot be upheld. It follows from the terms of the directive that the Member State is required to organise an appropriate institutional guarantee system. Under Art 5, the Member State has a broad discretion with regard to the organisation, operation and financing of the guarantee institutions. The fact, referred to by the Commission, that the directive envisages as one possibility among others that such a system may be financed entirely by the public authorities, cannot mean that the state can be identified as the person liable for unpaid claims. The payment obligation lies with the guarantee institutions, and it is only in exercising its power to organise the guarantee system that the state may provide that the guarantee institutions are to be financed entirely by the public authorities. In those circumstances the state takes on an obligation which in principle is not its own.

Accordingly, even though the provisions of the directive in question are sufficiently precise and unconditional as regards the determination of the persons entitled to the guarantee and as regards the content of that guarantee, those elements are not sufficient to enable individuals to rely on those provisions before the national courts. Those provisions do not identify the person liable to provide the guarantee, and the state cannot be considered liable on the sole ground that it has failed to take transposition measures within the prescribed period.

The answer to the first part of the first question must therefore be that the provisions of Directive 80/987 which determine the rights of employees must be interpreted as meaning that the persons concerned cannot enforce those rights against the state before the national courts where no implementing measures are adopted within the prescribed period.

Liability of the state for loss and damage resulting from breach of its obligations under Community law

In the second part of the first question the national court seeks to determine whether a Member State is obliged to make good loss and damage suffered by individuals as a result of the failure to transpose Directive 80/987.

The national court thus raises the issue of the existence and scope of a state's liability for loss and damage resulting from breach of its obligations under Community law.

That issue must be considered in the light of the general system of the Treaty and its fundamental principles.

(a) The existence of state liability as a matter of principle

It should be borne in mind at the outset that the EEC Treaty has created its own legal system, which is integrated into the legal systems of the Member States and which their courts are bound to apply. The subjects of that legal system are not only the Member States but also their nationals. Just as it imposes burdens on individuals, Community law is also intended to give rise to rights which become part of their legal patrimony. Those rights arise, not only where they are expressly granted by the Treaty, but also by virtue of obligations which the Treaty imposes in a clearly defined manner both on individuals and on the Member States and the Community institutions (see the judgments in Case 26/62 *Van Gend en Loos* [1963] ECR 1 and Case 6/64 *Costa v ENEL* [1964] ECR 585).

Furthermore, it has been consistently held that the national courts whose task it is to apply the provisions of Community law in areas within their jurisdiction must ensure that those rules take full effect and must protect the rights which they confer on individuals (see in particular the judgments in Case 106/77 *Amministrazione delle Finanze dello Stato v Simmenthal* [1978] ECR 629, para 16, and Case C–213/89 *Factortame* [1990] ECR I–2433, para 19).

The full effectiveness of Community rules would be impaired and the protection of the rights which they grant would be weakened if individuals were unable to obtain redress when their rights are infringed by a breach of Community law for which a Member State can be held responsible.

The possibility of obtaining redress from the Member State is particularly indispensable where, as in this case, the full effectiveness of Community rules is subject to prior action on the part of the state and where, consequently, in the absence of such action, individuals cannot enforce before the national courts the rights conferred upon them by Community law.

It follows that the principle whereby a state must be liable for loss and damage caused to individuals as a result of breaches of Community law for which the state can be held responsible is inherent in the system of the Treaty.

A further basis for the obligation of Member States to make good such loss and damage is to be found in Art 5 of the Treaty, under which the Member States are required to take all appropriate measures, whether general or particular, to ensure fulfilment of their obligations under Community law. Among these is the obligation to nullify the unlawful consequences of a breach of Community law (see, in relation to the analogous provision of Art 86 of the ECSC Treaty, the judgment in Case 6/60 *Humblet v Belgium* [1960] ECR 559).

It follows from all the foregoing that it is a principle of Community law that the Member States are obliged to make good loss and damage caused to individuals by breaches of Community law for which they can be held responsible.

(b) The conditions for state liability

Although state liability is thus required by Community law, the conditions under which that liability gives rise to a right to reparation depend on the nature of the breach of Community law giving rise to the loss and damage.

Where, as in this case, a Member State fails to fulfil its obligation under the third paragraph of Art 189 of the Treaty to take all the measures necessary to achieve the result prescribed by a directive, the full effectiveness of that rule of

Community law requires that there should be a right to reparation provided that three conditions are fulfilled.

The first of those conditions is that the result prescribed by the directive should entail the grant of rights to individuals. The second condition is that it should be possible to identify the content of those rights on the basis of the provisions of the directive. Finally, the third condition is the existence of a causal link between the breach of the state's obligation and the loss and damage suffered by the injured parties.

Those conditions are sufficient to give rise to a right on the part of individuals to obtain reparation, a right founded directly on Community law.

Subject to that reservation, it is on the basis of the rules of national law on liability that the state must make reparation for the consequences of the loss and damage caused. In the absence of Community legislation, it is for the internal legal order of each Member State to designate the competent courts and lay down the detailed procedural rules for legal proceedings intended fully to safeguard the rights which individuals derive from Community law (see the judgments in Case 60/75 *Russo v AIMA* [1976] ECR 45, Case 33/76 *Rewe v Landwirtschaftskammer Saarland* [1976] ECR 1989 and Case 158/80 *Rewe v Hauptzollamt Kiel* [1981] ECR 1805).

Further, the substantive and procedural conditions for reparation of loss and damage laid down by the national law of the Member States must not be less favourable than those relating to similar domestic claims and must not be so framed as to make it virtually impossible or excessively difficult to obtain reparation (see, in relation to the analogous issue of the repayment of taxes levied in breach of Community law, *inter alia* the judgment in Case 199/82 *Amministrazione delle Finanze dello Stato v San Giorgio* [1983] ECR 3595).

In this case, the breach of Community law by a Member State by virtue of its failure to transpose Directive 80/987 within the prescribed period has been confirmed by a judgment of the Court. The result required by that directive entails the grant to employees of a right to a guarantee of payment of their unpaid wage claims. As is clear from the examination of the first part of the first question, the content of that right can be identified on the basis of the provisions of the directive.

Consequently, the national court must, in accordance with the national rules on liability, uphold the right of employees to obtain reparation of loss and damage caused to them as a result of failure to transpose the directive.

The answer to be given to the national court must therefore be that a Member State is required to make good loss and damage caused to individuals by failure to transpose Directive 80/987.

Note

The principles of direct and indirect effects had limitations as suggested above in terms of securing compliance with EC law. The decision in *Francovich* provided a new and surer means of enforcing EC law as explained by Steiner below.

Josephine Steiner, 'From Direct Effects to *Francovich*: Shifting Means of Enforcement of Community Law' (1993) 18(3) *European Law Review* 9–12, 19–22

Assessment of Francovich

The decision in *Francovich* is undoubtedly consistent with, and a natural and logical extension of, the Court's case law. Having established that Community law can give rise to rights for individuals, and that national courts are obliged to ensure the full effectiveness of such provisions, it was but a small step to guarantee their full effect by holding states liable in damages for infringements of those rights for which they were responsible.

The breakthrough in *Francovich* lay not so much in the fact that individuals were held entitled to claim damages against the state – in the context of actions based on directly effective Community law against 'public' bodies that had long been possible [for example, *Bourgoin v Minister for Agriculture and Fisheries* [1985] 3 All ER 585, CA], but that their claim to compensation was independent of the principle of direct effects. Provided the criteria for *Francovich* are met, the individual may now proceed against the state for breach not of substantive, directly effective Community provisions, but for the state's primary failure to comply with its obligation to implement Community law. Although the Court found that the relevant provisions of Directive 80/987 were not directly effective, the criteria for liability under *Francovich* as regards the nature and content of the rights infringed are close to those for direct effects. The Court could, without difficulty, have found the provisions in question sufficiently precise and unconditional for direct effects, at least as regards the end to be achieved. It is submitted that it did not do so because it wished to establish a remedy for Member States' infringements of Community law which did not depend on the need to prove direct effects. In this way, the problems associated with directives arising from their lack of horizontal effect would be largely circumvented. If Community rights could not be enforced against private parties, compensation would at least be provided for individuals wrongfully deprived of their Community rights. At the same time the prospect of liability to all parties suffering damage as a result of their failures to implement Community law would provide states with a powerful incentive fully to comply with their community obligations.

A principle of state liability as applied in *Francovich* is arguably more legitimate as a means of enforcement of Community law than the principle of direct effects. Under the latter principle, Treaty provisions, the scope of which may not be clear (eg, Art 119), may be enforced against the legitimate expectations of 'private' parties. The majority of 'public' bodies, against which directives may be invoked, can hardly be seen as responsible for non-implementation. The element of public authority or control to which they are subject simply renders them liable by association. If that authority or control should have ensured compliance by the defendant organisation with the obligations imposed by directives and failed to do so, the fault lies less with the local authority or public enterprise than with the central authorities, the legislative or executive organs of the state.

If more legitimate than the principle of direct effects, a principle of state liability on the basis of *Francovich* is undoubtedly more legitimate than a principle of indirect effects. Given the nature of directives as binding on, and requiring implementation by, the state, it can be argued that individuals should not be required to comply with their provisions (albeit by means of 'interpretation' rather than direct effect) until they are implemented into national law. Only where domestic law is ambiguous and compatible with the directive, or has been expressly introduced in order to implement the directive [as in *Litster v Forth Dry Docks and Engineering Co Ltd* [1990] 1 AC 546, HL], should it be permissible to give indirect effect to Community law. The principles of direct and indirect effects were simply expedients designed to secure the enforcement of Community law precisely because states had failed to fulfil their obligations. The primary fault for non-compliance has always lain with the state. Since a principle of non-contractual liability of public authorities is recognised in all the Member States and, under Community law [Arts 178, 215(2) EEC], there seems no good reason why, in a case such as *Francovich*, the state should not be liable to individuals suffering damage as a result of its own failure to comply with Community law.

The problems: for what breaches will states be responsible?

The problem with *Francovich* lies not in the decision itself but in its implications. Although there may be difficulties in deciding, in the individual case, whether the content of a claimed right is sufficiently clear, or whether it was intended to benefit the plaintiff, or whether the required damage and causative link has been proved, the principal problem, and main focus of this article, lies in determining the meaning and scope to be attributed to this concept of failure.

First, although the ruling in *Francovich* concerned Member States' failure to implement a directive, the judgment was couched in the terms of the broadest principle: a Member State is 'liable to make good damage to individuals caused by a breach of Community law for which it is responsible' [at para 37]. As Advocate-General Mischo pointed out, this principle: 'is capable of being extended to cover any failure of Member States to observe Community law ..., whether the failure is in breach of the Treaty, regulations or directives, whether they have direct effect or not'.

Moreover, given the dual purpose of *Francovich*, that of protecting individuals' Community rights and ensuring the full effect of Community law there seems no reason in principle why *Francovich* should not apply to a failure by a Member State to fulfil any binding obligation of Community law. A principle of state liability is a powerful instrument in the enforcement of Community law; it is likely that the Court of Justice will seek to maximise its use.

Secondly, if Member States are to be liable for breach of any binding Community obligation, under what circumstances will they be liable? This question concerns the nature and gravity of the breach. In *Francovich*, Italy's breach of Community law was abundantly clear. They had made no attempt to implement the directive and the Court had given judgment to this effect. As Advocate-General Mischo commented: 'Rarely has our court had to give judgment in a case where the loss caused to individuals concerned by a failure to implement a directive has been as scandalous as here' [at para 1].

But *Francovich* will be invoked to support a claim in respect of other, lesser failures. A failure to fulfil a Community obligation can take many forms, embracing a broad spectrum of culpability. At its most blatant it can be a deliberate or knowing breach of Community law, for example a clear failure to implement an obligation, as in *Francovich* itself. It may be a partial failure, where implementation measures have been adopted, but they are faulty or inadequate. Such failures may be deliberate, knowing, negligent or innocent. Implementation measures may not have been adopted because existing national law was deemed to be adequate. Here the failure may be negligent or innocent.

The failures may be legislative or executive. They will normally comprise a wrongful act or omission; the enactment of measures, or failure to amend, repeal or introduce legislation, in breach of Community law. The failure may have been established directly by the Court of Justice under Arts 169 or 170 EEC [or under other enforcement provisions of the EEC Treaty, such as Arts 93(2), 100A(4)], or indirectly, via an interpretation of Community law in Art 177 EEC proceedings.

It is submitted that even where the other conditions for liability under *Francovich* are met, not all the above failures should give rise to non-contractual liability on the part of the state. They would not do so under the majority of laws of Member States, nor under the principles of Community liability.

For what kind of failures, then, should a state be liable? On what principles is this to be decided? And are these matters of national or Community law?

Principles applicable to liability

States' liability according to Community law

The Court of Justice has consistently held that, in the absence of Community rules, it is for the domestic system of each Member State to designate the courts having jurisdiction, and the procedural conditions governing actions at law, intended to ensure the protection of the rights which subjects derive from the direct effect of community law [*Rewe* Case 33/76 [1976] ECR 1989].

'It must be possible for every type of action provided for by national law to be available for the purpose of ensuring observance of provisions having direct effect on the same conditions as apply were it a question of observing national law.' [*Rewe* Case 158/80 [1981] ECR 1805]

Expressed originally in terms of directly effective Community rights, these principles were extended in *Francovich* to embrace the protection of 'all rights which parties enjoy under Community law'. States are obliged to make good the consequences of the damage caused 'within the context of national law on liability'.

However, the Court has also insisted that domestic law must not make it impossible in practice to exercise a Community right [*Comet* Case 45/76 [1976] ECR 2043]; national courts must guarantee 'real and effective protection' for individuals' Community rights [*Von Colson* Case 14/83 [1984] ECR 1891]. Since this is not always possible under national law, domestic courts have, on occasions, been obliged to adapt existing remedies and even provide new remedies to meet the demands of Community law [eg, *Factortame (No 2)* [1991] 1 All ER 106]. This will certainly be the case in the field of the Member States' non-contractual liability under *Francovich*. For, whilst all states provide for the non-contractual liability of public authorities, their law, in the vast majority of (perhaps all) cases, will be inadequate to provide effective protection for individual rights under *Francovich*. Moreover, national laws governing the non-contractual liability of public authorities differ considerably from state to state. Thus, if *Francovich* is to be fully and fairly applied in all Member States, it will be necessary to develop a framework of common community rules. ...

Direct and indirect effects: a residual role?

If *Francovich* is to be applied generally, to all breaches of Community law, on the principles suggested above, is there still a role for remedies based on direct or indirect effects?

The principle of state liability introduced in *Francovich* was laid down in the context of a Community provision which was not directly effective. In view of the difficulties facing individuals seeking to enforce directives, directly or indirectly, in horizontal situations, and the problem of establishing, in borderline cases, whether the defendant is a 'public' body, where the conditions for *Francovich* are met, *Francovich* will provide, in these sorts of circumstances, the surest, perhaps the only, remedy. But a remedy under *Francovich* is not excluded where the Community provisions (allegedly) breached are directly effective. The Court's reasoning, in terms of states' liability to make good damage caused to individuals by breaches of Community law for which it is responsible, can apply equally to directly effective provisions. A principle of state liability was simply 'particularly essential ...' where individuals were not entitled to rely on rights accorded to them by Community law before national courts [at para 34]. Advocate-General Mischo too suggested that the principle applied 'whether (the EC provisions in question) have direct effect or not' [at para 85].

The fact that the relevant provisions of Directive 80/987 (1980) OJ L283/23 were found by the Court of Justice not to be directly effective may seem to imply that the criteria for liability under *Francovich* are more generous than those for direct effect. If this were the case, a claim which failed under *Francovich* would be unlikely to succeed elsewhere. It is submitted that this is not the case. The criteria for direct effects are generous, and have usually been loosely applied. The Court's finding in *Francovich*, that the relevant provisions of the directive were not directly effective, was based on a technicality, and, as suggested above, for good reason. It wished to establish a principle of state liability which was independent of the principle (and the problems) of direct effects. In order to succeed under *Francovich* an individual must satisfy the three-fold criteria laid down by the Court, as well as the question of 'failure'. Even if the courts, both national and European, are lax in their approach to the three conditions, a plaintiff must still overcome the hurdle of proving failure. If the standard applied in determining the question of failure is as suggested above, requiring on the state's part at least constructive knowledge of the wrong, there will be times when a claim based on direct, and even indirect, effects may stand the greater chance of success. Individuals have succeeded in obtaining a remedy based on directly effective provisions of Community law when the state's breach of Community law was, at the time of breach, far from clear [eg, Case 152/84 *Marshall v Southampton AHA*; Case C 262/88 *Barber v Guardian Royal Exchange Assurance* [1990] ECR 1889]. Whilst it may not be consistent in principle to impose liability on a 'public' body based on directly effective Community law regardless of fault, and, in the same circumstances, to deny liability under *Francovich*, the distinction may be justified as a matter of policy. There is a difference of substance between liability in the individual case, on principles already established, and liability, with retrospective effect, to complainants at large.

Conclusion

... both the need for effective enforcement of individuals' rights and the need for uniformity require that the application of *Francovich* be subject to some common Community rules. These principles may be drawn from the law of Member States and from Community law [also from the Council of Europe's Recommendation R (84) 15], but they must reflect the special nature of Community law. As Schwarze suggests, the 'best' legal principles following a comparative analysis for the purpose of Community law 'are those which most closely correspond to the functional capacity and the goals of the Community'. Member States' obligations to implement Community law are not the same as public authorities' duties under national law; nor are they analogous to those of Community institutions. In implementing Community obligations Member States are carrying out a unique function, in a unique institutional context. These factors must therefore shape the appropriate rules.

However, if the nature of Community law, as 'binding' [Art 189 EEC] and 'supreme over national law' requires that states should not escape liability for damage caused by any wrongful acts, legislative or otherwise, both the nature of Community law and principles of certainty [an acknowledged principle of Community law; see Case 43/75 *Defrenne v Sabena* [1976] ECR 455] and equity demand that states should not, in this context, be liable in the absence of fault. To incur liability their failure to comply with Community law must be sufficiently clear; and, where Community law appears to allow for derogation, they must be free to exercise that discretion in good faith in the national interest.

Malcolm Ross, 'Beyond *Francovich'* (1993) 56 *Modern Law Review* 55, 58–62, 66–8, 71–2

... the *Francovich* judgment appears to open up a host of possible breaches by Member States of Treaty obligations which might lead to claims for damages by individuals.

A. The non-implementation by Member States of directives

This is, of course, the easiest scenario to contemplate since it essentially repeats the situation in *Francovich*. In the UK context, for example, there is a developing controversy surrounding the content of draft regulations which seek to implement the Health and Safety Framework Directive [89/391, OJ 1989 Ll83/1]. The general duty imposed upon employers by Art 5(1) of the directive is to ensure the safety and health of workers in every aspect related to the work. Art 5(4) allows for the possibility of Member States restricting or excluding employers' responsibility:

'where facts are due to circumstances unknown to them, exceptional and unforeseeable, or to exceptional events, the consequences of which could not have been avoided despite the exercise of all due care'.

Although not imposing an absolute obligation, the wording of this provision appears, at the very least, not to entertain any defences based on notions of cost effectiveness or practical difficulty. Nevertheless, the proposed regulations being drafted by the Health and Safety Executive to meet the directive in the UK contain what could be described as the traditional British approach, allowing employers to satisfy their responsibilities on the basis of steps which meet a 'reasonably practicable' criterion. It may well be that the UK is heading for a failure to implement the directive properly [compare the implementation of the Product Liability Directive in the Consumer Protection Act 1987].

[This example] contains an important complication absent in the *Francovich* situation itself. The presence of some purported implementing rules affords the opportunity of a *Marleasing* approach, whereas in *Francovich* a dismal failure to introduce any measures at all rendered it impossible to 'interpret' anything in the light of the directive. Hence the unsuccessful attempt in the alternative in *Francovich* to establish the directly effective nature of the relevant directive. Where an interpretative possibility exists in favour of the Community instrument, it must be considered whether this ousts the *Francovich* claim in damages or whether the plaintiff has a choice which might then be influenced by considerations of costs, procedures and solvency of defendants, such as might influence any decision to litigate.

It is suggested that, at least in this context, the plaintiff has a genuine choice in the same way that he or she might in other matters of non-contractual liability pursue any one of several joint defendants, but be only able to recover one sum for the loss involved. There is no justification for removing the *Francovich* claim against the state just because there might be an indirect action against the employer. ...

B. The use of Francovich *in the context of direct effect*

The clearest value of the remedy in *Francovich* is where the interest of the individual would not be protectable by other means; it thus provides a new weapon in areas where direct effect is lacking.

The key question is whether a directly effective Community law right carries with it an inherent entitlement to an appropriate remedy. Ever since *Factortame*, it seems out of the question that Community law could be restricted to the establishment of the directly effective right, leaving remedies entirely at the discretion of national courts. The position as clarified by *Factortame* would seem to have been that there is a Community law right to an appropriate remedy inherent in any directly effective right, but still leaving the national court to discern or create the remedy in question. By extending liability in *Francovich*, the Court has invented a Community law remedy for a particular type of breach of obligation by a Member State, but this does not mean that it supersedes the obligations on national courts that already exist.

Put in these terms, the relevance of *Francovich* depends upon whether the right to damages against the defaulting state derives from the individual's effective enjoyment of a substantive right to free movement of his goods under Art 30 EEC, or whether it is a specific, guaranteed remedy against any state default. Expressed in terms of the former classification, the plaintiff is still suing for breach of Art 30 by the named trustee of its obligations (the state); it so happens that damages are necessary to constitute effective enjoyment of the plaintiff's rights (as distinct, for example, from recourse to judicial review and the remedies associated therewith). The state becomes a defendant actor in just the same way that a private company might be sued for damages by the victim of an abuse of a dominant position under Art 86 [compare *Garden Cottage Foods Ltd v Milk Marketing Board* [1984] AC 130]. But if the alternative analysis above is applied, the action would arise against the state for failing to comply with the Treaty. There would be no question as to whether damages were the most appropriate or effective protection of the plaintiff's position; it would instead be the automatic consequence as a matter of Community law for a particular type of default. The directly effective nature of Art 30 would be irrelevant for this analysis. ...

It may therefore be that, in the context of directly effective rights, *Francovich* is no more than a specific, guaranteed element in the assurance of the fundamental principle of effective enjoyment. Its value is limited to articulating expressly what should already be the outcome of any proper application of that wider principle by a national court. However, its presence should mean that there need not be any lengthy anguishing by a national court as to what constitutes the inherent extent of a particular directly effective right claimed under Community law. Nor, as will be discussed, is the individual's right to a remedy to be hampered by the procedural dictates of national law.

C. Express obligations lacking direct effect

Article 5 EEC and the duty of solidarity

Is the far-reaching implication of *Francovich* that Art 5 can now give rise to directly effective rights for individuals? Such a view has not hitherto prevailed although the provision has become the *fons et origo* of several key extensions of Court jurisprudence [see *Factortame*; also Case C–234/89, *Delimitis v Henninger Brau* [1991] ECR 1–935 and Case C–143/88, *Zuckerfabrik Süderdithmarschen v Hauptzollamt Itzehoe*]. There is, of course, direct reference to Art 5 in the *Francovich* judgment, although put in terms that justification for the action can be found in the cornerstone principle of solidarity, rather than that the principle of damages flows directly from it. Framing the judgment expressly in terms of the direct effect of Art 5 would have been too adventurous a claim to be met with anything other than resistance from the Member States.

However, on closer scrutiny it may be argued that the effective application of the *Francovich* action achieves similar results. It is true that there are limiting criteria but it has already been seen that these are not elaborate obstacles to lawyers trained in Euro-interpretation and creative claims. The startling result that could follow is that the obligations arising from Art 5 would allow for actions that do not have any specific base elsewhere in the Treaty. Unlike the previous illustrations relating to the specific obligations contained in Arts 90(1) and 92–94, a dynamic approach to Art 5 allows any failure by a Member State to make at least the starting gate of litigation. Of course, it must then be evaluated against the three *Francovich* criteria. It remains to be seen whether the Court's future jurisprudence will elaborate upon these tests to allay conservative fears of an avalanche of open-ended and unjustified actions.

To identify the potential type of Art 5 claim, it is important to remember the fundamental, cohesive character of the provision as it has already been interpreted. The duty of solidarity, whilst express, is not specific. Its flexibility has allowed the creation of the very notion of effective protection, so unequivocally articulated previously in *Factortame*. Hence the suggestion put forward earlier in this paper that the failure of national courts to come up with adequate and sufficient remedies under national law for the protection of Community law rights would itself give rise to a claim under *Francovich*.

This approach raises a serious question as to the function of the limiting criteria adopted within the *Francovich* formula. It might be suggested that the requirement that individuals are affected and intended to be protected is only a particular expression of a fundamentality element as to the interests which can give rise to damages against the Member State. This approach would help clarify the ambiguous reference by the Court in *Francovich* to the significance of the nature of the breach when determining the conditions for state liability. It is suggested that it is the breach of a fundamental Community obligation which should be decisive, not the gravity of infringement. Moreover, the Court has on many occasions defended the initiation and expansion of the doctrine of direct effect as a necessary but natural response to the central position to be attached to individuals within most spheres of application of the Treaty. Art 5 may be seen as the archetypal expression of and vehicle for protection of the most important constitutional values. Therefore, the argument might run, it is for the entrenchment and emphasis of the fundamentality of certain rights that the presence of a *Francovich* action is most suited. Conversely, this same argument can be made to limit *Francovich* if it proves necessary to assuage fears that all defaults would render the Member State liable in damages. Only those breaches or lapses which are incompatible with fundamental rights could qualify as sufficiently important to be construed as affecting individuals.

Seen in these terms, an obvious candidate for *Francovich* protection is infringement by a Member State of human rights recognised as embodied within Community law. There could hardly be any argument against the 'individuality' of such claims; that is the very purpose of the protection demanded by codes of human rights. The adoption of *Francovich* remedies in this area would underline the importance to be attached to observance of these perceived cornerstones of individual entitlement. ... the Court would be in a position to consider the intrinsic protection afforded by human rights.

In essence, therefore, *Francovich* potentially creates two types of state liability. The first, and most easily identified, relates to breaches of express and specific duties contained in the Treaty and secondary legislation. These would be actionable according to the conditions laid down in *Francovich* without any additional requirements to be satisfied. The second type of liability concerns more nebulous claims, such as breach of an obligation created by general principles recognised by the Court to be generated by Art 5. Such actions would demand the additional requirement of fundamentality to render them specific enough. In other words, the capacity for a breach of Art 5 to trigger an action for damages by an individual would work in a similar fashion to the current operation of Art 90, that is, as a reference provision which depends for its availability to individuals upon the nature of the rule or principle which it seeks to underscore.

An intriguing scenario for Art 5 purposes may be conjured from developments under the Maastricht Treaty. The refusal of the British Government to sign up for the Social Chapter poses multifarious difficulties if and when ratification takes place. It will be recalled that the eleven states other than the UK signed a Social Protocol allowing for joint action and legislation on a range of issues, including health and safety and working conditions. There have already been suggestions that an employee in the UK deprived of the benefits which might accrue to him or her under legislation adopted under the Social Protocol might be able to demonstrate a distortion of competition by the UK contrary to one of the basic objectives of the Treaty.

Put into the terms of *Francovich*, the refusal of the UK to join the Social Protocol would be a breach of Art 5 in thwarting the attainment of Community objectives, namely a system of undistorted competition (or alternatively violating a principle of non-discrimination by creating a distorted set of employment conditions within the Community). This would be such a fundamental infringement so as to make it of relevance to individuals. The only remaining obstacle would be the question of causation. As argued previously in the context of Art 90, the plaintiff's claim might well point to the use in *Francovich* itself of the failure to implement as sufficient causation. Nevertheless, a narrow view might identify two stages in the present scenario, in order to distinguish it from a failure to implement legislation to which the defaulting Member State has been a party. In the first instance, there would be the refusal by the UK to participate; only then does there follow the actual enactment of legislation by the eleven which, it might be said, creates the disparity in social conditions to disadvantage the UK employee. However, it is submitted that the latter does not constitute a break in the chain of causation. The breach of Art 5 by the UK remains direct and its consequences for individuals in the event of the eleven choosing to act are eminently foreseeable. This type of difficulty nonetheless underlines the need for further refinement, as part of Community law, of the criterion of causation. Otherwise, haphazard application at national level seems inevitable. ...

E. Francovich: *a more radical view*

A more fundamental result and reappraisal of the regime of Community law is achieved if *Francovich* is interpreted as travelling at least some way down the path towards establishing and entrenching an individual right to have Member States observe their Community obligations. On this view, instead of making all provisions of the Treaty directly effective (which would not be tenable against the traditional criteria for determining direct effect), the Court has adopted in the guise of a remedy a principle which is itself also a right of action. Put another way, *Francovich* significantly expands the notion of effective protection. In this way, rather than simply introducing a guaranteed remedy of damages for breach of identified and predetermined rights under the Treaty, the judgment may be seen as enlarging the scope of what constitutes a protectable interest, so as to include a new set of individually-oriented rights which can be classified as fundamental. It is suggested that this approach is signalled by the effect the *Francovich* judgment may have on claims placed on the footing of Art 5. Put briefly, the long-lasting impact of *Francovich* seems to depend on which element of the concept of effective protection it is seen as developing. On the narrower view, the case refines what is meant by effective (in the form of a new remedy in Community law), whereas the more radical interpretation emphasises its effect on protection (by adding to the rights which can give rise to a remedy). What makes this potential development so important is that it treats the contribution of the case as one of substance as well as procedure. Instead of the effective enjoyment of specific rights, effective enjoyment of the sum total of Community law would be enforceable in national courts, so long as the interest was sufficiently fundamental and the causal link established.

Thus, in the longer term, it is suggested that the likeliest contribution of *Francovich* to the framework of Community law is constitutional in character. By describing the liability of Member States to individuals as 'inherent' in the Treaty, the Court has echoed its earlier attitudes towards direct effect [Case 26/62 *Van Gend en Loos*], effective protection [Case C-213/89 *Factortame*] and the uniform application of Community law [Case C-143/88 *Zuckerfabrik*]. The subtlety of the Court's approach lies in the manner in which Art 5 has been used to reveal these fundamental imperatives which are not deducible from any other text in the Treaties, thereby clothing its inventiveness with constitutional legitimacy. However, having found a plausible source for this policy of individual protection, the 'inherent' characteristic ascribed to these principles allows for unlimited creativity on the part of the Court. The Court thus seems to be declaring unilaterally a new set of 'super-rules' which outrank the basic institutional and legislative structure contained in the Treaties. To be able to rely on 'inherence' rather than reasoned justification is itself a revealing comment upon the confidence and status of the Court and the progress of the Community as a *sui generis* legal order. In effect, there has been a double layer of inventiveness at work in the Court's approach. Having created the doctrine of direct effect and established a set of inspirational general principles, the Court is disingenuous in *Francovich* in giving direct effect to some, at least, of those very principles. The judgment, whilst dramatically bolstering the scope of individual rights, is likely to inflame the political debate concerning the acceptable constitutional and democratic bases to the Community [see Lenaerts (1991) 28 CMLR 11]. But, it might be said, by conferring yet more rights of redress upon individuals enforceable in their national courts, the 'spirit of subsidiarity' is already at work.

Secretary of State for Transport, ex p Factortame (No 4) Joined Cases C-46/93 and C-48/93 [1996] 2 WLR 506, ECJ

51   Community law confers a right to reparation where three conditions are met: the Rule of Law infringed must be intended to confer rights on individuals; the breach must be sufficiently serious; and there must be a direct causal link between the breach of the obligation resting on the state and the damage sustained by the injured parties.

52   First, those conditions satisfy the requirements of the full effectiveness of the rules of Community law and of the effective protection of the rights which those rules confer.

53   Secondly, those conditions correspond in substance to those defined by the court in relation to Art 215 in its case law on liability of the Community for damage caused to individuals by unlawful legislative measures adopted by its institutions.

54   The first condition is manifestly satisfied in the case of Art 30 of the Treaty, the relevant provision in Case C-46/93, and, in the case of Art 52, the relevant provision in Case C-48/93. Whilst Art 30 imposes a prohibition on Member

States it nevertheless gives rise to rights for individuals which the national courts must protect: *Ianelli and Volpi SpA v Meroni* (Case 74/76) [1977] ECR 557, 575, para 13. Likewise, the essence of Art 52 is to confer rights on individuals: *Reyners v Belgian State* (Case 2/74) [1974] ECR 631, 651, para 25.

55   As to the second condition, as regards both Community liability under Art 215 and Member State liability for breaches of Community law, the decisive test for finding that a breach of Community law is sufficiently serious is whether the Member State or the Community institution concerned manifestly and gravely disregarded the limits on its discretion.

56   The factors which the competent court may take into consideration include: the clarity and precision of the rule breached; the measure of discretion left by that rule to the national or Community authorities; whether the infringement and the damage caused was intentional or involuntary; whether any error of law was excusable or inexcusable; the fact that the position taken by a Community institution may have contributed towards the omission, and the adoption or retention of national measures or practices contrary to Community law.

57   On any view, a breach of Community law will clearly be sufficiently serious if it has persisted despite a judgment finding the infringement in question to be established, or a preliminary ruling or settled case law of the court on the matter from which it is clear that the conduct in question constituted an infringement.

58. While, in the present cases, the court cannot substitute its assessment for that of the national courts, which have sole jurisdiction to find the facts in the main proceedings and decide how to characterise the breaches of Community law at issue, it will be helpful to indicate a number of circumstances which the national courts might take into account.

59   In Case C-46/93 a distinction should be drawn between the question of the German legislature having maintained in force provisions of the Biersteuergesetz concerning the purity of beer prohibiting the marketing under the designation 'bier' of beers imported from other Member States which were lawfully produced in conformity with different rules, and the question of the retention of the provisions of that same law prohibiting the import of beers containing additives. As regards the provisions of the German legislation relating to the designation of the product marketed, it would be difficult to regard the breach of Art 30 by that legislation as an excusable error, since the incompatibility of such rules with Art 30 was manifest in the light of earlier decisions of the court, in particular *Rewe-Zentral AG v Bundesmonopolverwaltung für Branntwein* (Case 120/78) [1979] ECR 649 and *Commission of the European Communities v Italian Republic* (Case 193/80) [1981] ECR 3019. In contrast, having regard to the relevant case law, the criteria available to the national legislature to determine whether the prohibition of the use of additives was contrary to Community law were significantly less conclusive until the court's judgment of 12 March 1987 in *Commission of the European Communities v Federal Republic of Germany* (Case 178/84) [1987] ECR 1227, in which the court held that prohibition to be incompatible with Art 30.

60   A number of observations may likewise be made about the national legislation at issue in Case C-48/93.

61   The decision of the UK legislature to introduce in the Merchant Shipping Act 1988 provisions relating to the conditions for the registration of fishing vessels has to be assessed differently in the case of the provisions making

registration subject to a nationality condition, which constitute direct discrimination manifestly contrary to Community law, and in the case of the provisions laying down residence and domicile conditions for vessel owners and operators.

62 The latter conditions are *prima facie* incompatible with Art 52 of the Treaty in particular but the UK sought to justify them in terms of the objectives of the common fisheries policy. In the judgment in *Secretary of State for Transport, ex p Factortame Ltd (No 3)* (Case C-221/89) [1992] QB 680, the court rejected that justification.

63 In order to determine whether the breach of Art 52 thus committed by the UK was sufficiently serious, the national court might take into account *inter alia*, the legal disputes relating to particular features of the common fisheries policy, the attitude of the Commission, which made its position known to the UK in good time, and the assessments as to the state of certainty of Community law made by the national courts in the interim proceedings brought by individuals affected by the Merchant Shipping Act.

64 Lastly, consideration should be given to the assertion made by Rawlings (Trawling) Ltd, the 37th applicant in Case C-48/93, that the UK failed to adopt immediately the measures needed to comply with the order of the President of the Court of Justice of 10 October 1989 *in Commission of the European Communities v United Kingdom of Great Britain and Northern Ireland* (Case 246/89R) [1989] ECR 3125, and that that needlessly increased the loss it sustained. If that allegation – which was certainly contested by the UK at the hearing – should prove correct, it should be regarded by the national court as constituting in itself a manifest and, therefore, sufficiently serious breach of Community law.

65 As for the third condition, it is for the national courts to determine whether there is a direct causal link between the breach of the obligation borne by the state and the damage sustained by the injured parties.

66 The aforementioned three conditions are necessary and sufficient to found a right in individuals to obtain redress, although this does not mean that the state cannot incur liability under less strict conditions on the basis of national law.

67 As appears from *Francovich v Italian Republic* (Joined Cases C-6 and 9/90) [1995] ICR 722, 772–773, paras 41–43, subject to the right to reparation which flows directly from Community law where the conditions referred to in the preceding paragraph are satisfied, the state must make reparation for the consequences of the loss and damage caused in accordance with the domestic rules on liability, provided that the conditions for reparation of loss and damage laid down by national law must not be less favourable than those relating to similar domestic claims and must not be such as in practice to make it impossible or excessively difficult to obtain reparation (see also *Amministrazione delle Finanze dello Stato v SpA San Giorgio* (Case 199/82) [1983] ECR 3595).

68. In that regard, restrictions that exist in domestic legal systems as to the non-contractual liability of the state in the exercise of its legislative function may be such as to make it impossible in practice or excessively difficult for individuals to exercise their right to reparation, as guaranteed by Community law, of loss or damage resulting from the breach of Community law.

69 In the Case C-46/93 the national court asks in particular whether national law may subject any right to compensation to the same restrictions as apply

where a law is in breach of higher-ranking national provisions, for instance, where an ordinary federal law infringes the *Grundgesetz* of the Federal Republic of Germany.

70   While the imposition of such restrictions may be consistent with the requirement that the conditions laid down should not be less favourable than those relating to similar domestic claims, it is still to be considered whether such restrictions are not such as in practice to make it impossible or excessively difficult to obtain reparation.

71   The condition imposed by German law where a law is in breach of higher-ranking national provisions, which makes reparation dependent on the legislature's act or omission being referable to an individual situation, would in practice make it impossible or extremely difficult to obtain effective reparation for loss or damage resulting from a breach of Community law, since the tasks falling to the national legislature relate, in principle, to the public at large and not to identifiable persons or classes of person.

72   Since such a condition stands in the way of the obligation on national courts to ensure the full effectiveness of Community law by guaranteeing effective protection for the rights of individuals, it must be set aside where an infringement of Community law is attributable to the national legislature.

73   Likewise, any condition that may be imposed by English law on state liability requiring proof of misfeasance in public office, such an abuse of power being inconceivable in the case of the legislature, is also such as in practice to make it impossible or extremely difficult to obtain effective reparation for loss or damage resulting from a breach of Community law where the breach is attributable to the national legislature.

74   Accordingly, the reply to the questions from the national courts must be that, where a breach of Community law by a Member State is attributable to the national legislature acting in a field in which it has a wide discretion to make legislative choices, individuals suffering loss or injury thereby are entitled to reparation where the rule of Community law breached is intended to confer rights on them, the breach is sufficiently serious and there is a direct causal link between the breach and the damage sustained by the individuals. Subject to that reservation, the state must make good the consequences of' the loss or damage caused by the breach of Community law attributable to it, in accordance with its national law on liability. However, the conditions laid down by the applicable national laws must not be less favourable than those relating to similar domestic claims or framed in such a way as in practice to make it impossible or excessively difficult to obtain reparation.

The possibility of making reparation conditional on the existence of fault (third question in Case C-46/93)

75   By its third question, the *Bundesgerichtshof* essentially seeks to establish whether, pursuant to the national legislation which it applies, the national court is entitled to make reparation conditional on the existence of fault (whether intentional or negligent) on the part of the organ of the state to which the infringement is attributable.

76   As is clear from the case file, the concept of fault does not have the same content in the various legal systems.

77   Next, it follows from the reply to the preceding question that, where a breach of Community law is attributable to a Member State acting in a field in which it has a wide discretion to make legislative choices, a finding of a right to reparation on the basis of Community law will be conditional, *inter alia*, on

the breach having been sufficiently serious.

78 So, certain objective and subjective factors connected with the concept of fault under a national legal system may well be relevant for the purpose of determining whether or not a given breach of Community law is serious: see the factors mentioned in paragraphs 56 and 57 above.

79 The obligation to make reparation for loss or damage caused to individuals cannot, however, depend on a condition based on any concept of fault going beyond that of a sufficiently serious breach of Community law. Imposition of such a supplementary condition would be tantamount to calling in question the right to reparation founded on the Community legal order.

80 Accordingly, the reply to the question from the national court must be that, pursuant to the national legislation which it applies, reparation of loss or damage cannot be made conditional on fault (intentional or negligent) on the part of the organ of the state responsible for the breach, going beyond that of a sufficiently serious breach of Community law.

The actual extent of the reparation (question (4)(a) in Case C-46/93 and the second question in Case C-48/93

81 By these questions, the national courts essentially ask the court to identify the criteria for determination of the extent of the reparation due by the Member State responsible for the breach.

82 Reparation for loss or damage caused to individuals as a result of breaches of Community law must be commensurate with the loss or damage sustained so as to ensure the effective protection for their rights.

83 In the absence of relevant Community provisions, it is for the domestic legal system of each Member State to set the criteria for determining the extent of reparation. However, those criteria must not be less favourable than those applying to similar claims based on domestic law and must not be such as in practice to make it impossible or excessively difficult to obtain reparation.

84 In particular, in order to determine the loss or damage for which reparation may be granted, the national court may inquire whether the injured person showed reasonable diligence in order to avoid the loss or damage or limit its extent and whether, in particular, he availed himself in time of all the legal remedies available to him.

85 Indeed, it is a general principle common to the legal systems of the Member States that the injured party must show reasonable diligence in limiting the extent of the loss or damage, or risk having to bear the damage himself: *Mulder v Council and Commission of the European Communities* (Joined Cases C-104/89 and C-37/90) [1992] ECR I-3061, 3136, 3137, para 33.

86 The Bundesgerichtshof asks whether national legislation may generally limit the obligation to make reparation to damage done to certain, specifically protected individual interests, for example property, or whether it should also cover loss of profit by the applicants. It stales that the opportunity to market products from other Member States is not regarded in German law as forming part of the protected assets of the undertaking.

87 Total exclusion of' loss of profit as a head of damage for which reparation may be awarded in the case of a breach of Community law cannot be accepted. Especially in the context of economic or commercial litigation, such a total exclusion of loss of profit would be such as to make reparation of damage practically impossible.

88 As for the various heads of damage referred to in the Divisional Court's

second question, Community law imposes no specific criteria. It is for the national court to rule on those heads of damage in accordance with the domestic law which it applies, subject to the requirements set out in paragraph 83 above.

89   As regards in particular the award of exemplary damages, such damages are based under domestic law, as the Divisional Court explains, on the finding that the public authorities concerned acted oppressively, arbitrarily or unconstitutionally. In so far as such conduct may constitute or aggravate a breach of Community law, an award of exemplary damages pursuant to a claim or an action founded on Community law cannot be ruled out if such damages could be awarded pursuant to a similar claim or action founded on domestic law.

Notes

1   Ross considers that *Francovich* may have very far-reaching implications in terms of affording 'direct redress in national courts against breaches by Member States of their specific obligations which comply with the three criteria laid down in [the decision]'. In other words, *Francovich* may not only allow an individual to claim redress where a *Marleasing* approach is not available, but also may allow such a claim under various Community instruments incapable of having direct effect.

2   In *Secretary of State for Transport, ex p Factortame (No 4)* (1996)[12] the ECJ provided some clarification of the application of the *Francovich* principle. Most significantly, it found that the *Francovich* principle of state liability held good whatever the organ of the state which was responsible for the breach; liability was not dependent on fault on the part of the relevant organ of the state, and exemplary damages could be awarded against the state in claims founded on Community law if they could be awarded in similar claims founded on domestic law. Guidance was given as to when a breach would be 'sufficiently serious' (the second *Francovich* criteria). Factors to take into account could include: the precision of the rule breached; the measure of discretion left to the national or Community authorities; whether the infringement and the damage caused was intentional or voluntary; and the adoption or retention of measures contrary to Community law. A breach of Community law would always be sufficiently serious if it persisted, despite a judgment finding the breach to be established. In *HM Treasury, ex p British Telecommunications plc* Case C-392/93 (1996)[13] the ECJ found that the failure of the UK to implement correctly Directive 90/531 did not involve a sufficiently serious breach of Community law since the directive was worded imprecisely and the Commission had not given guidance on the subject.

3   It appears that the rule from *Francovich* may co-exist with the doctrine of indirect effect. Therefore, a litigant seeking a remedy for breach of Community law rights by a private body in reliance on a directive which has not been adequately implemented by the state now appears to have two

---

12   Judgment of 5 March 1996; [1996] 2 WLR 506; *The Times*, 7 March 1996. For discussion see 146 NLJ 451.
13   *The Times*, 16 April 1996.

alternative possibilities to pursue: (i) a claim against the state for damages;[14] and (ii) a claim against the private body. However, if the directive has not been implemented at all, it would seem that the litigant has only one claim – against the state.

4   If a litigant seeks a remedy for breach of Community law rights by a private body in reliance on a directive which has been adequately implemented by the state, he or she can not rely on the *Francovich* rule but on the doctrine of indirect effects. This seems to create an anomaly since, to an extent, the litigant is in a less advantageous position if the state has implemented the directive adequately than if it has not. The possibly more advantageous route of suing the state is denied to him or her.

5   Ross suggests that, if a Member State infringes human rights recognised as embodied in Community law, a remedy might be available under the *Francovich* principle.[15] On the protection available for human rights under Community law, see further Part II, Chapter 3.

Questions

1   In what respects is the *Francovich* principle likely to produce more equitable results than the doctrines of direct and indirect effects?

2   The complexities of the doctrines of direct and indirect effects, of the *Francovich* principle, and the relationship between the three rules, could have been avoided if all Community law creating individual rights had been worded precisely and made directly effective in Member States in the same way as domestic law. Individuals could then have been certain that they could rely on Community rights regardless of the nature of the body providing the right. Why was this course not taken?

3   The European Convention on Human Rights is not directly enforceable in UK domestic law. Could a UK citizen rely on the *Francovich* rule to claim a remedy against the state for a breach of one of the Convention rights?

4   Ross considers that a UK citizen might be able to rely on the *Francovich* rule to claim a remedy against the UK in relation to its failure to implement the Social Protocol. What is the basis of this proposition?

THE DOCTRINES OF DIRECT AND INDIRECT EFFECTS IN THE UK COURTS

The UK courts have accepted that Treaty provisions will produce direct effects in UK courts; the problem has arisen in relation to directives.

Litster v Forth Dry Dock and Engineering Co Ltd [1990] 1 AC 546, 553-4, 558 HL

Lord Keith: ... In Pickstone v Freemans plc [1989] AC 66 there had been laid before Parliament under paragraph 2(2) of Schedule 2 to the European Communities Act 1972 the draft of certain Regulations designed, and presented

---

14   See further Lasok (1992) 5 ICCLR 186; Smith (1992) 3 ECLR 129.
15   See further Coppel and O'Neill (1992) LS 227; Grief (1992) PL 555.

by the responsible ministers as designed, to fill a lacuna in the equal pay legislation of the UK which had been identified by a decision of the European Court of Justice. On a literal reading the regulation particularly relevant did not succeed in completely filling the lacuna. Your Lordships, however, held that, in order that the manifest purpose of the regulation might be achieved and effect given to the clear but inadequately expressed intention of Parliament, certain words must be read in by necessary implication.

... it is the duty of the court to give to Regulation 5 a construction which accords with the decisions of the European Court upon the corresponding provisions of the directive to which the regulation was intended by Parliament to give effect. The precedent established by *Pickstone v Freemans plc* indicates that this is to be done by implying, in Regulation 5(3), words indicating that, where a person has been unfairly dismissed in the circumstances described in Regulation 8(1), he is to be deemed to have been employed in the undertaking immediately before the transfer or any of a series of transactions whereby it was effected.

My Lords, I would allow the appeal.

Lord Templeman: ...In *von Colson and Kamann v Land Nordrhein-Westfalen* (Case 14/83) [1984] ECR 1891, 1909 the European Court of Justice dealing with Council Directive 76/207/EEC0, forbidding discrimination on grounds of sex regarding access to employment, ruled that:

'the Member States' obligation arising from a directive to achieve the result envisaged by the directive and their duty under Art 5 of the Treaty to take all appropriate measures, whether general of particular, to ensure the fulfilment of that obligation, is binding on all the authorities of Member States including, for matters within their jurisdiction, the courts. It follows that, in applying the national law and in particular the provisions of a national law specifically introduced in order to implement Directive [(76/207/EEC)] national courts are required to interpret their national law in the light of the wording and the purpose of the directive in order to achieve the result referred to in the third paragraph of Art 189.'

Thus the courts of the UK are under a duty to follow the practice of the European Court of Justice by giving a purposive construction to directives and to regulations issued for the purpose of complying with directives. In *Pickstone v Freemans plc* [1989] AC 66, this House implied words in a regulation designed to give effect to Council Directive (75/117/EEC) dealing with equal pay for women doing work of equal value. If this house had not been able to make the necessary implication, the Equal Pay (Amendment) Regulations 1983 (SI 1983/1794) would have failed their object and the UK would have been in breach of its treaty obligations to give effect to directives. In the present case, in the light of Council Directive (77/187/EEC) and in the light of the ruling of the European Court of Justice in *Bork's* Case (1989) IRLR 41, it seems to me, following the suggestion of my noble and learned friend, Lord Keith of Kinkel, that paragraph 5(3) of the regulations of 1981 was not intended and ought not to be construed so as to limit the operation of Regulation 5 to persons employed immediately before the transfer in point of time. Regulation 5(3) must be construed on the footing that it applies to a person employed immediately before the transfer or who would have been so employed if he had not been unfairly dismissed before the transfer for a reason connected with the transfer ...

Finnegan v Clowney Youth Training Programme Ltd (1990) 2 AC 407, 415-7 HL

Lord Bridge of Harwich: ... [T]he relevant legislation by Order in Council applicable to Northern Ireland has been designed to reproduce precisely the substance of the legislation enacted by the Westminster Parliament. Thus, on turning to the Sex Discrimination (Northern Ireland) Order 1976, we find that Art 8 reproduces precisely the provisions of s 6 of the English Act of 1975 and in the Equal Pay Act (Northern Ireland) 1970, set out in Schedule 1 to the Order of 1976 as amended by that Order, s 6(1A) reproduces precisely the provisions of s 6(1A) of the English Act 1970. Similarly, following the *Marshall* case (1987) QB 401, appropriate amendments to the Order of 1976 were made by the Sex Discrimination (Northern Ireland) Order 1988 which precisely reproduced in Art 4 the provisions of s 2 of the English Act of 1986.

On the face of it, therefore, the enactment applicable to the circumstances of the present employee's claim is indistinguishable from the enactment which fell to be applied in *Duke v GEC Reliance Systems Ltd* [1988] AC 618 and would appear, therefore, to dictate the inevitable result that the appeal must fail. This was the view of the Court of Appeal in Northern Ireland. Counsel for the employee submits, however, that a crucial distinction is to be derived from the chronology, in that the English Act 1975 was passed before the Council of the European Communities adopted the Equal Treatment Directive, on 9 February, whereas the Order of 1976 was not made until July of that year. He referred us to a familiar line of authority for the proposition that the national legislation of a Member State of the European Community which is enacted for the purpose of implementing a European Council directive must be construed in the light of the directive and must, if at all possible, be applied in a sense which will effect the purpose of the directive: see *von Colson and Kamann v Land Nordrhein-Westfalen* (Case 14/83) (1984) ECR 1891; *Pickstone v Freemans plc* (1989) AC 66; *Litster v Forth Dry Dock and Engineering Co Ltd* (1990) 1 AC 546.

I entirely accept the validity of the proposition, but I do not accept that it has any application here. Before the decision in the *Marshall* case (1986) QB 401 it is apparent from the history I have recounted that neither the UK Parliament nor the UK Government perceived any conflict between the provisions of s 6(4) of the Sex Discrimination Act 1975 and s 6(1A) of the Equal Pay Act 1970 on the one hand, and the provisions of the European Equal Treatment Directive on the other hand, such as to call for amendment of the English statutes after the adoption of the directive. Accordingly, it would appear to me to be wholly artificial to treat the Order of 1976 enacting identical provision for Northern Ireland, because it was made after the directive, as having been made with the purpose of implementing Community law in the same sense as the regulation which fell to be construed in the *Pickstone* and *Litster* cases. The reality is that Art 8(4) of the Order of 1976 being in identical terms and in an identical context to s 6(4) of the English Act of 1975, must have been intended to have the identical effect. To hold otherwise would be, as in *Duke v GEC Reliance Systems Ltd* (1988) AC 618, most unfair to the employers in that it would be giving retrospective operation to the amending Order of 1988 and effectively eliminating the distinction between Community law which is of direct effect between citizens of Member States, and community law which only affects citizens of Member States when it is implemented by national legislation.

Alternatively, counsel for the employee invited us to depart from *Duke v GEC Reliance Systems Ltd* in pursuance of *Practice Statement (Judicial Precedent)* [1966] 1 WLR 1234. I need only say that, so far from being persuaded that the decision in that case was wrong, I entertain no doubt that it was right for the reasons so clearly set out in the speech of Lord Templeman.

We were further invited to make a reference to the European Court of Justice under Art 177 of the EEC Treaty. In my opinion, however, the determination of the appeal does not depend on any question of Community law. The interpretation of the Order of 1976 is for the UK courts and it is not suggested that the Equal Treatment Directive is of direct effect between citizens.

I would dismiss the appeal.

Appeal dismissed.

Erika Szyszczack, 'Sovereignty: Crisis, Compliance, Confusion, Complacency?' (1990) 15(6) *European Law Review* 483–7

Confusion

By adopting a narrow, literal interpretation of the direct effects of directives [Case 152/84, *Marshall*], the European Court left unresolved [the issue:] when may the provisions of a directive give rise to indirect effects by a purposive construction being given to national law deemed to implement the directive's obligations?

... in *Duke v GEC Reliance Ltd* [1988] AC 618 the House of Lords rejected the use of a purposive construction of s 6(4) of the Sex Discrimination Act 1975 since it pre-dated the directive. Therefore there was no discretion vested in the national courts to construe the Act in conformity with the directive which in this instance did not give rise to direct effects. Counsel for Ms Duke had argued that s 2(4) of the European Communities Act 1972 provided the legal basis for the purposive construction of the Sex Discrimination Act 1975 but this argument was rejected by Lord Templeman (with whom the rest of the House of Lords concurred):

> [Section 2(4)] does no more than reinforce the binding nature of legally enforceable rights and obligations imposed by appropriate Community law ... [It] does not ... enable or constrain a British court to distort the meaning of a British statute in order to enforce against an individual a Community directive which has no direct effect between individuals. Section 2(4) applies, and only applies, where Community provisions are directly applicable. [*ibid* at p680]

This decision was the subject of much academic criticism within the UK [Foster, (1988) 25 CML Rev 629: Arnull, (1988) 13 EL Rev 42: Fitzpatrick, (1989) 9 OJLS 336]. Central to the criticism was the failure of the House of Lords to apply the rulings of the European Court, whereby national courts are directed to interpret national implementing legislation in accordance with Community law. In *Von Colson* the European Court limited the purposive interpretation only to legislation enacted specifically to implement a directive. This may not have been a deliberate limitation since, in subsequent cases, the Advocates-General have argued that the obligation is wider, embracing more than implementing legislation [see Advocate-General Mischo in Case 80/86, *Criminal Proceedings against Kolpinghuis Nijmegen BY* [1987] ECR 3639; Advocate-General van Gerven in Case C–262/88, *Barber v Guardian Royal Exchange Assurance Group*]. This would seem to be a tenable position to take since Member States do not always need to introduce implementing legislation in order to comply with a directive. However, when informing the Commission, either under obligations to notify contained in a directive, or as part of the Commission's implementation review of a directive, a Member State is forced into a position of identifying the relevant national legislation it claims fulfils the Community obligations. It would be absurd to allow legislation predating a directive to be immune from the *Von Colson* principle of purposive interpretation, and a denial of Community obligations to prevent individuals from enforcing their Community rights, simply because there was no need for amendment of existing national legislation.

The case of *Finnegan v Clowney Youth Training Programme Ltd* [1990] 2 All ER 546, an appeal from the Northern Ireland Court of Appeal, provided the House of

Lords with the opportunity of extricating itself from the morass it had led itself into in *Duke*. The House of Lords chose not to grasp this opportunity. Ms Finnegan had been retired by her employers soon after her 60th birthday. The normal retirement age for men was 65. A Northern Ireland Industrial Tribunal upheld her complaint of sex discrimination by interpreting the parallel provisions to s 6(4) of the Sex Discrimination Act 1975, namely Art 8(4) of the Sex Discrimination (Northern Ireland) Order 1976, to comply with the Equal Treatment Directive as interpreted in *Marshall*. The decision was reversed by the Northern Ireland Court of Appeal, following the ruling in *Duke*. When the issue came before the House of Lords, their lordships could have seized upon two distinctions between the *Duke* and *Finnegan* litigation. First, the Northern Ireland Order 1976 had been enacted *after* the Equal Treatment Directive. Secondly, the European Court had already ruled in Case 222/84, *Johnston v Chief Constable of the Royal Ulster Constabulary* [1986] ECR 1651 that the Order should be interpreted in the light of the Equal Treatment Directive.

Despite these distinctions, the House of Lords held that the Northern Ireland Order merely enacted the provisions of the Sex Discrimination Act 1976 in Northern Ireland and that there was no material difference between the two pieces of legislation. Ignoring the *Johnston* ruling, the House of Lords reiterated its view from *Duke* that the purposive rule of construction contained in s 2(4) of the European Communities Act 1972 does not apply to legislation pre-dating a directive which was not designed to implement the directive. The mere accident of timing of the Northern Ireland Order 1976 was irrelevant. Furthermore, because the directive did not give rise to direct effects in this case, the House of Lords ruled that there was no point of Community law involved which would merit a reference to the European Court. To hold otherwise would be:

> most unfair to the employer in that it would be giving retrospective operation to the amending Order of 1988 and effectively eliminating the distinction between Community law which is of direct effect between citizens of Member States and Community law which only affects citizens of Member States when it is implemented by national legislation [*per* Lord Bridge at p551].

While the House of Lords may feel the need to maintain the distinction, its conclusion that no point of Community law arises is untenable. There may be doubts and misgivings over allowing the influence of Community law to permeate into the national legal system by the 'back door', but as Curtin points out, the European Court may have consciously adopted this distinction between horizontal direct effects and indirect effects in order to avoid the 'hostile reactions from national courts which the formal acceptance of horizontal direct effect would probably have brought in its wake'. Once this is grasped by the House of Lords, Lord Denning and the UK Government would have good reason to feel overwhelmed by the creativity of the European Court.

In two other cases the House of Lords has been more responsive in adopting a purposive construction to national legislation adopted after a Community directive. These cases reveal the confused thinking of the House of Lords as to the legal basis of a purposive construction. In *Pickstone v Freemans plc* [1989] AC 66 the House of Lords was invited to construe an amendment to the Equal Pay Act 1970 introduced to comply with the Equal Pay Directive and an infringement ruling by the European Court. Previously, the UK courts had adopted the convention that the national legislation should be ambiguous before resort was made to the international — or Community — law obligation underlying the legal claim [*Haughton v Olau Line (UK)* [1986] IRLR 465, CA]. Taking the unprecedented step of resorting to *Hansard* in order to determine the circumstances and motive for the national legislation, Lord Oliver had no hesitation in treating the issue as a question of construction, enabling the court to depart from the literal wording of the legislation ...

This purposive reasoning was extended one year later in *Litster v Forth Dry Dock and Engineering Co Ltd* [1989] 1 All ER 1134 to apply to Community obligations imposed as a result of the European Court's interpretation of the Transfer of Undertakings Directive.

In their enthusiasm to adopt this 'greater flexibility' in statutory interpretation, it seems to have escaped their lordships' attention that in this situation, like the situation in *Duke* and *Finnegan*, the directive only gave rise to indirect effects and not direct effects. The only difference between the two situations was that in *Litster* the directive had necessitated implementing legislation.

Notes

1   In *Finnegan* Lord Bridge did not allow the Equal Treatment Directive to have indirect effect since he considered that the Northern Ireland Order in question was not 'implementing legislation'. As Szyszczack suggests, this finding highlighted the anomalies created by the lack of a doctrine of horizontal direct effect.

2   It is not entirely clear how the UK courts will react to *Marleasing*; in certain decisions such as *Litster*, as discussed above, the courts have been prepared to derogate to a certain extent from the traditional theory of parliamentary sovereignty in giving an interpretation to UK legislation adopted to give effect to a directive which Parliament may not have intended. The courts have been prepared to disregard the possibility that Parliament deliberately set out to give effect to a directive in a minimalist fashion. However, to go further and give effect to a directive regardless of the wording of the domestic instrument purporting to implement it would be to bring about an extremely radical change in the balance of power between the judiciary and Parliament. If the courts refuse to take this stance, an individual may still be able to rely on the rule from *Francovich* to obtain redress.

Questions

1   In what sense can it be said that in refusing to find that legislation pre-dating a directive and not intended to implement the directive (in *Finnegan*) could be interpreted so as to allow the directive to have indirect effect, the House of Lords may have failed to understand the attitude of the ECJ to the possibility of horizontal direct effect?

2   Is the ruling in *Finnegan* as regards purposive construction inconsistent with that in *Litster*? Is it consistent with the finding of the ECJ in *Faccini Dori* (see above) that national courts must interpret national legislation, whether adopted before or after a directive, in the light of the directive so as to achieve the result it has in view?

3   What reasoning appears to underlie the refusal of the House of Lords in *Finnegan* and *Duke* to accept that a directive can have indirect effect through national legislation pre-dating the directive?

CHAPTER 3

THE EUROPEAN CONVENTION ON HUMAN RIGHTS

INTRODUCTION[1]

The European Convention on Human Rights was conceived after the Second World War as a means of preventing the kind of violation of human rights seen in Germany during and before the war. It has not generally been invoked in relation to large scale violations of rights, but instead has addressed particular deficiencies in the legal systems of the Member States which on the whole create regimes of human rights which are in conformity with the Convention. Drafted in 1949, it was based on the United Nations Declaration of Human Rights,[2] and partly for that reason, and partly because it was only intended to provide basic protection for human rights, it appears today as quite a cautious document, less far reaching than the 1966 International Covenant on Civil and Political Rights. Nevertheless, it has had far more effect on UK law than any other Human Rights Treaty due to its machinery for enforcement which includes a Court with the power to deliver a ruling adverse to the Government of Member States. Thus the machinery for the enforcement of the Convention is impressive compared to that used in respect of other human rights' treaties, particularly the 1966 International Covenant on Civil and Political Rights which, as far as the UK is concerned, has been enforceable only through a system of assessment of national reports.[3]

The Court insists upon the dynamic nature of the Convention and adopts a teleological or purpose-based approach to interpretation, which has allowed the substantive rights to develop until they may cover situations unthought of in 1949. At the same time, the Court is greatly influenced by general practice in the Member States as a body and will interpret the Convention to reflect such practice, so that a state which is clearly out of conformity with the others may expect an adverse ruling. Where practice is still in the process of changing and may be said to be at an inchoate stage as far as the Member States generally are concerned, it may not be prepared to place itself at the forefront of such changes. There is general agreement that its jurisprudence has had an enormous impact, not only through the outcome of specific cases, but in a general symbolic, educative and preventive sense.

The control mechanism for the Convention has been the subject of a certain amount of criticism. The immensely slow and difficult route to Strasbourg is

---

1   General reading, see: Merrills and Robertson, *Human Rights in Europe,* 3rd edn (1993); P Van Dijk and F Van Hoof, *Theory and Practice of the European Convention on Human Rights,* 2nd edn (1990); R Beddard, *Human Rights and Europe,* 3rd edn (1993); JES Fawcett, *The Application of the European Convention on Human Rights,* 2nd edn (1987); FG Jacobs, *The European Convention on Human Rights* (1975); Z Nedjati, *Human Rights under the European Convention* (1978); Harris, O'Boyle and Warbrick, *Law of the European Convention on Human Rights* (1995).

2   The declaration was adopted on 10 December 1948 by the General Assembly of the UN.

3   The optional protocol to the Covenant governs the right of individual petition. For comment on the general efficacy of the reporting system see HRLJ 1980, p136–170. For UK compliance with the covenant see DJ Harris and SL Joseph (eds), *The International Covenant on Civil and*

becoming more so due to the number of applications, despite improvements in the mechanisms for considering applications. The fact that an application may take five years to be heard is perhaps one of the main deficiencies of the Convention enforcement machinery; this chapter, therefore, devotes some time to explaining that process and the significant part played in it by the European Commission of Human Rights. Criticism has been levelled at the role of the Commission; this has led to the adoption of reforms which are considered below.

THE CONVENTION AND ITS PROTOCOLS

Currently the Member States are: Austria, Belgium, Bulgaria, Cyprus, Czech Republic, Denmark, Estonia, Finland, France, Germany, Greece, Hungary, Iceland, Ireland, Italy, Liechtenstein, Lithuania, Luxembourg, Malta, the Netherlands, Norway, Poland, Portugal, Romania, San Marino, Slovakia, Slovenia, Spain, Sweden, Switzerland, Turkey, the United Kingdom. The numbers have increased due to the disintegration of the Soviet Union and Yugoslavia.

Convention for the Protection of Human Rights and Fundamental Freedoms

The Governments signatory hereto, being Members of the Council of Europe,

Considering the Universal Declaration of Human Rights proclaimed by the General Assembly of the United Nations on 10 December 1948;

Considering that this Declaration aims at securing the universal and effective recognition and observance of the Rights therein declared;

Considering that the aim of the Council of Europe is the achievement of greater unity between its Members and that one of the methods by which that aim is to be pursued is the maintenance and further realisation of Human Rights and Fundamental Freedoms;

Reaffirming their profound belief in those Fundamental Freedoms which are the foundation of justice and peace in the world and are best maintained on the one hand by an effective political democracy and on the other by a common understanding and observance of the Human Rights upon which they depend;

Being resolved, as the Governments of European countries which are like-minded and have a common heritage of political traditions, ideals, freedom and the Rule of Law to take the first steps for the collective enforcement of certain of the Rights stated in the Universal Declaration,

Have agreed as follows:

Article 1

The High Contracting Parties shall secure to everyone within their jurisdiction the rights and freedoms defined in s1 of this Convention.

Section 1 Rights and freedoms

Article 2 Right to life

1. Everyone's right to life shall be protected by law. No one shall be deprived of his life intentionally save in the execution of a sentence of a court following his conviction of a crime for which this penalty is provided by law.

2. Deprivation of life shall not be regarded as inflicted in contravention of this Article when it results from the use of force which is no more than absolutely necessary:

    (a) in defence of any person from unlawful violence;

    (b) in order to effect a lawful arrest or to prevent the escape of a person lawfully detained;

    (c) in action lawfully taken for the purpose of quelling a riot or insurrection.

Article 3 Prohibition of torture

No one shall be subjected to torture or to inhuman or degrading treatment or punishment.

Article 4 Prohibition of slavery and forced labour

1. No one shall be held in slavery or servitude.

2. No one shall be required to perform forced or compulsory labour.

3. For the purpose of this Article the term 'forced or compulsory labour' shall not include:

    (a) any work required to be done in the ordinary course of detention imposed according to the provisions of Article 5 of this Convention or during conditional release from such detention;

    (b) any service of a military character or, in the case of conscientious objectors of compulsory military service;

    (c) any service exacted in case of an emergency or calamity threatening the life or well-being of the community,

    (d) any work or service which forms part of normal civic obligations.

Article 5 Right to liberty and security

1. Everyone has the right to liberty and security of person. No one shall be deprived of his liberty save in the following cases and in accordance with a procedure prescribed by law:

    (a) the lawful detention of a person after conviction by a competent court;

    (b) the lawful arrest or detention of a person for non-compliance with the lawful order of a court or in order to secure the fulfilment of any obligation prescribed by law;

    (c) the lawful arrest or detention of a person effected for the purpose of bringing him before the competent legal authority on reasonable suspicion of having committed an offence or when it is reasonably considered necessary to prevent his committing an offence or fleeing after having done so;

    (d) the detention of a minor by lawful order for the purpose of educational supervision or his lawful detention for the purpose of bringing him before the competent legal authority;

    (e) the lawful detention of persons for the prevention of the spreading of infectious diseases, of persons of unsound mind, alcoholics or drug addicts or vagrants;

    (f) the lawful arrest or detention of a person to prevent his effecting an unauthorised entry into this country or of a person against whom action is being taken with a view to deportation or extradition.

2. Everyone who is arrested shall be informed promptly, in a language which he understands, of the reasons for his arrest and of any charge against him.

3. Everyone arrested or detained in accordance with the provisions of paragraph 1(c) of this Article shall be brought promptly before a judge or other officer authorised by law to exercise judicial power and shall be entitled to trial within a reasonable time or to release pending trial. Release may be conditioned by guarantees to appear for trial.

4. Everyone who is deprived of his liberty by arrest or detention shall be entitled to take proceedings by which the lawfulness of his detention shall be decided speedily by a court and his release ordered if the detention is not lawful.

5. Everyone who has been the victim of arrest or detention in contravention of the provisions of this Article shall have an enforceable right to compensation.

Article 6 Right to a fair trial

1. In the determination of his civil rights and obligations or of any criminal charge against him, everyone is entitled to a fair and public hearing within a reasonable time by an independent and impartial tribunal established by law. Judgment shall be pronounced publicly but the press and public may be excluded from all or part of the trial in the interests of morals, public order or national security in a democratic society, where the interests of juveniles or the protection of the private life of the parties so require, or to the extent strictly necessary in the opinion of the court in special circumstances where publicity would prejudice the interests of justice.

2. Everyone charged with a criminal offence shall be presumed innocent until proved guilty according to law.

3. Everyone charged with a criminal offence has the following minimum rights:

    (a) to be informed promptly, in a language which he understands and in detail, of the nature and cause of the accusation against him;

    (b) to have adequate time and facilities for the preparation of his defence;

    (c) to defend himself in person or through legal assistance of his own choosing or, if he has not sufficient means to pay for legal assistance, to be given it free when the interests of justice so require;

    (d) to examine or have examined witnesses against him and to obtain the attendance and examination of witnesses on his behalf under the same conditions as witnesses against him;

    (e) to have the free assistance of an interpreter if he cannot understand or speak the language used in court.

Article 7 No punishment without law

1. No one shall be held guilty of any criminal offence on account of any act or omission which did not constitute a criminal offence under national or international law at the time when it was committed. Nor shall a heavier penalty be imposed than the one that was applicable at the time the criminal offence was committed.

2. This Article shall not prejudice the trial and punishment of any person for any act or omission which, at the time when it was committed, was criminal according to the general principles of law recognised by civilised nations.

Article 8 Right to respect for family and private life

1. Everyone has the right to respect for his private and family life, his home and his correspondence.

2. There shall be no interference by a public authority with the exercise of this right except such as is in accordance with the law and is necessary in a democratic society in the interests of national security, public safety or the

economic well-being of the country, for the prevention of disorder or crime for the protection of health or morals, or for the protection of the rights and freedoms of others.

Article 9 Freedom of thought, conscience and religion

1. Everyone has the right to freedom of thought, conscience and religion; this right includes freedom to change his religion or belief and freedom, either alone or in community with others and in public or private, to manifest his religion or belief, in worship, teaching, practice and observance.

2. Freedom to manifest one's religion or beliefs shall be subject only to such limitations as are prescribed by law and are necessary in a democratic society in the interests of public safety, for the protection of public order, health or morals, or for the protection of the rights and freedoms of others.

Article 10 Freedom of expression

1. Everyone has the right to freedom of expression. This right shall include freedom to hold opinions and to receive and impart information and ideas without interference by public authority and regardless of frontiers. This Article shall not prevent States from requiring the licensing of broadcasting, television or cinema enterprises .

2. The exercise of these freedoms, since it carries with it duties and responsibilities, may be subject to such formalities, conditions, restrictions or penalties as are prescribed by law and are necessary in a democratic society, in the interests of national security territorial integrity or public safety, for the prevention of disorder or crime, for the protection of health or morals, for the protection of the reputation or rights of others, for preventing the disclosure of information received in confidence, or for maintaining the authority and impartiality of the judiciary.

Article 11 Freedom of assembly and association

1. Everyone has the right to freedom of peaceful assembly and to freedom of association with others, including the right to form and to join trade unions for the protection of his interests.

2. No restrictions shall be placed on the exercise of these rights other than such as are prescribed by law and are necessary in a democratic society in the interests of national security or public safety, for the prevention of disorder or crime, for the protection of health or morals or for the protection of the rights and freedoms of others. This Article shall not prevent the imposition of lawful restrictions on the exercise of these rights by members of the armed forces, of the police or of the administration of the State.

Article 12 Right to marry

Men and women of marriageable age have the right to marry and to found a family, according to the national laws governing the exercise of this right.

Article 13 Right to an effective remedy

Everyone whose rights and freedoms as set forth in this Convention are violated shall have an effective remedy before a national authority notwithstanding that the violation has been committed by persons acting in an official capacity.

Article 14 Prohibition of discrimination

The enjoyment of the rights and freedoms set forth in this Convention shall be secured without discrimination on any ground such as sex, race, colour, language, religion, political or other opinion, national or social origin, association with a national minority, property, birth or other status.

Article 15 Derogation in time of emergency

1. In time of war or other public emergency threatening the life of the nation any High Contracting Party may take measures derogating from its obligations under this Convention to the extent strictly required by the exigencies of the situation, provided that such measures are not inconsistent with its other obligations under international law.

2. No derogation from Article 2, except in respect of deaths resulting from lawful acts of war, or from Articles 3, 4 (paragraph 1) and 7 shall be made under this provision .

3. Any High Contracting Party availing itself of this right of derogation shall keep the Secretary-General of the Council of Europe fully informed of the measures which it has taken and the reasons therefor. It shall also inform the Secretary-General of the Council of Europe when such measures have ceased to operate and the provisions of the Convention are again being fully executed.

Article 16 Restrictions on political activity of aliens

Nothing in Articles 10, 11 and 14 shall be regarded as preventing the High Contracting Parties from imposing restrictions on the political activity of aliens.

Article 17 Prohibition of abuse of rights

Nothing in this Convention may be interpreted as implying for any State, group or person any right to engage in any activity or perform any act aimed at the destruction of any of the rights and freedoms set forth herein or at their limitation to a greater extent than is provided for in the Convention.

Article 18 Limitation on use of restrictions on rights

The restrictions permitted under this Convention to the said rights and freedoms shall not be applied for any purpose other than those for which they have been prescribed.

First protocol (1952) Cmnd 9221

Article 1 Protection of property

Every natural or legal person is entitled to the peaceful enjoyment of his possessions. No one shall be deprived of his possessions except in the public interest and subject to the conditions provided for by law and by the general principles of international law.

The preceding provisions shall not, however, in any way impair the right of a State to enforce such laws as it deems necessary to control the use of property in accordance with the general interest or to secure the payment of taxes or other contributions or penalties .

Article 2 Right to education

No person shall be denied the right to education. In the exercise of any functions which it assumes in relation to education and to teaching, the State shall respect the right of parents to ensure such education and teaching in conformity with their own religious and philosophical convictions.

Article 3 Right to free elections

The High Contracting Parties undertake to hold free elections at reasonable intervals by secret ballot, under conditions which will ensure the free expression of the opinion of the people in the choice of the legislature.

Fourth protocol (1963) Cmnd 2309, entry into force 1968

[Securing certain rights and freedoms other than those already included in the Convention and in the first Protocol thereto]

Article 1 Prohibition of imprisonment for debt

No one shall be deprived of his liberty merely on the ground of inability to fulfil a contractual obligation.

Article 2 Freedom of movement

1. Everyone lawfully within the territory of a State shall, within that territory, have the right to liberty of movement and freedom to choose his residence.

2. Everyone shall be free to leave any country, including his own.

3. No restrictions shall be placed on the exercise of these rights other than such as are in accordance with law and are necessary in a democratic society in the interests of national security or public safety, for the maintenance of *ordre public*, for the prevention of crime, for the protection of health or morals, or for the protection of the rights and freedoms of others.

4. The rights set forth in paragraph 1 may also be subject, in particular areas, to restrictions imposed in accordance with law and justified by the public interest in a democratic society.

Article 3 Prohibition of expulsion of nationals

1. No one shall be expelled, by means either of an individual or of a collective measure, from the territory of the State of which he is a national.

2. No one shall be deprived of the right to enter the territory of the State of which he is a national.

Article 4 Prohibition of collective expulsion of aliens

Collective expulsion of aliens is prohibited.

Sixth protocol (1983) 5 EHRR 167, entry into force 1985

Article 1 Abolition of the death penalty

The death penalty shall be abolished. No one shall be condemned to such penalty or executed.

Article 2 Death penalty in time of war

A State may make provision in its law for the death penalty in respect of acts committed in time of war or of imminent threat of war such penalty shall be applied only in the instances laid down in the law and in accordance with the relevant provisions. The state shall communicate to the Secretary of the Council of Europe the relevant provisions of that law.

Article 3 Prohibition of derogations

No derogation from the provisions of this Protocol shall be made under Article 15 the Convention.

Article 4 Prohibition of reservations

No reservation may be made under Article 57 of the Convention in respect of the provisions of this Protocol.

Seventh protocol (1984) 7 EHRR 1, entry into force 1988

Article 1 Procedural safeguards relating to expulsion of aliens

1. An alien lawfully resident in the territory of a State shall not be expelled therefrom except in pursuance of a decision reached in accordance with law and shall be allowed:

(a) to submit reasons against his expulsion;

(b) to have his case reviewed; and

(c) to be represented for these purposes before the competent authority or a person or persons designated by that authority.

2. An alien may be expelled before the exercise of his rights under paragraph 1 (a), (b) and (c) of this Article, when such expulsion is necessary in the interests of public order or is grounded on reasons of national security.

Article 2 Right of appeal in criminal matters

1. Everyone convicted of a criminal offence by a tribunal shall have the right to have conviction or sentence reviewed by a higher tribunal. The exercise of this right including the grounds on which it may be exercised, shall be governed by law.

2. This right may be subject to exceptions in regard to offences of a minor character, as prescribed by law, or in cases in which the person concerned was tried in the first instance by the highest tribunal or was convicted following an appeal against acquittal.

Article 3 Compensation for wrongful conviction

When a person has by a final decision been convicted of a criminal offence and when subsequently his conviction has been reversed, or he has been pardoned, on the ground that a new or newly discovered fact shows conclusively that there has been a miscarriage of justice, the person who has suffered punishment as a result of such conviction shall be compensated according to the law or the practice of the State concerned, unless it is proved that the non-disclosure of the unknown fact in time is wholly or partly attributable to him.

Article 4 Right not to be tried or punished twice

1. No one shall be liable to be tried or punished again in criminal proceedings under the jurisdiction of the same State for an offence for which he has already been finally acquitted or convicted in accordance with the law and penal procedure of that State.

2. The provisions of the preceding paragraph shall not prevent the reopening of the case in accordance with the law and penal procedure of the State concerned, if there is evidence of new or newly discovered facts, or if there has been a fundament defect in the previous proceedings, which could affect the outcome of the case.

3. No derogation from this Article shall be made under Article 15 of the Convention

Article 5 Equality between spouses

1. Spouses shall enjoy equality of rights and responsibilities of a private law character between them, and in their relations with their children, as to marriage during marriage and in the event of its dissolution. This Article shall not prevent States from taking such measures as are necessary in the interests of the children.

European Convention for the Prevention of Torture and Inhuman or Degrading Treatment or Punishment (1987)

The member States of the Council of Europe, signatory hereto,

Having regard to the provisions of the Convention for the Protection of Human Rights and Fundamental Freedoms,

Recalling that, under Article 3 of the same Convention, 'no one shall be subjected to torture or to inhuman or degrading treatment or punishment';

Noting that the machinery provided for in that Convention operates in relation to persons who allege that they are victims of violations of Article 3;

Convinced that the protection of persons deprived of their liberty against torture and inhuman or degrading treatment or punishment could be strengthened by non-judicial means of a preventive character based on visits,

Have agreed as follows:

Chapter 1

Article 1

There shall be established a European Committee for the Prevention of Torture and Inhuman or Degrading Treatment or Punishment (hereinafter referred to as 'the Committee'). The Committee shall, by means of visits, examine the treatment of persons deprived of their liberty with a view to strengthening, if necessary, the protection of such persons from torture and from inhuman or degrading treatment or punishment.

Article 2

Each Party shall permit visits, in accordance with this Convention, to any place within its jurisdiction where persons are deprived of their liberty by a public authority.

Article 3

In the application of this Convention, the Committee and the competent national authorities of the Party concerned shall co-operate with each other.

Notes

1   Articles 8–11 have a second paragraph enumerating certain restrictions on the primary right. An exception may only be relied upon if it is 'prescribed by law'[4] and 'necessary in a democratic society'. The latter phrase was interpreted in the *Handyside* case[5] and the *Silver* case[6] as meaning that, to be compatible with the Convention, the interference must, *inter alia*, correspond to a pressing social need and 'be proportionate to the legitimate aim pursued'. The interests covered by the restrictions are largely the same in all these articles and, apart from the 'rights of others' exception, reflect general societal concerns.

2   The state is allowed a 'margin of appreciation' – a degree of discretion – as to the measures needed to protect an interest which falls within one of the exception clauses. The doctrine of the margin of appreciation was first adopted in respect of emergency situations, but it has gradually permeated all the Articles. It has a particular application with respect to paragraph 2 of Arts 8–11, but it can affect all the guarantees. In different cases a wider or narrower margin of appreciation has been allowed. In considering this area it should be borne in mind that, although the doctrine is well established, it has not been applied very consistently and therefore only indications as to its application will be given. A narrow margin may be allowed, in which

---

4   This phrase includes unwritten law; see *Sunday Times*, case judgment of 26 April 1979, A30.
5   Judgment of 7 December 1976, A24.
6   Judgment of 25 March 1983, A61.

case a very full and detailed review of the interference with the guarantee in question will be conducted. This occurred in *Sunday Times v UK* (1979);[7] it was held that Strasbourg review was not limited to asking whether the state had exercised its discretion reasonably, carefully and in good faith; it was found that its conduct must also be examined in Strasbourg to see whether it was compatible with the Convention. If a broader margin is allowed, Strasbourg review will be highly circumscribed. For example, the minority in the *Sunday Times* case (nine judges) wanted to confine the role of Strasbourg to asking only whether the discretion in question was exercised in good faith and carefully, and whether the measure was reasonable in the circumstances.

It is quite hard to predict when each approach will be taken, but it seems to depend on a number of factors. Some restrictions are seen as more subjective than others, such as the protection of morals. It is therefore thought more difficult to lay down a common European standard, and the Court and Commission have, in such instances, shown a certain willingness to allow the exceptions a wide scope in curtailing the primary rights. For example, Art 10 contains an exception in respect of the protection of morals. This was invoked in the *Handyside* case (1976)[8] in respect of a booklet aimed at schoolchildren which was circulating freely in the rest of Europe. It was held that the UK Government was best placed to determine what was needed in its own country in order to protect morals, and therefore no breach of Art 10 had occurred. Some restrictions, particularly national security, fall more within the state's domain than others, and therefore the Strasbourg authorities may think that the state authorities are best placed to evaluate the situation and determine what is needed. In *Civil Service Unions v UK* (1987)[9] the European Commission, in declaring the unions' application inadmissible, found that national security interests should prevail over freedom of association, even though the national security interest was weak while the infringement of the primary right was very clear; an absolute ban on joining a trade union had been imposed.

The margin of appreciation doctrine clearly has the power to undermine the Convention, and therefore its growth has been criticised. Van Dijk and Van Hoof have written of it as '... a spreading disease. Not only has the scope of its application been broadened to the point where, in principle, none of the Convention rights or freedoms are excluded, but also has the illness been intensified in that wider versions of the doctrine have been added to the original concept'.[10]

3   Further general restrictions on Convention rights are allowed under Arts 17, 15 and 64. In considering the restrictions Art 18 must be borne in mind. It provides that the motives of the national authority in creating the restrictions must be the same as the aims appearing behind the restrictions

---

7   2 EHRR 245. See further Part VI, Chapter 3, pp942–4.
8   1 EHRR 737. See further Part VI, Chapter 3, pp960–1.
9   10 EHRR 269.
10 Van Dijk and Van Hoof, p604.

when the Convention was drafted. Under Art 15(2), derogation is allowed in respect of most, but not all, of the rights. The non-derogability of certain rights, in particular the right to freedom from torture and inhuman or degrading treatment, implies that democracies would not violate them even in an emergency situation. In order to derogate the state in question must show that there is a state of war or public emergency, and in order to determine the validity of this claim two questions should be asked. Firstly, is there an actual or imminent exceptional crisis threatening the organised life of the state? Secondly, is it really necessary to adopt measures requiring derogation from the Articles in question? A margin of discretion is allowed in answering these questions because it is thought that the State in question is best placed to determine the facts, but it is not unlimited; Strasbourg will review it if the state has acted unreasonably.

The UK entered a derogation in the case of *Brogan* (1988)[11] after the European Court of Human Rights had found that a violation of Art 5, which protects liberty, had occurred. At the time of the violation there was no derogation in force in respect of Art 5 because the UK had withdrawn its derogation. This might suggest that there was no need for it or that the UK had chosen not to derogate, despite the gravity of the situation which would have justified derogation.[12] However, after the decision in the ECHR the UK entered the derogation stating that there was an emergency at the time. This was challenged as an invalid derogation but the claim failed on the basis that the exigencies of the situation did amount to a public emergency, and the derogation could not be called into question merely because the Government had decided to keep open the possibility of finding a means in the future of ensuring greater conformity with Convention obligations. The fact that the emergency measures had been in place since 1974 did not mean that the emergency was not still in being.[13] However, it may be argued that a state's failure to enter a derogation need not preclude the claim that a state of emergency did exist. If, whenever a state perceived the possibility that an emergency situation might exist, it felt it had to enter a derogation as an 'insurance measure', this would encourage a wide use of derogation.

In the *Greek* case[14] the Commission was prepared to hold an Art 15 derogation invalid. Greece had alleged that the derogation was necessary due to the exigencies of the situation; it was necessary to constrain the activities of Communist agitators due to the disruption they were likely to cause. There had been past disruption which had verged on anarchy. Greece therefore claimed that it could not abide by the Articles in question: 10 and 11. Apart from violations of those articles, violations of Art 3, which is non-derogable, were also alleged. The Commission found that the derogation was not needed; the situation at the decisive moment did not contain all the elements necessary under Art 15.

---

11 Judgment of 29 November 1988 (1989), A145; (1989) 11 EHHR 117.
12 See below, fn 13, para 47 of the judgment.
13 *Brannigan and McBride v UK* (1994) 17 EHRR 539.
14 Report of 5 November 1969, Yearbook XII.

4   Extracts from certain significant decisions of the Court and Commission regarding breaches of the substantive rights are set out, with criticism of them, in Part VI.

THE RIGHT OF COMPLAINT

Under Art 19 the Convention set up the European Commission of Human Rights and the European Court of Human Rights. The main role of the Commission is to filter out applications as inadmissible, thereby reducing the workload of the Court. However, it also has another role; it tries to reach a friendly settlement between the parties and can give its opinion on the merits of the case if it is not intended that a final judgement should be given. It can also refer the case to the Court or the Committee of Ministers for the final judgement. Creation of the Commission represented a compromise: when the Convention was drafted in 1949 it was thought too controversial merely to allow citizens to take their Governments before the Court. There was a feeling that a political body composed of Government representatives might be more sympathetic to states' cases; the state might feel less on trial than in the Court. Therefore the Commission was created as an administrative barrier between the individual and the Court and has been used as a means of filtering out a very high proportion of cases, thus considering far more cases than the Court.

The role of the Commission came under review for a number of reasons. It is barely able to deal with the number of applications it receives, and as states which used to be part of the Soviet Union or Yugoslavia become signatories to the Convention, this problem will be exacerbated, especially as such countries do not have a developed system for protection for human rights as the old Member States have and so will tend to use the Convention as a means of developing such protection. Thus, although a two-tier system involving two part-time bodies may have been an acceptable control mechanism when the Convention was drawn up, it has become much less appropriate. Moreover, although the notion of involvement of an administrative body in dealing with cases may have been acceptable in 1950, it arguably detracts from the authority of the Convention. The Parliamentary Assembly of the Council of Europe therefore recommended that the Commission and the Court should be merged into one body which would sit full time – a new Court of Human Rights.[15] It was proposed[16] that the new Court would come into operation in 1995, and that there would be a transitional period from 1995 to 2000 during which the old Commission and Court would hear cases already referred to them, while new cases would be referred to the new Court. On 11 March 1994 all but one of the contracting parties signed Protocol 11, which will greatly change the control mechanism when it comes into force.[17]

Under the present arrangements, if an application is found inadmissible the case will not reach the Court. If it is found admissible, but a friendly settlement is reached, the Court may not be required to decide on the application of the

---

15   See 'Reform of the Control Systems' 15 EHRR 321.

16   Recommendation 1194 adopted on 6 October 1992 by the Parliamentary Assembly of the Council of Europe.

Convention (see below). Thus, the admissibility criterion and the mechanism allowing for a friendly settlement are crucial within the system for enforcing the Convention. The main danger is, it will be suggested, that a lower standard of human rights than that allowed by the Convention may at times be enabled to prevail. In future, admissibility and the examination of the merits with a view to reaching a friendly settlement will be undertaken by the Court and therefore the system will less open to criticism since a judicial as opposed to an administrative body will be making the key decisions. However, the admissibility criteria remain unchanged under Protocol 11 and the manner of their application by the Court will play a part in determining the extent to which Convention standards are upheld.

The Court has jurisdiction under Art 45 of the Convention to consider all cases which raise issues as to the application of the Convention. Its constitution and jurisdiction are governed by the Convention Arts 19–56, but under Protocol 11, which is set out below, these Arts will be replaced by a revised Section II of the Convention (Arts 19–51). Under Protocol 11, Arts 27 and 28, judges of the Court will decide on admissibility. Art 25 (which will be replaced by Art 34) governs at present the right of individual complaint and it is therefore widely viewed as the most important article in the Convention. Under it, UK citizens can seek a remedy for a breach of Convention rights by petitioning the European Commission, although they have at present no right to bring a case before the Court. However, the position of the individual before the Court has greatly strengthened; as Janis, Kay and Bradley observe 'in practice and in principle it is the individual, not the commission, who is the true "party" before the court'.[18] On 1 October 1994, when Protocol 9 came into force for the 13 states which consented to it, the individual, or a group of individuals, was added to the bodies who can refer a case to the Court, under Arts 44 and 48.[19] The UK was not one of the consenting parties. Protocol 9 will be repealed by Protocol 11 which will in future govern the ability of individuals to refer cases to the court. Under Protocol 11, an individual will be able to take a case directly to the Court, under Art 34.

Protocol no 11 – ECHR (1994)

European Court of Human Rights

Article 27

Committees, Chambers and Grand Chamber

1.   To consider cases brought before it, the Court shall sit in committees of three judges, in Chambers of seven judges and in a Grand Chamber of 17 judges. The Court's Chambers shall set up committees for a fixed period of time.

---

17   Under Art 5 of the protocol it will come into force one year after it has been ratified by all the Member States. See (1994) 15 HRLJ 86. The merger procedure may take until the year 2000 to be completed. Adoption of Protocol 11 represents a very radical reform and many critics view it as a risk. See eg Schermers, 'The Eleventh Protocol to the European Convention on Human Rights' (1994) 19 EL Rev 367, 378 and (1995) EL Rev 3; Lord Lester of Herne Hill QC (1996) PL 5.

18   (1995) *European Human Rights Law*, p67.

19   Protocol 9, which has been available for Member States to ratify since November 1990, gives individuals, groups and non-governmental organisations the right to seize the court under Art 5.

2. There shall sit as an *ex officio* member of the Chamber and the Grand Chamber the judge elected in respect of the State Party concerned or, if there is none or if he is unable to sit, a person of its choice who shall sit in the capacity of judge.

3. The Grand Chamber shall also include the President of the Court, the Vice-Presidents, the Presidents of the Chambers and other judges chosen in accordance with the rules of the Court. When a case is referred to the Grand Chamber under Art 43, no judge from the Chamber which rendered the judgment shall sit in the Grand Chamber, with the exception of the President of the Chamber and the judge who sat in respect of the State Party concerned.

Article 28

Declarations of inadmissibility by committees

A committee may, by a unanimous vote, declare inadmissible or strike out of its list of cases an individual application submitted under Art 34 where such a decision can be taken without further examination. The decision shall be final.

Article 29

Decisions by Chambers on admissibility and merits

1. If no decision is taken under Art 28, a Chamber shall decide on the admissibility and merits of individual applications submitted under Art 34.

2. A Chamber shall decide on the admissibility and merits of inter-State applications submitted under Art 33.

3. The decision on admissibility shall be taken separately unless the Court, in exceptional cases, decides otherwise.

Article 30

Relinquishment of jurisdiction to the Grand Chamber

Where a case pending before a Chamber raises a serious question affecting the interpretation of the Convention or the protocols thereto or where the resolution of a question before it might have a result inconsistent with a judgment previously delivered by the Court, the Chamber may, at any time before it has rendered its judgment, relinquish jurisdiction in favour of the Grand Chamber, unless one of the parties to the case objects.

Article 31

Powers of the Grand Chamber

The Grand Chamber shall

a. determine applications submitted either under Art 33 or Art 34 when a Chamber has relinquished jurisdiction under Art 30 or when the case has been referred to it under Art 43; and

b. consider requests for advisory opinions submitted under Art 47.

Article 32

Jurisdiction of the Court

1. The jurisdiction of the Court shall extend to all matters concerning the interpretation and application of the Convention and the protocols thereto which are referred to it as provided in Arts 33, 34 and 47.

2. In the event of dispute as to whether the Court has jurisdiction, the Court shall decide.

Article 33

Inter-State cases

Any High Contracting Party may refer to the Court any alleged breach of the provisions of the Convention and the protocols thereto by another High Contracting Party.

Article 34

Individual applications

The Court may receive applications from any person, non governmental organisation or group of individuals claiming to be the victim of a violation by one of the High Contracting Parties of the rights set forth in the Convention or the protocols thereto. The High Contracting Parties undertake not to hinder in any way the effective exercise of this right.

Article 35 [at present admissibility is governed by Articles 26 and 27]

Admissibility criteria

1. The Court may only deal with the matter after all domestic remedies have been exhausted, according to the generally recognised rules of international law, and within a period of six months from the date on which the final decision was taken.

2. The Court shall not deal with any individual application submitted under Art 34 that

   a. is anonymous; or

   b. is substantially the same as a matter that has already been examined by the Court or has already been submitted to another procedure of international investigation or settlement and contains no relevant new information.

3. The Court shall declare inadmissible any individual application submitted under Art 34 which it considers incompatible with the provisions of the Convention or the protocols thereto, manifestly ill-founded, or an abuse of the right of application.

4. The Court shall reject any application which it considers inadmissible under this Article. It may do so at any stage of the proceedings.

Article 36

Third-party intervention

1. In all cases before a Chamber or the Grand Chamber, a High Contracting Party one of whose nationals is an applicant shall have the right to submit written comments and to take part in hearings.

Article 38 [which will replace Article 28]

Examination of the case and friendly settlement proceedings

1. If the Court declares the application admissible, it shall

   a. pursue the examination of the case, together with the representatives of the parties, and if need be, undertake an investigation, for the effective conduct of which the States concerned shall furnish all necessary facilities;

   b. place itself at the disposal of the parties concerned with a view to securing a friendly settlement of the matter on the basis of respect for human rights as defined in the Convention and the protocols thereto.

2. Proceedings conducted under paragraph 1.b shall be confidential.

Article 39

Finding of a friendly settlement

If a friendly settlement is effected, the Court shall strike the case out of its list by means of a decision which shall be confined to a brief statement of the findings and of the solution reached.

Article 40

Public hearings and access to documents

1. Hearings shall be public unless the Court in exceptional circumstances decides otherwise.

2. Documents deposited with the Registrar shall be accessible to the public unless the President of the Court decides otherwise.

Article 41

Just satisfaction

If the Court finds that there has been a violation of the Convention or the protocols thereto, and if the internal law of the High Contracting Party concerned allows only partial reparation to be made, the Court shall, if necessary, afford just satisfaction to the injured party.

Article 42

Judgments of Chambers

Judgments of Chambers shall become final in accordance with the provisions of Art 44, paragraph 2.

Article 43

Referral to the Grand Chamber

1. Within a period of three months from the date of the judgment of the Chamber, any party to the case may, in exceptional cases, request that the case be referred to the Grand Chamber.

2. A panel of five judges of the Grand Chamber shall accept the request if the case raises a serious question affecting the interpretation or application of the Convention or the protocols thereto, or a serious issue of general importance.

3. If the panel accepts the request, the Grand Chamber shall decide the case by means of a judgment.

Article 44

Final judgments

1. The judgment of the Grand Chamber shall be final.

2. The judgment of a Chamber shall become final

    a. when the parties declare that they will not request that the case be referred to the Grand Chamber; or

    b. three months after the date of the judgment, if reference of the case to the Grand Chamber has not been requested; or

    c. when the panel of the Grand Chamber rejects the request to refer under Art 43.

3. The final judgment shall be published.

Article 45

Reasons for judgments and decisions

1. Reasons shall be given for judgments as well as for decisions declaring applications admissible or inadmissible.

2. If a judgment does not represent, in whole or in part the unanimous opinion of the judges, any judge shall be entitled to deliver a separate opinion.

Article 46

Binding force and execution of judgments

1. The High Contracting Parties undertake to abide by the final judgment of the Court in any case to which they are parties.

2. The final judgment of the Court shall be transmitted to the Committee of Ministers, which shall supervise its execution.

Article 47

Advisory opinions

1. The Court may, at the request of the Committee of Ministers, give advisory opinions on legal questions concerning the interpretation of the Convention and the protocols thereto.

Notes

1 Art 34 (which will replace the present Art 25) refers to the *victim* of a violation of the Convention. However, the application can have a partly abstract character. In *Donnelly v UK* (1973)[20] the complaint concerned the allegation that the applicants had been tortured during their detention in Northern Ireland. They also wanted a full investigation of the whole system of interrogation employed by the security forces. It was found that, so long as the applicants had been 'affected', a more wide-ranging review was possible in the public interest; the complaint was admissible on that basis. A potential victim may make a complaint if the circumstances are such that the complainant is unsure whether or not he or she is a victim of a violation of a Convention right. This was found to be the case in a complaint concerning the possibility that the applicants' telephones were being tapped (*Klass v Federal Republic of Germany* (1979))[21] where, by virtue of the very nature of the action complained of, it was impossible for the applicants to be certain that they had been affected.

2 The application will be incompatible with the Convention if it claims violation of a right which is the subject of a derogation (Art 15) or reservation (Art 64) by the relevant Member State. Thus the right does appear in the Convention, but the state in question is not at present bound to abide by it.

3 Incompatibility will occur if the applicant or respondent are persons or states incompetent to appear before the Commission. The complaint must be directed against an organ of Government, not against individuals. However, the violation of the Convention by an individual may involve the responsibility of the state. The state may have encouraged the acts in question or failed to prevent or remedy them. Thus the condition will be fulfilled if the state is in some way responsible for the alleged violation. This is an aspect of the phenomenon known as *drittwürkung*, which means that

---

20 Appl 5577–5582/72 Yearbook XVI.
21 Judgment of 6 September 1978, A.28 (1979–80); 2 EHRR 214 ; see also (1980) 130 NLJ 999.

human rights provisions can affect the legal relations between private individuals, not only between individuals and the public authorities.[22]

4   The application will be incompatible with the Convention if it is aimed at the destruction or limitation of one of the rights or freedoms guaranteed by the Convention, and therefore conflicts with Art 17. The intention is to prevent an applicant claiming a right which would enable him or her to carry out activities which ultimately would lead to the destruction of the guaranteed rights. Therefore the Commission rejected the application of the banned German Communist party due to its aims (*Kommunistiche Partei Deutschland* (1957)).[23]

5   The applicant must provide *prima facie* evidence of exhaustion of domestic remedies. The burden then shifts to the state to show: that the remedy was reasonably ascertainable by the applicant; that the remedy does exist and has not been exhausted; and that the remedy is effective. The requirement that domestic remedies must have been exhausted means in practice the 'legal remedies available under the local law which are in principle capable of providing an effective and sufficient means of redressing the wrongs for which ... the respondent state is said to be responsible'.[24] If there is a doubt as to whether a remedy is available, Art 26 will not be satisfied unless the applicant has taken proceedings in which that doubt can be resolved. This generally means that judicial procedures must be instituted up to the highest court which can affect the decision, but also, if applicable, appeal must be made to administrative bodies.

6   The applicant only needs to exhaust those possibilities which offer an effective remedy, so if part of the complaint is the lack of a remedy under Art 13 then the application is not likely to be ruled inadmissible on this ground.[25] A remedy will be ineffective if, according to established case law, there appears to be no chance of success.[26] The Commission will decide whether a remedy did in fact offer the applicant the possibility of sufficient redress. If there is a doubt as to whether a given remedy is able to offer a real chance of success, that doubt must be resolved in the national court itself.[27] If more than one remedy is available, Art 26 may have been complied with if the applicant exhausts only the remedy likely to prove effective. It has been held that judicial review is a sufficient remedy.

7   The condition that the application must not be manifestly ill-founded hands very significant power to the Commission. Formally speaking the Commission should not decide on the merits of the application. Yet when it declares an application manifestly ill-founded, it is in fact pronouncing on

---

22 See Van Dijk and Van Hoof, Chapter 1, Part 6. For commentary on *drittwurkung* see EA Alkema, 'The Third Party Applicability or *Drittwurkung* of the ECHR in Protecting Human Rights', *The European Dimension* (1988), pp33–45.

23 Appl 250/57 Yearbook I (1955–57).

24 *Nielsen*, appl 343/57, Yearbook II (1958–59), p412.

25 *X v UK* (1981) appl 7990/77, D+R 24.

26 Appl 5874 172, Yearbook XBII (1974).

27 *Donnelly v UK* Nos 5577-5583/72.

the merits because it is determining whether or not a *prima facie* violation has taken place. Thus, this condition creates an extension of the role of the Commission behind the cloak of merely determining admissibility; it may in fact be taking the final decision on the merits.

8   The Commission finds an application ill-founded if the facts obviously fail to disclose a violation. In theory this ground will only operate if the ill-founded character of the application is clearly manifest. It has been said that, 'the task of the Commission is not to determine whether an examination of the case submitted by the applicant discloses the actual violation of one of the rights and freedoms guaranteed by the Convention, but only to determine whether it includes any possibility of the existence of such a determination.'[28] In practice the Commission goes further: the ill-founded character of the application may not always be clearly manifest. This is clear from the voting procedure. It is not necessary to have unanimity on this condition; a bare majority will be sufficient. It is arguable that it should have been necessary to have unanimity or a two-thirds majority as to manifest ill-foundedness, even though a bare majority would suffice in respect of the other conditions.

9   At present the procedure in the Court is covered by Arts 48–55. The Court is not bound by the report of the Commission or by its decision on admissibility. The proceedings before the chamber of seven judges will consist of a written stage followed by a hearing. An on-the-spot inquiry can be conducted by a delegate of the Court. The Court can also order a report from an expert on any matter. The Commission acts as an independent and impartial advisory organ in the proceedings. Although an applicant can be heard as a person providing clarification, the issue lies between the Court and the state to establish whether a violation has occurred. If it appears established, the state must attempt to demonstrate that the case falls within an exception to the right in question.

10   The procedure before the Court may conclude before the judgment on the merits if the state settles. However, the Court does not have to discontinue the procedure; it can proceed in the interests of the Convention and may give a declaratory judgment even though the state is now willing to settle. The judgment does not state what remedial measures should be taken; it is up to the state to amend its legislation or make other changes in order to conform with the judgment. Thus a response may well be in doubtful conformity with the Convention.[29] The Court is not ultimately a coercive body and relies for acceptance of its judgments on the willingness of states to abide by the Convention. The Court can award compensation under Art 50. The purpose of the reparation is to place the applicant in the position he would have been in had the violation not taken place. It will include costs

---

28   *Pataki*, appl 596/59, Yearbook III (1960).

29   The Contempt of Court Act 1981 may be said to represent such a response to the ruling of the Court in the *Sunday Times* case (1979) 2 EHRR 245 that UK contempt law violated Art 10. The Act preserved the common law discretion to punish for contempt which appears, especially since the decision in *AG v Newspaper Publishing plc* [1988] Ch 333 (see further, Part VI, Chapter 3, p951), to give insufficient weight to freedom of speech.

unless the applicant has received legal aid. It can also include loss of earnings, travel costs, fines and costs unjustly awarded against the applicant. It can also include intangible or non-pecuniary losses which may awarded due to unjust imprisonment or stress. For example, in the *Young, James and Webster* case (1981)[30] pecuniary and non-pecuniary costs were awarded: the Court ordered £65,000 to be paid.

11 The Committee of Ministers has jurisdiction to decide on violations of the Convention under Art 32; it is therefore a political body which is nevertheless performing a judicial role. Like the creation of the Commission, this is the result of a compromise; it was thought when the Convention was drafted that a Court of Human Rights with full compulsory jurisdiction would be too controversial and would therefore be unacceptable to all Member States. However, like the Commission, its role has been viewed with increasing dissatisfaction and, when the control mechanism is reformed under Protocol 11 and the new Court is established, the Committee will no longer discharge an adjudicatory function under Art 32. The Committee is also charged with the supervision of the execution of the judgment. This includes both the judgment on the merits and on compensation. The Committee notes the action taken to redress the violation on the basis of information given by the state in question. The Committee can publish the report of the Commission if a state does not take measures to address a breach of the Convention. This is a sanction: a degree of humiliation will flow from the declaration by all the Foreign Ministers of all the other Member States that a certain state has violated international human rights norms. Also, ammunition will thereby be offered to the opposition parties in the particular state. The final sanction will be expulsion from the Council of Europe. In practice, if the Commission has given its opinion that a violation has occurred, the state in question has usually taken measures to address the violation and the Committee has not had to give judgement. Doubts have been raised over the fitness of the Committee to oversee one of the key stages in the whole Convention process, namely the implementation of national law to bring it into line with the findings of the Court or Commission. It is apparent that a rigorous analysis of the changes that the offending state has made in its law would be desirable, to ensure that the judgement is fully implemented, and to make future similar breaches of the Convention by that state impossible. The Committee would not *prima facie* appear to be capable of carrying out such a quasi-judicial role. However, under Protocol 11 it will continue to supervise execution of the judgment under Art 54.

Questions

1 Will the new control mechanism be likely to inspire confidence in applicants?

2 Is further reform of the control mechanisms of the Convention needed? Examples might include abolition of the supervision of the Court's judgment by the Committee of Ministers with a view to ensuring more effective judicial supervision, or allowing the Court to fine Member States who failed to implement the judgment of the Court fully.

---

30 Judgment of 13 August 1981, A.44.

3   What significance may be found in the steady improvement in the position of the individual applicant in proceedings before the Court?

4   Why are Member States willing to submit to judgments of the Court of Human Rights which may require a radical change in national law? Is it appropriate that a group composed largely of foreign judges should continue to have a significant impact on UK law?

THE INFLUENCE OF THE CONVENTION IN THE EUROPEAN UNION

The influence of the Convention in EC law is becoming increasingly important due to acceptance of the principle enunciated in *Amministrazione delle Finanze dello Stato v Simmenthal* (1978)[31] and *Nold v Commission* (1974),[32] namely that respect for fundamental rights should be ensured within the context of the Community. The Convention has come into a closer relationship with Community law as the process of European integration has continued.

J Nold, Kohlen- und Baustoffgroßhandlung v Commission of the European Communities Case 4/73, ECJ

Judgment of the Court of 14 May 1974

Fundamental rights are an integral part of the general principles of law the observance of which the Court ensures. In safeguarding these rights the Court is bound to draw inspiration from the constitutional traditions common to the Member States and cannot uphold measures which are incompatible with the fundamental rights established and guaranteed by the constitutions of these states.

Similarly, international treaties for the protection of human rights, on which the Member States have collaborated or of which they are signatories, can supply guidelines which should be followed within the framework of Community law.

Johnston v Chief Constable of the RUC Case 222/84 [1986] ECR 1651, paras 17 and 18, ECJ

Art 6 of the [equal treatment] directive requires Member States to introduce into their internal legal systems such measures as are needed to enable all persons who consider themselves wronged by discrimination 'to pursue their claims by judicial process'. It follows from that provision that the Members States must take measures which are sufficiently effective to achieve the aim of the directive and that they must ensure that the rights thus conferred may be effectively relied upon before the national courts by the persons concerned.

The requirement of judicial control stipulated by that article reflects a general principle of law which underlies the constitutional traditions common to the Member States. That principle is also laid down in Arts 6 and 13 of the European Convention for the Protection of Human Rights and Fundamental Freedoms of 4

---

31   Case 106/77 [1978] ECR 629.

32   ECR 491. For discussion of such influence see P van Dijk and G van Hoof, Ch 8; Clapham, *Human Rights and the European Community: A Critical Overview* (1991); HG Schermers (1990) 27 CMLR 249; N Grief (1991) PL 555; J Coppel and A O'Neill [1992] 29 CMLR 669; N Foster (1987) 8 HRLJ 245; Lenaerts (1991) 16 ELR 367

November 1950. As the European Parliament, Council and Commission recognised in their joint declaration of 5 April 1977 (*Official Journal* Ch 103 p1) and as the court has recognised in its decisions, the principles on which that Convention is based must be taken into consideration in Community law.

Notes

1   The Treaty of European Union Art F2 states that the EU will respect fundamental rights as recognised by the Convention. The ECJ in Opinion 2/94 (28 March 1996)[33] has, however, held that the Community cannot accede to the Convention on the ground that an amendment to the Treaties would be required in order to bring about this change, since it would go beyond the scope of Art 235. The result of these developments is that, in all the Member States, implementation of Community measures in national law is clearly subject to respect for the Convention rights, although an individual cannot make an application to Strasbourg against the Union alleging that the Union has violated the Convention. Even though formal accession of the Union to the Convention has not yet occurred, the Convention will control Union conduct. Thus, the decision of the ECHR in *Rees* (1986)[34] was relied upon by the ECJ in deciding, in Case 13/14 *P v S and Cornwall CC* (1996),[35] that transsexuals fall within the Equal Treatment Directive. This was found on the basis that the directive was simply the expression of the principle of equality, which was one of the fundamental principles of European law.[36]

2   Pronouncements of the ECJ such as that in *Nold* suggest that protection for fundamental rights in the European Community is likely to increase due to the respect for such rights apparently evinced by the ECJ. Below, Coppel and O'Neill question this assumption.

J Coppel and A O'Neill, 'The European Court of Justice: Taking Rights Seriously?' (1992) 12(2) *Legal Studies* 227–30, 231–6, 244–5

1 Introduction

... References to fundamental rights are now being made by the court in order to extend its jurisdiction into areas previously reserved to Member States' courts and to expand the influence of the Community over the activities of the Member States. This shall be termed the 'offensive' use of fundamental rights, to be contrasted with the earlier 'defensive' use.

It will be argued that the court is using fundamental rights 'offensively' in two ways. On the one hand, it is extending the use of the concepts of fundamental rights in specific areas of Community law previously untouched by those concepts. On the other hand, it is undertaking a more general expansion of its jurisdiction, in the guise of fundamental rights protection, into areas previously the preserve of Member States, by means of subtle changes in its formulation of a crucial jurisdictional rule.

---

33   *The Times*, 16 April 1996.

34   9 EHRR 56.

35   Judgment of 30 April 1996; *The Times*, 7 May 1996.

36   These developments have particular significance in the UK since the Convention is not part of UK law. See further Part VI, Chapter 1.

With respect to both the offensive and defensive uses of fundamental rights, it must be questioned whether the court has ever been motivated by a concern for any supposed lack of adequate protection of fundamental rights within the European Communities. It is the argument of this paper that the court has employed fundamental rights instrumentally, so as to accelerate the process of legal integration in the Community. It has not protected these fundamental rights for their own sake. It has not taken these rights seriously.

2 The defensive use of human rights

Starting in the late 1960s, increasing concern was expressed in the courts in Germany and Italy on the question of whether or not the fundamental rights entrenched in their respective national constitutions were recognised and protected within European Community law [for a summary of the relevant German case law see especially Brinkhorst and Schermers *Judicial Remedies in the European Community*, 4th edn (1987), pp144–54]. Their fear was that these fundamental rights would gradually be eroded as the competences of the Community increased.

In response to the threat that national courts would resolve their dilemma by opting for the supremacy of their own national constitutional provisions on fundamental rights protection, the European Court discovered that the protection of fundamental rights was indeed a general principle of European Community law. This development contradicted its own previous case law rejecting the idea of fundamental rights protection within the Community legal order [See *Friedrich Stork and Co v High Authority of the ECSC* Case 1/58 [1959] ECR 17, *Geitling v High Authority of the ECSC* (Cases 36–8, 40/59) [1960] ECR 523; *Sgarlata v Commission of the EC* Case 40/64 [1965] ECR 215], and was effected notwithstanding the absence of any mention or list of fundamental rights within the texts of the Community treaties.

In a series of cases, in response to references from the German courts, the European Court began to use the vocabulary of fundamental rights protection.

Subsequent case law has shown that this particular strategy to defend the supremacy of Community law and of the European Court has been a largely successful one, despite initial caution on the part of the German courts [see *Wunsche Handelsgesellschaft* reported in [1987] 3 CMLR 225] and some continuing reservations from the Italian courts [see *Frontini v Ministero delle Finanze* Case 183/73, reported in [1974] 2 CMLR 383, 90]. The European Court's policy on fundamental rights appears, thus far, to have averted any significant damage by the courts of the Member States to the integrity, unity and supremacy of the Community legal order.

3 The offensive use of human rights

... In 1989 Mancini J of the European Court summarised the position the Court had achieved in relation to fundamental rights [Mancini, 'A Constitution for Europe' (1989) 26 CML Rev 595, 611]: 'Reading an unwritten bill of rights into Community law is indeed the most striking contribution the court made to the development of a constitution for Europe. This statement should be qualified in two respects. First ... that contribution was forced on the court from outside, by the German and, later, the Italian constitutional courts. Second, the Court's effort to safeguard the fundamental rights of the Community citizens stopped at the threshold of national legislations.'

One feature of the defensive use of fundamental rights was that these rights were applied only to Community acts. Initially, at least, human rights were not applied directly to the activities of Member States [see eg *Defrenne v Sabena* Case

149/77 [1978] ECR 1365, and *Demirel* Case 12/86 [1987] ECR 3719]. It is arguable that the Court no longer feels itself constrained to observe any distinction between Community acts and Member State acts, at least in relation to fundamental rights protection. The Court has increasingly been applying fundamental rights considerations to the acts of Member States.

The *Rutili* decision appeared to lay the foundations for this later development. The French Ministry of the Interior sought to restrict the movements of an Italian national within France, derogating from Art 48 of the EC Treaty on the free movement of workers. The grounds stated for such derogation were those set out in Art 48(3), namely 'public policy, public security and public health'. The court held that the scope of the public policy derogations could not be determined unilaterally by Member States, but was a matter to be determined by Community law.

However, the court went on to suggest that the limitations on Member State action under Community law were paralleled by certain provisions of the European Convention on Human Rights [para 32]: '[T]hese limitations ... are a specific manifestation of the more general principle enshrined in Arts 8, 9, 10 and 11 of the Convention for the Protection of Human Rights and Fundamental Freedoms ... which provides[s], in identical terms that no restrictions in the interests of national security or public safety shall be placed on the rights secured by the above quoted Articles other than such as are necessary for the protection of those interests "in a democratic society"'.

It is not until 1989 that the court was seen openly to take the step of assessing the validity of an act of a Member State on the basis of fundamental rights considerations [*Wachauf v Federal Republic of Germany* Case 118/75 [1976] ECR 1185, 1207 is discussed coming to the following conclusion].

The decision in *Wachauf* is of significance because, for the first time, the European Court applied fundamental rights principles to national acts formulated in implementation of Community legislation. The court held that, where a Community provision incorporates the protection of a fundamental right, national measures which implement that provision must give effect to the provision in such a way that the fundamental right is respected.

This may indeed be a conservative interpretation of the implications of *Wachauf*. The European Court itself, in the subsequent case of *Elleniki Radiophonia Tileorasi (ERT) v Dimotiki Etairia Pliroforissis* [Case 260/89 [1991] ECR 2925], interpreted *Wachauf* in broader terms [*ibid*, para 41]. '[M]easures which are incompatible with respect for human rights, which are recognised and guaranteed [in Community law], could not be admitted in the Community.' It is not clear from the terms of the judgment in *ERT* whether the court in this passage is referring to Community measures or Member State measures, but given that *ERT* concerned measures instituted by Greece, a Member State, in derogation from Community law, the latter conclusion is not unjustifiable.

Further, in *ERT* the court adopted a more forthright fundamental rights approach to the question of the admissibility of public policy derogations by Member States from Community law than is evidenced by *Rutili*. The court held [para 43] that: 'When a Member State invokes Arts 56 and 66 of the Treaty in order to justify rules which hinder the free movement of services, this justification, which is provided for in Community law, must be interpreted in the light of general principles of law, notably fundamental rights. The national rules in question may only benefit from the Art 56 and 66 exceptions insofar as they are compatible with fundamental rights, the observance of which the court ensures.' And, the court went on [para 45 – authors' translation]: 'The limitations imposed on the power of Member States to apply the provisions of Arts 66 and 56 of the treaty for reasons of public order, public security and public health must be understood in the light of the general principle of freedom of expression, enshrined in Art 10 of the European Convention.'

In *ERT*, the European Court is once more seen to be extending its jurisdiction in the matter of fundamental rights. The court is, in effect, applying the text of the European Convention not only to the acts of Community institutions but also to any attempts by Member States to derogate from the market freedoms assured by Community law. It is a development of *Rutili* precisely in that it uses the European Convention on Human Rights as an additional standard on the basis of which to judge Member State action, rather than, as in *Rutili*, merely a declaration which happens to echo general principles of existing Community law.

4 Changing formulations of the general jurisdictional rule

The line of cases from *Wachauf* through to *Grogan* also evinces an incremental expansion of the area of law and of Member State action which is subject to fundamental rights validation by the European Court of Justice.

In *Cinéthèque v Fédération nationale des cinémas français* Case 60/84 [1985] ECR 2605, para 26 the court stated [emphasis added]:

> Although it is true that it is the duty of this court to ensure observance of fundamental rights in the field of Community law, it has no power to examine the compatibility with the European Convention of national legislation which concerns, as in this case, an area which falls within the jurisdiction of the national legislator.

... the *Cinéthèque* formula was reworded in *Demirel v Stadt Schwaebisch Gmund* [Case 12/86 [1987] ECR 3719, 3754, para 28]: '[The Court] has no power to examine the compatibility with the European Convention on Human Rights of national legislation lying outside the scope of Community law'. This change of emphasis from that which is within the jurisdiction of the national legislator to that which is within the jurisdiction of Community law is a subtle one, but one which may nevertheless have revolutionised the impact of fundamental rights considerations on national administrative and legislative action. For one thing it paved the way for the decision in *Wachauf*, which applied fundamental rights standards to a Member State act in implementation of a Community rule. Such an act is one which clearly falls within the jurisdiction of the national legislator and also falls within the scope of Community law. The application of fundamental rights criteria in this case would not have been consistent with the reasoning of *Cinéthèque* but fell within the *Demirel* formulation.

In *ERT*, the court appeared to go further, stating the following [see note [24], para 42]: 'According to its jurisprudence [see the decisions in *Cinéthèque* and *Demirel*] ... the court cannot assess, from the point of view of the European Convention on Human Rights, national legislation which is not situated within the body of Community law. By contrast, as soon as any such legislation enters the field of application of Community law, the court, as the sole arbiter in this matter, must provide the national court with all the elements of interpretation which are necessary in order to enable it to assess the compatibility of that legislation with the fundamental rights – as laid down in particular in the European Convention on Human Rights – the observance of which the court ensures'.

The implication of the court is that it would examine all matters which did fall within the area of Community law. The only Member State actions which the court might decline to vet on human rights grounds are, therefore, those which occur in an area of exclusive Member State jurisdiction. This concept of exclusive Member State jurisdiction may itself be open to future redefinition by the court.

This implication was spelt out by Advocate-General Van Gerven in *Grogan* when he stated [see note [29] para 31 of the opinion of the advocate-general of 11 June 1991]: 'In [*Cinéthèque*] ... it was stated that the court's power of review did not extend to "an area which falls within the jurisdiction of the national legislator", a statement which, generally speaking, is true. Yet once a national rule is involved which has effects in an area covered by Community law (in this case Art 59 of the EEC Treaty) and which, in order to be permissible, must be able to be justified under Community law with the help of concepts or principles of Community law, then the appraisal of that national rule no longer falls within the *exclusive jurisdiction* of the national legislature'.

The court in *Grogan* did not expressly adopt the advocate-general's formulation, asserting [*ibid*, para 30 of the judgment of the court] that it was competent to pronounce on fundamental rights issues 'where national legislation falls within the field of application of Community law', but that 'the court has no such jurisdiction with regard to national legislation lying outside the scope of Community law.' Nevertheless, the implication as to the requirement of exclusive national jurisdiction remains. This represents, in practice, a major expansion of the *Cinéthèque* reasoning, and a doctrine of much wider application than the strict terms of the decision in *Wachauf*.

5 Conclusion

Given the jurisdictional expansion seen in the reformulation of the *Cinéthèque* dictum in *ERT* and *Grogan*, the court now sees itself as being able to review national legislation wherever this operates in an area touched by Community law. *ERT* reveals that such assessment of the validity of national law will be made from a point of view of its respect for human rights. Similarly, national courts would now seem to be obliged to give effect to the European Convention on Human Rights, as this would be interpreted by the European Court of Justice, if not the European Court of Human Rights in Strasbourg, in all questions before them which fall within the field of Community law [see Hall (1991) European L Rev 466]. Article F(2) of the common Provisions of the Maastricht Treaty may encourage this trend.

At times the court has seemed willing to apply human rights as if they were superior to (and hence grounds for invalidating) the acts of Member States. However, at the same time, it clearly subordinates human rights to the end of closer economic integration in the Community. In doing so the court has treated human rights, and in particular their place in any normative hierarchy, in a confused and ambiguous way.

Evidently it is economic integration, to be achieved through the acts of Community institutions, which the court sees as its fundamental priority. In adopting and adapting the slogan of protection of human rights the court has seized the moral high ground. However, the high rhetoric of human rights protection can be seen as no more than a vehicle for the court to extend the scope and impact of European law.

By using the term 'fundamental right' in such an instrumental way the court refuses to take the discourse of fundamental rights seriously. It thereby both devalues the notion of fundamental rights and brings its own standing into disrepute.

Questions

1 Coppel and O'Neill argue that in protecting rights the ECJ is motivated primarily by the desire to accelerate the process of legal integration in the Community. What limitations might this motivation impose on the level of rights protection provided by the ECJ?

2 Given the founding principles of the EU, would it be a legitimate development for it now to base its rights protection on any ground other than legal integration?

3 Bearing in mind that the Convention is not part of UK domestic law, what are the implications of the 'offensive' use of fundamental rights for the UK?

PART III
PARLIAMENT

CHAPTER 1

THE HOUSE OF COMMONS[1]

INTRODUCTION

This chapter considers the role of the House of Commons in the UK constitution in relation to the legislative process and scrutiny of the executive. Its emphasis will be on the constitutional relationship between the Commons and government; on the functions Parliament can realistically be attempted to perform, the extent of its domination by Government and an evaluation of its work. Proposals for reform will also be considered.

Some important changes to the House of Commons are considered below.

Michael Ryle, 'The Changing Commons', (1994) *Parliamentary Affairs* 647, 648–9, 654–5

The constitutional framework

... the constitutional setting of Parliament changes from time to time. There have been some important changes in the period under review which have had procedural consequences at Westminster.

It is worth remembering that proposed constitutional changes in the government of other parts of the UK were rejected when legislation brought forward by the Labour Government in 1977 and 1978 for Scottish and Welsh assemblies failed to become law. The only procedural fall-out at Westminster was the inclusion, among the new Select Committees set up in 1979, of the Scottish Affairs and Welsh Affairs Committees. The Scottish Grand Committee has also been given leave from time to time to sit in Edinburgh. ...

Much the most important constitutional change affecting Parliament in the last 50 years was Britain's entry into the European Communities on 1 January 1973. Under the Treaty of Rome and the European Communities Act 1972, Community law has effect in all Member States, and, for the first time in history, it is now possible (as the *Factortame* case showed) for an Act passed by the UK Parliament to be held by the courts to be of no effect. In practice, although the issue remains of hot political concern, there has been remarkably little difficulty in the working of Parliament as a result of this limitation of sovereignty. Successive Governments have sought to ensure that Britain is not in conflict with

---

1   General reading for this part (additional to that cited elsewhere in it) – relevant chapters in the following: Turpin, *British Government and the Constitution,* 3rd edn (1995); Home and Elliot, *Time for a New Constitution* (1988); IPPR, *The Constitution of the United Kingdom* (1991); SA De Smith, *Constitutional and Administrative Law,* 6th edn (1994); A Bradley and ECS Wade, *Constitutional and Administrative Law,* 11th edn (1993); O Hood Phillips, *Constitutional and Administrative Law,* 7th edn (1987); McEldowney, *Public Law* (1994); Pyper and Robins (eds), *Governing the UK in the 1990s* (1995) Part II; Griffith, *Parliamentary Scrutiny of Government Bills* (1974); Burton and Drewery, *Legislation and Public Policy* (1981); Walkland and Ryles, *The Commons Today* (1981); Erskine May, *Parliamentary Practice* (21st edn); Franklin and Norton, *Parliamentary Questions* (1993); Rush, *Parliamentary Government in Britain* (1981); Norton, *The Commons in Perspective* (1981); chapters in Harlow (ed), *Public Law and Politics* (1984); Constitution Unit, *Reform of the House of Lords* (1996); articles in *Parliamentary Affairs,* (see especially on 'sleaze' and members' interests, the Autumn 1995 issue); chapter in Keir and Lawson, *Cases in Constitutional Law* (1979); *Report of the Conference on Reform of the Second Chamber* (Cmnd 9038) of 1918.

Community obligations, and legislation has often had to be introduced to achieve this; much of our legislation is now Community-inspired. However, there remain many matters affecting UK citizens in which the European Union (as it now is) plays no part and in respect of which the powers and authority of Parliament are undiminished.

As a result, although the UK has to abide by the rules of the Community it has voluntarily joined, Parliament in no way behaves as a subordinate or constricted body. The main consequence of British membership for the practices and procedures of the Commons has been the creation of opportunities for the scrutiny and debate of Community law and other matters. ...

[An important change] was the passage of the House of Commons (Administration) Act 1978, under which the House of Commons Commission, chaired by the Speaker, plans and controls the House's own services and expenditure. Prior to 1978, the Treasury had to approve the House's estimates and could control every detail of Parliament's expenditure (even the appointment of a part-time cleaner needed the approval of some civil servant), and therefore the level and nature of services provided for the House to assist the scrutiny of the Government was directly determined by ministers themselves. Today the estimates for the House of Commons administration are laid before Parliament by the Speaker after examination by the Commission. Subject to Parliament's approval of the total, the expenditure, staffing and services of the House are therefore now decided by the House itself and controlled by the Commission on behalf of the House. Six heads of separate departments, chaired by the Clerk of the House, are responsible for advising the Commission and implementing its policies and decisions.

The use of time

There has been little change in the number of sitting days per session in the period under review. Apart from a slight rise in the length of sittings, total parliamentary time (excluding committee work, which has expanded enormously) has remained broadly constant. There has, however, been one welcome reform for many Members. After the War when much controversial business was being pushed through, the House sat late night after night and often all through the night. Since the 1960s, changes to standing orders have limited late debate on some types of business, the Whips have been willing to agree to avoid late sittings on other business and really late sittings are now relatively rare.

With one exception, the division of time on the floor of the House has not changed significantly: 50–55% of business is initiated by the Government; 10% is initiated by the official Opposition and 35–40% is initiated by back-benchers. Exceptionally, in the first few sessions after the War no time was allowed for private Members' bills and motions. Since 1951, however, at least 20 Fridays have been allotted in each normal length session for these proceedings and in recent sessions this has been increased to the equivalent of 24 Fridays by taking some private members' motions on Mondays.

A formal change in the rights of the Opposition was achieved by the creation in 1982 of Opposition days – at present 20 each session – when the matter for debate is chosen by one of the opposition parties. Until then, the Opposition were able to choose the subject for debate on supply days when, technically, the Government's estimates were before the House, but until 1967 even this was limited by the exclusion of various matters, especially legislative questions. The creation of Opposition days with almost no restrictions on the matters of debate is another change of constitutional significance. In the last century the opposition parties as such had no specified opportunities to initiate debate.

Notes

1   Philip Norton has summarised the four main changes to Parliament generally since the early 1970s as: increased independence (of back-bench MPs); greater professionalism (ie more MPs are now career politicians); increased specialisation (the introduction of permanent Select Committees has given MPs the opportunity to build up expertise in particular areas); greater accessibility (both greater visibility, through broadcasting of the Commons' proceedings, and a more active relationship between MPs and the public and pressure groups).[2]

2   One notable recent trend which dramatically illustrates Norton's first point, the increased independence of back-bench MPs, has been the phenomenon of such MPs switching parties or resigning the Whip. Two MPs have deserted the Conservative Party for its rivals: Alan Howarth for the Labour Party on 8 October 1995,[3] and Emma Nicholson for the Liberal Democrats on 31 December 1995. Peter Thurnham resigned the Conservative Whip to sit as an independent on 22 February 1996.

THE COMMONS AND LEGISLATION

Primary legislation

What is the proper legislative role of the Commons?

The doctrine of the Separation of Powers (first postulated by John Locke in 1690 and expanded by Montesquieu in the 18th century), which demanded that a body separate from the executive be vested with legislative power, has been extremely influential in general terms but seldom has a constitution been fashioned which accords with its precepts. At least in theory, Parliament is pre-eminently a legislative body, and as the dominant partner in Britain's tri-partite legislature,[4] the contribution of the Commons should be of great importance. It is, however, elementary that a Government with an overall majority will be able to ensure that the vast majority of its bills will reach the statute books, often with little modification. (In the 1985–86 parliamentary session, out of 50 Government bills, 48 became law). If Parliament is not in fact a separate legislature, what is its proper role? In order to be able to analyse properly the functions which the Commons performs in relation to legislation, it is necessary to place it into a comparative perspective, by examining how legislatures can be classified.

---

2   P Norton, 'Parliament's Changing Role' in Pyper and Robins (eds), *Governing the UK in the 1990s* (1995), esp pp85–95.

3   See *Observer*, 8 October 1995 for his resignation letter.

4   Commons, Lords, Monarch.

Philip Norton, 'Parliament and Policy in Britain: The House of Commons as a Policy Influencer' (1984) 13(2) *Teaching Politics* 198, 200–2

... I would distinguish between legislatures which have a capacity, occasionally or regularly exercised, for policy-making, for policy-influencing, and for having little or no policy impact.

1   *Policy-making* legislatures are those which can not only modify or reject Government measures but can themselves formulate and substitute a policy for that proposed by Government.

2   *Policy-influencing* legislatures can modify or reject measures put forward by Government but cannot substitute a policy of their own.

3   Legislatures with *little or no policy impact* can neither modify or reject measures, nor generate and substitute policies of their own.

'Policy' has been subject to different definitions. I would define it as a related set of proposals which compromise a recognisable whole, based ideally but not necessarily (in practice probably rarely) on conscious and tested assumptions as to costs, needs, end products and implications. 'Policy-making' is the generation of that recognisable whole. Once 'made', policy can then be presented for discussion, modification, acceptance or rejection, application and evaluation. 'Policy influence' can be exerted at these later stages. It may take the form of formal modification or even rejection. It may work through a process of anticipated reaction: that is, the policy-makers may be influenced by expectations of whether or not a particular policy will gain approval. In such instances, the 'making' of policy is influenced by, but is not in the hands of, the legislature. In cases of little or no policy impact, a legislature has no appreciable influence upon policy-making nor upon the later stages of the policy cycle.

If we liken policy to a small (or not so small) jigsaw the picture becomes clearer. Policy-makers put the jigsaw together. They may do so in a clumsy and haphazard manner. They may produce a well-structured piece. Whichever, the responsibility for putting it together is theirs. A policy-making legislature can modify or reject that jigsaw, substituting one it has compiled itself. A policy-influencing legislature can reject the jigsaw or, more likely, reject or move about some of the pieces, but has not the capacity to reconstruct it or create a new jigsaw. A legislature with little or no policy impact looks upon and approves the jigsaw, with or without comment.

This classification of legislatures has two advantages. Firstly, it provides a useful framework for distinguishing between the US and UK legislatures. Congress is a policy-making legislature. That is, not only can it amend or reject executive policy, it can – and occasionally does – substitute a policy of its own. It has the leadership capable of formulating a policy as a substitute to that of the executive. In the House of Commons, the equivalent leadership is the executive. Though it has the capacity, recently exercised, to modify and even reject executive proposals, the House does not have the capacity to generate alternative policies. It is a policy influencer, not a policy-maker. [One problem with this assertion arises in the context of private members' legislation. However, procedural and political constraints ensure that such legislation is not used as a major policy-making medium. ...] Secondly, the distinction is useful in helping understand recent developments ... To make sense of their impact upon the House of Commons it is helpful to draw the distinction between the making and the influencing of public policy. Without it, the changes of recent years may appear confused and shapeless. ...

Question

Elsewhere, Norton notes that his second category – policy influencing legislatures – is 'the most crowded of the three'; into it fall 'most legislatures of western Europe ... of the Commonwealth [and] of the new legislatures of east and central Europe' whilst the first category – policy making legislatures – 'is almost empty', its only members being the US Congress and the US state legislatures.[5] Why has Montesqueiu's model been so overwhelmingly rejected?

Notes

1   Norton states that the House of Commons does not have a leadership 'capable of formulating a policy as a substitute to that of the executive', but on one level this is inaccurate. The Opposition can and does formulate alternative policies. What it does not have is the administrative back-up (civil servants, parliamentary draftsmen) to allow it to produce a large volume of alternative legislation, though it could presumably produce some. The essential difference is that the Opposition will only rarely have a majority in the Commons whereas Congress is quite often (as at the time of writing) controlled by a party which does not also make up the executive.

2   Norton is here using the word 'policy' to mean actual measures passed; the term is also used to describe the mass of executive discretionary decisions which will be required to implement and run new legislative schemes in practice; a contemporary example relates to the allocation of funds raised by the National Lottery, currently attracting considerable criticism.[6]

3   Even if it is accepted that the legislative role of the Commons lies in *responding* to government measures, if it is thought that this role demands that the House provide independent assessment of the merit of government bills and make numerous amendments to them, then clearly it is not fulfilling this role. As Calvert puts it, 'the substantial task of legislating will have been largely discharged before the bill is read in the House', or again 'Before the formally dramatic part of the legislative process even begins almost all the terms of almost all [government] bills are settled'.[7]

However, on one view, the argument which states that the Commons is redundant because it is largely powerless to amend or reverse the Government's programme is wrongheaded; it is contended that the Commons would be undermining democratic accountability if it substantially changed Government bills, since the legislative programme of the party which attracted the greatest proportion of votes should be enacted, in accordance with the electorate's presumed wishes. This argument was undoubtedly what Professor Crick had in mind when he wrote '... the phrase "Parliamentary control" should not mislead anyone into asking for a

5   Philip Norton, *Does Parliament Matter?* (1993), pp50–1.
6   See eg, 'Tories deserve to suffer with this foolish lottery', *The Sunday Times*, 29 October 1995.
7   *British Constitutional Law* (1985), p84.

situation in which Governments can have their legislation changed or defeated ...'.[8]

4   At the time of writing, where the Government has a majority of only one, the force of Crick's argument is perhaps more apparent than usual. As a Governments' majority increases, it must, perforce have more regard to the views of its back-benchers. However, when a majority reaches a low enough level, small groups of dissident MPs become able to force the Government to depart from its pre-planned policy which was the platform on which it was elected. Of course, most of its legislative policies are not directly mandated (see below) but (to take the example of current Government policy on the European Union) the Government stood on a platform of a general attitude towards Europe which could perhaps be described as cautious scepticism. This was the publicly declared, official policy of the Conservative party. If a number of anti-EU MPs are able to force the Government into a far more thorough-going scepticism,[9] this could be viewed as a welcome example of greater Parliamentary control over the executive. But it may also be seen, in Crick's terms, as an undermining of the democratic mandate.

5   In another sense, it is of course wholly unrealistic to expect the House of Commons to subject Government bills to independent scrutiny. The Government is the Government precisely because it is the party with an overall majority in the Commons. Therefore, by definition, the majority of MPs in the House will be pre-disposed to support legislation introduced by the Government, so that it is built into the nature of the Commons that most of its members will precisely not be impartially minded. The House can be seen to be poised between two possible roles, fulfilling neither of them. Because, formally, the Commons is the law-making body, it must be composed of democratically elected members, ie those tied to political parties, thus ensuring that in practice the Cabinet legislates. But again, because MPs are tied to political parties they are unable to carry out

---

8   *The Reform of Parliament* (1964), p80. Crick's point of view is clearly open to a number of objections: it can be plausibly argued that many people vote, not after a careful assessment of which legislative programme they would like to see enacted, but on the basis of traditional loyalty, misinformation, misunderstanding or their reaction to politicians' perceived personalities. Further, it is undoubtedly true that people may vote for a party even though they may object to some of its specific legislative proposals (for general discussion of voting patterns see Dennis Kavanagh and Bill Jones, 'Voting Behaviour' in Jones (ed), *Politics (UK)* (1994)). Finally, Crick's argument applies in its purest form only to manifesto Government bills; as Zander notes (below) these form only a small percentage of enacted legislation; the argument is certainly wholly inapplicable to legislation which actually appears to reverse the policies which the electorate thought the party introducing it stood for: an example can be seen in the increases in taxation introduced by the Major administration subsequent to the 1992 general election in which a key Conservative campaigning theme was their opposition to the higher taxes which they alleged Labour would introduce (see Kavanagh and Jones, *op cit*, p195).

9   For example, the Government has at various points come under intense pressure from right wing back-benchers to take action against the EU over its ban on British beef and associated products (see for example the treatment of Douglas Hogg, the Agriculture Minister, on 1 May 1996, in which his call for further persuasion and negotiation was greeted with 'near derision' by back-benchers (see 'Back bench beef fury boils over', *Independent*, 30 April 1996). The Government did indeed adopt a policy of non-cooperation with the EU in retaliation for the ban, which did not, however, last very long.

properly the actual task of the House, scrutiny of legislation in a fair-minded and impartial manner. It is dissatisfactions such as these which have led some commentators to suggest removing the Commons formal legislative role all together.

Sir William Wade, *Constitutional Fundamentals* (1989), pp27–9

The technique of legislation is, I suppose, the subject of more abjuration and malediction by lawyers than any other aspect of their profession. In 1975 it was studied by a strong committee appointed by the Government and presided over by Sir David (now Lord) Renton [*The Preparation of Legislation*, cmnd 6053 (1975)]. They made 121 recommendations. In the aggregate these are of great importance and potential benefit, but none of them can be described as radical. Among the more notable were the recommendations that advice on draft bills should be sought from specialists in the relevant branches of law; that statements of principle should be encouraged; that earlier Acts should be amended by the textual rather than the referential method where convenience permits; and that the structure and language of statutes should be kept under continuous review by the Statute Law Committee, a Lord Chancellor's committee of eminent lawyers and experts which was first constituted over l00 years ago.

Perhaps the most shocking feature of our legislative process is the way in which parliamentary scrutiny is eliminated on the pretext of shortage of time. When the Scotland bill [to grant devolution] was before Parliament in 1978, 58 of its 87 clauses and 14 of its 17 schedules were passed over without discussion in the House of Commons, including all the financial clauses which of course the House of Lords could not discuss either. Yet this was revolutionary constitutional legislation – abortive though it proved in the end. It cannot be an adequate excuse to say that there is no time for proper consideration of important bills. Admittedly the party system has distorted the constitution to such an extent that most legislation could more accurately be said to be enacted by the Government than by Parliament. There is truth, unfortunately, in Lord Hailsham's charge that we have allowed the constitution to become an elective dictatorship [*Elective Dictatorship* (1976); *The Dilemma of Democracy* (1978), Ch 3]. If Parliament is no longer willing or able to give proper attention to legislation, we should perhaps consider whether some new body ought to be invented for this purpose. In France the vetting of draft legislation is an important function of the *Conseil d'Etat*, to which the Government is required by the constitution to submit its bills before introducing them in the legislature. The *Conseil d'Etat* will criticise provisions which are objectionable in principle, and also bad drafting. Government bills are thus vetted by an independent and highly professional body, and not merely by those who are in a hurry to push them through Parliament.

Notes

1   It should be borne in mind that the Commons still provides a constitutional safeguard, albeit one of mainly theoretical importance, in that Governments could presumably not rely on it to pass legislation which removed the basic liberties of the citizen.

2   McEldowney suggests that the main role of the Commons is to legitimise legislation (echoing Norton's view that most legislatures exist not to make laws but to assent to them) and also to provide the 'life blood of party

politics' through its 'debates, votes and censure[s]'.[10] This latter suggestion may be seen as a variant on the publicising role of Parliament suggested by some commentators (see below).

3 If it is accepted that due to its make-up and the party system the Commons cannot be expected either to take on the role of policy-maker or provide genuinely independent assessment of Government bills, by what criteria may it be assessed? Putting it another way, what can we reasonably expect it to do? It is suggested that four main functions may be identified. The first is the education of both Government and electorate through the publicising effects of debate in Parliament: the electorate will become aware of the issues surrounding a bill, whilst the reaction of newspapers, commentators and the public to debates on the proposed legislation will help keep the Government informed of the drift of public opinion. The second is the influence on the pre-legislative process which both back-benchers and Opposition MPs may have. The third is the limited amount of improvement and amendment which, despite the partisan nature of the Commons, still does take place. The fourth is the clarification as to the meaning and operation of a given piece of legislation which may take place during debate. These may, since *Pepper v Hart* (1993),[11] go to the interpretation a bill receives in the courts; they may also provide ammunition for future political attack if things do not go as planned. It is clear that in relation to the first, third and fourth of these functions, the amount of time and resources which Members have available to them to devote to scrutiny of legislation will be crucial; the importance of the second and third will be closely tied to the size of the Government's majority.

The legislative work of the Commons

The pre-legislative stage

With the above considerations in mind, the actual legislative work of the House may be considered in detail. The beginnings of the legislative process are considered below by Zander.

Michael Zander, *The Law-Making Process* (1994), pp2–3, 7–8, 10–11

Legislation – the Whitehall stage

Legislation takes the form either of public or private bills. Most Acts are public general Acts which affect the whole public. Private Acts ... are for the particular benefit of some person or body of persons such as an individual or company, or local inhabitants. (They must not be confused with private members' bills. ...) Private Acts sometimes deal with the affairs of local authorities and are then called Local Acts.

In addition to Acts of Parliament there are also very large numbers of statutory instruments (see further pp92–102 below). In the early years of this century the number of statutory instruments was in the hundreds; since the Second World War it has been in the thousands, and again the number of pages has been increasing greatly. Thus in 1951 there were 2,335 statutory instruments running to 3,523 pages. In 1986 there were 2,332, running to 9,048 pages.

---

10 *Public Law* (1994), p45.

11 1 All ER 42.

(a) The sources of legislation

The belief that most bills derive from a Government's manifesto commitments is mistaken. It has been estimated that only 8% of the Conservative Government's bills in the period from 1970 to 1974 came from election commitments and that in the 1974–9 Labour Government the proportion was only a little higher at 13% (Richard Rose, *Do Parties Make a Difference?*, 2nd edn (1984), pp72–3). The great majority of bills originated within Government departments, with the remainder being mainly responses to particular and unexpected events such as the Prevention of Terrorism (Temporary Provisions) Act 1974 in response to the Birmingham IRA bombings, or the Drought Act 1976.

A surprising number of bills derive from the recommendations of independent advisory commissions or committees. Some of these are ad hoc – such as Royal Commissions, departmental and inter-departmental committees. Others are standing bodies, such as the Law Reform Committee which advises the Lord Chancellor on civil law reform and the Criminal Law Revision Committee which advises the Home Secretary on reform of the criminal law. The most important standing body is the Law Commission. ...

Analysis has shown that as many as a quarter to a third of all statutes that could have been preceded by the report of an independent advisory committee or commission were the result of such a report. ...

(b) The consultative process

The Government department with responsibility for the legislative project will need to decide how much, if at all, to consult during the gestation process leading to the introduction of a bill in Parliament. Obviously, if the proposed legislation impinges on the responsibilities of other Government departments or governmental agencies they will have to be consulted. But there is also the question whether, if so, to what extent persons or bodies outside the governmental machine should be consulted.

The traditional Whitehall view has been that outside persons and bodies should not normally be consulted at this stage – that the time for consultation is later when the bill has been introduced in Parliament. The effect of this is that consultation only starts when it is generally too late to influence the basic shape of the legislation and all that can be achieved is adjustment at the margins. But in recent years consultation has become more common.

In an important and wide-ranging report on the legislative process *(Making the Law)* issued in 1992 the Hansard Society said that many organisations in their evidence to the society emphasised the fundamental importance of consultation. Some (English Heritage, the Bank of England, the Institute of Directors, the Association of Chief Police Officers) thought that it worked tolerably well. Some (such as the CBI, the Institute of Chartered Accountants and the National Consumer Council) said it worked better than in the past. Others (the Consumers' Association, the BMA, the TUC, local authority associations) were very critical of the lack of consultation. The Independent Television Commission said that the absence of any open inquiry before the introduction of the Broadcasting bill in 1989 led to many late changes.

Many organisations complained that when there was consultation the time allowed was frequently inadequate. The Consumers' Association said that six weeks was a reasonable time but that, of 100 consultation documents in 1990, 10% had allowed three weeks or less and another 20% allowed only four weeks.

Some organisations regretted that Royal Commissions or committees of inquiry were no longer appointed (Mrs Thatcher appointed no Royal Commission during the 13 years of her premiership). The local authority associations regretted a decline in the use of Green Papers and White Papers (see below). Also it regretted a change in the style of White Papers which it said had become glossy booklets promoting the Government's policy without reference to alternatives and with less discussion of issues than in former years. The consultation procedures of the Law Commission ... were commended as a model.

The report concluded that 'the overwhelming impression from the evidence is that many of those most directly affected are deeply dissatisfied with the extent, nature, timing and conduct of consultation on bills as at present practised' (p30).

The report recommended (pp29–40) that Government should so far as possible consult those with relevant interests or experience at the policy information stage. Consultative documents should be as precise as possible. Wherever possible, clauses, or even whole bills, should be published in draft for comment before introduction in Parliament. Government should draw up and publish guidelines to Government departments about consultation. ...

(d) Cabinet control

To what extent is the process of the preparation of legislation controlled or supervised by the Cabinet and its sub-committees? Little is known of this. But a rare glimpse of some of what goes on behind the scenes was given in a lecture in 1951 by the then First Parliamentary Counsel in charge of the office of parliamentary draftsmen (see below).

Sir Granville Ram, 'The Improvement of the Statute Book' (1951) *Journal of the Society of Public Teachers of Law*, NS, pp442, 447–9

> Under present arrangements the opening of a new session of an old Parliament normally takes place at the end of October or beginning of November; and about six weeks after the beginning of each session the Cabinet Office asks departments to send in lists of the bills likely to be required for introduction in the *next* session, together with their observations as to the urgency of any bill included in the lists, an estimate of its magnitude, and a forecast of the date on which instructions to Parliamentary Counsel can be ready.
>
> I must make it plain that all these proposals, observations and forecasts relate not to the session that has just begun but to the next one which will begin nearly 11 months later. When they have been received from departments they are collated and submitted to a Cabinet Committee, known as the Future Legislation Committee, which always includes in its membership the Leaders of both Houses and the Chief Whip, because the drawing up and control of the legislative programme must be closely related to the arrangement of Parliamentary business. Soon after Christmas the committee examines the department's proposals in detail, and draws up a tentative list of bills for discussion with the ministers who have put forward the proposals. The committee then holds a meeting at which those ministers are present, and after consultation with them and with the First Parliamentary Counsel, draws up a provisional list of bills for the session due to begin in the following autumn. This list is prepared with careful regard to the amount of time likely to be available for legislation during the session and, in drawing it up, the committee makes allowances for the subsequent inclusion of bills the need for which has not yet been foreseen, and for annual bills (such as Finance Bills, Army and Air Force (annual) Bills and Expiring Law Continuance Bills). The bills recommended for inclusion in the programme are placed in order of priority, having regard to the dates when instructions to Parliamentary Counsel can be ready, to the time that drafting may be expected to take, and to the Chief Whip's estimate of the approximate dates on which the bills must, respectively, be introduced in

order to pass through their successive stages under the arrangements he will have to make for the Parliamentary business of the session. The list is then submitted to the Cabinet, and when the Cabinet has approved the recommendations of the committee, with or without alterations, the bills remaining in the list become the Government's provisional programme of legislation for the following session.

The need for determining the lines of a session's programme so long before the session starts is obvious because bills take time to draft, but there remains much for the Future Legislation Committee to do before the programme is finally completed and its main features are announced in the King's speech at the opening of the new session. Between Easter and the summer recess the committee reviews the progress of the bills decided upon, and considers any proposals made by ministers for the addition to the programme of bills that have not been previously foreseen. Early in June departments will be asked by the Cabinet Office for particulars of any such bills, but the departments anticipate this request whenever possible by giving information to the Cabinet Office as soon as it becomes reasonably clear that any bill not already included in the provisional programme is likely to be wanted. During this period between Easter and the end of July the Future Legislation Committee also controls the flow of instructions to Parliamentary Counsel so as to secure, so far as possible, that it shall conform to the order of priority approved by the Cabinet. Finally, after the summer recess the Future Legislation Committee presents to the Cabinet, when they are considering the King's speech for the opening of Parliament, a complete classified programme.

Upon the opening of a new session, control of the programme for that session passes to another Cabinet Committee called the Legislation Committee. That committee performs functions in relation to the examination of draft bills which I will describe later, but it also exercises control over the programme for the current session, much in the same way as the Future Legislation Committee controls the programmes for future sessions. In this capacity it reviews every month the progress of all bills in the programme for the current session, and regulates both the flow of instructions to Parliamentary Counsel and the flow of bills to the two Houses according to the progress made. Applications for the admission of new bills to the programme are made to this committee through the Cabinet Office, and any necessary adjustments, whether by way of changes in priority or of addition to, or deletions from, the programme are authorised by the committee.

This machinery for obtaining a place in the programme is the product of many years of experience and has proved far more effective than anything previously devised. ...

Notes

1   Governments must take account of the likely response of its own back-benchers to legislation, as ascertained by the Whips, at the pre-legislative stage. If back-benchers are aware of widespread public discontent at proposed legislation this will be relayed to the Government which will wish to avoid the embarrassment of hearing its own supporters expressing public dissent – dissent which as Norton remarks, 'provides good copy for the press'.[12] The effect of this anticipated response may be to force the

---

12   *The Commons in Perspective* (1981), p119.

Government into modifying its proposals, the most dramatic example being the Labour Government's abandonment of its proposed industrial relations legislation in 1969 when it became clear to it that its own MPs did not support the measure. Similarly, in October 1992, John Major's administration was forced to abandon its plans for immediate closure of 31 coal pits in order to avoid near-certain defeat by Conservative back-benchers, whilst Michael Heseltine's plans to sell off the Post Office suffered a similar fate in 1994. See also the example of the Family Homes and Domestic Violence Bill (below pp323–4).

2   The ability of back-bench MPs to influence (and, at a later stage, amend) legislation is obviously dependent upon the degree to which (within the context of the basic loyalty which the party system demands) they are prepared to view their own party's policy with a critical eye, and vote against legislation it has brought forward. Philip Norton notes an interesting trend here.

Philip Norton, *Does Parliament Matter?* (1993), p21

The behaviour of MPs has changed in recent decades. Most significantly of all ... has been the change in behaviour in the division (voting) lobbies. Members have proved relatively more independent in their voting behaviour. As we have seen, cohesion was a marked feature of parliamentary life by the turn of the century. That cohesion has been maintained throughout the 20th century, reaching its peak in the 1950s. In the 1960s, one distinguished American commentator was able to declare that cohesion had increased so much 'until in recent decades it was so close to 100% that there was no longer any point in measuring it' (Beer, 1969: 350–1). Shortly afterwards, it did become relevant to measure it.

The early years of the 1970s saw a significant increase in cross-voting by Conservative MPs. They voted against their own leaders more often than before, in greater numbers and with more effect. On six occasions, cross-voting resulted in the Government being defeated. Cross-voting also became a feature of Labour MPs after the party was returned to office in 1974, contributing to most of the 42 defeats suffered by the Government in the 1974–79 Parliament. The number of defeats on the floor of the House, combined with defeats in standing committee, ran into three figures. Some degree of independent voting has been maintained in succeeding Parliaments. In 1986, the Government lost the second reading of the Shops Bill, the first time in the 20th century a Government with a clear overall majority had lost a second reading vote.

Notes

1   One recent display of apparent independent-mindedness by back-bench MPs resulted in a severe embarrassment to John Major's Government. The Prime Minister had decided to back the recommendation of the Conservative majority on the Committee of Privileges, which had come out against implementing the recommendation of the Nolan report that MPs should be required to disclose the amount of income they were earning from outside consultancies. John Major committed himself very publicly to this decision by defending it in Prime Minster's Questions on 2 November 1995.[13] Whilst the vote on the issue on Monday 6 November was technically a free one, there was no doubt that it had become a party political issue. In the event, a Labour amendment, calling for immediate disclosure of outside

earnings, was passed with a majority of 51; 23 Conservative MPs voted with Labour while another 31 abstained or did not vote. However, while this may be seen as a triumph of individual conscience over narrow party interest, there may be another story to tell. It appears that many Conservative MPs, particularly those in marginal seats, felt unable to face the anger of their local constituency parties and the damage to their personal reputation which they feared would have been caused had they been known to have voted against disclosure; a number of local Labour parties had run 'a huge ... propaganda campaign' over the weekend immediately prior to the vote, which had successfully publicised the issue.[14] The episode may therefore show the ability of back-benchers to act as conduits for public opinion as opposed to exemplifying their independent mindedness, though it does, of course, show that the direct force of public opinion may frighten MPs into 'independence' from Government policy.

2   The extent to which back-bench MPs consider themselves able to criticise their own leadership will obviously also be subject to short term political considerations. At the time of writing, it is noticeable that even leftist Labour MPs, influenced presumably by the proximity of the next general election and the fact that they seem to have their best chance of gaining power for 16 years, seem loath to criticise openly the leadership of their party, despite its marked shift to the centre.

3   The anticipation of criticisms by the Opposition may also exert some influence on the pre-legislative stage. The Commons acts as a forum in which the Opposition can express criticisms of legislation from many sources in society, including pressure groups and those who would be directly affected by the proposals. Government spokespersons will wish to know what these criticisms will be in order to be able to deploy counter-arguments. This is one of the factors which encourages the Government to engage in the consultation with such relevant groups which Zander noted above. Further, the Government will of course expect the Opposition to oppose its bill, but, if it is anticipated that Opposition criticism will have popular support, the Government may reconsider its proposals. As Ronald Butt puts it, 'If [the Government] suspects that the Opposition will have an attractive case, it will do its best, within broad limits, to make that case less attractive, or to steal and adapt the Opposition's clothes'.[15] This would be more likely to happen where the parties are ideologically fairly close, as at present, than where there are greater and more fundamental differences between them, as in the early and mid-1980s. Butt instances the extensive amending of the capital gains tax provisions of the 1964 Labour Government by the Chancellor, produced, he argues, by the exposure of weak elements in the Labour proposals by the Opposition.[16]

---

13   HC Deb 2 November 95, col 388.
14   'Tories routed on MPs' rules', Guardian, 7 November 1995.
15   *The Power of Parliament*, 2nd edn (1969), p317.
16   *Ibid.*

Legislation: through the House of Commons

Michael Zander, *The Law-Making Process*, pp53–7, 58–64

The sequence of events in the legislative process from the introduction of a bill to Royal Assent has been described by a senior member of the office of Clerk to the House of Commons, most kindly written for the second edition of this book:

A bill must be given 'three readings' in each House before it can be submitted for the Royal Assent. The first reading is purely formal when the Clerk of the House reads the title from a dummy bill and a day is named for second reading.

The debate on second reading is the main consideration of the general principles of a bill, at the end of which a vote [though it need not] be taken on the bill as a whole. Although a bill can be lost at many stages in its career, the second reading is undoubtedly the most important, and the vast majority of bills which get a second reading and proceed into committee also get on to the statute book. For Government bills, the minister in charge of the department concerned usually opens the debate, and one of his junior ministers replies at the end. Front bench Opposition speakers follow the ministerial opening, and precede the winding-up.

Unless a Member moves that the bill be sent to a committee of the whole House (or to a Select Committee if a detailed examination with witnesses is required or to a Special Standing Committee which combines both Select Committee and Standing Committee procedure) all bills after second reading (with the exception of certain financial measures) are automatically sent upstairs to a Standing Committee. These committees consist of from 16 to 50 Members and, in a session, over 500 Member are called upon to serve on them. Appointments to Standing Committee are made by a Select Committee, called the Committee of Selection, which is charged with having regard to the 'qualifications of those Members nominated and to the composition of the House'. The Government thus keeps its majority, but the opposition and minority parties so far as possible are fully represented. The chair is taken by a Member selected by the Speaker from a panel of chairmen, who maintains the same standard of impartiality in committee as the Speaker does in the House. The task of the committee is to go through the bill and amend it where desirable, bearing in mind that the general principle of the bill has been approved by the House.

A bill in committee is considered clause by clause and the question that the clause 'stand part of the bill' is put on each one. Before the question is put on a clause, however, amendments may be moved – provided that they are relevant, not 'wrecking', and conform to various technical requirements, such as the limitation imposed by any accompanying financial resolution passed by the House. Members of most Standing Committees are showered with suggestions for amendments from interested bodies to add to any ideas of their own for amendment of the bill. The Government's amendments are drafted by the Parliamentary Counsel who prepare their bills; the private member usually seeks the advice of the Public Bill Office. ...

A bill which has been considered by a committee of the whole House and emerges unamended goes straight on to third reading. Any other bill must have a consideration or 'report' stage, when further amendments may be moved, and attempts made either to restore parts lost in committee or to remove parts added. The Government frequently use the report stage to introduce, in a form acceptable to them, amendments the principle of which they have accepted in committee. The members who have been through the committee stage together very often dominate the debates on report stage. This is partly because many of the points at issue were postponed in the committee at the request of the Government, and partly because these members are by now (if they were not before) specialists in the subject, which may make it difficult for an 'outsider' to break in. The report stage is a useful safeguard, however, against a small committee amending a bill against the wishes of the House, and a necessary opportunity for second thoughts. The Speaker takes account of the time spent on amendments in committee when selecting what is to be discussed. A large bill may take two or even three days on report, amounting to 10 hours consideration or more.

There remains the third reading; and here, unlike the second reading, when a bill may be reviewed in the context of the subject to which it relates, debate must be confined to the contents of the bill. ... Since 1967, the third reading may be taken without debate unless at least six members table a motion, 'that the question be not put forthwith'. Although a vote may be called on a bill at this stage it would amount almost to a parliamentary accident for a bill which had been given a second reading to fall at this final stage.

Safely read the third time, a bill is endorsed *soit baille aux Seigneurs* and tied up in a green ribbon together with a message asking the Lords' concurrence. The Clerk of the House proceeds to the 'other place' and hands in the bill at the bar of the House. ...

After a Commons bill has been through the Lords, it is returned with the Lords amendments to it, which then must be considered in the House. On any bill, the two Houses must finally reach agreement on the amendments made by each other if the bill is not to fall during that session. Under the Parliament Acts 1911 and 1949, disagreement between the two Houses can delay a bill only for a year if the Commons persist with it; and in the case of a money bill, a bill passed by the Commons can go for Royal Assent after only one month's delay. Where one House cannot agree to the other's amendments, it sends a message to that effect giving reasons. A bill can go back and forth several times but it is only rarely that a bill has had to be reintroduced in a second session in order to become law, because of the failure of the two Houses to agree, the last occasion being the Aircraft and Shipbuilding Act in Session 1976–7.

The final stage in the enacting process is Royal Assent. Under the Royal Assent Act 1961, Royal Assent is given by notification, by which the short title of the bills which have received Royal Assent is read out in each House together with a formula signifying the fact of assent.

Apart from the usual course charted by a bill in the Commons, there are a number of other procedures. ...

After the second reading, a bill may be committed to a Special Standing Committee which, though nominated like a Standing Committee, acts for four sittings like a Select Committee, hearing evidence from interested parties and thereafter going through the bill in the same way as a normal Standing Committee. Although this procedure is still at an experimental stage it is a most significant development, since it brings into the parliamentary process consideration of the 'outside' points of view and interests that previously were confined to the Government's own pre-legislative consideration. Needless to say, such an evidence-taking stage is much easier to apply to bills where all Members are willing to co-operate to improve their provisions than they would be to bills which some Members consider should be opposed totally. Provision has also existed since 1967 under Standing Order no 78 for a bill which was considered by a Second Reading Committee (or the Scottish Grand Committee) on second reading to have its report stage taken in Standing Committee, but this Standing Order has been used only once.

From this account of the customary procedures for the passage of a bill, it will be seen that, if proper consideration is given at each stage to a substantial measure, whether or not it is opposed in principle, its passage takes a considerable time. In fact, major bills will take six months or more to pass. On the other hand a small bill can, if urgency requires it, pass through both Houses in a day. The Government business managers have to fit in an average of about 60 Government bills, including between 10 and 20 substantial bills, each session, almost all of which will get through to receive the Royal Assent. This contrasts with the 10 or so private members' bills enacted out of the more than 80 such bills which are presented each session. The key to the productivity of Parliament lies in control of the timetable of the House of Commons by the Government and the willingness of the House to entrust the Chair with discretion to select amendments for debate, and to accept or reject motions for the closure of debate.' ...

Note: legislation in haste

Sometimes the legislature moves with amazing, some would say indecent, haste. ...

The Official Secrets Bill passed all its stages in one day in August 1911. The junior minister responsible for piloting it through the House of Commons described the event nearly 20 years later [JEB Seely, *Adventure* (1930), p145 – cited by DGT Williams in 'Statute Law and Administrative Law' *Statute Law Review* (1984) 166]:

I got up and proposed that the bill be read a second time, explaining, in two sentences only, that it was considered desirable in the public interest that the measure should be passed. Hardly a word was said and the bill was read a second time; the Speaker left the Chair. I then moved the bill in committee. This was the first critical moment; two men got up to speak, but both were forcibly pulled down by their neighbours after they had uttered a few sentences, and the committee stage was passed. The Speaker walked back to his chair and said: 'The question is, that I report this bill without amendment to the House.' Again two or three people stood up; again they were pulled down by their neighbours, and the report stage was through. The Speaker turned to me and said: 'The third reading, what day?' 'Now, sir,' I replied. My heart beat fast as the Speaker said: 'The question is that this bill be read a third time.' It was open to anyone of all the members in the House of Commons to get up and say that no bill had ever yet passed through all its stages in one day without a word of explanation from the minister in charge. ... But to the eternal honour of those members, to whom I now offer, on behalf of that and all succeeding Governments, my most grateful thanks, not one man seriously opposed, and in a little more time than it has taken to write these words that formidable piece of legislation was passed.

(b) Interaction between interested parties during the legislative process

A description of the interaction between ministers, civil servants, MPs and outside interests in the legislative process emerged from an account of the background to the Criminal Justice Act 1972 in a BBC documentary broadcast on 16 September 1972. The presenter was Professor Anthony King of Essex University, who discussed what happened with the Conservative minister of state at the Home Office, Mr Mark Carlisle, with his opposite number in the Labour Opposition, Sir Elwyn Jones, with one of the senior civil servants involved, Mr Michael Moriarty of the Home Office, and with a back-bench MP,

Mr Edmund Dell. The transcript is taken from *Westminster and Beyond*, ed A King and A Sloman (1973), Chapter 12. ...

King: It's not generally realised that civil servants brief their ministers not just behind the scenes but while actual debates are going on the floor or in committee. Michael Moriarty was present during the second reading debate and I asked him, since he's not allowed to sit next to ministers on the front bench, how he went about communicating with them.

Moriarty: On the whole by rapidly scribbled notes, some of them things that we ourselves realise the minister is going to need from what we hear someone else saying or what we hear him saying, sometimes things that he asks us to produce.

...

King: Let's suppose an MP raises a point [in the committee stage] and the minister isn't quite sure how he's going to reply: will he in Standing Committee, actually there and then, turn to you and mutter something to you in order to get some help?

Moriarty: Yes, because of the geography, which it's slightly difficult to describe. We are, in fact, only a few feet away from the minister, so it's perfectly easy for a minister just to get up from his seat and take a couple of paces so that he can talk quietly to us, or he can even stage whisper from where he's sitting, or he can ask his parliamentary private secretary, sitting just behind him, to turn round and have a word with us. ...

King: ... Part of the job of civil servants working on a bill is to take all the amendments – on jury service suspended sentences and so on, and brief the minister on them, as Michael Moriarty explained.

Moriarty: This is the main task of officials during the committee stage. Each morning the Order Paper is brought down from the Parliamentary Section as early as they can, and one then drops everything else and sets to work looking at the amendments, trying to work out exactly what an MP is getting at – sometimes, of course, it's quite a job – and this may be because he is approaching something in a confused way or because he's just a lot cleverer than we are on a particular matter. And then one goes through the processes of deciding how far the objective is compatible with the objectives of the Government in the bill, and how far it's a sensible way of achieving it.

King: How far is it part of the job of a civil servant to warn a minister of unforeseen consequences of an amendment which he might perhaps be about to accept?

Moriarty: Oh, I think that is really part of the bread-and-butter of briefing on amendments. Of course, this question, I think, raises in turn the question where the initiative lies, and I suppose this is different on different occasions. In our case, the initiative I think lay with us in the first instance. We would usually tender some briefing and advice on an amendment and, if necessary, Mr Carlisle would discuss these with us, tell us if he saw it differently, and so on. But on the whole he let us get on with working out a brief before telling us what his own thoughts were. But one can certainly see if it worked the other way round: that, if it began with the minister saying what he thought, it would certainly be the task of the civil servant to say: 'Well, but have you considered A, B, and C?'

King: Back-benchers and Opposition MPs, however, lack that sort of professional assistance. Where do they get help from? How did Edmund Dell inform himself for purposes of taking part in the committee proceedings?

Dell: Well, here, of course, I have the great good fortune of having a wife who is very deeply acquainted with this whole area and who was therefore able to draw my attention to all the necessary material on every point on which I wanted to speak. So she was of enormous assistance.

King: So it was then a question of simply going to the library and reading the stuff up?

Dell: It was a matter of going to the library, reading the stuff up, preparing the speech, and putting the available information before the minister and the committee and saying: 'This is information which has obviously not been considered in preparing this bill.'

King: And in addition to what an MP can do on his own, there are also organisations willing to help him, as well as to press their views on him. I asked Sir Elwyn Jones where he and his colleagues got their information from.

Jones: Well, you will remember that there were the reports of committees, which were the foundation of the clauses in the bill, which we were able to call upon. But then in the background there are a large number of bodies, fortunately, in this country – this is one of our strengths as a democracy – like Justice, the British Section of the International Commission of Jurists, like the National Council for Civil Liberties, like the Howard League. There are half a dozen bodies at least who have worked on this sort of problem and whose reports and recommendations are available to us.

The time taken by parliamentary debates

Professor John Griffith has studied the time taken by debates on Government bills in three sessions of Parliament: 1967–8, 1968–9 and 1970–1. In the first session there were 60 bills which took an average of 23 hours each; in the second, 50 bills averaged 20 hours debate; in the third, 73 bills averaged 16 hours. The overall average was 19 hours 54 minutes. These figures cover the aggregate of time devoted to debates in both Houses (JAG Griffith, *Parliamentary Scrutiny of Government bills* (1974), pp15–16).

But out of the total of 183 bills no fewer than 74 (40%) were dealt with in less than five hours. At the other end of the spectrum, in each of the three sessions there were seven bills that absorbed over half of the total amount of time. These 21 bills averaged 96 hours of debating time (*ibid*).

The average distribution of time over the three sessions was:

Second reading	15%
Committee stage	65%
Report stage	15%
Third reading	2%
Lords' amendments in Commons	3%
Total 100%	

(Source: *ibid*, table 1.2, p17.)

In a later study conducted by Professor Griffith with Mr Michael Ryle, Clerk of Committees in the House of Commons, it was found [Griffith and Ryle, *Parliament*, pp310–13] that there were three main categories of bills. The first was the category of major policy bills of which there might be about 10 per session. They are debated on second reading on the floor of the House of Commons on one day for six hours, or sometimes over two days for 12 hours. A few are then taken in committee of the full House but most are sent to Standing Committee where they are debated for 50 or more hours. Most are then further debated on report, third reading and consideration of Lords' amendments.

The second group consists of some 20 or so policy bills which take up somewhat less time – say 30 or more hours in committee.

The third group consists of a further 20 or so bills which, for one reason or another, go through very quickly. Some are consolidation bills (see p65). Some small uncontentious bills are debated in Second Reading Committees off the floor of the House under Standing Order no 90. The debates average some 30 minutes, a few going through virtually 'on the nod'. Most of these bills are introduced in the Lords. Some of the bills in the group are consolidated fund and appropriation bills, the function of which is to 'raise supply' (ie moneys). Under Standing Order 54 these are not debated at all.

Thus in the two sessions 1984–85 and 1985–86 there were a total of 107 Government bills. Of these, 20% were not debated on the floor of the House of Commons at all; 19% were debated for under an hour; 11% were debated for 1–5 hours; 29% were debated for 5–13 hours, 10% for 13–20 hours, and 11% for more than 20 hours.

Note: some further relevant facts

A study by Ivor Burton and Gavin Drewry, *Legislation and Public Policy* (1981), of the years 1970–74, when Mr Edward Heath was Prime Minister, showed the following further facts that bore on the questions of parliamentary procedure: ...

(3) In 23 of the 185 bills (12%) the second reading in the House of Commons took under one hour. ...

(4) No less than 30% of Government bills were sent to a committee of the whole House of Commons rather than one of the Standing Committees.

(5) Standing Committees usually consisted of fewer than 20 Members, 16 being the standard size, but a few more important bills were sent to larger Standing Committees with up to 30 members (see p116).

(6) In a high proportion of cases, bills were dealt with by the committee at one sitting. ...

(7) In a high proportion of cases at the second reading the Opposition did not oppose the Government's bills. There was bipartisan support for 90 out of 185 (49%). In another 35 (19%) the Opposition were neutral or critical without however calling any division. In a further 22 (12%) there was either no debate on the floor of the House, or the second reading was not reached. In only 38 cases out of 185 (20%) was there any division on the second reading (table 4.15, p123).

Notes

1   Whilst Governments may sometimes be able to 'fast track' non-contentious bills through the House of Commons, this procedure can be sabotaged by back-benchers even at a late stage. A dramatic example of this appeared in the recently announced decision of the Major administration to withdraw the Family Homes and Domestic Violence Bill,[17] whose provisions would have given unmarried women living with men the same rights as wives to exclude violent partners from their homes. Eight Conservative MPs on the right of the party had expressed concern that the legislation would undermine the institution of matrimony. However, the impact of the back-bench intervention went well beyond merely affecting the parliamentary procedure adopted; the Lord Chancellor agreed to withdraw the bill

---

17   See eg, 'Cabinet backs down on violence bill', *Independent*, 27 October 1995.

altogether for reconsideration. It should be noted that the Labour and Liberal Democratic parties were broadly supportive of the measure, so it was not defeat in the Commons which the Government was seeking to avoid, but rather a public display of disunity. This may be in part have been attributable to short term electoral considerations, but nevertheless illustrates the powerful influence which the threat of adverse political publicity can exert, at least on a Government concerned about its level of public support.[18] The bill was modified and combined with proposed divorce legislation and re-introduced into the Commons, where Conservative Members were given a free vote on the measure, a move which was clearly intended to take the sting out of any possible rebellion which duly came. On 24 April, right-wing MPs forced a major change to the bill, against Government policy; the 'cooling off' period for the new no-fault divorce procedure was increased from a year to 18 months. Four leading Cabinet members voted with the rebels, including the Home Secretary, in a move which was perceived as increasing Government embarrassment.[19]

2   Clarification as to the meaning and implementation of a bill was instanced at the beginning of this chapter as a useful product of parliamentary debate; the recent passage of the Prevention of Terrorism (Additional Powers) Act 1996 is instructive in this respect. Despite the fact that the bill was guillotined (see below), a few important points emerged from the Home Secretary's speeches during the debate. The most controversial provision in the bill allowed for the police to stop and search persons for items related to terrorist offences without any reasonable suspicion. In response to numerous questions during the debate about the safeguards balancing the new power, two key points were made: first, guidance as to the operation of the powers will be issued by the Home Secretary to the police;[20] second, and more specifically, the Home Secretary will instruct the police to apply the PACE Code for Stop and Search to all searches under the new power.[21] The second point is particularly important, and given the silence of the new Act itself as to the applicability of the code, may enable the courts to decide, through perusal of *Hansard*,[22] that Parliament's intention was that the code should be applied. Thus, significant legal consequences could flow from this assurance.

3   The committee stage is often perceived as a time in which party loyalties are less strong and more constructive debate may take place. However, as appears from Zander's account, MPs lack the resources which would give them the expertise required to challenge increasingly complex Government legislation from a position of sufficient knowledge. As Griffith and Ryle

---

18   The last opinion poll taken before the decision to withdraw the bill was announced showed the Conservatives 30 points behind Labour (see *Sunday Times*, 22 October 1995).

19   See 'Divorce bill threatened by rebel vote', *Independent*, 25 April 1996.

20   HC Deb 2 April 1996, col 265.

21   *Ibid*. The code gives a number of important procedural safeguards; for details see Part VI, Chapter 4, pp973–5.

22   *Pepper v Hart* [1993] 1 All ER 42 provides that the court may look to *Hansard* to assist them in construing ambiguous statutes.

comment, 'the Opposition has no back up comparable to that of the minister's departmental staff'.[23] Norton, whilst noting that MPs' resources have increased dramatically since 1960, remarks that 'By international standards [their] office, secretarial and research facilities remain poor'.[24]

4   Adversarial debate may be used in committee as on the floor of the House and the style is particularly unsuited to examining the factual and technical background to the bill. Vernon Bogdanor has recently described Standing Committees as 'mere *ad hoc* debating committees within which second reading speeches are repeated at tedious length interspersed with the reading of well-rehearsed briefs helpfully supplied by interested organisations'.[25] The Study of Parliament Group recognised both this problem and that of the lack of sufficient information for MPs, and, on a very few occasions, the standing committees have been allowed to follow the recommendations of the group and call expert witnesses, ministers, and records before going on to the usual clause by clause examination of the bill and amendments. This procedure was followed during the passing of the Criminal Attempts Act 1981, and substantial changes were made during the committee stage.

5   In general, however, the committee stage results in the acceptance of Government amendments only because, as Griffiths' examination of standing committees found, 'party discipline is largely maintained'.[26] Further, many Opposition amendments are designed not to increase the effectiveness of the bill but to embarrass the Government; the political role of opposition MPs can prevent them undertaking *constructive* criticism. However, where they are able to offer such criticism, it may have an indirect effect; whilst nearly all Opposition amendments are rejected, 'Ministers in committee do agree to reconsider proposals from the Opposition (often in order to make progress), and this sometimes results in Government amendment at a late stage which more or less accept the Opposition's argument'.[27]

6   The Maastricht debate[28] showed the efficacy of the Commons as a means of publicising issues surrounding legislation. Because of the newsworthiness of the drama generated during the debates, the pros and cons of both Maastricht generally and the UK opt-out from the Social Protocol in particular were given a thorough airing. The greatest threat to the ability of the Commons to generate such publicity through debate (or to propose amendments) comes from the devices available to the Government to reduce the time available for debate. The use of the 'closure' allows debate to be simply cut off at the instance of Government Whips (if supported on a vote

---

23   *Op cit*, p316.
24   Norton, *Does Parliament Matter?* (1993), p20.
25   'The Westminster Malaise', *Independent*, 15 May 1996.
26   'Standing Committees in the House of Commons' in Walkland and Ryle, *The Commons Today* (1981), p130.
27   Griffiths and Ryle, *Parliament, Functions Practice and Procedures* (1989), p317.
28   For extended analysis of this debate see Rawlings, (1994) PL 258.

which must be passed with at least 100 members in favour), while the 'guillotine' allows the Government to allocates a set amount of time for each stage of debate. The use of these techniques is provided for by House of Commons Standing Orders.

House of Commons Standing Orders, nos 35, 36, 80 and 81

(1) The closure

35(1) After a question has been proposed a Member rising in his place may claim to move 'That the question be now put', and, unless it shall appear to the Chair that such motion is an abuse of the rules of the House, or an infringement of the rights of the minority, the question, 'That the question be now put', shall be put forthwith.

(2) When a question 'That the question be now put' has been decided in the affirmative, and the question consequent thereon has been decided, a Member may claim that any further question be put which may be requisite to bring to a decision any question already proposed from the Chair, and if the assent of the Chair, as aforesaid, be not withheld, any question so claimed shall be put forthwith.

(3) This order shall apply in committee only when the Chairman of Ways and Means or either Deputy Chairman is in the chair.

36 If a division be held upon a question for the closure of debate under Standing Order no 35 (closure of debate) or for the proposal of the question under Standing Order no 28 (powers of chair to propose question), that question shall not be decided in the affirmative unless it appears by the numbers declared from the chair that not fewer than 100 Members voted in the majority in support of the motion.

(2) The guillotine

80 There shall be a committee, to be called the Business Committee, consisting of the Chairman of Ways and Means, who shall be Chairman of the committee, and not more than eight other Members to be nominated by Mr Speaker in respect of each bill to which this order applies. The quorum of the committee shall be four. The committee:

(a) shall, in the case of any bill in respect of which an order has been made by the House, allotting a specified number of days or portions of days to the consideration of the bill in committee of the whole House or, on report, divide the bill into such parts as it may see fit and allot to each part so many days or portions of a day so allotted as it may consider appropriate; and

(b) shall report its resolution (or resolutions) to the House, and on a motion being made for the consideration of such report the question thereon shall be put forthwith, and on consideration of the said report the question 'That this House doth agree with the committee in its resolution (or resolutions)' shall be put forthwith and, if that question be agreed to, any such resolution shall have effect as if it were an order of the House.

Proceedings in pursuance of this sub-paragraph, though opposed, may be decided after the expiration of the time for opposed business.

81 If a motion be made by a minister of the Crown providing for an allocation of time to any proceedings on a bill, Mr Speaker shall, not more than three hours after the commencement of the proceedings on such a motion, put any question necessary to dispose of those proceedings.

Notes

1   Griffiths and Ryle note that requests for closure motions by Government Whips are rarely refused by the Speaker, but that this is partly due to the fact that the Whips tend to consult with the Speaker before proposing a closure; when they do so 'they are often told, privately, to wait a while'.[29] They further point out that the Speaker does exercise a real discretion; she will 'take into account the Members who have spoken and how many still wish to speak; particular regard will be had to whether the Government and Opposition spokesmen have been heard and whether minority opinion has been expressed [as well as] the length of debate and how much longer it could last'.[30] Their research shows that the use of the closure as a means of limiting the time for debate of Government bill has markedly declined; there were 11 divisions on closure motions in respect of such bills in 1947–48 and in 1961–62, falling to none in 1985–87 and three in 1987–88.[31]

2   Griffiths and Ryle find that the usage of the guillotine has remained fairly constant between 1974 and 1988, although in the 1987–88 session it was used six times, the greatest usage during this period. Finding also that 'since 1974–75, Governments have been reluctant to move for an allocation of time order until Standing Committee has sat for 70–80 hours, whereas less than 30 hours was common during the period 1946–47 and 1960–61', they conclude that its use has been 'fairly consistently restrained since 1945'. Nevertheless, it remains a useful tool for Government, since its use dramatically decreases the Opposition's power to delay legislation which may be seen as 'its strongest weapon',[32] since the threat of delay can force compromises from ministers.

3.   A recent use of the guillotine is illuminating. The legislation in question was the Prevention of Terrorism (Additional Powers) Act 1996 (above). Passed in the wake of the resumption of IRA violence, the measure was subject to a guillotine which enabled all of its stages to be taken in one day. The bill clearly had some impact on civil liberties, but the Opposition front bench agreed with the Government both on the need for the measure in principle and on the necessity of using a guillotine in order to make the new powers available to the police by the weekend. In the debate on the guillotine, Mr Newton spoke for the Government, and Mrs Taylor for the official Opposition.

HC Deb 2 April 1996, cols 159–66, 181

Mr A J Beith (Berwick-upon-Tweed): Could not what the Leader of the House wants have been achieved – even taking into account the Home Secretary's delay in producing the bill – if the Home Secretary had published the bill last week, and if each day this week, including Thursday, had been used to enable us to discuss separate stages on separate days? Consultation with outside bodies could have taken place between the sittings.

---

29   Griffith and Ryle, *op cit*, p223.

30   *Ibid*, p222.

31   *Ibid*, p301.

32   *Ibid*, p306.

Mr Newton: It has been necessary for full consideration to be given to these matters within Government. The policy was agreed collectively by the Government only last week. My right hon and learned friend the Home Secretary has acted with commendable speed in the wake of that, and as a result we need to transact the business in the way laid down in the motion.

Mr Max Madden (Bradford, West): First, what is the most recent precedent for the Government's recommendation of the procedure that we are being asked to follow? Secondly, can the Leader of the House explain – as the Home Secretary signally failed to do yesterday – the motivation for the bill's being rushed through the House in this way?

Mr Newton: I cannot immediately recall a precise precedent, but then I cannot recall precisely similar circumstances. Terrorism has been resumed in this country; the police have made clear their belief that they need these additional powers in order to have the maximum scope for combating further instances of that terrorism; and we are operating within a day or so of the Easter recess.

The hon. gentleman made the same point in response to my business statement yesterday. I thought that my right hon and learned friend made the case for the proposals absolutely clear in his own statement yesterday – and, indeed, that has been accepted by those on the Opposition front bench.

Mr Kevin McNamara (Kingston upon Hull, North): Everyone accepts that the bill is very important. How can the right hon gentleman justify having allowed less than five minutes for the discussion of each amendment – presuming that all were selected – quite apart from any time spent on voting?

Mr Newton: I defend it on the basis of my general judgment that the amount of time that we have provided for discussion of the bill and the motion – to which I shall refer in a moment – is appropriate for proper debate of the proposals in the particular circumstances, and against the background of a resumption of terrorism on the mainland.

Mr D N Campbell-Savours (Workington): Over the 16 years in which I have been in the House, I have noticed that when legislation is guillotined, it invariably goes wrong. Why can we not have real time in which to discuss what may – I do not know – be a perfectly valid bill?

Mr Newton: Let me repeat what I just said. I think that the motion provides appropriate time in the particular circumstances – Opposition front benchers have found that view persuasive on the basis of briefing that they have been freely given – and in view of the fact that the House is about to rise for the Easter recess. It will not surprise the House that, despite my support for the proposals of my right hon. and learned friend the Home Secretary, it gives me no pleasure whatever to be moving a timetable [guillotine] motion. It is in fact the first that I have moved for more than two years. I simply believe that, in the circumstances with which we are confronted, it is both sensible and necessary. ...

Mr Campbell-Savours: Is there not an immense principle involved here – that one should never guillotine legislation that has implications for civil liberties?

Mrs Taylor: There are always difficulties in saying never in politics. A balance must be reached in difficult situations such as this and people must weigh up competing claims, and that presents the House with an extra difficulty. That is why the time scale is providing so many difficulties and – if I may say so – so many suspicions on the part of hon Members who believe that the Home Secretary and the Government are bouncing the legislation through and that we are taking their word on its merits.

Mr Dennis Skinner (Bolsover): In answer to questions yesterday, the Home Secretary made clear that the stop and search measures are comprehensive and will not apply simply to the rounding up of alleged terrorists. The net result will be that anybody can be caught in the net, and that is a matter of civil liberties and justice. The Home Secretary made the game plan abundantly clear. Is my right hon. friend seriously happy with that?

Mrs Taylor: My hon friend the Member for Blackburn – the Shadow Home Secretary – has received significant assurances from the Home Secretary on such aspects as the monitoring of the workings of the new proposals, and he is satisfied with those assurances.

Mr McNamara: Is my hon friend aware that Home Office briefings, as reported by the media yesterday, said that the Home Office did not expect any particular problems over the coming weekend?

Mrs Taylor: I am not responsible for Home Office briefings; I am responsible for the collective decision of the Shadow Cabinet which was made on the basis of the overall briefings that we received. We face a real problem and a real danger. If the Government say that there is a significant risk and if the bill can minimise that risk and help to protect lives, we have a responsibility to facilitate its passage through the House. I hope that in view of all that has been said, we can have an explanation from the Home Secretary of why no indication whatever of the possibility of the changes was given during the recent debate on the Prevention of Terrorism Act just three weeks ago. It would have been wiser if the Home Secretary had given a proper indication that these changes were under consideration. We shall all have to make our own judgment about why he did not do so.

It is important that the House is consulted where possible. It is not just a matter of the pride of Members. It is a fact that the more Members who are consulted and involved in decision-making, the better the chances are that we shall get our legislation right and that the Government will not have to return to the House for further amendment because of deficiencies in the legislation.

In conclusion, we are not happy with the way in which the Government have forced such instant decisions upon the House, but, for the reasons that I gave earlier, we will not stand in the way of the bill or the proposed time scale. However we trust, and ask for an assurance, that the House will not be treated in such a cavalier way in future. ...

Mr Alan Beith [moving an amendment to increase the length of the committee stage]: ... Even if we take it as read that for the purposes of this weekend the police need the powers, it was open to the Home Secretary to ensure that they received adequate parliamentary debate. He could have brought the bill forward considerably earlier – even a week ago would have enabled its stages to be properly considered. The bill was in his hands last Thursday or Friday, if not before. He could have published it then so that interested organisations and bodies, especially those dealing with the courts, could have brought forward proposals for amendments. Having failed to do any of those things, he could yesterday have ensured that the procedure that the House followed would take as much time as was available this week so that it could be done properly.

There are a number of ways in which the procedures for the bill could have been dealt with [interruption]. Hon Members who seem to think that this is some kind of joke should realise that if there are no gaps between the stages of a bill, the people outside the House, who will have to live with the legislation – some of them will have to arrest people in the street on the basis of it – will not get the chance to consider it properly.

I made some inquiries outside the Metropolitan Police area and discovered that, in other police authority areas, chief officers were not familiar with what was going on, and did not know the precise content of the proposed powers. Those are the sort of people whom we would consult between the stages of the bill, to ensure that the powers reached the statute book in an appropriate form.

... There will be no report stage, because the Government will accept no amendments. I was struck by the fact that the Leader of the House spoke as if he had already accepted that there would be no report stage. He said something like, 'That will be an hour for third reading' – but actually the hour is for both report stage and third reading. The Leader of the House has already taken, as part of the scheme of things, the fact that the Government, however wrong they may be shown to be on detail, will not amend the bill in committee because they do not want a report stage. So we can forget about a report stage. And they will take the same altitude in another place [the House of Lords].

That is government by decree. The Government have already decided the precise form that the bill should take. Whenever Governments make such decisions they get things wrong. Even with the best will in the world, the best organised Government in the world, with the finest ministers and the finest civil servants, might still make mistakes. The present Government have a record of making mistakes. The Home Secretary and the Home Office certainly have a record of making mistakes about what the law is, and about the position in which they will be found in when the matter comes before the courts. The Home Secretary has made so many such mistakes that he should be bound to expect it to happen in this instance. ...

Mr Tony Banks (Newham, North-West): Legislation that is made on the hoof is invariably poor and defective. I assure the Home Secretary that I do not want to be blown up, either at Easter or at any other time; my constituents do not want to be blown up, and I am sure that he does not want to be blown up either. In fact, my constituents are probably more likely to be blown up than the Home Secretary, as was demonstrated by the cowardly attack that caused the explosion in the East End. Neither my constituents nor I can travel around in bullet-proof, chauffeur-driven limos.

When my hon. friend the Member for North-East Derbyshire (Mr Barnes) said that those who opposed the timetable motion or the bill would be accused of being soft on terrorism, I heard a sedentary 'Hear, hear' from one of the limo-occupiers on the Government front bench. That is a monstrous suggestion.

I do not want my civil liberties to be blown up either. I cannot agree to the speedy process because, frankly, it is leading the way to repenting at leisure. We are asked to put on the statute book legislation that is not temporary. We all know how the PTA came about. I would not mind what was going on if the Home Secretary told us that the measures would be implemented only for a set period and we could see an end. If measures needed to be passed urgently before Easter, I could understand the point made but I agree with my hon friend the Member for North-East Derbyshire that we do not have to go into recess. Easter does not start until Good Friday. I assume that that is the period that we are talking about. There is not a great deal of important business tabled for tomorrow, and Thursday we are in recess. Why can we not take more time?

Reasonable people will have to be convinced by the bill. If the Home Secretary can make a good case, why does he have to sacrifice and undermine it by ramming the bill through the House and the other place? That is why I am uneasy about it. I would like to hear more about the reasoning behind the bill and have more time to consider it. When dealing with civil liberties, we should not be so ready to be stampeded. There is a whiff of panic in the air, and that gets me. I always feel that the terrorists are winning when we turn ourselves inside out, brush aside all our normal procedures, ram things through override arguments and deride people who have a contrary point of view. We imprison ourselves, demean our institution, and the terrorist wins when we do such things in the Houses of Parliament.

Note

Despite such opposition, both the guillotine motion, and the bill itself were carried in the allotted time of one day. The episode vividly illustrates that if both main parties are behind a populist measure, scrutiny can be reduced to negligible proportions, leaving individual back-benchers largely impotent. Since, in fact, measures which are seen as 'tough' on crime or terrorism are likely in the future to have all party support, given their populist appeal, it can be seen how the party system not only facilitates executive dominance of the Commons at the expense of the Opposition, but perhaps as importantly can result in the almost total withdrawal of sustained back-bench scrutiny if such an action is perceived to be politically advantageous by the Opposition leadership.

Delegated legislation

The Parent Act

In a growing number of cases, Acts of Parliament do not specify precisely how a particular policy is to be put into effect, but rather grant broad enabling powers to the relevant minister to implement a certain policy at a time of his or her choosing, within the general parameters of the Act. Such an Act may also grant to the minister a discretion to delay bringing in the proposed new scheme until he or she thinks it appropriate to do so. What will be the position if the Secretary of State disregards the will of Parliament and decides not to bring in such a scheme at all, and without seeking to procure the repealing of the Act in question, attempts to implement an alternative policy, relying on his prerogative powers? In *Secretary of State for the Home Department, ex p Fire Brigades Union and Others* (1995),[33] the House of Lords upheld the finding of the Court of Appeal that the Home Secretary, Michael Howard, was wrong to decide not to bring into force the statutory scheme for criminal injuries compensation which had been laid down in the Criminal Justice Act 1988 and to bring in a 'radically different' tariff scheme.

The House of Lords was thus, as it were, enforcing the constitutional rights of Parliament against the executive, thus preventing the abuse of the latter's powers. In actual fact of course, it was the Conservative Government which had procured the passage the original legislation, and the same Conservative Government which later decided that it wished to disregard that legislation. The gap between constitutional theory and political reality can be seen in the fact that the majority of MPs, as Conservatives, probably regarded the decision of the House of Lords as an source of acute political embarrassment, rather than hailing it as a vindication of their constitutional rights.

---

33   2 WLR 464; for the case itself see Part IV, Chapter 1, pp508–11.

Scrutiny of delegated legislation: efficacy

Michael Zander, *The Law Making Process* (1994), pp92–7, 98–9, 100–1

Each year over 2,000 sets of rules and regulations are made by ministers or the Crown in Council or other central rule-making authorities – by comparison with less than 100 public Acts of Parliament. This form of legislation is under the authority of powers delegated by Parliament. (The residual power to legislate under royal prerogative is no longer of much importance.) The reason is usually to avoid having too much detail in the main Act and thereby to waste the time of parliamentarians in minutiae. The delegated power to make regulations also enables the responsible minister to respond to new circumstances by amplifying the original rules without troubling Parliament with matters of detail that are within principles dealt with in the original legislation. Sometimes, however, Parliament leaves to ministers power to issue regulations on matters of principle.

The most sweeping grant of delegated legislative power to the executive is undoubtedly that in s2(2) of the European Communities Act 1972, which permits Orders in Council and regulations by designated ministers and Government departments to be made to give effect to Community instruments and provisions of the treaties which do not have direct effect. The Act provides that such delegated powers are to have the effect of Acts of Parliament and can include any provision that could have been included in an Act of Parliament except that they may not impose or increase taxation; have retroactive effect; sub-delegate legislative powers; or create new criminal offences punishable with more than two years' imprisonment or fines of over £400.

For another remarkable example of delegated legislation see the Hallmarking Act 1973, s7(a) of which gives the Secretary of State, 'after consulting the Council and such other persons as he thinks fit', authority to 'make regulations wholly or partly varying, supplementing or replacing the provisions of the section'. The International Transport Conventions Act 1983, ss8 and 9, allows that statute to be amended by delegated legislation; so does the Transport Act 1985, s46. The Courts and Legal Services Act 1990, s125(4), gives the Lord Chancellor the power by order to 'make such amendments or repeals in relevant enactments as appear to him to be necessary or expedient in consequence of any provision made by Part II with respect to advocacy, litigation, conveyancing or probate services'. Such provisions giving ministers the power to amend and even to repeal statutory provisions by statutory instruments are known as 'Henry VIII clauses'.

Most delegated legislation is issued in the form of statutory instruments which are available from the Stationery Office. Their drafting is usually left to the legal advisers in departments – though in cases of particular importance or difficulty parliamentary counsel will be brought in. The process of outside consultation is usually more fulsome than is the case with legislation proper. The need for secrecy is less, since the principles of the new law have already been laid down and the department is therefore less reluctant to take advice on matters of implementation. Sometimes regulations are published in draft for comment. See for instance Law Society's *Gazette*, 29 October 1986, 3238. In some cases consultation is even mandatory. Thus procedural regulations for tribunals and inquiries must be submitted in draft to the Council on Tribunals (Tribunals and Inquiries Act 1971, ss10, 11).

Parliamentary scrutiny of delegated legislation is usually slight. Some statutory instruments, whose subject matter is not felt to be of importance, are simply laid before Parliament. There is no actual procedure for them to be discussed, though any MP who wishes can ask the responsible minister about it or can seek to raise the matter in debate. But more often the enabling Act states that instruments must be laid before Parliament and shall become law unless, within a period of a few days, a resolution is passed to annul it. This is known as the 'negative resolution' procedure. The period is usually 40 days. But even if a group of Members decide to challenge such an instrument (by what is called a 'prayer') there is no guarantee that the Government will provide time for a debate or the opportunity of a vote. The Opposition can use one of their own precious 'supply dates' for the debate. A debate is only guaranteed for the minority of statutory instruments which have to be passed by an affirmative resolution (as opposed to the normal 'negative resolution' procedure). But even then the statutory instrument cannot be amended in the course of the debate. It can only be approved, annulled or withdrawn. During the committee stage of the Courts and Legal Services Bill 1990 Lord Mackay, the Lord Chancellor, said that in future he would see that the affirmative resolution procedure would be used for all statutory instruments giving effect to 'Henry VIII clauses'.

Since 1973 there has been a Joint Select Committee on Statutory Instruments of both Houses to consider, *inter alia*, statutory instruments of a general character and those subject to the negative and affirmative resolution procedure. Its function is to review statutory instruments from a technical and not from a policy point of view. Its chairman, to emphasise this point, is a member of the Opposition rather than of the Government.

The function of the committee is to determine whether the special attention of each House should be drawn to an instrument on any of nine grounds:

(i)   that it imposes a tax or a charge;

(ii)   that it is made under primary legislation which expressly excludes the instrument from challenge in the courts;

(iii) that it purports to have retrospective effect where the enabling Act does not expressly provide for such effect;

(iv)   that there appears to have been unjustifiable delay in the publication of the instrument or in laying it;

(v)   that the instrument has come into operation before being laid and there appears to have been unjustifiable delay in sending notification of this as required by the Statutory Instruments Act 1946, s4(1);

(vi)   that it appears doubtful whether the instrument is *intra vires* the enabling statute, or the instrument appears to make some unusual or unexpected use of the powers in the enabling legislation;

(vii) that for any special reason the form or purport of the instrument calls for elucidation;

(viii) that the drafting of the legislation appears to be defective; and

(ix)   any other ground which does not impinge on the merits of the instrument or on the policy behind it.

In determining these matters the committee has the assistance of Counsel to the Speaker and Counsel to the Lord Chairman of Committees and, of course, takes written and oral evidence from the departments responsible for making the regulations.

As has been seen, the committee does not, however, consider the merits of statutory instruments or of the policies behind them. That is done either on the floor of the House or in the case of the House of Commons, in one of the standing committees on statutory instruments. These procedures are also defective. The debates on the floor of the House usually take place late at night and are poorly attended. Debates in standing committees are for up to one and half hours (T St John Bates, 'Parliament, Policy and Delegated Legislation', *Statute Law Review,* Summer 1986, p117).

See further JD Hayhurst and P Wallington, 'The Parliamentary Scrutiny of Delegated Legislation', *Public Law,* Winter 1988, pp547–76. The authors argue that the use of delegated legislation has changed significantly especially in the previous decade or so. 'It is no longer the technical implementation of detail in a legislative mosaic, although undoubtedly the majority of statutory instruments are in this category. More of the policy of a legislative proposal is likely to be delegated, the legislation being enabling not just at a specific but at the broadest level' (p573). They instanced the recasting of the supplementary benefit system done principally by regulations under the Social Security Act 1986. Other examples were the Legal Aid Act 1988 and the Education Reform Act 1988.

The last named Act was an example of the 'increasingly common practice' of conferring power to amend the Act itself and 'of the astonishingly detailed rule-making powers that may be given to a minister' (p574). They conclude: 'Delegated legislation, in other words, matters, and matters increasingly, and its scrutiny, whether by Parliament or the courts, is not just a tedious corner of the constitutional edifice' (*ibid*).

They were pessimistic about the prospects but they did find that the joint committee was working well. Its mere presence was helpful quite apart from the content of its reports.

The Hansard Society's 1992 report on the legislative process (*Making the Law*) said: 'We consider the whole of the approach of Parliament to delegated legislation to be highly unsatisfactory. The House of Commons in particular should give its procedures for scrutiny of statutory instruments a thorough review' (para 366, p90).

One proposal it made was that departmentally-related Select Committees might review statutory instruments in their field when they are laid before Parliament and report on those that raise matters of public importance.

The [Joint Committee on Statutory Instruments], it said, did valuable work. 'However some of its critical findings appear to be ignored by ministers. We heard from the chairman of the committee that some instruments on which his committee had reported adversely had not been debated. We also understand that debates on affirmative resolutions, approving instruments, are quite often held before the committee has had time to report' (para 370, p90). The Hansard Society report said: 'We find this very unsatisfactory. If the joint committee is to be effective, its reports must be heeded and ministers should be required to answer its criticisms in debate' (para 371, p91). It recommended (*ibid*) that no statutory instrument should be debated until the joint committee had reported. Where the joint committee reports that it finds an instrument to be defective a motion to approve the instrument should not be made without a resolution to set aside the committee's findings (this in effect is what happened in Australia.)

On the question of how statutory instruments are debated, the Hansard Society report said (para 372, p91): 'We see little merit in short debates late at night on the floor of the House with few Members taking part, as often happens now'. The report agreed with the report of the House of Commons Select Committee on Sittings of the House ('the Jopling report') [HC 20–I of 1991–92, paras 72–73.] that it was desirable to free the time of the House itself by sending most delegated legislation to Standing Committees for debate. It recommended that all statutory instruments requiring affirmative resolutions and all 'prayers' for the annulment of a statutory instrument should automatically be referred to Standing Committees for debate. Longer or more complicated statutory instruments which did not have to be approved in a hurry could sometimes be sent to a special Standing Committee which could hear evidence (para 373, p91). A prime objective, it suggested, was to make it possible for Members to play a constructive part in the work of Standing Committees on Statutory Instruments so that they would find it worthwhile to spend time on them. It made a number of other detailed recommendations:

- Before a committee started debating a statutory instrument, it should be able to question ministers on the purpose, meaning and effect of the instrument. This would follow the procedure established for European Community documents in Standing Committees which had proved helpful (para 375, p91).

- There should be a substantive motion to enable the committee to approve or reject it or otherwise express an opinion – as opposed to merely stating that it had considered the instrument (para 376, p92).

- Although the report did not recommend that the House or its committees should be given the power to amend statutory instruments, it should be possible for Members to move and vote on amendments without amending the instrument. This could be achieved if there were a motion to approve an instrument subject to specified amendments being made. If this passed, the minister could withdraw the instrument, amend it and bring it back for reconsideration (para 379, p92).

- Subject to general timetabling there should no longer be an arbitrary time-limit on debates on statutory instruments in Standing Committees (para 380, p93).

- Although not all 'prayers' against statutory instruments could be debated, at least those that are serious should be (in 1985–86, 69% were not debated; in 1990–91, 78% were not debated). The failure to debate 'prayers' was 'a major erosion of Parliament's rights and a potential weakening of the scrutiny of delegated legislation' (para 387, p94). ...

Delegated legislation – some Anglo-American comparisons

One strange fact is the difference in the interest in delegated legislation in England and the US. This was the subject of a fascinating comparative study by Professor Michael Asimow of the University of California ('Delegated Legislation in the United States and United Kingdom' (1983) 3 *Oxford Journal of Legal Studies* 253). His point of departure was the observation that 'In the USA the substance of regulations and the procedure by which they are made, present issues which generate enormous controversy in political, judicial and academic circles. In Britain, nearly everyone seems satisfied with (and hardly anyone seems interested in) procedural and substantive aspects of delegated legislation' (*ibid*, p253).

In the US, delegated legislation is the field of rule-making by regulatory agencies created by Congress to regulate a great variety of fields – airlines, trucking, roads, railways, radio and television, corporate securities, labour relations, energy pricing, business practices, financial institutions, etc. The agencies, in Asimow's phrase, 'generated a huge number of highly controversial regulations which attracted attention to the subject in legal and economic literature as well as in the popular press. A vast number of court decisions have focused on procedural requirements for making rules and clarification of the scope of the court's power to review the rules' (p254).

In the first part of his study Asimow drew a picture of the system in the US and in Britain. In the second half he offered some reflections on possible reasons why the subject was of such intense interest and controversy in the one country and so uncontroversial and almost uninteresting in the other.

He looked in turn at a number of possible explanations:

1   *Laying before Parliament* – It might be argued that, since delegated legislation generally had to be laid before Parliament, that might explain the British feeling that it was under control. But the explanation foundered in face of the fact that it was widely and indeed generally felt that parliamentary control of delegated legislation was superficial in the extreme and in practice virtually non-existent.

2   *The consultation process* – Insofar as Government departments consulted with interest groups it might be said that this defused potential controversy about the rules being made. But in practice such consultation was not very elaborate and often hardly took place at all. Moreover, it usually only involved those already known to the department and took place behind closed doors. In the US, by contrast, a proposed rule had to be published in the Federal Register and often this triggered 'an outpouring of responses'. The courts had laid down a rule that agencies had to respond to the material objections made by commentators in the statement of purpose which accompanied the eventual rule. In addition there were often oral hearings conducted by agencies to enable interested parties to articulate their criticisms of proposed rules. The American system 'thus enriches the quantity and quality of inputs available to decision-makers and is universally considered to enhance democratic values of public participation in the making of crucial decisions as well as to improve the acceptability of those decisions to persons affected by them' (p268).

...

4   *Importance of delegated legislation* – Britain has far fewer rules made through delegated legislation and on the whole they are less important than those in the US. Why then did Britain rely so relatively little on this technique? Both countries had to grapple with similar problems of 'controlling technology, ensuring environmental and industrial safety, regulating land use, providing telecommunication and public utility services, administering a welfare state, operating complex schemes of taxation, and so on' (p269).

Americans tended to seek solutions in regulation in the broad sense of governmental control of private sector economic behaviour which generally entailed regulation in the narrow sense of subordinate legislation. In the US the party battles in the Congress and the inability of the administration to have its way in the primary legislation meant that many issues were left to be resolved through subordinate legislation. In Britain by contrast the executive could get its policy enacted in the primary statute and therefore had less need to leave important details to the regulatory process.

... the most important British technique for controlling the private sector was through heavy reliance on official discretion to make individualised orders. Parliament would legislate, giving officials broad discretionary powers. Often the powers were loosely circumscribed by guidelines prepared by the Government department concerned.

Notes

1   In 1978 the Select Committee on Procedure 1977–78 warned, '... the system provides only vestigial control of statutory instruments and is in need of

complete reform'. The fundamental problem identified with the system was that instruments subject to negative affirmation were increasingly becoming law without ever having been debated by the Commons. Since that report, this phenomena increased sharply: in 1978–79, 71.7% of prayers for annulment were debated; in the 1985–86 session, this percentage had dropped to 30.6%. In practice it is the Government which determines how much time shall be made available for consideration of statutory instruments; it can thus limit scrutiny to negligible proportions.

2   The enactment of broad enabling powers by Parliament which give ministers *de facto* powers to legislate may also be seen as a significant erosion of parliamentary sovereignty. So-called 'Henry VIII' clauses, in giving ministers the power to amend primary legislation by regulations which may never be seen or debated by Parliament, offend against one of the fundamental principles of parliamentary sovereignty, that 'no person or body is recognised by the law of England as having a right to override or set aside the legislation of Parliament' (Dicey).[35] Further, it is arguable that there must come a point at which the provision Parliament enacts is so substanceless and hands over such enormous discretionary powers to ministers that it should be regarded as ineffective to pass the powers it purports to, due to its violation of fundamental constitutional principle. Suppose, for example, an Education Act were passed which stated simply 'The Secretary of State may make such regulations as she thinks fit for the provision and regulation of primary, secondary and higher education in the UK'. Such a provision would effectively hand to ministers the power to legislate in whatever manner they pleased on any aspect of education policy. The courts will apparently not allow Parliament to bind its successors on the ground that to do so would allow Parliament to subvert its own continuing sovereignty (see Part I, Chapter 4). By analogy, the courts should also refuse to allow Parliament to effectively hand over its legislative power to the executive. Whilst Parliament would still retain the power to repeal the Act, the erosion of parliamentary sovereignty that such an Act would constitute would be far greater than, for example, an attempt to bind future Parliaments as to the wording of subsequent legislation through the use of 'a notwithstanding clause'.

The legal force of the laying and publication requirements

Laying requirements

Section 4(1) of the Statutory Instruments Act 1946 (SIA) provides that where an instrument is required to be laid by the parent act the instrument 'shall be laid before ... Parliament and ... shall be so laid before coming into effect'. Section 4(1) does allow for an instrument to come into effect before laying if this is 'essential', provided that the Lord Chancellor and the Speaker are notified and the reason for the omission to lay is explained to them. Since the laying requirements represent the only measure of Parliamentary control over delegated legislation, it is of some importance to ask what will be the legal effect of a failure to comply with them?

---

35   AV Dicey, *An Introduction to the Study of the Law of the Constitution*, 10th edn (1959), ppxxxiv.

In decided cases on the legality of failure to comply with express procedural requirements, the courts have tended to classify such requirements as either mandatory or directory. A breach of a requirement seen as mandatory has led to the Authority's action being held invalid, while breach of a directory requirement has left the act or decision standing. In two 19th-century cases, *Bailey v Williamson* (1873)[36] and *Starey v Graham* (1899),[37] the requirement to lay was held to be directory. It can be noted, however, that in *Bailey* Parliament had intended the provision to be directory only in that particular instance; the case should not therefore be seen as having established any general principle that laying requirements are always directory. On the other hand, *Springer v Dorley* (1949),[38] a West Indian case, is persuasive authority to the effect that the requirements are directory only. Campbell (1983) PL 43 cites these authorities, statements made in the House during the passage of the SIA and the opinions of Erskine May, Allen and Graham-Harrison, First Parliamentary Counsel in 1932, as evidence for his view that the requirement is not mandatory.

There is no direct authority against this view but merely a number of persuasive indicators. First of all, there is *Sheer Metalcraft* (1954).[39] The case was mainly concerned with the publication of statutory instruments, and will be considered again in relation to that issue, but its full text is given here. It was brought by persons who had been prosecuted under an instrument, the Iron and Steel Prices Order, 1951, an important part of which consisted of a number of schedules setting out the maximum prices for different commodities of steel.

Sheer Metalcraft [1954] 1 QB 586, 588

> **Streatfield J:** The point which has been taken is that, by reason of the deposited schedules not having been printed and not having been certified by the minister as being exempt from printing, the instrument is not a valid instrument under the Statutory Instruments Act 1946 ['the SIA'].
>
> Section 1 [of the SIA] visualises the making of what is called a statutory instrument by a minister of the Crown; s2 visualises that after the making of a statutory instrument it shall be sent to the King's printer to be printed, except in so far as under regulations made under the Act it may be unnecessary to have it printed. It is said here that the minister did not certify that the printing of these very bulky deposited schedules was unnecessary within the meaning of regulation 7. It is contended, therefore, that as he did not so certify it, it became an obligation under the Act that the deposited schedules as well as the instrument itself should be printed under s2 of the Act of 1946, and in the absence of their having been printed as part of the instrument, the instrument cannot be regarded as being validly made.
>
> To test that matter it is necessary to examine s3 of the Act of 1946. By subsection (1): 'Regulations made for the purposes of this Act shall make provision for the publication by His Majesty's Stationery Office of lists showing the date upon which every statutory instrument printed and sold by the King's printer of Acts of Parliament was first issued by that office ...' There does not appear to be any

---

36   LR 8 QB 118.
37   1 QB 406.
38   (1950) 66 LQR 299.
39   1 QB 586.

definition of what is meant by 'issue', but presumably it does mean some act by the Queen's printer of Acts of Parliament which follows the printing of the instrument. That section, therefore, requires that the Queen's printer shall keep lists showing the date upon which statutory instruments are printed and issued.

Subsection (2) is important and provides: 'In any proceedings against any person for an offence consisting of a contravention of any such statutory instrument, it shall be a defence to prove that the instrument had not been issued by His Majesty's Stationery Office at the date of the alleged contravention unless it is proved that at that date reasonable steps had been taken for the purpose of bringing the purport of the instrument to the notice of the public, or of persons likely to be affected by it, or of the person charged.'

It seems to follow from the wording of this subsection that the making of an instrument is one thing and the issue of it is another. If it is made it can be contravened; if it has not been issued then that provides a defence to a person charged with its contravention. It is then upon the Crown to prove that, although it has not been issued, reasonable steps have been taken for the purpose of bringing the instrument to the notice of the public or persons likely to be affected by it.

I do not think that it can be said that, to make a valid statutory instrument, it is required that all of these stages should be gone through: namely, the making, the laying before Parliament, the printing, and the certification of that part of it which it might be unnecessary to have printed. In my judgment the making of an instrument is complete when it is first of all made by the minister concerned and after it has been laid before Parliament. When that has been done it then becomes a valid statutory instrument, totally made under the provisions of the Act.

The remaining provisions to which my attention has been drawn, in my view, are purely procedure for the issue of an instrument validly made – namely, that in the first instance it must be printed by the Queen's printer unless it is certified to be unnecessary to print it; it must then be included in a list published by Her Majesty's Stationery Office showing the dates when it is issued and it may be issued by the Queen's printer of Acts of Parliament. Those matters, in my judgment, are matters of procedure. If they were not and if they were stages in the perfection of a valid statutory instrument, I cannot see that s3(2) would be necessary, because if each one of those stages were necessary to make a statutory instrument valid, it would follow that there could be no infringement of an unissued instrument and therefore it would be quite unnecessary to provide a defence to a contravention of any such instrument. In my view the very fact that subsection (2) of s3 refers to a defence that the instrument has not been issued postulates that the instrument must have been validly made in the first place otherwise it could never have been contravened.

In those circumstances I hold that this instrument was validly made and approved and that it was made by or signed on behalf of the minister on its being laid before Parliament; that so appears on the face of the instrument itself. In my view, the fact that the minister failed to certify under regulation 7 does not invalidate the instrument as an instrument but lays the burden upon the Crown to prove that at the date of the alleged contravention reasonable steps had been taken for bringing the instrument to the notice of the public or persons likely to be affected by it.

Verdict: Guilty on all counts.

Notes

1　Whilst Streatfield J's comments on laying were, strictly, *obiter*, it is submitted that the whole manner in which he analysed the case, contrasting the actions which actually complete the instrument – making and laying – with the 'purely procedural' matter of publishing it, together with the fact that he chose to say that the instrument was complete 'after' it was laid, suggests that he regarded laying as a vital part of the process of creating a valid instrument.

2　Dr Campbell (*op cit*) disagrees with this argument: pointing out that the question before the judge was whether publishing was necessary to render the instrument valid, he argues that Streatfield J was merely confirming that the instrument before him was valid as it stood, before going on to consider the effect of publishing and was not intending to make any pronouncement on the necessity or otherwise of laying.

3　It is also arguable that the necessity perceived by Parliament of passing an Indemnity Act in 1944 in respect of *National Fire Service Regulations* which had not been laid, suggests that there was concern that the regulations were invalid due to the failure to lay. Speeches in the House recognised that it was for the courts to make an authoritative judgment on the issue, but the fact that parliamentary time was made available for the matter suggests that the House did not regard the possibility that the regulations were invalid as remote.

4　In considering the directory/mandatory issue, general principles used by the courts may be identified and applied. The courts tend to consider, *inter alia*, 'the importance of the provision that has been disregarded' (*Howard v Bodington* (1877)),[40] and the effect of non-compliance with the procedure as in *Coney v Choyce* (1975).[41] To assume that the judiciary would as a general rule hold the requirement to lay as directory only is to assume that they regard parliamentary control over delegated legislation, even in a case such as this one where Parliament had the power to annul the instrument, as of negligible importance. Some indication that they do not do so may be seen in the stress laid by Sir Thomas Bingham in *ex p Fire Brigades Union and Others* (1994) (above) on the 'overriding legislative role of Parliament'. This role cannot be limited only to the part played by Parliament in passing the parent Act; it clearly also extends to Parliament's scrutiny of delegated legislation, brought under that Act, to ensure that it conforms to the scheme which it had originally envisaged.

5　The approach taken in *Bailey v Williamson*[42] was to attempt to elucidate Parliament's intention as to whether the requirement to lay should be mandatory. It would be surprising if Parliament itself was of the opinion that its own scrutiny of delegated legislation was of such negligible importance that, as a general rule, a minister should be able to flout flagrantly the provisions for Parliamentary scrutiny, 'a constitutional

---

40　2 PD 203.

41　1 All ER 979.

42　(1873) LR 8; QB 118.

safeguard of some value'[43] and yet produce a perfectly valid order. The courts could note that the Parliamentary committee appointed to consider the efficacy of such scrutiny (the Select Committee on Procedure in the 1977–78), in producing a report which urged the vital need for reform clearly did not take this view. In the premises, it seems that a strong argument can be put forward that instruments which are subject to laying requirements will be of no effect unless those requirements are complied with.

Publication requirements

The question whether publication of delegated legislation is necessary for its validity has also been much debated. Since publication is the principle means by which such legislation is brought to the notice of those whom it may affect, adherence to the doctrine of the Rule of Law[44] (which, *inter alia*, requires that persons ought to be subject only to laws which are reasonably ascertainable) is in issue here.

If a person is charged with an offence under a statutory instrument which has not been published she will have a defence to the charge under s3(2) of the Statutory Instruments Act 1946 if she can show that at the date of the alleged offence the relevant instrument had not been issued by Her Majesty's Stationery Office. The generally accepted interpretation of s3(2) (the view acted on in *Sheer Metalcraft*)[45] is that the defence applies only to instruments which there is a duty to publish; that is, all those instruments which cannot be excused from publication by the minister certifying that they fall within one of the exceptions set out in the Statutory Instruments Regulations 1947, regs 5–8. DJ Lanham has, however, taken issue with this view, arguing that it can produce unjust results.

DJ Lanham, 'Delegated Legislation and Publication' (1974) 37 *Modern Law Review* 510, 521–2

To what kinds of statutory instrument does this provision apply? The most equitable construction would be that it applies to all statutory instruments which have not been issued at the date of the alleged contravention, whether or not there is a duty to publish the instrument in the statutory manner. This interpretation was urged on the court in *Defiant Cycle Co v Newell* (1953) [2 All ER 38], but it was not necessary to decide the matter and Parker J [*ibid*, at p43] left it open. Attractive though that interpretation may be, it seems improbable that it will be accepted because it fails to give any meaning to the word 'such'. A more plausible interpretation is that the defence applies whenever there is a duty to publish the instrument and the instrument is not published. This appears to be the interpretation acted on both in *Defiant Cycle Co v Newell* and *Sheer Metalcraft* (1954) [1 All ER 542]. This is a more literal construction, since it gives the word 'such' some employment but it produces a less satisfactory result. Consider the situation in *R v Sheer Metalcraft*. The Iron and Steel Order 1951 was a statutory instrument which contained bulky schedules. Under the Statutory Instruments Act and Regulations the minister could have exempted the schedules from the

---

43 De Smith, *op cit*, p148.

44 See Part I, Chapter 3.

45 See above.

requirement of publication by certificate [Statutory Instruments Regulations 1947, SI 1948/1, reg 7]. The minister did not do so and so the schedules fell into the category of statutory instruments which are required to be published in the statutory manner. They were not so published and the court held that this brought the s3(2) defence into play [the Prosecution was able to prove that some other form of publication had taken place and so, on the facts, the defence failed]. But suppose that the minister had given his certificate and no publication in any form had taken place at the time of the alleged contravention. On the footing of this second interpretation the s3(2) defence would not be available. It is true that under regulation 7 of the Statutory Instruments Regulations the minister is required to have regard to the steps which have been or may be taken to publicise the substance of the schedules before granting his certificate; but there is no suggestion that, in the event of a failure to publicise (perhaps through an oversight), the certificate would be invalid. On the assumption that a statutory instrument comes into force when made and that ignorance of the law is no defence, a person could be convicted of an offence under a schedule whose contents he could not possibly know – a curiously harsh and presumably unintended result.

Notes

1 Lanham agrees that it is 'improbable' that the defence applies even to instruments which have been exempted from publication by certificate, but goes on to construct an ingenious third interpretation of the defence (see pp522–3).

2 The Crown will defeat the s3(2) defence if it can show that, notwithstanding the failure to publish, reasonable steps had been taken to bring the instrument to the attention of those likely to be affected by it. Lord Goddard has considered this provision in the following case.

Defiant Cycle Co v Newell [1953] 2 All ER 38, 41

Lord Goddard: ... the Solicitor General has accepted the position that the result is that, if no certificate has been given exempting the Queen's printer from printing the whole of the order, while it does not affect the validity of the order itself, it throws on the Crown the burden of proving that, at the date of the commission of the offence, reasonable steps had been taken for the purpose of bringing the purport of the instrument to the notice of the public, or of persons likely to be affected by it, or the person charged. It is abundantly clear from the cases stated that there was no evidence before the justices that the steps required by s3(2) of the Act of 1946 to be proved by the prosecution had been taken, and that, therefore, the appellants were entitled to rely on that as a defence. No evidence was given on that point because, at the hearing, the Crown were relying on the letter (to which I have referred) as a certificate and as exempting them from the necessity of proving these facts. What was before the justices was evidence that an assistant secretary in the Ministry of Supply:

> whose duties included the making of arrangements for the printing of statutory instruments made by the minister, decided, having regard to the provisions of reg 7 of the Statutory Instruments Regulations, 1947, that the printing and sale of the said deposited schedules referred to in each of the said statutory instruments ... was unnecessary; that in so deciding she had regard primarily to the bulk of the schedules; secondly to the fact that copies thereof were to be made available through the regional offices; and, thirdly, to the fact (of which she was aware) that trade associations would be

distributing to the trade copies of the said deposited schedules or at least of such parts thereof as related to types of iron and steel most in demand.

No doubt, she thought that those things were to be done, and her anticipation may have been correct. It may be she knew enough to be satisfied that in due course these things would be done, but that does not discharge the burden which the statute places on the Crown in the event, as the Solicitor General has admitted, that there is no certificate exempting the Queen's printer from printing part of the order. The appellants contended that the Minister of Supply had not proved that at the date when he purported to issue the said statutory instruments he had taken reasonable steps to bring the purport of the said statutory instruments to the notice of the public, and, on the other hand, the Crown never contended that they had given any such evidence. The appellants were entitled to rely on the fact that this evidence had not been given, and, accordingly, the justices ought to have dismissed the information.

Question

What would be the position if persons other than the Crown, eg investigative journalists, had brought the instrument to the attention of the defendant?

Note

The statutory defence does not apply to all forms of delegated legislation. What therefore is the position at common law if a person is charged with an offence under delegated legislation which was unpublished at the time of the offence?

DJ Lanham, 'Delegated Legislation and Publication' (1974) 37 *Modern Law Review* 510–15

In constitutional terms the simplest case is one where there is no statutory requirement of any particular form of publicity and where the piece of delegated legislation does not specify the date on which it is to come into operation. Here there is clear authority that the legislation does not come into effect until published. In *Johnson v Sargant* (1918) [1 KB 101] an order, made by the Food Controller under the Defence of the Realm Regulations, in part required importers of beans to hold them at the disposal of the Controller unless they had been sold and paid for before the order took effect. The order was made on 16 May 1917, but was not published until 17 May. Bailhache J held that imported beans, which had been paid for on 16 May, were not caught by the order. His lordship said that he was unable to hold that the order came into operation before it was known and that it was not known until 17 May. ... It is suggested that the principle in *Johnson v Sargant* is that delegated legislation does not come into effect until it is published. ... Lanham goes on to consider possible authorities against this proposition:

> The first case usually relied on is *Jones v Robson* [1901] 1 KB 673. The Coal Mines Regulations Act 1906 empowered the minister to make orders prohibiting the use of certain kinds of explosives in mines. The Act also had provisions about giving notice of these orders. The minister made an order on 24 July 1899, to come into effect on 1 October 1899. No notice, in the form required by the Act, however, had been given. D was charged with breach of the order and argued in effect that the order was void because statutory notice had not been given. The Divisional Court held that the notice requirements were directory only and did not affect the validity of the order. The defendant did not deny that the Order had in fact been published or that he himself knew of the order. The situation was thus quite different from that in *Johnson v Sargant*. It is against these considerations that the *dictum* by Bruce J in *Jones v Robson* [1901] 1 KB 101, 680 must be judged:

'directions contained in the section about notice are directory only ... the order comes into force when it is made by the Secretary of State'.

The antithesis is between the making of an order (which had clearly been published) and statutory notice, not the making of an order and its publication. The other English case is explicable on similar grounds, though here the statutory requirement of publication was the more general one provided by s2 of the Statutory Instruments Act 1946. The case is *Sheer Metalcraft Ltd* [1954] 1 QB 586. Streatfield J, relying principally on the existence of the special defence in s3(2), distinguished between the making of a statutory instrument on the one hand and its issue to the Stationery Office for printing on the other: 'the making of an instrument is complete when it is first of all made by the minister concerned and after it has been laid before Parliament' [at 590]. In itself that is a harmless enough proposition and is certainly in line with cases like *Jones v Robson*. It by no means follows, however, that if an instrument is made and not published at all, or published only in part, a person will be guilty of an offence by unwitting contravention of the unpublished provision. Assuming the instrument does not state when it is to come into force, the potential defendant would in these circumstances have a defence under the rule in *Johnson v Sargant* [1918] 1 KB 101. The availability of the statutory defence under s3(2) of the 1946 Act may mask the common law defence of lack of publication but it does not invalidate that defence. This becomes important in those cases where the statutory defence does not apply.

All that has been contended so far is that a piece of delegated legislation which does not itself state a commencement date comes into effect on the date of publication, not that on which it was made. Both Wade [*Administrative Law*, 3rd edn, p335] and Halsbury [*Laws of England*, 3rd edn, vol 36, p494] treat *Johnson v Sargant* as authority for this somewhat limited proposition. It is suggested, however, that the case is authority for a more robust constitutional principle: that a piece of delegated legislation which states that it is to come into effect on a certain date but which is not published until a later date does not come into force until it is published. This interpretation appears to be accepted by Keir and Lawson [*Cases in Constitutional Law*, 5th edn, p38] and Griffith and Street [*Principles of Administrative Law*, 5th edn, p105] and it is supported by two Commonwealth cases, *Ross* (British Columbia) [1945] 1 WWR 590. See also *Minister of Mines v Harney* [1901] AC 347 (PC) (minister's decision to forfeit a lease not effective unless notified to lessee). Prerogative legislation by proclamation could not generally come into effect until published: *Chitty on Prerogative*, p106 and *Harla v State of Rajasthan* (India) AIR (1951) SC 467. In *Ross* an order prohibited hunting from 8 September. There was no evidence that the order had been published at all. It was held that the defendant who went hunting from 8–10 September could not be convicted. In the *Harla* case Bose J said [AIR (1951) SC 467, 468]: ' Natural justice requires that before a law can become operative it must be promulgated or published.'

The foundation for the presumption suggested above is the same as that for the presumption against retrospective legislation: that Parliament does not intend what is unjust [Maxwell, *Interpretation of Statutes*, 12th edn, p215]. There is no distinction in substance between a measure made and published on 10 January which states that it came into force on the preceding 1 January and a measure made on 1 January stating that it is to come into operation on that day but not published until 10 January. From the point of view of a person trying to discover his legal rights and duties on 9 January both kinds of legislation are equally obnoxious. Parliament can, of course, legislate retrospectively and can confer a power on its delegates to do so [Allen, *Law and Orders*, 3rd edn, p205]. But where

Parliament has not expressly or by necessary implication given its delegate power to legislate retrospectively, the presumption must surely be that Parliament did not confer such a power. In the words of Somervell LJ [sitting as an additional judge of the KBD in *Master Ladies Tailors' Organisation v Minister of Labour and National Service* [1950] 2 All ER 525, 528]. 'It has of course been laid down in the clearest possible terms that no statute or order is to be construed as having a retrospective operation unless such a construction appears very clearly or by necessary implication in the Act.'

Notes

1   Lanham argues that the *Sheer Metalcraft* decision is only authority for the proposition that an instrument is complete from the moment that it is made and laid, and does not show that persons can be convicted under legislation which has never been published (p512). However, this seems to ignore the simple fact that whatever Streatfield J said or did not say, the defendants in that case were convicted under an unpublished instrument (the statutory defence failed because the Crown had taken steps to bring the instrument to the attention of the defendants (p591)).

2   Later in his article Lanham offers an alternative view on the relationship between the common law and statutory defences. While Streatfield J considered the fact that it was thought necessary to include the statutory defence proof that there was no pre-existing defence of non-publication at common law, Lanham considers that the statutory defence was merely a – partial – declaration of the existing law, inserted during the passage of the SIA to allay the fears of MPs who had heard 'reports that magistrates courts were fining persons for offences against unpublished delegated legislation'. Parliament was therefore merely 'spell[ing] out the true position' (p523). The trouble with this argument is that if one accepts Lanham's premise that unpublished instruments are invalid at common law, the defence would, far from confirming the common law rule, have actually emasculated it by allowing the Crown to enforce liability under unpublished instrument if they had taken reasonable steps to publicise it in other ways. Lanham may have a reply to this: he states that where no definition of 'publication' is given, it may be taken to mean 'taking such steps as are reasonable ... to draw the citizen's attention to the legislation'. If this tentative definition is correct, then the statute would indeed have merely declared, and not emasculated the common law defence. However, Lanham concedes that his definition of 'publication' is offered 'in the absence of authority'[46] – it cannot therefore be confidently relied upon.

3   Dr Campbell is unconvinced by Lanham's argument. Citing *Jones v Robson*, and *Sheer Metalcraft*, in opposition to it, he then goes on to consider other evidence.

AIL Campbell, 'Publication of Delegated Legislation' (1982) *Public Law* 569, 570

In *Lim Chin Aik v R* [1963] 1 All ER 223 there was an argument that an order once made became part of the law of Singapore and ignorance of the law was no

---

46   All references are to p516.

excuse on a charge of contravention of the order. The Privy Council thought that, even if the making of the order was a legislative function, the maxim 'ignorance of the law is no excuse' was not applicable under Singapore law where there were no provisions in Singapore law for some kind of publication or other provision designed to enable a man to find out what law is, but they did not say that there was no validity to the order, and having made the point that the maxim was not applicable, still considered whether the order had been transgressed.

The Statutory Instruments Act 1946 also implies that instruments have validity without publication. The 1946 Act dropped the requirement of publicity before a rule came into operation, which indicates that, overall, publicity was not regarded as being needed for the validity of an instrument. Similarly, laying was not regarded as essential for validity [HC Deb, vol 417, cols 1103–1105; vol 417, col 1172 (1945–46)]. It provided for the publication of instruments after they are 'made', for the annulment of instruments laid before Parliament, before printing and issue, which implies that they are valid before printing and issue, and a defence in the case of non-issue of an instrument, which implies that it is valid and in operation [see ss2, 3 and 5].

It seems, therefore, that regulations do not require publication for their validity. But it has been argued that the common law rule was that publication was required, and that s3(2) of the 1946 Act, providing a defence if an instrument has not been issued, is declamatory of such a rule. There is one case which is cited for this argument, *Johnson v Sargant* [1918] 1 KB 101, where Bailhache J said that, in the absence of authority, he was unable to hold that an order had operation before it was known to a person charged with contravening it [*ibid*, p103]. It is to be noted that this ruling was 'in the absence of authority' and it cannot be regarded as being in itself of much weight, though the result, which no doubt determined the ruling, seemed just. It was subject to criticism and Sir William Graham-Harrison actually said of it: 'I am bound to say that ... the argument for the unsuccessful plaintiff seems to me right and the principle adopted by the judge wrong.' [*ibid*, citing his *Notes on the Delegation by Parliament of Legislative Powers* (1931), p84]. Of course, if Parliament when passing the Statutory Instruments Act 1946 regarded it as the law, one could argue that it was important. But Parliament then apparently regarded the law as uncertain. ... Thus, Brigadier Low said: 'I have been in some doubt, as I believe have all my learned friends on both sides of the House, as to the state of the law at the present time'. [HC Deb, vol 415, col 1136 (1945–46)]. ... Subsequently, when the Solicitor General introduced s3(2) at the report stage, he said that it was provided to remove uncertainty.' ... So, even if *Johnson v Sargant* [1901] 1 KB 101 could be regarded as then representing the common law, which must be doubtful, Parliament was not certain that it did. Furthermore, there was an earlier deliberate decision not to require that an instrument be printed before it be valid. ... When [the Solicitor General] brought in s3(2), he was then concerned with the problem of conviction, but not with validity. A limited defence only was provided and it was limited, possibly, so that emergency instruments could be passed [see HC Deb, vol 417, col 1135 (1945 46)]. A limited defence assumes the validity of an instrument which is not issued. It was earlier suggested, before s3(2) was introduced, that a general rule be adopted that instruments should not come into force until published or on sale [see HC Deb, vol 415, cols 1117, 1123, 1145 (1945–46); HC Deb, vol 417, col 1140 (1945–46)], but that kind of rule was not adopted. As Manningham-Buller said at the report stage: 'This new clause does not affect the coming into operation of the instrument ... The operation may take place before the instrument is issued' [HC Deb, vol 417, col 1134 (1945–46)].

In conclusion, delegated legislation can come into operation without publication There is scholarly authority for the proposition, and, in examination of the case law and statutes in the area, indicates that it is correct. An argument based on the 1946 Act and *Johnson v Sargant* (1901) 1 KB 101 does not properly establish a contrary conclusion. The proposition is also supported in practice. It would seem to be the view of the Joint Committee on Statutory Instruments. Recently, in special report [First Special Report of the Joint Committee on Statutory Instruments (1977–78)], it thought it notable that statutory instruments would become the 'law of the land' without being printed, given a principle that ignorance of the law is no defence to an allegation of a breach of it. The committee's own terms of reference also suggest that the proposition is valid, since the committee is to examine instruments with a view to drawing the attention of the House to an instrument on the ground that there has been unjustifiable delay its publication.

Note

Lanham has replied to this argument[47] citing, *inter alia*, the view of Barwick CJ in an Australian case:

> To bind a citizen by a law, the terms of which he has no means of knowing, would be a mark of tyranny ... [That] the law should operate before it is notified would be so fundamentally unjust that it is an intention I could not attribute to the Parliament unless compelled by intractable language to do so.[48]

It is submitted that this clear argument of principle is to be preferred, given the relative paucity of authority in the area.

THE COMMONS' ROLE IN RELATION TO THE EXECUTIVE

It is an axiom of any theory of responsible government that thorough scrutiny of the executive arm of the state is vital to a democratic system; an important part of this scrutiny is undertaken by Parliament, to which, at least theoretically, all ministers are responsible.[49] As Norton has pointed out, in the House of Commons 'Unlike [in] many legislatures, the Government of the day is obliged to explain its actions continually and open itself to constant criticism. The US President does not face a critical Congress and can even hide away from the press if he so chooses. The British Prime Minister, however, has to face the Leader of the Opposition twice a week over the despatch box.'[50]

---

47 (1983) PL 395.

48 *Watson v Lee* (1979) 144 CLR 374, 379.

49 It should be noted that changes in the organisation of the civil service, the 'Next Steps' initiative, and the rise in the number of Government services carried out by semi-autonomous agencies, has raised serious questions as to the extent to which Ministers in charge of the relevant departments can still be held accountable to Parliament. This issue is discussed in the chapter on the executive (Part IV, Chapter 2).

50 Norton, 'Parliament I: The House of Commons' in Jones (ed), *Politics UK*, 2nd edn (1994), p319.

Scrutiny on the floor of the Commons

As Michael Ryle points out, the opportunities for scrutiny in the Commons have increased markedly over the last 50 years.

Michael Ryle, 'The Changing Commons' (1994) *Parliamentary Affairs* 647, 658–9

In addition to their Opposition days, the official Opposition choose the subject for debate on all but the first of the five or six days debate on the Queen's speech at the beginning of each session. They have debates – in practice, less than one a session – on motions of censure. They can have debates on 'prayers' to annul statutory instruments on the floor of the House or in standing committees. They can apply for emergency debates (in recent years the Speaker has only allowed one or two such debates each session). Scottish and Welsh matters of the Opposition's choosing have, since 1957, been debated in the Scottish and Welsh Grand Committees. Opposition front bench spokesmen are asking an increasing number of private notice questions on urgent matters. And Prime Minister's Question Time is used increasingly by Leaders of the Opposition to give a public airing, at prime time for media attention, to matters of their choosing. In a wide range of ways, the opportunities for the Opposition to set the agenda have increased to some extent over the past 50 years.

Opportunities for back-benchers have expanded considerably more. Time for private members' bills and motions has been increased. Back-bench Members choose which European documents to debate. They can raise any matter for which ministers are responsible on numerous adjournment motions. They choose the subjects for estimate days. Back-benchers also bring in many more bills under the '10 minute rule', which permits a short speech at prime media time, than they did in the 1940s and 50s. Back-benchers also have many opportunities to raise matters without debate. Aided by their research assistants, Members have made fuller use of questions for written answer to obtain information and to press ministers for action, and the back pages of *Hansard* are a mine of information on an amazingly wide range of matters; that was not the case 40 or 50 years ago.

The conduct of Question Time itself has changed markedly. Far fewer questions are reached for oral answer: some 45–50 a day in the 1940s and 1950s; about 15 a day today. Oral questions have become broader and more political and Speakers have been willing to allow more supplementaries; today they are really opportunities for Members on both sides to make political points rather than to seek for information as originally conceived. There has also been the development of the syndication of questions, whereby Members – inspired, it may be thought, by their Whips – put down very similar questions on arranged topics in the attempt to get as many questions favourable to ministers, or hostile (as the case may be), high on the list and likely to be called.

Another development has been the adoption, since about 1977, of 'open' questions to the Prime Minister which enable Members to raise whatever matters they wish. Again, the tabling is often syndicated. Prime Ministers Question Time is covered live on television and Members – particularly the Leader of the Opposition – regularly seek to highlight current political issues of their choosing and hope to get coverage on the evening television news programmes. This is a far cry from the intimate, sometimes searching, sometimes lightly teasing, exchanges between Attlee and Churchill in the years after the war; quite often in those days there would be no questions to the Prime Minister (they only came up after 44 questions to other ministers) or there would be no supplementaries.

Other expanding opportunities for back-benchers include almost daily applications for emergency debates when a matter which a Member considers urgent may be given publicity, occasional private notice questions, and the right to table early day motions; little used until the mid-1960s, today up to 2,000 such motions are tabled each session. The Speaker tries to call as many Members as possible – certainly more than in the years up to 1983 – to speak in debates and to ask supplementary questions on ministerial statements. There has been one restriction of back-benchers' rights, however; because more and more Members want to speak in some important debates, it became necessary in 1984 to give the Speaker power to impose 10 minute limits on speeches for part of some debates.

Notes

1   Whilst the floor of the House now has increased potential as a forum for scrutiny of the executive, it is here that scrutiny can still sometimes be at its most ineffective. At the end of each day half an hour is set aside for adjournment debates. This provides opportunities for back-benchers to make extended criticisms of Government policy. Unfortunately, the House tends to be almost empty at this time, and very little publicity is afforded to these debates, which consequently lose much of their sting. Standing Order 20 in respect of emergency debates allows a further opportunity to raise urgent issues on the floor of the House, but requests for such debates are rarely granted. Similarly, Early Day Motions allow for cross-party expressions of concern or criticism of Government policy, but as the Commons Factsheet no 30 notes '... in the vast majority of cases there is no prospect of these motions ever being debated'.

2   Far more publicity is given to the questioning of ministers on the floor of the House; 45–50 minutes are set aside every day, except Friday, for oral answers to be given to Members' questions. Over 70,000 such questions were put down by MPs in the 1987–88 session, and the occasion is now often afforded live television coverage. Oral questions and their supplementaries tend to be used as an opportunity to probe ministers' grasp of their portfolios or attack Government policy. They thus have some effect in ensuring that ministers are kept up to the mark; they provide an opportunity for weak elements in Government policy to be publicly exposed, and are one of the few times in which ordinary back-benchers can raise matters directly with Cabinet ministers.

3   The ability of Members to put down really probing questions is reduced by the lack of information and support staff available to back-benchers. Ministers, by contrast, have the aid of a skilled team of civil servants who provide them with answers to the tabled questions and undertake research into the questioner's known interests and concerns in an attempt to anticipate and prepare the minister for possible supplementaries. (The cost of this preparation in officials' time amounts to an average of £75 per oral answer). This inequality has led some observers to call for the establishment of a Department of the Opposition to improve the efficiency of Opposition MPs by giving them a staff of civil servants which would go some way to redressing the imbalance between ministers and MPs. Needless to say, no such department has yet been created. However, various disadvantages might result from such a reform. Douglas Wass, in a lecture proposing a Department of the Opposition conceded that there were fears that the

department might inhibit the emergence of new parties, and that the department's civil servants might 'capture the minds' of the Opposition front bench, encouraging a drift to the middle ground commonly presumed to be favoured by the Civil Service.[51]

4   This is perhaps one area in which television coverage has, whilst being helpful in terms of publicity, perhaps given a misleading impression. The kinds of 'Commons clash' at Prime Minister's Question Time (PMQT) between the Leader of the Opposition and the Prime Minister which routinely gains television coverage may give the impression that ritual baiting, party point scoring, and above all, a complete lack of information transmission are the outstanding characteristics of Question Time. What needs to be borne in mind is that PMQT is by far the most politicised of all oral questioning of ministers. A more comprehensive examination of Prime Minister's Questions reveals that, whilst oral questions are often put and dealt with on a purely party political basis, they can yield useful results in terms of scrutiny as well. Information can be gained; useful concessions or statements of intent to which the Government can later be held are extracted; inadequacies in Government thinking are exposed. The following sample reveals both 'political' and 'scrutinising' questioning at work.

HC Deb 7 November 1995, col 726; 2 April 1996, cols 147–9; 8 February 1996 cols 466–7; 19 February 1996, col 4; 2 April 1996, cols 137, 144, 145

7 November 1995

Mr Prescott: [Following the Government's defeat on the Nolan report][52] Does the right hon gentleman accept that he and the Prime Minister were completely out of step with public opinion in wanting to keep the outside earnings of Members of Parliament secret? Does he share my sense of outrage that some Conservative Members are already making it clear that they will not observe the decision of the House? Will he make it clear that that would be totally unacceptable to him and the Prime Minister?

The Deputy Prime Minister: The right hon gentleman raises a most important question for the House. I can say unreservedly on behalf of the Prime Minister and myself, since he asked me specifically, that both of us believe that it is right for all right hon and hon Members to enter into the spirit of the letter of the decisions taken yesterday evening. That was the will of the House. As to what the House should determine to do in the event of any right hon and hon Member not making such a decision, that is properly a matter for the House of Commons.

2 April 1996

Mr Blair: Does the Prime Minister recall, in the days when he was flatly against a referendum on Europe, saying that referendums were introduced only to cover up divisions in the Cabinet and none such existed in his Cabinet? Are not those divisions precisely the reason why he is in favour of a referendum today?

The Prime Minister: I am surprised that the right hon gentleman should say that when he has just announced a referendum to sort out internal difficulties in his party about his policy. I have said that I will contemplate a referendum on a

---

51   Quoted in Turpin, *British Government and the Constitution*, 3rd edn (1993), p451.

52   For the Nolan report and the debate see Part III, Chapter 3, pp454–76.

particular issue of policy that has never occurred before. The right hon gentleman intends to ballot all his party members about Labour policy – which is a novel proposition: I am not entirely sure how one can ballot people about something that does not exist.

Mr Blair: I suspect that I shall have rather more support for my referendum than the Cabinet will give the right hon gentleman's. Why cannot the Prime Minister answer now the question that he was able to answer a few months ago? Has the Chancellor changed his mind – a nod or a shake of the head will do? We have paralysis in the Government – even the big man of the Cabinet cannot get his way. Is not the decision being taken only because the Government are weak, divided and are being pushed around by their factions? ...

Mr Marlow: While our masters in Brussels are deciding how to dispose of the British beef industry, will my right hon friend suggest to them that, if they are to slaughter perfectly healthy cattle, the beef would be better used as food aid rather than being incinerated? If people were faced with a one in three chance of dying of starvation or a one in 100 million chance of contracting Creutzfeldt-Jakob disease, surely they would eat the beef.

The Prime Minister: As my hon friend intimates, my right hon and learned friend the Minister of Agriculture, Fisheries and Food is in Luxembourg today trying to restore public confidence to the beef markets across Europe. He is making good progress and he will keep negotiating until a package of measures is agreed. It is no longer certain whether that will occur today; there is a long way to go in the negotiations and I anticipate that they will continue for many hours yet.

Mr Ashdown: Does the Prime Minister realise that, as we speak, jobs are being lost and small farms and small firms are going to the wall because of delay and indecision on BSE? Does he acknowledge that he could take some steps without waiting for Brussels? I shall suggest three: first, launch a British standard for quality British beef; secondly, launch a public information campaign to correct misrepresentation and misinformation, which is still widespread and damaging; and, thirdly, get together with the banks and put together a credit guarantee scheme to help small firms and farmers until compensation arrives. I beg the Prime Minister to act now, when he can, rather than stand there wringing his hands and waiting for Brussels to open the door.

The Prime Minister: The right hon gentleman's last sentence beggars belief, given his party's policy on the European Union, but I agree with him about the need to do whatever we can to help the beef industry. Nine or 10 measures have been taken already; a number are currently under consideration and more are under discussion in Brussels. The Agriculture Council is considering and discussing the possibility of extending the scope of intervention to deal with short-term confidence problems. That would clearly be of great benefit to many British farmers. We are also considering a package of measures to deal with BSE. We are discussing its funding and a number of other confidence-building measures for the market. The right hon gentleman knows that, although there are certain things that we can do in Britain, the fundamental decision needs to be a cross-European one, as he himself told the House the other day.

8 February 1996

Mr Blair: Does the Prime Minister agree that the Scott Inquiry was entirely fairly conducted and that no criticism can or should be made of its processes or procedures?

The Prime Minister: As I said in the House on previous occasions: 'I asked Sir Richard to carry out the report and I have every confidence that he will do so', and has done so, 'thoroughly'.

Mr Blair: I must press the Prime Minister on this because he will know that, in the past few days, there has been a concerted attempt to rubbish the inquiry. Will he say unequivocally that he accepts that it was entirely fairly conducted?

The Prime Minister: I just said to the right hon gentleman: 'I asked Sir Richard to carry out the report and I have every confidence that he will do so', and has done so, 'thoroughly'. The right hon gentleman is saying that neither he nor anybody else can comment fairly on the Scott report until people have had the opportunity to study it. I agree with that point, but it also applies to the past three years. It applies to the fact that the Opposition have made constant and blatant smears throughout those past three years without having had the evidence of the Scott report before them. If, in his question, the right hon gentleman was making it clear that he believes that those were unjustified attacks without any evidence, I would be pleased for him to withdraw them now and make it clear that he will repudiate them.

Mr Blair: The Prime Minister is not even prepared to say whether the report is fairly conducted. When he says that we should await the findings of the report, let me remind him that he and his ministers will have had the report for eight days, that four Government departments have units working on it and that we are to get it a few hours before publication. I am not asking him to comment on its findings, but on whether it was fairly conducted. He set up the inquiry. He chose Sir Richard Scott. Is he now prepared to state that he is confident that it was fairly conducted? If he does not say that, the final vestiges of respect will be removed from the Government.

The Prime Minister: I know that the right hon gentleman had carefully prepared his third sound-bite before my first answer, and I am tempted to refer him to the two answers I have just given. I made it clear that: 'I asked Sir Richard to carry out the report and I have confidence that he will do so', and has done so, 'thoroughly' [official report, 6 June 1995; vol 261, c 15]. I have now said that three times. Will the right hon gentleman now stop preparing his sound-bites in advance and listen to my answers before he prepares his questions?

Mr Illsley: To ask the Prime Minister if he will list his official engagements for Thursday 8 February [12662].

The Prime Minister: I refer the hon gentleman to the answer I gave some moments ago.

Mr Illsley: Why cannot the Prime Minister publish such an important document as the report of the Scott Inquiry a few days before the statement on it next week so that the Opposition, and indeed the House, can be properly informed? Is not it disgraceful that a few Conservative Members will have had that report for eight days, but the rest of the House will receive it on the day of the statement?

The Prime Minister: We plan to follow the precedents for a weighty report of this nature, and to permit Opposition spokesmen to see the report several hours before the statement is made. Of course, the House will also wish to study and comment on the report. That is why we propose to find time in Government time for an early debate on the report a few days after the statement has been made, once the whole House has had the opportunity to study the report and comment on it on the basis of detail, not of innuendo and smear, which has been the nature of the comments thus far from a number of Opposition Members.

19 February 1996

Mr Jon Owen Jones: To ask the Secretary of State for Wales what assessment his department has made of the effect a single European currency will have on the Welsh economy [14158].

Mr Hague: None.

2 April 1996

Mr Gapes: To ask the Secretary of State for Defence if he will make a statement on plans for the phased withdrawal of British troops from IFOR, and if Her Majesty's Government plan to keep any British forces in former Yugoslavia after 31 December [22310].

The Secretary of State for Defence (Mr Michael Portillo): Under the terms of the Dayton peace agreement, and UN Security Council resolution 1031, IFOR's mandate expires at the end of the year. The British contingent to IFOR will withdraw along with other IFOR forces. Planning the withdrawal is a matter for NATO - the UK is participating fully in this process.

Mr Gapes: I am grateful to the Secretary of State for clarifying that. Can he assure us that, this time next year, British forces in former Yugoslavia will not be trying to hold the ring in a possible three-way conflict in a resumed civil war while the US has cut and run, and pulled out to arm one side in that conflict?

Mr Portillo: I have said repeatedly that Nato has deployed together, is working together and will withdraw together. The hon gentleman has advocated the withdrawal of British troops for a long time. I well understand his reasons, but I believe that the performance of British forces in Bosnia under the UN and Nato has done a great deal to save lives and has brought enormous credit to our forces. ...

Mr Touhig: To ask the Secretary of State for Defence what is his department's estimate of the number of anti-personnel land mines in Bosnia [22317].

Mr Soames: IFOR estimates that up to 5 million land mines, including anti-personnel mines, may have been laid in Bosnia.

Mrs Mahon: Is it not obscene to carry on supporting the manufacture of land mines when the Overseas Development Administration spends millions of pounds on land mine clearance and in helping amputees? Do the minister and the Government feel any shame whatsoever when they see the limbless victims of this dreadful policy?

Mr Soames: The hon lady almost certainly is not aware that anti-personnel mines have not been exported from this country for many years. The UK, like many other countries, considers mines, including anti-personnel mines, to be legitimate defence weapons when used responsibly and in accordance with the laws of war. Our armed forces have and need these weapons – without them, they would be less effective.

Notes

1   It can be seen that the Deputy Prime Minister's reply to Mr Prescott contains a potentially useful assurance: if Government later shows a lack of zeal in supporting action against Conservative Members who fail to abide by the new disclosure rules, this view can be quoted against them. The exchange between Mr Blair and the PM is classic party political stuff; the PM's reply to Mr Ashdown re BSB reveals something of Government policy; the exchange over the Scott report with Mr Blair revealed Mr Major's unwillingness to give whole-hearted support to Scott's findings, while his reply to Mr Illsley

made apparent the relative weakness of the Government's argument justifying the lack of advance disclosure of the Scott report to the Opposition. The remainder of the questions are valuable in informational terms, and also in providing public assurances, against which Government action could later be tested.

2   As a method of obtaining information, questions requesting written answers are likely to be more effective.

HC Deb WA 4 July 1994

Lord Chancellor's Department

Recycled paper

Mr Ron Davies: To ask the Attorney-General what percentage of the Law Officers' Departments' (a) press releases and (b) written answers are printed on recycled paper.

The Attorney-General: Nil.

Foreign Affairs Council

Mr Bates: To ask the Secretary of State for Foreign and Commonwealth Affairs if he will make a statement on the outcome of the Foreign Affairs Council in Brussels on 18 and 19 July.

Mr Hurd: I attended the Council.

There was an open debate on the German presidency's programme. My intervention centred on the EU's relations with central and eastern Europe and making common foreign and security policy more effective.

The presidency and Commission briefed Member States on follow-up to the White Paper.

The Council discussed the establishment of the Consultative Commission on racism and xenophobia, as agreed at the Corfu European Council. The UK will nominate its representatives by the end of July. The chairman of the consultative commission will be decided when all UK members have been appointed.

The Council discussed a Commission paper on relations between the European Union and the countries of central and eastern Europe.

Ministers approved a declaration urging the parties to accept the contact group plan for a negotiated settlement in Bosnia. The presidency reported on plans to inaugurate the EU administration of Mostar on 25 July. Ministers also discussed the situation in the Croatian Krajina and the former Yugoslav republic of Macedonia.

The Council had a general discussion on a number of issues likely to be discussed with the European Parliament in the autumn.

The President of the Commission reported to the Council on the EU-Canada summit in Bonn on 6 July, and the EU-US summit in Berlin on 12 July.

The Council also discussed the outcome of the G7 summit in Naples.

On the Mediterranean, the Commission briefed ministers on the state of negotiations with Morocco, Tunisia and Israel on new partnership agreements. While those with Tunisia and Israel were making good progress, important differences with Morocco remained to be resolved. The Council agreed conclusions reaffirming the need to deepen EU-Mediterranean relations. ...

The Council agreed by qualified majority vote – with Spain, Portugal and Greece voting against – to an increase of just under 30% in the quota for imports from

China of stuffed toys, customs classification 9503 41, for the period March to December 1994. Proposals for similar increases in the quotas for non-stuffed toys representing animals or non-human creatures, 9503 49, and certain miscellaneous toys, 9503 90, were not agreed – Spain, Portugal, Greece and France voting against. The latter two proposals are to be considered further by COREPER.

The Commission reported on the progress of work on proposals to establish a common regime for the use of OPT — outward processing in the textile sector. It was agreed that, due to delays in agreeing the overall regime, the Commission would prepare a separate proposal to establish duty exemption for OPT conducted with the countries of central and eastern Europe.

The Council took note of a number *of* measures which will be introduced with the aim of improving the effectiveness of procedures in the common foreign and security policy inter-governmental pillar.

Free trade agreements were signed with Estonia, Latvia and Lithuania.

The Council agreed the conditions for the release of a 35m ECU balance of payments grant for Albania.

The Council agreed in principle to provide food aid to Armenia, Azerbaijan, Georgia, Kyrgyzstan and Tajikistan.

The Commission reported to the Council on the outcome of the OECD negotiations for an international shipbuilding agreement, which ended on 17 July. France indicated its opposition to the conclusion of the agreement in its present form and requested the Commission to continue negotiations. The Council will return to this issue at its meeting on 4 October.

HC Debs WA 19 February 1996, cols 10, 22, 41, 46; 1 April 1996, col 68; 2 April 1996, col 91

19 February 1996

Mortgages

Mr Frank Field: To ask the Secretary of State for Education and Employment how many heads of household below retirement age and available for work have mortgages [14300].

Mr Clappison: I have been asked to reply. The latest estimate for England is that 7,540,000 heads of household who are below retirement age, and were either in employment or seeking and available for work, have mortgages. This estimate is from the 1994–95 Survey of English Housing and is subject to sampling error.

Mr Lloyd: To ask the Secretary of State for Foreign and Commonwealth Affairs what assistance is currently provided by Her Majesty's Government to west African countries bordering Nigeria [15566].

Mr Hanley: Cameroon benefits from a bilateral aid programme, focused on conservation of forestry and bio-diversity and totalling some £2.3 million in 1995–96. Niger, Chad, and Benin also receive UK aid, most notably through the joint funding scheme – £0.41 million in 1994–95. The UK provides substantial assistance to all four countries through its contributions to multilateral aid, particularly EU aid, of which our share in 1994 was about £22 million.

Empty buildings

Dr Lynne Jones: To ask the Secretary of State for Education and Employment how many empty buildings her department currently owns; what is the cost of insuring and securing these buildings; how many were designed as residential properties; and what was the total amount spent by her department on empty property taxes in each of the last five years [14571].

Mr Robin Squire: The Department for Education and Employment and the Employment Service together currently own 26 freehold properties which are empty.

One property includes a hostel block for use by trainees and four terraced houses for the use of hostel supervisors.

Following general Government practice, the department and the ES bear the cost of their own property insurance.

The department and the ES together also hold 135 leasehold properties which are empty. None is designed for residential use.

In many leaseholds buildings, the landlord insures the building and recovers the cost through the overall service charge; it is not possible to disaggregate this charge without disproportionate time and cost.

The cost of security for empty buildings is also included In maintenance costs and it is therefore not possible to identify the separate total for security costs.

The department's contribution in lieu of rates on vacant properties for the current year ending March 1996 will be £170,900. The ES's CILOR on vacant properties in the year ended 31 March 1995 was £680,000. CILOR figures for previous years are included in overall running cost figures and cannot be separated out without disproportionate costs.

Mr Tipping: To ask the President of the Board of Trade:

(1) what assessment he has made of the research undertaken by Professor Denis Henshaw, a copy of which has been sent to him, on child leukaemia and electromagnetic fields; and if he will make a statement [15632];

(2) what research he has (a) commissioned and (b) evaluated into the link between electromagnetic fields and child leukaemia; if he will place copies of that research into the Library; and if he will make a statement [15631].

Mr Page [holding answer 16 February 1996]: My right hon friend the President of the Board of Trade receives advice from the National Radiological Protection Board on the issue of electromagnetic fields and any effects on human health, including the possibility of a link with childhood leukaemia.

Both the NRPB and other independent bodies conduct research into possible causes of leukaemia and other cancers, supported by funding from Government. An important five year study into possible causes of childhood leukaemia is at present being conducted by the UK Co-ordinating Committee on Cancer Research, due to be completed in about two years time. The Government are funding this research together with various bodies and when complete, it will be evaluated by NRPB and its advisory group on non-ionising radiation and the findings will be published.

NRPB acknowledges the link between radon deposition and electromagnetic fields but advise that the theory in recently published research, suggesting an increased risk of cancer due to the effects of fields on radon and its decay products, is speculative. There is still no convincing evidence that electromagnetic fields from power lines or domestic appliances are harmful to health and no biological mechanism has been established to change this view.

1 April 1996

Mr John D Taylor: To ask the Secretary of State for Northern Ireland how many people in Northern Ireland have contracted Creutzfeldt-Jakob disease in each of the past five years; and how many have died [22938].

Mr Moss: There have been three cases, all fatal, resulting in one death in each of the years 1992, 1993 and 1995.

2 April 1996

Mr Meale: To ask the Secretary of State for Foreign and Commonwealth Affairs if a meeting between the Chair of the Government Communications Staff Federation and civil service unions is permitted under the conditions laid down in GCHQ general notice – GN 100/84 [24395].

Mr Rifkind: GCHQ general notice GN 100/84 was superseded on 20 December 1995 by another notice, PCN 12/9S, which, in accordance with my written reply to the hon Member for Gravesham (Mr Arnold) on that day, *Official Report*, columns 1191–92, relaxed the restrictions on trade union membership at GCHQ while still upholding the Government's concerns regarding the protection of national security. Like GN 100/84, PCN 12/95 places no constraints on a meeting between the Chairman of the Government Communications Staff Federation and the Civil Service unions.

Notes

1   It can be seen that, in replying to written questions, particularly in sensitive areas like negotiations and decisions made in the Council of Ministers (Mr Hurd's reply), the answer can be couched in very general – therefore quite uninformative – terms, eg 'The Council discussed a Commission paper on relations between the European Union and the countries of eastern and central Europe'; 'the Council also discussed the outcome of the G7 summit …'. The fact that the minister can determine the level of detail disclosed, and cannot immediately be challenged on this, is obviously one major drawback in asking a question in writing. However, in other areas, it can be seen that very detailed and precise information is obtainable, making full use of the Government's formidable resources.

2   Ministers cannot in practice be compelled to answer any question: as Tomkin notes,[53] 'An answer to a question cannot be insisted upon if the answer is refused by a minister; the Speaker has refused to allow supplementary questions in these circumstances'. A list of some of the topics on which successive Governments have refused to answer questions appears below.

Appendix 9 to the Report from the Select Committee on Parliamentary Questions, HC 393 (1971–72)

(6) Refusal to answer

Attorney-General

Details of investigations by the Director of Public Prosecutions; Day to day administration of the Legal Aid Scheme; …

Defence

Details of arms sales; Operational matters; Contract prices; Costs of individual aircraft, etc; Details of research and development; Numbers of foreign forces training in the UK; Accident rates for aircraft.

Exchequer

Economic and budgetary forecasts; Exchange Equalisation Account; Government borrowing; Sterling balances; Tax affairs of individuals or companies; Day to day matters of the Bank of England.

---

53   'A Right to Mislead Parliament?' (1996) 16(1) LS 63, 81.

Home

Telephone tapping; Names of prohibited immigrants; Regional seats of government; Security service operations; Operational matters of the police.

Prime Minister

Telephone tapping; Cabinet Committees; Cost of the 'hot line'; Security arrangements at Chequers; Detailed arrangements for the conduct of Government business; List of future engagements; ...

Notes

1   In addition a minister may refuse to answer any question which would be likely to cost more than a certain amount (currently £450) to research. Nevertheless, despite these restrictions, MPs seem broadly satisfied with PQs as a method of obtaining information on government; Tomkin (*op cit*, p32) notes a study carried out in 1989 in which 72% of MPs said they were useful in this respect and 97% said written answers were useful in obtaining information that might be hard to obtain elsewhere.

2   Following the publication of the Scott report, with its findings that ministers had given a series of misleading answers to MPs on the question of the sale of defence-related equipment to Iraq, the Government promised a review of policy on refusal to answer questions in particular areas. The assurance was given in the debate on the Scott report; see HC Deb 26 February 1996, col 592. See further, Part IV, Chapter 2, pp590–92, 595.

3   Ministers' questions may have a more hidden but arguably very important result, as postulated by Sir Norman Chester.[54] He points out that many decisions in a department will be taken at a low level without the minister's actual accord or knowledge. The tabling of a question which queries this decision and the subsequent investigation by the minister and senior members of the department will bring the decision to the minister's attention. The minister will then either have to justify it, which will bring the decision to public attention, or modify departmental policy if it becomes apparent that it is evolving in a manner which was not originally intended. However, as mentioned above, for such questions to have this effect, back-benchers must have the means of gaining information about the day-to-day running of departments.

4   One further and rather important issue relating to parliamentary questions is the question mark over their truth and comprehensiveness. As the Scott report has revealed, it appears that ministers repeatedly at the very least answered questions in a way which they knew gave a misleading impression in answering questions on whether arms-related equipment was in fact being exported to Iraq, in breach of the Government's own guidelines and whether those guidelines had changed.

Richard Norton Taylor, *Truth is a Difficult Concept: Inside the Scott Inquiry* (1995), pp84–5

Confronted by tenacious questioning ... Civil Service witnesses to the inquiry admitted that ministers' replies to parliamentary questions were misleading,

---

54   'Questions in the House' (quoted in Walklands and Ryle *op cit*, pp188–9).

inaccurate, or simply wrong. Officials admitted that answers they drafted were misleading. They also blamed other officials for drafting misleading minutes. The FO's William Patey, for example, said the DTI's Tony Steadman's argument in a letter to the MoD's Alan Barrett that Matrix Churchill machine tools were 'not necessarily' going to be used by the Iraqis to make weapons was 'not accurate'. Patey said Barrett's advice to Lord Trefgarne that Whitehall officials were satisfied that the exports were for 'general industrial use' was 'clearly wrong'.

Ministers gave MPs a string of misleading answers:

On 20 April 1989, four months after the guidelines had been secretly relaxed, Alan Clark told MPs, 'Applications for such licences are examined against the guidelines on the export of defence equipment set out by the Foreign Secretary, Sir Geoffrey Howe, in 1985'.

On 3 May 1989, Waldegrave told the Labour MP, Nigel Griffiths, 'The Government has not changed their policy on defence sales to Iraq or Iran. These are governed by strict guidelines ...'

On 14 December 1989, six months after Whitehall officials warned that British equipment was helping to build up Iraq's arms industry, Lord Trefgarne told his fellow peers, 'We do not sell arms to Iraq ... The sale of such items to Iraq and Iran is subject to very close guidelines'.

On 1 July 1991, Archie Hamilton, Armed Forces Minister, told MPs, 'There were certainly no arms sales to Iraq from British firms. That is what I have always said and I confirm it absolutely'.

In answer to a question by the Labour MP, Ann Clwyd, on 14 March 1989, Eric Forth, Junior DTI Minister, referred her to an answer given by Alan Clark to the Tory MP, Teddy Taylor two months previous. Clark had told Taylor, 'The guidelines are being kept under constant review in the light of the cease-fire and developments in the peace negotiations'.

Tony Steadman, head of the DTI's Export Licensing Unit who advised Clark that publicity would make it 'more difficult' for machine tool companies seeking approval for exports to Iraq, admitted the answer was misleading. It made no mention of the Government's secret policy shift the previous December. Asked by Baxendale whether a full answer might have provoked criticism and a debate in Parliament, Steadman replied, 'I agreed we should have gone further.'

On 20 April 1989, Clark told the Labour MP, Chris Mullin, that the Government was still applying the 1985 guidelines. 'Licence applications', added Clark, 'are considered on a case-by-case basis, in accordance with stringent export control procedures which include, in particular, an assessment of the human rights record of the country concerned'.

'That's just wrong, isn't it?' asked the QC.

Eric Beston, Steadman's boss, agreed, adding, 'The avoidance of controversy was not an uncommon concern in the presentation of policy – or, in this case, the non-presentation of policy'.

Clark later admitted that Tim Sainsbury, the Trade Minister, misled Parliament on 5 December 1990, when he told MPs the Government had 'scrupulously followed' official guidelines on exports to Iraq. Sainsbury made his inaccurate statement after press reports that Clark had given companies a 'nod and a wink' encouraging them to sell weapons-making machinery to Iraq. Clark said Sainsbury's comment was the result of a departmental 'muddle ... lifting stuff from the word processor'.

Asked by Lord Justice Scott why he did not put the record straight, Mr Clark replied, 'It is not for me to say [to Mr Sainsbury] the whole department is ignorant and you haven't been properly briefed'.

... **Baxendale** asked Gore-Booth [a senior civil servant at the Foreign Office] about questions in Parliament: 'If there is a question, it should be fully answered, should it not? The answer should be sufficiently full to give a true meaning?'

Gore Booth: 'Questions should be answered so as to give the maximum degree of satisfaction possible to the questioner.'

Baxendale: 'I am not sure you really mean that, because that is rather like people just given you the answer you want to hear ... 'I do not think you quite mean that'.

Gore-Booth: 'No, it might be the answer you do not want to hear.'

Baxendale: 'That does not give you much satisfaction. Should the answer be accurate?'

Gore-Booth: 'Of course.'

Baxendale: 'And they should not be half the picture?'

Gore-Booth: 'They might be half the picture. You said, 'Should (they) be accurate?' And I said, 'Yes, they should'.'

Baxendale: 'Do you think that half the picture is accurate?'

Gore-Booth: 'Of course half a picture can be accurate.' ...

Notes

1   Theoretically, of course, proven and intentional misleading of the House would be a resignation matter for a minister.[55] But even if this was accepted as a reliable safeguard, three main concerns remain. The first is the idea that ministers regard replying to questions in sensitive areas as 'more of an art "form" than a means of communication';[56] ie even if they do not tell outright lies, they do not regard the occasion as a straightforward exercise in the giving of information. Secondly, there is the fact that in many areas, even if the House was misled, it would be unlikely that this would ever be known. The fact that misleading replies had been given re Iraq was only clearly established during the examination of witnesses and documents by the Scott Inquiry, which was a wholly exceptional event. Further, the powers of the inquiry were unprecedented; it could compel the attendance of witnesses, obtain sensitive documents and conduct thorough and expert cross-examination.[57]

2   The Clive Ponting episode in 1985 illustrates the same point. Mr Ponting, a civil servant, resigned because he considered that ministers had repeatedly misled the House over the sinking of the cruiser the *General Belgrano* during the Falklands conflict; he then gave to the press what he considered to be the true version of events. He was prosecuted under the Official Secrets Act and

---

55   See generally on this, Part IV, Chapter 2, pp592–97.

56   The view of a senior civil servant, quoted in Norton Taylor, *op cit*, p95. See, for a similar view, Part IV, Chapter 2, p595.

57   The other main way in which deception could be uncovered is by the discovery of documents in court as occurred in the Matrix Churchill case itself. However, the relevant documents were only discovered because the judge took the fairly rare step of refusing to follow the strong recommendation of ministers in their PII certificates that the documents should not be disclosed.

was clearly guilty under the terms of the Act, but despite the clearest possible summing up by the judge, the jury refused to convict.[58] In other words, when Ponting revealed the deception, he was risking near certain criminal sanctions. Not many will be prepared to do this.

3   The third concern is that ministers now apparently regard it as legitimate, even sometimes necessary, to mislead the House. This issue will be dealt with in terms of ministerial responsibility later in this book.[59]

4   Televised reporting of the House of Commons was introduced in 1989. Michael Ryle considers its impact below.

Michael Ryle, 'The Changing Commons'(1994) *Parliamentary Affairs* 647, 660–1

Sound broadcasting of the Commons was approved in 1977, and one of the most significant changes that has ever occurred in the life of the House of Commons was brought about when the televised reporting of the House was launched in 1989. All proceedings in the House are televised although the choice of what is actually broadcast lies with the BBC and other broadcasters. The broadcasters also decide what proceedings in committees they wish to televise, and there is regular coverage, especially on special parliamentary programmes, of the work of Select Committees. On one day recently there were three items relating to Select Committees on the BBC's Nine O'clock News.

The effect of television on the business and proceedings of the House has also been important. Somewhat surprisingly, it has had little impact, now that it is part of normal life, on the way Members speak in debate (though front bench speakers always include some carefully chosen quotable sentences which they hope may make the evening news programmes) or in the way they behave when listening to debates; even the notorious 'doughnuting' (gathering around the Member speaking) appears to have fallen out of fashion. On the whole, Members largely ignore the cameras and behave much as they did before they were brought in.

Collectively, as an institution, the House has, however, been changed by televising. Tactical and procedural jockeying to get the most favourable coverage has become important for all the parties and for some prominent individuals. There is now, for example, keen competition between the parties to get business of their choosing – perhaps a ministerial statement from the Government side or a private notice question or 'point of order' from the Opposition – before the House on Tuesdays, Wednesdays and Thursdays from after questions at 3.30 till 4pm, when the House is covered live on BBC television. And Select Committees like to choose inquiries or hearings that will be of interest to the broadcasters.

More generally, both MPs and the viewing public have become increasingly aware of the bond between them that television has forged. Members are conscious that the electorate is watching and listening to what is going on in Parliament. The viewers are conscious that they are being shown their own Parliament in action, and what it says and does influences their own political judgements – and their votes at the next election.

---

58   See generally, G Marshall, 'Ministers, Civil Servants and open Government' in Harlow (ed) *Public Law and Politics* (1986), pp86–9.

59   See Part IV, Chapter 2, pp592–95.

Notes

1   Norton's view is that 'Television has proved a powerful reinforcement to Parliament's capacity to ensure ministers explain their actions'. Clearly, its most significant effect has been to enhance significantly Parliament's publicising powers.

2   Whilst, in general, questions of ministers, speeches, and debates on policy may have little impact, they may on occasions be decisive. The careers of ministers, even Prime Ministers, can be severely damaged or destroyed during such occasions, whilst the reputation of an administration as a whole may be dented. One example is the famous speech of Norman Lamont, made after his forced resignation, in which he described the Major administration as giving the impression of being 'in office, but not in power'; a similarly wounding attack was made by Sir Geoffrey Howe on Mrs Thatcher in his unexpectedly ferocious resignation speech in November 1990. Conversely, if a minister manages to acquit him or herself with aplomb during a testing debate, his or her stature may be increased. Michael Howard's performance in the debate in October 1995 on his dismissal of the Director of the Prison Service, Derick Lewis (following the publication of the highly critical Learmont report on prisons) was widely regarded as a crucial moment in his career, given that he had been accused of misleading the House. The fact that he was generally regarded to have decisively rebutted the attack on him by Jack Straw, the Shadow Home Secretary in the debate – one verdict was that 'in ... one of the fiercest prize fights of recent years ... Howard wiped the floor with Jack Straw',[60] – apparently greatly increased his standing amongst Conservative MPs and party activists. [61]

3   Interestingly, however, the same episode demonstrates that such Parliamentary clashes apparently have more impact on ministers' standing in the parliamentary party than on the electorate at large; an opinion poll taken after the debate showed that, by a majority of two to one, those questioned thought that Michael Howard should resign;[62] this is not to say of course that Mr Howard may have commanded even less confidence in the country before the debate, merely that his Commons 'victory' may have had far less impact on the public than his colleagues may have thought.

4   The Government is of course generally as sure of winning votes taken after debates on policy as it is of carrying its own legislation. But just as with legislation, who wins the actual votes is not the end of the story. One of the most important policy debates in recent years was occasioned by the publication of the Scott report in February 1996. The main formal debate on Scott was in the form of an adjournment debate,[63] but was effectively one of confidence in the Government's record on the arms-to-Iraq affair and specifically in Sir Nicholas Lyell and William Waldegrave. Two Conservative MPs and all eight Ulster Unionists voted against the

---

60   'Bitter revenge of the uncivil servant', *Sunday Times*, 22 October 1995.
61   See *Sunday Times*, 15 October 1995.
62   NOP opinion poll, *Sunday Times*, 22 October 1995, p2.
63   HC Deb 26 February 1996, cols 589 *et seq.*

Government but it won the division by one vote. It seems therefore that in the final analysis, despite appeals to them by Robin Cook to see the vote as deciding not whether the Government was defeated but one which decided 'the quality of democracy in which we live', Conservative MPs perceived the occasion as ultimately a struggle between parties rather than between executive and back-bencher; as the Conservative Sir Michael Marsh saw it, "this debate has been a straight party political battle".[64]

5   However, quite apart from the narrowness of the result,[65] the outcome cannot be seen simply as a Government victory. The threat of rebellion, of possible defeat, had its impact: the Government made a 'massive last minute effort to secure the support of waverers and dissident MPs';[66] part of which involved a shift in the Government's public stance on Scott. Greater preparedness to admit that mistakes had been made became evident together with increased willingness to promise (albeit in fairly non-committal terms) to review areas of policy and practice criticised by Scott. The following extracts from this debate illustrate both this more emollient stance taken by Government ministers and the pressure they were put under by the preparedness of a few Conservative MPs to speak out against their own Government's record. Mr Lang and Mr Freedman spoke for the Government; all the other speakers quoted are back-bench Conservative MPs.

HC Debs 26 February 1996, cols 589, 592, 597–9, 636, 655–6, 663–4, 668, 684

Mr Lang: The report rightly focused on the serious and defamatory charges that had been made and of which the Government now stand acquitted. But in my statement 10 days ago, I also took care to draw attention to Sir Richard's criticisms, to which I referred repeatedly, and to his conclusions and recommendations on which I should like today to indicate more of the Government's thinking.

To recap on my earlier remarks, mistakes were made. There are lessons to be learnt. The Government have accepted the inquiry's criticisms concerning the distribution of intelligence material, and have already taken action to improve it. We have accepted the criticism about export controls and licensing procedures and have already undertaken to publish a consultation paper on that, as Sir Richard Scott recommends.

We have already undertaken to consider further and very carefully Sir Richard's comments on the use of wartime export control legislation. We accept the principle of the need now for greater supervision by the office of the Attorney-General of Customs and Excise prosecutions in relation to export control matters, and I shall say more on that. We also accept many of his other recommendations.

'Erskine May' sets out a number of subjects on which successive administrations have declined to answer questions on grounds of public policy. At present, those

---

64   *Ibid*, col 678.

65   This was generally emphasised in the broadsheet newspapers (which were broadly hostile to the Government on the issue). See for example 'Major scrapes in by a single vote' *Independent*, 27 February 1996.

66   *Ibid*.

include discussions between ministers, or between ministers and their official advisers; the proceedings of Cabinet, or its Committees; security matters; operational defence matters; and details of arms sales to particular countries.

Here I come to the particular point that Sir Richard Scott has raised in relation to parliamentary questions on the sale of arms or defence-related equipment. He said that the long-standing practice should be re-examined. The Government are content to do this and my right hon friend the Chancellor of the Duchy of Lancaster has today placed in the library of the House a document setting out the current position in relation to informing Parliament on the export of arms, together with an explanation of how that practice has evolved.

That is an important step forward and I hope hon Members will find that document a useful basis on which to take the discussion forward. Serious issues are involved.

The report also considered the position of Customs and Excise as an independent prosecuting authority, a role that has remained unchanged for very many years. It recommends the introduction of a formalised system of supervision by the Attorney-General of export control prosecutions. At the same time, Sir Richard affirms the important constitutional principle that a prosecuting authority should be independent and free from political direction. He considers the analogy with the Crown Prosecution Service and the Director of Public Prosecutions, both of which are subject to the superintendence of the Attorney-General, whereas the Customs and Excise prosecuting authority is not. Sir Richard notes that, acting in that capacity, the Attorney-General exercises a quasi-judicial role. His actions and decisions are not, for example, subject to Cabinet collective responsibility.

Although the analogy that Sir Richard draws with the CPS and the Serious Fraud Office is not exact, the Government accept that there are benefits in his recommendation: that in future the role of the Attorney-General should include the exercise of increased supervision of Customs and Excise prosecutions in relation to export control matters.

The Government are urgently developing proposals on the precise nature and scope of the increased supervision and my right hon and learned friend will be reporting further on that to the House as soon as possible.

In relation to the use of intelligence by Government departments, Sir Richard makes it clear that he does not feel qualified to make recommendations on how the various systems and procedures might be improved. He acknowledges that a number of improvements have been made and sets out a number of areas in which he considers that problems existed.

Since 1992, major reviews have taken place in the Foreign and Commonwealth Office, the Department of Trade and Industry, the Ministry of Defence and Customs and Excise. As a result, modern information technology systems have been introduced and new internal distribution arrangements have been adopted. In addition, the requirements of users are now more fully reflected in the intelligence-gathering process.

Sir Richard also makes a procedural recommendation, which he has not published for security reasons, concerning intelligence personnel, which will be discussed with the Chairman of the parliamentary Intelligence and Security Committee. The Government also propose to inform the Intelligence and Security Committee, chaired by my right hon friend the Member for Bridgwater (Mr King), of other improvements that have been made. I have no doubt that that committee, which was specially set up to deal with such matters, will want to be satisfied, and in due course to reassure the House, that an adequate response has been made to Sir Richard's observations.

The law on public interest immunity in civil and criminal cases is made by the courts, and Sir Richard Scott does not consider legislative intervention necessary or, at present, desirable. The Government, however will consider his recommendations in the light of developing case law – in particular, his view that the time is opportune for a collective reappraisal by ministers. As part of that consideration, the Government would welcome the views of hon Members and others on future developments in the use of PII certificates. ...

Mr Richard Shepherd (Aldridge-Brownhills): I first want to say how much I appreciate the fact that the Prime Minister set up the inquiry. I must be like the fellow in a Bateman cartoon – the only person on my side who believes parliamentary answers and who would have engaged in argument with my constituents about whether we supplied defence-related equipment during 1988 and 1989 that enhanced the capacity of Saddam Hussein. I was born when one anathema threatened Europe. Many people in this country are aware that Saddam Hussein is another anathema. Thanks to the Prime Minister, we have an account of how we enhanced the defence capacity of Iraq. I find that deeply and profoundly disturbing.

I have tried to list the instances in just the first volume of the report where Sir Richard Scott identified that the Government were intending to mislead or be less than candid with Parliament and the people of this country. I jotted down just a few of the references before I ran out of resources, time and patience. They include: D1.27, D1.151, D1.165, D2.35, D2.36, D2.432. It goes on; there are pages and pages of it.

In D4.3, on page 501, Scott alludes to the evidence of Mr Gore-Booth, and later to that of Sir Robin Butler. There we see clever men laying out an argument, the substance of which is to argue that half a picture may be an indication of the whole picture. We have to make it quite clear to Sir Robin Butler, Mr Gore-Booth – an honoured servant who I understand has been promoted to the High Commission in New Delhi – and such servants of the state that neither the House nor the country will be governed on the basis of half the picture.

That is profoundly important because as a back-bench Member of Parliament, I represent the constituency of Aldridge-Brownhills. In that I am equal to the highest in this land, those who govern us, who are dependent on the authority of their own electorate and answer directly through this House and at times of elections. I am profoundly disturbed that the intent behind the policy, if not to tell an untruth, was to give an impression that was designedly misleading. ...

Mr Quentin Davies: Let us ... not deceive ourselves. Let us not be carried away or allow ourselves to fall into the temptation of being diverted so comfortably into talking about something else so that we do not have to face the harsh reality before us. In that context, I hope that we hear nothing more about whether there was a change in the guidelines or whether the guidelines were simply being flexibly interpreted – because of course there was a change in the guidelines. ...

Let us also not talk about whether it is reasonable to make changes in arms sales policy – of course it is. No one is denying that; it is no problem at all. But it is very different to make changes and then pretend to the House that they have not been made. That is the point.

Let us also not fool ourselves and spend time talking about whether we perhaps should not have a policy on the disclosure of arms exports or whether we should have a policy of greater disclosure. I would perfectly accept arguments in the national interest that we should say nothing about our arms exports to the Middle East. I would have been perfectly happy to accept that, and if ministers had done that I would not have quarrelled with it, but they did not. They pretended that they were making statements that were relevant, true and informative to the House; the statements that they made were anything but that.

Let us also not spend too much time – although, of course, the point is important – discussing the integrity of my right hon friend the Chief Secretary [William Waldegrave]. I accept his integrity and that he did not wish to mislead the House. I entirely accept that he never thought, 'Wouldn't it be nice to mislead the House of Commons? How can I best do that?' I accept that entirely and I accept, as the judge did, his sincerity in that matter, but, whatever may have been his subjective sentiment at the relevant time, the objective fact – I shall prove it in a moment – is that he did mislead the House. Therefore, I am afraid that he has made a very serious mistake.

I have no wish at all to deprive the Government of an extremely able minister and a man for whom I have always had a high personal regard, but I am afraid that he must take responsibility for that mistake. Whatever happens tonight, it must be made clear that someone is taking responsibility and that the principle has been restored that ministers remain fully accountable to the House of Commons. ...

Mr Rupert Allason (Torbay): May I remind the House that one of the most important people involved in the debate today is Paul Henderson? He is a man who volunteered his services to the security service when he was travelling behind eastern Europe. He was subsequently recruited by the Secret Intelligence Service In my judgment, and, indeed, that of Mr T [a security services agent], who gave evidence for him at the Old Bailey, he is a very brave man, particularly as he was willing to go back to Baghdad after the execution of Farzad Bazoft.

In my judgment, officials in Whitehall would have been better off trying to find ways to get Mr Henderson a medal than trying to put him in prison. It is a fact that there was a conspiracy to put him in prison. If one reads volume 3, and all of section G, one will see that it is quite clear that every possible obstacle was put in the way of his defence. It is also perfectly clear that the support that was given, in terms of documents to the defence, was given grudgingly. That is also in the report. ...

I now deal with the conduct of the Attorney-General, whose integrity I do not doubt for one moment. The fact, however, is that he failed to stop the prosecution at an early stage. It is also the case that somebody somewhere failed to tell the judge of the President of the Board of Trade's reservations about the certificate that he had signed. Most significantly, the advice that the Attorney-General gave regarding PIIs and the duty of ministers was perceived by Lord Justice Scott to be wrong. If Scott is wrong, the offence is even greater because there was no even-handed approach to the suppression of the documents going to the defence because the PIIs were used only to disadvantage the defence.

The fact is that, even after calling in the Matrix Churchill papers, the Attorney-General still had no idea that Henderson was an SIS agent. The question that has yet to be addressed is why the Director General of the Security Service, Sir Patrick Walker, or the chief of the SIS, Sir Colin McColl, simply did not take a stroll down Whitehall to Buckingham Gate and tell the Attorney-General, 'This is our man'. What message does that give to other people who wish to assist our security and intelligence services?

As regards the future, I very much hope that we shall have a complete review of the way in which PIIs are used. ...

Mr Quentin Davies: I am sure that my right hon friend will agree that, if the policy was changed without proper authorisation from senior ministers, that compounds the offence rather than mitigating it.

Can my right hon friend think of a better documented case in the history of this Parliament of the House being misled? If he can, will he name it? Does he not share my fear that, if we do nothing about such a case as a result of tonight's debate, the most fearful constitutional precedent will be created?

Mr Allason: Will my right hon friend give an undertaking that the presumption in future will always be on disclosure and not suppression? Will he give an undertaking that there will never again be such an abuse of public interest immunity certificates granted on national security grounds?

Mr Freeman: The presumption should be disclosure and, when the judge read and interpreted the public interest immunity certificates in the Matrix Churchill trial, he made a positive decision on disclosure. I give my hon friend the undertaking I gave a few moments ago – the Government will ensure that an opportunity arises in Government time for that matter to be considered further.

Note

The concessions made by the Government were of course limited and (apart from the pledge as to greater supervision of C & E prosecutions) it remains to be seen whether any of the areas which they promised to examine will be reformed. See further on the Government's response to the Scott report Part IV, Chapter 2.

The Select Committees

It was precisely to give back-benchers more in-depth knowledge of Government departments that 14 Select Committees were set up in 1979, covering between them each of the major Government departments with the exception of the Law Officers' Department and the Lord Chancellor's Department which were brought within the system in 1991.

The committees were set up due to widespread dissatisfaction with procedures on the floor of the House of Commons as a means of scrutinising the workings of Government and a consequent perception that the balance of power between the executive and Parliament was not being maintained under the then current arrangements.

The new committees were better equipped and organised than their predecessors, set up in the 1966–70 Parliament. Their function was expressed to be 'to examine the expenditure, administration and policy of the principal Government departments'. The committees allow officials and ministers to be questioned in a systematic and searching manner which is not always possible on the floor of the House of Commons. Furthermore, the members of the committees are comparatively well informed and can call on the assistance of expert advisors. The published reports of committees constitute a significant and valuable source of information about the workings of Government. The committees show an impartiality remarkable in the contentious atmosphere of the Commons; they 'seek to proceed by a more non-partisan approach',[67]

---

67 Craig, *Administrative Law*, 2nd edn (1989), p69.

conducting their business in an inquisitorial as opposed to adversarial manner on party lines. This can be partly explained by the fact that the committees' members are chosen from the back-benches: no front bench spokesmen are appointed to them although former ministers may be.

The remit of the Select Committees

Second Report from the Select Committee on Procedure, HC 19–II (1989–90)

[14 March 1990]

5   The general terms of reference of these committees are as set out in Standing Order no 130. ... The committees are responsible for the interpretation of their own terms of reference. The committees are entitled to examine the expenditure, administration and policy of the principal Government departments, and also of their 'associated public bodies'. The terms of the standing orders do not define 'associated public bodies', but the then Chancellor of the Duchy of Lancaster said in his speech on 25 June 1979 that:

'The Government also accept the Procedure Committee's view that the committees must be able to look at the activities of some public bodies that exercise authority of their own and over which ministers do not have the same direct authority as they have over their own departments. The test in every case will be whether there is a significant degree of ministerial responsibility for the body concerned.'

Associated public bodies therefore include all nationalised industries, fringe bodies and other Governmental organisations within the responsibilities of the department or departments concerned for which ministers are ultimately answerable. They do not, however, include bodies for which ministers are not answerable to Parliament, even though these bodies may be in receipt of Government funds. There will no doubt be borderline cases, but in general the existing principles of Parliamentary accountability can be applied.

Powers of the committees

7   Select Committees (and their sub-committees) normally have the power to 'send for persons, papers and records'. This power is understood as a power to 'order' the attendance of persons and the submission of papers, but its interpretation and its application to ministers are examined in detail in the memorandum by the Clerk of the House which was reproduced at appendix C, to the First Report from the Select Committee on Procedure, session 1977–78 (HC 588–1).

8   Any official who appears before a Select Committee or who submits papers to it does so on behalf of his ministers. As the Procedure Committee emphasised in its report:

'The over-riding principle concerning access to Government information should be that the House has power to enforce the responsibility of ministers for the provision of information or the refusal of information. It would not, however, be appropriate for the House to seek directly or through its committees to enforce its rights to secure information from the executive at a level below that of the ministerial head of the department concerned (normally a Cabinet minister), since such a practice would tend to undermine rather than strengthen the accountability of ministers to the House.'

In practice, committees normally proceed on the basis of 'requests' for departmental witnesses and evidence rather than through the exercise of formal powers.

9 It should be noted that, in addition to examining the expenditure, administration and policy of Government departments and associated public bodies, Select Committees are free to seek evidence from whomsoever they please, and are entitled to require the production of papers by private bodies or individuals so long as these are relevant to the committees' work.

Summoning of named officials

10 Officials appearing before Select Committees do so on behalf of their ministers. It is customary, therefore, for ministers to decide which officials (including members of the armed services) should appear to give evidence. Select Committees have in the past generally accepted this position. Should a committee invite a named official to appear, the minister concerned, if he did not wish that official to represent him, might suggest that another official could more appropriately do so, or that he himself should give evidence to the committee. If a committee insisted on a particular official appearing before them – whether serving in the UK or overseas – they could issue a formal order for his attendance. In such an event the official would have to appear before the committee. In all circumstances, the official would remain subject to ministerial instructions as to how to answer questions.

...

Open sessions

13 Select Committees usually admit the public and press to hearings, and it is possible that proceedings may be broadcast. Departments may wish to ascertain from the Clerk to the Committee beforehand whether particular proceedings are to be recorded for broadcasting. Arrangements for the treatment of confidential information in oral evidence are referred to in paragraphs 49–51 below. Although the broadcasting authorities, not the Select Committees, control what recorded material is broadcast, it is up to the Select Committee to decide whether or not a session is a public or closed one, recording, of course, not being permitted in the latter.

...

17 ... The departmental committees have ... been given power to appoint specialist advisors either to supply information which is not readily available or to elucidate matters of complexity within the committee's orders of reference. ...

General

20 The general principle to be followed is that it is the duty of officials to be as helpful as possible to committees, and that any withholding of information should be limited to reservations that are necessary in the interests of good government or to safeguard national security. Departments should, therefore, be as forthcoming as they can (within the limits set out in this note) when requested to provide information whether in writing or orally. This will also help to ensure that the reports of committees are as soundly based on fact as possible. Oral evidence is recorded verbatim. When oral evidence is to be given, it is advisable for departments to send at least two witnesses so that they can divide between themselves the responsibility for answering questions. Because officials appear on behalf of their ministers, departments might want to clear written evidence and briefing with ministers. It may only be necessary for ministers to be consulted should there be any doubt among officials on the policy to be explained to the committee. However, ministers

are ultimately responsible for deciding what information is to be given and for defending their decisions as necessary, and ministers' views should always be sought if any question arises of withholding information which committees are known to be seeking. It should be remembered that an extended and unexplained delay in providing the evidence requested by a committee may be interpreted by them as a refusal. If departments are asked by committees to undertake research work or surveys on their behalf, it may be possible to meet such requests by the utilisation of existing information, modified as appropriate. But if the new work involved is likely to be substantial, and the committee has power to appoint its own specialist advisers (see para 17), it may be appropriate to suggest to the committee that it considers this alternative, or possibly the employment of private research agencies or universities.

Accuracy of evidence

21 Officials appearing before Select Committees are responsible for ensuring that the evidence they give is accurate. They are reminded to take particular care to see that they are fully and correctly briefed on the main facts of the matters on which they expect to be examined. Should it nevertheless be discovered subsequently that the evidence unwittingly contained errors, these should be made known to the committee at the earliest possible moment.

Informal discussions and social meetings

22 Some committees, in addition to taking formal evidence, occasionally conduct informal discussions or arrange to meet officials at social gatherings. When that occurs, officials should apply the same considerations as apply to formal evidence, because the supply of information informally can affect a committee's report as much as formal evidence.

Status of information supplied

23 Once information has been supplied to a committee, it becomes 'evidence' and, subject only to the conventions governing classified information (see para 48–51), it is entirely within the competence of the committee to report and publish it or to refrain from doing so. Departments may not themselves make public use of any evidence prior to its publication by the committee, without the permission of the committee. Committees frequently publish on a daily basis evidence given in public as well as publishing the evidence as a whole with their reports. Whether published as a 'daily part' or in collected form, the evidence may be quoted without risking a breach of parliamentary privilege, as may documents supplied to the committee are already in the public domain. Letters addressed to the Clerk to the Committee, however informal, are strictly speaking 'evidence' and liable to be published. Copies of evidence may also be sent by the committee which received it to other departmental committees which might have an interest in it.

Inter-departmental liaison

24 Generally speaking the subjects of inquiry by Select Committees will fall clearly within the responsibilities of particular departments. Occasionally, however, committees may enquire into subjects which span the work of more than one department, or where departmental responsibility is not self-evident. Inquiries by the Lords Science and Technology Committee are almost always 'multi-disciplinary' and it is important in these cases that one department takes the lead to ensure that the different departments give evidence which is consistent. The aim must be to ensure that committees

direct their questions on each aspect of such subjects to the department chiefly concerned with that aspect, and do not question departments whose role is that of co-ordination about matters which go outside that role. This indicates that where in such cases the committee needs a memorandum covering the interests of several departments, it may be better for this to be submitted by the department with the predominant role in the field concerned (rather than by a co-ordinating office such as the Cabinet Office). If the committee then asks that department questions (whether in writing or orally) proper to some other department, they can be re-directed.

...

Limitations on the provision of information

General

28 Committees' requests for information should not be met regardless of cost or of diversion of effort from other important matters. It might prove necessary to decline requests which appeared to involve excessive costs. However, requests for named officials who are serving overseas to attend to give evidence should not be refused on cost grounds alone. Most committees will be willing to arrange for evidence from these witnesses to be heard on a mutually acceptable date. If it is proposed to refuse a request ministers should be consulted.

Conduct of individual civil servants

28A Further supplementary guidance, principally concerning evidence on the 'conduct' of individual civil servants, was published in April 1987, following the Government's Response, entitled Accountability of Ministers and Civil Servants (Cm 78, February 1987) to the First Report from the Treasury and Civil Service Committee (session 1986/87, HC62) and to the First Report from the Liaison Committee (session 1986/87, HC 100). This supplementary guidance is attached at Annex A.

29 The Procedure Committee recognised that there may be occasions when ministers may wish to resist requests for information on grounds of national security ... a letter of 9 May 1967 to the chairmen of certain Select Committees from the then Lord President of the Council and Leader of the House, ... refers (among other limitations on the provision of information) to 'information affecting national security, which would normally be withheld from the House in the national interest'. Guidance to departments on the release of classified information to committees is given in the manual 'Security in Government Departments'. This manual is the overriding authority; what follows must be read subject to its guidance. Officials must not disclose information which the manual says must be withheld; they should consult their departmental security officers if in doubt.

30 Officials should not give evidence about or discuss the following topics:

(i) In order to preserve the collective responsibility of ministers, the advice given to ministers by their departments should not be disclosed, nor should information about inter-departmental exchanges on policy issues, about the level at which decisions were taken or the manner in which a minister has consulted his colleagues. Information should not be given about Cabinet Committees or their decisions (see paras 31–33).

(ii) Advice given by a Law Officer (see para 36).

(iii) The private affairs of individuals or institutions on which any information held by ministers or their officials has been supplied in confidence (including such information about individuals which is available to the Government by virtue of their being engaged in or considered for public employment).

Officials should also, where possible, avoid giving written evidence about or discussing the following matters. Where appropriate further guidance is provided in the succeeding paragraphs:

(iv) Questions in the field of political controversy (see paras 34–35).

(v) Sensitive information of a commercial or economic nature, eg knowledge which could affect the financial markets, without prior consultation with the Chancellor of the Exchequer, sensitive information relating to the commercial operations of nationalised industries, or to contracts; commercial or economic information which has been given to the Government in confidence, unless the advance consent of the persons concerned has been obtained (see para 53 for the provision of information by Government contractors).

(vi) Matters which are, or may become, the subject of sensitive negotiations with Governments or other bodies, including the European Community, without prior consultation with the Foreign and Commonwealth Secretary (see para 37), or, in relation to domestic matters, with the ministers concerned.

(vii) Specific cases where the minister has or may have a quasi-judicial or appellate function, eg in relation to planning applications and appeals, or where the subject-matter is being considered by the courts, or the Parliamentary Commissioner (see paras 38–39).

Where, exceptionally, matters such as (iv)–(vii) have to be discussed, application may be made for 'sidelining' (see para 51). There is no objection to saying in general terms why information cannot be given and it is very unusual for a committee to press an official who indicates that he is in difficulty on such grounds in answering a question. If however this happens, it may be best to ask for time to consider the request and to promise to report back. Paragraphs 7 and 8 should be referred to.

Collective responsibility

31 Departmental witnesses, whether in closed or open session, should preserve the collective responsibility of ministers and also the basis of confidence between ministers and their advisers. Except in a case involving an Accounting Officer's responsibility (see paras 9–11 and 17 of the Accounting Officers Memorandum, reproduced in para C4 of 'Government Accounting') the advice given to ministers which is given in confidence, should not therefore be disclosed, though departments may of course need to draw on information submitted to ministers. It is necessary also to refuse access to documents relating to inter-departmental exchanges on policy issues. Equally, the methods by which a current study is being undertaken should not normally be disclosed without the authority of ministers, unless they have already been made public. Nor should departments reveal the level at which decisions were taken. It should be borne in mind that decisions taken by ministers collectively are normally announced and defended by the minister responsible as his own decisions, and it is important that no indication should be given of the manner in which a minister has consulted his colleagues (see also para 36 on the special position of the Law Officers).

32 In no circumstances should any committee be given a Cabinet paper or extract from it, or be told of discussions in a Cabinet Committee. Nor should information be given about the existence, composition or terms of reference

of Cabinet Committees, or the identity of their chairmen, beyond that information disclosed by the Prime Minister in answer to a parliamentary question on 26 January 1988, and if witnesses are questioned on such matters they must decline to give specific answers. There is, however, no objection to pointing out in general terms that consultation between departments runs through the whole fabric of Government and occurs at all levels both official and ministerial.

...

Policy

34 Official witnesses, whether administrative, professional or services, should as far as possible confine their evidence to questions of fact relating to existing Government policies and actions. Officials should be ready to explain what the existing policies are and the objectives and justification, as the Government sees them, for those policies, and to explain how administrative factors may have affected both the choice of policy measures and the manner of their implementation. It is open to officials to make comments which are not politically contentious but they should as far as possible avoid being drawn, without prior ministerial authority, into the discussion of alternative policy. If official witnesses are pressed by the committee to go beyond these limits, they should suggest that the questioning be addressed, or referred, to ministers. If there is a likelihood of a material issue of policy being raised by a committee in its questioning of official witnesses, departments will wish to consult ministers beforehand (on appearance by ministers, also see paras 7–8).

...

International relations

37 Negotiations with other Governments are normally conducted in strict confidence. Officials should take care in discussing or giving written evidence matters which may affect relations with other Governments or bodies, including the European Community, or relations between British officials and those of other governments. Texts of communications between Governments, unless already made public, should be regarded as confidential and should not be submitted as evidence without prior approval of the minister concerned.

Matters sub-judice

38 Committees are subject to the rules by which the House regulates its own conduct and that of its Members.

Documents relating to the internal administration of Government

42 The Procedure Committee recommended that:

'Select Committees should regard any refusal by Government departments to provide information relating to departmental or inter-departmental organisation – unless fully explained and justified to their satisfaction – as a matter of serious concern which should be brought to the attention of the House.'

43 Requests for documents which go beyond a description of the existing organisation of a department and deal with methods of operation (eg, arrangements for formal and informal co-ordination or for delegation of authority) or with reviews of existing departmental organisation or methods, may raise more difficult questions, since these will frequently be internal working papers. Ministers should be consulted about any requests for

information of this kind, with the presumption that information on these matters should be provided, in an appropriate form, unless it would conflict with the guidance in paragraph 30 above. Except where particular arrangements have been made public, information about inter-departmental organisation may present more difficulty (see paras 31–32).

Documents of a previous administration

44   There are well-established conventions which govern the withholding of policy papers of a previous administration from an administration of a different political complexion. Since officials appear before Select Committees as representatives of their ministers and since Select Committee are themselves composed on a bipartisan basis, it follows that officials should not provide a Select Committee with papers of a previous administration which they are not in a position to show to present ministers. If such papers are sought, ministers should be consulted about the request. The general rule is that documents of a former administration which have not been released or published during the period of that administration should not be released or published by a subsequent Government. Where ministers propose to make an exception it would be necessary to consult a representative of the previous administration before showing the papers either to present ministers or, with ministers' agreement, releasing them to a Select Committee.

Treatment of evidence

Open sessions

45   Unclassified memoranda prepared by departments for a committee may be published by the committee before its full report is presented to the House, and may be available to the press and public at the time of the related session. Open sessions of committees often attract publicity since evidence before them may be reported forthwith by the press. Departments are in these circumstances free to comment immediately to the press on matters raised in their evidence. If a Select Committee takes evidence in public fron: a minister or senior official, therefore, it may be considered desirable for a press officer also to attend, so as to be able to answer press queries. Such press briefing should not, however, extend to comment on matters of policy since such comment might be regarded as impeding the committee in its task and hence as contempt. Care should be taken not to go beyond the evidence given by the minister or official in commenting on any suggestion made by another witness, eg the chairman of a nationalised industry, at the same hearing, or to disclose information not yet given publicly.

...

47   Evidence critical of a department or its agents may be given in open session by persons outside the department on occasions where departmental witnesses are not also present or at sessions held after the departmental evidence has been given. In these circumstances departments should not seek publicly to respond to such criticism outside the ambit of the committee. Instead, the chairman of the committee concerned may be asked to consider inviting the department to express their view or provide further comments to the committee as soon as possible.

Disclosure of confidential information in general

48   The general aim of departments should be to assist committees by disclosing to them whatever official information they may require for the carrying out of their Parliamentary functions, provided that there are no overriding reasons of security or other grounds for withholding such information. It

may be, however, that particular information requested by a committee, or other information which a department consider might have a relevant bearing on a committee's enquiries, should only be made available on the basis that it will not be published and will be treated in confidence. Where this is so, the department should inform the Clerk to the Committee that the information can be made available only on this basis, explaining the reasons in general terms. Such information should not be made available until the committee has agreed to treat it accordingly. ... In considering the submission of confidential evidence to a committee, departments should bear in mind that the final authority as to whether or not evidence shall be published rests with the committee.

...

Evidence from other bodies

52 Committees may, as stated in paragraph 5 above, call for evidence from non-departmental bodies for which departments have responsibility. If a department become aware that a non-departmental body for which they are responsible has been invited to give evidence, they may wish to consider whether it would be advisable to discuss the lines of evidence with the witnesses before the hearing. The department may also wish to seek the committee's agreement to their being represented at the hearing; whether this is allowed is entirely a matter for the committee.

...

55 Departments may also wish to ask non-departmental bodies for which they have responsibility to show them written evidence or replies in draft before submitting them. ... The bodies would, of course, remain free to express their independent views, subject to their statutory or contractual responsibilities and subject to there being no questions of security involved.

...

Annex A – Guidelines for officials giving evidence to departmental Select Committees

[These guidelines supplement, and should be read in conjunction with, the memorandum of guidance for officials appearing before Select Committees, and will be incorporated in future editions of that guidance.]

1 Officials who give evidence to departmental Select Committees do so on behalf of their ministers in accordance with the principles that civil servants are accountable to ministers, and that it is ministers who are accountable to Parliament. In giving evidence, civil servants are therefore subject to the instructions of ministers and remain bound to observe their duty of confidentiality to ministers.

2 In the course of Select Committee inquiries into the expenditure, administration and policies of departments and their associated bodies, the evidence given by officials will normally be concerned with explaining the policies and actions undertaken by ministers, and by departments on their behalf, and the reasons for those policies and actions. Sometimes, however, a Select Committee's inquiries may involve questions relating to what has been done by individual civil servants. On such occasions, the principles of ministerial accountability are still applicable, even if officials have acted outside or contrary to the authority given to them by ministers.

3 Subject to the general principles set out above, official witnesses should in all Select Committee inquiries be as helpful as possible in answering questions concerned with the establishment of the facts of what has occurred in the making of decisions or the carrying out of actions in the implementation of Government policies.

4   There may, however, be occasions where questions put by members of a Select Committee in the course of an inquiry appear to be directed to the 'conduct' of individual civil servants. 'Questions directed to the conduct' in this context means more than the establishing of facts about what has occurred; it carries the implication of allocating individual criticism or blame. In such circumstances, in accordance with the principles of ministerial responsibility, it is for the minister to look into the matter and if necessary institute a formal inquiry. Such an inquiry into the conduct and behaviour of individual civil servants and consideration of disciplinary action is properly carried out within a department according to established procedures designed and agreed for the purpose and with appropriate safeguards for the individual. It is then for the minister to be responsible for informing the committee of what has happened, and of what has been done to put the matter right and to prevent a recurrence. Evidence to a Select Committee on this should be given not by the individual civil servant or servants concerned, but by the minister or by a senior official specifically designated by the minister to give such evidence on his behalf. This would include the result of any disciplinary or other departmental proceedings against individual civil servants.

...

6   If, when officials are asked to give evidence to the Select Committee, it is foreseen that the inquiry may involve questions about the 'conduct' of the individual officials in question or about other individual named officials, it should be suggested to the committee that it would be appropriate for a minister or a senior official designated by the minister to give evidence, rather than the named officials in question. Any question which appears to relate to the 'conduct' of individual civil servants, such as the allocation of blame for what has occurred, can then be answered by the minister or designated senior official. If an official giving evidence to a committee is unexpectedly asked questions which he or she believes are directed at his or her individual 'conduct', or at the 'conduct' of another named individual civil servant, or if the official is uncertain whether or not questions fall into this category, the official should indicate that he or she wishes to seek instructions from his or her minister, and the committee should be asked to allow time for the minister's instructions to be sought.

28 April 1987

Notes

1   The power to question members of the executive is clearly crucial to the efficacy of the committees, and not surprisingly has caused controversy. As Tomkin notes (*op cit*, p75), whilst MPs and ministers can be required to attend by committees if an initial request is refused, and, in the last resort, ordered to attend by the House, no MP has been ordered to attend 'this century' and no minister has ever been ordered to attend. In 1979 the Leader of the House pledged that '... every minister ... will do all in his or her power to co-operate with the new system of committees'. Despite this promise the committees have sometimes found themselves frustrated when investigating areas of acute sensitivity by the refusal of certain key witnesses to attend. For example, in 1984 the Government would not allow the Director of Government Communications Headquarters to give evidence to the Select Committee on Employment which was enquiring into the trade union ban at GCHQ. Similarly, in 1986 the Defence Committee, in the course of its inquiry

into the Westland affair, wished to interview certain officials; again the minister in question would not allow them to attend.

2 This ability of ministers to control which of their officials appear before Select Committees is justified in terms of ministerial responsibility; since ministers, not civil servants, are responsible to Parliament and civil servants give advice only on behalf of ministers, it is for ministers to choose which civil servants they think are appropriate to 'represent' them. However, this interpretation of ministerial responsibility has recently run into renewed controversy. During the Scott Inquiry, two retired officials in the Ministry of Defence (MoD), Mr Primrose and Mr Harding, had important first-hand information about aspects of the Supergun affair, and the Trade and Industry Select Committee (TISC) which was investigating the affair, wished to interview them. The MoD refused to allow them to attend; the Scott report's findings on this incident follow:

Inquiry into Exports of Defence Equipment and Dual-Use Goods to Iraq and Related Prosecutions, HC 115 I (1995–96)

F4.61 Mr Bevan was asked by the Inquiry to explain why Messrs Primrose and Harding could not have been given access to departmental papers if necessary, and why it was inappropriate or likely to be unproductive for them to give oral evidence to TISC. Mr Bevan said:

> ... the advice given to ministers about the response to TISC's request to take evidence from Mr Primrose and Mr Harding was agreed by Sir Robin Butler and Sir Michael Quinlan. The rationale was as follows.

> Under the conventions that apply to the relationship between Select Committees and Government departments, officials give evidence on behalf of ministers and are responsible to ministers for their evidence. Evidence about the actions of departmental officials acting in their official capacity must be given on this basis. Messrs Primrose and Harding, being retired officials, were not responsible to ministers and could not therefore give official evidence on behalf of ministers. Their appearance was therefore regarded as inappropriate.

> Retired officials are not normally given access to departmental papers; evidence by Messrs Primrose and Harding without such access was thought likely to be unproductive. If they had been given access they would have been in a position to give full evidence about the MoD's actions without being responsible to ministers for their evidence. This would have been inconsistent with the established conventions. ...

F4.64 The Government's starting-point was that officials would have been giving evidence to TISC on behalf of MoD ministers. On that basis it was, in the Government's view, inappropriate for former MoD officials to give such evidence since they could no longer speak on behalf of MoD ministers. That would have been inconsistent with established conventions. But there was a different starting-point available to the Government. TISC was inquiring into the facts of a particularly sensitive export to Iraq. There was a strong argument in favour of the Government's facilitating the provision of relevant evidence to TISC if it lay within its power to do so. In that way TISC would have been better able to establish the relevant facts. The provision of evidence to establish the relevant facts ought not to have been regarded as a matter on which the officials with first hand knowledge of those facts would have been giving evidence 'on behalf of ministers'. On the contrary, Mr Primrose and Mr Harding were primary witnesses to the facts themselves. Far from being unproductive, their evidence would have been highly pertinent and helpful. Mr Harding made clear to the inquiry that he would have been prepared to give evidence to TISC. ...

F 4.66 A minister's duty to account to Parliament for what his department has done ought, in my opinion, to be recognised as extending (in the absence of any special limiting factors) to an obligation to assist an investigating Select Committee to obtain the best first hand evidence available on the matters being investigated. The refusal to facilitate the giving of evidence to TISC by Mr Harding and Mr Primrose may be regarded as a failure to comply fully with the obligations of accountability owed to Parliament.

Notes

1   Sir Richard Scott has recently commented[68] on the wider significance of this episode, turning on its head the notion that ministerial responsibility justifies this convention of this kind of control by ministers:

> Given that ministers have not got personal knowledge of a vast number of things that happen within their department ... their obligation I think is to facilitate the giving of information by those who do have personal knowledge of the matter. [Scott then goes on to note the Osmotherly rules – allowing ministers to prevent civil servants from giving evidence to Select Committees.] I think that ministerial accountability does require ministers to facilitate Select Committees obtaining first-hand evidence from those with first-hand knowledge of the matter in question.[69]

2   On the whole, Committees have not found Civil Service recalcitrance a serious handicap; for example, the Select Committee on Trade and Industry stated in its 2nd Report of 1985–86: 'In the vast majority of previous ... committees no serious problem has arisen'. The restrictions on the divulging of information and the refusal of persons to attend are both likely to hamper the committees in exposing major Government embarrassments but interfere little with their day to day scrutiny of the relevant departments.

3   In 1988 the Agriculture Select Committee wished to interview Edwina Currie after the salmonella-in-eggs affair and she was requested to attend its inquiry. When she refused, the Committee reiterated its request and stated its view that it was for the committee to determine whether or not her evidence was relevant. Eventually she did attend after the committee put down a motion ordering her attendance, but did not accept that the committee had power to compel her.

4   Failure to attend has generally less of a problem than failure to answer questions properly. As Norton puts it, 'Whilst the committees normally get the witnesses they want, they do not always get the answers they want ...'.[70] When Edwina Currie did finally attend the committee, she refused to add to her earlier statements about salmonella in eggs and 'under pressure from its Chairman, the committee did not press her' (Tomkin, *op cit*, p77). As the

---

68   See the minutes of evidence taken before the Public Services Committee on 8 May 1996, HC 313 (1995–96).

69   *Ibid*, QQ 394–397.

70   Norton, *Does Parliament Matter?* (1993), p108.

above extract made clear, the areas on which officials will refuse to answer questions are very wide, and constitute a severe restriction on freedom of information. Whilst some exceptions are relatively well defined, and aimed at protecting clear identifiable interests (eg collective ministerial responsibility (above, para 30(i)), others are unacceptably vague: for example, information may be withheld 'in the interests of good government' (para 20), a phrase, of which, Brazier comments, 'Sir Humphrey Appelby would be proud'.[71]

5   Even those exceptions aimed at presenting clear and dependable principles seem to go further than is needed. Would collective Cabinet responsibility *really* be threatened by Select Committees being told of the 'existence' of Cabinet Committees (p32)? Admittedly, since Cabinet Committees are often set up to discuss particular proposals by particular ministers, if a Select Committee was told that a Cabinet Committee had been set up to consider 'Mr Heseltine's proposal to do so and so', then, if the proposal was later dropped, a (not particularly important) breach of collective responsibility would have taken place. But committees could simply be told that a Cabinet Committee had been established to consider 'a proposal to do so and so', without revealing whose proposal it had been. To be sure, if the proposal was a very specific one, clearly within a given minister's portfolio, then the author of the proposal would be impliedly revealed, but this would not always be the case. To have a blanket prohibition on the revelation of even the *existence* of Cabinet Committees implies a presumption in favour of secrecy, unrebuttable even when the principle invoked to justify the secrecy (collective responsibility) was not at stake in a given particular instance. As part of John Major's modest moves towards open government, this exception was in fact recently abolished.

6   Further restrictions, of uncertain scope, exist in relation to the types of question to which civil servants will respond. The First Report from the Treasury and Civil Service Select Committee (session 1986–1987) drew a distinction between the 'actions' and 'conduct' of civil servants. 'Actions' would be assumed to be activities consistent with the policies of the minister in questions while 'conduct' would connote misconduct. The committee asserted a right in exceptional circumstances to consider the conduct of civil servants on the basis that to hold otherwise would be detrimental to the public interest. In making this distinction the committee referred to the speech made by Sir Maxwell Fyfe in the House of Commons after the Crichel Down affair in 1954. It was suggested that, where a civil servant acts in accordance either with an express order from the minister or with ministerial policy, the minister will be responsible for those actions. Again, where the civil servant has made a mistake which causes delay but which is not on a serious policy issue, the minister will accept responsibility and will deal with the mistake within the department. However, where a civil servant acts reprehensibly and out of accordance with the minister's wishes it was suggested that the minister need not endorse and defend the actions, although he will be expected to render an account of them to Parliament. It was the last situation with which the committee was concerned. In response,

---

71   Brazier, *Constitutional Practice* (1994), p227.

the Government amended the guidelines to be issued to civil servants on answering such questions. The guidelines advised that where 'conduct' of civil servants was or might be in question, the civil servant should seek advice from the minister as opposed to answering the question. The minister would take responsibility either for attending the committee or for ensuring that any necessary disciplinary measures were carried out within the department. See further on the conduct of civil servants before Select Committees, Part IV, Chapter 2, pp552–7, 558–65, 573–8, 597–9.

7 Select Committees have the formal power to send for papers; however, Parliament can compel the production of documents from a department headed by a Secretary of State (ie most departments) only through an address to the Crown.[72] Furthermore, as Tomkin notes (*op cit*, pp79–80) 'The 1994 draft of the Cabinet Office memorandum *Departmental Evidence and Response to Select Committees* contains guidelines [on this matter, which state, *inter alia*]:

> the Government's commitment to provide as much information as possible to Select Committees is met largely through the provision of memoranda and written replies ... it does not amount to a commitment to provide access to internal files, private correspondence ... advice given on a confidential basis or working papers (para 49).

> Cabinet and Cabinet Committee papers are, of course, never disclosed to Select Committees (para 71).

8 Clearly, scrutiny over the national finances is a vital link in the chain of Commons control of the executive; it is, however, patchy. As Colin Turpin comments, Government borrowing 'largely escapes scrutiny' while detailed parliamentary examination of departmental supply expenditure 'was abandoned long ago'.[73] However, in the area of verifying the authorisation of expenditure and ascertaining that value for money has been obtained, the Public Accounts Committee has been notably effective. It is, as De Smith notes, 'scrupulously non-partisan',[74] while the value of its investigations is greatly enhanced by the fact that the Comptroller and Auditor-General, an officer of the House and therefore independent from the Government and assisted by a staff of several hundreds, sits with it.

9 The PAC's remit is 'to see that public moneys are applied for the purposes prescribed by Parliament, that extravagance and waste are minimised and that sound financial practices are encouraged in estimating and contracting and in administration generally'.[75] The committee seeks to achieve proper accountability by asking for clear objectives to be set, for proper monitoring of programmes to be established from their outset, and by comparing achievement with expectation. In the early 1980s it exposed the inadequate notice given to the House of the spiralling costs of the Polaris Enhancement Project which had reached £1,000 million from an initial estimate of £175 million. The committee revealed how such information was being concealed

---

72 Erskine May, *Parliamentary Practice*, 21st edn, p630.
73 *British Government and the Constitution* (1990), p482.
74 *Op cit*, p287.
75 Erskine May, *op cit*, p661.

from the Commons and won the significant promise from the Government that the committee would in future be supplied with adequate financial information about defence costs. Serious criticism has been levelled by the committee at the production costs of defence in the session 1985–86, the efficiency of the nationalised industries in the session 1986–87 and, in the same session, the cost of storing EC food surpluses.

10 Whilst many Select Committee reports are unanimous, they are not invariably so. Griffith and Ryle have produced detailed figures on the number of divisions within a committee on aspects of its report[76] (recorded in the minutes of the proceedings of the committee, which are published with the report),[77] and find that divisions are often, though not always, along party lines. 'A clear example of dissension on party lines was provided by the Energy Committee on the structure and ownership of the coal industry. Altogether there were over 40 divisions, almost all dividing with the same five Conservative members defeating the same four Labour members. ... During the 1983–87 Parliament there were eight principal occasions on which committees divided on the motion that the draft report ... be the report of the committee to the House. ... The Home Affairs Committee had two dissentients, both Labour, on the report on the Special Branch ... Three Labour members dissented from the report ... on the 1987 Budget ...'. 'The Foreign Affairs Committee also, where it divided, tended to do so on party lines, as in its consideration in 1984–85 of the sinking of the *Belgrano*, and of UK-Soviet relations and the Single European Act in 1985–6'.[78]

11 However, it remains true that most committee reports are unanimous and many are critical of Government policy. The Social Services Committee, for example, brought out a report which was critical of the Government-introduced Social Fund shortly before the 1991 General Election. On 7 November 1995 the Defence Select Committee produced a strongly worded report which described the Ministry of Defence's investigation into the effects of the so-called 'Gulf War syndrome' on British veterans of that conflict as 'wholly inadequate'. The committee took the rare step of calling a press conference to publicise their findings; it described the Ministry's response to veteran's complaints as 'characterised throughout by scepticism, defensiveness and general torpor'.[79] On the same day, the Treasury and Civil Service Select Committee demonstrated its independence by producing a report which raised serious concerns about the adequacy with which the Bank of England performs its role of supervising the banking industry, following the collapse of Barings Bank.[80] Both of these reports received considerable media coverage.

---

76 Griffith and Ryle, *op cit*, p429.
77 For an explanation of the committees' method of preparing their reports see Griffith and Ryle, *op cit*, p285.
78 *Ibid*, p429.
79 'MoD accused of turning blind eye to stricken troops', *Independent*, 7 November 1995.
80 'MPs want re-think on Bank's role', *Independent*, 7 November 1995.

12 One disappointing feature of the system of committee reports is that so few of them are actually debated. Brazier notes that 'by June 1990, only seven had been debated substantively, from a total of 591, although many others had been relevant to the course of other debates. Gathering information is an important exercise, but unless the House finds time to debate such information and conclusions there is an obvious danger that Select Committee reports will merely take up shelf space in libraries'.[81]

The problem of self incrimination

Where the committees seek to question individuals about suspected serious wrongdoing, a conflict may arise between the public interest in seeking the information in question, and the individual privilege against self-incrimination. This problem arose out of the investigation by the Social Security Select Committee of the Maxwell pension fund. When the committee called Kevin and Ian Maxwell, both refused to answer certain key questions.

First Special Report from the Social Security Committee, HC 353 (1991–92)

...

8 During the meeting both QCs [representing the Maxwells] argued that the committee should not proceed with its questions. Mr Carman, in defending his client's right to silence, introduced the concept of a person being 'on the threshold of charges' [Q389]. He also said that Mr Kevin Maxwell had been 'advised by me and by others that imminently he faces the risk of a criminal prosecution'[Q384], and Mr Jarvis, with reference to Mr Ian Maxwell, argued that the committee should not proceed with its questioning. There was, they said, a very real possibility of charges being made in the near future and that a public, televised committee session could jeopardise the prospects of a fair trial. It was further argued that Mr Ian Maxwell and Mr Kevin Maxwell had a right in common law not to incriminate themselves, a possibility that might exist if they answered the committee's questions, and also that under the terms of the House's own *sub judice* rule the committee should agree to postpone the meeting. Mr Jarvis did say that Mr Ian Maxwell would be prepared to answer written questions provided that no public use was made of the answers (he later added that another condition was that the answers should not be released to the Serious Fraud Office) [QQ336, 405]. Mr Carman said that this was something that Mr Kevin Maxwell was also prepared to consider [QQ393–4]. The committee then went into private session to consider the points made.

9 The committee decided that it was reasonable for the meeting to continue and for questions to be put in public. We were quite clear that the House's *sub judice* rule was not brought into play by any current legal proceedings. It is also the case that there is no right to silence in front of a Select Committee, whatever the position in common law. We also believed that, despite the legal difficulties Mr Ian Maxwell and Mr Kevin Maxwell faced, there were questions that they could answer without there being any danger of them incriminating themselves.

10 The committee therefore proceeded to put a total of four questions to the two Mr Maxwells. The four questions were:

---

81 Brazier, *Constitutional Practice* (1993), p228.

(i) Did you make attempts to gain copies of those documents [which the committee had ordered them to bring to the meeting] even though you may not be in possession of the originals [QQ407–8]?

(ii) We are looking at the pension funds as they relate to MCC and Mirror Group Newspapers; can you tell the committee which pension trust funds you belong to and at what period [QQ409–10]?

(iii) Who owns BIM [QQ411–12]?

(iv) What advice do you have for the committee and therefore the Government about the policy of self-investment'? Do you think a rate of 5%, which is what is being talked about, is sensible or not [QQ413–14]?

They each declined to answer any of these questions. The committee saw little point in continuing in those circumstances and therefore the meeting was brought to a close.

11 Colleagues expressed two opposing points of view to us. There was the concern that either or both of the witnesses might incriminate themselves, or that the televising of the proceedings (over which the House has decided that Select Committees have no say) would prevent a fair trial taking place should Mr Carman's prediction of Mr Kevin Maxwell being on 'the threshold of charges' prove accurate. The opposing view was that the refusal of a witness to help a committee with its inquiry, if it went unpunished, might lead to a weakening of the whole Select Committee system.

12 The committee kept both of these considerations in its mind when making each of its relevant decisions. But against them the committee saw an even greater threat to the Select Committee system. To opt not to undertake an inquiry into the operation of pension funds in the wake of Robert Maxwell's plundering of the pension funds he controlled would not merely be a betrayal of those citizens who have lost or may still lose their pensions. We believe it would have struck the public as an example of politicians unwilling to grapple with difficult issues which are of major importance to them.

13 Alternatively, to have undertaken an inquiry, but to have ignored the Maxwell brothers, seemed to us the equivalent of suggesting to Shakespeare that he was mistaken to have included the prince in Hamlet. As in practically all political decisions the question of balance is crucial, and it is a proper balance which we have tried to maintain in all the decisions we have made.

14 The committee decided to send a questionnaire for written answer to all those who had been trustees of the various Maxwell pension funds since 1984, the year that Robert Maxwell bought Mirror Group Newspapers. When sending out these questionnaires, we made it clear that the answers would be made public. Recipients of the questionnaire were also asked to indicate if they would be prepared to answer supplementary oral questions at a public meeting.

15 As we have already mentioned, three people declined to answer the questionnaire. These were Mr M Stoney, Mr Ian Maxwell and Mr Kevin Maxwell. Mr Ian Maxwell's and Mr Kevin Maxwell's refusals once again came via their solicitors. The reasons they gave for not answering the questionnaire were the same as those that had been given at the meeting on 13 January. The committee rejected the proposals that it should meet in private and refuse to publish its Minutes of Evidence. While Members of the committee are confident that any commitment they gave not to disclose any of the information given at that meeting would be honoured, they would not, however, be the only parties to the agreement and therefore could not

guarantee that information presented to them would not be selectively leaked.

16 When the committee changed the terms of reference of its inquiry into ownership and control of pension funds in early December it was aware that, at the very most, it would have only six months before a general election had to be called. As events have turned out only three months were available for the committee to complete the initial stages of its inquiry. But from the outset the committee has attempted to take a longer term view, both of the nature and scope of its inquiry, and of the behaviour of some witnesses. Simultaneously, the committee has always been mindful that it needed to balance a free and uninhibited inquiry against its wish to do nothing which might be used by others to claim that its activities had prevented a fair trial. The committee was aware of course that how this balance is struck might change over time.

17 The committee is mindful that the primary task of the Serious Fraud Office is to collect evidence on whether the law has been broken and, if so, to press charges, rather than to trace the missing funds and to secure their return. From the outset, the committee therefore was anxious, not only to play the historic role given to the House of Commons of voicing the grievance of constituents (in this instance, the grievance naturally felt by those contributors to the pension schemes run by Mr Robert Maxwell who have been defrauded) but also to open up these events to public scrutiny.

18 It is in carrying out this side of its inquiry that the refusal of the Maxwell brothers to give evidence has been most harmful to the committee's activities. We have not been able to gain first hand information from Mr Ian and Mr Kevin Maxwell on the structure and control operated within the Maxwell 'empire'. Nor were we able to put questions on whether any of the missing pension funds are still held by privately owned Maxwell companies, or in private Maxwell bank accounts held in countries outside the UK jurisdiction. Similarly, the committee was not able to gain first hand evidence from the Maxwell brothers on how they saw their personal role as trustees, how they carried out their responsibilities, nor to discuss with them their qualifications on being appointed to undertake such a role. Nor was the committee able to talk to Mr Ian and Mr Kevin Maxwell about the role of those US investment banks which were involved in the alleged illegal operation to support MCC shares by routing share purchases through off-shore trusts. There were also many other matters on which Mr Ian and Mr Kevin Maxwell could have assisted the committee.

19 Those Members who have had a chance to read our report on the ownership of pension funds [Second Report from the Social Security Committee, The Operation of Pension Funds, HC 61-II, 1991–92] will realise that lack of time has prevented this committee from doing any more than make a start on its inquiries into the plundering of assets from pension funds run by Mr Robert Maxwell. While the committee cannot bind its successor, or judge whom the House may appoint to a newly constituted Social Security Committee, all the Members of the current committee are standing for re-election and are committed after the election to pursuing the issues raised in that report.

20 There is no doubt that to refuse to answer questions in front of a Select Committee is a serious matter. The House of Commons expressed its view in a resolution agreed *nem con* on the 12 August 1947 'that the refusal of a witness before a Select Committee to answer any question which may be put to him is a contempt of the House and an infraction of the undoubted right of

this House to conduct any inquiry which may be necessary in the public interest' [Commons Journal (1946–47), p378].

21 We hope our colleagues in the House support the longer term approach to our inquiry which we have adopted. Similarly, although we believe that Mr Ian Maxwell and Mr Kevin Maxwell should be brought before the House for their refusal to answer questions properly put to them by the Select Committee, this has to be a matter for our successor committee. In political activity the question of timing is often as important as the subject itself. We therefore hope that our colleagues in the House share our view on the long term nature of the inquiries which we began in early December. We also trust that they accept that there is a need for them to find an appropriate time to consider the question of Mr Ian Maxwell and Mr Kevin Maxwell's *prima facie* contempt of the House.

Notes

1 If a committee is seriously dissatisfied with a refusal to disclose information it could table a motion for a debate of the matter in the House which might make a finding of contempt of Parliament. In 1981 the Leader of the House gave a 'formal undertaking' that if a refusal to disclose legitimately sought information was causing widespread concern in the House, the Government would 'seek' to find time for debate of the matter in the House. Such a pledge clearly gave the committees far less certainty with respect to the enforcement of their powers than that sought by the Select Committee on Procedure 1977–78 which in its First Report stated its belief that 'a more effective last resort' should be available to committees frustrated in their quest for legitimate information, and proposed that Parliamentary time should be guaranteed for a debate on an order for return of papers if repeated requests by the committee for information were refused. Their proposals have never been enacted.

2 Committees have, however, showed themselves unwilling to evoke contempt proceedings, leaving bad publicity from a refusal to attend as the main persuasive sanction. With regard to the committees' powers to enforce production of papers, it could be noted that the First Report from the Select Committee on Procedure, 1977–78, stated the committees belief that 'a more effective last resort should be available to committees' frustrated in their legitimate investigations; they suggested a procedure, namely that after a number of requests and then an order had been refused by the department concerned, time would be compulsorily made available for a Commons debate on an order for return of papers (paras 7.23–7.27).

Evaluation of the Select Committees

The views of the Government on the functioning of the Select Committees are of interest.

Minutes of evidence taken before the Select Committee on Procedure, 13 December 1989, HC, 19-iii (1989–90), pp19–21

ii. Effectiveness of departmental Select Committees

10 ... If Select Committee inquiries are to make a positive contribution to the work of Government or the House, the *choice* of subjects for investigation

needs to be apt and well-defined; the *timetable* of the inquiry and degree of *detail* well matched to developments in the field concerned; and the committees themselves sufficiently *well-informed* to make the most of the opportunities afforded by the cross-examination of those giving oral evidence. These matters are discussed in more detail below. But much rests on the chairmen of committees, in particular, to ensure that the aspirations of 1979 are fulfilled in individual inquiries and a return achieved for the considerable investment of time and energy made by ministers, officials and other witnesses.

11   In particular, an inquiry needs to be sufficiently focused to allow an in-depth study that is not overtaken by events by the time it is complete. Quick investigations of topical events may place extra work on ministers and officials who are already very busy on a live issue and need to be particularly carefully mounted if committees are to make a contribution which is both timely and thoroughly researched.

12   The choice and type of inquiries must ultimately remain in the hands of the committees themselves and they will no doubt wish to retain a balanced mixture. A committee's work is likely to be of greater value in the long run, in the Government's view, if it concentrates mainly on authoritative and well researched reports on issues of genuine significance to the public at large, with a bias towards the quality of their reports rather than their quantity.

13   As stated above, the success of Select Committees should not be judged solely on the number of their recommendations accepted or rejected by Government. Committee views and those of Government should be expected often to coincide, given that they will both have given serious consideration to the same questions and to a similar factual base. It does not follow that Government policy in such situations derives from committee recommendations, any more than it follows that the committee's view was determined solely by persuasive Government evidence. Similarly, the rejection of recommendations by Government does not necessarily mean that a committee's report has no influence either on Government or on the subsequent development of Government thinking.

iii. Impact on Government: workload for departments

14   The Government wishes to reaffirm the undertaking given in 1979 by the then Leader of the House (*Hansard* 25 June 1979, col 45) that the Government will make available to Select Committees as much information as possible, subject to certain safeguards for both ministers and committees. What follows should be read as within this overall approach.

15   There is a demonstrable impact in terms of increased workload through supplying memoranda and oral evidence and preparing the necessary briefing. Available estimates of staff costs range from £5,000 to £26,000 per inquiry, with, for example, 360 staff hours in two weeks being required of the Inland Revenue and a similar effort from Customs and Excise for one recent inquiry. The increased scale and detail of committee inquiries also has a direct impact (for example, the number of memoranda sought from the Ministry of Defence has gone up ten-fold from five in 1984–85 to 53 in 1987–88). The direct cost of responding to Select Committee inquiries, although significant in absolute terms, is, however, small relative to the totality of public expenditure, or the totality of departmental running costs. For this reason, no new attempt has been made to assess the attributable costs in public expenditure terms of dealing with requests from committees for evidence. ...

20   The increased scale of Select Committee activity, and the consequently increased pressures on senior officials, mean that ministers continue to attach considerable importance to the well established convention (see eg para 7.8 of the Report of the Procedure Committee in 1977/8, and the memorandum by the Clerk of the House at Appendix C of that report) that they have discretion to decide which officials should give evidence on their behalf.

...

v. Possible changes in practice or procedure

22   The existing procedures and practices of departmental Select Committees vary significantly and a number of the following suggestions for consideration by the Procedure Committee would amount to the adoption generally of good practice already adopted by some committees.

23   Planning of inquiries. With the consolidation of the place of the departmental committees in the work of the House, and the growth in the scale and impact of their work, there is a case for the committees taking steps to plan their forward work programmes in a systematic fashion. This might contain the following elements:

(a)   committees could draw up forward work programmes each autumn for the session ahead, the details and timing of which could then be the subject of informal discussion with departments to mutual advantage, and the final versions forwarded to departments;

(b)   where committees wish to mount a potentially wide-ranging inquiry, there may be benefits in a two stage approach – an initial, fairly brief, inquiry across the whole range, followed by a second stage concentrating on a limited number of specific topics where a more in-depth scrutiny would be of greater value to both the House and the Government;

(c)   it is common current practice for officials to give evidence early in an inquiry and for ministers to do so towards the end. The Government would not wish to propose a universal rule in this area and indeed some inquiries proceed without ministerial evidence being taken at any stage. But where ministerial evidence is sought, there can be particular advantages in the practice of taking it in the final stages of an inquiry. This allows committees to explore apparent conflicts of evidence and criticisms of Government made by other witnesses, at a stage when the committee is close to formulating its conclusions and recommendations. Suggestions for future action made by others can also be tested out.

Such an approach would not, of course, rule out additional inquiries into subjects which gain prominence in the course of a year.

24   Control by committees of their work. In order to enable ministerial and official witnesses to be as helpful as possible to committees in their oral evidence and to keep related briefing focused on the essentials, the committee might wish to consider the following:

(a)   ministerial and official witnesses (and indeed other witnesses also) could be given a clear indication five or more days in advance of the main lines of questioning Members will wish to pursue;

(b)   if additional lines of questioning are pursued without such advance indications, committees may need to recognise that immediate answers may not be possible.

This approach would help to ensure that witnesses are able to answer the questions Members wish to ask and reduce wasted effort in departments preparing briefing on topics not raised.

vii. Overall Impact of the work of Select Committees on the House as a whole

33. This must be primarily for the House itself to judge. The Government's perception is that the work of Select Committees has helped to make the wider work of the House better informed and as such has been beneficial, but that improvements in the quality of Select Committee work are possible which would enhance their contribution further, both to the work of Government and the work of the House.

Question

This Government report appears to suggest general satisfaction with the present operation of the committees. Is this an indication that their impact has in fact been minimal?

Notes

1   The suggestion that Select Committees plan their work more systematically (para 23) is of interest. Whilst many commentators believe that the committees' work is insufficiently methodical, and driven by short term political considerations (see below pp395–7), to hear the suggestion of greater forward planning from the Government should make one pause. The suggestion made is that committees should confer with Government departments over subjects for discussion after drawing up forward work programmes (para 23a). The cynical-minded might suspect that Government departments would like to have advance notice of areas of their activities which will come under scrutiny, not so that they could co-operate more fully with the committees, but rather so that they could have time to prepare to give the committees a favourable impression, eg by concealing embarrassing policy blunders from scrutiny or preparing to give an impression of activity in a particular area where no real action is being taken.

2   Michael Ryle, in his evidence to the Select Committee on Procedure, also expressed broad approval of the present scheme.

Minutes of Evidence taken before the Select Committee on Procedure, HC 19-ii (1989–90)

Wednesday 6 December 1989

Memorandum by Mr Michael Ryle (SC 35)

1   Select Committees are instruments of Parliament. They cannot be designed, developed or assessed without regard to the functions of the House. Their value must be measured by the extent to which they assist the fulfilment of those functions.

2   At the heart of the functions of the House of Commons today lies the task of scrutinising the policies and acts of the Government. Ministers must explain and defend – or be prepared to explain and defend – everything they do or propose to do. Their principal critics, the Opposition parties, must equally explain and defend their alternative policies. Parliament is essentially a critical forum through which the powers of Government are exercised and in which they are publicly examined.

3   The influence of Parliament depends on the extent to which its critical process both reflects and conditions public opinion. To be effective the House of Commons must both listen to and speak to the people it represents.

4   This public criticism, to be effective, requires the use of procedures which enable ministers, civil servants and others to be examined in detail on their responsibilities, and, above all, which provide access to the information necessary to assets their conduct. The great growth in this century in the range, volume and complexity of modern government has meant that this criticism in depth can no longer be achieved by the simple process of debate followed by vote, and that there is not enough time for the actions of ministers to be fully considered on the floor of the House. Hence the development of a range of committee systems. ...

The departmentally-related Select Committees

6   I have long argued that if the House is effectively to get to grips with the policies and actions of ministers, this could only be done by specialist Select Committees concerned with the affairs of each Government department. In my view, with a few qualifications, the present system is well designed to do this and the present committees are, by and large, working very well. I would not wish to suggest any major changes in their powers or in the way they use them.

7   In my view the main achievements of the new Select Committees have been:

   (a) more frequent and systematic examination of ministers than can be achieved on the floor of the House;

   (b) the discovery and publication of much more information about the workings of Government, which has enriched public discussion of issues both inside and outside Parliament; this is reflected in the increasingly frequent references to Select Committees in the media and in debate in the House;

   (c) enhancement of contact between Parliament and the people by public examination of witnesses from outside Government, by visits around the country and by increased media coverage (the regular reporting of Select Committees on television may prove particularly significant);

   (d) the bringing into the open of arguments between Government and pressure or interest groups (or between such groups) previously largely conducted in private; and

   (e) the strengthening of the influence of Parliament on the formulation of Government policy. Committee reports and recommendations clearly have some influence; the very process of inquiry has more; but the potential of inquiry 'how will the committee react to this policy' in my opinion may be the most important factor of all. The Select Committees have added a new parliamentary dimension to the Government decision-taking process.

8   Against this background of relative success (of course not all committees have always succeeded) it would, in my view, be a grave mistake to interfere with the way these committees operate. One of the strengths of the new system has been the freedom left to committees to choose their subjects for inquiry. This has led to rich variety of investigations, employing different methods for different matters. It would, I believe, be damaging and restrictive if the House attempted to impose on these committees more specific duties to scrutinise particular issues or areas of business, or to standardise their working methods.

9   Having said that, I suggest a few points which I would be happy to amplify, if so requested, in oral evidence. ...

(b) means must be found to include the scrutiny of the Scottish Office within the scope of Select Committees;

(c) I do not believe that the present departmentally-related committees should be directly involved in the legislative process, but it might be desirable if committees were to review systematically how Acts of Parliament (including the relevant delegated legislation) are operating in practice within a few years of their coming into effect;

(d) the most significant decisions in the planning and control of public expenditure involve difficult choices and assessment of priorities; Governments have to make such choices, but the House rarely does. Select Committees could play a more active part in clarifying the nature of these choices, examining the consequences of alternative policies, and indicating their own preference. This should be done at both the macro-economic level – the choices between expenditures in major policy areas (between health and education, for example) – and in more detail by examining the balance of expenditure within individual policy areas (within the NHS for example); and

(e) Select Committees might profitably examine, in more detail than can be done in debates on the finance bills, the implications of various fiscal policies and detailed tax proposals.

Notes

1 Michael Ryle views Parliament as a 'critical forum through which the powers of Government are exercised and in which they are publicly examined'; this would seem to exclude any view of Parliament as a policy making or even policy influencing forum. This would not appear to be a view shared by the Chair of the Education, Sciences and Arts Committee, which reported in 1982–83: 'Our British Library report was immediately followed by a Government decision to build it, our higher education report led to the establishment of a National Advisory Body in the public sector, our Proms report restored the concerts to the Albert Hall, and our ICCRROM report re-established the British subscription to that organisation'.[82]

2 It can be difficult to assess the impact of the committees on departmental policy-making because committee reports may merely contribute to debate which is already taking place. One of the few examples of a Select Committee report apparently resulting in a clear change in Government policy can be seen in the decision to repeal the 'sus' law by means of the Criminal Attempts Act 1981 after a critical report from the Home Affairs Select Committee. It has to be conceded that such examples are very much the exception. Griffith and Ryle's blunt conclusion is that 'Select Committees have not made a general impact on Government polices'.[83] As Norton notes, they are essentially 'advisory bodies' only;[84] Gavin Drewry comments that the committees 'are in the business of scrutiny and exposure, not Government'.[85] Where their activities do impact on policy, this is more

---

82 HC 92 (1982–3), quoted in Griffith and Ryle, *op cit*, p432.

83 *Op cit*, p430.

84 *Does Parliament Matter?*, p108.

85 *The New Select Committees* (1989).

likely to happen in relatively 'non political' areas, as appears from the list of achievements cited by the Education, Sciences and Arts Committee above; to expect them to be able to change contentious party-driven policies is clearly unrealistic.

3   The Chairman of the Select Committees Liaison Committee, Terence Higgins, in a memorandum produced in 1990, makes a number of sensible suggestions for reform, and warns against assessing the success of the committees by reference only to their impact on Government policy.

Minutes of Evidence taken before the Select Committee on Procedure, HC 19-iv (1989–90)

Wednesday 17 January 1990

Memorandum by Rt Hon Terence L Higgins MP, Chairman of the Liaison Committee

The working of the Select Committee system

...

2   The experience of the last 10 years leads me to believe that the structure of the committee system established in 1979 was fundamentally right. I am not therefore in favour of any radical changes. On the contrary, I believe it is important to defend and re-affirm the basic principles which have become established. Nonetheless, this is clearly an appropriate moment to consider how the system could he improved in the light of experience.

5   There are two features of the 'new' Select Committee system set up in 1979 which I believe are fundamental and essential to its success. First, the committees are related to departments. Secondly, they operate on an all-party basis. I begin by discussing each of these, and then the work of the Liaison Committee, before turning to more detailed points and concluding with an appraisal of the present system's effectiveness.

The departmental relationship

6   The relationship of individual Select Committees to particular Government departments has meant that their Members have been able to build up specific expertise regarding that part of government whose expenditure, administration and policy it is their task to scrutinise. Over time, this has enabled them to establish a continuing relationship with ministers and officials, and over the lifetime of a Parliament members of a committee may indeed acquire more knowledge and experience of a department than those whose work they are monitoring. It is interesting to note that, contrary to the fears expressed by some commentators when the departmental committees were set up, they have not become too closely identified with the interests of their department.

The all-party approach

13   The fact that the committee system operates on an all-party basis has undoubtedly been one of its greatest strengths. To a remarkable extent committees have succeeded in producing unanimous reports and in general a non-partisan approach has been adopted when taking evidence in public. There can be no doubt that when committees do reach a consensus after investigating matters in depth, the impact of their reports is far greater than if they simply divide on party lines. The comments which I make on a number of specific issues are clearly important in ensuring that the committees continue to do their work on behalf of the House as a whole as impartially as possible.

Chairmen

14 I am convinced that if the system is to retain the respect it has built up over the last decade, it is most important that the chairmanships of the departmental committees should continue to be shared amongst the parties. The present Government deserves credit for recognising this through three successive Parliaments. There is, however, a danger after each general election, and particularly when there is a change of Government, that an incoming administration might be tempted to secure all the chairmanships for members of its own party. I hope that the Procedure Committee will recommend that the committee chairmanships should continue to be shared between the parties on the present basis (that is to say in relation to the main parties' representation in the House).

15 In general I believe that the Whips should be involved as little as possible in Select Committee affairs. However, I recognise that as each Select Committee has a majority of Government Members, they will not naturally elect chairmen from among their opposition Members. An agreement 'through the usual channels' is therefore necessary for some committees to be chaired by opposition Members. I recognise this is unavoidable if the present arrangement regarding chairmen is to be maintained.

Nomination of committees

16 I am somewhat concerned about the present arrangements for nomination of Select Committees. Debates on the floor of the House have given the impression that in some cases internal party discussions and the influence of the Whips may have had a decisive influence on the choices made by the Committee of Selection [for example 'it is for each party to decide which hon Members it will nominate' (HC Deb 1987–88, 125, c398) 3 HC (1981–82) 92, para 42]. The Procedure Committee may wish to examine whether this is a problem as far as all party Select Committees are concerned. The requirement for recommendations of the Committee of Selection to be endorsed by a debatable motion on the floor of the House, gives some protection against the packing of committees with party 'loyalists' or the exclusion of those of particularly independent views. But I am not convinced that this protection is adequate in all circumstances.

17 One of the strengths of the Select Committee system is that Members are nominated for a Parliament and except in the most exceptional circumstances cannot be removed. This is important as far as maintaining their independence is concerned and I strongly recommend that this should be preserved. However, this is difficult to achieve when adjustments are made to the parliamentary Select Committee system to conform with the departmental structure of Government. It is arguable that when an existing departmental Select Committee is divided because there has been a corresponding division in a Government department, members of the existing committee should be entitled to priority on one or other of the new divided committees. And when departments are merged members of the new, unified, committee should be drawn from the members of the existing committees.

...

Formal powers

39 The formal powers of the departmentally-related committees appear adequate. In particular the power to send for 'persons, papers and records' has secured for committees the evidence and information they need and use

of them has ensured the attendance of reluctant witnesses from outside the field of Government and Parliament when necessary.

40　The undertaking given by the then Leader of the House on 11 January 1981, that if there was widespread general concern in the House regarding an alleged ministerial refusal to appear or disclose information to a Select Committee, time would be provided for a debate on the matter, appears to be sufficient to protect the rights of Select Committees in relation to ministers.

41　Controversy has however arisen in two recent cases – the 'Westland' affair, and the reluctance of the Member for Derbyshire South [Edwina Currie] to appear before the Agriculture Committee.

42　Personally I consider the outcome of the whole series of reports by the Treasury Committee [HC (1985–86) 92 and (1986–87) 62], the Defence Committee [HC (1985–86) 519] and the Liaison Committee [HC (1986–87) 100], which began with the Treasury inquiry into the relationship between ministers and civil servants and continued in the specific case of 'Westland', the relevant replies by the Government [Cmnd 9841, 9916 and Cm 78] and the subsequent debate [HC Deb (1985–86) 103, cc339–416], was highly satisfactory. We now have the position established that if an official refuses to give evidence to a Select Committee on the grounds that this would raise questions about his 'conduct', he will not be questioned further but the minister to whom he is responsible can be required to investigate what has been going on and then inform the committee of the result of his investigations This is a significant improvement in Parliamentary accountability compared with what was thought to be the previous position.

43　The second case is rather different and raises the question of whether a Member of Parliament is entitled to refuse to give evidence to a Select Committee. I realise there are various opinions on this. Personally I believe Members have a duty to help any committee that the House has asked to carry out duties on its behalf. So I am glad that no precedent has recently been created which suggests a Member need not do so.

...

The effectiveness of the system

64　In general ministers, and to a significant extent civil servants, now face intensive interrogation in a way which was simply not achieved before the 1979–80 reforms. Debates on the floor of the House, interventions in speeches, parliamentary questions, valuable though they are, do not enable Members to get to the heart of a matter in as effective a way as they can in a lengthy and well organised committee session. However tested ministers may be on the floor of the House, appearance before a Select Committee is in many ways a far more rigorous exercise.

65　Another important distinction between business on the Floor of the House and proceedings in a Select Committee is that each committee chooses its own subjects for investigation, whereas business on the Floor of the House is largely dictated by the Government or the official Opposition, which tends to result in debates of immediate partisan interest. Furthermore, the system is flexible. A committee can carry out a study in depth over many months, or, if more appropriate, turn its attention at a few hours' notice to a matter which requires urgent investigation.

66　In appraising the success or otherwise of the committee system, it would be a mistake to concentrate too precisely on the extent to which committees' recommendations have been accepted or not accepted by the Government. In a great many cases, ministers do accept committee recommendations. Sometimes this means progress on a particular issue is more rapid than it would otherwise have been. It is naturally more difficult for a committee to persuade a minister that a whole policy should be reversed; but even this can and does happen. Similarly, it is important to note that while the number of debates on specific Select Committee reports is limited, there are now a considerable number of debates in which committee reports are 'tagged' on the order paper, thus enabling the House to consider matters in greater depth and better briefed (see also para 52).

67   The potential impact of a Select Committee inquiry is likely to be particularly effective whenever a minister is considering a change in policy. In addition to considering the reaction on the floor of the House, ministers and their advisers now have to take into account how the Select Committee will react and how they will explain and justify their decisions in detail.

...

69   The Select Committee system has also given new opportunities to those outside the House of Commons. They have increasingly provided a forum where pressure groups and other bodies outside Government have been able to bring their problems, requests and views before Parliament and to have them analysed. Much of the evidence given to committees comes from such bodies. It is valuable in enabling the committees to hear all points of view and to put often conflicting points to ministers and civil servants for comment. Additionally, the process of publication of evidence from such sources means that it can in its turn be tested or challenged; pressure groups' arguments are now subject to closer scrutiny.

Note

This broadly satisfied survey of the work of the committees may be contrasted with the critiques which follow. Pythian and Little note the ineffectiveness of the Select Committees in revealing covert Government policy on arms to Iraq; Giddings takes a generally critical overview.

M Pythian and W Little, 'Parliament and Arms Sales: Lessons of the Matrix Churchill Affair' (1993) 46(3) *Parliamentary Affairs* 293, 295–6

In principle the Select Committee system is supposed to act as some sort of a check on the actions of the executive. However, committees have limited resources and powers, and consequently rely heavily upon the co-operation of the departments which they oversee. Too aggressive an investigation may lead to co-operation being withdrawn (refusal to send key civil servants before the committee for example) and might even jeopardise future relations. Moreover, for superannuated back-benchers Select Committees offer a belated chance of a knighthood (or at least some overseas trips) and they are well aware that the Whips who control such patronage keep a close eye on their committee activities.

The House of Commons Trade and Industry Select Committee investigation of the Supergun affair illustrates some of these weaknesses. Initially set to investigate British arms sales to Iraq, it backed off when it discovered the enormity of the task and decided to concentrate solely on the Supergun affair. It then transpired that key officials had been prevented from giving evidence. For example, under cross-examination at the Old Bailey, Eric Beston admitted that he had been summoned by the committee but had been ordered by Peter Lilley (the minister) not to comply because of the risk that 'dirty washing' might be aired to the consequent embarrassment of the Government.

The committee did secure an apparent victory over the Department of Trade and Industry when it secured a comprehensive list of all products licensed for export to Iraq by the DTI between January 1987 and August 1990. While on the surface this may seem to prove that Parliament can effectively oversee this aspect of Government policy, the published list leaves a lot to be desired. The listing is of equipment type rather than specific equipment, and as such is not of as much use as it might at first seem. For instance, 'radar systems and equipment' is the entry which denotes the export of Thorn EMI's Cymbeline radar system without detailing its ability to locate enemy weapons, including artillery and helicopters, and direct the fire of mortars and guns. Neither does it record the quantity exported and over precisely what time period, nor the fact that Iraq was the world's largest user of the Cymbeline, nor that Iraqi servicemen were trained in its operation in Britain.

Furthermore, while the committee's published memoranda of evidence list all companies participating at the annual Baghdad Trade Fairs from 1980 to 1989, it fails to recognise the occurrence of perhaps the most significant of all the fairs held in Baghdad during this period – the one and only Baghdad International Military Exhibition, held in 1989 – let alone list the 17 British companies exhibiting there, nor the fact that a member of the MoD's sales department (DESO), David Hastie, attended – hence ensuring that he need not give evidence.

It should be no surprise, then, that the conclusions reached by the Select Committee are far less critical of departments of Government than could have been expected. In achieving this result, the Conservative majority on the committee vetoed references pointing to and critical of the role of the intelligence services, thus lending greater credence to the official line that the Supergun scandal was no more than a bureaucratic failing due to excessive compartmentalisation. On a number of occasions the Chairman, Kenneth Warren, used his casting vote to achieve this. His role also extended to meeting two witnesses critical of the Government – Gerald James and Christopher Cowley – prior to their appearance where he was able to preview their testimonies.

P Giddings, 'Select Committees and Parliamentary Scrutiny: *Plus ça change?*' (1994) 47(4) *Parliamentary Affairs* 668, 682–5

... taken as a whole the work of the committees has been unsystematic and its coverage of the work of Government patchy, not to say idiosyncratic. In spite of the existence of the Liaison Committee with a co-ordinating brief, each committee is a law unto itself in the choice of topics for investigation. And the same political dynamic is often evident in the pattern of questioning, which does not always follow a coherent strategy. Members are first and foremost political animals and generalists. They will pursue those topics and lines of inquiry which fit with their perception of the political needs of the moment, which may nor immediately relate to the requirements of rational or systematic analysis of policy issues, expenditure priorities or administrative systems, nor to the brief which has been put before them by the clerk.

Second, and really a particular instance of the first criticism, notwithstanding the terms of reference of the committees, repeated encouragement from the Liaison Committee, and even draft model questions from the Treasury Committee, expenditure has been largely neglected. Some committees have held hearings on their department's annual report and the Defence Committee, as already noted, has done considerable work on the procurement of some weapons systems, but the committees as a whole have not provided the systematic and comprehensive review of public expenditure which some had hoped to see. To a large degree, this simply reflects the fact that relatively few MPs are interested in this at the level of detail which is required for such investigations and, like departmental administration, it comes low in their priorities when compared with major items of policy.

Whilst the establishment of the departmentally-related Select Committees was the major development of the 1980s, it was not the only important one. Concern over the control of public expenditure led to an increase in the powers of the Public Accounts Committee, the House's most venerable Select Committee, in the National Audit Act, 1983 – passed in spite of strong Government opposition to its central features. The Act converted the old Exchequer and Audit Department to a new and independent National Audit Office (NAO) and extended its remit to cover 'value for money' investigations and the activities of any body (other than local authorities or nationalised industries) which receives more than half of its income from public funds. The enhanced independence and wider remit for the Comptroller and Auditor General and the NAO has given the PAC a renewed vigour, which it has most recently demonstrated with its report on the Conduct of Public Business. Although policy matters remain formally outside its remit, the value-for-money investigations in particular have taken the PAC into the heart of controversial areas of government activity, such as housing benefits, control of local authority spending, NHS costs and defence procurement.

Plus ça change ...

'The evolution of Select Committees has proceeded in a manner which maintains the continuity of institutional forms in the House of Commons. It has been a work of cautious adaptation, sensitive to the susceptibilities of those in Government but bringing renewed vitality to the traditional critical functions of Parliament'. That assessment in 1988 remains true today. Caution, continuity and adaptation have been hallmarks of the development of the Select Committee system in the last 50 years. ... Indeed, the principal features of that system remain untouched: the Chamber of the House of Commons remains the primary forum for debate and decision; the mode of behaviour and discourse in the House is still that of cohesive, adversarial parties; single party majority Government remains the norm; the executive is still dominant. *'Plus la même chose.'* Whilst Select Committees have grown and become more prominent, they do not provide an alternative career structure to ministerial office, even if they do provide a useful staging-post in the career of some ambitious younger MPs as well as for some of those whose ministerial days are over. On the other hand, they do provide an outlet for the increased professionalisation which has been so marked in British parliamentary politics in the last 30 years.

Although the fundamentals remain the same, change there has certainly been. Select Committees have grown in number and significance, particularly if one takes the quantity of activity and published output as an indicator. Scrutiny has been extended, accountability deepened and policy debate widened. A substantial and continuous process of explanatory dialogue between ministers and their officials on the one side and back-bench MPs on the other is taking place across the whole range of Government, absorbing a significant and growing amount of the energies and time of all concerned.

How might the Select Committee system develop? If, as seems most likely whilst the present party and electoral systems remain intact, they continue as scrutiny rather than decision-making committees, the obvious developments are those which would build upon the existing system. A further extension of the range of scrutiny, including, for example, the security services, is desirable. Deeper scrutiny of administration and expenditure would be possible with more staff resources and, in particular, if the services of the National Audit Office could be made more widely available and perhaps extended in coverage. The increased (but still relative) openness of Government which will result from the 1993 White Paper *Open Government* should provide plenty of material for committee members (and their advisers and assistants) to explore.

A more radical development would be for the committees to engage with the passage of parliamentary business, such as legislation or expenditure. One of the reasons for Governments' relatively benign attitude to Select Committees has been that, if necessary, they can afford to ignore them, at least as far as the dispatch of Government business is concerned. Whilst it is helpful for Governments to have the support of Select Committees (on which, of course, their nominal supporters are normally in a majority), it is not necessary. Adverse or critical reports from scrutiny committees are an irritant or an embarrassment, but no more. However, should the committees become engaged with the legislative or expenditure process, the Government – and hence the whips – would be bound to take a much closer interest in their work, and especially in their votes. This would undoubtedly lead to a very significant shift away from the consensual mode of Select Committee work towards the adversarial. The dispatch of business would become the priority. Such a development seems unlikely in present political circumstances: Governments, particularly Governments with small majorities, are not likely to add to the number of hurdles they have to clear in getting their programme through Parliament.

Two factors may, nevertheless, generate pressure for change. The first is the growing perception that the House of Commons is over-loaded. The difficulties encountered in setting up the European legislation committees and the responses to the Jopling Report both indicate that Members see themselves as over-burdened and are pressing for significant rationalisation. The growth of Select Committee activity has, of course, contributed to the pressure of business, but there is little sign so far that many Members are willing to countenance reducing Select Committee work as a way of cutting the burden. (Standing Committees would be a more popular choice for a reduced role.) But as the pressure for rationalisation becomes stronger, then the case for a more co-ordinated and systematic Select Committee structure – looking for example at whether departmentally-related committees should deal with European business, PCA and even NAO reports – will also grow, however much individual committees protest that they should be free to determine their own priorities. Such an outcome is unlikely, but there is no doubt that the signs of overload are there, for the House as well as the Government.

The second factor is the clear need for reform of the legislative process. Few, apart from Government business managers, find the present arrangements satisfactory, particularly in standing committees. The need for extensive Government amendments to legislation in the course of its passage, and increasingly after it has passed, has demonstrated the inadequacy of present scrutiny. This ground has been well worked over by the Rippon Commission's *Making the Law* (Hansard Society, February 1993). Legislative reform should be a priority for the House of Commons and it would not be surprising if Select Committees featured when it is considered – indeed, it would be astonishing if they did not. The case for using the committees for some form of pre-legislative hearings, the use of special standing committees and similar devices will all have their backers, no doubt. Reformers will need to beware how easily involving

Select Committees in the passage of business could destroy their present *raison d'être* as instruments of scrutiny.

Notes

1 There might seem to be a discouraging paradox at the heart of assessment of the committees. Giddings criticises the Select Committees for being too influenced by political considerations in their choices of subject for scrutiny. At the same time, however, many commentators would like to see the role of the committees strengthened. One obvious way to do this, as Giddings suggests, would be by giving the committees a role to play in the present, unsatisfactory system of passing legislation. However, as Giddings immediately concedes, making this change, or any other which made the committees more influential, would ensure greater attention from the Government and the Whips, leading, as he puts it, to 'a significant shift away from the consensual mode of [their] work towards the adversarial'. It is the non-partisan nature of the committees that most commentators would identify as one of their most valuable features. The conclusion seems to be that the committees cannot be strengthened without losing much of their value.

2 Professor Hennessey has recently argued[86] that, leaving aside formal changes to their powers and jurisdiction, the Select Committees could still achieve far more simply by being more bold in their aspirations:

> Now the problem with the Select Committees ... is really what Ernie Bevin once said of his beloved working class, that it is the 'poverty of their aspirations' that is so breathtaking and disappointing because they will not push things beyond a certain point. They will not keep at it. It is not entirely their fault ... in that you cannot talk to these people about this or talk about that because it is national security and so on and you cannot talk to the officials that actually did it ... Yet I have always thought that, in the end, if Select Committees really pushed this, perhaps having to go to votes in the House or orders from the floor and so on for people to attend, the whole climate would change. Apart from the Public Accounts Committee, you see, those who are steeped in executive convenience do not really walk in fear of these bodies like yours and they should do because, apart from anything else, you ... are all we have got and by 'we', I mean the Queen's subjects, not just this place.[87]

3 Important proposals by the Labour Party for reform of the House of Commons announced in a meeting with Charter 88 on 14 May 1996 revolve around giving greater powers to the Select Committees.[88] First, they would be given powers to examine proposed Chairs of executive agencies and quangos and be empowered to 'ratify senior public appointments, such as the Governor of the Bank of England'.[89] Second, echoing the suggestions put forward by Giddings, they would be given important new powers to

---

86 See the minutes of evidence taken before the Public Services Committee on 20 March 1996, HC 313 (1995–96).

87 *Ibid*, Q90.

88 The proposals are set out in a paper, called *New Politics, New Parliament* available from the Labour party. Vernon Bogdnaor's comments on the proposals given below are from his article, 'The Westminster Malaise', *Independent*, 15 May 1996.

89 *Ibid*.

examine legislation before it was formally introduced into Parliament. Committees in the relevant field would be able to call witnesses to comment on the desirability and workability of the proposed legislation, and examine Green and White papers and other materials, such as comments from interested parties, thereby inputting into the pre-legislative process and increasing potential for informed contributions to legislative debate. However, in discussing these proposals, Vernon Bogdanor reaches the same conclusion as Giddings: as long as Parliament continues to be dominated by an adversarial two party system (which Bogdanor considers could only be cured by reform of the electoral system), the increased power of the committees would simply attract the attention of the Whips, destroying the current relative independent-mindedness of the committees.[90] It was suggested by Ann Clwyd that this could be avoided by taking the Whips out of the selection of committee members, putting the decision in the hands of back-benchers only, but Bogdanor regards this as a 'Utopian hope'. The proposals are certainly an interesting suggestion, and if implemented would amount to the biggest change to the House since the introduction of the present Select Committee system in 1979.

Scrutiny of the executive: conclusions and proposals for reform

Two contrasting views appear below. McEldowney and McAuslan emphasise above all that Parliamentary scrutiny of an ever burgeoning executive depends upon the consent, good will and good faith of Government ministers and civil servants. They believe that such benign and co-operative attitudes towards parliamentary scrutiny on the part of the executive are by no means always evident.

McEldowney and McAuslan, 'Legitimacy and the Constitution: the Dissonance between Theory and Practice' in McAuslan and McEldowney (eds), *Law, Legitimacy and the Constitution* (1985), pp20–24

What has developed over the last two decades and particularly since 1979 is a multitude of Select Committees, established to increase the effectiveness of Parliamentary control over the executive, by increasing the opportunities for MPs to question, with the aid of specialist advisers, both civil servants and ministers, about policy and its implementation. A further step in the direction of increased financial control came with the National Audit Act of 1983 which expanded the powers of the Comptroller and Auditor-General to conduct value for money audits of Government departments and other public agencies, and affirmed his status as an officer of Parliament not of the Government. These steps could be regarded as off-setting trends noted earlier. Maybe there are less checks on Government outside Parliament and less commitment to participation, but the checking role of MPs has been boosted and their participation in useful fact-finding committees increased. This is precisely the development one should be looking for in a parliamentary democracy.

---

90 *Ibid.*

The establishment of committees is one thing; taking them seriously and facilitating their work another. The latter requires that information be released to committees and that ministers and civil servants appear before and answer questions fully and to the best of their ability. It requires, in short, the co-operation of the executive and to that extent is a species of auto-limitation. Auto-limitation via parliamentary Select Committees has then replaced or may be seen as a partial replacement for the potentially more effective checks on central Governmental power which large and well financed elected local Governments may ensure.

How has this species of auto-limitation worked? The committees have produced many reports, been responsible for the publication of a great deal of useful information given to them in evidence and have to that extent undoubtedly increased our general understanding and knowledge of the policy-making process and the forces and arguments that bear upon that process. But that is not their main function. In respect of that function, the checking and controlling of the executive, we cannot give such a sanguine verdict. Ministers from both Labour and Conservative Governments have been, at best, reluctant participants in the process and have instructed civil servants likewise. There have been well publicised occasions when information has been refused to committees. As the Ponting trial brought out, misleading information has been given to committees, information which by no stretch of the imagination could be claimed, as it was in that case, as being in need of protection because of national security. Nor has the enhanced status, powers and salaries of the Comptroller and Auditor-General and his staff resulted in any dramatic improvement in controlling the way central Government spends its money; waste still occurs and there remains the problem of ensuring that action is taken to meet the criticism of the Comptroller and the committee to which he reports. This is a problem which affects all the committees.

Again, it may be argued that this is carping criticism. The committees are in place and, despite some inevitable tension between them and the executive, are producing more information about what the Government is doing which is a major factor in increasing accountability. Even the discovery of false and misleading information which is given to committees is evidence of their success, as, without their perseverance, such behaviour might well not have been unearthed. No Government can or would hand over policy-making and implementation to the House of Commons and critics of the alleged ineffectiveness of the committees seem to assume that that is what should have happened. It is, *au fond*, a question of balance, of give and take, and overall, judged on that common-sense basis, the committees are a useful adjunct to the total process of ministerial responsibility.

We come back to our point made earlier. The committees exist to do more than provide more information about the policy-making process and, if that is all that can be claimed for them, then they cannot be accounted a success in the matter of controlling the executive. The issue may be put in this way. At a time when other checks are being done away with or made less effective, can we see the committees as effective replacements? Can we see any evidence that Government goes about its business in a positively better way because of the presence of the committees? If on the other hand the evidence is that policy-making is more secretive, implementation is more casual in matters of complying with law and fair administrative practices, the House of Commons is treated in a more cavalier fashion, then we would be forced to conclude with Ian Aitken that:

> It should by now be obvious ... that a system greeted with such fanfares of
> libertarian enthusiasm six years ago is little more than a sham unless it has

full powers to demand and to get the truth from public servants paid from the public purse ... If their [the MPs who created and believed in the committees] creation is worth keeping, it must have the powers to perform its investigative function ['Why Parliament should put Select Committees on trial' *Guardian*, 15 February 1985, p9].

The House of Commons is then being downgraded or by-passed as an effective check or control on the powers of central Government; a point made by commentators of all political hues for many years. This is quite simply because the effectiveness of the House of Commons depends ultimately upon the co-operation of the Government of the day with the members of the House, other than in those comparatively rare occasions when a Government has no majority in the House. A Government minded to get its way, and give nothing away, can reduce the House to comparative impotence. It will always be possible to point to some 'victories': concessions on legislation forced out of an unwilling Government running out of time in a session; admissions on misleading information, and an apology given to a Select Committee; the backing down on a policy initiative because of (Government) back-bench opposition. Examples of all of these can readily be found over the last five or six years; but at a time when effective extra-Parliamentary though lawful checks on Government power are being reduced, parliamentary checks need to be increased and that is not happening.

Note

By contrast, Bernard Crick, taking a rather more limited view of the proper role of the House of Commons, suggests that its powers cannot be increased markedly, that it should not attempt to escape from its inevitably political role; and that any idea of its sharing executive power with the Government should be firmly rejected. With these considerations very much in mind, he makes a series of practical suggestions.

B Crick, 'The Reform of Parliament', 2nd edn, (1964), pp278–85.

...

2   Governments must govern, but strong Government needs strong Opposition. Therefore, the procedures of Parliament need rethinking to fit the concept of 'equal access to the electorate' by the parties, and this for the whole life of a Parliament, not merely during the statutory campaign, since in a real sense Parliament is a continuous election campaign (but one which needs to be more fairly conducted). This concept is a more relevant key to parliamentary procedure than concepts of ministerial discretion and governmental secrecy, but it should complement, not threaten, the normal Government control of the House to put its business through. The facilities available to the Opposition and back-bench members in general should be greatly increased, particularly the expansion of the library into a Parliamentary workshop of research and investigation employing many trained research workers who could serve committees. There should thus be the deliberate creation of a 'counter-bureaucracy' to Whitehall, part complementary and part to break new ground, to obtain information for Parliament.

Failing all this, the opposition needs to shed the influence of the modern 'executive mind' and see itself again as an opposition whose primary duty is to oppose, not to preen and muzzle itself by too much conceit of being an 'alternative Government'.

...

5 Controls on any Government are all ultimately political. Therefore, it is ultimately vain to seek impartial adjudication of the exercise of ministerial discretion. At best such devices should be regarded as complementary to an increase in parliamentary scrutiny. But Governments, by the same token, need not fear the direct power of specialised committees, since party lines will hold, and ultimate political power is found only in the electorate (or, more subtly, in the self-control exercised by both Government and Opposition when they remind themselves, and are reminded, of how the electorate is likely to react: expectations are as important as experience). So, once again, all forms of 'control' as influence which can reach the ears of the electorate need strengthening.

6 No government can in fact be responsible or be held responsible for every error or act of maladministration. Therefore, we should accept the obvious, that ministers will not resign, nor ought they to, except occasionally when they are personally culpable. Then there would be no threat to 'ministerial responsibility' from almost any degree of parliamentary scrutiny and inquiry which stops short of sheer obstruction or endangering national security. Control of the administration should be seen as a joint task between ministers and committees of MPs. 'Ministerial responsibility' is, in fact, now a purely legal concept which defines who it is can use certain powers and to whom questions on them must be put; but the concept is misused as a kind of knock-down argument against any examination of a minister's use of his powers. The real meaning of the concept is simply political, indeed all ministers are collectively responsible to the electorate more than to Parliament. So ministerial or collective responsibility should never be invoked to refuse any form of parliamentary scrutiny and inquiry which does not threaten political control of Parliament. That proceedings in Parliament indirectly and ultimately threaten the Government's control of the electorate should be no argument against them, for Parliament should be a device (and easily could be) to ensure something like equality of access to the public between Government and Opposition.

7 Technical and expert advice is more and more necessary to modern government but is more and more open to opinion and interpretation. Therefore, such advice should be given (with as few exceptions as possible), openly, and the presumption should be for, not against, its coming through committees of Parliament. This would seem a protection for the Government as well as for the public. There are very few fields of applied knowledge where experts will not differ, on matters of priority if not on principle. Certainly, the Government must alone make the final decision and carry the responsibility; but decisions are likely to be more wise and rational if the issues have been openly canvassed. Everyone suspects, for instance, that the real area of defence secrets – whose discussion would endanger the safety of the state – is far smaller than any recent Government has allowed, even on the bleakest view of international relations and the lowest estimate of the efficiency of foreign intelligence services; a large part of what Professor Edward Shils called 'the torment of secrecy' is that so many of the secrets are not secret. At the very least Parliament, by developing the library of the House of Commons into a great research library, should offer alternative expert advice even if unasked. MPs will specialise more than they have done, but they will rarely be experts: they need regular access both to outside experts and to trained research workers (who would be employed by the library) and more experience in knowing how to use them. ...

9   Time and tide wait for no man and much of politics is the art of being present at the right time. Therefore, the time-span of the parliamentary session should be increased, though without necessarily increasing the number of days the whole House sits. From the end of July to the third week of October Britain is without a Parliament. There would be a great gain for the public interest and probably for the efficiency of Government if the House only rose for a month in the summer, but spread its sitting days far more thinly over the rest of the year, even (as others have suggested) adjourning on Wednesdays to give time for research, reading, political and public business, and general digestion of Monday and Tuesday and preparation for Thursday and Friday. Both ministers and back-bench MPs would be less frantically over-busy, as they often are, and the public would see more of them. There would seem no general objection to some committees seeking to continue their work during periods of recess.

10   British government and politics is *British* government and politics. Therefore, it is misleading (and usually deliberately so) to suggest that greater use of committees of advice, scrutiny, and investigation would lead to their controlling the policy of the executive, as happens in the US and in the France of the Third and Fourth Republics. No procedural changes in Parliament whatever could rewrite British social history which has created the two party system in its highly disciplined form. The constitutional arrangements of these other systems of government are entirely different, indeed they have (or had) written, fundamental constitutions which encourage deliberate divisions of power and formal checks and balances, unlike the British 'sovereignty of Parliament' (or complete executive power limited only by political considerations). Even further than this: such systems are as they are largely because they do not have parties as disciplined and political divisions so relatively clear-cut as in Britain.

Britain today suffers under the burden of three native curses: that of amateurism, that of 'inner circle' secrecy, and that of snobbery. All three serve to debase both the quality of political life and the energy of economic activity. The unreformed Parliament is more than a symbol of these things; it helps to perpetuate them by the most effective of all forces in politics and society – example. If Parliament were reformed, the whole climate of expectations could change, much of the sweet fog we muddle through might lift. ...

Question

Is Crick's vision of Parliament's role too limited?

Notes

1   Crick's prescription, that expert advice and research should be openly debated, with an acknowledgment that experts may differ, seems particularly relevant at the time of writing, shortly after the Government announced that there was, after all, the possibility of a link between BSE and Creutzfeldt-Jakob disease. The criticisms being made of the Government now is precisely that it relief far too heavily on the opinions of certain advisors and failed to publicise (even attempted to suppress?) rival studies.

2   Crick's conclusion, that secrecy is one of Britain's bedevilling 'native curses', can be seen to be supported by the same episode. Even though they are now supposedly strengthened by the Government's new Code of Practice on Open Government (see Part IV, Chapter 3), MPs generally and the Select

Committee on Agriculture failed to root out the Government's prevarication and withholding of information on BSE before the Government itself decided that it could no longer conceal the risk of a health threat to the general public.

CHAPTER 2

THE HOUSE OF LORDS

INTRODUCTION

This Chapter will consider the constitutional role of the House of Lords. It will examine its membership, its effectiveness in scrutinising legislation and policy, and the constraints, both legal and conventional, which restrict its powers. It will deal with the criticisms commonly levelled at the Lords, looking in particular at the extent to which it is controlled by party political interests, and it will consider proposals for reform.

Griffith and Ryle sketch the atmosphere and basic function of the Lords.

J A G Griffith and M Ryle, *Parliament: Functions, Practice and Procedures* (1989), p455

Despite many apparent similarities, there are essential differences between the two Houses of Parliament, which require that the House of Lords be considered separately. Writing over a century ago, Bagehot said that:

with a perfect Lower House it is certain that an Upper House would be scarcely of any value. But ... beside the actual House [of Commons] a revising and leisured legislature is extremely useful. [*The English Constitution* (1964), pp133-134.]

If true in 1867, this is all the more valid today. Great changes have taken place in the activity and tempo of the Lords since 1945, particularly in the increased flow of public legislation. As the weight of legislation has increased, neither Government nor the House of Commons have been able to prevent the onus of revision shifting increasingly onto the Lords.

The differences between the Houses derive from the source of political authority of the Lords – based on prescription and immemorial antiquity rather than popular election; the retention of its old procedures, which have not as yet been forced into radical change (as were those of the Commons in the late nineteenth century by the Irish Nationalists); the lack of a Speakership with effective powers; a continuing tendency towards one party, because of the hereditary peerage; an absence of priority for Government business; the maintenance of freedoms for the individual member, resulting from the comparative lack of pressures on the time of the House; the lack of power on financial matters; the presence of bishops, law lords and life peers and the consequent specialist experience of many members; and the distinctive and idiosyncratic contribution of the hereditary peerage. These factors contribute to the peculiar, indeed unique, quality of the House of Lords.

THE MAKE-UP OF THE HOUSE OF LORDS

Notes

1   On the face of it, the House of Lords constitutes an anomaly in a democracy: it participates in the legislative process and yet none of its members is elected. Its members are there either through birth, appointment or by virtue of the office they hold. Therefore they are not accountable to the electorate. The presence of hereditary peers who ensure the continuance of the

Conservative majority in the Lords is in general seen as particularly indefensible. Hereditary peers (over 750 of them) form the majority of those entitled to sit in the Lords although many of them do not attend.

2 To many commentators in this area, the most outstanding feature of the House of Lords is its wholly undemocratic character.

Donald Shell, 'The House of Lords: Time for a Change?' (1994) 47(4) *Parliamentary Affairs* 721, 721–3

It is ... appropriate to begin this article by drawing attention to the fundamentally unreformed nature of the House. Above all, it remains a predominately hereditary body. Over 60% of its members are there because they inherited this right. Of the remainder, not a single one is elected; all owe their position to the recommendation of successive Prime Ministers. The House of Lords remains an institution unscathed by democracy.

The unreformed House

Imagine the task of conducting around Westminster a delegation of officials from eastern Europe here in the UK to learn the ways of democracy. Explaining the House of Lords must present something of a challenge. That most of those entitled to sit, to speak, and to vote in the second chamber do so simply because they inherited this right seems extraordinary. That Britain, a country thought to have pioneered the development of democracy, should retain as part of its Parliament a second chamber still dominated by the aristocracy, seems paradoxical. That towards the close of the twentieth century, far from feeling embarrassed about this state of affairs, many seem to take pride in the continued existence of the House of Lords as a sort of tribute to English genius, or the triumph of English pragmatism, must surely bemuse overseas observers.

Having perhaps parried some difficult questions from those seeking know-how about democracy on the place of hereditary legislators, it would then have to be explained that the remaining members of the House are not elected, either directly or even indirectly, that they are not appointed by the House of Commons, or by local Councils, or even by a committee of any kind. Rather, every single one of them has become a member of the second chamber because the Prime Minister of the day had decided to recommend them for a peerage. Yes, the former Prime Minister, Baroness Thatcher had roundly declared at the opening of her maiden speech in the House of Lords (2 July 1992) that according to her own calculations she was responsible for the elevation of no fewer than 214 of those entitled to sit and listen to her. Mr Wilson could claim professional paternity for a slightly larger number.

Inquirers about the party breakdown in the House might be told that whatever the complexion of the government of the day, the Conservative Party always enjoys control in the House of Lords. At the end of the most recent session, of those eligible to turn up any time and speak or vote in the House, 453 were Conservative, 111 Labour, 56 Liberal Democrat, 256 cross-bench, with 55 in other categories. Conservative spokesmen may emphasise that their party does not have an overall majority, but with over 48% of the House taking the Conservative whip, and around 30% sitting on the cross-benches, Conservative preponderance is assured. When Prime Minister, Mrs Thatcher took care to recommend almost twice as many Conservatives as Labour party supporters for elevation to the House. Far from evening up the party balance in the House, she seemed determined to ensure an increased Conservative majority. That she was allowed to do this is surely curious; that no outcry greeted such behaviour is remarkable.

To say that such a House is deeply offensive to democratic values is surely a truism. But what is remarkable as the continued existence of the House is the fact that so much satisfaction is expressed with it and that so little public debate surrounds the survival of this feudal relic.

Notes

1   The presence of hereditary peers is objectionable on another ground: modern hereditary peerages do not descend to women unless there is an express provision in the letters patent creating the peerage for its inheritance by female heirs.

2   The membership of the House of Lords is drawn from a number of sources; by far the most important recent change in the composition of the house came with the creation of life peerages in 1958.

J A G Griffith and M Ryle, *Parliament: Functions, Practice and Procedures* (1989), pp458–64

Hereditary peers by succession

The holders by succession of an hereditary peerage of England (granted pre-1707), Scotland (up to 1707), Great Britain (1707–1800), and the United Kingdom (1801 to date) are the peers by succession, entitled as such to a writ of summons to Parliament from the Crown. Since 1963, it has been possible to disclaim an hereditary peerage for life, and at the end of 1988 there were 12 peers who had done so.

Peers by succession are still in the majority in the House. However, a greater proportion of regular attenders are life peers, so the domination of peers by succession is, in practice, reduced.

Hereditary peers of first creation

Until the passage of the Life Peerages Act 1958, all new members of the House were hereditary, except the law lords and bishops. A steady flow of new hereditary creations meant that the lay membership of the House increased from 270 in 1801 to 591 in 1901 and to 908 in 1960 but, after the 1964 election, Mr Wilson let it be known that he would recommend no more hereditary peerages (except for the Royal Family). This practice was followed by his three successors, and it had become accepted that the creation of hereditary peers was a thing of the past. However, in 1983, Mrs Thatcher surprised commentators by recommending the creation of two hereditary viscountcies 'in exceptional circumstances,' and a year later an hereditary earldom was also conferred.

But the vast majority of hereditary peers of first creation date back to before 1965, and this group is therefore declining in both numbers and significance.

Bishops: the Lords Spiritual

Twenty-six bishops of the Church of England have seats in the House of Lords: the Archbishops of Canterbury and York and the Bishops of London, Durham and Winchester *ex officio*, together with 21 other diocesan bishops by seniority of appointment. They hold their seats during the tenure of their sees, and retire at the age of 70. Historically, the House of Lords has consisted of the Lords Spiritual and Temporal.

Bishops are now appointed by the Crown on the advice of the Prime Minister, who makes the recommendation from candidates selected by the Church itself: they are no longer appointed on political grounds, and certainly feel no obligation to support the party under whom they were appointed. They speak and vote on many different subjects, especially those involving moral or social welfare, housing and education. The lay secretary to the Archbishop of Canterbury provides some organisation, so that there is a Church spokesman to take part in all debates on which a Church view is thought appropriate. But the bishops also speak in a personal capacity on social or moral questions of particular concern, and on local issues of concern to their sees. Although they used to refrain from speaking or voting on straight political issues, in recent years they have shown less readiness to regard themselves as political neuters, and have increasingly ranged themselves against Conservative opinions; for example, on television and broadcasting, capital punishment, homosexuality, immigration and inner-city housing problems.

Law Lords

The House of Lords is the final Court of Appeal for the United Kingdom in civil cases, and for England, Wales and Northern Ireland in criminal cases. The appellate jurisdiction of the House is largely exercised by the serving Lords of Appeal in Ordinary.

The serving Lords of Appeal in Ordinary are governed by a convention that they do not participate in debates on public party political controversy.

In recent years, the Law Lords have taken an active part in the House, speaking on legislation especially where points of law arise, and in debate, especially on law reform and on reports of royal commissions or other enquiries with which they have been connected. They also serve on committees.

Life peers

The Macmillan administration passed the Life Peerages Act 1958, which gave the Crown power to create men and women peers for life. ... Life peers have transformed the House. Instead of a House consisting predominantly of landowners and retired politicians (with a sprinkling of lawyers and bishops) the range of occupations and interests has been vastly increased. The numbers of life peers created has been large, and the variety of persons selected for life peerages has been extensive. The largest category is of politicians, whether ex-Ministers, ex-MPs or others active elsewhere in party politics, especially in local government. But the many other occupations honoured include businessmen, trade unionists, academics, civil servants and other public servants, diplomats, senior servicemen, industrialists, scientists, economists, journalists, newspaper proprietors, doctors, lawyers, farmers, technologists, actors and artists, clerics, accountants, nurses, social workers, and a composer. Those appointed are not representative in the sense that they are appointed to speak for their colleagues, but they do provide a wide spectrum of expertise.

Officers and office-holders

Lord Chancellor

The Lord Chancellor is *ex officio* the Speaker of the House of Lords, but his role is quite unlike that of other Speakers. He has no effective and controlling powers, and the standing orders of the House deny him power to maintain order. His role is 'ornamental and symbolic' [HL 9 of 1987–88, para 13]; the responsibility for maintaining order rests with the House as a whole.

Leader of the House and the Government Chief Whip

The Leader of the House is appointed by the Prime Minister, is a member of the Cabinet, and is responsible for the conduct of government business in the Lords. With the Speaker lacking effective powers of order, it is the Leader who advises the House on matters of procedure and order. He has a special part to play in

Creation of Life Peerages, 1958–1988 (excluding Law Lords)

Prime Minister	Cons	Lab	Lib/SDP	Crossbench	Total	Average per 12 months
Macmillan/Home 1958–64	17 (25)	29	1 (1)	18 (22)	65 (48)	17
Wilson 1964–70	11	78	6	46	141	25
Heath 1970–74	23	5	3	15	46	13
Wilson/Callaghan 1974–79	17	82	6	34	139	27
Thatcher 1979–88	77 (2)	39	9	37 (2)	162 (4)	17
Total	145	233	25	150	553	

Note   a) Resignation honours attributed to outgoing Prime Ministers.

b) Political affiliation is that of a Lord upon creation.

c) Figures in parentheses give the number of hereditary peerages awarded (excluding advancements).

expressing the 'sense of the House' and in drawing attention to transgressions or abuse of the rules. Essentially therefore, he has to play two roles: the first as the Leader of the Government in the Lords, and secondly as the shepherd of the House, the chief protector of its rights and privileges. These two functions can come into conflict, but there is an obvious advantage to the House in having a Government Minister as its champion. Occasional attempts to question the impartiality of the Leader or his independent role have been unsuccessful.

The Government Chief Whip is responsible for the detailed arrangement of government business, and for consultations with the other political parties on the business of the House. He also sends out a weekly 'whip' with underlinings, to members of his own party inviting their presence when divisions are expected; the other parties' whips do likewise.

Note

De Smith comments that 'the Life Peerages Act was passed mainly in the hope strengthening and broadening the composition of the House ...'.[1] As one commentator puts it:

What the introduction of the life peers has undoubtedly achieved is the revivification of the House of Lords, which if not moribund prior to their arrival, did seem somewhat somnolent. The 1968 White Paper dealing with reform of the House showed that the average daily attendance of peers for 1967–68 was 230 [House of Lords Reform (Cmnd 3799, 1968), para 11]; over the past four parliamentary sessions since 1979 it has, each year, fallen just short of 300. This compares with a figure of 140 for 1963 and 92 in 1954–55.[1a]

---

1   *Constitutional and Administrative Law*, 6th edn (1994), p322.
1a   B Hadfield, 'Whither or Whether the House of Lords' (1984) 35(4) NILQ 313, 320–1.

WHAT DOES THE HOUSE OF LORDS DO?

The work of the House and its effectiveness will be examined in this section. Broadly, the House has two roles, undertaking detailed scrutiny of both legislation and Government policy and administration. These roles include the House's important functions of initiating legislation and scrutinising and reporting on the policy and legislative output of the institutions of the European Union.[2]

Brigid Hadfield, 'Whither or Whether the House of Lords' (1984) 35(4) Northern Ireland Legal Quarterly 313, 324–326

The House of Lords–its functions

The White Paper of 1968 on reform of the Lords listed the following main functions–

(a) the provision of a forum for full and free debate on matters of public interest;

(b) the revision of public bills brought from the House of Commons;

(c) the initiation of public legislation, including in particular those Government bills which are less controversial in party political terms, and private members' bills;

(d) the consideration of subordinate legislation;

(e) the scrutiny of the activities of the executive; and

(f) the scrutiny of private legislation.

To this must now be added – most importantly – the scrutiny of (proposed) legislation emanating from the European Economic Community. Further, the very existence of the House of Lords enables certain powers of considerable constitutional importance – or potentially so – to be vested in it; already mentioned is the requirement that its consent must be obtained for any Prolongation of Parliament Bill. Also, the superior judges can only be removed from office on the presentation of a petition to the Sovereign from both Houses of Parliament. Finally, under the House of Commons Disqualification Act 1975, the maximum number of holders of paid ministerial office who may sit and vote in the House of Commons is fixed at 95 [s 2(1) and Schedule 2. See also s2(2).] This relates to the doctrine of collective responsibility and is aimed at trying to prevent excessive domination of the House by the executive, and more particularly by the Prime Minister, through the patronage power of the appointment of the executive. This means – as the size of any modern Government is always in excess of 95 – that some of its members must be drawn from the House of Lords. Whilst some of these appointments are necessary simply because there is a second chamber, this is by no means the explanation of all such appointments.

Whatever the quality of the Lords' work, one point is incontrovertible – the existence of a second chamber enables more time to be spent on parliamentary matters than would otherwise be the case. Over the past four sessions, the time spent on the floor of the House alone is as follows –

---

2   For a description of these institutions, see above, Part II, Chapter 2.

	1979–80	1980–81	1981–82	1982–83
No of sitting days	206	143	147	94
No of weeks during which the House sat	52	36	39	24
No of hours for which the House sat	268h 25m	919h 53m	930h 04m	619h 08m

The time of the House divided approximately as follows (%)–

	1979–80	1980–81	1981–82	1982–83
Starred questions	5.5	5.3	5.7	5.8
General debates	19.3	16.3	20.1	23.4
Debates on EC Committee Reports	2.6	3.7	2.7	3.2
Public Bills	49.2	58.1	50.9	46.2
(a)Lords Bills	8.3	26.0	17.4	26.4
Commons Bills	40.9	32.1	33.5	19.8
(b)Government Bills	45.3	50.9	43.5	39.9
Private Members Bills	3.9	7.2	7.4	6.3
Affirmative instruments	4.7	3.6	4.3	3.9
Negative instruments	0.1	0.2	0.8	0.6
Unstarred questions	8.0	4.7	7.8	9.0

To this should be added the following figures on questions asked in the House

	1979–80	1980–81	1981–82	1982–83
Number of starred questions	765	537	531	357
Number of unstarred questions	68	31	50	36
Number of questions for written answer	1,277	857	1,098	619
Number of private notice questions	16	2	6	2

The functions of the House may thus be classified into four broad categories: the legislative, scrutiny of the executive, the deliberative, and consideration of Community law, which last function takes place mainly in Committee and sub-committee rather than on the floor of the House.

Scrutiny of legislation

As the following table shows, the Lords amend a fair proportion of legislation originating in the Commons, often to an extensive degree.

J A G Griffith and M Ryle, *Parliament: Functions, Practice and Procedures* (1989), p352

Statistics of Amendments by the House of Lords to Public Bill originating in the House of Commons

Session	Government Bills originating in House of Commons	Number of Bills amended by the Lords	Number of amendments made by the Lords
1972–73	28 (10)[1]	11	884[2] (8)[3]
1973–74(Feb)	15 (4)	–	–
1974	21 (6)	4	259[4] (–)
1974–75	40 (10)	21	1,075[5] (154)
1975–76	35 (12)	17	703 (256)[6]
1976–77	26 (11)	11	81 (19)
1977–78	29 (6)	11	525 (157)[7]
1978–79	23 (6)	5	120 (1)
1979–80	46 (9)	18	971 (6)
1980–81	31 (8)	14	418 (1)
1981–82	29 (7)	8	842 (0)
1982–83 (June)	28 (5)	3	52 (0)

[1] The number in brackets is the number of money and/or supply bills.

[2] This figure includes 218 to the Water Bill.

[3] The figure in brackets is the number of amendments rejected by the Commons.

[4] This figure includes 156 to the Housing Bill.

[5] This figure excludes amendments and amendments to amendments etc made to the Trade Union and Labour Relations (Amendment) Bill.

[6] A large proportion of this figure is taken up by the Lords' unacceptable amendments to the aircraft and Shipbuilding Industries Bill, the Dock Work Regulation Bill and the Health Services Bill.

[7] A large proportion of this figure is taken up by the Lords' unacceptable amendments to the Scotland Bill and the Wales Bill.

Note

As indicated, the work of the House in considering public bills constitutes its single most time-consuming task, reflecting the fact that such scrutiny is generally regarded as the Lords' most important role. Philip Norton has suggested three main features of the House of Lords which render it 'particularly suitable' for the task of detailed consideration of legislation.

Philip Norton, 'Parliament II: The House of Lords' in Jones (ed), *Politics UK* (1994), p354

First, as an unelected House, it cannot claim the legitimacy to reject the principle of measures agreed by the elected House. Thus, basically by default, it focuses on the detail rather than the principle. Secondly, its membership includes people who have distinguished themselves in particular fields – such as the sciences, the law, education, industry industrial relations – who can look at relevant legislation from the perspective of practitioners in the field rather than from the perspective of party politicians. And, third, the House has the time to debate non-money bills in more details than is usually possible in the Commons – unlike in the Commons there is no provision for a guillotine and all amendments are discussed. The House thus serves as an important revising chamber, trying to ensure that a bill is well drafted and internally coherent. In order to improve the bill, it will suggest amendments, most of which will be accepted by the Commons. In terms of legislative scrutiny, the House has thus developed a role which is viewed as complementary to, rather than one competing with (or identical to) that of the Commons.

Notes

1   Two of the positive attributes which Norton identifies arise from the fact that the House is not elected; the first directly, the second from the fact that it cannot consider money bills, which is a reflection of its lower, because undemocratic, status. (Such a wide disability does not apply, for example, to the elected US Senate.) The paradoxical notion that much of the value which commentators perceive in the Lords is attributable to the one characteristic which most lays it open to attack – its un-elected status – is a recurring theme in the literature on the subject.

2   What is the *nature* of the legislative work of the Lords?

The legislative work of the Lords relates mainly to public Bills, on the consideration of which it expends half its time. The formal delaying power of the House is probably less important in real terms than the fact that its presence means a prolongation of the parliamentary consideration of Bills, providing opportunity for more detailed scrutiny and for second thoughts on the part of the Government, in the light of comments made both inside and outside Parliament. Also, its existence enables Bills to be initiated elsewhere than in the Commons, which tends to suffer from a glut of Bills at the beginning of a session (especially after a general election) and from the Finance Bill in the second part of a session.

... it would seem from a consideration of the 12 parliamentary sessions since 1972 that the Lords do have a valuable revising role, albeit a more limited role than is usually appreciated.

It should be noted, first, that many of the Commons' Bills go through the Lords 'on the nod'. This is probably best explained by the subject-matter of those Bills, although a partial explanation may be found in the fact that these Bills arrive in the Lords later rather than earlier in the parliamentary session. The conclusion is, however, that the Lords concentrate their revising efforts on only a limited number of Commons' Bills. Secondly, the majority of amendments proposed and accepted are of the technical or drafting kind; these cause no difficulties to any Government of any complexion and this is the main explanation for their high level of acceptability to the Commons. Some amendments are, however, of substantive importance.[3]

3   The picture that emerges is one of a House which is concerned not so much with the broad policy behind bills, but rather with ensuring that measures will be workable in practice. In this sense, the Lords may be seen as complementary to the House of Commons, which is regarded as unsuitable for the detailed scrutiny of legislation, due to its combative style of debate, and the fact that the Opposition will oppose much Government legislation

---

3   Hadfield, *op cit*, pp325, 326.

as a matter of course.[4] However, such a division of labour by the two Houses arguably leaves a lacuna in the scrutiny provided by Parliament as a whole: if the Commons Opposition attacks policy wholesale, whilst the Lords largely ignore it, measured and discriminating criticisms of policy may never receive consideration.

4   Clarke and Shell compare the ability of the House of Lords to revise and amend legislation with that of the Commons, in the context of the passage through the House of one piece of legislation.

DN Clarke and D Shell,'Revision and Amendment by the House of Lords: A Case Study' (1994) *Public Law* 409, 410–14

The House of Lords and government legislation

The Bryce Commission in 1918 identified as the first function of the House 'the examination and revision of Bills brought from the House of Commons' [Cd 9038, (1918), Report of the Conference on Reform of the Second Chamber]. The White Paper on reform of the House issued by the Wilson Government in 1968 following all party talks listed 'the revision of Bills brought from the House of Commons' as one of six functions carried out by the House. Increasingly in recent years attention has focused on the role of the House in making a seemingly ever growing number of amendments to an ever expanding quantity of legislation In the early 1950s the number of pages of primary legislation enacted each year rose to around 1000; by the 1970s it had reached almost 2000, and in the 1980s up to 1987 the average was over 2500, after which the page size for legislation altered, though it would seem volume continued to increase. Far from reducing the quantity of legislation, and improving its quality, as the Conservatives in opposition in the 1970s had argued was necessary, the Conservatives in office since 1979 steadily increased the quantity. Nor would many accept that there had been any improvement in quality in the sense of clarity and precision and the avoidance of unnecessary complexity and obscurity. It has been widely argued that this has been the main reason underlying the vast growth in the number of amendments made to Bills in the revising chamber. [In the three sessions 1970 to 1973 the House of Lords made (on average) some 950 amendments per session to Government Bills; by 1979 to 1982 the average had risen to almost 1,300 per session, but by 1987 to 1990 it had gone up to an average of over 2,600.] Overwhelmingly these were amendments introduced by ministers themselves, though many were of course responses to representations made to Government by the many interests typically affected by legislation, such representations being made both within and outside of parliament. Twenty years ago a major study of parliamentary scrutiny of legislation concluded that many Bills emerge from the House of Commons 'in a state unfit to be let loose on the public' [JAG Griffith, *Parliamentary Scrutiny of Government Bills* (1974), p231.] Since then the situation has deteriorated considerably. As a result the House of Lords sits longer hours and spends an increasing proportion of its time tidying up legislation brought to it from the Commons in a highly unsatisfactory form. In the 1992–93 session the House of Lords spent almost half its sitting time dealing with Government legislation, and made 2056 amendments to Government Bills, of which only 18 were subsequently rejected by the Commons.

Most of the work undertaken by the House of Lords in revising legislation is of a relatively apolitical character. But increasingly in the 1980s the House was

---

4   See Part III, Chapter 1.

spoken of as a chamber with a growing influence. This was not simply because it made large numbers of amendments to sometimes ill-thought-out legislation, but also because ministers often found it expedient to give way to pressure brought to bear on them in the upper House. Especially when the Thatcher Government had a very large majority in the Commons, from 1983 onwards, it began to appear easier to secure changes to Bills in the Lords than in the lower House. Though the Conservatives retained a considerable numerical superiority in the Lords, when all other parties and the large number of cross-bench peers combined against them the Government was liable to be defeated. Furthermore, Conservative peers were less susceptible to the threats or blandishments of the party whips than were their counterparts in the Commons. Generally the House was at its most influential when there was a whiff of rebellion within the Tory ranks on some measure. Not infrequently this would be first exposed in the House of Commons, with Conservative back-benchers expressing disquiet about some aspect of a Bill, perhaps by voting against the Government, perhaps only by speaking in Opposition to some proposal. When this happened and was followed by Government defeat in the Lords it could easily appear prudent to ministers to give way rather than face further difficulties when the Bill concerned returned once again to the Commons. A study of organised groups showed that those outside Parliament with an interest in legislation found the Lords almost as useful as the Commons as a chamber for securing adjustments to Bills [M Rush (ed), *Parliament and Pressure Politics* (1990); see especially Chapter 5 by N Baldwin] ...

The ability to revise and amend

... it is the way the legislative procedure operates in the Upper House which facilitates the submission and consideration of amendments. The student of Parliament is taught at an early stage that a Bill goes through the same stages in each House; a second reading to debate the principles of the Bill, a committee stage to consider the detail, a report stage to report on and consider final amendments before the third reading completes the process. The keen student may even take note that the Lords always sits as a committee of the whole house, the Commons rarely so. The reality is that the procedure is similar only in form. In the case of the passage of the [Leasehold Reform, Housing and Urban Development Act] through the Commons, for example, only 32 MPs were assigned to the Standing Committee. Though the report stage occupied about 10 hours, the third reading debate, following on immediately [the usual practice], lasted barely 40 minutes. Some of the themes and concerns that were to surface in the Upper House had an earlier rehearsal in the Commons – but by no means all. Amendments to the Bill in the Commons were few; at the committee stage, some threats were headed off by promises to reconsider and then by making no change at the report stage. Where divisions were called at report the House divided largely on party lines. This procedure is, in reality, highly ritualised. The Government has its majority, even in committee; the divisions called by the Opposition at report stage on the 1993 Act were set pieces on a few issues of principle. Where amendments were put down by Conservative back-bench opponents at the report stage, the arguments were largely markers for later debate in the Lords.

It is the different way the same format of committee stage, report, and third reading is used that permits the Lords to make the best use of the time to consider amendments. Since the committee stage involves the whole House and amendments are also allowed at the third reading stage in the Lords, [four and a half hours on the 1993 Act] any peer who has a concern can put down an amendment at the committee stage knowing that there are two further occasions to return to the issue. Indeed, many such amendments are acknowledged to be 'probing'; seeking to elucidate the meaning of a particular section; or to judge the Government's attitude to some change; or, by listening to other contributions to the debate, to gauge the degree of support from elsewhere in the House. Many amendments are withdrawn, with consent, without a vote thus enabling private discussions, redrafting and resubmission at report or third reading. These three genuine opportunities permit a process which allows proposals to be aired, reconsidered and reformulated in a way that is not possible in the Commons.

The Upper House is also jealous of the opportunity to debate those changes proposed by the Government itself. Thus Lord Williams of Elvel, for the Opposition, insisted upon an explanation of a Government change to the 1993 Act stating:

> It is part of the job of this House, as a revising chamber, ... to correct the Government when it tries to slide through amendments without any proper debate.

This can be compared, on this legislation, to a whole series of amendments at report stage in the Commons, not all of them technical, which received no explanation whatsoever. [*Hansard*, vol 218, cols 927–32. Given the decision in *Pepper v Hart* [1993] AC 593, allowing reference to statements in Parliament by the courts where legislation is ambiguous or obscure, it may be that there will be more chance of a relevant explanation by a Minister in the Lords being of relevance than in the Commons, where nothing may have been said.]

Questions

1 Which of the qualities of the House which make it suitable for the revision of legislation identified by Clarke and Shell are attributable to its procedure, and which to its composition?

2 Is the Lords' more flexible and informal procedure attributable to its make-up in any way?

Notes

1 Whilst the main task of the House of Lords can accurately be said to be improving, rather than radically changing Government Bills, a series of recent Government defeats by the House serve as a reminder that this is not its only task: the Lords will on occasions make changes to Government Bills on issues of principle. On 6 February 1996, the Lords inflicted a major defeat on the Government's Broadcasting Bill by voting by 223 to 106 (a majority of 117) to deny Sky Television exclusive rights to the eight most important sporting events of the year, including Wimbledon and the Olympic Games, ensuring that the majority of viewers who do not have Sky will be able to view the events on BBC or ITV. The department responsible – National Heritage – made it clear that the Government would accept the change, saying, 'We will want to consider how we might give effect to peers' wishes in a way that is enforceable and practicable'.[5] Whilst the fact that the Lords' amendment doubtlessly reflected popular opinion may have given the Lords comfort, the defeat undoubtedly represented a reversal for the

---

5 Quoted in 'Peers inflict huge defeat on TV Sports', *Independent*, 7 February 1996. In the following month, the Government announced that it would bring forward its own amendment to the Lords' wishes. (The announcement was made by Lord Ingelwood in an answer to a written question – see 'Bottomley retreats on "jewels in the crown",' *Independent*, 5 March 1996.)

Government's free market policy on broadcasting which is an important plank in its general pro-market philosophy. It therefore marked a clear rebuff by the Lords of a central and politically contentious strand of Government policy. Interestingly, there was no suggestion from the Government that the Lords had acted unconstitutionally in any way.

2   A similarly important and embarrassing defeat was inflicted on the Government's Family Law Bill at the end of February 1996. Despite 'intensive Government efforts to "whip" Conservative peers' into line,[6] 21 Conservative rebels, including former Government ministers joined with Labour peers to pass an amendment allowing divorcing couples to split their pensions at the time of divorce. The amendment illustrates not only the preparedness of the Lords to oppose the Government on matters of principle, but also the relative ineffectiveness of whipping in the Lords in comparison to the Commons.

3   The third victim of recent Lords activism was the Government's highly contentious policy of restricting the appeal and social security rights of asylum seekers to the UK, as set out in the Asylum Bill. The basic policy of the Bill is to draw up a 'white-list' of countries considered 'safe'; asylum seekers from these countries would face a presumption against their admittance and a 'fast track' procedure for determining their application which would limit their rights of appeal. The amendment carried in the Lords (on 23 April 1996) would exempt from the 'white-list' category applicants 'who can show a reasonable claim that [they] have been a victim of torture' in their own country and those 'claiming to fear persecution in a country which has a recently documented record of torture'[7] and would therefore considerably restrict the amount of applicants subject to the new provisions. The amendment thus represents a significant attack on the policy behind the Bill. The Government's response to the amendment has been ambiguous: it apparently accepts the principle that those with a well founded fear of torture should be not subject to the new procedure, but regards the present wording of the amendment as unacceptable. At the time of writing the Government apparently intends to bring forward its own amendment dealing with the position of possible torture victims at the report stage in the Lords.[8] Whether the amendment will accept the spirit of the Lords' amendment therefore remains to be seen.

4   Much of what has been said so far paints a favourable picture of the role of the Lords in improving Government Bills – a role which, as Clarke and Shell note, has become increasing significant in the last decade. But, as Clarke and Shell also noted, the reason for this increase in importance may lie as much with the Commons as the Lords; a point made elsewhere by Shell:

If the productivity of the House were to be measured in terms of the number of amendments passed, then its record is impressive. By the late 1980s some 2,000

---

6   'Tory defeat over wives' pension split', *Independent*, 1 March 1996.

7   Quoted in 'Lords' blow to Howard clampdown on asylum', *Independent*, 24 April 1996.

8   This will apparently not be till after Whitsun and no approximate date has yet been set. This and other information on the Government's response to the amendment was given by the Asylum Bill team at the Home Office in a telephone conversation with one of the authors on 15 May 1996.

amendments per session were being made to Government Bills. But such figures probably have more to do with the ill-thought-out nature of much legislation when first introduced than with any particular skill or diligence by peers. Some commentators saw a decline in consultation between Government and organised groups during the Thatcher years as correlated with a decline in the quality of legislation as first introduced to Parliament. This it was argued had led to the development of a legislate-as-you-go mentality, which in turn imposed increased burdens on the House as a revising chamber. Certainly, the House became during the 1980s the object of much greater attention from interest groups. From a practical point of view, many groups found that for securing detailed adjustments to Bills, the Lords was at least as useful as the Commons.9

Question

Even if Shell's account is correct, is it not the case that the Lords still deserves credit for showing themselves able to rise to the challenge of improving increasingly ill-thought-out legislation?

Notes

1   It is worth remarking that Shell's account does not detract from the reasons given by Norton for the particular effectiveness of the Lords.

2   Although the Lords may not always contrive to have their amendments accepted, they may eventually be accepted in modified form in the Commons. For example, an amendment to the Police and Criminal Evidence Act 1984 allowing evidence unfairly obtained to be excluded emanated in the Lords and eventually prompted the Government to put forward its own amendment which became s78 of the Act.

3   The legislative role of the House of Lords is not confined to scrutiny of measures originating in the Commons. Bills which are not seen as contentious in party political terms are regularly introduced into the Lords thus relieving pressure on the Commons. Examples include the National Heritage Bill (1980–81 session), the Data Protection Bill, and the Wildlife and Countryside Bill (1982–83 session). This work is by no means small in scale: Griffith and Ryle have compiled figures showing that in 1978, 58 Public General Acts were introduced, 60 in 1979, 67 in 1980 and 57 in 1982.10

4   From consideration of Acts from some sessions between 1978 and 1982, Hadfield has identified four (not exclusive) broad categories into which Public Bills introduced in the Lords can be placed:

   (a) law reform measures, including consolidating Acts and Acts dealing with the administration of justice; (b) international Acts, including the implementation of treaties; (c) Acts relating solely to Northern Ireland or Scotland; and (d) matters of non-controversial substance (in the party-political sense).11

5   Members of the Lords, unlike members of the Commons, are free to introduce Private Member's Bills into the House and there is usually enough time for them to be debated fully although of course if they are passed this does not ensure that time will be found for them in the Commons. As the

---

9   Donald Shell, 'The House of Lords: Time for a Change?' (1994) 47(4) PA 721 at 733.

10   Griffith and Ryle, *op cit*, p353.

11   Hadfield, *op cit*, p325. For an example of a legislative debate in the Lords see below, pp437–40.

Lords have no constituents to whom they are accountable they may feel free to bring forward Private Members Bills on emotive and contentious subjects such as homosexuality and abortion. The initiative for relaxing the law relating to homosexual conduct, which eventually resulted in the passing of the Sexual Offences Act 1967, came from the Lords, not the Commons. Similarly, the Anti Discrimination (No 2) Bill 1972–73 raised interest when being discussed by the Lords' Select Committee. This led to espousal of the Bill first by back-benchers and then by the Government. The eventual result was the Sex Discrimination Act 1975.

6 The House of Lords has recently created for itself an important new scrutinising mechanism for overseeing the use of delegated legislation, the scrutiny of which, as noted above, is generally thought to be inadequate in the Commons.[12] On 10 November 1992, the House of Lords decided to establish on a trial basis a new Select Committee on the Scrutiny of Delegated Powers ('DPSC'); the Committee produced its first report early in 1993 and the Lords agreed to give it permanent status on 2 November 1994. The remit of the Committee is 'to report whether the provisions of any Bill inappropriately delegate legislative powers; or whether they subject the exercise of legislative power to an inappropriate degree of parliamentary scrutiny';[13] the Committee itself has indicated that it will pay particular attention to bills containing 'Henry VIII' clauses (giving ministers powers to repeal or amend primary legislation) and skeleton legislation which in effect gives ministers power to 'legislate' their own chosen policy through secondary legislation. The Committee has expressed satisfaction with its own work; Government has co-operated with it by producing a memorandum for most pieces of delegated legislation, which explains the purpose of a given provision and why delegated legislation has been used for it. The Committee reports[14] some 'successes in securing parliamentary control where none had originally been provided' and in improving the level of scrutiny provided (eg by upgrading to the affirmative resolution procedure in one case), but also cases in which their proposals had been resisted by the Government and thus resulted in no change (Himsworth, p41). They did not confine their recommendations to the field of Parliamentary scrutiny, recognising that 'in some cases, extra-parliamentary scrutiny by consultation may be more significant' (*ibid*). In particular, the Committee singled out the Education Act 1994 and the Deregulation and Contracting-Out Bill for particular criticism, noting the almost unprecedentedly wide powers they gave ministers to legislate on matters of important principle and secured changes to the Bills, substantial in the case of the former. The Committee may be regarded as having made an

---

12 We give here only a very brief summary of the Committee's work, drawing on C Himsworth's interesting analysis, 'The Delegated Powers Scrutiny Committee' (1995) PL 34. All quotes in the text are from this article, unless otherwise indicated.

13 First Report of the Select Committee on the Procedure of the House HL 11 (1992-93) quoted *ibid*, p36.

14 Twelfth Report of the Select Committee on the Scrutiny of Delegated Powers HL 90 (1993-94).

important contribution to the scrutiny provided by the Lords, and to have provided a welcome focusing of attention on the increasing use of delegated legislation for matters of principle and substance.

7   In considering this issue, it is worth noting that the House of Lords has recently clearly rejected any idea that it may not vote to reject any item of subordinate legislation submitted to it for consideration.[15]

Scrutiny of EU policy and legislation

Given the ever-growing impact of EU legislation, this task is clearly of great importance, particularly as it has been suggested that the British MEPs in the European Parliament are not particularly effective in this role.[16] The main responsibility for this area of the Lords' work lies with the House of Lords Select Committee on the European Communities, considered by Bogdanor below.

V Bogdanor, 'Britain and the European Community' in Jowell and Oliver (eds), *The Changing Constitution*, 3rd edn (1994), pp10–13

The House of Lords Select Committee is a more influential body than its Commons counterpart. It is chaired by a salaried office-holder of the House, who as Principal Deputy-Chairman of Committees, ranks third in the Lords after the Lord Chancellor and the Chairman of Committees. Whereas in the Commons, the Committee before 1991 sifted legislation for the House as a whole to consider, in the Lords it is the Chairman of the Select Committee, assisted by a legal adviser and the Clerk, who sifts legislation for the Select Committee and its sub-committees to consider. This sift is later endorsed by the Select Committee itself. On average, around one-third of the Community documents received are selected for further consideration, and around one-tenth are the subject of reports to the House.

The House of Lords Select Committee calls upon a wide range of sources, including MEPs, for both written and oral evidence. MEPs giving evidence to the House of Lords Committee are not confined to those representing Britain, but will include members of other nationalities, so enabling the House of Lords Committee to establish links with the Rapporteur of the relevant Committee of the European Parliament. Moreover, the House of Lords Committee also takes evidence from Commission officials, and representatives of interest groups, academics, etc. in all the countries of the Community.

Around one-half of the reports from the House of Lords Committee are debated in the House. Since the Government does not enjoy control over the order paper in the House of Lords as it does in the Commons, the Select Committee could always, in the last resort, *insist* upon a debate. These debates are in no way dominated, as those in the Commons have been, by the division between pro- and anti-Community opinions, and a leading part is played in debates on the floor of the House by members of the Select Committee and the sub-committees. At the same time, the debates are of less importance in the Lords than in the Commons, for the reports of the Commons Select Committee are on limited and technical matters, and not wide-ranging as is the custom with the Lords

15   HL Deb 20 October 1994, col 356.
16   See V Bogdanor, 'Britain and the European Community' in Jowell and Oliver (eds), *The Changing Constitution*, 3rd edn (1994), pp18–19.

committee. In the Lords, it is the reports which are important, not least because they attract a wide readership throughout the Community and its institutions, and not the debates.

There is widespread agreement that the scrutiny procedures adopted by the Lords are amongst the most effective in the Community. In 1977, a Committee established by the Hansard Society for Parliamentary Government was 'struck by the relevance and businesslike nature of the results of the Lords' work in this field, and think it significant that the Commons, who are meant to represent the people of this country, have taken in contrast to the Lords, a largely inward-looking and conservative attitude where the opposite was required.' And in 1982 a Report of the Study Group of the Commonwealth Parliamentary Association on 'The Role of Second Chambers' concluded that the Lords offered 'the only really deep analysis of the issues that is available to the parliamentary representatives of the [then] ten countries in the Community. ... The Lords' reports are far more informative and comprehensive than those produced by the Commons committee on European legislation.' The Study Group attributed this to the greater specialist knowledge of peers and comparative absence of partisanship.

[The Committee] has the advantage, because of the system of nominating to life peerages men and women of eminence, of containing experts in almost every field covered by Community activity. Whether the subject-matter be agriculture, law, or economics, some of the leading authorities in the country will be found in the Lords; and since much Community legislation is technical, this means that the Lords is peculiarly suited to considering it. Thus the scrutiny procedures of the House of Lords owe their effectiveness to factors which it would be difficult to replicate in any legislature dominated primarily by party politicians. They depend upon the peculiarities of a chamber whose members are there either by hereditary right or by nomination.

Notes

1   Once again the conclusion is reached that the Lords' effectiveness in this area is strongly linked to its undemocratic nature. It is *not* of course dependent on the particular method for selecting life peers, ie Prime Ministerial patronage.

2   Philip Norton broadly concurs with Bogdanor's favourable assessment of the work of the Lords in this area:

The EC Committee has built up an impressive reputation as a thorough and informed body, issuing reports which are more objective and extensive than its counterpart in the Commons, and which are considered authoritative both within Whitehall and the institutions of the EC. The House, like the chambers of other national legislatures, has no formal role in the EC legislative process, and so has no power, other than that of persuasion, to affect outcomes. The significance of the reports, therefore, has tended to lie in informing debate rather than in changing particular decisions.[17]

Scrutiny of domestic administration and policy

The House also scrutinises, and occasionally influences, Government policy. Peers can debate policy in a less partisan atmosphere than the Commons and are not subject to the constituency and party influences that dominate in the elected

---

17   Philip Norton, 'Parliament II: The House of Lords' in Jones (ed), *Politics UK* (1994), p359.

House. They are therefore in a position to debate issues of public policy that may not be at the heart if the partisan battles and which, consequently, receive little attention in the Commons. Given their backgrounds, peers are also often – though not always – able to debate public policy from the perspective of those engaged in the subject. The House, for example, is able to debate science policy with an authority denied the lower House. The Lords contains several distinguished scientists; the Commons does not. When discussing education, the House will normally hear from peers who are professors, university chancellors, vice-chancellors, and former secretaries of state for education.[18]

Notes

1   Donald Shell has remarked, in relation to the House's non-legislative debates: 'Many of the debates held in the Lords can only be seen as occasions on which peers talk to each other. Most pass entirely unnoticed even in the 'quality' newspapers, and there is little evidence to show they have any impact elsewhere either.'[19] This is surely too sweeping a comment; whilst the views of hereditary peers with little expertise or general reputation may receive little attention, remarks made by, for example, the Law Lords will usually have some impact.

2   The Lords have other methods by which they scrutinise policy: questions of Ministers and Select Committees.

Philip Norton, 'Parliament II: The House of Lords', *op cit*, pp358–9

Questions

Questions in the Lords are of two types: starred and unstarred. The meanings are different to those employed in the Commons. In the Commons, starred questions are oral questions and unstarred questions are written questions. In the Lords, starred questions are non-debatable questions and unstarred questions are questions on which a short debate may take place. (Lords may also table questions for written answer, though the number tabled is not numerous: about half-a-dozen on any particular day.) At the beginning of each day's sitting, up to four 'starred' questions may be asked. These are similar to those tabled for oral answer in the Commons, though – unlike in the Commons – they are addressed to Her Majesty's Government and not to a particular minister (see example below). A peer rises to ask the question appearing in his or her name on the order paper, the relevant minister (or whip) replies for the Government, and then supplementary questions – confined to the subject of the original question – follow. This procedure, assuming as many as four questions are tabled (they usually are), is expected to last no more than 20 minutes. This allows for perhaps as many as four or five supplementaries on each question to be asked, the peer who tabled the motion by tradition being allowed to ask the first supplementary. Hence, though a shorter question time than in the Commons, the concentration on a particular question is much greater and allows for more probing.

At the end of the day's sitting, there is also usually an 'unstarred' question: that is, one which may be debated ... Peers who wish to speak do so and the appropriate minister responds. The advantages of such unstarred questions are similar to those of the half-hour adjournment debates in the Commons, except

---

18   Philip Norton, 'Parliament II: The House of Lords', *op cit*, p354.
19   Donald Shell, 'The House of Lords: Time for a Change?' (1994) 47(4) PA 721, 734.

that in this case there is a much greater opportunity for other members to participate. For example, when the Earl of Perth on 28 January 1993 asked what action the Government proposed to take on the devastation in Perthshire caused by the River Tay, no fewer than seven peers spoke – in addition to Lord Perth – before the minister rose to reply. The debate lasted more than one-and-a-quarter hours.

Note

The question for a written answer remains a versatile tool – the sample appearing below indicates the multiplicity of purposes for which a question can be put and the variety of uses which may be derived from the answers.

HL WA 73, 6 December 1994; WA 83 and 84, 7 December 1994; WA 1, 9 January 1995; WA 48, 3 April 1996

Baroness Jeger asked Her Majesty's Government:

How many appeals against council tax banding remain unanswered, and how many appellants have died while awaiting the outcome of appeals.

The Minister of State, Department of the Environment (Viscount Ullswater): As at the end of October, 275,231 and 19,212 initial period council tax banding appeals were outstanding in England and Wales respectively. There were 19,686 initial period appeals outstanding in Scotland at the end of September, the latest date for which figures are available. Information on the number of appellants who have died while awaiting the outcome of appeals is not collected.

Lord Avebury asked Her Majesty's Government:

What action they have taken on the findings in the report *Targeting Basic Assistance in Northern Iraq; Findings from a Household Expenditure Survey,* which they commissioned, and in particular on the fall in living standards suffered by the population as a whole, and the chronic energy deficiency shown by 12% of the female population.

Baroness Chalker of Wallasey: We received the report in September. Since then we have agreed to provide £365,000 to Save the Children Fund for a further village rehabilitation project, which includes special measures for assisting female-headed households, and for a pilot income-generation project for very poor urban households, many of which are headed by women. We have distributed the report widely to other aid agencies, in particular the UN agencies, who have welcomed it as a basis for targeting food aid and other assistance.

Lord Lester of Herne Hill asked Her Majesty's Government:

Whether they consider that Ministers and civil servants, in discharging their public functions, have a duty to comply with the European Convention on Human Rights and the International Covenant on Civil and Political Rights.

Baroness Chalker of Wallasey: International treaties are binding on states and not on individuals. The United Kingdom is party to both treaties and it must comply with its obligations under them. In so far as acts of Ministers and civil servants in the discharge of their public functions constitute acts which engage the responsibility of the United Kingdom, they must comply with the terms of the treaties.

Lord Lester of Herne Hill asked Her Majesty's Government:

Further to their Answer of 7 December 1994 (HL WA 84), whether they consider that local authorities, in discharging their public functions, have a duty to comply with the terms of the European Convention on Human Rights and the International Covenant on Civil and Political Rights; and ...

Further to their Answer of 7 December 1994 (HL WA 84), whether they consider that Her Majesty's judges, in discharging their public functions, have a duty to comply with the European Covenant of Human Rights and International Covenant on Civil and Political Rights.

The Minister of State, Foreign and Commonwealth Office (Baroness Chalker of Wallasey): As I stated in my Answer of 7 December, the treaties referred to, in common with treaties in general, are binding on States party to them and not individuals. The acts or omissions of public officers or authorities may engage the international responsibility of the United Kingdom in so far as they raise issues in respect of the fulfilment of the United Kingdom's obligations under the treaty. The position in international law in this regard is no different for the treaties referred to by the noble Lord than for other treaties. In the cases of the European Convention on Human Rights and the International Covenant on Civil and Political Rights, the determination whether a particular act or omission does engage the responsibility of the United Kingdom is specially entrusted (subject to the rules and procedures laid down in the treaties) to the supervisory bodies established by those treaties ...

Lord Bancroft asked Her Majesty's Government:

With reference to the Parliamentary Ombudsman's Annual Report for 1995, which records a further big increase in the total number of cases referred to him what further steps they are taking to bring to departments' notice the existence of the Code of Practice on Access to Government Information in relation to which (by contrast) very few complaints were referred.

The Parliamentary Under-Secretary of State, Ministry of Defence (Earl Howe): Liaison officers were appointed in each major department and body within the jurisdiction of the Parliamentary Commissioner for Administration when the Code of Practice on Access to Government Information was introduced in April 1994. They are responsible for raising awareness of the code and giving guidance on best practice within their respective departments. Many departments have also produced internal guidance manuals or leaflets relating to the Code of Practice on Access to Government Information.

In addition, the Office of Public Service (OPS) circulates epitomes of cases investigated by the Parliamentary Commissioner for Administration, and has made available to departments many thousands of copies of its leaflet explaining the Code of Practice on Access to Government Information. Training courses in Open Government are run for departmental staff at the Civil Service College.

OPS have also produced and distributed 14,000 copies of a booklet called *The Ombudsman In Your Files,* which is aimed at raising civil servants' awareness of the PCA's procedures and guiding them on how to avoid the malpractices that may lead to complaints. The booklet refers to the Code of Practice on Access to Government Information, and includes an Open Government case study.

Notes

1   Baroness Jeger's question illustrates the sheer usefulness of these questions as a means of obtaining information which could only be compiled by an individual at considerable time and expense. The information could also, of course, be used to attack the council tax politically. Lord Avebury's question is of the typical 'pressing for action' type, giving the peer the ability to put down an informed motion asking for more action to be taken, as possibly could Lord Bancroft's. Lord Lester's two questions are rather more sophisticated and significant, in that the questioner may have procured an important statement of principle from the Government which, in a recent

article[20] Lord Lester argues could give the citizen a legitimate expectation that civil servants and ministers will comply with the convention, giving rise to a possible action in judicial review if this expectation is not fulfilled. Lord Lester's question also indicates the kind of thoughtful attention to constitutional issues which is perhaps less likely to be displayed by Members of the more party-oriented House of Commons.

2   What of the Lords' Select Committees?

... the House has made increased use of select committees since the early 1970s. One of the first to be established examined a Private Member's Bill on sex discrimination in the 1972–73 session. It is ironic that despite peers' unwillingness to address this issue in respect of the hereditary membership of their own House in the 1990s, they did much to advance the anti-discrimination cause in the early 1970s. Subsequent *ad hoc* select committees dealt with a miscellany of topics with mixed results. A report on overseas trade in 1985 represented a powerful and much quoted indictment of Government policies. Inquiries into laboratory experimentation on animals and into charity law cleared the way to legislation in theses areas. Other select committee reports, such as one recommending the abolition of the mandatory life sentence for murder, met with less success.[21]

3   De Smith considers that although some useful work is done in the areas of legislation and scrutiny of policy and administration, the former is 'not very satisfactory in practice', the latter 'not performed adequately'. De Smith attributes these failures partly to the 'amateurish lack of organisation within the House' but also to its lack of real power and its Conservative-dominated ranks. This he suggests, not only means that the Lords 'can be overridden by the Commons' but also that, due to their undemocratic and partisan composition, they 'lack a firm basis of support' and, conscious of this, are 'very reluctant to exercise [their] suspensory power over legislation'.[22] It is upon these two issues, the extent of Conservative domination of the Lords, and the limitations of the powers of the House that the remainder of this chapter will concentrate.

PARTY ALLEGIANCE IN THE HOUSE OF LORDS

J A G Griffith and M Ryle, *Parliament: Functions, Practice and Procedures* (1989), pp465–6

Party allegiance

In 1988 the party allegiance of peers who attended the House was; Conservative 416, cross-bench or Independent 244 (excluding the Law Lords and bishops, numbering 60), Labour 119, Liberal 43, and SDP 43. These figures represent a

---

20   'Government Compliance with International Human Rights Law: A New Year's Legitimate Expectation' (1996) PL 187.

21   Donald Shell, 'The House of Lords: Time for a Change?' (1994) 47(4) PA 734.

22   De Smith, *op cit*, pp525 and 527. De Smith suggests that this reluctance applies mainly to legislation sponsored by a Labour Government, but, as will be evident, the Lords' reluctance extends to any major legislation, particularly if it was mandated by a party manifesto.

significant change in the political complexion of the House. By the end of the nineteenth century, there existed a large Conservative or Unionist majority in the Lords, and this permanent majority continued well into the twentieth century. The 1968 White Paper on House of Lords Reform stated that 'the Conservatives have always in modern times been able to command a majority,' [Cmnd 3799 para 18] and indeed one of the objectives of the reform then proposed was that 'no one party should possess a permanent majority.'

But, as recently said by the Government Chief Whip 'in almost every case and almost every way ... the Government do not have an overall majority in this House' [HL Deb, vol 471, cols 1506-1509 (17 May 1984)]. The following table shows that the Conservatives, although the largest party in the House, have not had an absolute majority in recent years.

Party composition of whole House (excluding peers without writs or on leave of absence)

	1968 (July)	1974 (July)	1983 (May)	1986 (Nov)	1989 (May)
Conservative	351	370	448	412	412
Labour	116	134	132	118	111
Liberal	41	37	41	43	–
SDP	–	–	–	43	23
Independent	281	291	315	331	284
Democrats	–	–	–	–	56
Total	789	832	936	947	885

Nonetheless, the party composition of the Lords normally gives the present Conservative Government a majority, [HL Deb, Vol 451, col 149 (26 April 1984)] unless the cross-benchers vote overwhelmingly with the Opposition parties. This majority is in doubt only if a significant number of Conservatives either vote with the Opposition, or abstain; either by failing to vote, or by staying away.

The ... table [overleaf] shows that there is a difference between the party political composition of the whole House, and of those who attend regularly (here and elsewhere taken as those who attend more than a third of the sittings of the House). 168 Conservative peers attended over a third of the sittings in session 1985–86, 88 Labour, 27 Liberal and 24 SDP, and a further 73 Independent or cross-bench make up the total of 380.

The table also distinguishes between peers by succession and created peers. Of the 177 peers by succession who attended regularly in 1987–88, 114 were Conservatives, seven Labour, 15 Democrats, four SDP and 37 Independents. Of the 222 created peers who attend regularly, 70 are Conservative, 84 Labour, 23 Democrat, 9 SDP and 36 Independent. At the time of the White Paper in 1968 there was a rough equality amongst those who attended regularly between peers by succession and created peers. Now a majority of regular attenders are created peers.

Although the majority of ministers sit in the Commons, some Cabinet ministers do sit in the Lords and every department is represented by a junior minister or spokesman.

Composition of the House
Working House: breakdown by party

Party		1967–68	1983–84	1984–85	1985–86	1986–87	1987–88
Conservative		125	167	170	168	173	184
	By Succession	87	100	106	101	110	114
	Created	38	67	64	67	63	70
Labour		95	98	91	88	82	91
	By Succession	14	7	8	7	7	7
	Created	81	91	83	81	75	84
Liberal or SLD		19	25	26	27	36	38
	By Succession	11	9	12	12	14	15
	Created	8	16	14	15	22	23
SDP		N/A	21	23	24	15	13
	By Succession		5	6	7	5	4
	Created		16	17	17	10	9
Independent		52	76	74	73	73	73
	By Succession	26	33	34	36	36	37
	Created	26	43	40	37	37	36
Total		291	387	384	380	379	399
	By Succession	138	154	166	163	172	177
	Created	153	233	218	217	207	222

Notes

1 The above illustrates the fact that it is the very low attendance of the hereditary peers which prevents greater Conservative dominance.

2 How does this in-built Conservative weighting affect the work of the Lords in practice? The Lords are clearly aware of the fact that if they were to create serious difficulties for Labour Governments, demand among Labour MPs for reform of the Lords would become more pressing. Commentators suggest that although the House is traditionally generally sympathetic to Conservative Governments, it tends to adopt an even-handed approach to legislation emanating from a Labour administration and is very reluctant to exercise its remaining suspensory powers over legislation.

3 More important in recent years has been the fact that the House's general sympathy towards Conservative administrations has not resulted in servile obedience to the governments of the last 16 years. Writing in 1985, Donald Shell found that the Lords were proving unexpectedly difficult for the Thatcher Government:

Donald Shell, 'The House of Lords and the Thatcher Government' (1985) *Parliamentary Affairs* 16, 28–29

There seems something paradoxical in a Conservative Government experiencing real difficulties with the House of Lords. After all, hereditary peers out-number created peers by almost two to one, and the Conservative Party remains far and away the largest single party in the House. Yet by Summer 1984 it was apparent that Mrs Thatcher's legislation was more at risk in the Lords than in the Commons. In particular, the defeat the peers inflicted on the Local Government

(Interim Provisions) Bill on 28 June obliged the Government fundamentally to alter its strategy for coping with the abolition of the Greater London Council. If this was the most prominent embarrassment suffered by the Government, it was by no means the only one. In the same month peers insisted on the principle of their amendments to the Housing and Building Control Bill, despite their rejection by the Commons. And on half a dozen other bills in the opening session of the 1983 Parliament Government suffered defeats in the Lords ...

In the 1983–84 session there were indications of a more determined and self-confident mood amongst peers. With a Commons majority of 146 and a leader more ascendant within the Conservative Party than for many years (perhaps since Disraeli), it was peers rather than MPs (either Government back-benchers or opposition MPs) who could exert parliamentary checks upon Government. Following the election, the Labour leader in the Lords emphasised that the House had a 'much heavier responsibility' because of the huge Government majority in the Commons and even though this view was firmly repudiated by the Lord Chancellor, peers were undoubtedly conscious that they could more readily oblige governments to reconsider legislative proposals than MPs could. As this situation became more widely recognised, peers were put on their mettle. 'It is an interesting constitutional situation that gives an unelected chamber a greater influence than the elected chamber to change the minds of the executive on legislation', bemoaned a senior Tory MP.

Shell goes on to find that the Lords' lack of obedience to the wishes of Conservative Governments is not simply due to the fact that there is no overall Conservative majority in the House.

Why, then, has the Thatcher Government found itself suffering major defeats with increasing frequency in the Lords? To some extent the answer to that question is implicit in what has already been written. There is firstly the fact that despite its preponderance, and it increased relative strength in recent years, the Conservative Party does not have a majority in the Lords. Thus whenever the Government manages to get the other three parties in the House and most of the cross-benchers (who usually give the Government support) lined up against it, there is the strong possibility of defeat.

But added to this is the fact that Conservative back-benchers in the House have on some issues proved unreliable. Such unreliability may be expressed by voting with the opposition (and on average in 22 major defeats from 1979–84, 154 Conservative peers did enter the opposition lobby), or by abstention or absence.

... there is nothing like the machinery for whipping which exists in the Commons: there are no 'area Whips' though subjects may be allocated as the special responsibility of certain individual whips. This is also true of the other parties, though they do use three line whips more frequently.

Whipping in the Lords remains essentially low-key. It may be possible to persuade peers, but they cannot be coerced, commanded or bullied. Apart from a handful of office-holders, they receive no salaries; the vast majority are part-timers in the House, and very few can have ambitions for office. In such circumstances heavy whipping is unlikely to be effective.

... once the Government has gone down to a clear defeat, a significant compromise will usually have to be made, as it was on the Local Government Paving Bill in 1984. If that compromise is again rejected, then the Government will probably have to give way, as it did on accommodation for the elderly in the 1984 Housing and Building Control Bill.

Notes

1 The Lords have not displayed any more obedience to the Major administration, as the examples given above of major Government defeats on televising of sport, splitting of pensions and rights of asylum seekers indicate.

2 Ultimately, however, major points of Government legislation can usually be carried, even if the Lords oppose them. This is due to a mixture of legal and conventional restraints on the powers of the House, which will be examined in the next section.

LIMITATIONS ON THE POWERS OF THE HOUSE OF LORDS

The most important limitation on the power of the Lords is the Parliament Act 1911, as amended by the Parliament Act 1949. As Bradley and Wade note, the Act of 1911 was brought in after the 'rather uncertain convention' that the Lords should give way to the Commons when the peoples' will was behind that body, broke down when the Lords rejected Lloyd George's budget in 1909.[23]

Parliament Act 1911

Powers of House of Lords as to Money Bills

1.–(1) If a Money Bill, having been passed by the House of Commons, and sent up to the House of Lords at least one month before the end of the session, is not passed by the House of Lords without amendment within one month after it is so sent up to that House, the Bill shall, unless the House of Commons direct to the contrary, be presented to His Majesty and become an Act of Parliament on the Royal Assent being signified notwithstanding that the House of Lords have not consented to the Bill.

(2) A Money Bill means a Public Bill which in the opinion of the Speaker of the House of Commons contains only provisions dealing with all or any of the following subjects, namely, the imposition, repeal, remission, alteration, or regulation of taxation; the imposition for the payment of debt or other financial purposes of charges on the Consolidated Fund, or on money provided by Parliament, or the variation or repeal of any such charges; supply; the appropriation, receipt, custody, issue or audit of accounts of public money; the raising or guarantee of any loan or the repayment thereof; or subordinate matters incidental to those subjects or any of them. In this subsection the expressions 'taxation,' 'public money,' and 'loan' respectively do not include any taxation, money, or loan raised by local authorities or bodies for local purposes.

(3) There shall be endorsed on every Money Bill when it is sent up to the House of Lords and when it is presented to His Majesty for assent the certificate of the Speaker of the House of Commons signed by him that it is a Money Bill.

Before giving his certificate, the Speaker shall consult, if practicable, two members to be appointed from the Chairmen's Panel at the beginning of each Session by the Committee of Selection.

---

23 See Bradley and Wade, *Constitutional and Administrative Law*, 11th edn (1993), p204.

Restriction of the powers of the House of Lords as to Bills other than Money Bills

2.–(1) If any Public Bill (other than a Money Bill or a Bill containing any provision to extend the maximum duration of Parliament beyond five years) is passed by the House of Commons in three successive sessions (whether of the same Parliament or not), and having been sent up to the House of Lords at least one month before the end of the session, is rejected by the House of Lords in each of those sessions, that Bill shall, on its rejection for the third time by the House of Lords, unless the House of Commons direct to the contrary, be presented to His Majesty and become an Act of Parliament on the Royal Assent being signified thereto, notwithstanding that the House of Lords have not consented to the Bill:

Provided that this provision shall not take effect unless two years have elapsed between the date of the second reading in the first of those sessions of the Bill in the House of Commons and the date on which it passes the House of Commons in the third of those sessions.

(2) When a Bill is presented to His Majesty for assent in pursuance of the provisions of this section, there shall be endorsed on the Bill the certificate of the Speaker of the House of Commons signed by him that the provisions of this section have been duly complied with.

(3) A Bill shall be deemed to be rejected by the House of Lords if it is not passed by the House of Lords either without amendment or with such amendments only as may be agreed to by both Houses.

(4) A Bill shall be deemed to be the same Bill as a former Bill sent up to the House of Lords in the preceding session if, when it is sent up to the House of Lords, it is identical with the former Bill or contains only such alterations as are certified by the Speaker of the House of Commons to be necessary owing to the time which has elapsed since the date of the former Bill, or to represent any amendments which have been made by the House of Lords in the former Bill in the preceding session, and any amendments which are certified by the Speaker to have been made by the House of Lords in the third session and agreed to by the House of Commons shall be inserted in the Bill as presented for Royal Assent in pursuance of this section:

Provided that the House of Commons may, if they think fit, on the passage of such a Bill through the House in the second or third session, suggest any further amendments without inserting the amendments in the Bill, and any such suggested amendments shall be considered by the House of Lords, and, if agreed to by that House, shall be by the House of Lords and agreed but the exercise of this power by The House of Commons shall not affect the operation of this section in the event of the Bill being rejected by the House of Lords.

Certificate of Speaker

3. Any certificate of the Speaker of the House of Commons given under this Act shall be conclusive for all purposes, and shall not be questioned in any court of law.

Parliament Act 1949

An Act to amend the Parliament Act, 1911 …

1. The Parliament Act, 1911, shall have effect, and shall be deemed to have had effect from the beginning of the session in references which the Bill for this Act originated (save as regards that Bill itself) as if–

(a) there had been substituted in subsections (1) and (4) of section two thereof, for the words 'in three successive sessions', 'for the third time', 'in the third of those sessions', 'in the third session', and 'in the second or third session' respectively, the words 'in two successive sessions', 'for the second time', 'in the second of those sessions', 'in the second session', and 'in the second session' respectively; and

(b) there had been substituted in subsection (1) of the said section two, for the words 'two years have elapsed' the words 'one year has elapsed':

Provided that, if a Bill has been rejected for the second time by the House of Lords before the signification of the Royal Assent to the Bill for this Act, whether such rejection was in the same session as that in which the Royal Assent to the Bill for this Act was signified or in an earlier session, the requirement of the said section two that a Bill is to be presented to His Majesty on its rejection for the second time by the House of Lords shall have effect in relation to the Bill rejected as a requirement that it is to be presented to His Majesty as soon as the Royal Assent to the Bill for this Act has been signified, and, notwithstanding that such rejection was in an earlier session, the Royal Assent to the Bill rejected may be signified in the session in which the Royal Assent to the Bill for this Act was signified.

Notes

1   The Acts allow the House of Commons to assert political supremacy over the Lords in two very important instances. Firstly, s2 of the Parliament Act 1911 makes various provisions to present a Bill for the Royal Assent against the opposition of the Lords. When a Bill has been passed by the Commons in two successive sessions and it is rejected for a second time by the Lords it can be presented on its second rejection for the Royal Assent. One year must elapse between the second reading of the Bill in the Commons at the first session and its passing in the Commons in the second.

2   Secondly, if a Bill is a money Bill as defined in s1(2) of the Parliament Act 1911, and is passed by the Commons but is not passed by the Lords without amendment within one month after they receive it, it shall be presented to the Queen for the Royal Assent and become an Act of Parliament. This provision, adopted with a view to stopping the Lords blocking the passing of essential financial legislation and contained in s1(1) of the 1911 Act, was brought forward after the Lords had rejected the Finance Bill 1909.

3   However, the limits on the Lords' power under the Parliament Acts are not as significant as may at first appear. Firstly, not all Bills are subject to the Parliament Acts. Exemption extends to private Bills, statutory instruments, Bills prolonging the life of Parliament and Bills originating in the House of Lords. Secondly, in practice the Government will not want to wait for over a year before securing the passage of its legislation and so will be prepared to accept compromise amendments.

4   As previously mentioned, the Lords are generally circumspect in the use of their formal powers. They will however on occasion use their powers of suspension fully as in relation to the Trade Union and Labour Relations (Amendment) Bill 1974–75. In the debate in the Lords in relation to their amendments to this Bill, Lord Carrington said:

In our system we have hitherto taken the view that the will of the elected house must in the end prevail, but that there should be a second House which has the opportunity ... to enforce a delay in which there can be reassessment by Government ... If we now decide to use that very limited power we are not thwarting the will of the people for, in so far as it is represented by the House of

Commons, it will and must prevail in a comparatively short time. [HL Deb, vol 365 col 1742 (11 November 1975).]

The Lords eventually allowed the Bill to go for Royal Assent only because the Government threatened to pass it under the Parliament Acts procedure. By delaying the Bill the Lords had opened up the possibility that it would receive greater scrutiny. The suspensory powers were again used to the full in relation to the War Crimes Bill 1991, which had actually to be passed under the Parliament Acts procedure.

5   The Lords accept a number of self-imposed informal constraints which have developed into conventions designed to avoid accusations that they are acting party politically. One of the most important conventions has been termed 'the doctrine of the mandate'. This doctrine was explained by Lord Salisbury in 1964: as a guiding principle, where legislation had been promised in the Party manifesto the Lords would not block it on the ground that it should be regarded as having been approved by the British people. [HL Deb, vol 261, col 66 (4 November 1964).] This doctrine was developed during the post-war Labour administration but now normally applies to 'mandated' Bills of either party. However, this doctrine does not mean that the Lords will refrain from insisting on an amendment to a Bill even though the effect will almost certainly be to kill it. This occurred in relation to the House of Commons (Redistribution of Seats) Bill in 1968–69. Lord Carrington recalls the evolution of the Salisbury Rules, and their application in the Lords during the period of Labour Government in the 1960s:

Lord Carrington, *Reflect on Things Past* (1988), pp77–8, 203–4

Cranborne [Leader of the House of Lords] reckoned that it was not the duty of the House of Lords to make our system of government inoperable. Nor, he considered, was it justified that the Opposition peers should use their voting strength to wreck any measure which the Government had made plain at a General Election that they proposed to introduce. He thus evolved guidelines, now unofficially known as the Salisbury Rules, which meant that the Lords should, if they saw fit, amend, but should not destroy or alter beyond recognition, any Bill on which the country had, by implication, given its verdict. The Lords, in other words, should not frustrate the declared will of the people.

I doubt if this amounted to a formal constitutional doctrine but as a way of behaving it seemed to be very sensible ... To this day the convention continues that the House of Lords may amend but does not reject Bills on matters of formal and declared Government policy which have received a second reading in the Commons.

To lead the Tories in the Lords when there was Conservative Government was a comparatively simple matter at that time, although there would always be some dissidents, or some who thought our policy inadequately robust. To lead them in Opposition, when they have a majority in the House and strongly objected to many of the Labour Government's measures, needed more delicate handling. ... The Prime Minister, Wilson, began by taking an attitude towards the Polaris project – that our nuclear armoury should not and would not be truly independent because of the American provenance of some of it – which I knew to be nonsense in logic and reckoned (and said) was a viewpoint advanced to placate the left wing of his own party, like much else. If we chose, our deterrent force would be entirely independent, because we would command and control it. But many issues were more controversial on our side.

I tried to apply the Salisbury Convention: and, like Salisbury, I found the greatest difficulty lay in striking a proper balance between, on the one hand, giving my troops a taste of battle, allowing enough uninhibited passion to find voice; and, on the other hand, keeping them sufficiently minded that it was not our job to provoke a constitutional crisis, that the House of Commons had been elected by the people, that the Government had a majority in that House and that Government must go on. Both sides of the balance were necessary. We had to behave responsibly; but I couldn't expect our supporters to lie down and be silent when something to which they took strong and principled objection was being proposed. Plenty of them felt that their right and their duty was to protest; and they could protest both with their voices and with their votes. The former need not be discouraged, but the latter need handling. On the whole, matters went tolerably well.

Notes

1   Lord Carrington provides an illuminating insight into the way in which in this area of the British constitution, as in so many others, informal guidelines, shared understandings and self restraint complement the bare statutory framework (in this case the Parliament Acts) and in fact become more important in practice: the Parliament Act procedure has only been used four times since it was introduced.

2   The Lords have recently indicated their reluctance to allow the development of further conventions governing the use of their powers to diminish their role still further. Up until recently, the Lords had not voted on any item of subordinate legislation submitted to them for consideration. However, when this was pointed out to them and it was suggested that a convention had come into being that the Lords would not vote down items of subordinate legislation, their Lordships' response was bullish: a motion by Lord Simon of Glaisdale to the effect that the House had unfettered free.lom to vote on any subordinate legislation before them was overwhelmingly approved.[24]

Question

Would it be desirable to replace this rather *ad hoc* system for restraining the suspensory power of the Lords with legislation which laid down in detail the situations in which the power could and could not be used? Would it be possible to frame such legislation?

Notes

1   When the Lords oppose a Bill sent up by the Commons they tend to propose amendments at the committee stage rather than vote against the second reading, but there is a convention that amendments at the committee stage should not re-open matters of principle already accepted by the Commons. The Lords will rarely insist on their amendments to a Government Bill if a compromise can be reached, although of course they may do so when the Government lacks an effective majority to ensure their rejection in the Commons. O Hood Phillips has also argued[25] that there is almost a convention that the Lords will not return a Government Bill to the Commons for reconsideration more than once.

---

24   HL Deb 20 October 1994, vol 559, col 356.

25   *Constitutional and Administrative Law*, 7th ed (1987), p148.

2 Donald Shell considers that the combined effect of these legal and conventional restraints on the Lords means that it is unable to provide an appreciable check on the Government-dominated Commons. The experience of the Thatcher Government is again used as an example.

To the Thatcher Governments of the 1980s the House was frequently an irritant but never a serious obstacle. In particular, legislation relating to local government and its various responsibilities, notably education and housing, was frequently amended against the will of the government. Ministers regularly gave ground to the Lords, with the House even being described as the real opposition during the 1983 Parliament when the Labour opposition in the Commons was at its lowest ebb. But in the late 1980s there appeared to a hardening of ministerial attitudes to the Lords, with the Government endeavouring wherever possible to overturn any defeat it suffered there. This culminated in the used of the Parliament Act procedures to pass the War Crimes Act of 1991, a Bill which the Government chose to persist with notwithstanding strong opposition in the Lords, not least from the judicial peers, as well as much opposition from within Conservative Party ranks. It was certainly not a manifesto Bill, and not at all the kind of legislation envisaged as appropriate for Parliament Act procedures when these had first been formulated. [26]

3 Shell's view here (expressed in 1994) that the Lords were 'an irritant, but never a serious obstacle' to the Thatcher Government seems at odds with his opinion in 1985 that the Government was then experiencing 'real difficulties' with the Lords (above, pp27–8). The inference is presumably that the 'more determined and self-confident mood amongst peers' in 1983 which he noted in his earlier article was a product of the peers' knowledge that the Commons Opposition was at that time relative ineffectual, given the huge Conservative majority after the 1983 General Election; and further that as the Conservatives' majority was progressively reduced in subsequent elections, the peers retreated towards a more facilitative and anodyne approach. If this explanation is correct, it may be concluded that the Lords are capable of taking a flexible approach towards their self-imposed restraints, adopting a more bullish approach when the political situation seems to demand it. This is one argument in favour of leaving such restraints on a self-imposed basis only.

4 However, any notion that as a Government's majority decreases[27] the House of Lords is content to leave real opposition to Government proposals to the Commons seems hard to square with the recent series of defeats inflicted by the Lords on Government legislation – defeats on matters of important and controversial policy relating to television rights to sport (described as 'the biggest Government upset in the Lords since 1988'),[28] pensions and rights of asylum seekers (see above). While it is tempting to try to formulate general rules about the behaviour of the Lords which relate it to the situation in the Commons, it is quite possible that the Salisbury Convention excepted[29] the most important factor in determining the assertiveness of the Lords is simply the nature of the legislation put before them.

---

26 Donald Shell, 'The House of Lords: Time for a Change?' (1994) PA 721, 733.

27 John Major's administration has a majority of just one at the time of writing.

28 'Peers inflict huge defeat on TV Sport', *Independent*, 7 February 1996. The defeat in 1988 referred to was the 133 vote defeat over the 'poll tax' in May of that year.

CONCLUSIONS AND DIRECTIONS FOR REFORM

It is interesting to begin this section with some self-evaluation: Brigid Hadfield has analysed comments made by peers which reveal their own perceptions of their role and effectiveness.

Brigid Hadfield, 'Whither or Whether the House of Lords' (1984) 35(4) *Northern Ireland Legal Quarterly* 313, 331–3

The best recent descriptions of the general extremities of the Lords' powers (other than under the Parliament Acts) were given by non-Government peers during the second reading debates on the Rates Bill and the Local Government (Interim Provisions) Bill. To the former the Opposition moved a reasoned amendment: in regard for the constitutional convention that 'we do not exercise our full parliamentary powers on the second reading of a Government Bill, especially if it appeared in the manifesto', [HL Deb vol 450, col 911 (9 April 1984), *per* Baroness Birk] no attempt was made to deny the Bill a second reading or to delay it. The justification given by Baroness Birk for tabling the reasoned amendment – in itself an unusual course of action – lay in the 'constitutional' nature of the Bill – it involved the relationship between central and local government the powers of local councillors and the extent of 'local democracy' –

> To say that an issue is constitutional does not mean that a change should never be made, but it should be made only with great care, great deliberation and great trepidation; and, too, only when a very strong case has been made out. *This supersedes any manifesto commitment* [emphasis supplied]. That case has not been made out.

Baroness Birk then referred to the opposition to the Bill (guillotined in the Commons where it was carried by 125 votes) from back-bench Conservative Members of Parliament, including a former Prime Minister and a former Secretary of State for the Environment, and continued –

> ... conventions do not require this Chamber to remain silent on issues that are of grave concern in this House, another place and even beyond. As we have always said from every Bench, this House is a guardian of our rights, constitution and civil liberties – and also the speed with which things are done in another place. [See n 56, *supra* cols 908–9 and 911.]

During the second reading of the Local Government (Interim Provisions) Bill, Lord Hooson said of the debate that it was crucial in terms of judging –

> how effective, if at all, is this House as a modifying and balancing factor against the unwarranted exercise of power by ... an elective dictatorship. In certain circumstances ... your Lordships' House has a clear constitutional duty to take appropriate steps to cause the executive to reconsider their position and the full implications of what they are doing. What has been doubted in many quarters is whether your Lordships' House is now sufficiently free from Party and political manipulation by the executive of whatever political colour, to perform any such function effectively. [HL Deb vol 452, col 897 (11 June 1984).]

Less heady assessments were made, during a debate on peers' rights, by Viscount Whitelaw, the Leader of the House, and Lord Cledwyn of Penrhos, the Leader of the Opposition. The latter referred to the 'important constitutional

---

29   See pp432–3 above.

safeguard' of the requirement of the Lords' consent to any Prolongation of Parliament Bill and, further, stated his belief that the Bryce exposition of the functions appropriate for a second chamber still held good for the Lords today. Indeed –

> the greater use of the guillotine in another place makes the work of revision more important and we can also add to Lord Bryce's list this House's European Communities Committee which has gained a first class reputation throughout Western Europe for the quality and importance of its work.

Question

The more grandiose aspirations of the Lords for a crucial role in the preservation of our constitutional liberties seem to sit oddly with the non-contentious, facilitative function they generally perform in practice in relation to legislation. Are such heady conceptions of their role anything more than a consolation for their lack of real power?

Note

Donald Shell argues that despite the usefulness of the work done by the House of Lords, its undemocratic nature is no longer tolerable in terms of political morality and, perhaps more importantly, serves to render the House ultimately ineffectual.

Donald Shell, 'The House of Lords: Time for a Change?' (1994) 47(4) *Parliamentary Affairs* 721, 735–6

Any examination of the functions of the House can point without too much difficulty to useful work performed by peers. It would be odd of this were not the case. The House of Commons is far from being a perfect legislature. There is plenty of work for a second chamber to do. And the House of Lords does contain within its ranks a great many highly experienced politicians as well as many others who have achieved distinctions in various walks of life. Other much less distinguished folk often represent a family tradition of public service. So one would expect some good to come from the Lords. The details of draft legislation are often debated in an unsatisfactory way in the Commons; the use of the guillotine is frequent, and the imperatives of party conflict take precedence over the need for careful and methodical scrutiny of legislation. Governments of all persuasions have found the House of Lords a necessary adjunct to the legislative process. Peers themselves have sought to enhance the effectiveness of their House by developing select committee work.

But whatever usefulness the present House possesses should not be taken as an excuse for avoiding the questions of reform. Reform is necessary because retaining the present House symbolises Britain's half-hearted commitment to democracy. Governments that urge upon other institutions the need for modernisation while ignoring the House of Lords lose credibility. To talk of developing a classless society while leaving the present House of Lords in place is a nonsense. Furthermore, the present composition of the House, including as it does a ridiculous imbalance in party strengths, ensures that governments need not take the House very seriously.

The House lacks the legitimacy to resist Government effectively. It would now be foolish to rely on the House to provide satisfactory protection for the fundamentals of the constitution. The House is too ready to settle for being mildly awkward to government when it ought to be persistently difficult. If the Government choose to reverse Lords' amendments to Bills, then peers prefer to give way rather than to sue their powers to hold up legislation. The only recent exception to this was the War Crimes Bill, which peers felt able to resist precisely because it was not a Bill upon which the Government could apply a whip in the Commons. On delegated legislation peers have in effect accepted a convention forbidding them from voting against statutory instruments, lest they accidentally use the veto power they still possess in this area.

Note

Shell's view that the Lord's lack of legitimacy means that 'it would now be foolish' to rely on the House to protect fundamental constitutional principles was arguably borne out by the response of the Lords in April 1996 to the Prevention of Terrorism (Additional Powers) Act which, *inter alia*, gives the police new powers to stop and search pedestrians to search for terrorist-related items, without having to have reasonable suspicion (s1). The fundamental principle at stake (it has of course been violated before) was that measures threatening the liberty of the subject should be given a decent period for scrutiny and that debate should not be subject to severe time constraints. The Act passed all its stages in the Commons in a single day and the Lords were requested by the Government to follow suit. As the extracts from the debate given below make clear, many peers expressed considerable disquiet at what they were being asked to do, but, ultimately appeared to think it their duty to acquiesce.

HL Deb 3 April 1996, vol 571, no 73, cols 298, 301–4, 337–8

Lord Rodgers of Quarry Bank: I shall make one further important point about our earlier discussion. I do not believe that what the noble Earl said represented the view of any party in this House. He argued that because consultation took place with opposition parties in another place, there was no need for it here. That is a very dangerous principle. I was very surprised to hear it from a Conservative Minister in particular. It is a principle which puts party above Parliament and assumes that relationships and communications between parties are more important than communications within a House between parties in the spirit of the remarks made by the noble Lord, Lord McIntosh of Haringey, about co-operation on issues of terrorism. I do not want to labour the point or ask for a lesson to be learnt. But I would not want it to stand on record – I do not believe that the noble Baroness would want it, either – that consultation between parties is at any time in any circumstances a substitute for consultation and communication between parties in this House or another place ...

Baroness Park of Monmouth: It has been asked why we should pass these extensions of that legislation now, and why so fast. We should perhaps remember that the IRA spent the whole time of the ceasefire collecting money for more arms and tried several raids on cash shipments in the Republic in recent months. They collected information on more possible targets and did their dummy run for Canary Wharf in December, well before the Mitchell Report put them in a corner and also provided their excuse for ending the ceasefire. From their point of view they were simply switching back to another military phase of the struggle after extracting the maximum benefit from a political phase ... I urge that we do not tie the hands of the police behind their backs. The victims of IRA bombs are innocent too. They have a right to protection. I share the hope of many noble Lords that there should be some review of this measure in due course – I welcome the promise of regular reports though I do not regard them as a substitute – and I believe very strongly that proper scrutiny is our right and our duty, but the IRA do not play by our rules. They know nothing about our procedures and care less. It would be irresponsible not to listen and to act in time when they make their own murderous intentions so clear.

Lord Stoddart of Swindon: My Lords, I decided to speak today not because I am necessarily opposed to the provisions of the Bill but because I am very concerned at the way in which it has been handled. Noble Lords should recall the experiences we have had with Bills which have been rushed through Parliament. We have learnt and lived to regret such Bills as time has gone on. Our experience of rushed Bills has not been a happy one.

The Minister will know that I cannot be accused of being a softie on crime or terrorism. I am, if anything, a hardliner. I am anti-criminal – very anti-criminal; I am victim friendly; I detest the terrorist murderers of the IRA and regret that, instead of being defeated and routed before the peace process, they were let off the hook and allowed to re-arm and regroup. So, basically, I am in favour of any measures to deal with the terrorists and to protect our own people from their activities. But, if we so bring in measures without proper democratic scrutiny then it is the terrorists who have won, particularly if these measures impinge on the freedom of our people to go about their business unhindered.

I believe that this point was raised by my noble friend earlier; namely, that there is a suspicion that the police asked for these powers some weeks ago in anticipation of problems arising around the 80th anniversary of the 1916 Easter Rising. If that is true, and perhaps the noble Baroness can tell us whether it is, why on earth was no legislation brought forward earlier so that we could indeed have had a proper discussion? But, even if the police did not ask for powers, the Government themselves should have shown intelligent anticipation after the ceasefire was so brutally ended, and asked Parliament to consider new measures, but again with adequate time for proper scrutiny of those measures. As it is, we have a raft of significant measures of which the House of Commons was given only one day's notice. The measures were railroaded through on a guillotine allowing only six hours for all stages of the Bill. That is hardly time to put forward any amendments in Committee, let alone at Report stage, and no time for consultation with, or representations from, individuals and organisations. Democracy means that people have the right of representation in Parliament and that their views can be considered and taken into account.

It is simply not good enough to say that the Official Opposition Front Bench is content to allow the Bill to be forced through Parliament without proper discussion. It really is intolerable that the Front Benches should behave in this way, particularly the Labour Front Bench in the House of Commons. As I said earlier, I have some sympathy with my noble friend Lord McIntosh, since he really has not had time to consider the matter properly. Nevertheless, I shall listen to his advice. The noble and learned Lord, Lord Hailsham, once referred to the House of Commons as an 'elected dictatorship'. I rather fear that things have moved on since then and that we now have a one-party state, certainly in respect of this Bill.

I now turn to the Bill itself. As has already been mentioned, clause 1 is the most onerous. Stop and search powers may very well be necessary, but Parliament is entitled to consider the implications and to consider them properly. The powers are bound to cause resentment. The Irish community and other minority communities, may very well fear that they will be unduly targeted. There is a risk that people will remonstrate with the police. If one is stopped in the street and asked to take off one's clothes, one's coat, gloves and hat, people may very well get angry and remonstrate with the police. The people will be very severely punished. We should understand that the penalties for obstructing the police are very severe. They are six months in prison or a fine of £5,000 or both. We are considering heavy penalties. We also have to have regard to the shame that people will feel on being stopped and body-searched in the street.

I ask the noble Baroness this question: what is the position of women in particular? Women do engage in terrorism and they are just as suspect as anyone else. Can I have an assurance from the Minister that those searches will be conducted by female officers? What about privacy? These are matters which should concern us. What is the position as regards juveniles? They can carry bombs, too, and they can have bombs planted on them by adults. The present position, as I understand it is that juveniles must be searched at the police station in the presence of a parent, guardian or a social worker. Do the provisions of clause 1 of the Bill transcend the protection of juveniles that we have at the present time? These are relevant matters which we would have wanted to explore in a reasonable Committee stage debate.

I nevertheless understand and accept the urgency of the measure and will certainly not seek to divide the House on Second Reading, even if that were to do any good anyway. I shall not seek to do it. I understand the need and the Government's position. However, to meet the points which I have raised, I have tabled an amendment by which the Government can redeem themselves and give Parliament the opportunity to give proper consideration to a replacement Bill after the Easter Recess. It is an amendment to allow the legislation to run for three months [only, after which it would be reviewed] ...

Lord MacIntosh of Haringey: ... I happen to think that my noble friend's amendment is mistaken. I think he is wrong to choose three months. That is too short a period. My noble friend is also wrong to suggest the stick of the Act ceasing to have effect. We have never suggested that the Act should cease to have effect before any further consideration takes place. However, the idea put forward by the noble Lord, Lord Jenkins, that there should be an opportunity for full parliamentary consideration of the provisions of this Act within the next year before the order comes up next March as a continuance order seems sensible. I speak personally, not having had the time to consult my honourable friends in another place. Indeed, it seems a more sensible suggestion than that put forward by my noble friend. On that basis and in the light of developments since my noble friend tabled his amendment, I hope that he may see fit to withdraw it.

Nevertheless, some further scrutiny will be required. It will have to be parliamentary scrutiny because I am sure that those who say that legislation brought forward in this way is almost bound to have defects are right. Indeed, my noble friend Lord Houghton of Sowerby has been in his seat twice during the past week to give proof of that when referring to the defects of the Dangerous Dogs Act 1991, which was rushed through in a similar way. We would do well to take account of the reconsideration of that Act which has been called for on many occasions and the amount of parliamentary time that has been devoted to such a reconsideration when we consider the possibility that we may have got something wrong in this legislation. I think that that is highly likely. The Government should recognise that fact and stretch out an olive branch to parliamentary reconsideration, which is what my noble friend Lord Stoddart is suggesting.

Earl Russell: This House is a revising Chamber. We live by the creed that, right or wrong, a Bill might as well be as well drafted as possible. Nobody's initial drafting is perfect, and even in the very brief Committee stage that we have had, we have detected one or two ways in which, if we discussed the Bill quietly around a table in private, we could succeed in improving it.

However, we have not succeeded in ventilating a number of other questions. In particular and for the benefit of those of us who are not quite up to pace, if I may put it like that, it would be nice to know exactly what the Bill adds – or what it does not add – to the existing powers of the police. For all those reasons, it would be an extremely good thing in matters where liberty may be at stake if we could consider the Bill together to make it as good as possible. We have not had the opportunity to do that today, but I hope that we shall have such an opportunity fairly soon.

Notes

1   Thus the House felt itself unable either to reject the Bill or to extend time for consideration, although peers clearly expressed a sense of constitutional impropriety in the way in which the matter had been handled.

2   The weaknesses of the House clearly extend beyond its inability to withstand the Commons. Brazier identifies three key problems:

> ... it could be argued that the House is weakened in three fundamental respects: it is anomalous, unrepresentative, and on an average day Conservative-led. No modern state seeking to create a new legislature would devise anything remotely resembling a House most of whose members may sit on the basis of hereditary while the rest of its members exist on the unrestricted patronage of the head of Government. Hereditary does occasionally provide young peers, and once even a Communist marquess, but such events are rather exceptional. The House is unrepresentative (or representative of only certain sections of society); former ministers and ex-MPs make up a sizeable proportion of the working House. And it cannot be right in principle that one party is permanently in a stronger position in the House of Lords than any other – even if that does not guarantee the sacrosanctity of all Conservative legislation in the House.[30]

3   In examining the various proposals for reform which have been put forward, the first question is obviously whether a second chamber is needed at all. Hadfield had no doubts on the matter:

> Unicameralism would enhance the powers of the executive, not of the Commons even if reformed. Arguments in favour of unicameralism are largely, in substance and in consequence if not in presentation, arguments in favour of autocracy and not (Parliamentary) democracy. It is too facile to quote Abbé Sieyes' dismissal of a second chamber–'if a second chamber dissents from the first it is mischievous; if it agrees, it is superfluous'. The saying largely fails to take into account that a Government may, when formulating its policies, respond in advance to the known opinions of those whom it has to persuade, cajole or 'whip' into support. A second chamber may agree because the Government has anticipated its likely response and formulated its policies in that light. Similarly, the saying largely ignores non-decisions which are as important as decisions–Governments may decide not to implement a particular policy at all knowing that it will face too hostile a reception. It is, further, hard to see why, in principle, it is mischievous to require a Government with, say, 40% of the popular vote, to subject its wishes to a prolonged and more considered

---

30   Ronald Brazier, *Constitutional Practice*, 2nd edn (1994), p259.

parliamentary process. It may be mischievous to obstruct a government if the 'obstructors' have no democratic foundation but this is a point in favour of a reformed second chamber and not unicameralism.

The four functions identified by the Bryce Committee as being appropriate for a second chamber, updated by reference to the scrutiny of European Community law have been shown by the work of the House of Lords to be necessary – necessary, in the sense that the Commons cannot discharge them all; necessary in the sense that if one adheres to the concept of a balanced constitution they should be done.[31]

4   If it is conceded that a second chamber is desirable, should reform concentrate on the membership of the House, its powers, or both?

5   Reform of the *powers* of the House of Lords, as opposed to its composition, leads back to the problem that it is an undemocratic institution. On the one hand the Lords performs some valuable functions and could be empowered to perform them more effectively. On the other, allowing the Lords increased power would be undesirable as it would result in an enhanced perception of its anomalous nature. Thus, reform of the Lords with a view to making it a more democratic institution is probably desirable but carries with it the difficulty that part of its value – as pointed out above – derives from the fact that it is *not* an elected body. Accountability to constituents and therefore the much greater influence of the party machine in the Lords would not appear likely to enhance its value.

6   In 1968 the Government introduced a Bill to reform the Lords. It would have introduced an attendance requirement in order to entitle members to vote. Inheritance of a peerage would no longer of itself have qualified for membership of the House. Members of the House would have been divided into two groups: those entitled to vote and those entitled to attend and speak but not vote. About 80 new Labour life peers would have had to be created in order to address the unfairness caused by the in-built Conservative majority. The Bill was defeated by an alliance of back-benchers.[32]

7   The 1968 Bill fudged the issue of the selection of life peers – leaving it in the hands of the Prime Minister of the day, but laying down some vaguely worded principles of uncertain status to guide the Prime Minister on selection. A more rigorous agenda for reform has been put forward by Brigid Hadfield.

Brigid Hadfield, 'Whither or Whether the House of Lords' (1994) 35(4) *Northern Ireland Legal Quarterly* 320, 348–51

It is the composition of a second chamber – for want of a better word, let it now be termed the Senate – that has been the greatest stumbling-block to reform. It is probably true to state that some of those in the abolitionist camp would be in favour of a reformed second chamber if one could be composed on a rational basis. The problem is as follows. The Senate would either have to be elected or

---

31   Hadfield, *op cit*, pp347–8.
32   O Hood Phillips, *op cit*, pp108–69.

non-elected. If the former, it would become a rival to the Commons and political impasse would inevitably result. On the other hand, a non-elected Senate founders both because the method of composition is deficient (the arguments on, for example, heredity and patronage need no exposition) and because a non-elected Senate would have no authority or justification for asserting itself against the Commons or Government. These arguments have consistently frustrated the high intentions of the Preamble to the Parliament Act 1911, and yet the force of the arguments largely depends upon the powers given to the Senate. A purely advisory Senate would scarcely need an impeccable electoral mandate. It is surely possible to achieve, more or less, a balance between the method of composition of the Senate and the powers with which the Senate is entrusted, and thereby to achieve (as Vincent would have it) an institutionalised secondary power of influence, exercised upon the primary power of government, by directive élites. So the following scheme is suggested. These would be removed completely from the Senate's powers: (a) all financial matters, including finance Bills, as currently defined under the Parliament Act 1911; (b) delegated legislation, the Commons procedure to be reformed ...; (c) Bills certified by the Government as being a matter of 'political confidence'; these would be considered and consented to by the Commons alone, subject to these reforms: full provision by the Government of explanatory memoranda, a certain amount of time to be allocated in advance to each part of the Bill so that no clause remains undiscussed by the Commons in Committee, and minimum intervals between each legislative stage; and (d) scrutiny of the executive, although the Senate may here play a subsidiary role through its Question Time and general debates, which would remain in existence.

As far as European Community matters are concerned – where there are no *powers* in the national Parliaments – the current division of labour between Commons and second chamber would remain. To the Senate would also be entrusted the two general powers of consent to a Prolongation of Parliament Bill and to the removal from office of the superior judiciary. The Senate's legislative powers would be (a) the power to initiate any Bill on which its consent is required; and (b) the power to revise and consent to all Bills coming to it from the Commons. As far as the first category is concerned, the Government, as at present, would decide which Bills to begin in the Commons and which in the Senate, but it is to be hoped that the Senate would, first 'inherit' the Lords expertise in law reform and regional matters and, secondly, would, where appropriate, take the Bill's Committee stage in its own newly-created Select or Special Standing Committee. All this would be without prejudice to the Commons' procedures over such Bills – for example, its committee stage may too be taken in Special Standing Committee. As far as Bills on which the consent of both Houses is required are concerned, the Senate would be given six months in which to consider the Bill; if agreement between the two Houses had not been reached within that time, [The Senate would be required to consider the Bill within that time; failure to do so would be implied consent] ... then the problematic clauses would be submitted to the vote of both Houses, voting separately but the votes to be totalled, the issue to be resolved by a simple majority of all votes cast (a split vote being resolved in the Government's favour). The consent of the Senate as such could not, however, be dispensed with. [Where a Bill is initiated in the Senate and is not agreed to, the Government would, if it wished to proceed further, have to 'restart' the Bill in the Commons and then send it to the Senate, when the six month rule would then operate.]

The size of the Senate is envisaged at somewhere around 400. This figure has not been chosen arbitrarily. The average daily attendance of the Lords is around 300;

and 81 of the 400 being recommended for membership of the Senate would have quite considerable commitment outside Parliament. These 81 are the United Kingdom members of the European Parliament (which sits for approximately 65 days each year) and it is recommended, in light of the extensive amount of European work the Senate will do, that MEPs should *ex officio* be members of the Senate (and, therefore, be disqualified from membership of the House of Commons). Of the remainder, 162 would be elected at the same time as the MEP-Senators, on the same (European) constituencies but by a system of proportional representation. This recommendation is designed to inject into the Senate both party political representation and regional awareness. From these 162 Senators alone the Government of the day would choose its leader of the Senate, departmental spokesmen and so forth. It is recommended that the Senate would operate, as does the House of Lords, with no guillotine and a freer atmosphere of debate than the Commons. These Senators could serve for a five-year fixed-term of office (as do the MEPs) or, if continuity is thought desirable, for ten years, which would maintain the coincidence of dates with European elections. The fact that such elections would (almost certainly) not be synchronised with Commons' elections would inject a desirable element of political disjunction.

The remaining Senators would, rather like some Irish Senators, represent certain functional or vocational interests. In Ireland, these are divided into five categories: (a) the cultural and educational; (b) the agricultural; (c) labour; (d) industrial and commercial; and (e) administrative, which includes public administration, the social services and voluntary social activities. As far as the United Kingdom is concerned (b) could be subsumed under (c) which would be labelled 'Trade Union' and then each of the four categories would be represented by 30 Senators, the method of selection and election to be as follows. Candidates could only be nominated by an 'accredited body' in their group, for example, university vice-chancellors, the Royal Academy, the Royal Society, a trade union, the Confederation of British Industry, (registered) charities and so forth (the list would clearly be quite lengthy). They would then be elected by Members of Parliament to serve for a term of five (or 10) years, on the day that the elections for the other Senators were held.

The current judicial work of the House of Lords would be given to either a reconstituted Judicial Committee of the Privy Council, or to a new statutory final Supreme Court of Appeal. All judges who have held high judicial office (say Court of Appeal and above) would on their retirement, but not before, become *ex officio* (or *functus officio*) members of the Senate. Whilst this would not inject a youthful element into the Senate, it would provide invaluable legal expertise, which would otherwise only be directly provided, if at all, by the 'cultural and educational interests'.

Penultimately, after each General Election, a maximum number of 15 political appointments may be made by the Government, after consultation with the leaders of all other political parties represented in the Commons, from amongst persons who have served a minimum of 10 years in the Commons. Such Senators would provide a certain amount of Commons 'awareness' for the Senate, and they would serve for life. The Government would not, however, be able to appoint such Senators as members of the Government; thereby fears of influential patronage would be minimised.

Finally, there is much in general terms to be said for the representation of Christian (and other religious) interests in the Senate; but it is clearly the responsibility of each faith to determine whether or not service in the Senate would be compatible with that faith. Those who concluded that such service was compatible would be enabled to nominate candidates for the Senate under category (a), the cultural and educational, which would then be appropriately renamed.

In order for the current experience of the House of Lords to be transmitted to the Senate, transitional arrangements would have to be made. For example, all those peers who have, over several sessions, regularly attended one-third or more of the sittings of the House should be for life (should they wish and should they not otherwise become qualified under another head) non-voting members of the Senate.

Note

Hadfield makes the essential connection between the powers of the Senate and its membership; the greater the former, the more concern will be expressed about the democratic credentials of the latter. However, it is not clear why she believes that it is necessary or desirable to remove the role of scrutinising executive policy and administration from the reformed House. Such scrutiny clearly does *not*, in Hadfield's words, require an 'impeccable electoral mandate', unlike for example the power to effectively 'kill' legislation passed by the elected House. Scrutiny of the executive can be undertaken by anyone with a critical intelligence and access to relevant information; it is carried on every day by un-elected journalists, academics and various 'watchdogs'. Given the preponderance of executive power over the legislature, and the secretive nature of much executive decision-making,[33] it seems odd to suggest removing one of the present sources of scrutiny, albeit one of limited effectiveness.

Question

Is it naïve to propose that the Government should be able to preclude consideration of certain bills by the Senate simply by certifying that they concern a matter of 'political confidence'? Should not such certification be subject to an affirmative resolution of the Commons, or be left to the Speaker's discretion?

Notes

1   It might be thought desirable that those Senators representing specific interest groups should utilise their backgrounds by bringing their expertise to bear for the good of all, not use Parliament as a means of advancing the position of their own particular group. For this reason, it might be a good idea if the term was made longer (10 years?) and re-standing was forbidden. This should prevent Senators seeking re-selection by aggressively pushing the interests of their selectors.

2   Hadfield's thoroughly worked out proposals may be contrasted with those put forward by the Institute for Public Policy Research (IPPR):

    [The IPPR] recommend that the Lords be replaced by an elected second chamber for a term of four years, 'but at a two-year interval from the elections to the Commons' [*A Written Constitution for the United Kingdom* (IPPR, 1991), Art 68.] Under such proposals the existing arrangements under the Parliament Acts 1911 and 1949, restricting the Lords powers over Money Bills would be retained. However, the terms of the present delaying powers of the Lords might be

---

33   See generally, Part IV, Chapter 3.

amended in line with the proposals contained in a 1969 Labour Government Bill, reducing the period of delay over Bills to 60 parliamentary days from the date of disagreement between the two Houses.

At the heart of any reform proposals, and there are wide variations on the IPPR proposals, is the idea of creating a more representative House of Lords, in line with general reforms of the electoral system in the United Kingdom. Electoral reform is intended to replace the current 'first past the post' electoral system with some form of proportional representation. This might suggest that reform of the Lords on its own is merely 'tinkering with the system', when a more radical rethink might be desired.[34]

4   The IPPR's proposals appear to ignore the correlation which Hadfield suggests should be borne in mind between powers and composition: they propose democratising the House, but weakening its powers (by reducing the delaying power). This reverses the usual argument for reform, which is that greater representativeness would justify the vesting in the new chamber of *increased* power. It is possible to argue that these proposals would result in the worst of both worlds: the replacement of the peers by professional politicians, more tied to the political parties and (as likely as not) with no particular expertise might well reduce the *quality* of the chamber's work, which, as argued, lies mainly in its capacity for informed and non-partisan scrutiny of legislation; at the same time, instead of this reduction in *quality* being compensated for by increasing the *power* of the second chamber to act as a check on the executive-dominated Commons, the reverse is proposed.

5   Simply removing the limitations on the power of the Lords under the Parliament Acts would be one way of strengthening the House. However, if they were removed, a convention would probably develop that the powers made once again available should not be used. It is apparent that restraints which have grown up under convention have a more constraining effect on the Lords than do the formal limits on their power. It is unlikely that the conventions will wither away; the reason for their continued existence is too cogent as they are ultimately a means of self preservation. Thus such conventions would only disappear if reform of the Lords were undertaken with a view to making it a democratic Chamber. However, if such reform were undertaken much of its value might be lost, in which case increased powers might even be harmful.

6   What is the likelihood of far-reaching reform, in practical terms? Ronald Brazier is not optimistic:

There is no political consensus over possible reforms. The Conservative government has no plans to alter the House of Lords in any way. From the late 1970s to the late 1980s the Labour Party was committed to the abolition of the House of Lords and to the transfer of necessary functions to the House of Commons. That flirtation with unicameralism was, however, overcome by 1989 when the party decided to advocate the replacement of the Lords by a second chamber, directly elected by proportional representation. [See *Meet the Challenge: Make the Change* (Labour Party, 1989), pp55–56.] The powers of that chamber would be limited. The Liberal Democrats want the House of Lords to be replaced

---

34   John F McEldowney, *Public Law* (1994), pp57–8.

by a Senate·of about 100 members, elected by proportional representation, and with *greater* powers than the present House.[35] Over the years the parties have thus scattered away from the virtual all-party agreement on reform which had been achieved in 1968.[36]

7 Given the difficulties in this area, and the lack of enthusiasm for making much parliamentary time available, Shell suggests that reformers could start with something simple:

> Labour might in the future carry [a] simple piece of legislation excluding all peers by succession, notwithstanding Conservative hostility. This at least could be achieved without any great expenditure of legislative time, and it would please the overwhelming majority of Labour supporters. Nor is such a change likely to meet with sustained opposition from the modern Conservative party. Such a step would clear the ground for further reform, most obviously the introduction of an elected element into the House.[37]

Questions

1 How far would this single reform go towards addressing the criticisms of the Lords discussed above?

2 Given that all life peers are appointed by the Prime Minister of the day, would this reform not actually *increase* executive influence over Parliament? Surely such a change *must* be coupled with a more satisfactory system for the selection of life peers?

Notes

1 At the time of writing, it is believed that the Labour Party, if they win the next general election, will introduce a very brief Bill to remove the voting rights of all hereditary peers. Legislation to *replace* the Lords with an elected Chamber would probably have to await a second term in government. Certain hereditary peers with a proven track record of parliamentary activity could be made life peers to enable them to carry on their work. See, for example, 'Blair to inflict instant curb on the Lords', *The Times*, 8 April 1996.

2 Some possible flesh to put on the bones of Labour's proposal has been suggested by the Constitution Unit,[38] which proposes that 63 new Labour peers should be created, to fulfil a suggested formula for party strengths which would give the Government of the day a 'majority of one over the nearest opposition party' (quoted *ibid*). The unit also recommends reform of the appointments system to refute charges that 'a giant quango' would be created.

---

35 See *Here We Stand: Proposals for Modernizing Britain's Democracy*, Liberal Democrat Federal White Paper No 6, p234.

36 Ronald Brazier, *Constitutional Practice,* 2nd edn (1994), pp259–61.

37 Donald Shell, 'The House of Lords: Time for a Change?' (1994) 47(4) PA 721, 736.

38 A left-leaning think-tank; its proposals are reported briefly in *Independent*, 25 April 1996 ('Blueprint drawn up for reform of the Lords').

3   In a recent article by Andrew Roberts, defending the hereditary peerages,[39] three main arguments against the Labour plan can be discerned amongst the rather rhetorical tributes to 'the natural romance and ancient elegance inherent in the hereditary principle'. First, he points out that the cross-benchers – the independent peers – are overwhelmingly the hereditary peers; therefore the effect of removing their rights would be to decrease the very comparative political independence which renders the Lords valuable; second, he argues that the work of many talented and distinguished peers (such as the Russell family) would be lost to the nation as a result of the Labour proposals. It should be noted that if a Labour Government were prepared, as indicated above, to award life peerages to outstanding hereditary peers, this point would be met, as would perhaps the first point as many of the present cross-benchers might remain in the House. Third, Roberts contends that with the passing of the hereditary peers, the House would lose much of its 'historical grandeur' and thus cease to have any attraction for 'ambitious and talented people' (ie life peers) who would presumably (although the point is not made explicit) participate less in the work of the House. This must count as pure speculation, and indeed, it is arguable that if the House of Lords were seen as less archaic and anomalous, greater enthusiasm for its work might result. Roberts' first point clearly raises the most serious concern and one which, it is suggested, could be met by fixing a quota for a substantial number of independent peers to be created and maintained, some of which could be hereditary peers who had formerly played an active role in the Lords.

---

39 'Farewell to the Lords', *The Sunday Times*, 11 February 1996. The article is one of the few recent full-blown defences of the *status quo*, so is of some interest.

CHAPTER 3

PARLIAMENTARY PRIVILEGE

INTRODUCTION

This Chapter will consider the privileges of Parliament. The examples used will mainly relate to the House of Commons, but the privileges of the two Houses are substantially identical. It will touch on all the main privileges, concentrating on freedom of speech as by far the most important and contentious privilege claimed. Conflict between Parliament and the courts will also be discussed and criticisms of the current state of affairs in this field will be considered.

Colin Munro considers the justification for privilege, and offers a definition.

Colin Munro, *Studies in Constitutional Law* (1987), pp134–6

'The sole justification for the present privileges of the House of Commons is that they are essential for the conduct of its business and maintenance of its authority', according to one clerk of the House of Commons. If the constant general purpose has been the maintenance of Parliament's independence, the threats to that independence have come from various quarters: at times from the ordinary courts seeking to enforce the general law of the land, at times from the Crown, at times from other persons or bodies, including the mass media. Sometimes the enemy is within, and then privilege enables the House to deal with members who abuse their office or seek to obstruct its business.

The Houses are able to deal with offenders and enforce their privileges because they are the High Court of Parliament, and so have an inherent jurisdiction. ... When any of the rights and immunities known as privileges are disregarded or attacked by anybody, the offence is called a breach of privilege, and is punishable under the law of Parliament. By virtue of the same jurisdiction, each House may punish offences against its authority or dignity, even if they do not involve breaches of specific privileges. Such offences are contempts of Parliament: the concept is analogous to contempt of court. The Houses' penal jurisdiction, or power to punish offenders, may be regarded as complementing their privileges, or as being itself an aspect of privilege.

Coke mentioned the *lex et consuetudo parliamenti*, and parliamentary privilege is regarded as part of the law and custom of Parliament. Its origin is customary; it is recognised as having the status of law; but it will be found, for the most part, not in statutes or cases, but in parliamentary proceedings. ... Since it is enforced primarily by the Houses themselves, it is defined principally in resolutions of the Houses and rulings by the Speakers.

Of course, like any other part of the law, parliamentary privilege is subject to the supremacy of Acts of Parliament. Acts have curtailed the scope of privilege, as for example when members' privilege of freedom from arrest was withdrawn from the servants of members, to whom it had previously extended (Parliamentary Privilege Act 1770). Again, Acts of Parliament may regulate the exercise of privilege. The determination of disputed elections for parliamentary constituencies, which lay within the Commons' privilege of regulating its own composition, has effectively been transferred by statute to judges of the ordinary courts. But it is also possible for statute to maintain or extend the scope of privileges. The privileges of freedom of speech and exclusive cognisance of internal proceedings were given a statutory foundation when included as Article

9 of the Bill of Rights: 'That the freedom of speech, and debates or proceedings in Parliament, ought not to be impeached or questioned in any court or place out of Parliament.'

We have reached a point where a definition of parliamentary privilege may be offered. It is that part of our constitutional law which consists of special rules developed by the Houses of Parliament so as to augment their dignity and independence, and in order to protect themselves collectively and their members when acting for the benefit of their House, against interference, attack or obstruction.

Notes

1   The justification for privilege offered by the clerk of the Commons cited by Munro offers a stringent test: only those matters which are 'essential' for the proper conduct of the business of the House should be claimed as privileges. The Committee of Privileges has given its own view of the *raison d'être* of Parliamentary privileges (in its report on the 'cash for questions affair'). They regard their purpose as 'not to protect individual Members of Parliament but to provide the necessary framework in which the House in its corporate capacity and its Members as individuals can fulfill their responsibilities to the citizens they represent'[1] a definition which also stresses that 'privileges' are not in fact to do with the personal aggrandisement of MPs but simply necessary adjuncts to their role as public servants. Given that one of the fundamental principles of the British Constitution is supposed to be equality before the law, it seems right that those who argue in favour of placing some in a uniquely privileged position should have to adduce compelling evidence that such protection is indeed necessary. It is worth bearing these tests in mind when examining the arguments put forward in cases in which the proper scope of privilege has been contested.

2   Munro's definition is somewhat more wide-ranging and imports the rather nebulous concept of 'dignity'; it will become apparent that the House of Commons sometimes appears to take a rather expansive view of what the protection of its dignity demands; a view which might be thought to sit rather uneasily with the sometimes childishly combative mode of debate which, as noted in Chapter 1 of this Part, is not unknown in that House.

THE 'INTERNAL' PRIVILEGES OF PARLIAMENT

The privileges in general

Many questions of privilege have been relatively uncontentious; those which affect only members of Parliament in their capacity as MPs, have been agreed by Parliament and the courts to be under the sole jurisdiction of Parliament. As Coleridge J said in *Stockdale v Hansard* (1839):[2]

> ... that the House should have exclusive jurisdiction to regulate the course of its own proceedings and animadvert upon any conduct there in violation of its rules or derogation from its dignity, stands upon the clearest ground of necessity.

---

1   Quoted in D Oliver, 'The Committee on Standards in Public Life: Regulating the conduct of Members of Parliament' (1995) PA 590, 596.

2   9 Ad & El at 233.

The case of *Bradlaugh v Gossett* (1884)[3] is also instructive; it was summarised in *Rost v Edwards* (1990).

Rost v Edwards [1990] 2 WLR 1280, 1287

In *Bradlaugh v Gossett* (1884) 12 QBD 271 the Parliamentary Oaths Act of 1866 required Charles Bradlaugh, who had been elected to Northampton as a Member of the House of Commons, to take the oath. The question had arisen whether Mr Bradlaugh was qualified himself to sit by making an affirmation instead of taking the oath. Subsequently, following re-election, he was prevented from taking the oath by order of the House. The sergeant was ordered to exclude him from the House until he undertook not to disturb the proceedings further. Mr Bradlaugh sought a declaration from the courts that the order of the House was *ultra vires* and also an injunction restraining the Sergeant at Arms from preventing him from entering the House and taking his oath. The court decided against Mr Bradlaugh, taking the view that what was in issue was the internal management of the House procedure and therefore the court had no jurisdiction. Lord Coleridge C J said at p275:

> What is said or done within the walls of Parliament cannot be inquired into in a court of law. On this point all the judges in the two great cases which exhaust the learning on the subject – *Burdett v Abbott* (1811) 14 East 1, 148 and *Stockdale v Hansard*, 9 Ad & El 1 – are agreed, and are emphatic. The jurisdiction of the Houses over their own members, their right to impose discipline within their walls, is absolute and exclusive. To use the words of Lord Ellenborough, 'They would sink into utter contempt and inefficiency without it'.

Note

As Munro notes, whilst disputed elections (an area previously falling within the House's right to regulate its own proceedings) are now determined by High Court judges, the 'form' of privilege is preserved, as their findings are merely certified to the Speaker for her to act as she thinks fit; in fact the findings of the court are invariably complied with. Despite this erosion of privilege in the area of elections, the question of whether a candidate may take his seat having been clearly elected still falls to be determined solely by the House,[4] as recent examples make clear.

Colin Munro, *Studies in Constitutional Law* (1987), pp142–5

... Mr Anthony Wedgwood Benn became Viscount Stansgate in succession to his father in 1960, his seat was declared vacant by the House of Commons and he was barred from the chamber (the law was subsequently changed to permit hereditary peerages to be disclaimed). Similarly, it is for the House of Lords to determine whether a peerage entitles the holder to sit in that House. A life peerage had been created for the judge Sir James Parke in 1855, presumably so as to strengthen judicial expertise in the House of Lords without at the same time diluting its ranks for the future with the descendants of lawyers. But the House decided that a peerage of that sort did not entitle the holder to sit in Parliament.

---

[3] 12 QBD 271.

[4] Munro, *op cit*, p134.

The House of Commons may also expel a member for grounds other than disqualification, if it considers him unfit to continue in that capacity A sufficient cause would be conviction of a criminal offence involving turpitude. In 1922 that engaging Edwardian rogue, Horatio Bottomley, was finally expelled by the House upon a conviction for fraud, having been unjustly acquitted on two earlier occasions. In 1947 when Garry Allighan was expelled, it was his gross contempt of the House which caused it. He had made unsubstantiated allegations that details of confidential party meetings, held within the precincts of Parliament, were being revealed by members to journalists for money or while under the influence of drink. He was himself receiving payments for doing just that, and had lied to the Committee of Privileges.

Indeed, if the Government were to use its majority in the House to vote to expel all members who opposed it, no objection could be heard by the courts in this country. It is usually said in response to this that there is nothing to prevent expelled members, if not disqualified from standing, from being re-elected, as John Wilkes was by the electors of Middlesex in the eighteenth century. That is true, but the real protection against abuse lies in conventional self-restraint. The calling of an election is itself at the wish of a Commons majority, for another aspect of privilege is the House's right to determine when casual vacancies will be filled. When a vacancy arises through a member's death, expulsion or disqualification, it is for the House to resolve that a writ be issued for the holding of a by-election.

Exclusive cognisance of internal affairs

Each House collectively claims the right to control its own proceedings and to regulate its internal affairs and whatever takes place within its walls. The claim was partly protected by the provision in the Bill of Rights to the effect that 'the freedom of speech and debates or proceedings in Parliament ought not to be impeached or questioned in any court or place out of Parliament', and so this aspect of privilege is linked to the freedom of speech. It is also linked to the privilege concerning composition, for the Houses regard their membership as their own affair.

The claim has been accepted by the courts, at least provided they can agree that 'internal concerns' are involved. 'Whatever is done within the walls of either assembly must pass without question in any other place', said Lord Denman in *Stockdale v Hansard* [at 114]. In *Bradlaugh v Gossett*, Stephen J observed that 'the House of Commons is not a court of justice, but the effect of its privilege to regulate its own internal concerns practically invests it with a judicial character', and held that 'we must presume that it discharges this function properly and with due regard to the laws, in the making of which it has so great a share' [at 285]. Indeed, the doctrines upon which claims to privilege are based, and upon which the jurisdiction of courts is denied or restricted have much in common with those which are expressed as the sovereignty of Parliament. When, for example, the validity of an Act of Parliament is challenged on the ground of alleged defects of parliamentary procedure, and the courts refuse to investigate, their refusal might be justified on grounds of sovereignty or privilege. In *British Railways Board v Pickin* [1974] 1 All ER 609, the sovereignty aspect was emphasised, but privilege was also adduced as a justification in the speeches of Lord Simon of Glaisdale and Lord Morris of Borth-y-Gest...

However, if matters happen 'within the walls', but are unconnected with the business of Parliament, the ordinary courts may be entitled to assume jurisdiction without being in breach of privilege, or at least are allowed to. 'I know of no authority for the proposition that an ordinary crime committed in the

House of Commons would be withdrawn from the ordinary course of criminal justice', said Stephen J in *Bradlaugh v Gossett* [at 283]. In practice it has been left to the ordinary authorities and courts to deal with incidents such as the killing of the Prime Minister by a madman in the lobby of the House of Commons (in 1812) and the projection of CS gas into the chamber by a protester in the public gallery (in 1970). Sometimes there would be concurrent jurisdiction, as where one member assaults another in the course of proceedings.

Notes

1   It is hard to see why the House requires its ability to allow or disallow Members at its pleasure. Apart from the hypothetical (but still disturbing) possibility that the House *could* resolve, quite legally, to expel all Opposition MPs, a more realistically concern relates to its power to determine when vacancies (caused by death or bankruptcy) should be filled. Complaints have been directed at Government dilatoriness in moving writs for by-elections at which they expect to be defeated, and it is not fanciful to suggest that a Government with a majority of only one (the position at the time of writing) could procure a delay in a by-election which could wipe out its majority so that the election only took place after a crucial Commons vote which was expected to be very close. There seems to be no reason why the law should not provide that all by-elections must take place within a fixed time of a seat becoming vacant.

2   A case which, as Munro puts it, took a 'generous' view of the scope of the House's internal affairs was *Graham-Campbell, ex p Herbert* (1935), in which the High Court considered whether a magistrate had been right in finding that he lacked jurisdiction to prosecute Members for selling alcohol without a licence in the Member's Bar.

Graham-Campbell, ex p Herbert [1935] 1 KB 594, 602

Lord Hewart CJ: Here, as it seems to me, the magistrate was entitled to say, on the materials before him, that in the matters complained of the House of Commons was acting collectively in a matter which fell within the area of the internal affairs of the House, and, that being so, any tribunal might well feel, on the authorities, an invincible reluctance to interfere. To take the opposite course might conceivably be, in proceedings of a somewhat different character from these, after the various stages of those proceedings had been passed, to make the House of Lords the arbiter of the privileges of the House of Commons.

Notes

1   This decision cannot be justified by arguing that the privilege found here to exist, of flouting the licensing laws,[5] was necessary to allow the House to carry on its business properly. (Such a notion could, for example justifiably be used to protect Members from criminal liability incurred by speeches or questions in the House.) Even if some notion of protecting the dignity of Parliament is invoked, it is hard to see how that is protected by shielding Members from the ordinary criminal law in a matter as unrelated to their constitutional activities as illegal drinking.

---

5   Note that Avory J also found that the Licensing Acts were not intended to apply to Parliament (at p603).

2   It seems almost certain that if more serious offences were committed, the House would hand over the matter to the courts, for as De Smith comments, its penal powers 'are inadequate to deal with ordinary crime';[6] in any event Parliament would be anxious to avoid the unfavourable publicity that would undoubtedly ensue from an attempt to protect such an offender through an assertion of immunity by virtue of privilege. In the unlikely event of such an assertion being made by the Commons, the outcome must be in doubt.

Members' financial interests: the Nolan Report and its aftermath

The problem of Members' outside interests

One further, important aspect of the Commons' internal regulatory rules lies in the regulations governing Members' financial interests. As Alan Doig notes, this issue has implications which go well beyond mere internal self-regulation.

Alan Doig, 'Full Circle or Dead End? What Next For The Select Committee on Members' Interests?' (1994) 47(3) *Parliamentary Affairs* 355, 356

It is generally accepted, and certainly among MPs, that MPs may have other occupations and sources of income in addition to their parliamentary salary. It is also not in dispute that in representing interests and opinions, MPs can help bridge the gap between government and organisations affected by its activities. Government policy-making and decision-taking need a continuing bilateral relationship of information, co-operation and mutual understanding, for example in the oil industry, it's not a case that we have a choice, the politics of energy and oil draw us into very close relationships with government. Such organisations, ranging from multinationals like ICI or British Airways to representative organisations like the National Farmers' Union or the Royal College of Nursing will have offices and staff to monitor, liaise with and report back on the decision-making processes of Whitehall and Westminster. Those without a permanent governmental relations office can hire professional lobbyists. Whatever the means, however, the purpose is to get that interest's message to the policymakers and the legislators.

Concern about the activities of interests and of professional lobbyists – and the involvement of MPs with those activities – has been growing. What MPs do in Parliament, or say to ministers or government departments, should be in accordance with their perceptions of the public or national interest, of the promises of party manifestos and of the expectations of their constituencies. At the same time, in representing the views of interests, what they say and do may be felt to be compromised because they are being paid to sell the interest's views to colleagues, ministers and civil servants, whether or not they themselves are convinced of the intrinsic value of that interest's case. The underlying expectations of political decision-making processes, and the public's acceptance of the outcomes, are not best served by suspicions or allegations of hidden influence, the exploitation of insider contacts and information, the role of money to secure privileged access to the decision-making procedures and, above all, the conflict of interest for MPs who may serve two masters.

---

6   *Constitutional and Administrative Law*, 6th ed (1994), p325.

Notes

1   A public perception that the existing rules on this matter were either inadequate or were being flouted with impunity arose after various incidents in which MPs were perceived as having used their office for improper gain attracted intense media interest. The most notorious event was the 'cash for questions' affair in which the *Sunday Times* reported[7] that two MPs had been willing to table questions in Parliament in return for payments of money. Another episode of concern was the tabling by one MP in another MP's name of an amendment which would have benefited an association for which he acted as a parliamentary adviser.[8]

2   As a result of this concern, a standing committee was set up to enquire generally into the issue of standards in public life (not into specific instances) under the chairmanship of Lord Nolan.[9] The political impetus behind the establishment of the Nolan Committee was the need of the Major Administration to de-politicise the damaging issue of 'sleaze' by handing over consideration of the issue to a neutral body; the move also afforded recognition to the need to implement changes to the rules governing member's interests in order to restore public confidence in the institutions of government.

3   The establishment of the Committee also answered to a more constitutional concern. As Dawn Oliver notes,[10] when the Committee of Privileges reported on the 'cash for questions' affair in 1995[11] it found that the conduct of the Members concerned 'fell short of the standards the House is entitled to expect of its Members' and the House of Commons passed resolutions to this when it debated the matter on 20 April.[12] But as Oliver goes on to point out, the Committee 'nowhere ... made clear' what these standards were, beyond a specific finding on the impropriety of certain short-term consultancies. The lack of an authoritative text[13] setting out such standards has serious implications: 'Accountability cannot be effectively imposed if the

---

7   10 July 1994.

8   See HC Deb 22 May 1995, col 612, for the MPs' apology.

9   Its members were appointed for three years in the first instance. On the Nolan Committee and the issue of standards in public life generally, see articles in *Parliamentary Affairs* 48(4) which is devoted to this issue; also Dawn Oliver, 'Standards of Conduct in Public Life – What Standards?' (1995) PL 497.

10   *Ibid.*

11   HC Deb 351, 1994–95.

12   HC Deb 20 April 1995, col 382

13   As Oliver notes (*ibid*), the only written guidance on standards is found in Erskine May and previous resolutions of the House; however, not only does this make it difficult for Members (and their critics for that matter) to find out what standards are expected of them, but also these standards may have become 'blurred' with the introduction of the requirement for registering interests, which might have been taken as signifying that as long as an interest is registered it does not matter how the Member acts in relation to it.

criteria against which conduct is to be measured ... are not made clear'.[14] Nolan was also therefore an opportunity for the introduction of some clarity as to standards: the rules were to be made both more accessible and more precise.

4   The first report of the Nolan Committee was published in May 1995[15] and dealt with MPs, ministers and civil servants, executive quangos and NHS bodies. We are concerned here only with the first of these matters. The Second Report from the Select Committee on Standards in Public Life[16] (hereafter 'the Standards Committee'), which was set up to consider Nolan's proposals, summarises the recommendations made by Nolan which were accepted in principle by the House of Commons, when the Report was debated on 19 July as follows: '...the Appointment of a Parliamentary Commissioner for Standards; the establishment, [from the 1995–6 session] of a new Select Committee of Standards and Privileges [replacing the old Committee on Members' Interests and the Committee of Privileges]; the introduction of a Code of Conduct, coupled with a review of the wording of the 1947 Resolution [see below]'.[17] We now turn to the two main areas of controversy: firstly, employment of members by outside bodies and its influence on their conduct; secondly the issue of disclosure of outside interests. These issues will be dealt with in turn.

Parliamentary consultancies – permissibility, payment for advocacy

In relation to this issue, Nolan first of all recommended that 'Members should remain free to have paid employment unrelated to their role as MPs'[18] and then went on to consider the thorny issue of Members entering into agreements with and receiving payment from lobbying firms and campaigning groups which were clearly related to their activates in Parliament.

First Report of the Committee on Standards in Public Life, Cm 2850

...

22. A more specific issue then arises as to whether some paid outside interests are less acceptable than others. As we have noted above, the greatest current concern about the independence of the House arises when organisations seek the services of a Member of Parliament specifically as a Parliamentary adviser or consultant.

26. In 1947 ... the House declared that:

> ... it is inconsistent with the dignity of the House, with the duty of a Member to his constituency and with the maintenance of the privilege of freedom of speech, for any Member of the House to enter into any contractual agreement with an outside body controlling or limiting the Member's complete independence and freedom of action in

---

14   Oliver, *op cit*, p497.
15   *First Report of the Committee on Standards in Public Life*, Cm 2850 (hereafter, 'the Nolan Report').
16   HC 816, (1994–95), para 3.
17   *Ibid.*
18   *Op cit*, para 21.

Parliament or stipulating that he shall act in any way as the representative of such outside body in regard to any matters to be transacted in Parliament; the duty of a Member being to his constituency and to the country as a whole, rather than to any particular section thereof. ...

29. The ... formal position ... has remained unchanged for 50 years, and perhaps even for 300 years. The resolution of 1947 remains binding on Members of Parliament, and is the most detailed statement of the Law of Parliament on this subject. However this resolution, which appears at first sight clear and unequivocal, contains within itself the seeds of the current problem.

30. The 1947 resolution was drawn up in response to concern about an outside body – a trade union, as it happens – attempting to instruct a Member. It clearly prohibits any contracts which in any way limit a Member's freedom of action in the House. Thus it prohibits a Member from entering into a consultancy agreement which imposes, in return for payment, a binding obligation to speak, lobby or vote in accordance with the client's instructions, or to act as the client's representative in Parliament.

31. Although the resolution therefore prohibits a Member of Parliament from entering into any agreement requiring action on behalf of an outside body 'in regard to any matters to be transacted in Parliament', it does not prohibit a binding obligation to advise the client on Parliamentary matters. The Member remains free to enter an agreement to act as an adviser or consultant about Parliamentary matters. On the face of it therefore, this resolution might appear to draw the clear line between paid advice and paid advocacy which very many people, in Parliament and outside, have told us would be appropriate...

Nolan then goes on to consider problems with the modern application of the resolution.

39. First, there has been a radical change in the nature of MPs' outside employment. Until recently, Members with paid outside employment typically pursued careers and occupations which, with the possible exception of journalism or the law, were largely unconnected with Parliament. Usually these were the same occupations that they had pursued before entering Parliament. Only a few Members were paid in connection with their Parliamentary duties. That position has now, however, been radically transformed. The proportion of Members pursuing careers largely unconnected with Parliament, such as farming, has fallen, while ... the proportion whose outside employment arises directly out of their Membership of the House of Commons has risen to a very significant level.

40. Second, the introduction of the Register of Members' Interests, designed to further the wholly admirable concept of disclosure of interests, has tended to create a false impression that any interest is acceptable once it has been registered, and so to add to the confusion which has developed.

41. Some of this confusion may stem from the 'defining purpose' of the Register as set out in the First Report of the Select Committee on Members' Interests 1991/92. This purpose is 'to provide information of any pecuniary interest or other material benefit which a Member receives which might reasonably be thought by others to influence his or her actions, speeches or votes in Parliament, or actions taken in his or her capacity as a Member of Parliament.'

42. In the 1995 edition of the Register of Members' Interests consultancy agreements come under the third of the listed categories of registrable interests. Under the heading 'clients' it provides that Members must disclose the names of clients 'for whom they provide services which depend essentially upon, or arise

out of, Membership of the House; for example sponsoring functions in the Parliamentary buildings, making representations to Government Departments or providing advice on Parliamentary or public affairs.'

43. The position is, therefore, that the 1947 resolution prevents a Member from agreeing to act for a client in Parliament, but the rules governing the Register of Members' Interests expressly contemplate that the Member may have received material benefits 'which might reasonably be thought by others to influence his or her actions, speeches or votes in Parliament' and which, in the case of consultancy agreements, may involve Members being paid for making representations to Government departments on issues which inevitably will normally be concerned with matters to be transacted in Parliament.

44. The contrast between the 1947 Resolution and the rules governing the Register is in our view totally unsatisfactory. It is small wonder that it has given rise to confusion in the minds of Members of Parliament themselves. We agree with the comment made by Madam Speaker on 12 July 1994 (*Official Report,* col 829) that there is an urgent need to clarify the law of Parliament in this area...

Nolan then goes on to consider the relationship between payments for advice and the possibility of paid advocacy.

48. If a Member is engaged to advise a client on Parliamentary matters affecting the client, and is at the same time free to speak, lobby and vote on those same matters in the House, it is not merely possible but highly likely that the Member will use Parliamentary opportunities in a way consistent with that advice.

49. It is more likely than not that Members who enter into consultancy agreements will do so with clients to whose viewpoints they are sympathetic, although Members who have such agreements have been at pains to tell us that they would not hesitate both to make clear to their clients where their views differed, and to express views in the House which their clients did not share. Nevertheless the impression can easily be gained, however unfair this may be in individual cases, that not only advice but also advocacy have been bought by the client. The evidence which we have received leaves us in little doubt that this is the impression which many people have. It is one of the most potent sources of public suspicion about the true motivation of Members of Parliament. In recent years Members have acquired paid consultancies on a large scale. Over the same period public scepticism about MPs' financial motives has increased sharply. It must be more likely than not that these two developments are related, but in any case their combination can only tend to undermine the dignity of Parliament as a whole.

50. We would consider it thoroughly unsatisfactory, possibly to the extent of being a contempt of Parliament, if a Member of Parliament, even if not strictly bound by an agreement with a client to pursue a particular interest in Parliament, was to pursue that interest solely or principally because payment, in cash or kind, was being made. A Member who believes in a cause should be prepared to promote it without payment; equally a Member ought not to pursue a cause more forcefully than might otherwise have been the case as a result of a financial interest. We believe that such action would breach the spirit if not the letter of the 1947 resolution, and we cannot be confident that all Members are as scrupulous in this respect as some have claimed to be.

51. With these factors in mind we have carefully considered whether we should recommend an immediate and total ban on all forms of advocacy in the House by Members pursuing the interests of those with whom they hold consultancy or sponsorship agreements. The effect of this would be to prevent Members with such interests from speaking, and perhaps from voting, when a relevant subject

was under consideration. We have little doubt that such a ban would receive not only widespread public support but also support from many Members. A number of MPs who gave evidence to us endorsed the principle that paid advice is acceptable but paid advocacy is not. There is also a substantial body of opinion which holds that it is wrong in principle for Members to accept money for any services, even purely advisory services rendered in their capacities as Members.

52. We have concluded, however, that an immediate ban in that particular form, would be impracticable. It would involve asking three-fifths of the Members of the House and their clients or sponsors to amend with immediate effect arrangements which have been made perfectly lawfully and are often of very long standing. Because so many Members have such interests, and so would be excluded from particular pieces of business, there would be a short term disruption of the business of the House. The impact on the income of many Members would have implications which could not be ignored. And the issues it would raise for the equilibrium of party political funding could only be addressed by a fundamental re-examination of that issue...

55. There is one area where we have no doubt that immediate action can and should be taken. Whatever arguments there may be in favour of Members who are retained as consultants by outside organisations acting as principals in their own right, we can see no justification for consultancy agreements between Members and public relations or lobbying firms, which are themselves acting as advisers and advocates for a constantly changing range of miscellaneous and often undisclosed interests. Similarly, it seems to us inappropriate for Members who are connected with legal and other professional firms which offer clients Parliamentary services of any type to retain that connection unless arrangements can be made to separate completely the Member's interest in the firm from that part of its work. We consider that this is precisely the situation which the Prime Minister has described as 'a hiring fair'. We believe that the House should act immediately to stop this practice by outlawing agreements which commit Members to giving Parliamentary advice for payment to multi-client lobbying organisations or to the clients of such organisations. We also believe that the House should prohibit Members from maintaining direct or active connections with firms, or those parts of firms, which provide paid Parliamentary services to multiple clients.

Note

Nolan thus decided against a ban on paid advocacy, but recommended the outright prohibition of Members' employment by certain types of organisations regardless of what kinds of activities the organisation wished the Member to engage in on their behalf. When the Standards Committee put forward its own recommendations on these matters, it came to somewhat different conclusions.

Second Report from the Select Committee on Standards in Public Life, HC 816 (1994–95)

9. The distinction [drawn by Nolan] between single and multi-client consultancies is ... difficult to understand. Public disquiet has arisen chiefly because of the perception that Members' services are 'for hire' to outside interests. In that context, the Nolan report particularly highlighted advocacy for multi-client lobbying firms. This is a cause of concern, but no more so than advocacy on behalf of lobbying companies acting for a single client. In any case it would not be difficult to devise a system whereby a multi-client organisation could operate through a series of single-client subsidiaries, thereby

circumventing any prohibition directed solely at lobbying companies with multiple clients.

10. Having wrestled with this problem at great length and in exhaustive detail we have been driven to the conclusion that the Nolan Committee's attempt to regulate merely *the types* of outside bodies with which Members should be allowed to have a paid relationship will not work. The difficulties of definition, and therefore of enforcement, are simply too great. Our alternative approach, which we explain in the following paragraphs, in fact goes significantly further than the Nolan recommendations. It would address Members' relations with both single client *and* multiclient consultancies, rather than singling out the latter.

11. The main source of public anxiety, as identified by Nolan, is the notion that influence, whether real or imagined, can be bought and sold through Members. This suggests that any remedial action, rather than seeking to draw a line of legitimacy between different types of outside body with which Members should or should not be allowed to have paid relationships, ought to concentrate on defining as closely as possible those *actions* by Members which, because they give rise to suspicions about the exercise – or attempted exercise – of improper influence, need to be prohibited.

13. We propose that the rules of the House should now distinguish between paid advocacy in Parliament (unacceptable for the reasons outlined above) and paid advice (acceptable provided it is properly registered and declared). Nolan considered the idea of separating advocacy from advice, but was not persuaded finally that the difference was sufficiently clear cut to be enforceable. We believe that we have addressed the definitional problems identified by Nolan which arise from making this fundamental distinction.

14. Our Report is based on a three-pronged approach:

– a prohibition on paid advocacy in Parliament;

– strict regulation governing paid advice;

– transparency in all paid activities related to Parliament.

15. It is not feasible, however desirable the greatest possible degree of clarity in any new rules, to provide for every conceivable eventuality in advance. Our task has been to recommend a framework to the House. It will be one of the key functions of the Parliamentary Commissioner for Standards and of the new Select Committee on Standards and Privileges to provide detailed guidance as cases of doubt arise.

l6. We have concluded that the most sensible and fruitful course – foreshadowed in our First Report and consistent with, but going well beyond, Nolan – would be to take up and build upon the 1947 Resolution, which, amongst other things, deals with the issue of advocacy for payment.

17. This Resolution represents a concise and well expressed statement of basic principles. However, whilst it describes the types of agreement which Members should not enter into on the grounds that their independence would thereby be fettered, it does not indicate the specific kinds of Parliamentary action which ought not to be undertaken, for payment, on behalf of outside bodies, whether or not they form the subject of a formal arrangement.

18. **We therefore recommend that the House be asked to agree to the following addendum to the 1947 Resolution:**

> *and that in particular no Member of this House shall, in consideration of any remuneration, fee, payment, reward or benefit in kind, direct or indirect, which the Member or any member of his or her family has received, is receiving or expects to receive–*

(i) advocate or initiate any cause or matter on behalf of any outside body or individual, or

(ii) urge any other Member of either House of Parliament, including Ministers, to do so, by means of any speech, Question, Motion, introduction of a Bill, or amendment to a Motion or Bill.

20. The specific activities included in the proposed addendum to the 1947 Resolution are those which ought to be presumed, *prima facie,* to constitute advocacy. The list should, however, be regarded as descriptive and illustrative rather than exhaustive. At the same time, we are concerned to ensure that no limitation on Members' freedom of action which we recommend interferes with their ability to inform themselves on matters of public concern, or with the performance of their paramount duty to represent the interests of their constituents and those of the public generally. The object of the prohibition contained in the Resolution is *paid* advocacy in Parliament. In their consideration of any complaint we would expect the Commissioner and the new Select Committee to have regard both to the nature and directness of the interest giving rise to any remuneration, and to how far the relevant Parliamentary activity could be regarded as conferring, or seeking to confer, a particular benefit on the interest in question.

SPECIFIC ACTIVITIES WITHIN THE HOUSE

(a) Speaking

21. No Member should take payment for speaking in the House. Such action would clearly be incompatible with the ban on paid advocacy which we have recommended. However, we recognise that speaking differs in a key respect from other forms of Parliamentary activity. The tabling of an Early Day Motion or of an amendment to a Bill, for example, is personal to the Member concerned and therefore undertaken for his own purposes or those of the cause he is espousing. A speech, by contrast, is a contribution to debate and therefore, in some sense, made for the benefit of the House as a whole; it can also be challenged or rebutted on the spot by other Members. Moreover, speaking in a debate involves participating in proceedings, as opposed, in most cases, to initiating them – a distinction to which we attach some importance. For this purpose speaking includes supplementary questions (of which, by definition, no written notice is given).

22. We are not, by proposing a ban on paid advocacy in Parliament, seeking to deprive the House of well-informed contributions from Members with experience or knowledge of direct value to the subject being debated. If the ban were applied to paid advisers in all circumstances, this could lead to an undesirable position in which the Members entitled to take part in a debate would be predominantly those with less direct acquaintance with the subject before the House. We note that Nolan himself accepted that: 'There can be few cases where any damage to the public interest can result from a Member who has declared an interest speaking in the House, even in a Second Reading debate on a relevant Bill or in a Committee of the Whole House'.

23. On the other hand, it is not practicable to lay down in advance, with the precision that a Resolution of the House would require, all the circumstances in which it would or would not be proper for a Member with a paid interest to take part in a debate. It will be one of the main functions of the Code of Conduct, which the House has already decided should be drawn up, to set out a series of general principles against which particular cases can be judged. Members who, having consulted the Code, are still in doubt about their own position will be

able to seek advice from the Parliamentary Commissioner on Standards or the Clerk of the House. ...

25. In making that judgement Members will need to bear in mind that the absolute requirement on them not only to register but also to declare their relevant financial interests will remain unchanged. If a complaint were made in an individual case, or if advice were sought in advance, we believe that the House would expect the Parliamentary Commissioner and the Select Committee to consider any individual speech against the criterion of whether it might bring particular benefit to the organisation or individual from which the Member received payment.

(b) Questions, Motions, Amendments to Bills, Introduction of Bills etc

27. There is, in our view, a distinction to be drawn between initiating proceedings and merely taking part in them. The terms of our proposed addendum to the 1947 Resolution emphasise the act of initiation. In particular, the tabling of questions, motions, and amendments to bills, the introduction of bills, and the seeking of a debate on the adjournment on a Wednesday morning or at the end of the day constitute the initiation of proceedings. Any Member who is a paid Parliamentary adviser, or who receives any form of remuneration from any outside body, should not initiate proceedings of this sort if they relate specifically and directly to the affairs and interests of that body. No doubt a Member contemplating such action will wish to reflect carefully as to whether, say, the tabling of a question asking for certain statistics might be held to bring a particular benefit to a body from which he receives payment. In any case, a Member's relevant interests will now be recorded on the Order Paper under the terms of the Resolution agreed by the House on 19 July 1995.

(c) Voting

29. The proposed list of Parliamentary activities capable of constituting advocacy does not include voting, ...

ACTIVITIES OUTSIDE THE HOUSE

30. Quite apart from any formal proceedings, there are many other ways in which Members may, and indeed should, quite legitimately pursue their Parliamentary duties. For example, rather than table a Parliamentary Question, a Member may prefer to write to the Minister concerned, seek to arrange a meeting to receive a deputation, or attend on a Minister himself as part of such a deputation. The House will recall that it is already a strict rule that in taking actions of this sort the Member must disclose to the Minister 'or any servant of the Crown' all relevant financial interests he may have. (For this purpose 'servant of the Crown' is deemed to cover both departmental officials and staff of executive agencies). Members of Parliament, by virtue of their office, are in a particularly privileged position, and there is a legitimate concern that this position should not be abused.

31. Transparency is of paramount importance in this area. Parliamentary proceedings are open; declarations and registration of interests are known to the House as a whole. This is not the case at present with activities outside the House, and consideration must be given to ways of reassuring the House and the public that the ban on paid advocacy is not being circumvented. **We therefore recommend that any deputations to Ministers or officials introduced or accompanied by a Member with a relevant declarable interest should be recorded in the Register alongside the initial declaration.**

SOURCES OF PAYMENT

33. The phrase 'any outside body or individual' in the proposed addendum to

the 1947 Resolution is, and is meant to be, comprehensive. There will be those who would wish to draw a distinction in this context between commercial organisations and charities; but the fact remains that paid advocacy is paid advocacy, whatever the source of remuneration. Any attempt to discriminate by defining some sources of payment as legitimate and others as illegitimate is fraught with difficulty, and would lead to endless argument. It is far better in our view to make the ban on paid advocacy universal and for Members to realise that if they enter into such a commitment on behalf of any cause, however worthy, they must suffer some necessary restrictions on their freedom of action, subject always to their overriding responsibility to represent their constituents without hindrance.

SPONSORSHIP

35. Sponsorship is an issue which the Select Committee on Members' Interests has already addressed and the outcome of its deliberations is reflected in the current rules on registration, the relevant sections of which read as follows:

> *Sponsorship (Category 4)*
>
> 24. This part of the form is divided into two main subsections. Subsection (a) relates to sponsorship or financial support of the Member as a candidate at the previous election: here the Member is required to register the source of any contribution to his or her election expenses in excess of 25 per cent of the total of such expenses.
>
> 25. Subsection (b) relates to other forms of sponsorship, which is interpreted to cover any regular or continuing support from companies or organisations from which the Member receives any financial or material benefit in support of his or her role as a member of Parliament. For example, it is necessary to register the provision of free or subsidised accommodation and the provision of the services of a research assistant free or at a subsidised salary rate. It is also necessary, in this subsection, to register any regular donation in excess of £500 per year made by an organisation or company to the Member's constituency party if the donation is linked directly to the Member's candidacy in the constituency or if he or she acted as an intermediary between the donor and the constituency party.
>
> 26. There is a third question in this category of the form, supplementary to subsection (b) and designed solely to elicit whether the Member benefits personally from any payment or material benefit registered in that subsection. In other words. its purpose is to distinguish clearly between benefits accruing directly to the Member and those accruing solely to the constituency party.
>
> 27. Trade union sponsorships will normally be registrable under both subsections (a) and (b), particularly if they are based on the Labour movement's 'Hastings Agreement' of 1933; but if trade union donations to a constituency party are not linked in any way to the Member's candidacy in a constituency and were not arranged or solicited by the Member, nor paid via him or her, they are exempt from registration. The same criteria for registration apply to regular donations made to a constituency party by any other organisation or company.

36. The key paragraph here is paragraph 27, which (in the case of trade union sponsorship) makes the test of registrability whether the donation to a constituency party is linked to the Member's candidacy and whether it was arranged or solicited by the Member or is paid via him or her. Since the purpose of registration is to record 'those pecuniary interests held by Members *which*

might reasonably be thought by others to influence their parliamentary conduct or actions' a Member should not be able to engage in advocacy on behalf of a sponsoring organisation, whether a trade union or a company, where the sponsorship is of a kind which already has to be registered. But no such prohibition should apply in respect of sponsorships which are not registrable under existing rules.

Notes

1   The recommendations of the Committee in this area, specifically the proposed addendum to the 1947 Resolution (motion no 1 in the debate) were accepted by the House on 6 November.[19] This reform is probably the most important change to the rules of the House resulting from the Nolan report. It will be policed by the new Standards Ombudsman and Select Committee (see below) but breaches of it will ultimately be a matter for the House.

2   A number of doubts were expressed by Members during the debate on the matter; the following brief extracts from *Hansard* illustrate both the actual width of the new restrictions and the confusion surrounding their meaning.

HC Deb, 6 November 1995, cols 614–17

Mr Marlow: I do not want to be controversial, but because of the way that the first resolution is written it appears that, for example, a farmer who is in receipt of money from Brussels through the common agricultural policy would not be able to discuss agricultural policy with the National Farmers' Union and then engage in debate in this House. That is one example, but many others flow from the resolution. I believe that it is far more far-reaching than my right hon friend thinks. Will he consider that matter very deeply before he replies to the debate?

Mr Newton: ... I believe that I can say reasonably authoritatively that what the Committee was concerned with, and what it believed the proposed resolution to be directed at, is the question of payment by someone in respect of an interest, not in respect of an interest that someone has through his own employment or occupation. None of us would envisage that, for example, a farmer would be prohibited from saying anything on agricultural policy – although, having declared the interest, he may wish to choose his words carefully, as I am sure Hon Members do at present.

...

Mr Banks: Will the Leader of the House explain what my situation would be? I receive support from the International Fund for Animal Welfare, in respect of which I employ an additional member of staff. If I continue to do so, would I be prevented by the amendment to the 1947 resolution from initiating debates, asking ... questions and introducing Bills or early-day motions? It is crucial to me to know the answer to that question.

Mr Newton: If the hon gentleman were receiving payment, or a benefit in kind such as the provision of payment for a research assistant, the answer to his question would be yes.

...

Mr Sims: I am grateful to my right hon friend. He will know that I raised a point on Thursday which he said that he would clarify today. He has not allayed my concerns. In its report, the Select Committee states:

---

[19]   HC Deb, cols 659–61.

we are not … seeking to deprive the House of well-informed contributions from Members with experience or knowledge of direct value to the subject being debated.

Is it not clear from what my right hon friend has just said that any Members with specialist knowledge cannot make such contributions if they are in receipt of any payment, be it from a trade association, a trade union, or, indeed, a campaigning organisation? That would restrict the ability of Members of Parliament to speak.

Mr Newton: … Our proposal is that the 1947 resolution should be extended to indicate specific kinds of parliamentary action which ought not to be undertaken for payment on behalf of outside bodies. These are advocacy by way of speech, question, motion, introduction of Bill or amendments to a motion or Bill. Nor should it be acceptable for one Member to encourage another to take those actions on his or her behalf – in other words, indirect advocacy in relation to payment. Benefit in kind is to be treated in the same way as cash. That covers the case of the research assistant of the hon Member for Newham, North-West (Mr Banks). Payments to a Member's family are to be treated in the same way as those to a Member.

This is a major extension of our rules. l do not disguise that. Everyone is aware of it – increasingly so, I think. The House will expect me to say a little more about what the Committee sees as the practical implications.

The key to our approach is that Members should not be paid to initiate parliamentary proceedings or initiate them on behalf of clients to whom they are paid advisers. In other words, they should not advocate in Parliament the cause of outside interests from which they receive remuneration.

I now come to the point made by my hon friend the Member for Chislehurst. This may reassure the hon Member for Newham, North-West as well. As Lord Nolan's report said, there will be a natural tendency for hon Members to advise outside bodies whose views, to a large extent, they share. For that reason, the prohibition on questions, motions and Bills applies only

> if they relate specifically and directly to the affairs and interests of that body.

However, we were concerned that such a prohibition should not prevent contributions from being made to debate by hon Members bringing the knowledge and experience gained by legitimate work as paid advisers, or in any other way. For that reason, in relation to speeches we have advised that it should remain entirely acceptable for hon Members to speak during debates on a matter that affects the interests of an outside body with which they have a paid connection so long as they do not initiate such a debate and, as now, fully declare their interest when they speak. The report also says that, in such circumstances, the hon Member will need to take care that his or her speech does not

> bring particular benefit to the organisation or individual from which the Member received payment.

I hope that that explanation is at least some help to my hon friend the Member for Chislehurst. …

Mr Sims: I am grateful to my right hon friend for his explanation. Although I understand the argument that hon Members should not initiate proceedings, surely the word 'advocate' means to speak in support of. To include the words 'advocate' and 'speech' in the resolution makes it appear to anyone reading it that an hon Member may not speak in support of a cause for which he or she is being paid.

Mr Newton: I assure my hon friend that that was not what the committee wished; nor is it what the committee regards the proposed resolution as meaning.

Mr Michael Fabricant (Mid-Staffordshire): On a point of order, Madam Speaker. If someone passes a motion in the House, what holds: the wording in the motion, or the intended meaning of the motion, as explained during the debate while that motion is taking place?

Madam Speaker: All hon Members of common sense will read carefully what the Leader of the House is saying as well as take into account the motion on the Order Paper. Ultimately, many of the resolutions, motions and amendments passed today may have to go to the special Select Committee for implementation.

Mr Newton: I am grateful to you, Madam Speaker for that explanation. That is, indeed, the position.

Note

It is to be presumed in the light of this last exchange that the new Select Committee of Standards and Privileges will interpret the advocacy ban in the manner suggested by Mr Newton. Thus Members with a financial interest in a given matter will be able to speak generally for or against a given bill, motion or amendment, (provided the speech doesn't bring any particular benefit to the sponsoring organisation) but not initiate any of these, nor ask any parliamentary question. As appears above, the ban will only apply if the question/motion etc 'relates specifically and directly to the affairs and interests of that body'. Clearly, the Committee and the Commissioner will have some work to do in clarifying the meaning of the phrase 'specifically and directly' which seems rich with ambiguity.

Disclosure of interests

Before the Nolan saga began, there was already in existence a Register of Members' Interests: in this, as from 1995, must be included details (not including the *amount* of renumeration) of 'all remunerated outside employment ... irrespective of whether it has any bearing on a Member's actions in Parliament'.[20] The question was whether the disclosure requirements should be extended.

First Report of the Committee on Standards in Public Life, Cm 2850

Disclosure of interests

60. The House has for long operated on the principle that transparency is in most cases the best safeguard against conflicts of interest. Sir Terence Higgins MP said in evidence to us:

> *Transparency is all important; wherever one draws the line on the issues you are considering, it is vital that there should be proper registration and it should be apparent both to the public, the House and Members themselves whether a person has an interest or not.*

61. When the Register of Interests itself was established in 1974, it did not supersede the practice of declaring an interest at appropriate times. In fact the House in setting up the Register took the opportunity to enshrine in a formal resolution the long-standing convention of declaring an interest:

---

20 *Second Report from the Select Committee on Standards in Public Life*, HC 816 (1994–95), para 39.

In any debate or proceeding of the House or its Committees or transactions or communications which a Member may have with other Members or with Ministers or servants of the Crown, he shall disclose any relevant pecuniary interest or benefit of whatever nature, whether direct or indirect, that he may have had, may have, or may be expecting to have.

This requirement casts its net wider than the Register, and it is not clear that its extent is always fully appreciated.

62. The House already goes to some lengths to ensure that Members of Select Committees know when to declare an interest. Declarations are required when putting a question to a witness and at deliberative meetings of the Committee. In addition, the Chairman is expected to seek declarations of interest immediately after the Committee is established, and to remind Members of their obligations from time to time.

63. There is much to be said for more systematic action to remind Members of their obligations to declare interests at other times. It is particularly important to emphasise that this obligation exists on each and every occasion when a Member approaches other Members or Ministers on a subject where a financial interest exists. Such contacts are often informal and private, and are therefore where the greatest risk of impropriety arises. It is clear that declaration at present is not always made in accordance with the rules, often through forgetfulness or misunderstanding. We have been told that Ministers always know when a Member who approaches them has a financial interest. But that is unlikely, especially given the number and extent of Members' financial interests. In any event the onus is on the Member to declare, not on the Minister to know. A Minister who discovers that an interest exists which has not been declared ought normally to consider whether the omission is sufficiently serious to report to the Select Committee on Members' Interests.

64. It has been suggested by some of our witnesses that the Register of Members' Interests is not particularly effective because it gives the appearance of declaration while permitting a form of declaration which may yield little information as to the true nature of the interest.

65. We agree. While the new 1995 register is an improvement on earlier editions, it lacks a standardised form of description and the nature of the interest is often difficult to discern. It is important that the Register should give a clear picture of the nature of the interest in question, and in particular of the nature of any activity that a Member is undertaking for payment, in order that a possible conflict of interest can be readily discerned. This is needed in respect of all declarable interests. At the same time, registration of minor interests, which obscure the real purpose of the register, should be discouraged.

66. Full declaration is especially important in respect of paid activities related to Parliament. We consider that in those cases, because the risk of impropriety is greater, it is essential that the full terms of all consultancy and sponsorship agreements, if not already in writing, should be reduced to writing and deposited along with the Register, so as to make them open for public inspection in full.

67. The need to deposit the contract in full is illustrated by the recent 'cash for questions' case. At several places in the evidence there is discussion of the form of entry which would have been put in the Register, and it is clear that whether or not payment was being made for a single question, or for a consultancy, the entries would have been wholly uninformative. One example will suffice. The Cash for Questions Report contains the following exchange. Mr John Morris says:

.... Mr Calvert asks ,'How much information will you have to give when' ... You reply, 'What I shall say is something like this. I would put July 1994, consultancy project carried out for Mr Jonathan Calvert.'.

Mr Riddick responds:

May I point out that this is how the Registrar had suggested to me that I register this.

68. The Registrar is not blamed for suggesting an uninformative description, because the Member did not go into detail with him. But it is clearly unsatisfactory that such opaque descriptions are routinely being entered so that there is disclosure in appearance but not in practice.

69. Depositing the agreement will inevitably involve disclosure of the remuneration. We believe that the public, and in particular Members' constituents, have a right to know what financial benefits Members receive as a consequence of being elected to serve their constituencies. We consider it right, therefore, that remuneration should be disclosed in these cases. We also believe that information about the remuneration or other financial consideration received by a Member for Parliamentary services, or by way of sponsorship, should be entered in the register itself, possibly in banded form. It has been argued that actual remuneration is irrelevant, and that the mere existence of a financial relationship is what matters. That argument is not at all convincing. A Member who gets £1,000 a year as a Parliamentary adviser is less likely to be influenced by the prospect of losing that money than one who receives £20,000 a year. The scale of the remuneration is in practice relevant to a full understanding of the nature of the service expected. We have noted that several MPs with whom we raised this issue did not object to disclosure of remuneration so long as this related strictly to Parliamentary services.

70. We are aware that in a number of other countries the practice is to require full disclosure of [all] assets and income. But it is by no means clear that full disclosure of financial matters unrelated to Parliamentary business is relevant to the public interest. No-one has put a convincing case to us as to why that might be necessary.

Notes

1   The House of Commons accepted in the 6 July debate 'the extension of the requirement for ... relevant interests to be declared by means of symbols on the Order Paper, previously applied only to the proposers of Early Day Motions, to all written Parliamentary Proceedings except Division lists' also recommended by Nolan.[21] In political terms, this was seen as uncontroversial, as merely extending the range of a given type of disclosure to encompass other activities. In fact, this was quite an important change, allowing possible motivations behind the initiation of written Parliamentary proceedings to be immediately ascertained.

2   The proposal that agreements with outside bodies relating to parliamentary activities should be put in writing – in particular that the amounts earned should be revealed – was thought to require further consideration by the Standards Committee which deals with Nolan's recommendations in the extract below. Of this extract, paragraphs 38–42 of the Committee were

---

21   As summarised in the *Second Report from the Select Committee on Standards in Public Life*, para 3.

uncontroversial and were agreed unanimously by the members of the committee; paras 43–49 occasioned dispute within the Committee and became its official report only after a division, which the Conservative majority on the Committee won by one vote. The motion which follows these paras represents the unsuccessful attempt of Opposition Members to procure a report by the Committee which supported Nolan's recommendations on this matter.

Second Report from the Select Committee on Standards in Public Life, HC 816 (1994–95), paras 38–49 and ppxx–xxi of the Minutes of the Committee's Proceedings

38. We support Nolan's view that agreements relating to Parliamentary activities should be put in writing. We deal later in this Report with the question of how far such agreements should be disclosed. We accept the Nolan recommendation that there is no need for disclosure of employment agreements unrelated to a Member's role in Parliament.

...

40. If our recommendation that paid advocacy in Parliament should be prohibited altogether is adopted by the House, it is essential that no future agreements should require Members to take part in activities which can be described as advocacy.

41. The new requirement for employment agreements to be put in writing will apply principally to any arrangement whereby a Member may offer advice about parliamentary matters. We think it right, however, that it should also include frequent, as opposed to merely occasional, commitments outside Parliament which arise directly from membership of the House. For example, a regular, paid newspaper column or television programme would have to be the subject of a written agreement, but *ad hoc* current affairs or news interviews or intermittent panel appearances would not.

42. It may not always be immediately obvious whether a particular employment agreement arises directly from, or relates directly to, membership of the House. At one end of the spectrum are those Members whose outside employment pre-dates their original election, whilst at the other extreme are those who have taken up paid adviserships since entering the House. In between there will be many cases which are difficult to classify. Some Members, for example, may provide advice on Parliamentary matters incidentally as part of a much wider employment agreement covering matters wholly unrelated to the House. In these circumstances, it would be for an individual Member to decide how far it would be proper to isolate the Parliamentary services within a separate, depositable agreement; in reaching that decision he may wish to consult the Commissioner.

V. DISCLOSURE OF AGREEMENTS AND AMOUNTS RECEIVED, ETC

43. The concern which the Nolan Report as a whole sought to address was the perception – albeit stimulated by a small number of cases – that outside interests are able to buy influence in the House. We have set out our reasons for believing that the better course is to go further than Nolan suggested, and straightforwardly to ban agreements involving paid advocacy. In these cases, therefore, the question of disclosure would no longer arise.

44. As we have made clear, other agreements relating to Parliament should be put into writing and deposited with the Parliamentary Commissioner for Standards, to ensure both that they are within the rules and that the ban on

advocacy is effective. Where any doubt arises, the Commissioner will of course be able to pursue the matter with the Member and, if necessary, the Select Committee.

45. Given the ban on paid advocacy, which was not envisaged by Nolan, we are not persuaded that it should be a requirement to disclose the amount of remuneration paid in respect of deposited agreements.

46. Nolan refers to the declaration of the 'financial benefits Members receive as a consequence of being elected to serve their constituents'. In practice, many of the consultancy agreements which are at present registered and which are in future likely to be deposited with the Commissioner do not arise because the individual had become a Member of the House but are a continuation of a previous occupation. Some of the consultancies, and in particular non-executive directorships, may not arise from membership of the House at all and affairs in the House will rarely or never be relevant to them.

47. The Nolan report seemed to imply that the amount paid should be declared as an indication of how much time was being spent on outside activity rather than on the duties of a Member. But in reality any payment made will reflect not the amount of time spent in providing the advice, but the resources of the client and the quality of the advice.

48. Moreover, Nolan's reference to the 'financial benefits Members receive as a consequence of being elected' would in practice, if it were to be fairly applied, range far more widely than the Nolan Committee itself appeared to envisage. It would, for example, be hard to argue that most payments for broadcasting, newspaper articles and interviews, lecturing etc, would not be embraced.

49. In reality we judge that the real choice is between the view that compulsory disclosure of remuneration for legitimate activity is an unjustified intrusion, and the view that full disclosure of all income – in effect, the publication of the tax return – should be required. Nolan concluded that 'no-one has put a convincing case' for full disclosure. We agree.

Minutes of proceedings

Motion made and Question put, that paragraphs 43 to 49 be left out and that the following paragraphs be inserted:

> On the assumption that the House agrees to our recommendation that all agreements for Members to act as paid advisers to any outside body or individual should be put in writing, we now turn to the question of how far such agreements should be made available in whole or in part to the public or to the Parliamentary Commissioner for Standards, rather than, as at present, being entirely a private matter between the Member and the body concerned, with the House being aware through the Register simply that such a contract or agreement exists.

> Nolan clearly recommended that all agreements under which Members acted as paid advisers to any outside body or individual be made available to the general public as part of the Register, with the fees or benefits disclosed in bands. His argument, and we agree, is that Members' constituents have a right to know what financial benefits Members receive, that the actual amount is significant since a Member getting £1,000 a year is less likely to be influenced by the prospect of losing that money than one who receives £20,000 a year, and that the scale of the remuneration is in practice relevant to a full understanding of the nature of the service expected.

> **We therefore recommend that a copy of any agreement which involves the provision to any outside body or individual of the services of a Member in**

his capacity as a Member of Parliament should be deposited with the Parliamentary Commissioner for Standards, available for public inspection, and that the amount of any fee or benefit received should be disclosed in bands of: up to £1,000, £5,000–£10,000, and thereafter in bands of £5,000. [*Mrs Ann Taylor.*]

The Committee divided.

Ayes 5	Noes 5
Mr John Evans	Mr Quentin Davies
Mr Robert Maclennan	Mr Iain Duncan Smith
Mr John Morris	Sir Archibald Hamilton
Mr Stanley Orme	Sir Terence Higgins
Mrs Ann Taylor	Sir Geoffrey Johnson Smith

Whereupon the Chairman declared himself with the Noes.[21a]

Question put, That paragraphs 43 to 49 stand part of the Report.

The Committee divided.

Ayes 5	Noes 5
Mr Quentin Davies	Mr John Evans
Mr Iain Duncan Smith	Mr Robert Maclennan
Sir Archibald Hamilton	Mr John Morris
Sir Terence Higgins	Mr Stanley Orme
Sir Geoffrey Johnson Smith	Mrs Ann Taylor

Whereupon the Chairman declared himself with the Ayes.[21b]

Notes

1   The Standards Committee thus re-awakened the party political aspect of the debate by splitting sharply on party lines on this issue, an aspect of its deliberations which was emphasised in the extensive media coverage of its findings;[22] the party political aspect of the debate was further accentuated when the Prime Minister publicly gave his support to the view of the Conservative majority on the Committee.[23]

2   In the Commons debate, Labour motions were put forward on the same lines as that put forward and rejected in the Committee, calling for the copies of the consultancy agreements to include details of the amount earned through them and for the agreements to be open to inspection by the public.

HC Deb, 6 November 1995, cols 614–17

Mrs Taylor: The Select Committee points out that Members of Parliament receive such payments only by virtue of their positions in this place: they would not receive them if they were not Members of Parliament. Therefore, our constituents have a right to know about the payments and they should be made public. If

---

21a The motion was therefore defeated.

21b The motion therefore passed.

22   See, for example 'Tories block Nolan plan for disclosure of earnings', *Guardian*, 1 November 1995.

23   In Question Time on 2 November, HC Deb, cols 387–9.

there is a distinction to be made, it is the one that has been drawn already – and that the Leader of the House commended to the House – between those agreements that relate to parliamentary activity and the independent work that some hon Members perform. No further distinction needs to be made in order to implement the amendments that stand in my name.

The Nolan Committee recommendations state that the amount of money that Members of Parliament receive is relevant because whether an hon Member receives £1,000 or £20,000 from an organisation may influence that hon Member when it comes to disagreeing with that organisation. That point is fundamental to our argument and to our amendments. Some Conservative Members are concerned about the long-term consequences of going down the disclosure path. There have been many scares about tax returns and I hope that the Leader of the House has calmed some of the hysteria with his answer to my intervention. The scares about hon Members' income tax returns being made public are no more than smokescreens and diversions from the central issue. I would go further and say that there is far more chance of seeing a real campaign to make hon Members' tax returns public if my amendments are defeated this evening than if they are carried.

Mr Morris: Some hon Members will say that what they decide to keep secret about their outside earnings for parliamentary work is their business, and their business alone: that it has nothing to do with the *Sun*, with hon Members who take a different view or with anyone else. I implore them to think again before we vote tonight. In particular, I ask them to stop being so self-indulgent to the detriment not only of parliamentary colleagues but of the institution of Parliament itself. Taking and concealing money for parliamentary favours is demeaning to us all and puts an undoubted stain on the reputation of this House. That is why what they do in the matter that we are debating today is our business too.

I find it a matter for deep regret that the decision by the Special Select Committee on full disclosure of earnings that arises from membership of the House was taken by a casting vote and that members of the Committee divided wholly on the basis of party allegiance.

I hope that after this debate the divide on full disclosure will no longer be one between right and left but will be seen in all parts of the House as one between right and wrong. It is not too late now for us to unite in the cause of open dealing and restoring the reputation of this honourable House.

Sir Edward Heath: ...

I adhere to all the points that I made in my earlier speech and, in particular, to what I said about the appointment of a commissioner. I do not think that the House altogether recognises the problems that will face him. Any political agitator in the country will be able to write to him making allegations about Members' conduct in the economic sphere, and the commissioner will be bound to investigate them. In the course of that, all the allegations will become public.

Mrs Ann Taylor: No.

Sir Edward Heath: Of course they can become public. The hon Lady cannot simply think that when the commissioner starts investigating, the chap who put the allegations will not give it to the press. It will all come out and be published. If the allegations are irresponsible, there is no reason why they should be thrown to the public, and that is the problem that the commissioner will face ...

I say to the Liberal Democrat spokesman, the hon Member for Caithness and Sutherland (Mr Maclennan), that the proposed bands if incomes are reviewed are absolute nonsense. What justification could there be for that? Are we to say that if an hon Member is only mildly dishonest we should do so and so but that if he is tremendously dishonourable we should take certain other actions? The hon Gentleman is also wrong to say that if an hon Member had only his parliamentary income to live on and is offered £1,000 or £2,000 that is important to him. If he is a barrister earning £250,000 a year from fees, £20,000 is neither here nor there. We cannot categorise people's morality and honesty by trying to move financial barriers up and down. That is a great failure of his argument.

The argument with which I agreed was about the difficulties of industry, and in some cases the professions, in dealing with the Government. In this country there is an enormous gap between them, and people in industry do not know how to deal with Government Departments. I discovered that 30 years ago in the European negotiations when I found out how close businesses in the other European Union countries were to their Governments and Ministers. Businessmen flew to Brussels to brief them while they were carrying on negotiations. If I mentioned that I was going to Brussels businessmen would ask, 'What for? Where is Brussels anyway?' ... That is why business takes the view, 'These people can help us and advise us and tell us how to do things.' ...

I shall now deal with the question of the public having a right to know. Of course people have a right to know about our public salaries, but we have a right to privacy. Why should people have a right to know about the financial rewards for our individual private activities? That does not stand up to any examination. It has just become a cry, 'They have a right to know about us.' The public have a right to know about our public position and public rewards, but not about our private activities – *[Interruption.]* That argument has gone out of the window. What is the point of publishing the private income of hon Members?[24]

Note

At the vote, the Labour amendments were carried, by 322 votes to 271 (on disclosing amounts) and by 325 votes to 202 (on making the agreements open to inspection by the public).

Enforcement of the new rules – the new mechanisms and compliance by MPs

As noted above, the House voted to put in place new mechanisms to police adherence to the new rules; these were a new Committee on Standards and Privileges and a new Parliamentary Commissioner for Standards. The text of the Standing Orders setting up these bodies is as follows.

HC Deb, 6 November 1995, cols 610–12

Standing Order (Committee on Standards and Privileges)

(1) There shall be a select committee, called the Committee on Standards and Privileges—

(a) to consider specific matters relating to privileges referred to it by the House;

(b) to oversee the work of the Parliamentary Commissioner for Standards; to examine the arrangements proposed by the Commissioner for the

---

[24] Some confusion appears to arisen at this point: whilst all of a Member's outside interests have to be declared in the Register, the requirement to disclose the *amount* of income received would apply only to employment undertaken by a Member which involved him providing his services 'in his capacity as a Member of Parliament'; thus purely 'private income' relating to private activities would not have to be disclosed.

compilation, maintenance and accessibility of the Register of Members' Interests and any other registers of interest established by the House; to review from time to time the form and content of those registers; and to consider any specific complaints made in relation to the registering or declaring of interests referred to it by the Commissioner; and

(c) to consider any matter relating to the conduct of Members including specific complaints in relation to alleged breaches in any code of conduct to which the House has agreed and which have been drawn to the committee's attention by the Commissioner; and to recommend any modifications to such code of conduct as may from time to time appear to be necessary.

(2) The committee shall consist of 11 Members, of whom five shall be a quorum.

(3) Unless the House otherwise orders, each Member nominated to the committee shall continue to be a member of it for the remainder of the Parliament.

(4) The committee shall have power to appoint sub-committees consisting of no more than seven Members, of whom three shall be a quorum, and to refer to such sub-committees any of the matters referred to the committee; and shall appoint one such sub-committee to receive reports from the Commissioner relating to investigations into specific complaints.

(5) The committee and any sub-committee shall have power to send for persons, papers and records, to sit notwithstanding any adjournment of the House, to adjourn from place to place, to report from time to time and to appoint specialist advisers either to supply information which is not readily available or to elucidate matters of complexity within the committee's order of reference.

(6) The committee shall have power to order the attendance of any Member before the committee or any sub-committee and to require that specific documents or records in the possession of a Member relating to its inquiries, or to the inquiries of a sub-committee or of the Commissioner, be laid before the committee or any sub-committee.

(7) The committee shall have power to refuse to allow proceedings to which strangers are admitted to be broadcast.

(8) Mr Attorney General, the Lord Advocate, Mr Solicitor General and Mr Solicitor General for Scotland, being Members of the House, may attend the committee or any sub-committee, may take part in deliberations, may receive committee or sub-committee papers and may give such other assistance to the committee or sub-committee as may be appropriate, but shall not vote or make any motion or move any amendment.

Standing Order (Parliamentary Commissioner for Standards)

(1) There shall be an officer of this House, called the Parliamentary Commissioner for Standards, who shall be appointed by the House.

(2) The principal duties of the Commissioner shall be—

(a) to maintain the Register of Members' Interests and any other registers of interest established by the House, and to make such arrangements for the compilation, maintenance and accessibility of those registers as are approved by the Committee on Standards and Privileges or an appropriate sub-committee thereof;

(b) to provide advice confidentially to Members and other persons or bodies subject to registration on matters relating to the registration of individual interests;

(c) to advise the Committee on Standards and Privileges, its sub-committees and individual Members on the interpretation of any code of conduct to which the House has agreed and on questions of propriety;

(d) to monitor the operation of such code and registers, and to make recommendations thereon to the Committee on Standards and Privileges or an appropriate sub-committee thereof; and

(e) to receive and, if he thinks fit, investigate specific complaints from Members and from members of the public in respect of—

(i) the registration or declaration of interests, or

(ii) other aspects of the propriety of a Member's conduct,

and to report to the Committee on Standards and Privileges or to an appropriate sub-committee thereof.

(3) The Commissioner may be dismissed by resolution of the House.

Notes

1   The Commons appointed Sir Gordon Downey to act as the first Commissioner. The procedure will thus be that a complaint will in the first instance be made to the Commissioner; he will then make a recommendation to the Committee, which will then report to the House. It is to be presumed that the Committee will be reluctant to overturn findings made by the Commissioner, particularly where doing so would lay it open to charges of party political bias. It may be noted that the Commissioner is given no powers to send for persons or papers, though he will, presumably be able to call upon the assistance of the new Standards Committee in this respect. In the first case under the new regime, Sir Gordon recommended that Jonathan Aitken should apologise to the House for failing to register a £10,000 pa directorship of Astra Defence Systems. Mr Aitken did so, and the Committee confirmed that he had infringed the registration requirements. Whilst this is encouraging, it remains to be seen whether any convention of respect for the Commissioner's findings will grow up. As Oliver notes, in the May debate on Nolan 'some hostility [was shown by Members] directed mainly to concern that the House's "sovereignty" might be undermined if independent outsiders were involved in policing conduct';[25] this suggests that at least some members may be minded to view the work and findings of the Commissioner with a sceptical eye. This leads on to the question whether the new standards are likely to be complied with and whether the House will make any substantial effort to enforce them.

2   As has been seen, the rationale adopted by Nolan for recommending disclosure of amounts earned demanded that the requirement to disclose be limited only to remuneration which the MP acquires as a result of being an MP. As is readily apparent however, whether a particular source of remuneration is from an occupation unrelated to a Member's activities is an issue which is open to debate – the Standards Committee noted that 'there will be many cases which are difficult to classify'[26] – and following the vote on 6 November there were immediate signs that a number of MPs (mainly from the Conservative benches) were planning to exploit the ambiguity in the rules in order to avoid full disclosure; others hinted at open defiance.[27]

---

25   Dawn Oliver, *op cit*, p499.

26   *Op cit*, para 42.

27   See 'Commons vote to disclose earnings', *Guardian*, 7 November 1995.

3   Fears of recalcitrance were borne out when the new Register was published
    on 7 May 1996; between 30 and 40 MPs declared only some of their earnings;
    principle amongst the refusenik MPs were Sir Edward Heath, who claimed
    that most of his earnings were related only to his previous post as Prime
    Minister, and David Mellor, who claimed that his earnings were also
    unrelated to his work as an MP.

FREEDOM OF SPEECH

The general parameters of the privilege

In terms of creating conflict outside the political realm it is, not surprisingly,
those privileges which in their exercise can affect the legal rights of those *outside*
Parliament which have caused difficulties. Principle amongst these is freedom
of speech, considered below by Colin Munro.

Colin Munro, *Studies in Constitutional Law* (1987), pp137–41

Freedom of speech

This may be considered the most important privilege. Parliament is a
deliberative and legislative assembly, and it may be regarded as an essential
characteristic of a free legislature that its members are able to perform their
duties without fear of penalty. ...

The privilege ... was effectively secured at the Revolution. Its inclusion in the Bill
of Rights gave it a statutory foundation. Article 9 of the Bill of Rights proclaimed:
'That the freedom of speech, and debates or proceedings in Parliament ought not
to be impeached or questioned in any court or place out of Parliament'. This was
primarily declaratory of the existing law, and Erskine May [20th edn (1983), p89]
is careful to note that 'it may prove to be the case that the law is wider than
Article 9'. Be that as it may, it is plain that the interpretation and implications of
Article 9 are of great importance.

Article 9 applies equally to both Houses, and its effect is that no action or
prosecution can be brought against a Member for anything said or done in the
course of proceedings in Parliament. The most important application of this is
that it invests members with an immunity from the law of defamation, when
they are speaking in Parliament and on some other occasions. So, when an action
for defamation was brought against a Member of the Commons for words
spoken in the House, the court recognised that it had no jurisdiction in the
matter, and ordered that the writ should be removed from the records [*Dillon v
Balfour* (1887) 20 LR Ir 600]. In the same way, the courts would be unable to
entertain prosecutions or actions of other kinds. In 1938, when Mr Duncan
Sandys raised a matter of national security in a parliamentary question, and
refused to reveal the sources of his information, a prosecution on an Official
Secrets charge was threatened. The House asserted its privilege in order to avert
the threat [HC 146 (1937–38), HC 173 (1937–38)]. In 1977, at a trial on Official
Secrets Act charges, a judge had allowed a witness, an officer in the Security
Services, to be identified only as 'Colonel B'. When some organs of the press
referred to the officer by his real name, in disregard of the judge's wishes,
proceedings for contempt of court were brought against them. However, four
Members of the Commons, who named the officer during questions in the
House, were, under the shelter of privilege, immune from such proceedings
themselves. Article 9 also means that matters arising in the course of

parliamentary proceedings cannot be relied on for the purpose of supporting an action or prosecution based on events occurring elsewhere. For example, the Church of Scientology, bringing a libel suit against an MP for remarks made in a television interview, was unable to refer to his speeches in the House of Commons in seeking to prove his malice [*Church of Scientology of California v Johnson-Smith* [1972] 1 QB 522, [1972] 1 All ER 378].

How far the protection of parliamentary privilege extends is not entirely clear. Article 9 refers to 'speech' and 'debates', categories which obviously overlap. Together they would seem to cover all the oral business of the Houses and their committees, and protect not only members and officers but also, for example, members of the public giving evidence before a committee [*Goffin v Donnelly* (1881) 6 QBD 307]. The difficulty really arises over what may be counted as 'proceedings in Parliament'. Something is not a 'proceeding in Parliament' merely because it happens there. A defendant's defamatory statements about his former wife, put in letters to MPs, were not protected by reason of having been posted within the Palace of Westminster [*Rivlin v Bilankin* [1953] 1 All ER 534]. Even a conversation between Members, if on private affairs, would probably not be privileged [HC 101 (1938–39)]. Rather the phrase seems intended to cover what is the business of Parliament or its Members. A committee once provided an explanation:

It covers both the asking of a question and the giving written notice of such question, and includes everything said or done by a Member in the exercise of his functions as a Member in a committee of either House, as well as everything said or done in either House in the transaction of Parliamentary business [*Ibid*, pv].

That is a helpful formulation, but still leaves some areas of uncertainty. The London Electricity Board case in 1958 was on the borderline. Mr George Strauss MP, in a letter written to a minister, described the Board's practices in selling scrap metal as 'a scandal which should be instantly rectified'. The letter was passed on to the Board, which threatened to sue Mr Strauss for libel. The House determined that the letter was not a 'proceeding in Parliament', although the Committee of Privileges had taken the opposite view [HC 305 (1956–57), HC 227 (1957–58), 591 HC *Official Report* (5th series), col 208]. However, it is difficult to infer much from this, for the vote was narrow and the decision is not binding on the House. It may too have been significant that the subject of the letter (being a matter of day-to-day administration of a nationalised industry) was not within ministerial answerability, and therefore could not have formed the basis of a parliamentary question. The Speaker ruled that if a Member tabled a question, and a minister invited him to discuss it with him, the correspondence or discussions were covered by privilege [591 HC *Official Report* (5th series), col 808]. Indeed, if the test is whether a matter is connected with, or a preliminary to, actual business of the whole House or a committee, it is arguable that even unsolicited correspondence is covered, if it is immediately related to a question or motion already tabled or a pending debate. But, in most circumstances at least, letters from the public to MPs and letters from MPs to the public, would appear not to be 'proceedings in Parliament'.

Parliament's official reports and papers enjoy a corresponding privilege. Following *Stockdale v Hansard* [(1839) 9 Ad & El 1], the Parliamentary Papers Act 1840 was passed, which bars proceedings, criminal or civil, against persons for the publication of papers or reports printed by order of either House of Parliament, or copies of them. ...

Something else which may be treated as a breach of privilege or contempt is the impeaching or questioning of privileged proceedings elsewhere. Article 9 implies as much. In the London Electricity Board case, it was taken for granted in parliamentary discussion that the commencement of proceedings in a court in respect of a 'proceeding in Parliament' was in itself a breach of privilege. That assumption may be criticised, and the assumption that a mere threat to institute proceedings amounts to a breach of privilege is even more doubtful. It may be noted too that the Select Committee on Parliamentary Privilege recommended in 1967 that, save in exceptional circumstances, such matters should be left to the ordinary processes of the courts [HC 34 (1967–68)]. But it is by no means certain that the House might not take a similar view again.

There is another implication also to be drawn from Article 9. Members' freedom is only put beyond question 'out of Parliament'. Nothing prevents the House from itself punishing a Member on account of his words or actions, and if it were thought that a member was abusing his privilege by, for example, using it in order to make unjustified attacks on individuals, such a response would be possible.

When Members of Parliament are not clothed by parliamentary privilege, they may benefit from some other privilege or defence. For example, under the Parliamentary Commissioner Act 1967, communications between MPs and the Parliamentary Commissioner for Administration are protected by absolute privilege (which is a defence to actions for defamation). Actions by Members in pursuit of their parliamentary duties would seem generally to be protected by qualified privilege, which is a defence in the law of defamation unless lost by proof of malice. In *Beach v Freeson* [[1971] 2 All ER 854], an MP's letters to the Lord Chancellor and to the Law Society, reporting complaints about a solicitors' firm in his constituency, were held to be so protected. Had the London Electricity Board gone on to sue Mr Strauss, which they did not, he would have been protected as well. By statute, a similar defence applies to the publication of extracts from, or abstracts of, parliamentary papers, and by common law to the fair and accurate reporting of parliamentary proceedings [Parliamentary Papers Act 1840, s3, Defamation Act 1952, s9; *Wason v Walter* (1868) LR 4 QB 73].

Notes

1 Whilst extracts from *Hansard* will be covered by s3 of the Parliamentary Papers Act, protection does not extend to headlines under which the extract appears (*Mangena v Lloyd* (1908)).[28]

2 A parliamentary sketch will be covered by qualified privilege if it is fair and accurate and published without malice (*Cook v Alexander* (1974)).[29]

3 A recent example of the dramatic use of Parliamentary privilege to shield an MP from the ordinary criminal law was seen in the use by Brian Sedgemore MP of an Early Day Motion to name a mother and child who had been the subject of a so-called 'Mary Bell Order' – an order which forbids all publicity about the child in question.[30] But for the cloak of parliamentary privilege, naming the subjects of the order would have been a contempt of court. At the time of writing, it is believed that no action has been taken by the House

---

[28] 99 LT 824.

[29] 1 QB 279.

[30] The child was the illegitimate daughter of a well-known politician. For details, see the *Observer*, 28 January 1996.

of Commons against Mr Sedgemore for misuse of privilege. The case can be regarded as a naked use of privilege to undermine the Rule of Law (a view taken by certain newspapers for example).[31] However it is also a classic instance in which the privilege of free speech was deployed to allow uninhibited discussion by the legislative body of a serious issue: Sedgemore believed that the court order wrongly denied the mother the chance to use publicity to raise funds for her daughter's education (the child is handicapped and has special educational needs, and the mother is taking her case to the European Commission of Human Rights under Article 10 of the Convention which guarantees freedom of expression): the motion called for a 'change in the law to prevent [such] gross denial[s] of human rights'.[32]

Areas of uncertainty and controversy

Wason v Walter (1868)[33] confirmed that Article 9 provides complete civil and criminal immunity for members in respect of words spoken by them during proceedings in Parliament.[34] This is a remarkably wide privilege, considering the numerous constraints on freedom of expression of the rest of the population.[35] Regrettably however, as was evident from the above, the scope of the privilege is by no means clear. This is partly due to the fact that, as Munro noted, the phrase, 'proceedings in Parliament' is of uncertain meaning. The matter has been considered by the Commons, but decisions by the House on matters of privilege set no binding precedent. So for example in the *Strauss* case, whilst the Commons at the time found that the letter was not covered by privilege, (reversing the finding of the Committee of Privilege), subsequent events have suggested that the matter would now be differently decided: in 1967 the Select Committee on Parliamentary Privilege strongly recommended that legislation be enacted to reverse the Commons decision in *Strauss* (1970); the Joint Committee on Publication of Proceedings in Parliament proposed a definition of 'proceedings in Parliament' which *included* letters sent between MPs for the purpose of allowing them to carry out their duties. Their proposed definition was subsequently approved by the Faulks Committee on Defamation 1975, and the Committee of Privileges 1976–77. Further, in the *Strauss* case, the vote on whether the Electricity Board had committed a breach of privilege, which went against Strauss, an Opposition MP, divided substantially along party lines. This phenomena was seen even more clearly in the recent report of the Committee of Privileges on implementation of the Nolan Committee's recommendations: both the Committee and the House as a whole split on

---

31 See, eg 'Respect the Rule of Law', *Daily Telegraph*, 31 January 1996.

32 Quoted in the *Observer, op cit*.

33 QB 73.

34 Note, however, the interesting comment of Laws J on Article 9 (speaking extra-judicially): 'I am not myself convinced that if [an MP] were motivated by reasons of actual personal malice to use his position to defame, in the course of debate, an individual outside Parliament, he should not as a result be subject to the ordinary laws of defamation, and Article 9 could readily be construed comfortably with such a state of affairs' (The Hon Sir John Laws, 'Law and Democracy' (1995) PL 72, 76, n 14).

35 See Part V, Chapter 2.

clearly defined party lines.[36] If the Commons is going to be influenced by party political principles when making such determinations, this will clearly hinder any attempt to deduce a set of consistent principles from its decisions.

The problem of whether a particular speech or letter is covered by absolute privilege assumes a more pressing aspect when a litigant sues in defamation in respect of words which Parliament has deemed to be absolutely privileged, that is, immune from civil or criminal proceedings. When this happens, Parliament can regard the action as a contempt and attempt to prevent the litigant from exercising his legal right to sue and enforce the judgment of the court.

This was illustrated in 1839 in the case of *Stockdale v Hansard*;[37] Stockdale brought an action in respect of allegedly defamatory words in a report of prison inspectors published by Hansard, by order of the Commons. When the action was tried, the court decided that Hansard's reports were not covered by absolute privilege, so that Stockdale could proceed. Parliament, however refused to accept this judgment and so an impasse developed (see below), which was finally resolved only when the Parliamentary Papers Act was passed. Alternatively, as in the *Church of Scientology* case mentioned above, the issue can arise where a defendant to a libel action wishes to defend the proceedings brought against him by referring to matters which have taken place in Parliament: is this 'questioning' of 'proceedings in Parliament'? This issue arose in *Rost v Edwards* (1990), which affords some limited judicial guidance on the interpretation to be given to the words 'proceedings in Parliament'.

Rost v Edwards [1990] 2 WLR 1280, 1289–1291, 1293

The plaintiff, a Member of Parliament and a consultant to two organisations concerned with energy, brought an action for libel arising out of an article published in a national newspaper which he alleged meant that he was improperly seeking to sell privileged and confidential information obtained by him as a member of the House of Commons Select Committee on Energy to Danish companies. The plaintiff wished to call evidence that as a result of the article he had been de-selected from membership of the Standing Committee of the Electricity Privatisation Bill and had not been appointed chairman of the Select Committee on Energy. He further sought to adduce evidence as to the criteria for registration in the Register of Members' Interests, the nature of his consultancies and reason why he had not registered his interest. The defendants, the journalist, editor and publisher of the article in the newspaper, wished by way of justification to rely on the failure to register.

...

Popplewell J: The result of the principles upon which the Solicitor General relies, if correct, will prevent the plaintiff without leave of the House from calling any

---

36 As noted above, the issue which split the parties was the proposed disclosure of the *amount* of outside earnings. All of the Conservative Members on the Committee voted against the proposal, whilst all Opposition Members voted in favour. In the Commons vote on the issue, 33 Conservative MPs voted with the Opposition and a further 31 abstained or did not vote. The rest (around 220) followed the Prime Minister's lead and voted against the proposal. The Opposition was united behind support for the proposal. For the debate, see HC Deb, 6 November 1995, cols 608–682; the crucial divisions showing how the Committee and the House voted see *Second Report from the Select Committee on Standards in Public Life*, HC 816 (1994–95), ppxx-xxi and HC Deb, *op cit*, cols 661–662 respectively.

37 9 Ad & El 1.

evidence as to his appointment or de-selection as a member of the standing committee. Nor, if he is right, can the plaintiff simply say I was appointed; on the day of the article I was de-selected; and invite the jury to draw the inference for which the plaintiff contends.

The reason for the de-selection would involve discussing and examining the proceedings of the House because the appointment and de-selection of members of a committee of the House forms part of the proceedings of that House. Likewise in relation to the anticipated election of the plaintiff to be chairman of the Select Committee on Energy, that would constitute a direct inquiry into an examination and discussion of the appointment of a member of a committee of the House and inferences about that could also not be drawn. Additionally there is the difficulty evidentially that one member of the committee would not be a proper person to give evidence of the views of the whole committee.

For the reasons that I have given above I am clearly of the view that if Mr Hartley wishes to call evidence at the trial in relation to the appointment and de-selection of the plaintiff in relation to the Standing Committee of the Electricity Privatisation Bill and in relation to his appointment in relation to the chairmanship of the Select Committee Energy it will be necessary for him to petition the House. The Solicitor General rightly did not make any commitment as to the likely result of that exercise. ...

The [next] issue which arises for consideration is the letter written by one of the Opposition members both to the plaintiff and to the Speaker in relation to questions which he subsequently raised in the House about the plaintiff's conduct. I have already ruled that the questions asked by Members of Parliament are inadmissible. In my judgment the letters themselves add nothing to the evidence in this case, whether covered by privilege or not. If I have to decide whether the letters are governed by parliamentary privilege I have no hesitation in saying that they are.

I turn now to the question of the Register of Members' Interests. ... The Solicitor General observed that the expression 'proceedings in Parliament' has not yet been defined either by statute or by case law in this jurisdiction, though he referred me to section 16(2) of the Australian Parliamentary Privilege Act 1987. However he submitted that it embraced the various forms of business in which either House takes action and the whole process by which either House reaches a decision in particular debate. He also submitted that it embraced things said or done by a Member of Parliament in the exercise of his function as a member in a committee of either House; and everything said or done in either House in the transaction of Parliamentary business, whether by a member of either House or by an officer of either House. In particular he said it embraced the regulation by either House of its proceedings, for example the practice and procedure relating to the Register of Members' Interests. ...

[Counsel for the Defendant] pointed out [that] there are plenty of areas which are not covered by 'proceedings in Parliament.' It is clearly not possible to arrive at an exhaustive definition. Mr Browne referred by way of example to *Stockdale v Hansard*, 9 Ad & El, 1 where it was held that no privilege attached at common law to a report by the Inspector of Prisons even though the publication of the report had been made by order of the House of Commons. As a result the Parliamentary Papers Act 1840 had to be passed. This is an example, says Mr Browne, of what is ancillary to the operation of Parliament. I need not cite all the examples or analogies put forward at the Bar. A line has to be drawn somewhere. As Lord Pearce once said: 'I do not know, I only feel.'

In the result, I conclude that claims for privilege in respect of the Register of Members' Interests does not fall within the definition of 'proceedings in Parliament ...

Questions

1   Does Popplewell J adduce any cogent reasons for finding some of the activities in question to be 'proceedings in Parliament' and others not?

2   What principles can be deduced from the case to assist in interpreting the phrase in future?

Notes

1   It will be seen that on the question (at issue in the *Strauss* case and discussed above) as to whether letters between Members on official business are covered by the privilege, Popplewell J had 'no hesitation' in saying (*obiter*) that they were covered, but cited no authority, and indeed no argument of principle to support his view.

2   The issue arose again in *Prebble v Television New Zealand Ltd* (1994);[38] in that case, since the matters to which the defendant wished to refer in his plea of justification were clearly 'proceedings in Parliament', parts of his defence were struck out.

3   It seems clear that a letter from a constituent to a Member will not amount to a proceeding in Parliament, and thus not be absolutely privileged, but will it be afforded the more limited protection of qualified privilege?

Rule [1937] 2 KB 375, 380

The appellant wrote to the Member of Parliament for his constituency two letters containing defamatory statements about a police officer and a justice of the peace for the place where he resided. He was charged with publishing defamatory libels and pleaded that the libels were published on a privileged occasion. The trial judge ruled that the occasion was not privileged and the appellant was convicted. ...

It is sufficient for the purpose of this case to say that in our judgment a Member of Parliament to whom a written communication is addressed by one of his constituents asking for his assistance in bringing to the notice of the appropriate Minister a complaint of improper conduct on the part of some public official acting in that constituency in relation to his office, has sufficient interest in the subject-matter of the complaint to render the occasion of such publication a privileged occasion. When once it is seen that a decision favourable to the appellant requires no more than this limited assertion of the interest of a Member of Parliament in the welfare of his constituents, it appears to us impossible to resist the conclusion that the conviction cannot be supported.

'Impeached or questioned'

It is not merely the phrase 'proceedings in Parliament' which has caused disagreement. Article 9 of the Bill of Rights states that freedom of speech, debates and proceedings in Parliament ought not to be 'impeached or questioned in any court or place outside Parliament'. It is accepted that this means that no legal liability may arise in respect of words spoken in Parliament, but what further meanings do the words have? Do they mean that words spoken, or matters taking place in Parliament cannot even be adduced in

---

38   3 All ER 407, PC; an extract from the case appears below at pp485–9.

evidence? Or that they may be so adduced, but cannot be subject to *critical* scrutiny? In *Rost v Edwards*, an argument for the latter interpretation was considered.

Rost v Edwards [1990] 2 WLR 1280, 1289, 1290

Mr Hartley [for the Plaintiff] argued that, although the courts appeared to have given a wide interpretation to the word 'questioned,' on analysis of the cases it was in fact used in the context of 'attributing an improper motive' or 'adversely questioning' and not used synonymously with 'examining.'

There is nothing, says Mr Hartley, to support on the simple construction of the Bill of Rights the contention that 'questioned' means 'examined.' If it was intended simply to prevent any discussion about what was said in Parliament it would have been quite unnecessary to use the word 'impeach.' He observed that all the cases cited involved some criticism either of individual Members of Parliament or the Houses of Parliament as a whole. Thus in *Bradlaugh v Gossett*, 12 QBD 271 what was sought to be impugned was an order of the House on the ground that it was beyond their power and jurisdiction to grant the order. In *Dingle v Associated Newspapers Ltd* [1960] 2 QB 405, what was being sought was to attack the report of the Select Committee on the ground of some defect of procedure. In the *Church of Scientology* case [1972] 1 QB 522, what was being suggested was some improper motive on the part of a Member of Parliament and in *Secretary of State for Trade, ex p Anderson Strathclyde Plc* [1983] 2 All ER 233 what was being sought was in some way adversely to criticise what the Secretary of State had said in the House of Commons.

Mr Hartley says that he does not wish in this case to criticise anybody. He simply wants to call as a factual witness a chairman of the Committee of Selection to say (a) that the plaintiff had been selected to sit on the Standing Committee and (b) that as a result of the article he had been de-selected. He is not asking the court to draw any inference; he is merely seeking to lead evidence of fact which in no possible sense could affect the dignity of the House or infringe the right of free speech in proceedings in the House. He accepted however that, if his submission was right and he was entitled to call the evidence, it would not be open to Mr Browne to suggest to the chairman that it was for some totally different reason that the plaintiff had been de-selected. That, said Mr Hartley, was an unavoidable consequence of the previous decisions. He adopted what the Attorney General had said in the *Scientology* case [1972] 1 QB 522, 527:

'The court should in any event strictly limit the use of *Hansard* to prove the fact that a particular person at a particular date had referred to particular matters in the House of Commons. The extracts should be used solely to prove these facts and they should not be used to prove inferences which would reflect on the maker of any statement in the House.'

Mr Hartley says now that extracts from *Hansard* can be put before the court without the leave of the House he is entitled simply to put the fact of selection and de-selection and to call a witness to support it.

He drew my attention to the decision of *Blackshaw v Lord* [1984] QB 1 where a plaintiff had been awarded damages which included damages in relation to the mention of the article in Parliament. Part of the claim for damages was based on an answer given in the House of Commons. The Court of Appeal could find nothing wrong with the judge's direction, which had included reference to that evidence. Mr Hartley says that this is authority for the proposition that in relation to a claim for damages there is nothing to stop a plaintiff giving evidence as to what happened in Parliament. He distinguishes his position from that which obtained in the *Scientology* case [1972] 1 QB 522 and says that he is relying on what happened in Parliament not in support of a cause of action but in relation to damages.

I have some sympathy for Mr Hartley's interpretation of the word 'questioned' and if I were faced for the first time with interpreting the word 'questioned' in the Bill of Rights I confess that I might well have concluded that it involved some allegation of improper motive. But what is clear is that, given the views of the large number of judges (and, more particularly, their quality) who have interpreted the Bill of Rights, it is simply not open to this court to take that view. ... I have to say that the weight of authority is such that if it is now sought to challenge the unanimous view of those judges who have expressed their views on this subject it can only be resolved by a court at a higher level than this one.

Notes

1 Thus the decision was that the courts were unable simply to hear factual evidence about what had gone on in Parliament, without that body's permission. Whether the evidence should be admitted would therefore be decided by a resolution of the House of Commons, which could be subject to party political considerations. It seems far from satisfactory that matters of admissibility of evidence should be decided by such a partisan body.

2 It is hard to see what conceivable detriment could accrue to Parliament by a neutral examination of its affairs in court. There therefore seems to be nothing to weigh in the balance against the undoubted infringement of the plaintiff's right to present his case fully and freely. Of this right it was said in *The Five Ailsbury Men* (1705) 2 Salk 503: 'It is the birthright of every Englishman who apprehends himself to be injured, to seek for redress in your Majesty's court of justice; and if there ... any power can control this right and can prescribe when he shall and when he shall not be allowed the benefit of the laws he cease to be a free man and his liberty and property are precarious'. This *dicta*, though adverted to in *Rost*, seems to have borne little weight. The decision is hard to defend on principled grounds, and indeed was clearly decided on the basis of precedent only; Popplewell J himself opined, when expressing his hope that Parliament would allow the evidence to be adduced, that 'neither freedom of speech, nor the dignity of the House' would be affected by the evidence in question (at p1291).

3 The Privy Council has since said (in *Prebble v Television New Zealand Ltd* (1994)[39] that 'It is questionable whether *Rost* ... was rightly decided', commenting that such decisions 'betray some confusion between the right to prove the occurrence of parliamentary events and the embargo on questioning their propriety' (at p418). From this *dicta*, and the House of Lords' finding in *Pepper v Hart* (1993)[40] that the courts may, contrary to a long-standing prohibition, consult *Hansard* as an aid to statutory interpretation, one may tentatively conclude that the type of non-critical examination of affairs in Parliament at issue in *Rost* do not, after all, fall within the prohibition on 'questioning' in Article 9 and are therefore not a breach of privilege.

---

[39] 3 All ER 407.
[40] 1 All ER 42.

4   In *Prebble* itself, the defendant, Television New Zealand, made certain allegations of impropriety in a broadcast against the fourth Labour Government of New Zealand which were alleged by the plaintiff, a minister within that Government, to carry a meaning defamatory of him. In libel proceedings in New Zealand the defendant alleged, *inter alia*, that the defamatory meanings were mostly true. Certain of the particulars of the justifications relied on statements and actions which took place in Parliament. The plaintiff applied to strike out those particulars which concerned matters taking place in the House and which were therefore, under Article 9 of the Bill of Rights 1689, subject to Parliamentary privilege. The judge agreed that the particulars should be struck out and the Court of Appeal upheld that decision but considered it unjust that the plaintiff should be able to continue the action given that the defendant's ability to substantiate his justification plea was thereby substantially impaired, and so ordered a stay of proceedings until the Committee of Privileges could determine whether the privileges protected by Article 9 could be waived.

The plaintiff appealed against the stay of proceedings and the defendant against the decision to strike out the particulars.

The questions for decision by the Privy Council were:

(i) would the allegations, if pursued, infringe Article 9;

(ii) if so, should a stay have been ordered?

The defendants' submission was that even critical scrutiny of parliamentary proceedings ought to be permitted, where the interests of justice so demanded.

Prebble v Television New Zealand Ltd [1994] 3 All ER 407, 414–19

Lord Browne-Wilkinson: The defendants submit, first, that [parliamentary privilege] only operates to protect the questioning of statements made in the House in proceedings which seek to assert legal consequences against the maker of the statement for making that statement. Alternatively, the defendants submit that parliamentary privilege does not apply where it is the Member of Parliament himself who brings proceedings for libel and parliamentary privilege would operate so as to prevent a defendant who wishes to justify the libel from challenging the veracity or *bona fides* of the plaintiff in making statements in the House.

The first of those submissions is based on the decision in the New South Wales Supreme Court: *Murphy* (1986) 5 NSWLR 18. In that case a judge was being prosecuted for an alleged offence. The principal Crown witness had previously given evidence to a select committee of the Senate relating to matters in issue in the trial. The question arose whether, in the course of the criminal trial, the witness's earlier evidence to the select committee could be put to him in cross-examination with a view to showing a previous inconsistent statement. Hunt J held that Art 9 did not prohibit such cross-examination, even if the suggestion was made that the evidence given to the select committee was a lie. He further held that the statements of the select committee could be used to draw inferences, could be analysed and be made the basis of submissions. Almost immediately Commonwealth legislation, the Parliamentary Privileges Act 1987, made it clear that *Murphy* did not represent the law of the Commonwealth. Section 16 of that Act provides 'for the avoidance of doubt' in relation to proceedings of the Parliament of the Commonwealth as follows:

(3) In proceedings in any court or tribunal, it is not lawful for evidence to be tendered or received, questions asked or statements, submissions or comments made, concerning proceedings in Parliament, by way of, or for the purpose of –

(a) questioning or relying on the truth, motive, intention or good faith of anything forming part of those proceedings in Parliament;

(b) otherwise questioning or establishing the credibility, motive, intention or good faith of any person; or

(c) drawing, or inviting the drawing of, inferences or conclusions wholly or partly from anything forming part of those proceedings in Parliament.

That Act, therefore, declares what had previously been regarded as the effect of art 9 and subs (3) contains what, in the opinion of their Lordships, is the true principle to be applied.

It is, of course, no part of their Lordships' function to decide whether, as a matter of Australian law, the decision of Hunt J was correct. But Art 9 applies in the United Kingdom and throughout the Commonwealth. In their Lordships' view the law as stated by Hunt J was not correct so far as the rest of the Commonwealth is concerned. First, his views were in conflict with the long line of *dicta* that the courts will not allow any challenge to what is said or done in Parliament. Second, as Hunt J recognised, his decision was inconsistent with the decision of Browne J in *Church of Scientology of California v Johnson-Smith* [1972] 1 All ER 378, [1972] 1 QB 522 (subsequently approved by the House of Lords in *Pepper v Hart* [1993] 1 All ER 42, [1993] AC 593) and *Comalco Ltd v Australian Broadcasting Corp* (1983) 50 ACTR 1, in both of which cases it was held that it would be a breach of privilege to allow what is said in Parliament to be the subject matter of investigation or submission.

Finally, Hunt J based himself on a narrow construction of Art 9, derived from the historical context in which it was originally enacted. He correctly identified the mischief sought to be remedied in 1688 as being, *inter alia*, the assertion by the King's courts of a right to hold a Member of Parliament criminally or legally liable for what he had done or said in Parliament. From this he deduced the principle that Art 9 only applies to cases in which a court is being asked to expose the maker of the statement to legal liability for what he has said in Parliament. This view discounts the basic concept underlying Art 9, *viz* the need to ensure so far as possible that a member of the legislature and witnesses before committees of the House can speak freely without fear that what they say will later be held against them in the courts. The important public interest protected by such privilege is to ensure that the Member or witness at the time he speaks is not inhibited from stating fully and freely what he has to say. If there were any exceptions which permitted his statements to be questioned subsequently, at the time when he speaks in Parliament he would not know whether or not there would subsequently be a challenge to what he is saying. Therefore he would not have the confidence the privilege is designed to protect.

Moreover to allow it to be suggested in cross-examination or submission that a Member or witness was lying to the House could lead to exactly that conflict between the courts and Parliament which the wider principle of non-intervention is designed to avoid. Misleading the House is a contempt of the House punishable by the House: if a court were also to be permitted to decide whether or not a Member or witness had misled the House there would be a serious risk of conflicting decisions on the issue.

The defendants' second submission [is] that the rules excluding parliamentary material do not apply when the action is brought by a Member of Parliament ... their Lordships ... cannot accept that the fact that the maker of the statement is the initiator of the court proceedings can affect the question whether Art 9 is infringed. The privilege protected by Art 9 is the privilege of Parliament itself. The actions of any individual Member of Parliament, even if he has an individual privilege of his own, cannot determine whether or not the privilege of Parliament is to apply. The wider principle ... prevents the courts from adjudicating on issues arising in or concerning the House, *viz* whether or not a Member has misled the House or acted from improper motives. The decision of an individual Member cannot override that collective privilege of the House to be the sole judge of such matters.

Their Lordships are acutely conscious (as were the courts below) that to preclude reliance on things said and done in the House in defence of libel proceedings brought by a Member of the House could have a serious impact on a most important aspect of freedom of speech, *viz* the right of the public to comment on and criticise the actions of those elected to power in a democratic society: see *Derbyshire CC v Times Newspapers Ltd* [1993] 1 All ER 1011, [1993] AC 534. If the media and others are unable to establish the truth of fair criticisms of the conduct of their elected Members in the very performance of their legislative duties in the House, the results could indeed be chilling to the proper monitoring of Members' behaviour. But the present case and *Wright's* case illustrate how public policy, or human rights, issues can conflict. There are three such issues in play in these cases: first, the need to ensure that the legislature can exercise its powers freely on behalf of its electors, with access to all relevant information; second, the need to protect freedom of speech generally; third, the interests of justice in ensuring that all relevant evidence is available to the courts. Their Lordships are of the view that the law has been long settled that, of these three public interests, the first must prevail. But the other two public interests cannot be ignored and their Lordships will revert to them in considering the question of a stay of proceedings.

For these reasons (which are in substance those of the courts below) their Lordships are of the view that parties to litigation, by whomsoever commenced, cannot bring into question anything said or done in the House by suggesting (whether by direct evidence, cross-examination, inference or submission) that the actions or words were inspired by improper motives or were untrue or misleading. Such matters lie entirely within the jurisdiction of the House, subject to any statutory exception such as exists in New Zealand in relation to perjury under s108 of the Crimes Act 1961.

However, their Lordships wish to make it clear that this principle does not exclude all references in court proceedings to what has taken place in the House. In the past, Parliament used to assert a right, separate from the privilege of freedom of speech enshrined in Art 9, to restrain publication of its proceedings. Formerly the procedure was to petition the House for leave to produce *Hansard* in court. Since 1980 this right has no longer been generally asserted by the United Kingdom Parliament and their Lordships understood from the Attorney General that in practice the House of Representatives in New Zealand no longer asserts the right. ...

Since there can no longer be any objection to the production of *Hansard*, the Attorney General accepted (in their Lordships' view rightly) that there could be no objection to the use of *Hansard* to prove what was done and said in Parliament as a matter of history. Similarly, he accepted that the fact that a statute had been passed is admissible in court proceedings. Thus, in the present action, there cannot be any objection to it being proved what the plaintiff or the Prime Minister said in the House (particulars 8.2.10 and 8.2.14) or that the State-Owned Enterprises Act 1986 was passed (particulars 8.4.1). It will be for the trial judge to ensure that the proof of these historical facts is not used to suggest that the words were improperly spoken or the statute passed to achieve an improper purpose.

It is clear that, on the pleadings as they presently stand, the defendants intend to rely on these matters not purely as a matter of history but as part of the alleged conspiracy or its implementation. Therefore, in their Lordships' view, Smellie J was right to strike them out. But their Lordships wish to make it clear that if the defendants wish at the trial to allege the occurrence of events or the saying of certain words in Parliament without any accompanying allegation of impropriety or any other questioning there is no objection to that course.

Stay of proceedings

The Court of Appeal, whilst upholding the decision of Smellie J to strike out the allegations in the defence which infringed Art 9, stayed the plaintiff's action unless and until the privilege was effectively waived both by the House itself and by any individual Member concerned. The House of Representatives has taken the view that it cannot waive the privilege. Therefore the stay effectively prevents the plaintiff from establishing, if he can, that he has been most seriously defamed. ...

The majority of the Court of Appeal took the view that the allegations struck out were 'very close to the core of this highly political case' (*per* Sir Robin Cooke P) and that without regard to such allegations the court could not adequately 'consider a substantial plea of justification or ... properly quantify damages' (*per* Richardson J). Therefore the dispute was, in their view, incapable of being fairly tried and should be stayed. McKay J took the view that the allegations struck out would not be determinative of the defence of justification and would have refused a stay.

Their Lordships are of the opinion that there may be cases in which the exclusion of material on the grounds of parliamentary privilege makes it quite impossible fairly to determine the issue between the parties. In such a case the interests of justice may demand a stay of proceedings. But such a stay should only be granted in the most extreme circumstances. The effect of a stay is to deny justice to the plaintiff by preventing him from establishing his good name in the courts. There may be cases, such as the *Wright* case, where the whole subject matter of the alleged libel relates to the plaintiff's conduct in the House so that the effect of parliamentary privilege is to exclude virtually all the evidence necessary to justify the libel. If such an action were to be allowed to proceed, not only would there be an injustice to the defendant but also there would be a real danger that the media would be forced to abstain from the truthful disclosure of a Member's misbehaviour in Parliament, since justification would be impossible. That would constitute a most serious inroad into freedom of speech.

But their Lordships do not agree that the present case falls into that extreme category. Mr Galbraith for the plaintiff submitted, and Mr Tizard for the defendants had difficulty in denying, that the allegations struck out were comparatively marginal. The burden of the libel relates to acts done by Members of the Government out of the House to which questions of parliamentary privilege have no application. There were six matters upon which the defendants were seeking to rely and which consisted of statements made in the House. Those allegations relate to the plea that the alleged conspiracy was kept secret. Apart from these six allegations, there is a large number of other matters relied upon in the defence in support of the allegation of secrecy, eg statements made outside Parliament to the same effect as those made in the House. Although the defendants will be handicapped on this aspect of the case by the exclusion of matters stated in the House, the impact on their case will only be limited. As to the allegations that certain parliamentary processes were done in implementation of the alleged conspiracy, although the defendants will be precluded from alleging that the necessary legislation was improperly procured, the actual sales of the state-owned assets and all other allegations relating to the impropriety of the transactions remain open and can be ventilated in court.

For these reasons, their Lordships are unable to agree with the majority of the Court of Appeal that the interests of justice demand a stay. Although (as in all cases where parliamentary privilege is in issue) the court will be deprived of the full evidence on these issues, the plaintiff is entitled to have his case heard and the defendants are able to put forward the overwhelming majority of the matters upon which they rely in justification of the alleged libel.

Notes

1   Their Lordships give two reasons as to why critical scrutiny of proceedings in Parliament cannot take place. One was that, if the courts found that the Member had lied to the House (a contempt of Parliament) but Parliament found he had not, there would be a conflict between Parliament and the courts. But all the serious conflicts which have arisen between the courts and Parliament (see below) have arisen because the courts have tried to attach *legal liability* to things done or said in Parliament and Parliament has sought to protect its Members from such liability. No such liability was in question in this case. The second reason given was that, if Members anticipated that their statements made in the House would later be subject to 'challenge' or questioning, they would not have the confidence to speak out freely. Two things may be said about this. Firstly, it seems, with respect, simply incorrect. If a Member is telling the truth, or giving his honest opinion, why should the realisation that his statements may later be scrutinised inhibit him from speaking? Maybe such a realisation would inhibit him from telling lies, but is this a bad thing? Presumably, no one wishes to encourage Members to be dishonest. But secondly, what Members say in the House is *already the subject of critical and probing scrutiny*, as carried on by journalists and political commentators. What possible justification is there for saying that a Member who may be savaged in the Press for misleading the House – as William Waldegrave has repeatedly been[41] in respect of misleading answers given by him to the House on selling arms in relation to Government policy on arms to Iraq, but that such a Member must be exempt from such criticism if it would be voiced by a barrister in a courtroom? In neither case is he in danger of incurring legal liability for what he says.

2   The Bill of Rights states that freedom of speech, debates and proceedings in Parliament ought not to be 'impeached or questioned in any court or *place outside Parliament*' (emphasis added). Why is such questioning permitted by the press?

3   For a similar English case in which the defendant newspaper wished to rely upon pleading impropriety connected with the handling of certain early day

---

41   See eg 'Five steps to save us from the contempt of our rulers', *Independent*, 16 February 1995.

motions in Parliament in defending an action brought by an MP, see *Allason v Haines* (1995).[42] The defence was found to be contrary to Article 9, but it was held that since the defence pleaded was the only one available to the defendant, it would be manifestly unfair to allow the action to proceed; it was therefore struck out.

4   The injustice which appears to arise from privilege where the person claiming privilege is the one who has made the defamatory statements concerned was adverted to in a recent Australian decision.

Wright and Advertiser Newspapers Ltd v Lewis (1990) 53 SASR 416, 421–2

King CJ: A Member of Parliament could sue for defamation in respect of criticisms of his statements or conduct in the Parliament. The defendant would be precluded however from alleging and proving that what was said by way of criticism was true. This would amount to a gross distortion of the law of defamation ... [which] in law is by definition an *untrue* imputation against the reputation of another ... If the defendant were precluded from proving the truth of what is alleged, the Member of Parliament would be enabled to recover damages ... for an imputation which was perfectly true [King CJ went on to consider how the defences of fair comment and qualified privilege might well also not be available in such a situation]. If this is the true legal position, it is difficult to envisage how a court could apply the law of defamation in a rational way to an action by a Member of Parliament in respect of an imputation relating to his statements or conduct in the House, or could try such an action fairly.[Original emphasis.]

Notes

1   Parliament itself is supposed to regulate and punish misuses of its privilege of free speech. For example, if a Member repeated unfounded accusations relating to another member the House might regard this as a misuse of privilege and therefore a contempt. However, in the *Colonel 'B'* case[43] in 1978, Parliament took no action against MPs who had used their privilege of freedom of speech to break the *sub judice* rule and thus commit a clear contempt of court with impunity. In 1984, a member committed a breach of the privilege of freedom of speech in seeking to limit the freedom of action of other members by words spoken in debate (*Bank's* case[44]). The Committee of Privileges recommended that no action be taken against the Member.

2   The position with respect to Article 9 and defamation has undergone an important change. During the third reading of the Defamation Bill in the Lords on 7 May 1996, an amendment which would allow an MP to waive privilege in relation to defamation proceedings was carried by a large majority.[45] It was subsequently passed by the Commons. The amendment was designed to remedy the apparent injustice which occurs when MPs are forced out of office as a result of allegations relating to their parliamentary

---

42   *The Times*, 25 July 1995.
43   (1978) HC 667 (1977–78); HC 222 (1978–79).
44   Unreported.
45   See Hudson, 'Parliamentary Privilege' (1996) NLJ, 17 May, 719.

conduct, but have no way of clearing their name through defamation proceedings (any action would be struck out as contrary to Article 9). The case of Neil Hamilton, forced to resign his position as a junior minister after 'cash for questions' allegations were made against him, was a recent example much in peers' mind.

3   Whilst MPs and peers might welcome this change[46] if it becomes law, two clear objections to it are apparent. The first is the apparent unfairness of the new position: if an MP is defamed about his parliamentary activities, he or she can lift the cloak of privilege to sue. By contrast, a newspaper or journalist defending an action brought by an MP, who needs to adduce evidence as to proceedings in Parliament as part of his defence (as in *Prebble*) will find that privilege will prevent him from doing so. In addition, of course, citizens defamed by MPs will continue to be unable to clear their names as only MPs will be able to waive privilege.

4   Arguments in favour of the asymmetry of the proposed new position attempt to justify it by reference to the public interest in freedom of speech in Parliament which requires immunity for MPs but not for those who defame them. This may partly answer criticisms of the situation whereby citizens are not able to sue MPs, but it does not tell us why journalists who *prima facie* defame MPs should not be able to defend themselves by adducing evidence of proceedings in Parliament in order to prove the truthfulness of what they said. This aspect of privilege still stands to be justified by the reasons put forward in *Prebble*, which as argued above, seem manifestly unpersuasive.

5   The second main objection to the change was argued by Lords Lester and Richards in the debate; as the former put it, 'The immunities written into Article 9 were not included simply for the personal ... benefit of Members ... but to protect the integrity of the legislative process by ensuring the independence of individual legislators'.[47] Since the rationale for privilege is supposed to be its necessity to each House as a whole, it follows that waiver of its protection should be a matter for the House only, not a power in the hands of individual Members, to be used for their personal benefit.

CONFLICT BETWEEN PARLIAMENT AND COURTS

One peculiar characteristic of parliamentary privilege is the fact that both the courts and Parliament have at times claimed the right to determine what is the law in this area. As P Leopold puts it, in the context of the scope of the privilege of free speech: 'the problem is that [a ruling on the matter] could be made by both Parliament and the courts with not necessarily the same result' ((1990) PL 30). Should conflict flow from such a different result, the outcome remains uncertain, as illustrated by a case already mentioned, *Stockdale v Hansard*.[48] This convoluted and colourful litigation is described by Erskine May.

---

46   Not all welcomed it – see below.
47   Quoted *ibid*.
48   9 Ad & El 1.

Erskine May, *Parliamentary Practice* 20th edn (1983), pp151–154

Messrs Hansard, the printers of the House of Commons, had printed by order of that House a report made by an inspector of prisons against which a Mr Stockdale brought an action for libel. The court did not consider Messrs Hansard's proof of the House's order to print a sufficient defence. Lord Denman CJ observed that the House's direction to publish all parliamentary reports was no justification for Hansard or anyone else.

[The House passed resolutions] declaring that the publication of parliamentary reports, votes and proceedings was an essential incident to the constitutional functions of Parliament; that the House had sole and exclusive jurisdiction to determine upon the existence and extent of its privileges; that to dispute those privileges by legal proceedings was a breach of privilege; and that for any court to assume to decide upon matters of privilege inconsistent with the determination of either House of Parliament was contrary to the law of Parliament.

... Messrs Hansard in this case relied entirely upon the privileges of the House and its order to print. The defence was unsuccessful. The Attorney General argued the case for regarding the High Court of Parliament as a superior court of exclusive jurisdiction binding on other courts, and its law a separate law. Each House separately, it was contended, possessed the whole power of the mediaeval High Court of Parliament, and so subordinate were the courts of law to each that a writ of error ran from them to Parliament. Furthermore, were the privileges of the Commons subject to review by the courts, the Lords would be the arbiter not only of their own privileges but also of those of the Commons. Once again, an appeal was made to the principle that the constitution supposed that the *lex parliamenti*, like the law administered in equity, ecclesiastical and admiralty courts, was a system different from the common law, the judges of which had no means of arriving judicially at knowledge of it. In such circumstances the courts must respect the general rule that they should follow the law of the court of original jurisdiction. Finally, the Attorney General cited instances of the Commons exercising its inquisitorial powers as a court by examining and committing judges.

The court rebutted nearly all these contentions. It was accepted that over their own internal proceedings the jurisdiction of the Houses was exclusive: but it was (in Lord Denman's view) for the courts to determine whether or not a particular claim of privilege fell within that category. Though the Commons had claimed that the publication of certain types of papers was essential to its constitutional functions, and the Attorney General argued that the court was bound to accept such a declaration as evidence of the law, Lord Denman held that the court had a duty to inquire further. There was, in his opinion, no difference between a right to sanction all things under the name of privilege and the same right to sanction them by merely ordering them to be done. This would amount to an 'arbitrary and irresponsible' superseding of the law.'

... Lord Denman denied further that the *lex parliamenti* was a separate law, unknown to the judges of the common law courts. Either House considered individually was only a part of the High Court of Parliament, and neither could bring an issue within its exclusive jurisdiction simply by declaring it to be a matter of privilege. Any other proposition was 'abhorrent to the first principles of the constitution'. The declaration of the House ... was not the action of a court, legislative, judicial or inquisitorial, so that the superiority of the House of Commons over other courts had nothing to do with the question. In any case, there was, it seemed to the judges, no basis for regarding the courts of law as in principle incapable of reviewing any decision of the House of Commons. Conversely, there was no parliamentary revision of court judgments for error. The Commons was not a court of law in the sense recognised in the courts, and was unable to decide a matter judicially in litigation between parties, either originally or by appeal.

Having received an unfavourable verdict, the House of Commons, again despite their strong view expressed in the resolutions referred to above, ordered to be paid the damages and costs for which Messrs Hansard were declared liable. It was however agreed that, in case of future actions, the firm should not plead and that the parties should suffer for their contempt of the resolutions and defiance of the House's authority.

When therefore a third action was commenced for another publication of the original report, judgment was given against Messrs Hansard by default. Damages were assessed and the sheriffs of Middlesex levied for the amount, though they delayed paying the money to Stockdale for as long as possible. In 1840, the Commons committed first Stockdale and then the sheriffs, who had declined to repay the money to Messrs Hansard. Proceedings for the sheriff's release on a writ of *habeas corpus* proved unsuccessful. Howard, Stockdale's solicitor, was also proceeded against, but escaped with a reprimand.

While in prison, the persistent Stockdale commenced a fourth action, for which both he and Howard were committed. Messrs Hansard were again ordered not to plead, and judgment was entered against them. At this point, the situation was in part resolved by the introduction of what became the Parliamentary Papers Act 1840, affording statutory protection to papers published by order of either House ...

The case of *Howard v Gosset* (1845) may be viewed however as a continuation of the conflict in some of its aspects. Howard, Stockdale's solicitor, brought an action against the Serjeant at Arms and others for having taken him into custody and committed him to prison in obedience of the House's order and the Speaker's warrant. ... Leave to appeal was given to the defendants and the Attorney General was directed to defend them. The court favoured the plaintiff, on the grounds of the technical informality of the warrant. The judges proceeded on the principle that the warrant might be examined with the same strictures as if it had issued from an inferior court ... while at the same time concluding that they might adjudge it to be bad in form 'without impugning the authority of the House or in any way disputing its privileges'.

A select committee roundly condemned this doctrine, but advised the House 'that every legitimate mode of asserting and defending its privileges should be exhausted before it prevented by its own authority, the further progress of the action'. [Select Committee on Printed Papers, 2nd Report, HC 397 (1845), pvi.] The House accepted the advice and an appeal was lodged. In order, however, to avoid submission to any adverse judgment on appeal, the Serjeant was not authorised to give bail and execution was levied on his goods. In the event, the decision of the lower court was overturned, and the court found that the privileges involved were not in the least doubtful. The warrant of the Speaker was valid as a protection to the officer of the House, and the warrant should be construed as if it were a writ from a superior court.

Notes

1   In giving a return which did not state the facts upon which the allegation of contempt was based, Parliament had clearly learned from *Paty's case*

(1704)[49] in which the Speaker gave the grounds for the finding of contempt: one of the judges (Holt CJ) hearing the application for *habeas corpus* dissented from the finding that the writ could not be granted, stating that where the reasons given could not amount in law to a breach of privilege or contempt, *habeas corpus* ought to be granted.

2 It is not certain that the matter could again be resolved as it was in *Stockdale*;[50] Calvert considers it uncertain '... that a court of law would meekly accept a general return to a writ' in similar circumstances.[51] Keir and Lawson, in contrast, take the view that the courts 'yielded the key to the fortress'[52] by refusing to question the legality of imprisonment for contempt where no reason is given, implying that a precedent has been set. Further, if the House of Lords (Judicial Committee) was asked to grant a writ of *habeas corpus* it could not avoid questioning the Common's actions on the grounds that the Commons was a superior court. An appeal was in fact made to the Lords in *Paty's case*, but the counsel preparing it was promptly imprisoned by the Commons.

3 In *Bradlaugh v Gossett*[53] Stephen J said that, '... the principal result of [*Stockdale*] is to assert in the strongest way the right of the Court of Queen's Bench to ascertain in case of need to the extent of the privileges of the House and to deny emphatically that the court is bound by resolution of the House declaring any particular matter to fall within their privilege ...'. More recently in *Rost v Edwards* the question of the courts' role as determiner of the boundary of privilege was addressed:

> The approach I have to this aspect of the case is this. There are clearly cases where Parliament is to be the sole judge of its affairs. Equally there are clear cases where the courts are to have exclusive jurisdiction. In a case which may be described as a grey area a court, while giving full attention to the necessity for comity between the courts and Parliament, should not be astute to find a reason for ousting the jurisdiction of the court and for limiting or even defeating a proper claim by a party to litigation before it. If Parliament wishes to cover a particular area with privilege it has the ability to do so by passing an Act of Parliament giving itself the right to exclusive jurisdiction. Ousting the jurisdiction of the court has always been regarded as requiring the clearest possible words.[54]

Notes

1 How should this conflict be resolved? De Smith has suggested that jurisdiction over breaches of privilege and contempts should be handed over to the courts.[55] It seems clear that the present state of affairs is unsatisfactory. It has been noted that the present competition for

---

49 2 Ld Raym 1105.
50 9 Ad& EI 1.
51 *British Constitutional Law* (1985), p115.
52 *Cases in Constitutional Law*, 6th edn (1979), p225.
53 12 QBD 271, 279.
54 2 WLR 1280, 1293.
55 *Constitutional and Administrative Law*, 6th edn (1994), p332.

jurisdictions makes for uncertainty in this area, whilst the view that the party political nature of the Commons renders it unsuitable for deciding what are in effect legal issues has also been touched on. It is clear from the recent vote on the implementation of the Nolan report's recommendations (above) that the mere fact that questions of privilege are being considered and that consequently the House has a technically free vote will not preclude the intrusion of party interests. One could envisage such considerations intruding themselves in the case of, for example, a senior Government figure sued for libel; in determining whether the Minister's publishing of the libel was covered by privilege, Government MPs might well be more concerned with possible embarrassment for the government than with following expert recommendation.

2   But dissatisfaction with the Commons as a decision-making body does not stop there. If a question of privilege arises, the Committee of Privileges will consider the matter and make a recommendation to the Commons. Unfortunately, the Commons does not always follow the Committee's recommendations, nor is it bound by its previous decisions, drawbacks illustrated by the case of GR Strauss 1958,[56] previously considered. Whilst the Commons as a whole is not ideally suited to make the final decisions on matters of privilege, the Committee of Privileges itself has been subject to criticisms as a forum for trying issues which, at least theoretically, could result in the imprisonment of those it finds to have been in breach of privilege or to have committed contempts. Firstly, it is nominated in proportion to party strengths; it is, as De Smith notes, (p320) unusual for it to divide along party lines, but it did so in the WJ Brown case (1947),[57] in delivering a verdict which favoured the Government MP concerned, and recently, as described above, split dramatically over the Nolan report. Secondly, in denying alleged contemners the right to legal representation, and on occasion condemning them without giving them the opportunity to put their case (the Electricity Board were condemned unheard in the Strauss case) the Committee is open to the charge of breaching the rules of natural justice. The justice of this second criticism was recognised by the 1967 Select Committee on Parliamentary Privilege which recommended a number of procedural changes aiming at giving those at risk of condemnation a right to put their case in a proper manner; their proposals have not yet been enacted. The changes proposed included giving those involved in a charge of contempt a right to appear at its hearings, give evidence, call, examine and cross examine witnesses; it was also suggested that those attending should be able to ask the Committees leave to be legally represented and to apply for legal aid. These proposals have not yet been enacted.

3   However, as Munro notes, 'the central criticism',.that the House acts as a judge in its own case, 'would only be met if the contempt jurisdiction were transferred to another body, such as the ordinary courts.[58] Such a transfer (from it should be excluded Parliament's power to punish Members for purely internal breaches of privilege) seems a desirable but, at the moment, unlikely course of action.

---

[56]   See report of Committee of Privileges, HC 308 (1956–57).

[57]   HC 188 (1946–47).

[58]   Munro, *op cit*, p151.

PART IV
THE EXECUTIVE

CHAPTER 1

PREROGATIVE POWERS[1]

INTRODUCTION

In his *Commentaries on the Laws of England,* Blackstone wrote that the prerogative is 'that special pre-eminence which the King has, over and above all other persons, and out of the ordinary course of the common law, in right of his royal dignity'. The term 'prerogative', then, refers to powers which are unique to the sovereign and which s/he has by common law as opposed to statute. Prerogative powers are sometimes referred to as the 'Royal Prerogative'; this is technically correct, as in law these powers belong to the Monarch. However, by convention, they are in practice exercised by the Prime Minister; in some cases by the Cabinet. However, certain prerogatives remain which are generally exercised by the Monarch personally. These are sometimes known as the 'personal prerogatives' and will be examined below.

This Chapter first considers the nature of prerogative powers, in particular the concept of an 'act of state', and examines the more important prerogatives: the power to dissolve Parliament, to assent to Bills, to declare war, to dismiss and appoint ministers; personal prerogatives of the monarch: various immunities such as the Queen's personal immunity from suit or prosecution, and property rights. Secondly, it considers matters the courts have traditionally considered in relation to the prerogative: its existence and extent, its relationship with statute and the duty of the Crown to compensate citizens affected by prerogative powers.

THE NATURE AND EXTENT OF THE PREROGATIVE

Colin R Munro, *Studies in Constitutional Law* (1987), pp159–61

The royal prerogative may be defined as comprising those attributes peculiar to the Crown which are derived from common law, not statute, and which still survive.

Some of these points need to be amplified, so that we may see what sort of creature we are dealing with. First, notice that the prerogative consists of legal

---

1 General reading for this part (additional to that cited elsewhere): Brazier, *Constitutional Practice* (1994),; Jenkins, *Accountable to None: The Tory Nationalisation of Britain* (1995); Pyper and Robins (eds), *Governing the UK in the 1990s* (1995), Part I; Macintosh, *The British Cabinet* (1977); Baroness Thatcher, *The Downing Street Years* (1993); Lawson, *The View from No 11* (1992); Crossman, *Diaries of a Cabinet Minister* (1975); chapters in Harlow (ed), *Public Law and Politics* (1984); articles generally in *Parliamentary Affairs*; Marshall, *Constitutional Theory* (1971); Marshall and Moodie, *Some Problems of the Constitution* (1971); Jennings, *The Law and the Constitution,* 5th edn (1959) and *Cabinet Government* (1959); essays in McEldowney and McAuslan, *Law, Legitimacy and the Constitution* (1985); Turpin, *British Government and the Constitution,* 3rd edn (1995); IPPR, *The Constitution of the United Kingdom* (1991); Greer, 'The Next Steps Initiative [etc]' (1992) *Political Quarterly* 63; Dicey, *The Law of the Constitution,* 10th edn, (1959); SA De Smith, *Constitutional and Administrative Law,* 6th edn (1994); A Bradley and ECS Wade, *Constitutional and Administrative Law,* 11th edn (1993); O Hood Phillips, *Constitutional and Administrative Law,* 7th edn (1987); H Barnett, *Constitutional and Administrative Law* (1995).

attributes, not matters merely of convention or practice. The courts will recognise, in appropriate cases, that these attributes exist, and, when necessary, enforce them. So, when a university archaeological team excavated a treasure hoard from St Ninian's Isle in the Shetlands, an action was brought to establish that the treasure belonged to the Crown. [*Lord Advocate v University of Aberdeen* 1963 SC 533.] The courts will rule, in other cases, that a prerogative which has been claimed does not exist or that Government action falls outside the scope of the prerogative. In 1964, a court had to decide whether the Crown's monopoly over the printing of Bibles applied to the new translation, the New English Bible, and held that it did not. [*Universities of Oxford and Cambridge v Eyre and Spottiswoode Ltd* [1964] Ch 736, [1963] 3 All ER 289.]

Strictly speaking, the prerogatives are recognised, rather than created, by the common law, for their source is in custom. By origin, royal prerogatives were attributes which of necessity inhered in kings as the governors of the realm. It is natural to think of the prerogative as composed of powers, for it is in the exercise of the Crown's discretionary powers, and the control of that exercise, that our chief interest lies. But rules affected the Crown in a variety of ways. Some gave rights to the Crown, such as the right to treasure trove. Some gave immunities, such as the Crown's immunity from being sued. Some even imposed duties, such as the Crown's duty to protect subjects within the realm.

It is with rules peculiar to the Crown that we are concerned. In owning property or entering into contracts, the Crown is doing nothing which an ordinary person might not do. The word 'prerogative', however, aptly describes only something over and above the ordinary, as Blackstone emphasised:

> It signifies, in its etymology (from *prae* and *rogo*) something that is required or demanded before, or in preference to, all others. And hence it follows, that it must be in its nature singular and eccentrical; that it can only be applied to those rights and capacities which the king enjoys alone, in contradistinction to others, and not to those which he enjoys in common with any of his subjects; for if once any one prerogative of the Crown could be held in common with the subject, it would cease to be prerogative any longer. [*Commentaries*, I, p239.]

Properly, then, the prerogative is confined to matters, such as the power to declare war or the power of creating peerages, which are peculiar to the Crown ... These special legal attributes are a residue, a remnant of what was possessed by medieval kings and queens. What remains is left to the executive by the grace of Parliament, for Parliament can abrogate or diminish the prerogative, like any other part of the common law.

The prerogatives that remain are relics. But they are not unimportant relics.

Notes

1 Munro admits that there is more than one view on the scope of the prerogative but arguably understates the definitional vacuum surrounding the term. Moreover, it is not as if there has not been more than adequate time for clarification. As McEldowney and McAuslan put it, 'Notwithstanding that the royal prerogative as a source of power of the Government antedates Acts of Parliament, has been at the root of a civil war and a revolution in England and has been litigated about on countless major occasions in respect of its use both at home and overseas, its scope is still unsure'.[2]

---

2 'Legitimacy and the Constitution: The Dissonance Between Theory and Practice' in McAuslan and McEldowney, *Law, Legitimacy and the Constitution* (1985), p12.

2 Professor Wade believes that this lack of clarity (for which he partly blames Dicey – see below) has resulted in many exercises of power being wrongly labelled as examples of the prerogative. He notes a number of examples of Government actions which have been misdescribed by the courts as acts of 'prerogative' power.

HWR Wade, *Constitutional Fundamentals* (1989), pp58–66

But what does 'prerogative' mean? I have felt disposed to criticise the use of this term in some recent judgments and other contexts where, as it seemed to me, no genuine prerogative power was in question at all. If prerogative power is to be brought under judicial control, and if ministers are to be condemned for abusing it unlawfully, it is worth finding out what it really is. In the first place, the prerogative consists of legal power – that is to say, the ability to alter people's rights, duties or status under the laws of this country which the courts of this country enforce. Thus when Parliament is dissolved under the prerogative it can no longer validly do business. When a man is made a peer, he may no longer lawfully vote in a parliamentary election. When a university is incorporated by royal charter, a new legal person enters the world. All these legal transformations are effected in terms of rights, duties, disabilities, etc, which the courts will acknowledge and enforce. The power to bring them about is vested in the Crown by the common law, so it clearly falls within the definition of the royal prerogative as 'the common law powers of the Crown'. But when the Government cancels the designation of Laker Airways by making a communication to the Government of the United States under the terms of an international agreement, that has no effect under the law of this country whatsoever and has nothing to do with any power conferred by common law or recognised by British courts. It may be, as the Court of Appeal held, an act prohibited by a British statute. But it is not an act of power in any British constitutional sense, since it involves no special power that a British court will recognise. Whatever powers the Government may have had under the Bermuda Agreement were powers in the sphere of international law, and their capacity to make the Agreement came not from common law but from their status in international law as an international person. In the Laker Airways case the Attorney General claimed that the Crown was entitled to cancel the designation under the royal prerogative, and there was much talk about prerogative in the judgments. But if there was no power, in the correct legal and constitutional sense, there was no prerogative either. There was merely a piece of administrative action on the international plane.

Another example shows another species of inaccuracy. The Criminal Injuries Compensation Board is an instance of the practice, dear to the administrative heart, of doing things informally and extra-legally if means can be devised. This Board pays out several million pounds of public money annually to the victims of violent crime. But until recently it had no statutory authority. [The Board was made statutory by the Criminal Justice Act 1988.] Parliament simply voted the money each year, and the Board dispensed it under the rules of the scheme, which were laid before Parliament by the Home Secretary but had no statutory force. Nevertheless, by a feat no less imaginative than in the Laker Airways case, the courts assumed jurisdiction to quash decisions of the Board which did not accord with the rules of the scheme. In doing so, they described the Board as 'set up under the prerogative' [*Criminal Injuries Compensation Board, ex p Lain* [1967] 2 QB 864 at 881, 883]. But one essential of 'prerogative', if I may be forgiven for saying so, is that it should be prerogative. Its etymology means that it should be some special power possessed by the Crown over and above the powers of an ordinary person, and by virtue of the Crown's special constitutional position.

... Now if we apply this test to the constitution of the Criminal Injuries Compensation Board, it is surely plain that the Government, in establishing it, was merely doing what ... any of us could do if we had the money ready to hand. We could set up a board, or a committee, or trustees with authority to make grants according to whatever rules we might please to lay down. Thousands of foundations or trusts have been set up in the exercise of exactly the same liberty that the Government exercised in the case of the criminal injuries scheme. So far as the Crown came into the picture at all, it was exercising its ordinary powers as a natural person, which of course include power to transfer property, make contracts and so on. [In *Panel on Take-overs and Mergers, ex p Datafin plc* (1987) QB 815 at 848, Lloyd LJ expressed his agreement with this argument.] Blackstone was quite right, in my opinion, in saying that such powers are not prerogative at all.

Much the same might be said of other powers of the Crown which writers on constitutional law are fond of cataloguing as prerogative, without regard to Blackstone's doctrine. The power to appoint and dismiss ministers, for instance, appears to me to be nothing else than the power which all legal persons have at common law to employ servants or agents, so that it lacks any 'singular and eccentrical' element. Ministers as such have no inherent powers at common law and must therefore be counted as ordinary servants. It is otherwise with judges, who have very great legal powers, and their appointment and dismissal were undoubtedly within the true prerogative before Parliament gave them a statutory basis. I will not go through the whole catalogue of the powers commonly classed as prerogative in textbooks and elsewhere, though I suspect that a number of them would not pass the Blackstone test. A collector's piece comes from a hopeless case of 1971. Mr Clive Jenkins, the trade union leader, sued the Attorney General in an attempt to stop the Government from distributing a free pamphlet on the Common Market at a cost to the taxpayer of £20,000. The judge is reported to have held that the issue of free information is 'a prerogative power of the Crown' which the court cannot question [*Jenkins v Att Gen* 115 Sol Jo 674]. Since all the Crown's subjects are at liberty to issue as much free information as they like (and many of them issue much too much of it), I offer you this as a choice example of a non-prerogative.

The truth seems to be that judges have fallen into the habit of describing as 'prerogative' any and every sort of Government action which is not statutory. It may be, also, that the responsibility for this solecism can be loaded onto that popular scapegoat, Dicey. For his well known definition of prerogative is 'the residue of discretionary power left at any moment in the hands of the Crown'. He makes no distinction between the Crown's natural and regal capacities, indeed at one point he says [*The Law of the Constitution* (10th edn), p425]:

> Every act which the executive Government can lawfully do without the authority of an Act of Parliament is done in virtue of this prerogative.

So the judges and authors whose wide statements I have ventured to criticise could quote Dicey against me. But if we match Dicey against Blackstone, I think that Blackstone wins. Nor do I think that the criticism is mere pedantry. The true limits of the prerogatives of the Crown are important both in constitutional and in administrative law. This is all the more so now that the courts are showing signs, as in the Laker Airways case, of bringing the exercise of the prerogative under judicial control. It may well be easier to extend control to the few genuine prerogative powers which may possibly admit it, for example an improper use of *nolle prosequi*, if the court is not by the same token committed to extend it to all

sorts of pretended prerogatives, such as the control of the civi
making of contracts or treaties.

PASSPORTS AND THE RIGHT TO TRAVEL

There is another area where the term prerogative is loosely used ..ɪe, in
addition, an infusion of law is badly needed. This is the matter of passports, or
perhaps I should call it the citizen's right to travel. For many years the
Government has claimed an unfettered discretion to grant, deny or cancel a
passport without reasons given or fair procedure or right of appeal or legal
remedy, and in the past this supposed power has been used arbitrarily to restrict
the rights of British subjects to leave the country and also, it seems to re-enter it.
The Immigration Act 1971 made a minor change by providing that a patrial who
has the right to leave and enter the realm freely must on proper request show a
passport or other satisfactory evidence of his identity and nationality. [Sched 2,
para 4(2)9(a).] But he may still be unable to enter other countries without a
passport and the denial of it may in practice deny him freedom of travel.

In principle it is highly objectionable that the executive should claim this power
of administrative punishment, but there is no doubt that it does. A typical
statement comes from the *Report of the Committee of Privy Councillors on the
Recruitment of Mercenaries* of 1976, when there was concern over British
mercenaries fighting in countries such as Angola. The Committee said [Cmnd
6569 (1976), para 18, quoting 881 HC Deb (Written Answer 265)]:

> The issue of a passport is an exercise of the royal prerogative and the
> document, when issued to its holder, nevertheless remains the property of
> the Crown. No United Kingdom citizen has a right to have a passport issued
> to him and the Foreign Secretary, by whom the prerogative is exercised, can
> withhold or withdraw a passport at his discretion.

They then quoted a parliamentary answer enumerating the types of person to
whom it was the practice to refuse passports, one of which was 'in very rare
cases':

> a person whose past or proposed activities are so demonstrably undesirable
> that the grant or continued enjoyment of passport facilities would be contrary
> to the public interest.

This is a polysyllabic way of describing any one whose activities are disapproved
of by the Government.

My first comment, which may not now come as a surprise, is that I question
whether passports have anything to do with the royal prerogative in its proper
sense. A passport as such has no status or legal effect at common law whatever.
It is imply an administrative document. On its face it is an imperious request
from the Foreign Secretary that all whom it may concern shall allow the bearer to
pass freely without let or hindrance and shall afford him assistance and
protection. In reality it is an international identity card, certifying that a traveller
is accepted by this country as one of its nationals. A United Kingdom national's
passport does not have the slightest effect upon his legal rights, whatever they
may be, to go abroad and return. Those rights are a matter of common and
statute law, which the Crown has no power to alter. The Committee on
Mercenaries very rightly said that the withholding or withdrawing of passports
as a means of preventing United Kingdom citizens from leaving the country
could not be justified either pragmatically or morally – and that what effect it
might have would be based on bluff, relying on the citizen's ignorance of his
right at common law to leave the kingdom and return to it. Since it has no effect
on legal rights, the grant or withdrawal of a passport is not an exercise of legal

power and cannot therefore represent the exercise of prerogative power. Formerly the Crown did possess the power to prevent a subject from leaving the realm by issuing the writ *ne exaet regno*, which was once a favourite instrument for preventing the clergy from resorting to Rome. That had legal effect, and was therefore a true prerogative power, but it is now held to be obsolete except when granted by the court to a creditor against an absconding debtor. According to Blackstone, if I may invoke him again, 'by the common law, every man may go out of the realm for whatever cause he pleaseth, without obtaining the King's leave.' [*Commentaries*, I, p265.] Passports do not enter into the legal picture at all.

Notes

1   As Wade notes, later in his argument, the courts have since held that the refusal of a passport is subject to judicial review;[3] therefore, presumably refusal to grant a passport on grounds of mere Government disapproval of the applicant's political views or activities could be challenged as (a) taking into account an irrelevant consideration, or (b) as 'pure' *Wednesbury* unreasonableness. It would also be open to the court in considering whether the reasons advanced by the minister justified the abrogation of the important human rights in question (freedom to travel and, in some cases, freedom of expression) to take into account both Articles 2 and 3 of the Fourth Protocol to the European Convention on Human Rights and Article 10, as well as the weight of these rights as common law principles. (See generally, Part V, Chapter 2.)

2   Wade's contention that 'Ministers as such have no inherent powers at common law' is perhaps open to question. Whilst theoretically all prerogative powers are vested in the sovereign, the courts recognise clearly enough that the powers are in fact exercised by ministers: in *Secretary of State for the Home Department, ex p Northumbria Police Authority* (1988)[4] (discussed below), the court referred to 'the prerogative powers available to the Secretary of State [for the Home Department] to do all that is reasonably necessary to preserve the peace of the nation' (at p609). Nor is this a case where the courts were mistakenly labelling 'prerogative' a power in fact belonging to any ordinary citizen.

3   The prerogative covers a quite startlingly wide range of areas. Harry Calvert gives a useful list.

Harry Calvert, *An Introduction to British Constitutional Law* (1985), pp163–5

The potential range of prerogative powers is ... enormous and no attempt will be made to set out a comprehensive list of them. Some are, however, more important or, at all events, better known than others.

For purposes of description, it is helpful to list individual prerogative powers in this way and convenient, also, to classify them as, eg legislative, executive and judicial. This process of rationalisation is aided by the work of commentators and judges in examining the scope and nature of the prerogative. The reality, however, is that the prerogative is residual and unsystematic.

---

3   *Secretary of State for Foreign and Commonwealth Affairs, ex p Everett* [1989] 1 All ER 655.
4   2 WLR 590.

Amongst the best-known examples are the following:

(a) The power to summon, prorogue and dissolve Parliament ('proroguing' being the act of adjourning a Parliament at the end of a session).

(b) The power to declare war and peace, not legally a prerequisite to the institution or termination of hostilities, but having legal consequences (such as rendering certain persons 'enemy aliens' and thus subjecting them to certain legal disabilities, eg in relation to trade).

(c) The prerogative of pardon – the dispensing power of the power to release a particular individual from the obligation to obey a particular law, was the subject of great controversy in the seventeenth century and the Bill of Rights 1689 contains a dubious partial prohibition of it. The power, however, to erase a conviction after the event survived and may be exercised absolutely, as is most common today, or conditionally, as was formerly common where a person convicted of murder and sentenced to death was reprieved and the sentence commuted to one of life imprisonment. This power remains peculiar in that it is exercised, in England, on the advice not of the Prime Minister but of the Home Secretary.

(d) The power to confer peerages and other honours – the vast majority of peerages (and few hereditary ones are created) are today almost invariably created on the advice of the Prime Minister, the most common occasions by far being those of the Birthday Honours and New Year's Honours lists. Exceptionally, the monarch may confer a peerage without advice and certain honours are in the gift of the monarch personally.

(e) The power to conclude treaties. This is merely a particular, though important, facet of the power of the Crown in relation to foreign affairs. Its exercise is commonplace; each year the United Kingdom becomes a party to a host of international arrangements simply by the exercise of the prerogative power and without any need for endorsement by Parliament. Amongst the most striking exercises of this power in recent years have been the acceptance by the United Kingdom of the compulsory jurisdiction of the Commission and Court established under the European Convention of Human Rights and Fundamental Freedoms ... and accession to the Treaty of Rome leading to United Kingdom membership of the European Community.

Whilst the exercise of the prerogative power in this way effectively renders the United Kingdom a party to such a treaty in the eyes of international law, one extremely important limitation on effectiveness should be noted. Notwithstanding that it is the clear purport of the treaty in question to confer rights or to impose obligations on the individual subject within the realm, mere accession to it by the Crown in the exercise of its prerogative power will not, by itself, have this effect, a point vividly illustrated in a number of cases such as *Civilian War Claimants Association Ltd v The King* [1932] AC 14, where the treaty in question had as its clear purport the provision of compensation for individuals suffering loss or injury as a result of the actions of the Axis powers during the First World War and where the funds for this purpose were actually handed over to the Crown. This, however, by itself conferred no right to compensation upon particular persons allegedly so injured.

A corollary of this doctrine is that individual subjects within the United Kingdom have no means of enforcing, as of right, an award in their favour by the organs of the European human rights regime established under the Convention above, under United Kingdom law. They may confidently expect compliance by

Her Majesty's Government for the Government will not wish to court the consequences of non-compliance, the ultimate sanction of which is expulsion from the Council of Europe. Until Parliament legislates so as to provide otherwise, however, the individual has a mere spes, rather than a right, that he will benefit.

It follows that if it is intended to implement a treaty regime into the domestic law of the United Kingdom so as to affect the rights and duties of the subject, Parliament must intervene. Thus, although the United Kingdom acceded to the Treaty of Rome by prerogative act, and thus became a member of the European Community in the eyes of European and international law, Parliamentary action was necessary if that membership was to be more than a sham. It is a central feature of the European Community that its laws apply to individuals in respect of their legal relationships within the Community. If subjects in the United Kingdom were to be able to assert their rights under or be fixed with obligations arising out of Community law, that law had to be incorporated into the domestic law of the United Kingdom by Act of Parliament and this end was achieved by the European Communities Act 1972.

The surviving prerogative powers of the Crown extend over an area vastly more wide than is indicated in this short list of examples. The power to declare war and peace, for example, may be viewed as merely a particular aspect of a wider prerogative concerning, amongst other things, the conduct of war, control over the armed forces generally (in so far as this is not now regulated by statute) and, incidentally thereto, the requisitioning and even destruction of property for these purposes. The treaty-making power relating to the conduct of foreign and colonial affairs involving matters such as the recognition of foreign states and governments, the organisation of diplomatic services and the reception and accreditation of the representatives of foreign states.

Notes

1 To Calvert's list, one could add (as Munro[5] and Heuston[6] point out), the fact that the assent of the monarch is a necessary element in legislation.

2 Calvert's concentration on the treaty-making aspect of the prerogative's ambit in foreign affairs deflects attention from the rather more drastic actions which may be taken in under it. Heuston quotes Bagehot on the subject: 'I said in this book it would very much surprise people if they were really told how many things the Queen could do without consulting Parliament. Not to mention other things, she could disband the army ... dismiss all the officers from the General commanding-in-chief downwards ... [and] all the sailors too; she could sell off all our ships of war and all our navy stores; she could make a peace by the sacrifice of Cornwall and begin a war for the conquest of Brittany ... She could make every parish in the United Kingdom a university ... In a word, the Queen could by prerogative upset all the action of civil government'.[7] Of course, these powers are, by convention, exercised on the advice of ministers, but since conventions are not enforced by the courts,[8] it is still correct to say that the Queen *could*, as a matter of strict legal theory, do all the above.

5 *Op cit*, p160.
6 *Essays in Constitutional Law* (1964), p66.
7 Walter Bagehot, *The English Constitution*, pp282–284, quoted in Heuston, *op cit*, p72.
8 See Part I, Chapter 2.

PREROGATIVE AND STATUTE: EXCLUSION OR CO-EXISTENCE?

A key issue in relation to the prerogative is its relationship with statute. What happens when an area formerly regulated by the prerogative becomes covered by a statute?

Attorney General v De Keyser's Royal Hotel Ltd [1920] AC 508, 526, 539, 575

> **Lord Dunedin**: 'Inasmuch as the Crown is a party to every Act of Parliament it is logical enough to consider that when the Act deals with something which before the Act could be effected by the prerogative, and specially empowers the Crown to do the same thing, but subject to conditions, the Crown assents to that, and by that Act, to the prerogative being curtailed.'

> **Lord Atkinson:** It is quite obvious that it would be useless and meaningless for the Legislature to impose restrictions and limitations upon, and to attach conditions to, the exercise by the Crown of the powers conferred by a statute, if the Crown were free at its pleasure to disregard these provisions, and by virtue of its prerogative do the very thing the statutes empowered it to do. One cannot in the construction of a statute attribute to the Legislature (in the absence of compelling words) an intention so absurd. It was suggested that when a statute is passed empowering the Crown to do a certain thing which it might theretofore have done by virtue of its prerogative, the prerogative is merged in the statute. I confess I do not think the word 'merged' is happily chosen. I should prefer to say that when such a statute; expressing the will and intention of the King and of the three estates of the realm, is passed, it abridges the Royal Prerogative while it is in force to this extent: that the Crown can only do the particular thing under and in accordance with the statutory provisions ... and subject to all the limitations, restrictions and conditions by [them] imposed.

> **Lord Parmoor**: 'The constitutional principle is that when the power of the executive to interfere with the property or liberty of subjects has been placed under Parliamentary control, and directly regulated by statute, the executive no longer derives its authority from the Royal Prerogative of the Crown but from Parliament, and that in exercising such authority the executive is bound to observe the restrictions which Parliament has imposed in favour of the subject.'

Notes

1   In the *Northumbria Police Authority* case (1988) 2 WLR 590 the court had to consider whether s4 of the Police Act 1964, which authorised Police Authorities to maintain vehicles, apparatus and equipment required for police purposes, effectively granted them a monopoly of this power, so that the Home Secretary had had his pre-existing prerogative power to keep the peace (which included the power to maintain and supply equipment to the police) abridged by the statute. Purchas LJ held that s4 '[fell] short of an express and unequivocal inhibition sufficient to abridge the prerogative powers'. The approach therefore seemed to be that statutes only abridged the prerogative if they expressly and unequivocally indicated that such was their intention. This appears to make the prerogative *harder* to 'repeal' than legislation, which can of course be implicitly repealed. Croom Johnson LJ thought that s4 'does not expressly grant a monopoly' and that in the circumstances 'there [was] every reason not to imply' such a monopoly,

which does at least appear to admit of the possibility that the monopoly necessary to oust the prerogative could have been impliedly granted. Clarity appears to be lacking in this case, but the impression gained is that the courts were reluctant to allow erosion of the prerogative in the absence of a clear intent (express *or* implied?) to do so. In other words, any ambiguity – and there clearly was ambiguity in this case – seems to be resolved in favour of preservation of the prerogative.

2   Munro considers that the effect of a statute is only to abridge the prerogative *temporarily*, so that 'if the statute is later repealed the prerogative will still exist as it did before the statue was existed'. Of course, as he notes in the same essay, 'There is no doubt that Parliament may expressly abolish or restrict the prerogative'.[9] But suppose that the Act which abolished the prerogative was itself repealed? Would the abolished prerogative spring back to life?

3   Will the disabling of the prerogative by statute still take effect even where the statute in question only gives 'enabling' powers, allowing a scheme under the statutory provisions to be set up in the future? If it does not, could the Government set up an alternative scheme, inconsistent with the statutory one, acing under the prerogative? These were the issues which the House of Lords had to consider in the following case.

Secretary of State for the Home Department, ex p Fire Brigades Union [1995] 2 All ER 244, 252–6

The Criminal Justice Act 1988 ss108–117 and Scheds 6 and 7 provided for a statutory scheme to replace the old non-statutory scheme for compensating victims of violent crime. The statutory scheme would have compensated victims under the tort measure of damages. Section 171 of the Act permitted the Secretary of State for the Home Department to choose when the scheme was to come into force. He decided not to bring it in and instead set up a tariff system (acting under the prerogative) which was radically different from the scheme envisaged by the Act. Lord Browne Wilkinson found that the Home Secretary did not have an absolute duty to bring the scheme in, but then continued as follows:

> **Lord Browne Wilkinson:** It does not follow that, because the Secretary of State is not under any duty to bring the section into effect, he has an absolute and unfettered discretion whether or not to do so. So to hold would lead to the conclusion that both Houses of Parliament had passed the Bill through all its stages and the Act received the royal assent merely to confer an enabling power on the executive to decide at will whether or not to make the parliamentary provisions a part of the law. Such a conclusion, drawn from a section to which the sidenote is 'Commencement', is not only constitutionally dangerous but flies in the face of common sense. The provisions for bringing sections into force under s171(1) apply not only to the statutory scheme but to many other provisions. For example, the provisions of Pts I, II and III relating to extradition, documentary evidence in criminal proceedings and other evidence in criminal proceedings are made subject to the same provisions. Surely, it cannot have been

---

9   *Op cit*, pp172 and 170, respectively.

the intention of Parliament to leave it in the entire discretion of the Secretary of State whether or not to effect such important changes to the criminal law. In the absence of express provisions to the contrary in the Act, the plain intention of Parliament in conferring on the Secretary of State the power to bring certain sections into force is that such power is to be exercised so as to bring those sections into force when it is appropriate and unless there is a subsequent change of circumstances which would render it inappropriate to do so.

If, as I think, that is the clear purpose for which the power in s171(1) was conferred on the Secretary of State, two things follow. First, the Secretary of State comes under a clear duty to keep under consideration from time to time the question whether or not to bring the section (and therefore the statutory scheme) into force. In my judgment he cannot lawfully surrender or release the power contained in s171(1) so as to purport to exclude its future exercise either by himself or by his successors. In the course of argument, the Lord Advocate accepted that this was the correct view of the legal position. It follows that the decision of the Secretary of State to give effect to the statement in para 38 of the 1993 White Paper (Cm 2434) that 'the provisions in the 1988 Act will not now be implemented' was unlawful. The Lord Advocate contended, correctly, that the attempt by the Secretary of State to abandon or release the power conferred on him by s171(1), being unlawful, did not bind either the present Secretary of State or any successor in that office. It was a nullity. But, in my judgment, that does not alter the fact that the Secretary of State made the attempt to bind himself not to exercise the power conferred by s171(l) and such attempt was an unlawful act.

There is a second consequence of the power in s171(1) being conferred for the purpose of bringing the sections into force. As I have said, in my view, the Secretary of State is entitled to decide not to bring the sections into force if events subsequently occur which render it undesirable to do so. But if the power is conferred on the Secretary of State with a view to bringing the sections into force, in my judgment, the Secretary of State cannot himself procure events to take place and rely on the occurrence of those events as the ground for not bringing the statutory scheme into force. In claiming that the introduction of the new tariff scheme renders it undesirable now to bring the statutory scheme into force, the Secretary of State is, in effect, claiming that the purpose of the statutory power has been frustrated by his own act in choosing to introduce a scheme inconsistent with the statutory scheme approved by Parliament.

THE LAWFULNESS OF THE DECISION TO INTRODUCE THE TARIFF SCHEME

The tariff scheme, if validly introduced under the Royal Prerogative, is both inconsistent with the statutory scheme contained in ss108 to 117 of the 1988 Act and intended to be permanent. In practice, the tariff scheme renders it now either impossible or at least more expensive to reintroduce the old scheme or the statutory enactment of it contained in the 1988 Act. The tariff scheme involves the winding up of the old Criminal Injuries Compensation Board together with its team of those skilled in assessing compensation on the common law basis and the creation of a new body, the Criminal Injuries Compensation Authority, set up to assess compensation on the tariff basis at figures which, in some cases, will be very substantially less than under the old scheme. All this at a time when Parliament has expressed its will that there should be a scheme based on the tortious measure of damages, such will being expressed in a statute which Parliament has neither repealed nor (for reasons which have not been disclosed) been invited to repeal.

My Lords, it would be most surprising if, at the present day, prerogative powers could be validly exercised by the executive so as to frustrate the will of Parliament expressed in a statute and, to an extent, to pre-empt the decision of

Parliament whether or not to continue with the statutory scheme even though the old scheme has been abandoned. It is not for the executive, as the Lord Advocate accepted, to state as it did in the White Paper (para 38) that the provisions in the 1988 Act 'will accordingly be repealed when a suitable legislative opportunity occurs'. It is for Parliament, not the executive, to repeal legislation. The constitutional history of this country is the history of the prerogative powers of the Crown being made subject to the overriding powers of the democratically elected legislature as the sovereign body. The prerogative powers of the Crown remain in existence to the extent that Parliament has not expressly or by implication extinguished them. But under the principle in *A-G v De Keyser's Royal Hotel Ltd* [1920] AC 508, [1920] All ER Rep 80 if Parliament has conferred on the executive statutory powers to do a particular act, that act can only thereafter be done under the statutory powers so conferred: any pre-existing prerogative power to do the same act is *pro tanto* excluded ...

In his powerful dissenting judgment in the Court of Appeal, Hobhouse LJ decided that, since the statutory provisions had not been brought into force, they had no legal significance of any kind. He held, in my judgment correctly, that the *De Keyser* principle did not apply to the present case: since the statutory provisions were not in force they could not have excluded the pre-existing prerogative powers. Therefore the prerogative powers remained. He then turned to consider whether it could be said that the Secretary of State had abused those prerogative powers and again approached the matter on the basis that since the sections were not in force they had no significance in deciding whether or not the Secretary of State had acted lawfully. I cannot agree with this last step. In public law the fact that a scheme approved by Parliament was on the statute book and would come into force as law if and when the Secretary of State so determined is in my judgment directly relevant to the question whether the Secretary of State could in the lawful exercise of prerogative powers both decide to bring in the tariff scheme and refuse properly to exercise his discretion under s171(1) to bring the statutory provisions into force.

I turn then to consider whether the Secretary of State's decisions were unlawful as being an abuse of power. In this case there are two powers under consideration: first, the statutory power conferred by s171(1); second, the prerogative power. In order first to test the validity of the exercise of the prerogative power, I will assume that the 1988 Act, instead of conferring a discretion on the Secretary of State to bring the statutory scheme into effect, had specified that it was to come into force one year after the date of the royal assent. As Hobhouse LJ held, during that year the *De Keyser* principle would not apply and the prerogative powers would remain exercisable. But in my judgment it would plainly have been an improper use of the prerogative powers if, during that year, the Secretary of State had discontinued the old scheme and introduced the tariff scheme. It would have been improper because in exercising the prerogative power the Secretary of State would have had to have regard to the fact that the statutory scheme was about to come into force: to dismantle the machinery of the old scheme in the meantime would have given rise to further disruption and expense when, on the first anniversary, the statutory scheme had to be put into operation. This hypothetical case shows that, although during the suspension of the coming into force of the statutory provisions the old prerogative powers continue to exist, the existence of such legislation basically affects the mode in which such prerogative powers can be lawfully exercised.

Does it make any difference that the statutory provisions are to come into effect, not automatically at the end of the year as in the hypothetical case I have put, but on such day as the Secretary of State specifies under a power conferred on him by Parliament for the purpose of bringing the statutory provisions into force? In my judgment it does not. The Secretary of State could only validly exercise the prerogative power to abandon the old scheme and introduce the tariff scheme if, at the same time, he could validly resolve never to bring the statutory provisions and the inconsistent statutory scheme into effect. For the reasons I have already given, he could not validly so resolve to give up his statutory duty to consider from time to time whether to bring the statutory scheme into force. His attempt to do so, being a necessary part of the composite decision which he took, was itself unlawful. By introducing the tariff scheme he debars himself from exercising the statutory power for the purposes and on the basis which Parliament intended. For these reasons, in my judgment the decision to introduce the tariff scheme at a time when the statutory provisions and his power under s 171(1) were on the statute book was unlawful and an abuse of the prerogative power.

Notes

1   The House of Lords held by a majority of three to two (Lord Keith and Lord Mustill dissenting) that it was an abuse of power for the Home Secretary to purport to use the prerogative to set up a scheme inconsistent with the statutory one. The decision to do so was therefore unlawful.

2   It will be noted that notwithstanding the view of Professor Wade (above) that the whole Criminal Injuries Compensation Scheme had nothing to do with the prerogative, it was common ground that the prerogative was in fact being used.

3   One important argument of the dissenting minority was that, since any scheme the minister put in place could be changed (albeit with difficulty) by Parliament in the future, the minister could not be said to be frustrating Parliament's intent as he had not put an end to the statutory scheme, something only Parliament itself could do (*per* Lord Mustill at p267). With respect, this view seems to be clearly mistaken. By bringing in a scheme which differed radically from that envisaged by Parliament, the minister was clearly contravening their will: the fact that such contravention could later be reversed is beside the point. Lord Mustill seems to think that Parliament's will is not frustrated as long as it is not permanently frustrated.[10]

PERSONAL PREROGATIVES

Some of the more important prerogatives which the monarch may exercise personally relate to her powers over Parliament and the appointment of a Prime Minister. Sir Ivor Jennings notes, 'There are, however, certain prerogative powers which the Queen exercises on her own responsibility, and which may fitly be called "the personal prerogatives". Exactly what they are is by no means clear; for there are differences of opinion in respect of several of them. There is no controversy that she need not accept advice as to the appointment of a Prime Minister or as to the creation of peers so as to override the opposition of the House of Lords. There is controversy as to whether she can dismiss a Government or dissolve Parliament without advice, or whether she can refuse

---

10   For further comment on the decision, see TRS Allan (1995) 54(3) CLJ 491.

to dissolve Parliament when advised to do so.'[11] The power to dissolve Parliament, independently of a request to do so by the Prime Minister is by no means obsolete.

R Brazier, *Constitutional Texts* (1990), pp438–9

In the wholly unlikely events of a Government losing a vote of confidence in the House of Commons but refusing either to recommend a dissolution or to resign, or of a Government which tried improperly to extend the life of Parliament beyond the statutory maximum of five years, the Queen would be justified in insisting on an immediate dissolution. There has been royal insistence on a dissolution twice this century in the context of the Prime Minister's request to create peers so as to coerce the House of Lords: in both cases the Prime Minister unreservedly acquiesced.

(1) EDWARD VII

'He began by saying', Nash recorded, 'that the King had come to the conclusion that he would not be justified in creating new peers (say 300) until after a second general election and that he, Lord Knollys, thought you should know of this now, though, for the present he would suggest that what he was telling me should be for your ear only. The King regards the policy of the Government as tantamount to the destruction of the House of Lords and he thinks that before a large creation of peers is embarked upon or threatened the country should be acquainted with the particular project for accomplishing such destruction as well as with the general line of action as to which the country will be consulted at the forthcoming election.'

[Note made on 15 December 1909 of a conversation between Asquith's secretary, Vaughan Nash, and the King's Private Secretary, Lord Knollys, quoted in Roy Jenkins, *Asquith* (London: Fontana edn, 1967), p225.]

(2) GEORGE V

Mr Asquith did not ask for an immediate reply. It seems, however that King George and his private secretary misunderstood the purport of the discussion. Mr Asquith intended to prepare the King for the advice which he would subsequently receive from the Cabinet, while the King thought that no guarantee for the creation of peers would be sought before the election. Three days later Lord Knollys discovered that the King was mistaken, and Sir Arthur Bigge was instructed to telegraph that it would be impossible for the King to give contingent guarantees. The King 'much resented the implication' that in the event of a Liberal Government being returned he might fail to act constitutionally; and he considered that Mr Asquith was seeking to use his name to secure a Liberal victory. On 15 November the Cabinet gave the following advice in a formal minute:

> An immediate dissolution of Parliament – as soon as the necessary parts of the Budget, the provision of old age pensions, and one or two other matters have been disposed of. The House of Lords to have the opportunity, if they demand it, at the same time, but not so as to postpone the date of the dissolution, to discuss the Government Resolution. HM ministers cannot, however, take the responsibility of advising a dissolution unless they may understand that in the event of the policy of the Government being approved by an adequate majority in the new House of Commons, HM will

---

11 *Cabinet Government*, 3rd edn (1959), p394, quoted in R Brazier, *Constitutional Texts* (1990), p437.

be ready to exercise his constitutional powers (which may involve the prerogative of creating peers) if needed to secure that effect shall he given to the decision of the country.

HM ministers are fully alive to the importance of keeping the name of the King out of the sphere of party and electoral controversy. They take upon themselves, as is their duty, the entire and exclusive responsibility for the policy which they will place before the electorate. HM will doubtless agree that it would be inadvisable in the interest of the State that any communication of the intentions of the Crown should be made public unless and until the actual occasion should arise.

Mr Asquith and Lord Crewe (as leader of the House of Lords) saw the King on the following day. The King, after much discussion, 'agreed most reluctantly to give the Cabinet a secret understanding that, in the event of the Government being returned with a majority at the general election, I should use my prerogative to make peers if asked for. I disliked having to do this very much, but agreed that this was the only alternative to the Cabinet resigning, which at this moment would be disastrous.'

[Jennings, *Cabinet Goverment*, pp440-1.]

Note

For the powers of the monarch in relation to Parliament and the Prime Minister see further Part I, Chapter 2 on Constitutional Conventions.

CONTROL OF THE PREROGATIVE BY THE COURTS

Two key questions clearly arise here. First, will the courts be prepared to make a finding as to whether the prerogative claimed actually exists in law; secondly, will they be prepared to adjudge whether an admittedly existent power was properly exercised? The courts have clearly answered the first question in the affirmative. Furthermore, they are reluctant to allow new prerogatives to be created although they may allow a recognised prerogative to broaden in adapting itself to new situations. In *BBC v Johns* [1964] 1 All ER 923 the BBC claimed that a new prerogative had come into existence; in response Diplock LJ said 'It is 350 years and a civil war too late for the Queen's courts to broaden the prerogative. The limits within which the executive Government may impose obligations or restraints on the citizens of the United Kingdom without any statutory authority are now well settled and incapable of extension' (at 941). However, Lord Diplock's statement must be treated with some caution: in *Malone v Metropolitan Police Commissioner* [1979] Ch 344 the assertion that a prerogative power existed to authorise telephone tapping was based on the argument that no new power was being created although an old one was being extended to a new situation. It could be argued that the boundary between creating a new power and adapting an old one is not always clear, and that *Malone's* case is an example of an instance in which it is arguable that a new power was being claimed since it was very doubtful whether a prerogative power to intercept communications between citizens had ever existed.

It appears that in other areas the courts may approach the question of whether a prerogative to do a certain act exists not by considering whether it is authorised by some clearly defined and specific aspect of the prerogative but rather by first accepting the presence of a rather expansive and broadly defined general prerogative power and then finding that the specific act in question falls within that broad power:

Secretary of State for the Home Department, ex p Northumbria Police Authority [1988] 2 WLR 590, 609–10

Mr Keene referred us to *Chitty's Prerogatives of the Crown* (1820) for the purposes of demonstrating that there was then no recognisable 'prerogative to provide or equip a police force.' With respect to Mr Keene, in my judgment this argument begs the question. One is not seeking a prerogative right to do this. The prerogative power is to do all that is reasonably necessary to keep the Queen's peace. This involves the commissioning of justices of the peace, constables and the like. The author clearly identifies the prerogative powers inherent in the Crown in relation to the duty placed on the Sovereign to protect his dominions and subjects ...

After considering the principle and transcendent prerogatives with respect to foreign states and affairs, as supreme head of the church as the fountain of justice the author turns to the question of the protection of the realm in these terms, at p71:

> The duties arising from the relation of sovereign and subject are reciprocal. Protection, that is, the security and governance of his dominions according to law, is the duty of the sovereign; and allegiance and subjection, with reference to the same criterion, the constitution and laws of the country, form, in return, the duty of the governed, as will be more fully noticed hereafter. We have already partially mentioned this duty of the sovereign, and have observed that the prerogatives are vested in him for the benefit of his subjects, and that His Majesty is under, and not above, the laws.

The up-to-date position is summarised in *Halsbury's Laws of England* (4th ed, 1981), vol 36, p200, para 320:

> General functions of constables. The primary function of the constable remains, as in the 17th century, the preservation of the Queen's peace. From this general function stems a number of particular duties additional to those conferred by statute and including those mentioned hereafter. The first duty of a constable is always to prevent the commission of a crime. If a constable reasonably apprehends that the action of any person may result in a breach of the peace it is his duty to prevent that action. It is his general duty to protect life and property. The general function of controlling traffic on the roads is derived from this duty.

... In my judgment, the prerogative powers to take all reasonable steps to preserve the Queen's peace ... include the supply of equipment to police forces which is reasonably required for the more efficient discharge of their duties.

Notes

1 It is clear, that where a statute expressly preserves an immunity of the Crown or the exercise of a prerogative power, the courts will have to determine the scope of the power or immunity in question. Section 28(1) of the Crown Proceedings Act 1947, which provides that the Court can make an order for discovery of documents against the Crown and require the Crown to answer interrogatories, is qualified by s28(2) which preserves Crown privilege to withhold documents on the grounds of public interest in a variety of cases. It was therefore thought in 1947 and for some time afterwards, that s28(2) created important qualifications arising from the

prerogative: it did not prevent the withholding of documents or refusal to answer questions on the ground that disclosures would be injurious to the public interest. Certain cases demonstrate the development there has been in determining the scope of this privilege.

2   In *Duncan v Camell Laird & Co* [1942] 1 KB 640 the House of Lords held that documents otherwise relevant to judicial proceedings are not to be produced if the public interest requires that they be withheld. Crown privilege as formulated here was an exclusionary rule of evidence based on public interest and the minister was deemed the sole judge of what that constituted. In *Ellis v Home Office* [1953] 2 QB 135, a prisoner on remand, who was severely injured by a mentally disturbed prisoner in the prison hospital, sued the Crown for negligence. Privilege was claimed to prevent the disclosure of medical reports on his assailant and so the action had to fail. However, in *Conway v Rimmer* [1968] 1 All ER 874 a police constable was prosecuted for theft. The charge was dismissed but he was dismissed from the police force. He brought an action for malicious prosecution against his former superintendent but the Home Office objected to the disclosure of reports relevant to the case. The House of Lords in a landmark decision overruled the minister's claim of Crown privilege and ordered disclosure. This substituted judicial discretion for executive discretion regarding disclosure of documents.

3   As to our second question, the traditional view was that the *exercise* of prerogative power was not subject to review, as Colin Munro indicates.

Colin Munro, *Studies in Constitutional Law* (1987), p175

From cases such as *Darnel's Case* [(1627) 3 St Tr 1] (where the king's warrant for detention of a prisoner, although giving no reasons, was accepted as conclusive) and the *Case of Ship Money* [(1637) 3 St Tr 826] (when the king's judgment as to the existence of an emergency was held to be unchallengeable), was derived a view that courts lacked jurisdiction to review the manner of exercise of prerogative powers, or the adequacy of the grounds upon which they had been exercised.

This view survived the Revolution, and found judicial acceptance long afterwards. In *Allen* [(1862) 1 B & S 850, 121 ER 929], it was argued that the Attorney General had entered a *nolle prosequi* irregularly because he had failed to give the prosecutor and the accused the opportunity to state their views. The court was not interested. 'The power ... is entrusted to the Attorney General who is the great law officer of the Crown', said Blackburn J, 'and whether he is right or wrong this court cannot interfere' [(1862) 121 ER 929 at 932]. In *Engelke v Musmann* [[1928] AC 433, HL], the House of Lords, accepting that the recognition of envoys of foreign states was a matter for the Crown, ruled that a ministerial certificate as to the entitlement of an individual to claim diplomatic privilege was conclusive. In *Chandler v DPP* [[1964] AC 763, [1962] 3 All ER 142, HL], supporters of the Campaign for Nuclear Disarmament had been convicted of conspiracy to commit a breach of section 1 of the Official Secrets Act 1911 by entering a prohibited place 'for any purpose prejudicial to the safety or interests of the state'. They had undoubtedly plotted to enter Wethersfield air base in rural Essex and immobilise it by sitting down on the runways. But was their purpose prejudicial to the interests of the state? The trial judge had not allowed them to call evidence to argue otherwise, and the House of Lords held that this was right. Lord Reid said:

It is ... clear that the disposition and armament of the armed forces are and for centuries have been within the exclusive discretion of the Crown and that no one can seek a legal remedy on the ground that such discretion has been wrongfully exercised (at 791).

Notes

1   In some areas, this traditional reluctance to subject the prerogative to scrutiny has been maintained: the courts will continue to accept as conclusive Foreign Office certificates in various areas including the entitlement of individuals to claim diplomatic immunity, the recognition of foreign states or governments or the existence of a state of war: *Bottrill, ex p Kuechenmeister* [1947] KB 41.

2   Acts under the prerogative which are termed acts of state are non-justiciable. The expression 'act of state' has no precise definition but it is generally used to describe 'an act done by the Crown as a matter of policy in relation to another state or to an individual who is not within the allegiance to the Crown'.[12] Acts of state may tend to be performed outside Her Majesty's dominions but this factor is not a definitional element of the concept as it includes actions within the dominions such as the detention of an enemy alien in wartime as in *Vine Street Police Station Superintendent, ex p Liebmann* [1916] 1 KB 168. Unfortunately the only recent authority, *AG v Nissan* (1970),[13] has not cleared up uncertainty as to the meaning of the concept; De Smith called it 'a disaster for students of the law'. It has been argued that the flexibility of this concept has contributed to concern that it is incompatible with the Rule of Law.

3   Acts of state appear to fall into two groups. First, they may be acts in relation to foreign states such as the declaration of war (as in *Lynch* (1903))[14] or the annexation of territory. Secondly, in certain classes of case an act of sovereign power relating to an individual may be claimed to be an act of state in order to prevent the aggrieved person claiming redress for damage done. The classes include aliens outside or inside British territory. A friendly alien within Her Majesty's dominions is entitled to protection so that act of state cannot be used as a defence to a claim brought in respect of a tortious act done to him on the authority of the Crown: *Johnstone v Pedlar* (1921).[15]

In *Bottrill, ex p Kuechenmeister* (1947)[16] a German national was interned during the war; his application for a writ of *habeas corpus* failed as such detention was held to constitute an act of state. In *Buron v Denman* (1848)[17] an act of state was successfully advanced as a defence to an action in tort brought by an enemy alien on the ground that the action was subsequently ratified by the Crown. *Dicta* in *Nissan* even suggest that injury directly inflicted on British subjects may be justified under the plea of act of state. Clearly the above examples merely indicate situations in which the courts

---

12   O Hood Phillips, *Constitutional and Administrative Law*, 7th edn (1987), p278.
13   AC 179.
14   1 KB 444.
15   2 AC 262.
16   KB 41.
17   2 Ex 167.

will allow an 'act of state' to be asserted. It is unlikely that a precise definition of the concept will emerge from case law due to an executive-minded reluctance on the part of members of the judiciary to attempt it; Lord Pearson in *Nissan* said: 'it is necessary to consider what is meant by the expression 'act of state', even if it is not expedient to attempt a definition'.

4   Actions of this nature may appear to conflict with the Rule of Law, in particular, its insistence that the law, particularly that part of it affecting individual liberty, should be reasonably certain, and that where the law confers wide discretionary powers there should be adequate safeguards against their abuse. Uncertainty as to the scope of acts of state and as to the persons to whom they apply means that citizens cannot know beforehand what their rights are. For example, *dicta* in *Nissan* suggest, as noted above, that in some circumstances direct injury inflicted on British citizens may be justified under the plea of act of state. Only Lord Reid rejected this view completely. It might further be pointed out in this context that the Crown servant perpetrating the purported act of state may not know at the time whether it can be so classified because it may not have been authorised by the Crown. Acts of state can be retrospectively validated; the Captain in *Buron v Denman* who captured a Spanish ship did not know with certainty that he was acting under the defence of act of state until the action was subsequently ratified.

5   Furthermore, although it appears that 'act of state' is not in general available as a defence to a tortious action done to a British citizen with the authority of the Crown either outside or inside Her Majesty's dominions (*Walker v Baird* (1892)),[18] it is unclear what is meant in this context by the term 'British citizen'. In *Nissan*, a number of definitions were put forward. As Hood Phillips notes (*op cit*, p283), Lord Morris 'wondered' whether the term meant 'those owing allegiance to the Crown'. Lord Pearson was 'uncertain' as to whether the term included all those within the wide definition contained in s1 of the British Nationality Act 1948. Thus the concept of an 'act of state' infringes the principle that the law should be certain. As Lord Diplock said in *Merkur Island Shipping Corpn v Laughton* (1983),[19] 'Absence of clarity is destructive of the Rule of Law'.

6   The imprecise nature of acts of state may suggest that arbitrary power is being exercised: in a particular instance there may be uncertainty as to whether authority allows an action to be classified as an act of state. Clearly the concept of the Rule of Law does not mean that servants of the Crown must always point to lawful authority for their actions; if so the Crown would be placed in a disadvantageous position in comparison with citizens in general which would infringe the principle of equality before the law. A comparison between *Malone v Metropolitan Police Commissioner* (1979)[20] and *Entick v Carrington* (1765)[21] may be thought to illustrate the point. In *Malone* no tort was committed because there is no tort of invasion of privacy; therefore as it is accepted that in England everything which is not forbidden

---

18   AC 491 (PC).
19   2 AC 570.
20   Ch 344.
21   19 St Tr 1029.

is permitted, the state could claim that it did not need specific lawful authority to tap telephones. In contrast, in *Entick*, the state needed lawful authority which it lacked (due to the general nature of the search warrant) in order to perpetrate an otherwise tortious action (trespass). Under the principle from *Entick*, when a Crown servant does an action which, without lawful authority, would be criminal or tortious, he or she should be able to point to such authority which should clearly exist. If its existence is in doubt as it may be due to the nebulous nature of the concept of 'act of state', arbitrary action on the part of Crown servants is not precluded.

7   The principle of equality before the law is infringed because, unlike the ordinary citizen, the Crown may not have to pay for what it takes. This may even be the case in respect of the seizure of British-owned property if such seizure was connected with an act of state (*Secretary of State for India v Kamachee Boye Sahaba* (1859))[22] although it is probable that today a court would not accept such argument. Although acts of state appear to represent an exercise of the prerogative they are exempt from the general principle, deriving from *Burmah Oil Co v Lord Advocate* (1965),[23] that compensation is payable in respect of actions under the prerogative which cause damage.

8   A further conflict between act of state and the Rule of Law arises due to the lack of safeguards which might act as a check on the use of these powers of uncertain scope. Acts of state are non justiciable. In *Salaman v Secretary of State for India* (1906)[24] it was held that 'an act of state is essentially an act of sovereign power and hence cannot be challenged, controlled or interfered with by municipal courts'. This does not mean that a mere assertion of the defence will suffice to oust the jurisdiction of the courts. The Crown must specifically plead 'act of state' and the court can then consider whether the particular action does fall within that concept. This was precisely the issue which fell to be determined in *Nissan*; unfortunately the judgments in that case as already indicated were not very helpful for those who find a precise definition of the concept desirable.

Nissan, a citizen of the UK and colonies, was a lessee of a hotel in Cyprus which was requisitioned and used by British troops engaged in a peace-keeping operation. Nissan brought an action against the Crown in England claiming that he was entitled to compensation for damage to the contents of the hotel and destruction of stores. The Crown argued that because the actions of the troops were acts of state, no compensation was payable. The case came before the House of Lords on the preliminary question whether this assertion was correct. It was determined that although the agreement of the British Government with the Cyprus Government to send peacekeeping forces was almost certainly an act of state, not all actions occurring as a result of that agreement could be classified as acts of state. The decision suggests, then, that only acts which are part of or necessarily incidental to high level policy decisions will be properly classifiable as acts of state.

---

22   13 Moo PC 22.

23   AC 75.

24   1 KB 613.

Insofar as this decision can be said to have narrowed down the concept of an act of state it is to be welcomed as cutting down the area of non-justiciable action. However, once it has been determined that an action *is* an act of state it will be impossible to review it in the courts. The procedure adopted in carrying it out will be entirely the concern of the Crown. Acts of state are therefore distinct from some other exercises of the prerogative.

9   In relation to prerogative powers which are not classifiable as acts of state, before the decision in the *GCHQ* case (below), the most important revision of the non-reviewability principle was made by Lord Denning in the following case.

Laker Airways Ltd v Department of Trade [1977] QB 643, 705

Lord Denning: ... The prerogative is a discretionary power exercisable by the executive Government for the public good, in certain spheres of governmental activity for which the law has made no provision, such as the war prerogative (of requisitioning property for the defence of the realm), or the treaty prerogative (of making treaties with foreign powers). The law does not interfere with the proper exercise of the discretion by the executive in those situations: but it can set limits by defining the bounds of the activity: and it can intervene if the discretion is exercised improperly or mistakenly. That is a fundamental principle of our constitution. It derives from two of the most respected of our authorities. In 1611 when the King, as the executive Government, sought to govern by making proclamations, Sir Edward Coke declared that: 'the King hath no prerogative, but that which the law of the land allows him': see the *Proclamations Case* (1611) 12 Co Rep 74, 76. In 1765 Sir William Blackstone added his authority, *Commentaries*, vol I, p252: 'For prerogative consisting (as Mr Locke has well defined it) in the discretionary power of acting for the public good, where the positive laws are silent, if that discretionary power be abused to the public detriment, such prerogative is exerted in an unconstitutional manner'.

Question

This *dictum* was cited with approval by Purchas LJ in *Secretary of State for the Home Department, ex p Northumbria Police Authority* (see above) at p603. His comment was, 'The question whether once the power exists the courts will interfere with its exercise is still open'. If this is correct, should not Purchas LJ have expressly overruled at least part of what Lord Denning said?

Note

Did GCHQ leave this question open? In the case, the House of Lords had to consider a challenge to an Order in Council made by the Prime Minister which prevented staff at GCHQ belonging to national trade unions. Six members of staff and the union involved applied for judicial review of the Prime Minister's instruction on the ground that she had been under a duty to act fairly by consulting those concerned before issuing it. It had first to be determined whether the decision was open to judicial review. In general a person affected by a decision concerning public law matters made under statutory powers may challenge it by way of judicial review.

CCSU v Minister for Civil Service [1985] AC 374, 417–8, HL

Lord Roskill: ... In short the orthodox view was ... that the remedy for abuse of the prerogative lay in the political and not in the judicial field. But fascinating as it is to explore this mainstream of our legal history, to do so in connection with the present appeal has an air of unreality. To speak today of the acts of the sovereign as 'irresistible and absolute' when modern constitutional convention requires that all such acts are done by the sovereign on the advice of and will be carried out by the sovereign's ministers currently in power is surely to hamper the continual development of our administrative law by harking back to what Lord Atkin once called, albeit in a different context, the clanking of mediaeval chains of the ghosts of the past: see *United Australia Ltd v Barclays Bank Ltd* [1941] AC 1, 29. It is, I hope, not out of place in this connection to quote a letter written in 1896 by the great legal historian FW Maitland to Dicey himself: 'The only direct utility of legal history (I say nothing of its thrilling interest) lies in the lesson that each generation has an enormous power of shaping its own law': see Richard A Cosgrove, *The Rule of Law: Albert Venn Dicey, Victorian Jurist* (1980), p177. Maitland was in so stating a greater prophet than even he could have foreseen for it is our legal history which has enabled the present generation to shape the development of our administrative law by building upon but unhampered by our legal history.

My Lords, the right of the executive to do a lawful act affecting the rights of the citizen, whether adversely or beneficially, is founded upon the giving to the executive of a power enabling it to do that act. The giving of such a power usually carries with it legal sanctions to enable that power if necessary to be enforced by the courts. In most cases that power is derived from statute though in some cases, as indeed in the present case, it may still be derived from the prerogative. ... If the executive in pursuance of the statutory power does an act affecting the rights of the citizen, it is beyond question that in principle the manner of the exercise of that power may today be challenged on one or more of the three grounds which I have mentioned earlier in this speech. If the executive instead of acting under a statutory power acts under a prerogative power and in particular a prerogative power delegated to the respondent under article 4 of the Order in Council of 1982, so as to affect the rights of the citizen, I am unable to see, subject to what I shall say later, that there is any logical reason why the fact that the source of the power is the prerogative and not statute should today deprive the citizen of that right of challenge to the manner of its exercise which he would possess were the source of the power statutory.

In either case the act in question is the act of the executive. To talk of that act as the act of the sovereign savours of the archaism of past centuries.

But I do not think that that right of challenge can be unqualified. It must, I think, depend upon the subject matter of the prerogative power which is exercised. Many examples were given during the argument of prerogative powers which as at present advised I do not think could properly be made the subject of judicial review. Prerogative powers such as those relating to the making of treaties, the defence of the realm, the prerogative of mercy, the grant of honours, the dissolution of Parliament and the appointment of ministers as well as others are not, I think, susceptible to judicial review because their nature and subject matter are such as not to be amenable to the judicial process. The courts are not the place wherein to determine whether a treaty should be concluded or the armed forces disposed in a particular manner or Parliament dissolved on one date rather than another.

In my view the exercise of the prerogative which enabled the oral instructions of 22 December 1983 to be given does not by reason of its subject matter fall within what for want of a better phrase I would call the 'excluded categories' some of which I have just mentioned. It follows that in principle I can see no reason why those instructions should not be the subject of judicial review. ...

I find considerable support for the conclusion I have reached in the decision of the Divisional Court (Lord Parker CJ, Diplock LJ (as my noble and learned friend then was) and Ashworth J in *Criminal Injuries Compensation Board, ex p Lain* (1967) 2 QB 864, the judgments in which may without exaggeration be described as a landmark in the development of this branch of the law.

Notes

1   The House of Lords went on to find that the applicants had had a legitimate expectation that they would be consulted, and that the Prime Minister had, *prima facie* 'acted unfairly'[25] in failing so to consult, but that reasons of national security justified the failure. McEldowney and McAuslan note that the national security ground was not advanced by the Prime Minister 'until she had lost at first instance'.[26]

2   The principle affirmed in the *GCHQ* case was followed in *Secretary of State for Home Affairs, ex p Ruddock* (1987) 2 All ER 518. CND brought a High Court action challenging the decision to tap phones of its members on the ground that the Government had aroused a legitimate expectation through published statements that it would not use tapping for party political purposes. The action failed but did establish the principle that the courts were entitled to review unfair actions by the Government arising from failure to live up to legitimate expectations created in this way. The judge, Mr Justice Taylor, also stated that the jurisdiction of the courts to look into such a complaint against a minister should not be totally ousted, rejecting the argument put forward on behalf of the Crown that the Court should not entertain the action because to do so would be detrimental to national security.

3   *Secretary of State for Foreign and Commonwealth affairs, ex p Everett* (1989)[27] also showed a willingness to review the exercise of prerogative powers which related this time to the Secretary of State's power to issue passports. Passports are issued by the Passport Office, a department of the Home Office, under the royal prerogative. A passport was defined in *Brailsford* (1905)[28] as a 'document issued in the name of the Sovereign ... to a named individual ... to be used for that individual's protection as a British subject in foreign countries.' The Home Secretary can therefore exercise a discretion to withhold a passport where a person wishes to travel abroad to engage in activities which are politically deplored although legal. Because these powers arise under the royal prerogative it was thought that they would not be open to review until the ruling in *Council for Civil Service Unions v Minister for the Civil Service* (the *GCHQ* case) (1984).[29] The Court of Appeal held that review was available of a refusal to issue a passport to a British citizen living in Spain. Thus refusal or withdrawals of passports must be made fairly and reasonably although the merits of such decisions cannot be considered.

---

25   *Per* Lord Scarman at p949.
26   *Op cit*, p31.
27   QB 811.
28   2 KB 730, 745.
29   3 All ER 935.

4 In spite of this welcome recognition by the courts that the mere fact that a power can be labelled 'prerogative' does not immediately oust their jurisdiction to consider the legality of its exercise, the degree of judicial control in this area should not be exaggerated. The *Malone* case[30] demonstrates a willingness on the part of the courts to recognise the existence of prerogative powers of doubtful origin, whilst as Birkinshaw notes, '... it is ironic to realise that the exercise of some of the most important prerogatives is devoid of any control save political rebellion or insurrection – declaration of war for instance or the appointment of a Prime Minister'.[31] Munro, commenting on the *GCHQ* decision, and the *obiter* remarks made in it about excluded categories of prerogative powers (above), concludes that it seems, 'the propriety of most exercises of prerogative power will still continue to be unsusceptible to challenge in the courts' and that although the case is 'Interesting in terms of principle, it would be a mistake to overrate its practical consequences.'[32] His view is perhaps a little pessimistic, and was made without the benefit of studying the recent decision in *Ministry of Defence, ex p Smith and others* (1995)[33] The case concerned a challenge to the ban on homosexuals serving in the armed forces, a policy which it was found was maintained by the prerogative. It was argued for the Ministry of Defence that (*inter alia*) the case was 'concerned with the exercise of a prerogative power in an area – the defence of the realm – recognised by the courts to be unsuitable for judicial review' (at p441). This contention was directly addressed by the court of first instance, as follows.

Ministry of Defence, ex p Smith and others [1995] 4 All ER 427, 445, 446.

Simon Brown LJ: In so far as Mr Richards [for the MOD] relies upon this being an irrationality challenge to the exercise of the prerogative – which I am satisfied it is, the broad statutory framework being to my mind immaterial in identifying the true source of this power – Mr Pannick [for the applicants] points to a series of cases since *CCSU* in which, despite Lord Diplock's doubts, the courts have accepted the reviewability on *Wednesbury* grounds of decisions taken in the exercise of prerogative power: see in particular *Secretary of State for Foreign and Commonwealth Affairs, ex p Everett* [1989] 1 All ER 655, [1989] QB 811 (a Court of Appeal decision concerning passports), *Secretary of State for the Home Dept, ex p Bentley* [1993] 4 All ER 442, [1994] QB 349 (a decision of the Divisional Court with regard to the prerogative of mercy), and *Criminal Injuries Compensation Board, ex p P* (1995) 1 All ER 870, [1995] 1 WLR 845 (where the Court of Appeal by a majority found the CICB scheme reviewable even though it involved the distribution of 'bounty' on behalf of the Crown). True, only in *Bentley* did the applicant succeed, and even then only on a narrow issue concerning the scope of the prerogative. But it can no longer be suggested that the exercise of prerogative power is on that ground alone outside the court's supervisory jurisdiction.

As to Mr Richards' reliance on Parliament's examination and implicit approval of the existing policy, Mr Pannick reminds us that the executive decision under challenge in *Brind* had itself been debated in both Houses of Parliament, a

---

30 *Malone v Metropolitan Police Commissioners* (1979) Ch 344.
31 'Decision-Making and its Control' in McEldowney and McAuslan, *op cit*, p152.
32 Munro, *op cit*, p182.
33 4 All ER 427, QBD; (1996) 1 All ER 257, CA.

consideration that did not deflect the House of Lords from considering the competing arguments on irrationality.

Brind is also the decision upon which Mr Pannick most heavily relies in response to Mr Richards' submissions on the particular nature of the policy here sought to be impugned – a military judgment upon the requirements of the armed services and thus a decision affecting the defence of the realm. *Brind* too, Mr Pannick stresses, involved policy considerations as to the way in which the United Kingdom should respond to the terrorist threat in Northern Ireland – a highly sensitive political issue affecting the security of the state. *Brind*, moreover, as many of the speeches emphasised, involved only the most limited interference with freedom of speech (a restriction ultimately found insufficient even to get past the admissibility threshold at Strasbourg); contrast the substantial interference with the right of privacy in the present case.

Mr Pannick refers us also to the Divisional Court's judgment in *Army Board of the Defence Council, ex p Anderson* [1991] 3 All ER 375, [1992] QB 169 in which a decision of the Secretary of State for Defence was held reviewable in relation to a complaint of racial discrimination in the army, albeit on the ground of unfair procedure and not irrationality.

It is time to state my conclusions on these issues.

(1) I have no hesitation in holding this challenge justiciable. To my mind only the rarest cases will today be ruled strictly beyond the court's purview – only cases involving national security properly so-called and where in addition the courts really do lack the expertise or material to form a judgment on the point at issue. This case does not fall into that category. True, it touches on the defence of the realm but it does not involve determining 'whether ... the armed forces [should be] disposed of in a particular manner' (which Lord Roskill in *CCSU* thought plainly unreviewable – as indeed had been held in *China Navigation Co Ltd v A-G* [1932] 2 KB 197, [1932] All ER Rep 626). No operational considerations are involved in this policy. Now, indeed, that the 'security implications' have disappeared, there appears little about it which the courts are not perfectly well qualified to judge for themselves.

Note

Having found the issue justiciable, the court went on to find that the policy of excluding homosexuals could not be held to be *Wednesbury* unreasonable. Clearly, the last part of the judge's remarks were *obiter*; when the Court of Appeal heard the appeal of the servicemen and women it made no such general remarks about the availability of review against the prerogative but nor did they disapprove of Smith Brown LJ's comments, and indeed appeared to take it for granted that the issue was justiciable. Clearly, therefore, *ex p Smith* indicates that the unreviewable areas of the prerogative were perhaps smaller than had been previously thought, whilst Simon Brown LJ's *dicta* that only 'the rarest cases' will be non-justiciable is in stark contrast to Munro's prediction that 'most' exercises of prerogative will be unreviewable. In any event, is the existence of the prerogative itself satisfactory? If not, what is to be done?

Colin Munro, *Studies in Constitutional Law* (1987), p183–4

A couple of examples will serve to show the desirability of change. Consider first the prerogative power of dissolving Parliament. A statute puts the maximum duration at five years, but within that period a Parliament may be dissolved, and a general election held, at any time. The prerogative, nominally exercised by the

Crown, is in reality exercised on the Prime Minister's advice, at least in the ordinary course of events. This effectively enables the Prime Minister to choose the date of the next general election, and it is notorious that the choice is influenced not by considerations of the public interest but by calculations of party advantage. That is surely an abuse of power, but it is a power the exercise of which cannot be effectively challenged. It is one of the subjects, as noted earlier, on which Governments simply refuse to submit themselves to parliamentary questioning, and it is, according to Lord Roskill's guidance, unamenable to challenge in the courts. The force of any public criticisms which opposition parties might tender is undercut by their own past record. Only legislation could remove the opportunity for abuse, for example by providing for a fixed term, although legislation would require a Government sufficiently disinterested to embark on it.

Then consider the surviving prerogative immunity, that the Crown is not bound by statutes, unless it is so provided. This might not have mattered so much in the seventeenth century, but in the twentieth century the Government is a very large employer, an important landowner, an owner of factories, prisons, and hospitals, a manufacturer, a builder, a landlord, and much more besides. Even so, legislation which imposes requirements or controls or penalties in the interests of health, hygiene, or safety, or in protection of employees, consumers or tenants, or for the sake of the environment, is presumed not to apply to the Government unless there is a clear indication to the contrary. In fact, important pieces of legislation are sometimes made applicable to the Government, and sometimes not. Unfair dismissal legislation applies to the Government, but Government employees do nor enjoy the protection provided by the Contracts of Employment Act 1972. The Occupiers' Liability Act 1957 applies, but the Health and Safety at Work etc. Act 1974 does not. The Town and Country Planning Act 1971 does not, in spite of the significance for the environment of some Government activities. It is difficult to justify the exemption of the Government from any of these laws, and the removal of the immunity by statute would be desirable, as it would throw the onus of proof on those who argue for special treatment. The issue came to public notice in 1986, when a food poisoning outbreak at the Stanley Royal Hospital in Wakefield resulted in 19 deaths, but the immunity from the food hygiene laws attaching to NHS hospitals prevented any prosecutions. The Government responded to criticisms by agreeing to make hospitals subject to the hygiene laws, not by sweeping away the immunity altogether.

If some prerogatives are ripe for abolition, there are others which must either remain or be replaced. There must be some legal powers for the regulation of the Civil Service, the control of the armed forces, and the conduct of foreign policy. But there would be several advantages in replacing the existing prerogatives with statutory powers, such as the Government more usually acts under. If that were done, the purposes and extent of the powers could be clearly set out, whereas much of the law concerning the prerogative is obscure and derived from ancient precedents. Supervision of the exercise of the powers could be more efficiently carried out in Parliament and by the courts. The opportunity for members of Parliament to consider and debate the appropriate limits of such powers would also provide an occasion for other arrangements to be mooted. It is not self-evident, for example, that the Government should be involved in the appointment of archbishops and bishops in the Church of England; nor is it obvious that the honours system is best, or most appropriately, administered by the Government. These last may be thought relatively minor issues. What is more important is that behind the phrase 'Royal Prerogative' lie hidden some issues of great constitutional importance, which are insufficiently recognised.

Question

Are there any arguments *against* replacing prerogative powers with statutory provisions?

CHAPTER 2

THE CENTRAL EXECUTIVE: STRUCTURES AND ACCOUNTABILITY

INTRODUCTION

This chapter does not attempt a description of the everyday workings of the institutions which make up the central executive, for that would amount to a description of a system of government, rather than an analysis of the constitution. Insofar as a distinction can be maintained,[1] a work on the constitution should be looking for a normative framework within which government is supposed to be carried on; simply describing the practice of government *per se* is not therefore the aim. What we are looking for are informing and pervasive ideas and conventions which purport to regulate Government activity according to an idea of constitutionalism.[2] Since the core of the notion of constitutionalism is the idea of limited Government, of checks on Government power, and on the accountability of Government, these themes determine the topics considered here. Attention will focus therefore on two main areas; first, the increased concentration of power both into central Government generally and into a few hands within Government; and secondly, a cluster of concepts about responsibility and accountability: the responsibility of ministers for their departments, their responsibility to be open with Parliament and not to mislead it; the responsibilities of civil servants to ministers and possibly to Parliament. The impact on traditional notions of accountability of the 'Next Steps' reforms will be considered in depth; the whole topic of accountability will be informed by the evidence thrown up by the Scott Inquiry and its conclusions which will be given extensive coverage.

THE PRIME MINISTER AND THE CABINET

Three main issues will be discussed here. First, the debate as to the actual importance of the Cabinet in the system of government; second, and clearly connected to the first matter, the ways in which the Prime Minister can (a) control and manipulate, and (b) effectively bypass Cabinet; third, the relevance of collective responsibility to these first two issues. We start with a brief outline of the position of the Cabinet and the manner of the appointment of a Prime Minister.

Harry Calvert, *An Introduction to British Constitutional Law* (1986), pp146, 150–1, 155

> ... the Cabinet, as an institution, does not rest on parliamentary authority but rather on practice developed over the centuries. It is true that the existence of the Cabinet is now acknowledged in parliamentary legislation – the Parliamentary Commissioner Act 1967, for example, creates a privilege for Cabinet papers in

---

1   There is at present some debate as to what matters properly belong in a work on constitutional law; for a critical analysis of recent trends in this respect see FF Ridley, 'There is no British Constitution: A Dangerous Case of the Emperor's Clothes' (1988) 41 PA 340, esp pp342 *et seq*.

2   See Part I, Chapter 1.

connection with proceedings before the 'ombudsman' – but this no more puts the Cabinet on a statutory, legal, basis than does the Dogs Act create dogs.

Important consequences attend the fact that the composition, powers and procedures of the Cabinet are not fixed by law. ... It may meet more or less regularly; it may discharge business in plenary session or sit in committees. We are told that decisions are usually arrived at by consensus, but there is nothing to stop a vote being taken, or simply for the Prime Minister to divine the 'sense of the meeting' and proceed accordingly. ...

Calvert then goes on to consider the increased power of modern Prime Ministers, starting with the manner of their appointment.

Appointment of a Prime Minister

Legally, the position is simple. The monarch may, if he wishes, appoint any number of persons he likes to be 'Minister of the Crown' and may, if he wishes, appoint one of them to be his 'Prime' Minister. Acts of Parliament assume but do not require that there will be a 'Prime Minister'.

The efficient functioning of the constitution, however, does require that there should be a Prime Minister and, since any Government is heavily dependent upon Parliament, and particularly the House of Commons, especially for the authority to raise taxes, it follows that if a Prime Minister is to do the job properly, he must be a person who enjoys the confidence or support of a stable majority of the House of Commons. Under the modern party system, a party leader is that party's candidate for the office of Prime Minister and when, in a general election, the electorate returns to the House of Commons a majority of members of a particular party it in substance elects a Prime Minister. The words 'in substance' have been used because formally the choice remains that of the monarch but the constitutional role of the monarch in this regard is now accepted as being nothing more than formally appointing the person who commands a majority in the House of Commons, and in the usual situation above envisaged there will be no room for doubt on the matter. The electorate will have made it abundantly clear who should be appointed.

In exceptional situations, however, it may be less clear. Suppose:

... a Prime Minister resigns or dies in office and the majority party is divided as to who his successor shall be; or

although a particular party secures a majority in a general election, its leader is defeated.

Who is to be appointed?

For the monarch, the basic criterion remains the same. He must seek to ensure that he appoints a person who will enjoy the confidence of a majority of Members of the House of Commons. Usually, the monarch will be spared a controversial decision. All major political parties now have procedures for electing a leader and would, if circumstances compelled it, find ways of removing an old one and appointing a new. Once the leaders of the various factions are identified, then either one commands a majority, in which case, the problem disappears; or, if there is no majority, a wise monarch will await reliable information as to what has emerged as a result of the horsetrading and dealing which would inevitably attend the business of trying to form a coalition or, at least, a minority Government with the tacit support of a majority.

There is no 'proper' course for a monarch in such unusual circumstances, there is merely a prudent course. If the monarch made the 'wrong' choice, ie appointed a person who, in the event, could not command the support of a majority in the

House of Commons, that appointment would nevertheless remain valid although effective government would be impossible and crisis would result. The monarch would then have to consider a dissolution if advised or, if not, consider whether to dismiss the Prime Minister wrongly chosen and appoint another in his place, or to muddle on. Controversy would attend any chosen course of action and the stature of the monarch would be demeaned. In an extreme case, the existence of the monarchy itself would be threatened.

These considerations effectively mean that in exceptional cases, the monarch's role might well go beyond simply doing what he is told. There can be room for substantial individual judgment by a monarch and if caution does not attend its exercise, crisis with unpredictable consequences may result.

Notes

1   See further on the monarch's powers in relation to the choice of a Prime Minister Part I, Chapter 3.

2   Bagehot, writing in 1867, called the Cabinet 'the most powerful body in the nation' (*The English Constitution* (1963 edn)) and considered that collective responsibility meant that every member of the Cabinet had the right to take part in Cabinet discussion but was bound by the decision eventually reached. In contrast John Mackintosh in *The British Cabinet* (1977) wrote: 'the principal policies of a government may not be and often are not originated in Cabinet'.

3   A number of writers, including Richard Crossman, have considered that Cabinet government has shown signs of developing into Prime Ministerial government and that therefore collective decision-making has suffered (see for example his *Diaries of a Cabinet Minister* (1975)). Crossman argued that the power of the Prime Minister to sack Ministers, to determine the Cabinet agenda and the existence and membership of Cabinet committees meant that his or her control over the Cabinet was the most important force within it. Mrs Thatcher, Prime Minister between 1979 and 1990, is generally considered to have (at least temporarily) increased the power of the Prime Minister by using the available power to the full.

4   However, other commentators point out that in diluting and fragmenting the power of the Cabinet in this fashion it might be argued that Mrs Thatcher was merely taking further a process which had already begun. The use of gatherings other than Cabinet to make decisions – inner Cabinets, Cabinet committees, ministerial meetings – had been growing for the last 30 years and had arguably undermined the Cabinet as a decision-making body, though many considered this inevitable. In what follows, by discussing the three issues outlined at the start of this section,[3] we will attempt to reach some balanced conclusions on these matters and root out their significance in constitutional terms.

The changing role of the Cabinet

As Brazier notes, 'Meeting only once a week for a couple of hours ... and being composed entirely of Ministers with heavy departmental responsibilities, the Cabinet could not possibly now be the forum either for the close control of

---

3   The importance of Cabinet; Prime Ministerial control over it; collective responsibility.

activities of government or for the co-ordination of the departments of state'.[4] Neither, clearly does it have time to either formulate, approve or even discuss much policy. 'Since the Second World War all but a tiny proportion of decisions have been taken by individual ministers, by correspondence and by committees'.[5] These last have assumed an increasingly important role: much of the major policy-making work of Government which requires either the co-operation of more than one department or is so important that it requires wider discussion, has long been carried out through the Cabinet Committee system which in its formal guise 'has been in existence since the First World War, [compromising] some 30 to 40 standing committees ... and well over 100 *ad hoc* committees' which both settle points of detail and isolate fundamental question for decision by cabinet.[6] What has been the effect of the growth of this system on the Cabinet?

S James, 'The Cabinet System Since 1948: Fragmentation and Integration' (1994) 47(4) *Parliamentary Affairs* 613, 619–20

From 1945 until the arrival of Mrs Thatcher, Cabinet meetings followed a standard format: first came a standing item on parliamentary business, under which the Leaders of both Houses would detail business for the following week; then a report on overseas developments, in which the Foreign Secretary sketched out the dominant issues of the moment. The rest of the agenda consisted of items referred up by committees. Occasionally these came because, although the Committee supported the proposal unanimously, the issue was so important that it was felt Cabinet should look at the subject. But in most cases ministers had disagreed at committee and the chairman had allowed an appeal. Most of these appeals were straightforward arbitration exercises: the ministers who had argued the issue in committee would rehearse their cases, and in effect appeal to the judgement of their colleagues who had not been there and who were asked to screen the proposal, not from an expert point of view but for its good sense and public acceptability in a sort of political litmus test.

Although the Cabinet's court of appeal role gave it a say on some key decisions, the system had serious faults. The Cabinet became almost entirely reactive to the proposals of ministers and committees. There was little discussion of general political developments. There was no item of 'any other business' to allow discussion of other issues that might be worrying ministers. The Cabinet's role was essentially negative: it could block, amend or qualify proposals, but of itself did not initiate policy. It was a brake, not a dynamo. Furthermore, by the time an issue reached it, it had often gained irreversible momentum. Hailsham observed, after serving under Macmillan and Heath: 'The ground has usually carefully been prepared by discussion between civil servants, correspondence between ministers, in formal meetings, Cabinet committee meetings ... By the time the Cabinet is brought in as a whole, it may be that only one decision is possible even when, had it been consulted at the outset, the policy would have been unacceptable.'

---

4   Brazier, *Constitutional Practice*, 2nd edn (1994), p104.

5   S James, 'The Cabinet System Since 1948: Fragmentation and Integration' (1994) 47(4) PA 613, 619.

6   Brazier, 'Reducing the Power of the Prime Minister' (1991) 44(4) PA 453, 456.

Note

Some correctives will need to be made to this view below, but for now it is sufficient to note the Cabinet's relative lack of importance, except perhaps *in extremis*. What are the consequences of this for the exercise of power within Government?

Prime Ministerial control over Cabinet and Government

Two main issues are in play here: first, the Prime Minister's power of patronage; secondly, his control over the agenda and meeting of Cabinet and its committees – crudely speaking, over who discusses what and when.

Prime Ministerial Patronage

Whilst the Queen formally appoints all Ministers of the Crown, this power is of course exercised in practice by the Prime Minister who has the absolute power of appointment and dismissal of ministers.[7] The Prime Minister's freedom to choose who they want will be limited by the need to maintain some sort of balance in the Cabinet between different wings of the parties and to appease powerful personalities in it, but still the Prime Minister, and the Prime Minister alone makes this decision. Similarly, the Prime Minister may – subject to political constraints – get rid of any ministers they do not want at any time; they may do this in response to major mistakes made by that minister or simply because they find the views of the particular minister uncongenial. This is of course normally achieved through 're-shuffling' rather than outright dismissal, which is comparatively rare. The skill and judgment – and ruthlessness – of a Prime Minister in exercising this power is of key importance: Clement Atlee famously observed that a vital characteristic of any Prime Minister was the ability to be a good butcher.

The political constraints on this power are most marked in one area; as James remarks, 'This discretion [to dismiss or reshuffle] may be less when dealing with the most senior two or three members of the Cabinet who can more or less insist on one of the top jobs. For something like two-thirds of the post-war era, the Exchequer and the Foreign Officer have been held by party magnates who were effectively irremovable. Once someone has reached that level in the Cabinet, there are few other places to which they can be transferred'.[8]

Nevertheless, in spite of this exception (which is not absolute – both Mrs Thatcher and Mr Major managed to lose Chancellors from Government) the Prime Minister, if determined enough, can make quite extensive use of this power in order to achieve a Cabinet which reflects the Prime Minister's particular political outlook. Mrs Thatcher, as is well known, made particular use of this power; as James Prior notes, she came to power in 1979 with a Cabinet initially based on a balance between moderates and Thatcherites.

---

7   Note, though, that Prime Ministers will generally leave junior appointments to the minister at the head of the department concerned, through lack of knowledge if nothing else.

8   James, *op cit*, p625.

James Prior, *A Balance of Power* (1986), pp114–18

The power of a modern Prime Minister is awesome, particularly when it comes to the power of appointment and dismissal of ministers. But the Leader of any party in power will know that there has to be some sort of balance in a Cabinet, between right and left, youth and age, different backgrounds and so on.

The balance of the Cabinet looked better for our wing of the Party than I had dreamt possible. Looking round the table at our first Cabinet meeting, I saw that most of us had worked together in the Shadow Cabinet and had managed to restrain Margaret from pursuing her more extreme instincts.

The only major changes from the Shadow Cabinet were the introduction of Christopher Soames, Peter Walker, George Younger and Humphrey Atkins, who had been Chief Whip in Opposition and became Secretary of State for Northern Ireland following Airey Neave's assassination on the eve of the election campaign.

However, the composition of the economic team at the Treasury and the other economic Departments obviously showed [Thatcher] was going to have her own way as far as she possibly could. Margaret's main supporters at the outset in Cabinet were Geoffrey Howe, her Chancellor, Keith Joseph at Industry, John Nott at Trade, David Howell at Energy, Patrick Jenkin at Social Services, Angus Maude as Paymaster-General and John Biffen as Chief Secretary to the Treasury – not a very impressive bunch, and with little experience at the centre of Government. In addition, the three 'territorial' ministers, Nick Edwards at the Welsh Office, George Younger at the Scottish Office, and Humphrey Atkins at Northern Ireland, in the early days all generally supported the Prime Minister's line.

I was the only minister in the economic team with whom she was likely to have any difficulties. In some respects I was surprised to be offered Employment. After all, I had not had a very easy run with the Party in Opposition but I think Margaret felt to have changed me then would have signified too dramatic a shift in policy, and in any case what else was she likely to have offered me? The writing may already have been on the wall, but it did not seriously worry me to start with, because I assumed she would take things gradually, bearing in mind the experience of Ted's Government some five years before.

The dissenters in the Cabinet included Peter Carrington at the Foreign Office, myself at Employment, Peter Walker at Agriculture, Mark Carlisle at Education, Michael Heseltine at the Environment, Norman St John Stevas as Leader of the House, and Gilmour as Lord Privy Seal and Carrington's deputy.

This left a powerful foursome of Willie Whitelaw at the Home Office, Hailsham as Lord Chancellor, Francis Pym at Defence, and Christopher Soames as Leader of the Lords, who were less openly in one camp or the other. This foursome nearly always split equally, with the former two supporting the Prime Minister.

...

Margaret found for the first time that she really did have the levers of power in her hands, and my goodness she was going to exercise them. From day one in Cabinet she was very much more determined and gave a far stronger lead than she ever gave in opposition. The full extent of the power of a modern Prime Minister, who has the support of the Cabinet Office and Number Ten itself, is still not fully appreciated. Nothing really happens in Whitehall unless the central driving force of Number Ten or the Cabinet Office has approved it. In Opposition, Margaret's tendency to the extreme had been tempered by her need to carry colleagues with her and her need not frighten people into believing there would be chaos if she were elected. The belief then that Britain was ungovernable was never far below the surface. But, once in power, Margaret turned this belief to her advantage, for it could then be used to support her argument that strong government was what the country really needed. I am sure that by 1979 people were looking for new courage and a fresh determination in tackling Britain's problems. Margaret showed at once that she was tough and not likely to be shaken off once she had made up her mind. More than ever I think that has been her greatest asset.

Those of us in Cabinet who were out of sympathy with Margaret's views grossly under-estimated her absolute determination, along with Geoffrey and Keith, to push through the new right-wing policies.

Note

By 1981 Mrs Thatcher had shuffled five of the seven moderates out of her Cabinet, leaving her with one which reflected her own political convictions pretty closely.[9] But this cannot be put down merely to the excesses of an extreme ideology. As Brazier notes,[10] there were clear precedents for this type of behaviour: Neville Chamberlain in particular when he came to power in 1937 ruthlessly excluded from his Cabinet anyone who was opposed to his policy of appeasing the European dictators. This power that the Prime Minister has over the careers of ministers obviously gives the Prime Minister enormous influence over ministers, aware as they are that their continuing in office is, broadly speaking, dependant upon their retaining the Prime Minister's favour.

Prime Ministerial allocation of Government business

The Prime Minister can determine what the Cabinet discusses, both specifically, in that its written agenda for its weekly meetings is set by him or her, and more generally, through the manipulation of Cabinet committees. As well as using the official Cabinet committees, which have formal procedures and are serviced by the civil service in respect of minutes, agendas etc, the Prime Minister can make use of *ad hoc* informal groups of ministers, convened to discuss a particular issue. Meetings of these groups will not be attended by civil servants and they will often not have formal agendas or minutes. The use of the formal committees is, as noted above, well established, and, given that they allow proper discussion of the issue by a fair number of ministers, are generally seen as a necessary and reasonable way of doing business. Thus, as a former minister recalls, when an issue already discussed by a committee (relating to British military presence in Suez and defence procurement) was put before the Cabinet in 1966:

It soon became clear that all the details were now cut and dried ... so the whole thing was fixed. All Cabinet could do was express opinions and influence to some extent the general tone of the white paper by drafting amendments. Of course there were some ministers like Barbara Castle who took up postures of protest. But the rest of us felt that there was nothing we could do and that the procedure under which we had been excluded was not unreasonable. Fourteen of our twenty-three members of Cabinet are members of the Cabinet committee. To the preparation of this white paper this fourteen had devoted nineteen meetings and two Chequers weekends. After all this, it was natural enough that they should expect Cabinet to give formal authorisation to the recommendations that they had worked out.' [11]

---

9   See Brazier, *Constitutional Practice*, 2nd edn (1994), p79.

10   *ibid*, pp72–3.

11   Crossman, *Diaries of a Cabinet Minister: Minister of Housing 1964–66* (1975), pp455–6.

By contrast, the heavy use made by Mrs Thatcher of *ad hoc* groups of ministers to discuss key issues raised more concern.

M Doherty, 'Prime Ministerial Power and Ministerial Responsibility' (1988) 41(1) *Parliamentary Affairs* 49, 54

The role of the Cabinet under Mrs Thatcher is to endorse rather than to make decisions. This was evident in a statement by Geoffrey Howe, Secretary of State for Foreign and Commonwealth Affairs since 1983, during an interview with the *Daily Mail* on the 6th February 1984. When asked whether or not the full Cabinet had discussed the decision to ban trade unions at the Government Communication Headquarters at Cheltenham, he replied, 'No. It was discussed, as almost every Government decision is discussed, by the group of ministers most directly involved. There are very few discussions of Government decisions by full Cabinet'. Mrs Thatcher favours decision-making by means of informal *ad hoc* sessions at Number 10. The behaviour of a Cabinet committee, led by Lord Whitelaw, at the time Lord President of the Council and from 1979–1983 Home Secretary, which was set up in 1985 to consider the teachers' pay dispute, is informative. Instead of making a report to the Cabinet, it reported back to the Prime Minister at a meeting she chaired at Number 10. James Prior, who was Secretary of State for Employment (1979–81) and Secretary of State for Northern Ireland (1981–84), tells us that the use of such groups developed gradually; that she used the formal machinery of Cabinet government at first, but then, 'after a few years, the formal Cabinet committees were very much downgraded and she began to operate much more in small groups dominated by her "cronies"'.

Notes

1   The use of such informal groups was not an innovation of Thatcher's, as James notes:[12] 'In the 1960s and 70s ... [Prime Ministers] managed [issues] by secret committees. Barbara Castle's diaries recorded that for years Wilson prevented his Cabinet from discussing Rhodesia and devaluation; similarly the head of Callaghan's policy unit recalls his Prime Minister running economic policy through a secret committee called "the seminar"'.

2   Mrs Thatcher appears to have taken this technique further, by making much greater use of such groups as a deliberate way of disabling the views of those opposed to her policies. In one sense, this more ruthless procedural style was the natural corollary of her more radical policies; the greater than usual internal dissent and opposition caused by the latter necessitated either the more domineering style she adopted or the abandonment or dilution of the more radical aspects of her New Right programme, which Mrs Thatcher was not prepared to countenance. She thus made use of informal groups quite specifically in order to ensure that particular issues were handled by groups sympathetic to her. Because Prime Ministers can hand-pick these groups, they can (within limits) ensure that a given sensitive issue is discussed only by those ministers whom they wish to discuss it. Thus, for example, in the early 1980s Michael Heseltine put forward proposals for a radical programme of investment in the inner cities, to tackle the poverty, unemployment and crime which was causing serious social unrest. Mrs Thatcher, who was opposed to the plan, convened a special group of ministers to discuss it, selecting ministers she knew would be hostile to

---

12   *Op cit*, p621.

Heseltine's proposals; the group duly came up with recommendations which involved nothing like the investment Heseltine had proposed.[13]

3   But whatever the procedural imperatives of her radical policies, the point is that Mrs Thatcher's way of doing business starkly illustrated the enormous powers which the flexible nature of the Cabinet and committee system gives to *any* Prime Minister. As Brazier notes, the power to decide 'whether to set up a committee and when to dissolve it ... its terms of reference ... members and chairman [and to] lay down rules which restrict appeal to the full Cabinet' means that 'Significant parts of the British machinery of Government are...within the personal control of the Prime Minister ...'.[14] The treatment of the budget provides a vivid illustration of this point.

> ... the Chancellor's budget proposals are of major economic and political importance, but they arrived at in great secrecy in the Treasury, in consultation with the Prime Minister. Individual ministers can and do make representations to the Chancellor ... which may or may not be heeded. But the first which the Cabinet hears of the detail of the budget are on the morning ... the Chancellor presents it to the House [by which time] it is obviously too late...for ministers to be able to insist on more than minor changes. This astonishing procedure is justified by the need for secrecy [to prevent] damaging leaks.[15]

4   Brazier notes that the 'details' of the budget are not revealed prior to Budget Day. Once again, Mrs Thatcher took this practice further as a former member of her Government notes:

> The 1981 Budget was rigidly deflationary and thus highly controversial at a time of deep recession, yet the strategy behind it was never discussed in Cabinet and was only revealed to the full Cabinet on Budget Day itself. One can guess the reason: the Chancellor and the Prime Minister concluded that the Cabinet might well insist on some changes. But this is why the Cabinet exists – to make collective decisions on important issues that face individual departments, and thus affect the government as a whole. Collective responsibility is based on collective decision-making. Margaret Thatcher is not the first Prime Minister to circumvent her colleagues, nor will she be the last, but this habit is not the sign of a happy or healthy government.[16]

5   Two correctives to the picture of Prime Ministerial power being painted should be noted: first of all, their power depends greatly on (a) the size of their majority in Parliament, and (b) their perceived popularity and the popularity of their policies. Secondly, the powers outlined above do not mean that the Prime Minister has the capacity to control the detailed policy making and day-to-day administration of all Government departments. Simple lack of knowledge and insufficient time precludes this.

6   Nevertheless, despite this caveat, this ability to bypass Cabinet has a wider significance: its adverse affect on two important aspects of Government. First, there is internal consultation and scrutiny: if an issue is discussed in a small, informal and carefully selected group, the number of people – and

---

13   See Henessy, *Cabinet* (1986), p102.
14   Brazier, 'Reducing the Power of the Prime Minister', *op cit*, pp456–7.
15   *Ibid*, p456.
16   Francis Pym, *The Politics of Consent* (1984), p18.

particularly unpersuaded, possibly sceptical people – to whom proposed Government policy has to be explained is decreased, as is the variety of critical perspectives which have the chance of influencing that policy. This might be seen as a negative effect in constitutional terms since the effect is that power is concentrated in fewer hands and policy (arguably) becomes less honed and tested. However, the corollary of this process is a reduction in the risk of leaks, and a decrease in the chances of controversial policies suffering modification or even abandonment – ie a gain in political terms. Clearly, as we have seen, these political considerations tend to trump the constitutional ones. This is not surprising, given that the person who manipulates, who determines the particular system of Government used the Prime Minister, is before all else a politician. The second aspect of Government adversely affected is the notion of collective responsibility, a notion to which we now turn.

Prime Minister, Cabinet, and collective responsibility

Collective responsibility as an aspect of Government accountability will be considered briefly below. Here, its significance in relation to the issues discussed above is considered.

According to Ronald Brazier:

> The doctrine of collective ministerial responsibility requires that all ministers, and usually parliamentary private secretaries, must accept Cabinet decisions, or dissent from them privately while remaining loyal to them publicly, or dissent publicly and resign, unless collective responsibility is waived by the Cabinet on any given occasion. If a minister does not resign over an issue of policy or procedure he will be collectively responsible for it, in the sense that he will have to support it publicly through his votes in Parliament and through his speeches.[17]

An example of the enforcement of the doctrine by the Prime Minister appears below, in a statement by Harold Wilson which was read to his Cabinet on 3 April 1969 and then released to the press; general discussion of collective responsibility by Colin Turpin follows.

> The Prime Minister said that there had for some time been a growing tendency for some ministers to act in ways which called in question the collective responsibility of the Cabinet, in so far as they had apparently felt free, in their personal dealings both with members of the PLP (Parliamentary Labour Party) and with the Press, to dissociate themselves from certain of the Government's policies and to allow this to be known to outside bodies, particularly the trade unions, with whom their colleagues were often conducting difficult and delicate negotiations in the name of the Government as a whole. Before a decision was reached on any item of Government policy a minister was entitled to defend his own point of view within the Cabinet as strongly and persuasively as he wished. But once a decision had been taken the principle of collective responsibility required every member of an Administration to endorse it and to defend it to any outside body on any occasion, whether private or public. This remained true even if the minister was himself a member of the outside body concerned. There was no objection in principle to ministers retaining affiliations of this kind

---

17 *Constitutional Practice*, 2nd edn (1994), pp129–30.

provided that no conflict of interest or allegiance resulted. But this proviso was especially important in the case of ministers who were members of the National Executive Committee of the Labour Party (NEC), where any clash of loyalties was liable to be particularly embarrassing. It had to be recognised that the NEC's concept of its relationship to the Parliamentary Party had changed since the Labour Party became the Government Party. During the Labour Government of 1945–51 the executive would never have sought to enforce a decision of the annual conference of the Party on the Government. And even in 1960, when the Labour Party were in Opposition, the executive had refused to try to impose the decisions of the conference on the PLP. Now, however, it was seeking to assert a right to withhold support from the Government on issues on which the annual conference had not yet expressed a view.

It would be unfortunate if circumstances developed, perhaps later in the year, in which it proved impossible to deal with this situation except by means of a ruling that no member of the Cabinet might offer himself for election to the NEC. He himself would greatly regret it if he were forced to give such a ruling, since the result would be not only to weaken the links between the Government and the NEC but also to reduce the latter to a body which was competent merely to discuss and to protest but not to exercise influence or to accept responsibility. Nevertheless, this situation could be avoided only if ministers themselves recognised and accepted that, where any conflict of loyalties arose, the principle of the collective responsibility of the Government was absolute and overriding in all circumstances and that, if any minister felt unable to subscribe to this principle without reservation, it was his duty to resign his office forthwith.[18]

Colin Turpin, 'Ministerial Responsibility' in Jowell and Oliver (eds), *The Changing Constitution*, 3rd edn (1994), pp147–50

Since the implementation of policies often requires joint action by several departments, and policies can have ripple effects that spread throughout the administration, ministerial solidarity is a necessary condition of the working of Cabinet government. 'There is no other condition', wrote Laski, 'upon which that teamwork which is of the essence of the Cabinet system becomes possible.' [Laski, *Parliamentary Government*, p256]. The interdependence of Government departments is greater today than when Laski wrote, and departments have now also to co-ordinate their policies with the decisions of EC institutions.

Collective responsibility in this aspect of ministerial solidarity is not, however, of unqualified public benefit. Parliament and the public are presented with the appearance of an 'improbable harmony' where disagreement may be sharp and unreconciled, a state of affairs which, in the view of one MP, has 'fertilized the distrust with which the public regards politicians', giving 'the perfect alibi to the lackey and the time server' [Mr Neil Kinnock, *The Times*, 18 April 1974 (letter to the editor)]. Criticisms of this sort have particular force in respect of the extension of collective responsibility to discussions and argument which precede the taking of decisions: here the 'privatisation' of conflict between decision-makers prevents the focusing of public opinion upon issues until after decisions have been announced. Paradoxically, collective responsibility can provide a shield for the Government against parliamentary scrutiny. The positions taken by different departments, the pressures resisted or accommodated, are concealed from Parliament in a contrived unanimity. ...

The rigour of collective responsibility is, as is well known, mitigated by the

---

18 Quoted in Brazier, *Constitutional Texts* (1990), pp350–1.

practice of 'unattributable leaking' by ministers to the press, in this way rallying support outside for their position in arguments within Government, or letting it be known that they have opposed a decision unwelcome to sections of their party or to interest groups. Gordon Walker defended this practice as necessary to the preservation of collective responsibility [*The Cabinet* (1972), p32]. It has not diminished in frequency since his time and must be counted an established, if not entirely 'correct', feature of the constitutional system. Prime Ministers try to curb the practice, but have been known to resort to it themselves.

A more radical remedy for the strains which may be caused in party and government by the demands of collective solidarity is the *suspension* of the obligation, so as to allow open dissent, within specified limits, on a strongly contested question. The 1932 'agreement to differ' was seen as something unique until collective responsibility was again suspended in 1975 for the referendum campaign on membership of the European Communities, and in 1977 for the second reading of the European Assembly Elections Bill. There are those who deprecate this sort of expedient as undermining the basis of parliamentary government, but it is questionable whether the public interest is always well served by the concealment of differences on policy within government. In particular, when the Opposition leadership is in agreement with the official Government view on an important issue facing the country, public debate is devalued if the dissenting opinions of senior politicians on both sides are stifled by insistence on collective responsibility.

In any event it may be impossible to maintain a public show of ministerial solidarity when there are sharp ideological differences, or an especially keen contest on some particular question of policy, between Cabinet ministers. This became evident in the periods of Labour government in the 1960s and 1970s. In the earlier years of Mrs Thatcher's premiership there were ministers who openly expressed their disagreement with Government policies and who were not, with one or two exceptions, visited with immediate loss of office as a result. Leading dissentients were, however, progressively removed in Cabinet reshuffles and dissension became less persistent – but when it occurred, was more portentous. The Westland Affair in 1985–6 brought to public notice a striking degree of dissension between ministers and the pursuit of contradictory policies by different departments. Collective responsibility appeared to be dissolving but, in the result, was vindicated by the dramatic resignation of the dissenting minister, Mr Heseltine. In justifying his resignation, Mr Heseltine declared that there had been a lack of proper, collective discussion of the matter in contention, which had 'broken the workings of the constitution'. This tangled affair did at all events emphasise the link between collective decision-making and collective responsibility. Again, when Mr Nigel Lawson resigned as Chancellor of the Exchequer in 1989, he did so on the ground that the exchange-rate policy he was seeking to further was not being supported by the Prime Minister, who was instead giving rein to the contrary opinions of her personal economic adviser, Sir Alan Walters, Mr Lawson too, in his resignation speech, insisted on the need for the collective resolution of policy differences in government. Disagreement between ministers on policy towards the European Community precipitated the resignation in 1990 of Sir Geoffrey Howe, Leader of the House of Commons and Deputy Prime Minister, who protested in his letter of resignation that 'Cabinet government is all about trying to persuade one another from within' [*The Times*, 2 November 1990].

Despite the recurring note struck by these three ministers in their public statements, they did not resign for the purpose of defending a constitutional principle of collective decision-making, but for a variety of convoluted and partly unavowed reasons. Nevertheless that principle is essential to the effective working of Cabinet government. Although, as we have seen, the responsibility of ministers does not depend on their having taken part in the making of the decision or policy in question, the convention of collective solidarity finds its most secure anchorage, and its most convincing justification, in executive arrangements which allow for full discussion and the representation of contrary viewpoints. A style of administration – like that of Mrs Thatcher's premiership – which is not favourable to collective decision-making may be seen as undermining the basis of the convention.

Notes

1   As Turpin notes, collective responsibility implies not only a duty of public acquiesence to official Government policy but, as a corollary of this, a reasonable chance for Government ministers to at least discuss key policies which the convention will demand they later defend. As James notes, the lesson of the Heseltine affair is that 'the enforcement against ministers of the rule of collective responsibility implies an obligation on the Prime Minister ... to ensure that colleagues are consulted, at least on major issues'.[19] The problem is that these two basic aspects of the convention derive unequal levels of support from the political imperatives of Government. Whilst, with exceptions, the basic survival of Government depends upon the first aspect,[20] giving maximum incentive for its enforcement by the Prime minister, by contrast, as discussed above, the Prime Minister may often have strong reasons *not* to allow fulfilment of the second, since denial of full ministerial participation in policy formation will clearly assist a Prime Minister bent on forcing through controversial policies. Further, the first half of the convention arguably provides a disincentive for honouring the second: the Prime Minister's motivation for allowing full participation is hardly increased by his knowledge that (provided things are not pushed too far) ministers will have to support a given policy regardless of whether they supported, opposed or even discussed it. Once again in an important aspect of British governmental practice, politics may be seen to trump constitutionalism.

2   Two further aspects of collective responsibility are perhaps worth noting. One is that the convention – which obviously requires that disagreements amongst ministers be concealed from Parliament and the public – helps ensure a lack of transparency in the decision-making process. The other is that in general it increases the power of dominant groups in Government over weaker voices: those who have lost the battle over a policy in Cabinet are obliged to support the policy of the powerful, which becomes (subject to leaks) the only policy known to the public. Collective responsibility can thus be seen as another device which, if not exactly centralising power, concentrates it further in a few hands.

---

19   James, *op cit*, p627.
20   The persistent, long-standing unpopularity of the conspicuously divided Conservative party at the time of writing (it has trailed Labour badly for over a year in opinion polls and by-elections) is, by common consensus, a case in point.

3 Of course, in a sense, some version of collective responsibility is a prerequisite for any kind of recognisable government. Any collection of individual people is inevitably going to disagree over at least some important issues, and if all those disagreements were on public show, if ministers could constantly disclaim responsibility for decisions they did not like, then we would hardly have recognisable 'Government' policy at all – only different policies, held by different individuals. But it is important nevertheless to recognise clearly all the implications and consequences of the convention, necessary as it may be to an extent.

CENTRALISATION

Before turning to look at accountability, another topic – the issue of centralisation of power – merits consideration. Whilst it is a significant issue in its own rights, it is strongly related to the accountability issue. For if, as the writers presented below argue, the last 16 years have seen a dramatic convergence of power in the hands of central Government, it becomes of even greater importance to see how effective controls over central Government are, given that they have a more important role to play than ever before. Patrick Birkinshaw traces the historic rise in the power of the state in the 20th century.

P Birkinshaw, 'Decision-Making and its Control' in McAuslan and McEldowney *Law, Legitimacy and the Constitution* (1985), pp154–5

The gradual compenetration throughout the nineteenth and twentieth centuries of State and Civil Society as the State assumed increasing regulatory powers to redress the excesses and imbalances caused by market forces and the State's own 'neutrality' in the governance of human affairs is well documented. Increasing regulation of the erstwhile private economy; introduction of institutional machinery to help assuage the ruptures caused by conflict between the forces of capital and labour; the impact of 'war efforts' upon the State's assumption of greater responsibility for control of essential industries as well as its increasing responsibility for organising public health and welfare, education and regulation of the environment are all well catalogued. These interventionist and centralising tendencies transformed the classical model of a balanced representative democracy beyond recognition. Not only did the official organs of authority – the departments of state, local authorities, public boards and corporations – grow enormously in terms of manpower, expenditure and powers but there emerged a bewildering arabesque of non-departmental bodies, governmental agencies, tribunals, intermediary organisations representing the interests of particular groups or clienteles to the governors as well as a host of private organisations which were allowed to regulate their domestic affairs and members in return for basic compliance with the governmental will. By the middle of the twentieth century, the degree of compenetration and interdependence defied compete attempts to distinguish the private and public realms successfully.

All of this increased enormously the power of Government, or more specifically the ministers. The shell of power was in parliamentary legislation, its substance was in statutory instruments, departmental rules, codes of practice, ministerial circulars and letters, White Papers, statements of intent, government contracts and in the informal deals struck between mighty departments and their client groups. All the features, in other words, of government by dominion through the power of the public purse, government by enormous delegation to official, quasi official and 'private' self-regulating bodies.

Question

But is this rise in state power a development to be deplored, as upsetting the 'balance' of the constitution?

AW Robson, *Public Administration Today* (1948), pp16–17[21]

I have little sympathy with those who declare ... that the balance of the constitution is upset ... because the executive is called upon to play a much greater part than it did 50 or 100 years ago. There is no ideal pattern which can serve as a permanent model of constitutional development. The true balance of a polity is to be tested by the extent to which it succeeds in meeting all the needs of the people who live under it ... If a constitution is able to provide broadly satisfactory results over the whole field of contemporary demand ... then we can say it is in a state of balance. To reserve that word for a particular set of relationships between the legislature, the executive and the judiciary which happened to emerge in the seventeenth century and which suited the conditions of the eighteenth and early nineteenth century is to display symptoms of chronic nostalgia which are unlikely to be of any help in solving the problems of our own time. These problems demand new ideas, new institutions and new relationships.

Note

Whilst Robson is clearly right to protest against a nostalgic adherence to outmoded constitutional conceptions, his proposed test seems to propound an over-simplistic formula itself. Constitutional analysts will generally lack the empirical data to establish whether a given set of arrangements satisfies the needs of all citizens, and in any event, whether these needs are met will in large part depend on the social and economic policies which are propagated *through* the structures under consideration. In what follows, the writers quoted are concerned more with the fact that certain sets of arrangements may make it *more difficult to tell* whether needs are being met, by removing possibilities for feedback and representation by those affected by policies and also that certain constitutional arrangements may make any given policy *less likely* to be satisfactory in practice by removing local control over decision-making.

The emasculation of local government

In what follows, McAuslan and McEldowney argue that the Conservative Governments since 1979 have viewed other fora for political legitimacy and the exercise of legitimated political power as potential rivals which must be dismantled altogether, or at least subject to rigorous centralised control. G W Jones examines the destruction of the financial independence of local government in particular.

P McAusland and J McEldowney, 'Legitimacy and the Constitution: The Dissonance Between Theory and Practice' in McAuslan and McEldowney, *op cit*, pp15–20

Elected on a 43.4 per cent minority of votes in 1979, and a slightly smaller percentage in 1983, the Conservative Governments, of which incidentally Lord

---

21 Quoted in Loughlin, *Public Law and Political Theory* (1992), p200.

Hailsham is a senior member, as Lord Chancellor, and with comfortable majorities in the House of Commons, have consciously set about a course of radical social and economic change. Such changes departed from the existing political consensus of successive Governments since 1945 on how and in accordance with what principles the country should be governed, and when these programmes of change have been opposed by elected and appointed representatives of other parties and groups within the community, they have set about dismantling the institutions from which opposition has come and curbing their independence.

Policy which has been pursued consistently since 1979 via legislation and administration has been to whittle down, reduce or eliminate the role of local electoral institutions; local participation in the administration of services affecting local areas; and local opposition, lawfully expressed, to central government policies. All these practices, to be discussed briefly below, are good examples of that centralised democracy or elective dictatorship which is counterpoised to limited government.

Take first, the assault on local elected government. We do not pretend that local government is without faults, some of them indeed – secretiveness, denial of rights to the opposition, waste and petty abuses of power – going to the question of the legitimacy of its existence or activities, but it has three crucial features which are vital attributes in that diffusion and limitation on central government power which the concept of limited government necessarily involves. These features are: localness, the elective principle, and an independent taxing power. These characteristics are interrelated and fundamental because between them they virtually guarantee that at any time in the history of the state there will be alternative policies and spending patterns being pursued by alternative elected governments, local governments, to those being pursued or desired by central governments. And the maintenance of such alternative governments, however inconvenient, foolish or inefficient they may be is essential to the continuance of a system of limited government. Any central government, intent on increasing its own powers and decreasing opportunities for dissent from or alternative approaches to its politics, will sooner or later feel the need to attack and emasculate these alternative governments, these alternative centres of power, at their electoral and financial roots.

The authors then survey increased financial control over local authorities and go on:

The next step, duly proceeded to in legislation passed in 1985 was to abolish certain elected local governments and transfer their functions either to other existing elected local governments or to central government appointed bodies or bodies with a mixture of central and local government appointees or joint boards of local government members. The initial argument in favour of this 'reorganisation', that it would be more efficient and save ratepayers money, did not stand up to independent private sector financial scrutiny. [Coopers & Lybrand Associates produced two reports in early 1984. They estimated a range from an annual saving over the then current costs of the Metropolitan County Councils of 0.25 per cent, to an annual cost of 3.25 per cent. The Government's own estimate was a saving of 7.5 per cent.] Alternative arguments that abolishing upper-tier authorities would bring government closer to the people and thus be more democratic and remove a source of conflict and tension were belied by the plethora of non-directly elected bodies, especially in London, that were provided for in the legislation to replace the directly elected Greater London Council and the metropolitan counties that were being abolished.

At the root of the abolitionist case was the political fact that the local Governments scheduled to be abolished were controlled by the Labour Party, in some cases aggressively so, and as upper-tier authorities they could both obtain funds from and influence policies in lower-tier authorities controlled by the Conservative Party, and could act, and particularly in the case of the GLC and the South Yorkshire Metropolitan County did act as focal and effective points of opposition to the Government. This the Government was not prepared to countenance, especially in London which was the seat of national government. Rather than wait for or use the democratic electoral process to try and displace their political opponents, the usual tactic in a democratic society supporting a system of limited government – the Government decided to abolish these centres of opposition – quite possibly only temporary centres – altogether.

Carol Harlow quotes Bagehot's aphorism that elections are a buckle between people and power. They provide a means for maintaining a democratic check on power, for changing those wielding power and for informing those wielding power of the reaction of the people over whom power is being wielded. The democratic ethic behind the electoral process provides too the rationale for the greater involvement of people in the process of government not only through elections but through service on public bodies which are involved in the process of governing. This greater involvement in government brings a greater commitment to the whole constitutional process. For many commentators as Harlow points out, a major problem in Government today is that there is, despite some gains in some areas, notably planning, still too few opportunities for participation in Government and too little meaning to elections. Successive Governments, prior to 1979, were at best lukewarm towards the arguments and reluctant to take action for greater participation. But only since 1979 has there been positive hostility towards greater participation in Government Specific action has been taken or planned to cut down on participation, on elections and on the institution of local government, the standard-bearer for greater participation in Government. In their place, have come greater centralisation of power, greater secrecy over how decisions on rates, formerly open to local electors to see and comment on, are made; and greater efforts to appoint the 'right' sort of person – 'one of us' – to quangos rather than ensure a representative cross-section of the community on such bodies. In a sentence, government is withdrawing from the people – not in the sense of becoming smaller but in the sense of becoming less open to persuasion, more authoritarian – and the buckle between people and power is being loosened.

G W Jones, 'The Relationship between Central and Local Government', in Harlow (ed), *Public Law and Politics* (1986), pp68,70,71,77

In the past governments sought to *influence* local authority spending: now they seek to *control* it. This change was embodied in the Local Government Finance Act 1982, which gave retrospective legal validity to the centre to fix expenditure targets for each local authority, and empowered it to penalise those who went over those targets by withdrawal of grants. ... The Government expected conformity by local authorities with these targets, centrally determined, indeed predetermined. This approach was radically different from that of the past [in which Government merely sought to *persuade* local authorities to adhere to its spending proposals]. ...

Mrs Thatcher once claimed that her Government would hold what she regarded as monopolies at arm's length, and she included alongside trades unions, opticians and lawyers, elected local authorities. She did not recognise that as elected bodies they had any distinctive constitutional legitimacy. They seemed to be conceived as partial interest which had to be subordinated on all issues to the views of the central Government which represented the superior national interest. In this Government there was no place for constitutional thinking about the need to diffuse power between institutions of government and to erect a system of checks and balances. This monocentric perspective explains why the Government has rejected the previous mode of consulting with local government in favour of taking unilateral, one-sided decisions, ... As a result the figures produced by the Government as its target for local Government expenditure were felt by local Government to be totally impossible to achieve: hence the divergence between targets and out-turn since 1979. ...

Local authorities had traditionally been able to fix the tax at whatever level they wished. But by the Rates Act 1984 the Government has the power to determine the rate for a specific number of authorities and to determine it for a far wider number by the general rate capping powers. John Griffith has seen this change as transforming local Government into local administration. Some regard it as the fundamental change, or greater constitutional significance than the abolition of councils, since it ended the right of local authorities to be responsible decision-makers accountable for their policies to their own voters. ...

[Furthermore,] an increasing effort will be made to make local authorities conform to central priorities in policy for particular services. ... There will be further extensions of specific grants, whereby Government grants will be directed to be spent as the centre wants and not left for local determination, as in spending on inner-city projects, in-service training and vocational and technical education. The other protective strategy will be to remove services from local Government and put them in appointed bodies, more amenable to central Government's pressures than elected local authorities, such as the police, fire and transport boards in the metropolitan areas, the urban development corporations in London and Merseyside, the Arts and Sports Councils, the Historic Buildings and Monuments Commission and the Manpower Services Commission. As their functions grow so local Government is eroded. ...

Jones then considers the subjugation of local authorities to the discipline of the market.

Here again, in a kind of neo-Marxist approach, the Conservative Government makes no distinction between central and local government: both are parts of a single state. Local government is seen as but the local branch of the state apparatus. It, too, must curtail its scope, or, if it will not do so itself, then the central Government must impose the reduction on it. Thus councils have had to sell off their council houses, run their direct labour organisations as businesses, put more and more of their functions out to competitive tender, and follow 'business practices' in the management of their staff. To achieve this decentralisation to the market, and thus to individual consumers who express their preferences through their purchases rather than their votes or political lobbying, the Government has taken extreme centralising measures, extending the powers of the central government and local government, using hierarchy to attain markets.

Note

McAuslan and McEldowney noted the trend of passing local government functions to appointed boards and committees, which gives central government considerable powers of patronage. Weir, writing in 1995, notes how closed to local participation these bodies ('extra governmental organisations' – 'EGOs') are, compared to local government, and identifies a similar trend in relation to regional governance.

Quangos: patronage and openness

Stuart Weir, 'Quangos: Questions of Democratic Accountability' (1995) 48(2) *Parliamentary Affairs* 306, 315–16

The host of local EGOs are far less open to local residents than local Government. Local authorities are obliged to keep a public register of members' interests; all authority meetings are open to the public; and there are public rights of access to agendas, minutes and background papers for all council meetings. Further, local authorities are obliged to publish locally both auditors' criticism and sets of performance indicators on housing, refuse collection, schools, etc. They must also consider an auditors' public interest report at a meeting open to the public and press, and make the report publicly available. There is no such requirement on any executive body, national or local, not even those which provide the same services (housing, schools, etc) as local authorities, to publish either auditors' findings or performance indicators. From 1995, the Audit Commission will publish local authority performance figures nationally. There exists no uniform requirement to publish similar information for any EGOs (where performance indicators are largely for purposes of internal control).

The Department of City and Regional Planning at the University of Wales has published an analysis of the 'governance question' in Wales. The analysis is confined to the relationship between the Welsh Office and recognised NDPBs [Non-Departmental Public Bodies] and NHS bodies, which doubled in number from 40 in 1979 to 80 in 1991. Executive NDPBs are established within a clear policy context; they frame their corporate plans in accordance with current policy, and these plans are submitted annually to the Welsh Office in draft form for approval. The Welsh Secretary appoints most chairpersons and members and meets the former regularly; this department holds regular meetings with their chief executives and finance officers. This is a highly secretive process, and will remain so under the Government's 'Open Government' code. Many quangos do not publish their corporate plans because they may contain 'commercial sensitive information'. The Commons Welsh Affairs Committee took odds with this position, arguing: 'We do not accept that the requirement for confidentiality is sufficient justification for publishing no information on future proposals and activities. In the absence of published political and operational guidelines ... the responsibility falls more heavily on NDPBs to explain how they propose to spend the public money by which they are financed.' Party-political patronage is freely exercised in Wales. The Welsh study delineates a systematic network of interlocking appointees, who have ties with the Conservative Party, at the heads of key EGOs.

Note

The first Nolan report investigated the issue of patronage. It found the charge of political patronage in appointments not proven[22] but made a series of recommendations on ensuring that appointment was on the basis of merit only, all of which were accepted by the Government. It also considered the issue of openness in quangos, hearing submissions which 'highlighted the refusal of some public bodies to provide information even where it had previously been in the public domain; the excessive use of commercial confidentiality to justify

---

22 *First Report of the Committee on Standards in Public Life*, Cm 2850, pp70–1.

withholding information and difficulty in finding where information could be obtained'.[23] It did not think a common statutory framework for openness practicable and instead recommended a Code of Best Practice, which the Government accepted. The text of this appears below, following the report's sample of submissions on this issue.

First Report of the Committee on Standards in Public Life, Cm 2850, pp 93, 95

'Public scrutiny of what people do is probably the most powerful pressure towards probity of conduct' (The Audit Commission, written evidence).

'The general rule for the conduct of NDPBs should be transparency except in cases of commercial or personal confidentiality. Minutes of decisions taken should be available to the public' (Demos, written evidence).

'At a local level, quangos affect crucial areas of people's lives. Local editors ... say that there is a growing feeling that people are alienated and feel powerless to influence the decision making of such bodies ... One of the reasons is the secrecy with which quangos are shrouded' (Santha Rasaiah, Parliamentary and Legal Committee, Guild of Editors).

'... the public are not only consumers of, but shareholders in public services. They should expect standards of disclosure and accountability no less than shareholders would have in respect of the board of a commercial organisation. At the moment these fall a long way short ...' (Anne Caldwell, correspondent).

A Standard of Best Practice for Openness in Executive NDPBs & NHS Bodies

Access to information

- Adoption of a specific code on access to information incorporating the Government's code,[24] and building on it where possible.
- Clear and published procedures for implementing the code, including:
  - well defined criteria for information that will be withheld, which should be cited whenever a request for information is refused;
  - standards for speed of response to enquiries (eg information to be provided normally within 21 days or correspondent informed of likely date);
  - an appeal mechanism, within the organisation initially and then either to the Ombudsman, or (where the body does not come under the Ombudsman's jurisdiction) to another independent person appointed for the purpose;
  - a policy on charging for information provided (with requests requiring only a reasonable amount of work incurring no charge).

Meetings

- Opening meetings to the public or making minutes of meetings (and main committees) available for public inspection or describing key discussions and decisions in newsletters etc after each meeting. Some items may be deemed confidential, but the criteria for doing so should be published.
- A well publicised Annual General Meeting open to public and media, allowing an opportunity to question the board members on the performance and activities of the body.

---

23 *Ibid*, p 92, para 117.
24 This is a reference to the Government's Code of Practice for openness in central government which appears in Chapter 3 of this Part.

- Other opportunities taken to involve and inform the public and organisation with a major interest, through consumer groups or user forums; or public meetings on major issues.

Publications

- Annual Report & Accounts, including information on the role and remit of the body, long term plans or strategy; membership of the board, performance against key targets; targets for the forthcoming year; their commitment and approach to open government; and where further information can be obtained (including how to inspect the register of board members interests and how to pursue complaints).

- Other important information to be routinely published. Depending on the body this might include key statistics; the results of consultation exercises; details of key procedures (eg criteria for allocating public funds); reports of regulatory investigations etc.

- All publications should be made as widely available as possible, such as through public libraries, and all annual reports & accounts should be deposited in the parliamentary libraries.

Note

The second report, which dealt with 'not for profit local bodies' such as Training and Enterprise Councils (TECs), Local Enterprise Councils (LECs) and grant maintained schools, considered openness and local involvement in relation to these bodies.

Second Report of the Committee on Standards in Public Life, Cm 3270–1, paras 29, 30, 253–258, Recommendations 33 and 34

29. The most powerful tool for ensuring that public business is transacted with propriety is openness. In our first report, we recommended a code of practice on openness for executive non-departmental public bodies.

30. The evidence we received shows that, while many of the elements of that code are in place in local public spending bodies, there is a good deal of variation in practice and progress can still be made.

...

253. The concern that TECs and LECs are secretive organisations has been tackled in recent years by the organisations themselves, the Enterprise Agencies, the TEC National Council and Government (and there is a contractual requirement for them to pay due regard to the Government's Openness Code of Practice). There is however a widespread view among TECs and LECs that the efforts they have made to improve their openness have not won recognition, particularly from the media. This may change over time.

254. There remain some areas in which progress has been slow. The first is publication of contracts made with organisations in which directors have an interest ... The other area, and one on which there is considerable reluctance by both TECs and LECs to take a more open stance, is the publication of board papers, including agendas and minutes. It is argued that publication would drive the decision-making process into smaller sub-groups, and make the work of the whole board much more difficult and less effective. While we recognise that this is a danger, we believe it should be possible to develop practices ... to allow greater disclosure. Even where confidentiality is necessary, it can frequently be subject to a defined time limit. In practice, some TECs have found it possible to make papers available. Lincoln TEC told us:

board minutes and supporting papers [are] placed in the public domain by library services including [a] quarterly performance report

255. Highlands and Islands Enterprise told us about an intermediate stage to the publication of papers. Their LECs provide a summary of board assistance decisions to the media and, where there is further interest, offer a more detailed briefing. We commend this process, but we consider that it could be used in parallel with a system of more open access to board papers and minutes.

R33. All TECs and LECs should seek to adopt good practice by opening as many board papers as possible (including agendas and minutes) to public scrutiny and briefing the media and other interested parties on the outcome of board discussions.

256. Both TECs and LECs are required by their contracts to have one annual public meeting each year. Most, if not all, go further. In addition to formal consultative meeting many organise open meetings by sector or subject; others, serving a variety of discrete communities, organise roadshows, or other events, in those communities. Disappointingly, these events tend to be costly and not very well attended. Many TECs and LECs are seeking ways to address that problem.

257. TECs and LECs believe that their consultative and open meetings are often an important opportunity for interested parties to contribute to the preparation of their strategic plans. These are then discussed in draft with the funding agency or Department. Because the final detail of the plan will depend on the outcome of funding discussions, we recognise there may be difficulties in publishing them more widely in draft form, but we believe that there is much to be gained in terms of actual and perceived local accountability by being more open about the process. Although both government and enterprise agencies lay considerable stress on taking local views into account, we think that there is a need to go further by reviewing the scope for publishing all or part of TEC and LEC strategy documents on a consultative basis.

258. More generally, we believe that TECs and LECs need to do much more to explain locally their policies on accountability, propriety, governance and openness. All produce annual reports, but the information provided is not always as extensive as is found in the best company annual reports. We believe more effort to improve practice is needed, perhaps through an award such as exists for housing associations. Thought should also be given to providing key information in a form that can easily and cheaply be reproduced and updated.

R34. TECs and LECs should make available (and update annually) a statement of their policies in relation to local accountability, propriety, governance and openness.

Quangos: control by central government

The proliferation of quangos has not just effected local democracy. In theory, quangos have been set up because they can run the area remitted to them better than politicians. This should result in a decrease in central Government powers, though at the expense of a democratic deficit in these areas. However, Weir finds that the claim of most quangos to independence from central government is at best exaggerated. He begins by examining the enormous financial powers of these bodies.

Stuart Weir, 'Quangos: Questions of Democratic Accountability' (1995) 48(2) *Parliamentary Affairs* 306, 307–8, 312–13

As [the table below shows,] there are 5,573 'extra governmental' organisations, or EGOs, in the United Kingdom. Of these, there are 44 at national level; 355 at regional level; and 4,775 at local level. The great mass of these – 4,586 – are bodies which are not recognised by government in its own figures for quangos – they are thus classified as 'non-recognised' bodies. The full breakdown is as follows:

Recognised executive NDPBs	350
'Non-recognised' NI NDPBs	8
NHS bodies	629
'Non-recognised' bodies:	
Grant-maintained schools	1,025
City technology colleges	15
Further education corporations	557
Higher education corporations	164
Registered housing associations	2,668
Training and Enterprise Councils	82
Local Enterprise Companies	23
Police Authorities	52
Total	5,573

In 1992–93, the last year for which reliable figures are available, Britain's non-elected executive bodies (EGOs) were responsible for £46.65 billion of public expenditure ... [representing] nearly a third – 30% – of total central Government public expenditure, a more useful measure than the widely-used estimate of a fifth of public expenditure. It dwarfs the £12 billion expenditure that the Government owned up to – the official figure for expenditure on all recognised NDPBs.

The size of this expenditure on public goods is not in itself a cause for reproach; few would quarrel with increases in expenditure on health services or social housing. The point is that the bodies spending this huge tranche of public money are under the control of an appointed and self-appointing magistracy in a multiplicity of bodies. In 1993, this magistracy amounted to between 57,000 and 63,000 people (see Table 2).

2   EGOs, the New Local Magistracy and Elected Councillors

	Exec NDPs	NHS Bodies	Non-Rec EGOs	Total	Cllrs	Local Magistracy
England	234	557	3,981	4,772	20,852	51,148–55,953
Scotland	47	23	304	374	1,977	3,325–3,843
Wales	23	33	158	214	1,682	1,707–1,967
Northern Ireland	54	16	91	161	582	1,117–1,357
Total	358	529	4,534	5,521	25,093	57,296–63,120

Members of the new magistracy continually assert their independence of Government in media interviews. This is assumed to be a public good, though the exercise of independent powers by unelected bodies would subvert basic principles of democracy. The reality, however, is that EGOs possess scarcely any independent room for manoeuvre. They have specifically been created, or adapted, to act as dependent agencies within parameters of policy and resources set by Government.

For example, the Housing Corporation was originally set up to promote the voluntary housing movement. But as it has become the main channel for public investment in housing, David Edmonds, a former chief executive, recently observed, 'Its role is perhaps too important for the Department of the Environment fully to respect the original statutory functions'. In evidence to the Select Committee on the Environment, the Corporation said that it saw its role as an executive, carrying out government policy. Senior officials, according to Edmonds, have used the phrase, 'We are a government agency'; board members 'have often queried their role when all main decisions are taken by ministers, civil servants and Corporation staff'; and 'the DOE and its regional structure duplicates and double-checks much of the Corporation's work' (*The Guardian*, 10.9.93). Active members of Housing Association boards complain about the absence of consultation downwards to them; as one recently wrote, 'take it or leave it' is the implicit attitude (*The Guardian*, 21.1.94).

Consider also the TECs [Training and Education Councils], which as private companies run by local businessmen would at first sight seem to possess independence from Government. In fact, their operating framework is dictated by the Government's priorities and they work within sets of parameters laid down by contractual obligations and enforced by intrusive departmental regulations and financial incentives and penalties. In the absence of independent sources of funds they are driven by the invisible hand of Government – by cash and contracts, not by their directors. It is a system within which, according to one private-sector chair, 'civil servants remain the puppet master and TECs become mere puppets in all practical terms'. TECs were set the task of developing a strategic vision for local economies and employment markets, but the Government soon obliged them to concentrate on make-work schemes for unemployed workers during the recession. A survey and editorial in the *Financial Times* (10.5.93) concluded that TECs were 'being paid huge sums of money to do a task they do not much rate, while being denied freedom and funds to get on with the things their leaders think are most important'.

Note

The findings of the second Nolan report[25] were to a similar effect:

A constant complaint from all the bodies we have been examining is that they are subject to excessively detailed central control. Good auditing of the new service providers ... is essential. But detailed local control should not be replaced with detailed central control. Instead the bodies need to be given as much freedom of action as possible within clear policy guidelines and operating boundaries, supported by strong and well-understood sanctions. Regulation needs to be clear and explicit.[26]

---

25 *Second Report of the Committee on Standards in Public Life*, Cm 3270–1.
26 *Ibid*, Chapter 1, para 4.

GOVERNMENT ACCOUNTABILITY

Once the charge of centralisation is made out,[27] attention naturally shifts to those mechanisms by which the exercise of this vastly increased power may be scrutinised and made accountable. The traditional panacea for all ills is the convention of the accountability of ministers to Parliament. The detailed *mechanisms* by which the actions of ministers and their departments are scrutinised (Parliamentary Questions, Select Committees, etc) are examined in Part III, Chapter 1. The normative content of the convention itself, and sanctions for its breach are examined here.

This is a complex area. Essentially the idea of ministerial responsibility involves two concepts: first, the duty of ministers to give an account and explanation of their actions and of the decisions taken by their department to Parliament; secondly, the obligation to accept responsibility for mistakes made personally by them or by their department. A corollary of both these aspects of the doctrine is the duty of ministers not to mislead Parliament. The above summary indicates the order in which the various elements to this topic will be considered.

We start then with the duty to give an account; the traditional doctrine will be considered first; possible modification of it in the light of the increasing complexity of Government business and the 'Next Steps' reforms will then be noted; finally, areas of uncertainty and difference of opinion relating to the 'new' position will be considered.

The duty to give an account

It should be noted that the difficulties in this area commence at once, with terminology. In the above introduction, we have distinguished between what we have called 'the duty to give an account' and the 'obligation to accept responsibility'. This broadly follows a distinction in terminology put forward by Sir Robin Butler, Head of the Home Civil Service and accepted by the Government (see below) in which 'accountability' denotes the duty to explain, whilst 'responsibility' means the obligation to accept personal blame for error. Unfortunately, Turpin, in an important essay on this topic[28] written before Sir Robin's suggested information treats the two terms as 'synonymous' whilst noting that others treat the imposition of sanctions on a minister for his personal fault as a strong form of responsibility sometimes described as 'accountability'. The matter is further confused by the fact that 'ministerial responsibility' or 'individual responsibility of ministers' is generally used as a shorthand to denote both aspects of the doctrine. In what follows, the terminology put forward by Sir Robin Butler (though not necessarily the propositions lying behind it) is followed.

---

27 For a detailed (and controversial) exposition of this claim, see Jenkins, *Accountable to None: The Tory Nationalisation of Britain* (1995).

28 'Ministerial Responsibility' in Jowell and Oliver (eds), *The Changing Constitution*, 3rd edn (1994), p112.

The traditional position

We need to ask, what exactly is a minister accountable for? Theoretically, the answer is, everything that goes on in his or her department. That this obligation is indeed formally present can be seen in the official Government definition of ministerial responsibility, which we will return to again later in this Chapter. That definition is as follows:

> Each minister is responsible to Parliament for the conduct of his or her department, and for the actions carried out by the department in pursuit of Government policies or in the discharge of responsibilities laid upon him or her as a minister. Ministers are accountable to Parliament, in the sense that they have a duty to explain in Parliament the exercise of their powers and duties and to give an account to Parliament of what is done by them in their capacity as ministers or by their departments.

This is the position as set out in *Questions of Procedures for Ministers* ('QPM') a booklet produced by Government, intended as guidance for Ministers which was only made public in the 1990's. It should be noted that, whilst as the Nolan report remarked, 'QPM has no particular constitutional status'[29] Professor Henessey, giving evidence to the Public Service Committee in April[30] described QPM as the 'strand of DNA which determines the proper conduct of central government ... as both the Nolan and Scott Inquiries discovered as they went along ...'. QPM is also a useful starting point, partly because it gives the Government view of its own responsibility and partly because it is interesting to note what it leaves unsaid. As a matter of fact and common sense, clearly a minister will not be able to give an account of everything going on within a large and complex Government department in which hundreds of decisions may be taken every day by civil servants, often at quite a low level. But QPM does not say how this affects the minister's accountability. Presumably, a minister is accountable for the actions of civil servants in that he can be required to investigate a matter and report to the House on it; but can their be a parallel accountability of the civil servants themselves? In the chapter on House of Commons (Part III, Chapter 1) the restrictions on what kinds of questions civil servants would respond to when being questioned by Select Committees – restrictions which suggested that they did not need to account for their decisions – were noted and will not be re-rehearsed here (see above, pp371–2, 375–80). As the Government sees the position from the point of view of the convention of ministerial responsibility, the idea is that the civil servant is accountable not to Parliament but to the minister. This view is summed up in the following important select committee report.

Fifth Report from the Treasury and Civil Service Select Committee, HC 27 (1993–94), para 120, pxxxv

> 120. The Government's interpretation of the principles of ministerial accountability and of responsibility has been set out in recent years in the Armstrong Memorandum and in the Memorandum of Guidance for Officials

---

29 *First Report of the Committee on Standards in Public Life*, Cm 2850-I, Chapter 3, para 9 (p92).
30 HC 313-1 (1995–96), Minutes of Evidence, 20 March 1996, Q66.

appearing before Select Committees, known after its original author as the *Osmotherly Rules*. The Government, and Sir Robin Butler in particular has sought to restate the existing Government position, albeit with greater clarity of terminology than in the past. In recent pronouncements the Government has sought to draw a distinction between accountability and responsibility. According to the Government, ministerial accountability to Parliament is a minister's ultimate duty to account to Parliament for the work of his department: 'the minister in charge of a department is the only person who may be said to be ultimately accountable for the work of his department'. In the Government's view, it means that 'in the last resort ... ministers can be challenged about any action of the Civil Service'. The Government contends that since civil servants act on behalf of ministers – except in specified cases where statutes confer powers or responsibilities directly upon civil servants ministers alone are accountable to Parliament. In the view of the Government, civil servants are accountable to ministers, and when they give evidence to select committees, they do so 'on behalf of ministers'. According to the Armstrong Memorandum, even the appearance of Accounting Officers before the Committee of Public Accounts is 'without prejudice to the minister's responsibility and accountability to Parliament in respect of the policies, actions and conduct of his department'.

Note

The issue of the non-accountability to Parliament of civil servants and possible changes to this principle will be returned to below. There follows an extract from a Government memorandum[31] submitted to the Committee: the document made it clear that the Government does not accept that the fact of delegation reduces accountability, though (using the distinction outlined above) it did reduce ministerial responsibility. An indication of the Committee's and Sir Robin Butler's views on the issue then follows.

Minutes of Evidence taken before the Treasury and Civil Service Select Committee on 26 April 1994, HC 27 (1993–94), p189 and QQ 2094–95

9. A distinction between being accountable and being responsible, in the sense of being personally responsible and blameworthy, is one that Sir Robin Butler has made on several occasions to distinguish between the constitutional fact of ministerial accountability for all that a department does, and the limits to the direct personal responsibility (in the sense of personal involvement) of ministers for all the actions of their departments and agencies, given the realities of delegation and dispersed responsibility for much business.

10. The distinction becomes of more than academic importance when it is argued that trends in modern administration have opened an 'accountability gap' in which ministers have distanced themselves from their traditional full accountability for their departments, without a growth in alternative mechanisms by which it could be ensured that some other person is accountable for matters which the minister has delegated. The Government does not accept such an analysis because it does not accept that delegation diminishes ministerial accountability to Parliament, or that it creates a new form of direct accountability to Parliament for civil servants. Delegation helps to make clear, however, the limits to ministers' personal involvement in the actions of their Departments.

---

31 Memorandum submitted by the Office of Public Science and Service.

2094. [Questioning of Sir Robin Butler];... the Chancellor of the Duchy of Lancaster [William Waldegrave] is quoted as saying: 'The essence is to clarify the distinction between responsibility for the provision of services, which can – and often should – be devolved, and accountability for policy'– which you yourself have just referred to – 'which remains firmly with the minister.' Now could I quote you briefly what Sir Brian Cubbon said to us in his memorandum about this. He said: 'Ministers are concerned with far more than policy. Ministers deal with a seamless robe of decisions and matters which cannot be dignified with the word policy': the details of legislation, individual cases and incidents, appointments, influencing other people's decisions, EU matters, etc.' and then later: 'This seamless robe now covers an increasingly corpulent frame. The ministerial workload is determined, not by statute or convention or long-term Government strategies, but by the shifting spotlight of public attention. In the name of accountability, a minister can be asked about practically anything, and at all times of the day and night. Ministers say, reasonably, that if they are going to be held accountable for virtually everything, they are going to control virtually everything,' and he went on to say to me that when Sir Leon Brittan was Home Secretary, Sir Leon had said to him, 'If I am going to be accountable, I am going to be in charge.' So my question to you, Sir Robin, is this: if the Secretary of State is in charge, is he not therefore responsible and is not the distinction which you sought to draw between accountability and responsibility largely semantic?

Sir Robin Butler: The minister is in charge but in a complex department no minister can be in charge of everything. Just to take as it were an example absurdly, when Sir Leon Brittan was Home Secretary he may have been in charge. He could not have been responsible for the quality of lunch every day in Brixton Prison; he could not have been having reports on what was on the menu that day or on the cleanliness of the kitchens because that is simply not humanly practicable. But somebody ought to be responsible for that and the person who ought to be responsible for it ought to be the Governor and that ought to be made clear. So the distinction I have tried to draw between accountability and responsibility, and that the Chancellor of the Duchy takes up in his speech, is that Sir Leon Brittan, as Sir Brian Cubbon said, is accountable for everything. He can be asked in the House of Commons, he can be asked by the press, about the quality of food at Brixton Prison and could be required to give an answer, but to say that he can be day-to-day responsible for that is false and it is damagingly false. It is, therefore, important to make clear which official is responsible. The Home Secretary is always accountable but somebody else has to be responsible and responsible to the Home Secretary.

2095. And it is this thinking which led you to write in paragraph 9 the distinction about what is blameworthy and what is not?

Sir Robin Butler: Yes.

Notes

1   It is apparent that the duty to explain extends to answering criticisms, to defending the record of the department in question, even to promising investigation and remedial action if necessary. The duty to explain therefore goes beyond mere the neutral transmission of information: 'accountability' means not only 'giving an account' but also 'being held to account' with the proviso that this kind of being held to account does not include the

---

32   Minutes of Evidence Taken Before the Public Service Committee, HC 313, (1995–96), 3 April 1996, QQ 115. Lord Armstrong is a former Secretary to the Cabinet, and Head of the Home Civil Service. He held these positions during the launch of the 'Next Steps' initiative.

acceptance of personal fault by the minister. (Acceptance of such fault means acceptance of 'responsibility' and resignation may then become an issue – a matter we will examine below). Therefore, 'accountability' in the Government sense also covers what Turpin described as 'strong responsibility' – the ability for redress (short of personal redress) to be exacted by Parliament. Lord Armstrong recently explained it thus to the Public Service Committee: in cases in which the minister cannot fairly be held to be personally responsible,

...the responsibility of the minister is to take the action which is required to ensure that it does not happen again. I do not think the minister is exempted from a measure of responsibility. I do not think that responsibility is necessarily a resigning matter for the minister concerned, but I think he is responsible for taking action which will both deal with the situation that has occurred and make sure that, as far as possible, it is not repeated in the future.[32]

2   The Treasury and Civil Service Select Committee did not in fact accept the Government's postulated distinction between accountability and responsibility as an authoritative statement of the constitutional convention of individual responsibility.[33] They also noted that whilst they disagreed with the notion that civil servants should be debarred from answering any questions which might imply accountability to Parliament,

... it would not be appropriate for Select Committees to seek to negotiate new rules to replace the Osmotherly Rules, because they are only to be regarded as the Government's opening negotiating position in its dealings with Select Committees.

and concluded

The precise implications of the doctrine of ministerial accountability for the conduct of civil servants in relation to Select Committees is unlikely to be agreed between the Government and Select Committees (*ibid*).

3   The new Civil Service Code,[34] (see further below), appears, mainly by omission, to preserve the existing position. Apart from a mention of the 'accountability of civil servants to the minister' (para 4) and an instruction that they 'should not deceive or knowingly mislead ... Parliament or the public' it is silent on the issue.

4   Is the present position satisfactory? Dawn Oliver thinks not.

Ministerial responsibility, it is suggested, has become a governmental defence against accountability instead of a weapon against government and a mechanism for accountability. Civil servants remain for the most part anonymous, without personal responsibility to members of the public with whom their departments deal or, most importantly, to Parliament and its select committees. They can never express their own views about Government action, for which ministers alone are 'responsible'. Nor do ministers have to answer questions about these matters, because they are Members of Parliament and MPs cannot be compelled by select committees to answer questions. Hence Parliament encounters barriers against the effective investigation of areas of Government activity because of the

---

33   *Op cit*, paras 121–123.

34   This came into force on 1 January 1996; its full text appears in *Hansard* HL Deb 9 January 1996, WA 21.

doctrine of ministerial responsibility and its flipside – parliamentary government.[35]

5   Interestingly, there is evidence that civil servants themselves consider the present position unsatisfactory.

Minutes of Evidence Taken Before the Public Service Committee, HC 313 (1995–96), 20 March 1996; Memorandum submitted by the Association of First Division Civil Servants[36]

43. ... The civil servant is accountable to his or her minister, who is in turn accountable to Parliament. But does that mean that the civil servant has no direct duty to Parliament or indeed to the public?

44. In 1990 the FDA raised questions with Sir Robin Butler about a separate duty over and above the duty of accountability and responsibility to ministers, that an individual civil servant might, in some circumstances, have towards Parliament. Sir Robin Butler said:

> This is not the constitutional position. Neither the Code (Civil Service Pay and Conditions of Service Code) nor the Armstrong Memorandum recognise such a direct duty to Parliament. It is not acceptable for civil servants to seek to frustrate the policies or decisions of ministers by unauthorised disclosure of information, and it is for ministers rather than civil servants to bear political responsibility and to be accountable to Parliament.

45. At that time the duty of the civil servants was to give their loyalty and confidential service for 'all practical purposes' to the government of the day, as set out in the Civil Service Code at paragraph 9904. So no other answer was possible for most civil servants – although of course the duties of Accounting Officers and their accountability to the Public Accounts Committee, and thus to Parliament, have been long-established.

46. However, the Civil Service Code changed on 1 January 1996. The 'all practical purposes' clause was removed. Under the new Civil Service Code, the civil servant has a duty to make all information relevant to a decision available to ministers.

47. What is still unclear is the practical impact of those changes. In short, has the duty of the civil servant changed as a result? In theory, probably not, because the supposition both is and was that a civil servant is accountable to the minister who is in turn accountable to Parliament. Moreover, a civil servant's responsibility to the public and to Parliament are, so the argument goes, subsumed by the responsibilities that a minister has to Parliament and the public. So in discharging the duty to ministers, the civil servant discharges any duty to Parliament and the public; to do otherwise, is to elevate the judgment of what is in the public interest as assessed by the non-elected public servant above the judgment of the elected public servant.

48. But if ministers are no longer to hold these responsibilities, in the way argued by Mr Howard, Sir Robin Butler and now Sir Richard Scott, if indeed those responsibilities are by implication more properly and more reasonably placed upon civil servants' shoulders, who is accountable to Parliament for the actions of the civil servants?

49. Increasingly in the real world the general public and the press demand that questions they raise about the running of government are answered clearly. Is it

---

35   Oliver, 'Parliament, Ministers and the Law' (1994) 47(4) PA 630 at 643.
36   The Association represents the interests of senior civil servants.

practicable for one person to be responsible and another accountable? Is this not a recipe for civil servants being publicly blamed for what has gone wrong, to shoulder that responsibility, and then be given no opportunity to give their account of what has really happened? Whilst Government ministers claim the credit when things go well, nobody can accuse them of the same enthusiasm when things go badly. Thus, the civil servant may be asked to accept the blame for what has gone wrong, whilst the minister is the only person to explain the reason why, and the civil servant remains bound by the conventions when they appear in public as before Select Committees, of only answering questions within the confines of Government policy and without criticising the ministers concerned. That is hardly a recipe for sound government.

50. Our convoluted system does not lend itself easily to reform on a piecemeal basis. Possibly, if we were starting with a blank sheet of paper we would all know what the answers are, but so many pieces of sticking plaster have been applied to the system as and when it has sprung a leak, that nothing short of a wholesale review of openness and accountability will meet the need.

The impact of Next Steps

The term 'Next Steps' refers to the changes in the organisation of certain Government departments which came out of proposals put forward by the Prime Minister's Efficiency Unit in the late 1980s. The nature of the reforms themselves will first of all be considered; we will then turn to their impact on ministerial accountability.

Next Steps: the nature of the reforms

A Gray and B Jenkins, 'The Management of Central Government Services' in Jones (ed), *Politics UK* (1994), pp433–4

One of the most frequent complaints of managers in the UK civil service has been of the hierarchical financial regimes in which they have had to operate. Purchasing, appointing temporary staff and even painting the office often seemed impossible without reference to principal finance officers. More fundamentally, the annual limits on the budget and controls over capital investment decisions hampered efficiency and effectiveness. The Financial Management Initiative, with its philosophy of accountable management, was intended to move departments from this position, and the Next Steps to take these changes in delegation and financial freedom even further.

There is no doubt that these developments are crucial in shaping the management regimes negotiated in framework documents. Twelve agencies, for example, are now treated as trading funds, ie as commercial businesses with concomitant accounting practices and financial freedoms over capital investment. Such bodies are those with identifiable products and markets (eg Her Majesty's Stationery Office, the Royal Mint and the Vehicle Inspectorate). However, financial freedoms are not the only management systems of importance. Encouraged by the Treasury's policy of local rather than national pay bargaining, agencies are developing their own personnel management regimes. Thus, from April 1994, all agencies with over 2,000 staff have responsibility for their own pay bargaining. The Treasury has also urged that all new systems link pay with performance. Meanwhile, in the wider field of human resource and personnel management, the Civil Service (Management Functions) Act, passed in December 1992, has given scope for the Treasury to delegate to agencies powers to alter the terms and conditions of staff without further reference to the centre.

Notes

1   After an initially hesitant start, the reforms have gathered pace. As Gray and Jenkins note:

> By the autumn of 1993, a total of 89 agencies, as well as similar units in Customs and Excise and the Inland Revenue, employing over 350,000 civil servants (nearly two-thirds of the total), had been established. Numbers of employees ranged from the 64,215 in the Social Security Benefits Agency to the 25 in the Wilton Park Conference Centre. The plan is to launch the remaining agencies by April 1995 by which time 75 per cent of civil service personnel will be employed in agencies.[37]

(This target was not met: in response to a recent Parliamentary Question Mr Heseltine gave the percentage of civil servants working in executive agencies as 67% as at 1 April 1995.)[38]

2   A key quote from the report which inspired the reports makes their aim clear:

> The aim should be to establish a quite different way of conducting the business of government. The central civil service should consist of a relatively small core engaged in the function of servicing ministers and managing departments, who will be the 'sponsors' of particular government policies and services. Responding to these departments will be a range of agencies employing their own staff, who may or may not have the status of Crown servants, and concentrating on the delivery of their particular service, with clearly defined responsibilities between the Secretary of State and the Permanent Secretary on the one hand and the Chairmen or Chief Executives of the agencies on the other. Both departments and their agencies should have a more open and simplified structure. [39]

3   The key question surrounding the introduction of the reform from the constitutional point of view was what effect they would have on the traditional accountability of ministers to Parliament for the work of their departments. If ministers were no longer running the departments, who would answer to Parliament for their work? The original Next Steps report recognised that the issue was of concern.

Next Steps: the impact on accountability

Prime Minister's Efficiency Unit, *Improving Management in Government: The Next Steps* (1988), Annex A

Annex A Accountability to Ministers and Parliament on operational matters

> 1 Evidence we gathered in the scrutiny suggested that when individuals had to answer personally to Parliament, as well as to ministers, their sense of personal responsibility was strengthened. The accountability of permanent secretaries to the Public Accounts Committee, as accounting officers, is long established. It includes direct personal accountability for financial propriety. Another instance

---

37   *Ibid*, p432.
38   HC Deb WA 30 October 1995, cols 7–8.
39   Prime Minister's Efficiency Unit, *Improving Management in Government: The Next Steps* (1988), para 44.

of officials having specific functions which may require them to answer directly to Parliament (though on behalf of their minister) is the case of principal officers, and of bodies with independent or delegated authority, answering to the Select Committee on the Parliamentary Commissioner for Administration.

2 In paragraph 23 we point out that if the concept of agencies developed in the report is to succeed, some extension of this pattern of accountability is likely to be necessary. The principal reasons are, first, that the management of an agency is unlikely in practice to be given a realistically specified framework within which there is freedom to manage if a minister remains immediately answerable for every operational detail that may be questioned; and second, that acceptance of individual responsibility for performance cannot be expected if repeated ministerial intervention is there as a ready-made excuse.

3 The precise form of accountability for each agency would need to be established as part of drawing up the framework for agencies. Any change from present practice in accountability would, of course, have to be acceptable to ministers and to Parliament. It is axiomatic that ministers should remain fully and clearly accountable for policy. For agencies which are Government departments or parts of departments ultimate accountability for operations must also rest with ministers. What is needed is the establishment of a convention that heads of executive agencies would have delegated authority from their ministers for operations of the agencies within the framework of policy directives and resource allocations prescribed by ministers. Heads of agencies would be accountable to ministers for the operations of their agencies, but could be called – as indeed they can now – to give evidence to Select Committees as to the manner in which their delegated authority had been used and their functions discharged within that authority. In the case of agencies established outside departments, appropriate forms of accountability to ministers and to Parliament would need to be established according to the particular circumstances.

4 There is nothing new in the suggestion that ministers should not be held answerable for many day-to-day decisions involving the public and public services. Apart from services delivered by local authorities, there are large numbers of central Government functions carried out at arm's length from ministers. The main categories are:

– decisions on individual cases, where these need to be protected from the risk of political influence, eg tax cases, social security cases;

– some management and executive functions, eg in Customs and Excise, Regional and District Health Authorities, Manpower Services Commission (MSC);

– quasi-judicial or regulatory functions, eg Office of Fair Trading, Immigration Appeals;

– nationalised industries.

5 A variety of different structures exist to cover these functions, for example:

– Customs and Excise and the Inland Revenue are non-ministerial departments with boards which have defined statutory responsibilities;

– the MSC and the other main bodies in the Employment Group (Health and Safety Executive, and ACAS) are non-departmental public bodies. The Chairman of the MSC is Accounting Officer for the MSC's expenditure;

– HMSO and some other internal services bodies (eg Crown Suppliers) are established as trading funds and work on a commercial basis;

– the PSA, the Procurement Executive and the NHS Management Board are agencies within departments;

– a range of quasi-judicial functions is carried out by a statutory tribunals (eg Rent Tribunals, Industrial Tribunals).

6 Agencies outside departments generally operate within a statutory framework which lays down the constitution of the particular agency and the powers of ministers in relation to it. In answer to Parliamentary Questions about matters within the control of the agency, ministers often preface their reply by saying 'I am advised by the Chairman of the Board that … '. Most operations currently carried out within departments operate under statute. Where it is necessary to change the arrangements for formal accountability for operations currently carried out within departments, legislation (normally primary legislation) would generally be required, and in instances where this is needed it should be considered. Provided that the objective of better management is clearly explained and understood, and that an appropriate form of accountability to ministers and to Parliament is retained, the Government should be able to present such proposals in a positive light.

7 As regards the Public Accounts Committee, as explained in paragraph 22 of the report, the modification of accountability we propose should not immediately affect accountability to the PAC. This would remain, as now, with the Accounting Officer, who may still be, but need not be, the Permanent Secretary. (Of the 76 Accounting Officers appointed by the Treasury, only 18 are First Permanent Secretaries.) However, the practice might develop of the Accounting Officer being accompanied at a PAC hearing by the manager of the agency. The Accounting Officer would answer questions about the framework within which the agency operated; the manager would answer questions about operations within the framework. This would give the PAC the ability to question in detail the person who had firsthand knowledge of the particular operation. It would also in the process put a clear pressure on the agency head to be responsible for his or her agency and to strive for good value from his or her spending.

8 In the case of other select committees it is existing practice for officials with operational responsibility to give evidence before them. It would be normal in the future for the agency head to give evidence before a select committee about operational matters within his or her responsibility.

9 The powers of the Parliamentary Commissioner for Administration could continue to apply to agencies.

10 Quite apart from the issue of improving Civil Service management, there is a good case for trying to reduce the degree of ministerial overload that can arise from questions about operations, as distinct from policy. For example, Social Security Ministers receive about 15,000 letters a year from MPs, many of which are about individual cases. In the future, MPs could be asked to write about operational matters directly to the Chairman of the Board or the local office manager. Arrangements of this sort could be promulgated by a letter from the relevant minister or the Leader of the House to all MPs. (In the past the Chancellor of the Exchequer has written to all MPs asking them to refer questions about constituents' tax to local tax offices, and the Secretary of State for Social Services has written similarly about referring social security cases to DHSS local office managers.) If an MP writes to an operational manager about matters which are essentially political, it is already normally practice for the manager to refer the letter to the minister.

11 It would be part of the framework drawn up between the department and the agency to have specific targets for promptness in dealing with correspondence with MPs. It should be possible for MPs to get a quicker answer when dealing direct with the responsible person, because the intermediate stage of a

headquarters branch calling for a report from a local manager before drafting a reply for the minister will have been cut out.

Notes

1 How have these suggested new arrangements for scrutiny of the agencies been realised in practice and what impact have these changes had? A parliamentary question which is perceived as raising matters within the remit of the Chief Executive of an agency will be answered by the Executive, and his answers have (from October 1992) been printed in *Hansard*. Chief Executives give evidence to the Public Accounts Committee in relation to their Agency's accounting policies. But what exactly *is* the allocation of responsibility between minister and Chief Executive, and does the fact that the Chief Executive has taken on greater levels of responsibility than civil servants were ever admitted to have relieve the minister of accountability for those areas? The Government position is reiterated in the 1995 Next Steps Review:[40]

> The introduction of Next Steps agencies has not changed the normal framework of ministerial accountability to Parliament. Ministers account to Parliament. The Next Steps programme has, however, built on the conventional relationships between ministers and those carrying out the executive functions of Government. The aim is that operational responsibilities should be clearly delegated, with the Chief Executive being personally responsible to the minister for the management and performance of the agency. The form and extent of this delegation is determined case by case in published framework documents. However, for ministers to provide an adequate account to Parliament and others, they need to keep in touch and do, of course, retain the right to look into, question and even intervene in the operations of an agency if public or Parliamentary concerns require it.

2 The Government considers that the reforms have 'emphasised delegation and clarity of responsibility' and thus 'strengthened accountability'.[41] The Treasury and Civil Service Select Committee has given extensive consideration to this issue. Selections from its minutes of evidence and its report appear below, starting with the issue of whether the Next Steps agencies have in fact improved accountability.

Minutes of Evidence taken before the Treasury and Civil Service Select Committee on 23 November 1993, HC 27 (1993–94), QQ 1365 and 1366, and on 26 April 1994, QQ 2103 and 2104; Fifth Report, paras 163, 166–7, 170–1

Sir Robin Butler: I believe that [the Next Steps reforms] do increase accountability to Parliament for this reason: that, in the past, whereas the minister was accountable, and still is accountable, for the operation of every executive agency, below that it was a little difficult to see who was responsible for the quality of the services. Now there are Chief Executives who are appointed with terms of reference that are published; they publish their corporate plans; they publish their results; they can be called before select committees of Parliament, and are; and in my view that greatly increases the total accountability of the system ...

---

40 Cm 3164, piv.

41 Memorandum submitted by the Office of Public Science and Service, *op cit*, para 12.

Sir Robin Butler: I think in no case are [the agencies] independent of ministers. A minister can always intervene with the agencies. Similarly, any Member of Parliament who is dissatisfied with the way in which an agency is performing, and the answer that they get from a Chief Executive, can take it up with the minister. In a sense there are two opportunities for Members of Parliament or the public to test these agencies...

Sir Robin Butler: I think there is a misunderstanding, particularly about Next Steps Agencies. People often refer to them as quasi-autonomous. They are not. They are part of the Civil Service. The Chief Executive of a Next Steps Agency is a civil servant like anybody else, responsible to the minister, and the minister is accountable for him. That is not often widely understood and that is part of the reason, part of the misunderstanding, why people have talked about an accountability gap. I say there is no accountability gap because a minister is accountable, in the sense that he can be called to account for everything that goes on in his Department; every exercise of the powers that Parliament has given to him.

Chairman

2104. It might be a responsibility gap.

Sir Robin Butler: There might be a responsibility gap, but that is what we have sought to close in the Next Steps arrangement by defining the responsibility of Chief Executives and civil servants down the line. So my whole argument about Next Steps is that it is an improvement in accountability because we have both retained the fact that Parliament can always ask a minister about anything under his control, but can recognise that some powers have, in a complex society, to be delegated.

[Fifth Report]

163. The second main area of debate about the progress of the Next Steps programme relates to accountability and responsibility, both in terms of the means by which an account of the operations of agencies was given to Parliament and the public and in terms of the wider allocation of responsibility. In the last Parliament our predecessors expressed concern that the practice of ministers of asking Chief Executives to reply to Parliamentary questions on operational matters which were not then published would limit Parliamentary and public access to information on the work of agencies. They also noted inconsistencies between departments in the division of Parliamentary answers between ministers and Chief Executives. Since then, the Government has accepted a recommendation from the Procedure Committee which was supported by our predecessors that all replies to Parliamentary questions from agency Chief Executives should be published in the Official Report (*Hansard*). The Benefits Agency detailed the arrangements for handling Parliamentary business in its own case. The Chief Executive responded to questions about individual cases, local issues and the day-to-day operation and performance of the agency. Ministers replied to questions relating to policy, reporting national statistics or with a policy input. They also replied to inform Members that information was not readily available and could only be obtained at disproportionate cost. The Chief Executive replied to nearly two thirds of questions. Mr Bichard believed these arrangements had 'worked well', enabling Members to receive quick and effective responses. The Next Steps Project Manager also emphasised the advantages of the new arrangements. He said that the Next Steps Team monitored the division of responsibility for answering questions. He admitted that there was a 'grey area' between policy and operations and said that in such cases the minister should reply. Like Mr

Bichard, he emphasised that Members retained the right to call ministers to account if dissatisfied with a response from an agency Chief Executive ...

Mr Vernon Bogdanor argued that this change in practice should be mirrored by a change in theory: 'the *actual* responsibility of the Chief Executive for the work of his or her agency should be accompanied by a direct *constitutional* responsibility for his work'. To give effect to this, ministers should state that the Osmotherly Rules did not apply to agency Chief Executives. The idea of giving agency Chief Executives greater authority personally to account for their actions gained wide support, including that of Sir Peter Kemp. The original Next Steps Report envisaged that legislation might be necessary to enable agencies to operate with sufficient independence and accountability. Several observers felt that the time had now arrived to give statutory backing to executive agencies, endowing their agreements with ministers with legal force. It was suggested that this would strengthen the division of responsibility between ministers and Chief Executives, facilitate improved public and Parliamentary scrutiny and make it more difficult to 'shift the goal posts' ...

167. The Government argued that the establishment of executive agencies left the traditional doctrine of ministerial accountability unimpaired while increasing 'the accountability of whole areas of Civil Service work, through greater openness and clearer lines of responsibility'. According to the Government, Agencies did not 'undermine the key constitutional principle that it is ministers who are accountable to Parliament for all that their Departments do'. The Government emphasised the marked growth of information about the internal operations of Government available to Parliament and the public as a result of Next Steps and argued that the creation of agencies made accountability 'more effective' through enhanced transparency in Government. Mr Waldegrave described the previous arrangements for ministerial replies on operational matters as 'a fiction', a view which has also been expressed by another minister. The Government saw the new arrangements as an improvement on previous practice, because a Member of Parliament had an opportunity both to receive a reply from the responsible civil servant and to seek a reply from a minister if he remained dissatisfied. Mr Waldegrave added that it was important that a minister or his office scanned replies to ensure that issues were not emerging which related to policy ...

170. **We support the arrangements for Parliamentary questions on operational matters within the ambit of an executive agency to be referred in the first instance to agency Chief Executives and we welcome the fact that their answers are now published in the Official Report.** The extent to which Chief Executives provide answers should, by and large, be seen as a welcome sign of the extent of their devolved responsibilities and need not of itself be a cause for concern. We nevertheless regard it as important that ministers maintain an engagement with individual cases raised by way of Parliamentary questions. We suspect that the scope for active ministerial involvement in individual cases raised in this manner under the previous arrangements would not be universally regarded as 'a fiction'. We believe that ministerial intervention will sometimes be desirable, particularly in individual cases, and is a necessary part of a minister's role. **Ministers should always respond where Members of Parliament consider the response by an agency Chief Executive to be unsatisfactory.**

171. We do not believe that ministerial power to intervene in the actions and decisions of agencies justifies the retention of ministerial accountability for the actions and decisions of agencies for which Chief Executives are responsible. The theoretical separation of accountability and responsibility is nowhere more untenable than in the operation of agencies; continued adherence to the theory

behind such a separation might jeopardise the durability of the delegation at the heart of Next Steps. The delegation of responsibility should be accompanied by a commensurate delegation of accountability. **We recommend that agency Chief Executives should be directly and personally accountable to select committees in relation to their annual performance agreements. Ministers should remain accountable for the framework documents and for their part in negotiating the annual performance agreement, as well as for all instructions given to agency Chief Executives by them subsequent to the annual performance agreement. To this end, we recommend that all such instructions should be published in agency annual reports, subject only to a requirement to preserve the personal confidentiality or anonymity of individual clients.**

Notes

1   It will be seen that the Select Committee made quite a radical proposal – to end the ministerial obligation to answer for all operational matters. This would be replaced by a parallel obligation of the Chief Executive which would be enforced by select committees, in effect ending the 'parallel' system of accountability which currently exists.[42] The proposal was rejected by the Government on the grounds that it would undermine ministerial accountability. Recently, in evidence before the Public Service Committee, Peter Hennessey said:

> I actually think the ... Committee was right to say that agency Chief Executives would come and give evidence ... in their own right. ... If you have got named responsibilities in framework documents ... publicly-assigned responsibilities, you have got to be publicly accountable for them, no caveats ... . If you really are going to follow through the logic of the Next Steps, you have to go that far ... .[43]

The issue of the blurring of responsibility between Chief Executive and minister will be returned to below when we consider the issue of ministerial resignation.

2   The situation as it relates to accountability therefore seems to be this; Chief Executives will answer parliamentary questions on operational matters and give evidence to Select Committees, but the minister can be asked all the same questions as the Chief Executive, if Parliament is dissatisfied with the latter's replies. Also, the minister can intervene in any aspect of the running of agencies, though the expectation is that s/he will not do so and as we shall see, when errors and blunders in operational matters come to light, ministers will often distance themselves from mistakes which they claim are due to mistakes in running the agencies, not in the original policies themselves. Only the minister can be asked about matters of high policy. Although the Chief Executive gives an account to Parliament about operational matters, any disciplinary action against the Chief Executive is a matter for the minister only, not Parliament.

---

42   It is worth noting the interestingly comments of the Association of First Division in this regard. Civil servants noting the Select Committee's proposals they go on: 'This will inevitably mean considering the possibility ... of making civil servants both responsible and accountable in certain areas of government work ... It has been suggested that such consideration should be limited only to agency chief executives. But it is not logical to begin such a review on that basis. The whole machine needs to be reviewed...'. Minutes of Evidence Taken Before the Public Service Committee, HC 313 (1995–96), (20 March 1996); Memorandum submitted by the Association of First Division Civil Servants, para 53.

43   Minutes of Evidence Taken Before the Public Service Committee, HC 313 (1995–96), (20 March 1996), Q 92.

3   Is this a logically satisfactory position? Arguably not. The whole point of these agencies is that they are supposed to operate with a large degree of independence from ministers; thus they can determine their own spending priorities, and negotiate pay levels with the civil servants they employ. This is supposed to lead to greater efficiency, better delivery of public services, since the agencies will be run on much more business-like lines and be free from constant political interference by ministers.

As Lord Armstrong, recently said in evidence before a select committee,[44]

> It seemed to me absolutely clear at [the time the first agencies were set up] that ... Chief Executives were going to be given responsibility for day to day management ... and they would be left to get on with it and the letters of complaints ... and that kind of thing would be dealt with by the Chief Executive and the minister would not expect to be involved.

Given that this is the whole point of the changes, it seems somewhat futile to still maintain that the minister should be accountable for everything going on in the agencies. See, for the latest exchanges between the Public Service Committee and the Government, the Committee's Second Report (HC 313–I (1995–96)) and the Goverment's response (HC 67 (1996–97)).

4   Oliver has gone further and alleges that there are reasons of principle, as well as internal consistency for discarding, or at least radically revising, the doctrine of ministerial accountability.

Dawn Oliver, 'Parliament, Ministers and the Law' (1994) 47(4) Parliamentary Affairs 630, 644–5

> ... Ministers and MPs cling to the idea that ministerial responsibility is crucial to the constitution. It is suggested that the time has come to dare to think the unthinkable and accept that ministerial responsibility can only offer a marginally effective, last resort, solution to problems of bad government. Indeed, it actually inhibits the targeting of criticism and thus enables bad government and bad decision-making to be perpetuated.

> We need to face up to the fact that alternatives are needed, are possible, are being devised and could be developed, as far better checks on government than ministerial responsibility can ever be. This is not to argue for an end to parliamentary government (though the Liberal Democrats' 1993 paper *Here We Stand: Proposals for Modernising Britain's Democracy* suggested relaxing the requirement that all ministers be members of one or other of the Houses of Parliament: perhaps even this constitutional principle is not immutable?). Nor is it to exonerate ministers from responsibility for their own acts and policies or those of their departments. It is an argument for accepting explicitly the need to supplement existing arrangements with legally based, non-parliamentary mechanisms of control and accountability, and acknowledging that there are situations where ministerial responsibility can be involved inappropriately to protect Government against accountability rather than to expose Government to it.

> There is not the space here to develop a programme for a set of supplements to or alternatives for ministerial responsibility. Much work needs to be done on the subject. But the possibilities can be mapped out. There are civilised countries in the world with comparable levels of development and sophisticated political

---

44 Public Service Committee, *op cit*, 3 April 1996, QQ 109. Lord Armstrong was Cabinet Secretary and Head of the Home Civil Service during the launch of the Next Steps initiative.

cultures (and the British political culture is sophisticated, even if part of the sophistication lies in the scepticism of Britons about Government, anti-intellectualism and deep indifference to matters of governance) which manage, indeed are relatively effectively governed, without our level of reliance on this convention, our rejection of legal regulation in central government (local government is quite another matter in the UK) and our tendency to reject fully-fledged or full-blooded alternatives.

In New Zealand for example – the closest relative of the United Kingdom system – much of the public sector has been corporatised in state owned enterprises independent of ministers, thus breaking the unity of the Crown. Almost the whole of the remaining civil service is organised into executive agencies and ministers are responsible for formulating the policy within which these operate. Ministers, not Chief Executives, are responsible to Parliament. Appointments of Chief Executives and staff are on the recommendation of the State Services Commission, which is independent of the Government department, by the Governor General in Council – effectively the Cabinet; the Chief Executive is the employer of agency staff. There is an Official Information Act 1982 and a Bill of Rights Act 1990. In Sweden executive agencies are independent of Government, they have representative boards, they report directly to Parliament and they are subject to audit by a range of independent auditing agencies. Ministers are not responsible to Parliament for them, although Sweden has a parliamentary executive. Sweden has a freedom of information regime. The United States, without a parliamentary executive, adopts a quite different model for controlling Government, with regulatory agencies concerned with rule-making and adjudication, and functions conceived quite differently from our framework of policy making, administration and management. There, too, is a government in the sunshine act.

In a typically Jourdainian way – unwittingly – we may be moving away from the parliamentary executive and ministerial responsibility in the UK. Clearly, with majority voting now widely provided for in the European Union Council of Ministers, ministerial responsibility cannot operate in relation to Union matters. The statutory initiatives discussed above establish the beginnings of non-parliamentary mechanisms of accountability. The executive agencies remove much administration, in practice if not in theory, from the scope of ministerial responsibility save as a last resort. The link between Parliament and redress of grievances is almost broken in appointments such as the Revenue Adjudicator, and the Government has promised a number of lay adjudicators under the Citizen's Charter to deal with grievances which will further weaken these links. If such officers proliferate and arc successful, the redress of grievance function of Parliament can be expected to atrophy. And we can expect alternatives to develop as the ineffectiveness of Parliament over what both ministers and their departments do creates problems for which solutions are essential.

Note

Derek Lewis (former Director General of the Prison Service) has recently made proposals[45] to alter radically the status and organisation of certain politically contentious Government agencies, in particular the prison service; his proposals reflect elements of Oliver's analysis. Key features of the new arrangements would be:

- an independent board, established by statute, which would have responsibility for oversight of the prison service and for its management through a Chief

---

45 Minutes of Evidence Taken Before the Public Services Committee on 22 May 1996, HC 313 (1995–96).

Executive and management board that it would appoint (and if necessary remove);

- policy would be set by ministers through secondary legislation; ... this would ensure there was absolute clarity about what was policy and Parliament would be given a proper opportunity to scrutinise and take action on policy changes;
...
- the sponsoring department would have the responsibility for monitoring efficiency through systematic and rigorous performance audits conduced by an independent inspectorate ... with powers for the sponsoring department to intervene in the case of serious deficiencies.

The accountability of quangos

What about the scrutiny of quangos – boards and bodies which are not formally part of Government, as the Next Steps agencies are? Who is there to explain their actions, to promise to look into problems, to implement remedial action in response to criticism? Two views may be contrasted below. Stuart Weir produces a swingeing critique of the present position; extracts from the second Nolan report reveals a perhaps more measured assessment.

Stuart Weir, *Quangos: Questions of Democratic Accountability* (1995) 48(2) *Parliamentary Affairs* 306, 319–20

If appointed boards are not made accountable through the variety of old and new mechanisms, then the question has to be asked: where does democratic accountability for the myriad policies and decisions they make actually lie? The only answer is through ministers to Parliament. It is an answer that is profoundly unsatisfactory for a variety of reasons, the chief of which is that Britain is governed through Parliament not by it. The traditional doctrine of ministerial responsibility has long since become a political myth. If it stands for anything, it is not Government's responsibility to but its assertion of independence from Parliament. Equally the principle that ministers are responsible for every act of their civil servants has decayed over time. Ministers no longer accept political responsibility for the bad judgement or major mistakes of their officials, while the officials themselves are protected from scrutiny by the continuing fiction that they have no identity other than through their ministers. Moreover, as senior officials are responsible to ministers alone, they give evidence to Parliament on ministers' terms. They are forbidden under the Osmotherly Rules from discussing policy options or decisions and from commenting on 'questions in the field of political controversy'. The entire bureaucratic structure, including public bodies of all kinds, is almost entirely detached from democratic control by the secrecy of the system.

The government's solution to the *de facto* weaknesses of the discredited system of ministerial responsibility has been internal to the administrative system – framework agreements, performance indicators, Charters, targets and audit. The purpose is to replace notional responsibility at ministerial level with managerial responsibility. But the Government's managerial reforms apply weakly and unevenly, and especially so to EGOs. Even if the reforms eventually improve the managerial performance and responsiveness of all such bodies, there will remain a major accountability gap. The Government presents the public with a false choice between, on the one hand, effective performance and responsive services and, on the other, democratic accountability. Both are required, but at the moment neither at national nor local level are there effective mechanisms for making the policies and decisions of EGOs democratically accountable.

'Reinvented' Government, in effect, leaves accountability standing at best on one leg only. It does nothing to introduce real accountability for policies and decisions, which remain in the fictional realm of ministerial responsibility to Parliament. EGOs are, in effect, accountable solely to ministers and their departments. Ministerial responsibility works to block effective parliamentary scrutiny and control of the policies and decisions of ministers and senior officials.

So far as the public accountability of EGOs and other public bodies are concerned, it fails in two other important ways too – the first a matter of principle, the second practical. First, it is a deceit to suggest that a general vote – 'a distant and diffuse one at that' (to quote Waldegrave again) – every four or five years can give Government ministers and their officials the democratic authority to decide highly specific issues in all significant public services in every part of the country; and it is absurd to suggest that a national Parliament is the proper arena for making Government accountable for this local universe of decision-making. Secondly, even if the public found such a highly centralised system of accountability desirable, it is anyway a practical impossibility. The seven major departments of state, and the host of agencies and advisory bodies attached to them, constitute a vast and complex range of responsibilities that ministers simply cannot begin to oversee. Not since the Crichel Down Affair in 1954 have ministers of either party shown an inclination to accept responsibility for the mistakes of their own departments. But the logic of the Government's reforms, the disabling of local government and proliferation of EGOs is to make ministers virtually the single ultimate point of responsibility for the billions of spending and policy decisions of a host of EGOs, 94 executive agencies and 439 local authorities. A very modern ideology has produced a practical nonsense.

Second Report of the Committee on Standards in Public Life, Cm 3270-I

18. Consumers may have the opportunity to influence the service providers through local consultation arrangements. The main real sanction which consumers tend to have against the funders, however, is through the electoral process. But national general elections are a very weak and ineffectual mechanism for seeking to influence the provision of local services. The sanctions which the electorate collectively can exercise over national Government will seldom be sufficiently targeted to address specific local problems. The ability of the electorate to influence non-departmental public bodies, such as the Housing Corporation or the Funding Agency for Schools, is particularly limited. There is no effective local sanction which can be used to oblige these bodies to respond to local priorities, however much they may seek to be responsive to them.

19. As we noted in our first report, it is not for this committee to enter into the argument of whether or not local services should be run under the auspices of elected local authorities, rather than those of the elected national Government. Yet when local bodies are ultimately accountable to central Government, the intermediate mechanisms which enable proper accountability to be secured, and to be seen to operate, need to be very carefully constructed. In particular, there is a responsibility on national Government, and on its agencies and regulators, to ensure that centrally funded bodies are able to respond to local needs and concerns, and have arrangements in place which enable local concerns to be raised.

The obligation to accept responsibility for errors and failures

The constitutional position

Here we examine how developments in the duty to explain has affected responsibility for error and whether as many commentators argue, a contraction of responsibility has occurred. As seen above, ministers are now considered by the Government not to have to accept personal blame – and therefore possibly resign – unless matters of policy are involved. Certain it is that resignations in the absence of such fault have always been few and far between.

The resignation of Sir Thomas Dugdale in respect of the Crichel Down Affair in 1954 is usually cited as an example of a resignation due to responsibility accepted by the minister for departmental errors. Land in Devon was acquired by compulsory purchase in 1938 for use as a bombing range. After it was transferred to the Ministry of Agriculture and by them to the Commissioners for Crown Lands who let it to a tenant of their choice. The former owner of the land was denied the right to buy it back and neighbouring landowners who had been led to believe that they would be able to bid for it were denied the opportunity to do so. When these events led to an inquiry it was concluded that civil servants in the Department of Agriculture had acted in a deceitful and high-handed manner. The Minister for Agriculture then resigned and said in the House: 'I as Minister must accept full responsibility to Parliament for any mistakes or inefficiency of officials in my Department'. In fact this example of the operation of the doctrine may not be as clear cut as this suggests: it became apparent that the minister had played a personal part in the decisions made.

One rare example of a ministerial resignation in the absence of personal fault was Lord Carrington's, in the aftermath of the Argentinian invasion of the Falkland Islands in 1982.

Lord Carrington, *Reflect on Things Past* (1988), pp368–71

On Friday 2 April Argentina invaded the Falkland Islands. On Monday 5 April I surrendered to the Queen at Windsor my seals of office as Foreign and Commonwealth Secretary.

It was a difficult as well as a painful decision and it was entirely my own. There was a good deal of pressure on me to remain at my post. I was grateful for the confidence and kindness this implied but I could not agree that it would be right. It was a great additional sadness to me that Humphrey Atkins, Lord Privy Seal and my number two in the Foreign Office, as well as Richard Luce, decided they should go as well.

As to the responsibility for the invasion itself, in the sense of having left undone something we should have done which would have pre-empted it, I could not with honesty and soul-searching feel much. To have prepared and sailed the sort of military force which could physically have prevented invasion, which could have defeated the attempt, was not a decision it was at any time rational for the Government to have taken before the event on the information they possessed ... As to whether we might – or British intelligence might – have discerned earlier the actual intention to invade, I doubt it. Plans, even detailed plans, are one thing: firm decisions quite another. It was rumoured afterwards that American satellite Intelligence had disclosed everything, and been rejected by us – rumours without a breath of truth.

Stories which were later given currency that we in the Foreign Office ignored warnings from our Embassy in Buenos Aires were totally without foundation. The basic criticism levelled at us was, of course, miscalculation – we miscalculated that the Argentinians would invade. Certainly we did: we miscalculated Argentine folly. And history will record that the fundamental miscalculation was General Galtieri's.

It was not a sense of culpability that led me to resign – a subjective judgement, of course, but one which was later to find confirmation in the Franks Report. The logic of my resignation was different, and I had two principal reasons, one general and one more particular.

The general reason was my sympathetic understanding that the whole of our country felt angry and humiliated. I felt that myself. British territory had, without warning, been invaded. There were hysterical outbursts in Parliament and yells of 'betrayal', and although these were inaccurate and offensive they were understandable. Inhabitants of a British colony – men and women of British blood – had been taken over against their will. Diplomacy had failed to avert this. Military reinforcement had not been tried. Deterrence had been exposed as a bluff. Our hand had apparently been called. There was never the slightest doubt that, with Mrs Thatcher at the head of the Government, we wouldn't take this lying down, and we didn't. But the first shock and fury were felt throughout Britain, and in those circumstances – with people very naturally turning on the Government and accusing it of mismanagement – it is right, in my judgement, that there must be a resignation. The nation feels that there has been a disgrace. Someone must have been to blame. The disgrace must be purged. The person to purge it should be the minister in charge. That was me. I was also very aware my membership of the Lords was at that moment an embarrassment to the Prime Minister, and a weakness. In the Commons Humphrey Atkins was first-class, as was Richard Luce, but when there's a real political crisis it is in the House of Commons that the life and death of Government is decided and I bitterly regretted that I could not face that House at Margaret Thatcher's side.

The more particular reason was my awareness that the Government was in for a hard time and that my presence would make it not easier but harder. We were now assembling a task force and sailing to the South Atlantic – an action with which I wholeheartedly agreed. During the time it would take – a matter of weeks, not days – it was going to be difficult to keep Parliament and country sufficiently united behind our actions, and unity is essential in war. My departure would put a stop to the search for scapegoats. It would serve the cause of unity and help turn the eyes of all from the past to the immediate future. With John Nott, I had attended a fairly disagreeable meeting of the 1922 Committee and although nobody shouted for my resignation I knew that within the Conservative Party itself my remaining in office was not going to help the Prime Minister with her own supporters.

Notes

1 It will be seen that Carrington's decision was taken at least partly for political reasons – to assist the Government in the difficult times ahead. In any event, if there ever was a time when ministers accepted that they should resign for atone for mistakes which are not their own, the time is certainly passed. The Government's present position has been summarised thus: [46]

The Government contended that 'It has never been the case that ministers were required or expected to resign in respect of any and every mistake made by their

---

46 *Fifth Report from the Treasury and Civil Service Select Committee*, HC 27 (1993–94), para 121.

departments, though they are clearly responsible to Parliament for ensuring that action is taken to put matters right and prevent a recurrence'. The resignation of Sir Thomas Dugdale over the Crichel Down Affair in 1954 was held to be the exception that proved the rule. The notion of ministers resigning for the mistakes of others was seen by Mr Waldegrave as 'a bad doctrine'. Mr Waldegrave suggested that in cases which might possibly entail resignation, Select Committees might inquire into whether ministerial accountability was matched by actual ministerial responsibility for mistakes. The Government's position was broadly consistent with that outlined by Sir David Maxwell-Fyfe in the Crichel Down debate in July 1954. He listed categories of actions or events for which, in the view of the Government, it would and would not be appropriate to hold a minister responsible. He contended that 'a minister is not bound to defend action of which he did not know, or of which he disapproves', but he concluded that a minister 'remains constitutionally responsible to Parliament for the fact that something has gone wrong, and he alone can tell Parliament what has occurred and render an account of his stewardship'. Lord Jenkins and Lord Callaghan endorsed the Government's view that ministers should not be expected to resign for administrative failures in which they are not directly involved, the latter remarking that 'if we were to apply Thomas Dugdale's approach today we would not have the same Cabinet for three weeks running'.

2 The 'new' doctrine of responsibility for policy only appears to be gaining ground: not only has the Government repeatedly asserted it, but Parliament now seems to accept it. As Woodhouse notes,[47] when the 'new' doctrine was put forward by the then Home Secretary James Prior in 1983, after a break-out from the Maze Prison by IRA prisoners, in response to calls for his resignations, many MPs were not impressed. For example, Enoch Powell protested that the minister could not say to the House and to the public that the policy was excellent and was his, but that the execution was disastrous or defective and had nothing to do with him. However, when Kenneth Baker put forward the same argument in a similar situation in 1984, 'the House seemed to accept his division between policy and administration and the corresponding limitation of his responsibility'.[48] Lord Justice Scott also indicated in his report that he accepted the 'new' doctrine saying he found it 'difficult to disagree' with Sir Robin Butler's view that:

the conduct of government has become so complex and the need for ministerial delegation of responsibilities to and reliance on the advice of officials has become so inevitable as to render unreal the attaching of blame to a minister simply because something has gone wrong in the department of which he is in charge.[49]

3 The following questions are raised by the 'new' position on responsibility: (a) is the operational/policy division sustainable; (b) is it liable to be abused by ministers anxious to avoid responsibility; (c) how should persons other than ministers be held responsible? These issues will be looked at in turn.

---

47 'When do Ministers Resign?' (1993) 46 (3) PA 277, 286–87.

48 *Ibid*, p287.

49 *Inquiry into Exports of Defence Equipment and Dual-Use Goods to Iraq and Related Prosecutions*, HC 115-I (1995–96), para K8.15.

The operational/policy divide

This issue has arisen mainly in the context of defining the different responsibilities of Chief Executives and ministers; below the Treasury and Civil Service Select Committee considers the present position, finds it unsatisfactory, and suggests reform.

Fifth Report from the Treasury and Civil Service Select Committee, HC 27 (1993–94)

165. In 1990 Sir Peter Kemp, the then Next Steps Project Manager, said that 'it is part of the purpose of Next Steps to try and distinguish just whose fault it is. If, in fact, the shortcoming is such that it was the fault of the lack of resources or legislation which was not within the power of the Chief Executive, the transparency of the system should enable that to be seen. If, on the other hand, it was simple bad management on the part of the Chief Executive then that should be seen too and the man should be held to account accordingly.' Much evidence questioned whether the Next Steps programme was providing such opportunities in practice. Our predecessors set store by the view that agency Chief Executives who failed could be more readily dismissed than other civil servants, yet Professor Eric Caines argued that 'Nobody is sacked for making mistakes, the deal being that if ministers are to protect Chief Executives, they for their part must shield ministers'. He alleged that 'a compact of sorts has been struck between ministers and Chief Executives which ensures that neither of them assumes the ultimate risk'. A Chief Executive was required to accept limited freedom and the need to keep ministers out of political trouble in return for job security. Others suggested that the framework documents and other publicly available information on the operation of agencies did not provide sufficient clarity for outsiders to determine the allocation of responsibility. There was a blurring of responsibilities which made it impossible to distinguish between policy and operations. Ministers might pass the buck for policy failures, and disclaim responsibility for operational activities. There was a 'bureaucratic Bermuda Triangle' in which accountability disappeared. The difficulties in drawing a clear line of responsibility between policy and operations noted in the Trosa Report were observed by others. The extent to which agency Chief Executives were bound by decisions on the level of resources on which they could not comment publicly was seen as typifying the fact that they had 'responsibility but no authority'.

167. ... The Government ... challenged the notion that responsibility in practice was too diffuse, Mr Waldegrave considering that it was perfectly possible under the present arrangements for an agency Chief Executive to be dismissed if he made 'a pig's ear of managing the Agency'. With regard to the criticism that agency Chief Executives were unable to comment on their resource levels, Mr Michael Bichard did not believe that an agency Chief Executive would be able to retain his credibility if he criticised the resources framework within which he was required to operate. The Government saw no case for giving statutory form to the relationship between ministers and Chief Executives, believing the general quality of agreements reached between Departments and Agencies was 'levelling up'. The Inland Revenue's Management Plans for 1994–95 to 1996–97 include for the first time a purchaser/provider contract, agreed with the Financial Secretary to the Treasury, setting out the operational targets and objectives which the Department is expected to meet in the year 1994–95 in return for the resources provided to it. The Chairman of the Board of Inland Revenue considered this to be 'an important development'; although targets were not new, the contract

formalised them in a new way. It would provide a firmer basis for accountability. The Inland Revenue was 'pioneering a contract' of this kind within the British Civil Service. Mr Waldegrave commended this endeavour, which he expected other Departments to follow.

169. ... We consider that the delegation of freedom to manage to executive agencies has not been as thorough and as complete as is desirable, and that this reflects real uncertainties about the division of responsibilities between ministers and parent Departments on the one hand and agencies and their Chief Executives on the other, uncertainties which arise in part from difficulties in identifying and agreeing upon the dividing line between policy and operations. As a solution to these difficulties, it is necessary to base the accountability of Executive Agencies on a distinction which is more tangible: that between decisions made by the agency and decisions made by the minister or parent Department. To this end, **we recommend that the process of target-setting is replaced by annual performance agreements between ministers and agency Chief Executives.** The new performance agreements would be different in character from the current target setting process and would have the following characteristics: they would arise from a process of formal negotiation and require the active agreement of the agency Chief Executive as well as the minister; they would prescribe a minimum of financial controls, ideally setting a single financial target or laying down unit costs for agency services; they would be subject to an evaluation at the end of the year to be undertaken by a body outside the Department. Where a minister or parent Department wished to give an instruction to an agency on a matter within the terms of the performance agreement, or to request the agency to carry out work outside the terms of the performance agreement, this should be done in writing and with financial terms specified as appropriate. It would be for the agency Chief Executive to determine whether such a written instruction was necessary. Although the scope for ministerial and departmental intervention would not be subject to any enforceable restraint, we believe that this requirement, coupled with proposals below relating to accountability, would represent important restraints on unnecessary interference. We do not think that the introduction of legislation need be necessary for such annual performance agreements. They should be made under the terms of revised framework documents.

Ministerial abuse of the operational/policy divide?

The committee found that there was room for doubt in trying to locate the operational/policy divide. Without being unduly cynical, it might be suggested that ministers are happy to leave the matter vague, in order to give themselves maximum scope for argument when faced with criticisms about failures in their department. When William Waldegrave was pressed by the committee as to exactly when a minister should take responsibility, his replies did not suggest anxiety to clarify the position.[50]

1894. When Sir Robin appeared in front of the Scott Inquiry he drew a distinction between ministerial accountability and ministerial responsibility. Do you draw the same distinction and, if so, could you define each?

Mr Waldegrave: I find all these words quite difficult because they are bound to overlap in ordinary language I think. There is a real sense in which ministers are

---

50 Minutes of Evidence Taken Before the Treasury and Civil Service Select Committee on 26 April 1994, HC 27 (1993-94) QQ, 1894–97.

accountable to Parliament and the electorate for policy, but are not responsible for every action taken in a common sense way by the thousands of people ultimately working within that policy. They are accountable for the structures, for the appointments, for the policy and accountable if they do not put things right properly when serious things go wrong and they are accountable if a lot of little things continuously go wrong and they do not see that something is done about that. However, I think there is a proper sense in which somebody carrying out a day to day policy can be said to be responsible for actually carrying out those things he has agreed to carry out.

Chairman

1895. So who is responsible then? If the minister is not responsible, then who is responsible?

Mr Waldegrave: The minister is ultimately accountable for everything.

1896. But you said he or she is not necessarily responsible? Who is responsible?

Mr Waldegrave: Again, you are going to have to take resort in common sense. It depends on the extent and importance and if something has gone wrong, and it is a serious thing, then committees like this inquire into whether it would be plausible to say the minister should have seen in advance that it was going to go wrong and should have done something in advance about it. If it is something that goes wrong, as things will go wrong in life with the best of intentions, then has he done something to put it right, if it is important? Or is it actually a matter of how that office is organised or how that delegated thing is carried out, in which case, in the first instance at least, it might be right to say this is within the normal conscientious carrying out of the duty by this agency head or civil servant of one kind or another, and part of his normal conscientious work would have been for him to get that right and it is unfair to blame the minister? It is terribly difficult to make general rules. Ultimately, of course, the minister is accountable to Parliament for everything.

Sir Thomas Arnold

1897. For you personally does accountability as a concept lack a blame element? This seems to be the principal point of distinction which was in Sir Robin's mind if I understood his evidence to Scott correctly.

Mr Waldegrave: I think you have again to look at individual cases. I find them rather difficult to categorise.

Notes

1   The advantages of this confusion to beleaguered ministers anxious to stay in Government seems to be twofold. First, it will very often by arguable as to whether failures in a given area are due to policy or its implementation; as Professor Hennessey recently pointed out[51] 'There is not actually a proper division between [the two] ... These are seamless garments. If operationally you hit real trouble, it is usually because the policy is flawed'. However, in the common case in which both policy and its application are at fault, ministers, because the control the flow of information to Parliament, can ensure that only evidence of *administrative* failings reach Parliament. Civil servants may know first hand that policy was to blame as well, but will be unable to bring this to Parliament's attention against the wishes of their minister. As the FDA very recently pointed out,

---

51   *Op cit*, QQ 93.

Operational failures ... could all be laid at the door of Government agencies failing to deliver Government policies ... At the same time, policy failures and the reasons for them, for example lack of resources, remaining impenetrable because of the confidentiality which binds a civil servant to ensure that any difference in the advice which she or he gives the Minster and the Government's ultimate decision is never revealed'.[52]

2   Derek Lewis, in a memorandum recently submitted to the Public Services Committee,[53] has voiced similar concerns. Noting that, at present, 'in speaking publicly about agencies, Chief Executives are either required to avoid comment on ... policy or to expound the policy of the Government of the day' he goes on to argue that the Chief Executive should be permitted to comment publicly and to Parliament on policy:

If this is not permitted, the principle of ministerial responsibility is seriously distorted. Ministers would be free to impose half-baked impractical policies or to set wholly unrealistic performance targets, and then simply load the blame onto those running the agency for any failure to implement or achieve as a mere operational matter.

He notes by way of example that both chief constables of police and the Chair of the Bank of England are able, within limits, to express their views on Government policies which they are actively involved in implementing, and expresses the view that, far from merely provoking 'destructive and intolerable conflict' between Chief Executives and ministers, allowing such 'reasoned public debate' would improve the quality of our democracy.[54]

3   Lord Justice Scott made an important point which addressed precisely this concern; noting Sir Robin Butler's distinction between 'accountability' and 'responsibility' he argues that it has:

... an important bearing on the obligation of ministers to provide information to Parliament. If ministers are to be excused blame and personal criticism on the basis of the absence of personal knowledge or involvement, the corollary ought to be an acceptance of the obligation to be forthcoming with information about the incident in question. Otherwise Parliament (and the public) will not be in a position to judge whether the absence of personal knowledge and involvement is fairly claimed or to judge on whom responsibility for what has occurred ought to be placed. Any re-examination of the practices and conventions relied on by Government in declining to answer, or to answer fully, certain Parliamentary Questions should, in my opinion, take account of the implications of the distinction drawn by Sir Robin between ministerial 'accountability' and ministerial 'responsibility' and of the consequent enhancement of the need for ministers to provide, or to co-operate in the provision of, full and accurate information to Parliament.[55]

4   The second advantage to ministers of the ambiguity surrounding the operational policy divide is this: because ministers have repeatedly asserted

---

52   Minutes of Evidence Taken Before the Public Service Committee (Memorandum), HC 313-1, (1995–96), 20 March 1996, para 24.

53   Minutes of Evidence Taken Before the Public Services Committee (Memorandum), 22 May 1996, HC 313, (1995/96).

54   Ibid, paras 10–12.

55   Inquiry into Exports of Defence Equipment and Dual-Use Goods to Iraq and Related Prosecutions, HC 115-I,(1995–96), para K8.16.

(particularly in relation to the Next Steps agencies) that operational matters are not their primary responsibility, it appears that they can have the best of both worlds. They can interfere with the day-to-day running of the agency in order to satisfy short term political imperatives, but then if things go wrong step back and rely on the principle that policy only is their concern to deflect criticism on to the Chief Executive concerned. To many this is what the Derek Lewis saga illustrates. When the highly critical Learmont Report on the state of Britain's prisons came out in October 1995, Michael Howard, the Home Secretary, found that all the problems identified therein were due not to his policies but to the way they had been put into practice by the head of the Prison Service, Derek Lewis, whom he promptly sacked. Lewis complained in vain that in fact much of his day-to-day work had been directed and controlled by Michael Howard and launched an action for wrongful dismissal against the Home Office which it eventually settled, paying the claimed damages in full.

5   There was evidence that Howard had in fact intervened in matters of day-to-day running. The Learmont Report contained a section devoted to the difficulties encountered by the Prison Service because of the political demands made on Lewis. The report found that 'ways and means must be found to overcome the problem' and that a new relationship was needed to 'give the Prison Service the greater operational independence that agency status was meant to confer.'[56] A newspaper reported a prison governor as saying, 'The idea that Howard has not been meddling is just nonsense ... We all know he's been messing everywhere'.[57] In an interview[58] Lewis claimed that documents which he would demand from the Home Office to support his action would prove extensive ministerial interference: 'Lewis is calling for minutes of meetings which he says will show how he was summoned virtually every day to the Home Office by one minister or another, interfering in operational matters'. Examples he gave include the personal intervention of Mr Howard to try and procure the movement of Private Lee Clegg (the soldier convicted of murder following a shooting at a security checkpoint in Northern Ireland) to an open prison after a campaign on his behalf by the right-wing press. Further allegations were that 'ministers challenged the punishments meted out to particular prisoners – a matter that is the sole legal prerogative of prison governors' and also decisions on home leave for prisoners and the disciplining of staff.[59] When the Learmont Report came out, and the Opposition called for Mr Howard's head, politically Howard was protected by the support of his party and the Prime Minster, whilst constitutionally he was assisted in making his claim that the mistakes did not concern him by the presumption that operational matters were always the sole concern of Chief Executives. The problem is that the type of interference described above will often be covert: Parliament will not usually have access to the evidence which would reveal it.

---

56   Quoted in 'Bitter Revenge of the Uncivil Servant', *Sunday Times*, 22 October 1995.
57   *Ibid.*
58   'My Life with Michael Howard', *Independent*, 3 June 1996.
59   *Ibid.*

6 Most interestingly, Lord Armstrong, giving his views on these matters before the Public Service Committee[60] in April 1996 said:

> I think that if you had asked me that day before I retired whether I thought the Prison Service should be made into an agency, I would have doubted it, because I should have felt that not only the objectives and the budget are matters of great political moment but there are many aspects of day to day management which inevitably become politically controversial ...

He contrasts the Prison Service with the Driver and Vehicle Licence Centre (DVLC) which was ideal because its work was only 'management activity'. The highly political nature of all aspects of penal policy and practice make it inevitable that ministers will be unable to resist the pressure to intervene in day-to-day management decisions, thus both undermining the basis of the Next Steps principle and creating confusion about responsibility and accountability.

How should persons other than ministers be held responsible?

This penchant of ministers to attribute failure not to their policy but to operational matters, and thus to officials, raises a question as to whether Parliament should have any part to play in protecting officials in danger of being scapegoated by ministers or even in disciplining them itself. Civil servants are employed under the royal prerogative which, as the FDA recently noted,[61] 'legally ... gives the right to dismiss a civil servant at will and without compensation ... The Government in practice exercises [that] right'.

The FDA went on to voice its concern over the manner in which Derek Lewis was dismissed:

> The Home Secretary dismissed Mr Lewis summarily, for no stated disciplinary reasons and outside the terms of the Civil Service Management Code and departmental procedures. Mr Lewis was given no notice of his dismissal [ibid].

We have already seen how the Treasury and Civil Service Select Committee suggested that Chief Executives should be directly accountable to them for their performance and Scott's suggestion that ministers must provide full information about any incident in respect of which they propose to 'delegate blame' to civil servants, which would undoubtedly assist the latter. A more interesting and radical proposal was considered by the Treasury and Civil Service Select Committee but dropped. It appears below.

Minutes of Proceedings of the Treasury and Civil Service Select Committee HC 27 (1993–94), ppcxix–cxxx

... In our view, in the first instance, in principle, both accountability and responsibility to Parliament should always rest with the minister. Where the minister believes others, perhaps civil servants or the Chief Executive of an agency, have in reality been responsible, he should be able to indicate to Parliament who he believes was responsible and the reasons why he takes that view. It will then be a matter for Parliament to determine whether it accepts the minister's interpretation of events or whether it believes that responsibility should remain with the minister.

---

60 *Op cit*, QQ 109–11, 116–20.
61 *Ibid*, para 10. For the preogative generally, see Chapter 1 of this Part.

This new doctrine of ministerial responsibility could have implications for the anonymity of civil servants. They would become personally responsible for decisions that they take on the interpretation and implementation of policy. To ensure that their position is protected from arbitrary transfer of responsibility by a minister, we believe that such designation of an individual or group of civil servants should always be a decision of the Government as a whole, rather than one minister. Thus, any designation of a person other than the minister should have the prior approval of, at least, the Prime Minister and, preferably, the Cabinet. Ministers should only ever be able to pass on responsibility where they can show that, firstly, they were not involved in a policy decision which resulted in the creation of the situation which concerns Parliament; secondly, that they did not know of its existence when any unacceptable behaviour occurred and it was reasonable for the minister not to have been aware of it, and, thirdly, if they had known, they would have stopped it. If ministers cannot show each of these things, then they should accept responsibility and where appropriate they should resign.

Note

It is not perhaps realistic to look for the implementation of such a change, at least not in the near future.

Ministerial resignation in practice

It is important to note that it would be naive to talk of the above factors as if they were determinative of a minister's decision whether or not to resign. Whether or not a resignation actually occurs will of course depend upon a wide variety of other factors, and the actual record of resignations will not be seen to marry well with any constitutional theory which supposedly dictates when resignation should occur. One well known empirical study of resignations was Finer's:[62]

> S E Finer's classic analysis on this subject shows that three variables have to come into alignment: the minister must be compliant, the Prime Minister firm, and the party clamorous. Finer suggests that this conjunction is rare – and is quite fortuitous. Furthermore, from a normative (or constitutionalist) viewpoint, it is also indiscriminate in the sense that which ministers escape and which are caught has very little to do with the gravity of the offence.[63]

Notes

1   A more recent study,[64] citing a number of cases (Edwina Currie, David Mellor, Cecil Parkinson) in which the Prime Minister of the day tried unsuccessfully to hang on to the minister in question suggests that Finer's second requirement is not always necessary.

2   As is well known, there were no resignations over the Scott report, despite the findings that Sir Nicholas Lyell was 'personally at fault' and William Waldegrave had signed a string of untrue letters and deliberately chosen not to inform Parliament of the change in policy on arms-related exports to Iraq (see below). Clearly, John Major (and the Conservative party generally) regarded the matter from the outset as a party political battle. The stream of

---

62   S E Finer, 'The Individual Responsibility of Ministers' (1956) 34 *Public Admin* 377.
63   Loughlin, *Public Law and Political Theory* (1992), pp52–3.
64   Woodhouse, 'When do Ministers Resign?' (1993) 46(3) PA 277.

criticisms from former senior Government ministers directed at Scott's procedures,[65] the pointed failure of the Prime Minster to declare his confidence in the fairness of Scott's procedures,[66] and the presentation of the report to the press, using carefully prepared – and misleading – press briefings[67] whilst the Opposition had had only a few hours to read the report, had pre-figured this. The behaviour of Conservative MPs in the initial debate on Scott, described in one report as 'rall[ying] noisily round John Major and his ministers'[68] after having only 10 minutes to read the report suggests that for them, simple party loyalty rather then what Scott actually said dictated their response to his findings. As discussed in the House of Commons chapter, the substantive debate on the report was won by the Conservatives, admittedly only by one vote but with only two Conservative rebels.

3   However, a further factor which may have saved ministers, noted by commentators at the time, was the fact that Scott found, sometimes rather confusingly, that there had been no bad faith amongst ministers involved. As Andrew Neil commented in the *Sunday Times*,[69] 'The convoluted, often contradictory manner in which Scott has chosen to construct his report has proved a godsend for those charged with damage limitation'. Similarly, the *Independent*,[70] commenting on the initial Scott debate on 15 February, noted, 'it was looking increasingly likely that Sir Richard's decision not to accuse the two ministers directly of bad faith will endure their survival'. Andrew Neil instanced the treatment of Waldegrave: 'Plain folk will not easily understand why the report says that Waldegrave ... "designedly" and "deliberately" misled Parliament and public about the changes of policy ... yet absolves him of any "duplicitous intention".'

Another article in the *Sunday Times* (on the same day) quotes a minister as saying, 'He doesn't go for the jugular. There are enough ifs and buts to get our people off the hook'.

4   So, even though there were no resignations, the point about the constitutional factors discussed above is that the Government still has to justify a refusal to accept responsibility to the public and to Parliament in normative, constitutional terms. It does not say, 'We really don't care whether the minister should, constitutionally speaking, resign. We've decided it would be better for political reasons for the minister to brazen it out'. Instead, as with Scott, it argues why the minister does not need to resign: their was no intention to mislead Parliament; the Attorney-General's advice on PII's is a matter of legal opinion. The constitutional convention thus sets the parameters for the debate. Further, whilst a minister may cling

---

65   See 'Furious Scott takes on Tory "smear campaign" ', *Independent*, 8 February 1996.

66   HC Deb 8 February 1996, cols 466–67.

67   See for example, 'Blind to blame', *Sunday Times*, 18 February 1996. Andrew Neil described the 'rigging' of the presentation of the report 'an awesome disgrace to democracy'. See 'Weasel words let guilty wriggle off Scott's hook', *Sunday Times*, 18 February 1996.

68   'Secretive, incompetent, chaotic', *Independent*, 18 February 1996.

69   'Weasel words let guilty wriggle off Scott's hook', *op cit*.

70   *Op cit.*

on to power, if the Government is seen to have a weak case in constitutional terms this will be apparent to the public, which will draw conclusions accordingly.[71]

The duty to give information and not mislead Parliament

Until November 1995 – and therefore during the time in which the events which gave rise to the Scott Inquiry took place – *Questions of Procedure for Ministers* had this to say about the duty not to mislead Parliament:

> [Minister's responsibility for their department] includes the duty to give Parliament...and the public as full information as possible about the policies, decisions and actions of the Government, and not to deceive or mislead Parliament and the public. [para 27].

The importance of the obligation to give full and truthful information to Parliament is clear, as noted in the Scott report:[72]

> D4.58 The importance, if ministerial accountability is to be effective, of the provision of full and adequate information is, in my opinion, self-evident. If, and to the extent that, the account given by a minister to Parliament, whether in answering PQs, or in a debate, or to a Select Committee, withholds information on the matter under review, it is not a full account, and the obligation to account for what has happened, or for what is being done, has, *prima facie*, not been discharged. Without the provision of full information it is not possible for Parliament, or for that matter the public, to hold the executive fully to account. It follows, in my opinion, that the withholding of information by an accountable minister should never be based on reasons of convenience or for avoidance of political embarrassment and should always require special and strong justification.

The findings of the Scott report

By far the most comprehensive and authoritative inquiry into the compliance by Government with this practice in the context of a controversial defence exports policy, an inquiry which had unique access to highly confidential Government papers and to Government officials, was that undertaken by Lord Justice Scott into the export of defence-related equipment to Iraq. The report's[73] conclusion was that:

> Government statements made in 1989 and 1990 about policy on defence exports to Iraq consistently failed ... to comply with the standard set by paragraph 27 of [QPM] and, more important, failed to discharge the obligations imposed by the constitutional principle of ministerial accountability.[74]

In this section, the findings of the Scott report which support this conclusion will be given; the significance of the justifications by the Government for the – at the least – incomplete disclosure to Parliament of this policy will be explored;

---

71 Opinion polls taken shortly after the Scott report showed that majorities of over 60% thought Waldegrave and Lyell should resign.

72 *Inquiry into Exports of Defence Related Equipment and Dual-Use Goods to Iraq and Related prosecution* HC 115 I (1995–96).

73 *Ibid.* For articles generally on the Scott report see the Autumn 1996 edition of *Public Law*, and I Leigh and L Lustgarten (1996) 59(5) MLR 695.

74 *Op cit*, para D4.63.

questions will be asked about the position of civil servants in this respect; parliamentary and governmental reaction to the report's findings will be analysed.

The factual background to the Scott Inquiry

In order to understand Scott's condemnation of the Government, the circumstances leading to the setting up of the Scott Inquiry and the Government's changing policy on arms to Iraq needs to be understood. In what follows, Ian Leigh explains the background to the inquiry.

Ian Leigh, 'Matrix Churchill, Supergun and the Scott Inquiry' (1993) Public Law 630–631

The establishment of the Scott Inquiry followed the collapse in November 1992 of the trial of executives from the machine tools company Matrix Churchill, charged with deception in obtaining export licences. Matrix Churchill had been part of a network of European companies acquired by the Iraqis in an attempt at covert armaments procurement. The prosecution was halted after Alan Clark, the former Minister of State at the Department of Trade and Industry and Defence Procurement Minister, confirmed under cross-examination the defendant's defence that there was no deception, because the Government was fully aware of the intended use (in armaments manufacture) of the machine tools which had been the subject of the licence application. The judge had earlier partially quashed public interest immunity certificates served by the prosecution, designed to suppress evidence about intelligence sources, about information held by the Security Services (MI5) and the Secret Intelligence Service (MI6), and high level inter-departmental and ministerial contact over the licence application.

Note

The granting of export licences for sale of defence related equipment to both Iran and Iraq was governed by guidelines which aimed to restrict the sale of such equipment. The parts of the Scott report with which are of relevance here concern the manner in which these guidelines were changed, or re-interpreted and the information which was given by ministers to Parliament about the changing face of Government policy under the guidelines. The guidelines as originally drafted are described here by Richard Norton-Taylor.

Richard Norton-Taylor, *Truth is a Difficult Concept*: *Inside the Scott Inquiry* (1995), pp40–2

The export guidelines which were to cause the Government so much anguish were drawn up in 1984, ironically in an attempt to make it easier for ministers to defend their policy in public. 'The Iran–Iraq war', William Waldegrave, former minister of state at the Foreign Office, was to tell the inquiry, 'was turning out to be a really major war. It was not just an incursion. Persians and Arabs had been squabbling with each other for 8,000 years, but this was turning out to be a really major war with hundreds of thousands of people killed'.

They were prompted by Sir Richard Luce, one of Waldegrave's predecessors at the FO, and one of the few members of the Government who expressed real anxiety about selling arms-related goods to Iraq and Iran. He was the only witness at the Scott Inquiry who suggested that British policy should involve considerations of morality.

On November 13, 1984, he wrote a memo to Lord Howe, then Foreign Secretary. Headed 'Sales of Defence Equipment to Iran and Iraq', it began: 'You need no reminding about the amount of time we have devoted to this complicated subject and the difficulties it has presented to both of us, both in conducting our relations with the two sides in the conflict – other Arab States and the Americans – and in presenting a sufficiently clear and robust defence of our policy to Parliament, the press and British public.'

What became known as the Howe guidelines were designed to unravel the knots tying up the Government over attempts to draw distinctions between 'lethal' and 'non-lethal' exports. They stated:

(i)   We should maintain our consistent refusal to supply any lethal equipment to either side.

(ii) Subject to that overriding consideration, we should attempt to fulfil existing contracts and obligations.

(iii) We should not, in future, approve orders for any defence equipment which, in our view, would significantly enhance the capability of either side to prolong or exacerbate the conflict.

(iv) In line with this policy, we should continue to scrutinise rigorously all applications for export licences for the supply of defence equipment to Iran and Iraq.'

Three weeks later, on December 4, 1984, Howe minuted Lady Thatcher. Echoing Luce, he said the guidelines would make it easier to defend the Government's position 'in public and in Parliament'. In a phrase which was to provoke hours of debate in Whitehall and yet more hours of exchanges at the Scott Inquiry, Howe told the Prime Minister that guideline (iii) 'enables us to retain a modicum of flexibility'.

Despite the stated purpose of the guidelines – to make it easier publicly to defend government policy – Howe nevertheless told Thatcher, 'I do not believe ... that it will be appropriate to seek an opportunity to seek a high-profile announcement of the new arrangements in Parliament. Rather, we should allow the new guidelines to filter out through answers to parliamentary questions and inquiries from the media'.

It took ten months before the Government finally decided to publish the guidelines – on October 19, 1985 – in answer to a question from the Liberal Democrat MP, Sir David Steel. 'It did trickle out', explained Howe to the inquiry. 'David Steel was the recipient of the last gulp of the trickle.' ...

So what did the guidelines amount to? Scott and Baxendale caught out Howe as he tried to downplay their importance. After explaining they constituted an 'inhibition' rather than 'a prohibition', he was reminded that in a letter to Lord Mottistone in November 1988 – just as the Government was planning to relax controls on exports to Iraq – he said the guidelines 'prohibit the export to either country [Iraq or Iran] of any equipment which would significantly enhance the capability of either side to prolong or exacerbate the conflict'. Howe was also reminded that in July 1986 Peter Collecott of the FO's Middle East Department, wrote in an official minute: 'The ministerial guidelines for exports to Iran and Iraq are intended to stop the flow of defence-related equipment'. And while, on the one hand, Howe minimised the significance of the guidelines, he was also quick to claim that they amounted to 'a huge national sacrifice'.

Note

When Iran and Iraq declared a ceasefire in 1988, the British Government was eager to seize the 'big prize' of renewed exports sales to Iraq in particular. At this point, therefore a relaxed version of guideline (iii) was put forward (on 21 December). In future, defence equipment which *'would be of direct and significant assistance to either country in the conduct of offensive operations in breach of the ceasefire'* was not to be exported; the significance of this change is considered below. However, what happened next was the Iranian *fatwa* (sentence of death) against Salman Rushdie, which dealt such a blow to British-Iranian relations, that it became politically impossible to export any defence related equipment to Iran. A further modification of the policy was therefore agreed upon; at the same time it was also agreed that neither modification would be announced to Parliament. Scott traces the unfolding of Government policy starting with the decision to adopt the new guideline (iii).[75]

Inquiry into Exports of Defence Equipment and Dual-Use Goods to Iraq and Related Prosecutions, HC 115-I (1995–96)

D3.65 The state of affairs, therefore, that had been reached by the end of February 1989 was (i) that the Ministers of State at the FCO, the MOD and the DTI had agreed that a more liberal policy towards defence equipment sales to Iraq and Iran should be implemented; (ii) that at MODWG and IDC level the liberal policy was being implemented by the application of the revised form of guideline (iii) 'on a trial basis for the time being'; and (iii) that it had been agreed that no public announcement of these changes would be made. These changes were regarded as temporary or provisional, pending final agreement being reached on the form the new, more liberal, policy should take. ...

D3.42 Accordingly, Mr Waldegrave replied to Mr Clark by a letter dated 7 February 1989 from his Private Secretary to Mr Clark's Private Secretary. The letter said that '... DTI, MOD and FCO officials have agreed that the form of words tabled on 21 December [revised guideline (iii)] appears after all to meet our joint requirements, and should continue to be used on a trial basis for the time being' and that 'Mr Waldegrave is content for us to implement a more liberal policy on defence sales, without any public announcement on the subject'.

Following the 'tilt' to Iran, Mr Waldegrave set out in a letter of 27 April 1989 the new policy:

We agreed [*ie* at a meeting of junior ministers on 24 April] that we should continue to interpret the guidelines more flexibly in respect of Iraq, as we have done in practice since the end of last year; but that we should revert to a stricter interpretation for Iran, along the lines which operated before the ceasefire. This would, in effect mean, that we would not contemplate a major sale of defence equipment to the Iranian Armed Forces. This need not in principle preclude all sales to the Iranian Navy or to the IRGC, although in present circumstances I find it extremely difficult to envisage any major exports to those organisations.

Mr Waldegrave's letter then repeated the agreed form of answer to be used 'if we are now pressed in Parliament over the guidelines', namely:

---

75 The Scott report uses a number of abbreviations. The most important are as follows: FCO – Foreign and Commonwealth Office; MOD – Ministry of Defence; DTI – Department of Trade and Industry; MODWG – Ministry of Defence Working Group; ELA – Export Licence Applications.

'The Guidelines on the export of defence equipment to Iran and Iraq are kept under constant review, and are applied in the light of prevailing circumstances, including the ceasefire and developments in the peace negotiations.'

D3.84 The essence of the agreement reached between the ministers at their 24 April 1989 meeting, as described in Mr Waldegrave's letter, was, so far as Iraq was concerned, that they would 'continue to interpret the guidelines more flexibly. ... as we have done in practice since the end of [1988]'. The 'flexible interpretation' since the end of 1988 had consisted, in practice, of the application of the revised guideline (iii) to Iraqi ELAs and AWP applications. This practice was, therefore, to continue ...

D3.89 The MODWG met on 10 May 1989. Lieut-Colonel Glazebrook's manuscript notes, made on the agenda for the meeting, record what the MODWG members were told about the ministerial agreement:

'1. IRAQ. new relaxed Guidelines

2. IRAN. apply stringent Guidelines.'

D3.90 On 15 June 1989 Mr Barrett followed up the remarks made at the 10 May MODWG meeting by sending a note to all MODWG members in order 'to confirm in writing the interpretation of the guidelines which ministers had agreed we should now use when considering ELAs and AWP applications for Iran and Iraq.' The written confirmation was as follows:

'2. For both countries the normal security considerations should continue to apply. In addition the existing guidelines in respect of lethal equipment will still apply. For non-lethal equipment the following will apply:

a. Iran. – The existing guidelines strictly interpreted in the way that they were being used at the height of the conflict. There should not, however, be a blanket embargo against the Iranian Navy or IRGC; we should stop anything which we believe would pose a direct threat to the Armilla Patrol.

b. Iraq. – We should refuse applications only if they would be of direct and significant assistance in the conduct of offensive operations in breach of the ceasefire.'

Note

This then was the new policy agreed upon by ministers. It is worth noting the view of 'one of the MoD [Ministry of Defence's] most experienced assessor of weapons systems responsible for vetting arms exports'[76] (Lieutenant-Colonel Glazebrook) on what kind of equipment was actually cleared for export to Iraq under this new, undeclared policy:

... in his view, and that of his military colleagues, Matrix Churchill machine tools were 'lethal' and should never have been cleared for exports. Glazebrook was so concerned about the 'whittling away' of export controls that, in June 1989, he drew up a report to warn ministers of how 'UK Ltd is helping Iraq, often unwittingly, but sometimes not, to set up a major indigenous arms industry'. Britain's contribution to Iraq, he said, included setting up a major research and development facility to make weapons, machinery to make gun barrels and shells, and a national electronics manufacturing complex. Taken together, the exports represented 'a very significant enhancement to the ability of Iraq to manufacture its own arms and thus to resume the war with Iraq'. Export guidelines should be tightened, he said, 'from the point of view of both military and security concerns. (*ibid*).

---

76 Norton-Taylor, *op cit*, p52.

Scott's findings: the failure to disclose shifts in policy; the Government's explanations

As Scott found, 'A conscious decision was taken by the junior ministers that there should be no public announcement [of the new policy]'. He goes on to note that 'As a consequence of this decision, answers given by ministers to Parliamentary Questions ['PQ's'] and [their] letters ... to MPs ... were decidedly uninformative'.[77] In another part of the report he states, ' ... The answers to PQs ... failed to inform Parliament of the current state of Government policy on non-lethal arms sales to Iraq. This failure was deliberate ...'.[78]

The following extracts from the report show first, Scott's analysis of this failure as displayed in certain ministerial letters to MPs[79] and second his discussion of three different rationale offered by various Government spokespersons for the way in which the Government handled replies to MPs on this issue.

Inquiry into Exports of Defence Equipment and Dual-Use Goods to Iraq and Related Prosecutions, HC 115-I (1995–96)

D4.1 Over the period February 1989 to July 1989, a number of letters, signed mainly by Mr Waldegrave but a few by Lord Howe, were sent to MPs whose constituents had asked questions about Government policy on defence sales to Iraq. ...

D4.2 A form of response to be incorporated in the letters sent to the MPs in question was settled in the FCO. The response included the following two sentences (or the gist of them):

'British arms supplies to both Iran and Iraq continue to be governed by the strict application of guidelines which prevent the supply of lethal equipment or equipment which would significantly enhance the capability of either side to resume hostilities. These guidelines are app'ied on a case by case basis.'

D4.3 Letters to MPs incorporating these sentences and signed by Mr Waldegrave numbered some seven in March 1989, five in April, twenty-three in May, one in June and two in July. Lord Howe signed two similar letters in May and two in July. In one of the April letters and in each of the May, June and July letters the formula was preceded by the statement that: 'The Government have not changed their policy on defence sales to Iraq or Iran.'

In one letter there was a reference to 'our firm and even-handed position over arms sales to Iran and Iraq'.

D4.4 The reference in each of these letters to the criterion that governed the supply of non-lethal defence equipment to Iraq was not accurate. Since the end of February 1989 the criterion for Iraq had been the new formulation, namely, that there would be no supply of equipment which would be of direct and significant assistance to Iraq in the conduct of *offensive* operations in breach of the ceasefire. The inaccuracy should have been noticed by Mr Waldegrave, who had been one of the midwives at the birth of this new formulation. Lord Howe, on the other hand, had not been informed of the junior ministers' agreement on the new formulation.

---

77 *Op cit*, para D3.107.

78 *Ibid*, para D4.42.

79 Replies to PQs are analysed in Part III, Chapter 1, pp358–60.

D4.5 The statement in the letters that 'The Government have not changed their policy on defence sales to Iraq or Iran' was untrue. ...

D4.6 Mr Waldegrave knew first hand, the facts that, in my opinion, rendered the 'no change in policy' statement untrue. I accept that, when he signed these letters, he did not regard the agreement he had reached with his fellow ministers as having constituted a change in policy towards Iraq. In his evidence to the inquiry, he strenuously and consistently asserted his belief, in the face of a volume of, to my mind, overwhelming evidence to the contrary, that policy on defence sales to Iraq had, indeed, remained unchanged. I did not receive the impression of any insincerity on his part in giving me the evidence he did. But it is clear, in my opinion, that policy on defence sales to Iraq did not remain unchanged.

D4.7 The proposition that the Government's position over 'arms sales to Iran and Iraq' was 'even-handed' had been untrue ever since the decision, taken as a consequence of the Rushdie affair, to 'return to a more strict approach to Iran.'

This differential policy was already being implemented by 17 April. I could well understand that the reference in the letter to Mr Curry to the 'even-handed position' may have been an overlooked refugee from a common form sentence that would, two months earlier, have been unexceptional. But the proposition that on 17 April, the date of the letter, it was a true statement is not, in my opinion, remotely arguable ...

D3.4 It has been strenuously argued by a number of ministers and officials who have given evidence to the inquiry that the many statements to the effect that Government policy remained unchanged after the ceasefire and that the Guidelines announced in 1985 remained in force were not invalidated by the fact of the changes that were agreed upon by the junior ministers in the period preceding July 1990. The essence of the argument proceeded on these lines:

(i) Government policy, of which the Howe Guidelines announced in October 1985 were an important part, had been established by senior ministers with the concurrence of the Prime Minister.

(ii) It was not open to junior ministers on their own authority to alter the policy thus established.

(iii) Junior ministers could, within the bounds of their own ministerial authority, make decisions as to the manner in which in changing circumstances the established policy would be applied.

(iv) Changes in the manner in which established policy would be applied were, inevitably, necessitated by the ceasefire and by other events. But these changes did not, and could not, constitute any change in the established policy itself. They exemplified no more than a flexible application, geared to the new circumstances, of the established policy.

I accept ... that in deciding that the agreed approaches to defence exports to Iraq and Iran respectively could be described as being interpretations of the 1985 Guidelines, the junior ministers believed that they were avoiding a formal change of the 1985 Guidelines. But, however the agreement reached by the junior ministers be described, if the substance of the agreement was to change the criterion that would be applied to applications for licences to export defence equipment to Iraq, they were, in any ordinary use of language, agreeing on a change of policy. I regard the explanation that this could not be so because the approval of the senior ministers and the Prime Minister had not been obtained as sophistry ...

D4.52 A frank and sustained defence of the divergence between the Government's actual policy and the various ministerial statements of policy, whether in letters or in answers to PQs, was offered by Lord Howe in his oral evidence to the inquiry. He said:

> ... there is nothing necessarily open to criticism in incompatibility between policy and presentation of policy ... It [ie the Government] is not necessarily to be criticised for a difference between policy and public presentation of policy.

He explained:

> The fact is that, as soon as you are embarked upon the necessary policy, in competition with other nations, of enhancing a commercial position, a commercial position which is more inhibited than other nations, for reasons we have investigated, any attempt to enlarge that base is capable of being criticised by others ...
>
> Q. Can this not be explained to the public in a manner the public would understand?
>
> A. Not easily, not if you visualise, as the *Independent* pointed out, the extremely emotional way in which such debates are conducted in public ... if you look at the various reasons given by colleagues for caution in relation to the shifting nuances of policy, in the Spring of 1989, they all add up to a very good reason for not volunteering this, because the scope for misunderstanding is enormous.
>
> ... Q. [So the Government's approach was] 'We know what is good for you. You may not like it and, if you were made aware of it, you might protest, but we know what is best'?
>
> A. It is partly that, but it is partly 'If we were to lay specifically our thought processes before you, they are not just going before you; they are laid before a worldwide range of uncomprehending or malicious commentators'. This is the point. You cannot choose a well balanced presentation to an elite Parliamentary audience.

In relation to the circumstance that, as a result of the re-formulation of guideline (iii) and the decision to apply the re-formulated guideline to Iraq but not to Iran, policy was no longer even-handed or impartial as between the two countries Lord Howe said: 'It cannot be seen like that. That is the point.' And

> Frankly the inaccuracy is intrinsic in the policy position that we are presenting. If you are saying that the Guidelines are still in place and being applied directly to Iran without any qualification, and being applied with modification to Iraq, then that is the thing you cannot disclose and you have to head back to 'The Guidelines are in place'. That is the point. The Guidelines are in place because the basic policy has not changed.

...

D3.121 I have referred earlier in this section of the report to arguments that have been put forward in support of the proposition that the Guidelines, as announced in 1985, remained in force and unchanged notwithstanding the agreement reached by the junior ministers over the period December 1988 to May 1989. For a number of reasons I do not accept that proposition or the arguments.

D3.122 First, it is argued that the relaxation of the Guidelines agreed upon by the junior ministers did not constitute a change in the Guidelines but was no more than a liberal, relaxed interpretation, or implementation, of them. ...

This 'interpretation' is said to be consistent with the flexibility inherent in the Guidelines from their inception. It was this 'interpretation' that had been applied to Iraq since February 1989 and was confirmed for Iraq at the end of April 1989. In Mr Waldegrave's written comments, the use of revised guideline (iii) is described as follows:

> The revised form of guideline (iii) was used by the MODWG and IDC in January and February 1989 as a temporary working premise on a trial basis. After the *fatwa*, ministers decided that the suggested change in the guidelines should not go ahead and that instead the original guidelines were to be applied with flexibility. Thereafter, the MODWG and IDC applied the original guidelines restrictively for Iran and liberally for Iraq. In the case of Iraq, this meant in practice that those groups used the suggested revised form of guideline (iii) as an interpretative gloss on the original guidelines.

D3.123 The viewpoint expressed in the passage from Mr Waldegrave's letter that I have cited, and exemplified in the passage cited from his written comments, is one that does not seem to me to correspond with reality. The revised formulation of guideline (iii) was intended to do two things; first. it was intended, in view of the termination of the conflict, to restate guideline (iii) in a manner that could make sense; second, it was intended to release from the guidelines non-lethal equipment whose military value was primarily defensive. If that second purpose had not been present, the reference to 'offensive operations in breach of the ceasefire' would not have been included and the limiting adjective 'direct' would not have been necessary. To describe this revised formulation as no more than an interpretation of the old, is, in my opinion, notwithstanding the many advocates who espoused the thesis, so plainly inapposite as to be incapable of being sustained by serious argument. In my opinion, the agreement to which Mr Waldegrave referred in his 28 March 1989 letter was, on any ordinary use of language, an agreement to adopt a new and more liberal policy towards sales of non-lethal defence equipment than had been in place during the conflict and to do so by applying a revised formulation of guideline (iii) in place of the original. The intended effect of applying the revised guideline was to release a certain class of non-lethal defence equipment from the Guidelines.

D3.124 I accept that Mr Waldegrave and the other adherents of the 'interpretation' thesis did not, in putting forward the thesis, have any duplicitous intention and, at the time, regarded the relaxed interpretation, or implementation, of guideline (iii) as being a justifiable use of the flexibility believed to be inherent in the Guidelines. But that that was so underlines, to my mind, the duplicitous nature of the flexibility claimed for the guidelines. Flexibility that reflects the differences of opinion that may arise whenever an attempt is made to apply a criterion that depends upon a value judgment is inevitable and desirable. For example, whether an enhancement of military capability is 'significant' is a matter on which opinions may differ. If opinions do differ, a decision falling within the spectrum created by those differences can legitimately be described as an application of the criterion. Guideline (iii) had, thus, an inherent and entirely acceptable flexibility. But the removal from the scope of guideline (iii) of non-lethal defence equipment of a primarily defensive nature is not a 'flexible interpretation' of the Guidelines. It is a decision that the Guidelines will not be applied so as to restrict the sale of a certain class of defence equipment. The description of that decision as being merely a flexible interpretation, or flexible implementation, of the Guidelines is bound to be misleading to anyone who does not know the substance of the decision.

D4.42 ... Having heard various explanations as to why it was necessary or desirable to withhold knowledge from Parliament and the public of the true nature of the Government's approach to the licensing of non-lethal defence sales to Iran and Iraq respectively, I have come to the conclusion that the overriding and determinative reason was a fear of strong public opposition to the loosening of the restrictions on the supply of defence equipment to Iraq and a consequential fear that the pressure of the opposition might be detrimental to British trading interests.

Note

It is worth commenting briefly on the differing justifications[80] put forward. The first one, that no change took place because no change was approved at a high level was described by Alan Clark as a 'slightly *Alice in Wonderland* suggestion' where '... because something was not announced, it could not have happened'.[81] In effect, one of the most disturbing aspects of the whole affair, that this important change in policy was never approved at a senior level is being used to *defend* a failure to be open with Parliament. Nevertheless, the capacity of Government ministers to indulge in such mental acrobatics is important, given the new subjective formulation of the duty not to mislead Parliament, considered below. The second justification, put forward by Lord Howe is frankly paternalistic; it is significant in revealing a clear rejection by a former senior Government figure of the basic principle of democratic accountability based upon the provison of full information to the public, not because that information would (say) threaten national security but simply because the public is not deemed to be capable of considering it in a sensible, rational way. The third is perhaps the most important: it rests on the notion that because only a minor change (a new interpretation of declared policy) had taken place and the main policy had already been declared, it was not necessary to declare any change, since Parliament already had most of the information.

After the Scott report: the duty not to mislead Parliament

The remainder of this chapter will discuss what, post-Scott, appears to be the extent of the obligation not to mislead Parliament; this will not involve any attempt to find a consensus between the various differing viewpoints as to the extent of this obligation, for none presently exists. Rather, it will sketch the various positions taken in the new parameters of the debate. The findings of Scott take us to five key questions at the heart of the current debate over the duty not to mislead Parliament. The first is whether the current list of topics on which the Government will refuse to supply information should be reviewed; the second is the question whether and if so when the giving of incomplete information is to be regarded as misleading; the third is the issue of when, if ever, it may be right to lie to Parliament; the fourth is the significance of the minister's own belief as to whether he is saying something misleading; and the fifth is the constitutional position of civil servants who are asked to co-operate with the misleading of Parliament or become aware that it is occurring.

---

80 Another put forward was that if Iran heard of the 'tilt to Iraq', this could cause a further deterioration in Britain's relations with that country and thus put British hostages under the control of Iran at risk (*Ibid*, paras 3.107–3.108). Scott finds that the contemporary documentation reveals no evidence that this was a 'significant factor' in the decision to conceal the change in policy from Parliament (*ibid*).

81 Norton-Taylor, *op cit*, pp68–9.

On 2 November 1995, a change which could have a bearing on at least four of the above was announced. Paragraph 27 of QPM (noted above) had been revised to read as follows:

> Ministers must not knowingly mislead Parliament and the public and should correct any inadvertent errors at the earliest opportunity. They must be as open as possible with parliament and the public, withholding information only when disclosure would not be in the public interest, which should be decided in accordance with established Parliamentary convention, the law, and any relevant Government code of practice.[82]

The significance of this new wording will be one of the main focuses of the discussion below.

Areas in which Government refuses to supply information

Two points emerge here: first of all, the refusal of successive administrations to disclose information on the sale of defence equipment; secondly, the discretion left to ministers in the new formulation of QPM to withhold information 'in the public interest'. These will be treated together in the materials which follow, which start with extracts from a recent Select Committee report and the Scott report dealing with the particular issue of information relating to exports of military equipment.

Fourth Special Report from the Defence Select Committee, HC 407 (1995–96)

9. We recommend that answers to parliamentary questions about specific exports, specific companies and specific countries should be answered fully *unless* there are compelling reasons of national security, commercial confidentiality or relations with foreign states which would rebut the presumption in favour of publication.

10. We recommend that the decision whether to withhold information should be taken by ministers on the specific facts of each case and not by the application of a general civil service rule.

11. If a minister decides a parliamentary question should not be answered fully, the answer should indicate not a blanket formula but the reason for that refusal ,eg:

- the information is commercially confidential (it would be against the financial interests of the UK company concerned to disclose this matter)
- the information is classified (but not specifying whether restricted, confidential, secret or top secret)
- the information relates to matters which are treated as confidential between Governments.

The reply should also give an indication (most likely in the case of commercially confidential matters) of the timescale over which it is likely to remain confidential. ...

DIFFICULT CASES

12. There will be cases where there is a conflict between a minister's duty to the House and the need to preserve the confidentiality of certain information. If a

---

82 HC Deb 2 November 1995, col 456. Professor Hennessey in his opinion (given below) refers to this as 'the new front-end of QPM'.

minister decides not to give a full answer to a parliamentary question or in debate he should give details of the background in confidence to the chairman of the relevant departmental select committee (and of the Public Accounts Committee in matters involving expenditure). This would be analogous to the confidential procedure used when a Government department incurs a contingent liability which it does not wish to publish.

Inquiry into Exports of Defence Equipment and Dual-Use Goods to Iraq and Related Prosecutions HC 115-I (1995–96)

K8.10 Commercial confidentiality may, in many cases, continue to constitute a valid reason for refusal by ministers to supply the names of the exporters of arms and defence-related equipment, or the contract prices applicable to the exports, or the value of the exported goods, or information relating to the specification and performance characteristics of the goods. It is not, however, apparent why commercial confidentiality should bar the provision of any other information about the export of arms or defence-related equipment. In particular, it is not apparent why Parliamentary Questions seeking information about the quantities of the goods exported to particular countries and the extent to which public funds have been used to provide credit support far the sales should not be answered ...

K8.13 In my opinion, the time is ripe for Parliament and the Government to conduct a comprehensive review of the 'previous practice' whereunder information on exports of arms and defence-related goods need not be given by ministers. Is it any longer satisfactory that Parliament and the British public are not entitled to be told to which countries and in what quantities goods such as artillery shells, land mines and cluster bombs have been licensed for export? The limitations that the public interest requires to be placed on the obligations of accountability owed by ministers need, I respectfully suggest, to be urgently re-thought.

K8.14 This urgency is underlined by the indications that have been given that the Government have in mind the re-formulation of paragraph 27 of *Questions of Procedure for Ministers*. It seems the Government's Response to the Nolan Committee's First Report suggests that the obligation on ministers to supply information to Parliament (and the public) will not extend to information the disclosure of which 'would not be in the public interest'. Would it be said that, because a purchaser of arms or defence-related equipment from the United Kingdom would be displeased if the sale became public knowledge (and as a consequence might place elsewhere future orders), it 'would not be in the public interest' for the British public to be informed of the sale? Past experience suggests that that might well be the Government response. I have in mind the generally uninformative nature of the Government responses to Parliamentary Questions about arms sales to Iraq in the period covered by my terms of reference as well as submissions made to me by Government regarding publication of certain passages in this report. The extent to which information on the export of arms and defence-related goods from this country can 'in the public interest' properly be withheld from the public of this country is a matter that should be the subject of public debate and further Government clarification.

Notes

1   These two recommendations both clearly have a potential impact which goes beyond the particular case of defence exports in the approach they advocate, and indicate a growing momentum towards placing the onus on ministers to justify disclosure. Professor Hennessey has recently opined that

the new formulation of QPM has 'a fistful of weasel words'; he expressed particular concern, echoing Scott, over the words 'public interest' and 'Parliamentary Conventions':

Sir Frank Cooper, a very formidable operator in his day in Whitehall said ... last week about public interest that this was the red rag to the bull to him because, 'I have never discovered who is the guardian of the national interest'. It has very rarely got to do with the national interest ... but it has to do with the people advocating a particular interest'. Now that is an insider talking ... I think Parliamentary conventions are almost as worrying because we have not had an updated list that I know of ... of the banned Parliamentary Questions since 1978 ...

His advice was that the Public Service Committee, which has the remit of addressing the issues of ministerial accountability and responsibility in the light of the Scott report should formulate a rigorous re-draft of the obligation to give information which 'reduces those caveats and the let-outs to an absolute minimum ... and places firmly within ... QPM ... an onus to disclose ... mak[ing] it a positive obligation'.[83] As can be seen, the Select Committee on Defence has already made a start in that direction in relation to one specific area. A suggested redraft submitted by Professor Hennessey to the Committee appears below. The Government has very recently accepted (see HC 67 (1996–97) pvii) that the phrase 'parliamentary conventions' should be deleted from QPM.

2   Sir Richard Scott's contributions to this debate,[84] in evidence before the Public Service Committee has been twofold: first he has stressed that the categories of excluded areas do require 'serious and urgent revision'. Secondly, he has called for debate on whether an independent officer of the House – someone 'like the Comptroller and Auditor General' – should be given the power to examine claims made by Government to be witholding evidence 'in the public interest' by examining the relevant background papers; the officer could report regularly to the House on whether the exceptions to disclosure were being fairly and reasonably used.

'Ministers must not knowingly mislead Parliament'

Here we examine issues 2–4 above.

Fifth Report from the Treasury and Civil Service Select Committee, HC 27 (1993–94), paras 124–26; Minutes of Proceedings of the same, 8 March 1994, QQ 1840, 1843, 1906, 1907 and 24 April 1994 Q2148 (Sir Robin Butler)

124. ... There has been considerable concern recently about the adequacy of, and adherence to [the guidance in *Questions of Procedure for Ministers re* openness with Parliment].

125. Sir Robin Butler informed the Scott Inquiry that there was a category of Parliamentary answers 'where it is necessary to give an incomplete answer, but one should, in these circumstances, seek not to mislead'. Mr Waldegrave, in evidence to the sub-committee, vividly asserted the need, in certain circumstances, not to disclose all relevant information: 'There are plenty of cases

---

83   Minutes of Evidence, *op cit*, Q 66.
84   Minutes of Evidence, HC 313 (1995–96) (8 May 1996), QQ 412–14.

over the years, with both Governments, where the minister ... will not mislead the House and will take care not to mislead the House, but may not display everything he knows about that subject ... Much of Government activity is much more like negotiation, much more like playing poker than it is like playing chess. You do not put all the cards up all the time in the interests of the country'. The necessity for non-disclosure has been asserted in the past, even in the case of civil servants appearing before select committees. In 1985 the then Head of the Home Civil Service said that, taking 'an extreme case', when a decision had been made to devalue the pound, a minister could instruct a civil servant appearing before a select committee not to reveal that devaluation in advance. Sir Robin Butler reaffirmed this in 1990, while emphasising that that 'would not extend to the minister instructing the civil servant to mislead the committee; that would be improper'. There is self-evidently a problem in determining the line between non-disclosure which is not misleading and a misleading answer or statement. This problem is more acute for ministers than for civil servants, since a civil servant appearing before a select committee can refer a committee to a minister. Both Mr Waldegrave and Sir Robin Butler gave examples of answers which they held to be incomplete but not misleading. In such cases there was a general duty 'to make clear that you have information which you cannot disclose', although there were circumstances when even this would not be appropriate. Even in the latter circumstances, ministers and civil servants had to 'frame their answer in a way which avoids misleading, if they possibly can'.

126. Sir Robin stressed that it was wrong for a minister or a civil servant to lie, to mislead intentionally or to give an answer which was known to be false. The Prime Minister has made it clear in a letter to the Chairman of the Sub-Committee that, in such circumstances, a minister would usually be expected to relinquish his office. However, Sir Robin Butler and Mr Waldegrave also contended that there were 'very rare occasions' when the wrong of lying to the House would be outweighed by the greater wrong consequent upon not lying. Three instances were adduced in support of this contention. First, Sir Stafford Cripps did not mislead Parliament over devaluation but said after the devaluation in 1949 that, if he had been asked just before devaluation whether he was going to devalue he would have told a lie to Parliament. Second, Mr Peter Thomas gave an untrue answer about whether Mr Greville Wynne, who had just been arrested by Soviet authorities, was working for British Intelligence; this was untrue but was considered necessary to save Mr Wynne's life. Finally, both Sir Robin Butler and Mr Waldegrave alleged that, on 16 November 1967, the then Mr James (now Lord) Callaghan gave an answer which was 'false'. Mr Waldegrave did not dissent from the proposition that Lord Callaghan had lied to the House. Sir Robin Butler, who had worked in the Treasury as Secretary to the Budget Committee at the time, argued that when Lord Callaghan said in answer to a question from Mr Stanley Orme about devaluation 'I have nothing to add to or subtract from anything I have said on previous occasions on the subject of devaluation' he was misleading the House since his previous answers had been that assertions that the Government was not going to devalue the pound and he therefore did have something to subtract from previous statements. He accepted that Lord Callaghan did not have an intention to mislead and was thus not 'deliberately lying to the House of Commons', but argued that he had made a 'slip', which Sir Robin Butler implied Lord Callaghan had acknowledged. In reply, Lord Callaghan vigorously contested Mr Waldegrave's implication that he had lied to the House, stating that 'none of my answers supports Mr Waldegrave's assertion that I lied to the House of Commons'. He did not admit to a false answer to Mr Orme, referring to 'one *possible* slip (which was not intended to deceive) in the reply I gave to Mr Orme'. He repudiated 'the attempt

to put a construction on my replies by Sir Robin Butler and Mr Waldegrave, twenty five years after the event, that no one who was present ever did either at the time or later'. ...

134. Effective accountability depends in considerable measure upon adherence by ministers and civil servants to the duty set out in *Questions of Procedure for Ministers* to give Parliament, including its Select Committees, and the public as full information as possible about the policies, decisions and actions of the Government, and not to deceive or mislead Parliament and the public'. We are aware of considerable public cynicism about the honesty of politicians generally and in this context concern about the honesty and integrity of ministerial statements to and answers in Parliament might seem misplaced. However, the knowledge that ministers and civil servants may evade questions and put the best gloss on the facts but will not lie or knowingly mislead the House of Commons is one of the most powerful tools Members of Parliament have in holding the executive to account. Not only is the requirement laid down clearly in Government guidance to ministers, it is a requirement which the House of Commons itself expects from all its Members, departure from which standard can be treated as a contempt. We accept that the line between non-disclosure and a misleading answer is often a fine one, not least because the avoidance of misleading answers requires not only strict accuracy but also an awareness of the interpretations which could reasonably be placed upon an answer by others, but ministers should be strengthened in their determination to remain the right side of that line by certainty about the consequences of a failure to do so. **Any minister who has been found to have knowingly misled Parliament should resign.**

[Evidence of Mr Waldegrave and Sir Robin Butler]

Mr Waldegrave: There are plenty of cases over the years, with both Governments, where the minister – and it very often has happened in relation particularly to diplomatic matters, but not only to diplomatic matters – will not mislead the House and will take care not to mislead the House, but may not display everything he knows about that subject, but he will answer the question accurately.

Chairman

1843. Let me get this right. You are saying, if a minister is criticised or found to be misleading the House, he or she should not necessarily resign?

Mr Waldegrave: There is a full range, is there not, from very serious things to totally trivial things. Far the best judge of this is surely the House at the time. ...

1906. Referring to Sir Robin Butler's answer, he went on to refer to a 'wider category of cases where it is necessary to give an incomplete answer'. The devaluation case is cut and dried, but I am interested in this wider category of cases where it is necessary to give an incomplete answer. Can you imagine circumstances where a minister could give an incomplete answer where he should actually have to resign?

Mr Waldegrave: It would depend again on whether the effect had been to seriously mislead the House about an important matter.

1907. So you can foresee that an incomplete answer would be a resignation issue?

Mr Waldegrave: You have to look at what the outcome would ultimately be for the House and for the judgment of the House. We had an example of what was alleged to be – I was not in the House at the time – an incomplete answer which the House accepted in relation to Northern Ireland [*re* whether the Government was making covert contacts with IRA/Sinn Fein] and the House very easily accepted that; both sides of the House accepted that. ...

Sir Robin Butler: The position is that the duty of ministers is always to give full and truthful information to Parliament and not to lie or to mislead. The duty of civil servants is the same. Only in the most exceptional circumstances – so exceptional, you may say, as to be virtually theoretical and of which I have quoted examples – can an even greater damage be done by telling the truth ...

Notes

1   A senior member of the FDA in evidence to the Public Service Committee commented that: '... there is a commonly accepted culture that the function of [an answer to a PQ] is to give no more information than the minister thinks will be helpful to him or her, the minister, in the process of political debate in the House.'[85]

2   The giving of selective information is thus routine. During the Scott Inquiry, Sir Gore-Booth [a very senior civil servant] opined, in a similar manner to Sir Robin Butler and William Waldegrave, that giving such incomplete information was not necessarily misleading – 'half a picture can be true'. Scott's comment on this view is as follows:

D4.55 The problem with the 'half a picture' approach is that those to whom the incomplete statement is addressed do not know, unless it is apparent from the terms of the statement itself, that an undisclosed half is being withheld from them. They are almost bound, therefore, to be misled by the statement, notwithstanding that the 'half a picture' may, so far as it goes, be accurate. The proposition is not that a statement to Parliament must include each and every fact relating to the subject in order to avoid being misleading. Such a requirement would clearly be impracticable. A fair summary of the 'full picture' would often, depending on the question that had been asked and the apparent purpose of the statement, be a complete and sufficient response. The proposition is that if part of the picture is being suppressed and the audience does not know it is being suppressed. the audience will be misled into believing the half picture to be the full picture.[86]

3   However, Scott was unworried about the reformulation of QPM noted above:

K8.5 The qualification of 'mislead' by the addition of the adverb 'knowingly' does not, to my mind, make any material difference to the substance of the obligation resting on ministers not to mislead Parliament or the public. It must, I believe, always have been the case that misleading statements made in ignorance of the true facts were not regarded as a breach of a minister's obligation to be honest with Parliament and the public. Questions might, of course, arise as to why the minister was ignorant of the true facts and thus unable to have rendered to Parliament an accurate account of his stewardship.'[87]

---

85   *Minutes of Evidence Taken Before the Public Service Committee*, HC 313 (1995–96) (20 March 1996), Q 21.

86   *Scott report*, para D4.55.

87   *Ibid*, para K8.5.

4   Arguably, Scott is a little too sanguine here. A genuinely inadvertent mistake of fact should arguably not be viewed as serious misconduct (though as Scott notes, it may raise issues of competence) but the addition of the word 'knowingly' could have far wider consequences than this. In is worth remembering the case of Waldegrave himself: Scott found that he persisted in his view that the Guidelines had not changed 'in the face of overwhelming evidence to the contrary'. The position potentially is, therefore that minister who holds an honest but manifestly unreasonable – even bizarre – view that Government policy has not changed is entitled simply to tell Parliament that there has been no change. Clearly the risk is that a minister will be able to refute charges of knowingly misleading the House as long as he is able to make up some argument, however flimsy, that he didn't *realise* that that was what he was doing. The duty ought surely to be based on a the requirement for a more objective assessment by the minister. To take the example of the change in the export guidelines: if the minister realised or ought to have realised that despite their honest belief that Government policy had not changed, others might well take a different view, the information which gives rise to the possible inference that there has been a change ought to be disclosed to Parliament. Parliament can then make its own judgement on the matter. In short, ministers' duty should be to neither knowingly *or recklessly* mislead Parliament.

5   The FDA certainly saw difficulties with the new subjectivist formulation:

38. The new Civil Service Code makes it clear that Parliament must not *knowingly* be misled. Equally, in his evidence to the Scott Inquiry, and indeed to the Select Committee, Sir Robin Butler indicated that both ministers and civil servants may be justified in giving only half the picture. He did not confine such withholding of information to questions of national security, matters affecting the national economy, nor foreign affairs. The implication is that ministers may withhold information, provided that the answer that they give is not misleading.

39. But Sir Richard takes the argument further. He says ministers deliberately withheld information and that in his judgment the reason for this was a fear of public opposition to what was really happening. However, he does not say Parliament was deliberately misled.

40. The question is how this position can sit alongside the duty clearly laid out in *Questions of Procedure* to give Parliament, including its Select Committees and the public, as full information as possible about the policies, decision and actions of the Government, and not deceive or mislead Parliament and the public.

41. There may, as one cynical civil servant put it recently be three drafts in future placed before all ministers:

— The complete answer in accordance with *Questions of Procedure for Ministers;*

— The answer which deliberately withholds information, but does not knowingly mislead; and

— The answer which designedly leads Parliament to believe one policy is in place where the overwhelming evidence is to the contrary, but does so unintentionally.'[88]

---

88   HC 313 (1995–96) (20 March 1996); FDA memorandum, paras 38–41.

6   So what would a really rigorous obligation on ministers to be open with parliament entail? Professor Hennessey produced a suggested new formulation of QPM for the Public Service Committee to consider:

> Ministers must not knowingly mislead Parliament and the public and should correct any inadvertent errors at the earliest opportunity. Statements and Parliamentary answers must be based on the fullest and best information available to the Government at the time. Ministers must be as open as possible with Parliament and the public. Withholding information must be restricted to those matters and such occasions where demonstrable harm might occur to especially sensitive state actions, activities, and relationships to a degree that would clearly override the obligation to disclose. It is the duty of the Prime Minister to ensure that in all the Government's dealings with Parliament and the public, the onus will normally be on full and timely disclosure. On matters in which Parliament has shown an interest where full disclosure might incur serious harm, ministers should make the case for confidentiality privately either to the Leaders of the Opposition parties on a privy counsellor basis or to the chair of the relevant House of Commons or House of Lords Select Committee. It will be for the Prime Minister to ensure that ministers live up to their responsibilities in this area and to set an example himself/herself. It will be for officials to follow the lead of their ministers.
>
> These principles and the obligations that derive from them represent the pillars of ministerial life and public service. It will be for individual ministers to judge how best to act in order to uphold the highest standards. It will be for the Prime Minister to determine whether or not they have done so in any particular circumstances. Any adverse findings about the conduct of his/her colleagues on the part of the Prime Minister must be reported to Parliament.[89]

Misleading Parliament: the position of civil servants

Two questions arise here. First, what does a civil servant do if he or she is asked to draft answers to Parliamentary Questions which s/he considers misleading, or is instructed to withhold certain information from Select Committees? Secondly, if civil servants willingly collude with ministers to mislead Parliament, can they be brought to account? One of the extremely rare cases in which a civil servant actually went public with allegations of ministerial deception of parliament was the celebrated case of Clive Ponting.

Geoffrey Marshall, 'Ministers, Civil Servants, and Open Government', in C Harlow (ed), *Public Law and Politics* (1986), pp86–9

> Mr Ponting, a civil servant in the Ministry of Defence, was charged with disclosing to a Member of Parliament official information without authority, the information in question being two documents about the conduct of naval operations in the South Atlantic and the sinking of the Argentinian cruiser *General Belgrano* in May 1982. It was conceded by the prosecution that national security had not been prejudiced by the communication of the documents. An argument about national security was however involved in the issue between Ponting and his ministerial superiors since it was a potential danger to national security that the Secretary of State eventually relied upon as his reason for declining to answer questions put by Mr Tam Dalyell MP, and it was Ponting's

---

89   Minutes of Evidence, *op cit.*

disagreement with his minister on the question of danger to national security that persuaded him that ministers were unnecessarily and improperly concealing the truth from the House of Commons.

The factual members that were the subject of the alleged deception of the House were, on the face of it and in isolation, not of great moment. They related to the details of the *Belgrano*'s course at various times in relation to the British task force, the precise date at which the submarine *Conqueror* sighted the *Belgrano* and the making of certain changes in the naval rules of engagement, not revealed at the time they were made. In order to answer Mr Dalyell's questions, Mr Ponting was asked to draft replies for the minister. His draft replies were not used. In his book Mr Ponting notes that as a civil servant he was accustomed to having drafts rejected or modified. That was 'a fact of life in a bureaucracy'. But in this case ministers, he thought, had decided to mislead Parliament. Errors had been made in the statements given on the points raised in Mr Dalyell's question and the minister, instead of conceding them, was intending to choke off further inquiries and the junior minister, Mr John Stanley, was claiming erroneously that none of the questions could be answered on grounds of national security. It was, Mr Ponting relates, against all his training to disclose Government information. Yet as a civil servant he could not be a party to the deliberate deception of Parliament. He therefore sent Mr Dalyell an unsigned note saying that the information he sought was unclassified and that he should press his questions and later he sent the two documents. Mr Dalyell passed the documents to the Chairman of the Foreign Affairs Committee, who returned them to the Ministry of Defence, and the Attorney-General, with no prompting from Mr Heseltine or Mrs Thatcher, instituted proceedings.

... What then should Mr Ponting have done other than what he did? In describing his moment of truth he said that he wondered about appealing to someone outside the department since he saw that ministers were not likely to change their minds and accept his advice and since no other senior civil servant in the department had protested about the ministers' conduct, and 'I had received no support from those high up in the Department'. There is no suggestion in his book however that he had explicitly asked for support on the issue as it finally presented itself to him. As to the external appeal (to the Head of the Home Civil Service perhaps) he remarks that all the methods of effective protest were cut off by people already involved in the cover up. The manner in which this 'cutting off' took place however is not detailed. Mr Ponting added that he remembered a note by the Treasury to the Public Accounts Committee saying that an officer who without authority corrected misleading evidence by publishing the true facts to the Committee or to the House would not be in breach of the Official Secrets Act since the publication would amount to a proceeding in Parliament and be absolutely privileged. That makes it somewhat harder to understand why Mr Ponting, if no one in the civil service would listen to him, did not approach the Foreign Affairs Committee or its chairman directly asking them to investigate the allegations, if necessary saying publicly that he had done so. Given that in Mr Ponting's belief at the time there was no major departmental plot or sinister cover up, he was dealing with a ministerial misjudgement about the need to classify information. So leaking to Mr Dalyell or to some other opponent of the Government if it had been Mr Ponting's last desperate throw need not have been his first.

Notes

1   Until very recently, civil servants owed no general duty to Parliament or the public to see that they were not being misled. For the first time, in the New

Civil Service code, it is stated (para 5) that they 'must not knowingly mislead Parliament or the public'.[90] Nevertheless, it is clear that, as Ms Symons (director of the FDA) noted[91] if they asked to do so, or are aware of deception by ministers, they are in 'no circumstances' to go public with this information: 'the civil servant should not leak information to the British public'. Instead, they have the right under the Code to appeal ultimately to the Civil Service Commissioners (paras 11 and 12) but only after departmental procedures have failed to resolve the issue. As Mr Dunabin explained,[92] civil servants do see this as a 'very substantial benefit ... because one cannot suppose that the ... Commissioners will turn down such an appeal simply because they think that the information which is not being released is embarrassing to ministers and their party policy ... [but only] if they [thought] ... it was not in the public interest, properly so defined for that information to be released'.

2 Whether the new procedure will be used remains to be seen. During Sir Robin Butler's time as Head of the Home Civil Service (formerly the ultimate point of appeal), he reported that only one complaint was made to him in nine years. The FDA considers that civil servants often fear the displeasure of senior management if they make a formal complaint. No formal complaints by civil servants were made during the arms to Iraq episode.

3 Of course, if civil servants do not complain, this may not always be for fear of the consequences to them. They may simply not be concerned about whether Parliament is being misled or not, as long as they are carrying out instructions. Civil servants interviewed by Scott were quite blunt about where their loyalties lay. Mark Higson, for example, said, 'It was simply a matter of us not telling the truth, of knowingly not telling the truth to the public and Parliament. The policy was bent and we concealed that policy'. In such cases, civil servants' lack of accountability to Parliament means that they can effectively escape being brought to account in any way for colluding with ministers to deceive. Under the present constitutional understanding, only ministers, not Parliament, can 'punish' civil servants. But whilst ministers may be prepared to discipline civil servants for errors of administration, they are hardly likely to punish civil servants for carrying out their instructions to draft incomplete or misleading answers to questions. Another lacuna in Parliamentary accountability is thus apparent.

---

90 This came into force on 1 January 1996; its full text appears at HL Deb 9 January 1996, WA 21.

91 Before the Public Service Committee, HC 313 (1995–96), (20 March 1996), QQ 33–35.

92 *Ibid*, Q 35.

CHAPTER 3

OFFICIAL SECRECY AND ACCESS TO INFORMATION

INTRODUCTION[1]

It has often been said that the UK is more obsessed with keeping Government information secret than any other Western democracy.[2] It is clearly advantageous for the party in power to be able to control the flow of information in order to prevent public scrutiny of certain official decisions and in order to be able to release information selectively at convenient moments. The British Government has available a number of methods of keeping official information secret, including use of the doctrine of public interest immunity, the deterrent effect of criminal sanctions under the Official Secrets Act 1989, the Civil Service Conduct Code,[3] around 80 statutory provisions engendering secrecy in various areas, and the action for breach of confidence (discussed in Part VI Chapter 3). The justification traditionally put forward for maintaining a climate of secrecy, which goes beyond protecting specific public interests such as national security, is that freedom of information would adversely affect 'ministerial accountability'. In other words, ministers are responsible for the actions of civil servants in their departments and therefore must be able to control the flow of information emanating from the department in question. However, it is usually seen as essential to democracy that Government should allow a reasonably free flow of information so that citizens can be informed as to the Government process and can therefore assess Government decisions in the light of all the available facts, thereby participating fully in the workings of the democracy. A number of groups therefore advocate freedom of information and more 'open' government in Britain, as in most other democracies. They accept that certain categories of information should be exempt from disclosure but argue that those categories should be as restricted as possible compatible with the needs of the interest protected and that the categorisation of any particular piece of information should be open to challenge.

---

1 General reading, see: T Hartley and J Griffiths, *Government and Law*, 2nd edn (1981), Chapter 13; DGT Williams, *Not in the Public Interest* (1965); D Leigh, *The Frontiers of Secrecy – Closed Government in Britain* (1980); J Michael, *The Politics of Secrecy* (1982); KG Robertson, *Public Secrets* (1982); D Wilson, *The Secrets File* (1984); D Wass, *Government and the Governed* (1984) p81 *et seq*; P Birkinshaw, *Freedom of Information*, 2nd edn (1996); Ewing and Gearty, *Freedom Under Thatcher* (1990), Chapter 6; P Birkinshaw, *Government and Information* (1990); D Feldman, *Civil Liberties and Human Rights in England and Wales* (1993), Chapter 14; Bailey, Harris and Jones, *Civil Liberties: Cases and Materials*, 3rd edn (1995), Chapter 7; JD Baxter, *State Security, Privacy and Information* (1990); S Shetreet (ed), *Free Speech and National Security* (1991); P Gill, *Policing Politics: Security, Intelligence and the Liberal Democratic State* (1994); L Lustgarten and I Leigh, *In From the Cold: National Security and Parliamentary Democracy* (1994).

2 For example, Robertson, *Freedom, the Individual and the Law* (1989), pp129–31.

3 See Drewry and Butcher, *The Civil Service Today* (1991). It should be pointed out that the Civil Service Code which came into force on 1 January 1996 contains a partial 'whistle-blowing' provision in paras 11 and 12; for discussion see below.

The citizen's 'right to know' is recognised in the USA, Canada, Australia, New Zealand, Denmark, Sweden, Holland, Norway, Greece and France. In such countries the general principle of freedom of information is subject to exceptions where information falls into specific categories. Perhaps responding to the general acceptance of freedom of information, there has been a shift in the Government attitude to freedom of information in the UK recently: that is, the principle appears to have been accepted but the traditional stance as to the role of the law has hardly changed. The UK has always resisted freedom of information legislation and until 1989 criminalised the unauthorised disclosure of any official information at all, however trivial, under s2 of the Official Secrets Act 1911, thereby creating a climate of secrecy in the civil service which greatly hampered the efforts of those who wished to obtain and publish information about the workings of government.

OFFICIAL SECRECY

Introduction

During the 19th century, as Government departments grew larger and handled more official information, the problem of confidentiality grew more acute. Internal circulars such as the Treasury minute entitled 'The Premature Disclosure of Official Information' 1873 urged secrecy on all members of Government departments and threatened the dismissal of civil servants who disclosed any information; a Treasury minute issued in 1875 warned civil servants of the dangers of close links with the press.[4] The perceived need to enforce secrecy led to the passing of the Official Secrets Act 1889 which made it an offence for a person wrongfully to communicate information obtained owing to his employment as a civil servant. However, the Government grew dissatisfied with this measure; under its terms the state had the burden of proving both *mens rea* and that the disclosure was not in the interests of the state. It was thought that a stronger measure was needed and eventually the Government passed the Official Secrets Act 1911, s2(1) of which provided:

> ... If any person having in his possession or control [any information ...] which has been entrusted in confidence to him by any person holding office under His Majesty or which he has obtained [or to which he has had access] owing to his position as a person who is or has held of office under His Majesty, or as a person who holds or has held a contract made on behalf of His Majesty, or as a person who is or has been employed under a person who holds or has held such an office or contract ... (a) communicates the [code word, pass word,] sketch, plan, model, article, note, document, or information to any person, other than a person to whom he is authorised to communicate it, or a person to whom it is in the interest of the state his duty to communicate it, ... that person shall be guilty of a misdemeanour.

The criticism frequently levelled at s2 was that it lacked any provision regarding the substance of the information disclosed, so that technically it criminalised, for example, disclosure of the colour of the carpet in a minister's

---

4 See Robertson, *Public Secrets* (1982), p53.

office. There were surprisingly few prosecutions under s2; it seems likely that it created an acceptance of secrecy in the civil service which tended to preclude disclosure. In one of the few cases which did come to court, *Fell* (1963),[5] the Court of Appeal confirmed that liability was not dependent on the contents of the document in question or on whether the disclosure would have an effect prejudicial to the interests of the state.

The decision in *Ponting* (1985)[6] is usually credited with finally bringing about the demise of s2.[7] Clive Ponting, a senior civil servant in the Ministry of Defence, was responsible for policy on the operational activities of the Royal Navy at a time when Opposition MPs, particularly Tam Dalyell, were pressing the Government for information relating to the sinking of the *General Belgrano* in the Falklands conflict. Michael Heseltine, then Secretary of State for Defence, decided to withhold such information from Parliament and therefore did not use a reply to Parliamentary questions drafted by Ponting. He used instead a much briefer version of it and circulated a confidential minute indicating that answers on the rules of engagement in the Falklands' conflict should not be given to questions put by the Parliamentary Select Committee on Foreign Affairs. Feeling that Opposition MPs were being prevented from doing their job of scrutinising the workings of Government, Ponting sent the unused reply and the minute anonymously to the Labour MP, Tam Dalyell, who disclosed the documents to the press.

Ponting was charged with the offence of communicating information under s 2. His defence rested on the provision in s2(1)(a) of the 1911 Act that the information had been communicated 'to a person to whom it is in the interests of the state his duty to communicate it, or to a person to whom it is in the interests of the state his duty to communicate it'. The judge directed the jury that duty meant official duty, meaning the duty imposed upon Mr Ponting by his position. In relation to the words, 'in the interests of the state', the judge said:

> I direct you that these words mean the policies of the state as they were in July 1984 ... and not the policies of the state as Mr Ponting, Mr Dalyell, you or I might think they ought to have been ... The policies of the state mean the policies laid down by those recognised organs of Government and authority ...' While it has [the support of a majority in the House of Commons], the Government and its policies are for the time being the policies of the state.

The judge in *Ponting* effectively directed the jury to convict. Despite this direction they acquitted, presumably feeling that Ponting should have a defence

---

5 Crim LR 207. See David Hooper, *Official Secrets* (1987) for history of the use of s2.

6 Crim LR 318; see also (1985) PL 203 at 212 and (1986) Crim LR 491.

7 It may be noted that, although a conviction was obtained in *Tisdall* (1984), in *The Times*, 26 March the decision created some adverse publicity for the Government due to what was perceived as a draconian use of s2. Sarah Tisdall worked in the Foreign Secretary's private office and in the course of her duties came across documents relating to the delivery of cruise missiles to the RAF base at Greenham Common. She discovered proposals to delay the announcement of their delivery until after it had occurred and to make the announcement in Parliament at the end of question time in order to avoid answering questions. Considering that this political subterfuge was morally wrong, she leaked the documents to the *Guardian* but they were eventually traced back to her. She pleaded guilty to an offence under s2 and received a prison sentence of six months – an outcome which was generally seen as harsh: see Y Cripps, 'Disclosure in the Public Interest: The Predicament of the Public Sector Employee' (1983) PL 600.

if he was acting in the public interest in trying to prevent Government suppression of matters of public interest. The prosecution and its outcome provoked a large amount of adverse publicity, the public perceiving it as an attempt at a cover-up which had failed, not because the judge showed integrity but because the jury did.[8]

The outcome of the *Ponting* case may have influenced the decision not to prosecute Cathy Massiter, a former officer in the security service, in respect of her claims in a Channel 4 programme screened in March 1985 (*MI5's Official Secrets*) that MI5 had tapped the telephones of trade union members and placed leading CND members under surveillance.[9] Section 2's perceived lack of credibility may also have been a factor in the decision to bring civil as opposed to criminal proceedings against the *Guardian* and the *Observer* in respect of their disclosure of Peter Wright's allegations in *Spycatcher*: civil proceedings for breach of confidence were in many ways more convenient and less risky than a s2 prosecution (see Part VI, Chapter 3).

There is a long history of proposals for the reform of s2. The Franks Committee, which was set up in response to Caulfield J's comments in *Aitken* (1971), recommended that s2 should be replaced by narrower provisions which took into account the nature of the information disclosed.[10] The Franks proposals formed the basis of the Government's White Paper on which the Official Secrets Act 1989 was based. There were various other attempts at reform; those put forward as Private Member's Bills were the more liberal. For example, Clement Freud MP put forward an Official Information Bill[11] which would have created a public right of access to official information, while the Protection of Official Information Bill[12] put forward by Richard Shepherd MP in 1987 would have provided a public interest defence and a defence of prior disclosure.

The Official Secrets Act 1989[13]

Once the decision to reform the area of official secrecy had been taken, an opportunity was created for radical change which could have included freedom of information legislation along the lines of the instruments in America and

---

8   For comment on the case see C Ponting, *The Right to Know* (1985); G Drewry, 'The Ponting Case' (1985) PL 203.

9   The IBA banned the programme pending the decision as to whether Massiter and the producers would be prosecuted. The decision not to prosecute was announced by Sir Michael Havers on 5 March 1985. An inquiry into telephone tapping by Lord Bridge reported on 6 March that all authorised taps had been properly authorised. This of course did not address the allegation that some tapping had been carried out, although unauthorised.

10   Report of the Committee on s2 of the Official Secrets Act 1911, Cmnd 5104; see W Birtles, 'Big Brother Knows Best: The Franks Report on s2 of the Official Secrets Act' (1973) PL 100.

11   1978–79 Bill 96.

12   1987–88 Bill 20.

13   For comment on the 1989 Act see S Palmer, 'The Government Proposals for Reforming s 2 of the Official Secrets Act 1911' (1988) PL 523; W Hanbury, 'Illiberal Reform of s2' (1989) 133 Sol Jo 587; S Palmer, 'Tightening Secrecy Law' (1990) PL 243; J Griffith, 'The Official Secrets Act 1989' (1989) 16 *Journal of Law and Society* 273; D Feldman, *Civil Liberties and Human Rights* (1993), Chapter 14.3.

Canada. However, it was made clear from the outset that the legislation was unconcerned with freedom of information.[14] It de-criminalises disclosure of some official information, although an official who makes such disclosure may of course face an action for breach of confidence as well as disciplinary proceedings, but it will not allow the release of any official documents into the public domain. Thus claims made, for example, by Douglas Hurd (the then Home Secretary) that it is 'a great liberalising measure' clearly rest on other aspects of the Act. Aspects which are usually viewed as liberalising features include the categorisation of information covered, the introduction of tests for harm, the *mens rea* requirement of ss5 and 6, the defences available, and decriminalisation of the receiver of information. In all these respects the Act differs from its predecessor, but the nature of the changes has led commentators to question whether they will bring about any real liberalisation.[15] Other features of the Act have also attracted criticism: the categories of information covered are very wide and do not admit of challenge to the categorisation; the Act contains no defences of public interest or of prior disclosure, and no general requirement to prove *mens rea*.

Official Secrets Act 1989

Security and intelligence

1.–(1) A person who is or has been –

    (a)   a member of the security and intelligence services; or

    (b)   a person notified that he is subject to the provisions of this subsection,

is guilty of an offence if without lawful authority he discloses any information, document or other article relating to security or intelligence which is or has been in his possession by virtue of his position as a member of any of those services or in the course of his work while the notification is or was in force.

(2) The reference in subsection (1) above to disclosing information relating to security or intelligence includes a reference to making any statement which purports to be a disclosure of such information or is intended to be taken by those to whom it is addressed as being such a disclosure.

(3) A person who is or has been a Crown servant or government contractor is guilty of an offence if without lawful authority he makes a damaging disclosure of any information, document or other article relating to security or intelligence which is or has been in his possession by virtue of his position as such but otherwise than as mentioned in subsection (1) above.

(4) For the purposes of subsection (3) above a disclosure is damaging if –

    (a)   it causes damage to the work of, or of any part of, the security and intelligence services; or

    (b)   it is of information or a document or other article which is such that its unauthorised disclosure would be likely to cause such damage or which falls within a class or description of information, documents or articles the unauthorised disclosure of which would be likely to have that effect.

---

14   See White Paper on s2, Cmnd 7285; Green Paper on Freedom of Information, Cmnd 7520; White Paper, Reform of the Official Secrets Act 1911, Cmnd 408.

15   For example, Ewing and Gearty (1990), p200.

(5) It is a defence for a person charged with an offence under this section to prove that at the time of the alleged offence he did not know, and had no reasonable cause to believe, that the information, document or article in question related to security or intelligence or, in the case of an offence under subsection (3), that the disclosure would be damaging within the meaning of that subsection.

(6) Notification that a person is subject to subsection (1) above shall be effected by a notice in writing served on him by a Minister of the Crown; and such a notice may be served if, in the Minister's opinion, the work undertaken by the person in question is or includes work connected with the security and intelligence services and its nature is such that the interests of national security require that he should be subject to the provisions of that subsection.

(7) Subject to subsection (8) below, a notification for the purposes of subsection (1) above shall be in force for the period of five years beginning with the day on which it is served but may be renewed by further notices under subsection (6) above for periods of five years at a time.

(8) A notification for the purposes of subsection (1) above may at any time be revoked by a further notice in writing served by the Minister on the person concerned; and the Minister shall serve such a further notice as soon as, in his opinion, the work undertaken by that person ceases to be such as is mentioned in subsection (6) above.

(9) In this section 'security or intelligence' means the work of, or in support of, the security and intelligence services or any part of them, and references to information relating to security or intelligence include references to information held or transmitted by those services or by persons in support of, or of any part of, them.

Defence

2.–(1) A person who is or has been a Crown servant or government contractor is guilty of an offence if without lawful authority he makes a damaging disclosure of any information, document or other article relating to defence which is or has been in his possession by virtue of his position as such.

(2) For the purposes of subsection (1) above a disclosure is damaging –

(a) it damages the capability of, or of any part of, the armed forces of the Crown to carry out their tasks or leads to loss of life or injury to members of those forces or serious damage to the equipment or installations of those forces; or

(b) otherwise than as mentioned in paragraph (a) above, it endangers the interests of the United Kingdom abroad, seriously obstructs the promotion or protection by the United Kingdom of those interests or endangers the safety of British citizens abroad; or

(c) it is of information or of a document or article which is such that its unauthorised disclosure would be likely to have any of those effects. (3) It is a defence for a person charged with an offence under this section to prove that at the time of the alleged offence he did not know and had no reasonable cause to believe, that the information, document or article in question related to defence or that its disclosure would be damaging within the meaning of subsection (1) above.

...

(4) In this section 'defence' means –

(a) the size, shape, organisation, logistics, order of battle, deployment, operations, state of readiness and training of the armed forces of the Crown;

(b) the weapons, stores or other equipment of those forces and the invention, development, production and operation of such equipment and research relating to it;

(c) defence policy and strategy and military planning and intelligence;

(d) plans and measures for the maintenance of essential supplies and services that are or would be needed in time of war.

International relations

3.–(1)A person who is or has been a Crown servant or government contractor is guilty of an offence if without lawful authority he makes a damaging disclosure of –

(a) any information, document or other article relating to international relations; or

(b) any confidential information, document or other article which was obtained from a state other than the United Kingdom or an international organisation,

being information or a document or article which is or has been in his possession by virtue of his position as a Crown servant or government contractor.

(2) For the purposes of subsection (1) above a disclosure is damaging if –

(a) it endangers the interests of the United Kingdom abroad, seriously obstructs the promotion or protection by the United Kingdom of those interests or endangers the safety of British citizens abroad; or

(b) it is of information or of a document or article which is such that its unauthorised disclosure would be likely to have any of those effects.

(3) In the case of information or a document or article within subsection (1)(b) above –

(a) the fact that it is confidential; or

(b) its nature or contents, may be sufficient to establish for the purposes of subsection (2)(b) above that the information, document or article is such that its unauthorised disclosure would be likely to have any of the effects there mentioned.

(4) It is a defence for a person charged with an offence under this section to prove that at the time of the alleged offence he did not know, and had no reasonable cause to believe, that the information, document or article in question was such as is mentioned in subsection (1) above or that its disclosure would be damaging within the meaning of that subsection.

(5) In this section 'international relations' means the relations between states, between international organisations or between one or more states and one or more such organisations and includes any matter relating to a state other than the United Kingdom or to an international organisation which is capable of affecting the relations of the United Kingdom with another state or with an international organisation.

(6) For the purposes of this section any information, document or article obtained from a state or organisation is confidential at any time while the terms on which it was obtained require it to be held in confidence or while the circumstances in which it was obtained make it reasonable for the state or organisation to expect that it would be so held.

Crime and special investigation powers

4.–(1)A person who is or has been a Crown servant or government contractor is guilty of an offence if without lawful authority he discloses any information, document or other article to which this section applies and which is or has been in his possession by virtue of his position as such.

(2)This section applies to any information, document or other article –

    (a) the disclosure of which –

        (i)   results in the commission of an offence; or

        (ii) facilitates an escape from legal custody or the doing of any other act prejudicial to the safekeeping of persons in legal custody; or

        (iii) impedes the prevention or detection of offences or the apprehension or prosecution of suspected offenders; or

    (b) which is such that its unauthorised disclosure would be likely to have any of those effects.

(3)This section also applies to –

    (a) any information obtained by reason of the interception of any communication in obedience to a warrant issued under section 2 of the Interception of Communications Act 1985, any information relating to the obtaining of information by reason of any such interception and any document or other article which is or has been used or held for use in, or has been obtained by reason of, any such interception; and

    (b) any information obtained by reason of action authorised by a warrant issued under section 3 of the Security Service Act 1989, any information relating to the obtaining of information by reason of any such action and any document or other article

which is or has been used or held for use in, or has been obtained by reason of, any such action.

(4)It is a defence for a person charged with an offence under this section in respect of a disclosure falling within subsection (2)(a) above to prove that at the time of the alleged offence he did not know, and had no reasonable cause to believe, that the disclosure would have any of the effects there mentioned.

(5)It is a defence for a person charged with an offence under this section in respect of any other disclosure to prove that at the time of the alleged offence he did not know, and had no reasonable cause to believe, that the information, document or article in question was information or a document or article to which this section applies.

(6)In this section 'legal custody' includes detention in pursuance of any enactment or any instrument made under an enactment.

Information resulting from unauthorised disclosures or entrusted in confidence

5.–(1) Subsection (2) below applies where –

    (a) any information, document or other article protected against disclosure by the foregoing provisions of this Act has come into a person's possession as a result of having been –

        (i)   disclosed (whether to him or another) by a Crown servant or government contractor without lawful authority; or

        (ii) entrusted to him by a Crown servant or government contractor on terms requiring it to be held in confidence or in circumstances in which the Crown servant or government contractor could reasonably expect that it would be so held;

      (iii)   disclosed (whether to him or another) without lawful authority by a person to whom it was entrusted as mentioned in sub-paragraph (ii) above; and

   (b) the disclosure without lawful authority of the information, document or article by the person into whose possession it has come is not an offence under any of those provisions.

(2) Subject to subsections (3) and (4) below, the person into whose possession the information, document or article has come is guilty of an offence if he discloses it without lawful authority knowing, or having reasonable cause to believe, that it is protected against disclosure by the foregoing provisions of this Act and that it has come into his possession as mentioned in subsection (1) above.

(3) In the case of information or a document or article protected against disclosure by sections 1 to 3 above, a person does not commit an offence under subsection (2) above unless –

   (a) the disclosure by him is damaging; and

   (b) he makes it knowing, or having reasonable cause to believe, that

it would be damaging; and the question whether a disclosure is damaging shall be determined for the purposes of this subsection as it would be in relation to a disclosure of that information, document or article by a Crown servant in contravention of sections 1(3), 2(1) or 3(1) above.

(4) A person does not commit an offence under subsection (2) above in respect of information or a document or other article which has come into his possession as a result of having been disclosed –

   (a) as mentioned in subsection (1)(a)(i) above by a government contractor; or

   (b) as mentioned in subsection (1)(a)(iii) above, unless that disclosure was by a British citizen or took place in the United Kingdom, in any of the Channel Islands or in the Isle of Man or a colony.

(5) For the purposes of this section information or a document or article is protected against disclosure by the foregoing provisions of this Act –

   (a) it relates to security or intelligence, defence or international relations within the meaning of section 1, 2 or 3 above or is such as is mentioned in section 3(1)(b) above; or

   (b) it is information or a document or article to which section 4 above applies and information or a document or article is protected against disclosure by sections 1 to 3 above if it falls within paragraph (a) above.

(6) A person is guilty of an offence if without lawful authority he discloses any information, document or other article which he knows, or has reasonable cause to believe, to have come into his possession as a result of a contravention of section 1 of the Official Secrets Act 1911.

Information entrusted in confidence to other states or international organisations

6.–(1) This section applies where –

   (a) any information, document or other article which –

      (i)   relates to security or intelligence, defence or international relations; and

      (ii) has been communicated in confidence by or on behalf of the United Kingdom to another state or to an international organisation, has come into a person's possession as a result of having been disclosed (whether to him or another) without the authority of that state or organisation or, in the case of an organisation, of a member of it; and

(b) the disclosure without lawful authority of the information, document or article by the person into whose possession it has come is not an offence under any of the foregoing provisions of this Act.

(2) Subject to subsection (3) below, the person into whose possession the information, document or article has come is guilty of an offence if he makes a damaging disclosure of it knowing, or having reasonable cause to believe, that it is such as is mentioned in subsection (1) above, that it has come into his possession as there mentioned and that its disclosure would be damaging.

(3) A person does not commit an offence under subsection (2) above if the information, document or article is disclosed by him with lawful authority or has previously been made available to the public with the authority of the state or organisation concerned or, in the case of an organisation, of a member of it.

(4) For the purposes of this section 'security or intelligence', 'defence' and 'international relations' have the same meaning as in sections 1, 2 and 3 above and the question whether a disclosure is damaging shall be determined as it would be in relation to a disclosure of the information, document or article in question by a Crown servant in contravention of sections 1(3), 2(1) and 3(1) above.

(5) For the purposes of this section information or a document or article is communicated in confidence if it is communicated on terms requiring it to be held in confidence or in circumstances in which the person communicating it could reasonably expect that it would be so held.

Authorised disclosures

7.–(1) For the purposes of this Act a disclosure by –

(a) a Crown servant; or

(b) a person, not being a Crown servant or government contractor in whose case a notification for the purposes of section 1(1) above is in force,

is made with lawful authority if, and only if, it is made in accordance with his official duty.

(2) For the purposes of this Act a disclosure by a government contractor is made with lawful authority if, and only if, it is made –

(a) in accordance with an official authorisation; or

(b) for the purposes of the functions by virtue of which he is a government contractor and without contravening an official restriction.

(3) For the purposes of this Act a disclosure made by any other person is made with lawful authority if, and only if, it is made –

(a) to a Crown servant for the purposes of his functions as such; or

(b) in accordance with an official authorisation.

(4) It is a defence for a person charged with an offence under any of the foregoing provisions of this Act to prove that at the time of the alleged offence he believed that he had lawful authority to make the disclosure in question and had no reasonable cause to believe otherwise.

(5) In this section 'official authorisation' and 'official restriction' mean, subject to subsection (6) below, an authorisation or restriction duly given or imposed by a Crown servant or government contractor or by or on behalf of a prescribed body or a body of a prescribed class.

(6)In relation to section 6 above 'official authorisation' includes an authorisation duly given by or on behalf of the state or organisation concerned or, m the case of an organisation, a member of it.

Prosecutions

9.–(1)Subject to subsection (2) below, no prosecution for an offence under this Act shall be instituted in England and Wales or in Northern Ireland except by or with the consent of the Attorney General or, as the case may be, the Attorney General for Northern Ireland.

(2)Subsection (1) above does not apply to an offence in respect of any such information, document or article as is mentioned in section 4(2) above but no prosecution for such an offence shall be instituted in England and Wales or in Northern Ireland except by or with the consent of the Director of Public Prosecutions or, as the case may be, the Director of Public Prosecutions for Northern Ireland.

Penalties

10.–(1) A person guilty of an offence under any provision of this Act other than section 8(1), (4) or (5) shall be liable –

(a) on conviction on indictment, to imprisonment for a term not exceeding two years or a fine or both;

(b) on summary conviction, to imprisonment for a term not exceeding six months or a fine not exceeding the statutory maximum or both.

(2)A person guilty of an offence under section 8(1), (4) or (5) above shall be liable on summary conviction to imprisonment for a term not exceeding three months or a fine not exceeding level 5 on the standard scale or both.

Arrest, search and trial

11.–(4) Section 8(4) of the Official Secrets Act 1920 (exclusion of public from hearing on grounds of national safety) shall have effect as if references to offences under that Act included references to offences under any provision of this Act other than section 8(1), (4) or (5).

'Crown servant' and 'government contractor'

12.–(1) In this Act 'Crown servant' means –

(a) a Minister of the Crown;

(b) a person appointed under s8 of the Northern Ireland Constitution Act 1973 (the Northern Ireland Executive, etc.);

(c) any person employed in the civil service of the Crown, including Her Majesty's Diplomatic Service, Her Majesty's Overseas Civil Service, the civil service of Northern Ireland and the Northern Ireland Court Service;

(d) any member of the naval, military or air forces of the Crown including any person employed by an association established for the purposes of the Reserve Forces Act 1980;

(e) any constable and any other person employed or appointed in or for the purposes of any police force (including a police force within the meaning of the Police Act (Northern Ireland) 1970);

(f) any person who is a member or employee of a prescribed body or a body of a prescribed class and either is prescribed for the purposes of this paragraph or belongs to a prescribed class of members or employees of any such body;

(g) any person who is the holder of a prescribed office or who is an employee of such a holder and either is prescribed for the purposes *of* this paragraph or belongs to a prescribed class of such employees.

(2)In this Act 'government contractor' means, subject to subsection (3) below, any person who is not a Crown servant but who provides, or is employed in the provision of, goods or services –

(a) for the purposes of any Minister or person mentioned in paragraph (a) or (b) of subsection (1) above, of any of the services, forces or bodies mentioned in that subsection or of the holder of any office prescribed under that subsection; or

(b) under an agreement or arrangement certified by the Secretary of State as being one to which the government of a state other than the United Kingdom or an international organisation is a party or which is subordinate to, or made for the purposes of implementing, any such agreement or arrangement.

Lord Advocate v Scotsman Publications Ltd [1989] 2 All ER 852, 859, 860, 861, HL

Lord Templeman: My Lords, in this appeal the Lord Advocate, acting on behalf of the Crown, claims to restrain the respondent newspapers and television companies from disclosing certain information contained in a book written by one Cavendish, that information having been obtained by him in the course of his employment with the British security and intelligence services.

Any such restraint is an interference with the right of expression safeguarded by the Convention for the Protection of Human Rights and Fundamental Freedoms, Article 10 ...

The question ... is whether the restraint sought to be imposed on the respondents is 'necessary in a democratic society in the interests of national security' [para 2 of Article 10]. Similar questions were considered in *AG v Guardian Newspapers Ltd (No 2)* [1988] 3 All ER 345, [1988] 3 WLR 776 (the *Spycatcher* case) but at that time Parliament had not provided any answer to the questions posed by the conflict between the freedom of expression and the requirement of national security.

In my opinion it is for Parliament to determine the restraints on freedom of expression which are necessary in a democratic society. The courts of this country should follow any guidance contained in a statute. If that guidance is inconsistent with the requirements of the convention then that will be a matter for the convention authorities and for the UK Government. It will not be a matter for the courts.

The guidance of Parliament has now been provided in the Official Secrets Act 1989, which was enacted on 1 May 1989 and will be brought into force on such date as the Secretary of State may by order appoint. By the 1989 Act certain categories of persons will be guilty of a criminal offence if they disclose information relating to security or intelligence in the circumstances specified in the Act but not otherwise. In my opinion the civil jurisdiction of the courts of this country to grant an injunction restraining a broach of confidence at the suit of the Crown should not, in principle, be exercised in a manner different from or more severe than any appropriate restriction which Parliament has imposed in the 1989 Act and which, if breached, will create a criminal offence as soon as the Act is brought into force. ...

In my opinion the respondents fall into the category described by s5 notwithstanding that Cavendish had retired from his employment and was not a Crown servant at the date when information protected against disclosure was disclosed by Cavendish and came into the possession of the respondents. The restrictions imposed by the 1989 Act on third parties are less onerous than the restrictions placed on Cavendish and other security employees. By s5(2), subject to s5(3), a third party into whose possession confidential information has come:

> is guilty of an offence if he discloses it without lawful authority knowing, or having reasonable cause to believe, that it is protected against disclosure by the foregoing provisions of this Act and that it has come into his possession as mentioned in subsection (I) above.

In the present case the respondents are well aware that the information derived from Cavendish is protected against disclosure and came into their possession as a result of a disclosure by Cavendish. But by s5(3):

> In the case of information or a document or article protected against disclosure by ss1–3 above, a person does not commit an offence under subsection (2) above unless (a) the disclosure by him is damaging; and (b) he makes it knowing, or having reasonable cause to believe, that it would be damaging …

By s1(4) the disclosure by the respondents of the protected information derived from Cavendish will be damaging if:

(a) it causes damage to the work of, or of any part of, the security and intelligence services; or

(b) it is of information or a document or other article which is such that its unauthorised disclosure would be likely to cause such damage or which falls within a class or description of information, documents or articles the unauthorised disclosure of which would be likely to have that effect.

The information derived from Cavendish which the respondents may wish to publish and disclose is information embedded in a book of memoirs by Cavendish. Part of that book relates to the period between 1948 and 1953 when Cavendish was a security employee and is protected against disclosure by s1 of the 1989 Act. The Crown concedes, however, that publication of that information by the respondents will not cause or be likely to cause damage to the work of the security or intelligence services, presumably because the information is inaccurate or unenlightening or insignificant. The information itself does not fall within a class or description of information the unauthorised disclosure of which would be likely to be damaging. Nevertheless, the Crown contends that it is entitled to restrain the respondents from publishing this harmless information because the information is contained in the memoirs of a security employee. It is said that the publication of harmless information derived from a former security employee and protected by s1 against disclosure by him, though not damaging in itself, would cause harm by encouraging other security employees to make disclosures in breach of s1 of the 1989 Act and by raising doubts as to the reliability of the security service.

My Lords, it is well known, at home and abroad, that every security service suffers from time to time from an employee who is disloyal for ideological or other reasons which may derive from the desire for profit or notoriety. The motives of Cavendish are irrelevant if he is in breach of the duty of lifelong confidence of security employees accepted in the *Spycatcher* case and imposed by s1 of the 1989 Act. If the 1989 Act had been in force when Cavendish circulated his book to a chosen band of readers, he would have committed an offence under s1 of the Act notwithstanding that the information disclosed in his book is harmless. But it does not follow that third parties commit an offence if they disclose harmless information. Were it otherwise, the distinction between an offence by a security employee and an offence by a third party which appears from the 1989 Act would be eradicated. A security employee can commit an offence if he discloses any information. A third party is only guilty of an offence if the information is damaging in the sense defined by the Act.

If the Crown had asserted that future publication by the *Scotsman* would be likely to damage the work of the security services, then difficult questions might have arisen as to the nature of the damage feared, whether an injunction was necessary within the meaning attributed to that expression by the European Court of Human Rights and whether the restriction on freedom of expression constituted by the injunction sought was 'proportionate to the legitimate aim pursued' as required by the European Court of Human Rights in *Handyside v UK* (1976) 1 EHRR 737 and *Sunday Times v UK* (1979) 2 EHRR 245. These difficult questions do not, however, arise since the Crown conceded that future publication would not be likely to cause damage other than the indirect damage which I have already rejected.

In the present case the respondents did not instigate or encourage or facilitate any breach by Cavendish of his obligations. They did not solicit a copy of the Cavendish book or any information from him or derived from him. They did not commit an offence at common law in connection with an offence or attempted offence by Cavendish. It may be that there are circumstances in which a third party might be liable to be restrained from publishing protected information even though the publication by the third party might itself be harmless. It is unnecessary, however, to consider this possibility in the present instance.

I would affirm the decision of the Court of Session and dismiss the appeal of the Crown.

Notes

1 Section 1(1) is intended to place members or former members of the security services under a lifelong duty to keep silent any information related to the services even though their information might reveal serious abuse of power in the security service or some operational weakness. There is no need to show that any harm will or may flow from the disclosure and so all information, however trivial, is covered.

2 Section 1(3), however, is only satisfied if harm results from the disclosure, but taken at its lowest level it is clear that this test may be very readily satisfied: it is not necessary to show that disclosure of the actual document in question has caused harm or would be likely to cause harm, merely that it belongs to a class of documents disclosure of which would be likely to have that effect. Disclosure of a document containing insignificant information and incapable itself of causing the harm described under s1(4)(a) can therefore be criminalised, suggesting that the importation of a harm test for Crown servants as opposed to members of the security services may not in practice create a very significant distinction between them. However, harm must be likely to flow from disclosure of a specific document where, due to its unique nature, it cannot be said to be one of a class of documents. The ruling of the House of Lords in *Lord Advocate v Scotsman Publications Ltd* (1989) suggests that the test for harm under this subsection may be quite restrictively interpreted.[16]

---

16 For criticism of the ruling see Walker (1990) PL 354.

3   The harm test under s2 is potentially extremely wide due to its open-textured wording. It states, in effect, that a disclosure of information in this category is damaging if it causes damage to the area of Government operation covered by the category. No clue is given as to what is meant by 'damage'; in many cases it would therefore be impossible for a Crown servant to determine beforehand whether or not a particular disclosure would be criminal.

4   The harm test under s3(1)(b) contained in s3(3) is somewhat curious; once the information is identified as falling within this category, a fiction is created that harm may automatically flow from its disclosure.

5   Section 4(3) covers information obtained by use of intercept and security service warrants. There is no harm test under this category. It therefore creates a wide exception to the general need to show harm under s1(3) when a Crown servant who is not a member of the security services makes a disclosure about the work of those services.

6   Section 5 does not refer to a new category of information. The section is primarily aimed at journalists who receive information leaked to them by Crown servants, although it could of course cover anybody in that position. In contrast to disclosure of information by a Crown servant under one of the six categories, s5 imports a requirement of *mens rea* under s5(2). This provision affords some recognition to media freedom; nevertheless the burden of proof on the prosecution would be very easy to discharge if the information fell within ss1(3), 3(1)(b) or 4(3) due to the nature of the tests for damage included in those sections; it would only be necessary to show that the journalist knew that the information fell within the category in question. Another apparent improvement in terms of media freedom is the decriminalisation of the receiver of information. However, this improvement might be said to be more theoretical than real in that it was perhaps unlikely that the mere receiver would be prosecuted under the 1911 Act even though that possibility did exist. The fact that journalists were included at all in the net of criminal liability under s5 has been criticised on the basis that some recognition should be given to the important role of the press in informing the public about government actions.[17] A comparison could be drawn with the constitutional role of the press recognised in America by the *Pentagon Papers* case.[18]

7   The Act appears to provide three defences for Crown servants: first that the defendant did not know and had no reasonable cause to believe that the information fell into the category in question; secondly that he or she did not realise that the information would cause harm; and thirdly that he or she believed that he had lawful authorisation to make the disclosure and had no reasonable cause to believe otherwise (s 7). However, the first two defences may be conflated in certain categories, largely because the second defence is intimately tied up with the harm tests and therefore, like them, operates on a

---

17   See, eg Ewing and Gearty, pp196–201.

18   *New York Times Co v US* 403 US 713 (1971): the Supreme Court determined that no restraining order on the press could be made so that the press would remain free to censure the Government.

number of levels. Where there is no harm test, as under ss1(1) or 4(3), only the first defence is available. Under ss3(1)(b), since the test for harm may be satisfied merely by showing that the information falls within the subsection the second defence may be more apparent than real. Under s1(3) the second defence may be of limited value to defendants. It would not necessarily avail the defendant to prove that it was known before the disclosure took place that it would not cause harm if the prosecution could prove a likelihood that harm would be caused from disclosure of documents falling into the same class.

8   The Act contains no public interest defence. Thus, the situation of the civil servant in the UK who believes that disclosure as to a certain state of affairs is necessary in order to serve the public interest may be contrasted with the situation of his of her counterpart in the USA where he or she would receive protection from detrimental action flowing from whistle-blowing[19] under the Civil Service Reform Act 1978. However, the Civil Service Code, which came into force on 1 January 1996, contains a partial 'whistle-blowing' provision in paragraphs 11 and 12 (see *Hansard,* HL Deb 9 January 1996). The duty of civil servants remains not to disclose any information to which they have acquired access as civil servants, without authorisation (para 10 of the code). However, paras 11 and 12 provide that if a civil servant believes that he or she is being asked to act in a way which *inter alia* is improper, unethical or which raises fundamental issues of conscience, he or she should report the matter in accordance with departmental guidance (para 11). If the matter has been reported in this manner and the civil servant does not believe that a response is a reasonable response, he or she should report the matter to the Civil Service Commissioners (para 12). Where the matter cannot be resolved by resort to these procedures the civil servant should either resign or carry out his or her instructions.[20] This is therefore a very limited provision since it only allows ultimate disclosure of information to the Civil Service Commissioners. No protection is offered in the code if the disclosure is to an Opposition MP, as in *Ponting.*

9   No express defence of prior publication is provided by the 1989 Act; the only means of putting forward such a defence would arise in one of the categories in which it was necessary to prove the likelihood that harm would flow from the disclosure; the prosecution might find it hard to establish such a likelihood where there had been a great deal of prior publication because no further harm could be caused. Prior publication would be irrelevant under s1(1). Thus where a member of the security services disclosed information falling within s1 which had been published all over the world and in the UK, a conviction could still be obtained. If such publication had occurred but the information fell within s1(3), the test for harm might be satisfied on the basis that, although no further harm could be

---

19   For discussion of the situation of UK and USA civil servants and developments in the area, see Y Cripps (1983) PL 600; Zellick (1987) PL 311–13; Starke (1989) 63 ALJ 592–594.

20   It may be noted that when the questions of procedure for ministers are next revised, they will be brought into harmony with the Civil Service Code (see *Hansard,* HL Deb 29 November 1995).

caused by disclosure of the *particular document*, it nevertheless belonged to a class of documents disclosure of which was likely to cause harm. Where harm flowing from publication of a specific document is relied on, *Lord Advocate v Scotsman Publications Ltd* (1989) (below) suggests that a degree of prior publication may tend to defeat the argument that further publication can still cause harm. However, this suggestion must be treated with care as the ruling was not given under the 1989 Act and the link between the Act and the civil law of confidence may not form part of its ratio.[21]

Questions

1 Has the 1989 Act afforded any recognition to the important constitutional role of the journalist?

2 As things stand, a journalist who repeated allegations made by a member of the security services as to corruption or treachery in MI5 could be convicted if it could be shown, first, that he or she knew that the information related to the security services and, secondly, that disclosure of that type of information would be likely to cause damage to the work of the security services, regardless of whether the particular allegations would cause such damage. What would be the position under the Act of a journalist who repeated allegations made by a future Cathy Massiter after they had been published in other countries?

Public interest immunity

Discovery may be needed by one party to an action of documents held by the other in order to assist in the action or allow it to proceed. Where a member of the Government or other state body is the party holding the documents in question it may claim that it is immune from the duty to make such disclosure, asserting public interest immunity, a privilege based on the royal prerogative.[22] The immunity is expressly preserved in the Crown Proceedings Act 1947, but this means that the courts have had to determine its scope. Section 28(1) of the 1947 Act, which provides that the court can make an order for discovery of documents against the Crown and require the Crown to answer interrogatories, is qualified by s28(2) which preserves Crown privilege to withhold documents on the grounds of public interest in a variety of cases.

Certain decisions demonstrate the development there has been in determining the scope of this privilege. The House of Lords in *Duncan v Camell Laird and Co* (1942)[23] held that documents otherwise relevant to judicial proceedings are not to be disclosed if the public interest requires that they be withheld. This test may be found to be satisfied either (a) by having regard to the contents of the particular document, or (b) by the fact that the document

---

21 Only Lord Templeman clearly adverted to such a link.

22 See Cross and Tapper, *Cross on Evidence*, 7th edn (1990) Chapter XII; (1942) 1 All ER 587. For a discussion of the legal and historical background; Jacob, 'From Privileged Crown to Interested Public' (1993) PL 121; Bradley, 'Justice, Good Government and Public Interest Immunity' (1992) PL 514; Ganz, 'Matrix Churchill and Public Interest Immunity' (1993) 56 MLR 564; Allan, 'Public Interest Immunity and Ministers' Responsibility' (1993) CLR 661.

23 [1942] AC 624.

belongs to a category which, on grounds of public interest, must as a class remain undisclosed.[24] Crown privilege as formulated here was an exclusionary rule of evidence based on public interest and the minister was deemed the sole judge of what that constituted. In *Ellis v HO* (1953),[25] a prisoner on remand who was severely injured by a mentally disturbed prisoner in the prison hospital, sued the Crown for negligence. Privilege was claimed to prevent the disclosure of medical reports on his assailant and so the action had to fail. The danger clearly arose that, since the executive was the sole judge of what was in the public interest, matters embarrassing to Government might be concealed. In *Conway v Rimmer* (1968)[26] the speeches in the House of Lords revealed the degree of concern which had arisen in the judiciary as to the danger of injustice created by the use of this privilege by ministers. In that case a police constable was prosecuted for theft. The charge was dismissed but he was dismissed from the police force. He brought an action for malicious prosecution against his former superintendent but the Home Office objected to the disclosure of reports relevant to the case. The House of Lords, in a landmark decision, overruled the minister's claim of Crown privilege and ordered disclosure.

This decision substituted judicial discretion for executive discretion regarding disclosure of documents. However, the judges have tended to exercise this discretion cautiously. Disclosure is unlikely to be ordered unless the party seeking it can show: first, that the material is clearly relevant to a specific issue in the case; secondly that it will be of significant value in the fair disposal of the case; and thirdly, following *Air Canada v Secretary of State for Trade (No 2)* (1983) that it will assist the case of that party. The main issue for determination in *Air Canada* concerned the conditions which have to be satisfied before a court will inspect documents for which public interest immunity is claimed. If the court does not inspect it cannot order disclosure. The court considered that the documents were relevant in the case and necessary for its fair disposal. However, this did not lead the majority to find that inspection was necessary in order to determine whether non-disclosure would prevent the court from judging the issues. Instead, the majority found that the party seeking disclosure must show that 'the documents are very likely to contain material which would give substantial support to his contention on an issue which arises in the case'.[27] As Zuckermann points out below, this created a very serious obstacle to disclosure. Lord Scarman dissented from this view, although he agreed that inspection was unnecessary; extracts from his dissenting judgment are set out below.

Air Canada v Secretary of State for Trade (No 2) [1983] 1 All ER 910, 923–25, HL(E)

> **Lord Scarman:** My Lords, others of your lordships have analysed the issues, and narrated the facts, of this complex litigation. I shall, therefore, confine my speech to the narrow issue which we have to decide. The appeal raises an issue, not

---

24 *Ibid* at 592.
25 [1953] 2 QB 135.
26 [1968] AC 910.
27 *Per* Lord Fraser [1983] 1 All ER 917.

previously explored by the House, arising on the discovery of documents which belong to a class in respect of which the Crown has made a powerful claim in proper form for immunity from production in the public interest. The appeal illustrates, if illustration be needed, that the House's decision in *Conway v Rimmer* [1968] AC 910 was the beginning, but not the end, of a chapter in the law's development in this branch of the law.

The issue is specific and within a small compass. The Crown having made its objection to production in proper form. In what circumstances should the court inspect privately the documents before determining whether they, or any of them, should be produced?

The court, of course, has a discretion: but the discretion must be exercised in accordance with principle. The principle governing the production of disclosed documents is embodied in RSC, Ord 24, r 13. No order for the production of any documents for inspection or to the court shall be made unless the court is of the opinion that the order is necessary either for disposing fairly of the cause or matter or for saving costs: r 13(1). And the court may inspect the document for the purpose of deciding whether the objection to production is valid: r 13(2). The rule provides a measure of protection for a party's documents irrespective of their class or contents and independently of any privilege or immunity. While the existence of all documents in a party's possession or control relating to matters in question in the action must be 'discovered', that is to say disclosed, to the other party (or parties), he is not obliged to produce them unless the court is of the opinion that production is necessary.

Faced with a properly formulated certificate claiming public interest immunity, the court must first examine the grounds put forward. If it is a 'class' objection and the documents (as in *Conway v Rimmer* [1968] AC 910) are routine in character, the court may inspect so as to ascertain the strength of the public interest in immunity and the needs of justice before deciding whether to order production. If it is a 'contents' claim, eg a specific national security matter, the court will ordinarily accept the judgment of the minister. But if it is a class claim in which the objection on the face of the certificate is a strong one — as in this case where the documents are minutes and memoranda passing at a high level between ministers and their advisers and concerned with the formulation of policy – the court will pay great regard to the minister's view (or that of the senior official who has signed the certificate). It will not inspect unless there is a likelihood that the documents will be necessary for disposing fairly of the case or saving costs. Certainly, if, like Bingham J in this case, the court should think that the documents might be 'determinative' of the issues in the action to which they relate, the court should inspect: for in such a case there may be grave doubt as to which way the balance of public interest falls: *Burmah Oil Co Ltd v Governor and Company of the Bank of England* [1980] AC 1090, 1134–1135, 1145. But, unless the court is satisfied on the material presented to it that the documents are likely to be necessary for fairly disposing of the case, it will not inspect for the simple reason that unless the likelihood exists there is nothing to set against the public interest in immunity from production.

The learned judge, Bingham J, correctly appreciated the principle of the matter. He decided to inspect because he believed that the documents in question were very likely to be 'necessary for the just determination of the second and third issues in the plaintiffs' … case'. Here I consider he fell into error. For the reasons given in the speech of my noble and learned friend, Lord Templeman, I do not think that the appellants have been able to show that the documents whose production they are seeking are likely to be necessary for fairly disposing of the issues in their 'constitutional' case. Indeed, my noble and learned friend has demonstrated that they are unnecessary. Accordingly, for this reason, but for no other, I would hold that the judge was wrong to decide to inspect the documents.

On all other questions I find myself in agreement with the judge. In particular, I am persuaded by his reasoning that the public interest in the administration of justice, which the court has to put into the balance against the public interest immunity, is as he put it:

> In my judgment, documents are necessary for fairly disposing of a cause or for the due administration of justice if they give substantial assistance to the court in determining the facts upon which the decision in the cause will depend.

The learned judge rejected, in my view rightly, the view which has commended itself to the Court of Appeal and to some of your lordships, that the criterion for determining whether to inspect or not is whether the party seeking production can establish the likelihood that the documents will assist his case or damage that of his opponent. No doubt that is what he is seeking; no doubt also, it is a very relevant consideration for the court. But it would be dangerous to elevate it into a principle of the law of discovery. Discovery is one of the few exceptions to the adversarial character of our legal process. It assists parties and the court to discover the truth. By so doing, it not only helps towards a just determination: it also saves costs. A party who discovers timeously a document fatal to his case is assisted as effectively, although less to his liking, as one who discovers the winning card; for he can save himself and others the heavy costs of litigation. There is another important aspect of the matter. The Crown, when it puts forward a public interest immunity objection, is not claiming a privilege but discharging a duty. The duty arises whether the document assists or damages the Crown's case or if, as in a case to which the Crown is not a party, it neither helps nor injures the Crown. It is not for the Crown but for the court to determine whether the document should be produced. Usually, but not always, the critical factor will be whether the party seeking production has shown the document will help him. But it may be necessary for a fair determination or for saving costs, even if it does not. Therefore, although it is likely to make little difference in practice, I would think it better in principle to retain the formulation of the interests to be balanced which Lord Reid gave us in *Conway v Rimmer* [1968] AC 910, 940:

> It is universally recognised that here there are two kinds of public interest which may clash. There is the public interest that harm shall not be done to the nation or the public service by disclosure of certain documents, and there is the public interest that the administration of justice shall not be frustrated by the withholding of documents which must be produced if justice is to be done.

And I do so for the reasons given by Lord Pearce in the same case. Describing the two conflicting interests, he said of the administration of justice, at p987, that the judge:

> can consider whether the documents in question are of much or little weight in the litigation, whether their absence will result in a complete or partial denial of justice to one or other of the parties or perhaps to both, and what is the importance of the particular litigation to the parties and the public.

Basically, the reason for selecting the criterion of justice, irrespective of whether it assists the party seeking production, is that the Crown may not have regard to party advantage in deciding whether or not to object to production on the ground of public interest immunity. It is its duty to bring the objection, if it believes it to be sound, to the attention of the court. It is for the court, not the Crown, to balance the two public interests, that of the functioning and security of the public service, which is the sphere within which the executive has the duty to make an assessment, and that of justice, upon which the executive is not competent to pass judgment.

For these reasons I would dismiss the appeal.

Chief Constable of West Midlands Police, ex p Wiley, Chief Constable of Nottinghamshire Police, ex p Sunderland (1995) 1 AC 274[28] 281, 291–306

Mr Wiley was charged with robbery but at his trial the prosecution offered no evidence. He made a formal complaint against certain members of the West Midlands police force and he later commenced a civil action against the Chief Constable of the West Midlands force. Mr Sunderland was charged with assault but at his trial also the prosecution offered no evidence. He made a formal complaint that he had been assaulted by police officers and he indicated his intention to commence a civil action against the Chief Constable of Nottinghamshire Police. It was thought by lawyers acting for Mr Wiley and Mr Sunderland (following *Neilson v Laugharne* (1981))[29] that the documents compiled for the complaint which would come into the hands of the chief constables would attract public interest immunity. Therefore in contesting the civil actions the chief constables could make use of the information contained in them but Mr Wiley and Mr Sunderland would not be able to do so. The lawyers therefore required the chief constables to give undertakings that the information would not be so used. The chief constables refused to do so and declarations were granted that they had acted unlawfully in so refusing; the chief constables appealed against grant of these declarations to the House of Lords.

All the parties concerned argued that public interest immunity did not attach to documents coming into existence during a police complaints investigation. The House of Lords had to consider whether *Neilson v Laugharne* and the decisions following it were wrongly decided. In *Neilson* Lord Oliver had determined that a class immunity should attach to police complaints documents on the basis that the police complaints procedure would be placed in jeopardy if that was not the case.

Lord Templeman: ... I consider that when a document is known to be relevant and material, the holder of the document should voluntarily disclose it unless he is satisfied that disclosure should voluntarily disclose it unless he is satisfied that disclosure will cause substantial harm. If the holder is in any doubt he may refer the matter to the court. If the holder decides that a document should not be disclosed then that decision can be upheld or set aside by the judge. A rubber stamp approach to public interest immunity by the holder of a document is neither necessary nor appropriate. ...

Lord Woolf: ... I turn to the decision of the Court of Appeal in *Neilson v Laugharne* [1981] QB 736. The case involved proceedings which have been commenced by the plaintiff in the county court claiming damages from a chief constable after the plaintiff had made a complaint which had resulted in the chief constable instituting the complaints procedure under section 49 of the Police Act 1964, which was the predecessor to the procedure which is now contained in Part IX of the Act of 1984. In the course of discovery the chief constable objected to the production of the documents on the ground that their production would be

---

28   (1995) 1 Cr App R 342.

29   [1981] QB 736.

injurious to the public interest and on the ground that they were covered by legal professional privilege. The judge upheld the claim that the documents were covered by legal professional privilege. The Court of Appeal did not accept this was the case but dismissed the plaintiff's appeal on the grounds that the documents were entitled to public interest immunity on a class basis.

[Oliver LJ found]

> What, as it seems to me, one has to look at is the likely consequences of a general right to disclosure in civil litigation in the context of the statutory purpose sought to be achieved by the section ...

I do not see any objection in having regard to the statutory purpose of the legislation as long as care is exercised not to attach too much importance to this. If the legislation does not provide expressly for immunity for documents created in order to achieve the statutory purpose the courts should be slow to assume this was required by Parliament. Oliver L J ... then went on to consider whether the liability to disclose the documents in civil proceedings would adversely affect the attainment of the legislative purpose and having done so came to the conclusion that it would in a number of ways; which he identified [1981] QB 736, 752–753. The first was that police officers who are asked to co-operate in the inquiry would clearly be disinclined to provide statements which might subsequently be used to found civil claims against them. ... He also referred to the position of relatives, associates or neighbours of the complainant and asked whether such persons were:

> likely to be willing to offer free and truthful co-operation in investigations under the section if they know that any statements which they make are liable to be disclosed to the complainant in any civil proceedings which he may be minded to commence?

Finally, Oliver LJ referred to the position of the complainant himself, that he might be deterred from making a statement if it could be quoted against him in any civil proceedings which he had in contemplation. In addition, Oliver LJ referred to the burden which would be placed upon the police authority if they were placed in the position of having to scrutinise every statement made on an inquiry under the section so as to ascertain whether or not it should be the subject matter of a contents claim ...

As to the reasoning of Oliver LJ, the first thing which has to be said is that the only evidence in support of the claim was apparently an affidavit of a deputy chief constable to the effect that an inquiry would be prejudiced if persons approached to make statements thought that such statements might be used in civil litigation and *revealed* to the parties. It was insubstantial material on which to establish a new class claim to public interest immunity. It was certainly not self-evident that the adverse consequences to which Oliver LJ referred would follow without establishing a new class claim. Oliver LJ accepted that the fact that the documents would not be immune in disciplinary or criminal proceedings undermined a case for immunity on the basis of confidentiality but somewhat surprisingly did not consider that this did not also undermine the case based upon lack of co-operation. If there were disciplinary or criminal proceedings then the fellow officer or the witness would be well aware of the part which the witness had played. As to the complainant, the point was weakened by the fact that, founding himself upon what was said by Lord Cross of Chelsea in *Alfred Crompton Amusement Machines Ltd v Customs and Excise Commissioners (No 2)* (1974) AC 405, 434, he accepted that the complainant's statement could be included in counsel's brief and may form the basis of cross-examination although it could not be used as evidence to controvert anything Which the complainant's witnesses might say.

Finally, the administrative burden which might be placed upon the police of scrutinising the documents to see whether a contents claim for immunity could be justified provides no proper foundation for establishing a class basis for immunity ... It is now necessary to refer to the cases in which *Neilson v Laugharne* [1981] QB 736 had not only been followed but also had been given an extended application ...

[In *Makanjuola*] Bingham LJ, after he had expressed his conclusion, went on to make the following comments [1992] 3 All ER 617, 623, which have since attracted considerable attention and probably explain why the case was belatedly reported:

> I would, however, add this. Where a litigant asserts that documents are immune from production or disclosure on public interest grounds he is not (if the claim is well founded) claiming a right but observing a duty. Public interest immunity is not a trump card vouchsafed to certain privileged players to play when and as they wish. It is an exclusionary rule, imposed on parties in certain circumstances, even where it is to their disadvantage in the litigation. This does not mean that in any case where a party holds a document in a class *prima facie* immune he is bound to persist in an assertion of immunity even where it is held that, on any weighing of the public interest, in withholding the document against the public interest in disclosure for the purpose of furthering the administration of justice, there is a clear balance in favour of the latter. But it does, I think, mean: (1) that public interest immunity cannot in any ordinary sense be waived, since, although one can waive rights, one cannot waive duties; (2) that, where a *litigant* holds documents in a class *prima facie* immune, he should (save perhaps in a very exceptional case) assert that the documents are immune and decline to disclose them, since the ultimate judge of where the balance of public interest lies is not him but the court; and (3) that, where a document is, or is held to be, in an immune class, it may not be used for any purpose whatever in the proceedings to which the immunity applies, and certainly cannot (for instance) be used for the purposes of cross-examination. (Emphasis added.)

This is a very clear statement as to the nature of public interest immunity, most of which I would unhesitatingly endorse ... I would be surprised if Bingham LJ was intending by these remarks to extend principles of public interest immunity or to make their application any more rigid than was required as a result of the previous authorities. I would certainly not regard them as being of general application without hearing fuller argument as to this being appropriate. It is to be noted that the *Makanjuola* case was not one involving a department of state. If a Secretary of State on behalf of his department as opposed to any ordinary litigant concludes that any public interest in documents being withheld from production is outweighed by the public interest in the documents being available for purposes of litigation, it is difficult to conceive that unless the documents do not relate to an area for which the Secretary of State was responsible, the court would feel it appropriate to come to any different conclusion from that of the Secretary of State. The position would be the same if the Attorney-General was of the opinion that the documents should be disclosed. It should be remembered that the principle which was established in *Conway v Rimmer* [1968] AC 910 is that it is the courts which should have the final responsibility for deciding when both a contents and a class claim to immunity should be upheld. The principle was not that it was for the courts to impose immunity where, after due consideration, no immunity was claimed by the appropriate authority. What was inherent in the reasoning of the House in that case was that because of the conflict which could exist between the two aspects of the public interest involved, the courts, which have final responsibility for upholding the Rule of Law, must equally have final responsibility for deciding what evidence should be available to the courts of law in order to enable them to do justice. As far as contents of documents are concerned, I cannot conceive that their Lordships in *Conway v Rimmer* would have anticipated that their decision could be used, except in the most exceptional circumstances, so that a department of state was prevented by the courts from disclosing documents which it considered it was appropriate to disclose. As to class claims, it is interesting to note that Lord Reid in his speech in *Conway v Rimmer* referred to the announcement of the then Lord Chancellor in the House of Lords in June 1956 that in future reports of witnesses to accidents, medical reports and other documents which were previously the subject of a claim to privilege on a class basis would in future be disclosed. Again, recently the Government itself has been reviewing what documents can be disclosed in the furtherance of open government and as a result of that review, documents are now being made available which in the past have been the subject of claims to immunity. Compare the present policy in regard to minutes of meetings between the Chancellor of the Exchequer and the Governor of the Bank of England with the decision of this House in *Burmah Oil Co Ltd v Governor and Company of the Bank of England* [1980] AC 1090. I doubt whether the courts would ever interfere with governmental decisions of this nature.

Where, however, parties other than government departments are in possession of documents in respect of which public interest immunity could be claimed on a class basis, there are practical difficulties in allowing an individual to decide that the documents should be disclosed. The indiscriminate and, indeed, any disclosure, of documents which are the subject of a class claim to immunity can undermine that class. If the reason for the existence of the class is that those who make the statement should be assured that the statement will not be disclosed, the fact that in some cases they are disclosed undermines the assurance. The assurance can never be absolute because of the residual power of the court to order disclosure in the interest of the administration of justice. However, if the assurance is to have any value the cases where disclosure occurs have to be restricted to situations where this is necessary. Here the court may have to intervene to protect the public interest ...

The next case to which it is necessary to refer is the decision of the court of Appeal in *Halford v Sharples* [1992] 1 WLR 736 ... it was conceded in this case by all parties and accepted by the court, as a result of the *Hehir* [1982] 1 WLR 715 and *Makanjuola* [1992] 3 All ER 617 decisions (a transcript of the *Makanjuola* decision was available to the court), that if documents were protected from disclosure in the public interest, the chief constable was not entitled to make any *use* of information contained in the documents. It made no difference that both parties were well aware of the contents of the documents. They were not even entitled to rely on secondary evidence of the documents ... The case was one in which counsel for the Secretary of State appeared to assist the court. It is of interest to note the debatable approach which counsel for the Secretary of State considered it was appropriate to adopt having regard to the authorities. In the words contained in the judgment of Sir Stephen Brown J, at p745:

He accepted that there is a general duty to disclose everything that is relevant except that which the law prohibits. He explained that the Secretary of State's position was, and always has been, that it is not in the public interest that complaints and discipline files should be disclosed. He said that the Secretary of State was not making policy in taking the view but was *merely obeying the law*. The test was not 'Will it do any harm in this case?' The emphasis should be placed upon integrity of the files. Contributors to section 49 procedures were entitled to know and to be assured that what they had contributed will not be seen by anybody including the Inspectorate or the Secretary of State. He said that in this case the Secretary of State had not seen the files in question. (Emphasis added.)

If counsel was seeking to indicate that the Secretary of State no longer had responsibility for considering and assisting the court if necessary by providing evidence as to where the public interest lay, then I would disagree ...

The judgments in this case

In the Court of Appeal it was common ground that in civil proceedings public interest immunity applies on a class basis to the file of documents that came into existence as a result of the investigation into the complaints which had been made. The Court of Appeal therefore focused on the question whether the chief constables were entitled to use the information contained in the documents to assist their cases in the civil proceedings ... Nolan LJ, at p127, relied on the submissions which were made by counsel on behalf of the authority, that the use by chief constables of complaints investigation material in preparing their defence had 'a very detrimental effect on the important public interest of speedy and effective investigations into alleged police misconduct' ... Nourse LJ, at p128, was of the same opinion as Staughton and Nolan LJJ and shared the view of Popplewell J that the half-way house contended for by the chief constables 'has no logic'. The appeal was therefore unanimously dismissed.

Between the hearing in the Court of Appeal and the hearing before this House, as already indicated, the authority has accepted that in general the class immunity created by the *Neilson* decision can no longer be justified. However, in my opinion, this is the case, not because of any change in the balance of public interest or change in attitudes since the *Neilson* decision but because establishing a class of public interest immunity of this nature was never justified. This lack of justification is part of the explanation for the problems which the courts have since had in finding a logical limit to the application of the class and creating a sensible balance between the interest of those involved in subsequent legal proceedings and the interest of those responsible for conducting the investigations into police complaints.

The recognition of a new class-based public interest immunity requires clear and compelling evidence that it is necessary. Yet as the present case had demonstrated, the existence of this class tends to defeat the very object it was designed to achieve. The applicants only launched their proceedings for judicial review to avoid the existence of a situation where their position would be prejudiced as a result of their not being given access to material to which the police had access. Their non co-operation was brought about because of the existence of the immunity. Mr Reynold, on behalf of the applicants, made it clear that if there were to be disclosure of documents which came into existence as a result of the investigation, it would be inappropriate to grant injunctive relief. The restrictive nature of any assurance which could be given to a potential witness in relation to civil proceedings meant that it was unlikely to have significant effect on their decision as to whether to co-operate or not. The class was artificial in conception and this contributed to it having to be rigidly applied. The comments of Lord Taylor of Gosforth CJ in *Ex p Coventry Newspapers Ltd* [1993] QB 278, 292–3, which have already been cited, are likely to be equally appropriate in the great majority of cases. While I agree with Lord Hailsham of St Marylebone's statement in *National Society for the Prevention of Cruelty to Children* [1978] AC 171, 230, that: 'The categories of public interest are not closed, and must alter from time to time whether by restriction or extension as social conditions and social legislation develop' in my opinion no sufficient case has ever been made out to justify the class of public interest immunity recognised in *Neilson*.

The *Neilson* case [1981] QB 736 and the cases in which it was subsequently applied should therefore be regarded as being wrongly decided. This does not however, mean that public interest immunity can never apply to documents that come into existence in consequence of a police investigation into a complaint. There may be other reasons why because of the contents of a particular document it would be appropriate to extend immunity to that document. In addition, Mr Pannick submitted that the report which comes into existence as a result of a police investigation into a complaint is a candidate for public interest immunity on a narrower class basis. Mr Pannick did not, however have available the evidence which would be needed to succeed on this submission. Although I have considerable reservations as to whether it would be possible to justify a class claim to immunity as opposed to a contents claim in respect of some reports, it would not be right to close the door to a future attempt to establish that the reports are subject to class immunity.

The fact that documents coming into existence as a result of a police investigation are not entitled to public interest immunity from disclosure means that the decision of Popplewell J and that of the Court of Appeal (1994) 1 WLR 114 were wrong in these cases and the declarations and the injunction should not have been granted.

AAS Zuckerman, 'Public Interest Immunity – A Matter of Prime Judicial Responsibility' (1994) 57 Modern Law Review 703, 704, 705, 707–9, 714, 715, 717–20, 722–5

A Introduction – protecting private and public interest in litigation

The *Matrix Churchill* case, in which ministerial claims for public interest immunity were rejected and the accused acquitted, has given rise to an intense controversy concerning ministers' responsibilities in connection with public interest immunity. In addressing the issues raised by this case, we should not allow ourselves to be distracted from one fundamental and uncontroversial principle: that all relevant evidence is not only admissible but is also compellable.

The disclosure of the whole truth is as important to the administration of justice as it is to individual litigants. A judgment which is known to have been given, not on the basis of all the available evidence but on only part thereof, cannot inspire confidence in its correctness. ...

There is, however, one exception to this observation: public interest immunity. An examination of judicial decisions in this area provides ample reason for doubting the courts' adherence to the idea that it is in the interests of justice that all relevant evidence should be made available in civil or criminal proceedings.

The doctrine that the courts are the sole arbiters of whether and when suppression of evidence is in the interests of justice has, paradoxically, encouraged ministers and public bodies to pay little or no regard to the interests of justice. Government ministers and other officials could legitimately reason that it is not for them but for the courts to decide whether justice required disclosure. Their task is limited to expressing the view that disclosure would be deleterious to the public interest. On their part, the courts have declined to place such claims under searching scrutiny, preferring to accept them at face value. Furthermore, the courts have shown a remarkable reluctance to investigate the effects that the withholding of evidence might have on the prospects of a litigant to prove his case and on their own ability to render correct judgments. These judicial attitudes have created fertile conditions for practices of the kind which the Scott Inquiry has been investigating.

B The judicial assumption of responsibility for the public interest

[In *Conway v Rimmer*] the House of Lords established three principles of great constitutional importance.

First, it held that the responsibility for deciding whether or not evidence should be withheld from a court of law rested with the courts and not the Crown. It was for the courts to determine whether the public interest necessitated suppression of evidence and, therefore, the matter was not one of Crown privilege. ...

Second, the House of Lords laid down the process of reasoning which should be followed in the exercise of the judicial discretion to sanction the withholding of evidence. In arriving at its decision, the court has to weigh the public interest in the suppression of evidence against the public interest that the administration of justice shall not be frustrated. This balancing exercise requires the court to place on one side of the scales the potential harm to the public from the disclosure of the evidence in question. On the other side of the scales, the court has to place the consequences to the court's ability to administer justice, if the evidence were to be suppressed. This last aspect requires the court to take account two separate, if closely related, factors. It requires the court to consider the likely effect that the absence of the evidence might have on the court's facility to ascertain the true facts. It also requires the court to take into account the effect that the withholding of the evidence will have on the appearance of justice and on confidence in the judicial system. It has been insufficiently appreciated that the need to conduct a balancing act in respect of every claim for immunity has greatly reduced the significance of the distinction between contents claims and class claims. Whether it is claimed that the contents of a particular document is sensitive and its disclosure would, *per se*, be harmful, or whether it is claimed that, notwithstanding the innocuousness of the information, it is desirable to maintain the confidentiality of the class to which it belongs, the court must consider whether the actual information in question is of importance to the determination of truth before it can allow the information to be withheld.

The third principle has to do with inspection. As we have just observed, the balancing exercise necessitates an assessment of the effect that the absence of a piece of information might have on the determination of truth. This raises the question: how is the court to determine the likely effect that the evidence would or would not have if it has been withheld? Mindful of this difficulty, the House of Lords held that a court was entitled to inspect in private materials for which immunity has been claimed for the purpose of deciding whether or not their suppression would have an adverse effect on the ascertainment of truth.

The *Conway v Rimmer* decision represents a bold and progressive step in the direction of establishing government accountability for the suppression of evidence ... The assumption of responsibility for deciding whether evidence should be withheld has had crucial implications for ministerial responsibility.

When a minister's certificate was conclusive, the minister had to consider, at least in theory, what effect his certificate would have on the administration of justice. Under the new dispensation, ministers are relieved of this responsibility. For them it is only to decide whether they believe that the disclosure of the evidence would be harmful to the public interest. If it would be, they may claim immunity. It is then for the court to decide whether to accept the claim or overrule it, depending on the outcome of the balance of interests carried out by the judge. Ministers who appeared in the Scott inquiry were therefore correct in asserting that the responsibility for the suppression of evidence rested with the courts. Their task has been confined to determining whether there are grounds for believing that disclosure would be injurious to the public interest and to asserting that this is the case by issuing a certificate to this effect.

C Receding judicial scrutiny of claims for immunity

Blanket immunity

As we have seen, it was an important aspect of the decision in *Conway v Rimmer* that immunity from production in evidence should not be extended on an *a priori* basis to certain classes of documents. According to that decision, claims for immunity have to be balanced, in each individual case, against the interests of the administration of justice. This exercise necessitated consideration of the effect that the withholding of evidence would have on the court's ability to determine the factual issues in question. Notwithstanding the fact-dependent nature of the balancing test, the courts were soon tempted to extend blanket immunity to whole classes of documents and forgo altogether a case-by-case balancing exercise in respect of these classes. ...

In relation to national security, blanket immunity subsisted both before and after *Conway v Rimmer*. In *Conway v Rimmer* itself there were *dicta* that could be interpreted as saying that decisions to withhold evidence on grounds of national security must be left to ministerial discretion [[1968] 1 All ER 874, 880, 888, 890]. Later, this view was clearly spelt out by the House of Lords in *Council of Civil Service Unions v Minister for the Civil Service* [1984] 3 All ER 935 where Lord Fraser stated:

> The decision on whether the requirements of national security outweigh the duty of fairness in any particular case is for the Government and not for the courts; the Government alone has access to the relevant information, and in any event the judicial process is unsuitable for reaching decisions on national security [[1984] 3 All ER 944; see also *per* Lord Diplock at 952].

Recently, this policy has been reiterated by Russell LJ, who held that 'once there is an actual or potential risk to national security demonstrated by an appropriate certificate, the court should not exercise its right to inspect' [*Balfour v Foreign and Commonwealth Office* [1994] 2 All ER 588 at 596]. Thus, the words 'national security' need only be uttered by a minister for the information in question to become inaccessible even in the interests of justice. In the United States, by contrast, the courts have kept the jurisdiction to judge claims of privilege on grounds of national security firmly in their hands [*United States v Reynolds* 345 US 1 (1953)].

Acceptance of the argument from candour

The principle in *Conway v Rimmer* has been eroded, not only by the granting of blanket immunity, but also, and perhaps more significantly, by a ready acceptance of the argument from candour. It stands to reason that, for instance, it is in the public interest that military secrets should be kept inviolable. But what justification is there for according public interest immunity to, say, statements in the course of a police inquiry under s49 of the Police Act 1964? Or, to take another example, what justification is there for according immunity to correspondence between social workers? The argument from candour provides the justification.

The argument from candour has two facets: internal and external. The internal facet proceeds as follows. For public institutions, such as government departments and local authority welfare agencies, to function properly, their officers must not be inhibited from expressing their candid professional views. In the absence of immunity, civil servants and other public employees would be inhibited in the expression of opinion. *Ergo,* immunity is in the public interest. The external facet proceeds on two assumptions: first, that to fulfil their functions, public bodies, such as the police, social workers or child welfare organisations, require information from the public. Second, if members of the public thought that such information might be made public, they would be reluctant to come forward. *Ergo,* immunity is necessary in order to encourage the divulgence of information. ...

Obstacles to inspection

The conditions that have to be fulfilled before a court would inspect documents were more fully considered in *Air Canada v Secretary of State for Trade* [1983] 1 All ER 910.

The House of Lords proceeded from the assumption that it was in the public interest to protect from disclosure Government papers concerned with the workings of the Cabinet and with the formulation of Government policy. The court then turned to consider the other side of the scales. The documents were clearly relevant. Further, it was accepted that they were necessary for disposing fairly of the cause [[1983] 1 All ER 915]. But the court still had to determine whether non-disclosure would have a deleterious effect on the ability of the court to judge the issues fully and adequately. Bingham J felt, as we have seen, that he could not come to a decision on this point unless he looked at the documents, but the House of Lords thought otherwise.

It was not enough for the party seeking disclosure to show that the documents would help establish the truth one way or the other. The party seeking discovery it was held, must show that the documents are likely to assist his own case [*per* Lords Wilberforce, Edmund-David and Fraser; Lords Scarman and Templeman disagreeing].

This requirement presents a major obstacle to overcoming a claim for public interest immunity for, clearly, the party seeking disclosure has no access to the documents, does not know their contents and, ordinarily, cannot prove that the documents are likely to affect the outcome of the case, let alone that they would assist his own case. Carol Harlow and Richard Rawlings describe this as a '"Catch 22" dilemma: without the evidence the case cannot be won; without the case the evidence cannot be secured' [*Pressure Through Law* (1992), p175].

This decision, perhaps more than any other decision, has seriously eroded the principle of judicial scrutiny of claims for public interest immunity propounded by *Conway v Rimmer*. It also amounts to a reversal of the principle that the party seeking to withhold documents from discovery bears the burden of showing that the public interest so requires [*D v NSPCC* [1977] 1 All ER 589 at 619]. Judicial scrutiny has been thus emasculated, not by an open change of policy, but by means of a technical ploy. *Conway v Rimmer* decided that no order should be made for the disclosure of documents in respect of which a *prima facie* valid claim for immunity has been made, except where the court is satisfied that disclosure is necessary in the interests of justice. To be so satisfied the court needs to inspect the documents to find out what they contain. Yet, on the *Air Canada* ruling, no inspection may take place unless the party seeking disclosure has shown that the documents will assist his case. Since, in the majority of cases, the party seeking disclosure is ignorant of the contents of the documents, this requirement is a bar to inspection, without which no order for disclosure can be made. It follows, in effect, that once a claim for immunity has been made, which is valid on the face of it, this is the end of the matter. Further, the rule in *Air Canada* has not remained confined to Cabinet papers and high level policy-making communications. It has even been applied where a citizen sued the police for wrongful arrest and false imprisonment [*Evans v Chief Constable of Surrey Constabulary (Attorney General intervening)* [1989] 2 All ER 594].

Not only did *Air Canada* undermine the *Conway v Rimmer* policy of judicial scrutiny of ministerial claims, it also tends to undermine the public interest in the administration of justice, which *Conway v Rimmer* set out to promote. Lord Wilberforce, this time a member of the majority in *Air Canada*. had this to say of the idea that it was in the interests of justice that judgments should be given on the basis of all existing and available evidence:

> In a contest purely between one litigant and another, such as the present, the task of the court is to do and to be seen to be doing, justice between the parties, a duty reflected in the word 'fairly' in the rule [RSC, Ord 24, r 13]. There is no higher additional duty to ascertain some independent truth. It often happens, from the imperfection of evidence, or the withholding of it sometimes by the party in whose favour it would tell if presented, that an adjudication has to be made which is not, and is known not to be, the whole truth of the matter: yet, if the decision has been in accordance with the available evidence and with the law, justice will have been fairly done [[1983] 1 All ER 919].

This reasoning is suspect. For while it is true that in an adversary system the court has no obligation, indeed no power, to seek to ascertain the facts independently of the evidence that the parties choose to present to it, it does not follow that the court has no duty to assist a party to obtain evidence relevant to the issue before the court. As has already been suggested, a court that is not prepared to assist a party to obtain relevant evidence fails in its obligation to afford that party an opportunity to prosecute his cause, because the facility of obtaining and presenting evidence is essential to the establishment of one's legal rights. The decisions in *Burmah Oil Co* and *Air Canada* place a clog on the administration of justice and should be reconsidered, especially now that the Court of Appeal has held that a claim for public interest immunity in criminal trials cannot be properly determined without inspection of the material in question [see *Keane* [1994] 2 All ER 479].

D Public interest immunity in criminal proceedings

In *Matrix Churchill*, itself a criminal prosecution, the court was concerned with the operation of public interest immunity in criminal proceedings. The position in criminal cases is, fundamentally, no different from that in civil proceedings [*Governor of Brixton Prison, ex p Osman (No 1)* [1992] 1 All ER 108]. The interests at stake are, however, very different because, in criminal prosecutions, the accused runs the risk of punishment which may involve loss of liberty, of property and of reputation. Nevertheless, the balancing test of *Conway v Rimmer* is perfectly capable of according adequate weight to the interest of protecting the innocent from conviction [see *eg Keane* [1994] 2 All ER 478, 485]. ...

E Conclusion – prime judicial responsibility

The *Matrix Churchill* case has given rise to a lively debate concerning ministers' position with regard to the issue of public interest immunity certificates. The

Attorney-General has stated that ministers have a duty to claim public interest immunity [House of Commons, 10 November 1992]. Some commentators have questioned this assertion. Others have advanced the view that, as the law stands at present, the Attorney-General was right in asserting that ministers have a duty to claim immunity [Smith, 'Public Interest Immunity in Criminal Cases' (1993) 52 CLJ 1; Tomkins, 'Public Interest Immunity after Matrix Churchill' (1993) PL 530; Allan, 'Public Interest Immunity and Ministers' Responsibility' (1993) CLR 661]. The commentators seem, however, to be united in the view that it is undesirable that ministers should claim immunity from disclosing evidence in criminal proceedings and their criticism has been tinged with a note of condemnation of the ministerial practices in the *Matrix Churchill* case.

In condemning ministers, critics have overlooked the role played by the courts in this regard. The courts have made it the law of the land that the responsibility for deciding whether evidence should be given in legal proceedings lies with judges and not with ministers. The role of ministers, it has been held, is confined to informing the courts by means of public interest immunity certificates, of the adverse consequences which may result from the disclosure of documents or information for which ministers are responsible. It is not for ministers to decide whether evidence should be disclosed in legal proceedings, nor do they possess the information necessary for such a decision.

In the field of public interest immunity, ministerial practices and judicial policies feed upon each other. Both, however, have to use statute as their starting point and take on board entrenched conventions of public administration. The law concerning public interest immunity has evolved against the background of the notorious catch-all provision of s2 of the Official Secrets Act 1911. Although this provision has now been abolished and replaced by the more guarded and liberal provisions of the Official Secrets Act 1989, the administrative philosophy continues to embrace the tenet that secrecy is in the interest of good government. This philosophy has received judicial approval on countless occasions as many of the cases mentioned in this article demonstrate. In *Conway v Rimmer* itself. Lord Reid said:

> The business of government is difficult enough as it is, and no Government could contemplate with equanimity the inner workings of the Government machine being exposed to the gaze of those ready to criticise without adequate knowledge of the background and perhaps with some axe to grind. That must in my view also apply to all documents concerned with policy making within departments ... Further, it may be that deliberations about a particular case require protection as much as deliberations about policy [[1968] 1 All ER 888].

Accordingly, David Williams' description of the situation is as valid today as it was 30 years ago:

> A steady repetition of arguments about the need for frankness about the value of confidential relationship between minister and civil servant, about the criteria of administrative efficiency, and so forth, has certainly helped the official view ... It has shifted the onus of proof. Those who wish to support publicity wherever possible have been thrown on the defensive. It seems to have been forgotten that in a democratic country the onus should be on those who support secrecy to justify their case [*Not in the Public Interest* (1965), pp57–58].

'In this country,' Carol Harlow and Richard Rawlings write [*Pressure Through Law* (1992)], 'a wall of silence blocks public access to information. Britain is almost alone in the Western world in possessing neither freedom of information legislation nor a general right to access to data held in official files.' On their part, the judiciary have shown remarkable willingness to bolster this wall of silence by placing their trust in the ability of ministers to judge what is in the public interest, as Stephen Sedley has recently pointed out ['The Sound of Silence: Constitutional Law Without a Constitution' (1994) 110 LQR 270]. Indeed, the courts have shifted the burden of proof with regard to public interest immunity. Once a claim for immunity has been made, which is within the accepted range of claims, the onus is on the party seeking disclosure to persuade the court that the interest in non-disclosure may be overcome. To make things worse, the ruling in the *Air Canada* case ensures that, in civil litigation, this onus is practically impossible to discharge.

Surely, when ministers read judicial decisions that exalt the importance of maintaining the secrecy of Cabinet papers, of promoting the confidentiality of advice given by civil servants to ministers, of screening high level policy-making processes from the public gaze, they are entitled to feel persuaded that they are rendering an important public service when they issue public interest immunity certificates. In some situations, the courts did not even require the advice of ministers in order to conclude that secrecy is important to the proper functioning of government and of other social organisations. Many decisions have involved no ministerial claim and no public interest immunity certificates.

One final point needs to be made in order to avoid misunderstanding. It is not suggested that the practices that have been developed since *Conway v Rimmer* are desirable or defensible. On the contrary, they are harmful to a healthy administration of justice and are inimical to good government in a democratic society. More specifically, they have undermined the sensible and enlightened principles of *Conway v Rimmer*. What is suggested, instead, is that ministers do not bear a major responsibility for this state of affairs. They have followed well-established practices which have had the courts' seal of approval. Further, if ministers were to be made the sole culprits in the aftermath of the Scott Inquiry, only limited progress will have been made, for the law will have been left unchanged. The courts would remain free to continue granting licence for suppression of evidence in all but criminal prosecutions. Stephen Sedley has recently written that 'it has taken the *Matrix Churchill* affair and the Scott Inquiry to compel serious scrutiny of the assumptions about the competence of ministerial and departmental government which have underlain the courts' willingness to accept public interest immunity certificates from ministers' [(1994) 110 LQR]. Clearly, then, if we are seriously interested in the reform of the law on public interest immunity, we must start by acknowledging that the judiciary are primarily responsible for the present state of affairs and not shrink from putting the courts themselves on trial and not just ministers.

Inquiry into Exports of Defence Equipment and Dual-Use Goods to Iraq and Related Prosecutions, HC 115 I (1995–96)

Below are extracts from the Report of an Inquiry chaired by Sir Richard Scott, into government policy in relation to export of arms to Iraq. Directors of the company Matrix Churchill were accused of exporting arms to Iraq in breach of export regulations. They faced criminal proceedings although they alleged that government ministers had known of the exports. In the criminal trial ministers put forward public interest immunity certificates claiming that matters relevant to the defendants' defence should not be revealed. Mr Clarke's certificate made an exception for one witness who was to be called for the prosecution. The judge in the case ruled that a number of the matters covered by the PII certificates should be revealed and this led to the collapse of the case. The case caused a public and parliamentary outcry since it created the impression that government had been prepared to allow three innocent men to be imprisoned rather than reveal its policy in relation to selling arms to Iraq. Sir Richard Scott was therefore appointed to head an Inquiry into the matters at issue. The extracts set out below relate only to the claims of Public Interest Immunity made by the ministers in question.

The first extract relates to the attitude of ministers and of the Attorney-General to signing the certificates.

G13.61 Mr Heseltine was of the clear view that the DTI documents ought not to be withheld from the defence. [Transcript, Day 69, pp70–71: 'My view was that the documents should be released. If there was injury for the reasons that would flow from their class category, that, in my view, should be overwhelmed by the justice argument.] He accepted that, in forming this view, he was exercising an element of judgment. He did not take the view that Category B and C class claims were unimportant. He believed that 'there is a relationship between civil servants and their ministers, which is unusual, as it is *sui generis*, and the fact that there are security interests involved that are not disclosed, seem to me to provide ... a legitimate case ...' for PII claims. [*Ibid*, pp78–79.] But he was not prepared to assert the claim in a manner that might damage the conduct of the defence in the Matrix Churchill case. In his written evidence to the Inquiry, he said that his concern was 'that the trial judge must have the clearest signal that anything of relevance to the trial must be disclosed' and was 'to make clear to the judge that if he considered that all or any part of the papers was relevant to the proceedings then [he] was exercising no constraint on him in making them available.'[Written Statement of Mr Heseltine dated 24 February 1994, p10, para 4.] The point was not put to Mr Heseltine explicitly, but I infer from his evidence that the views he was expressing would have been applicable to any criminal case, and that if documents were of relevance to the defence they ought not on Category B class claim grounds to be withheld. He did, moreover, make clear in his oral evidence that he did not regard there as being any significant difference, so far as his role as a Minister in making the PII claim was concerned, between the DTI Category B and the DTI Category C documents, [Transcript, Day 69, pp86–88] and, further, that his view was not dependent on the issue arising in a criminal trial: 'I would have taken the same view in a civil case,' he said. [*Ibid*, p98.]

G13.69 Mr Heseltine signed the Certificate in its redrafted form. Before doing so he read with some care the *All England Report* of the *Makanjuola* judgment and marked the passage at p623 between g and h. The sentence '...the ultimate judge of where the balance of public interest lies is not him [*ie* the minister] but the Court' was, said Mr Heseltine, 'the clinching part as far as I was concerned'. [Transcript, Day 69, p112.]

G13.71 There is, in my opinion, no doubt whatever but that Mr Heseltine signed the re-drafted Certificate on the footing that he had a duty in law to claim PII class protection for the DTI documents. He had been so advised by the Attorney-General. He had not been informed that if he took the view that the case for disclosure to the defence was a clear one, it was open to him to agree to the disclosure of the documents. He had signed the Certificate in the belief that the judge would be aware that in his (Mr Heseltine's) view some of the documents ought to be disclosed to the defence.

G13.100 The Attorney-General expressed the firm opinion that a minister's function in claiming PII was to decide whether documents placed before him fell into a PII class of documents that the Courts had in previous cases recognised as attracting PII. If a minister did not feel able to subscribe to the view that disclosure of a class of documents would be injurious to the public interest, it would be his duty to use language in the Certificate to which he could conscientiously subscribe or raise the matter with ministerial colleagues for a collective ministerial decision [Paragraph A.11.3(i) of Sir Nicholas Lyell's written statement dated 2l March 1994.] In the case of a class claim, the Attorney-General said, the damage to the public interest 'caused by disclosure of an individual document ... flows from the fact that the document forms an integral part of a class which requires protection, rather than from the specific contents of that document or the specific damage that would be caused by disclosure of that document individually.'[Paragraph A.11.1(v) of Sir Nicholas Lyell's written statement (*ibid*).] It followed that it was not, in the Attorney-General's view, necessary for the minister to ask himself whether disclosure of the documents to the defence would be damaging to the public interest. If the Courts had, in previous cases, allowed PII claims in respect of documents falling within the class in question, then the minister had a duty to claim PII for such of his documents as he thought fell within the class. It was not, in the Attorney-General's view, for the minister to decide to disclose the documents to the defendant on the ground that the requirements of justice outweighed the damage to the public interest that might be caused by that disclosure. So to decide would be to perform the 'balancing' exercise that was, in the Attorney-General's view, the prerogative of the Courts.

G13.102 In the application to the Matrix Churchill case of the views described in the previous paragraphs, it was the Attorney-General's view:

(i) that each of the ministers (including Mr Heseltine) who signed a PII Certificate had been under a duty to claim PII for his department's documents falling within Categories B and C regardless of whether the minister thought that disclosure of the documents to the defendants would in fact be damaging to the public interest; and

(ii) that since Mr Alan Moses QC had not advised (and if asked would not have advised) in respect of any of the documents that Judge Smedley would be bound to order disclosure to the defence, it was not open to Mr Heseltine to treat the case as a clear one in which the interests of justice required the disclosure of the documents to the defence.

The PII Certificates: Summary

G13.103 It may be convenient to summarise the position regarding the PII Certificates that had been prepared for use at the trial. It is also convenient to deal with Mr Lilley's certificate prepared for, but not used at, the committal.

(i)(a) The Home Office Certificates, signed by Mr Clarke, sought to protect documents relating to intelligence matters emanating from the SIS or from the Security Service and to protect oral evidence relating to the operations or personnel of the two services. The exception, expressed in the first Certificate, related to the evidence in Mr T's witness statement and 'any oral evidence arising therefrom provided no further disclosure of information falling within the categories in paragraph 6 [of the Certificate] is made.' [See para G13.13 above.] Mr Clarke regarded himself as having a discretion to authorise the giving of evidence, oral or documentary, notwithstanding that it would have qualified for PII protection. It was on that footing that he had given the authority referred to regarding Mr T's evidence. Mr T was proposed to be called as a witness by the prosecution. Whether Mr Clarke would have given the like authority in regard to evidence necessary for the purposes of the defence was not a point to which his attention was directed at the time (ie September 1992). Even if it had been, he did not have sufficient details of the likely lines of defence to have permitted him to consider exercising the discretion. He was content to leave the defendants' interests in obtaining disclosure to be dealt with by the judge.

(ii)(a) The DTI Certificate signed by Mr Lilley protected sixteen documents of the Category B type. Mr Lilley believed that there was a need to protect the confidentiality of documents within Category B in order to ensure that officials were candid in the advice which they gave. [See para G13. 3 above.] In his view, Category B covered documents concerned with the formulation and development of policy, as long as policy involved 'people at a high level at some stage in its formulation or development'. The class could, in his view, include documents concerned with application of policy in cases where policy was developed by its application, but would not otherwise include purely routine documents.

(b) The DTI Certificate signed by Mr Heseltine protected a large number of Category B documents and some Category C ones. It was Mr Heseltine's view that at least some of these documents, if not all, ought to be disclosed to the defence. He believed that his opinion to that effect, which he supposed he had made known to the Attorney-General (he could not have anticipated that his letter of 11 September would be left unread by the Attorney-General), would be communicated to the judge who would rule on disclosure. Mr Heseltine did not understand that he had any discretion to authorise disclosure to the defendants of documents qualifying for PII 'class' protection. He had not been told of the 'clear case' exception. If he had known he had discretion to authorise disclosure of DTI documents if he considered there to be a clear case in the interests of justice for such disclosure, he would have exercised it.

The Public Interest Immunity Claims

G18.43 The Public Interest Immunity claims that were made in the Matrix Churchill case raise the following issues:

(i) The claims made for PII included class claims of two separate varieties, namely, the Categories B and C described in Mr Garel-Jones' Certificate, as well as contents claims to cover the redacted parts of the Category C documents. The character of the documents for which Category B and Category C class claims were made raise the question whether class claims are appropriate in criminal cases, and, if so, whether the making of class claims with as wide a catchment net as the Treasury Solicitor's Department, and Mr Leithead in particular, appear to have regarded as necessary and proper can be justified.

(ii) What is the proper function of the minister (or senior official) who, by signing a PII Certificate, makes the claim for PII? Is it his function to exercise his judgment as to whether the public interest would suffer any significant damage if the documents in question were disclosed to the defence? If so, then, presumably, a minister must refrain from signing a Certificate unless he is so satisfied. Or is the minister's function to do no more than satisfy himself that the documents fall into the described class? If so, why is it necessary for a minister, as opposed to a departmental lawyer or official, to sign the certificate?

(iii) To what extent is it open to a minister, or to counsel, to authorise to be disclosed to the defence documents which are of the same general class or description as documents that in a previous case have been the subject of a successful PII claim?

Some of these questions are answered by the speeches in the House of Lords in *Chief Constable of the West Midlands Police, ex p Wiley* [1994] 3 All ER 420. Since, however, this case post-dated by some two years the PII decisions that were taken in the *Matrix Churchill* case, the justification for those decisions must be tested by reference to the case law as it stood at the time.

G18.44 The class claims made in the *Matrix Churchill* case were claims that, according to the Attorney-General and to Mr Leithead in the Treasury Solicitor's Department, it was the legal duty of the respective ministers to make. The ministers were not entitled, it was said, to exercise any judgment as to whether or not the class claims should be made or as to whether the damage that might be caused to the public interest by disclosure of the contents of the documents to the defence was of sufficient gravity to justify withholding from the defence documents that would otherwise have been disclosable.

G18.54 The proposition that a minister is ever under a legal duty to claim PII in order to protect documents from disclosure to the defence notwithstanding that in the minister's view the public interest requires their disclosure to the defence is, in my opinion, based on a fundamental misconception of the principles of PII law. To the extent that the proposition is sought to be supported by reference to Lord Justice Bingham's judgment in *Makanjuola*, it is based in my opinion, on a misreading of that judgment.

G18.67 ... Ministers had been accustomed, in civil cases at least, to claim PII without necessarily having had regard to the consequences on the administration of justice of their doing so. It does not, however, follow that a minister, with perhaps more of an instinct for justice than some of his fellows, might not from time to time have taken account of the requirements of justice before making a PII claim. Lord Reid's point was not that ministers were not entitled, or were not able, to take some account of the requirements of justice, but that they did not have a duty to do so. The contention that ministers are not entitled to take into account, or are not capable of taking into account, the requirements of justice seems to me, besides being an improbable one, to be contradicted by the submissions made in *Conway v Rimmer* by counsel for the Home Secretary. It was the Home Secretary who was objecting to the production of the documents on the ground that they fell within a class of documents the production of which would be injurious to the public interest. Counsel said this:

> In a conflict between the public interest in good government and the public interest in the administration of justice as between private litigants, the last word in the resolution of the conflict must lie with the executive and not with the judiciary which is not equipped to assess the effect of the production [of the documents]. [*Ibid*, p926.]

Counsel putting forward this submission was the Attorney-General, Sir Elwyn Jones (later Lord Chancellor). In contending for the right of ministers to the last word in resolving the conflict between the two public interests, the Attorney-General (and the Home Secretary on whose behalf he was speaking) must have regarded ministers as capable of attributing some weight to the public interest in the administration of justice. If that was so in 1967, it is difficult to see why ministers' ability and willingness to do so should have in the meantime disappeared. It is, of course, the case that ministers and officials without any detailed knowledge of the issues in a case cannot weigh with any accuracy the extent to which the documents in question will, or may, assist the party claiming discovery. But they will at least know that the documents are within the criteria of relevance that would normally require their disclosure for the purposes of the litigation.

The second extract relates to the use of PII certificates in criminal cases.

K6.12 As to the documents whose potential to assist the defence is apparent, could a situation ever arise in which disclosure could properly be refused on PII grounds? This is not a question which needs to be asked in civil cases. In civil cases, where private interests are in competition, the interests in the litigation of one party may from time to time be required to be subordinated to the greater public interest. I have already cited passages in *Duncan v Cammell Laird* and *Conway v Rimmer* to that effect. Can there be any such subordination of the interests of a defendant in a criminal trial? In my opinion, there cannot. In civil cases, the weight of the public interest factors against disclosure may justify a refusal to order disclosure notwithstanding that without disclosure an otherwise sound civil action might fail. But, for the purposes of criminal trials, the balance must always come down in favour of disclosure if there is any real possibility that the withholding of the document may cause or contribute to a miscarriage of justice. The public interest factors underlying the PII claim cannot ever have a weight sufficient to outweigh that possibility. In a civil case, the heavier the weight of the public interest factors underlying the PII claim, the less likely it will be that the balance will come down in favour of disclosure. But if the fundamental principle underlying the rules of disclosure of documents in criminal cases is that documents should be disclosed 'in order to prevent the possibility that a man may ... be deprived of the opportunity of casting doubt on the case against him' (*per* Lord Lane in *Hallett*), it must follow that a document which might assist a defendant in a criminal trial cannot be withheld on the ground of some greater public interest. In criminal trials, once it has been decided that a document might be of assistance to the defence, that should be the end of the PII claim. If that is so, then there is no real balance to be struck. The only issue for decision is whether the document might be of assistance to the defence.

K6.18 For the reasons given above, the approach to PII claims in criminal trials should be as follows:

(i) If documents are not within the criteria of relevance established by *Keane* and *Brown (Winston)*, they need not be disclosed.

(ii) PII claims on a class basis should not in future be made. PII contents claims should not be made in respect of documents which it is apparent are documents which might be of assistance to the defence.

(iii) Before making a PII claim on a contents basis, consideration should be given to the use of redactions. The PII claim can then be confined to the redacted parts of the documents.

(iv) PII claims on a contents basis should not be made unless in the opinion of the Minister, or person putting forward the claim, ' ... disclosure will cause substantial harm' (*per* Lord Templeman in *ex p Wiley*).

(v) A PII claim should not be made if the responsible minister forms the opinion that notwithstanding the sensitivity of the documents the public interest requires that the documents should be disclosed.

(vi) Save where the circumstances render it impracticable, a minister who is asked to sign a PII certificate should always be given adequate time to reflect upon the weight of the public interest factors alleged to require that the documents in question be not disclosed and on the relevance, so far as it is known, of the documents to the defence. It is undesirable that any minister should be placed in the position, in which, for example, Mr Garel-Jones was placed, of having to reach a decision overnight as to whether PII should be claimed.

(vii) If a disclosure issue in respect of documents the subject of a PII claim is referred to the judge, the judge should, unless the parties are in agreement on the point, be invited to rule, first, whether the documents are within the criteria of materiality so as to be disclosable.

(viii) If the documents are within the criteria of relevance established by *Keane* and *Brown (Winston)*, the judge should be asked to decide whether the documents might be of assistance to the defence. If a document satisfies this test, the document ought not to be withheld from a defendant on PII grounds. There is no true balance to be struck. The weight of public interest factors underlying the PII claim is immaterial. However, existing authority, with its apparent endorsement of the 'balancing exercise' while at the same time requiring the disclosure of any document which 'may prove the defendant's innocence or avoid a miscarriage of justice', suffers, in my opinion, from some degree of ambiguity. It would be important, in my opinion, if disclosure of a material document is to be withheld, that the defendant should know whether the decision was based on the judge's conclusion that the document would not be of any assistance to the defence or on the judge's conclusion that, despite meeting that test, the weight of public interest factors precludes disclosure. The latter conclusion would, in my opinion, be wrong in principle and contrary to authority.

(ix) For the purposes of any argument on the assistance that a document might give the defence, the defendant should specify the line or lines of defence which, in the defendant's contention, give the document its requisite materiality.★

(x) If the documents, although relevant and *prima facie* disclosable, do not appear to be documents that might assist the defence, the judge may conclude that in view of the public interest factors underlying the PII claim, the documents need not be disclosed.

★ As to this, reference should be made to paragraph 40 of the Joint Opinion dated 9 October 1995 of Treasury Counsel, Mr Stephen Richards and Mr A W H Charles, which was provided to Government for the purposes of advising on PII practice post *ex p Wiley*. Counsel made a very similar recommendation to that contained in sub-paragraph (vii) above. It should be noted also that, at the time of publication of this Report, consideration is being given to the question whether there should be a statutory obligation imposed on the Defence to provide advance disclosure of its defence. See in this connection, the Report of the Royal Commission on Criminal Justice (paragraph 57 *et seq*) (Cmnd 2263); Home Office Consultation Papers on Disclosure (Cmnd 2861) and on Pre-Trial Hearings (Cmnd 2924): the Justice response to the consultation paper entitled 'Disclosure: A consultation paper, The JUSTICE Response' – September 1995. A Bill entitled 'The Criminal Procedure and Investigations Bill', containing relevant proposals, is currently before Parliament. See also paragraph K5.2 above.

Notes

1   After *Air Canada*, in effect, three tests had to be satisfied before disclosure could be ordered. The documents in question must be relevant to the case; they must be of assistance in disposing of it and the party seeking disclosure must show that they will assist his or her own case. As Zuckermann points out, this means that if the party seeking disclosure does not know in detail what the documents contain he or she will not be able to satisfy the third test and the court will therefore refuse to inspect the documents to see if the second test is satisfied. The second test mentioned above has received an interpretation restrictive of disclosure; the need to show that the material in question will be of *substantial* assistance to the court was emphasised in *Bookbinder v Tebbit* (No 2) (1992).[30] Even where these three tests may be satisfied discovery may be refused due to the nature or 'class' of the material in question even where it clearly falls outside the protected categories covered by the Official Secrets Act 1989. In *Halford v Sharples* (1992)[31] the applicant claimed sex discrimination in that she had not been recommended for promotion, and sought discovery of documents from *inter alia* the police authority which had failed to interview her and the chief constable of her own force. The Court of Appeal found that all documents of any type relating to internal police inquiries were protected by public interest immunity and therefore production of the files would not be ordered. It also found that immunity from disclosure was also an immunity from use. Thus no use at all could be made of the information contained in the documents in question regardless of the fact that both parties were aware of their contents.

The House of Lords in *Wiley* considered that there was insufficient evidence to support Lord Oliver's conclusion in *Neilson* as to the need for a new class claim to public interest immunity. Thus it was found that *Neilson* must be regarded as wrongly decided but that did not mean that public interest immunity would never attach to police complaints documents: whether it did or not would depend on the particular contents of the document.[32] This decision emphasises that a clear case must be made out for use of a broad class claim to public interest immunity and as far as documents in the hands of public authorities are concerned it is preferable that each case be considered on its own facts and not on the basis of a class claim. Moreover, it is to be welcomed in the interests of justice as going some way towards ensuring that civil actions against the police are not undermined by claims that relevant information cannot be disclosed.

2   One of the most controversial assertions of public interest immunity occurred in the *Matrix Churchill* case,[33] as AAS Zuckermann indicates.

---

30   [1992] 1 WLR 217.

31   [1992] 3 All ER 624.

32   See *Taylor v Anderton* [1995] 2 All ER 420.

33   See Leigh, *Betrayed: The Real Story of the Matrix Churchill Trial* (1993); Tomkins, 'Public Interest Immunity after Matrix Churchill' (1993) PL 530.

Zuckermann observes that, after *Conway v Rimmer*, ministers were relieved of the responsibility of considering suppressing evidence by way of public interest immunity certificates on the administration of justice. On this basis, the responsibility for the suppression of evidence lies with the courts, not ministers, and therefore Zuckermann does not condemn the ministerial practices revealed in the Scott report (see further Part IV, Chapter 2). He ends by arguing that the courts, 'not just ministers', should be put on trial for their part in the *Matrix Churchill* affair. On this view, judicial responsibility for the suppression of evidence, claimed in *Conway*, is in a sense a double-edged sword; on the one hand it allows the judges to provide a check on the actions of the executive, but on the other it frees the executive from keeping a check on itself as regards the potential effect of a PII certificate on the administration of justice. Zuckermann assumes that the only public interest which ministers can be expected to understand and evaluate – in the light of judicial approval of 'closed' government – is the interest in secrecy. Once that interest is established they can and perhaps should close their eyes to the likely consequences attendant on issuance of the certificate, such as the possibility that an innocent person might be convicted, even where such a possibility is self-evident due to the nature of the material sought to be suppressed (as it seems to have been in the *Matrix Churchill* case), and despite their knowledge of judicial timidity and reluctance to resist PII claims, especially in national security cases. Possibly, Zuckermann's understandable eagerness to condemn judicial bolstering of the 'wall of silence blocking access to public documents' has led him to accept too readily ministerial claims of inability to understand or take any responsibility for the requirements of the interests of justice so long as a public interest in non-disclosure can be made out. Possibly, he also displays a readiness to accept that ministers are seeking to act in the public rather than the Government interest when a claim for suppression of evidence is made. In the light of Lord Templeman's comments in *Wiley*, above, it is suggested that both ministerial and judicial responsibility for creating 'the wall of silence' should be clearly condemned.

3   Zuckermann's conclusions as regards the use of PII certificates generally, and as regards their use in the *Matrix Churchill* case in particular, do not harmonise with those of Sir Richard Scott in the Scott Report. Scott found that the Government attitude 'to disclosure of documents to the defence was consistently grudging. The approach ought to have been to consider what documents the defence might reasonably need and then to consider whether there was any good reason why the defence should not have them ... the actual approach ... seems to have been to seek some means by which refusal to disclose could be justified'.[34] The danger in the argument, reiterated by Lord Scarman in *Air Canada* (above), that judges take the responsibility for considering the effect of suppression of evidence on the administration of justice, is that both judiciary and ministers succeed in shuffling off the responsibility for such suppression. The judges accept, as ministers strongly

---

34   Section G of the Scott report. See also the debate in Parliament on the Scott Report, *Hansard* HC Deb 26 February 1996; HC Deb, vol 272, no 51, in particular col 612.

demand they should, that matters of public safety can be judged only by the executive, while ministers hide behind the fiction that the judiciary will weigh up the interest in such matters against the interest in justice. Thus, ministers are able to adopt the convenient constitutional position of demanding on the one hand that the judiciary should not look behind PII claims based on national security interests, and on the other that if judges accede to such demands they must take the responsibility for doing so. Clearly, there is a strong argument that judges should be less timid when faced with such claims, but there also appears to be merit in Scott J's argument (see para G18.67 of the Scott report) that ministers must take some responsibility for putting them forward, bearing in mind ministerial responsibility for upholding the proper administration of justice. It is suggested that the creation of a dichotomy between ministerial and judicial responsibility in this matter, in order to ensure that the latter prevails, is unnecessary and leads to situations such as the one which arose in *Matrix Churchill*. Thus, in the light of *Matrix Churchill* there is arguably a need for greater regulation of the issue of PII certificates which would be based on the acceptance of initial ministerial responsibility for their potential effects on justice, although the judiciary should remain the final arbiters in the matter.[35]

4   The argument, criticised by Scott J, that before signing a PII certificate ministers need do no more than satisfy themselves that documents fall into a prescribed class may be based partly on 'entrenched conventions of public administration' including the rule that 'secrecy is in the interests of good government'. In future this argument may become less sustainable in the face of the new culture of openness depending from the 1994 Code of Practice on Access to Government Information (see below). Although the Code excludes many matters from its ambit, including categories of information which would be likely to be the subject of PII claims, it is based on the principle that responsibility for ensuring access to official information lies with departments, not with the judiciary, thus suggesting not only that good government requires a degree of openness, but that it accepts sole responsibility for ensuring that openness is maintained. It may also be noted, in support of this point, that the duties and responsibilities of ministers set out in *Questions of Procedure for Ministers* include: 'the duty to give Parliament and the public as full information as possible about the policies, decisions and actions of the Government and not to ... knowingly mislead Parliament and the public ... [and] the duty to ... uphold the administration of justice.'

Questions

1   'While the courts bear, and should bear, the ultimate responsibility for considering the effect of suppression of evidence on the administration of justice, ministers can nevertheless be expected, within current constitutional conventions, to take responsibility for considering the public interest in such administration in conjunction with the public interest in secrecy, when considering the issuance of a PII certificate.' Have the courts accepted this

35   See further I Leigh, 'Reforming Public Interest Immunity' *Webb JCLI* (1995) (2) 49–71.

argument, or have they clearly taken the position that judicial responsibility for determining when evidence should be given precludes acceptance of initial ministerial responsibility?

2 To a layperson it might seem strange to assert that ministers should not balance the interests of justice against the need for secrecy in a particular sphere of Government operation. This is tantamount to asserting that ministers are not responsible for the miscarriages of justice which may result from this policy. What is the basis for making this claim?

3 What constitutional and civil libertarian objections are there to view that ministers have a duty and not a discretion to claim PII?

FREEDOM OF INFORMATION[36]

Almost all democracies have introduced freedom of information legislation[37] within the last 30 years. For example, Canada introduced its Access to Information Act in 1982 while America has had such legislation since 1967. In this section we will look briefly at the US freedom of information legislation and will go on to consider the current arrangements for the release of Government documents to the public in the UK.

Freedom of information in the US

Freedom of Information Act 1967 (US)

5 US Code §552

§ 552.(a) Each agency shall make available to the public information as follows:

(1) Each agency shall separately state and currently publish in the Federal Register for the guidance of the public –

   (A) descriptions of its central and field organisation and the established places at which, the employees (and in the case of a uniformed service, the members) from whom, and the methods whereby, the public may obtain information, make submittals or requests, or obtain decisions;

   (B) statements of the general course and method by which its functions are channelled and determined, including the nature and requirements of all formal and informal procedures available;

   (C) rules of procedure, descriptions of forms available or the places at which forms may be obtained, and instructions as to the scope and contents of all papers, reports, or examinations;

   (D) substantive rules of general applicability adopted as authorised by law, and statements of general policy or interpretations of general applicability formulated and adopted by the agency; and

   (E) each amendment, revision, or repeal of the foregoing.

---

36 See generally P Birkinshaw, *Freedom of Information*, 2nd edn (1996); *Government and Information* (1990); *Reforming the Secret State* (1990).

37 See T McBride, 'The Official Information Act 1982' (1984) 11 NZULR 82; LJ Curtis, 'Freedom of Information in Australia' (1983) 14 Fed LR 5; HN Janisch, 'The Canadian Access to Information Act' (1982) PL 534; For America, see M Supperstone, *Brownlie's Law of Public Order and National Security* (1982), pp270–87; P Birkinshaw *Freedom of Information*, 2nd edn 91996), Ch 2.

(3) Except with respect to the records made available under paragraphs (1) and (2) of this subsection, each agency, on request for identifiable records made in accordance with published rules stating the time, place, fees to the extent authorised by statute, and procedure to be followed, shall make the records promptly available to any person. On complaint, the district court of the United States in the district in which the complainant resides, or has his principal place of business, or in which the agency records are situated, has jurisdiction to enjoin the agency from withholding agency records and to order the production of any agency records improperly withheld from the complainant. In such a case the court shall determine the matter *de novo* and the burden is on the agency to sustain its action. In the event of non-compliance with the order of the court, the district court may punish for contempt the responsible employee, and in the case of a uniformed service, the responsible member. Except as to causes the court considers of greater importance, proceedings before the district court, as authorised by this paragraph, take precedence on the docket over all other causes and shall be assigned for hearing and trial at the earliest practicable date and expedited in every way.

(4) Each agency having more than one member shall maintain and make available for public inspection a record of the final votes of each member in every agency proceeding.

(b) This section does not apply to matters that are –

(1) specifically required by executive order to be kept secret in the interest of the national defence or foreign policy;

(2) related solely to the internal personnel rules and practices of an agency;

(3) specifically exempted from disclosure by statute;

(4) trade secrets and commercial or financial information obtained from a person and privileged or confidential;

(5) inter-agency or intra-agency memorandums or letters which would not be available by law to a party other than an agency in litigation with the agency;

(6) personnel and medical files and similar files the disclosure of which would constitute a clearly unwarranted invasion of personal privacy;

(7) investigatory files compiled for law enforcement purposes except to the extent available by law to a party other than an agency;

(8) contained in or related to examination, operating, or condition reports prepared by, on behalf of, or for the use of an agency responsible for the regulation or supervision of financial institutions; or

(9) geological and geophysical information and data, including maps, concerning wells.

(c) This section does not authorise withholding of information or limit the availability of records to the public, except as specifically stated in this section. This section is not authority to withhold information from Congress.

Note

The US Freedom of Information Act applies to all parts of the Federal Government unless an exemption applies. Exempted categories include information concerning defence, law enforcement and foreign policy. The exemptions can be challenged in court and the onus of proof will be on the agency withholding the information to prove that disclosure could bring about the harm the exemption was intended to prevent. A number of reforms have been suggested since 1980 and in 1986 a major Freedom of Information Act reform was passed which extended the exemption available to law enforcement practices.

P Birkinshaw, *Freedom of Information* 1st edn, (1988), pp36–8

Freedom of information — overseas experience

The USA has possessed a Freedom of Information Act (FOIA) since 1966. Previous statutes had only allowed public access to Government documents if a 'need to know' was established, and they allowed agencies to withhold information for 'good cause'. All agencies in the executive branch of the federal government, including administrative regulatory agencies, are subject to FOIA. Excluded from the operation of the Act are the judicial and legislative branches of government. So too are members of the President's immediate personal staff, whose sole function is to give advice and assistance to the President. State government and local and city government are not included in this legislation.

The aim of the Act, as amended in 1974, is to provide public access to an agency's records if it is covered by the Act. An applicant does not have to demonstrate a specific interest in a matter to view relevant documents – an idle curiosity suffices.

Exemptions

Although the basic thrust of the Act is positive and supportive of openness, there are nine exemptions from the FOIA which include national defence or foreign policy information that is properly classified. An executive order of 1982 reversed the trend of relaxation of security classifications and 'broadened the discretion to create official secrets' since any form of unspecified damage may be used to justify exemption. Mandatory secrecy requirements rather than permissive ones have become more common, the 'balancing test' requiring the weighing of public access against the government need for secrecy has been eliminated, and systematic declassification has been cancelled. The order allows for its own mandatory 'review requests' of classified information as an alternative to FOIA actions. Internal rules and practices of an agency will be exempt but not the manuals and instructions on the interpretation of regulations. Other important exemptions include: trade secrets; commercial and financial information obtained by the Government that is privileged or confidential; inter- or intra-agency memoranda or letters which are not available by law; information protected by other statutes; personnel or medical files disclosure of which would constitute an invasion of privacy; and investigatory records compiled for law enforcement purposes if disclosure would result in certain types of harm. Reliance by an agency on an exemption is discretionary and not mandatory.

Challenging a refusal

Where there is a refusal to supply information, appeal procedures are specifically provided in each agency's FOIA regulations. A denial letter will inform the applicant of a right of appeal – usually within 30 days. The official refusing the appeal must be identified, and the exemption and reasons for refusal must be given.

UK freedom of information: the Public Records Acts

Public Records Act 1958

General responsibility of the Lord Chancellor for public records

1.–(1)The direction of the Public Record Office shall be transferred from the Master of the Rolls to the Lord Chancellor, and the Lord Chancellor shall be generally responsible for the execution of this Act and shall supervise the care and preservation of public records.

(3)The Lord Chancellor shall in every year lay before both Houses of Parliament a report on the work of the Public Record Office, which shall include any report made to him by the Advisory Council on Public Records.

...

Access to public records

5.–(1)Public records in the Public Record Office, other than those to which members of the public had access before their transfer to the Public Record Office, shall not be available for public inspection until they have been in existence for 50 years or such other period, either longer or shorter, as the Lord Chancellor may, with the approval, or at the request, of the Minister or other person, if any, who appears to him to be primarily concerned, for the time being prescribe as respects any particular class of public records.

(2)Without prejudice to the generality of the foregoing subsection, if it appears to the person responsible for any public records which have been selected by him under section three of this Act for permanent preservation that they contain information which was obtained from members of the public under such conditions that the opening of those records to the public after the period determined under the foregoing subsection would or might constitute a breach of good faith on the part of the Government or on the part of the persons who obtained the information, he sha'l inform the Lord Chancellor accordingly and those records shall not be available in the Public Record Office for public inspection even after the expiration of the said period except in such circumstances and subject to such conditions, if any, as the Lord Chancellor and that person may approve, or, if the Lord Chancellor and that person think fit, after the expiration of such further period as they may approve.

(3)Subject to the foregoing provisions of this section, subject to the enactments set out in the Second Schedule to this Act which prohibit the disclosure of certain information obtained from the public except for certain limited purposes) and subject to any other Act or instrument whether passed or made before or after this Act which contains a similar prohibition, it shall be the duty of the Keeper of Public Records to arrange that reasonable facilities are available to the public for inspecting and obtaining copies of public records in the Public Record Office.

...

First Schedule

Definition of public records

Departmental records

2.–(1) Subject to the provisions of this paragraph, administrative and departmental records belonging to Her Majesty, whether in the United Kingdom or elsewhere, in right of Her Majesty's Government in the United Kingdom and, in particular, –

(a) records of, or held in, any department of Her Majesty's Government in the United Kingdom; or

(b) records of any office, commission or other body or establishment whatsoever under Her Majesty's Government in the United Kingdom,

shall be public records.

Public Records Act 1967

1. In subsection (1) of section 5 of the Public Records Act 1958 (which provides that public records in the Public Record Office, with certain exceptions, shall not be available for public inspection until they have been in existence for 50 years or such other period as the Lord Chancellor may, in accordance with that subsection, prescribe as respects any particular class of public records) for the words 'until they have been in existence for 50 years or such other period', there shall be substituted the words 'until the expiration of the period of 30 years beginning with the first day of January in the year next after that in which they were created, or of such other period'.

Notes

1 Robertson has suggested that information is withheld to prevent embarrassment to bodies such as the police or civil servants rather than to descendants of persons mentioned in it; and in support of this he cites examples such as police reports on NCCL (1935–41), flogging of vagrants (1919), decisions against prosecuting James Joyce's *Ulysses* (1924) as instances of material which in January 1989 was listed as closed for a century.[38]

2 In 1992–93 a review was conducted of methods of ensuring further openness in government and its results were published in a White Paper on Open Government (Cm 2290). The White Paper stated that a Code of Practice on Access to Information would be adopted (the code is discussed below) and there would be a reduction in the number of public records withheld from release beyond 30 years. A review group established by Lord Mackay in 1992 suggested that records should only be closed for more than 30 years where their disclosure would cause harm to defence, national security, international relations and economic interests of the UK; information supplied in confidence; personal information which would cause substantial distress if disclosed. Under s3(4) of the 1958 Act records may still be retained within departments for 'administrative' reasons or for any other special reason.[39]

UK freedom of information: the Code of Practice on Access to Information

The attitude to secrecy exemplified by US freedom of information legislation, which is founded on the presumption that information must be disclosed unless specifically exempted, may be contrasted with that in the UK which takes the

---

38 See *Media Law* (1990), p338.

39 The White Paper proposals in relation to public records are considered by Birkinshaw, 'I Only Ask for Information' – the White Paper on Open Government' (1993) PL 557.

opposite stance. No general provision is made for such disclosure; the starting point is to criminalise disclosure in certain categories of information. American freedom of information provision can in particular be contrasted with provision under the UK Public Records Act 1958. Considering all the various and overlapping methods of preventing disclosure of official information in the UK and bearing in mind the contrasting attitude to this issue evinced in other democracies, it may appear that the UK is being increasingly isolated in its stance as a resister of freedom of information legislation.

There have been certain recent developments which suggest that a gradual movement towards more open government has been taking place in the UK over the last decade. The Data Protection Act 1984 allows access to personal information held on computerised files. The Campaign for Freedom of Information has, from 1985 onwards, brought about acceptance of the principle of access rights in some areas including local Government. Disclosure of a range of information was decriminalised under the Official Secrets Act 1989. After the 1992 election the Prime Minister promised a review of secrecy in Whitehall to be conducted by William Waldegrave, the minister with responsibility for the Citizen's Charter, which would concentrate on the large number of statutory instruments which prevent public disclosure of government information in various areas, with a view to removing those which did not appear to fulfil a pressing need. It was also promised that a list of secret Cabinet committees with their terms of reference and their ministerial membership would be published. Reform of the Official Secrets Act 1989 would be undertaken so that disclosure of a specific document would be criminalised as opposed to disclosure of a document belonging to a class of documents which might cause harm. A White Paper on Open Government (Cm 2290) was published in July 1993.

A new Code of Practice on Access to Government Information was introduced from April 1994 as promised in the White Paper. The Code provides that certain Government departments will provide information on request and will volunteer some information. The White Paper describes the role of the PCA as follows:

> The Parliamentary Commissioner for Administration (PCA), the Parliamentary Ombudsman, has agreed that complaints that departments and other bodies within his jurisdiction have failed to comply with this code can be investigated if referred to him by a Member of Parliament. When he decides to investigate he will have access to the department's internal papers and will be able in future to report to Parliament when he finds that information has been improperly withheld. The Select Committee on the PCA will then be able to call departments and ministers to account for failure to supply information in accordance with the code, as they can now call them to account for maladministration or injustice. The ombudsman has the confidence of Parliament and is independent of the Government. Parliamentary accountability will thus be preserved and enhanced. Ministers and departments will have a real spur to greater openness, and citizens will have an independent investigator working on their behalf.

However, no legal remedies are provided for citizens if the Code is breached and a number of matters were excluded from it as set out below.

Code of Practice on Access to Government Information (1994)

Part I: *Purpose*

1   This Code of Practice supports the Government's policy under the Citizen's Charter of extending access to official information, and responding to reasonable requests for information, except where disclosure would not be in the public interest as specified in Part II of this Code.

2   The aims of the Code are:

- to improve policy-making and the democratic process by extending access to the facts and analyses which provide the basis for the consideration of proposed policy;

- to protect the interests of individuals and companies by ensuring that reasons are given for administrative decisions, except where there is statutory authority or established convention to the contrary; and

- to support and extend the principles of public service established under the Citizen's Charter.

These aims are balanced by the need:

- to maintain high standards of care in ensuring the privacy of personal and commercially confidential information; and

- to preserve confidentiality where disclosure would not be in the public interest or would breach personal privacy or the confidences of a third party, in accordance with statutory requirements and part II of the Code.

Information the Government will release

3   Subject to the exemptions in Part II, the Code commits departments and public bodies under the jurisdiction of the Parliamentary Commissioner for Administration (the Ombudsman) [in Northern Ireland, the Parliamentary Commissioner for Administration and the Commissioner for Complaints]:

(i)   to publish the facts and analysis of the facts which the Government considers relevant and important in framing major policy proposals and decisions; such information will normally be made available when policies and decisions are announced;

(ii)   to publish or otherwise make available, as soon as practicable after the Code becomes operational, explanatory material on departments' dealings with the public (including such rules, procedures, internal guidance to officials and similar administrative manuals as will assist better understanding of departmental action in dealing with the public) except where publication could of the Code;

(iii) to give reasons for administrative decisions to those affected [subject to statutory provision or established convention: see para 2 above];

(iv) to publish in accordance with the Citizen's Charter full information about how public services are run, how much they cost, who is in charge, and what complaints and redress procedures are available: full and, where possible, comparable information about what services are being provided, what targets are set, what standards of service are expected and the results achieved;

(v)   to release, in response to specific requests, information relating to their policies, actions and decisions and other matters related to their areas of responsibility.

4   There is no commitment that pre-existing documents, as distinct from information, will be made available in response to requests. The Code does not require departments to acquire information they do not possess, to provide information which is already published, to provide material which the Government did not consider to be reliable information, or to provide information which is provided as part of an existing charged service other than through that service.

Part II : Reasons for confidentiality

The following categories of information are exempt from the commitments to provide information in this Code. The exemptions will not be interpreted in a way which causes injustice to individuals. References to harm include both actual harm and risk or reasonable expectation of harm.

(i) Defence, security and international relations

Information whose disclosure would harm national security or defence.

Information whose disclosure would harm the conduct of international relations or affairs.

Information received in confidence from foreign governments, courts or international organisations.

(ii) Internal discussion and advice

Information whose disclosure would harm the frankness and candour of internal discussion, including:

- proceedings of Cabinet and Cabinet committees;
- internal opinion, advice, recommendation, consultation and deliberation;
- projections and assumptions relating to internal policy analysis; analysis of alternative policy options and information relating to rejected policy options;
- confidential communications between departments or public bodies including regulatory bodies.

(iii) Communications with the Royal Household

Information relating to confidential communications between Ministers and Her Majesty the Queen or other Members of the Royal Household, or relating to confidential proceedings of the Privy Council.

(iv) Law enforcement and legal proceedings

Information whose disclosure could prejudice the administration of justice, including fair trial and the enforcement or proper administration of the law.

Information whose disclosure would be likely to prejudice the prevention, investigation or detection of crime, the apprehension or prosecution of offenders, or the security of any penal institution.

Information covered by public interest immunity or legal professional privilege, or which could prejudice legal proceedings, public inquiries or other formal investigations or proceedings (whether actual or prospective) or whose disclosure is, has been or is likely to be addressed in the context of such proceedings. This includes information relating to proceedings which have been completed or discontinued, or relating to investigations which have or might have resulted in proceedings.

Information whose disclosure would harm public safety or public order.

Information which could endanger the life or physical safety of any person, or identify the source of information given in confidence for law enforcement or security purposes.

Information whose disclosure would increase the likelihood of damage to the environment, or rare or endangered species and their habitats.

(v) Immigration and nationality

Information relating to immigration, nationality, consular work and entry clearance cases.

(vi) Effective management of the economy and collection of tax

Information whose disclosure would harm the ability of the Government to manage the economy, prejudice the conduct of official market operations, or could lead to improper gain or advantage.

Information whose disclosure would prejudice the assessment or collection of tax or duties, or assist tax.

(vii) Effective management and operations of the public service

Information whose disclosure could lead to improper gain or advantage or could reasonably be expected to prejudice:

- the competitive position of a department or other public authority;
- negotiations or the effective conduct of personnel management, or commercial or contractual activities;
- the awarding of discretionary grants.

Information whose disclosure would harm the proper and efficient conduct of the operations of a department or other public body or authority, including regulatory bodies and NHS organisations.

(viii) public employment, public appointments and honours

Personnel records (relating to public appointments as well as employees of public authorities) including those relating to recruitment, promotion and security vetting.

Information, opinions and assessments given in confidence in relation to public employment and public appointments.

Information, opinions and assessments given in relation to recommendations for honours.

(ix) Unreasonable, voluminous or vexatious requests

Requests for information which are manifestly unreasonable or are formulated in too general a manner, or which (because of the amount of information to be processed or the need to retrieve information from files not in current use) would require unreasonable diversion of resources.

(x) Publication and prematurity in relation to publication

Information which is or will soon be published, or whose disclosure would be premature in relation to a proposed announcement or publication.

(xi) Research, statistics and analysis

Information relating to incomplete analysis, research or statistics, or information whose disclosure could be misleading or deprive the holder of priority of publication or commercial value.

Information held only for preparing statistics or carrying out research, and which relates to individuals or companies who will not be identified in reports of that research or in published statistics.

(xii) Privacy of an individual

Unwarranted disclosure to a third party of personal information about any person (including a deceased person) or any other disclosure which would constitute or could facilitate an unwarranted invasion of privacy.

(xiii) Third party's commercial confidences

Information including commercial confidences, trade secrets or intellectual property whose unwarranted disclosure would harm the competitive position of a third party.

(xiv) Information given in confidence

Information held in consequence of having been supplied in confidence by a person who:

- gave the information under a statutory guarantee that its confidentiality would be protected; or

- was not under, and could not have been put under, any legal obligation to supply it; and

- has not consented to its disclosure.

Information provided in confidence by a medical practitioner who has expressed the view that disclosure of the information would be injurious to the person's health or welfare.

(xv) Statutory and other restrictions:

Information whose disclosure is prohibited by or under any enactment, regulation, European Community law or international agreement.

Information which could not be sought in a Parliamentary Question, or whose release would constitute a breach of Parliamentary Privilege.

3 In investigating complaints that departments or public bodies within his jurisdiction have failed to observe the provisions of the Code of Practice on Government Information, the Parliamentary Commissioner will follow the same procedures as for other complaints investigated under the Act: ...

(viii) the commissioner has full discretion to set out the facts of the investigation, to explain his reasons for finding maladministration (if he upholds the complaint), to analyse and comment upon any disputed points about the interpretation of the code, to recommend what information should be published, to criticise the department (if appropriate), and otherwise to provide a full report on his investigation in accordance with his powers under the Parliamentary Commissioner Act;

(ix) at present, where maladministration has led to unremedied injustice, the role of the commissioner is to recommend redress, but the giving of redress is normally a matter for the department; where a department accepts that maladministration has occurred — and even in those cases where it does not accept that charge — it is often possible for redress to be provided before the full process of investigation and report has been completed. By analogy, in cases relating to the Code of Practice, departments may similarly be able to provide information to the satisfaction of the person making a complaint once the commissioner has indicated that he is going to investigate or during the course of an investigation. In cases where the information in dispute has not been so provided by the department, the commissioner (in the light of sub paragraph (x) below) will not normally look to provide the redress himself by seeking to disclose the disputed information in his reports; if exceptionally he were minded to do so, he would first of all inform the principal officer of his intention;

(x) Section 11(3) of the Act confers on ministers a power to give notice in writing to the commissioner with respect to any document or information or class of documents specified in the notice, that disclosure 'would be prejudicial to the safety of the state or otherwise contrary to the public interest' and where such a notice is given nothing in the Act shall be construed as authorising or requiring the commissioner or his staff to communicate to any person or for any purpose any document or information specified in the notice, or a document or information of a class so specified. Indiscriminate use of section 11(3) could inhibit the ability of the commissioner to carry out effective review of complaints relating to the Code of Practice on Government Information. Without fettering the discretion of ministers to use this power if the circumstances so demand, or of the commissioner to carry out his functions under the Act, neither the commissioner nor departments will act in such a way as to make the use of section 11(3) the usual means of resolving differences of opinion between the commissioner and departments. Normally the commissioner will make reasoned recommendations in his report without the specific information which is in dispute thereby being disclosed. Ministers will remain accountable to Parliament for the actions taken or refused in the light of the Parliamentary Commissioner's recommendations;

(xi) the report mentioned above includes as appropriate:

- the report of the results of the investigation the commissioner is required to send to the Member of the House of Commons (or if he is no longer a Member of the House to such other Member as he thinks appropriate) by whose request the investigation was made (s10(1));

- the special report to Parliament that may be made as the commissioner thinks fit under s10(3) of the Act if, after conducting an investigation, it appears to the commissioner that injustice has been caused to the person aggrieved in consequence of maladministration (in these cases usually by a failure to provide information) and that the injustice has not been, or will not be, remedied; and the annual and other reports made under s10(4) of the Act.

(For the purpose of the law of defamation, publications mentioned in s10(5) of the Act are absolutely privileged.)

(xii) once a report under s10(3) or 10(4) has been laid before Parliament, it is then a matter for the House, or more usually in the first instance the Select Committee for the Parliamentary Commissioner for Administration, to consider that report and the action to be taken in the light of it. The commissioner would expect to take account of the views expressed by the Select Committee though he is not statutorily bound by them.

Appendices to the Minutes of Evidence taken before the Select Committee on the PCA, session 1993–1994, HC 33 (1993–94), Vol II, p258

Memorandum submitted by the Campaign for Freedom of Information (M31)

I am writing with the comments of the Campaign for Freedom of Information on the proposed role of the Parliamentary Ombudsman under the Open Government White Paper (Cm 2290).

We regard the central proposal of the White Paper, the proposed Code of Practice on disclosure, as extremely disappointing. We do welcome some of the

White Paper's proposals, particularly the proposed statutory rights to personal files and health and safety information. However, we believe that the factors that led the Government to propose broad statutory rights in these areas apply equally across the public sector and should have led the Government to accept the case for freedom of information legislation.

One aspect of the Code of Practice – the proposal that an independent arbitrator, the Parliamentary Ombudsman, should be able to investigate complaints – is a valuable step forward. But the Code nevertheless suffers from weaknesses of such a fundamental nature that they cast doubt on whether it is capable of achieving its objectives. These features inevitably have implications for the work of the Ombudsman.

In particular we are concerned about:

- the limited scope of the disclosure Code, which is restricted to those areas subject to the Ombudsman's jurisdiction. These exclude many important parts of government;

- the lack of enforcement provisions. We recognise the value of the Ombudsman's approach However, overseas experience with disclosure of information suggests that persuasion and reason are not enough – a legal remedy is also necessary;

- the fact that the Code only promises to answer applicants' questions – not allow them to see copies of documents. This is a fundamental flaw, which undermines the credibility of the proposals. It will generate considerable public suspicion and unnecessary work for the Ombudsman;

- the potentially large volume of complaints, and the possibility that the Ombudsman's office will not receive the resources to handle them efficiently. Long delays in dealing with complaints may frustrate applicants as effectively as outright refusals to disclose.

Scope

In our view the scope of the disclosure scheme is distorted by limiting it, as far as central government is concerned, to bodies subject to the Parliamentary Ombudsman's jurisdiction. We understand the practical reasons for this, but in terms of the scheme's objectives it is very unsatisfactory. It reinforces the case for removing many of the limitations on the Ombudsman's jurisdiction.

The restrictions mean that parts of government which should be subject to any new access arrangements – and which are covered by freedom of information laws overseas – are excluded for essentially arbitrary reasons.

It may or may not have been justified to exclude from the Ombudsman's remit those bodies which have little direct dealings with individual members of the public – and therefore offer little scope for complaints of maladministration. But this cannot be a proper basis for exempting such bodies from an open government policy, particularly as they may be responsible for policies of great public interest. The promotion of 'informed policy making' is an explicit objective of the White Paper [para 1.7].

Most of the exclusions from the Ombudsman's jurisdiction set out in Schedule 3 of the Parliamentary Commissioner Act 1967 are inappropriate as exemptions to a disclosure scheme. No one setting out to create such a scheme from first principles would exclude subjects as important as foreign relations, the government's actions overseas (presumably including the Falklands and Gulf wars), the administration of overseas territories (eg Hong Kong), nationalised industries such as the Post Office, British Rail and British Coal, the BBC, the Civil Aviation Authority, most of the Cabinet Office's functions, the work of the police, the Home Office's crime prevention functions, the Crown Prosecution Service, the Bank of England, Government departments' commercial transactions, personnel matters, the treatment of members of the armed services, and so on.

Some information in these areas may of course need to be withheld. The scope of the Code's proposed exemptions more than adequately provide for any such necessary confidentiality.

The scope of the Code is limited in an even more surprising way. Information about immigration, nationality, consular work and entry clearance is excluded from it altogether [p76] despite the fact that these topics largely *are* subject to investigation by the Ombudsman. The draft Code of Practice already contains exemptions for law enforcement and national security which adequately protect information whose disclosure might undermine efforts to control illegal immigration or suspected terrorists. We find it difficult to understand why the subject of immigration, *per se*, should be treated as taboo. This further reinforces the impression of a scheme whose scope has been determined in an arbitrary manner.

Enforcement

In our view an effective disclosure scheme requires an effective enforcement mechanism.

This is not to underestimate the value of a relatively informal remedy such as that offered by the Ombudsman. A complaint to the Ombudsman costs the applicant nothing and may, through a combination of persuasion and the threat of adverse publicity, often secure disclosure. However, it is unsatisfactory to rely exclusively on such an approach.

Many overseas freedom of information laws combine strict enforcement in a court or tribunal with the alternative of complaint to an ombudsman. In Australia, Denmark and Sweden the citizen has the choice of either remedy; in Canada, an ombudsman (the Information Commissioner) provides the first stage of an appeal process, with a remedy in the court thereafter. In these countries the ombudsman is often favoured because this avoids legal costs. But the legal remedy is available if government refuses to comply, if there are irreconcilable differences of opinion, or where the issue is essentially of legal interpretation.

Injustice

Section 5(1) of the Parliamentary Commissioner Act 1967, allows the Ombudsman to take up a complaint only if it has come from a member of the public who 'claims to have suffered injustice in consequence of maladministration'. The complainant must allege both maladministration and injustice. Section 6(2) provides that the injustice must have been suffered by the complainant him or herself – a complaint may not be made about an injustice inflicted on the community generally.

However, the White Paper suggests that for complaints under the Code of Practice the Ombudsman will take a relaxed view of this requirement:

'the Ombudsman ... has said that, in the context of a failure to provide information in accordance with the Code, this would not mean that the person bringing a complaint would necessarily have to show some demonstrable injury or disadvantage arising from refusal of information. It would be enough to found a complaint that the person or persons concerned had not been given information which, in accordance with the Code of Practice to which the Government is committed, they believed they were entitled to have' [para 4.19].

This is a significant move from the conventional requirement. Maladministration complaints sometimes do involve access to information. But they are normally upheld only if the complainant can show that he or she was disadvantaged by the withholding of information – for example if the person was not informed of the existence of a right of appeal against a decision, and was thereby deprived of the opportunity to exercise it.

The Ombudsman's reported views appear to suggest that the denial of information requested under the Code will in itself be considered to be an injustice – even, presumably, if there is no disadvantage to the applicant other than the frustration of his or her desire for information. We welcome this.

More importantly, the relaxation of the 'injustice' test means that complaints to the Ombudsman under the Code will be very different from conventional complaints – both as to the topics involved, and nature of the complainants.

In his conventional role, the Ombudsman usually deals with ordinary citizens who have fallen foul of the bureaucracy in the course of their private lives – for example, in the handling of their pensions, tax or benefits. Most are bystanders, who probably want nothing to do with the government, except for it to treat them fairly and leave them alone.

Secrecy cases are likely to bring in an entirely different constituency: those primarily interested in policy issues. They may be monitoring, probing, seeking to question, influence, improve or challenge government proposals; or to expose what they regard as complacency or malpractice. Requesters may include journalists, pressure groups, professional bodies, trade associations, campaigning organisations, local authority associations, academics, local politician, political researchers and perhaps even MPs themselves.

These groups will have been enfranchised by the relaxation of the requirement that they demonstrate injustice to themselves. Their complaints are therefore far more likely to involve matters of public interest or contention. These in turn are more likely to provoke a defensive response from government.

The defensive approach may extend to the Government's dealings with the Ombudsman, particularly if his recommendation favours disclosure on a controversial issue on which the Government feels vulnerable. Decision-makers use secrecy to protect themselves from criticism and challenge. Something more than persuasion and rational discussion may be needed for them to relinquish it.

The absence of precedent

Moreover, in handling disclosure cases the Ombudsman will be working in a new field, without the benefit of the long history of precedent and 'case law' built up under conventional maladministration cases. The meaning of the two key terms, 'maladministration' and 'injustice', have been repeatedly elaborated and clarified over the last 25 years and now rest on well-documented foundations, reducing the scope for disagreement over interpretation.

But the exemptions described in the disclosure Code involve a multitude of new and undefined terms, for which no body of precedent exists. Complaints to the Ombudsman will constantly raise issues of interpretation – but there will be no court to issue authoritative judgements.

Interpreting exemptions

All the Code's exemptions raise definitional problems. Will a disclosure, in the words of the Code, 'harm defence', 'harm national security', 'harm the conduct of international affairs', 'prejudice the proper administration of the law', 'prejudice public inquiries', 'prejudice other formal proceedings', 'harm public safety', 'prejudice the conduct of official market operations', 'lead to improper gain or advantage', 'prejudice negotiations', 'prejudice the effective conduct of personnel management', 'harm the proper and efficient conduct of the operations of a department', constitute 'an unwarranted disclosure [which] would harm the competitive position of a third party'.

These terms are not clearly defined; their extent and limitations are not obvious; they are all potentially contentious. We accept that it will be possible for many disputes to be resolved by discussion, particularly where in the circumstances a department has no vested interest in concealment. Departments will wish to avoid criticism by the Ombudsman, and will attempt to respond positively. But where the information is potentially embarrassing, and a department fears that a disclosure will expose it to serious criticism – for example by contradicting the evidence it has relied on to justify a key policy – it may be tempted to reject the Ombudsman's recommendation.

We doubt whether departments will find it difficult, or even embarrassing, to put forward and defend a different interpretation from the Ombudsman's. The broad exemptions provide ample, indeed almost unlimited, scope for differences of interpretation. The department need only explain that this is a matter of which there are legitimate differences of opinion; and that while it understands and respects the contrary view, it has the responsibility of deciding and feels obliged to follow its own judgment.

In the absence of a body capable of delivering and enforcing authoritative judgements we believe that it will be relatively easy for government departments to take this view and continue, in Mr Waldegrave's words 'to use secrecy for convenience if they can get away with it' [*Hansard*, 19 February 1993, col 598].

The exclusion of documents

The Code itself suffers from a weakness which fundamentally undermines the value of the whole exercise and seems likely to generate significant problems for the Ombudsman.

The White Paper makes it clear that the government intends to release information, not copies of original documents: 'The Code creates a commitment to give access to information rather than particular pre-existing documents' [para 4.8]; 'There is no presumption that pre-existing documents, as distinct from information, will be made available' [p73].

What is apparently envisaged is that people will be supplied with a letter setting out the information they have requested, but will not be given access to existing reports or documents. In effect the government is promising to do no more than answer the public's questions. We are not clear whether this necessarily represents an advance on existing practice.

Moreover, since the Code provides that applicants will in future have to pay for information, the Code may in some respects be a retrograde step.

The restriction on access to documents also distinguishes the Code from overseas freedom of information laws, which are typically based on a right to existing records.

We are not convinced by the White Paper's justification:

The Code creates a commitment to give access to information rather than particular pre-existing documents. People will in general find it easier to describe the information they seek, rather than the documents they wish to see. Attempts overseas to provide the public with a full guide to the filing systems of departments have not by most accounts been successful ... [para 4.8].

This paragraph misunderstands the operation of overseas freedom of information laws. In practice, requesters are not obliged to itemise each individual *document* to which they seek access. Instead, they describe in as precise terms as possible the specific information, or the topic on which information is sought. Departments are then obliged to take reasonable steps to locate documents containing the requested information.

A letter from the department summarising the facts, but withholding the report from which they are taken, will not be favourably received by requesters. It is not difficult to imagine the suspicion that will follow. How fairly has the information been edited? Has the department left out what it considers is not relevant? Has it excluded inconvenient or contradictory data?

We suspect that departments will find it all too easy to 'launder' the information that is released, and we ourselves view with suspicion the Government's reluctance to contemplate the disclosure of actual documents.

The White Paper fuels such concerns. It states that 'material which the Government did not consider to be reliable information' will be withheld [p73] and that 'information whose disclosure could be misleading' will also not be released [p78]. We are not aware of comparable provisions in any overseas freedom of information law, nor in any existing UK access law.

P Birkinshaw, ' "I Only Ask for Information" – the White Paper on Open Government' (1993) *Public Law* 557, 559, 560

Analysis

In a government tradition that has been steeped in secrecy the White Paper on Open Government (WP) [Cm 2290] is a remarkable document. Remarkable both for announcing a significant *point de depart* from the culture of secrecy that has characterised the conduct of British Government – though it is well to remember that all Governments are secretive by nature, the British only more transparently so than most – and remarkable also for marking that departure, not in the form of legislation on freedom of information or open government, but largely through non-enforceable 'grace and favour' provisions. Access to government information, it should be emphasised, not papers, will be dependent upon the discretion of officials who will be guided by a Code in the exercise of their discretion: 'the Code does not itself provide access to any particular document or paper' (para 4.20). There will, however, be statutory rights to health and safety information and personal information. The Government is additionally proposing liberalisation of access to public records under the 30 year (or more) rule and 'relaxation' of the laws prohibiting disclosure, largely in line with the 1989 Official Secrets Act (OSA). ...

Maintaining confidentiality

All FOI statutes exempt and sometimes exclude certain information. The WP specifies in Chapter 3, and the Code in Part II, the reasons and grounds for holding back public access for reasons of confidentiality. Some of the exemptions require a harm test to justify exemption; some do not, eg confidential communications between ministers and the Royal household, or information which could not be sought in a Parliamentary Question [prompting Maurice Frankel to write: 'Civil servants who have spent a lifetime perfecting techniques of evading MPs' questions, will now be free to practise on the general public' (*Secrets*, August 1993)], and information relating to immigration and nationality. The areas requiring a harm test cover such items as defence and national security; international relations; law enforcement and legal proceedings; proceedings of Cabinet and Cabinet committees; internal discussion, opinion and advice; management of the economy and collection of taxes; effective management of the public service; damage to public authorities' commercial and negotiating interests; and the competitive position of a third party. References to harm include both actual harm and risk or reasonable expectation of harm. Personal privacy, information given in confidence, unreasonable or voluminous requests, disclosure which would be premature or information which is already in the public domain are also grounds for refusing access.

In the WP's discussion of law enforcement and legal proceedings, public interest immunity is raised as an exception to the general presumption of openness in legal proceedings. In a way, the whole weakness of the voluntary nature of the Government's proposals is highlighted by events surrounding the Matrix Churchill trial concerning the three executives who were tried for breaching arms' export embargoes to Iraq. Public interest immunity certificates were signed as a matter of course which, had they been successful, would have helped to conceal that relevant guidelines had in fact been relaxed but that Parliament had been misinformed of this and, through Parliament, the public. In this case, judicial vigilance dramatically exposed the discreditable secrecy of ministers and officials, although we have to await the report of the Scott Inquiry for the full details. In cases where PII is claimed, the court is the final arbiter on where the public interest lies. The Government has been careful to avoid such a role for the courts and has recommended that the PCA should investigate complaints where there is a refusal to provide information.

The exemption concerning the confidentiality of internal discussion, opinion and advice has caused much debate. This exemption seeks to protect the position of civil servants in their role as neutral advisers to Government. Were the advice revealed, civil servants would be reluctant to advise in complete candour fearing that their advice and their name could be used by the Opposition in attacking Government policies, or an incoming Government of a different party would single out civil servants with whom they could not work because of the tenor of their advice. The confidentiality of the relationship between ministers and civil servants would be eroded (para 3.15). As such it has long been supported by the First Division Association of Civil Servants and even included in Bills drafted or supported by the Freedom of Information Campaign. However, that campaign has drawn a distinction between policy advice and factual advice – as in the USA – and between policy advice and expert advice, ie advice offered on the basis of expertise and qualifications on a specific subject, very commonly of a scientific or economic nature [see *Secretary of State for Health, ex p US Tobacco Inc* [1992] 1 All ER 212 (QBD)]. What is common elsewhere is that factual evidence and expert evidence are available, as indeed are many forms of information once the policy-making process is over. The Freedom of Information Bill sponsored by Mark Fisher MP in the 1992/93 session, which was 'talked out' at report stage by the Government, would have allowed access to scientific and expert advice. Such advice would help to assess the strength of the options to the policies adopted by a Government. The WP is in fact very protective of all forms of advice given in the policy-making process. It recommends protection of advice not only by 'generalist' civil servants but also by experts, be they presumably civil servants or outsiders. Furthermore, such advice should be protected not only where it falls within the policy-making process: 'Internal candour may be just as important in assessing the effects of existing policies' (para 3.16).

One suspects an overkill in civil service sensitivity here. The WP dismissed the anonymising of papers when publishing them as 'not credible' without offering explanation (para 3.16). Where it is obvious who the adviser is, a lack of published documents will lead to ill-informed speculation about the nature of the advice which could be far more damaging to an individual. The reasoning is redolent of government sensitivity rather than civil service sensitivity.

Minutes of Evidence Taken Before the Treasury and Civil Service Committee, 8 March 1994, HC 27 (1993–94), Vol II, p176

Mr Davies:

1911. Mr Waldegrave, I would like to ask you one or two questions if I may about open government and start by congratulating you on the very considerable progress you have made in publishing this White Paper and indeed in releasing a lot of documents from the Public Record Office. There has been an unprecedented move forward, I think, in that field since you have been in your present office. Would you describe this White Paper and the draft Code as a reasonable compromise between the present position and the full Freedom of Information Act regime which applies in some other western countries?

Mr Waldegrave: Yes, I would, for the following reason. Presuming I get legislative time in a reasonable sense soon for the statutory things that need to be done in relation to personal records and health and safety records, if you look at the things which are then covered by statute and then you take that template and you say: 'Let's look at America. What are things about which people actually ask questions under the Freedom of Information Act?' about 80% of what in America or Canada is requested under the Freedom of Information Act will actually be statutorily based here. You are then left with the 20% or so which deals with central Government work and so on. It is possible, of course, as the Chairman very well knows, to have an Act covering that area too. I happen to think that the ombudsman route, policing a Code, is potentially a very swift and powerful and cheap way, both of improving the behaviour within the bureaucracies themselves and of giving a readier access, in terms of complaint to the citizen, without having to go through the courts. In this one area, the ombudsman holds the redress in his own hands; he sees the information. I think it will make much more of a change than people have yet realised.

1912. So you would see this really as a final solution, not just as a step along the road to full open Government?

Mr Waldegrave: Well, never say never, but I believe a real chance of doing what people want and if it does work it has the great merit of being cheaper, quicker and more accessible for the people who want to make a complaint.

1913. Do you accept, as a fundamental principle in a democracy where power by definition derives from the people, that all information should be open unless there are specific reasons to restrict the access to particular pieces of information?

Mr Waldegrave: I certainly do and some words very like those open the White Paper.

1914. Right. I wonder if I could come on to the issue of the role of the ombudsman? You describe the role of the ombudsman in very positive terms in contrast to Freedom of Information regimes around the world, but can we have your assurance that if the ombudsman rules that a piece of information should be revealed then the government department concerned will accept that ruling in all cases?

Mr Waldegrave: The Government has never, except in one very early case which it gave in on, tried to withstand the ombudsman. That is the first thing to say. The second thing to say is, as I said earlier, if a government was so silly then the ombudsman has the power – because he has the information – to take further steps. He has said himself that he would at that point try to negotiate, which would be sensible. He would try and say to the department: 'Come on'; that would be his first reaction, to say: 'Don't be so foolish'. In this case it is unlike other kinds of redress where you might have to order a bureaucracy to pay money or something. He actually holds the redress in his own hands. He has the bits of paper in his own hands.

Minutes of Evidence Taken Before the Public Service Committee, HC 313 (1995–96), 3 April 1996

128. ... Under what circumstances do you see that the Freedom of Information Act would be a sensible policy for Britain?

Lord Armstrong of Ilminster: I think one of the problems about phrases like 'freedom of information' and 'open government' is that they are as long as a piece of string. I think there may well be a case for an Act, whatever it is called, which gives the individual greater right of access to information held about him within government. That needs to be circumscribed in the case of the security and intelligence agencies. Where I do not think a Freedom of Information Act has a part to play is in exposing the processes of decision-making in government before a decision happens and that was the issue I was trying to take in the House of Lords on that occasion. I do think that the processes by which, under present arrangements, decisions are explained to the public and justified to the public, lack something of fullness. That is perhaps inevitable because where a major decision is being announced, for instance, by way of a Parliamentary statement you know much better than I do the restrictions in terms of time that are available for a Parliamentary statement or an answer to a Parliamentary Question and inevitably it is not possible for a minister making such a statement to give full exposition of the facts and the figures and the arguments that lie behind the decision that is taken. There may be political considerations as well but we will leave those aside as I am a non-political civil servant, or was. It has always seemed to me that the form of openness that would best suit that sort of situation is not the kind of openness which would reveal all the processes of advice to ministers and all the information raw, as it were, but a process where by when a decision is announced (it may well be announced by a statement in the House or by an answer to a Parliamentary Question) that there should be made available as well to the House of Commons and to the public a much fuller account of the facts and the figures that are taken into account in making the decision and the arguments and considerations which have led to the decision being taken as it was. I think that would be beneficial to an understanding of what the decision is about and why it was taken as it was, so I think it would be a more open, more transparent, form of justification, if you like, of government decisions to Parliament and to the public. I also think it might well make for better decision-making because if it was known that such a document had to be produced and would have to be produced at the end of the day, the likely contents of that document would be in people's mind while the decision was being processed and I think that would have a healthy effect on decision-making itself. I think if you try to deal with this process by means of statute, which requires publication of certain types of documents, the effect will simply be to drive the process into channels which the Act cannot reach. Things will be done on the back of envelopes. Things will be done behind the Speaker's chair orally late at night and not done through the usual process. That would not be good ...

Parliamentary Commissioner for Administration's Annual Report for 1995, Cm 296

6. Two other investigations involved DSS. One [*Ibid*, p3.] brought out that, despite the department's reminders, there are still staff at local office level who

do not know about the obligations to release information under the Code. A woman who had sought access to a report of a visit made to her by a departmental official met with a refusal, even though she cited the Code to the local office. Happily the department gave the information as soon as I intervened. In the second case [PCA: Eighth Report, 1994–95, HC 606, p7.] a man sought access to a report to the Secretary of State for Social Security made by the person who had been appointed under section 17(4) of the Social Security Administration Act 1992 to hold an inquiry into the man's NIC position. For a long time the department claimed that Exemption 4(d) (covering information subject to legal professional privilege) applied. After research I established that there was no question of such privilege. The department eventually agreed to make available a copy of the report to the man in question. They also agreed to inform those appointed to hold such enquiries in the future that copies of their reports would be released to the individuals on request.

7. Three other investigations raised interesting and challenging issues. In the first [PCA: Ninth Report, 1994–95, HC 758, p11.] the Treasury who have approached open government in a positive way, as illustrated by their releasing the minutes of the monthly meetings between the Chancellor of the Exchequer and the Governor of the Bank of England, refused to make available a 1994 report on frauds in Whitehall (one of an annual series) which they had prepared from departmental returns. When I took up the complaint they reconsidered the request. They then decided that, subject only to very minor excisions to avoid prejudice to investigations or legal proceedings, the report could be released. Better still, they promised to release all future such reports, a promise they honoured in December 1995. I did not find all other departments as open-minded. In another case [PCA: First Report, 1995–96, HC 86, p1.] MAFF at first refused to release any information to a man who had bought at auction an imported heifer which had later had to be slaughtered after it had tested sero-positive for foot and mouth disease. They maintained that, irrespective of the Code, they owed the importer a common law duty of confidentiality – on the facts of the case I did not find that argument persuasive. After the referring Member's and my interventions, bit by bit all the information sought was released, except the name of the importer. I accepted that the name could be withheld under Exemption 13 of the Code (covering information whose unwarranted disclosure would harm the commercial confidence of a third party). In the course of that investigation I also found that, although MAFF had decided in principle to accept *ex gratia* compensation claims from the owners of such slaughtered cattle, they had never made that fact publicly, known. At my prompting they put that omission right. The third case [PCA: Ninth Report, 1994–95, HC 758, p1.] involved DNH who were faced with a request that they should release information about the repeal of the broadcasting restrictions governing the interviewing of members of certain organisations in Northern Ireland. The complainant concerned felt strongly that the public interest in disclosure would outweigh any harm that would arise, but DNH refused the request relying on Exemption 2 of the Code (covering information whose disclosure would harm the frankness and candour of internal discussion). Having studied what was contained in the relevant Departmental papers I had no hesitation in upholding the department's view.

8. In two other cases in contrast, the first concerning DOE [PCA: First Report, 1995–96, HC 86, p8.] and the second [*Ibid*, p8.] the Charity Commission, I had no doubt that the information sought should be released. In the former case a man wanted information about the composition and membership of various working parties which had been helping to formulate guidance on best available air

pollution control techniques for certain prescribed industrial and other processes. I found that while departmental officials had tried to be helpful within their understanding of what could be released they had been wrong not to release the information sought. In the latter case, the Charity Commission had simply failed to take action on a man's request for some information about a long-established charity. They remedied that after I had intervened.

9. The one investigation which I discontinued [PCA: Ninth Report, 1994–95, HC 758, p13.] concerned a request made to HO to disclose information in their possession about records held by the Security Service. I decided to discontinue the investigation after the Permanent Secretary had confirmed to me that the decision not to release the information sought had been taken for the purposes of protecting the security of the State. That took the matter outside my jurisdiction (although I had come to the view that the existing wording in the Code did not match what was said to have been the Government's intentions) ...

10. Of the 15 Exemptions listed in Part II of the Code under which a refusal to release information may be justified it is already apparent that several feature relatively frequently and others hardly at all as grounds for refusing a request. Exemption 2, covering internal discussion and advice; Exemption 4, covering law enforcement and legal proceedings; and Exemption 13, covering third parties' commercial confidences, are emerging as areas where refusal decisions are liable to be challenged. It is those Exemptions, coupled with the 'harm' test (the test under which harm to be expected from disclosure should be weighed against the public interest in making information available), which are becoming the issues around which my exchanges with departments turn. There is a large overlap between certain of the Exemptions and thought could usefully be given to a more clear delineation between the areas they cover. I have had cases in which four or more different Exemptions have been put to me as reasons for not releasing the information sought. That strikes me as over-defensive.

11. Despite concerns expressed when and after the Code first came into force, complaints about departments' charges for information or complaints that inaccurate information may have been supplied have not featured strongly, (though both arise in a few of the complaints which I am currently investigating). What remains by far the most surprising feature is that even now, nearly two years after the Code came into force, the public's use of it remains minimal. That might change if more publicity were given to the existence of the Code.

12. What other lessons can be drawn from what is still a very limited number, and therefore not necessarily representative pattern, of complaints? First, departments make no difficulties in providing me with the information they are seeking to withhold. Secondly, my intervention frequently prompts a change of heart. It may be the threat of involving my aid has a similar effect in cases which do not reach me. Thirdly, so far at least I have had no real problems in getting my decisions accepted, even where release has been stoutly resisted by the department in question up to the time when I reach a decision. Some departments, relying on the letter of the Code, are still coy about releasing documents, even though paradoxically it can be more troublesome to them (and to me) to summarise information and release that summary. It would help departments and inquirers if internal documents are presented in a way which separates policy advice from factual matters. What I have found disappointing are signs that, even within departments, knowledge of the Code's obligations can fall of quite rapidly as one moves away from those officials who have specific responsibilities in connection with information release; also there is a tendency in some departments to use every argument that can be mounted, whether legally-based, Code-based or at times simply obstructive, to help justify a past decision that a particular document or piece of information should not be released instead

of reappraising the matter in the light of the Code with an open mind. I have found it time-consuming to have to consider a whole series of different defences, even when many of them prove to have no real foundation. That is one reason why it has taken longer than I would wish to complete my investigations during 1995. The other reason has been the complexity of some of the cases themselves. Some of them have been seen by the complainants and by the departments as test cases. Test cases make slow progress. In that sense they have not been typical information requests.

13. As my monitoring of the Code has developed, I have been encouraged to see signs of a change in the attitude to the release of information which the Code has produced. I have noticed this with reference to the Treasury, the Inland Revenue and DSS. No doubt other departments have also made progress but I have detected in some departments an unawareness of the implications of the existence of the Code and an impermeability to its influence. It may encourage departments generally if I quote from the report of the Ombudsmen in New Zealand for the year ended 30 June 1995. In it they comment on 12 years of the Official Information Act which they describe as an integral part of the public sector operational environment. I commend what they say in the following passage:

> Information management techniques should have regard to the Act by increasing progressively the availability of information while at the same time protecting information which needs to be withheld. There is a need for well structured reports which identify the issue, set out the options for addressing it and the advice offered on the options. This approach will ensure the separation of the factual information from advice and will enable information to which one of the withholding provisions may apply to be identified much more easily. Many reports currently contain an unclear mixture of fact and advice making application of the withholding provisions difficult and time consuming. This often results in frustration for the requester's expectation for the early release of the requested information. There is a need for the public sector to review the structure of reports so that the spirit and intent of the official information legislation can be more effectively implemented.

To my mind those sentiments could well apply in the UK with reference to the current Code.

14. Finally, I record certain other relevant developments. In the spring of 1995 the Cabinet Office produced a report [*Open Government: Code of Practice on Access to Government Information*, 1994 Report – Cabinet Office, March 1995.] on the experience of departments, agencies and other public bodies in implementing the Code during the first nine months of its existence. Although there were some uncertainties over the statistics, what came out from that report was the low number of requests for information under the Code which had been made to departments. In other words, the low level of complaints to me cannot be taken to show that there is a high level of satisfaction with regard to requests for the release of information; it is simply a consequence of the fact that relatively few requests to departments are being made ...

Second Report from the Select Committee on the Parliamentary Commissioner for Administration, HC 84 (1995–96), Open Government

The Effect of the Ombudsman

...

34. The Ombudsman has concluded that the Code 'offers members of the public genuine benefits in terms of obtaining information'. [Second Report of the PCA

Session 1994–95. *Access to Official Information: The First Eight Months*, HC 91, p7.] The Campaign for Freedom of Information also described its preliminary experience of the Code positively, 'it is capable of eliciting information which would previously not have been disclosed. The prospect of an investigation by the Ombudsman does appear to make departments whose objections to disclosure are not well-founded think again. The release of internal guidelines is likely to be valuable to individuals in their dealings with government and to organisations which advise them'. [Evidence p37.] **We conclude that the Code has been an important and valuable contribution to more open government.**

The Immigration and Nationality Exemption

40. The substantive reason for the exemption of this information is the fact that much of the information may be 'sensitive information provided in confidence by individuals and organisations'. There are, however, exemptions already in place to deal with these quite proper concerns – Exemption 12 exempts information whose release would involve 'an unwarranted invasion of privacy' and Exemption 14 concerns 'Information given in confidence'. These two exemptions appear to meet this concern. The OPS add arguments relating to the amount of extra work involved and the explanations and reasons already offered for decisions. The fact that reasons are to be given for decisions has not meant in any other area that the Government has ruled out access to information under the Code. Requests for information might involve extra work. This does not, however, seem an adequate reason for such a blanket exemption. Open government has its costs, one of them being in labour and resources. No doubt such costs are to be kept to a minimum and in certain instances recovered. But to deny to one group access to information on that basis appears to undermine the Government's insistence that access to personal information is an important personal right and that openness can improve standards of administration. One is left with the sense of an exemption included as a result of special pleading from one department and with the suspicion that there is something to hide. The best way to dispel such assumptions would be to remove the Exemption. **We recommend that Exemption 5 'Immigration and Nationality' be removed from Part II of the Code.**

Frankness and Candour

41. Another exempted area on which some initial comment is appropriate is Exemption 2 'Internal discussion and advice' ...

42. We have already stated clearly that this is a legitimate area to exempt from unrestricted access. Constitutional traditions of Cabinet collective responsibility and a non-political civil service might be impaired were deliberation and advice to be released. It should be noted, however, that this is not an absolute exemption. There is a harm test to be applied and, therefore, also a further public interest test. Thus the documents listed are not automatically exempted from release. Moreover, the Exemption deals with subjective matters such as the effect on frankness and candour. This effect may well vary between ministers and civil servants. It depends also, we suspect, on the robustness of the political culture in which FOI operates.

43. One issue to be considered is the availability of factual analysis and research whether conducted internally or commissioned by the Government from outside sources. The Code commits the Government 'to publish the facts and analysis of the facts which the Government considers relevant and important in framing major policy proposals and decisions; such information will normally be made available when policies and decisions are announced'. [Code – Annex, pxlix.] The Guidance adds, 'Departments should plan from the earliest stages of policy preparation which factual and analytical information is to be published when the

policy is announced', [Guidance, p5.] are under an absolute, or 'class', exemption. The Code makes quite clear that they are subject to the same harm and public interest tests as the other categories in this Exemption. Mr Reid said, 'I have detected some discrepancies between what is in the Code and what is in the Guidance on the Code'. [Q 38.] He would operate according to the contents of the Code. **We recommend that the Guidance be amended to make clear that the harm test applies to the first two categories listed in Exemption 2.**

Publicity and the Office of Public Service

50 ... The Open Government 1994 Report gave statistics on the number of Code request so made to Departments. The total to the end of 1994 (a nine month period) was 2600 requests. There are significant doubts as to the reliability of this statistic, to which we shall return. Any revision would only make it lower. The fact therefore remains that the number of requests in comparison with other countries is very low ...

59. We criticise the meagre publicity for government openness. We do so, not merely for the sake of an ironic turn of phrase but because the vigour with which the Government publicises the Code is a key test of the sincerity of its concern for openness. Is open government regarded as an enthusiastic initiative or a grudging concession? The facts to date suggest a Government machine suspicious of its own Code and unwilling to encourage its use. Mr Freeman promised to look again at the level of funding for Code publicity. [Q417.] He agreed that 'I need to look again at the total resources devoted and the mechanisms by which this is communicated, and that will include talking to departmental colleagues'. [Q423.] We welcome this commitment and **we recommend that there be a considerable increase in the funds devoted both at central and departmental level to the publicising of the Code.**

79. There has been criticism,of the Code's refusal to grant a right of access to documents. The Campaign described this as "a potentially overwhelming defect: the opportunities for selective editing are obvious ..."

81. In the Ombudsman's opinion to ask for all the information in a document can usually only be met by the provision of the document. This is in effect to weaken the distinction he Government has attempted to maintain between information and documents and allow an effective right of access to documents, subject to the exemptions of the Code. We welcome this development. There are already a number of statutory rights to documents in the United Kingdom ... Moreover, the refusal of a document can engender unnecessary suspicion. This is exemplified in Case No A 3/94, a Highways Agency case involving 'Failure to supply a third party information relating to a submission to the European Commission'. This complaint disputed the fullness of the information disclosed rather than any refusal of the information itself. The Ombudsman concluded that 'All the information [the complainants] have sought has been disclosed to them ... Since that it is so it is paradoxical that the term of the letter sent to the complainants ... left the impression that information might be being held back. [Eighth Report of the PCA, Session 1994–95, Selected Cases 1995 – *Volume 3: Access to Official Information*, HC 606, paras 8–9.]

82. We also accept the claim that there will always be a possibility, whether by design or oversight, that significant aspects of a document are removed or obscured in any paraphrase sent to a requester ...

83. It is apparent that the Ombudsman considers that, subject to the exemptions and requirements of the Code, requesters should have a right of access to documents. It is also apparent that Government has some sympathy with this view. That being the case, the current wording of the Code and Guidance is

unnecessarily restrictive and negative. **We recommend that the wording of the Code and the accompanying Guidance be amended to assert of right of access to documents, subject to the exemptions of the Code.**

External Review and the Ombudsman

96. Most FOI systems make provision for the external and independent review of a request for information. Such impartial scrutiny is perhaps particularly important in the case of FOI where the release of information can possibly be most inconvenient or embarrassing for a Government.

1. The Tribunal

97. Tribunal hearings are somewhat less adversarial than a court's and the tribunal is not bound by the normal rules of evidence. The Administrative Appeals Tribunal (AAT) is the main external review body for FOI matters at Commonwealth level in Australia ...

2. The Court

98. In FOI regimes established by statute the court will always have a residual role through the possibility of judicial review of administrative decisions or appeal on a point of law (it is worth pointing out that even the United Kingdom's Ombudsman is susceptible to judicial review). In some instances, such as the Ontario legislation, it is made explicit that the courts cannot undertake *de novo* consideration of the case but only judicial review. Courts might also be involved as a means of enforcing the decision of the external review body. This is the case in Canada and Quebec.

99. There are also FOI regimes in which the court is the principle mechanism of external review. This is the case in the United States but is not common in Westminster-style systems. In Canada the court handles all cases claiming exemption on the grounds of commercial confidentiality. The third party concerned can take the matter to court in an attempt to block the release of information. In New South Wales and in South Australia it is possible to appeal either to the Ombudsman or to the District Court. A third type of court involvement is as a final mechanism of appeal after the applicant has gone to an Ombudsman/Information Commissioner for external review.

3. The Ombudsman/Information Commissioner

100. The third model for external review is that of the Ombudsman/Information Commissioner. In New Zealand the Ombudsman was given sole responsibility for the external review of FOI decisions. In Australia the Ombudsman has external review powers but a complainant can also go to the AAT. Ombudsmen usually have power only to make recommendations ...

Comparison of Options for External Review

101. In Australia the AAT was criticised for the inconsistency of its judgements. This was because FOI was only one of the areas covered by the Tribunal and it was very possible for a FOI case to come before someone with little experience of such matters. This was obviously a disadvantage when the AAT was supposed to be establishing a jurisprudence on FOI matters. Critics considered it too formal and adversarial.

102. In New South Wales we heard that the Court process was extremely slow, costly, formal and inexperienced in issues of administrative law. Some to whom we spoke in Australia doubted whether it was helpful for the two parties to a FOI dispute to have to be litigants in either court or tribunal. There seems to be a general conclusion that court are often not best placed to give reasoned and consistent judgements on FOI that they are formal, expensive and slow.

103. The Government has preferred the Ombudsman as the method of external review. Mr Waldegrave, then Chancellor of the Duchy of Lancaster, explained the reasons for this very clearly in his opening remarks at the Open Government Seminar organised by the Campaign for Freedom of Information which took place on 21 October 1993. His words merit quotation at length:

> For whatever reason, the states which have most recently enacted FOI laws in Australia have given the job of enforcement to an Ombudsman or Information Commissioner rather than to the courts. In Queensland the Ombudsman expressed the advantages of this approach in these terms:
>
> > *In summary I see the Ombudsman, because of his experience, currently existing powers, cheapness, flexibility, informality and non-confrontational approach, as ideally placed to serve as the external review mechanism [for FOI]*

104. The Government's arguments in favour of an Ombudsman, as opposed to a court or tribunal, can be summed up as follows:

—there are no costs to the complainant

—the investigation is quicker than a legal process

—the Ombudsman investigation avoids a confrontational and adversarial approach

—there is greater flexibility of approach than in a legal system

—the Ombudsman is already part of this country's political fabric, enjoying the respect of government departments and agencies

—the Ombudsman is able to make general recommendations for procedural improvements.

109. We find the arguments of the Government in favour of an Ombudsman or Information Commissioner to be persuasive, although we recognise that there will be continuing debate about the respective merits of the Ombudsman and Tribunal systems. The more recent FOI regimes established abroad have followed the Ombudsman model, we presume for similar reasons to those outlined by the Government. Moreover, we have an Ombudsman institution which has over its 29 year history achieved an influential, respected and highly effective place in our administrative life. **We recommend that the Ombudsman/Information Commissioner model remain the external review mechanism for the consideration of FOI complaints.**

The Jurisdiction of the Ombudsman

112. Although there are strong arguments in favour of the Ombudsman/Information Commissioner model for external review, there are problems with the Government's strategy of adding on FOI to the Ombudsman's other responsibilities without any change to his powers. The Ombudsman drew the Committee's attention to the current restrictions to jurisdiction, a matter which we discussed in detail in our Report on 'The Powers, Work and Jurisdiction of the Ombudsman' [*First Report from the Select Committee on the PCA*, Session 1993–94, HC 33, paras 45–51.] We there recommended that the 1967 Act be amend so as to specify exclusions rather than inclusions to the Ombudsman's jurisdiction. The Government accepted this recommendation but has yet to act on it. The introduction of FOI responsibilities makes the need for this amendment all the more acute. There are certain departments and agencies, such as the Cabinet Office, currently exempt from the Ombudsman's remit most probably because they had minimal administrative dealings with the public. The likelihood, therefore, of maladministration leading to injustice was very remote. Once Whitehall acquires responsibilities to provide information these

departments are susceptible to requests as any other and should come within the Ombudsman's jurisdiction. There are also Non-Departmental Public Bodies and quangos outside jurisdiction. The Campaign identified the current limits to the Ombudsman's jurisdiction as one of the drawbacks of the Code, 'important areas of the public service sector fall outside the scope of any code'. [Evidence p37: see also Evidence p107.] Among the bodies excluded are the Atomic Energy Authority, the Monopolies and Mergers Commission, the Civil Aviation Authority, the Crown Prosecution Service, the Bank of England, the National Curriculum Council, the Broadcasting Standards Council and Training and Enterprise Councils. As the Campaign put it, 'it is unlikely that anyone devising an open government scheme from first principles would exclude [such bodies] from its scope'. [Evidence p45.]

113. In addition to the restrictions placed on the Ombudsman's jurisdiction by the framing of Schedule 2 to the 1967 Act, there are also restrictions on the subject-matter he can investigate found in Schedule 3. There are similar restrictions within the body of the, Act. The Campaign gave an example of a request which had been foiled by such a restriction. The Campaign had applied to the Lord Chancellor's Department for the report of an interdepartmental working group which had considered the implications of a legal ruling (*Pepper v Hart*) of some constitutional significance. The request was refused by the Department, citing Exemption 2. The Campaign appealed to the Ombudsman who accepted their complaint for investigation. However, 'the investigation was abruptly discontinued after the Lord Chancellor's Department refused to supply the requested report to the Ombudsman. Although the Ombudsman has wide powers of access to departmental information, section 8(4) of the Parliamentary Commissioner Act 1967 expressly denies him the right to obtain information or documents "relating to proceedings of the Cabinet or of any committee of the Cabinet" '. [Evidence p48.] The case raised a serious anomaly – as was pointed out earlier, Cabinet papers are not automatically exempted under the Code from release. A harm test applies. Yet the Ombudsman, the Government's preferred route of external appeal, cannot adjudicate in such cases because he has no access to the relevant documents. This is clearly unacceptable. **We note the recommendation previously made by this Committee in 1978 that 'no harm would be done by allowing the Commissioner access to Cabinet or Cabinet committee papers in the very rare cases where he considered it necessary, except where the Attorney-General certified that such access would itself be "prejudicial to the safety of the State or otherwise contrary to the public interest" '.** [*Fourth Report from the Select Committee on the PCA*, Session 1977–78, HC 615, para 34; see Evidence p107.] **This is also our view and we recommend to this effect.**

114. There is pressing need for the reform of the 1967 Act. Previous recommendations of this Committee, on the appointment and financing of the Ombudsman and on the redrafting of Schedule 2, still await enactment and are all the more urgent in the light of the Ombudsman's new FOI responsibilities. To these reforms we would add the removal of the absolute ban on access to Cabinet papers and a review of the provisions of Schedule 3 to the Act. Mr Freeman accepted that reform of the Ombudsman's jurisdiction was a 'third candidate' for legislation, along with two new proposed statutory rights, and he hoped to make progress. [Q458.] The Government should conduct a thorough review of the current legislation along the lines we have indicated. **We recommend the thorough revision of the 1967 Act to remove the omissions in the Ombudsman's current jurisdiction, to implement the past recommendations of the Committee on the extension of his jurisdiction, and to ensure that the**

Ombudsman has comprehensive and effective powers in his consideration of FOI disputes.

118. In its emphasis on the importance of the enforceability of Ombudsman decisions the Government clearly accepts that the decisions of an independent external adjudicator need at least to be *de facto* binding. This seems at present to be the case. We have stated above our preference for the Ombudsman to remain the external adjudicator in FOI cases. To give him powers to enforce his decisions on all matters investigated, both FOI and other cases of maladministration, would be a departure from the traditional concept of the Ombudsman and grant a general power that no one has asked for. It would upset a constitutional arrangement which over the last 29 years has been remarkable for its effectiveness and success.

119. An alternative approach is that adopted in New Zealand where the Ombudsman has binding powers only on FOI matters, these binding powers only being overruled by a Cabinet order. On other issues he relies on the customary powers of recommendation and persuasion. We consider, however, that there are advantages in the Ombudsman retaining an integrated approach to all complaints. We have previously made clear our determination to ensure that all recommendations of the Ombudsman are complied with. Our judgement is that there is at present no problem with compliance with Ombudsman decisions (albeit such compliance on rare occasions takes time to achieve). As has been pointed out, in FOI cases the Ombudsman has the power of redress himself in that he has access to the disputed information. **We do not, therefore, recommend any change to the Ombudsman's enforcement powers, considering current powers to be adequate. We would, however, make clear that should problems of compliance arise the Committee will have no hesitation in reviewing this conclusion and, if necessary, recommending binding orders.**

A Freedom of Information Act

121. We have already discussed one advantage of a Freedom of Information Act, namely the publicity attending its preparation and passage through Parliament and the consequent public awareness of their access rights. Publicity alone, however, is not enough to justify primary legislation and any shortfall in publicity could be compensated by a determined effort from Government. A more powerful reason given for a statute by those we met when we visited Australia and New Zealand was the need to change governmental culture from one of secrecy to one where openness is accepted and there is a willingness to allow the public to participate to a greater degree in the processes of government ...

122. The Government has made clear that it remains opposed to a single Freedom of Information Act. Mr Freeman explained why:

> First of all, I think the system we have at present, which is a Code plus a number of specific Bills which are now on the statute book ... provides a much more flexible system. We can amend the Code and we can extend the Code far quicker than we can with legislation; we can be more responsive. Secondly, I think our procedure is cheaper and quicker in delivering action. I think to have the Ombudsman pursue individual concerns that remain after the department has considered a request which has not been immediately met provides a free, sensible and very efficient service. Thirdly, and finally, I think that to introduce the courts with a general remit to safeguard the provision of information disclosure and transparency would in some way confuse and diminish the accountability of ministers and departments to Parliament.

123. Often the argument against a Freedom of Information Act is framed in term of the disadvantages that would spring from the involvement of the courts. There are now plenty of examples, cited above, of FOI regimes established by statute with an Ombudsman or Commissioner rather than the court as the external appeal mechanism. There may well be recourse to the courts on a point of law or as a form of judicial review but such recourse need not be common. To introduce a statute with the Ombudsman as the final appeal process (apart from the possibility of judicial review) would seem to meet Mr Freeman's concern to avoid the court and retain the Ombudsman as the form of external review.

124. As to the objection of inflexibility, some might see the ease with which the Code can be amended by Government to be a disadvantage, rather than an advantage, of the current system. There has been no parliamentary approval or sanction given to the contents of the Code. Furthermore, such a Code is extremely vulnerable to slight amendments at the behest of departments finding the Code uncomfortable to live with. Thus the purpose of the Code might be wholly negated. But even taking Mr Freeman's point, if Parliament thought it appropriate it could legislate in such a way that later changes could be made by secondary legislation, which would preserve parliamentary approval whilst providing a fairly speedy mechanism for amendment.

125. The arguments of publicity and effect on civil service culture may not in themselves be enough to justify primary legislation. A more compelling argument, however, follows from the Government's advocacy of the advantages of the Ombudsman. The Government is, however, planning to remove from the Ombudsman's FOI jurisdiction all requests for personal information (which account for a high percentage of requests in other FOI regimes). The suggestion in the White Paper is that such requests come under the remit of the Data Protection Registrar who will thus become our version of a Privacy Commissioner. In New Zealand the Ombudsman previously had responsibility for personal information requests but they have recently been taken over by the Privacy Commissioner. In Australia the Privacy Commissioner defers on personal information matters to the Ombudsman. Other FOI regimes combine an Information and Privacy Commissioner in a single office ... To include personal information within a privacy statute while retaining other access rights in a Code is to put the Ombudsman and open government concerns at a disadvantage. They can always be overruled by privacy considerations which have statutory authority. It is, however, difficult always to judge where privacy considerations end and public interest considerations begin.

126. The Government also proposes that environmental and health and safety information be removed from the Ombudsman's jurisdiction, being placed on a statutory footing, perhaps with a tribunal as an external appeals mechanism. It is hard to reconcile this with the advantages elsewhere cited for an Ombudsman scheme. Neither the Data Protection Registrar nor the envisaged tribunals would be as able to encourage the extension of good practice in open government, which is one of the benefits of the Ombudsman's new role. Moreover, with at least three different access regimes in place the dissemination of clear and consistent precedents for the consideration of access requests will be undermined with such complex issues as candour, harm, confidentiality, public interest being differently interpreted by different authorities. The Ombudsman and the Code would be left with the 'rump' of government information, sometimes obstructed or overruled by the impinging of statutory judgements on their own remit. This system seems complicated and effectively to cancel the very advantages for the Ombudsman's involvement which the Government advanced. We have recently seen in the Health Service a complicated complaints mechanism, established

piecemeal over the years, reformed in favour of a comprehensive and unitary system. It would be unfortunate at this crucial moment to make a similar mistake, only to unravel it in a few years. It is precisely because we accept the arguments advanced by the Government for an Ombudsman supervision that we conclude that there should be a single Freedom of Information Act encompassing all access rights. This would preserve the Ombudsman's important role, maintain the consistency of open government judgements and ensure that the various considerations that inform any decision on access all carry similar statutory weight. It would also give Parliament the opportunity to approve in detail the contents of the Code. We are convinced that on balance the advantage lies in favour of legislation. **We recommend, that the Government introduce a Freedom of Information Act.**

Notes

1   One of the key criticisms of the Code relates to the extensiveness of the list of exemptions and their breadth. Compare, for example, the confidentiality provision in the code (14a) with the equitable doctrine of confidence. The key difference is that under the latter, before the publication of the information concerned can be actionable, the plaintiff must show that disclosure would cause him some kind of detriment.[40] Additionally, the defendant may still defeat the plaintiff's claim if he can show that publication would be in the public interest, a defence which appears to have widened in scope recently,[41] thus affording more recognition to freedom of speech and of information. The Code does not require the department concerned to show that any detriment would flow from the requested disclosure, nor is there any public interest exception. This provision in the Open Government Code thus affords freedom of information less recognition than the existing law. Not only are the exemptions very broad, they are likely to give rise to grave difficulties of interpretation. If a department considers, on its interpretation of one of the exempting provisions, that the exemption applies, although the information seeker and Ombudsman disagree, the department cannot be compelled to release the information. No avenue of challenge to the exclusions from the Code is available.

2   Where an exemption clearly does not apply, a department cannot be forced to disclose the information. If the Ombudsman recommends that a department should reveal information and the department does not accept the recommendation, it may be called upon to justify itself before the Select Committee on the Parliamentary Commissioner for Administration (PCA). However, this will not have the same impact as if the enforcement mechanism for the Code were to be legally binding since the committee cannot compel a department to release information. If the Code is amended, as the Select Committee on the PCA recommends, it may allow access to more sensitive matters. The need for an enforcement mechanism available through the courts rather than the PCA may then become more apparent. See Note 5 below.

---

40   See, for example the well known exposition of the doctrine in *Coco v A N Clark (Engineers) Limited* (1969) RPC 41 at 47. Some doubt has been expressed as to whether detriment is a necessary ingredient of the action (*dicta* of Lord Keith in *A-G v Guardian Newspapers (No 2)* [1988] 3 All ER 545 at 640), but the orthodox view remains that it is.

41   See for example *Lion Laboratories v Evans and Express Newspapers* [1985] QB 526 and *W v Egdell* [1990] Ch 359.

3   The Code is apparently based on the presumption that all useful government information will be released unless there are pressing reasons why it is in the public interest that it should remain secret. This is the general principle on which freedom of information is based. However, in relation to major policy decisions (Part I s3(i)) the Code only relates to information considered 'relevant' by the Government. In countries which have FOI, the usefulness or relevance of documents containing information is determined by the person who seeks it rather than by government ministers or civil servants. Usefulness is not an objective quality but depends on the purposes of the seeker which only he or she can appreciate. Further, the Code promises only to afford release of information as opposed to documents. As pointed out in the memorandum submitted by the Campaign for Freedom of Information, and endorsed in the *Second Report from the Select Committee on the PCA*, the information seeker will be unable to ensure that all significant parts of the document in question have been disclosed. Thus, both these limitations undermine the principle of 'openness' and add to the number of avenues available to a department which is subject to the Code to use in order to avoid complying with it in relation to sensitive information.

4   As the Select Committee on the PCA points out, the Government has made little effort to publicise the Code and this may be one reason for the lack of interest shown in it by individual citizens (see further the *Second Report of the Parliamentary Commissioner for Administration*, HC 91 (1994–95), para 5). Individual citizens who are aware of its existence may be deterred from using the Code due to the charges which have been imposed for providing information, which have in some instances been excessive.[42]

5   Under the Parliamentary Commissioner Act 1967 s5(1) the Ombudsman can take up a complaint only if the citizen has suffered injustice as a result of maladministration; both maladministration and injustice must be shown and there must be a causal link between them. These requirements will be relaxed in relation to complaints relating to the Code of Practice. In relation to the Ombudsman's wider role in combatting maladministrative secrecy – where the Code makes no commitment to release particular information – these requirements must of course be met.

6   The Second Report from the Select Committee concludes that the Ombudsman should not be given binding powers in relation to the FOI aspects of his role but should maintain an integrated approach (para 119). The Committee notes that in New Zealand the Official Information Act is enforced by an Ombudsman but the recommendations on disclosure were made legally binding unless vetoed by an Order in Council within 21 days. This suggests that the traditional, recommendatory approach of the Ombudsman was seen as inappropriate in relation to freedom of information. The Committee rejects this model. However, it is suggested that the Committee gives insufficient consideration to the possibility of providing binding powers for the Ombudsman in relation to the Code. Its grace and favour basis is arguably inappropriate in relation to freedom of

---

42   See further the Citizen's Charter report on the operation of the Code, *Open Government* (1994).

information, although the recommendatory nature of the PCA's role may be appropriate in relation to his main function.

7   Certain matters set out in Schedule 3 of the Parliamentary Commissioner Act 1967 are excluded from the investigation by the PCA. These include extradition and fugitive offenders, the investigation of crime by or on behalf of the Home Office, security of the state, action in matters relating to contractual or commercial activities, court proceedings and personnel matters of the armed forces, teachers, the civil service or police. The Government has always resisted the extension of the Ombudsman system into these areas. The Code at present takes these exclusions into account and goes even further than they do in exempting a number of matters from the access which are within the jurisdiction of the PCA. Future review of the Code may consider narrowing down the exemptions from the Code but the question would remain whether the PCA's supervision should be allowed to extend into areas from which, traditionally, he has been excluded.

8   Criticism can also be made of the use of the MP filter in relation to Code-based complaints (for discussion and criticism of this aspect of the PCA's role in relation to his main function see Part V, Chapter 3). Citizens who need to obtain access to the Ombudsman system may not be able to do so because having contacted an MP with a complaint, the MP may decide not to refer the complaint on to the PCA. Furthermore, MPs may appear to be hampered by their political allegiance in contrast to the Ombudsman who is independent. Although MPs may not know the political allegiance of a constituent who makes a complaint regarding a refusal of access to politically sensitive information, and might in any event be uninfluenced by it, the constituent might assume that the complaint would be more forcibly pursued by an Opposition MP. In some instances MPs may have an interest in seeing that the information is withheld and therefore may face a conflict of interests.

9   It is of particular importance to note that findings and recommendations made by the PCA are not enforceable in law, so that the adverse publicity which would be generated by a refusal to comply with a recommendation is the only sanction for non-compliance. However, research indicates that the influence of the PCA is far greater in practice than his limited formal powers might suggest. Rodney Austin notes that 'Whitehall's record of compliance with the non-binding recommendations of the ombudsman is actually outstanding; on only two occasions have Government departments refused to accept the PCA's findings, and in both cases the PCA's recommendations were [nevertheless] complied with'. However, Austin goes on to note that 'compliance with the PCA's recommendations usually involves the payment of an *ex gratia* compensation, or an apology, or the reconsideration of a prior decision by the correct process. Rarely does it involve reversal on merits of an important policy decision. Governments will fight tenaciously to preserve secrets which matter to them ... there is little ground for optimism that in a crucial case the Government would not choose to defy the PCA ...'.[43]

---

43   'Freedom of Information: The Constitutional Impact', in J Jowell and D Oliver (eds), *The Changing Constitution* (1994), p443.

If the PCA's ability to underpin the Code were enhanced by making the Ombudsman's recommendations enforceable in the courts as in New Zealand, a number of problems would remain. The complainant would not be able to enforce the Code in person. Many avenues of escape from it would still exist due to the limitations of the Ombudsman's jurisdiction. The Ombudsman might eventually find that he was almost unable to cope with the volume of complaints under the Code, and this situation would probably be exacerbated if he was also involved in litigation in attempting to enforce recommendations. Enhancing the role of the Ombudsman along New Zealand lines might amount merely to tinkering with the problems.

10 Should the Code therefore be replaced by a broad statutory right of access to information, enforceable through the courts? The present Government has no plans to enact such legislation. General statutory rights of access to personal information and to health and safety information were proposed in the White Paper. The Select Committee therefore concludes that statutory freedom of information is needed covering both these areas and those which will remain within the Ombudsman's remit with the Ombudsman as the final appeals process in relation to all areas. However, this would mean that rights of access to personal information and to health and safety information would be unenforceable. In a sense this is an argument for 'levelling down'. The fact that rights of access to information within certain areas will be made available and will apparently be enforced by mechanisms external to the Ombudsman might instead lead to the conclusion that access to information generally should be made enforceable either through the courts or by recourse to a tribunal ('levelling up').

11 Many commentators consider that one of the messages of the Scott report published in February 1996 is that the UK needs a Freedom of Information Act. The report tellingly reveals the lack of 'openness' in government: the system appears to accept unquestioningly the need to tell Parliament and the public as little as possible about subjects which are seen as politically sensitive. It would not appear that the voluntary Code can provide a sufficient response to the concerns which the report has aroused. The *Matrix Churchill* affair which led to the Scott Inquiry would not, it seems, have come to the attention of the public but for the refusal of the judge in the *Matrix Churchill* trial to accept that the information covered by the public interest immunity certificates, relating to the change in the policy of selling arms to Iraq, could not be revealed. As the Select Committee on the PCA points out in its Second Report, a freedom of information Act would tend to change the culture of secrecy in Government departments.

12 It is Labour Party policy to enact a freedom of information Act. Assuming that Labour form the next Government and pass such an Act how far would freedom of information be assured? The experience of other countries which have Freedom of Information Acts suggests that the practical problems which already lessen the efficacy of the Code, as the Select Committee pointed out in its Second Report, would also affect the Act, and that some new ones might arise. Assuming that the Act referred to 'documents' as opposed to 'information' the ordinary citizen seeking to use it might find that he or she could not frame the request for information specifically

enough in order to obtain the particular documents needed. The request might be met with the response that one million documents were available touching on the matter in question; the citizen might lack the expert knowledge needed to identify the particular document in question. The ability of the ordinary citizen to use the Act would also be affected by the cost of searches for information and the arrangements for meeting such cost. If the citizen had to meet most of it the likelihood is that many searches would not be initiated or would not be pursued. Government departments might tend to respond to the passing of the Act by moving from formal documentation of meetings and decisions to informal meetings without minutes, thereby evading the Act. (As the Select Committee Report suggested, this may be occurring already under the voluntary Code.)

The exceptions under a future UK Freedom of Information Act, while perhaps likely to be less wide ranging than those under the Code, might nevertheless mean that sensitive matters of great political significance remain undisclosed. In particular, the breadth and uncertainty of the term 'national security' may allow matters which fall only doubtfully within it to remain secret. Had such an Act been in place at the time of the change in policy regarding arms sales to Iraq, the subject of the Scott report, it is likely that information relating to it would not have been disclosed since it could have fallen within the exception clauses. The whole subject of arms sales would probably fall within a national security exception and possibly within other exceptions as well.[44] Thus, while it is suggested that a Freedom of Information Act, enforceable through a tribunal or the courts, would be a clear improvement on the current Code, its role in bringing about 'open government' should not be exaggerated.

Questions

1 What avenues are available to a department which is subject to the Code to use in order to avoid complying with it in relation to embarrassing information?

2 If, contrary to Austin's prediction, above, the PCA's recommendations are invariably complied with, will the proposed system be a satisfactory substitute for a Freedom of Information Act?

3 Now that the Code is in place, could it be argued that the UK citizen is in roughly the same position as regards gaining access to official information as the US citizen?

4 Consider the findings of the Scott report (see Part IV, Chapter 2, pp580–92) and relate them to the case for placing freedom of information on a statutory basis, along US lines.

5 The Scott report revealed weaknesses in the doctrine of ministerial accountability to Parliament. Is the Code on Access to Information likely to remedy the situation?

---

44 See further the Minutes of Evidence before the Public Service Committee, HC 313-1, (1995–96), QQ 66 *et seq.*

PART V

ADMINISTRATIVE LAW[*]

[*] General reading for this part (additional to that referred to in within it): relevant chapters in TRS Allan, *Law Liberty and Justice* (1995); Craig, *Administrative Law*, 3rd edn (1994); Wade and Forsyth, *Administrative Law*, 7th edn (1994); De Smith, *Judicial Review of Administrative Action*, 4th edn (1980); Foulkes, Administrative Law, 7th edn (1995); Supperstone and Goudie (eds), *Judicial Review* (1992); Law Commission, *Judicial Review and Statutory Appeals* (1994), no 226; Sunkin, *Judicial Review in Perspective* (1984); Law Commission, *Remedies in Administrative Law* Cmnd 6407; JUSTICE-All Souls Report on Administrative Law (1988); JUSTICE, *The Citizen and the Administration, Report of the Inquiry into Local Government Business (The Widdecombe Report)* Cmnd 9767; Birkinshaw and Lewis, *When Citizens Complain* (1993); Lewis *et al*, *Complaints Procedures in Local Government* (1988); chapters in A Bradley and ECS Wade, *Constitutional and Administrative Law*, 11th edn (1993); O Hood Phillips, *Constitutional and Administrative Law*, 7th edn (1987); H Barnett, *Constitutional and Administrative Law*, (1995).

CHAPTER 1

JUDICIAL REVIEW: AVAILABILITY, APPLICABILITY, PROCEDURAL EXCLUSIVITY

INTRODUCTION

Judicial review is the procedure whereby the High Court is able, in certain cases, to review the legality of decisions made by a wide variety of bodies which affect the public, ranging from Government ministers exercising prerogative[1] or statutory powers, to the actions of certain powerful self-regulating bodies. In Part V, Chapter 2 the principles which the courts apply in making this assessment are considered. This Chapter is concerned with the principles which determine whether review will be available or whether the complainant must rely on private law remedies; it examines the important procedural implications for the complainant which result from this public/private divide. The issue of who may apply for review is also given thorough discussion, with particular reference to the position of campaigning groups, which are increasingly turning to legal methods as a way of attacking decisions to which they are opposed. Related matters such as the circumstances in which review may be excluded and the relationship with tribunals are also explored.

IS JUDICIAL REVIEW AVAILABLE? THE PUBLIC/PRIVATE DIVIDE

Not all decisions which are disliked by citizens or groups of citizens are reviewable. Three main factors are used to decide whether aggrieved persons can challenge decisions. First, is the body which had made the decision one which it is appropriate to subject to review? Secondly, even if the body is in general terms subject to review, is the particular decision complained of reviewable? Thirdly, does the person who seeks to challenge the decision have standing (*locus standi*) to do so? Finally, what is the procedural relevance for the applicant of answers to the above questions? Does he or she have to proceed in a particular way depending on whether review is available? What will be the consequences for the applicant's case if she uses a procedure deemed inappropriate by the court for challenging the decision in question? These issues will be examined in turn.

What kinds of bodies are susceptible to review?

Not all decision-making bodies will be subject to review. There are clear examples of those which are. Many applications for judicial review are concerned with bodies such as local authorities carrying out statutory duties, which are quite clearly subject to public law remedies. The fact that a body derives its authority from statute will generally be conclusive. Problems tend to

---

1   For discussion specifically of the courts' ability to review the exercise of the prerogative, see Part IV, Chapter 1.

arise in the case of bodies which are created in some other way such as self regulatory bodies set up by persons with a common interest. The classification of one such body was considered by the Court of Appeal in *City Panel on Takeovers and Mergers, ex p Datafin plc* (1987). The Court of Appeal had to consider whether the Panel on Takeovers and Mergers, a self-regulating body without statutory, prerogative or common law powers, was subject to the supervisory jurisdiction of the high court as performing a public function. The Panel operated a Code regulating takeovers and mergers in the City.

City Panel on Takeovers and Mergers, ex p Datafin plc [1987] 2 WLR 699, 702–5, 712–5

> **Sir John Donaldson MR** [quoting from the Introduction to the Code]: The code has not, and does not seek to have, the force of law, but those who wish to take advantage of the facilities of the securities markets in the United Kingdom should conduct themselves in matters relating to take-overs according to the code. Those who do not so conduct themselves cannot expect to enjoy those facilities and may find that they are withheld. ... The provisions of the code fall into two categories. On the one hand, the code enunciates general principles of conduct to be observed in take-over transactions: these general principles are a codification of good standards of commercial behaviour and should have an obvious and universal application. On the other hand, the code lays down a series of rules; some of which are no more than examples of the application of the general principles whilst others are rules of procedure designed to govern specific forms of take-over. Some of the general principles, based as they are upon a concept of equity between one shareholder and another, while readily understandable in the City and by those concerned with the securities markets generally, would not easily lend themselves to legislation. The code is therefore framed in non-technical language and is, primarily as a measure of self-discipline, administered and enforced by the panel, a body representative of those using the securities markets and concerned with the observance of good business standards, rather than the enforcement of the law ...

'Self-regulation' is an emotive term. It is also ambiguous. An individual who voluntarily regulates his life in accordance with stated principles, because he believes that this is morally right and also perhaps, in his own long term interests, or a group of individuals who do so, are practising self-regulation. But it can mean something quite different. It can connote a system whereby a group of people, acting in concert, use their collective power to force themselves and others to comply with a code of conduct of their own devising. This is not necessarily morally wrong or contrary to the public interest, unlawful or even undesirable. But it is very different.

The panel is a self-regulating body in the latter sense. Lacking any authority *de jure*, it exercises immense power *de facto* by devising, promulgating, amending and interpreting the City Code on Take-overs and Mergers, by waiving or modifying the application of the code in particular circumstances, by investigating and reporting upon alleged breaches of the code and by the application or threat of sanctions. These sanctions are no less effective because they are applied indirectly and lack a legally enforceable base. Thus, to quote again from the introduction to the code:

> If there appears to have been a material breach of the code, the executive invites the person concerned to appear before the panel for a hearing. He is informed by letter of the nature of the alleged breach and of the matters which the director general will present. If any other matters are raised he is allowed to ask for an adjournment. If the panel finds that there has been a breach, it may have recourse to private reprimand or public censure or, in a more flagrant case, to further action designed to deprive the offender

temporarily or permanently of his ability to enjoy the facilities of the securities markets. The panel may refer certain aspects of a case to the Department of Trade and Industry, the Stock Exchange or other appropriate body. No reprimand, censure or further action will take place without the person concerned having the opportunity to appeal to the appeal committee of the panel.

The unspoken assumption, which I do not doubt is a reality, is that the Department of Trade and Industry or, as the case may be, the Stock Exchange or other appropriate body would in fact exercise statutory or contractual powers to penalise the transgressors. Thus, for example, rules 22 to 24 of the Rules of the Stock Exchange (1984) provide for the severest penalties, up to and including expulsion, for acts of misconduct and by rule 23.1:

> Acts of misconduct may consist of any of the following ... (g) Any action which has been found by the Panel on Take-overs and Mergers (including where reference has been made to it, the appeal committee of the panel) to have been in breach of the City Code on Take-overs and Mergers. The findings of the panel, subject to any modification by the appeal committee of the panel, shall not be re-opened in proceedings taken under rules 22 to 24.

The principal issue in this appeal, and only issue which may matter in the longer term, is whether this remarkable body is above the law. Its respectability is beyond question [and] ... I am content to assume for the purposes of this appeal that self-regulation is preferable in the public interest. But that said, what is to happen if the panel goes off the rails? Suppose, perish the thought, that it were to use its powers in a way which was manifestly unfair. What then? Mr Alexander submits that the panel would lose the support of public opinion in the financial markets and would be unable to continue to operate. Further or alternatively, Parliament could and would intervene. Maybe, but how long would that take and who in the meantime could or would come to the assistance of those who were being oppressed by such conduct?

A somewhat similar problem confronted the courts in 1922 [in relation to a similar self-regulatory body, the Refined Sugar Association] ... The matter came before a Court of Appeal consisting of Bankes, Atkin and Scrutton LJJ: see *Czarnikow v Roth, Schmidt & Co* [1922] 2 KB 478. The decision has no direct application to the present situation, because the court was concerned with the law of contract, but its approach was ... significant ... Bankes LJ said, at p484:

> To release real and effective control over commercial arbitration is to allow the arbitrator, or the arbitration tribunal, to be a law unto himself, or themselves, to give him or them a free hand to decide according to law or not according to law as he or they think fit, in other words to be outside the law. At present no individual or association is, so far as I am aware, outside the law except a trade union. To put such associations as the Refined Sugar Association in a similar position would in my opinion be against public policy. Unlimited power does not conduce to reasonableness of view or conduct.

Sir John went on to consider the facts of the case and then continued:

> ... No one could have been in the least surprised if the panel had been instituted and operated under the direct authority of statute law, since it operates wholly in the public domain. Its jurisdiction extends throughout the United Kingdom. Its code and rulings apply equally to all who wish to make take-over bids or promote mergers, whether or not they are members of bodies represented on the panel. Its lack of a direct statutory base is a complete anomaly, judged by the experience of other comparable markets world wide.

The issue is thus whether the historic supervisory jurisdiction of the Queen's courts extends to such a body discharging such functions, including some which are quasi-judicial in their nature, as part of such a system. Mr Alexander, for the panel, submits that it does not. He says that this jurisdiction only extends to bodies whose power is derived from legislation or the exercise of the prerogative. Mr Lever for the applicants, submits that this is too narrow a view and that regard has to be had not only to the source of the body's power, but also to whether it operates as an integral part of a system which has a public law character, is supported by public law in that public law sanctions are applied if its edicts are ignored and performs what might be described as public law functions.

In *Criminal Injuries Compensation Board, ex p Lain* [1967] 2 QB 864, 882, Lord Parker CJ, who had unrivalled experience of the prerogative remedies both on the Bench and at the Bar, said that the exact limits of the ancient remedy of *certiorari* had never been and ought not to be specifically defined. I respectfully agree and will not attempt such an exercise. He continued, at p882:

> They have varied from time to time being extended to meet changing conditions. ... The only constant limits throughout were that it was performing a public duty. Private or domestic tribunals have always been outside the scope of *certiorari* since their authority is derived solely from contract, that is, from the agreement of the parties concerned... We have as it seems to me reached the position when the ambit of *certiorari* can be said to cover every case in which a body of persons of a public as opposed to a purely private or domestic character has to determine matters affecting subjects provided always that it has a duty to act judicially. Looked at in this way the board in my judgment comes fairly and squarely within the jurisdiction of this court. It is, as Mr Bridge said, 'a servant of the Crown charged by the Crown, by executive instruction, with the duty of distributing the bounty of the Crown.' It is clearly, therefore, performing public duties.

Diplock LJ, who later was to make administrative law almost his own, said, at pp884–885:

> If new tribunals are established by acts of Government, the supervisory jurisdiction of the High Court extends to them if they possess the essential characteristics upon which the subjection of inferior tribunals to the supervisory control of the High Court is based. What are these characteristics? It is plain on the authorities that the tribunal need not be one whose determinations give rise directly to any legally enforceable right or liability. Its determination may be subject to *certiorari* notwithstanding that it is merely one step in a process which may have the result of altering the legal rights or liabilities of a person to whom it relates. It is not even essential that the determination must have that result, for there may be some subsequent condition to be satisfied before the determination can have any effect upon such legal rights or liabilities. That subsequent condition may be a later determination by another tribunal (see *Postmaster-General, ex p Carmichael* [1928] 1 KB 291; *Boycott, ex p Keasley* [1939] 2 KB 651). Is there any reason in principle why *certiorari* should not lie in respect of a determination, where the subsequent condition which must be satisfied before it can affect any legal rights or liabilities of a person to whom it relates is the exercise in favour of that person of an executive discretion, as distinct from a discretion which is required to be exercised judicially?

Ashworth J said at pp891–892:

> It is a truism to say that the law has to adjust itself to meet changing

circumstances and although a tribunal, constituted as the board, has not been the subject of consideration or decision by this court in relation to an order of *certiorari*, I do not think that this court should shrink from entertaining this application merely because the board had no statutory origin. It cannot be suggested that the board had unlawfully usurped jurisdiction: it acts with lawful authority, albeit such authority is derived from the executive and not from an Act of Parliament. In the past this court has felt itself able to consider the conduct of a minister when he is acting judicially or quasi-judicially and while the present case may involve an extension of relief by way of *certiorari* I should not feel constrained to refuse such relief if the facts warranted it.

The Criminal Injuries Compensation Board, in the form which it then took, was an administrative novelty. Accordingly it would have been impossible to find a precedent for the exercise of the supervisory jurisdiction of the court which fitted the facts. Nevertheless the court not only asserted its jurisdiction, but further asserted that it was a jurisdiction which was adaptable thereafter. This process has since been taken further in *O'Reilly v Mackman* [1983] 2 AC 237, 279 *(per* Lord Diplock) by deleting any requirement that the body should have a duty to act judicially; in *Council of Civil Service Unions v Minister for the Civil Service* [1985] AC 374 by extending it to a person exercising purely prerogative power; and in *Gillick v West Norfolk and Wisbech Area Health Authority* [1986] AC 112, where Lord Fraser of Tullybelton, at p163F and Lord Scarman, at p178F–H expressed the view *obiter* that judicial review would extend to guidance circulars issued by a department of state without any specific authority. In all the reports it is possible to find enumerations of factors giving rise to the jurisdiction, but it is a fatal error to regard the presence of all those factors as essential or as being exclusive of other factors. Possibly the only essential elements are what can be described as a public element, which can take many different forms, and the exclusion from the jurisdiction of bodies whose sole source of power is a consensual submission to its jurisdiction.

In fact, given its novelty, the panel fits surprisingly well into the format which this court had in mind in the *Criminal Injuries Compensation Board* case. It is without doubt performing a public duty and an important one. This is clear from the expressed willingness of the Secretary of State for Trade and Industry to limit legislation in the field of take-overs and mergers and to use the panel as the centrepiece of his regulation of that market. The rights of citizens are indirectly affected by its decisions, some, but by no means all of whom, may in a technical sense be said to have assented to this situation, eg the members of the Stock Exchange. At least in its determination of whether there has been a breach of the code, it has a duty to act judicially and it asserts that its *raison d'être* is to do equity between one shareholder and another. Its source of power is only partly based upon moral persuasion and the assent of institutions and their members, the bottom line being the statutory powers exercised by the Department of Trade and Industry and the Bank of England. In this context, I should be very disappointed if the courts could not recognise the realities of executive power and allow their vision to be clouded by the subtlety and sometimes complexity of the way in which it can be exerted ...

Notes

1   Sir John Donaldson also considered whether the panel could be controlled by the use of private law remedies. Since it was clear that it could not be, he and the other members of the Court of Appeal took the view that the panel was subject to judicial review for the reasons given.

2   It appears clear, at any rate that the fact that the source of a body's power is non-statutory should not be decisive (a finding confirmed by *Royal Life*

Saving Society, ex p Howe etc (1990) COD 499). Two crucial criteria appear to be: first, whether the exercise of the body's power would affect the interests of substantial numbers of the public, particularly their legal rights, and secondly, whether persons aggrieved would have some other, private law remedy, for example in contract. Thus, in *Code of Practice etc, ex p Professional Counselling Aids* (1990),[2] the fact that the Code of Practice Committee played a part in a system that operated in the public interest rendered it subject to review, while in *Football Association of Wales, ex p Flint Town United Football Club* (1991),[3] the existence of a contractual relationship between the Club and the Association was decisive in the court's decision that judicial review would be inappropriate.

3   However, it appears that a body can be one which affects the interests of the public and one against which no contractual remedy can be sought and yet remains not subject to review.

Football Association Ltd, ex p Football League Ltd [1993] 2 All ER 833, 848–9

Rose J: I have crossed a great deal of ground in order to reach what, on the authorities, is the clear and inescapable conclusion for me that the FA is not a body susceptible to judicial review either in general or, more particularly, at the instigation of the League, with whom it is contractually bound. Despite its virtually monopolistic powers and the importance of its decisions to many members of the public who are not contractually bound to it, it is, in my judgment, a domestic body whose powers arise from and duties exist in private law only. I find no sign of underpinning directly or indirectly by any organ or agency of the state or any potential government interest, as Simon Brown J put it in [*Chief Rabbi of the United Hebrew Congregations of GB and the Commonwealth, ex p Wachmann* [1993] 2 All ER 249, [1992] 1 WLR 1306], nor is there any evidence to suggest that if the FA did not exist the state would intervene to create a public body to perform its functions.'

Notes

1   Considering the finding in the *Datafin* decision, that to be reviewable, a body needs to have 'a public element' or be under some 'public duty' S Fredman and G S Morris comment,[4] 'even a cursory look at this formulation demonstrates that the dividing line between public and private remains elusive. What, after all is a 'public element' or 'public duty?' They go on to note that the test developed in later cases (and deployed by Rose J above) that the body 'should be governmental in nature so that if it did not exist the Government would be likely to step in and create a replacement' is 'singularly difficult to apply with any degree of certainty' because of the 'lack of consensus as to the proper functions of government'.[5] Fredman and Morris are arguably understating the matter here: there is not so much a

---

2   *The Times,* 7 November 1990.

3   COD 44.

4   'The Costs of Exclusivity: Public and Private Re-examined' (1994) PL 69. The article is quoted below, see pp701–2, 709–11.

5   *Op cit,* p72.

'lack of consensus' as to the proper functions of Government, as a heated political debate. As Lord Woolf has recently noted (speaking extra-judicially):[6] 'Increasingly services which, at one time, were regarded as an essential part of Government are being performed by private bodies'.[7] This growth in the 'contracted-out state' has caused intense controversy. In the same article, Lord Woolf impliedly disapproves the 'governmental' test.[8]

2   The lack of clarity which pervades this area can be seen in *Jockey Club, ex p Aga Khan* (1993) in which the Jockey Club was found not to be susceptible to review.

Jockey Club, ex p Aga Khan [1993] 2 All ER 853, 866–87

Lord Justice Bingham MR: ... I have little hesitation in accepting the applicant's contention that the Jockey Club effectively regulates a significant national activity, exercising powers which affect the public and are exercised in the interest of the public. I am willing to accept that if the Jockey Club did not regulate this activity the Government would probably be driven to create a public body to do so.

But the Jockey Club is not in its origin, its history, its constitution or (least of all) its membership a public body. While the grant of a royal charter was no doubt a mark of official approval, this did not in any way alter its essential nature, functions or standing. Statute provides for its representation on the Horseracing Betting Levy Board, no doubt as a body with an obvious interest in racing, but it has otherwise escaped mention in the statute book. It has not been woven into any system of governmental control of horse racing, perhaps because it has itself controlled horse racing so successfully that there has been no need for any such governmental system and such does not therefore exist. This has the result that while the Jockey Club's powers may be described as, in many ways, public they are in no sense governmental.

I would accept that those who agree to be bound by the Rules of Racing have no effective alternative to doing so if they want to take part in racing in this country. It also seems likely to me that if, instead of Rules of Racing administered by the Jockey Club, there were a statutory code administered by a public body, the rights and obligations conferred and imposed by the code would probably approximate to those conferred and imposed by the Rules of Racing. But this does not, as it seems to me, alter the fact, however anomalous it may be, that the powers which the Jockey Club exercises over those who (like the applicant) agree to be bound by the Rules of Racing derive from the agreement of the parties and give rise to private rights on which effective action for a declaration, an injunction and damages can be based without resort to judicial review. It would in my opinion be contrary to sound and long-standing principle to extend the remedy of judicial review to such a case.

Question

Lord Justice Bingham finds (a) that the Jockey Club exercises powers 'which affect the public and are exercised in the interests of the public'; (b) that it is in practice impossible to take part in racing in Britain unless one accepts the jurisdiction of the club; (c) that the Government would have to do the job the Club does now if the Club did not; but that (d) whilst the Club's powers are

---

6   '*Droit Public* – English Style' (1995), PL 57.

7   *Ibid*, at p63.

8   He suggests a test for determining the public/private divide which leaves the issue entirely out of the account; *ibid* at p64.

'public' they are not 'governmental'. He therefore concludes that it is not subject to public law. Can any coherent set of factors to determine the private/public issue be derived from these findings?

Notes

1   One clear point which appears to emerge from the decision is Bingham LJ's finding that access to private rights will preclude the availability of public law remedies. This point has not met with universal acclaim:

> The reliance on contract as the key to the availability or lack of availability of the Order 53 procedure in relation to regulatory bodies has some serious drawbacks. First, it distinguishes somewhat arbitrarily between those non-statutory bodies whose source of power is derived from contract and those whose power is not so derived. However, it is difficult to see why such bodies should be public while others with regulatory functions of similar significance should be private. Secondly, and more importantly, the equation of contract with private law is based upon the misguided belief in the voluntary, consensual nature of contract, obscuring the reality of underlying power relations. ...

> The second context in which contract has been deployed in order to prevent the use of the Order 53 procedure relates to bodies who, despite having an avowedly public character, have exercised their powers through the medium of contract. [This] equation of contract with private law reveals a further problem; it implies that even avowedly public bodies have 'private lives' which are beyond the scrutiny of the courts in their public-law jurisdiction.[9]

2   Lord Woolf[10] has suggested that the existence of a private law remedy should not by itself exclude judicial review; rather the test should be whether the issue in respect of which review is sought is '*satisfactorily protected* by private law' (emphasis added). This seems a more sensible test as it would take into account the cases in which a contract may be theoretically present but in which it would be either impractical or ineffective to sue on it.

3   In what follows, David Pannick considers the compatibility of the contract-private law equation with the *Datafin* decision and its application in other cases before going on to consider the coherence of this area of law in general.

David Pannick, 'Who is Subject to Judicial Review and in Respect of What?' (1992) *Public Law* 1, 2–6

That public law does not regulate the decisions of bodies with which the applicant has voluntarily entered into a consensual relationship is well established. As Lord Parker CJ explained in 1967, 'private or domestic tribunals have always been outside the scope of *certiorari* since their authority is derived solely from contract, that is, from the agreement of the parties concerned' [*ex p Lain* [1967] 2 QB 86 at 882B–C]. Some of the recent cases have badly misunderstood this principle.

In the first *Jockey Club* case, *ex p Massingberd-Mundy* Neill LJ concluded that although many aspects of the work of the Jockey Club were 'in the public domain' and many of its functions were 'at least in part public or quasi-public functions,' still it was not subject to judicial review because the authorities established that a consensual submission to jurisdiction was inconsistent with judicial review. Here, 'owners,

---

9   Fredman and Morris, *op cit*, pp74 and 76.
10   *Op cit*, p64.

trainers and riders of horses as well as executives of the various racecourses have a contractual relationship with the Jockey Club and have agreed to be bound by the Rules of Racing' [(1990) 2 Admin LR 609 at 626B]. He cited two cases, *Law v National Greyhound Racing Club Ltd* [[1983] 1 WLR 1302 (CA)] and *Calvin v Carr* [[1980] AC 674 PC] as compelling this conclusion...

The *Calvin* case is irrelevant for present purposes: it was not concerned with the scope of the procedure of application for judicial review, but the content of the principles of natural justice. The decision in the *Law* case was based on the fact that the powers of the National Greyhound Racing Club were not said to be other than contractual: there was no suggestion that they were monopolistic powers with which the complainant had no choice but to comply. No doubt this was because *Law* was decided before *Datafin* and therefore did not focus on the new criteria for the application of judicial review. Since *Datafin* the issue for public lawyers is not whether one can identify a private law agreement in order to exclude judicial review, but whether the respondent body (as the Divisional Court acknowledged was the case in relation to the Jockey Club) has such a *de facto* monopoly over an important area of public life that an individual has no effective choice but to comply with their rules, regulations and decisions in order to operate in that area. In *Datafin* itself, the powers of the Panel were, in part, consensual – in the sense that companies choose to comply. But the reality is that there is no effective choice: either you comply, or you do not do business in the City. Indeed, self-regulation (that is, the exercise of powers without statutory functions) depends on at least a degree of voluntary submission by those who are regulated.

For these reasons, in the second *Jockey Club* case, *ex p RAM Racecourses Ltd*, Simon Brown J expressed his disagreement with the approach taken by the Divisional Court in *ex p Massingberd-Mundy* on the issue of consensual submission. As he explained, the issue in relation to a body with monopolistic powers is not whether the applicant has consented to the jurisdiction of the body – he will have no choice – but whether those powers are sufficiently public to attract the interest of judicial review (as he concluded was the case in relation to at least some types of decisions made by the Jockey Club) [(1990) 3 Admin LR 265 at 292–4, *ibid* at 286–91]. The other judge hearing *ex p RAM Racecourses Ltd*, in the Divisional Court, Stuart-Smith LJ, recognised the force of the criticisms of *ex p Massingberd-Mundy*. Apart from that authority, he would have held that the decisions of the Jockey Club were amenable to judicial review, but he was not prepared to depart from it.

In the third *Jockey Club* case, *ex p the Aga Khan* [31 July 1991], Woolf LJ (giving the judgment of the Divisional Court) accepted that the Jockey Club has monopoly powers such that 'if a person wishes to take part in any aspect of racing, then they have no alternative but to accept the jurisdiction of the Jockey Club' and that the manner in which these powers are exercised is a matter of 'public interest and public importance'. However, in the light of the earlier two cases he concluded that at the level of the Divisional Court, any application for judicial review of the Jockey Club had to be dismissed.

The Court of Appeal will have to sort out this confusion. It is to be hoped that they will echo the views of Simon Brown J in *ex p RAM Racecourses Ltd* and in *ex p Wachmann* [(1991) COD, 309]. In the latter case, he rightly rejected an argument that the Chief Rabbi is not subject to judicial review because 'no one is compelled to be a Jew, or Orthodox Jew, still less a Rabbi'. As he explained, 'an Orthodox Rabbi is pursuing a vocation and has no choice but to accept the Chief Rabbi's disciplinary decisions' [3 July 1991; transcript at p8B–D]. Judicial review should not be excluded for reasons of 'consensual submission' where the relevant body has *de facto* monopolistic powers which the complainant has no practical choice but to acknowledge, whether by contract or otherwise, if he wishes to participate in the area of life governed by the body in question. The crucial issue is whether such a body (not empowered by statute, statutory instrument or the prerogative) has *de facto* monopolistic powers such as to constitute it a public body susceptible to judicial review.

Public element

The requirement that there must be a 'public element' before the decisions are subject to judicial review is not satisfied simply because the public is interested in the result. As Simon Brown J explained in *ex p Wachmann,* [transcript at p11D] 'whether or no a decision has public law consequences must be determined otherwise than by reference to the seriousness of its impact upon those affected.'

The courts have adopted a simple test of 'public element' in relation to a body which does not act pursuant to powers conferred by statute, statutory instrument or the prerogative: but for the existence of that body, would the state be likely to have enacted legislation to confer statutory powers on a comparable body to regulate the area of life over which the body has *de facto* control? Glidewell LJ (for the Divisional Court) concluded that, but for the existence of the Advertising Standards Authority, its functions 'would no doubt be exercised by the Director General of Fair Trading' [*ex p Insurance Service plc* (1990) 2 Admin LR 77 at 86C]. By contrast, there was, in the judgment of Rose J, no 'evidence to suggest that if the Football Association did not exist the State would intervene to create a public body to perform its functions' [*ex p Football League Ltd*, 31 July 1991; transcript at p29C–D]. Simon Brown J concluded that the decisions of the Chief Rabbi were not subject to judicial review because 'his functions are essentially intimate, spiritual and religious, functions which the Government could not and would not seek to discharge in his place were he to abdicate his regulatory responsibility' [transcript at pp10G–11A]. There are, in this respect, close analogies between the scope of judicial review and the test adopted by the European Court of Justice for deciding whether a respondent is a state body in respect of which a directive should have direct effect: the Community law principle applies to

> a body, whatever its legal form, which has been made responsible, pursuant to a measure adopted by the state, for providing a public service under the control of the state and has for that purpose special powers beyond those which result from the normal rules applicable in relations between individuals... [*Foster v British Cas plc* (1991) 1 QB 405 at 427G–H (ECJ)].

The question with which the Court of Appeal and the House of Lords will eventually have to grapple is: why should the jurisdiction of the court depend on a hypothesis as to what Parliament would do but for the existence of the body in question? Assuming that the powers of that body are monopolistic, such that they effectively govern an area of life in the United Kingdom, due either to a positive decision by Parliament or the absence of parliamentary intervention, it is difficult to see why public law should not impose on the substance and procedure of decision-making in that context certain minimum standards and ask, as did Lord Donaldson MR for the Court of Appeal in *Panel on Take-overs and Mergers, ex p Guinness plc*, 'whether something has gone wrong of a nature and degree which required the intervention of the court...' [[1990] 1 QB 146 at 178G–H].

There are, as Simon Brown J recognised in *ex p RAM Racecourses*, 'many different types of institution – often of an increasingly monopolistic nature – ruling various aspects of our national life. Some flexibility of response by the Courts is surely required' [at p294B]. The extent to which public law will intervene will continue to depend on the nature and scope of those powers, any public policy considerations and the type of decision which is impugned.

Note

Lord Woolf has proposed a more flexible approach to this area.[11]

> ... the Law Commission should make two principles clear. The first is that judicial review is a remedy of last resort, and it should not be available if there is some suitable alternative remedy. The second principle is subject to the first principle. It is that a body should be subject to judicial review if it exercises authority over another person or body in such a manner as to cause material prejudice to that person or body and, if judicial review were available, that person or body could show the decision-maker had acted unlawfully.

> This would be a *wide* jurisdiction. It would mean that the fact that the decision-making body was exercising its powers in the world of sport or within a religious community, would not necessarily exclude the jurisdiction of the court. The jurisdiction would, however, be subject to the discretion of the court as to whether a remedy should be withheld. It would have the great benefit that if, for example, a sportsman or a rabbi were unlawfully deprived from earning his living in his chosen profession, he might have a remedy in judicial review if he was not entitled to any other form of redress. If he had another remedy, there would be no need for judicial review. If he has no other remedy, he should be able to obtain justice on judicial review. Why should a policeman be in a better position than a sportsman or a minister of religion?

What kinds of decisions are subject to review?

Even where it is clear that the decision-making body may be described as a public body, particular decisions made by it may not be susceptible to judicial review if they are not seen to have a clear 'public' element. This issue was considered in *East Berkshire Health Authority, ex p Walsh* (1985) in relation to dismissal of an employee of the Health Authority.

East Berkshire Authority, ex p Walsh [1985] QB 152, 161–2, 164–6

> **Sir John Donaldson MR:** I now return to the main issue, namely whether the applicant's complaints give rise to any right to judicial review. They all relate to his employment by the health authority and the purported termination of his employment and of his contract of employment. Essentially they fall into two distinct categories. The first relates to Miss Cooper's power to act on behalf of the authority in dismissing him. The second relates to the extent to which there was any departure from the rules of natural justice in the procedures which led up to that dismissal. Both fall well within the jurisdiction of an industrial tribunal. The first goes to whether or not the applicant was dismissed at all within the meaning of section 55 of the Employment Protection (Consolidation) Act 1978. The second goes to whether the dismissal, if such there was, was unfair. Furthermore, both are issues which not uncommonly arise when the employer is a company or individual, as contrasted with a statutory authority. However, this only goes to the exercise of the court's discretion, whether or not to give leave to apply for and whether or not to grant judicial review. As the authority seek to have the proceedings dismissed in limine, if they are to succeed they can only do so on the basis that, accepting all the applicant's complaints as valid, the remedy of judicial review is nevertheless wholly inappropriate and the continuance of the application for judicial review would involve a misuse – the term 'abuse' has offensive overtones – of the procedure of the court under RSC, Ord 53.

---

11 'Judicial Review: A Possible Programme of Reform' (1992) PL 221, at 235.

The remedy of judicial review is only available where an issue of 'public law' is involved, but, as Lord Wilberforce pointed out in *Davy v Spelthorne Borough Council* [1984] AC 262, 276, the expressions 'public law' and 'private law' are recent immigrants and, whilst convenient for descriptive purposes, must be used with caution, since English law traditionally fastens not so much upon principles as upon remedies. On the other hand, to concentrate on remedies would in the present context involve a degree of circularity or levitation by traction applied to shoe-strings, since the remedy of *certiorari* might well be available if the health authority is in breach of a 'public law' obligation, but would not be if it is only in breach of a 'private law' obligation ... I have therefore to consider whether and to what extent the applicant's complaints involve an element of public law sufficient to attract public law remedies, whether in the form of *certiorari* or a declaration. That he had the benefit of the general employment legislation is clear, but it was not contended that this was sufficient to attract administrative law remedies. What is relied upon are statutory restrictions upon the freedom of the authority to employ senior and other nursing officers on what terms it thought fit. This restriction is contained in the National Health Service (Remuneration and Conditions of Service) Regulations 1974 (SI 1974 No 296), which provides by regulation 3(2):

> Where conditions of service, other than conditions with respect to remuneration, of any class of officers have been the subject of negotiations by a negotiating body and have been approved by the Secretary of State after considering the result of those negotiations, the conditions of service of any officer belonging to that class shall include the conditions so approved.

The conditions of service of, *inter alios*, senior nursing officers were the subject of negotiations by a negotiating body, namely the Whitley Council for the Health Service (Great Britain) and the resulting agreement was approved by the Secretary of State. It follows, as I think, that if the applicant's conditions of service had differed from those approved conditions, he would have had an administrative law remedy by way of judicial review enabling him to require the authority to amend the terms of service contained in his contract of employment. But that is not the position. His notification of employment dated 12 May 1975, which is a memorandum of his contract of employment, expressly adopted the Whitley Council agreement on conditions of service.

When analysed, the applicant's complaint is different. It is that *under* those conditions of service Miss Cooper had no right to dismiss him and that *under* those conditions he was entitled to a bundle of rights which can be collectively classified as 'natural justice'. Thus he says, and I have to assume for present purposes that he is correct, that under section XXXIV of the Whitley Council's agreement on conditions of service, his position as a senior nursing officer is such that his employment can only be terminated by a decision of the full employing authority and that this power of dismissal cannot be delegated to any officer or committee of officers. I do not think that he relies upon any express provision of those conditions when claiming the right to natural justice, but if he has such a right, apart from the wider right not to be unfairly dismissed which includes the right to natural justice, it clearly arises out of those conditions and is implicit in them.

The ordinary employer is free to act in breach of his contracts of employment and if he does so his employee will acquire certain private law rights and remedies in damages for wrongful dismissal, compensation for unfair dismissal, an order for reinstatement or re-engagement and so on. Parliament can underpin the position of public authority employees by directly restricting the freedom of the public authority to dismiss, thus giving the employee 'public law' rights and at least making him a potential candidate for administrative law remedies. Alternatively it can require the authority to contract with its employees on specified terms with a view to the employee acquiring 'private law' rights under the terms of the contract of employment. If the authority fails or refuses to thus create 'private law' rights for the employee, the employee will have 'public law' rights to compel compliance, the remedy being *mandamus* requiring the authority so to contract or a declaration that the employee has those rights. If, however, the authority gives the employee the required contractual protection, a breach of that contract is not a matter of 'public law' and gives rise to no administrative law remedies.

At one stage in the argument, I did wonder whether the issuing of the 'personal policy' document whereby the authority authorised district nursing officers, such as Miss Cooper, to 'hire and fire' senior nursing officers, such as the applicant, could be regarded as a breach of the 'public law' duty of the authority but came to the conclusion that it could not. If the applicant is right in his claim to be dismissible only by the authority itself, the issuing of this document was an anticipatory breach of his contract of employment which became a final breach when Miss Cooper acted on it. I say this because the authority was not purporting to vary his conditions of service, but only to act consistently with them. In any event, no relief was claimed by the applicant in respect of the issuing to this policy document.

I therefore conclude that there is no 'public law' element in the applicant's complaints which could give rise to any entitlement to administrative law remedies. I confess that I am not sorry to have been led to this conclusion, since a contrary conclusion would have enabled *all* National Health Service employees to whom the Whitley Council agreement on conditions of service apply to seek judicial review. Whilst it is true that the judge seems to have thought that this right would be confined to senior employees, I see no grounds for any such restriction in principle. The most that can be said is that only senior employees could complain of having been dismissed in the exercise of delegated authority, because it is only senior employees who are protected from such dismissal. *All* employees would, however, have other rights based upon the fact that Parliament had intervened to specify and, on this view, protect those conditions of service as a matter of 'public law'.

In my judgment, this is not therefore a case for judicial review.

Question

Would it be unduly cynical to suggest that, in reality, the fact that this decision prevented thousands of NHS employees from being able to apply for judicial review was not a fortunate by-product of the judge's decision but one of the reasons for it?

Notes

1   The decision was therefore that a failure to grant the applicant the private law rights flowing from a given set of contractual conditions ordered by Parliament[12] to be given to the applicant would be a public law matter, but a breach of the conditions once granted was a private matter only. The issuing of the 'personal policy' document (which may have wrongfully delegated powers to dismiss) was seen as only an anticipatory (private law) breach of contract. Such an improper delegation of power (if such it was) is clearly distinguishable from the individual decision to sack one employee and in terms of simplicity and efficiency, allowing the legality of that decision to be adjudicated upon when it happened instead of forcing all employees sacked by the delegatee to then bring individual actions on the point would seem

---

12   Or, presumably, any other body (eg a minister) exercising statutory or prerogative powers.

preferable. For further comment on public employee cases see Lord Woolf (1991) 107 LQR 298.

2   In the following case it was the gravity of the effects of the complained-of decision on the applicant which was decisive, rather than more technical issues arising from the 'public/private' divide. The applicant was seeking judicial review of the magistrates' decision to commit him for full trial, on the basis that they had erred in law in allowing certain key evidence to be admitted.

Neill v North Antrim Magistrates' Court and another [1992] 4 All ER 846, 856, 857

Lord Mustill: That committal proceedings are in principle susceptible to judicial review is beyond doubt, and the fact that *certiorari* will lie in cases of procedural irregularity in such proceedings is I believe also quite clear ... The question is, however, whether the reception of inadmissible evidence will found this remedy. As with many problems of judicial review, this question does not admit of an outright answer. Everything depends on the circumstances.

Lord Mustill then went on to find that magistrates were entitled to make a finding on the admissibility of evidence. He went on (at p857) ...

It is however one thing to hold that it is for the magistrates to rule on admissibility, if invited to do so, so that a decision on the issue must in principle be reviewable, and quite another to say that the grant of relief should follow as a matter of course. I wholly share the sentiments of those who, over the years, have exclaimed in dismay at the vision of the streams of applications by persons committed for trial seeking to put off the evil day by drawing attention to supposed errors in the application at the committal stage of the highly technical rules of criminal evidence. It is only in the case of a really substantial error leading to a demonstrable injustice that the judge in the Divisional Court should contemplate the granting of leave to move.

I believe, however, that the House is faced in the present appeal with just such a situation. I have pointed out the consequences of the resident magistrate's decision to allow the statements to be read. These went beyond the mere receipt of inadmissible evidence, for the appellant lost the opportunity to have the eyewitnesses' mental state, or their substantive testimony, or both, subjected to scrutiny. True it is, as counsel reminded us in argument, that if attempts had been made to secure the attendance of the boys by a witness summons the prosecution might very well have decided to withdraw the boys' statements, as they were entitled to (see *Epping and Harlow Justices, ex p Massaro* [1973] 1 All ER 1011, [1973] QB 433), and could have sought a committal on the remainder of the evidence. What would then have happened we do not know. The appellant might still have called for the attendance of the boys under art 34(2), which unlike its English analogue is not confined to the production in court of witnesses whose statements have been tendered in evidence. And, if in the event there had been no evidence in any form from the boys, it is impossible now to say whether the resident magistrate would have chosen to commit.

Finally, l must refer to *Barnet Justices, ex p Wood* [1992] Crim LR 312, a case brought to light after the conclusion of the argument which is very close to the present. In the course of an old-style committal the prosecution tendered the statement of a medical expert under r 120 of the Magistrates' Courts Rules 1981. The accused objected, at a very late stage of the hearing, to the admission of the statement, and invited the court to adjourn under r 7c(3) so as to enable the expert to be called. The court refused, no doubt influenced by the lateness of the application. On an application to quash the committal counsel for the prosecution conceded that the application must succeed, because once the objection to the statement had been made it ceased to be admissible and only the oral evidence of the expert could be employed. The Divisional Court held that the concession was rightly made. Since the case proceeded on a concession it has no direct authority and in any event was concerned with a rule that is not in issue here. But I draw reassurance from the fact that the very experienced members of the court considered that the committal should be quashed because there had been 'admitted to evidence a vital statement when what ought to have happened, according to law, was the calling of the maker of that statement, so that he could give oral evidence and be cross-examined on it'.

Accordingly, in the special circumstances of this case I consider that the admission of inadmissible evidence was not a harmless technical error, but was an irregularity which had substantial adverse consequences for the appellant, and that accordingly the court should have intervened to quash the committal.

Note

It appears that certain areas of jurisdiction of bodies generally subject to review may also be excluded, either because of a particular line of slightly eccentric authorities or because the area of law is seen as being outside the ordinary law of the land. Professor Wade reviews a case in this mould.

HWR Wade, 'Visitors and Errors of Law' (1993) 109 *Law Quarterly Review* 155, 156–9

Mr Page, a lecturer in philosophy in the University of Hull, was dismissed for redundancy at three months' notice. His letter of appointment had stated that the appointment was terminable by either party at three months' notice, but he claimed protection from the statutes of the university which provided that university officers 'may be removed by the Council for good cause' and that 'subject to the terms of his appointment no member of the teaching [staff] shall be removed from office save upon the grounds specified ... ,' which were not applicable to Mr Page. On a petition to the Queen as visitor the Lord President of the Council, advised by Lord Jauncey of Tullichettle, held that the dismissal was lawful. That decision was quashed by the Divisional Court (Taylor LJ and Rougier J) who held first that the visitor's decision was reviewable for error of law and secondly that it must be quashed as erroneous. The Court of Appeal (Lord Donaldson of Lymington MR, Staughton and Farquharson LJJ) affirmed on the first point but reversed on the second. Finally the House of Lords, by a three to two majority, held that all the judges below had been wrong on the one point on which they had been unanimous and that a visitor's determination on a point of law was not amenable to judicial review. The minority view was that judicial review was available but that the visitor's decision was right. All five opinions thus upheld Mr Page's dismissal.

In a lucid account of visitatorial jurisdiction Lord Browne-Wilkinson, with whom Lord Keith of Kinkel and Lord Griffiths agreed, emphasised the consistent judicial policy over 300 years in refusing to review visitors' decisions on their merits. *Mandamus* would lie to compel a visitor to adjudicate and prohibition would restrain him from acting outside his jurisdiction, but *certiorari* would never issue for mere error. The reason was, as explained by Lord Holt CJ in his classic judgment in *Philips v Bury* (1694) Holt KB 715, that an eleemosynary corporation is governed by a system of private law which is not of 'the common known laws of the kingdom' but is prescribed by the founder. This hallowed argument, now reaffirmed on the highest authority, is not however very convincing, for there would seem to be no reason why the courts should not interpret university and college charters and statutes as readily as they interpret private wills, settlements and contracts. Once that shibboleth is discarded, there arises the question which motivated Lord Slynn's dissent, in which

Lord Mustill joined: why should not the exemption of visitors, however old and traditional, be jettisoned, as so much else has been jettisoned, in the new era of judicial review which began some 40 years ago? Is it right to preserve what Lord Holt CJ called 'an arbitrary sentence,' neither appealable or reviewable, when appeal and review are intensively imposed upon other inferior jurisdictions? Even though, as Lord Griffiths said, 'the chances are that the visitor probably will get it right,' academics whose livelihood may depend upon what Lord Slynn called 'a clearly recognisable employment law question' may lay fair claim to the same sort of protection as is afforded so liberally to commercial employees. Since the majority speeches allow that visitors' decisions are reviewable for abuse of power and violation of natural justice, it is not obvious why they should not be brought within the full ambit of the *Anisminic* revolution in the gospel according to Lord Diplock.

According to that gospel, proclaimed first in a lecture and then in the two important judgments ..., all error of law by an inferior tribunal or court amounts to excess of jurisdiction, thus making redundant both the old distinction between jurisdictional and non-jurisdictional error of law and also the doctrine of error of law on the face of the record ... The weaker form of statutory protection, that a determination shall be 'final and conclusive,' has generally been held to bar any appeal but not to bar judicial review: *Medical Appeal Tribunal, ex p Gilmore* [1957] 1 QB 574. Without mentioning that authority, and although no such clause was in issue, the House of Lords now holds that a 'final and conclusive' clause will bar judicial review, at least in cases where Parliament may be thought to have intended to confer power to make final decisions. But whether this ruling is confined to inferior courts, as opposed to tribunals, is not entirely clear.

In the same context it is curious that the majority of the House of Lords claim to be upholding the dissenting judgment of Geoffrey Lane LJ in *Pearlman v Keepers and Governors of Harrow School* [1979] QB 56, a judgment notable for its sound logic but notable also for its incompatibility with what the House of Lords have now decided. It is true that in that case there was a 'final and conclusive' clause but it was conceded that (as mentioned above) such a clause would not protect a decision made in excess of jurisdiction. Lord Denning MR held that all error of law was excess of jurisdiction and that the county court judge's error was therefore reviewable. Geoffrey Lane LJ held that the judge kept within his jurisdiction and that therefore his error was not reviewable. Geoffrey Lane LJ was applying exactly the old jurisdictional distinction which the House of Lords purported to apply in *Anisminic* but which Lord Diplock later converted to his own use. The House of Lords have now sided with Lord Denning and Lord Diplock and they cannot have it both ways.

Procedural implications of the public/private divide

Applications for judicial review follow a procedure which differs in many important respects from the ordinary civil procedure. Applications are governed by Order 53 of the Rules of the Supreme Court, set out below.

Supreme Court Act 1981, s31

Application for judicial review

31.–(1) An application to the High Court for one or more of the following forms of relief, namely—

(a) an order of *mandamus*, prohibition or *certiorari*;

(b) a declaration or injunction under subsection (2); or

(c) an injunction under section 30 restraining a person not entitled to do so from acting in an office to which that section applies, shall be made in accordance with rules of court by a procedure to be known as an application for judicial review.

(2) A declaration may be made or an injunction granted under this subsection in any case where an application for judicial review, seeking that relief, has been made and the High Court considers that, having regard to—

(a) the nature of the matters in respect of which relief may be granted by orders of *mandamus*, prohibition or *certiorari*;

(b) the nature of the persons and bodies against whom relief may be granted by such orders; and

(c) all the circumstances of the case,

it would be just and convenient for the declaration to be made or the injunction to be granted, as the case may be.

(3) No application for judicial review shall be made unless the leave of the High Court has been obtained in accordance with rules of court; and the court shall not grant leave to make such an application unless it considers that the applicant has sufficient interest in the matter to which the application relates.

(4) On an application for judicial review the High Court may award damages to the applicant if—

(a) he has joined with his application a claim for damages arising from any matter to which the application relates; and

(b) the court is satisfied that, if the claim had been made in an action begun by the applicant at the time of making his application, he would have been awarded damages.

(5) If, on an application for judicial review seeking an order of *certiorari*, the High Court quashes the decision to which the application relates, the High Court may remit the matter to the court, tribunal or authority concerned, with a direction to reconsider it and reach a decision in accordance with the findings of the High Court.

(6) Where the High Court considers that there has been undue delay in making an application for judicial review, the court may refuse to grant—

(a) leave for the making of the application; or

(b) any relief sought on the application,

if it considers that the granting of the relief sought would be likely to cause substantial hardship to, or substantially prejudice the rights of, any person or would be detrimental to good administration.

(7) Subsection (6) is without prejudice to any enactment or rule of court which has the effect of limiting the time within which an application for judicial review may be made.

Rules of the Supreme Court, Order 53, rr3–4

Grant of leave to apply for judicial review

3.–(2) An application for leave must be made *ex parte* to a judge …

(3) The judge may determine the application without a hearing, unless a hearing is requested in the notice of application, and need not sit in open court; in any case, the Crown Office shall serve a copy of the judge's order on the applicant.

(4) Where the application for leave is refused by the judge, or is granted on terms, the applicant may renew it by applying—

(a) in any criminal cause or matter, to a Divisional Court of the Queen's Bench Division;

(b) in any other case, to a single judge sitting in open court or, if the Court so directs, to a Divisional Court of the Queen's Bench Division;

Provided that no application for leave may be renewed in any non-criminal cause or matter in which the judge has refused leave under paragraph (3) after a hearing...

(10) Where leave to apply for judicial review is granted, then—

(a) if the relief sought is an order of prohibition or *certiorari* and the Court so directs, the grant shall operate as a stay of the proceedings to which the application relates until the determination of the application or until the Court otherwise orders;

(b) if any other relief is sought, the Court may at any time grant in the proceedings such interim relief as could be granted in an action begun by writ.

Delay in applying for relief

4.–(1) An application for leave to apply for judicial review shall be made promptly and in any event within three months from the date when grounds for the application first arose unless the Court considers that there is good reason for extending the period within which the application shall be made.

(2) Where the relief sought is an order of *certiorari* in respect of any judgment, order, conviction or other proceedings, the date when grounds for the application first arose shall be taken to be the date of that judgment, order, conviction or proceeding.

(3) The preceding paragraphs are without prejudice to any statutory provision which has the effect of limiting the time within which an application for judicial review may be made.

Practical procedural differences

The procedure for judicial review, as well as the draconian three-month time limit differs in two important respects from an ordinary civil action. Instead of discovery of documents and cross-examination of witnesses being the norm, they will be ordered only in strictly limited, exceptional circumstances. As to the former, Lord Diplock had this to say in the leading case in the area.

O'Reilly v Mackman [1983] 2 AC 237, 282–3

Lord Diplock: It may well be that for the reasons given by Lord Denning MR in *George v Secretary of State for the Environment* (1979) 250 EG 339, it will only be upon rare occasions that the interests of justice will require that leave be given for cross-examination of deponents on their affidavits in applications for judicial review. This is because of the nature of the issues that normally arise upon judicial review. The facts, except where the claim that a decision was invalid on the ground that the statutory tribunal or public authority that made the decision failed to comply with the procedure prescribed by the legislation under which it was acting or failed to observe the fundamental rules of natural justice or fairness, can seldom be a matter of relevant dispute upon an application for judicial review, since the tribunal or authority's findings of fact, as distinguished from the legal consequences of the facts that they have found, are not open to review by the court in the exercise of its supervisory powers except on the principles laid down in *Edwards v Bairstow* (1956) AC 14, 36; and to allow cross-examination presents the court with a temptation, not always easily resisted, to substitute its own view of the facts for that of the decision-making body upon whom the exclusive jurisdiction to determine facts has been conferred by Parliament. Nevertheless having regard to a possible misunderstanding of what was said by Geoffrey Lane LJ in *Board of Visitors of Hull Prison, ex p St*

Germain (No 2) (1979) 1 WLR 1401, 1410 your Lordships may think this an appropriate occasion on which to emphasise that whatever may have been the position before the rule was altered in 1977, in all proceedings for judicial review that have been started since that date, the grant of leave to cross-examine deponents upon applications for judicial review is governed by the same principles as it is in actions begun by originating summons; it should be allowed whenever the justice of the particular case so requires.

Note

As to discovery, the importance for the applicant of being able to obtain sight of certain documents was emphasised by Lord Diplock in the same case. Referring to the *Anisminic* case he noted that it was only through discovery that 'the minute of the Commission's decision which showed that they had asked themselves the wrong question was obtained'. It was the fact that the Commission had asked itself the wrong question which established that they had erred in law and thus exceeded their jurisdiction.[13] Discovery therefore played a vital role in that case. Nevertheless, as the following decision makes plain, discovery will rarely be ordered. The applicant was seeking discovery of the minutes of certain meetings: summaries of those minutes had been set out in affidavits filed on behalf of the respondent. The applicant argued that only disclosure of the minutes themselves would reveal fully the grounds on which the decision being challenged (to grant aid to fund the Malaysian Pergau Dam project) had been made.

Secretary of State for Foreign Affairs, ex p the World Development Movement [1995] 1 All ER 615, 620–2

Rose LJ: As to disclosure of the two minutes of February 1991, it was common ground that in judicial review proceedings general discovery is not available as it is in a writ action under Ord 24, rr 1 and 2, that an application can be made under Ord 24, r 3, which by virtue of Ord 24, r 8 will be refused if discovery is not necessary for disposing of the case fairly, and that the judgments of the Court of Appeal in *Secretary of State for the Environment, ex p Islington London BC* (1991) *Independent*, 6 September are pertinent. In that case Dillon LJ said:

> In the case of *Secretary of State for the Home Dept, ex p Harrison* [1988] 3 All ER 86 ... this court ... accepted two submissions of Mr Laws, which are referred to as his 'narrower argument' and his 'wider argument'. The wider argument is stated ... to have been that an applicant is not entitled to go behind an affidavit in order to seek to ascertain whether it is correct or not unless there is some material available outside that contained in the affidavit to suggest that in some material respect the affidavit is not accurate. Without some *prima facie* case for suggesting that the affidavit is in some respects incorrect it is improper to allow discovery of documents, the only purpose of which would be to act as a challenge to the accuracy of the affidavit. With that I would, in general, agree – and indeed the decision binds us. But I would add the qualification that if the affidavit only deals partially, and not sufficiently adequately, with an issue it may be appropriate to order discovery to supplement the affidavit, rather than to challenge its accuracy. That must depend on the nature of the issue.

---

13   For the decision itself, see Chapter 2 of this Part, pp731–3.

The narrower argument referred to in that passage is not relevant for present purposes.

McCowan LJ said:

> The second matter which emerges from the authorities is that unless the applicant in judicial review is in a position to assert that the evidence relied on by a minister is false, or at least inaccurate, it is inappropriate to grant discovery in order to allow the applicant to check the accuracy of the evidence in question.

Mr Pleming [for the applicant] submitted that the evidence for the Foreign Secretary in the affidavit of the Foreign Secretary himself, and of Mr Manning, demonstrates, particularly when compared with the far fuller summaries of the minutes exhibited elsewhere in the evidence, that the affidavit summaries are at best incomplete, and at worst misleading. The material evidence is, in these terms, in para 4 of the Foreign Secretary's affidavit:

> The Accounting Officer of the Overseas Development Administration told me that, given its price, the project was premature by several years and that the extra cost of building it now could well exceed the value of the large sum of British taxpayers' money which the project required.

Mr Meaning's affidavit is in these terms, at para 35:

> ... Sir Tim Lancaster advised that the provision of aid funds for Pergau would not be consistent with his responsibility to ensure that aid funds were administered in a prudent and economic manner, and that he would wish to have an instruction from the Minister or from the Secretary of State if ODA were to incur expenditure on the project.

Mr Pleming submitted that it is no sufficient answer to a claim for discovery to make a bare assertion that the summaries provided are accurate and complete. The court should exercise its power, which is not enjoyed by House of Commons committees, to compel disclosure. This, he submitted, was not a fishing exercise or a 'Micawber' application, and discovery was sought in relation to only two documents. If the summary of the minutes provided to the Foreign Affairs Committee was accurate and complete, there was no reason why the minutes should not be disclosed. If it was inaccurate, the minutes should be disclosed.

Mr Richards [for the respondent], at the outset of his submissions, drew the court's attention to the terms of a letter dated 11 May 1994, sent by the Foreign Secretary personally to the Foreign Affairs Committee, which contained the unambiguous assurance that the summaries of the minutes which had been provided to that committee and which are, or will be exhibited to affidavits before this court, are full and accurate. He submitted that, in the light of ex p Islington London BC there was no basis for going behind the evidence or the summaries and looking at the minutes themselves.

In my judgment, although the affidavits of the Foreign Secretary and of Mr Manning give manifestly incomplete summaries of the minutes (to which indeed neither of them refers) and of the advice tendered to the Foreign Secretary, the Foreign Secretary's letter of 11 May 1994 provided, in the circumstances of this case, an effective answer to the claim for discovery when taken in conjunction with the summaries of the minutes exhibited elsewhere in the evidence. There appeared no basis, looking at this total picture, for questioning the accuracy of those summaries which, in the light of ex p Islington London BC, seems to be a necessary prerequisite for granting discovery of original documents. Furthermore, the summaries, in my view, provided the applicants with highly valuable ammunition to which it seemed unlikely that the minutes themselves would materially add. I was, therefore, wholly unpersuaded that disclosure of these minutes was necessary for the fair disposal of the issues in this case. It was for these reasons that indicated at an earlier stage that disclosure would not be ordered.

Procedural exclusivity

Other than these fairly straightforward matters, the public/private divide has a far more important procedural implication. If the applicant for judicial review is complaining about the decision of a body which is not susceptible to review at all (eg the Jockey Club) it will be clear that judicial review is wholly inappropriate, and that proceeding by way of an ordinary writ action is the only possible course. However, in the cases considered in the section above, in which the body is clearly 'public', but the decision which the applicant seeks to challenge may not be, the question arises, does the applicant have to use the specialised judicial review procedure? The leading authority in the field is the House of Lords decision in the following case, in which prisoners at Hull Prison, alleging that decisions made by the prison's Board of Visitors were bad for want of natural justice attempted to proceed by way of writ or originating summons, rather than under Order 53.

O'Reilly v Mackman (1983) 2 AC 237, 283–5

Lord Diplock: The power of Boards of Visitors of a prison to make disciplinary awards is conferred upon them by subordinate legislation: the Prison Rules 1964 made by the Secretary of State under ss6 and 47 of the Prison Act 1952. The charges against the appellants were of grave offences against discipline falling within r 51. They were referred by the governor of the prison to the Board under r 51(1). It thereupon became the duty of the Board under r 51(3) to inquire into the charge and decide whether it was proved and if so to award what the Board considered to be the appropriate punishment. Rule 49(2) is applicable to such inquiry by the Board. It lays down expressly that the prisoner 'shall be given a full opportunity of hearing what is alleged against him and of presenting his own case.' In exercising their functions under r 51 members of the Board are acting as a statutory tribunal, as contrasted with a domestic tribunal upon which powers are conferred by contract between those who agree to submit to its jurisdiction.

His Lordship then surveyed the expansive development of judicial review.

… Order 53 since 1977 has provided a procedure by which every type of remedy for infringement of the rights of individuals that are entitled to protection in public law can be obtained in one and the same proceeding by way of an application for judicial review, and whichever remedy is found to be the most appropriate in the light of what has emerged upon the hearing of the application, can be granted to him. If what should emerge is that his complaint is not of an infringement of any of his rights that are entitled to protection in public law, but may be an infringement of his rights in private law and thus not a proper subject for judicial review, the court has power under r 9(5), instead of refusing the application, to order the proceedings to continue as if they had begun by writ. There is no such converse power under the RSC to permit an action begun by writ to continue as if it were an application for judicial review; and I respectfully disagree with that part of the judgment of Lord Denning MR which suggests that such a power may exist; nor do I see the need to amend the rules in order to create one.

My Lords, at the outset of this speech, I drew attention to the fact that the remedy by way of declaration of nullity of the decisions of the board was discretionary – as are all the remedies available upon judicial review. Counsel for the plaintiffs accordingly conceded that the fact that by adopting the procedure of an action begun by writ or by originating summons instead of an application for judicial review under Ord 53 (from which there have now been removed all those disadvantages to applicants that had previously led the courts to countenance actions for declarations and injunctions as an alternative procedure for obtaining a remedy for infringement of the rights of the individual that are entitled to protection in public law only) the plaintiffs had thereby been able to evade those protections against groundless, unmeritorious or tardy harassment that were afforded to statutory tribunals or decision-making public authorities by Ord 53, and which might have resulted in the summary, and would in any event have resulted in the speedy disposition of the application, is among the matters fit to be taken into consideration by the judge in deciding whether to exercise his discretion by refusing to grant a declaration; but, it was contended, this he may only do at the conclusion of the trial.

[But] to delay the judge's decision as to how to exercise his discretion would defeat the public policy that underlies the grant of those protections: *viz* the need, in the interests of good administration and of third parties who may be indirectly affected by the decision, for speedy certainty as to whether it has the effect of a decision that is valid in public law. An action for a declaration or injunction need not be commenced until the very end of the limitation period; if begun by writ, discovery and interlocutory proceedings may be prolonged and the plaintiffs are not required to support their allegations by evidence on oath until the actual trial. The period of uncertainty as to the validity of a decision that has been challenged upon allegations that may eventually turn out to be baseless and unsupported by evidence on oath, may thus be strung out for a very lengthy period, as the actions of the first three appellants in the instant appeals show. Unless such an action can be struck out summarily at the outset as an abuse of the process of the court the whole purpose of the public policy to which the change in Ord 53 was directed would be defeated.

My Lords, Ord 53 does not expressly provide that procedure by application for judicial review shall be the exclusive procedure available by which the remedy of a declaration or injunction may be obtained for infringement of rights that are entitled to protection under public law; nor does s31 of the Supreme Court Act 1981. There is great variation between individual cases that fall within Ord 53 and the Rules Committee and subsequently the legislature were, I think, for this reason content to rely upon the express and the inherent power of the High Court, exercised upon a case by case basis, to prevent abuse of its process whatever might be the form taken by that abuse. Accordingly, I do not think that your Lordships would be wise to use this as an occasion to lay down categories of cases in which it would necessarily always be an abuse to seek in an action begun by writ or originating summons a remedy against infringement of rights of the individual that are entitled to protection in public law.

The position of applicants for judicial review has been drastically ameliorated by the new Ord 53. It has removed all those disadvantages, particularly in relation to discovery, that were manifestly unfair to them and had, in many cases, made applications for prerogative orders an inadequate remedy if justice was to be done. This it was that justified the courts in not treating as an abuse of their powers resort to an alternative procedure by way of action for a declaration or injunction (not then obtainable on an application under Ord 53), despite the fact that this procedure had the effect of depriving the defendants of the protection to statutory tribunals and public authorities for which for public policy reasons Ord 53 provided.

Now that those disadvantages to applicants have been removed and all remedies for infringements of rights protected by public law can be obtained upon an application for judicial review, as can also remedies for infringements of rights under private law if such infringements should also be involved, it would in my view as a general rule be contrary to public policy, and as such an abuse of the process of the court, to permit a person seeking to establish that a decision of a public authority infringed rights to which he was entitled to protection under public law to proceed by way of an ordinary action and by this means to evade the provisions of Ord 53 for the protection of such authorities.

My Lords, I have described this as a general rule; for though it may normally be appropriate to apply it by the summary process of striking out the action, there may be exceptions, particularly where the invalidity of the decision arises as a collateral issue in a claim for infringement of a right of the plaintiff arising under private law, or where none of the parties objects to the adoption of the procedure by writ or originating summons. Whether there should be other exceptions should, in my view, at this stage in the development of procedural public law, be left to be decided on a case to case basis – a process that your Lordships will be continuing in the next case in which judgment is to be delivered today [*Cocks v Thanet District Council* [1983] 2 AC 286].

In the instant cases where the only relief sought is a declaration of nullity of the decisions of a statutory tribunal, the Board of Visitors of Hull Prison, as in any other case in which a similar declaration of nullity in public law is the only relief claimed, I have no hesitation, in agreement with the Court of Appeal, in holding that to allow the actions to proceed would be an abuse of the process of the court. They are blatant attempts to avoid the protections for the defendants for which Ord 53 provides.

I would dismiss these appeals.

Note

The doctrine of 'procedural exclusivity' expounded in *O'Reilly* has been widely criticised, firstly for flawed reasoning, secondly for its tendency to lead to meritorious cases being struck out simply because the wrong procedure has been used. Fredman and Morris consider that 'the public/private barrier articulated in *O'Reilly* cannot be defended' and has produced 'deleterious consequences'. Their critique of the decision follows.

S Fredman and GS Morris, 'The Costs of Exclusivity: Public and Private Re-examined' (1994) *Public Law* 69, 70–1, 80–1

In asserting that the new Ord 53 procedure was mandatory for public law cases, Lord Diplock in *O'Reilly* argued that this was necessary to prevent litigants from evading the procedural protections built into that procedure. Short time-limits, leave requirements and limitations on fact-finding facilities are, on this view, essential to protect public authorities in the exercise of their public duties. However, there are two main problems with this rationale. First, it is not clear that public authorities necessarily and invariably need such protection. There may certainly be situations in which this is the case, planning law being a good example. However, it is unclear why public authorities are thought to need this protection in relation to judicial review and not, for example, in relation to claims in tort and contract an argument which is further strengthened by the more flexible approach to the divide articulated in *Roy v Kensington and Chelsea and Westminster Family Practitioner Committee*, [[1992] 1 All ER 705] discussed below. Secondly it fails entirely to explain the many cases in which, far from evading the procedural protections, litigants have chosen to surmount the hurdles to a claim under Ord 53. In such cases, the courts have almost invariably assumed that, just as the Ord 53 procedure is mandatory for public-law issues, so, conversely, it is barred for those classified as private. Little clear justification for this symmetry has been offered, although some reasons are hinted at. Some judges have voiced their fears of opening the floodgates to applications under

Ord 53. Another issue has been concern with remedies; the prerogative orders have never been applied to powers derived from contract and it has thereby been assumed, without foundation, that the Ord 53 procedure is co-extensive in its scope with these orders. In general, however, the existence of a procedural divide based on a public-private distinction has become almost axiomatic, with scant discussion as to why it should be maintained, although in some recent cases the higher judiciary has shown impatience with its constraints. A further rationale – the desire to limit judicial review to a specialist cadre of judges – seems scarcely relevant in the light of the multiplicity of judges now involved in some aspect of decision-making in relation to judicial review applications.

... Recent cases demonstrate yet more strongly that the doctrine of procedural exclusivity makes it likely that meritorious claims will fail for no reason other than the wrong choice of procedure [Note that there is no provision for changing from the writ procedure to Ord 53]. One way in which this is manifested is in the fact that litigants are tempted to use the confusion for tactical advantage. The public employment cases again are a good example. The Crown has been a prime mover in this regard. In a series of cases begun by civil servants by an application for judicial review, the Crown argued that leave should not be granted on the grounds that civil servants had contracts of employment and therefore the issue was private [*Civil Service Appeal Board, ex p Bruce* [1988] 3 All ER 686]. At the same time, the Crown has applied to strike out cases begun by civil servants under the writ procedure on the grounds that these employees did not have contracts and therefore the issue was one of public law [*McLaren v Home Office* [1989] ICR 824]. A similar point can be made in respect of the voluntary regulation cases. Thus in *Law*, the applicant was content with the writ procedure, but the Greyhound Racing Club asserted the public nature of its function in order to block the claim at the threshold. In *ex p Aga Khan*, the converse was the case: the Jockey Club asserted the private nature of its functions in order to block the Aga Khan's attempt to use public law. This phenomenon is not always deliberate: the luckless applicant in *Ali* could be forgiven for assuming that his remedy lay in private law. Yet his of all cases appears on the face of it meritorious: how could it not be unreasonable to allocate a sixth-floor flat to a disabled person?

Possibly more problematic still is the recognition in recent cases of the possibility of pursuing substantially the same argument but in a different forum. Thus, as noted above, the Court of Appeal which refused to consider the Aga Khan's claims of breach of natural justice in public law was willing to concede that the same claim could have been entertained as a private-law claim of breach of an implied term in the contract. The only difference it seems, lies in the nature of the remedies. The result is inordinate cost and expense, with case after case being struck out or refused leave for no reason other than that the incorrect procedure had been chosen. Indeed, if the courts are truly concerned at the risk of blocking up the system, this must be at least one contributing factor.

Notes

1   Anthony Tanney has pointed out numerous difficulties for the aggrieved citizen arising from the complexities inherent in the procedural exclusivity principle;[14] a particularly striking one is noted here. Tanney points out that where a person has a possible statutory right to a benefit (eg housing), if she is found to satisfy the relevant criteria she will have a private right to the

---

14   'Procedural Exclusivity in Administrative Law' (1994) PL 31.

benefit; however, a decision that the criteria are *not* satisfied is a matter of public law only and may be challenged only by the judicial review procedure.[15] As Fredman and Morris note, in *Ali v Tower Hamlets* (1992)[16] a 'third dimension was added': whilst the applicant had a private law right to accommodation if he wished to challenge the *type* of accommodation offered, his remedy lay only in public law (*ibid*).

2   By contrast, Lord Woolf comments that he 'would be loath to see the effect of [the] decision undermined'[17] and mounts a spirited defence of the principle it embodies.

Lord Woolf, 'Judicial Review: A Possible Programme for Reform' (1992) *Public Law* 221, 231–2

O'Reilly v Mackman

... It did, and still does, seem to me to be illogical to have a procedure which is designed to protect the public from unnecessary interference with administrative action, and then allow the protection which is provided to be by-passed. However, it is quite wrong to assume that the necessary price of that decision is drawn-out litigation over issues as to whether a particular action has been commenced in the wrong court. In his speech in *O'Reilly v Mackman*, Lord Diplock was careful to refer to a 'general rule'. If a litigant who has a valid claim *bona fide* but wrongly regards a case as not falling within *O'Reilly v Mackman* when it does, the principle should not be allowed to embarrass him. The court in such a situation can take the necessary steps to ensure that it can still deal with the merits of the case. Sometimes additional pleadings may be necessary. At present, Ord 53 expressly allows only for proceedings to go from judicial review (ie public law proceedings), to proceedings begun by writ, and not vice versa. This is a matter where amendment to the rules would improve the situation. However, even without such an amendment a little judicial ingenuity can overcome the problem as long as the case is one which has merit [see, eg *Chief Adjudication Officer v Foster* [1992] 1 QB 31 and *Secretary of State for the Home Department, ex p Muboyayi* [1991] 3 WLR 442]. If it has no merit, then it is important for the safeguards provided by judicial review to be utilised if it is a public law case.

It is true that there is still the problem of deciding whether or not the case is a public law case and that there is a grey area where it is difficult to decide this question. However, if, as has now become the position with regard to substantive law, there are real differences between the position of a litigant in public law and his or her position in private law, this difficulty is one which we cannot avoid. It is, however, the responsibility of the courts to chip away at the grey area by successive decisions. For an example of what can be achieved by judicial ingenuity to reduce the procedural problems, there is the Master of the Rolls' judgment in the recent case of *Chief Adjudication Officer v Foster*. In that case the Master of the Rolls on a statutory appeal was able to come to the conclusion that, although the court had no jurisdiction to deal with the statutory appeal, the appeal could be treated as though it were a hearing of a case of judicial review and disposed of accordingly. Procedural formalities were very properly kept in their proper place. They were not allowed to interfere with the performance of justice. That does not mean, of course, that it

---

15   As Fredman and Morris put it (commenting on *Cocks v Thanet*) 'the ... decision as to whether an applicant was homeless was a public discretion, but once the discretion had been exercised in the applicant's favour it became a private right', *ibid*, at p80.

16   3 All ER 512.

17   'Judicial Review: A Possible Programme for Reform' (1992) PL 221, 231.

would not be preferable for the need for additional flexibility to be embodied in an amended Ord 53.

Notes

1   One important problem which arises for the applicant from the public/private divide – the possibility of having a claim struck out because it was commenced using the wrong procedure – may in the future be removed. At the time of writing, Lord Woolf has just published his report on Access to Justice;[18] this proposes that all types of civil proceedings should commence in the same way, it being up to the court to allocate the action to the appropriate list. This will not of course abolish the public/private divide, nor remove all problems for applicants (eg a person could find his action struck out or refused because it was found by the court to be a public action which had been commenced after three months) but it will at least relieve the applicant from having to decide whether to proceed by way of an action for judicial review or whether to issue a writ or originating summons.

2   As Loughlin points out,[19] the debate about procedural exclusivity may be seen to relate back to the old Diceyan preoccupation with the desirability or otherwise of a separate system of administrative law. Loughin quotes Professor Wade on the subject:

> To impose a dichotomy would be to take a step backwards to the bad old days of the forms of action ... I remain of the opinion ... that the right policy was to fit the prerogative remedies into the mechanism of an ordinary action, so that there would be no dichotomy and no dilemma for the litigant.

Loughlin comments that this opinion reveals Wade's adherence 'to Dicey's view that the Rule of Law is founded on the supremacy of ordinary law universally applied by the ordinary courts'.[20]

3   The most important decision in this area since *O'Reilly* was that of the House of Lords in *Roy v Kensington and Chelsea and Westminster Family Practitioner Committee* (1992),[21] in which the House of Lords appeared to show some concern to restrict the *O'Reilly* principle.

Peter Cane, 'Private Rights and Public Procedure' (1992) *Public Law* 193–7

For present purposes, the facts of *Roy v Kensington and Chelsea Family Practitioner Committee* can be stated briefly. Dr Roy was a general practitioner providing general medical services within the NHS. The Committee, acting under statutory powers, withheld a proportion of his basic practice allowance on the ground that he had not been devoting a substantial amount of his time to his practice. Under the relevant statutory rules, the full rate of the allowance was payable only if in the opinion of the Committee he was so devoting a substantial amount of his time. Dr Roy issued a writ claiming, *inter alia*, payment of the withheld sum, contending that he *had* devoted himself to his practice as required by the regulations. The Committee applied to have the action struck out as an abuse of the process of the court on the ground that Dr Roy should have proceeded by way of an application for judicial review under RSC

---

18   For preliminary reports on Lord Woolf's findings, see, eg, *The Times*, 27 July 1996.
19   *Public Law and Political Theory* (1992), p189.
20   *Ibid*.
21   1 All ER 705.

Ord 53. The Committee's application failed in the House of Lords ... Lord Lowry was inclined to limit the impact of *O'Reilly* by giving it a restrictive interpretation according to which the exclusivity principle enunciated in that case would apply *only* when the interest which the applicant was seeking to protect by litigation was one which had no basis in private law. He was not happy about treating *O'Reilly* as laying down a rule that Ord 53 procedure has to be used in all cases involving challenges to 'public law acts or decisions', subject to exceptions to deal with cases involving private law rights. The importance of this preference for a restricted interpretation of *O'Reilly* (which Lord Bridge, who gave the only other substantial judgment, seemed to share) is probably more ideological than practical since under the other approach the exceptions could be framed widely enough to achieve a similar result to that which Lord Lowry favoured in adopting the restrictive interpretation of *O'Reilly*. But Lord Lowry's approach sets the tone for future developments in this area.

Action by writ or application for judicial review?

Lord Lowry gave several reasons why, in his opinion, it was right to allow Dr Roy to bring his claim by writ rather than by application for judicial review. The most important of these reasons were that: (1) Dr Roy was seeking to protect private law rights (this was also the basis of Lord Bridge's speech in Dr Roy's favour); (2) those private law rights 'dominate[d] the proceedings'; (3) the remedy sought by Dr Roy, namely an order for the payment of money due, could not be granted under Ord 53; and (4) if Dr Roy's complaint against the Committee succeeded, he would be *entitled* to the payment of the money withheld, and a person should not be required to use Ord 53 to claim a non-discretionary remedy.

Taking reason (4) first, it is by no means clear that the procedural limitations inherent in Ord 53 should not apply to any case in which a person seeks a non-discretionary remedy. The arguments in favour of requiring leave and imposing a short time-limit are not obviously inapplicable to all such cases; and, as Lord Lowry recognises, not all claims for non-discretionary remedies raise factual issues unsuited for resolution by Ord 53 procedure. Indeed, Dr Roy's claim raised no such issues. In fact, the distinction between discretionary and nondiscretionary remedies seems to be a surrogate for the distinction between public law rights and private law rights rather than a distinction with independent force.

Reason (3) raises a very important issue about the interpretation of Ord 53, r 7 and the Supreme Court Act 1981, s31(4). These provisions allow an award of 'damages' to be made on an application for judicial review provided the court 'is satisfied that, if the claim had been made in an action begun by the plaintiff at the time of making his application, he would ['could' in Ord 53, r 7(1)] have been awarded damages.' Lord Lowry assumes that these provisions would not have applied to Dr Roy's case [at 261G]; and yet it follows from the court's decision in *Roy* that if Dr Roy had made an application for judicial review of the Committee's decision and, at the same time, had commenced an action by writ claiming payment of the withheld portion of his practice allowance, he could have been awarded the sum due in the latter action (and would have been if his challenge to the committee's decision had been successful). So the reason why an order for payment of a sum due could not have been made on an application for judicial review must be that any such order would not be an 'award of damages.' As a matter of normal usage, an order for the payment of a liquidated sum due to the plaintiff is, indeed, not an award of damages. But is there any good reason why the term 'damages' as used in Ord 53 should be interpreted in this way? If damages can be awarded on an application for judicial review, why should the making of an order for the payment of money wrongfully withheld not also be within the power of the court on such an application?

A similar issue arises out of the recent case of *Woolwich Equitable Building Society v Inland Revenue Commissioners* [[1991] 3 WLR 790]. In earlier proceedings [*IRC, ex p Woolwich Equitable BS* [1990] 1 WLR 1400], the Society successfully challenged the validity of regulations under which it had been charged an amount of tax; the Revenue repaid the moneys, but the Society then made a claim for interest on the moneys calculated from the date they were paid, on the basis that from that date it had a common law right to restitution of the amount unlawfully demanded. The Court of Appeal found in favour of the Society. What would the position have been if the Society had expressly claimed the interest in the judicial review proceedings? On a literal interpretation of Supreme Court Act 1981, s31(4), an award of interest could not have been made in those proceedings (nor, indeed, could an order for repayment of the tax have been made) But what possible justification is there for such a position? Either the word 'damages' should be interpreted to cover any monetary remedy which satisfies the requirements of the subsection, or the provision ought to be amended to cover any monetary claim. Given that s31(4) does not alter the substantive law governing entitlement to monetary awards, there is no good reason why the procedural simplification it effects should not be extended to cover any monetary remedy which an applicant for judicial review is in a position to claim.

Consideration of the *Woolwich* case raises another query. Suppose the Society had expressly claimed repayment of the moneys and interest in the same proceedings in which it challenged the validity of the regulations. Could it, by so doing, have by-passed Ord 53? ... Conversely, if Dr Roy had claimed only a declaration that the Committee's decision to abate his practice allowance was invalid, could he still have made his claim by private law procedure? It is suggested that the answer to both of these questions depends, under the present law, on a consideration of the first two reasons given by Lord Lowry for allowing Dr Roy to sue in private law. These reasons, it will be recalled, were that Dr Roy was asserting private law rights, and that those rights 'dominated the proceedings.' It appears that if a plaintiff claims a private law remedy, that is a declaration, an injunction or a *(quaere,* non-statutory) monetary award, in aid of private law rights, then the claim need not be made by way of an application for judicial review unless, perhaps, the private rights in issue are not predominant. But this last qualification is very vague; and consideration of a case such as *Wandsworth LBC v Winder,* [[1985] AC 461], in which the only live issue was the validity of the challenged resolution, leads one to suspect that any relevant private law right would be held to be predominant over any public law issue. So the answer to both of the questions posed earlier in this paragraph would appear to be 'yes'!

What are 'private law rights'?

Does *Roy* cast any light on the definition of 'private law right'? Contractual and property rights are obviously private law rights, as are rights to obtain monetary awards for private law wrongs or to obtain restitution on some other basis than wrongful conduct (such as mistake of fact). The really difficult cases are those in which the right in question arises out of a statutory provision. Dr Roy's right was such: the Court of Appeal held that there was a contract between Dr Roy and the Committee [(1990) J Med LR 328]. but the House of Lords declined to decide this issue and instead treated Dr Roy's right as a private law statutory one. Are all statutory 'rights' private law rights? Surely not! It is quite clear that not all statutory duties are actionable in private law. We know from *Cocks v Thanet DC* [(1983) 2 AC 286] that the statutory right of certain homeless persons to be housed by a local authority is a private law right; and we know from Roy that the statutory right of a registered GP, under certain circumstances, to receive a full basic practice allowance is a private law right. But just as the courts have found it impossible to provide much guidance in general terms on the question of which statutory duties are actionable in the tort of breach of statutory duty, so it seems unlikely that much general guidance will ever be available on the question of which rights are private law rights for present purposes.

Notes

1   Fredman and Morris see four main advantages to the approach of the House of Lords in *Roy*:[22] first, the explicit recognition of the fact that a single claim could (as in *Roy* itself) contain a mixture of public and private law elements in the claim; secondly, the 'move away from procedural rigidity' represented by the Lords' preparedness to allow a writ action in a case concerning some public law elements, provided the private elements dominated; thirdly, the recognition that the choice of procedure should be at least partly dictated by whether it would be suitable for the type of claim in question; fourthly, the move away from contract as a key factor for locating the public private divide. They consider the first point to be the most important in that it recognises and allows for the complexity of a mixed case to be accommodated within a single action: 'having begun his action by writ, Dr Roy's case may then depend upon invoking public law principles in order to establish his private rights and obtain a private law remedy' (p82).

2   The third point they mention appears to have received some recognition in the recent House of Lords decision in *Mercury Communications v Director General of Telecommunications* (1995).[23] In refusing to strike out Mercury's application challenging decisions of the Director General relating to its operational agreement with BT brought by originating summons on the grounds that Mercury should have proceeded by way of an application for judicial review (AJR) the House of Lords stated *inter alia* that: (a) a crucial question was whether the proceedings constituted an abuse of the procedures of the court and (b) that in determining (a) it should be borne in mind that the procedure selected by Mercury was at least as well suited and possibly better suited for determining the issues raised than an AJR. This seems to represent a move towards a pragmatic view of procedure, based on efficacy and convenience rather than some elusive public/private divide.

The future of the public/private divide

In what follows, two different views are given as to the direction the law should take in this area. Anthony Tanney considers the basic soundness or otherwise of the *O'Reilly* principle and the question whether a degree of reform which left the core principle of a procedural divide untouched could be successful. Fredman and Morris then set out their arguments for abolition of the procedural divide and consider the issues raised by a single procedure.

Anthony Tanney, 'Procedural Exclusivity in Administrative Law' (1994) *Public Law* 51, 62–4, 65

How, then, are the problems just described to be addressed? It is important to emphasise at this point that *O'Reilly* is in some respects an inevitable product of the protection features of Ord 53 – in the words of Professor Wade [*Administrative Law*

---

22   *Op cit*, pp82–3.

23   1 All ER 575, HL.

(1988), p677] '[once Ord 53 had been reformed] how could it make sense to allow a choice of procedures for obtaining the same remedies under which the restrictions of one could simply be evaded by recourse to the other?' This argument has considerable logical force. The implication, indeed, would seem to be that to abandon exclusivity requires the dismantling of the restrictive/protective features of Ord 53 [Wade's preferred solution – see *Administrative Law*, p681]. Alternatively, if it were thought that public authorities did need protection against unfounded or dilatory challenges, *O'Reilly*-type problems might be tolerated as the price of that protection.

As to removing the special protection features of Ord 53, it seems to be agreed that provisions of some kind are needed to deal with dilatory applications. In the words of the Law Commission, 'We do not consider that the abandonment of [special time limits ... is a practical or desirable option. The principle of certainty (sc. that authorities need to know that after a period a decision will no longer be susceptible to legal challenge] ... tend[s] to justify the provision of special time limits for initiating legal challenges to administrative acts.'

There is much less agreement on the issue of whether the requirement that an applicant seek leave to bring an AJR should be retained. In fact, it may be that the issues of leave and the time-limit cannot be considered separately – it is conceivable that the presence of a short time limit actually encourages applications, giving added significance to the leave filter. Arguments from principle and pragmatism have been invoked by those advocating the removal of the leave stage. However, these arguments need not be evaluated here. My present aim can be achieved by stating the view of Le Sueur and Sunkin [(1992) PL 102 at 104] that, whatever the merits of the arguments against the leave stage, it is unlikely to be abolished, and that reform is likely to be directed to the formulation of principles governing the granting or withholding of leave. If this view be correct, and it is respectfully submitted that it is (the leave stage has influential judicial support from Lord Woolf and its retention is favoured by the Law Commission [para 5.8, 5.9]), some requirement of exclusivity would follow for reasons stated above. It would seem more worthwhile, therefore, to focus attention on whether the consequences for litigants of such a regime might be tolerated, and if not, mitigated.

Doubtless the problems for litigants of the *O'Reilly* rule as presently applied are more difficult to accept because in many cases actions have been struck out in circumstances that plainly do not offend against the 'protective' rationale behind the rule. This might be because the claim is plainly not frivolous and leave would surely have been granted under Ord 53. Alternatively, the claim, though brought outside the Ord 53 time-limit, may not relate to a decision on whose speedy immunisation from legal challenge an authority might need to rely. Doubtless there would be acute problems of definition in formulating a rule that operated only in circumstances where protection was *necessary* – as there has been in a rule which takes 'public law' as its starting point. However, if the striking out rule were to be confined to circumstances of necessity, instead of to civil actions raising issues of purely public law, any problems for litigants in ascertaining the scope of that rule might attract less criticism.

However, it is admitted that the prospects for formulating a striking out rule which is not 'public law driven' would seem to be slender if, as has been suggested above, a leave requirement continues to figure in the Ord 53 procedure. This requirement has come to be inextricably associated with the vindication of public law rights and it is difficult to imagine the courts not insisting on its observance *in general* in such cases. Yet in *mixed* cases raising issues of public law the courts have stated that the presence of a private law element to a claim provides a sufficient reason for allowing it to proceed by action. Why, then, might not another exception to exclusivity be fashioned which would allow a claim to continue where the plaintiff genuinely believed the case to involve wholly or partly private law? Indeed Lord Diplock specifically did not rule out further case by case exceptions to his general rule. In other words, even if exclusivity is to apply in general in public law claims, why not confine its effects to 'blatant attempts' [*O'Reilly* at p285] to raise a purely public law claim by action. Of course, details of any such rule would have to be worked out – eg would it be for the plaintiff to prove the *bona fide* nature of the error on an application by the authority to strike out the claim, or would it be for the authority to disprove it? Would the plaintiff have to demonstrate that the error was reasonable as well as genuine? Were the courts to have applied such an approach in *Cocks* and *Ali*, those claims would surely have been allowed to proceed … It has been suggested [Emery (1992) CLJ 344] that, in cases where public-law issues are intermingled with other types of legal issue, a form of reference procedure, modelled loosely on that contained in Article 177 EEC, might be deployed to separate the different strands of a claim and channel them into appropriate courts. The scheme envisaged is designed to deal with the fact that even in such 'mixed' cases, inferior courts do not have jurisdiction to resolve all public-law issues necessary to the disposal of a case. For example, magistrates' courts do not have an unlimited jurisdiction to strike at by-laws where the invalidity of the by-laws is raised as a defence to a prosecution for their breach. This proposal is, with respect, sensible, though it might be suggested at the same time that the procedure be invoked according, for example, to the degree of difficulty or importance of the public law point, rather than according to the way in which the jurisdictional boundary is currently drawn.

S Fredman and GS Morris, 'The Costs of Exclusivity: Public and Private Re-Examined' (1994) *Public Law* 69, 81–2, 83–5

It has been argued above that procedural exclusivity has proved to be unworkable. The original rationale given in *O'Reilly* does not justify the insistence that the Ord 53 procedure cannot be used in 'private cases', nor is it always true that public authorities need protection from the writ procedure. In addition, the conceptual apparatus of 'public' and 'private' is not sufficiently developed to sustain a rigid distinction, and the equation of contract with private law means that executive powers exercised by means of contract may not be properly supervised. In any case, the doctrine of procedural exclusivity has failed to recognise that a single case may present issues of both a private and a public character which need to be considered in the same forum, the possibility of which will increase in the 'contract State'. Finally, it can be self-defeating by creating more expensive and time-consuming litigation than is necessary.

What then is the way ahead? There are two possibilities. One is to retain the public-private divide, but allow flexibility in its application, an approach which may prove useful in cases which contain both public and private elements. The second possibility is to abandon the divide and allow a unified procedure, thus allowing all issues to be considered in the same forum. An important step in the direction of the first approach was made by the House of Lords in *Roy v Kensington and Chelsea and Westminster FPC* However, *Roy* did not go far enough in reappraising the public-private divide, as is evidenced by later cases, such as *Ali v Tower Hamlets*.

The authors then consider the decision in *Roy* and having noted its advantages (described above) go on:

[However] … the decision in *Roy* has some important disadvantages. First, their Lordships did not take the opportunity to examine *O'Reilly v Mackman* more radically; Lord Bridge specifically upheld its essential principle and Lord Lowry disclaimed any intention of discussing its proper scope. Thus, procedural exclusivity survives for certain types of case, presumably those which concern 'pure' public law, or which contain a non-dominant private law element. This leaves a fertile field for litigation. There is no further indication in the case itself of what might amount to a 'pure' public-law matter; or indeed, what a 'public-law' matter might be at all. Secondly, it remains unclear whether there is a genuine choice of procedure. Could Dr Roy have proceeded by Ord 53 if he had begun along that route? If so, why could not Walsh [East Berks AHA, ex p Walsh [1985] QB 152] and Bruce [Civil Service Appeal Board, ex p Bruce [1988] ICR 649] and Nangle [Lord Chancellor's Dept, ex p Nangle [1992] 1 QB 897]? It is likely that the courts will continue to prevent public employees at least from pursuing this route. The fear of opening the floodgates remains acute and the belief that alternative remedies are more appropriate is still strong. More worrying is the fact that Roy leaves open the possibility that contract will continue to play a central role. Although, in this case, the House of Lords were not prepared to hold that absence of a contract meant that Dr Roy could not pursue the writ procedure, they did not say explicitly that had Dr Roy clearly had a contract, he could have pursued a claim under Ord 53. Indeed, the more recent cases show that the existence of a contract remains a bar to Ord 53. This still leaves unsupervised the large body of executive powers now exercised by contract.

A single procedure

The more flexible approach to the public-private divide demonstrated by the House of Lords in Roy, whilst welcome, still leaves many problems unresolved. For the reasons we have indicated, we would therefore argue that the best solution to the difficulties of classification posed by the modern State is to abandon the divide altogether and replace it with a unified procedure. This would not imply that there is no conceptual difference between public and private-law grounds of challenge, merely that consideration of the substantive issues should not be obstructed by argument as to the proper form of proceedings. To those who argue that public authorities need protection against vexatious litigants we would respond that the striking-out procedure is sufficient to prevent wholly unmeritorious claims. In some cases this will prove burdensome for the respondent public authority who must initiate the striking-out procedure. However, this should be counterbalanced by the cost and time saved by removing leave requirements, which can use up valuable judicial resources even in the most meritorious claim. Indeed, research [Sunkin and Le Sueur (1992) PL 102] has shown that the leave procedure operates, at best, erratically. Moreover, abandoning the need for leave may encourage earlier internal review of claims. As far as time-limits are concerned, these could be geared to the specific context. Employment law has operated subject to relatively short time-limits even in the statutory context; in this context, for example, the six-month time-limit for applications suggested by the Law Commission would seem appropriate. In other contexts, such as planning, a shorter time-limit may be required. Moreover, a unified procedure would not necessarily imply a uniform approach to discovery; within that procedure the distinctive position of the Crown and the greater likelihood of public interest immunity claims arising in relation to the prerogative orders could still be accommodated.

Conclusion

In this article we have argued that the distribution of power within the contemporary State necessitates the abolition of the public-private divide established in O'Reilly v Mackman in favour of a unified procedure. This would avoid sterile and costly disputes over the proper form of proceedings and allow the courts to deal more efficiently with cases which contain both public and private elements, an eventuality which is likely to increase as the 'contract State' advances. Moreover, it would give the courts much greater flexibility to impose constraints upon the exercise of power where this was deemed appropriate regardless of whether that power lay with public or with private bodies. In 1986, Woolf LJ, as he then was, remarked;

[t]he interests of the public are as capable of being adversely affected by the decision of large corporations and large associations, be they of employers or employees, and should they not be subject to challenge on *Wednesbury* grounds if their decision relates to activities which can damage the public interest? [(1986) PL 220].

This theme was echoed by Sir Gordon Borrie in 1989 in stating '[a]s power shifts from the public sector to the private sector, it seems to be desirable that the instruments of control and accountability forged to ensure that the public sector behaves itself are considered for appropriate adaptation to the private sector'[(1989) PL 552]. At a time when significant areas of public power are being recharacterised as private, such exhortations become more pressing. Privatised prisons provide a clear example of the issues raised by the recharacterisation process. Had the fact situation in *O'Reilly v Mackman* itself occurred in a private prison, would the court have held that the Ord 53 procedure was not appropriate, thus depriving the applicants of any ground of challenging their treatment? If the notion of the prisoner's 'contract' suggested by the Woolf Inquiry [Cm 1456] were adopted, would it give rise to legitimate expectations which could be relied upon in judicial review proceedings by those held in public but not in private prisons? The courts have acknowledged that some private bodies, such as trade unions, wield power of a nature which requires supervision by the courts and the courts may exercise their private supervisory jurisdiction to extend the principles of good administration more widely. In the light of the convergence of public and private law in this respect, the maintenance of the divide does not preclude the supervision of public power in private hands. However, it still requires the proper forum for proceedings to be determined, an otiose requirement when the substantive result is the same in either. The exclusivity principle is based upon a simplistic and anachronistic model of the exercise of public power; attempts by the courts to operate the principle can only become increasingly contorted if it survives the extension of the 'contract State'.

WHO MAY APPLY FOR JUDICIAL REVIEW?

Locus standi

Persons seeking leave to apply for judicial review will only be granted it if they can show that they have 'sufficient interest in the matter to which the application relates'.[24] This requirement is unproblematic if the applicant is individually and directly concerned with the decision she disputes, for example if it relates to her employment (as in *Roy*) or application for housing (as in *Ali v Tower Hamlets* (1992)).[25] The controversial issue in this area is whether groups or individuals with no personal concern in the decision in question (eg pressure groups, local associations, etc) have standing to question it.[26]

It was found in *Secretary of State for the Environment, ex p Rose Theatre Trust Co* (1990)[27] that pressure groups whose only interest in a decision is concern about the issues involved will not in general have *locus standi* to challenge the decision. The law has moved on considerably from that position, partly as a

---

24   Supreme Court Act 1981, s31(3).

25   3 All ER 512.

26   For an interesting and in-depth analysis of this issue see Hilson and Cram, 'Judicial Review and Environmental Law – Is There a Coherent View of Standing?' (1996) 16(1) LS 3.

27   1 All ER 754.

result of an approach derived from *IRC, ex p National Federation of Self Employed* (1982).[28] In that case, their Lordships were unanimous in stressing that the question of standing is inextricably linked with the substantive merits of the application.

IRC, ex p National Federation of Self Employed [1982] AC 617 649–50, 653–5

The appellants were a body of taxpayers who wished to challenge arrangements made by the Inland Revenue for the taxation of casual employees of certain Fleet Street newspapers, which *inter alia* involved a partial amnesty on previous tax evasion. The appellants argued that the arrangements treated the employees in question in an overly generous manner, and that they had never been given such concessions. The issue for the House of Lords was whether the appellants had standing to challenge the IR's decision and seek an order for *mandamus* compelling the Inland Revenue to collect taxes in the usual way.

> **Lord Scarman:** ... I pass now to the ... nature of the interest which the applicant has to show. It is an integral part of the Lord Advocate's argument that the existence of the duty is a significant factor in determining the sufficiency of an applicant's interest.
>
> The sufficiency of the interest is, as I understand all your Lordships agree, a mixed question of law and fact. The legal element in the mixture is less than the matters of fact and degree: but it is important as setting the limits within which, and the principles by which, the discretion is to be exercised. At one time heresy ruled the day. The decision of the Divisional Court in *Lewisham Union Guardians* [1897] 1 QB 498 was accepted as establishing that an applicant must establish 'a legal specific right to ask for the interference of the court' by order of *mandamus: per* Wright J at p500. I agree with Lord Denning MR in thinking this was a deplorable decision. It was at total variance with the view of Lord Mansfield CJ. Yet its influence has lingered on, and is evident even in the decision of the Divisional Court in this case. But the tide of the developing law has now swept beyond it, as the Court of Appeal's decision in *Greater London Council, ex p Blackburn* [1976] 1 WLR 550 illustrates. In the present case the House can put down a marker buoy warning legal navigators of the danger of the decision. As Professor Wade pointed out in *Administrative Law*, 4th ed (1977), p610, if the *Lewisham* case were correct, *mandamus* would lose its public law character, being no more than a remedy for a private wrong.
>
> My Lords, I will not weary the House with citation of many authorities. Suffice it to refer to the judgment of Lord Parker CJ in *Thames Magistrates' Court, ex p Greenbaum,* (1957) 55 LGR 129, a case of *certiorari*; and to words of Lord Wilberforce in *Gouriet v Union of Post Office Workers* [1978] AC 435, 482, where he stated the modern position in relation to prerogative orders: 'These are often applied for by individuals and the courts have allowed them liberal access under a generous conception of *locus standi*'. The one legal principle, which is implicit in the case law and accurately reflected in the rule of court, is that in determining the sufficiency of an applicant's interest it is necessary to consider the matter to which the application relates. It is wrong in law, as I understand the cases, for the court to attempt an assessment of the sufficiency of an applicant's interest without regard to the matter of his complaint. If he fails to show, when he applies for leave, a *prima facie* case, or reasonable grounds for believing that there has been a failure of public duty, the court would be in error if it granted leave. The curb represented by the need for an applicant to show, when he

---

28   AC 617.

seeks leave to apply, that he has such a case is an essential protection against abuse of legal process. It enables the court to prevent abuse by busybodies, cranks, and other mischief-makers. I do not see any further purpose served by the requirement for leave.

But, that being said, the discretion belongs to the court: and, as my noble and learned friend, Lord Diplock, has already made clear, it is the function of the judges to determine the way in which it is to be exercised.

Lord Scarman then went on to find that in fact, the appellant had failed to make out a *prima facie* case that the IRC had acted unfairly. He also noted that the Court of Appeal had been 'misled' into treating *locus standi* as an issue separate from the merits.

The federation, having failed to show any grounds for believing that the revenue has failed to do its statutory duty, have not, in my view, shown an interest sufficient in law to justify any further proceedings by the court on its application. Had they shown reasonable grounds for believing that the failure to collect tax from the Fleet Street casuals was an abuse of the revenue's managerial discretion or that there was a case to that effect which merited investigation and examination by the court, I would have agreed with the Court of Appeal that they had shown a sufficient interest for the grant of leave to proceed further with their application. I would, therefore, allow the appeal.

Notes

1 On the question of the standing of individual tax-payers to challenge decisions of the Inland Revenue, see further *HM Treasury, ex p Smedley* [1985] 1 All ER 589 at 594, 595 [1985] QB 657, 670, 667 *per* Slade LJ and Donaldson MR.

2 The courts appeared to move beyond the position taken in *Rose Theatre* in *Inspectorate of Pollution, ex p Greenpeace Ltd (No 2)* (1994)[29] discussed here by Ivan Hare. Greenpeace were seeking review of the decision of Her Majesty's Inspectorate of Pollution (HMIP) to allow testing at the THORP nuclear reprocessing plant without further consultation.

... Greenpeace sought to impugn the substantive decision to vary BNFL's authorisation on the ground that an entirely new authorisation was required before testing at THORP could lawfully commence. This application was also dismissed but of general importance was the rejection of BNFL's claim that Greenpeace lacked sufficient standing to initiate the proceedings. In accepting that Greenpeace had *locus standi*, Otton J was influenced by a number of factors including the international reputation of the group and its significant local membership in the affected area. He also stressed that Greenpeace represented the best, and possibly the only, means by which the issues raised by the application could be addressed by a court. Two further points require some comment. First, Otton J took account of the fact that Greenpeace was seeking an order of *certiorari* and held that 'if *mandamus* were sought that would be a reason to decline jurisdiction'. In other words, the test of standing will vary according to the remedy sought by the applicant. This statement was purportedly based on the decision of the House of Lords in *IRC, ex p National Federation of Self-Employed and Small Businesses Ltd* [1982] AC 617. In fact, Lord Wilberforce was the only member of the House to adopt a clear position in favour of this view with Lord Diplock equally clearly opposed to it and the other Lords appearing to express somewhat equivocal support for Lord Diplock's position. There

---

29   4 All ER 329.

is a very strong argument that the purpose of the introduction of the unified Ord 53 procedure was to remove exactly this sort of distinction between the different forms of relief. Any return to the adjectival complexity of the prerogative orders is to be regretted.

Secondly, the court expressly declined to follow *Secretary of State for the Environment, ex p Rose Theatre Trust Co* (1990) 1 QB 504, a case which many feared marked a rejection of the prevailing liberal attitude to *locus standi*. Some have explained the courts' occasional reluctance to grant standing to pressure groups on the basis that the function of such bodies is essentially that of the lobbyist and to allow them to litigate their concerns would risk transforming judicial review into a mode of redress for political rather than legal grievances. The judgment in the present case is an affirmation of the advantages of allowing pressure groups to contribute their expertise to the forensic process. Otton J emphasised that Greenpeace, 'with its particular experience in environmental matters, its access to experts in the relevant realms of science and technology (not to mention the law), is able to mount a carefully selected, focused, relevant and well-argued challenge'.

This aspect of the cases is to be welcomed but they also reveal that, notwithstanding that the present judicial review procedure has been in operation for almost two decades, doctrinal confusion has yet to be eliminated. [30a]

3　Another issue of importance in the case was the fact that the interest Greenpeace had in the matter went clearly beyond the merely ideological. Otton J stressed the local health interest of the 2,500 supporters in the Cumbria region, whose health might be effected by emissions from the nuclear plant.[30] Thus members of the group had a personal interest in a matter of substantial general concern – public health. Thus although the court expressly declined to follow *Rose Theatre,* the decision was clearly distinguishable anyway: in the earlier case the group seeking to challenge the decision not to list the theatre site was only interested in the case because of its general concern about the preservation of this country's historical heritage. As Hilson and Cram remark, 'Had a substantial number of the individuals in the [Rose Theatre pressure group] lived locally, the position might well have been different'.[31]

4　A similar approach was adopted in *Secretary of State for the Environment, ex p Friends of the Earth* (1994)[32]; the group and its director were granted leave to challenge a decision related to the quality of drinking water in certain specified areas. The fact that the director lived in one of those areas – London – gave him a personal local interest in the matter.

5　However, in other cases involving decisions of *national* importance the courts have been prepared to move beyond this stance and allow challenges by persons whose only concern with the decision is intellectual or ideological. The rationale appears to be that in these cases, there is no one who will be personally affected and who therefore could claim a greater interest in the matter than the applicant. The result would therefore be that if the applicant were denied leave, no one else would be able to come

---

30a　I Hare, (1995) 54(1) CLJ 1, 2–3.

30　Hilson and Cram, *op cit*, p18.

31　*Ibid*, p19.

32　[1994] 2 CMLR 760.

forward to challenge the decision so that the courts would have no opportunity to test the legality of an important decision, a position that the courts seem increasingly minded to avoid. Thus, for example, in *Secretary of State for Foreign and Commonwealth Affairs, ex p Rees-Mogg* (1994)[33] it was found that the applicant had standing 'because of his sincere concern for constitutional issues'. (Compare the remarks of Donaldson MR in *ex p Argyll Group plc* [1986] 2 All ER 257, 265–6.)

6   *Secretary of State for Employment, ex p EOC* (1994)[34] concerned in part the standing of the Equal Opportunities Commission (EOC), a quango with the remit of curbing discrimination, to challenge statutory provisions. Certain provisions of the Employment Protection (Consolidation) Act 1978 governed the right not to be unfairly dismissed, compensation for unfair dismissal and the right to statutory redundancy pay. These rights did not apply to workers who worked less than a specified number of hours a week. The EOC considered that since the majority of those working for less than the specified number of hours were women, the provisions operated to the disadvantage or women and were therefore discriminatory.

It was held (*inter alia*) that the EOC was entitled to bring judicial review proceedings in order to secure a declaration that UK law was incompatible with EC law. Declarations were made that the conditions set out in the provisions in question were indeed incompatible with EC law. The case also illustrates the point that where both an individual *and* a group have an interest in a given decision, the courts may favour the group.[35]

7   In *Secretary of State for Foreign Affairs, ex p the World Development Movement* (1995)[36] the question was whether the pressure group concerned had standing to challenge an allegedly unlawful grant of foreign aid.

Secretary of State for Foreign Affairs, ex p the World Development Movement [1995] 1 All ER 611, 618–20

Rose LJ: Internationally, [the World Development Movement] has official consultative status with UNESCO and has promoted international conferences. It has brought together development groups within the OECD. It tends to attract citizens of the United Kingdom concerned about the role of the United Kingdom Government in relation to the development of countries abroad and the relief of poverty abroad.

Its supporters have a direct interest in ensuring that funds furnished by the United Kingdom are used for genuine purposes, and it seeks to ensure that disbursement of aid budgets is made where that aid is most needed. It seeks, by this application, to represent the interests of people in developing countries who might benefit from funds which otherwise might go elsewhere.

If the applicants have no standing, it is said that no person or body would ensure that powers under the 1980 Act are exercised lawfully. For the applicants Mr Pleming QC submitted that the Foreign Secretary himself, in a written statement of 2 March 1994, has expressly accepted that the matter is '... clearly of public and

---

33   1 All ER 457.

34   2 WLR 409.

35   See further on this issue, Hilson and Cram, *op cit*, pp21–5.

36   1 All ER 611.

Parliamentary interest'. It cannot be said that the applicants are 'busybodies', 'cranks' or 'mischief-makers'. They are a non-partisan pressure group concerned with the misuse of aid money. If there is a public law error, it is difficult to see how else it could be challenged and corrected except by such an applicant. He referred the court to a number of authorities: *IRC v National Federation of Self-Employed and Small Businesses Ltd* [1981] 2 All ER 93, [1982] AC 617, in particular the speech of Lord Wilberforce ([1981] 2 All ER 93 at 96, [1982] AC 617 at 630) and the speech of Lord Diplock, where there appears this passage :

> It would, in my view, be a grave lacuna in our system of public law if a pressure group, like the federation, or even a single public spirited taxpayer, were prevented by outdated technical rules of *locus standi* from bringing the matter to the attention of the court to vindicate the Rule of Law and get the unlawful conduct stopped. The Attorney General, although he occasionally applies for prerogative orders against public authorities that do not form part of central Government, in practice never does so against Government departments. It is not, in my view, a sufficient answer to say that judicial review of the actions of officers or departments of central Government is unnecessary because they are accountable to Parliament for the way in which they carry out their functions. They are accountable to Parliament for what they do so far as regards efficiency and policy, and of that Parliament is the only judge; they are responsible to a court of justice for the lawfulness of what they do, and of that the court is the only judge. (See [1981] 2 All ER 93 at 107, [1982] AC 617 at 644.)

... The question of lawfulness being for the court, Mr Pleming submitted that the court in its discretion should accept the standing of the applicants. If they cannot seek relief, he said, who can? Neither a Government nor citizen of a foreign country denied aid is, in practical terms, likely to be able to bring such a challenge ... Mr Richards [for the Secretary of State] accepted that the requirements of standing will vary from case to case and that the court may accord standing to someone who would not otherwise qualify where exceptionally grave or widespread illegality is alleged. He referred to that part of Lord Diplock's speech in *IRC v National Federation of Self-Employed and Small Businesses Ltd* [1981] 2 All ER 93 at 101, [1982] AC 617 at 637 which shows that his comments which I have read are *obiter*. He referred to the speeches of both Lord Wilberforce and Lord Fraser, to the effect that a United Kingdom taxpayer's interest, which is no more than that of taxpayers in general, is insufficient to confer standing, save in an extreme case (see [1981] 2 All ER 93 at 98–9, 108, [1982] AC 617 at 633, 646). If no United Kingdom taxpayer could raise the matter, this not being an exceptional case, the applicants, submitted Mr Richards, cannot be in a better position.

For my part, I accept that standing (albeit decided in the exercise of the court's discretion, as Donaldson MR said) goes to jurisdiction ... But I find nothing in *IRC v National Federation of Self-Employed and Small Businesses Ltd* to deny standing to these applicants. The authorities referred to seem to me to indicate an increasingly liberal approach to standing on the part of the courts during the last 12 years. It is also clear from *IRC v National Federation of Self-Employed and Small Businesses Ltd* that standing should not be treated as a preliminary issue, but must be taken in the legal and factual context of the whole case (see [1981] 2 All ER 93 at 96, 110, 113, [1982] AC 617 at 630, 649, 653 *per* Lord Wilberforce, Lord Fraser and Lord Scarman).

Furthermore, the merits of the challenge are an important, if not dominant, factor when considering standing. In Professor Sir William Wade's words in *Administrative Law* (7th edn, 1994), p712:

> ...the real question is whether the applicant can show some substantial default or abuse, and not whether his personal rights or interests are involved.

Leaving merits aside for a moment, there seem to me to be a number of factors of significance in the present case: the importance of vindicating the Rule of Law, as Lord Diplock emphasised in *IRC v National Federation of Self-Employed and Small Businesses Ltd* [1981] 2 All ER 93 at 107, [1982] AC 617 at 644; the importance of the issue raised, as in *ex p Child Poverty Action Group*; the likely absence of any other responsible challenger, as in *ex p Child Poverty Action Group* and *ex p Greenpeace Ltd*; the nature of the breach of duty against which relief is sought (see *IRC v National Federation of Self-Employed and Small Businesses Ltd* [1981] 2 All ER 93 at 96, [1982] AC 617 at 630 *per* Lord Wilberforce); and the prominent role of these applicants in giving advice, guidance and assistance with regard to aid (see *ex p Child Poverty Action Group* [1989] 1 All ER 1047 at 1048, [1990] 2 QB 540 at 546). All, in my judgment, point, in the present case, to the conclusion that the applicants here do have a sufficient interest in the matter to which the application relates within s31(3) of the 1981 Act and Ord 53, r 3(7).

It seems pertinent to add this, that if the Divisional Court in *ex p Rees-Mogg* eight years after *ex p Argyll Group* was able to accept that the applicant in that case had standing in the light of his 'sincere concern for constitutional issues', *a fortiori*, it seems to me that the present applicants, with their national and international expertise and interest in promoting and protecting aid to underdeveloped nations, should have standing in the present application.

Notes

1　On the position of pressure groups, see also *Secretary of State for Social Services, ex p Child Poverty Action Group* [1989] 1 All ER 1047.

2　The case is clearly not a charter for the tiresomely officious: the applicants were a body whose work was of international repute and whose concern for the issue in hand was genuine.[37] Further, the fact that there was no one more closely affected by the decision in question who could have brought the case was clearly instrumental in the court's finding. The requirement that no such person or persons be available to mount a challenge will often operate to protect what Hilson and Cram term 'local autonomy';[38] the idea is that if a particular community or individual is content to acquiesce in a decision, it would show disrespect for their autonomy if other bodies, not affected by the decision, were to be allowed to challenge it. Thus it is argued that in the case of decisions which are *only* of local significance, the courts are right to insist as they do that any challenger must have a local interest.[39] By contrast, in cases in which decisions have particular local interest but are also of national significance (eg the *Rose Theatre* case itself), it is argued that

---

37　See also the finding that Rees-Mogg's concern for constitutional issues was 'sincere' and that Greenpeace was genuinely exercised about testing at THORP.

38　*Ibid*, especially pp10–12 and 15–21.

39　*Ibid*, p17. For an example, see *Covent Garden Community Association v Greater London Council*, (1981) JPL 183. Of course, if no members of the local community are prepared to come forward, a position may result in which a decision which represents an abuse of power goes unchallenged. This obviously offends against the Rule of Law model of judicial review (as Hilsom and Cram note), in which its primary purpose is seen as being to enforce strict boundaries of legality against the executive, thereby upholding the law and the citizen's general liberty (threatened by arbitrary power). Such a model would probably require no rule of standing at all. Any concern to protect autonomy will be bound to come into conflict with the Rule of Law model and it is thought that instances in which only *local* interests are threatened are cases in which the balance can reasonably be struck in favour of autonomy.

'the autonomy of those personally affected or locally connected ought to be overridden and standing granted to those with [only] a general interest'.[40] This does not however represent the current legal position.[41]

3   While this current generous view of standing is in some respects welcome, since it will allow pressure groups with particular expertise in the relevant area to raise issues of general public importance, it will tend to introduce, it is suggested, further uncertainty into the area of judicial review. Instances may tend to arise which fall on the borderlines suggested by these recent rulings; in particular it may be hard to lay down coherent and clear principles which can be used to determine whether or not an issue is sufficiently significant to fall within the rule from the *World Development Movement* decision.

4   The Canadian Supreme Court has recently developed a 'twin track' approach to the question of standing, as noted by Lord Woolf:

The Canadian Supreme Court over the last few years has considered a quartet of cases dealing with this subject and it has now moved forward to the position where in *Finlay v Minister of Finance* (1986)[42] it adopted a two-track approach. The first track covers those cases where it is now well established that a litigant would have standing; where he or she has personally been adversely affected by the decision which is the subject of the complaint. The other track is a discretionary track. In determining whether someone who is unable to use the first track is entitled to use the second track, the court will take into account various considerations which the Supreme Court of Canada has identified as reflecting what is understood to be the purpose of rules as to *locus standi*. These considerations are:

(i) the allocation of scarce judicial resources;
(ii) the need to screen out the mere busybody;
(iii) the concern that in the determination of issues the courts should have the benefit of the conflicting points of view of those most directly affected by them; and finally,
(iv) the concern as to the proper role of the courts and their constitutional relationship to the other branches of government.

Whether or not the precedent provided by the Canadian Supreme Court is thought to have merit, the Law Commission might conclude that this is one of the aspects of judicial review where it is now possible to identify in the rules situations where a litigant would be taken to have sufficient interest, and then leave it to the court to determine those situations which are in the grey area.[43]

5   It should be noted that there has been some judicial inclination to separate the determination of standing into two distinct stages can be seen in the case law. The following comments are representative.

---

40   *Ibid*, pp15–16 and see pp19–20.
41   *Rose Theatre*; *Poole Borough Council, ex p Beebee* [1991] JPL 643.
42   2 SCR 607.
43   *Op cit*, pp232–3.

Monopolies and Mergers Commission, ex p Argyll Group plc [1986] 1 WLR 763, 773

The first stage test, which is applied on the application for leave, will lead to a refusal if the applicant has no interest whatsoever and is, in truth, no more than a meddlesome busybody. If, however, the application appears to be otherwise arguable and there is no other discretionary bar, such as dilatoriness on the part of the applicant, the applicant may expect to get leave to apply, leaving the test of interest or standing to be re-applied as a matter of discretion on the hearing of the substantive application. At this second stage, the strength of the applicant's interest is one of the factors to be weighed in the balance.

Note

The Law Commission has recently brought forward proposals for reform of the law of standing.[44] The main proposal is for a scheme which would give the applicant two alternative routes to standing. The first is uncontroversial: the applicant would have standing if she 'had been or would be adversely affected' by the decision in question. But secondly, standing would be granted if the court considered that 'it is in the public interest for an applicant to make the application'. Cane (*ibid*) makes a number of criticisms of this second test, of which perhaps the most important is the fact that the Commission has indicated that it should be at the discretion of the court, a notion, which, given the importance of the area, he considers 'extremely undesirable'.

CAN JUDICIAL REVIEW BE EXCLUDED?

It is a fundamental principle of English law that the courts always have a duty to ensure that a body exercising power does so within the parameters set for it in the provisions (often primary legislation) which established it or gave it power in the area under consideration. In *Anisminic Ltd v Foreign Compensation Commission* (1969)[45] it was held that this power of the court to keep the deciding body within the remit defined in the Act which gave it its powers could not be excluded, despite apparently clear words in a statute to the contrary. To allow the court's supervisory jurisdiction to be ousted would be to accede to the proposition that the body in question had arbitrary powers, and the court was not prepared to believe that such powers are ever granted, since the grant of them would undermine the basic principle of the Rule of Law.

Anisminic Ltd v Foreign Compensation Commission [1969] 2 AC 147, 170

Lord Reid: ... Let me illustrate the matter by supposing a simple case. A statute provides that a certain order may be made by a person who holds a specified qualification or appointment, and it contains a provision ... that such an order made by such a person shall not be called in question in any court of law. A person aggrieved by an order alleges that it is a forgery or that the person who made the order did not hold that qualification or appointment. Does such a provision require the court to treat that order as a valid order? It is a well established principle that a

---

44 Law Com No 226, para 5.41. For discussion, see P Cane, 'Standing up for the Public' (1995) PL 276, 285–6.

45 2 AC 147.

provision ousting the ordinary jurisdiction of the court must be construed strictly – meaning, I think, that, if such a provision is reasonably capable of having two meanings, that meaning shall be taken which preserves the ordinary jurisdiction of the court.

Statutory provisions which seek to limit the ordinary jurisdiction of the court have a long history. No case has been cited in which any other form of words limiting the jurisdiction of the court has been held to protect a nullity. If the draftsman or Parliament had intended to introduce a new kind of ouster clause so as to prevent any inquiry even as to whether the document relied on was a forgery, I would have expected to find something much more specific than the bald statement that a determination shall not be called in question in any court of law. Undoubtedly such a provision protects every determination which is not a nullity. But I do not think that it is necessary or even reasonable to construe the word 'determination' as including everything which purports to be a determination but which is in fact no determination at all. And there are no degrees of nullity. There are a number of reasons why the law will hold a purported decision to be a nullity. I do not see how it could be said that such a provision protects some kinds of nullity but not others: if that were intended it would be easy to say so.

Notes

1 The basic idea behind the *Anisminic* decision is that by making an error in law, the body asked itself the wrong question, determined a point it was not authorised to decide and thus exceeded its *vires*. Its decision is therefore *ultra vires* and a nullity. The idea of a body being empowered to err within certain limits was rejected.

2 Section 12(1) Tribunals Act 1992 now provides that the supervisory functions of the superior courts will not be excluded by Acts passed prior to 1 August 1958. This or course implies that effect may be given to ouster clauses in later statutes.

Tribunals and Enquiries Act 1992

12.–(1) As respects England and Wales–

(a) any provision in an Act passed before 1st August 1958 that any order or determination shall not be called into question in any court, or

(b) any provision in such an Act which by similar words excludes any of the powers of the High Court,

shall not have effect so as to prevent the removal of the proceedings into the High Court by order of *certiorari* or to prejudice the powers of the High Court to make orders of *mandamus*.

Supervisory functions of superior courts not excluded by Acts passed before 1 August 1958.

Notes

1 It may be pointed out that in cases involving national security the court will find either that review is not available or that it is very marginal. It seems to follow from *ex p Cheblak* (1991)[46] that although the decision to exclude persons from the UK is non-justiciable there may be some review of preconditions and procedures.[47] It appears to be unclear whether decisions

---

46 2 All ER 319.

47 See Walker, *The Prevention of Terrorism in British Law*, 2nd edn (1992),pp90–2.

to exclude persons under the Prevention of Terrorism Act 1989 are subject to judicial review. In *Secretary of State for the Home Department, ex p Stitt* (1987),[48] it was found that considerations of national security and confidentiality made review inappropriate.

2　Moreover, in the area of exclusion of persons under the PTA 1989, since the courts have decided that the minister is not obliged to give them reasons for his decisions, they have made it effectively impossible for them to determine whether the minister had acted within his powers, for example whether he had some evidence for his decision and had taken into account the proper considerations. In practice, therefore, though not in theory, review by the courts will be limited to cases in which the order given is bad on its face, because, for example it purports to exclude a suspect for more than the legislation allows. To assert that the courts would not have the power to quash such an order through the writ of *certiorari* would be tantamount to asserting that the minister has been endowed with an unlimited and arbitrary power in which case, by definition, the power would not be a legal one. It is submitted therefore that the courts retain the power of supervisory review of exclusion orders, but that in practice review will be impossible except in the improbable case of an order which palpably purported to exceed the powers given to the minister under the Act.

3　In deportation cases the courts appear content to allow the Home Secretary a wide margin of discretion. In *Brixton Prison Governor, ex p Soblen* (1963),[49] a deportation order was challenged on the grounds that the Secretary of State had acted for an improper purpose – allegedly in order to comply with a request from the United States for S's return made in order to circumvent the non-availability of extradition proceedings which were not possible due to the nature of S's offences (espionage). The Court of Appeal upheld the deportation order on the basis that the Secretary of State could act for a plurality of purposes. The fact that this might be termed extradition by the back door did not affect the validity of the order. The Court considered that the need to serve the public good by the removal of S need not be the dominant motive in making the order although the minister must have a genuine belief that removal was necessary on that basis. It did not matter if the minister's main motive for acting might have been to comply with the request from the USA.

4　A number of statutes governing national security concerns contain exclusion clauses. These include the Intelligence Services Act 1994 and the Interception of Communications Act 1985. The Security Services Act 1989 contains such a clause in s5(4). If a member of the public has a grievance concerning the operation of the 1989 Act complaint to a court is not possible: under s5 it can only be made to a tribunal and under s5(4) the decisions of the tribunal are not questionable in any court of law. The provision of s5(4) was criticised in 1992 by Mr Justice Kennedy in refusing an application for review of the Security Service Tribunal's decision not to investigate allegations that MI5 is still holding files on Harriet Harman, the Shadow Health Minister;[50] he

---

48　*The Times*, 3 February 1987.

49　2 QB 243.

considered that in some circumstances the courts certainly would have jurisdiction to intervene. In the following case, which concerned telephone tapping authorised by ministerial *fiat* (the Interception of Telecommunications Act not then being in force), the court took a similarly robust stance in dealing with the argument that national security considerations effectively ousted its jurisdiction.

Secretary of State for the Home Department, ex p Ruddock [1987] 2 All ER 518, 526–7

Taylor J: ... In effect the plea amounts to this: the Secretary of State invariably maintains silence in the interests of national security on issues such as are raised here. The court in its discretion should do likewise, and since making findings to decide the case may break that silence, the court should, in Lord Scarman's phrase, abdicate its judicial function. I cannot agree with that, either as a general proposition or in this particular case. I do not accept that the court should never inquire into a complaint against a minister if he says his policy is to maintain silence in the interests of national security. To take an extreme and one hopes unlikely example, suppose an application were put before the court alleging a warrant was improperly issued by a Secretary of State against a political opponent, and suppose the application to be supported by the production of a note in the minister's own hand acknowledging the criteria did not apply by giving instructions that the phone be tapped nevertheless to see if anything discreditable could be learnt. It could not be sensibly argued that the department's invariable policy of silence should require the court meekly to follow suit and decline to decide such a case. At the other extreme, I recognise there could occur a case where the issue raised was so sensitive and the revelations necessarily following its decision so damaging to national security that the court might have to take special measures (for example sitting *in camera* or prohibiting the mention of names). Conceivably (although I would reserve the point) in an extreme case the court might have to decline to try the issues. But in all such cases, cogent evidence of potential damage to national security flowing from the trial of the issues would have to be adduced, whether in open court or in camera, to justify any modification of the court's normal procedure. Totally to oust the court's supervisory jurisdiction in a field where *ex hypothesi* the citizen can have no right to be consulted is a draconian and dangerous step indeed. Evidence to justify the court's declining to decide a case (if such a course is ever justified) would need to be very strong and specific.

Note

Whilst this insistence that the court will not allow its supervisory jurisdiction to be ousted without 'cogent evidence' is clearly heartening to proponents of the Rule of Law, see by contrast decisions made under more overtly exclusionary legislation, eg *Secretary of State for the Home Department, ex p McQuillan* (1995). [51]

JUDICIAL REVIEW; APPEAL; TRIBUNALS

As McEldowney notes, judicial review and appeal can appear to perform similar functions for the citizen, but are aimed at remedying different grievances:

---

50   See *Guardian*, 15 February 1992.
51   4 All ER 400.

The Law Commission has noted that many judicial review applications were initiated as desperate and ill-disguised attempts to appeal against the decision in question. Conversely, appeals may be widely interpreted to include matters that could be reviewed. Occasionally the courts have accepted a wider remit to the appeal system even where it may overlap with the application for judicial review.

Appeals are not normally provided against discretionary decisions involving ministers or policy matters involving the allocation of resources or the implementation of Cabinet decisions. The absence of an appeal structure may be due to the political nature of the policy where the appropriate forum is in Parliament. However, this may not be a satisfactory reason to cover all cases where there is no appeal. In the previous chapter, criticisms made by the Council on Tribunals of the lack of a proper appeals system following the replacement of supplementary benefit payments by payments from the social fund made by social fund officers under the Social Security Act 1986, were noted. The absence of an appeal procedure was perceived as creating unfairness. The Council on Tribunals view judicial review as an inappropriate means of appeal from tribunal decisions. For example, instead of judicial review of immigration cases the Council on Tribunals favoured the introduction of an appeal on a point of law from the Immigration Appeal Tribunal, now to be found under the Asylum and Immigration Appeals Act 1993.[52]

Notes

1   The presence of an appeals procedure may influence the court against allowing the applicant leave to apply for judicial review. In *ex p Swati* (1986),[53] the Court of Appeal refused a would be visitor to the UK leave to apply for review of the Immigration Officer's decision to refuse him entry into the country, partly on the grounds that he there was a statutory procedure for appeal against the decision, even though this could only be exercised after Swati had left the country.

2   Michael Loughlin asks whether a sociological analysis of such decisions might not prove illuminating. He notes[54] that 'civil applications for judicial review more than doubled between 1981 and 1985 and that on average immigration cases constituted around 40 per cent of these applications, and in 1986 ... nearly 60%. Given the strain of this caseload on the courts, might not the *Swati* decision, effectively removing the remedy of judicial review in the largest category of immigration cases, best be viewed as an administrative or managerial response ... to this situation?' Whilst such an interpretation of the particular case might strike many as simplistic and implausible, the point is well taken that, particularly in examining the tortuous and changeable areas of *locus standi*, the public/private divide, and the procedural hurdles imposed on applicants for judicial review, illuminating insights may be gained through looking beyond purely legal considerations.

3   The relationship between tribunals (which usually deal with the merits of a decision) and the courts (which in judicial review proceedings are purportedly concerned with only the legality of it) is a complex and untidy one. Lord Woolf sketches a critique and some proposals for reform.

---

52   John F McEldowney, *Public Law* (1994), pp451–2.

53   1 All ER 717.

54   *Public Law and Political Theory* (1992), p55.

Lord Woolf, 'Judicial Review: A Possible Programme for Reform' (1992) *Public Law* 221, 228–31

There are ... a great many ... cases in which other tribunals could perform satisfactorily the role now performed by High Court judges. There are also situations where a very powerful argument can be made for suggesting that a tribunal could be better qualified than the High Court to perform the High Court's existing role. ...

What has been shown already by our extensive administrative tribunal system is that as long as tribunals are subject as a last resort to the supervision of the High Court or the Court of Appeal, they can provide a method of disposing of disputes in many areas to the satisfaction of the vast majority of the multitude of litigants who have resort to them. They can provide a forum where restrictions as to *locus standi* and representation need not apply. They should have an informality and flexibility of procedure which accord with the needs of the litigants. There should be more and better tribunals.

The relationship between courts and tribunals

However, the relationship between the courts and tribunals requires attention. There is the need for a proper structure. This is already recognised by the Law Commission and is to receive their attention. At the present time, there is a bewildering variety of ways in which proceedings can progress from tribunals to the High Court and the Court of Appeal. Statutory applications, statutory appeals, direct appeals to the Court of Appeal and, as a last resort, judicial review. The time limits for making applications and for appealing are not consistent. There is surely a case for trying to produce order out of this confusion. ... There should be an appeal from all decisions of a court or tribunal in civil matters to the Court of Appeal, with leave of the lower body or the Court of Appeal. Otherwise, matters should come to the High Court on judicial review. Criminal matters, wherever possible, should go by way of case stated to a single judge, with leave of the High Court or the court below; otherwise they should come on judicial review to a single judge. If a case is of especial importance, it can be heard by a two-judge court.

It could also be an advantage if tribunals were more closely integrated with the High Court. Both the tribunals and the High Court could benefit from an ability to refer cases one to the other. High Court and other judges should sit in tribunals more extensively than they do at present. They would ensure proper legal standards and the independence of tribunals. They would also develop greater experience of the process of administrative decision-making. A greater demand for discovery and cross-examination on applications for judicial review than exists at present is likely to develop. The European dimension could well act here as a catalyst. For example, in *ex p Factortame Ltd (No 2)*, the European Court made it clear that it is for

> the national court ... to ensure the legal protection which persons derive from direct effects of provisions of the Community law /and that any provision of a national legal system ... and judicial practice which might impair the effectiveness of Community law by withholding from the national court having jurisdiction to apply such law a power to do everything necessary at the moment of his application to set aside national legislative provisions ... are incompatible with those requirements [which are the very essence of Community law] [[1991] 1 AC 603, 643–4, emphasis supplied]

The experience of this country before the European Court of Human Rights, indicates that judges from countries with a different system from our own do not readily understand the extent of the safeguard provided for the public by judicial review. The Luxembourg Court, like the Human Rights Commission and the Strasbourg Court, could well wish to see built into our judicial review process a greater readiness to allow discovery and cross-examination. This could also become necessary because of the range of public bodies subject to judicial review. At the present time, most litigants are prepared to accept without investigation the evidence of central Government. However, this may not be the attitude of large public companies attacking public bodies. There could therefore be an advantage in the High Court having the ability to remit issues requiring the investigation of facts to an appropriate tribunal, where they could be investigated in a more appropriate manner than is possible in adversarial proceedings before the High Court.

The way forward over a period of time should thus involve creating a unified system of tribunals for resolving administrative disputes, with the High Court and Court of Appeal required to resolve only difficult problems of law and points of principle and policy of high importance to the development of administrative law. Again a precedent can be found in what has happened in Australia, where the system of tribunals and the Administrative Appeals Tribunal perform something of this role. Our existing tribunals could become, with other new tribunals, specialist sections of a new tribunal system presided over by an Administrative Appeal Tribunal. Within the tribunal system, there could be deployed skills and disciplines which at present play no part in our review process. The Lands Tribunal already makes the use of members from professions other than the law. An Environmental Tribunal would certainly need to do so. Why not a multi-skilled Administrative Appeal Tribunal? A policy along these lines would avoid the High Court being overburdened, and would avoid more and more judges having to be appointed to deal with an ever-increasing number of applications. The High Court and the Court of Appeal would play their role by ensuring that the tribunal system maintains correct standards.

CHAPTER 2

GROUNDS FOR JUDICIAL REVIEW

INTRODUCTION: THE JUSTIFICATION FOR REVIEW

The system of judicial review allows the judges to interfere, some would allege rather arbitrarily, in the machinery of government and administration. Using this self-made weapon, judges have struck down numerous important decisions, from the policy of the Greater London Council to reduce public transport fares in the capital by 25%,[1] to the recent decision of the Home Secretary to introduce a new, non-statutory criminal injuries compensation scheme.[2] What is the justification for this interference?

TRS Allan argues that far from being an instrument of unjustified interference, the operation of judicial review may forge an alliance between the judges and Parliament, thereby preventing subversion of the latter's sovereignty.

TRS Allan, 'Legislative Supremacy and the Rule of Law' (1985) 44 *Cambridge Law Journal* 111, 130–1

> ... In seeking to apply those common standards of morality which are taken for granted in the community – the judge respects the natural expectations of the citizen. Since he is bound to administer justice *according to law,* including legislation of which he may disapprove, he must faithfully accord every Act of Parliament its full and proper application. But in administering *justice* according to law he can hardly be indifferent to the expectations and aspirations of the governed – those from whom, in our political theory, all governmental authority is ultimately derived. Hence the importance of those presumptions of legislative intent which operate to exclude harsh and retrospective changes in the law in the absence of clear and unambiguous enactment. The Rule of Law therefore assists in preventing the subversion of the political sovereignty of the people by manipulation of the legal sovereignty of Parliament. But there is no opposition in this scheme between Parliament and the judiciary: it is an alliance against the executive. This alliance is most clearly and obviously threatened, and the political supremacy of the electorate subverted, when a judge attempts to ascertain, and give effect to, the wishes and intentions of a minister or government department in sponsoring legislation. It is not governmental intentions which count in interpreting statutes granting coercive powers to public officials: only the intention of Parliament as a whole in so far as that may be collected from a genuine attempt to construe the language of the statute in its legal, social and moral context.
>
> Judicial deference to the Rule of Law as a constitutional principle, therefore, operates to strengthen democracy by helping to ensure that the powers of government, democratically derived, are applied with proper respect for the legitimate expectations of the governed. The ultimate sovereignty of the people demands that their representatives, through Parliament, should have the last word. But the importance of the Rule of Law in reconciling the immediate political concerns of government, and the concomitant grants and exercise of powers, with the traditional, constitutional values of our society should not be

---

1   *Bromley LBC v GLC* [1983] AC 768.
2   *Secretary of State for the Home Dept, ex p Fire Brigades Union and others* [1995] 2 All ER 244, HL.

underestimated. It is, of course, the, field of administrative law that has witnessed the most recent and challenging development of the principle of the Rule of Law. The doctrine of *ultra vires* has emerged as a powerful weapon to fight abuse of discretionary powers granted by statute. The courts have rediscovered their supervisory jurisdiction over inferior tribunals in order to provide a remedy for errors of law. The attempt has been made to insist, in the interests of citizens affected, on the closest scrutiny of the conduct of public bodies compatible with the proper fulfilment of their statutory functions. It is not the function of the courts to interfere with the formation and execution of policy which Parliament has entrusted to administrative agencies: but those agencies must remain within the law, including the law governing their own jurisdiction and powers.

Note

The idea that the exercise of judicial review represents a judicial alliance with Parliament has recently come under critical scrutiny.

The Hon Sir John Laws, 'Law and Democracy' (1995) *Public Law* 72, 78

Lord Diplock's judicial review criterion of illegality is plain enough: no subordinate body may exceed the express bounds of its statutory power: that is, the power which on its proper construction the Act confers. But what of the other heads of review, *Wednesbury* unreasonableness and procedural unfairness? They are now as elementary as illegality. In the elaboration of these principles the courts have imposed and enforced judicially created standards of public behaviour. But the civilised imperative of their existence cannot be derived from the simple requirement that public bodies must be kept to the limits of their authority given by Parliament. Neither deductive logic nor the canons of ordinary language, which are the basic tools of statutory construction, can attribute them to that ideal, since although their application may be qualified by the words of any particular statute, in principle their roots have grown from another seed altogether. In some formulations, it is true, they have purportedly been justified by the attribution of an intention to the legislature that statutory decision-makers should act reasonably and fairly; but this is largely fictitious. In recent times, before *Ridge v Baldwin* it was not generally thought (to put it crudely) that administrative, nonjudicial, bodies owed such duties as to hear the other side. Before *Padfield* it was not generally thought that it was an enforceable function of every statute conferring public power that it only justified action to promote the distinct purposes of the Act, even though the Act did not state them. Before the concept of legitimate expectation assumed the status of a substantive legal principle (whose precise date may be nicely debated), it was not generally thought that decision-makers should be prevented from departing from previous assurances as to their actions without giving those affected an opportunity to make representations. *Wednesbury* itself reaches back to older law; but its fruition and its maturity came 20 years and more after it was decided. It cannot be suggested that all these principles, which represent much of the bedrock of modern administrative law, were suddenly interwoven into the legislature's intentions in the 1960s and 70s and onwards, in which period they have been articulated and enforced by the courts. They are, categorically, judicial creations. They owe neither their existence nor their acceptance to the will of the legislature. They have nothing to do with the intention of Parliament, save as a fig-leaf to cover their true origins. We do not need the fig-leaf any more.

Notes

1   For criticism of Laws' view see Christopher Forsyth, 'Of Fig-leaves and Fairy Tales: The *Ultra Vires* Doctrine, the Sovereignty of Parliament and Judicial

Review' (1996) CLJ 122, esp 127–40; for further discussion of these issues see Jeffrey Jowell, 'The Rule of Law Today' in Jowell and Oliver (eds), *The Changing Constitution*, 3rd edn (1994), pp73–75, P Craig, *Administrative Law*, 3rd edn (1994), pp3–40 and Wade *Administrative Law*, 7th edn (1994), Chapters 1 and 2. We now turn to the substantive principles of judicial review itself.

2   Judicial review is to be distinguished from review of the merits of the decision itself. It is concerned only with the legality of the decision, which will itself depend on whether it falls within any of the three main heads of review discussed below. Sir John Laws[3] gives a clear explanation as to why constitutional principle makes the simultaneous demand that judges ensure decisions are made legally but do not assess their merits:

[This demand] arises as a matter of definition from the very nature of the public power respectively lying in the hands of the courts and those whom they review. The paradigm of a public body subject to the public law jurisdiction is one whose power is conferred by statute. The statute is logically prior to it; and by the constitution it is for the courts to police the statute. But they do not act under the statute. They are altogether outside it. Their power is not derived from it, nor ultimately from any Act of Parliament. This state of affairs has two consequences. First, the judges have to see that the power given by the statute is not transgressed by its donee; secondly, they have no business themselves to exercise the powers conferred by it, precisely because they are not the donee. Hence the essence of the judicial review jurisdiction. It vindicates the Rule of Law not only by confining statutory power within the four corners of the Act, but also ensuring that the statute is not usurped by anyone – including the courts themselves.[4]

3   If it is found, upon review, that an authority has acted unlawfully, there are a number of remedies that can be granted. Discussion of these lies outside the scope of this book;[5] a very brief summary only will be given. The following are known as the prerogative remedies:

(1) *certiorari*: quashes an unlawful decision;

(2) *prohibition*: prohibits an authority from an unlawful act it was proposing to commit;

(3) *mandamus*: compels an authority to perform a particular act;

Prerogative remedies may not be granted against the Crown, though they can be granted against individual Government ministers; additionally, they have not been used in relation to delegated legislation found to be unlawful.

4   In addition, the following remedies, which are non-prerogative (and not unique to judicial review) may be sought:

(1) *injunctions*: restrain an unlawful action, and may be interim or final; for their use against the Crown and against Government ministers

---

3   'Law and Democracy' (1995) PL 72.

4   *Ibid*, pp77–78. Laws' analysis is not applicable in terms to cases in which the body which the court is reviewing does not receive its powers from statute, but it can apply by analogy; whichever source of power gave the jurisdiction to the decision-making body, it did not give a simultaneous jurisdiction to the courts.

5   Readers are referred to the relevant chapters in Craig, *Administrative Law*, 3rd edn (1994); Wade and Forsyth, *Administrative Law*, 7th edn (1994); Foulkes, *Administrative Law*, 7th edn (1995) or De Smith, *Judicial Review of Administrative Action*, 4th edn (1980) for a full exposition.

see *Re M* (1993)[6] and *Secretary of State of Transport, ex p Factortame (No 2)* 1990;[7]

(2) *declarations*: an authoritative statement by the court, eg that a given act is unlawful; often used in relation to the Crown, or delegated legislation;

(3) *damages*: available only if the applicant has claimed one of the above remedies *and* if she can show that the authority has committed a breach of contract or a tort.

5 In *Council of Civil Service Unions v Minister for Civil Service* (1985)[8] Lord Diplock summed up the grounds for judicial review in the following statement:

CCSU v Minister for Civil Service [1985] AC 374, 410

Lord Diplock: Judicial review has I think developed to a stage today when without reiterating any analysis of the steps by which the development has come about, one can conveniently classify under three heads the grounds upon which administrative action is subject to control by judicial review. The first ground I would call 'illegality,' the second 'irrationality' and the third 'procedural impropriety.' That is not to say that further development on a case by case basis may not in course of time add further grounds. I have in mind particularly the possible adoption in the future of the principle of 'proportionality' which is recognised in the administrative law of several of our fellow members of the European Economic Community; ...

ILLEGALITY

Established principles

As Lord Diplock explained it in the *GCHQ* case, 'By 'illegality' as a ground for judicial review I mean that the decision-maker must understand correctly the law that regulates his decision-making power and must give effect to it.'[9] This can mean simply that the decision-maker has made a mistake in interpreting (say) the statute by which his powers are governed. But it can also have a much wider meaning: it covers the situation where the decision maker does something which he is not in the simplest sense empowered to do, such as establishing a commercial laundry when empowered only to provide municipal wash houses (*Attorney General v Fulham Corp* (1921).[10] It also covers a number of ways in which a decision-maker can fail to exercise a discretion properly, such as taking into account improper considerations, or fettering the exercise of discretion by wrongly holding oneself to be bound by a previous policy. The head of 'illegality' is therefore the most broad and flexible head of judicial review.

---

6   3 WLR 433, HL; see Part I, Chapter 3, pp68–70 for an extract from the case.
7   1 AC 603.
8   AC 374.
9   *Ibid*, p410.
10 1 Ch 440.

Are all errors of law reviewable?

An important preliminary question which has arisen is whether any error of law made by the decision maker will result in it being held to have exceeded its jurisdiction.

The issue is that there may be mistakes which a body is entitled to make in coming to a decision – mistakes which do not render its decision unlawful. As we shall see, if the decision-making body – a tribunal – makes a 'mistake' in the sense that it gives more weight to a particular consideration than the court would have, or if it makes a mistake as to whether a fact is proven or not, the courts will view such mistakes as being within the tribunal's jurisdiction. But are mistakes as to the law which governs a tribunal ever of this type? Or do all errors of law made by a tribunal mean that it has exceeded its rightful jurisdiction? The leading case in this area is *Anisminic* (1969).

Anisminic Ltd v Foreign Compensation Commissioners **[1969] AC 147, 171–175.**

Anisminic Ltd had had certain of its property sequestered by the Egyptian Government, and had later sold it to TEDO, an Egyptian organisation, for considerably less than its actual value. Anisminic applied for compensation to the Foreign Compensation Commission, which had the duty, under Art 4 of the Foreign Compensation etc Order 1962, of distributing compensation to business such as Anisminic which had suffered loss by virtue of the confiscation of their property. Article 4 stated that the Commission was to treat a claim as good if they were satisfied of the following:

(a)   the applicant was the person referred to in the relevant part of Annex E of the Order as 'the owner of the property or ... the successor in title of such a person'; and

(b)   the person referred to in that part of Annex E 'and any person who became successor in title of such person ... were British Nationals'.

The Commission's initial finding was that Anisminic Ltd was not entitled to compensation because TEDO (its successor in title) was not a British national.

> **Lord Reid:** It has sometimes been said that it is only where a tribunal acts without jurisdiction that its decision is a nullity. But in such cases the word 'jurisdiction' has been used in a very wide sense, and I have come to the conclusion that it is better not to use the term except in the narrow and original sense of the tribunal being entitled to enter on the inquiry in question. But there are many cases where, although the tribunal had jurisdiction to enter on the inquiry, it has done or failed to do something in the course of the inquiry which is of such a nature that its decision is a nullity. It may have given its decision in bad faith. It may have made a decision which it had no power to make. It may have failed in the course of the inquiry to comply with the requirements of natural justice. It may in perfect good faith have misconstrued the provisions giving it power to act so that it failed to deal with the question remitted to it and decided some question which was not remitted to it. It may have refused to take into account something which it was required to take into account. Or it may have based its decision on some matter which, under the provisions setting it up, it had no right to take into account. I do not intend this list to be exhaustive. But if it decides a question remitted to it for decision without committing any of

these errors it is as much entitled to decide that question wrongly as it is to decide it rightly.

I can now turn to the provisions of the Order under which the commission acted, and to the way in which the commission reached their decision. ... The effect of the Order was to confer legal rights on persons who might previously have hoped or expected that in allocating any sums available discretion would be exercised in their favour. ...

The main difficulty in this case springs from the fact that the draftsman did not state separately what conditions have to be satisfied (1) where the applicant is the original owner and (2) where the applicant claims as the successor in title of the original owner. It is clear that where the applicant is the original owner he must prove that he was a British national on the dates stated. And it is equally clear that where the applicant claims as being the original owner's successor in title he must prove that both he and the original owner were British nationals on those dates, subject to later provisions in the article about persons who had died or had been born within the relevant period. What is left in obscurity is whether the provisions with regard to successors in title have any application at all in cases where the applicant is himself the original owner. If this provision had been split up as it should have been, and the conditions to be satisfied where the original owner is the applicant had been set out, there could have been no such obscurity.

This is the crucial question in this case. It appears from the commission's reasons that they construed this provision as requiring them to inquire, when the applicant is himself the original owner, whether he had a successor in title. So they made that inquiry in this case and held that TEDO was the applicant's successor in title. As TEDO was not a British national they rejected the appellants' claim. But if, on a true construction of the Order, a claimant who is an original owner does not have to prove anything about successors in title, then the commission made an inquiry which the Order did not empower them to make, and they based their decision on a matter which they had no right to take into account. If one uses the word 'jurisdiction' in its wider sense, they went beyond their jurisdiction in considering this matter. It was argued that the whole matter of construing the Order was something remitted to the commission for their decision. I cannot accept that argument. I find nothing in the Order to support it. The Order requires the commission to consider whether they are satisfied with regard to the prescribed matters. That is all they have to do. It cannot be for the commission to determine the limits of its powers. Of course if one party submits to a tribunal that its powers are wider than in fact they are, then the tribunal must deal with that submission. But if they reach a wrong conclusion as to the width of their powers, the court must be able to correct that – not because the tribunal has made an error of law, but because as a result of making an error of law they have dealt with and based their decision on a matter with which, on a true construction of their powers, they had no right to deal. If they base their decision on some matter which is not prescribed I for their adjudication, they are doing something which they have no right to do and, if the view which I expressed earlier is right, their decision is a nullity. So the question is whether on a true construction of the Order the applicants did or did not have to prove anything with regard to successors in title. If the commission were entitled to enter on the inquiry whether the applicants had a successor in title, then their decision as to whether TEDO was their successor in title would I think be unassailable whether it was right or wrong: it would be a decision on a matter remitted to them for their decision. The question I have to consider is not whether they made a wrong decision but whether they inquired into and decided a matter which they had no right to consider.

I have great difficulty in seeing how in the circumstances there could be a successor in title of a person who is still in existence. This provision is dealing with the period before the Order was made when the original owner had no title to anything: he had nothing but a hope that some day somehow he might get some compensation. The rest of the article makes it clear that the phrase (though inaccurate) must apply to a person who can be regarded as having inherited in some way the hope which a deceased original owner had that he would get some compensation. But 'successor in title' must I think mean some person who could come forward and make a claim in his own right. There can only be a successor in title where the title of its original possessor has passed to another person, his successor, so that the original possessor of the title can no longer make a claim, but his successor can make the claim which the original possessor of the title could have made if his title had not passed to his successor. The 'successor' of a deceased person can do that. But how could any 'successor' do that while the original owner is still in existence? One can imagine the improbable case of the original owner agreeing with someone that, for a consideration immediately paid to him, he would pay over to the other party any compensation which he might ultimately receive. But that would not create a 'successor in title' in any true sense. And I can think of no other way in which the original owner could transfer *inter vivos* his expectation of receiving compensation. If there were anything in the rest of the Order to indicate that such a case was intended to be covered, we might have to attribute to the phrase 'successor in title' some unusual and inaccurate meaning which would cover it. But there is nothing of that kind. In themselves the words 'successor in title' are, in my opinion, inappropriate in the circumstances of this Order to denote any person while the original owner is still in existence, and I think it most improbable that they were ever intended to denote any such person. There is no necessity to stretch them to cover any such person. I would therefore hold that the words 'and any person who became successor in title to such person' in art 4 (1)(b)(ii) have no application to a case where the applicant is the original owner. It follows that the commission rejected the appellants' claim on a ground which they had no right to take into account and that their decision was a nullity. I would allow this appeal.

Notes

1   McEldowney considers how *Anisminic* has fared in subsequent decisions:

In *Pearlman v Keepers and Governors of Harrow School* [[1979] QB 56], Lord Denning explained that any such distinction between errors which are jurisdictional and those that are not are so fine that the distinction may be discarded. Pearlman was a tenant who had installed central heating. He applied to the county court for a declaration that it constituted a 'structural alteration' of the premises. The county court decided that it did not and Pearlman sought certiorari to quash this decision in the High Court, notwithstanding the fact that the county court decision was by statute 'final and conclusive'.

Lord Denning's attempts to render obsolete the distinction between errors within jurisdiction and those that were outside jurisdiction was rejected in the Privy Council case of *South East Asia Fire Bricks v Non-Metallic Mineral Products* [[1981)]AC 363] by Lord Fraser. Lord Diplock in *O'Reilly v Mackman* believed that there was still an important distinction to be drawn between those bodies where error of law within jurisdiction remained relevant and bodies where it had become an unnecessary distinction. Inferior courts fell within the category of review such as tribunals and administrative agencies, while the ordinary courts such as the county court in *Pearlman* were entitled to rely on the distinction between errors within jurisdiction which are not reviewable and errors outside jurisdiction which are subject to review.[11]

2   It should be noted that Professor Wade[12] supports Lord Denning's view and Diplock's in *Re Racal* (1981).[13] In another essay, he explains Lord Diplock's view on the meaning of jurisdiction, first expounded in the *Anisminic* decision.

Lord Diplock's doctrine, as Lord Browne-Wilkinson explained very clearly, was an extension of the doctrine of *ultra vires*. 'Thence forward it was to be taken that Parliament had only conferred the decision-making power on the basis that it was to be exercised on the correct legal basis: a misdirection in law in making the decision therefore rendered the decision *ultra vires* ... a tribunal or inferior court acts *ultra vires* if it reaches its conclusion on a basis erroneous under the general law.' This is classical constitutional logic and it has rounded off the doctrine of *ultra vires* by eliminating the one recognised exception. The revival of the power to quash for *intra vires* error of law on the face of the record in *Northumberland Compensation Appeal Tribunal, ex p Shaw* [1952] 1 KB 338 was hailed as a great leap forward 40 years ago and led to many decisions about the content of the record, etc. But it can now be seen as a formalistic doctrine which can deservedly be consigned to oblivion. The same fate has overtaken the distinction between jurisdictional and non-jurisdictional law – except, of course, in the case of visitors. Of the large area within which tribunals were formerly allowed to err, only non-jurisdictional fact remains. There have been strong hints that that also may not long survive (*Secretary of State for Education and Science v Tameside MBC* [1977] AC 1014 at 1030, 1047) and its extinction may confidently be predicted when an occasion presents itself.

A paradoxical result is that *Anisminic is* now held to have destroyed the logic on which the decision itself was based. When the House of Lords invalidated the tribunal's decision which, by statute, 'shall not be questioned in any court of law', they did so under the long-established doctrine that a clause of that kind would protect errors of law which were *intra vires* but not those which were *ultra vires*, since Parliament could not be supposed to have intended to give any tribunal power to determine its own jurisdiction. But now that all errors of law are *ultra vires*, there is nothing left upon which the clause can operate, so that for a court to refuse to apply it, as was done in *Anisminic*, can now only be naked disobedience of Parliament. The obituary notice for yet another historic doctrine may have been written.[14]

Note

The historic doctrine here referred to is, of course, parliamentary sovereignty – the idea that the judges must unhesitatingly obey any and every Act of Parliament.

Ways of acting 'illegally': exceeding powers, irrelevant consideration

There are occasions where decision-makers have been found to have acted outside their powers in the simplest sense, sometimes with dramatic results.

---

11   McEldowney, *op cit*, pp470–1.
12   See *Constitutional Fundamentals* (1989), p82.
13   *Re Racal Communications Ltd* [1981] AC 374.
14   (1993) 109 LQR 158.

Laker Airways v Dept of Trade [1977] QB 643, 704, CA

Laker Airways had been granted a licence by the Civil Aviation Authority ('CAA') under statutory authority. As a result of a change in Government, and consequent change in policy, the Secretary of State issued 'guidance' to the CAA as he was entitled to; the guidance, however instructed them to revoke Laker's licence. Laker sought judicial review of the decision.

> **Lord Denning MR:** The first [question] is whether the Secretary of State was acting beyond his lawful powers when he gave the new policy guidance to the Civil Aviation Authority.
>
> In determining this point, I have found much help from the well reasoned decisions of the Civil Aviation Authority, not only in 1972, when they granted the licence to Laker Airways, but also in 1975 when they refused to revoke it. It is plain that they applied most conscientiously and sensibly the four general objectives set out in s3(1)(a), (b), (c) and (d) of the statute, as amplified and supplemented by the 1972 policy guidance. The new policy guidance of 1976 cuts right across those statutory objectives. It lays down a new policy altogether. Whereas the statutory objectives made it clear that the British Airways Board was not to have a monopoly, but that at least one other British airline should have an opportunity to participate, the new policy guidance says that the British Airways Board is to have a monopoly. No competition is to be allowed. And no other British airline is to be licensed unless British Airways had given its consent. This guidance was not a mere temporary measure. It was to last for a considerable period of years.
>
> Those provisions disclose so complete a reversal of policy that to my mind the White Paper cannot be regarded as giving 'guidance' at all. In marching terms it does not say 'right incline' or 'left incline'. It says 'right about turn'. That is not guidance, but the reverse of it.
>
> There is no doubt that the Secretary of State acted with the best of motives in formulating this new policy – and it may well have been the right policy – but I am afraid that he went about it in the wrong way. Seeing that the old policy had been laid down in an Act of Parliament, then, in order to reverse it, he should have introduced an amending Bill and got Parliament to sanction it. He was advised, apparently, that it was not necessary, and that it could be done by 'guidance.' That, I think, was a mistake. And Laker Airways are entitled to complain of it, at any rate in its impact on them. It was in this respect *ultra vires* and the judge was right so to declare.

Note

The principle that where an authority is endowed with power for one purpose, it must not use it for another applies even where the statute sets out no apparent purpose. In such instances, as the following case illustrates, the courts are prepared to infer a purpose from the general scheme of the legislation and then hold a decision *ultra vires* for failing to conform with that purpose.

Padfield v Minister of Agriculture, Fisheries and Food [1968] AC 977, 1029–32, 1034

Section 19 of the Agricultural Marketing Act 1958 provided that if persons complained to the Secretary of State about relevant matters, he could refer the complaints to a Committee of Investigation. The plaintiffs, whose complaint had not been so referred, sought judicial review of the decision not to refer their complaint.

Lord Reid: The question at issue in this appeal is the nature and extent of the minister's duty under s19(3)(b) of the Act of 1958 in deciding whether to refer to the committee of investigation a complaint as to the operation of any scheme made by persons adversely affected by the scheme. The respondent contends that his only duty is to consider a complaint fairly and that he is given an unfettered discretion with regard to every complaint either to refer it or not to refer it to the committee as he may think fit. The appellants contend that it is his duty to refer every genuine and substantial complaint, or alternatively that his discretion is not unfettered and that in this case he failed to exercise his discretion according to law because his refusal was caused or influenced by his having misdirected himself in law or by his having taken into account extraneous or irrelevant considerations.

In my view, the appellants' first contention goes too far. There are a number of reasons which would justify the minister in refusing to refer a complaint. For example, he might consider it more suitable for arbitration, or he might consider that in an earlier case the committee of investigation had already rejected a substantially similar complaint, or he might think the complaint to be frivolous or vexatious. So he must have at least some measure of discretion. But is it unfettered?

It is implicit in the argument for the minister that there are only two possible interpretations of this provision – either he must refer every complaint or he has an unfettered discretion to refuse to refer in any case. I do not think that is right. Parliament must have conferred the discretion with the intention that it should be used to promote the policy and objects of the Act; the policy and objects of the Act must be determined by construing the Act as a whole and construction is always a matter of law for the court. In a matter of this kind it is not possible to draw a hard and fast line, but if the minister, by reason of his having misconstrued the Act or for any other reason, so uses his discretion as to thwart or run counter to the policy and objects of the Act, then our law would be very defective if persons aggrieved were not entitled to the protection of the court. So it is necessary first to construe the Act.

When these provisions were first enacted in 1931 it was unusual for Parliament to compel people to sell their commodities in a way to which they objected and it was easily foreseeable that any such scheme would cause loss to some producers. Moreover, if the operation of the scheme was put in the hands of the majority of the producers, it was obvious that they might use their power to the detriment of consumers, distributors or a minority of the producers. So it is not surprising that Parliament enacted safeguards.

The approval of Parliament shows that this scheme was thought to be in the public interest, and in so far as it necessarily involved detriment to some persons, it must have been thought to be in the public interest that they should suffer it. But in ss19 and 20 Parliament drew a line. They provide machinery for investigating and determining whether the scheme is operating or the board is acting in a manner contrary to the public interest.

The effect of these sections is that if, but only if, the minister and the committee of investigation concur in the view that something is being done contrary to the public interest the minister can step in. Section 20 enables the minister to take the initiative. Section 19 deals with complaints by individuals who are aggrieved.

I need not deal with the provisions which apply to consumers. We are concerned with other persons who may be distributors or producers. If the minister directs that a complaint by any of them shall be referred to the committee of investigation, that committee will make a report which must be published. If they report that any provision of this scheme or any act or omission of the board and is contrary to the interests of the complainers *and is* not in the public interest, then the minister is empowered to take action, but not otherwise. He may disagree with the view of the committee as to public interest, and, if he thinks that there are other public interests which outweigh the public interest that justice should be done to the complainers, he would be not only entitled but bound to refuse to take action. Whether he takes action or not, he may be criticised and held accountable in Parliament but the court cannot interfere.

I must now examine the minister's reasons for refusing to refer the appellants' complaint to the committee. I have already set out the letters of March 23 and May 3, 1965. I think it is right also to refer to a letter sent from the Ministry on May 1, 1964, because in his affidavit the minister says he has read this letter and there is no indication that he disagrees with any part of it. ...

The first reason which the minister gave in his letter of March 23, 1965, was that this complaint was unsuitable for investigation because it raised wide issues. Here it appears to me that the minister has clearly misdirected himself. Section 19 (6) contemplates the raising of issues so wide that it may be necessary for the minister to amend a scheme or even to revoke it. Narrower issues may be suitable for arbitration but s19 affords the only method of investigating wide issues. In my view it is plainly the intention of the Act that even the widest issues should be investigated if the complaint is genuine and substantial, as this complaint certainly is.

Then it is said that this issue should be 'resolved through the arrangements available to producers and the board within the framework of the scheme itself'. This re-states in a condensed form the reasons given in paragraph 4 of the letter of May 1, 1964, where it is said 'the minister owes no duty to producers in any particular region', and reference is made to the 'status of the Milk Marketing Scheme as an instrument for the self-government of the industry', and to the minister 'assuming an inappropriate degree of responsibility'. But, as I have already pointed out, the Act imposes on the minister a responsibility whenever there is a relevant and substantial complaint that the board are acting in a manner inconsistent with the public interest, and that has been relevantly alleged in this case. I can find nothing in the Act to limit this responsibility or to justify the statement that the minister owes no duty to producers in a particular region. The minister is, I think, correct in saying that the board is an instrument for the self-government of the industry. So long as it does not act contrary to the public interest the minister cannot interfere. But if it does act contrary to what both the committee of investigation and the minister hold to be the public interest the minister has a duty to act. And if a complaint relevantly alleges that the board has so acted, as this complaint does, then it appears to me that the Act does impose a duty on the minister to have it investigated. If he does not do that he is rendering nugatory a safeguard provided by the Act and depriving complainers of a remedy which I am satisfied that Parliament intended them to have.

... As the minister's discretion has never been properly exercised according to law, I would allow this appeal. It appears to me that the case should now be remitted to the Queen's Bench Division with a direction to require the minister to consider the complaint of the appellants according to law. The order for costs in the Divisional Court should stand. The appellants should have their costs in the Court of Appeal but, as extra expense was caused in this House by an adjournment of the hearing at their motion, they should only have two-thirds of their costs in this House.

Notes

1 Wade notes that in this case, the House of Lords emphasised 'in broad terms that unfettered discretion is something which the law does not admit. If it were otherwise, everyone would be helpless in the face of the unqualified powers which ministers find it so easy to obtain from Parliament'.[15]

2 Despite such approving views, the courts have been accused of using their practice of inferring a purpose as a means whereby to interfere with policy. Often the purpose inferred is uncontroversial or the courts only go so far as stating – in effect – that whatever the purpose of the body's power may be, it is not to enable it to do the act complained of (as in the well known case of *Barnsley MBC, ex p Hook* (1976)[16] (discussed below). In other cases, however, the judiciary has been accused of inferring an unwarrantably narrow purpose from an Act which appears to grant broad discretion, and then holding a decision unlawful because it is not in conformity with this purpose. Arguably, this technique was adopted by the Lords in *Bromley London Borough Council v GLC* (1983)[17] discussed by Jeremy Waldron below.

Jeremy Waldron, *The Law* (1990), pp117–9

The 'Fares Fair' case

'Within six months of winning the election, Labour will cut fares on London Transport buses and tubes by an average of 25%.' The Labour Party made that commitment in its manifesto for the 1981 elections to the Greater London Council (GLC). It won the election and within six months bus and tube fares were reduced as promised. The move necessitated an increase in the rates (*ie* property taxes) levied on the London boroughs, Bromley (a Conservative-controlled council), brought an action in the High Court to challenge the decision. The GLC did not take the challenge very seriously, and were not surprised when the High Court judge rejected the Bromley application.

A few weeks later, the Bromley council appealed, and three judges sitting in the Court of Appeal reversed the original decision and upheld the Bromley challenge. The judges condemned the fare reduction as 'a crude abuse of the poor' and they quashed the supplementary rate that the GLC had levied on the London boroughs to pay for it. The GLC appealed to the House of Lords, the highest court in the land, but to no avail.

The Law Lords held unanimously that the GLC was bound by a statue requiring it to 'promote the provision on integrated, efficient *and economic* transport facilities and services in Greater London', and they interpreted this to mean that the bus and tube system must be run according to 'ordinary business principles' of cost effectiveness. The Labour council, they said, was not entitled to lower the fares and increase the deficit of London Transport in order to promote their general social policy, and they were certainly not entitled simply to shift a large percentage of the cost of travel in London from commuters to ratepayers.

The fact that the policy had been announced in advance and had secured majority support, carried little weight with the courts. According to the Law Lords and the judges in the Court of Appeal, members of the GLC should not

15 Wade, *op cit*, pp53–4.
16 1 WLR 1052.
17 1 AC 768.

have treated themselves as 'irrevocably bound to carry out pre-announced policies contained in election manifestos', particularly when it became apparent that central Government would penalise the move to bodies like the GLC. So, though the voters had supported in their thousands, the fare reduction was reversed, the supplementary rate quashed, and the policy frustrated, by the order of five judges.

It is fair to say the GLC and their lawyers were taken aback by the Court of Appeal and House of Lords decisions – 'shell-shocked' as the term one lawyer used. ... More than anything else, the Labour councillors were flabbergasted by the Law Lords' intrusion into a decision so clearly legitimated by electoral democracy:

> For generations in local government were understood that if you put something in your manifesto and got elected, you got on and did it. We cherished the belief that people believe in democratic government. If you got a popular vote you could do it.

As they saw it, the electorate had been given a choice: to subsidise London Transport in the interest of social and environmental policy or to persist with the existing fare structure. The electorate had made their choice, and councillors couldn't understand why the judges – who knew almost nothing about the detailed policy issues involved – would want to overturn their decision. Council solicitors were at a loss to explain the vehement unanimity of the Lords' decision: 'There is always room for argument where there is discretionary power'. The only thing they could see was that the courts were indulging in a gut-level reaction to Labour policy, to the beginning of some apprehended revolutionary socialist challenge.

Notes

1   The decision is often cited by leftist commentators as a paradigmatic example of conservative judicial bias, a subject which will be returned to below.

2   Ambiguity as to whether a decision is tainted with illegality through the influence of 'improper purposes' can arise in the case of decisions made for a plurality of purposes – some proper, some improper, as in the following case.

ILEA, ex p Westminster Council [1986] 1 All ER 19

The Inner London Education Authority ('ILEA') was opposed to government policy on rate-capping which it believed would adversely affect education provision in London. It was empowered by statute (s 142(2) of the Local Government Act 1972) to incur expenditure in the course of publicising matters within its area of information on matters relating to local government. The case arose from the decision of ILEA to retain an advertising agency in order to mount a campaign to generate 'awareness of the authority's views of the needs of the education service and to alter the basis of public debate about the effect of ... government actions'. ILEA admitted that the campaign had the dual purpose of educating the public and persuading them to share ILEA's opposition to rate-capping.

> **Glidewell J:** ... if a local authority resolves to expend its ratepayers' money in order to achieve two purposes, one of which it is authorised to achieve by statute but for the other of which it has no authority, is that decision invalid?

I was referred to the following authorities: (i) *Westminster Corporation v London and North Western Railway Co* [1905] AC 426.

Glidewell J considered the decision and concluded:

> This suggests that a test for answering the question is, if the authorised purpose is the primary purpose, the resolution is within the power. ...

(ii) More recently in *Hanks v Minister of Housing and Local Government* [1963] 1 QB 999, Megaw J did have to deal with a case in which it was alleged that a compulsory purchase order had been made for two purposes, one of which did not fall within the empowering Act.

At p1019, he quoted part of the dissenting judgment of Denning LJ in *Earl Fitzwilliam's Wentworth Estates Co Ltd v Minister of Town and Country Planning* [1951] 2 KB 284, 307:

> If Parliament grants a power to a government department to be used for an authorised purpose, then the power is only validly exercised when it is used by the department genuinely for that purpose as its dominant purpose. If that purpose is not the main purpose, but is subordinated to some other purpose which is not authorised by law, then the department exceeds its powers and the action is invalid.

It had been submitted to Megaw J that, although Denning LJ had dissented from the decision of the majority, this passage in his judgment did not differ from the view of the majority. Megaw J went on [[1963] QB 999, 1020]:

> I confess that I think confusion can arise from the multiplicity of words which have been used in this case as suggested criteria for the testing of the validity of the exercise of a statutory power. The words used have included 'objects', 'purposes', 'motives', 'motivation', 'reasons', 'grounds' and 'considerations'. In the end, it seems to me, the simplest and clearest way to state the matter is by reference to 'considerations'. A 'consideration', I apprehend, is something which one takes into account as a factor in arriving at a decision. I am prepared to assume, for the purposes of this case, that, if it be shown that an authority exercising a power has taken into account as a relevant factor something which it could not properly take into account in deciding whether or not to exercise the power, then the exercise of the power, normally at least, is bad. Similarly, if the authority fails to take into account as a relevant factor something which is relevant, and which is or ought to be known to it, and which it ought to have taken into account, the exercise of the power is normally bad. I say 'normally' because I can conceive that there may be cases where the factor wrongly taken into account, or omitted, is insignificant, or where the wrong taking into account, or omission, actually operated in favour of the person who later claims to be aggrieved by the decision. ...

I have considered also the views of the authors of text books on this. Professor Wade in *Administrative Law*, 5th ed (1982), under the heading 'Duality of Purpose' says, at p388:

> Sometimes an act may serve two or more purposes, some authorised and some not, and it may be a question whether the public authority may kill two birds with one stone. The general rule is that its action will be lawful provided that the permitted purpose is the true and dominant purpose behind the act, even though some secondary or incidental advantage may be gained for some purpose which is outside the authority's powers.

Professor Evans, in *de Smith's Judicial Review of Administrative Action*, 4th ed (1980), p329, comforts me by describing the general problem of plurality of purpose as 'a legal porcupine which bristles with difficulties as soon as it is touched'. He distils from the decisions of the courts five different tests upon which reliance has been placed at one time or another, including, at pp330–2:

> (1) What was the *true purpose* for which the power was exercised? If the actor has in truth used his power for the purpose for which it was conferred, it is immaterial that he was thus enabled to achieve a subsidiary object ... (5) Was any of the purposes pursued an unauthorised purpose? If so, and if the unauthorised purpose has materially influenced the actor's conduct, the power has been invalidly exercised because irrelevant considerations have been taken into account.

These two tests, and Professor Evans's comment upon them, seem to me to achieve much the same result and to be similar to that put forward by Megaw J in *Hanks v Minister of Housing and Local Government* [1963] 1 QB 999, in the first paragraph of the passage I have quoted from his judgment. That is the part that includes the sentence – 'In the end, it seems to me, the simplest and clearest way to state the matter is by reference to 'considerations'. I gratefully adopt the guidance of Megaw J, and the two tests I have referred to from *de Smith's Judicial Review of Administrative Action*.

It thus becomes a question of fact for me to decide, upon the material before me, whether in reaching its decision of 23 July 1984, the staff and general sub-committee of ILEA was pursuing an unauthorised purpose, namely, that of persuasion, which has materially influenced the making of its decision. I have already said that I find that one of the sub-committee's purposes was the giving of information. But I also find that it had the purpose of seeking to persuade members of the public to a view identical with that of the authority itself, and indeed I believe that this was a, if not the, major purpose of the decision. In reaching this decision of fact, I have taken into account in particular the material to which I have referred above in AMV's 'presentation' of 18 July 1984, the passages I have quoted from the report of the Education Officer to the sub-committee, particularly the reference to 'changing the basis of public debate', and the various documents which have been published by AMV since 23 July with the approval of ILEA. I accept that some of these documents do inform, but in my view some of them contain little or no information and are designed only to persuade. This is true in particular, in my view, of the poster slogan 'Education Cuts Never Heal' (skilful though I think it is) and it is also true of the advertisement 'What do you get if you subtract £75 million from London's education budget?'

Adopting the test referred to above, I thus hold that ILEA's subcommittee did, when making its decision of 23 July 1984, take into account an irrelevant consideration, and thus that decision was not validly reached.

Notes

1   Glidewell J thus found that a decision would be unlawful if 'materially influenced' by an unauthorised purpose. Purchas LJ put forward an arguably less strict test in *Simplex GE (Holdings) Ltd v Secretary of State for the Environment* (1988)[18] where he held that, on the issue of whether an unauthorised purpose had influenced a decision the applicant did not need to show that the decision maker 'would or even probably would have come

---

18   COD 160. The facts of the case appear below.

to a different conclusion [if he had not been influenced by the improper purpose]. He has only to exclude the ... contention ... that the [decision-maker] necessarily would still have made the same decision'. This test implies that once an unauthorised consideration can be shown to have been present, the onus of proof shifts to the decision-maker to show that he would clearly have made the same decision without taking account of that consideration; Glidewell's test seemed to envisage that it was for the applicant to show 'material influence' by the consideration. De Smith's legal porcupine continues to bristle.

2   A recent case involving the grant of foreign aid for development purposes shows both that the courts may not allow themselves to be troubled overmuch by arcane distinctions between 'purposes' and 'considerations' and will also brush aside the difficulties Glidewell J encountered if it is clear that a consideration was material. The main issue in the case was whether the Secretary of State had erred in law in deciding to grant financial aid to Malaysia to assist in the Pergau Dam project.

Secretary of State, ex p World Development [1995] 1 All ER 611, 625–7

Mr Richards [for the Secretary of State] submitted that the decision to furnish assistance in connection with the Pergau project fell squarely within the power conferred by s1(1). In particular: (a) it was furnished for a purpose specified, namely a developmental purpose, and (b) the Secretary of State was entitled to take account of wider purpose, and economic considerations. It is common ground that assistance must be furnished for the relevant purpose. But, submitted Mr Richards, there is no real distinction between 'assistance' and 'project', because in the absence of exceptional features, if the project is for promoting development, the assistance must be also. It is also, it has to be said, common ground that a decision-maker can take into account political and commercial considerations, provided that there is a sufficient substantive power within s1 of the 1980 Act.

Mr Richards submitted that this decision was taken by the Foreign Secretary personally and his thinking is of decisive importance in determining the purpose for which the assistance was furnished. The Foreign Secretary plainly considered, from the terms of his affidavit, that the assistance was for a developmental purpose, and he also took into account additional considerations. Mr Richard submitted further that the applicants' argument that an unsound development cannot furnish a purpose within s1 should be rejected. First because the word 'sound' does not appear in the 1980 Act. What the statute requires is a developmental purpose within the broad terms of s1(1), and the statutory power cannot be limited by the adoption of 'soundness' by an ATP scheme or anything else. Secondly, submitted Mr Richards, the Foreign Secretary (the decision-maker) took the view that the project was for a developmental purpose ... The project was of undoubted benefit because it met a need for electricity, and it does not negative a purpose within the section that that need could have been met in other ways. He submitted that the Malaysian Government was committed to the project, that the only effect of the grant of aid was to bridge the gap between the cost of Pergau and other cheaper means of generating electricity, and that this did not give rise to cost penalty. ...

Mr Richards further submitted that the sole purpose for which assistance was furnished was the developmental purpose. The wider political and economic considerations taken into account by the Foreign Secretary were not 'purposes' for which assistance was furnished, but were 'considerations' that the Secretary of State was entitled to take into account. Alternatively, if the wider 'considerations' are to be regarded as 'purposes' for which assistance was furnished, the existence of subsidiary purposes does not invalidate the decision, provided that those subsidiary purposes are not themselves irrelevant considerations.

For my part, I am unable to accept Mr Richards's submission that it is the Secretary of State's thinking which is determinative of whether the purpose was within the statute and that therefore para 3 of his affidavit is conclusive. Whatever the Secretary of State's intention of purpose may have been it is, as it seems to me, a matter for the courts and not for the Secretary of State to determine whether, on the evidence before the court, the particular conduct was, or was not, within the statutory purpose.

As to the absence of the word 'sound' from s1(1), it seems to me that if Parliament had intended to confer a power to disburse money for unsound developmental purposed, it could have been expected to say so expressly. And I am comforted in this view by the way in which the successive ministers, guidelines, governments and white papers identified by Mr Pleming have, over the years and without exception, construed the power as relating to economically sound development.

... As to Mr Richards' submission that the dam was of undoubted benefit because it met the need for electricity, this, as it seems to me, begs the question of whether there was a need for energy generated at substantially greater cost than by any other means, and the Malaysian Government's determination to go ahead with the scheme does not, as it seems to me, advance the argument. Such a determination is no doubt a necessary prerequisite for the granting of any overseas aid.

Accordingly, where, as here, the contemplated development is, on the evidence, so economically unsound that there is no economic argument in favour of the case, it is not, in my judgement, possible to draw any material distinction between questions of propriety and regularity on the one hand and questions of economy and efficiency of public expenditure on the other. It many not be surprising that no suggestion of illegality was made by any official, or that the Secretary of State was not advised that there would, or might be, any illegality. No legal advice was ever sought.

The Secretary of State is, of course, generally speaking, fully entitled when making decisions to take into account political and economic considerations such as the promotion of regional stability, good government, human rights and British commercial interest. In the present case, the political impossibility of withdrawing the 1989 offer has been recognised since mid-April of that year, and had there in 1991 been a developmental promotion purpose within s1 of the 1980 Act, it would have been entirely proper for the Foreign Secretary to have taken into account also the impact which withdrawing the 1980 offer would have had both on the United Kingdom's credibility as a reliable friend and trading partner and on political and commercial relations with Malaysia. But for the reasons given, I am of the view, on the evidence before this court, that there was, In July 1991, no such purpose within the section. It follows that the July 1991 decision was, in my judgment, unlawful.

Notes

1 Sedley J thus took a subtle approach towards the other considerations – human rights, diplomatic relations etc – to which the minister had had

regard. He did not rule that these reasons were irrelevant *per se*. Rather the finding was that these considerations could not be *substitutes* for the main criteria as to whether aid should be granted: whether it would promote sound development. If that criteria was not satisfied – as the judge found it was not – then these other purposes, *which could in other circumstances have been relevant*, could not justify this particular decision. There would be of course, though, be many cases where aid *would* assist in sound development. Once this condition precedent was fulfilled, then the other considerations could come in, to assist the minister in deciding as a matter of policy, which amongst many possible aid recipients (all legitimate under the statute) should be chosen.

2 Lord Irvine QC has criticised this decision,[19] arguing that Sedley J's approach is an example of 'elevating what is in truth a mere relevant consideration into *a* or *the* purpose of [the] statutory provision.' But surely, in deciding that promoting sound economic development was not merely a relevant consideration but the basic purpose of the statute, Sedley J was merely engaging in statutory interpretation, which even on the most minimalist view of the role of judicial review he is clearly entitled to do. Lord Irvine claims that the decision was made only 'under the mantle' of construction, but, when analysed this seems to mean nothing more than that he thinks that the judge's construction was wrong. (When Lord Irvine says that sound development was 'in truth' only a consideration, presumably 'in truth' can only mean, 'under a true construction of the statute'.) If the judge did indeed misconstrue the statute, he may have erred in law but he did not stray beyond the orthodox limits of judicial review.

3 Failure to have regard to purposes which the court finds to be impliedly relevant under the enabling statute continues to be a common ground for successful review. In *Somerset County Council, ex p Fewings* (1995),[20] the local authority banned stag-hunting on an area of its land, which, under s10(2)(b) of the Local Government Act 1972, they were to manage 'for the benefit of their area'. The decision was found to be unlawful on the grounds that (*inter alia*) :

(a) the councillors, in making their decision, at no point had their attention drawn to the governing statutory provision; and

(b) that they had made their decision largely on the basis that they considered stag-hunting cruel and morally repulsive, a consideration which, though relevant, was not the only factor they should have considered under the test.

4 In *Wealden District Council, ex p Wales* (1995),[21] a number of persons who were encamped on land had been given removal directions by two councils under s77 of the Criminal Justice and Public Order Act 1994 (which is basically aimed at giving local authorities the power to remove gypsies and new age travellers from their land). It was held that, in making decisions as

---

19 'Judges and Decision-Makers: The Theory and Practice of *Wednesbury* Review' (1996) PL 59, 68–9.

20 3 All ER 20, CA; for comment, see G Nardell (1995) PL 27.

21 *The Times*, 22 September 1995.

to the making of such orders and their enforcement, local authorities had to have regard to a variety of humanitarian factors, (some of which were contained in circulars from the Home Office). One council had entirely failed to take account of these, and its decision was quashed; the other had done so, but at the wrong stage – a declaration would be granted to this effect. The decision is interesting, because it laid a legal obligation on the council to give consideration to various factors which had only been expressed as 'guidance' by the Home Office.

Other types of illegality

This head also covers effectively failing to exercise a statutory discretion by applying a policy rigidly in every case or by improperly delegating the decision to another body or person (*Secretary of State for the Environment, ex p Brent LBC* (1982)[22] and *Ellis v Dubowski* (1921)[22a] respectively). The leading case on delegation of powers follows.

Carltona Ltd v Works Comrs [1943] 2 All ER 560, 563

The Commissioners of Works had power under wartime regulations to requisition property, and Carltona's factory was requisitioned. A requisition notice in respect of Carltona's factory was made by a civil servant, of the rank of assistant secretary, for and on behalf of the Commissioners of Works (at the head of which was a minister).

> **Lord Greene MR:** In the administration of Government in this county the functions which are give to ministers (and constitutionally properly given to minister because they are constitutionally responsible) are functions so multifarious that no minister could ever personally attend to them ... It cannot be supposed that [the regulation in question] meant that, in each case, the minister in person should direct his mind to the matter. The duties imposed upon ministers and the powers given to ministers are normally exercised under the authority of the ministers by responsible officials of the department. Public business could not be carried on if that were not the case. Constitutionally, the decision of such an official is of course the decision of the minister, the minister is responsible. It is he who must answer before Parliament for anything his officials have done under his authority and if for an important matter he selected an official of such junior standing that he could not be expected competently to perform the work, the minister would have to answer for that in Parliament.

Note

The *Carltona* principle is still alive and well; as McEldowney notes:

> ... In *ex p Oladehinde* [[1991] 2 AC 254] the House of Lords upheld the lawfulness of the Home Secretary's common practice to delegate to senior officials, namely immigration officers, his powers under the Immigration Act 1971 to serve notices of deportation. In such instances of delegation the House of Lords noted that care should be taken not to widen the delegation of powers unduly. Some caution must be exercised to establish that the officials are sufficiently senior and that they possess the necessary experience to carry out the statutory duties under the 1971 Act. The *Carltona* principle is applied to central government departments and the devolution of functions to civil servants.

---

22   QB 593.
22a 3 KB 621.

In local government, s101 of the Local Government Act 1972 permits the delegation of wide powers to officials to carry out specific functions of the local authority. The nature of any delegated power must be given close scrutiny. If the power rests with an officer who may consult with members of the council, it is wrong for the powers to be actually exercised by the councillor rather than the officer [see *Port Talbot Borough Council, ex p Jones* (1988) 2 All ER 207.][23]

Illegality: areas of particular uncertainty

Can decisions be reviewed for errors of fact?

T Jones, 'Mistake of Fact in Administration' (1990) *Public Law* 507, 512–25 (extracts)

It is possible to differentiate between two general approaches to whether mistake of fact should be recognised as a separate principle of administrative law. These might be termed the *expansive* and *limited* models of judicial review. The ensuing discussion proceeds under these two headings. The expansive review model would find its justification in the observation of Sir William Wade that 'decisions based upon wrong facts are a cause of injustice which the courts should be able to remedy' [*Administrative Law*, 6th edn (1988), p329]. Advocates of the limited review model would regard with favour the view expressed by Brandeis J in *St Joseph Stock Yards Co v United States*:

> [S]upremacy of law does not demand that the correctness of every finding of fact to which the Rule of Law is applied shall be subject to review by a court. If it did, the power of the courts to set aside findings of fact by an administrative tribunal would be broader than their power to set aside a jury's verdict' [298 US 38 84 (1936)].

The point being made is that the decisions of administrators should, because of their expertise in their field, be subject to a lesser degree of review than those of a jury.

A. Expansive review

It will come as no surprise that Lord Denning should be associated with the suggestion that an administrator's mistake of fact could form a ground for judicial review.

Jones then cites *Secretary of State for Employment v ASLEF (No 2)* [1972] 2 QB 455, *Laker Airways v Department of Trade*, and *Smith v Inner London Education Authority* [1978] 1 All ER 411 in which Lord Denning appeared to suggest that mistake of fact could be reviewable but then goes on:

> It would be a mistake to read too much significance into [these] suggestions. His observations to this effect appear in what are patently over-generalised summaries of the principles of judicial review. Nevertheless, similar suggestions appear in the judgments of both the Court of Appeal and the House of Lords in the *Tameside* case. Of particular significance is the judgment of Lord Wilberforce, which includes the following passage:
>
> > In many statutes a minister or other authority is given a discretionary power and in these cases the court's power to review any exercise of the discretion, though still real is limited. In these cases it is said that the courts cannot substitute their opinion for that of the minister: they can interfere on such

---

23 McEldowney, *Public Law* (1994), pp465–6. For recent discussion of the *Carltona* principle and its application to modern government executive agencies, see M Freedland (1996) PL 19.

grounds as that the minister has acted right outside his powers or outside the purpose of the Act, or unfairly, or upon an incorrect basis of fact' [[1977] AC 1014 at 1047].

Similarly, in the Court of Appeal, Scarman LJ felt that 'misunderstanding or ignorance of an established and relevant fact' was within 'the scope of judicial review'[*Ibid* at 1030].

... There are very few English cases where mistake of fact has been accepted as a ground for judicial review, and an even smaller number which appear to have been decided on this ground alone. Further, a close examination reveals that at least one case which appears to support mistake of fact as a ground for judicial intervention was decided on another basis.

In *Mason v Secretary of State for the Environment and Bromsgrove District Council*, [[1984] JPL 332] David Widdicombe QC, sitting as a judge of the Queen's Bench Division, was of the firm opinion that 'there could be no doubt that a mistake of fact *might vitiate a* decision'. On this point he found persuasive the judgment of Cooke J in *Daganayasi v Minister of Immigration* [(1980) 2 NZLR 130]. The learned deputy judge stressed that 'to vitiate a decision the mistake of fact had to be material, that was, there must be grounds for thinking that the decision might have been different if the mistake had not been made'. However, in this *case the mistake* of *a* planning inspector as to the calculation of a distance between two properties was held to be immaterial and not to have affected the planning decision. Nevertheless, the principle of material mistake of fact as a ground for judicial review was accepted. ...

An equally radical approach can be found in a second case ... *Hollis v Secretary of State for the Environment* [(1989) 47 P & CR 351]. The mistake at issue here was that of a planning inspector who wrongly concluded that a piece of land had never had green belt status. The conclusion of Glidewell J was that this incorrect finding of fact had been material to the decision reached. ... it is treated as self-evidence that the decision could be quashed because of the mistake of fact ... there is no discussion of this point. ...

A more ambiguous case is that of *Secretary of State for the Home Department, ex p Awuku*, [*The Times*, 3 October 1987] wherein McCowan J found unsatisfactory an immigration officer's reasons for a refusal of entry to the United Kingdom to three refugees from Ghana. He observed that there had been material errors of fact, such as a disbelief in a further period of detention (and in one case of any period of detention) suffered by the applicants just before they fled Ghana. It could not be said that that mistake of fact had not affected the views of the immigration officers and the Home Office thereafter. To an advocate of expansive review, this is a clear-cut case. The three refugees had in fact been detained, so it could not be possible to reach a valid decision on the basis that they had not. However, the actual basis of the ruling of the court to quash the three immigration decisions was somewhat different: that to decide against the applicants on the basis of matters on which they had been given no opportunity to comment was unfair and contrary to natural justice.

Ex p Awuku is illustrative of a general problem in articulating mistake of fact as a separate principle of administrative law. Even those judges who have taken an expansive approach to judicial review and are prepared to talk in terms of mistake of fact, are reluctant to cross the Rubicon and say that they can vitiate an administrative decision on this basis *alone*. ...

B. Limited review

A succinct summary of the philosophy underlying the limited approach to review of administrative fact-finding is provided by the following observation of

Lord Brightman in *Pulhofer v Hillingdon London Borough Council*:

> Where the existence or non-existence of a fact is left to the judgment and discretion of a public body ... it is the duty of the court to leave the decision of that fact to the public body to whom Parliament has entrusted the decision-making power save in a case where it is obvious that the public body, consciously or unconsciously, are acting perversely [[1986] AC 484, 518].

This approach does not necessarily close the door on a case such as *Jagendorf and Trott* or *Hollis*, because one might want to say that a decision based on the premise that a black wall was in fact white is perverse. We may recall, however, that the suggestion in *Jagendorf and Trott*, contrary to that of Lord Brightman, was that something less than *Wednesbury* unreasonableness could suffice to vitiate a decision on the basis of a mistake of fact. Lord Brightman's comment also illustrates the weakness of the deputy judge's attempt in *Jagendorf and Trott* to seek to found his approach on Parliament's presumed intent. Lord Brightman concludes that it can be presumed to be quite the opposite and that the conferment of a discretionary power includes the power to get a decision 'wrong'. ...

At root it is a question of policy and whether the courts wish to become involved in the supervision of administrative fact-finding. A separate question is that even if this is felt to be desirable on occasion, is it necessary for there to be a separate ground of review or are the existing principles governing judicial intervention adequate? These issues are addressed further in the next section.

ALTERNATIVE GROUNDS FOR JUDICIAL INTERVENTION

There are two realistic possibilities to discuss:

(1) that the decision-maker took into account an irrelevant consideration; and

(2) that the decision was reached upon no or insufficient evidence ...

(1) Mistake of fact as an irrelevant consideration

... How can a mistake of fact by an administrative decision-maker fall to be regarded as the taking into account of an irrelevant consideration? An obvious point to make is that the two concepts are closely related. This can be illustrated by referring to the decision of the Court of Appeal in *Simplex GE (Holdings) Ltd v Secretary of State for the Environment and the City of St Albans District Council* [1988] COD 160] which provides a clear example of an error of fact being treated as an irrelevant consideration. The part of this case which is relevant to the present discussion arose by way of an appeal (under s245 of the Town and Country Planning Act 1971) whereby Simplex sought the quashing of a decision by the minister to reject its appeal against deemed refusals by the district council to grant outline planning permission in respect of a particular site. The mistake made by the minister was that he thought that a study recommended by a planning inspector relating to the question of whether the site should be retained in the green belt had formed the basis of the council's decision, when no study had been carried out by the time of the minister's decision. (In any event, this study was concerned with the narrower issue of use within the green belt designation.) The contention of Simplex was that, as a result of his mistake, the minister had taken into consideration matters which he was not entitled to take into account. The Court of Appeal agreed, concluding that the mistake had been a significant factor in the minister's decision. It was sufficient for the appellant to show, as had been done in this case, that the decision might have been different had the irrelevant consideration not been taken into account.

(2) Mistake of fact and the no evidence rule

... The no evidence rule is targeted at administrative decisions which go against the weight of evidence before the decision-maker. In this sense, it is complementary to the doctrine of reasonableness, whereby a decision may be challenged on the ground that it was one that no reasonable administrator could have made. In contrast, the no evidence rule appears to permit a particular decision to be challenged, without asking a court to castigate the decision-maker as unreasonable. As Lord Wilberforce stated in *Tameside*: 'If a judgment requires, before it can be made, the existence of some facts then, although the evaluation of those facts is for the Secretary of State alone, the court must inquire whether those facts exist ...' [[1977] AC 1014, 1047].

Jones goes on to note the difficulties with the 'no evidence' rule and continues:

... But even accepting that a court can review the evidence on which a ... decision is based and assess its sufficiency, it is debatable whether this would always encompass a mistake of fact. The typical mistake of fact case is not concerned with finding whether an administrative decision was made against the weight of the evidence. The concern is whether he might have made a different decision had he not made a mistake about the facts. The ground of irrelevant consideration therefore provides a firmer and more accurate basis for challenging a ... decision ...

POLICY ARGUMENTS

... Mistake of fact as a ground for judicial intervention would appear to cut across the traditional distinction between appeal, which is concerned with the merits or correctness of a decision, and review, which is concerned with legality. As one Australian judge has declaimed:

The limited role of a court reviewing the exercise of an administrative discretion must constantly be borne in mind. It is not the function of the court to substitute its own decision for that of the administrator by exercising a discretion which the legislature has vested in the administrator. Its role is to set limits on the exercise of that discretion, and a decision within those boundaries cannot be impugned [*Minister for Aboriginal Affairs v Peho-Walbech* (1985–86) 162 CLR 24, 40–41].

CONCLUSION

Adopting the working hypothesis that mistake of fact can act as a vitiating factor precipitating judicial intervention, it is suggested that the doctrine possesses the following characteristics:

(1) It applies only where there has been a material or, as it might more accurately be called, a *cardinal* mistake of fact; that is, where the administrator has made a decision which he would or might not have made but for the error. There is no unrealistic expectation that an administrative decision-maker should get every fact right. In particular, as Bristow J explained in the course of a judgment which appears to accept that a mistake of fact could form the basis of a successful challenge to an administrative decision:

an obvious silly mistake can be added to glaring inaccuracies or obvious clerical error as an illustration of the sort of innocuous defect in ... a decision that does not amount to an error of law because it does no harm and produces no doubt as to whether the decision has been reached according to law or not [*Elmbridge Borough Council v Secretary of State for the Environment* (1980) 39 P&CR 543].

(2) The fact about which the decision-maker is claimed to have been mistaken must be 'an established and relevant' [[1977] AC 1014 at 1030 (Scarman LJ)] one before a court can review the decision. If two interpretations of the fact can reasonably be held, it is not a mistake to adopt one in preference to another.

(3) A court is going to be most prepared to intervene where the mistake is not only a material one, but is due to an administrative deficiency which indicates a failure on the part of the decision-maker to fulfil his legal duties. It is in this case that the argument for judicial intervention is at its strongest: where the issue is recognisably one of administrative law, rather than a purely factual one.

Notes

1   As Jones notes, making a decision on no, or insufficient evidence may be an error of law. However, there is some doubt as to whether such an error is justiciable. Lord Sumner in the *Nat Bell* case clearly saw the error of making a finding on no evidence as being non-reviewable. However, as Emery and Smythe point out,[24] this opinion was 'strictly *obiter*' and the matter was left open by the Court of Appeal in *Lincolnshire Justices, ex p Brett* (1926) 2 KB 192. Further, if a finding of fact on no evidence is an error of law, and if Lord Diplock in *Re Racal* is followed, then '*any* error of law ... made by ... [an authority] in the course of reaching their decisions on *matters of fact* ... would result in ... the decision they reached [being rendered] a nullity' (emphasis added). There seems to be no compelling reason to pick out the 'no evidence' error of law as the only such error which is not jurisdictional. It must be conceded, however, that the weight of authority directly on the issue, if not of academic opinion, is to the effect that such errors are not subject to review.

2   Another uncertain area lies in the defining of possible errors of law made in applying the law to the facts or drawing inferences. A distinction has been drawn between making a mistake in drawing those inferences which only a lawyer could draw – such a mistake being always an error of law (eg *Watson v Holland* [1985] 1 All ER 290) – and making a mistake in drawing inferences which could be drawn as well by a layman as by a lawyer. The second type of mistake can amount to an error of law *or* fact: the test in *Edwards v Bairstow* (1956)[25] must be applied. It will be convenient to employ a hypothetical example to explain this test, namely that of a body which must determine whether or not a piece of land is 'woodland', before exercising some power over it. *Edwards* makes clear that as long as the body selects land which a superior court would consider *could* sensibly be described as woodland, it does not matter if the superior court would *itself* have described it as such. In other words, as long as a body's decision is within the often large area within which opinions can legitimately differ, it cannot be said to have erred in law.[26]

Is there a duty to give reasons for decisions?

As appears from cases cited above, in many cases the courts will need to know the reasons for the decision in order to be able to assess its legality, for example

---

24   *Judicial Review* (1986).

25   AC 14.

26   For criticism of the *Edwards* test, see J Beatson, 4 Ox J Leg Stud 22.

so that they can tell whether a decision has been influenced by an irrelevant consideration, or with the aim of furthering an improper purpose. Additionally, in many cases a person who wishes to contest a decision *internally* will need to know the case against him, that is the reason for the decision against him, so that he or she can prepare their defence. This question is therefore also of relevance to the issue of procedural fairness (below).

In *Lambeth London Borough Council ex p Walters* (1993)[27] the applicant, who had a handicapped son, was offered accommodation by her local authority, Lambeth Borough Council, in discharge of its duties under s64 of the Housing Act 1985. However, she and her doctor considered the accommodation unsuitable due to her son's condition. She submitted a letter from her doctor to that effect to the authority and later appealed against the decision to offer the accommodation. Her appeal was dismissed on the basis that the accommodation was suitable, although no reasons were given for this finding. She applied for judicial review of the local authority's decision to dismiss her appeal.

It was found that where an administrative body was obliged under statute to afford fair treatment to those potentially affected by its actions it would come under a general duty to give reasons for its decisions to such persons. Part III of the Housing Act imported a concept of fairness throughout its provisions; a duty to give reasons therefore arose but no reasons at all had been given for rejecting the applicants appeal. Therefore the decision to reject the appeal was unlawful and would be quashed.

The leading case in this area is now *Secretary of State for the Home Dept, ex p Doody*.

Secretary of State for the Home Department, ex p Doody and others [1994] 1 AC 531, 565

The applicants wished to challenge decisions made by the Home Secretary about the length of their sentences; the Home Secretary had given no reasons for his decision and in particular had not informed the applicants whether the judges with whom he was obliged to consult had recommended a different term from that which he had fixed. (The full facts appear below at p773.) Having found that reasons should be given for reasons of procedural fairness, Lord Mustill continued as follows:

My Lords, I can moreover arrive at the same conclusion by a different and more familiar route, of which *ex p Cunningham* [1991] 4 All ER 310 provides a recent example. It is not, as I understand it, questioned that the decision of the Home Secretary on the penal element is susceptible to judicial review. To mount an effective attack on the decision, given no more material than the facts of the offence and the length of the penal element, the prisoner has virtually no means of ascertaining whether this is an instance where the decision-making process has gone astray. I think it important that there should be an effective means of detecting the kind of error which would entitle the court to intervene, and in practice I regard it as necessary for this purpose that the reasoning of the Home Secretary should be disclosed. If there is any difference between the penal

---

27   *The Times*, 6 October 1993.

element recommended by the judges and actually imposed by the Home Secretary, this reasoning is bound to include, either explicitly or implicitly, a reason why the Home Secretary has taken a different view.

Notes

1   As Campbell observes,[28] with Craig,[29] this 'justification [for requiring reasons] could apply to all administrative decisions potentially susceptible to ... judicial review'. Campbell continues: 'It must be compared with the House of Lords' previous view on this issue, expressed by Lord Keith in *Lonrho plc v Secretary of State for Trade and Industry* [[1989] 2 All ER 609 at 620]:

> The only significance of the absence of reasons is that if all other known facts and circumstances appear to point overwhelmingly in favour of a different decision, the decision-maker, who has given no reasons cannot complain if the court draws the inference that he had no rational reason for his decision.

On this previous view, the absence of reasons was irrelevant unless the decision was *prima facie* unreasonable'.[30] Campbell concludes that the law has 'now progressed' beyond the *Lonhro* position, though how far remains uncertain.

2   Campbell goes on to propose tentatively that *Doody* may now be taken to require reasons to be given in all cases by the authorities when making decisions which directly affect the liberty of the applicant, instancing *Secretary of State for the Home Dept, ex p Duggan* (1993)[31] in which it was held that a category A prisoner was entitled to be given reasons for the decision that he should remain in this category and therefore remain very unlikely to be released on licence. In decisions lacking such implications for personal liberty 'it is suggested that the duty to provide reasons may arise only where, because of the circumstance of the decision [it] is in particular need of explanation'.[32]

3   He also gives three such exceptional instances:[33]

First, a decision is in particular need of explanation where, by itself, it is *prima facie* unreasonable. This may arise because all the known facts point to a decision different from that reached by the decision-maker [as] in *Sinclair* [*The Times*, 5 February 1992].

... *Prima facie* unreasonableness may also arise where a decision is substantially different from that which the applicant reasonably or legitimately expected [as in] *Cunningham* [[1991] 4 All ER 310].

... Secondly, a decision may be in particular need of explanation where, by itself, it is *prima facie* unlawful [as in] *Northavon District Council, ex p Smith* [[1993] 3 WLR 776 (CA)].

... Thirdly, a decision may be in particular need of explanation where there is some conflict of evidence, and it is unclear what view of the evidence the

---

28   N R Campbell, 'The Duty to Give Reasons in Administrative Law' (1994) PL 184.
29   (1994) 110 LQR 12.
30   Campbell, *op cit*, p186.
31   3 All ER 277.
32   Campbell, *op cit*, p188.
33   Only the skeleton of Campbell's argument is given here; *ibid* at 188–9.

decision-maker has taken in reaching its conclusion. Without knowledge of those factual conclusions a person adversely affected by the decision may be unable to determine whether the decision-maker has acted lawfully or reasonably, and thus whether there are grounds for review. So much seems implicit in *Criminal Injuries Compensation Board, ex p Cummins* [*The Times*, 21 January 1992].

4   Compare the classes of case where reasons may be required given by Sedley J in *Higher Education Funding Council, ex p Institute of Dental Surgery* (1994):[34]

1   There is no general duty to give reasons for a decision, but there are classes of case where there is such a duty.

2   One such class is where the subject matter is an interest so highly regarded by the law – for example personal liberty – that fairness requires that reasons, at least for particular decisions, be given as of right.

3   Another such class is where the decision appears aberrant. Here fairness may require reasons so that the recipient may know whether the aberration is in the legal sense real (and so challengeable) or apparent ... this class does not include decisions which are themselves challengeable by reference only to the reasons for them.

5   Doody appears to move English law closer to imposing a general duty to give reasons for administrative decisions. However, *Higher Education Funding Council* (1994) in which the duty was found not to be present, demonstrates that much will depend on the particular circumstances of the case.

Higher Education Funding Council ex p Institute of Dental Surgery [1994] 1 All ER 651, 667–9, 670

The applicant institution wished to challenge the decision of the HEFC to award it a lower-than-hoped-for rating for its research, likely to result in a £270,000 cut in its funding.

Sedley J: ... That an apparently inexplicable decision is not ... a general requisite for leave or for relief is now clear from the decision of the House of Lords in Doody's case, where the length of the actual tariff periods set by the Home Secretary when matched against the facts of appellants' crimes formed no part of the grounds for requiring reasons in the interests of fairness. It follows that an apparently inexplicable decision may be a sufficient but is not a necessary condition for requiring reasons; it may equally be fair to require them on other grounds. It is arguable that since the decision in *Doody's* case the role of the inexplicable decision is to be regarded as evidential rather than legal, bearing principally on the discretionary decisions whether to grant leave and whether to grant relief by pointing to the need for reasons in the particular case. But we prefer the view that in the present state of the law there are two classes of case now emerging: those cases, such as *Doody's* case, where the nature of the process itself calls in fairness for reasons to be given; and those, such as Cunningham's case, where (in the majority view) it is something peculiar to the decision which in fairness calls for reasons to be given. This does not mean that differing tests of fairness are to be applied; only that, as always, the requirements of fairness will vary with the process to which they are being applied. In this context we unhesitatingly reject Mr Beloff's submission that the judicial character of the Civil Service Appeal Board and the quasi-judicial function of the Home Secretary

---

34   1 All ER 651, 671–2.

in relation to life sentence prisoners distinguish the cases requiring reasons from cases of purely administrative decisions such as the present one. In the modem state the decisions of administrative bodies can have a more immediate and profound impact on people's lives than the decisions of courts, and public law has since *Ridge v Baldwin* [1963] 2 All ER 66, [1964] AC 40 been alive to that fact. While the judicial character of a function may elevate the practical requirements of fairness above what they would otherwise be, for example by requiring contentious evidence to be given and tested orally, what makes it 'judicial' in this sense is principally the nature of the issue it has to determine, not the formal status of the deciding body.

The first limb of [counsel for the applicant's] submission is accordingly that the decision of the respondent was of a kind for which fairness requires that reasons be given. His written contention is that this will be the case –

> when the relevant decision has important consequences for the individual or body concerned, especially if the absence of reasons makes it very difficult for the applicant and the court to know whether the respondent has acted by reference to irrelevant factors, and especially if there is no justification for withholding reasons.

In our view this formula will not do. The absence of reasons always makes it difficult to know whether there has been an error of approach. The question of justification for withholding reasons logically comes after the establishment of a *prima facie* duty to give them. Neither can therefore add to the principal ground advanced, which is of such width that it would make a duty to give reasons a universal rule to which the only exception would be cases of no importance to anybody. There are certainly good arguments of public law and of public administration in favour of such a rule, but it is axiomatically not, or not yet, part of our law.

The chief benchmark of significance which we have at present in this setting *is* *Doody's* case. There the applicant knew the evidence on which he had been convicted but little else, while a considerable body of highly relevant matter had accumulated in the hands of the decision-maker and was going to affect many years of his liberty. If the Home Secretary were then to depart from the judicial view of tariff, it is not easy to think of a stronger case for the disclosure of reasons not merely to the applicant but to all mandatory life sentence prisoners, to each of whom the result of the case will necessarily apply. Equally here the argument, it seems to us, must be good for all applicants, not just disappointed ones, if they want to know why they have been rated as they have been. One would like to be able to hold that for all such applicants, disappointed or not, the importance of the decision alone was enough. But to do so would generalise the duty to give reasons to a point to which this court, at least, cannot go.

We must therefore look also at the other indicia: the openness of the procedure, widely canvassed in advance and published in circular form, the voluntary submission of self-selected examples of work; the judgment of academic peers. These, it seems to us, shift the process substantially away from the pole represented by *Doody's* case, not on mere grounds of dissimilarity (there will be many dissimilar cases in which reasons are nevertheless now required) but because the nature of the exercise was that it was open in all but its critical phase, and its critical phase was one in which, as Professor Davies deposes, 'the grade awarded to a particular institution was not determined by a score against specific features'. We shall return to this, which we find remarkable, but it is a fact and not one which Mr Pannick has been able to assault on legal grounds. In the result, the combination of openness in the run-up with the proscriptively oracular character of the critical decision makes the respondent's allocation of grades inapt, in our judgment, for the giving of reasons, notwithstanding the undoubted importance of the outcome to the institutions concerned.

... purely academic judgments, in our view, will as a rule not be in the class of case, exemplified (though by no means exhausted) by *Doody's* case, where the nature and impact of the decision itself call for reasons as a routine aspect of procedural fairness. They will be in the *Cunningham* case class, where some trigger factor is required to show that, in the circumstances of the particular decision, fairness calls for reasons to be given.

Is there then such a trigger factor here? The second limb of Mr Pannick's submission is that the applicant institute has been confronted with a decision which, on the evidence, is inexplicable: the institute's excellence is widely acknowledged and attested ... We lack precisely the expertise which would permit us to judge whether it is extraordinary or not. It may be a misfortune for the applicant that the court, which in *Cunningham's* case could readily evaluate the contrast between what the board awarded and what an industrial tribunal would have awarded, cannot begin to evaluate the comparative worth of research in clinical dentistry; but it is a fact of life. The applicant's previous grading, the volume and frequency of citation of its research and the high level of peer-reviewed outside funding which it has attracted, to all of which Mr Pannick points, may well demonstrate that the applicant has been unfortunate in the grading it has received, but such a misfortune can well occur within the four corners of a lawfully conducted evaluation.

Note

TRS Allan has criticised this decision; he notes that 'the court rejected the council's stated objections to giving reasons' – that it would undermine the assessment exercise – as 'casuistic and disingenuous'.[35] The judge could not see why distinguished academics were unable to give reasons for their individual and collective judgements. The judge also found the procedure for assessment to be somewhat defective. Noting this, and the fact that 'the importance of the rating to the Institute's standing and morale could scarcely be exaggerated', Allan concludes that 'the court's refusal to require the council to explain its decision seems hard to justify'.[36]

PROCEDURAL IMPROPRIETY

Procedural impropriety is one of the three main grounds of review identified by Lord Diplock in *Council of Civil Service Unions v Minister for the Civil Service* (1984);[37] it can denote both a failure to observe express procedural requirements (most commonly consultation) and a breach of the common law rules of natural justice.

When dealing with the effects of failure to undertake statutory consultation, the courts have tended to classify such requirements as either mandatory or directory. Breach of a mandatory requirement will render the decision or act in question invalid, in contrast to breach of a directory requirement which will not.

---

35   (1994) 52(2) CLJ 207, 209.

36   *Ibid.*

37   (1985) AC 374; (1984) 3 All ER 935.

The courts' pragmatic approach to such classification exemplified by the modern tendency to show a readiness to classify on the basis of the effect of non-compliance with the requirement (as in *Coney v Choyce* (1975),[38] has left the area in 'an inextricable tangle of loose ends'.[39] It could be noted that the factors employed to draw the distinction include the 'relation of the provision to the general object intended to be secured by the Act' (*Howard v Bodington* (1877)),[40] whether prejudice will be caused by the proposed action to those supposed to be consulted, and whether the failure to (for example) give reasons for an act can be remedied in some other way (as in *Howard v Secretary of State for the Environment* (1975)).[41]

Much of the responsibility for this uncertainty must be borne by Parliament which, as Emery and Smythe note, does not specify the consequences of a breach of the requirement imposed 'in the vast majority of cases'.[42] Indeed, it is arguable that by constantly leaving the matter open in the knowledge that the status of the requirements will be determined by the judiciary, Parliament is signalling its acquiescence in the court's tendency to take a pragmatic and flexible approach at the expense of certainty.

However, the judiciary are perhaps open to criticism for having failed to resolve uncertainty as to the fundamental rationale for intervening in this area; the case law seems to reveal substantial disagreement on this point. In *Secretary of State etc, ex p Association of Metropolitan Authorities* (1986),[43] the court refused to quash delegated legislation it had found to be unlawful on the ground that to do so would cause great administrative inconvenience. This decision seems to imply that the courts' role is that of a pragmatic administrative facilitator; in stark contrast, Lord Denning has said that 'Even if chaos should result, still the law must be obeyed' (*Bradbury v Enfield* (1967))[44], a statement which seemed to be advocating an absolutist enforcement of the law for its own sake. Thus as the basic justification for intervention is the subject of dispute there can be little prospect of consistency in intervention.

What will be the position if there are no statutory requirements about consultation or if there are provisions but these do not state what kind of consultation must take place? In other words, when must a person affected by a decision be consulted about it (and allowed to make representations, in whatever form) and what kind of consultation must take place? These questions will be addressed in turn.

When is consultation required?

For much of the first half of this century the courts drew a distinction between administrative decisions and 'judicial' type decisions, allowing the right to a

---

38 1 All ER 979.

39 De Smith, *Judicial Review of Administration Action* (1980), p142.

40 2 PD 203, 211.

41 QB 235.

42 *Judicial Review* (1986), p208.

43 1 WLR 1.

44 3 All ER 434.

hearing, or consultation, only in the latter type of case. This distinction was largely swept away by the decision in *Ridge v Baldwin*, described by Wade as 'the turning point of judicial policy'.[45]

Ridge v Baldwin [1964] AC 40, 64–5, 71–2, 132

By s191 of the Municipal Corporations Act 1882 the watch committee had power to 'at any time suspend and dismiss any borough constable whom they think negligent in the discharge of his duty or otherwise unfit for the same'. After the appellant was acquitted of certain charges in a trial during which unflattering remarks were made about him by the judge, he was dismissed by the committee. No specific charge was formulated against the appellant; his only opportunity to make representations was a meeting (on 18 March) at which his solicitor made representations on his behalf. The appellant sought from the court, *inter alia*, a declaration that his dismissal was illegal and *ultra vires*.

> **Lord Reid:** ... The appellant's case is that in proceeding under the Act of 1882 the watch committee were bound to observe what are commonly called the principles of natural justice. Before attempting to reach any decision they were bound to inform him of the grounds on which they proposed to act and give him a fair opportunity of being heard in his own defence. The authorities on the applicability of the principles of natural justice are in some confusion, and so I find it necessary to examine this matter in some detail. The principle *audi alteram partem* goes back many centuries in our law and appears in a multitude of judgments of judges of the highest authority. In modern times opinions have sometimes been expressed to the effect that natural justice is so vague as to be practically meaningless. But I would regard these as tainted by the perennial fallacy that because something cannot be cut and dried or nicely weighed or measured therefore it does not exist. The idea of negligence is equally insusceptible of exact definition, but what a reasonable man would regard as fair procedure in particular circumstances and what he would regard as negligence in particular circumstances are equally capable of serving as tests in law, and natural justice as it has been interpreted in the courts is much more definite than that. It appears to me that one reason why the authorities on natural justice have been found difficult to reconcile is that insufficient attention has been paid to the great difference between various kinds of cases in which it has been sought to apply the principle. What a minister ought to do in considering objections to a scheme may be very different from what a watch committee *ought* to do in considering whether to dismiss a chief constable ...

> **Lord Hodson:** ... The matter which, to my mind, is relevant in this case is that where the power to be exercised involves a charge made against the person who is dismissed, by that I mean a charge of misconduct, the principles of natural justice have to be observed before the power is exercised.

> One of the difficulties felt in applying principles of natural justice is that there is a certain vagueness in the term, and, as Tucker LJ said in *Russell v Duke of Norfolk*: 'There are ... no words which are of universal application to every kind of inquiry and every kind of domestic tribunal. The requirements of natural justice must depend on the circumstances of the case, the nature of the inquiry, the rules under which the tribunal is acting, the subject-matter under consideration and so forth'. If it be said that this makes natural justice so vague as to be inapplicable, I

---

45   *Constitutional Fundamentals* (1989), p79.

would not agree. No one, I think, disputes that three features of natural justice stand out – (1) the right to be heard by an unbiased tribunal; (2) the right to have notice of charges of misconduct; (3) the right to be heard in answer to those charges. The first does not arise in the case before your Lordships, but the two last most certainly do, and the proceedings before the watch committee, therefore, in my opinion, cannot be allowed to stand.

Note

Ridge thus made it clear that it was not so much the type of decision being made, or the status of the person making it that was important so much as asking whether fairness demanded consultation. In what circumstances, then will consultation be required? One principle developed by the courts in response to this question has been the notion of legitimate expectation.[46] This notion was first formulated by Lord Denning MR in *Schmidt v Home Secretary* (1969)[47] and its principles clarified in the *GCHQ* case, in which the Civil Service unions sought review of the decision, made by the Prime Minister without consultation, to ban trade unions at GCHQ.

Council of Civil Service Unions v Minister for the Civil Service [1985] AC 374, 400–1, 412–13

Lord Fraser: Mr Blom-Cooper [for the applicants] submitted that the minister had a duty to consult the CCSU, on behalf of employees at GCHQ, before giving instruction on 22 December 1983 for making an important change in their conditions of service. His main reason for so submitting was that the employees had a legitimate, or reasonable, expectation that there would be such prior consultation before any important change was made in their conditions.

It is clear that the employees did not have a legal right to prior consultation.

Lord Fraser explained why, and went on:

But even where a person claiming some benefit of privilege has no legal right to it, as a matter of private law, he may have a legitimate expectation of receiving the benefit or privilege, and, if so, the courts will protect his expectation by judicial review as a matter of public law.

[Such] expectation may arise either from an express promise given on behalf of a public authority of from the existence of a regular practice which the claimant can reasonably expect to continue ... The submission of behalf of the appellants is that the present case is of the latter type. The test of that is whether the practice of prior consultation of the staff on significant changes in their conditions of service was so well established by 1983 that it would be unfair or inconsistent with good administration for the Government to depart from the practice in this case. Legitimate expectations such as are now under consideration will always relate to a benefit or privilege to which the claimant has no right in private law, and it may even be to one which conflicts with his private law rights. In the present case the evidence shows that, ever since GCHQ began in 1947, prior consultation has been the invariable rule when conditions of service were to be significantly altered. Accordingly in my opinion if there had been no question of national security involved, the appellants would have had a legitimate expectation that the minister would consult them before issuing the instruction of 22 December 1983 ...

---

46 See generally on legitimate expectation, the very useful analysis by Craig, (1992) 108 LQR 79.
47 2 Ch 149.

Lord Diplock: My Lords, in the instant case the immediate subject matter of the decision was a change in one of the terms of employment of civil servants employed at GCHQ. That the executive functions of the minister for the Civil Service, in her capacity as such, included making a decision to change any of those terms, except in so far as they related to remuneration, expenses and allowances, is not disputed. It does not seem to me to be of any practical significance whether or not as a matter of strict legal analysis this power is based upon the rule of constitutional law to which I have already alluded that the employment of any civil servant may be terminated at any time without notice and that upon such termination the same civil servant may be re-engaged on different terms. The rule of termination of employment in the civil service without notice, of which the existence is beyond doubt, must in any event have the consequence that the continued enjoyment by a civil servant in the future of a right under a particular term of his employment cannot be the subject of any right enforceable by him in private law; at most it can only be a legitimate expectation.

Prima facie, therefore, civil servants employed at GCHQ who were members of national trade unions had, at best in December 1983, a legitimate expectation that they would continue to enjoy the benefits of such membership and of representation by those trade unions in any consultations and negotiations with representatives of the management of that Government department as to changes in any term of their employment. So, but again *prima facie* only, they were entitled, as a matter of public law under the head of 'procedural propriety', before administrative action was taken on a decision to withdraw that benefit, to have communicated to the national trade unions by which they had therefore been represented the reason for such withdrawal, and for such unions to be given an opportunity to comment on it.

Notes

1   Their Lordships went on to find that, though the failure to consult had been unfair, the decision was justified on national security grounds.

2   The requirement that if a practice is to give rise to legitimate expectation, the fact that it must be regular was stressed in the case. As Baldwin and Horne note:[48]

> It is to be anticipated, therefore, that where a body is engaged in irregular, non-recurring forms of decision-making it will be deemed less likely to create expectations than where it deals with a series of similar decisions. Accordingly, in the planning case of *Enfield London Borough Council v Secretary of State for the Environment* [[1975] JPL 155] it was argued that the Secretary of State had acted unfairly in making a decision on the basis of a new policy rather than the existing development plan. In the High Court, however, Melford Stevenson J could find no implied representation that the Secretary of State would adhere to the original plan.

3   In the *GCHQ* case, the legitimate expectation arose from a regular practice but it was acknowledged of course that an express undertaking could also give rise to the expectation. One such case, described by Baldwin and Horne[49] was *Liverpool Corporation, ex p Liverpool Taxi Fleet Operator's Association* ([1972] 2 WLR 1262):

---

48   (1986) 49 MLR 685, 700.

49   *Ibid*, at 699.

The corporation had limited the number of taxi-cab licences in Liverpool to 300 and had assured the owners that they would not change the policy without hearing representations. When the corporation resolved to increase the number, the Court of Appeal said that this could not be done without hearing the owners. The basis of the decision was fairness rather than either estoppel or a general duty to consult when rule-making. An expectation (and, it seems, one that had been relied upon) could not be dashed with impunity, especially one accompanied by an undertaking to pursue a particular course of action or procedure.

4   A useful attempt at setting out the law in this area in a systematic way can be found in the recent cases of *Devon County Council, ex p Baker* and *Durham County Council, ex p Curtis* (1995) heard together in the Court of Appeal. The cases concerned decisions by the two councils to shut down certain residential homes for the elderly. Devon had engaged in fairly extensive consultation with the residents; Durham only specifically made the residents aware of the plan five days before the final decision was made to go ahead with it. Residents from both homes claimed that they had had a legitimate expectation of proper consultation, which had been frustrated by the councils' actions. Simon Browne LJ found that cases of legitimate expectation could be broken down in four different categories. The first was substantive expectation (see below). He then went on to consider the others.

Devon County Council, ex p Baker; Durham County Council ex p Curtis [1995] 1 All ER 73, 88–91

(2) ... the concept of legitimate expectation is used to refer to the claimant's interest in some ultimate benefit which he hopes to retain (or, some would argue, attain). Here, therefore, it is the interest itself rather than the benefit that is the substance of the expectation. In other words the expectation arises not because the claimant asserts any specific right to a benefit but rather because his interest in it is one that the law holds protected by the requirements of procedural fairness; the law recognises that the interest cannot properly be withdrawn (or denied) without the claimant being given an opportunity to comment and without the authority communicating rational grounds for any adverse decision. Of the various authorities drawn to our attention, *Schmidt v Secretary of State for Home Affairs* [1969] 1 All ER 904, [l969] 2 Ch 149, *O'Reilly v Mackman* [1982] 3 All ER 1124, [1983] 2 AC 237 and the recent decision of Roch J in *Rochdale Metropolitan BC, ex p Schemet* (1993) 1 FCR 306 are clear examples of this head of legitimate expectation.

(3) Frequently, however, the concept of legitimate expectation is used to refer to the fair procedure itself. In other words it is contended that the claimant has a legitimate expectation that the public body will act fairly towards him. As was pointed out by Dawson in *A-G for New South Wales v Quin* (1990) 93 ALR at 39 this use of the term is superfluous and unhelpful: it confuses the interest which is the basis of the requirement of procedural fairness with the requirement itself:

No doubt people expect fairness in their dealings with those who make decisions affecting their interests, but it is to my mind quite artificial to say that this is the reason why, if the expectation is legitimate in the sense of well founded, the law imposes a duty to observe procedural fairness. Such a duty arises, if at all, because the circumstances call for a fair procedure and it adds nothing to say that they also are such as to lead to a legitimate expectation that a fair procedure will be adopted.

(4) The final category of legitimate expectation encompasses those cases in which it is held that a particular procedure, not otherwise required by law in the protection of an interest, must be followed consequent upon some specific promise or practice. Fairness requires that the public authority be held to it. The authority is bound by its assurance, whether expressly given by way of a promise or implied by way of established practice. *Re Liverpool Taxi Owners' Association*, [1972] 2 QB 299 and *A-G of Hong Kong v Ng Yuen Shiu* [1983] 2 All ER 346, [1983] 2 AC 629 are illustrations of the court giving effect to legitimate expectations based upon express promises; *Council of Civil Service Unions v Minister for the Civil Service* an illustration of a legitimate expectation founded upon practice albeit one denied on the facts by virtue of the national security implications.

The judge went on to find that the appellants in the *Devon* case had had full opportunity to make representations in favour of their case.

It is when one turns to the *Durham* case that the issue of consultation arises in its sharpest form, no promises or practice of consultation here being asserted by the appellants, no actual process of consultation being in fact afforded by the council. The *Durham* case, in short, on the facts, could hardly be more unlike the *Devon* case.

The legitimate expectation argument in the *Durham* case is advanced in these terms:

> The County Council's decision deprived the appellants of a benefit or advantage which they had hitherto been permitted by the County Council to enjoy and which they could legitimately expect either to continue indefinitely, or at least to continue unless and until the County Council communicated to them some rational ground for withdrawing the benefit on which they were given an opportunity to comment.

This, of course, is asserting a legitimate expectation in category 2. Certainly, Mr Bradley disavows, as inevitably he must, any attempt to assert a legitimate expectation in category 1 [*ie* a substantive right to carry on living in the residential homes].

As stated, the second category of legitimate expectation comprises those interests which the law recognises are of a character which require the protection of procedural fairness. What then is the touchstone by which such interests can be identified? It cannot be merely that the law insists they be not unfairly denied else there would be no point in introducing the concept of legitimate expectation in the first place; one would simply look at the decision in question and ask whether the administrator acted fairly in taking it.

I turn to the well-known passage in Lord Diplock's speech in *Council of Civil Service Unions v Minister for the Civil Service* [1984] 3 All ER 935 at 949, [1985] AC 374 at 408 where he describes the two situations in which, by reference to their consequences, decisions will be held susceptible to review, the second situation (class (b)) being the one involving what he called a legitimate expectation. Class (b) arises, he said, when a decision affects someone –

> by depriving him of some benefit or advantage which ... he has in the past been permitted by the decision-maker to enjoy and which he can legitimately expect to be permitted to continue to do until there has been communicated to him some rational grounds for withdrawing it on which he has been given an opportunity to comment ...

(I cite only class (b)(i). Class (b)(ii) depends upon an assurance and is therefore my category 4.)

Thus the only touchstone of a category 2 interest emerging from Lord Diplock's speech is that the claimant has in the past been permitted to enjoy some benefit or advantage. Whether or not he can then legitimately expect procedural fairness, and if so to what extent, will depend upon the court's view of what fairness demands in all the circumstances of the case. That, frankly, is as much help as one can get from the authorities. Lord Diplock's analysis supersedes, as I believe, all earlier attempted expositions of this doctrine such as that found in *Mclnnes v Onslow Fane* [1978] 3 All ER 211, [1978] 1 WLR 1520.

In short, the concept of legitimate expectation when used, as in the *Durham* case, in the category 2 sense seems to me no more than a recognition and embodiment of the unsurprising principle that the demands of fairness are likely to be somewhat higher when an authority contemplates depriving someone of an existing benefit or advantage than when the claimant is a bare applicant for a future benefit. That is not to say that a bare applicant will himself be without any entitlement to fair play. On the contrary, the developing jurisprudence suggests that he too must be fairly dealt with, not least in the field of licensing.

With these thoughts in mind I return to the *Durham* case. That the appellants have hitherto been enjoying some benefit or advantage of which the county council now proposes to deprive them cannot be doubted. On the authorities they accordingly get to first base in terms of asserting a legitimate expectation of some procedural fairness in the decision-making process. But it is no good pretending that the authorities carry them or the courts a single step further than that. The fact is that it still remains for the court to say, unassisted by authority save only in so far as there may exist other cases analogous on heir facts, whether that legitimate expectation ought to be recognised and, if so, precisely what are the demands of fairness in the way of an opportunity to comment and so forth.

As stated, I share Dillon LJ's view on the facts of this case that five days' notice of the proposed closure of Ridgeway House gave the residents wholly insufficient opportunity to make such representations as they would have wished to make in favour of their home being kept open in preference to others.

Note

It is interesting to note Simon Browne LJ's frankness as to the limited amount of precise guidance which can be gained from the authorities: his judgment amounts to an assertion that the courts can merely apply common sense and reasonableness, unencumbered – and un-assisted – by any more detailed guidance.

Legitimate expectation: procedural *and* substantive?[50]

The question here is whether legitimate expectation only gives one the right to be fairly heard (procedure), or whether it can actually extend to expectation that the benefit itself will not be withdrawn at all without good reason. Baldwin and Horne note some significant pointers:

In *O'Reilly v Mackman* Lord Diplock stated that the prisoners had no right to remission of sentence but had a 'legitimate expectation' that general past practice on remissions would be adhered to in the absence of a reason to the contrary. As one commentator put it: 'In effect the "legitimate expectation" is that official powers shall not be used arbitrarily: it is *ultra vires* to do so' [K Davies, *All England Law Reports: Annual Review of Administrative Law* (1984), p5].

---

50 On this issue generally see P Craig (1996) 55 CLJ 289.

Lord Diplock amplified his position in the *GCHQ* case, a decision located at the point where the line between expectations and forfeitures becomes very faint. He said that to qualify as a subject for review a decision must have consequences that impact upon other persons, either by affecting that person's rights as enforceable in private law, or,

> by depriving him of some benefit or advantage which either (i) he has in the past been permitted by the decision-maker to enjoy and which he can legitimately expect to be permitted to continue to [enjoy] until there has been communicated to him some rational ground for withdrawing it on which he has been given an opportunity to comment, or (ii) he has received assurance from the decision-maker [that benefits and advantages] will not be withdrawn without giving him first an opportunity of advancing reasons for contending that they should not be withdrawn [3 All ER 955 at 949].

The seeds of the substantive right can be seen in both the expectation and forfeiture cases. Where there is a past practice, right or benefit plus a legitimate or reasonable expectation, it is *not* the case that the public body can freely deprive a person so long as it follows the appropriate procedure (eg by communicating grounds and giving an opportunity to comment). There is a further test: there must exist 'rational' grounds. Thus an expectation is substantively protected to the extent that rational grounds must exist and be demonstrated before interference with the expectation will be allowed.[51]

The authors go on to note that the House of Lords decision in *Findlay v Secretary of State for the Home Department* (1985)[52] demonstrates that the courts had not at that time 'fully arrived at this position'.[53]However, since this piece was written there has been further judicial consideration of whether procedural legitimate expectation can take on a more substantive form: Laws and Sedley JJ have clashed directly over the issue in the following two cases. In the first, the facts are not particularly material. The second concerned a case in which the owner of a ship *The Nellie* claimed he had a legitimate expectation that he would be granted a fishing licence which had been dashed by the introduction of a new policy on the issuing of such licences; comment by C Himsworth follows.

Secretary of State for Transport, ex p Richmond upon Thames London Borough Council [1994] 1 All ER 577, 596

Laws J: ... there is no case so far as I am aware (certainly none was cited to me) in which it has been held that there exists an enforceable expectation that a policy will not be changed *even though* those affected have been consulted about any proposed change. And this is no surprise: such a doctrine would impose an obvious and unacceptable fetter upon the power (and duty) of a responsible public authority to change its policy when it considered that that was required in fulfilment of its public responsibilities. In my judgment the law of legitimate expectation, where it is invoked in situations other that one where the expectation relied on is distinctly one of consultation, only goes so far as to say that there may arise conditions in which, if policy is to be changed, a specific person or class of persons affected must first be notified and given the right to be heard. The extent to which, case by case, this principle applies may be affected by the important distinction between situations where the class of persons in

---

51 Baldwin and Horne, *op cit*, 705–6.
52 AC 318, HL.
53 Baldwin and Horne, *op cit*, 706–7.

question have specific expectations for the determination of their individual cases (as in *ex p Khan*) and others where the policy is of a more general nature which does not involve the resolution of any individual claims of right or status. But it is unnecessary for present purposes to go deeper into such and antithesis.

Mr Gordon relies upon particular words used by Parker LJ in *ex p Khan*. He said ([1985] 1 All ER 40 at 46, [1984] 1 WLR 1337 at 1334):

> There can, however, be no doubt that the Secretary of State has a duty to exercise his common law discretion fairly. Furthermore, just as, in the *Liverpool Taxi Owners* case, the corporation was held not to be entitled to resile from an undertaking and change its policy without giving a fair hearing so, in principle, the Secretary of State, if he undertakes to allow in persons if certain conditions are satisfied, should not in my view be entitled to resile from that undertaking without affording interested persons a hearing and then only if the overriding pubic interest demands it.

It is these last words that are stressed by Mr Gordon. He would set them alongside a passage from the judgment of Lord Denning MR in *Re Liverpool Taxi Owners' Association* [1972] 2 QB 299 at 308 where he said:

> At any rate they ought not to depart from it [ie an undertaking] except after the most serious consideration and hearing what the other party has to say; and then only if they are satisfied that the overriding public interest requires it. The public interest may be better served by honouring their undertaking than by breaking it.

Mr Gordon's submission is that these references to the 'overriding public interest' imply that where a public authority has effectively given an assurance that it would continue to apply a policy which it has adopted, there are two conditions which must be fulfilled before it may lawfully change tact: not only that a right to be heard must be accorded to those affected, but also that the change must be justified by reference to 'the overriding public interest'. But this latter condition would imply that the court is to be the judge of the public interest in such cases, and thus the judge of the merits of the proposed policy change. Thus understood, Mr Gordon's submission must be rejected. The court is not the judge of the merits of the decision-maker's policy.

Ministry of Agriculture, Fisheries and Food, ex p Hamble Fisheries [1995] 2 All ER 714, 723–4

The first question under this head, posed by Mr Paines [for the respondent], is whether there can in law be a legitimate expectation of anything more than a procedural benefit or protection. There is no doubt that the expectation to which Mr Green [for the applicant] lays claim is of a substantive benefit or advantage, not merely a procedural one. Mr Paines relies upon a passage in the decision of Laws J in *Secretary of State for Transport, ex p Richmond upon Thames London Borough Council* [1994] 1 All ER 577 at 594–6, [1994] 1 WLR 74 at 92–4. The respect to which this passage is entitled is not diminished by the fact that it is *obiter*, the decision having turned upon an unrelated point. But I regret to say that I disagree with significant elements of Laws J's reasoning, although not with its starting and finishing points. The subject matter was a submission of Mr Richard Gordon QC that the applicant local authority had acquired a legitimate expectation that policy would not be shifted in any circumstances beyond a certain point. Laws J's conclusion that neither precedent nor principle could carry Mr Gordon that far is one with which I would entirely agree. But, in order to develop his submission, Mr Gordon had contended that the law now recognised not only procedural but substantive legitimate expectations. Laws J said, 'This is an antithesis which is liable to cause confusion ...' (see [1994] 1 All ER 577 at 595, [1994] 1 WLR 74 at 92). This too I would respectfully indorse, as I would Laws J's conclusion of principle ([1994] 1 All ER 577 at 595, [1994] 1 WLR 74 at 93):

> I consider that the putative distinction between procedural and substantive rights in this context has little (if any) utility: the question is always whether the discipline of fairness imposed by the common law, ought to prevent the public authority respondent from acting as it proposes.

But it is for precisely this reason that I would not accept Laws J's further proposition that neither precedent nor principle goes further than the enforcement of legitimate procedural expectations. *Secretary of State for the Home Dept, ex p Ruddock* [1987] 2 All ER 518, [1987] 1 WLR 1482, which it was the privilege of Laws J and myself to argue at the Bar before Taylor J, was precisely a case legitimate expectation of a substantive benefit, namely that individuals not falling within the Government's publicised criteria for telephone surveillance would not have their telephones tapped by the security services. Taylor J held [1987] 2 All ER 518 at 531, [1987] 1 WLR 1482 at 1497):

> ... I conclude that the doctrine of legitimate expectation is essence imposes a duty to act fairly. Whilst most of the cases are concerned ... with a right to be heard, I do not think the doctrine is so confined ... Of course, [a promise or undertaking given by a minister as to how he will proceed] must not conflict with his statutory duty ... the Secretary of State ... cannot fetter his discretion. By declaring a policy he does not preclude any possible need to change it.

In so deciding, Taylor J founded upon the speech of Lord Scarman in *Findlay v Secretary of State for the Home Dept* [1984] 3 All ER 801, [1985] AC 318 in which the possibility of a substantive legitimate expectation was recognised.

In my respectful view, principle as well as precedent points to these conclusions. As Law J points out in the passage I have cited, the real question is one of fairness in public administration. It is difficult to see why it is any less unfair to frustrate a legitimate expectation that something will or will not be done by the decision-maker than it is to frustrate a legitimate expectation that the applicant will be listened to before the decision-maker decides whether to take a particular step. Such a doctrine does not risk fettering a public body in the discharge of public duties to stand still or be distorted because of that individual's peculiar position. As I hope to show in what follows, legitimacy is itself a relative concept, to be gauged proportionately to the legal and policy implications of the expectation. This, no doubt is why it has proved easier to establish a legitimate expectation that an applicant will be listened to than that a particular outcome will be arrived at by the decision-maker. But the same principle of fairness in my judgment governs both situations.

C Himsworth, 'Legitimately Exceeding Proportionality?' (1996) *Public Law* 46, 49

Sedley J poses the question: 'What then is the legal alchemy which gives an expectation sufficient legitimacy to secure enforcement in public law?' (at p728). In what circumstances does fairness demand that, at the point where a public body is considering making a change of policy which it is, in other respects, entitled to make, an exception should be made to give recognition to an expectation which has been raised? The answer, it is explained, is that a balance has to be struck. Legitimacy is 'not an absolute. It is a function of expectations induced by Government and of policy considerations which militate against their fulfilment' (p731). In the case of *The Nellie* [the *MAFF* case], it was held that the balance had been struck correctly. Whilst admitting other exceptions to the new licensing policy, the minister had acted neither irrationally nor unfairly in not extending the exceptions as far as to encompass those in the wider and more open-ended category of licence-holders which included *The Nellie's* owner. To have done so would have risked the eventual subversion of the new policy. *The Nellie's* owner should be regarded as having had 'a hope rather than an expectation' (p735).

Note

In *ex p Baker* and *ex p Curtis* (1995),[54] the Court of Appeal made some helpful *obiter* comments on the area of substantive legitimate expectation, seeming to incline more toward Sedley J's view. Simon Browne LJ said:[55]

These various authorities show that the claimant's right will only be found established when there is a clear and unambiguous representation upon which it was reasonable for him to rely. Then the administrator or other public body will be held bound in fairness by the representation made unless only its promise or undertaking as to how its power would be exercised is inconsistent with the statutory duties imposed upon it. The doctrine employed in this sense is akin to an estoppel. In so far as the public body's representation is communicated by way of a stated policy, this type of legitimate expectation falls into two distinct sub-categories: cases in which the authority are held entitled to change their policy even so as to affect the claimant, and those in which they are not. An illustration of the former is *Torbay Borough Council, ex p Cleasby* [1991] COD 142; of the latter, *ex p Khan*.

Other ways of establishing a right to consultation

A person affected by a decision may also be able to claim a right to a hearing or consultation simply by virtue of the importance of the decision for his livelihood, reputation or some other vital interest of his. The following well-known case illustrates the principle well.

Barnsley Metropolitan Borough Council, ex p Hook [1976] 1 WLR 1052, 1055–57

Lord Denning MR: [The plaintiff] is a street trader in the Barnsley market. He has been trading there for some six years without any complaint being made against him; but, nevertheless, he has now been banned from trading in the market for life. All because of a trifling incident. On Wednesday, 16 October 1974, the market closed at 5.30. So were all the lavatories, or 'toilets' as they are now called. They were locked up. Three-quarters of an hour later, at 6.20, Harry Hook had an urgent call of nature. No one was about except one or two employees of the council, who were cleaning up. They rebuked him. He said: 'I can do it here if I like'. They reported him to a security officer who came up. The security officer reprimanded Harry Hook. We are not told the words used by the security officer. I expect they were in language which street traders understand. Harry Hook made an appropriate reply. Again we are not told the actual words, but it is not difficult to guess. I expect it was an emphatic version of 'You be off'. At any rate, the security officer described them as words of abuse.

On the Thursday morning the security officer reported the incident. The market manager thought it was a serious matter. So he saw Mr Hook the next day, Friday 18 October. Mr Hook admitted it and said he was sorry for what had happened. The market manager was not satisfied to leave it there. He reported

---

54   1 All ER 73.

55   *Ibid*, at 88.

the incident to the chairman of the amenity services committee of the council. He says the chairman agreed 'that staff should be protected from such abuse'. That very day the market manager wrote a letter to Mr Hook, banning him from trading in the market. ...

So there he was on Friday, 18 October, dismissed as from the next Wednesday, banned for life.

He was, however, granted a further hearing. On the next Thursday, 24 October, he was allowed to state his case before the chairman of the amenity services committee, the vice-chairman, the amenities officer and the market manager himself. He went there accompanied by the president of the Barnsley Market Traders' Union. The matter was discussed. the council people saw no reason to alter the decision, but told Mr Hook that he could be heard further by the indoor services subcommittee. This met on the following Wednesday, 30 October. Mr Hook went there with a young articled clerk from his solicitors and the trade union representative. The committee met at 10 am but Mr Hook and his representatives had to wait for an hour before they were allowed in. Then the articled clerk and the union representative went in. But Mr Hook himself did not go in. He stayed outside in the corridor. The articled clerk and the union representative were allowed to address the committee, but they were not given particulars of the charge or of the evidence against Mr Hook. At that meeting the market manager was present and was in a position to tell the committee his view of the evidence. After Mr Hook's representatives has been heard, that subcommittee discussed the case (with the market manager still present) and decided to adhere to the original decision ...

I do not think that the right of a stallholder arises merely under a contact or licence determinable at will. It is a right conferred on him by the common law under which, so long as he pays the stallage, he is entitled to have his stall there; and that right cannot be determined without just cause. I agree that he has to have the permission of the market-holder to start with. But once he has it and has set up his stall there, then so long as he pays the stallage, he has a right to keep it there. It is not to be taken away except for just cause and then only in accordance with the provisions of natural justice. I do not mind whether the market-holder is exercising a judicial or an administrative function. A stallholder counts on this right in order to enable him to earn his living. ...

Note

Such principles may also apply where a licence has been refused in the first place, rather than revoked. The following case illustrates how the courts are reluctant to exclude the right to be heard, even in the face of some evidence that such was not the intention behind the relevant statute.

Huntingdon District Council, ex p Cowan [1984] 1 WLR 501, 502–3, 504, 506–8

Glidewell J: This is an application by way of judicial review for an order of *certiorari* to quash the decision of the Huntingdon District Council refusing to grant a licence for public entertainment for premises known as 'Cuddles', St Neots, and for *mandamus* directed to the council requiring them to hear the application according to law.

Under the legislation formerly in force, there was not merely a liquor licence for the sale of intoxicating liquor on the premises, but also a music and dancing licence. Indeed that was renewed, after Whitbreads purchased the premises, each year. But in fact there was no music or dancing at the premises until, in

December 1982, it was decided by Messrs Whitbreads to open at the premises a discotheque, that is to say, an establishment with dancing to recorded music. Thereafter – and I am not concerned with the detail of this – there is evidence of some complaints from people living in the locality.

On 14 March 1983, the Local Government (Miscellaneous Provisions) Act 1982, which now governs the grant of what are called 'public entertainment licences', had come into force. On that date. Whitbreads applied, through Mr Cowan, for an entertainment licence for these premises. The district council, whose function it now is to consider and make a decision upon that application, received observations upon it from the chief officer of police and the fire authority, though it seems that the observations from the latter authority were not in the form of objections. They also received a petition from a number of members of the public, presumably in opposition either to the licence being granted or to the hours at which the premises were open for public entertainment, I know not which.

Whitbreads were not informed by the local authority that any objectives had been received. They were not informed that there was opposition. It follows that they were not informed of the substance of the observations of the terms or substance of the petition. They were given no opportunity to comment upon what objectors had said either by way of oral hearing or in writing ...

Mr Richardson, for the applicants, submits that where an objector has made representations to the local authority, or where the local authority itself has some reason to believe that there is doubt about whether it should grant the application – in other words it has some point in mind of its own – then it is under a duty to give notice to the applicant, either by sending a copy of the representations or objections, or at least giving the substance to them, or if it is its own point, telling the applicant what the point is. Then it must, says Mr Richardson, give the applicant the opportunity to make representations in answer, to seek to deal with the objection or the point, and it may be that this needs to be by way of oral hearing ...

In reply, Mr Steel for the district council, accepts that the authority has a duty to act fairly but he does not accept that that extends to disclosing the objections or giving any opportunity for reply. He maintains that the authority is perfectly entitled to act as it has done. Indeed, as I apprehend it, this is a matter of principle upon which the authority is interested in being guided. Mr Steel submits that local authorities have many administrative or quasi-administrative functions where there is no duty to give information to applicants or to give applicants any right to make representations..

What seems to me to be Mr Steel's strongest argument, however, is this, that the other Parts of the Act of 1982, which are dealing with different sorts of licensing, do provide detailed procedures for the making of objections; the notification of objections to the applicant; for representations to be made by the applicant; and indeed, for a hearing ...

Mr Steel submits that this is one Act, and a normal principle of statutory construction is that an Act must be construed as a whole. It follows, he says, that where you have in relation to two similar subjects dealt with by the Act, detailed provisions providing for objections, notification, representations by an applicant and a hearing, and no such provisions in relation to entertainment licences, that can only be because Parliament intended that those provisions should not apply to entertainment licences.

The question which has exercised my mind is, does the fact that in the other Parts of the Act to which I have referred, specific provision is made for those features, whereas no such provision is made in Schedule 1, mean that Parliament intended that that rule of natural justice should not here apply? I have come to the conclusion that I ought not to draw that deduction.

It is true, as Mr Steel submitted, that these Parts of the Act are all dealing with licensing functions in one way or another. But from the way in which the various Parts have been drafted, it looks very much as though they have been separately drafted, almost as thought they were parts of separate statutes, certainly as though they were separate codes without reference one to the other. ...

Accordingly, in my judgment, a local authority is under a duty, when dealing with entertainment licences, first, to inform the applicant of the substance of any objection or of any representation in the nature of any objection (not necessarily to give him the whole of it, not to say necessarily who has made it, but to give him the substance of it); and, secondly, to give him an opportunity to make representations in reply.

Notes

1 In the field of prisoner's rights, the courts have built up a formidable jurisprudence which has progressively infiltrated requirements of fairness into the disciplinary process. In *Board of Visitors of Hull Prison, ex p St Germain (No 1) (1979)*[56] certain prisoners complained that the disciplinary proceedings which followed the Hull Prison riots were not conducted in accordance with the principles of natural justice. At that time prisoners' disciplinary hearings were conducted either by the Board of Visitors or the governor depending on the seriousness of the offence. The punishments available included loss of privileges, cellular confinement and loss of remission. The governor is empowered under r 50 of the Prison Rules to punish less serious offences but can award loss of up to 28 days remission. The Board of Visitors hears more serious charges and can award a loss of remission of up to 120 days under r 51.

The Court of Appeal, in the first such ruling since *Ridge v Baldwin (1964)*,[57] held that prisoners only lose those liberties expressly denied them by Parliament – otherwise they retain their rights under the law. 'The rights of the citizen, however circumscribed by penal sentence or otherwise, must always be the concern of the courts unless their jurisdiction is expressly excluded by statute' (Shaw LJ). There was nothing in the Prison Act 1952 or the Prison Rules made under it to take away the jurisdiction of the courts, and the Board of Visitors was discharging a quasi-judicial function. Thus it was found that the decision in question must be open to review and that boards of visitors must act in accordance with the rules of natural justice. However, it was determined that there must be substantial unfairness if a decision was to be quashed. This ruling was confined to Board of Visitors' hearings, however, and did not apply to those of governors' because it was thought that Boards of Visitors were more like an independent tribunal, that they conducted their proceedings more formally and, importantly, dealt with more serious matters and could award more serious punishments.

---

56 QB 425.

57 AC 40.

2 The courts have viewed the disciplinary function exercised by the governor of the prison and the disciplinary function administered by Boards of Visitors as two separate processes because the punishments available for each differ in degree of seriousness. There are far more governors' hearings,[58] and until very recently it was thought that no possibility of judicial review could arise in respect of such hearings due to the administrative inconvenience which review might entail. The cases already considered did not address the question whether governors' hearings should be open to review (apart from *dicta* in St Germain). In *Deputy Governor of Camphill Prison, ex p King* (1985)[59] the Court of Appeal took the view that although the deputy governor had misconstrued a prison rule and interpreted it out of line with the general principles of criminal law,[60] it had no jurisdiction to entertain an application for judicial review of the Prison Governor's adjudication on the prisoner. It based this decision on the difference between the functions of governors and of Boards of Visitors; the governor has a managerial as well as a disciplinary function and it was thought that this dual function might be adversely affected if the courts could question governors' decisions. Therefore the Court decided the case on policy grounds on the basis that it did not want to undermine the governor's authority in a volatile situation. It was pointed out that prisoners can petition the Secretary of State, and that judicial review of the Home Secretary's decision would be available.

3 This ruling was considered by the House of Lords in *Deputy Governor of Parkhurst Prison, ex p Leech, Deputy Governor of Long Lartin Prison, ex p Prevot* (1988).[61] Leech was punished for having a pen case adapted for smoking cannabis. He was awarded 28 days loss of remission at a governor's hearing and claimed that he was given no opportunity to cross-examine prison officers and in general had had no opportunity to put his defence. Prevot was punished because it was alleged that he had been masturbated by his wife during a prison visit. He claimed that he was given no opportunity to call his wife as a witness or any of the prisoners in the room at the time. He was awarded 21 days loss of remission at a governor's hearing.

It was considered whether prison governors' decisions should be open to judicial review, bearing in mind the recent recognition that Boards of Visitors' hearings should be so open. Could the two types of hearing be properly distinguished? Governors could also affect the rights of prisoners in that they could award loss of remission; it had already been accepted that prisoners had a legitimate expectation of receiving remission. Moreover, the governor had a duty to act in accordance with natural justice which was spelt out in the Prison Rules (r 49). Thus it was hard to find a logical distinction between the two disciplinary functions. *Dicta* in *St Germain (No 1)*

---

58 In 1989 95% of hearings were governor's hearings (*Prison Discipline Statistics 1989*, p8, Table 3).

59 1 WLR 36 (also see (1984) PL 513–18).

60 He had misinterpreted the meaning of 'possession' as connoting merely control as opposed to knowledge and control.

61 2 WLR 290, 1 All ER 485; for comment see (1988) 51 MLR 525; (1988) PL 183; (1988) CLJ 165; (1989) 23 CT 85.

pointed the way to this conclusion: Shaw LJ said, 'I do not find it easy, if at all possible to distinguish between disciplinary proceedings conducted by a Board of Visitors and those carried out by a prison governor ... the essential nature of the proceedings ... is the same. So in nature if not in degree are the consequences to a prisoner'. The House of Lords was not prepared to find a distinction on policy grounds. The argument put forward by the Court of Appeal in *Camphill* as to the indivisibility of the managerial function and the judicial role of governors was considered and it was thought that judicial review of the governor's judicial role would not undermine the managerial role but that the reverse would be the case; injustice perpetrated by the governor would be more likely to foment unrest, whereas if a prisoner was able to pursue a grievance by legal means that would calm the situation. The argument that an alternative remedy existed – petitioning the Secretary of State – was considered but it was thought that the existence of another remedy should only exceptionally oust the courts' jurisdiction. Unless judicial review was expressly denied it should be granted. In any event the possibility of petitioning existed in respect of Board of Visitors' hearings but had not precluded the availability of judicial review in such instances.

It was therefore concluded that hearings before governors should be conducted in accordance with the principles of natural justice. However, the point still stands that *all* governor's hearings may not be open to review. In some governors' disciplinary hearings loss of privileges may be awarded; it could be argued that such hearings would not be open to review on the basis that a loss of privileges is different in kind, not just in degree from a loss of remission. It could be argued that such consequences for a prisoner of a finding against him in a governor's hearing are much less serious than those which may normally flow from a Board of Visitors' hearing. In *Aston University, ex p Rothy* (1969)[62] it was held that natural justice would apply although there was no kind of legal right in the question; it was necessary to look at all the circumstances – the expectation of a fair hearing and the serious consequences which would follow from the decision. Perhaps a loss of privileges might not alone be sufficiently serious to warrant the application of the principles of natural justice but might be so if coupled with a loss of earnings – deprivation of a legal right. The point has not yet been resolved.

4   However, where national security is in play, the courts have been far more cautious in the requirements they have imposed on the decision maker concerned. In deportation cases there is a right to an *ex gratia* hearing before the three advisers. The procedure was described by a Home Secretary as follows: 'The person concerned ... will be given such particulars of allegations as will not entail disclosure of sources of evidence. He will be notified that he can make representations to the three advisers. The advisers will ... allow him to appear before them, if he wishes ... As well as speaking for himself he may arrange for a third party to testify on his behalf. Neither the sources of evidence nor evidence that might lead to disclosure of sources can be revealed to the person concerned but the advisers will ensure that the

---

62   2 QB 538.

person is able to make his points effectively. Since the evidence against a person necessarily has to be received in his absence, the advisers in assessing the case will bear in mind that it has not been tested by cross-examination and that the person has not had the opportunity to rebut it. ... On receiving the advice of the advisers the Secretary of State will reconsider his original decision but the advice given to him will not be revealed'.[63]

Mark Hosenball challenged this procedure in respect of the decision to deport him on grounds of national security (see *SSHD, ex p Hosenball* (1977) above) on the basis that it did not comply with the principles of natural justice as he had not been given adequate particulars of the allegations against him. The Court of Appeal, while acknowledging that the principles of natural justice would normally require that such particulars would be given, said that in cases where national security is involved, 'the rights of the individual [including his entitlement to natural justice] must be subordinated to the protection of the realm' (*per* Geoffrey Lane LJ). Lord Denning considered that in such cases it was not the proper role of the courts to attempt to determine the proper balance between the requirements of national security and the claims of the individual; this role fell correctly within the ambit of the Home Secretary's responsibilities.

Despite Lord Denning's view of the need to secure the interests of national security at the expense of individual rights, it must be questioned whether it would not be possible to put in place various means of protecting national security while giving greater weight to the right to a fair hearing. Other hearings concerning national security matters are heard in camera and the identity of witnesses is protected; it would not be impossible at least to improve the quality of deportation hearings just as the courts have improved the quality of prison disciplinary hearings.

What is required for a fair hearing?

Two points will be in issue here. The first is the manner in which a person affected by a decision must be permitted to make his case. The second is the rule against bias in the decision maker. These will be dealt with in turn.

What sorts of procedures are necessary?

The basic rule here is the maxim of *audi alteram partem* – hear the other side. The person affected by a decision should be given a fair chance to make representations upon it. We will turn in a moment to the detailed aspects of a fair hearing – witnesses, cross-examination and the like – but it should first be noted that a condition precedent for the ability of a person to be able to argue against an adverse decision, or to prepare their defence is the giving to them, in sufficient detail, of the reasons behind the decision which they wish to challenge. This was recognised to an extent in *Ridge v Baldwin* (above) but where the demand was not so much a statement of the case against someone as the giving of reasons for a decision affecting them, the courts have been slower to grant the right requested. The leading decision in this area is now *Doody* (1993).

---

63   HC Deb WA 15 June 1971, vol 819, col 376.

Secretary of State for the Home Department, ex p Doody and others [1994] 1 AC 531, 560–5

The four applicants had each received mandatory life sentences for murder. The Home Secretary, after consulting with the Lord Chief Justice and the trial judge (referred to in the judgement as 'the judges') had set the 'penal element'[64] in the sentence, which reflected the demands of retribution and deterrence. Once the penal part of the sentence had been served, the case would then go to the Parole Board who could then recommend whether it was safe to release the prisoner on licence or whether further imprisonment was needed to protect the public from the prisoner (referred to as 'the risk element'). In this case, the Home Secretary determined the penal period without consulting the prisoners; he then informed them of his decision, but did not give them any reason for it, or tell them whether he had fixed a period which differed from that recommended by the judges. The applicants sought, *inter alia*, declarations that (1) they were entitled to make representations to the Home Secretary on the matter; (2) that the Home Secretary was required to inform them what period had been recommended by the judges and their reasons; (3) that he was also required to inform them, if he had differed from the judges, of his reasons for so doing. On appeal, the first two declarations were granted by the Court of Appeal. The Home Secretary appealed to the House of Lords and the applicants cross-appealed.

> **Lord Mustill:** … Although it is tempting to approach the question of disclosure and reasons as if it were the judges' opinions to which the applications for judicial review are directed this is mistaken. It is the decision of the Home Secretary which vitally affects the future of the prisoner, and it is the openness of this decision which is essentially in dispute … The only issue is whether the way in which the scheme is administered falls below the minimum standard of fairness.
>
> What does fairness require in the present case? My Lords, I think it unnecessary to refer by name or to quote from, any of the often-cited authorities in which the courts have explained what is essentially an intuitive judgment. They are far too well known. From them, I derive that (1) where an Act of Parliament confers an administrative power there is a presumption that it will be exercised in a manner which is fair in all the circumstances. (2) The standards of fairness are not immutable. They may change with the passage of time, both in the general and in their application to decisions of a particular type. (3) The principles of fairness are not to be applied by rote identically in every situation. What fairness demands is dependent on the context of the decision, and this is to be taken into account in all its aspects. (4) An essential feature of the context is the statute which creates the discretion, as regards both its language and the shape of the legal and administrative system within which the decision is taken. (5) Fairness will very often require that a person who may be adversely affected by the decision will have an opportunity to make representations on his own behalf either before the decision is taken with a view to producing a favourable result; or after it is taken, with a view to procuring its modification; or both. (6) Since the person affected usually cannot make worthwhile representations without knowing what factors may weigh against his interests fairness will very often require that he is informed of the gist of the case which he has to answer.
>
> I … begin by … inquiring what requirements of fairness, germane to the present appeal, attach to the Home Secretary's fixing of the penal element. As general background to this task, I find in the more recent cases on judicial review a

---

64   Also referred to as the 'tariff sentence'.

perceptible trend towards an insistence on greater openness, or if one prefers the contemporary jargon 'transparency', in the making of administrative decisions. This tendency has been accompanied by an increasing recognition, both in the requirements of statute (cf s1(4) of the Act of 1991) and in the decisions of the Criminal Division of the Court of Appeal, that a convicted offender should be aware what the court has in mind for his disposal. Whilst the current law and practice concerning discretionary life sentences conform entirely with this trend the regime for mandatory life prisoners conspicuously does not. Should this distinction be maintained in its entirety? Contending on behalf of the Secretary of State that matters should be left as they are, Mr Pannick first points to the creation by Parliament of express statutory rights similar to those which might otherwise have come into existence through an implied obligation of fairness, and maintains that these leave no room to imply any further rights. Thus, the prisoner was entitled under s59 of the Act of 1967 (now obsolete and repealed) to make representations to the Parole Board in relation to his release on parole, either orally through the medium of an interview with a member of the local review board or in writing. Furthermore, in relation to his recall from licence the prisoner is still enabled to make representations and to know the reasons for the revocation of his licence: see s39(3) of the Act of 1991, re-enacting provisions of the Act of 1967.

The logic of this argument appears to demand that the prisoner's right to make representations is excluded in all cases except those just mentioned, an extravagant proposition for which the Secretary of State does not contend. But in any event I find it impossible to accept that these limited and fragmentary statutory rights demonstrate a Parliamentary intention to exclude all other aspects of fair treatment, the more so since the provisions originate in an Act passed 16 years before the formal separation of the penal and risk elements, and the ascription to the former of such a decisive influence on the future of the prisoner.

A similar argument is advanced on the broader ground that since Parliament has by s34 established a regime which assures discretionary life prisoners of important rights, whilst leaving untouched the Home Secretary's much more general powers in relation to mandatory prisoners, no new rights in this field should be created by judicial implication. The Secretary of State calls up the decision of the House of Lords in *Re Findlay* [1985] AC 318, which was concerned with another aspect of Mr Brittan's change in policy, to emphasise how careful the courts must be not to impose on a statutory general discretion constraints which Parliament has chosen not to create. Whilst I bear this warning carefully in mind, I cannot accept the argument. Even in relation to discretionary life prisoners, s34 does not exhaust the rights stemming from the general principle of fairness: as witness *Parole Board, ex p Wilson* [1992] QB 740 the reasoning of which I adopt in full.

My Lords, thus to reject the arguments advanced by the Secretary of State does not in itself mean that the respondents are entitled to succeed on the first three issues: it merely leaves the ground clear to consider what fairness demands. Starting with the first issue, we encounter no problems. It would be impossible nowadays to imagine that a prisoner has no right to address to the Home Secretary reasons why the penal term should be fixed at a lower rather than a higher level, and it is now accepted that the prisoner does have this right. Indeed, the Secretary of State has gone further, by very properly undertaking through counsel that a statement of this effect will be included in the next edition of *'Life Sentence: Your Questions Answered'*, the excellent booklet issued to persons serving life sentences.

[Turning to the second and third issues] it must now be asked whether the prisoner is entitled to be informed of that part of the material before the Home Secretary which consists of the judges' opinion and their reasons for it. It has frequently been stated that the right to make representations is of little value unless the maker has knowledge in advance of the considerations which, unless effectively challenged, will or may lead to an adverse decision. The opinion of the Privy Council in *Kanda v Government of Malaya* [1962] AC 322, 337 is often quoted to this effect. This proposition of common sense will in many instances require an explicit disclosure of the substance of the matters on which the decision-maker intends to proceed. Whether such a duty exists, how far it goes and how it should be performed depend so entirely on the circumstances of the individual case that I prefer not to reason from any general proposition on the subject. Rather, I would simply ask whether a life prisoner whose future depends vitally on the decision of the Home Secretary as to the penal element and who has a right to make representations upon it should know what factors the Home Secretary will take into account. In my view he does possess this right, for without it there is a risk that some supposed fact which he could controvert, some opinion which he could challenge, some policy which he could argue against, might wrongly go unanswered.

In the present instance, the opinion of the judges (or opinions, if the Lord Chief Justice differs from the charge judge) are weighed in the balance when the Secretary of State makes his decision. Beyond the fact that the opinion is not invariably decisive (as witness the statistics previously cited) there is no means of knowing how it figures in the Home Secretary's reasoning. That it does so figure is quite plain from the statements by successive ministers from which I have quoted. This being so, I think it clear that the prisoner needs to know the substance of the judges' advice, comprising not only the term of years which they recommended as the penal element, but also their reasons: for the prisoner cannot rationalise his objections to the penal element without knowing how it was rationalised by the judges themselves.

This does not mean that the document(s) in which the judges state their opinion need be disclosed in their entirety. Those parts of the judges' opinions which are concerned with matters other than the penal element (for example any observation by the judges on risk) need not be disclosed in any form, and even in respect of the relevant material the requirement is only that the prisoner shall learn the gist of what the judges have said. This will not necessarily involve verbatim quotation from the advice, although this may often be convenient. If the Home Secretary's duty is approached in this way I doubt whether the fact that in the past the advice has been given in documents intended to be confidential will often prove to be troublesome; and in the few cases where problems do arise it may well be that, upon request, the judges are prepared to waive the confidentiality of the documents.

In these circumstances I agree with the Court of Appeal on the second as well as the first of the issues. I do, however, have the misfortune to differ on the third.

I accept without hesitation, and mention it only to avoid misunderstanding, that the law does not at present recognise a general duty to give reasons for an administrative decision. Nevertheless, it is equally beyond question that such a duty may in appropriate circumstances be implied, and I agree with the analyses by the Court of Appeal in *Civil Service Appeal Board, ex p Cunningham* [1991] 4 All ER 310 of the factors which will often be material to such an implication.

Turning to the present dispute I doubt the wisdom of discussing the problem in the contemporary vocabulary of 'prisoner's rights', given that as a result of his own act the position of the prisoner is so forcibly distanced from that of the ordinary citizen, nor is it very helpful to say that the Home Secretary should out of simple humanity provide reasons for the prisoner, since any society which operates a penal system is bound to treat some of its citizens in a way which would, in the general, be thought inhumane. I prefer simply to assert that within the inevitable constraints imposed by the statutory framework, the general shape of the administrative regime which ministers have lawfully built around it, and the imperatives of the public interest, the Secretary of State ought to implement the scheme as fairly as he can. The giving of reasons may be inconvenient, but I can see no ground at all why it should be against the public interest: indeed, rather the reverse. This being so, I would ask simply: Is refusal to give reasons fair? I would answer without hesitation that it is not. As soon as the jury returns its verdict the offender knows that he will be locked up for a very long time. For just how long immediately becomes the most important thing in the prisoner's life. When looking at statistics it is easy to fall into the way of thinking that there is not really very much difference between one extremely long sentence and another: and there may not be, in percentage terms. But the percentage reflects a difference of a year or years: a long time for anybody, and longer still for a prisoner. Where a defendant is convicted of, say, several armed robberies he knows that he faces a stiff sentence: he can be advised by reference to a public tariff of the range of sentences he must expect; he hears counsel address the judge on the relationship between his offences and the tariff; he will often hear the judge give an indication during exchanges with counsel of how his mind is working; and when sentence is pronounced he will always be told the reasons for it. So also when a discretionary life sentence is imposed, coupled with an order under s34. Contrast this with the position of the prisoner sentenced for murder. He never sees the Home Secretary; he has no dialogue with him: he cannot fathom how his mind is working. There is no true tariff, or at least no tariff exposed to public view which might give the prisoner an idea of what to expect. The announcement of his first review date arrives out of thin air, wholly without explanation. The distant oracle has spoken, and that is that.

My Lords, I am not aware that there still exists anywhere else in the penal system a procedure remotely resembling this. The beginnings of an explanation for its unique character might perhaps be found if the executive had still been putting into practice the theory that the tariff sentence for murder is confinement for life, subject only to a wholly discretionary release on licence: although even in such a case I doubt whether in the modern climate of administrative law such an entirely secret process could be justified. As I hope to have shown, however, this is no longer the practice, and can hardly be sustained any longer as the theory. I therefore simply ask, is it fair that the mandatory life prisoner should be wholly deprived of the information which all other prisoners receive as a matter of course. I am clearly of the opinion that it is not.

Notes

1   For recent cases on the scope of the duty to give reasons see *Secretary of State for the Home Department, ex p Moon* (1995)[65] and *Lawrie v Commission for Local Authority Accounts* (1994).[66] It will be noted that, at two points in his judgment, Lord Mustill (with whom the other judges agreed) adopted the test of 'simply' asking: 'is [the procedure under review] fair?' Such explicit judicial reliance on 'fairness' as a test, at the highest level, arguably gives

---

65   *The Times*, 8 December 1995. For further discussion of *Doody*, see P Craig (1994) 53(2) CLJ 282.

66   SLT 118.

more force to the principle criticism of the law in this area, namely that, in adopting a test like 'fairness', which is not only imprecise in meaning in the first place but which avowedly demand widely different levels of consultation, etc, in different circumstances, the courts have made the law intolerably uncertain. A well-known exposition of this point is Rawlings':[67]

Flexible natural justice, or 'fairness' has come to have no fixed or settled content that an administrator should know must be observed ... All he knows ... is that he must be 'fair', and what 'fairness' requires in the particular circumstances he can only ultimately find out when the court, on judicial review, tells him that he has, or has not been fair ... As guidance to administrative practice [this test] is hopelessly imprecise from the point of view of those who want to know what procedural requirements the law lays down for them to observe.[68]

Arguably, Rawlings is overstating his case somewhat. If an administrator's type of procedure is covered by existing case law he *will* know more or less what is required of him; an arguably more accurate formulation of the critique would have pointed out that the test is inadequate because does not enable the administrator to work out, by analogy, what will be required of him in situations as yet not considered by the courts.

2   The courts *have* developed quite detailed rules as to the requirements of fairness in the context of prison disciplinary hearings in relation to the calling of all or any of the witnesses requested by the prisoner, cross-examination of witnesses, the general conduct of the proceedings and legal representation.

3   In *Board of Visitors of Hull Prison, ex p St Germain (No 2)* (1979)[69] it was held that a Boards of Visitors must be able to exercise a discretion to refuse a prisoner's request for witnesses if it is felt that he is purposely trying to obstruct or subvert the proceedings by calling large numbers of witnesses or if, where the request is made in good faith, it is felt that the calling of large numbers of witnesses is unnecessary. However, mere administrative inconvenience would not support a decision to refuse such a request and so if the only reason for the refusal was, for example, the inconvenience involved in recalling the witnesses from other prisons that would be insufficient. The principles established in the above case were confirmed in *Board of Visitors for Nottingham Prison, ex p Moseley* (1981);[70] it was held that if it were established that a prisoner had asked for and been refused permission to call witnesses that would, *prima facie*, be unfair.

In many instances it would seem essential that a prisoner should be able to call witnesses in order to challenge the evidence against him. Moreover, it may be unlikely that a case will often be so straightforward as to require only one witness for the defence. Therefore, if a prisoner can demonstrate that calling more than one witness was necessary due to the nature of his defence, it would follow that he should have been allowed to call them. In *St Germain (No 2)*, Lane LJ also considered whether the prisoners must be

---

67   See his 'Judicial Review and the Control of Government' (1986) 64 *Public Administration* 135.

68   *Ibid*, at 140–1.

69   3 All ER 545.

70   *The Times*, 23 January 1981.

allowed to cross-examine those who had given evidence against them, or whether such evidence could be given by way of written statements only.

Board of Visitors of Hull Prison, ex p St Germain (No 2) [1979] 3 All ER 545, 552–3

... It is clear that the entitlement of the board to admit hearsay evidence is subject to the overriding obligation to provide the accused with a fair hearing. Depending upon the facts of the particular case and the nature of the hearsay evidence provided to the board, the obligation to give the accused a fair chance to exculpate himself, or a fair opportunity to controvert the charge – to quote the phrases used in the passages cited above – or a proper of full opportunity of presenting his case – to quote the language of s47 or r 49 – may oblige the board not only to inform the accused of the hearsay evidence but also to give the accused a sufficient opportunity to deal with that evidence. Again, depending upon the nature of that evidence and the particular circumstances of the case, a sufficient opportunity to deal with the hearsay evidence may well involve the cross-examination of the witness whose evidence is initially before the board in the form of hearsay.

We again take by way of example the case in which the defence is an alibi. The prisoner contends that he was not the man identified on the roof. He, the prisoner, was at the material time elsewhere. In short the prisoner has been mistakenly identified. The evidence of identification given by way of hearsay may be of the 'fleeting glance' type as exemplified by the well-known case of *Turnbull* [1977] QB 224. The prisoner may well wish to elicit by way of question all manner of detail, eg the poorness of the light, the state of the confusion, the brevity of the observation, the absence of any contemporaneous record, etc, all designed to show the unreliability of the witness. To deprive him of the opportunity of cross-examination would be tantamount to depriving him of a fair hearing.

We appreciate that there may well be occasions when the burden of calling the witness whose hearsay evidence is readily available may impose a near impossible burden upon the board. However, it has not been suggested that hearsay evidence should be resorted to in the total absence of any first-hand evidence and this is the usual practice. Accordingly where a prisoner desires to dispute the hearsay evidence and for this purpose to question the witness, and where there are insuperable or very grave difficulties in arranging for his attendance the board should refuse to admit that evidence, or, if it has already come to their notice, should expressly dismiss if from their consideration. ...

Notes

1   The refusal of witnesses and of cross examination led to the quashing of six findings of guilt by way of *certiorari*.

2   In *Board of Visitors of Gartree Prison, ex p Mealy* (1981)[71] it was held that the accused should have been allowed to ask questions of a defence witness. On this basis it may be argued that a prisoner should in general be able to cross-examine prison officers. The refusal of witnesses and of cross examination led to the quashing of six convictions in *St Germain (No 2)*.

3   Proceedings have been found to have been unfair for because they disadvantaged the accused in other ways. *Board of Visitors of Gartree Prison,*

---

71   *The Times,* 14 November 1981.

ex p Mealy (1981)[72] arose because when Mealy came to answer the charges against him in a disciplinary hearing before the Board of Visitors he found that the order of the proceedings had been changed and he considered that this had adversely affected his ability to defend himself. It was accepted that a substantial unfairness had occurred which amounted to a breach of natural justice. It was further found that if necessary the chairman or woman of the Board should guide the prisoner through the proceedings. This finding implied that the Board of Visitors must seek to ensure equality between the parties.

4   In *Fraser v Mudge* (1975)[73] the Court of Appeal determined that a prisoner had no *right* to legal representation. The applicant had sought an injunction to delay a Board of Visitors' hearing so that representation could be obtained, but it was held on policy grounds that to allow the application would be prejudicial to maintaining order because discipline needs to be expeditious. Similarly, in *Maynard v Osmond* (1977)[74] it was held that it would not be normal to have such a right although a friend or helper might be permitted to be present.

However, in *Secretary of State for the Home Dept, ex p Tarrant* (1985),[75] although it was accepted, following *Fraser v Mudge*, that a prisoner could not claim a *right* to legal representation, it was ruled that a Board of Visitors must exercise a *discretion* as to its grant. The court then suggested certain factors which a board could properly take into account. These included: the seriousness of the charge and of the penalty, the likelihood that points of law might be likely to arise, the ability of the prisoner to conduct his own case; and the need for speed in making the adjudication. It was found that any Board of Visitors which had taken these factors into account would in the proper exercise of its discretion have granted legal representation. The decision of the Board was therefore quashed.

This decision may have been influenced by the expected outcome in *Campbell and Fell v UK* (1984)[76] in the European Court of Human Rights, which found that Art 6 of the European Convention had been breached by a failure to allow legal representation to a prisoner in a disciplinary hearing.

The House of Lords considered the issue afresh in *Board of Visitors of HM Prison, the Maze, ex p Hone* (1988)[77] but determined that legal representation in prison disciplinary hearings would remain discretionary. The applicant had been convicted of assaulting prisoner officers at a hearing in which he had had no legal representation. He appealed to the House of Lords on the question whether legal representation should be available as of right due to the requirements of natural justice and Art 6. In holding that the position would remain as in *Tarrant* the House of Lords took into account the delay

---

72   *Ibid.*

73   1 WLR 1132.

74   QB 240.

75   2 WLR 613; for comment see (1987) 38 NILQ 144.

76   Eur Court HR, Series A, Vol 80, judgment of 28 June 1984, 5 EHRR 207.

77   AC 379, [1988] 2 WLR 177, 1 All ER 321; for comment see [1988] 51 MLR 525; (1989) 40 NILQ 71.

and cost of obtaining legal advice which the House thought would be prejudicial to the administration of discipline in the prison, and also that, once granted, it would be difficult to deny the right in governors' hearings. If legal advice were imported into governors' hearings it was thought that difficulties would arise as such hearings would not be sufficiently expeditious. It is thus clear that the requirements of a fair hearing will vary quite substantially depending on the type of hearing.

5   For recent cases on natural justice see *Huntley v Attorney General of Jamaica* [1995] 2 WLR 114; *Ealing Justices, ex p Fanneran, The Times,* 9 December 1995 (both on the right to make representations); *Secretary of State for the Home Department ex p Hickley (No 2)* [1995] All ER 490 (on the requirement to disclose evidence on which a decision adversely affecting the applicant has been made); *Errington v Wilson, The Times,* 2 June 1995 (a Scottish case in which cross-examination of expert witnesses was found to be required in the case of a cheese producer whose cheese was ordered to be destroyed on health and safety grounds).

The rule against bias

One of the two rules of natural justice, *nemo judex in causa sua,* is commonly expressed to forbid bias on the part of the decision maker. This may include personal animosity towards the applicant by the decision maker. In cases where the decision maker has a non-pecuniary interest in the outcome, it will not be *assumed* that the decision maker is biased; what must be shown in these cases is that a reasonable man observing the proceedings would think that there was a 'real likelihood of bias' or would have a 'reasonable suspicion' of bias.

Metropolitan Properties Co (FGC) Ltd v Lannon [1969] 1 QB 577, 598–600

The issue was whether Mr Lannon, whose father (with whom he lived) was challenging the rent fixed for his residence, could sit on a rent review committee to adjudicate upon a case concerning the landlord with whom his father was in dispute.

> **Lord Denning MR:** A man may be disqualified from sitting in a judicial capacity on one of two grounds. First, a 'direct pecuniary interest' in the subject-matter. Second, 'bias' in favour of one side or against the other. ... So far as bias is concerned, it was acknowledged that there was no actual bias on the part of Mr Lannon, and no want of good faith. But it was said that there was, albeit unconscious, a real likelihood of bias. This is a matter on which the law is not altogether clear: but I start with the oft-repeated saying of Lord Hewart CJ in *Sussex Justices, ex p McCarthy:* ([1924] 1 KB 256 at 259].
>
>> It is not merely of some importance, but is of fundamental importance that justice should not only be done, but should manifestly and undoubtedly be seen to be done.
>
> In *Barnsley Licensing Justices, ex p Barnsley and District Licensed Victuallers' Association* [[1960] 2 All ER 703 CA], Devlin J appears to have limited that principle considerably, but I would stand by it. It brings home this point: in considering whether there was a real likelihood of bias, the court does not look at the mind of the justice himself or at the mind of the chairman of the tribunal, or

whoever it may be, who sits in a judicial capacity. It does not look to see if there was a real likelihood that he would, or did, in fact favour one side at the expense of the other. The court looks at the impression which would be given to other people. Even if he was as impartial as could be, nevertheless if right-minded persons would think that, in the circumstances, there was a real likelihood of bias on his part, then he should not sit. And if he does sit, his decision cannot stand: see *Huggins* [[1895] 1 QB 563]; and *Sunderland Justices* [[1901] 2 KB 357, CA], *per* Vaughan Williams LJ [*ibid* at 373]. Nevertheless there must appear to be a real likelihood of bias. Surmise or conjecture is not enough: see *Camborne Justices, ex p Pearce* [[1954] 2 All ER 850, DC], and *Nailsworth Licensing Justices, ex p Bird* [[1953] 2 All ER 652, DC]. There must be circumstances from which a reasonable man would think it likely or probable that the justice, or chairman, as the case may be, would, or did. favour one side unfairly at the expense of the other. The court will not inquire whether he did, in fact, favour one side unfairly. Suffice it that reasonable people might think he did. The reason is plain enough. Justice must be rooted in confidence: and confidence is destroyed when right-minded people go away thinking: 'The judge was biased'.

Applying these principles, I ask myself: Ought Mr John Lannon to have sat? I think not. If he was himself a tenant in difference with his landlord about the rent of his flat, he clearly ought not to sit on a case against the selfsame landlord, also about the rent of a flat, albeit another flat. In this case he was not a tenant, but the son of a tenant. But that makes no difference. No reasonable man would draw any distinction between 1968 him and his father, seeing he was living with him and assisting him with his case.

... No man can be an advocate for or against a party in one proceeding, and at the same time sit as a judge of that party in another proceeding. Everyone would agree that a judge, or a barrister or solicitor (when he sits *ad hoc* as a member of a tribunal) should not sit on a case to which a near relative or a close friend is a party. So also a barrister or solicitor should not sit on a case to which one of his clients is a party. Nor oɪ a case where he is already acting against one of the parties. Inevitably people would think he would be biased.

I hold, therefore, that Mr John Lannon ought not to have sat on this rent assessment committee. The decision is voidable on that account and should be avoided.

Question

Does the decision establish that the test for bias is a reasonable suspicion test?

Notes

1 Denning made reference to the view of Devlin J in *ex p Barnsley*, which differed from his own. Devlin LJ's view was as follows (at p187):

> We have not to inquire what impression might be left on the minds of the present applicants or on the minds of the public generally. We have to satisfy ourselves that there was a real likelihood of bias – not merely satisfy ourselves that that was the sort of impression that might reasonably get abroad.

2 If we are to consider what the reasonable man would have thought, looking at the situation, it obviously becomes crucial to ask, what is the extent of his knowledge? In *Pearce* itself it was said that the reasonable man is presumed to be in possession of such knowledge as he might readily have ascertained. The ruling in *Bremer Handelsgesellschaft mbh v Ets Soules et Cie* (1985)[78]

---

78 1 Lloyd's Rep 160.

provides some support for this view: 'the apparent fairness of the process must be judged in the light of the facts as they would have appeared to the reasonable man *at the time when they mattered, ie when the procedure was in progress'* (emphasis added). However, in *Steeples v Derbyshire County Council* (1985), the court stated that the reasonable man, in making his judgement, knows all relevant matters whether available to the public or not.

3   It is submitted that the view in *Bremer*, which was affirmed by the Court of Appeal, is to be preferred. The notion that fairness should be judged by facts generally known at the time of the hearing is in line with the well established notion that justice must not only be done, but must be seen to be done.

4   The decision in *Gough* (1993)[79] seems to go a long way towards resolving uncertainty as to the test for bias. The case arose from the discovery (after the trial) by a member of the jury in the trial of the appellant that she lived next door to the appellant's brother. Lord Goff considered whether the authorities established that there were two rival and alternative tests for bias which could be termed the reasonable suspicion test and the real likelihood test.

Gough [1993] AC 646, 668, 670

Lord Goff: In my opinion, if, in the circumstances of the case (as ascertained by the court), it appears that there was a real likelihood, in the sense of a real possibility, of bias on the part of a justice or other member of an inferior tribunal, justice requires that the decision should not be allowed to stand. I am by no means persuaded that, in its original form, the real likelihood test required that any more rigorous criterion should be applied. Furthermore the test as so stated gives sufficient effect, in cases of apparent bias, to the principle that justice must manifestly be seen to be done, and it is unnecessary, in my opinion, to have recourse to a test based on mere suspicion, or even reasonable suspicion, for that purpose. Finally there is, so far as I can see, no practical distinction between the test as I have stated it, and a test which requires a real danger of bias, as stated in *Spencer* [1987] AC 128. ...

In conclusion, I wish to express my understanding of the law as follows. I think it possible, and desirable, that the same test should be applicable in all cases of apparent bias, whether concerned with justices or members of other inferior tribunals, or with jurors, or with arbitrators. Likewise I consider that, in cases concerned with jurors, the same test should be applied by a judge to whose attention the possibility of bias on the part of a juror has been drawn in the course of a trial, and by the Court of Appeal when it considers such a question on appeal. Furthermore, I think it unnecessary, in formulating the appropriate test, to require that the court should look at the matter through the eyes of a reasonable man, because the court in cases such as these personifies the reasonable man; and in any event the court has first to ascertain the relevant circumstances from the available evidence, knowledge of which would not necessarily be available to an observer in court at the relevant time. Finally, for the avoidance of doubt I prefer to state the test in terms of real danger rather than real likelihood, to ensure that the court is thinking in terms of possibility rather than probability of bias. Accordingly, having ascertained the relevant

---

79   AC 646.

circumstances, the court should ask itself whether, having regard to those circumstances, there was a real danger of bias on the part of the relevant member of the tribunal in question, in the sense that he might unfairly regard (or have unfairly regarded) with favour, or disfavour, the case of a party to the issue under consideration by him; though, in a case concerned with bias on the part of a justices' clerk, the court should go on to consider whether the clerk has been invited to give the justices advice and, if so, whether it should infer that there was a real danger of the clerk's bias having infected the views of the justices adversely to the applicant.

Note

The rule against bias is commonly thought to be an absolute; that this is not so can be seen by the recent decision of the Court of Appeal in *Avon County Council, ex p Crabtree* (1995).[80] In this case, the applicant sought review of the decision of a fostering panel not to re-register him as a foster carer. His complaint was that the panel included persons against whom he had made complaints in the past. The court found that the rule against bias, in common with other rules of natural justice, had to be applied flexibly, as the circumstances demanded, and that, given the administrative-like nature of the panel, and the type of decision being made, there had been no unfairness to the applicant.

'IRRATIONALITY'

The conceptual basis of the doctrine

It must be stated at the outset that some confusion exists as to whether this is a kind of mixed-bag category, which encompasses a number of diverse matter such as improper considerations, basing a decision on no evidence, etc or properly speaking is only 'pure unreasonableness'. Indeed, this may be because, in fact, unreasonableness or irrationality as a wholly separate head arguably has no independent conceptual life, and, unless made more substantive in its scope,[81] may as well be subsumed into 'illegality', a point returned to below. Lord Diplock's formulation of this head in the *GCHQ* case (in which he referred to it as 'irrationality' was as follows:

> By 'irrationality' I mean what can by now be succinctly referred to as 'Wednesbury unreasonableness' *(Associated Provincial Picture Houses Ltd v Wednesbury Corporation* [1948] 1 KB 223). It applies to a decision which is so outrageous in its defiance of logic or of accepted moral standards that no sensible person who had applied his mind to the question to be decided could have arrived at it.[82]

The notion of unreasonableness, as Lord Diplock indicated, found its genesis in the following decision.

---

80 *Independent*, 29 November 1995.

81 See below.

82 [1985] AC 374, 410.

Associated Provincial Picture Houses v Wednesbury Corporation [1948] 1 KB 223, 228–229, 231, CA

The Wednesbury Corporation had power to grant licences for the opening of cinemas on Sundays 'subject to such conditions as the authority think fit to impose'. The Corporation imposed a condition in a Sunday licence that no children under 15 should be admitted to the cinema.

Lord Greene MR: ... When discretion of this kind is granted the law recognises certain principles upon which that discretion must be exercised, but within the four corners of those principles the discretion, in my opinion, is an absolute one and cannot be questioned in any court of law.

It is true the discretion must be exercised reasonably. Now what does that mean? Lawyers familiar with the phraseology commonly used in relation to exercise of statutory discretions often use the word 'unreasonable' in a rather comprehensive sense. It has frequently been used and is frequently used as a general description of the things that must not be done. For instance, a person entrusted with a discretion must, so to speak, direct himself properly in law. He must call his own attention to the matters which he is bound to consider. He must exclude from his consideration matters which are irrelevant to what he has to consider. If he does not obey those rules, he may truly be said, and often is said, to be acting 'unreasonably'. Similarly, there may be something so absurd that no sensible person could ever dream that it lay within the powers of the authority.

It appears to me quite clear that the matter dealt with by this condition was a matter which a reasonable authority would be justified in considering when they were making up their mind what condition should be attached to the grant of this licence. Nobody, at this time of day, could say that the well-being and the physical and moral health of children is not a matter which a local authority, in exercising theirs powers, can properly have in mind when those questions are germane to what they have to consider. Here Mr Gallop [for the plaintiff] did not, I think, suggest that the council were directing their mind to a purely extraneous and irrelevant matter, but he based his argument on the word 'unreasonable', which he treated as an independent ground for attacking the decision of the authority; but once it is conceded, as it must be conceded in this case, that the particular subject-matter dealt with by this condition was one which it was competent for the authority to consider, there, in my opinion, is an end of the case. Once that is granted, Mr Gallop is bound to say that the decision of the authority is wrong because it is unreasonable, and in saying that he is really saying that the ultimate arbiter of what is and is not reasonable is the court and not the local authority. It is just there, it seems to me, that the argument breaks down. It is clear that the local authority are entrusted by Parliament with the decision on a matter which the knowledge and experience of that authority can best be trusted to deal with. The subject-matter with which the condition deals is one relevant for its consideration. They have considered it and come to a decision upon it. It is true to say that, if a decision on a competent matter is so unreasonable that no reasonable authority could ever have come to it, then the courts can interfere. That, I think, is quite right; but to prove a case of that kind would require something overwhelming, and in this case, the facts do not come anywhere near anything of that kind. I think Mr Gallop in the end agreed that his proposition that the decision of the local authority can be upset if it is proved to be unreasonable, really meant that it must be proved to be unreasonable in the sense that the court considers it to be a decision that no reasonable body could have come to. It is not what the court considers unreasonable, a different thing altogether. If it is what the court considers unreasonable, the court may very well have different views than that of a local authority on matters of high public policy of this kind. Some courts might think that no children ought to be admitted on Sundays at all, some courts might think the reverse, and all over the country I have no doubt on a thing of that sort honest and sincere people hold different views. The effect of the legislation is not to set up the court as an arbiter of the correctness of one view over another. It is the local authority that are set in that position.

The court is entitled to investigate the action of the local authority with a view to seeing whether they have taken into account matters which they ought not to take into account, or, conversely, have refused to take into account or neglected to take into account matters which they ought to take into account. Once that question is answered in favour of the local authority, it may be still possible to say that, although the local authority have kept within the four corners of the matters which they ought to consider, hay have nevertheless come to a conclusion so unreasonable that no reasonable authority could ever have come to it. In such a case, again, I think the court can interfere.

Note

Another important case in this area is *Wheeler v Leicester City Council* (1985) which concerned the decision of Leicester City Council to withdraw certain facilities from Leicester City Football Club on the ground that it had failed to condemn the 1984 Rugby Tour of South Africa or to discourage its members from playing. The Council had asked the club four questions: does the club support the Government's opposition to the tour?; does the Club agree that the tour is an insult to the large proportion of the Leicester population?; will the Club press the RFU to call off the tour?; will the Club press the players to pull out of the tour? The Council made it clear that only an affirmative answer to all four questions would be acceptable. The stance of the club was that it was a matter of opinion whether a sporting boycott assisted in breaking down apartheid, and that it was a matter of individual conscience for its members whether they took part in the tour.

Wheeler v Leicester City Council [1985] AC 1054, 1077–79, HL

Lord Roskill: The council's main defence rested on s71 of the Race Relations Act 1976. That section appears as the first section in Part X of the Act under the cross-heading 'Supplemental'. For ease of reference I will set out the section in full:

> Without prejudice to their obligation to comply with any other provision of this Act, it shall be the duty of every local authority to make appropriate arrangements with a view to securing that their various functions are carried out with due regard to the need –
>
> (a) to eliminate unlawful racial discrimination; and
>
> (b) to promote equality of opportunity, and good relations, between persons of different racial groups.

His Lordship considered argument on the construction of the statute and concluded:

> I do not doubt that the council were fully entitled in exercising their statutory discretion under, for example, the Open Spaces Act 1906 and the various Public Health Acts, which are all referred to in the judgments below, to pay regard to what they thought was in the best interests of race relations.

The only question is, therefore, whether the action of the council of which the club complains is susceptible of attack by way of judicial review. It was forcibly argued by Mr Sullivan QC for the council, that once it was accepted, as I do accept, that s71 bears the construction for which the council contended, the matter became one of political judgment only, and that by interfering the courts would be trespassing across that line which divides a proper exercise of a statutory discretion based on a political judgment, in relation to which the courts must not and will not interfere, from an improper exercise of such a discretion in relation to which the courts will interfere. ...

To my mind the crucial question is whether the conduct of the council in trying by their four questions, whether taken individually or collectively, to force acceptance by the club of their own policy (however proper that policy may be) on their own terms, as for example, by forcing them to lend their considerable prestige to a public condemnation of the tour, can be said either to be so 'unreasonable' as to give rise to 'Wednesbury unreasonableness' (Associated Provincial Picture Houses Ltd v Wednesbury Corporation (1948) 1 KB 223) or to be so fundamental a breach of the duty to act fairly which rests upon every local authority in matters of this kind and thus justify interference by the courts.

I do not for one moment doubt the great importance which the council attach to the presence in their midst of a 25% population of persons who are either Asian or of Afro-Caribbean origin. Nor do I doubt for one moment the sincerity of the view expressed in Mr Soulsby's affidavit regarding the need for the council to distance itself from bodies who hold important positions and who do not actively discourage sporting contacts with South Africa. Persuasion, even powerful persuasion, is always a permissible way of seeking to obtain an objective. But in a field where other views can equally legitimately be held, persuasion, however powerful, must not be allowed to cross that line where it moves into the field of illegitimate pressure coupled with the threat of sanctions. The four questions, coupled with the insistence that only affirmative answers to all four would be acceptable, are suggestive of more than powerful persuasion. The second question is to my mind open to particular criticism. What, in the context, is meant by 'the club?' The committee? 90 playing members? 4,300 non-playing members? It by no means follows that the committee would all have agreed on an affirmative answer to the question and still less that a majority of their members, playing or non-playing, would have done so. Nor would any of these groups of members necessarily have known whether 'the large proportion', whatever that phrase may mean in the context, of the Leicester population would have regarded the tour as 'an insult' to them. ...

I greatly hesitate to differ from four learned judges on the Wednesbury issue but for myself I would have been disposed respectfully to do this and say that the actions of the club were unreasonable in the Wednesbury sense.

Lord Roskill went on to find that, in any event, the decision was bad for procedural unfairness.

Lord Templeman: My Lords, in my opinion the Leicester City Council were not entitled to withdraw from the Leicester Football Club the facilities for training and playing enjoyed by the club for many years on the council's recreation ground for one simple and good reason. The club could not be punished because the club had done nothing wrong. [The decision of Leicester City Council was quashed.]

Note

The following case concerned a challenge by Nottinghamshire County Council to a decision of the Secretary of State for the Environment relating to the rate support grant for the authority. One ground of challenge was that the decision was unreasonable because it was disproportionately disadvantageous to a small group of authorities.

Nottinghamshire County Council v Secretary of State for the Environment [1986] 2 AC 240, 246–50

Lord Scarman: My Lords, in December 1984 the Secretary of State for the Environment laid before the House of Commons the Rate Support Grant Report (England) for the year 1985–86. In due course the report was approved by resolution of the House. The Secretary of State included in the report (additionally to the matters which he was required by law to specify therein) expenditure guidance to local authorities for that year. ...

[His Lordship considered the *Wednesbury* submission of the applicants which was] that, even if the guidance complies with the words of the statute, it offends a principle of public law in that the burden which the guidance imposes on some authorities, including Nottingham and Bradford, is so disproportionately disadvantageous when compared with its effect upon others that it is a perversely unreasonable exercise of the power conferred by the statute upon the Secretary of State. The respondents rely on what has become known to lawyers as the '*Wednesbury* principles' – by which is meant the judgment of Lord Greene MR in *Associated Provincial Picture Houses Ltd v Wednesbury Corporation* [1948] 1 KB 223, 229. ...

The submission raises an important question as to the limits of judicial review. We are in the field of public financial administration and we are being asked to review the exercise by the Secretary of State of an administrative discretion which inevitably requires a political judgment on his part and which cannot lead to action by him against a local authority unless that action is first approved by the House of Commons.

The Secretary of State's guidance which is challenged was included in the Rate Support Grant Report for 1985–86 which was laid before and approved by the House of Commons: no payment of grant, and no reduction in the amount of grant by the Secretary of State applying a multiplier pursuant to s59 of the Act, can be made unless covered by the report or by a supplementary report and approved by the House of Commons. ...

My Lords, I think that the courts below were absolutely right to decline the invitation to intervene. I can understand that there may well arise a justiciable issue as to the true construction of the words of the statute and that, if the Secretary of State has issued guidance which fails to comply with the requirement of subs (11A) of s59 of the Act of 1980 the guidance can be quashed. But I cannot accept that it is constitutionally appropriate, save in very exceptional circumstances, for the courts to intervene on the ground of 'unreasonableness' to quash guidance framed by the Secretary of State and by necessary implication approved by the House of Commons, the guidance being concerned with the limits of public expenditure by local authorities and the incidence of the tax burden as between taxpayers and ratepayers. Unless and until a statute provides otherwise, or it is established that the Secretary of State has abused his power, these are matters of political judgment for him and for the House of Commons. They are not for the judges or your Lordships' House in its judicial capacity.

For myself, I refuse in this case to examine the detail of the guidance or its consequences. My reasons are these. Such an examination by a court would be justified only if a *prima facie* case were to be shown for holding that the Secretary of State had acted in bad faith, or for an improper motive, or that the consequences of his guidance were so absurd that he must have taken leave of his senses. The evidence comes nowhere near establishing any of these propositions. Nobody in the case has ever suggested bad faith on the part of the Secretary of State. Nobody suggests, nor could it be suggested in the light of the evidence as to the matters he considered before reaching his decision, that he had acted for an improper motive. Nobody now suggests that the Secretary of State failed to consult local authorities in the manner required by statute. It is plain that the timetable, to which the Secretary of State in the preparation of the guidance was required by statute and compelled by circumstance to adhere, involved him necessarily in framing guidance on the basis of the past spending record of authorities. It is recognised that the Secretary of State and his advisers were well aware that there would be inequalities in the distribution of the burden between local authorities but believed that the guidance upon which he decided would by discouraging the high spending and encouraging the low spending authorities be the best course of action in the circumstances. And, as my noble and learned friend, Lord Bridge of Harwich, demonstrates, it was guidance which complied with the terms of the statute. This view of the language of the statute has inevitably a significant bearing upon the conclusion of 'unreasonableness' in the *Wednesbury* sense. If, as your Lordships are holding, the guidance was based on principles applicable to all authorities, the principles would have to be either a pattern of perversity or an absurdity of such proportions that the guidance could not have been framed by a *bona fide* exercise of political judgment on the part of the Secretary of State. And it would be necessary to find as a fact that the House of Commons had been misled: for their approval was necessary and was obtained to the action that he proposed to take to implement the guidance.

In my judgment, therefore, the courts below acted with constitutional propriety in rejecting the so-called '*Wednesbury* unreasonableness' argument in this case. ...

To sum it up, the levels of public expenditure and the incidence and distribution of taxation are matters for Parliament, and, within Parliament, especially for the House of Commons. If Parliament legislates, the courts have their interpretative role: they must, if called upon to do so, construe the statute. If a minister exercises a power conferred on him by the legislation, the courts can investigate whether he has abused his power. But if, as in this case, effect cannot be given to the Secretary of State's determination without the consent of the House of Commons and the House of Commons has consented, it is not open to the courts to intervene unless the minister and the House must have misconstrued the statute or the minister has – to put it bluntly – deceived the House. The courts can properly rule that a minister has acted unlawfully if he has erred in law as to the limits of his power even when his action has the approval of the House of Commons, itself acting not legislatively but within the limits set by a statute. But, if a statute, as in this case, requires the House of Commons to approve a minister's decision before he can lawfully enforce it, and if the action proposed complies with the terms of the statute (as your Lordships, I understand, are convinced that it does in the present case), it is not for the judges to say that the action has such unreasonable consequences that the guidance upon which the action is based and of which the House of Commons had notice was perverse and must be set aside. For that is a question of policy for the minister and the Commons, unless there has been bad faith or misconduct by the minister. Where Parliament has legislated that the action to be taken by the Secretary of State must, before it is taken, be approved by the House of Commons, it is no part of the judges' role to declare that the action proposed is unfair, unless it constitutes an abuse of power in the sense which I have explained; for Parliament has enacted that one of its Houses is responsible.

Note

The approach of Lord Templeman clearly seems to indicate that in cases such as the one before him, the court should apply a higher threshold of unreasonableness, making it harder for the decision to be found unlawful. Indeed, reading his judgment carefully, it sounds as if even an outrageously immoral or illogical decision would not be subject to review, provided that Parliament had properly approved it and the decision was made in good faith. In *Secretary of State for the Environment, ex p Hammersmith LBC* (1991),[83] another case on economic policy, Lord Bridge held that the decision 'was not open to challenge on grounds of irrationality short of the extremes of bad faith, improper motive or manifest absurdity'. Have these cases laid down that in certain areas of decision making – eg matters of economic policy which had been approved by Parliament – a 'super *Wednesbury*' test should be applied? In the recent case of *Ministry of Defence, ex p Smith and others*,[84] which concerned a challenge by homosexual servicemen and women to the ban on homosexuals serving in the armed forces, Simon Browne LJ, without commenting on whether 'super *Wednesbury*' was a legitimate development, considered that it would not in any event apply in a case where like the instant, human rights were at stake; he appeared to believe that national economic policy issues could raise the reasonableness threshold but that the mere fact that the policy in question had been debated by Parliament would not.[85] When the case came to the Court of Appeal, Sir Thomas Bingham MR took a clear stance on the matter.

Ministry of Defence, ex p Smith and others [1996] 1 All ER 257, 264, CA

Sir Thomas Bingham MR: ... It was argued for the ministry, in reliance on *Nottinghamshire CC v Secretary of State for the Environment* [1986] 1 All ER 199, [1986] AC 240 and *Hammersmith and Fulham London BC v Secretary of State for the Environment* [1990] 3 All ER 589, [1991] 1 AC 521, that a test more exacting than *Wednesbury* was appropriate in this case (see *Associated Provincial Picture Houses Ltd v Wednesbury Corp* [1947] 2 All ER 680, [1948] 1 KB 223). The Divisional Court rejected this argument and so do I. The greater the policy content of a decision, and the more remote the subject matter of a decision from ordinary judicial experience, the more hesitant the court must necessarily be in holding a decision to be irrational. That is good law and, like most good law, common sense. Where decisions of a policy-laden, esoteric or security-based nature are in issue, even greater caution than normal must be shown in applying the test, but the test itself is sufficiently flexible to cover all situations.

Notes

1   Lord Irvine QC[86] considers any attempt in the *Nottinghamshire* case, to establish 'super *Wednesbury*' to be misguided. Lord Bridge's judgement (above) he comments, 'suggests that there is a level of irrationality short of manifest absurdity which may found judicial review *in the ordinary case*' whereas, he goes on, Lord Diplock's *GCHQ* formulation of irrationality

---

83   1 AC 521.
84   [1995] 4 All ER 427; [1996] 1 All ER 257, CA; the phrase 'super *Wednesbury*' originated in this case.
85   4 All ER 427, 447.
86   (1996) PL 59, 66–7.

clearly defined it as manifest (moral or logical) absurdity therefore leaving 'no room' for 'super *Wednesbury*'.

2 Aside from the confusion over 'super *Wednesbury*' this head of review is, it is submitted, in an unsatisfactory state. Both ways of expressing it appear to, reveal muddled judicial thinking. Lord Diplock's definition of irrationality in *Council of Civil Service Unions v Minister for Civil Service* (1985)[87] (above) is arguably essentially redundant; it is hard to visualise circumstances in which a decision which is outrageously immoral or illogical would not in any event be seen by the judiciary as being outside the purposes of the Act, and therefore *ultra vires*. The head of irrationality is alternatively expressed as referring to decisions which are so unreasonable that no reasonable man could come to them. Three comments can be made about this definition. First, such decisions would again surely be outside the purpose of the parent act; secondly, as Jowell and Lester argue,[88] the definition is tautologous (a decision is unreasonable if a reasonable man could not have made it). Thirdly, the definition seems to be merely another way of saying that the decision has fallen foul of the test in *Edwards v Bairstow*; in other words the decision-maker has come to a conclusion which is not *capable* of being considered correct. It therefore seems arguable that the doctrine of unreasonableness as presently understood adds nothing to the law of judicial review. The case dealt with in the following note reveals the apparent limitations of the head.

3 In *Secretary of State for the Home Dept, ex p Chahal* (1995),[89] the Secretary of State had made a determination that deportation of the applicant would be conducive to the public good and therefore he was liable to be deported under s3(5)(b) of the Immigration Act 1971. However the applicant claimed asylum in the UK on the basis that he was a refugee within the meaning of the Convention relating to the Status of Refugees 1951 as recognised in the Immigration Rules 1990 r 173. The Secretary of State maintained that the question whether he was a refugee was irrelevant once the decision to deport had been made. The applicant sought judicial review of the decision to deport him on the basis that his status as a refugee should have been taken into account.

The main question at issue was whether a balancing exercise between the threat to the security of the UK posed by the applicant and the threat to the life or freedom of the applicant if deported to the country in question (India) should have been carried out. It was found that the combined effect of the Convention and the 1990 Rules required that it should have been. However, although the Secretary of State had not deemed such an exercise necessary there was no evidence that it had not been carried out. The court was not able to determine whether, after carrying out such an exercise, the Secretary of State's decision could be called irrational, since while there was a great deal of evidence as to the risk to the applicant there was no evidence as to the risk to national security in the UK which he posed. However, the court

---

87 AC 374.
88 (1987) PL 368.
89 1 All ER 658, CA.

could consider whether the Secretary of State had been correct in his assessment of the risk to the applicant if returned to India. The Secretary of State had observed that under the Indian Constitution the applicant could come to harm only if convicted of a crime by due process and in accordance with the law. That still left open the possibility of informal ill treatment; nevertheless there were not sufficient grounds for finding that the Secretary of State had made an irrational or perverse decision in determining that the applicant's claim for asylum status was not made out.

Cases of 'total unreasonableness'

In the rare cases in which total unreasonableness is apparently used by the courts to strike down a decision, what appears to be the substantive content of the doctrine? What clues are there as to how the court will apply the doctrine in practice? The following two cases provide some illumination.

Hall & Co Ltd v Shoreham-by-Sea Urban District Council [1964] 1 WLR 240, 248, 250–1

Local planning authorities were empowered by statute to grant planning permission subject to such conditions as the council thought fit. The applicant was granted planning permission to develop land for a sand and gravel business, subject to the following condition: 'The applicants shall construct an ancillary road over the entire frontage of the site at their own expense, as and when required by the local planning authority, and shall give right of passage over it to and from such ancillary roads as may be constructed on the adjoining land'.

The court found as a fact that Hall would suffer from having to implement this condition in two ways: first the road would be likely to be damaged by huge increases in traffic from the rapidly developing area and Hall would be unable to get any compensation for this. Secondly, the council could decided at any time to close this road and Hall would then have to seek other means of access to the main roads which might not be forthcoming, due to development. Willmer LJ considered three main points on the question whether the conditions imposed were *ultra vires* the statute. The first was whether the conditions fundamentally altered the general law relating to the rights of the parties without clear and express words. The judge found that they did not (at p247). The second was whether the conditions 'fairly and reasonably related to the permitted development' (*ibid*). On this point, the judge said:

> **Wilmer LJ:** '[A] planning authority must necessarily take into consideration the effects of the granting of such permission on the development of adjoining properties. Bearing this in mind, it seems to me impossible to say that the conditions relating to the construction of the ancillary road are not 'in connection with the development authorised'. It is not sufficient merely to say that the conditions are unreasonable or unduly onerous, for that would properly be the subject for appeal. ... [Thirdly, Willmer LJ considered the *Wednesbury* unreasonableness point]:In order to justify the court in granting a declaration that the conditions are ultra vires it must be shown that they are so unreasonable that no reasonable council could have imposed them. [The judge found that the object sought to be attained by the defendants was a 'perfectly reasonable one' (at p249). Under the conditions sought to be imposed] the defendants would ... obtain the benefit of having the road constructed for them at the plaintiff's

expense, on the plaintiff's land, and without the necessity for paying any compensation in respect thereof ... It seems to me that this result would be utterly unreasonable and such as Parliament cannot possibly have intended'.

Hillingdon London Borough Council, ex p Royco Homes Ltd [1974] QB 720, 730, 732

Royco Homes applied for planning permission from the council to develop land for planning purposes. The council had broad statutory powers to grant permission 'subject to such conditions as they [thought] fit'. Permission was granted, subject to a number of conditions, two of which were objected to by Royco. The first was the requirement that the house should be occupied by persons who were on the council's housing waiting list. The second was that for 10 years the houses should be occupied by persons who had rights of security of tenure and rent control under the Rent Acts. Lord Widgery CJ found that the words in the statute (above) were 'too wide to bear their literal meaning' (at p729) and must 'fairly and reasonably relate to the permitted development', not be used to further some ulterior purpose. He then went on to consider the allegation that the condition had indeed been imposed for such a purpose:

> **Lord Widgery CJ:** ... to ensure that if a private developer was allowed to develop this land, he should have to use it in such a way as to relieve the council of a significant part of its burden as a housing authority to provide houses for the homeless, and, whether they are put as being conditions which are unreasonable or not related to the development or for an ulterior purpose, they are *ultra vires* ... [Having examined *Hall's* case, his Lordship then went on to find that the conditions were] the equivalent of requiring the applicants to take on their own expense a significant part of the duty of the council as housing authority. However well intentioned and however sensible such a desire on the part of the council may have been, it seems to me that it is unreasonable in the sense in which Willmer LJ was using that word in *Hall's* case.

Note

It appears, therefore, that a decision which is 'well intentioned' and 'sensible' may still be *Wednesbury* unreasonable. Is this finding compatible with Lord Diplock's test for irrationality in the *GCHQ* case? Neil Hawke offers some comments on this area, starting with Lord Green MR's *dicta* in *Wednesbury* that 'if a decision on a competent matter is so unreasonable that no reasonable authority could ever come to it, then the courts can interfere'.

Neil Hawke, 'Total Unreasonableness' (1985) *Public Law* 26–30

Total Unreasonableness

... Lord Greene's reference to a decision on a 'competent' matter indicates that the court's review function begins at a point within the powers of the administrative agency and begs the question whether it has '... nevertheless come to a conclusion so unreasonable that no reasonable authority could ever have come to it' [at p234]. One necessarily extreme example of this wider form of unreasonableness is found in *Backhouse v London Borough of Lambeth* (1972) 116 SJ 802. The case arose from the council's attempts to avoid rent increases for many tenants by virtue of the Housing Finance Act 1972. In order to avoid such increases, the council took one of its houses and raised the rent from £30.84 per month to an artificial £18,000, the amount which would have been yielded had the tenants been subject to the required increases. It was held that the council's resolution effecting the increase was totally unreasonable and therefore *ultra vires*: Parliament could never have intended that the Housing Finance Act should be used in this way. The decision depends on the assumption that an increase in rent is per se a competent, *intra vires* transaction which is rendered *ultra vires* only when taken to extremes. Clearly, the court's dilemma is in determining the point at which the extreme becomes unlawful. If the court pitches its conclusion too short, it will be rightly accused of departing from its function of judicial review to become a court of *appeal*.

One of the clearest examples form a limited number of cases in this context of total unreasonableness is the Court of Appeal decision in *Hall v Shoreham Urban District Council* [1964] 1 WLR 240. [It was found that] the authority's condition requiring the provision of a road indicated concern for a legally relevant matter in planning terms whereas the requirement that a public right of way be provided represented an extreme and totally unreasonable requirement beyond the lawful stipulation providing for the road. The decision therefore represents a powerfully defined limit on Parliament's supposed intentions for the legislation. Whether the court was justified in this instance in limiting the scope of the court was justified in this instance in limiting the scope of the statutory powers is doubtful. Nevertheless, the Court of Appeal's approach found favour in another significant planning case, *London Borough of Hillingdon, ex p Royco Homes Ltd* ... Despite references here to the total unreasonableness according to the narrower *Wednesbury* principle in so far as the council was using its planning powers for improper housing purposes. ...

More recently, there have been two further decisions which examine the possibilities for judicial review by reference to the concept of total unreasonableness. Both decisions are of the Court of Appeal: *London Borough of Ealing, ex p Richardson* [1983] JPL 533; and *London Borough of Haringey, ex p Barrs* (1983) *The Times*, 1 July 1983.

In *Richardson*, the applicant was a private, monthly tenant concerned about the state of repair of his house. On a complaint about the state of the house made to the local authority, the authority commissioned an inspection of the premises and concluded that they were unfit for human habitation and not repairable at reasonable expense. As a result, the authority served a closing order. The applicant had no statutory right to appeal against the order, so proceeded to the High Court on this application for judicial review ... It was held by the Court of Appeal that the local authority had adopted a wholly incorrect approach to the requirement that premises, to be subject to a closing order, should be incapable of repair at reasonable expense. The criterion of reasonable expense is defined by s39 of the Housing Act 1957, which states that 'In determining ... whether a house can be rendered fit for human habitation at a reasonable expense, regard shall be had to the estimated cost of the works necessary to render it so fit and the value which it is estimated that the house will have when the works are completed'. The local authority's surveyors estimated the cost of repairs at £3,000 and concluded that the value of the house with a sitting tenant, unrepaired, was £3,300 and £4,000 with a sitting tenant, repaired. These valuations were matched by figures produced by independent valuers commissioned by the applicant, who quoted from £6,000 to £7,200 and from £7,250 to £9,170 respectively. The local authority's valuation decision was condemned by the Court of Appeal on the ground that it was based, not on the value of the house, but on its rental income. Consequently, the cost of repairs was reasonable when set against the more objective values of the independent valuers.

Lord Lane CJ was '... frankly bewildered by the making of the closing order. This property undoubtedly needs work done on it but basically this is a perfectly good family house which is a very saleable asset. I cannot think that the council were aware of the true position as the value of the property and/or the extent and cost of repairs. The cost of repairs is, in my view, modest in relation to the value of the house (whichever value one takes and any reasonable owner would consider the house worth preserving) ... [N]o excuse or explanation and no justification [for the wide discrepancy in values] was proffered. It seems to me that the whole foundation of that conclusion, that the premises were not capable of being rendered fit at a reasonable cost, is shown to be wrong ... [I]t seems to me that the conclusion which was reached was falsified ...' The Court of Appeal quashed the closing order.

The decision in *Richardson* ... raises some doubts ... The applicant in that case did not have a right of appeal to the county court in respect of the closing order, hence the need to rely exclusively on judicial review. Normally, a landlord would expect to overturn a closing order in an appeal to the county court on the ground of 'reasonable expense' where the facts are as they are in *Richardson*. Without wishing to doubt the justice of the Court of Appeal's decision in favour of the applicant in this case, it is difficult in the more theoretical environment to justify a conclusion that the same facts can be treated as the proper subject for an appeal on one case and as the proper subject for review in another, according to the difference in status of the applicant and the availability of remedies on review and appeal. Consequently, this is one of two areas where the wider conception of *Wednesbury* unreasonableness is capable of distorting important areas of administrative law. The other area was referred to previously in relation to the implications of the decision in *Hall v Shoreham Urban District Council* where the Court of Appeal appears to have drawn the supposed limits of an Act of Parliament. Overall, therefore, it can be appreciated that this wider conception of *Wednesbury* unreasonableness is a potent weapon in the hands of the judiciary, enabling a measure of interference which is always capable of distorting Parliament's legislative intentions.

Note

Hawke's conclusion naturally leads one to concern about the role played by judges. If they have a 'potent weapon' in their hands capable of overriding the will of Parliament, does this mean they are immersed in politics? As Waldron pointed out earlier, the traditional view, as expressed by Mrs Thatcher after the *Bromley* case, was that judges of course do not involve themselves in political questions, they 'merely' apply the law. But are the judges really usurping the political role here?

'Irrationality', politics and the judiciary

Two eminent writers offer their views on this subject in the following extracts. What is interesting is that the political stance of each is markedly different: Wade has been described as 'the pre-eminent contemporary writer within the tradition of conservative normativism'[90] whilst Waldron's writings have a distinctly more realist, leftist cast. Nevertheless both agree that the traditional view is inadequate. Waldron first attempts to clear up some confusion about 'politics' and the judiciary.

---

90 Loughlin, *Public Law and Political Theory* (1992), p184.

Jeremy Waldron, *The Law* (1990), pp117–19

... it is hard to evaluate the claim that judges act politically, when the term 'political' is as ambiguous as it is. There are at least six different senses of the term that might be relevant in this context.

(i) 'Political' may mean nothing more than 'part of the political system'. In this sense, it is obvious that courts are political institutions and judges play a political role. They are part of the system of politics in this country, because they are part of the overall apparatus which we are governed.

(ii) 'Political' may mean ' their decisions make a difference to the allocation of power, liberty, and resources in society'. Someone once defined the great issue of politics as 'who gets what when and how'. Again it is undeniable that judges' decisions are political in this sense. ... That is simply another way of saying that courts are part of the political system. (iii) 'Political' may mean 'involved directly in political interaction with others'. This is a more subtle sense of politics. 'Politics' can refer not only to the great processes of society, but also to face-to-face interactions among small groups of people. We talk about the politics of the committee room, the politics of a family, or the politics of a Government department, meaning the way people struggle for influence, persuade one another, or make threats and offers of various sorts to get their way. There is no reason why we shouldn't talk about the politics of the judiciary, in the same sense. In an appellate court, there are usually several judges sitting on each panel, and they will attempt to influence one another, as well as the barristers and parties who appear before them. There are also questions like the influence which the Lord Chancellor has on the rest of the judiciary (promotion, appointment to particular panels, etc) as well as the interactions between courts at different levels and between judges and non-judicial actors, such as academics, practising lawyers, politicians, and so on. Once again, judicial behaviour is clearly 'political' in this sense.

(iv) 'Political' may mean 'biased towards one side or another in a partisan dispute'. That was the allegation made by many Labour supporters in the 'Fares Fair' case. They thought, as we have seen, that judges were influenced by the mood of the press, by a red scare, by inherent antipathy to socialist policies. The bias may or may not have been conscious, and it may or may not have been articulate. But – so the allegation goes – judges' class background disposes them to respond more favourably to some arguments than others, or to side more readily when they can with some causes rather than others. Even if they try to be 'neutral' and 'impartial', they can't help being influenced by their background and by the conservative ethos of their office. And usually, it is alleged, they don't even try. This claim is more controversial.

(v) 'Political' may mean 'consciously motivated by ideological or moral beliefs'. This is more specific: It claims not only that judges are politically biased, but that they deliberately use political premises in their decision-making. Judges would be political in this sense if, in their decisions, they decided to take a stand in favour of things like individual liberty, Christian values, *laissez-faire*, or social democracy. If that were the case, their actions would be based on political values just as much as those of a statesman. Like all politicians, they would be motivated by some vision of how society should be organised. The only difference would be that judges have to organise their decision-making around statues they did not make and precedents of previous courts; they would be more constrained in the realisation of their vision than elected politicians are. But in their interpretation of the law, they would be displaying their own values, their own ideology, their own policy aims, and their own principles.

(vi) 'Political' may mean 'motivated by ambition or the desire to stay in office'. This is the most sordid sense of the term. For example, many of Richard Nixon's actions in the course of the Watergate affair were political in this sense, rather than sense (v).

Note

Waldron concludes that it is inevitable and desirable that judges should be political in sense (v). Professor Wade agrees.

H W R Wade, *Constitutional Fundamentals* (1989), pp95–100

Whenever there is discussion of any extension of judicial review the objection is raised that it will bring the judges into politics. We must, it is said, at all costs avoid a politicised judiciary. I have never found it easy to give weight to this argument in its context, which is now usually that of a Bill of Rights. For as with policy, so with politics. The judges are already immersed in it, and have no hope of getting out if it. Books, articles and letters in the newspapers analyse their education and social backgrounds, accuse them of political prejudice, call their neutrality a pretence, and insinuate bias because, in selected instances, plaintiffs with bad cases lose them. The judges in the *Tameside* and *Laker* cases are said to have been motivated not by the need to control arbitrariness but by their aversion to certain political policies (Griffith, *The Politics of the Judiciary*, 3rd edn, p232). The fact that all this is accompanied by much misrepresentation is neither here nor there. The reality is that the judges are under a barrage of political fire. They are constantly having to decide cases which involve politics as well as law, some of which I have criticised myself – but in one of which would I accuse any one of bias or insincerity. That, again, is neither here nor there. The simple fact is that, like every one else, judges live in a world in which brickbats of all kinds are flying in all directions.

Yet among the judges themselves the fear of politicisation is strong. Lord Denning, not normally to be found among the timorous souls, said in a speech in the House of Lords that if judges were given power to overthrow Acts of Parliament they would become politicised, their appointments would be based on political grounds, and their reputation would suffer accordingly. [HL Deb 797 (25 March 1976)] ... But other eminent judges think differently, and in the same debate Lord Hailsham made an effective reply, ... instancing some of the more sensational judicial exploits, he said of the opposing judges:

> They are under the curious illusion that the judges are not already in politics. Lord Diplock, as one of the authors of the *Anisminic* decision, practically abolished an Act of Parliament about the Foreign Compensation Commission. What about *Gouriet*? Tameside education dispute? What about the decision invalidating Mr Roy Jenkins' policy on wireless licences? How about the various decisions of this House and the Court of Appeal on the Race Relations Act? And what about their recent decisions on the trade union legislation? ... If they [the judges] assume jurisdiction they are in politics; if they decline jurisdiction they are in politics. All they can hope to be is impartial ... [HL Deb 1382 (29 November 1978)].

This is a graphic and rhetorical version of the point which I made prosaically at the beginning of this lecture, when I stressed the wide range of alternative policies between which judges have to choose. If their primary object was to keep out of politics, they would have had to surrender to the executive in all the cases mentioned by Lord Hailsham and in many others. They would be confined to the literal interpretation of Acts of Parliament purporting to give ministers unfettered discretion, and the development of administrative law would be impossible. The law would be back in the shameful position in which it languished 30 years ago.

The extremist critics of the judges do not, I think, allow for the unenviable tasks which they have been given by Parliament. If certain organisations or individuals are given a statutory right to commit torts and other wrongs, which others are not allowed to commit, the judges have to decide where the limits of these of these immunities lie, often with nothing to guide them but imprecise phrases of elastic meaning, such as 'in contemplation and furtherance of a trade dispute'. Then, in borderline cases, they have to choose between rival interpretations. It is surely to be expected that immunities from the general law will not be interpreted in the widest possible sense, but will be kept within bounds, subject always to fair reading of the Act. Otherwise if I may use Lord Scarman's words, 'there will arise a real risk of forces of great power in our society escaping from the Rule of Law altogether'. It is surely right that the judicial instinct should be to minimise that disaster. My purpose now, however, is not to join in the political fray, but to illustrate how deeply the judges are embroiled in it willy-nilly. All that they can do is to grow thicker skins, in a sadly deteriorating climate. To expect them to change their spots is neither practicable nor right.

Note

To those who subscribe to the jurisprudential theory of realism, or its modern variant, critical legal studies, the law does not determine the decision the judges make, due to its inherent indeterminacy. Instead, it acts merely as a cloak under which judges can make decisions (whether consciously or not) on the basis of their own political opinions. If one believes that this doctrine has some useful insights, would it render the study of judicial review futile? Jones[91] does not think so. He quotes Levin on the subject:

> [The] commitment to articulating the appropriate boundaries of judicial review is a way of emphasising that society imposes certain duties and certain constraints upon its judges, just as it does upon other officials. ... [O]nly with a prescriptive approach can one hope to provide guidance to scrupulous judges ...[Levin 'Identifying Questions of Law in Administrative Law' (1985) GLJ 1, 15].

One can take the view that the courts decide whether or not to review a particular administrative decision capriciously, unrestrained by any shared understanding as to the appropriate standards of review. Under the guise of crude realism one can identify cases where judges appear to have manipulated the principles of administrative law in order to decide a case according to their own value judgments. However, to quote Levin again:

> ... too much cynicism about judicial review may ultimately discourage constructive evaluation of the courts' performance and thus become a self-fulfilling prophecy. One task of the scholar is to try to ensure that the realist thesis turns out to be no more true than it has to be [*Ibid* p16].

THE DEVELOPMENT OF JUDICIAL REVIEW

Liberal commentators have asked whether if it is indeed inevitable that judges must bring a package of substantive values to their task of supervisory review,

---

91 'Mistake of Fact in Administrative Law' (1990) PL 507, 525.

then could indeed *should* not those values be the fundamental human rights which the common law has always purported to protect?

In a well-known article, two leading constitutional lawyers suggest that the courts must move beyond the inadequate and misleading *Wednesbury* test to grasp the nettle of more substantive, rights-based principles.

J Jowell and A Lester 'Beyond *Wednesbury*: Substantive Principles of Administrative Law' (1987) *Public Law* 368, 369–70, 372–3, 374

Lord Diplock's third ground of review, 'irrationality', identifies a ... way in which the substance of official decisions may be challenged by the courts. By separating irrationality from illegality, he made the point that even though a decision may be legal (in the sense of being within the scope of the legislative scheme), it may nevertheless be substantively unlawful. In other words, he recognised that the courts may strike down a decision because it offends substantive principles, independent of those provided for by the statute in question. Lord Diplock said as much, defining irrationality as applying to 'a decision which is so outrageous in its defiance of logic or of accepted moral standards that no sensible person who had applied his mind to the question to be decided could have arrived at it'.

With rationality now standing on its own feet as an independent ground of review, the *GCHQ* decision clears the way for the courts to develop general principles of substantive administrative law based upon what Lord Diplock called 'accepted moral standards'.

The authors then go on to consider the unsatisfactory nature of *Wednesbury* as presently understood, concluding that it often disguises the true reason for judicial intervention.

We have already referred to the *Hall* case where *Wednesbury* unreasonableness disguised the true reason for quashing the condition, which was the breach of an accepted principle that property may not be taken without fair compensation. Had this principle been more openly admitted the clarity of the decision, as well as its integrity, would have been enhanced ...

THE CONTENT OF SUBSTANTIVE PRINCIPLES

Where do we discover any principles of substantive review? Look carefully and we find them even now lurking within the underbrush of *Wednesbury*. As we have seen, decision-makers far from senseless have been reviewed by the courts in generating principles which, although not often overtly expressed, nevertheless pray in aid Lord Diplock's 'accepted moral standards' ... the existing case law shows that for many years English judges have been stating principles of substantive review of administration without knowing or, more likely, admitting it. ...

The principle of proportionality

The principle of proportionality has already been recognised by the Court of Appeal in the extreme circumstances of *Barnsley Metropolitan BC, ex p Hook* (disproportionate administrative penalty), and by Lord Widgery CJ in the 'Crossman Diaries' case [*Att-Gen v Jonathan Cape Ltd* [1976] QB 752] (disproportionate restriction upon freedom of expression), and by Browne-Wilkinson J in the Employment Appeal Tribunal (employer's economic justification for unequal pay for work of equal value) [*Jenkins v Kingsgate (Clothing Productions) Ltd* [1981] 1 WLR 1485]. It seems so characteristically English to require that the means employed by the decision-maker must be no more than is reasonably necessary to achieve his legitimate aims – that he should not use a sledgehammer to crack a nut – that there should be no difficulty in absorbing the concept of proportionality into the English judicial process ...

The principle of legal certainty

In the words of the European Court of Human Rights,

> the law must be adequately accessible; the citizen must be able to have an indication that is adequate to a given case. Secondly, ... he must be able to foresee, to a degree that is reasonable in the circumstances, the consequences which a given action may entail [*Sunday Times v UK* (1979) 2 EHRR 245, at 271].

This approach is well recognised as essential to ensure legal certainty under Community law as well as under the European Convention...

The principle of consistency

The principle of consistency is applied without hesitation in Community law. It was confirmed at least tentatively in English law in *HTV Ltd v Price Commission* [[1976] 1 CR 170, CA] and in *Re Preston, Preston Group* [[1985] AC 835, HL], where it was acknowledged that fairness requires officials to follow their rules in like cases and not to breach their own contracts or representations. In the recent case of *Secretary of State for the Home Department, ex p Khan* [[1984] 1 WLR 1337] the Court of Appeal held that the Home Office was bound by the terms of a circular although there was no prejudicial reliance upon it.

Fundamental human rights

... We have referred in the section above to the principle of just compensation for expropriation lurking in the *Hall* case, and to Browne-Wilkinson LJ's reference in *Wheeler* to 'fundamental freedoms of speech and conscience' as basic rights inherent in the English legal system. In *Secretary for the Home Department, ex p Herbage (No 2)* [1987] 1 All ER 324, CA], Purchas LJ derived from the English Bill of Rights of 1688 a 'fundamental right' not to be inflicted with 'cruel and unusual punishments' which 'goes far beyond the ambit of the prison rules'. He stated that

> if it were established that a prison governor was guilty of such conduct it would be an affront to common sense that the court would not be able to afford relief under RSC, Order 53.

Incidentally, the Court of Appeal could also have gained support for this general principle from Art 3 of the European Convention on Human Rights which forbids torture, or inhuman or degrading punishment or treatment at the hands of the state or its agents.

Finally, as mentioned above, the House of Lords has recently invoked the rights to life and liberty as principles requiring particularly anxious scrutiny of the decisions of immigration officials about refugees seeking political asylum in the United Kingdom.

The European Court of Justice has frequently relied upon the doctrine of fundamental rights and has drawn upon the European Convention as a source of the general principles of law which must guide Community officials in exercising their powers, as well as in interpreting Community legislation. It is open to the English courts to adopt a similar approach.

Notes

1   In *Secretary of State for Home Dept, ex p Anderson* (1984)[92] the prisoner applicant wished to have a visit from his solicitor to discuss an action for assault he wanted to bring, but was refused permission. He sought judicial review of the decision to refuse permission. The court considered *Golder* and applied *Raymond v Honey* (1983) which had determined that a prisoner still retained a basic right of access to a court. According to *Golder* this right included as an integral part access to a solicitor. It was found that if prisoners had to register a complaint internally before communicating with a solicitor this would constitute an impediment; an inmate might hesitate to make an internal complaint because he could lay himself open to a disciplinary charge. This would be the offence of making a false and malicious allegation against a prison officer. (This has now been abolished by the Prison Amendment Rules 1989.) The Court held that the restriction placed on him by the simultaneous ventilation rule was *ultra vires* because it conflicted with this fundamental right – a right so fundamental that it could only be taken away by express language. *Anderson* is an interesting decision because it provides an instance of a domestic decision going beyond the rights provided by the European Convention on Human Rights.

2   Jowell and Lester's call for the development of judicial review went largely unheeded until recently. However, in 1993, a subtle and persuasive account of how judicial review could afford far greater protection for fundamental rights was put forward by Laws J, speaking extra-judicially, and appears to have gained some judicial recognition. His account strongly relates the proposed developments in the law back to well established principles, and may be attractive to the judiciary partly for that reason. Finding first that attempting to incorporate the ECHR judicially would be unconstitutional, Laws J goes on as follows.[92a]

Laws J, 'Is the High Court the Guardian of Fundamental Rights?' (1993) *Public Law* 59, 69–74

... the true route is, conceptually at least, surprisingly simple, consisting as it does in a recognition of the obvious. What I have in mind is this: the greater the intrusion proposed by a body possessing public power over the citizen into an area where his fundamental rights are at stake, the greater must be the justification which the public authority must demonstrate. If this seems a proposition of child-like simplicity, see what it means for the operation in practice of substantive, as opposed to procedural, juridical review. It means that the principles by which it is conducted are neither unitary not static, it means that the standard by which the court reviews administrative action is a variable one. It means, for example, that while the Secretary of State will largely be left to his own devices in promulgating national economic policy (as in the community-charge-capping case), of *Secretary of State for the Environment, ex p Hammersmith* [1991] 1 AC 521 the court will scrutinise the merits of his decisions much more closely when they concern refugees or free speech. This would represent a conceptual shift away from *Wednesbury* reasonableness: or, if that is too startling a description, at any rate a significant refinement of it. Irrationality is monolithic,

---

92 [1984] 2 WLR 725. (Also see (1984) PL 341–3.)

92a This article (including some of the part appearing below) is also quoted in Part VI, Chapter 1 in relation to protection of civil liberties under the British constitution.

and is for that reason an imperfect and inappropriate mechanism for the development of differential standards in judicial review.

Such an approach is, I believe, no more a usurpation of constitutional propriety than is the conventional *Wednesbury* approach itself. No one suggests, nowadays, that the courts behave improperly in requiring a minister to bring a rational mind to bear on a question he has to decide. In doing so, the court imposes a judge-made standard on the decision-maker. To bring forward a more exacting standard where the decision-maker proposes to prohibit the citizen from expressing his opinions or communicating information in his possession is not in principle a different exercise.

The fact is that just as the judges have evoked the *Wednesbury* doctrine, so they can refine it, and build differential principles within it. They may accord a place in our public law to the principle of proportionality, to which I shall come in a moment; and in doing so they may go further in articulating a doctrine by which substantive judicial review bears more closely on the decision-maker in some areas than in others. What I am at pains distinctly to emphasise is that in developing the law in this way they are as free to consider ECHR texts as any other legal text; that there is nothing which ought to discourage their saying so by explicit reference and that all of this, important as it is if fundamental rights are to be safeguarded, is conceptually no different from what the courts have already done in evolving standards of administrative conduct within the four corners of conventional judicial review. The prospect of judicial examination of public decisions to test their reasonableness has none of the arresting quality of a Batman cartoon; it is regarding as an elementary necessity, a function of the Rule of Law itself. But just as the citizen is entitled to expect that those having administrative power over him will bring a rational mind to bear on the subject in hand, whatever it is, so should he enjoy the assurance that where the subject matter engages fundamental rights such as freedom of speech and person, or access to the courts, any decision adverse to him will only survive judicial scrutiny if it is found to rest on a distinct and positive justification in the public interest.

The Third Position: Development of Public Law in Practice by Reference to the ECHR

Now I shall turn to see how these ideas may be applied in practice. I do not propose to attempt a lexicon of all the varying situations in which public law cases might be decided differently if the court systematically adopted the approach I am putting forward. More modestly, I shall concentrate on three notions, which in the present state of our law, I believe may be enlisted as important mechanisms for the development of substantive judicial review along the lines I have been discussing these are: proportionality, the giving of reasons, and the *Padfield* doctrine.

Proportionality

... The distinction is between two variants, or applications, of the irrationality rule. There is first the case where the decision under review is a finding of fact, and the complaint is that there was no evidence capable of justifying the finding. This sort of challenge is seen from time to time for instance in appeals on law by case stated from subordinate tribunals, or on statutory appeals against Inspectors' (or the Secretary of State's) decisions under the planning, eg *Coleen Properties v Minister of Housing and Local Government* [1971] 1 All ER 1049, and similar, legislation. This category of review is to be contrasted with and distinguished from those cases where the subject-matter of the challenge is the exercise of a discretion. In the latter instance, more often than not, there is no dispute about the primary facts. The complaint is as to the way the facts have been perceived by the decision-maker, the order of importance he has attached to them; or it may be against the policy which he has brought to bear on the facts.

The significance of this distinction for my argument is this. In the fact-finding case, irrationality occupies a natural and easily understood position: where the subordinate body's task is to ascertain past facts by the appreciation of evidence, it is self-evidently unreasonable for him to reach a conclusion which the evidence cannot support; he has manifestly failed to bring a rational mind properly to bear on the subject. But this is very rarely an apt model by which to characterise substantive review in a discretion case, Sometimes, of course, such a case succeeds when the decision-maker falls foul of that other arm of *Wednesbury*, the requirement to have regard to all relevant considerations, and to nothing else. Even there, since Lord Scarman's endorsement of the *CREEDNZ* case what *are* relevant considerations will often be for the decision-maker himself to decide, unless of course the empowering statute has laid it down for him. But, at any rate where the decision is taken by a public body with a sophisticated bureaucracy in support – typically Government – it will be relatively hard to find a case where a relevant consideration has literally been altogether left out of account, and even harder to find one where the decision cannot be supported by any rational process of thought whatever.

The truth is that the most interesting, and important, types of challenge to discretionary decisions – certainly those involving fundamental rights – are not usually about simple irrationality, or a failure to call attention to relevant matters. They are much more likely to be concerned with the way in which the decision-maker has ordered his priorities; the very essence of discretionary decision-making consists, surely, in the attribution of relative importance to the factors in the case. And here is my point: this is precisely what proportionality is about. There is no room for it at all in the fact-finding case; but if we are to entertain a form of review in which fundamental rights are to enjoy the court's distinct protection, the very exercise consists in an insistence that the decision-maker is not free to order his priorities as he chooses, confined only by a crude duty not to emulate the brute beasts that have no understanding, an insistence that he accord the first priority to the right in question unless he can show a substantial, objective, public justification for overriding it. Proportionality is surely the means of doing this. It is a ready-made tool in our hands.

It will be said that this approach falls foul of one of the received nostrums in our public law, one which time and again is successfully deployed by respondents facing challenges where the real complaint is only about the merits of what has been done; the rule that the relative weight to be accorded to the factors in play is always and only for the decision maker to decide. Again, this negative principle is correctly in place where the case concerns the decision-maker's appreciation of factual evidence. In discretion cases, it is obviously and rightly in place where the subject-matter is economic policy, as the charge-capping litigation shows, and no doubt in other instances where fundamental rights are not involved. But if the issue is freedom of speech, or person, or the like, the application of this principle would mean that the decision-maker is at liberty to accord a high or low importance to the right in question, as he chooses. This cannot be right.

What is therefore needed is a preparedness to hold that a decision which overrides a fundamental right without sufficient objective justification will, as a matter of law, necessarily be disproportionate to the aim in view. It will be misleading and unhelpful, not to say something of an affront to the decision-maker, to categorise these cases in conventional *Wednesbury* terms. Despite their primacy, fundamental rights may occupy different places in the hearts of different reasonable people. If a government or a local authority, perhaps too much in love with a particular policy objective, were to take a decision which curtails free speech for no very convincing reason, to excoriate it as having lost its senses looks a little too much like sending people with unacceptable politics to the psychiatric hospital. The deployment of proportionality sets in focus the true nature of the exercise: the elaboration of a rule about permissible priorities.

Notes

1   Laws J adverts to the fact that an argument very similar to his was rejected in the *Brind* case. However he considers that this was because the submission made in that case was that their Lordships should make such a presumption (in this case that free speech would not be infringed) because of Art 10 of the ECHR. He argues that this is a mistaken approach as it amounts to an attempt to incorporate the ECHR through the back door which the courts rightly resist as it offends constitutional principles. Instead he urges that the correct approach would be to argue that the norms implicit in the ECHR are already reflected in the common law – an approach which gains some support from the House of Lords decision in the *Derbyshire* case[93] – and that it is the importance the common law consequently attaches to fundamental rights which makes a presumption that statutes do not intend to override the a justifiable one.

2   There are signs that Laws J's thesis has gained some recognition by the judiciary: in *Secretary of State for the Home Department, ex p McQuillan* (1995)[94] a case involving human rights in an exclusion order context, Sedley J expressly followed Laws J's approach, but was unable to find for the applicant because of the statutory framework. In *Ministry of Defence, ex p Smith* (1995),[95] Laws' approach appeared to find partial acceptance: Sir Thomas Bingham MR accepted the following submission of David Pannick QC: '...the more substantial the interference with human rights, the more the court will require by way of justification before it is satisfied that the decision is reasonable...'.[96] This sounds almost like an echo of Laws' prescription. But the sting lies in the meaning of the word 'reasonable'; it denotes only a decision which is 'within the range of responses open to a reasonable decision-maker' (*ibid*). In other words, the prescription adopted seems to be this: the decision maker is required to take account of human rights in appropriate cases; further, he must have a more convincing justification the more his decision will trespass on those rights. But that decision remains primarily one for the decision maker. The courts will only intervene if the decider has come up with a justification which no reasonable person could consider trumped the human rights considerations – a position which seems to take us almost back to classic *GCHQ Wednesbury* irrationality, since fundamental human rights may reasonably be taken to be at least some of the 'accepted moral standards' referred to by Lord Diplock in *GCHQ* (1985).[97] It therefore remains to be seen whether Laws J's approach

---

93   *Derbyshire County Council v Times Newspapers* [1993] AC 534.

94   3 All ER 400.

95   1 All ER 257. For comment see I Hare (1996) 55 CLJ 180–2.

96   *Ibid*, at 263.

97   AC 374, 410; see above, p730.

will become anything more than a gloss only superficially overlaying traditional principles.

3   At the time of writing, the only case in which the Laws approach actually determined the (pro-rights) outcome of a case was one where Laws J himself was presiding; his decision was swiftly overturned by the Court of Appeal. A notable feature of the case was the fact that the Court of Appeal took a wholly different approach from Laws J, a fact which leads one commentator to question whether judicial review, which is of course supposed to be represent the practical application of the Rule of Law is in fact offending against the doctrine by virtue of its increasing uncertainty.

R Mallender, 'Judicial Review and the Rule of Law' (1996) 112 *Law Quarterly Review* 182–4

Judicial review is centrally concerned with vindicating the ideal of the Rule of Law. To this end, judges determine whether the decision-making powers of public bodies have been exercised in a way which satisfies the discretion-constraining requirements of administrative law. But what if both the sources of and the interpretation to be placed upon the norms applied by judges in judicial review proceedings are matters of considerable uncertainty'? Do not adjudicators then exercise a discretion which is not bridled by publicly ascertainable legal norms and which hence, runs counter to the very ideal that provides the *raison d'être* of their activities? These questions are raised by the recent case of *Cambridge Health Authority, ex p B* [1995] TLR 159, QBD and [1995] WLR 898 CA, in which the respondent health authority's decision not to allocate funds for the potentially life-sustaining treatment of, B, a 10-year-old victim of acute myeloid leukaemia was reviewed. The case prompts these questions in that the judgments of Laws J (in the Queen's Bench) and Sir Thomas Bingham MR (who delivered the leading judgment in the Court of Appeal) diverge in two crucial respects. First, in regard to the relevance of the fundamental right to life to B's application and, secondly, with respect to the question as to whether the decision could properly be attacked on the ground of unreasonableness (which is defined in *Associated Provincial Picture Houses v Wednesbury Corporation* [1948] 1 KB 223, as involving the making of a decision which no reasonable public body could make).

Laws J takes the novel step, in his judgment, of treating the fundamental right to life as providing a constraint upon the health authority's decision-making discretion. To justify doing so, he, first, expresses 'the greatest doubt' as to *Wednesbury's* adequacy as a standard of review (on account of its uncertainty) and, secondly, notes that, where such uncertainty exists, there are *dicta* which support the view that fundamental rights (*viz*, those occupying a place of central importance in the European Convention for the Protection of Human Rights and Fundamental Freedoms (Cmnd 8969) can be invoked in order to resolve uncertainties in the common law. (These *dicta* can be found in *Secretary of State for the Home Department, ex p Bugdaycay* [1987] 1 AC 514 at p531 and *Secretary of State for the Home Department, ex p Brind* [1991] 1 AC 696, at pp748–9). With this justification for invoking the right to life in place, he determines that the health authority's decision constitutes an interference with it and addresses the question as to whether they have provided a substantial public interest justification for doing so. This question he answers in the negative, rejecting both their argument that further remedial treatment would not be in B's interests (because of the suffering to which it would expose her) and their argument that funding the treatment would not be an effective use of their limited resources. In the light of these findings, he concludes that B's right to life has been violated and quashes the respondent's decision. While the bulk of the judge's analysis concerns the right to life, he, nonetheless, states that the same result can be reached by applying *Wednesbury* and identifies four forms of unreasonableness manifested by the health authority: *viz*, failure to consider the wishes of B's family, wrongly characterising the treatment sought as 'experimental', failure to explain the priorities that led to the decision not to provide it, and an inaccurate estimate of its cost.

In contrast to the judgment of Laws J, the right to life plays no part in that of Bingham MR, notwithstanding his observing both that 'our society is one in which a very high value is put on human life and that no decision affecting human life ... can be regarded with other than the greatest seriousness'. While, in the light of these comments, the Master of the Rolls' decision not to invoke the right to life might seem surprising, his not doing so can be explained by reference to his commitment to the principle that, in judicial review proceedings, judges must merely scrutinise the lawfulness of a public body's decision and must not adjudicate upon its merits – a commitment to which he gives emphatic expression thus: 'we have one function only, which is to rule upon the lawfulness of decisions. That is a function to which we should strictly confine ourselves'. It is, hence, unsurprising to find him basing his decision not on the right to life but, rather, on the ground of *Wednesbury* unreasonableness, which specifies a modest standard of review and, thus, leaves public bodies with broad scope for making discretionary decisions. The interpretation placed by Bingham MR on *Wednesbury* diverges radically from that of Laws J: he rescinds the judge's quashing order, identifying as unsustainable all four of the grounds on which the latter found the health authority's denial of treatment to be unreasonable.

Notes

1   The author goes on to find that in fact, on a more general jurisprudential level, both approaches 'reveal an intention to give effect to recognisably legal values' which restrains the discretion of both of them. Nevertheless, given that the two courts differed so markedly as to which (legal) matters were (a) relevant and (b) determinative of the matter in hand it seems apparent that the rapidly development of this area of law will inevitably entail a period of considerable uncertainty as to the content and scope of its core principles.

2   In a very recent decision of the Court of Appeal,[98] which received a good deal of publicity, it appeared that the grave implications for basic human rights involved were perhaps the decisive factor. The facts appear in the judgment.

Secretary of State for Social Security, ex p Joint Council of Welfare of Immigrants (1996) New Law Journal, 5 July 1985

In order to speed up the process of resolving the claims of persons seeking asylum in the UK (of which only 25% were ultimately found to be genuine refugees) and to reduce the expenditure on benefits, the respondent Secretary of State for Social Security made the Social Security (Persons from Abroad) Miscellaneous Amendment Regulations 1996, SI 1996/30 which removed all entitlement to income-related benefit from asylum seekers who failed to claim

---

98   The case was not fully reported at the time of writing.

asylum immediately on arrival in the UK (subject to a limited exception) and those whose claims had been rejected by the Home Secretary but who then appealed to the independent appellate authorities. The effect of the regulations was that a significant number of genuine asylum seekers were faced with the choice either of remaining in the UK destitute and homeless until their claims were finally determined, or of abandoning their claims and returning to face the persecution they had fled. The applicants sought judicial review of the regulations on the ground that they were *ultra vires* the enabling power. The application was dismissed by the Divisional Court. The applicants appealed.

Simon Brown LJ: ... The regulations are said to be *ultra vires* because of implied restrictions in the enabling power. Two central arguments are advanced. The first and wider one is that the regulations are inconsistent with the Asylum and Immigration Appeals Act 1993 in the sense that they create various sub-categories of asylum seekers in a way that the 1993 Act itself does not. ...

Secondly, and more narrowly, the applicants submit that the regulations materially interfere with the exercise of rights by asylum seekers under the 1993 Act (the conflict argument).

... For my part I would reject [the first argument]. The responsibility for the benefit budget lies with the Secretary of State and not with the Home Secretary. Subject always to the conflict argument, the Secretary of State is perfectly entitled to reach his own decision as to how asylum seekers should be treated and as to whether all should be treated in the same way. The enabling power is amply wide for these purposes. ... He is under no obligation to align the benefit scheme to the approach adopted in the 1993 Act.

... [On the conflict argument] powerful arguments are advanced on both sides. The *Leech* principle [see *Secretary of State for the Home Department, ex p Leech* [1993] 4 All ER 539 where the Court of Appeal struck down a prison rule giving an unrestricted power to read correspondence, including that between a prisoner and his solicitor, on the ground that it conflicted with the prisoner's basic rights of legal professional privilege] is undoubtedly of assistance to the appellants, and yet the analogy with *Leech* is not, as it seems to me, exact. ... I for my part have no difficulty in accepting the Secretary of State's right to discourage economic migrants by restricting their benefits. That of itself indicates that the regulations are not invalid merely because of their 'chilling effect'. ...

It is, moreover, as I recognise, one thing, as in *Leech*, to condemn direct interference with the unquestioned basic rights there identified; another to assert that the Secretary of State here is bound to maintain some benefit provision to asylum seekers so as to ensure that those with genuine claims will not be driven by penury to forfeit them, whether by leaving the country before their determination or through an inability to prosecute them effectively.

The present challenge, I therefore acknowledge, involves carrying the *Leech* principle a step further and this, moreover, in a field where Parliament has been closely involved in the making of the impugned regulations.

I have nevertheless concluded that it is a step the court should take. Parliamentary sovereignty is not here in question; the regulations are subordinate legislation only. The *Hammersmith* approach [see *Hammersmith and Fulham London Borough Council v Secretary of State for the Environment* [1990] 3 All ER 589 where the Secretary of State had been acting within a carefully defined system of parliamentary scrutiny and control in an important area of the national economy and with the legitimate aim of removing an unwarranted burden on public funds, so that the court was yet more reluctant than usual to interfere with governmental action] cannot, in my judgment, avail the Security of State [in the instant case]; it applies only once the court has determined that the regulations do not contravene the express or implied requirements of a statute – the very question here at issue. Parliament for its part has clearly demonstrated by the 1993 Act a full commitment to the UK's Convention obligations [see the Geneva Convention relating to the Status of Refugees 1951]. ...

The 1993 Act confers on asylum seekers fuller rights than they had ever previously enjoyed, the right of appeal in particular. And yet these regulations for some genuine asylum seekers at least must now be regarded as rendering these rights nugatory. Either that, or the regulations necessarily contemplate for some a life so destitute that, to my mind, no civilised nation can tolerate it. So basic are the human rights here at issue that it cannot be necessary to resort to the European Convention of Human Rights to take note of their violation. ... True, no obligation arises under ... the 1951 Convention until asylum seekers are recognised as refugees. But that is not to say that, up to that point, their fundamental needs can properly be ignored. I do not accept they can. Rather, I would hold it unlawful to alter the benefit regime so drastically as must inevitably not merely prejudice, but on occasion defeat, the statutory right of asylum seekers to claim refugee status. ... I for my part regard the regulations now in force as so uncompromisingly draconian in effect that they must indeed be held *ultra vires*. ...

Waite LJ delivered a concurring judgment. Neill LJ delivered a dissenting judgment.

Note

Potential for greater protection of human rights is not the only possible development in judicial review showing recent signs of life. The notion of proportionality, as Himsworth argues, may not have been laid to rest in *Brind* after all, as a careful examination of *Ministry of Agriculture, Fisheries and Food, ex p Hamble* (1995)[99] reveals.

C Himsworth, 'Legitimately Excluding Proportionality?' (1996) *Public Law* 46–7, 50–1

The case arose from the minister's refusal of a particular type of fishing licence – a licence which would permit beam trawl fishing of pressure stock (ie, stock subject to protection by quota under the EC fishing regime) – to *The Nellie*, a vessel whose owner was the applicant company in these proceedings. The refusal flowed in turn from a licensing policy change and the failure of *The Nellie* to qualify for a licence under either the new principal rules themselves or under designated exceptions to the rules formulated in such a way as to authorise the grant of a licence to boats which had a 'track record' of relevant fishing or which were in certain categories of 'pipe-line' vessels already, prior to the announcement of the change of policy, being built or converted with the genuine intention of use for North Sea beam trawling. The applicant's complaint, based on a rather complicated account of the history of *The Nellie* and preparations already in hand for her use under earlier licensing regimes, was that its 'legitimate expectation' of the grant of a North Sea licence had been dashed by the introduction of the new policy and, within that policy, the failure to permit exceptions which would accommodate *The Nellie*.

... A provocative twist in the judgment is Sedley J's incorporation into the analysis of legitimate expectation of a doctrine of proportionality; At one point,

---

99   2 All ER 714.

he says that 'legitimacy is a relative concept, to be gauged proportionately to the legal and policy implications of the expectation' (p724). And, in his closing approval of the minister's decision, he writes that the 'means adopted bore a fair proportion to the end in view, both in respect of what was included in, and of what was excluded from, the pipeline provisions' (p735). What is happening here is that a requirement of proportionality, despite its clear rejection as a self-standing ground of review by the House of Lords in *Brind*, is being woven back into the fabric of British judicial review as simply one aspect of an expanding doctrine of 'fair administration' – which has already accommodated the familiar concepts of fairness as natural justice, fairness as procedural propriety in general, and fairness as honouring legitimate expectations. Another requirement of fair administration now becomes proportionality of decision-making and that too becomes subject to the scrutiny of the courts. But if proportionality is a standard to be applied by courts as they review the balancing of interests relevant to the legitimacy of an expectation, it is difficult to see how they can do other than insist on proportionality in the weighing of considerations deemed to be relevant to any policy decision in Government. Is not an asserted 'legitimate expectation' a 'relevant consideration' like any other? If so, this should, once again, not be a surprising advance at the hand of a judge committed to a general expansion of judicial review. More importantly, it is a development entirely in line with the European approach already adopted to legitimate expectation. Despite the Lords in *Brind*, what we have seen is a growing need for the British courts to make use of the doctrine of proportionality where the EC context of a case has demanded it. But this, of course, has opened up a 'drift' between those cases and the remainder of non-EC judicial review which is anchored to *Brind* and indeed this is one of the examples cited by van Gerven himself [(1992) 32 CML Rev 679] of areas requiring consequential change to preserve the homogeneity of national law. There have been earlier straws in the wind and, quite independently of any EC pressures, there has been a long-running domestically-driven campaign towards bringing proportionality into the net of mainstream judicial review whilst, from the bench, Laws J has been making some tentative inroads and Sedley J has himself used the language of proportionality in the context of the judicial balancing of executive action against those rights (above all, the right to life) treated as fundamental. There can be little doubt, however, that *The Nellie* has, through its explicit emphasis upon EC harmonisation on the related front of legitimate expectation and its careful integration of proportionality into fair administration, fished in important new waters.

CHAPTER 3

OMBUDSMEN

INTRODUCTION

The first ombudsman was the Parliamentary Commissioner for Administration; that office was set up under the Parliamentary Commissioner Act 1967. Since then the system has been extended to other areas, suggesting that it has shown itself to be of value. It is important to bear in mind the role the PCA was set up to fulfil. Pre-existing judicial and parliamentary remedies did not, it appeared, provide adequate redress for members of the public who had suffered as a result of maladministration in central government. The Crichel Down Affair in 1954 had provided a particularly prominent example of such conduct. Defective administrative action was going unremedied either because it fell outside the jurisdiction of the courts or because MPs did not have sufficient powers to investigate it satisfactorily. In providing a further means of investigating complaints, the intention was that the PCA would not only uncover maladministration, but would also enable civil servants wrongly accused of maladministration to clear their names.

There will be some overlap between the range of administrative actions the ombudsman can consider and those which can be considered where there is a statutory right of appeal or in judicial review proceedings. A court can intervene in judicial review proceedings only where a decision is *ultra vires*, where it is considered *Wednesbury* unreasonable or where there has been a breach of natural justice. In a number of respects the ombudsman system may be more effective as a means of providing redress for the citizen mistreated by government authorities than judicial and Parliamentary remedies. However, it should be borne in mind that the ombudsman system was not set up as a replacement for other remedies, but in order to remedy their deficiencies and to fill gaps they created.

The table below, from evidence given to a Select Committee demonstrates the growth of the ombudsman system. It also shows that there has been a similar growth of other bodies dealing with citizens' complaints.

Evidence taken before the Select Committee on the PCA, HC 42 (1993–94), vol II

Ombudsmen

Public sector

Parliamentary Commissioner for Administration

Health Service Commissioner for England, Scotland, Wales

Commission for Local Administration in England

Commission for Local Administration in Wales

Commissioner for Local Administration in Scotland

NI Parliamentary Commissioner for Administration and Commissioner for Complaints

Prisons 'Ombudsman' England and Wales (from end of 1993)

Statutory
Central government
NHS
Local government
Northern Ireland
Private sector
Banking Ombudsman
Building Societies Ombudsman
Ombudsman for Corporate Estate Agents
Insurance Ombudsman
Investment Ombudsman
Legal Services Ombudsman
Legal Services Ombudsman for Scotland
Pensions Ombudsman

THE ROLE AND WORK OF THE PCA

Role of the PCA

Parliamentary Commissioner Act 1967

Departments and authorities subject to investigation

4.–(1) Subject to the provisions of this section and to the notes contained in Schedule 2 to this Act, this Act applies to the Government departments and other authorities listed in that Schedule.

(2) Her Majesty may by Order in Council amend the said Schedule 2 by the alteration of any entry or note, the removal of any entry or note or the insertion of any additional entry or note; but nothing in this subsection authorises the inclusion in that Schedule of any body or authority not being a department or other body or authority whose functions are exercised on behalf of the Crown.

(3) Any statutory instrument made by virtue of subsection (2) of this section shall be subject to annulment in pursuance of a resolution of either House of Parliament.

(4) Any reference in this Act to a Government department or other authority to which this Act applies includes a reference to the ministers, members or officers of that department or authority.

Matters subject to investigation

5.–(1) Subject to the provisions of this section, the commissioner may investigate any action taken by or on behalf of a Government department or other authority to which this Act applies, being action taken in the exercise of administrative functions of that department or authority, in any case where–

(a) a written complaint is duly made to a member of the House of Commons by a member of the public who claims to have sustained injustice in consequence of maladministration in connection with the action so taken; and

(b) the complaint is referred to the commissioner, with the consent of the person who made it, by a member of that House with a request to conduct an investigation thereon.

(2)Except as hereinafter provided, the commissioner shall not conduct an investigation under this Act in respect of any of the following matters, that is to say–

(a) any action in respect of which the person aggrieved has or had a right of appeal, reference or review to or before a tribunal constituted by or under any enactment or by virtue of Her Majesty's prerogative;

(b) any action in respect of which the person aggrieved has or had a remedy by way of proceedings in any court of law;

provided that the commissioner may conduct an investigation notwithstanding that the person aggrieved has or had such a right or remedy if satisfied that in the particular circumstances it is not reasonable to expect him to resort or have resorted to it.

(3)Without prejudice to subsection (2) of this section, the commissioner shall not conduct an investigation under this Act in respect of any such action or matter as is described in Schedule 3 to this Act.

(4)Her Majesty may by Order in Council amend the said Schedule 3 so as to exclude from the provisions of that Schedule such actions or matters as may be described in the Order; and any statutory instrument made by virtue of this subsection shall be subject to annulment in pursuance of a resolution of either House of Parliament.

(5)In determining whether to initiate, continue or discontinue an investigation under this Act, the commissioner shall, subject to the foregoing provisions of this section, act in accordance with his own discretion; and any question whether a complaint is duly made under this Act shall be determined by the commissioner.

Provisions relating to complaints

6.–(1)A complaint under this Act may be made by any individual, or by any body of persons whether incorporated or not, not being–

(a) a local authority or other authority or body constituted for purposes of the public service or of local government or for the purposes of carrying on under national ownership any industry or undertaking or part of an industry or undertaking;

(b) any other authority or body whose members are appointed by Her Majesty or any minister of the Crown or Government department, or whose revenues consist wholly or mainly of moneys provided by Parliament. ...

(3)A complaint shall not be entertained under this Act unless it is made to a member of the House of Commons not later than 12 months from the day on which the person aggrieved first had notice of the matters alleged in the complaint; but the commissioner may conduct an investigation pursuant to a complaint not made within that period if he considers that there are special circumstances which make it proper to do so. ...

Procedure in respect of investigations

7.–(1)Where the commissioner proposes to conduct an investigation pursuant to a complaint under this Act, he shall afford to the principal officer of the department or authority concerned, and to any other person who is alleged in the complaint to have taken or authorised the action complained of, an opportunity to comment on any allegations contained in the complaint.

(2) Every such investigation shall be conducted in private, but except as aforesaid the procedure for conducting an investigation shall be such as the commissioner considers appropriate in the circumstances of the case; and without prejudice to the generality of the foregoing provision the commissioner may obtain information from such persons and in such manner, and make such inquiries, as he thinks fit, and may determine whether any person may be represented, by counsel or solicitor or otherwise, in the investigation.

(3) The commissioner may, if he thinks fit, pay to the person by whom the complaint was made and to any other person who attends or furnishes information for the purposes of an investigation under this Act–

(a) sums in respect of expenses properly incurred by them;

(b) allowances by way of compensation for the loss of their time;

in accordance with such scales and subject to such conditions as may be determined by the Treasury.

(4) The conduct of an investigation under this Act shall not affect any action taken by the department or authority concerned, or any power or duty of that department or authority to take further action with respect to any matters subject to the investigation; but where the person aggrieved has been removed from the United Kingdom under any Order in force under the Aliens Restriction Acts 1914 and 1919 or under the Commonwealth Immigrants Act 1962, he shall, if the commissioner so directs, be permitted to re-enter and remain in the United Kingdom, subject to such conditions as the Secretary of State may direct, for the purposes of the investigation.

Evidence

8.–(1) For the purposes of an investigation under this Act the commissioner may require any minister, officer or member of the department or authority concerned or any other person who in his opinion is able to furnish information or produce documents relevant to the investigation to furnish any such information or produce any such document.

(2) For the purposes of any such investigation the commissioner shall have the same powers as the Court in respect of the attendance and examination of witnesses (including the administration of oaths or affirmations and the examination of witnesses abroad) and in respect of the production of documents.

(3) No obligation to maintain secrecy or other restriction upon the disclosure of information obtained by or furnished to persons in Her Majesty's service, whether imposed by any enactment or by any Rule of Law, shall apply to the disclosure of information for the purposes of an investigation under this Act; and the Crown shall not be entitled in relation to any such investigation to any such privilege in respect of the production of documents or the giving of evidence as is allowed by law in legal proceedings.

(4) No person shall be required or authorised by virtue of this Act to furnish any information or answer any question relating to proceedings of the Cabinet or of any committee of the Cabinet or to produce so much of any document as relates to such proceedings; and for the purposes of this subsection a certificate issued by the Secretary of the Cabinet with the approval of the Prime Minister and certifying that any information, question, document or part of a document so relates shall be conclusive.

(5) Subject to subsection (3) of this section, no person shall be compelled for the purposes of an investigation under this Act to give any evidence or produce

any document which he could not be compelled to give or produce in proceedings before the Court.

Obstruction and contempt

9.–(1)If any person without lawful excuse obstructs the commissioner or any officer of the commissioner in the performance of his functions under this Act, or is guilty of any act or omission in relation to an investigation under this Act which, if that investigation were a proceeding in the Court, would constitute contempt of court, the commissioner may certify the offence to the Court. ...

Reports by Commission

10.–(1)In any case where the commissioner conducts an investigation under this Act or decides not to conduct such an investigation, he shall send to the member of the House of Commons by whom the request for investigation was made (or if he is no longer a member of that House, to such member of that House as the commissioner thinks appropriate) a report of the results of the investigation or, as the case may be, a statement of his reasons for not conducting an investigation.

(2)In any case where the commissioner conducts an investigation under this Act, he shall also send a report of the results of the investigation to the principal officer of the department or authority concerned and to any other person who is alleged in the relevant complaint to have taken or authorised the action complained of.

(3)If, after conducting an investigation under this Act, it appears to the commissioner that injustice has been caused to the person aggrieved in consequence of maladministration and that the injustice has not been, or will not be, remedied, he may, if he thinks fit, lay before each House of Parliament a special report upon the case.

(4)The commissioner shall annually lay before each House of Parliament a general report on the performance of his functions under this Act and may from time to time lay before each House of Parliament such other reports with respect to those actions as he thinks fit.

(5)For the purposes of the law of defamation, any such publication as is hereinafter mentioned shall be absolutely privileged, that is to say–

(a) the publication of any matter by the commissioner in making a report to either House of Parliament for the purposes of this Act;

(b) the publication of any matter by a member of the House of Commons in communicating with the commissioner or his officers for those purposes or by the commissioner or his officers in communicating with such a member for those purposes;

(c) the publication by such a member to the person by whom a complaint was made under this Act of a report or statement sent to the member in respect of the complaint in pursuance of subsection (1) of this section;

(d) the publication by the commissioner to such a person as is mentioned in subsection (2) of this section of a report sent to that person in pursuance of that subsection.

[For Schedule 2 see below pp819–20.

Notes

1 The citizen must have suffered injustice as a result of maladministration. There are clear advantages for the aggrieved citizen in using the

ombudsman rather than relying on an MP to resolve the problem. Although MPs are of course able to hear a wide range of complaints, their powers of investigation are limited. The PCA in contrast has broad powers of investigation. Under s7 of the Act he may examine all documents relevant to the investigation, and the duty to assist him overrides the duty to maintain secrecy under the Official Secrets Act 1989. The PCA does not, however, have access to Cabinet papers; the courts on the other hand claim the power to order such access.

2   Parliamentary procedures such as Questions and Select Committees operate within the doctrine of ministerial responsibility; in other words the expectation is that the minister in question will remedy matters. As Harlow[1] points out, the doctrine 'may actually shelter more administrative blunders than it exposes'. The PCA can be more effective in practice as he on the other hand looks behind that expectation and considers the workings of the administrative body itself. The PCA's procedure can be more flexible than that of a Select Committee due to its informal, private nature and may get closer to the root of a problem.

3   The PCA was given the ability to investigate a wider range of complaints than could be investigated in a court and given greater investigative powers than those available to MPs. In some instances of maladministration there may be a statutory right of appeal to a tribunal. Where a court or tribunal could consider such defective administration the PCA will not investigate the matter unless it would not be reasonable to expect the complainant to seek redress in litigation. He is empowered to consider 'maladministration' under s10(3) of the Act as opposed to illegality. 'Maladministration' has been described by Richard Crossman in the debate on the Parliamentary Commissioner Bill 1967 as 'bias, neglect, inattention, delay, incompetence, ineptitude, perversity, turpitude, arbitrariness and so on'.

4   Although maladministration is a wide concept it does mean that the PCA is concerned with procedural defects rather than with the merits of a decision. This distinction is contained in s12(3) of the Act which provides that the PCA may not investigate the merits of a decision taken without maladministration. However, the distinction between substance and procedure is not always easy to draw (as appears from the contrast between the judgment of Nolan J at first instance and that of Lord Donaldson in the Court of Appeal in *Local Commissioner, ex p Eastleigh Borough Council* (1988),[2] see below), and the PCA has complied with the demand from the Parliamentary Select Committee on the PCA to interpret his role widely. Therefore this apparent limitation on the PCA's remit is less significant than may at first appear.

5   The third report from the Select Committee on the PCA for the session 1993–94 noted that the PCA has produced an expanded list of forms of maladministration.

---

1   'Ombudsmen in Search of a Role' (1978) 41 MLR 452.
2   3 WLR 116.

Third Report from the Select Committee on the Parliamentary Commissioner for Administration, HC 345 (1993–94)

Maladministration

10 ... The commissioner has always made clear his preference for the term 'maladministration', included in the statute without definition, in that it gives him considerable freedom and flexibility in interpretation. ... At paragraph 7 of his annual report Mr Reid produced 'an expanded list ... in the language of the l990s'[PCA Annual Report for 1993, para 7]:

- rudeness (though that is a matter of degree);
- unwillingness to treat the complainant as a person with rights;
- refusal to answer reasonable questions;
- neglecting to inform a complainant on request of his or her rights or entitlement;
- knowingly giving advice which is misleading or inadequate;
- ignoring valid advice or overruling considerations which would produce an uncomfortable result for the overruler;
- offering no redress or manifestly disproportionate redress;
- showing bias whether because of colour, sex, or any other grounds;
- omission to notify those who thereby lose a right of appeal;
- refusal to inform adequately of the right of appeal;
- faulty procedures;
- failure by management to monitor compliance with adequate procedures;
- cavalier disregard of guidance which is intended to be followed in the interest of equitable treatment of those who use a service;
- partiality;
- failure to mitigate the effects of rigid adherence to the letter of the law where that produces manifestly inequitable treatment'.

11 Mr Reid emphasised that he was not seeking to define maladministration, 'seeing strength in the fact that there is no statutory definition' of the word. It was hoped that the new list might, however, aid Whitehall in analysing PCA cases and circulating general lessons for the benefit of all departments and agencies. The list might also form a basis for a useful analysis of complaints in future PCA reports. We particularly welcome the relating of maladministration to the rights and proper expectations of the citizen in dealing with the executive. We learned with concern that departments will not infrequently respond to a draft report on an investigation with the argument that, to quote the commissioner, 'what has happened is not as bad as I have said it is and should not be termed as maladministration' [Q42]. We trust the further explanation here offered by the commissioner might in future reduce such special pleading. It is a matter of regret that at a time when the Citizen's Charter is meant to have changed attitudes in Whitehall to standards of service, some parts of the public sector seem still to lack an appropriately self-critical spirit.

Notes

1 In investigating maladministration the ombudsman system may have some advantages over a court hearing. Its informality in investigation may be

more effective at times in discovering the truth than the adversarial system in the courts. Moreover, in court the Crown may plead public interest immunity to avoid disclosing documents whereas the PCA can look at all departmental files. Such flexibility is also reflected in the fact that the ombudsman procedure is not circumscribed by rules as regards time limits and therefore may provide a remedy in instances which cannot be considered by a court. The *Ostler* case (1977)[3] illustrates the advantage of such flexibility in comparison with judicial agreement between the department concerned and a third party. The court also introduced changes in its procedures in order to deal with his court costs.

2 Whilst the jurisdiction of the PCA is, strictly speaking, limited to investigating specific cases of maladministration, he can and does make general findings and recommendations to improve the administration of a given department. In his most recent annual report,[4] the PCA appears to be widening his remit still further, to include criticisms of actual Government policies. The report claims that the policy of slimming down the Civil Service (reduced to under 500,000 in 1996 for the first time in over 50 years) has resulted in an upsurge in complaints, up 28% from the previous year in 1995. It went on, 'There is a risk that fewer staff will lead to slower service and more mistakes, because civil servants will have less time for thought to enable them to pursue considered and prudent action. I doubt whether automation and technology will compensate fully for cuts in human resources. I foresee more, not less, maladministration, despite the references to efficiency savings'.[5]

3 When the PCA upholds a complaint, the type of remedies recommended by him vary. *Ex gratia* payments to individuals adversely affected by maladministration appear to be made in roughly half of the cases in which the PCA makes a finding of maladministration (in 92 out of 177 cases in 1992 and in 108 out of 236 cases in 1995). Apologies, re-consideration of an individual case and/or changes to administrative rules and procedures may also result. Remedies may also be offered to other members of the public known to have been affected by a problem similar to that of the complainant.

4 Findings and recommendations made by the PCA are not enforceable in law. Thus the adverse publicity generated by a refusal to comply with a recommendation is the only sanction for non-compliance. However, it appears that the influence of the PCA is far greater in practice than his formal powers. Rodney Austin, considering what the PCA is likely to be able to achieve in policing the Government's new code on Open Government notes that:

Whitehall's record of compliance with the non-binding recommendations of the ombudsman is actually outstanding: on only two occasions[6] have Government

---

3   QB 122.

4   Cm 296.

5   *Ibid*, p2 para 6.

6   Now three: the third case was the Channel Tunnel rail link case – see pp846–7 below. For the code on Open Government, see Part IV, Chapter 3.

departments refused to accept the PCA's findings, and in both cases the PCA's recommendations were [nevertheless] complied with.'[7]

The success rate of the PCA is indicated by the fact that only twice since his institution has he had to make a special report to Parliament (under s10(3) of the PCA Act 1967) following initial rejection of his recommendations by the Government.

5 However, as Austin goes on to note, 'compliance with the PCA's recommendations usually involves the payment of an *ex gratia* compensation or an apology or the reconsideration of a prior decision by the correct process. Rarely does it involve reversal on merits of an important policy decision.'[8] Indeed, in certain cases the Government will explicitly state that it does not accept the PCA's finding of maladministration but is prepared to offer payment or an apology as a gesture of goodwill or out of respect for the PCA (as in the Channel Tunnel rail link case – see below).

6 Although the PCA's lack of formal powers might appear to weaken the PCA severely, it has been argued that the need for such a limitation is inherent in his role. If the PCA could award compulsory remedies it would be necessary to give the Department complained about a full and formal opportunity to answer the allegations made. Probably some of the procedure would have to be conducted in public. The fact that the PCA operates informally and privately has been thought to enhance his powers of persuasion. Where a particular complaint seems to be merely symptomatic of a deep-seated problem in a department, the PCA can sometimes persuade it to change its general procedure. This occurred in the *Ostler* case (1977): the Department of the Environment was persuaded to introduce new procedures in order to prevent a repetition of the situation which led to Ostler's complaint. Thus this apparent weakness in the PCA's powers may underlie one of his main strengths.

7 On the other hand, the lack of a power to award a remedy may in some situations appear to amount to a weakness in the PCA system. In *Congreve v Home Office* (1976),[9] the applicant succeeded in showing that the Home Office had acted unlawfully as regards television licence fees and a refund was awarded. The situation had already been investigated by the PCA which had found inefficiency on the part of the Home Office but had not recommended a remedy for licence holders.

---

7 'Freedom of Information: the Constitutional Impact', in J Jowell and D Oliver (eds), *The Changing Constitution* (1994), p443.

8 *Ibid.*

9 2 QB 629.

NUMBER OF CASES INVESTIGATED

Appendix to the Minutes of Evidence Taken Before the Select Committee on the PCA, HC 42 (1993–94), vol II

Table 1. Number of cases handled by the Parliamentary Ombudsman since the introduction of his office

Year	No of complaints			% of complaints	
	referred	investigated	upheld	rejected	upheld
1967	1,069	188	19	82.4	10.1
1968	1,120	374	38	66.6	10.2
1969	761	302	48	60.3	15.9
1970	645	259	59	59.8	22.8
1971	548	182	67	66.7	36.8
1972	573	261	79	59.4	30.3
1973	571	239	88	58.1	36.8
1974	704	252	94	64.2	37.3
1975	928	244	90	73.7	36.9
1976	815	320	139	60.7	43.4
1977	901	312	111	65.4	35.6
1978	1,259	341	131	72.9	38.4
1979	822	223	84	72.9	37.7
1980	1,031	225	107	78.2	47.6
1981	917	228	104	75.1	45.6
1982	838	202	67	75.9	33.2
1983	751	198	83	73.6	41.9
1984	837	183	81	78.1	44.3
1985	759	177	75	76.7	42.4
1986	719	168	82	76.6	48.8
1987	677	145	63	78.6	43.5
1988	701	120	59	82.9	49.2
1989	677	126	61	81.4	48.4
1990	704	177	74	74.9	41.8
1991	801	183	87	77.2	47.5

Source of figures: Parliamentary Commissioner for Administration, annual reports 1967–92.

Second Report from the Select Committee on the Parliamentary Commissioner for Administration, HC 64 (1993–94)

...

4 Referrals of complaints to the Commissioner rose by 18% from 801 in 1991 to 945 in 1992. There was a sharper increase in the number of cases accepted for investigation, from 215 cases in 1991 to 269 cases in 1992, an increase of 25%. More cases were completed than in any year since 1983, 190 reports being issued. We welcome this increase in activity, all the more surprising in an election year. The Committee has always been of the view that, with publicity, more investigable complaints could reach the ombudsman. The figures for 1992 suggest that both the public and Members are becoming more aware of the nature and extent of the commissioner's work and jurisdiction. It is particularly gratifying to note the greater number of cases being accepted for investigation. ...

7   One result of the continuing surge of complaints was that the number of
     outstanding cases undergoing investigation at the end of 1992 was 260, 73
     higher than the 1991 figure. Forecasts of future workload in the Management
     Plan included in the Annual Report had, since publication, 'been revised
     sharply upwards' [Q3]. The number of investigating units had been increased
     from six to eight to meet the increasing workload. This required further
     recruitment of staff and training. Mr Reid stressed that 'This is a major
     operation and my office is going through a period of considerable change'
     [Q3]. We are confident that the Commissioner's office will avoid the failures
     and deficiencies too often associated with organisational change in the bodies
     he investigates. *We also reiterate our concern that he should continue to be granted
     adequate funds and resources for the task assigned him by Parliament.*

Note

The most recent report by the PCA[10] show that the steady upsurge in
complaints is accelerating: in 1995, 1,706 complaints were referred to Mr Reid by
MPs, a 28% increase over 1994.

JURISDICTION: ARGUMENTS ABOUT EXCLUDED AREAS

Parliamentary Commissioner Act 1967, Schedules 2 and 3

Departments and authorities subject to investigation

Ministry of Agriculture, Fisheries and Food
Charity Commission
Civil Service Commission
Commonwealth Office
Crown Estate Office
Customs and Excise
Ministry of Defence
Department of Economic Affairs
Department of Education and Science
Export Credits Guarantee Department
Foreign Office
Ministry of Health
Home Office
Ministry of Housing and Local Government
Central Office of Information
Inland Revenue
Ministry of Labour
Land Commission
Land Registry
Lord Chancellor's Department
Lord President of the Council's Office
National Debt Office
Ministry of Overseas Development
Post Office
Ministry of Power
Ministry of Public Building and Works
Public Record Office

---

10 *Annual Report for 1995*, Cm 296, para 2, p65.

Public Trustee
Department of the Registers of Scotland
General Register Office
General Register Office, Scotland
Registry of Friendly Societies
Royal Mint
Scottish Office
Scottish Record Office
Ministry of Social Security
Social Survey
Stationery Office
Ministry of Technology
Board of Trade
Ministry of Transport
Treasury
Treasury Solicitor
Welsh Office ...

Schedule 3

Matters not subject to investigation

1   Action taken in matters certified by a Secretary of State or other minister of the Crown to affect relations or dealings between the Government of the United Kingdom and any other Government or any international organisation of states or Governments.

2   Action taken, in any country or territory outside the United Kingdom, by or on behalf of any officer representing or acting under the authority of Her Majesty in respect of the United Kingdom, or any other officer of the Government of the United Kingdom.

3   Action taken in connection with the administration of the Government of any country or territory outside the United Kingdom which forms part of Her Majesty's dominions or in which Her Majesty has jurisdiction.

4   Action taken by the Secretary of State under the Extradition Act 1870 or the Fugitive Offenders Act 1881.

5   Action taken by or with the authority of the Secretary of State for the purposes of investigating crime or of protecting the security of the state, including action so taken with respect to passports.

6   The commencement or conduct of civil or criminal proceedings before any court of law in the United Kingdom, of proceedings at any place under the Naval Discipline Act 1957, the Army Act 1955 or the Air Force Act 1955, or of proceedings before any international court or tribunal.

7   Any exercise of the prerogative of mercy or of the power of a Secretary of State to make a reference in respect of any person to the Court of Appeal, the High Court of Justiciary or the Courts-martial Appeal Court.

8   Action taken on behalf of the Minister of Health or the Secretary of State by a Regional Hospital Board, Board of Governors of a Teaching Hospital, Hospital Management Committee or Board of Management, or by the Public Health Laboratory Service Board.

9   Action taken in matters relating to contractual or other commercial transactions, whether within the United Kingdom or elsewhere, being transactions of a Government department or authority to which this Act applies or of any such authority or body as is mentioned in paragraph (a) or *(b)* of subsection (1) of s6 of this Act and not being transactions for or relating to:

(a) the acquisition of land compulsorily or in circumstances in which it could be acquired compulsorily;

(b) the disposal as surplus of land acquired compulsorily or in such circumstances as aforesaid.

10 Action taken in respect of appointments or removals, pay, discipline, superannuation or other personnel matters, in relation to –

(a) service in any of the armed forces of the Crown, including reserve and auxiliary and cadet forces;

(b) service in any office or employment under the Crown or under any authority listed in Schedule 2 to this Act; or

(c) service in any office or employment, or under any contract for services, in respect of which power to take action, or to determine or approve the action to be taken, in such matters is vested in Her Majesty, any minister of the Crown such authority as aforesaid.

11 The grant of honours, awards or privileges within the gift of the Crown, including the grant of Royal Charters.

Note

It may be helpful to consider the evidence heard by the Select Committee on the PCA, which give the reasons for various exclusions.

Evidence Taken Before the Select Committee on the PCA, HC 64 (1993–94), vol II, Annexes A and B

Annex A

PCA: examples of bodies outside jurisdiction

Certain departments of state

For example Cabinet Office, Law Officers' Department, Prime Minister's Office, Privy Council Office.

Reason for exclusion: Not carrying out functions which it was thought necessary (or appropriate) for PCA to investigate.

Certain court staff

For example Scottish courts, magistrates' courts.

Reason for exclusion: Originally all court and tribunal staff were excluded from PCA's jurisdiction on the grounds that PCA was not a judicial authority and was not concerned with the operations of the judiciary. The Courts and Legal Services Act 1990, which extended PCA's jurisdiction, covered only the staff of those courts and tribunals for which the Lord Chancellor's Department was directly responsible. ...

Educational organisations

For example Higher Education Funding Council for England, National Curriculum Council, School Examinations and Assessment Council.

Reason for exclusion: Direct impact on the public was considered to be insignificant and thus inappropriate to be within PCA's jurisdiction. ...

Nationalised industries

For example British Coal Corporation, British Railways Board, Civil Aviation Authority, the Post Office.

Reason for exclusion: Originally it was considered unnecessary and to be a threat to the efficient conduct of their business on commercial lines for them to be within jurisdiction. In recent years the Government has observed that nationalised industries should be subject to commercial disciplines and are in no sense a part of the administrative apparatus of government. Referring specifically to the CAA, the Government noted that it was a nationalised industry, that its air navigation and air traffic control services were trading activities which ought to be treated on the same basis as other nationalised activities and that its regulatory activities were subject to scrutiny by the Council on Tribunals.

Annex B

PCA: subject areas outside jurisdiction

Means of referring a complaint (s 5(1))

Implications of s5(1) are that it excludes from jurisdiction (a) bodies which are distinct entities from those in Schedule 2 and which are exercising functions of their own, and (b) legislative, judicial and quasi-judicial functions.

Direct access from members of the public is excluded because PCA was envisaged as a means of assisting MPs in one aspect of their functions; it was considered important to provide no means by which PCA might be an alternative to an MP as a source of protection against unjust administration by the executive.

Right of appeal to tribunal (s 5(2)(a))

Any action in which a right of appeal to a tribunal exists is excluded. A tribunal is not defined in the Act. They were considered outside the scope of PCA at the outset, because (a) their functions are quasi-judicial, not administrative, and (b) they are distinct from departments listed in Schedule 2 and exercise functions of their own. This was seen to conform with the underlying policy of the Act, that PCA was not to replace existing institutions or safeguards, but to supplement them by providing protection for the citizen in his/her dealings with the executive where otherwise they do not exist.

Legal remedy (s 5(2)(b))

Actions where a legal remedy exists are excluded, again reflecting the principle that PCA should not usurp the functions of existing institutions which provide protection for the citizen. (The proviso to the clause recognised the fact that there are few situations where there is ground for complaint of maladministration and where legal proceedings in some form or another cannot be instituted.)

Contractual or commercial transactions (Schedule 3, para 9)

The original reason for this exclusion was that PCA was intended to operate in the field of relationships between the Government and the governed. Commercial judgments are by nature discriminatory, so the justification ran, and so allowing the commercial judgments of departments to be open to examination by private interests while leaving those interests themselves free from investigation would amount to putting departments, and with them the taxpayer, at a disadvantage.

In its response to the fourth report of the select committee 1979–80, the Government repeated this argument in rejecting the Committee's conclusion that the continued exclusion of these matters would not be justified, and stated more generally that only these activities unique to Government should be subject to PCA. (The committee felt that all Government activities should be examinable unless there was a compelling argument otherwise.) ...

Exercise of extradition orders (Schedule 3, para 4)

In the exercise of extradition orders, the Secretary of State is acting in a quasi-judicial capacity as a final appellate authority. Adding, in effect, a further appeal – an investigation by PCA – would, the argument ran, be inappropriate and inconsistent with the Government's responsibility for compliance with international obligations.

Power of Secretary of State to intercept communications and withhold or withdraw passports when investigating crime (Schedule 3, para 5)

The exclusion of complaints relating to the above was justified because (a) the use of the power ought to be kept secret, and (b) its use must form part of criminal investigations which are not, in other respects, a matter for central government and thus outside PCA's scope.

Note

Most controversial has been the exclusion from the PCA's remit of contractual and commercial matters. The Government's justification for the exclusion, as appearing above, is based both on a theoretical contention that such matters are not in themselves governing activities, but only incidental to them, and also on the more practical ground that such scrutiny would place Government departments at a commercial disadvantage, compared to the private interests which would not be open to scrutiny in the same way. The exemption clearly excludes a potentially wide range of decisions from the ambit of the PCA, though as Seneviratne notes, it has in practice '... accounted for few rejections, perhaps because its scope has been limited by successive PCA's, who have decided that a service does not become commercial [merely] because a charge is made for it'.[11] The fourth report from the Select Committee on the PCA 1979 considered *inter alia* that the exclusion of commercial matters was unjustified.

Fourth Report from the Select Committee on the PCA, HC 593 (1979–80)

...

4   In his evidence the commissioner placed much emphasis on a point made by the Select Committee in 1978, namely that s5 of the Parliamentary Commissioner Act provided that the commissioner would not take up a case where a legal remedy was available, save in exceptional circumstances, and so if [the commercial exclusion were abolished] there would still be no danger of the commissioner being involved in disputes about the performance of contracts. He believed, as his predecessors had, that paragraph 9 was ' unnecessary and undesirable ... in addition to s5, and by its sweeping scope has had the effect of excluding many complaints which may have been found on investigation to be entirely justifiable'. What he was concerned about was 'the way in which a department conducted the administrative side of Government buying and selling', where there was considerable scope for maladministration that could not be brought before the courts. He cited the case of a small office cleaning company, which had as the mainstay of its business a contract with a Government department; when the contract came up for renewal the company was not invited to tender, and on making enquiries it was told that another Government department had communicated confidential information of a damaging nature about the

---

11   M Seneviratne, *Ombudsman in the Public Sector* (1994), p23.

company to the department with which it had held the contract. The commissioner told us that he could investigate a complaint about the communication of confidential information because that was an administrative matter, but he would not be able to look into whether the information was used to remove the company from the list of tenderers for the contract because that was a commercial matter excluded by paragraph 9 of the Schedule.

5   The commissioner also argued that the distinction between those forms of industrial assistance which he could investigate and those which he could not was illogical. As for the Government's contention that departments ought not to be subject to investigation of their commercial activities when other organisations were not so subject, the commissioner suggested that the Government disposed of such large amounts of money that its position was unique.

6   The Financial Secretary to the Treasury said in evidence that although the issue was finely balanced, the arguments for the exclusion of contractual and commercial matters from the Parliamentary Commissioner's jurisdiction remained valid. The Government's activities as a buyer of goods and services were quite different from those of its operations which were subject to the commissioner's scrutiny; they, by contrast, were 'of the very nature of Government'. It was the job of the Exchequer and Audit Department and the Public Accounts Committee, not the Parliamentary Commissioner, to ensure that the Government got value for its money. The Financial Secretary agreed that the loss of a Government contract could have serious consequences for a company but so could the loss of a contract with a firm in the private sector, and he suggested that if complaints from aggrieved would-be contractors were to be investigated the result would be frustration and a lot of wasted effort. He accepted that there would be considerable reason for disquiet if public purchasing policy were used to further a political objective such as an incomes policy, but he assured us that the present Government had no intention of using it in such a way. ...

8   We do not accept the Government's contention that only those activities which are unique to the function of government should be subject to review by the Parliamentary Commissioner; rather we believe that in principle all areas of government administration should be investigable by him unless in particular cases a compelling argument can be made out for their exclusion. Accordingly the claim that the Government's commercial activities should be exempt from examination because private contractors are exempt is in our view beside the point. The Government has a duty to administer its purchasing policies fairly and equitably, and if those policies are the subject of complaint then the complaints should be investigated; this is particularly important if any future Government were again to use the award of contracts as a political weapon. Section 12(3) of the Act would prevent the commissioner from questioning a *bona fide* commercial decision to purchase goods or services from one firm rather than another, or the legitimate exercise of a department's discretion to give selective assistance to one firm or one industry rather than another, but if decisions of this kind are taken with maladministration then it is right that they should be reviewed. It was suggested in evidence that the commissioner would not be able to decide whether maladministration had been committed, but we note the commissioner's view that that is the kind of judgment that he and his officers are making 'every day of the week.' In any case, a belief that the commissioner might have difficulty in making such a decision may be

thought to be poor ground for refusing him the right to try. It is true that any commercial maladministration by a department can be investigated by the Exchequer and Audit Department and censured by the Public Accounts Committee, but neither of these bodies is primarily concerned, as the Parliamentary Commissioner is, with any injustice a complainant might have suffered as a result. When the principle of this exclusion is applied to the field of local government the arguments in favour of it are, if anything, still weaker: that the Local Ombudsmen should be debarred from investigating complaints about the administration of schemes relating to concessionary fare-passes for old people and the allocation of market stalls seems to us little short of absurd. We are satisfied that ss5 and 12(3) of the Parliamentary Commissioner Act are sufficient on their own and that the further exemption from investigation conferred by paragraph 9 of Schedule 3 is not justified.

Notes

1   It is apparent that one of the main fears of the Committee in relation to the commercial exclusion was that the Government's immense public purchasing power could be used as a political weapon; for example, it could 'reward' business which were pursuing policies in line with Government recommendations (eg on wage levels) with lucrative contracts. The reassurance offered by the Government witnesses on this point seems weak: Nigel Lawson simply said that 'the present Government had no intention' of using their purchasing power in this way. This does not even amount to an undertaking; it also leaves wholly unanswered the questions of how a change of Government intention could be detected, still less remedied, if the PCA cannot investigate.

2   The committee also complained about the exclusion of public personnel matters, which, as Mary Seneviratne notes[12] are within the remit of both MPs in their individual capacity and of ombudsmen in other countries. The Government does have a clear argument of principle here, namely that it would be unfair to give public servants special protection which is denied to other employees. The PCA's reply, that the Government, as the country's largest employer should set a good example may seem unpersuasive: it could be argued that the Government could set its example simply by being a scrupulously fair and thoughtful employer, not by giving its employees special protection which is unavailable to others.

ACCESS TO THE PCA

Complaints cannot be made directly to the PCA by a Member of Parliament. Under s5(1) of the 1967 Act, the PCA may investigate a written complaint made by a member of the public to a Member of Parliament, if the complaint is referred by the MP and both he and the complainant agree to investigation by the PCA. This 'filter' role played by MPs has been the subject of much controversy. It is interesting to note, first of all, the views of MPs themselves on the problems with the present system, and the justifications for it.

---

12   *Ibid.*

First Report from the Select Committee on the PCA, HC 33 II (1993–94)

Summary of objections to the MP filter

65 Objections to the MP filter can be summarised as follows:

(1) The public should have direct access to the commissioner as a matter of right.

(2) The filter is an anomaly, almost unknown in other ombudsman systems. No such requirement exists, for instance, in the case of the Health Service Commissioner.

(3) Individuals with complaints may be unwilling to approach an MP, while desiring the ombudsman's assistance.

(4) The filter means that the likelihood of individuals' cases being referred to the commissioner will largely depend on the views and practice of the particular constituency MP. Some look with more favour on the Office of the commissioner than others.

(5) The filter acts as an obstacle to the commissioner effectively promoting his services.

(6) The filter creates an unnecessary bureaucratic barrier between the complainant and the commissioner involving considerable paperwork for MPs and their offices.

The unheard complaint

'... in the absence of a reliable crystal ball, predictions about the consequences of removing the MP filter amount to little more than guesswork' [Evidence, p144].

66 The central thesis of all arguments against the MP filter is that it is denying the public access to the commissioner and the opportunity for him to investigate appropriate complaints. Various statistical arguments are adduced to support this contention. One is a comparison of the number of complaints received by the Parliamentary Ombudsman with the number received by foreign ombudsmen. In Australia in 1991–92, for instance, the Commonwealth Ombudsman received 17,153 oral and written complaints. This compares with the UK's Parliamentary Ombudsman receiving 945 complaints in 1992 [*Fifth Report of the PCA*, session 1992–93, HC 569, para 10]. It is, however, difficult to compare ombudsman systems in this regard. Jurisdictions vary widely as does the role of Members of Parliament. The greater number of complaints can in certain circumstances, for instance, be attributed to the fact that the ombudsman 'is often the aggrieved person's first and only port of call outside of the organisation concerned' [Gregory and Pearson, *The Parliamentary Ombudsman After Twenty-Five Years*, p473].

67 A second statistical argument used to support the theory of a mass of unheard complaints is the experience of the Local Government Ombudsman after the introduction of direct access in May 1988. Until then members of the public had to approach the Local Government Ombudsman through the 'Councillor Filter'. Since May 1988 the public had the choice of either approaching the Local Government Ombudsman directly or through a Councillor. The memorandum from Dr David Yardley, Chairman of the Commission for Local Administration in England, charts the subsequent growth in the number of complaints:

'The average annual increase each year between the time the Commission was established in 1974 and the financial year 1988–89 had been 9 per cent. In 1988–89 the increase was 44 per cent, and this high level continued in 1989–90 when the increase was 24 per cent. In 1990–91 the increase returned to a more usual figure of 5 per cent... In the first year following the introduction of direct access 72 per cent of complaints were sent direct to the Local Government Ombudsman, and this figure had increased to 92 per cent by the end of 1992–93.' ...

71   It is difficult to quantify the number of complaints never heard because the complainants do not approach an MP. We do, however, have more information on how Members use the MP filter. The numbers of MPs referring cases in the last five years are as follows:

   1988: 359

   1989: 361

   1990: 371

   1991: 432

   1992: 460

We are pleased to note the recent increase in the number of Members referring cases to the ombudsman. This suggests that the efforts of the ombudsman to publicise his work among Members are bearing fruit. It may also relate to the growing awareness of the ombudsman among new MPs during the course of a Parliament.

72   Mr Reid pointed out that 'if an individual Hon Member decides not to use my services he is in effect denying potential redress to his constituents'. It is undoubtedly the case that the operation of the filter depends to a great degree on the activity of the Member. Although it is possible for a complaint to be referred from a Member other than the constituency MP, the results of the Questionnaire suggest that this rarely happens and that many Members would be extremely reluctant to refer a non-constituency complaint. Moreover, a majority of MPs rarely if ever suggest to the complainant a reference to the ombudsman and in our survey 45% of Members reported that they seldom or never referred complaints to the ombudsman. Yet the exercise of individual discretion by the Member on whether or not to refer a complaint is precisely the function of the filter. ... Although the evidence suggests that the use of the filter is variable, it does not necessarily suggest significant numbers of those who approach their MP are dissatisfied or denied appropriate redress. It does suggest, however, that those who stress the importance of retaining the filter need also to give attention to the way in which the filter is working and how its operation may be improved.

Direct access

73   We have seen that many propose the introduction of direct access as a means of ensuring that 'unheard complaints' reach the ombudsman. Concern was expressed by the Centre for Ombudsman Studies and by some Members at the effect this would have on the workload of the ombudsman's office. The Centre warned that 'if a system of direct access were to result in a high ratio of 'inappropriate' to 'appropriate' cases reaching the PCA, with very large numbers of the former type of complaint occupying the attention of the Office. amending the 1967 Act in this sense might prove to be one of those legislative changes, not unknown in recent years, which quickly comes to be a matter of considerable regret.

74   We believe that the abolition of the MP filter would result not only in unheard complaints being heard for the first time but in some complaints reaching the ombudsman's office which would previously have been more appropriately resolved by a Member. The effect of this will be either to increase unnecessarily the resources allocated to the ombudsman's office or

to cause a decline in the thoroughness of the ombudsman's investigations as his office struggles to cope with the increased volume of work. ...

75 The most important issue in deciding the fate of the MP filter remains a constitutional one. Will direct access undermine the constitutional role of Members in taking up the grievances of their constituents? Should the Parliamentary Ombudsman remain an 'instrument' of MPs or should access to his services now be seen as a right of the citizen? It is clear that the majority of Members appreciate the filter. We continue to believe that the Member of Parliament has an irreplaceable role in pursuing complaints of the public against the executive, notwithstanding the development within public bodies of an array of direct access complaint and redress mechanisms for the citizen. We note that since the introduction of direct access in the case of the Local Government Ombudsman the proportion of cases referred by Councillors has declined from 28% in the first year of direct access to 8% by the end of 1992–93. Moreover only approximately 5% of cases are referred by MPs to the Health Service Ombudsman where direct access applies. Direct access, it appears, may well result in fewer MPs being involved in the ombudsman's work.

76 The work of the Parliamentary Ombudsman, acting at the behest of MPs and reporting to them the details of his investigations, has a vital role in equipping the Member for the tasks of Parliament. The knowledge of the details of and problems in administration has an important part in any effective scrutiny of the executive. The publication of anonymised reports can never be a genuine substitute for direct involvement in the case which the Member has referred. Direct access will result in the denial to Members of expertise in the problems facing their constituents as they come into contact with the executive. This is to impoverish parliamentary, and thus political, life. We recommend that the MP filter be retained but coupled with concerted attention to the means whereby access to the ombudsman can be strengthened and enlarged.

77 We consider that the retention of the MP filter in its current form is preferable to the 'compromise proposal' of a right of appeal from MPs to the ombudsman in certain circumstances. This amounts to an attempt to retain the 'filtering' advantages of the Member while denying him the power of veto over a further reference to the ombudsman should the complainant remain dissatisfied. We consider that this merely places the ombudsman in the invidious position of acting as a court of appeal against the decisions of Members.

Notes

1 There is wide variation among MPs as to the number of complaints they submit each year to the PCA. In 1986, for example, 40% of MPs submitted no complaints. Therefore the availability of the PCA service may depend on where a complainant happens to live. For general discussion of the relationship between the PCA and MPs, see G Drewry and C Harlow, 'A Cutting Edge? The Parliamentary Commissioner and MPs' (1990).[13]

2 As appears from the above, the primary concern of MPs about removing their screening function is the fear that allowing direct access would undermine their constitutional role as defenders of the citizen against the

---

13   53 MLR 745.

executive. Apart from any symbolic undermining, the concrete threat, according to the Select Committee, appears to boil down to the fear that 'Direct access will result in the denial to Members of expertise in the problems facing their constituents ... This is to impoverish parliamentary, and thus, political life'. A number of points may be made in response to this. First of all, the argument, even if sound, seems rather self-serving. One may fairly predict that most constituents would consider that gaining a more efficient system for remedying their grievances easily outweighed this rather speculative harm. Secondly, the argument seems flawed in its own terms: it fails to recognise that direct access by the public to the PCA need not necessarily cause any decrease at all in either the involvement of MPs in the matters raised or in the flow of information to them, the second of which is certainly vital to their role as scrutinisers of the executive. The Committee says, 'the publication of anonymised reports can never be a genuine substitute for direct involvement in the case which the Member has referred'. But this is not the only alternative to the present system. If direct access were introduced, the continued involvement and knowledgability of MPs could be ensured very simply; the PCA would simply copy the appropriate MP in with any complaint received, and with news of the investigation of the complaint (if s/he decided to take it up) as it proceeded. It does not seem clear that MPs' constitutional role necessarily demands that they should have to make the *decision* as to whether a complaint should be investigated, particularly as it may reasonably be feared that their political allegiance could distort their judgement in sensitive cases. Thirdly, MPs would, of course, continue to receive numerous complaints on a variety of matters, many of which would be outside the PCA's jurisdiction.

3   Some amelioration of this system of making complaints has occurred; since 1978, where the PCA receives a complaint directly from a member of the public, the complainant's MP will be contacted and, if he or she is in agreement, the PCA will investigate. This system does not however encourage citizens to complain directly to the PCA and due to his low profile, many will in any event be unaware that complaint is possible. In New South Wales, where complaints can come directly from the public or from MPs, the vast majority of complaints come directly from the public. The British system, as JUSTICE pointed out in 1979,[14] weakens the PCA because he is unable to publicise himself as available directly to receive complaints when he is not so available.

4   The number of complaints may suggest to the general public that most administrative decisions are acceptable; thus the PCA may play a more important role in legitimising such decisions than in providing a means of redress for the victims of maladministration. These issues are considered below.

---

14   JUSTICE report, HC 593 (1979–80).

Appendix to the Minutes of Evidence Taken before the Select Committee on the PCA, HC 64 (1993–94), vol II

3.7 The MP filter

The number of complaints received by the Parliamentary Ombudsman is far lower than envisaged when the Parliamentary Ombudsman was introduced. The level is still more surprising when compared with the number of complaints received by ombudsmen in other countries. For example figures for 1991 show:

Danish ombudsman	5 million population:	2,000 complaints
Swedish ombudsman	8 million population:	4,000 complaints
British ombudsman	55 million population:	766 complaints

The jurisdiction and constitutional position of the Scandinavian ombudsmen is very different from the Parliamentary Ombudsman. Even so, the number of complaints received by the ombudsmen in this country still appears low. ...

When the introduction of the Parliamentary Ombudsman was first discussed in Parliament, MPs expressed concern that their role in dealing with constituents' grievances would be superseded by this new office and that this would leave them out of touch with their constituency and the problems facing it. They were concerned about their role as 'constituency ombudsmen'. For this reason, the MP filter, originally proposed by JUSTICE as a temporary measure lasting for about five years, was included in the Act. Twenty six years later, it is still in place.

The Parliamentary Ombudsman is the only ombudsman to whom consumers are denied direct access in the UK. There is no filter of complaints to either the Health Service Ombudsmen or Northern Ireland Ombudsman. The idea of an MP filter is almost unique. With the exception of the *mediateur* in France, we know of no other ombudsman in the world in which an MP filter operates.

The low level of complaints received by the Parliamentary Ombudsman is, by definition, determined by the low number of referrals MPs make to him. The Parliamentary Ombudsman's annual reports illustrate that referrals from MPs to the Parliamentary Ombudsman fluctuate somewhat from year to year (see appendix 2). The referral range ranges from a low of only 548 (in 1971) to a relative high of 1,259 (in 1978). These referral rates seem very low given estimates that MPs receive 250,000–300,000 complaints of all kinds each year. ...

From available data it appears that MPs very rarely take the initiative of suggesting to a complainant that his or her complaint be referred to the Parliamentary Ombudsman. There is evidence that some MPs have actually discouraged complainants from seeking to have their complaints referred to the ombudsman. In 1977 and 1978, 1,066 and 443 direct complaints respectively, came in from the public. Sir Idwal Pugh, then Parliamentary Ombudsman, referred these complaints back to the complainant for permission to submit to the relevant MP. Only 1 in 14 of these complaints were subsequently resubmitted by MPs to the ombudsman.

These figures demonstrate that it is extremely difficult for consumers to gain access to the Parliamentary Ombudsman. Complainants must know of the existence of the office. Secondly, they must know the process for persuading the MP to refer the complaint – a letter to an MP requesting that he or she refers the complaint to the ombudsman. Thirdly, they must persuade the MP that the complaint should be investigated by the Parliamentary Ombudsman.

Very little research or information is publicly available about how the MP filter works. The limited information which is available indicates that, from the consumer's perspective, the MP filter operates inequitably. A complainant's chance of having a grievance dealt with by the Parliamentary Ombudsman seems to depend on the approach of individual MPs.

3.8 MPs referrals to the Parliamentary Ombudsman (1986 figures):

263 MPs	(40.5%)	referred no complaints
200 MPs	(51.7%)	referred one complaint
102 MPs	(26.4%)	referred two complaints
43 MPs	(11. I%)	referred three complaints
30 MPs	(7.8%)	referred four complaints
7 MPs	(1.8%)	referred five complaints
4 MPs		referred six complaints
1 MP		referred seven complaints

These figures show that in one year, as many as four out of 10 MPs refer a single complaint to the Parliamentary Ombudsman; 85 MPs were responsible for 315 (44%) of referrals.

The existing system puts the interest of MPs above the interests of individual consumers with a grievance. If the MP filter does serve the interests of MPs, it does so at the expense of individual consumers and citizens for whom it constitutes a barrier to accessing a very important system of redress.

The emphasis should be on making the Parliamentary Ombudsman as accessible as reasonably possible. The complete removal of the MP filter is one way to do this. The Select Committee may resolve that the Parliamentary Ombudsman should continue primarily to serve the interests of MPs, even if that risks making the ombudsman less accessible. If so, the Select Committee should consider the compromise advocated by Sir Cecil Clothier which was that the individual consumer should first ask his or her MP to take up their grievance with the department or agency concerned. If they are dissatisfied with the response, he or she may then refer the complaint directly to the ombudsman.

In effect, the Parliamentary Ombudsman would require individuals to exhaust any complaints procedure provided by the relevant department or agency, and the services of their MP, in his or her role as complaints chaser.

The MP could, of course, refer the consumer's grievance to the Parliamentary Ombudsman. If the consumer is still dissatisfied, and their MP has not referred the grievance to the ombudsman, it seems proper to allow the consumer to do so on their own initiative. Such a system would not undermine the role of the MP as grievance-chaser. If anything, it would strengthen it.

Note

It seems clear that increasing knowledge by both MPs and consumers of the existence and worth of the PCA is the key to increasing his practical accessibility to the public. It appears that the PCA and Government departments covered by his work are making much greater efforts in this respect.

First Report of the Select Committee on the PCA, HC 112 (1994–95),

8   In its report on 'The Powers, Work and Jurisdiction of the Ombudsman' the Committee recommended the retention of the MP filter 'coupled with concerted attention to the means whereby access to the ombudsman can be strengthened and enlarged' [*First Report of the Select Committee on the PCA*; session 1993–94, HC 33, para 76]. This year Mr Reid sent a copy of his annual report to every Member of Parliament. We welcome this concern to remind

Members of his work. We were told that the number of Members who referred cases in 1993 was, at 429, 31 fewer than in 1992. In this Parliament, however, only 82 Members have never referred a case to the Parliamentary Commissioner and some of those have referred cases to him as Health Service Commissioner. We are encouraged by this evidence that the vast majority of Members both know of the commissioner's work and find it valuable. We would encourage further initiatives to contact both Members and their secretaries and research assistants with information. The commissioner also produced a new leaflet with, for the first time, detachable *pro formas* which complainants could use to contact their MP. Leaflets were sent to Citizens Advice Bureaux, public libraries, solicitors' and accountants' practices and many other organisations.

9   Perhaps most important of all is the publicising of the commissioner by the bodies he investigates. In its report on the Parliamentary Commissioner's annual report for 1992 the Committee made clear its expectation 'that any departmental literature on complaints should make clear the possibility of recourse to the ombudsman, as an independent mechanism for complaint' [*Second Report of the Select Committee on the PCA*, session 1993–94, HC 64, para 6]. In evidence on the 1993 report it became clear that the literature of some departments still leaves much to be desired. We were pleased to be told that the Inland Revenue had responded to previous criticisms from this committee [*First Report of the Select Committee on the PCA*; session 1992–93, HC 387, para 17] by including mention of the Parliamentary Commissioner in all relevant literature. MAFF had, since the middle of 1993, ensured that all complaints documents drew attention 'to the possibility of complaint to the commissioner' [Q197]. The Lord Chancellor's Department has introduced a Courts Charter, however, which makes no mention of the existence of the ombudsman. Sir Thomas Legg, Permanent Secretary to the Lord Chancellor, accepted that this was unsatisfactory and undertook to remedy this deficiency when the Court Service Agency was launched in April 1995 [Q366].

Note

One measure recently introduced aims to raise the level of awareness amongst civil servants of the PCA's work. A booklet called *The Ombudsman in Your Files*, which explains the role and procedures of the PCA, was published in December 1995 by the Cabinet Office. In his latest report,[15] the PCA 'welcome[s] this measure, though Mr Reid notes that the Cabinet Office did not publicise the booklet'.

ACCOUNTABILITY OF THE PCA

Parliamentary accountability

Appendix to the Minutes of Evidence Taken before the Select Committee on the PCA, HC 64 (1993–94), vol II

3.9 Accountability of the ombudsmen

One advantage of the present schemes is that the ombudsmen are accountable to

---

15   *Annual Report for 1995*, Cm 296, p2, para 5.

the Select Committee for their working practices. This is clearly a powerful tool. However, much of the public accountability of the ombudsmen depends on how far the Select Committee will raise issues with the ombudsmen which affect consumers. While the number of cases investigated and the time taken to complete investigations is assessed, these are 'throughput measures'. Such efficiency measures have little meaning for consumers unless effectiveness is also included in the equation.

Therefore the accountability of the ombudsman services would be improved if more information about service-targets and standards were made publicly available. The Parliamentary Ombudsman and the Health Services Ombudsman should set service targets or standards and report their performance against them. In addition to the information they already provide, they each should account for their performance in the following areas:

(i) Consumer satisfaction: how satisfied are complainants with the way the ombudsman handled their complaint?

(ii) Efficiency: how long it takes the ombudsmen to get Government departments and agencies to respond to requests for information and how long does it take for the ombudsman to complete an investigation?

(iii) Effectiveness: to what extent Government departments and agencies comply with the ombudsmen's recommendations?

(iv) Complaints not investigated: details about the number and types of complaints which are not investigated, why they were not investigated, and what alternative dispute resolution process was available to the complainant, if any?

The ombudsmen should consider producing a Citizen's Charter style document or 'Standards Statement', which would contain many of the above features.

Note

As well as being accountable to Parliament, the decisions of the PCA have been found to be subject to judicial review; the relevant decision is discussed below by Norman Marsh.

Judicial control

N Marsh, 'The Extent and Depth of Judicial Review of the Decisions of the Parliamentary Commissioner for Administration' (1994) *Public Law* 347–50

In *Parliamentary Commissioner for Administration, ex p Dyer* [[1994] 1 WLR 621, DC] ... the High Court declined to grant judicial review of the report of the Parliamentary Commissioner. [The applicant for judicial review, Miss Dyer, had had her previous complaint about the DSS dealt with by the PCA; Miss Dyer had received an apology and a £500 *ex gratia* payment to cover her expenses, an outcome which the PCA had described as 'satisfactory'.] The particular interest of the case lies in the legal issues which Simon Brown LJ discussed in connection with the three grounds on which Miss Dyer challenged the Parliamentary Commissioner's report. These grounds were: first, that the commissioner had not dealt with some of Miss Dyer's complaints; secondly, that although the commissioner had sent a copy of his draft report to the Department of Social Security, thus enabling them to point out any inaccuracies, no such copy was similarly sent to Miss Dyer; thirdly, that the commissioner had refused to reopen the case to deal with her complaints after he had, in accordance with s10 of the Parliamentary Commissioner Act 1967, sent a copy of his report to the Member of Parliament by whom the request for an investigation had originally been made.

Counsel for the Parliamentary Commissioner ... argue[d] that the courts' supervisory jurisdiction by way of judicial review was not applicable to the activities of the Parliamentary Commissioner. ... This argument was 'unhesitatingly' rejected by Simon Brown LJ who ... also rejected the less far-reaching proposition of counsel for the Parliamentary Commissioner to the effect that, even if as a general principle the functioning of the Parliamentary Commissioner is subject to judicial review, the courts were restricted in their review of the exercise of discretion conferred upon the commissioner by legislation. He distinguished the discretions exercised by the Parliamentary Commissioner, which were those relevant to the present case, and decisions regarding the formulation and implementation of national economic policy and relating to matters 'depending essentially on political judgment' which, as Lord Bridge of Harwich said in *Secretary of State for the Environment, ex p Hammersmith and Fulham London Borough Council* [[1991] AC 521 at 597] are not susceptible to review by the courts, 'short of the extremes of bad faith, improper motive or manifest absurdity'.

Nevertheless, Simon Brown LJ emphasised that the court was not 'readily to be persuaded to interfere with the exercise of the commissioner's discretion'. Indeed he went so far as to 'wonder whether in reality the end result is much different from that arrived at' [[1994] 1 WLR 621, 626] by Lord Bridge of Harwich in the *ex p Hammersmith and Fulham* case cited above. By this standard he had no difficulty in regarding the first of Miss Dyer's complaints, namely that the Parliamentary Commissioner had not dealt with all the matters of which she had complained, as unfounded. He held that 'the commissioner was entitled in the exercise of his discretion to limit the scope of his investigation, to be selective as to just which of Miss Dyer's many detailed complaints he addressed, to identify certain broad categories of complaint ... and investigate only those. Inevitably such an approach carried the risk that some of the problems which Miss Dyer complained of having experienced with the local office would continue ... But investigation should not be expected to solve all problems for all time'[*ibid* 628].

... The way in which Simon Brown LJ dealt with Miss Dyer's complaint that the Parliamentary Commissioner's draft report was sent to the Department of Social Security for comment on the facts but not to her is much less satisfying. He began by stating that the commissioner's practice had existed for 25 years and was 'known to have been acquiesced in by the select committee [of Parliament]'. However, it may be doubted whether the complainants prompting those investigations over those 25 years in all cases knew of the practice, and in any event the relevant question in the instant case was whether it was 'fair' to Miss Dyer, having in mind the classic test of Lord Loreburn LC in *Board of Education v Rice* [(1911) AC 179 at 182]:

> They (ie 'departments or officers of state [with] the duty of deciding or determining questions or various kinds') can obtain information in any way they think best, *always giving a fair opportunity to those who are parties in the controversy for correcting or contradicting any relevant statement prejudicial to their view* [emphasis added].

Simon Brown LJ, however, took the view that the practice of issuing his report in draft to give an opportunity for inaccuracies to be corrected was only relevant for the Government department in question, because 'it is the department rather than the complainant who may subsequently be called upon to justify its actions before the select committee and, if it is shown the draft report and does not point out any inaccuracy, it will then be unable to dispute the facts stated in it'[(1994) 1 WLR 621, 629].

This ignores the possibility that there may be inaccuracies of fact in the draft report which relate to the case made by the complainant. The impression given by this part of Simon Brown LJ's judgment is almost that the underlying purpose of the Parliamentary Commissioner Act is to give Government departments a better opportunity to refute accusations of maladministration made against them. 'It should be borne in mind', he says, 'that it is the department and not her [ie Miss Dyer] which is being investigated and which is liable to face public criticism for its acts'. Surely, what has to be borne in mind is that the purpose of the promoters of the Parliamentary Commissioner Act 1967 was to provide a new kind of remedy for the citizen against governmental maladministration, to which a fair procedure for the Governmental department is only a corollary, although a necessary one. ...

The other alleged justification given by the Parliamentary Commissioner (and, like the first, apparently accepted by Simon Brown LJ) was that s11(3) of the 1967 Act 'affords the department an opportunity to give notice in writing to the commissioner of any document or information the disclosure of which, in the opinion of the relevant minister, would be prejudicial to the safety of the state or otherwise contrary to the public interest'. As, according to the same subsection, 'nothing in the Act shall be considered as authorising or requiring the commissioner or any officer of the commissioner to communicate to any person or for any purpose any document or information specified in the notice, or any document of a class so specified', the draft report cannot be shown to the complainant before it has been 'vetted' in this respect by this department. But would it be an utterly unreasonable addition to the present practice to enable the complainant to see the report in draft after the security vetting has taken place?

THE PCA AND THE CITIZEN'S CHARTER

One of the more important aspects of the PCA's work is his role of scrutinising adherence by Government departments and agencies to the standards set out in the Citizen's Charter 1991.[16] The charter sets out performance standards for the delivery of a variety of public services and thus provides, *inter alia*, a yardstick by which the PCA can determine whether a given department's performance falls short of what may reasonably be expected. The PCA's role in relation to the charter is considered in the following select committee report.

First Report of the Select Committee on the PCA, HC 112 (1994–95)
Maladministration and redress
The principles of redress

4 The Citizen's Charter commits itself to an improvement in redress – 'At the very least, the citizen is entitled to a good explanation, or an apology. He or she should be told why the train is late, or why the doctor could not keep the appointment. There should be a well-publicised and readily available complaints procedure. If there is a serious problem, it should be put right.

---

16 Cm 1599.

And lessons must be learnt so that mistakes are not repeated. Nobody wants to see money diverted from service improvement into large-scale compensation for indifferent services. But the Government intends to introduce new forms of redress where these can be made to stimulate rather than distract from efficiency' [Citizen's Charter 1991, p5].

5   We are not aware of any concerted attempt, however, when the Citizen's Charter was published, either to revise the guidance to departments on the granting of compensation or to enunciate a philosophy of redress. We comment in detail on sections of the current guidance throughout this report. To begin with our conclusion, *current guidance on redress in cases of maladministration is out-dated, directed more towards the protection of the public purse than to the rights of the complainant. We welcome the announcement by Mr Nelson MP that guidance on redress and on ex gratia compensation is under review [QQ298–299]. We expect the conclusions of this report to be taken into account.*

6   Guidance to departments and agencies on the granting of redress concentrates on the question of *ex gratia* financial compensation. There is no unifying principle of redress. Any statements of principle are usually of a negative type:

'... departments should be guided by the general principle that the Government does not as a rule reimburse people's costs in establishing their claims for grants, subsidies, allowances, etc' [DAO (GEN) 15/92 para 15].

'Departments should remember that by definition the complainant has no legal right to any compensation at all' [DAO (GEN) 15/92 para 24 – see also para 20 for an example of such guidance].

7   There is a need for a clear principle to inform Government consideration of redress. We cannot improve on that stated by the ombudsman at the outset of the inquiry:

'... *the person who has suffered injustice as a result of maladministration should be back in the same position as he or she would have been had things gone right in the first place' [Q8].*

8   We were pleased to note the agreement of other witnesses with this principle. Sir Michael Partridge considered that his department's main aim was 'to put right the complainant's loss' [Q36]. The National Consumer Council supported the ombudsman's statement of principle as did Mr Nelson and Mr Hunt. *We recommend that this principle be formally incorporated into future guidance on the granting of redress in cases of maladministration.*

9   Departments and agencies have a duty to grant redress when their maladministration has resulted in injustice to the citizen. We have in the past come across cases where the department is unwilling to admit that 'maladministration' has occurred. This results in a refusal to grant appropriate redress. Similarly, the ombudsman criticised the Inland Revenue for too restrictive an interpretation of what constitutes 'serious or persistent' error. ...

24   ... The evidence suggests that thinking on redress remains far too Treasury-dominated. We believe that the Charter Unit must take on a far more active role in monitoring redress to ensure consistency of practice. The unacceptable variations in practice, revealed in our evidence, point to the failure of the Treasury to promote a positive and consistent ethic of redress within the Civil Service.

25   *We recommend that a 'Redress Team' be established within the Charter Unit to monitor and advise on the granting of redress within departments and agencies.*

There would clearly need to be Treasury representation on such a team, although we do not believe that such representation should account for more than 50% of its membership. Such a body would be able to advise on improvements in charter standards and conduct selective and specific audits of departmental practice. On occasions, to be specified below, departments and agencies would be obliged to refer cases to the Redress Team for a decision as to whether compensation is justifiable and, if so, at what amount. On other occasions there would be an obligation merely to consult on the appropriate amount of compensation, the final decision remaining with the department. We envisage all departments taking advantage of the expertise and overview enjoyed by the Redress Team, being willing to consult on difficult cases. We consider the establishment of such a team combines the advantage of a consistent approach to redress throughout the Civil Service with the decision-making on particular cases taking place as close as possible to the point at which the services were delivered.

26   Government Accounting warns departments to 'avoid the codification of rules (or the definition of precedents) in forms which, over a period of time, might come to be regarded as applicable to cases removed from the original justification. An unduly liberal regime of compensation would impose an administrative burden on departments and involve expenditure which would be unlikely to be adequately reciprocated by debtors to the Crown. Departments needing to distribute codified internal guidance on *ex gratia* payments, in order to permit a measure of delegated authority to local staff, should design it to be exclusive to closely defined cases'. Decisions on *ex gratia* cases should be based 'on the facts of cases' [Government Accounting para 36.3.4].

27   Despite this guidance there are schemes in place which grant *ex gratia* payments on a codified basis. The Department of Social Security operates a compensation scheme in cases of delayed payment modelled on the statutory scheme of the Inland Revenue. In the case of new claims for benefit, the delay must be of more than six months plus the relevant target clearance time subject to a maximum of 12 months. In the case of current benefits the delay must be of more than three months. These periods were recently reduced as a result of the recommendations of the ombudsman in his report on delays in the handling of disability living allowance. If the department is significantly at fault, no attempt is made to distinguish between those periods in the delay in which the department was at fault and delay attributable to other factors. Sir Michael Partridge considered this 'a simple rule of thumb. It is easy to apply. It is arguably generous but I think it gives quick compensation to people. There are always swings and roundabouts in a broad-brush scheme like that' [Q37].

28   We were assured by Mr Martin, Second Treasury Officer of Accounts, that 'the new ... agreement of the complainant to a proposed amount does not in any sense remove the department's obligation to re-consider the redress at the suggestion of the ombudsman'. The ombudsman is often in a better position to know whether the complainant is being short-changed than the complainant himself, who might never before have had such dealings with a department of state. Similarly, advice from the Redress Team should not overrule the ombudsman's views. Instead, we expect the Redress Team to be informed of any occasion when the ombudsman questions the fairness of compensation proposed by a department and agreed by the Team.

Complaints adjudicators

61   A recent development in the consideration of complaints and the offering of redress is the appointment of complaints adjudicators within Government departments and agencies. The Inland Revenue appointed a 'Revenue Adjudicator', Mrs Elizabeth Filkin, who recently published her first annual report, for the year 1993–94. The aim of such adjudicators is to provide a more impartial element to the internal complaints mechanism. In its third report of session 1993–94 the Committee noted the views of Mrs Strachan, Chairman of HM Customs and Excise, that 'if we could introduce some more independent element into our complaints handling that would be better' [Third Report of the Select Committee on the PCA, session 1993–94, HC 34S, para 19]. Customs and Excise have since decided to ask Mrs Filkin also to act as Adjudicator for Customs and Excise complaints. We were pleased to note the agreement of the Government with past recommendations of the Committee on the prerequisites of any complaints adjudicator system.

62   Mr Hunt welcomed the introduction of independent adjudicators, believing that the Revenue Adjudicator's Office would be a 'model for other departments and agencies of even how a difficult and rather complex department like the Revenue ... can be handled without the necessity of referring them to Mr Reid' [Q356]. We have previously encouraged other departments and agencies with extensive contacts with the public to consider the establishment of such adjudicators. We acknowledge that the Revenue Adjudicator would provide an excellent model for other adjudicator schemes to imitate. *We do, however, also see the need for clear central guidance from the Redress Team as to the essentials of any adjudicator scheme.* Our previous recommendations were designed to protect the rights of the public to learn of and approach the ombudsman. There are other issues of impartiality, investigative powers and procedure which need to be addressed. It would be unacceptable for there to be no policing of the term 'complaints adjudicator'. The public should be able to make certain assumptions about the way their complaint is to be handled when they come across the phrase.

63   We have already come across some worrying inconsistencies. Companies House has also decided to appoint a complaints adjudicator. We welcome this initiative given the many thousands of complaints and queries which have arisen since the introduction of late filing penalties. In examining the terms of reference of the complaints adjudicator for Companies House we were surprised to note the stipulation that the adjudicator should not inform the complainant directly of his or her findings but rather communicate them in confidence to Companies House for the agency's consideration. This practice contrasts with that of the Revenue Adjudicator who informs the complainant directly of her findings. The explanation given for this practice was that the Companies House Adjudicator was unfamiliar with the Treasury/OPSS guidance on compensation and *ex gratia* payments. It is in our view important that an adjudicator should be familiar with this guidance. It does not warrant the censorship of his findings by such a restrictive requirement being included in terms of reference.

Note

The Government's response to this report was published by the Select Committee on 15 March 1995;[17] Mr Reid's views on the Government's response appear below.

Parliamentary Commissioner for Administration, *Annual Report for 1995*, Cm 296, pp1–2

2   In my report for 1994 I referred to the outcome of the thematic inquiry by the Select Committee on the Parliamentary Commissioner for Administration into the practice of redress among Government departments. Their report, entitled 'Maladministration and Redress', was published on 11 January 1995. On 15 March 1995 the Select Committee published the Government's response [SC: Second Special Report 1994–95, HC 316] which largely accepted the Select Committee's recommendations. In particular, the Government accepted that the Treasury guidance on redress was out-dated and confirmed that it was being revised; agreed that departments and agencies which provide services to the public should produce internal written guidance on the consideration of redress in maladministration cases; affirmed the principle that departments and agencies should seek to identify all those affected by maladministration and offer appropriate redress; accepted that departments and agencies should have systems in place to prevent the recurrence of administrative failings; acknowledged the desirability of greater consistency among departments in the granting of redress, including, where appropriate, rates of interest; and accepted that financial compensation for worry and distress should be available in exceptional cases. I noted with approval that, by the end of the year, both the Inland Revenue and the Department of Social Security were reviewing their internal guidance on the consideration of redress, and that departments were being consulted on the proposed revision of Treasury guidance on redress in maladministration cases.

3   Another element of the Government response was its agreement 'that staff instructions should emphasise that, where mistakes have been made, the priority of the organisation will be to avoid a "blame culture"; but instead to encourage the ready admission of mistakes, the provision of swift and effective redress and steps to ensure that a similar failure does not recur'. I welcome that approach. It encourages prompt, polite and positive handling of complaints at local level. It avoids fostering the attitude that a complaint is a personal affront. It shows that a complaint provides an opportunity to improve standards of service, for the complainant and other members of the public, and for those who deliver a service 'to perceive and know what things they ought to do and ... have grace and power faithfully to fulfil the same'.

4   A further aspect of the Select Committee's inquiry which I regard as being of particular importance is the emphasis on the procedural changes and improvements which may be stimulated by complaints and by their investigation, whether internally or by me. Redress for the individual complainant is important, but measures to avoid or reduce the recurrence of maladministration are to my mind of equal significance. Many of the cases listed in appendix A to this report resulted in better practices, procedures or internal guidance, whether nationally or locally. It is my hope that all departments, agencies and other bodies within my jurisdiction should be aware of the shortcomings which my reports identify, so that they may strive to avoid similar failings in their own dealings with the public. I have therefore been glad that the Office of Public Service (formerly the Office of Public Service and Science) have circulated summaries of the reports of·

---

17   *Second Special Report of the Select Committee on the PCA*, HC 316 (1994–95).

selected cases which I have published, together with notes drawing civil servants' attention to the lessons of general application which can be learned from them. That practice implements one of the recommendations of the report of the Select Committee on their inquiry into the work of the Northern Ireland Parliamentary Commissioner and myself published in November 1993.

Notes

1 The charter itself makes only brief references to the ombudsmen, and the recognition that the charter had significant implications for them came from the PCA, not the Government. Some commentators have perceived, in certain aspects of the charter scheme, a threat to the position of the ombudsmen. The PCA Select Committee considered that the charter scheme of putting in place lay adjudicators, who would provide an external avenue for complainants who were dissatisfied with the internal handling of their complaint, 'could undermine the ombudsman's role'.[18] The committee also feared that 'the sheer variety of complaint mechanisms [put in place by the charter] could divert attention' away from the PCA.[19]

2 In general, however, it is thought that the philosophy behind the Citizen's Charter should assist the ombudsmen in their work, both in terms of standard setting and in generating a culture in which consumer rights are elevated above administrative convenience. In addition, as Seneviratne points out,[20] the emphasis in the Charter on effective internal complaints procedures, and the response which it states should be forthcoming when a complaint is found to be justified, namely an apology and redress where appropriate, should lead to a greater number of complaints being resolved at departmental level, taking some pressure off the PCA.

3 However, in a recent study of a major investigation by the PCA the authors[21] found that the Government's response to Mr Reid's recommendations revealed that the Charter was by no means a panacea for all ills:

Evidence to the Select Committee and recent reports of the Ombudsman have revealed inadequacies in much of the redress offered by many departments and agencies, through unwillingness to admit fault, refusal to apologise and failure to identify and compensate those affected by maladministration, as well as unacceptable inconsistencies in departmental practice, all of which highlight the need for reinforcement of the principles of the Citizen's Charter to improve administrative standards.[22]

CASES HANDLED BY THE PCA: SOME EXAMPLES

In order to give a flavour of the actual day-to-day work of the PCA, samples of his reports appear below. The first, an extract from a full length report, concerns an investigation of a complaint that the Department of Health had refused to

---

18 See Seneviratne, *op cit*, p55.

19 *Ibid*, p56.

20 *Ibid*.

21 R James and D Longley, 'The Channel Tunnel Rail Link, the Ombudsman and the Select Committee' (1996) PL 38. See further on this issue, pp846–7 below.

22 *Ibid*, at p45.

supply certain information to which the complainant thought he was entitled under the Government's policy on open Government. This policy is discussed in full in Part IV, Chapter 3; in brief, the policy calls for Government departments to be generally willing to disclose information, subject to certain exceptions. The PCA has been given the role of interpreting the code in disputed cases, and , if an allegation of unjustified non-disclosure is received by him, to investigate the case and make a recommendation as to whether a given piece of information should be released or not. The report appearing below is his first on a case concerning the new policy.

First Report of the Parliamentary Commissioner for Administration, HC 14 (1994–95)

1   The complainant had sought from the Department of Health (DH) information about discussions which were said to have taken place between DH and representatives of the pharmaceutical industry over the disclosure of pharmaceutical safety information. His request for information was made in the light of:

(a)   comments made in Parliament by the Parliamentary Under Secretary of State (PUSS) for Health who, in April 1993, in the course of the report stage of the Medicines Information Bill had said: 'We have begun to discuss with the pharmaceutical industry a new voluntary code of practice to increase the amount of information that they give the public'; and

(b)   a sentence in the 'Open Government' White Paper of 15 July 1993 (Cm 2290) which read: 'The Department of Health is currently discussing a code of practice on access to information with the pharmaceutical industry' (para 6.20).

Background

2   The complainant wrote to the PUSS on 9 May 1994 asking for more details about the discussions that were said to have taken place. He questioned if a dialogue had started by either of the dates referred to above and asked specifically: (i) what discussions had taken place before 15 July 1993; (ii) what form those discussions had taken; and (iii) who was involved in them and on what dates the discussions had occurred. When replying, on 27 May, the PUSS said that the pharmaceutical industry's code of practice for the disclosure of pharmaceutical data represented a voluntary initiative by the industry and that the information the complainant had sought was outside the scope of the Government's own code; nor did the PUSS think that cataloguing that information would be helpful on a matter which was the responsibility of the pharmaceutical industry rather than the Government. The complainant was not satisfied with that reply.

3   After the referral of the complaint to me I sought the comments of the Permanent Secretary of DH as envisaged in s7(1) of the Parliamentary Commissioner Act 1967. The Permanent Secretary pointed out in response that the department had not yet had the opportunity, in the light of the complainant's dissatisfaction with the PUSS's reply, to carry out an internal review as was normally envisaged under the code. I therefore suspended my investigation temporarily to allow DH to reconsider their decision not to release the information sought.

4   On 27 July the Permanent Secretary wrote to the complainant giving the results of the department's internal review. He reported that the PUSS had

concluded that it would be proper to disclose that discussions of an informal nature had taken place with the Association of British Pharmaceutical Industries (ABPI) during the second half of January 1993 and that one of the matters discussed had been the prospect of an industry voluntary code of practice on the disclosure of information to the public.

Departmental reasons for refusing access

5   In the same letter the Permanent Secretary identified three specific refusing access exemptions under the code which, in the department's view, justified their continuing refusal to release the remainder of the information which the complainant had sought. Those exemptions were exemptions 7(a) and (b) which cover:

'(a) Information whose disclosure could lead to improper gain or advantage or would prejudice:

● the competitive position of a department or other public body or authority;

● negotiations or the effective conduct of personnel management, or commercial or contractual activities;

● the awarding of discretionary grants'; and

'(b) Information whose disclosure would harm the proper and efficient conduct of the operations of a department or other public body or authority, including NHS organisations, or of any regulatory body';

and exemption 14(b) which covers:

'(b) Information whose disclosure without the consent of the supplier would prejudice the future supply of such information.'

Since I refer later to exemption 14(a) I include here for completeness the full terms of that exemption.

'(a) Information held in consequence of having been supplied in confidence by a person who:

● gave the information under a statutory guarantee that its confidentiality would be protected; or

● was not under any legal obligation, whether actual or implied, to supply it, and has not consented to its disclosure.'

6   I subsequently received from the Permanent Secretary more details of the department's objections to releasing information beyond that which it had disclosed, namely the form of the discussions (informal conversations with ABPI), the period when they took place (the second half of January 1993) and one of the matters discussed (the prospect of an industry voluntary code of practice on the disclosure of information to the public). Those objections were that discussions on a private basis between representatives of Government and outside organisations and individuals were clearly protected by specific exemptions in part II of the code. Disclosure of information about such discussions would make such outside bodies and individuals reluctant to discuss confidential business with departments in the future, and also inhibit officials and ministers from entering into such discussions. That would prejudice the proper and efficient conduct of the operations of Government and put at risk the supply of information and advice. It would harm the process of formulating advice to ministers and therefore be contrary to the public interest. The Permanent Secretary also said that the department had taken into account the fact that ABPI were a trade body with whom DH had a negotiating relationship, for example on the arrangements for the control of

prices charged by the industry for drugs used by the NHS, and a consultative relationship on the regime for the licensing and control of medicines. It would not be conducive to the conduct of negotiations and consultations with ABPI and other bodies if the department were to be seen to be revealing the details of private conversations. In any negotiations the parties needed to be sure of confidentiality which could not be assured if the Government were to be obliged to make disclosures under the code. He added that the department had considered whether it would be appropriate to override those considerations on the grounds of the public interest in the disclosure of the information which the complainant had sought. Ministers had decided in 1993 that disclosure of the fact that discussions were taking place with the pharmaceutical industry should be made in view of the public interest of the House of Commons having a proper picture of the various options that there were during its consideration of the legislation that was then before it. In view of that disclosure the department had thought it right to provide extra information in order to amplify the remarks already made but they did not believe that they should add further to it.

7   For his part the complainant wrote to me amplifying the reasons why he still considered that more of the information he had sought should be disclosed. He said that information as to the precise date or dates of the discussions had been withheld, as had information on their form and the identities of the participants. He questioned whether, in the light of what had been disclosed, it could properly be said as the White Paper had done that DH were at the time of the White Paper's publication currently discussing a code of practice of access to information with the pharmaceutical industry. He disputed the relevance of exemption 7(a) of the code saying that, for that exemption to be relevant, some form of negotiation needed to have taken place and that, in any case, the limited disclosure which he sought was not capable of prejudicing such negotiations as there might have been. He also disputed the relevance of exemption 7(b) saying that disclosure of the limited information he had sought would not undermine the department's ability to conduct discussions. He disputed the relevance of exemption 14(b), arguing that the information sought was not information which had been obtained by the department from a third party. Its disclosure therefore could not be capable of prejudicing the future supply of such information. Lastly, he maintained that if, though that was not his view, the information he had sought fell within the exemptions in part II of the code it should nevertheless be released since the public interest in making the information available would outweigh any harm or prejudice arising from its disclosure. The information concerned had acquired a significance purely because of the possibility that it contradicted a statement made by a minister to Parliament and repeated in a White Paper. He said that a refusal to disclose in full the information sought could only reinforce suspicions that Parliament and the public had been misled by spurious references to discussions which were not in fact taking place and that it was in the public interest that, one way or another, those suspicions should be dispelled or confirmed. ...

Assessment

9   There is no doubt that the Government's code is intended to protect information given in confidence. It includes provisions to give effect to that intention. I also do not doubt, having had the opportunity to study the relevant papers, that the basis of the contacts which occurred 'during the second half of January 1993' to adopt the department's phrasing was one of confidentiality. The fact that the veil was to an extent lifted by the PUSS's

comments in Parliament in April in 1993 and lifted rather further when the Permanent Secretary wrote to the complainant on 27 July 1994 does not mean that the claim to confidentiality can be said to have been abandoned altogether. I am satisfied that all that information not already disclosed which can fairly be said to be information supplied by ABPI is covered by exemption 14 of the code.

10   Is the information the complainant is still seeking information of that kind? The information still sought is the precise date or dates of the discussions which occurred, the form of those discussions and who was involved in them on the Government's side and on the ABPI side. Of those items only the very last – who was involved on the ABPI side – can, in my view, fairly be categorised as information supplied by ABPI and therefore as information falling within exemption 14 (that would be both exemption 14(a) and 14(b)) of the code).

11   To what extent, if any, do exemptions 7(a) or 7(b) justify the non-disclosure of information not covered by exemption 14? DH have argued that, because on some matters they are in a negotiating and consultative relationship with ABPI, the non-disclosure of the information which the complainant seeks is justified by exemption 7(a) and that, were that information to be disclosed, the conduct of future negotiations and consultations, both with ABPI and with other bodies, would be put at risk. Given the facts, should I accept that argument as valid? There is no suggestion that any negotiations took place in this case, while DH have been keen to stress that what is involved is a voluntary industry initiative. The fact that, under the code, DH like other departments are committed to releasing information which does not fall within the code's exemptions, is not of itself a matter likely to prejudice future negotiations or consultations, any more than has the PUSS's disclosure in Parliament that discussions with the pharmaceutical industry had begun. I do not consider that the information currently being sought can fairly be represented as the details of private conversations; it is the detail surrounding those conversations which is the object of the complainant's enquiries.

12   Would the disclosure of the information sought harm the proper and efficient conduct of the operations of the department (exemption 7(b))? That is a question the answer to which needs to be considered against the background of the information which has already been disclosed. I readily accept, for example, that there will be occasions when to reveal that any discussions have taken place will cause such harm. In this case that disclosure has already been made to Parliament. I am not of the view, given the information already provided, that the non-disclosure either of the precise dates of the discussions or of more information about their form can be justified under exemption 7(b). Who speaks for a department and within what limits of authority and with whom they have spoken are central to the proper and efficient conduct of the operations of the public service. I accept that, in certain cases, the identities of representatives may properly be withheld from third parties under the code. I also accept that, under exemption 7(b), a claim for withholding the names of the participants can, in this case, properly be made.

13   Exemptions 7(b) and 14(b) are, however, both subject to a harm test (though exemption 14(a) is not). Under the harm test it is necessary to consider whether the public interest in making available the information sought outweighs any harm or prejudice arising from the disclosure of that information even though it comes within the ambit of those exemptions. The

complainant has suggested that, should I conclude that the exemptions apply, I should nevertheless conclude that the information sought should be released because the public interest in its release will outweigh any harm or prejudice that would arise. That is not my view. DH have already acknowledged that they and ABPI were represented in the discussions referred to by the PUSS. That being so, I am not persuaded that the public interest requires releasing the specific identities of those involved.

14   There is one further point. It seems to me good practice that, when a department refuses a request for information under the code, the specific exemptions under part II of the code on which they rely and (where applicable) any tests of harm they have applied in reaching their judgment should be identified from the outset. That will help dissatisfied applicants to make an informed judgment as to whether or not they have grounds for requesting a review or asking a Member of Parliament to refer their complaints to me. The department's first reply to the complainant made no reference to any code exemptions; I am glad to see that they subsequently cited the code exemptions.

Conclusion

15   I therefore invited the Permanent Secretary to reconsider the decision not to release the precise date of the discussion or discussions and more information about their form. He told me in reply that, in the light of my views, the department had agreed that more information should be released. He observed that the department had taken the complainant's request for information about what discussions had taken place as going beyond what I have described as 'the detail surrounding the conversations' (para 11) to include matters of substance. He said that that interpretation had coloured the original response to the complainant; I can understand how that interpretation came to be made.

16   I note with approval that the department do not dispute my view that certain additional information should be disclosed to the complainant. The department have told me that they will be writing to tell him that:

(a)   there was an informal meeting on 26 January 1993 between an official of the department and a representative of the ABPI at which one of the matters discussed was the possibility of an industry voluntary code of practice on the disclosure of information;

(b)   there was further contact by letter on 1 February 1993;

(c)   between these dates there was contact on the telephone on one or two occasions of which no written record was kept.

I see this as a suitable outcome.

27 October 1994

Notes

1   The information the complainant was requesting was limited; he did not request details of the substance of the discussions, only information as to the personnel involved and the relevant dates. The fact that he was found not to be entitled even to these details indicates the breadth of the excluded categories of information under the code. Further, the consensual approach of the PCA, which comes across strongly in this report, may mean that he will be unable to wring maximum disclosure from even the limited provisions of the code. Such a non-contentious approach is probably essential, however, to avoid alienating the departments on whose goodwill

the effectiveness of his work is largely dependent; as De Smith comments, 'The PCA has placed a very high priority on cultivating good relations with heads of departments, so as to obtain their co-operation in his investigations ...'.[23]

2   The most important recent investigation by the PCA concerned a number of complaints by those whose property has been affected by the Channel Tunnel rail link.[24] The investigation was notable in being the largest ever undertaken by the PCA;[25] it also involved the PCA in the unusual step of examining the department's[26] handling of the project as a whole, albeit in the context of five individual complaints. The problems generated concerned peoples' homes, the value of which had been blighted by the prospect that the rail link would run past or near them. The PCA's report[27] found that there had been maladministration, causing widespread blight for which the Government had not, in line with existing policy, made any provision; however it also found that there were a number of cases of exceptional hardship, in respect of which it recommended that compensation should be offered. The Select Committee on the PCA backed the PCA's findings and recommendations.[28] The department denied that there had been any maladministration, and, unusually, refused to implement the PCA's recommendations. Neither the PCA nor the Select Committee were impressed by the department's arguments; in particular both denied strongly that in asking the department to look again at exceptional cases, they were criticising the general Government policy of not offering compensation for generalised blight. On this point, the Select Committee said:

'At the heart of this debate is a definition of maladministration found in the [PCA's 1993 Annual Report] – "failure to mitigate the effects of rigid adherence to the letter of the law where that produces manifestly inequitable treatment" ... The definition, which we fully support, implies an expectation that, when an individual citizen is faced with extraordinary hardship as a result of strict application of law or policy, the executive must be prepared to look again and consider whether help can be given.'[29]

The department, faced with the embarrassing prospect of a debate in the Commons on the matter, in which it would have been opposed by a unanimous, cross-party Select Committee, eventually agreed to look again at the possibility of a compensation scheme for those affected to an exceptional or extreme degree by the generalised blight. However, the Government made it clear that it agreed to this 'only out of respect for the PCA Select Committee and the office of Parliamentary Commissioner, and without

---

23   De Smith, *Constitutional and Administrative Law*, 6th edn (1994), p703.
24   See generally on this, R James and D Longley, 'The Channel Tunnel Rail Link, the Ombudsman and the Select Committee' (1996) PL 38. We are indebted to the authors for the discussion that follows.
25   *Annual Report of the PCA for 1995*, Cm 296, p3, para 7.
26   The department concerned was Transport.
27   *Fifth Report of the PCA*, HC 193 (1994–95).
28   *Sixth Report of the Select Committee on the PCA*, HC 270 (1994–95).
29   *Ibid*, para 20; quoted in James and Longley, *op cit*, p42.

admission of fault of liability', a concession described by James and Longley as 'grudging'.[30] Nevertheless, in terms of winning compensation, the PCA had prevailed again.

3   A wider sample of recent cases handled by the PCA and their outcomes appears below in the form of case summaries. It will be noted that, in many cases, the PCA's findings were followed by changes to the rules or procedures which had given rise to the original complaint.

Parliamentary Commissioner for Administration, *Annual Report for 1995*, Cm 296, pp69–70

Lord Chancellor's Department (LCD)

C.426/93– Mishandling by county court staff of a legal action and the initial refusal of LCD to pay compensation to the defendant. *Ex gratia* payment of £35,000 made for legal costs, loss of value of house when the complainant was unable to obtain a mortgage for a new one, and distress.

C.537/93 – Mishandling of a case by staff from three county courts and an incorrect notification of judgment to the Register of County Court Judgments. *Ex gratia* payment of £1,000 made and new procedures introduced.

C.694/93 – Mishandling of a case by staff at two county courts and the failure of the Courts Administrator to pay adequate compensation. *Ex gratia* payment of £196 for wasted costs offered to complainant.

C.812/93 – Complaint about mishandling and delays by staff serving the Immigration Appellate Authorities in dealing with the appeal of a man's wife against refusal of entry clearance into the UK and the refusal of LCD to pay compensation for wasted costs. LCD made *ex gratia* payment of £625 and agreed to reconsider their procedures.

Department of Social Security (DSS)

C.207/91 – Delay and mishandling of claims for attendance allowance and industrial injuries disablement benefit. *Ex gratia* payment of £5,902.65 made as compensation for late payment of attendance allowance and £195.13 for late payment of industrial injuries disablement benefit.

C.341/92 – Inadequate advice given about claiming attendance allowance. Arrears of £9,300.34 paid with an *ex gratia* payment of £6,976.04 as compensation for late payment of benefit.

C.780/92 – Mishandling of claim for IS [income support], and conduct of fraud investigation. *Ex gratia* payments totalling £111.77 made to reimburse extra mortgage interest charges and telephone costs.

C.87/93 – Mishandling of claims to IS, leading to loss of benefit and mortgage arrears. ES paid benefit arrears of £104.50 with an *ex gratia* payment of £11.76 to compensate for the delay in payment, and DSS made an *ex gratia* payment of £43.46 to compensate for mortgage interest charges. (See also under ES.)

C.133/93 – Misleading and inadequate advice about a claim to sickness benefit. Comprehensive revision of practice, and amendments to staff instructions and forms.

C.212/93 – Mishandling of claims for war pension and severe disablement allowance. *Ex gratia* payment of £167.99 in compensation for late payment of benefit.

---

30   *Op cit*, p44.

C.277/93 – Mishandling of claim for mobility allowance. *Ex gratia* payment of £468.27 made as compensation for late payment of benefit.

C.444/93 – Delay in the payment of sickness benefit and invalidity benefit. *Ex gratia* payments made totalling £41.20 for delay in payment of benefit; a refund of overpaid NICs made totalling £40.05; and the recovery of an overpayment of IS totalling £232.59 waived. DSS undertook to improve communications between BA and CA in cases involving benefit.

C.470/93 – Misdirection about possible entitlement to invalid care allowance and attendance allowance; failure to give advice about disability premium; and mishandling of claim for home responsibilities protection. Extra-statutory payments of attendance allowance, disability premium, carer premium and Christmas bonuses made totalling £12,811.15. *Ex gratia* payments of £3,254.22 made as compensation for the late payment of benefits. Class I NIC credits awarded from December 1987.

REFORM OF THE PCA

First Report of the Select Committee on the Parliamentary Commissioner for Administration, **HC 33 II (1993–94)**

Options for change

15   There is much in the existing legislation which has stood the test of time. There is little in the Office's experience to suggest the need to change ... PCA's ... existing powers or discretion to determine how investigations are conducted. Unless the ombudsman concept is to be fundamentally altered, the limitations on the PCA's remit to administrative actions (ie excluding legislative content and the need for changes to it, the merits of policies and decisions of a judicial or quasi-judicial character) should continue to apply – though where a decision has been reached maladministratively PCA remains in a position to say so. Experience over the years suggest that no new mechanism to secure implementation of the recommendations of PCA ... is needed. The Select Committee's own existence has meant that, unlike some other ombudsmen, the PCA ... has [not] experienced particular difficulties in securing redress felt to be due.

Note

The Committee then went on to consider various options for reform of the PCA (and also the Health Service Commission); these options, with the Government's and PCA's response to them, are discussed below by Phillip Giddings and Roy Gregory.

P Giddings and R Gregory, 'Auditing the Auditors: Responses to the Select Committee's Review of the United Kingdom Ombudsman System 1993' (1995) *Public Law* 46–51.

After a far-reaching inquiry into the powers, work and jurisdiction of the ombudsman, the Select Committee's report of January 1994 made 36 recommendations designed to 'broaden the scope of the ombudsman's work, secure greater access to and publicity for it, and ensure that the office secures adequate funds and resources' [*First Report from the Select Committee*, HC 333, 1993–94]. Thirty recommendations were directed to the Government, whose reply was set out in a memorandum appended to the Select Committee's report published in July 1994, and six to the ombudsman offices.

The Government's response

Scope

The Government agreed to look carefully at the committee's recommendation that the Parliamentary Commissioner Act should be amended so as to specify exclusions from, rather than inclusions within, the ombudsman's jurisdiction, but it will first examine whether publicity could achieve the objective of reducing confusion about whether particular bodies fall within the ombudsman's remit. ...

Access

Agreeing with the committee's view that the 'MP filter' should be retained, the Government undertook to play its part in enlarging access to the office by ensuring that the relevant Citizen's Charter literature states clearly what people can do if things go wrong, and that, if they remain dissatisfied, they can ask an MP to raise their case with the ombudsman. In cases where charter documents do not already contain such information it will be added at the earliest opportunity.

Publicity

The committee pointed out that public awareness is vital to the effectiveness of the ombudsman. Concerned at evidence that many people were ignorant of the ombudsman's services, the committee made two recommendations which the Government has accepted:

(i) that at the earliest opportunity the relevant statutes be amended to refer to the 'Parliamentary Ombudsman' and the 'Health Service Ombudsman' (HSO);

(ii) that a newsletter summarising cases of interest in a more popular and easily accessible form be produced.

A third recommendation – that a debate be held on the ombudsman in each Parliamentary session – was rejected by the Government, which argued that there was no widespread demand for it from Members and that the suggested newsletter could be a better way of keeping MPs informed. ...

Quality and impact: time taken in investigations

The committee considered that, notwithstanding recent progress on this front, investigations still take too long, and every effort should be made to meet the nine months target originally set in 1988. To this end the committee recommended, and the Government agreed, that the PCA should deal directly with complainants when requesting further information, while keeping the referring Member fully informed, as already happens in Northern Ireland.

Quality and impact: independence

The Government accepted the committee's recommendation that, in order to undergird the ombudsmen's independence and impartiality, legislation be introduced to provide:

(i) that the Parliamentary and Health Service Ombudsmen be appointed by the Crown, on an address of the House of Commons, no motion being made for such an address except by the Prime Minister with the agreement of the chairman of the Select Committee and the Leader of the Opposition;

(ii) that the expenses of the ombudsman offices be met from moneys voted directly by Parliament on estimates prepared by a new 'Public Administration Commission', consisting of the chairman of the Select Committee, the Leader of the House of Commons and seven non-ministerial MPs, one of whom would be chosen as chairman.

However, given the different structures and circumstances in Northern Ireland, the Government felt the application of those recommendations inappropriate there. The proposed Public Administration Commission, it added, should be required to have regard to any advice given by the Treasury.

Quality and impact: improvements in public administration

The Government broadly accepted three recommendations made by the committee, designed to enable the ombudsmen to promote 'good administration':

(i)   as with HSO reports, the Office of Public Service and Science (OPSS) should circulate epitomes of the Parliamentary Ombudsman's reports to all Government departments, drawing civil servants' attention to matters of concern and examples of good practice;

(ii)   public bodies and departments reported upon should be required to publish a report to the ombudsman describing ways in which the maladministration and failures of service identified had been rectified;

(iii) OPSS should produce a booklet for civil servants on the work of the ombudsman.

Other recommendations relating to the improvement of administration were less well received. The Government saw difficulties in the committee's suggestion that the ombudsman should be able to conduct administrative audits of the bodies within his jurisdiction, pointing out that the PCA himself had noted the possibility that his independence in investigating complaints could be prejudiced if a complaint concerned an organisation whose administrative procedures he had 'approved' in some way. The Government was also concerned that a formal power to audit could duplicate the work of other agencies; the NHS, it pointed out, is already subject to various forms of audit, both internal and external, eg the National Audit Office (NAO), the Audit Commission and the Health Advisory Service.

The Government also rejected the committee's recommendation that legislation be introduced to enable the ombudsman to initiate investigations where the committee had raised the matter informally with the ombudsman as a matter of concern. The Government felt that this would represent a fundamental change from the concept that his basic role is to investigate and suggest redress for people's grievances.

Provision of adequate funds and resources

The Government responded to the committee's concern about the resources necessary for the ombudsman's enlarged responsibilities by pointing out that the PCA's cash limit had already been increased by £659,000 to £5,123,000 in 1993–94 to provide for additional staff and accommodation, and that for 1994–95 an increase of 86% to £9,504,000 on the forecast out-turn for 1993–94 had been agreed specifically to take account of the PCA's enlarged responsibilities.

Ombudsman responses

The PCA has reported that, of the six recommendations addressed to himself, he has already started to implement two. In the interests of speed, once an MP has referred a complaint to him, he will now deal with the complainant directly, while keeping the referring Member in touch. He is continuing to work at reducing throughput times and will look again at the way those times are calculated and reported. He will consider the implications of the proposed public awareness and consumer satisfaction surveys when he makes his annual bid for resources. His thoughts on good administration are likely to be incorporated in the booklet *The Ombudsman in Your Files* which OPSS will produce for Government departments.

The Select Committee rejoinder

In its report of July 1994 the committee welcomed the Government's agreement to many of its recommendations but felt that some other responses merited further comment.

The committee argued that the Government's rejection of an annual debate on the ombudsmen failed to address the parallel between their work and that of the Comptroller and Auditor General (C and AG). Both, the committee pointed out, are officers of the House of Commons, entrusted with vital work in examining the performance of Government departments and agencies. Both report to the House the findings of their investigations. It was anomalous that the work of the C and AG is debated annually while the reports of the ombudsmen are not. Recent ombudsmen reports had highlighted the need for effective scrutiny of standards of administration in the public service. ...

Comment

The Government's response to the Select Committee's report may be regarded as largely supportive. Only seven recommendations were wholly rejected. Of particular significance was the acceptance of the need for legislation putting the appointment and financing of the ombudsman on a more explicitly independent footing. How long it will take for such legislation to find a place in the Parliamentary programme remains to be seen.

... The need for an annual debate on the work of the ombudsmen is also likely to continue to exercise the committee. It was raised by several members in the debate on the PCA's work in December 1994.

But if a good deal remains unresolved, the outcome of the Select Committee's 1993 review clearly represents a further step in the development of the UK's ombudsman system into an effective mechanism for dealing with maladministration and the redress of grievances.

Notes

1 One reform to the PCA's powers came with the passing of the Parliamentary Commissioner Act 1994, which extends the jurisdiction of the PCA to cover 'actions taken in exercise of administrative functions by administrative staff of certain tribunals' (introduction to the Act).

2 What direction should reform of the PCA take? It is sometimes argued that if the PCA were to appear too demanding and *a fortiori* if he were afforded coercive powers he might exacerbate the very problems he is expected to solve. Administrators might be reluctant to take bold decisions for fear of the consequences; 'defensive administration' might be undertaken; time wasting procedures designed not to further administrative efficiency but to deflect criticism. However, against this it could be argued that administrators take the benefit of a courageous decision which turns out well in the form of promotion and will therefore accept the risk that it will turn out badly.

3 Probably the need to appear reasonably emollient is inherent in the role of the PCA as currently conceived, but it is arguable that it is not a necessary part of it. If, for example, members of the public could contact the PCA directly, and if his role was given greater publicity, he might feel more able

to incur the displeasure of Government departments because he would be more supported by public opinion.

4 Thus, although the PCA at present has arguably evolved a limited role for himself as a gentle instrument of change which may represent a departure from the role it was hoped he would fulfil, it is submitted that this was not inevitable but occurred due to some of the constraints which were externally imposed. In this respect, a distinction should be drawn between allotting the PCA formal powers to award coercive remedies which, as argued above, might well detract from his efficacy, and removing certain of the limitations on him particularly as regards direct public access. The removal of such limitations would, it is submitted, lead to a more bold approach and would benefit the persons he is expected to serve.

THE LOCAL OMBUDSMEN

The ombudsman system has proved very popular: it was extended to the Health Service with the establishment of three Health Service Commissioners in 1972 and 1973, to Northern Ireland under the Commissioner for Complaints Act (Northern Ireland) 1969, and to local government [the 'LGO'] under the Local Government Act 1974. In 1990 a Legal Services Ombudsman was set up. A number of ombudsmen have also been established in the private sector (see the table above). Consideration of most of the other ombudsmen is outside the remit of this book, but brief consideration will be given to the worth of the LGO.

The basic work of the Local Government Ombudsmen

LGO's do not have complaints referred to them by MPs (and indeed are not accountable to Parliament like the PCA); members of the public may take complaints directly to an LGO. They have no power to initiate investigations on their own initiative. Their powers of investigation are the same as those of the PCA as noted by McEldowney:

> The jurisdiction of the LGO is similar to the 1967 Act and the PCA, and the powers of investigation are the same as the PCA. The LGO may investigate complaints where a member of the public has 'sustained injustice in consequence of maladministration'. The number of complaints has steadily increased over the years. In 1983–84 there were approximately 3,000 complaints but in 1990/91 the number had increased to over 9,000. Originally there was a councillor filter equivalent to the MP for the PCA discussed above. The Widdecombe report [Cm 9797] recommended, and the Government accepted, the desirability of allowing direct access and this was granted under the Local Government Act 1988. In terms of jurisdiction, in common with the PCA, the LGO may not enquire into contractual and commercial matters. ...
>
> Maladministration is interpreted by the LGO in a similar way to the PCA. In *Local Commissioner for Administration for the North and East Area of England, ex p Bradford Metropolitan City Council* [1979] QB 287 Lord Denning considered that the [LGO] is concerned in matters of maladministration with the manner in which decisions are reached and the manner in which they may or may not be implemented. The nature, quality and reasonableness of the decision are not part of the LGO remit. The subject matter of investigations conducted by the LGO covers a wide cross-section of local authority activities; housing, planning and

education comprise large proportion of the case-load of the LGO. Sections 266–269 and Schedule 16 of the 1993 Education Act extend the LGO's remit to appeal committees in grant-maintained schools. Complaints are made within 12 months from the day the complainant has notice of the matter complained of, although there is a discretion to investigate complaint out of time.

[The LGO] may not investigate a complaint which effects all or nearly all of the inhabitants of a local authority. Complaints about public passenger transport and the internal management of local authority schools are also excluded from this jurisdiction.[31]

Notes

1   Seneviratne notes that the following bodies are subject to investigation by the Local Government Ombudsmen (LGO): 'district, borough, city, or county councils (not town or parish councils); the Commission for New Towns or new town development corporations (housing matters only); housing action trusts; police authorities; fire authorities; any joint board of local authorities, including the National Park Boards; the National Rivers Authority (flood defence and land drainage matters only) [and] the Broads Authority'. In practice, 'the vast majority of investigations involve local councils ...'.[32]

2   The LGO has a dual role: the redress of individual grievances and the achievement of better administration. However 'the great bulk of the work ... does centre on individual grievance handling';[33] one role is clearly subordinate to the other. For discussion of the potentiality of the LGO to improve administration generally, see C Crawford, 'Complaints, Codes, and Ombudsmen in Local Government'.[34]

3   The LGO has responded to its (subordinate) role as general advice giver in a number of ways. One is the preparation of guidance notes for local authorities on a wide variety of topics, including disposal of land, declaration of interests, and repair and improvement of council houses.[35] Another lies in their practice of making general recommendations on good administrative practice when dealing with an individual complaint, with the aim of preventing such complaints recurring. Seneviratne notes how 'In a recent case (CLA case report 89/A/939), the LGO felt that the council had failed to conform to some basic standards of good administration in dealing with an application for housing, and they took the trouble to itemise in the annual report four basic axioms of good administration. These are, first, that although it is not wrong it itself for a council to discriminate for or against certain classes of applicants, such discrimination must be made for proper reasons and be seen to be fair. Second, that when allocating housing, and ... when making many other decisions, proper criteria should be used. Third,

31   McEldowney, *Public Law* (1994), pp440–1.
32   Seneviratne, *Ombudsman in the Public Sector* (1994), p85.
33   *Ibid*, p86.
34   (1988) PL 246.
35   Seneviratne, *op cit*, p117.

that reasons should be given for administrative decisions; and last, that such reasons should be noted in writing' (CLA annual report 1990–91:14).[36]

4   Seneviratne comments that this role of improving administrative practice may not always sit easily with the LGOs' primary function of investigating individual complaints. 'There is some tension between [the two roles]. They can result in a different relationship with local government, which may be happy to co-operate with individual grievance redress, but not so happy to see the [LGO] having a roving commission to comment upon their procedures. Too much emphasis on the second role could mean the commission would become too much like management consultants.'[37]Nevertheless, the two roles are clearly closely linked, as appears from the above CLA report.

Number of cases investigated, and success rate of the LGO

DCM Yardley, 'Local Ombudsmen in England: Recent Trends and Developments' (1983) Public Law 522, 525–7, 529–31

In broad terms, the records show that complaints are rejected in about 70% of all cases properly referred to the commission. This figure is reached by adding together the complaints which are rejected at an early stage for such reasons as that they are outside jurisdiction, that the complainant has failed to show that he has been personally affected by what he is complaining about, or that the matter complained about is clearly of no substance or has already been cured, and those which are rejected somewhat later after some interviews have been conducted and inquiries made. For example, it is quite common for a council tenant to complain that his landlord council have failed to keep up with their repairing and maintenance obligations. As soon as the complaint has been received, a letter is sent to the council asking them to comment on it, and if the resulting comments show clearly that the council have now cured the defect complained about and have already apologised to the tenant for any delay in doing so, it then becomes obvious that there is little else which the ombudsman could usefully do as a result of any further investigation. Accordingly the complaint will be rejected by way of a letter signed by the ombudsman himself, and giving a full explanation of the reasons for the rejection.

A good number of the remaining complaints result in local settlements. These are cases where the local authority are prepared to admit some fault and to provide what is seen by the Local Ombudsman as a suitable remedy, thus obviating the need for a full report to be published. ...

The annual Reports over the years since 1974 have shown that it is only in about 10–15% of all complaints that a full report is necessary. The highest percentage was in 1979–80, with 18%, and the lowest in 1981–82, 10.3%. Again in broad terms it is only in about two-thirds of these full reports that there is a finding of maladministration against the local authority. Thus by including the figures for local settlements it transpires that local authorities are found to be to some extent at fault in about 25% of all cases referred, and that such a finding is reached in a formal report in about 10% of all cases referred (in the most recent annual report for 1982–83, the figure was about 8%). The 75% success rate of local authorities, if

---

36   Quoted *ibid*.
37   *Op cit*, p116.

it is put that way, is reached by adding together the rejections and the average 5% of all complaints which result in full reports that do not find in favour of the complainant. But it would not be accurate to assume that local authorities are without fault in all such cases, for many of them are cases in which there is found to be some fault, though it is comparatively small and not sufficiently substantial to warrant a finding of maladministration. For example, to take the illustration of a housing issue again, it is not uncommon to find that there had indeed been undue delay in effecting repairs but that this had been partly exacerbated by the difficulty in gaining access to the premises because the tenant had been away from home, and that despite the delay the comfort and interests of the complainant had not been unduly prejudiced. In such a case there is little to be gained by making formal finding of maladministration.

Year after year it has been shown that about one-third of all complaints are upon housing matters, another one-third on planning issues, and the remaining one-third cover all the rest of local government services. ...

4 The possible introduction of enforcement powers

Along with many other ombudsmen throughout the world, the Local Commissioners have no power to enforce their decisions. If all Local Ombudsman reports were invariably accepted by the local authorities, no one would be likely to feel that there was anything lacking in the system, but unfortunately the 'success rate' has not been quite as good as that. Under the 1974 Act it is the duty of the authority, in any case where the Local Ombudsman has found that injustice has been caused to the person aggrieved in consequence of maladministration, to consider the report and to notify the Local Ombudsman of the action which they have taken or propose to take [Local Government Act 1974, s31(1)]. If the Local Ombudsman does not receive any such notification within a reasonable time, or is not satisfied with the action which the authority concerned have taken, or does not within a reasonable time receive confirmation from the authority concerned that they have taken action which satisfies him, he must make a further report stating this, and this further report must also be considered by the authority. But the issue of a further report is the final sanction which can be imposed by a Local Ombudsman and he can do no more in relation to any complaint thereafter.

The great majority of local authorities respond promptly, willingly and positively to reports issued by the Local Ombudsman, and it is not often necessary to issue further reports. But in 1982–83, there were 20. The practice has been to make them fairly short and sharp, with only a brief recital of the findings in the first report, followed by a clear statement of why the Local Ombudsman is dissatisfied with the actions of the authority, and what the authority should now do to put the matter right. Often this is salutary, and the matter is at last sensibly concluded. But there remains a hard core of resistance in some local authorities which for various reasons take the view that in the cases concerned they have acted rightly, and that the Local Ombudsman's findings do not persuade them to the contrary. Up to and including the end of the year 1982–83, there had been 78 cases all told in which local authorities had rejected the report of the ombudsman finding against them or simply failed to act upon it to his satisfaction. In the space of eight-and-a-half years, 78 failures is perhaps not disastrous, particularly if we bear in mind that many local authorities have since 1974 made praiseworthy efforts to introduce a proper complaints procedure into their own internal administrative machinery, with the result that the Local Ombudsmen tend far more than in earlier years to have to deal with the more difficult or contentious cases. But even one failure is one too many, for it represents a case of injustice perpetuated and not cured. ...

The regrettable record of failures in a small number of cases has led to a progressively strengthening movement in favour of some sort of power to compel authorities to comply with Local Ombudsman decisions. The matter has been raised several times by MPs in the House of Commons during the past year, and newspapers, journals and pressure groups such as the National Consumer Council have joined the campaign. Some writers have drawn attention to the provisions in the Commissioner for Complaints Act (Northern Ireland) 1969 whereby the person aggrieved may, on a finding by the commissioner of injustice caused by maladministration, apply to the county court for damages or a mandatory or other injunction if the authority have not complied with the report. Little use has been made of this provision in practice, but some think that it would act powerfully upon the will of local authorities to comply with reports which are adverse to them.

It is probably not a sufficient counter to the arguments for strengthening Local Ombudsmen's powers that the PCA has no power of enforcement, for his office is backed by the influence of a House of Commons Select Committee, which performs a function in supporting him which is in no way resembled by the representative body in relation to the commission. But the fact remains that ombudsmen normally work entirely by persuasion, backed by the force of publicity and parliamentary criticism. It is my view and that of my colleagues that this is how we should continue to work, and for the present we are agreed that our practice of talking to authorities and their leaders and chief executives, and of seeking to persuade them, is preferable to a relationship of policeman and potential offender and we hope that we shall be able to keep our functions truly extra-judicial. But we recognise that if the number of 'failures' increases, or if the recalcitrant authorities become more determined in their rejection of adverse criticism from Local Ombudsmen, Parliament may well find the movement for the introduction of more teeth into the powers of the Commission becomes irresistible. This would be one more nail in the coffin of local government independence, and we should regret it. Independence can only be maintained if it is enjoyed and exercised responsibly, and with a suitably sensitive reaction to the constructive criticisms made from time to time by the statutory ombudsmen who are charged with the duty to offer it.

Notes

1   Seneviratne notes that, by 1992, the total number of cases in which 'the local authority has not provided a satisfactory remedy after a finding of maladministration and injustice' amounted to 186, 'about 6% of all cases of maladministration and injustice'. She concludes that 'Non-compliance is therefore a serious problem ... [as] recognised by JUSTICE, which felt that it was bringing the LGO into disrepute'.[38] Dr Yardley rejects the proposal of giving the LGO power to enforce his findings in the County Court and states that he sees the need to reconsider the possibility only 'if the number of failures increases'. As Jones notes[39] (writing in 1994) 'the Commissions have now abandoned attempts at moral persuasion supported by JUSTICE, and the Widdecombe Committee has called for the 1974 Act to be amended along the lines of the legislation in force in Northern Ireland' (mentioned by Yardley above). Yardley's grounds for opposing the proposal to give the

---

38   Seneviratne, *op cit*, pp98–99.
39   'The Local Ombudsman and Judicial Review' (1994) PL 608.

LGO more teeth seem curiously weak; nowhere does he say that he thinks that using the courts would not work or explain how it would harm local authorities, apart from saying that it would be 'another nail in the coffin of [their] independence', a fear which it is hard to understand. It is not readily apparent how the ability of local authorities to flout the findings of an independent investigator that they have been guilty of maladministration is necessary for their independence.

2   Dr Yardley's other objection to the proposal to give LGOs the ability to enforce their findings in court seems to be simply that it would represent a change of the status quo: 'Ombudsmen normally work entirely by persuasion, backed by the force of publicity and parliamentary criticism'. Again, this argument seems to lack force. First, one argument for giving the LGO such powers relies precisely on the fact that since local authorities are *not* accountable to Parliament, the LGO is actually in a weaker position than the PCA, as confirmed by their greater 'failure' rate. Secondly, Dr Yardley seems simply to *assume* the inherent value of the persuasive tradition without explaining *why* it is valuable; still less does he demonstrate why the tradition is so valuable that the detriment caused by emasculating it should outweigh the undoubted benefit of giving the LGO power to provide a remedy to complainants in cases in which local authorities reject their findings.

3   A more persuasive argument in this respect is put forward by P Birkinshaw and N Lewis in *When Citizens Complain* (1993). They considered that giving the LGO such powers would imperil their relationship with local authorities, which, they feared, would become defensive and 'minimalist' in their responses to LGO recommendations. The current practice of negotiating the response of the authorities in a consensual and informal way would be placed in jeopardy (p39). This view can, of course, be challenged; it could be argued that, even if the LGO was given enforcement powers, consensual methods would still be used; that they would still be, and would be presented as being, very much the norm; that court action would be kept very much out of mind, seen as an exceptional and rarely resorted-to last resort. It must be borne in mind that arguments as to the harm which might be caused by the introduction of enforcement powers are in the end speculative hypotheses which must be weighed against a concrete harm – the 6% of LGO findings which are currently going unenforced.[40]

4   Although the distinction between policy (which the LGO may not question) and administration is generally maintainable it has on occasion caused disagreement. The distinction is clearly of the greatest importance in terms of defining the proper ambit of the LGOs' investigations; it arose for consideration in *Local Commissioner, ex p Eastleigh Borough Council* (1988),[41] considered below by Michael Jones.

---

40   For a full discussion of this issue see, C Himsworth (ed), *Judicial Teeth for Local Ombudsman?* (1985)

41   3 WLR 116.

M Jones, 'The Local Ombudsmen and Judicial Review' (1988) *Public Law* 608

Eastleigh's first importance, perhaps, is that it helps to clarify the impact which s34(3) of the 1974 Act has upon the scope of the commissioners' jurisdiction. ... In *Eastleigh*, the court's interpretation of s34(3) affirms the orthodox view, and the legislature's intent, that the commissioners ought not to usurp the policy-making discretions of democratically elected authorities; by s26(1) of the 1974 Act, they are directed to investigate 'action taken in the exercise of [the] administrative functions of [an] authority'. The justification for the exclusion of policy-oriented complaints is clear:

> Legislators, local as well as national, regard policy as the area where they alone are sovereign, where their decisions of principle must not be constitutionally questioned except by themselves in their own chamber. To allow an ombudsman to enter would be to diminish that prerogative of rulership [Glasser, *Town Hall*, (1984), p159].

But how far does the prohibition in s34(3) extend? At one point in his speech in *Eastleigh*, Lord Donaldson appeared to suggest that it would prevent the commissioners from examining any policy or discretionary decision which a local authority may make: 'Administration and maladministration have nothing to do with the nature, quality or reasonableness of [a] decision ...' [(1988) 3 WLR at 119]. The better view, it is submitted, was taken by Parker LJ who recognised that the immunity conferred by s34(3) is not absolute: '... the terms of s34(3) do not preclude the ombudsman from questioning the merits of all discretionary policy decisions, but only those taken without maladministration ...' [*ibid*, at 123]. In other words, the local ombudsmen (and their parliamentary colleague) may continue to find maladministration in the processes by which discretionary decisions are made upon grounds which closely resemble the *Wednesbury* principles of review employed by the courts – relevancy, proper purposes and so on. And there may still be room for a finding of maladministration where a commissioner considers that the terms of an authority's policy transcend the bounds of reasonableness, and step into perversity, capriciousness, or what the courts now term 'irrationality'. After all, the Parliamentary Commissioner, prompted by his Select Committee, has developed the analogous concept of the 'bad rule'.

PART VI

THE CITIZEN AND CIVIL LIBERTIES

CHAPTER 1

THE PROTECTION OF CIVIL LIBERTIES IN BRITAIN AND THE BILL OF RIGHTS ISSUE

INTRODUCTION[1]

In most Western democracies the rights of citizens are enshrined in a constitutional document sometimes known as a Bill or Charter of Rights. Britain, however, has no Bill of Rights in the modern sense, and therefore in order to discover which freedoms are protected and the extent of that protection, it is necessary to examine the common law, statutes and the influence of treaties to which Britain is a party, especially the European Convention on Human Rights. Certain particular characteristics of British constitution determine the means of protecting fundamental freedoms in the UK. The doctrine of the supremacy of Parliament means that constitutional law can be changed in the ordinary way – by Act of Parliament. Thus Parliament has the power to abridge freedoms which in other countries are seen as fundamental rights. It follows from this that all parts of the law are equal – there is no hierarchy of laws and therefore constitutional law cannot constrain other laws. Further, there is no judicial review of Acts of Parliament: a judge cannot declare a statutory provision invalid simply on the grounds that it conflicts with a fundamental right. Thus, if, for example, a statute is passed containing a provision which constrains freedom of speech, a judge must merely apply it, whereas in a country with a Bill of Rights the provision might be struck down as unconstitutional. However, there is a constraint on this process: if the judge considers that the provision in question is ambiguous he or she may interpret it in such a way that freedom of speech is maintained, either by relying on the common law doctrine of respect for fundamental rights or on the European Convention on Human Rights.

Thus, civil liberties in Britain are in a more precarious position than they are in other democracies, although this does not necessarily mean that they are inevitably less well protected: some bills of rights may offer only a theoretical protection to freedoms which is not reflected in practice. Civil liberties are residual, not entrenched as in other countries: they are the residue of freedom left behind after the legal restrictions have been defined. Civil liberties may be seen as areas of freedom of action surrounded by legal constraints which press upon them: they can exist only in the interstices of the law.

The main purpose of Part VI is to identify and examine certain of these areas of freedom but in order to do so it is necessary to say something more about the

---

1   General reading: Sir Leslie Scarman, *English Law: The New Dimension* (1974); P Wallington and J McBride, *Civil Liberties and a Bill of Rights* (1976); Bailey, Harris and Jones *Civil Liberties: Cases and Materials* (1995) Chapter 1; J Jaconelli, *Enacting a Bill of Rights* (1980); M Zander, *A Bill of Rights* (1985); R Dworkin, *A Bill of Rights for Britain* (1990); K Ewing, *A Bill of Rights for Britain* (1990); D Feldman, *Civil Liberties and Human Rights* (1993), Chapter 2; 'Do We Need a Bill of Rights?' (1976) 39 MLR 121; 'Should We Have a Bill of Rights?' (1977) 40 MLR 389; 'Britain's Bill of Rights', 94 LQR 512; 'Legislative Supremacy and the Rule of Law' (1985) CLJ 111; 'Incorporating the Convention' LAG, April 1990, 25; 'Fundamental Rights: The UK Isolated?' (1984) PL 46; PP Craig, *Public Law and Democracy in the United Kingdom and the United States of America* (1990); J Waldron, 'A Rights-based Critique of Constitutional Rights' (1993) 13 OJLS 18; C Adjei, 'Human Rights Theory and the Bill of Rights Debate' (1995) 58 MLR 17.

context within which they should be placed. The intention in this Chapter is to do this by looking first at the traditional constitutional arrangements for protecting civil liberties. Secondly, consideration will be given to the influence of the European Convention on Human Rights on domestic law will be considered and thirdly to the argument for importing the Convention into British law in order to provide more certain protection for civil liberties. The main argument in favour of a Bill of Rights is that government cannot be fully trusted to place restraints upon its own use of power. The restraint created by Parliament may not be effective so long as the Government commands a majority of votes in Parliament. A Bill of Rights may create, or help to create, a protected area surrounding citizens' rights.

THE PROTECTION OF CIVIL LIBERTIES UNDER THE BRITISH CONSTITUTION

The Diceyan tradition

A V Dicey, *The Law of the Constitution* (1959), pp197–8

The Rule of Law: Its Nature and General Applications

There is in the English constitution an absence of those declarations or definitions of rights so dear to foreign constitutionalists. Such principles, moreover, as you can discover in the English constitution are, like all maxims established by judicial legislation, mere generalisations drawn either from the decisions or *dicta* of judges, or from statutes which, being passed to meet special grievances, bear a close resemblance to judicial decisions, and are in effect judgments pronounced by the High Court of Parliament. To put what is really the same thing in a somewhat different shape, the relation of the rights of individuals to the principles of the constitution is not quite the same in countries like Belgium, where the constitution is the result of a legislative act, as it is in England, where the constitution itself is based upon legal decisions. In Belgium, which may be taken as a type of countries possessing a constitution formed by a deliberate act of legislation, you may say with truth that the rights of individuals to personal liberty flow from or are secured by the constitution. In England the right to individual liberty is part of the constitution, because it is secured by the decisions of the courts, extended or confirmed as they are by the Habeas Corpus Acts. If it be allowable to apply the formulas of logic to questions of law, the difference in this matter between the constitution of Belgium and the English constitution may be described by the statement that in Belgium individual rights are deductions drawn from the principles of the constitution, whilst in England the so-called principles of the constitution are inductions or generalisations based upon particular decisions pronounced by the courts as to the rights of given individuals.

This is of course a merely formal difference. Liberty is as well secured in Belgium as in England, and as long as this is so it matters nothing whether we say that individuals are free from all risk of arbitrary arrest, because liberty of person is guaranteed by the constitution, or that the right to personal freedom, or in other words to protection from arbitrary arrest, forms part of the constitution because it is secured by the ordinary law of the land. But though this merely formal distinction is in itself of no moment, provided always that the rights of individuals are really secure, the question whether the right to personal freedom or the right to freedom of worship is likely to be secure does depend a good deal upon the answer to the inquiry whether the persons who consciously or unconsciously build up the constitution of their country begin with definitions or declarations of rights, or with the contrivance of remedies by which rights may be enforced or secured. Now, most foreign constitution-makers have begun with declarations of rights. For this they have often been in no wise to blame. Their course of action has more often than not been forced upon them by the stress of circumstances, and by the consideration that to lay down general principles of law is the proper and natural function of legislators. But any knowledge of history suffices to show that foreign constitutionalists have, while occupied in defining rights, given insufficient attention to the absolute necessity for the provision of adequate remedies by which the rights they proclaimed might be enforced.

T R S Allan, 'Constitutional Rights and Common Law' (1991) 2 *Oxford Journal of Legal Studies* 453, 456–60

Rights and Liberties at Common Law

Contemporary reluctance to view the common law as a source of constitutional rights may be partly the consequence of defective legal analysis. At the root of common misunderstanding lies a confusion about the residual nature of liberty.

If common law liberty is merely residual, it is argued, it may be eaten away by ever-encroaching restrictions and restraints until deprived of all substance. The argument benefits here from the failure to distinguish between liberty and liberties.

Ronald Dworkin has repudiated altogether the idea of a general right to liberty. He insists that if someone has a right to something – in any useful sense of that expression – it must be wrong for the Government to deny it to him even though it would be in the general interest to do so. In this anti-utilitarian sense of 'right', there can be no general right to liberty. A great many laws which diminish one's liberty may be properly justified on utilitarian grounds, as being in the general interest or in the general welfare: they do not thereby infringe one's rights, merely on account of their necessary curtailment of freedom. The notion of rights implies that some special justification is needed for Government action which overrides them, even if that action is taken in the general interest. It is in that sense that we generally recognise rights to specific liberties, such as freedom of speech or religion or political activity. Dworkin denies that such liberties may be derived from a more general right to liberty. There must be independent criteria of the value of different sorts of liberty. He suggests that rights to specific liberties may be derived from a more fundamental concept of equality, that every citizen has a right to equal respect and concern [*Taking Rights Seriously* (1977), Chapter 12].

It is as important to make the distinction between liberty and liberties in understanding the common law. The common law does, of course, recognise a general right to liberty – in the sense that every encroachment by the state (or by another) on one's freedom must be justified. There need not be special moral justification of the kind which permits restriction of a basic liberty, such as freedom of speech. But there must be lawful *authority* for coercive action, and legislative restrictions on individual freedom must be duly enacted in the appropriate constitutional manner. If, then, liberty is residual, in the sense that everything which is not expressly forbidden the individual is permitted, the *foundation* of constitutional rights is laid. The burden is on the government or public authority to justify coercion. This is the aspect of the Rule of Law illuminated by *Entick v Carrington* [(1765) 19 St Tr 1029]: every coercive act of Government which is not shown to be authorised is automatically illegal.

But the common law is also solicitous of liberties: it acknowledges the importance of freedoms of speech and assembly, as well as of liberties of the person and rights of property. The case-law is replete with references to the significance of freedom of expression and freedom of conscience as public interests which deserve judicial protection [see Alan Boyle, 'Freedom of Expression as a Public Interest in English Law' (1982) PL 574]. A constitutional right at common law is a product of these two interacting faces of the Rule of Law. My right to freedom of speech is the outcome, first, of my undifferentiated residual liberty – whose restriction needs lawful authority and thereby moral (albeit utilitarian) justification – and secondly, of the court's attachment to the value of free speech, which is anti-utilitarian in character (in Dworkin's sense) and is of critical importance in determining the scope and effect of purported restrictions on my liberty.

In his dissenting judgment in the Court of Appeal in *Wheeler v Leicester City Council* [(1985) AC 1054 (see further my notes at (1985) 48 Mod LR 448; (1986) 49 Mod LR 121], Browne-Wilkinson LJ recognised that freedoms of speech and conscience were fundamental – and so immune from interference without express parliamentary sanction – despite the absence of a written constitution. He noted that modern polarisation of political attitudes had diminished the effectiveness of conventions which protected individuals from discriminatory action by the majority. But he did not suggest that, with the erosion of convention, the common law was helpless. Citing *Verrall v Great Yarmouth Borough Council* [[1981] 1 QB 202] to illustrate the importance accorded to freedom of speech, he concluded that 'it is undoubtedly part of the constitution of this country that, in the absence of express legislative provisions to the contrary, each individual has the right to hold and express his own views'.

Browne-Wilkinson LJ's approach demonstrates the basic dynamic of constitutional rights at common law. The positive value accorded to freedoms of speech and conscience was harnessed to the general principle of residual liberty to protect the applicant from oppressive treatment by the local authority. The authority had required the applicant's rugby club to endorse its views on sporting links with South Africa, as a condition of permission to use a local recreation ground for practice. It had thereby unlawfully interfered with the 'fundamental right of the club and its members to freedom of speech and conscience'. The intrinsic importance of the freedom justified a jealous and critical scrutiny of a claim to statutory support for encroachment on residual liberty. It could not assist the local authority that their stance in respect of apartheid was part of their policy of promoting good race relations; and that the Race Relations Act 1976, s71 imposed a duty to ensure that their functions were exercised with due regard for such an objective. Although the Act made racially discriminatory actions unlawful, it conferred no power to penalise individuals for holding particular views:

Basic constitutional rights in this country such as freedom of the person and freedom of speech are based not on any express provisions conferring such a right but on freedom of an individual to do what he will save to the extent that he is prevented from so doing by the law. Thus, freedom of the person depends on the fact that no one has the right lawfully to arrest the individual save in defined circumstances. The right to freedom of speech depends on the fact that no one has the right to stop the individual expressing his views, save to the extent that those views are libellous or seditious. These fundamental freedoms therefore are not positive rights but an immunity from interference by others. Accordingly, I do not consider that general words in an Act of Parliament can be taken as authorising interference with these basic immunities which are the foundation of our freedom. Parliament (being sovereign) can legislate so as to do so; but it cannot be taken to have conferred such a right on others save by express words [(1985) AC 1054 at 1065].

The speeches in the House of Lords, which affirmed Browne-Wilkinson LJ's conclusions, were less convincing because more loosely argued. Lord Roskill chose to frame his objection to the authority's conduct in terms of 'procedural impropriety' or unfairness; and his refusal to endorse Browne-Wilkinson LJ's 'somewhat wider ground' surely betrayed a weaker grasp of constitutional doctrine. Lord Templeman, though his speech failed to address the level of principle demanded by the freedoms in issue, gave at least general support to the correct approach. 'A private individual or a private organisation cannot be obliged to display zeal in the pursuit of an object sought by a public authority and cannot be obliged to publish views dictated by a public authority [ibid at 1080].'

The case is a good illustration of the dispiriting but notorious tendency of British judges to prefer pragmatism over principle [see further my 'Pragmatism and Theory in Public Law' (1988) 104 LQR 422]. Browne-Wilkinson LJ's principled judgment is conspicuous for its contrasting approach, but that hardly denies its value as an example. The broadly stated grounds of judicial review of administrative action sometimes conceal as much as they reveal. If a case involves questions of constitutional rights – or basic constitutional values – they should be openly confronted. And we should not mistake the deficiencies of particular judgments – even in the House of Lords – or the inadequacy of their reasoning, for inherent defects of 'constitutional' adjudication at common law.

If the speeches of the House of Lords in the 'Spycatcher' litigation were also somewhat disappointing, its result also shows that analysis of the right to freedom of expression as purely residual is incomplete. In some circumstances, at least, protection of the freedom is perceived as a public interest or value entitled to independent weight in a balance of argument to be struck between disclosure and secrecy. The House of Lords refused to grant a final injunction restraining the Sunday Times, the Guardian and the Observer newspapers from publishing extracts from Spycatcher, the book of memoirs of a retired intelligence officer published abroad in breach of his duty of confidentiality owed to the Crown [AG v Guardian Newspapers (No 2) (1990) AC 109]. Affirming that the 'general rule is that anyone is entitled to communicate anything he pleases to anyone else, by speech or in writing or in any other way', Lord Keith rejected the Crown's submission that whenever a Crown servant had made a wrongful disclosure, anyone to whom knowledge of the information came and who was aware of the breach of confidence came under a duty not to communicate it to anyone else [ibid at 256–7]. He cited the decision of the High Court of Australia in Commonwealth of Australia v John Fairfax, in which Mason J emphasised the court's duty to determine the Government's claim to confidentiality in the light of the public interest in open discussion of public affairs. Confidentiality would be upheld only where disclosure would be inimical to the public interest because national security, relations with foreign countries or the ordinary business of government would be prejudiced [(1980) 147 CLR 39, 51–2].

Admittedly, Lord Keith chose to ground his decision on the view that all possible damage to the interest of the Crown had already been done by publication of the book abroad: he was unwilling to engage in any balancing of public interests or to base his decision on any considerations of freedom of the press. Nonetheless, it is clear that the intrinsic importance of freedom of political speech – concerning matters of Government and public affairs – played an important role in limiting the principle protecting confidentiality. Moreover, Lord Goff envisaged a balancing operation, in which the court would weigh the public interest in maintaining the confidence against a countervailing public interest favouring disclosure. In order to restrain disclosure of Government secrets, the Crown must show that restraint was in the public interest. Confidentiality alone was not sufficient justification 'because in a free society there is a continuing public interest that the workings of government should be open to scrutiny and criticism' [[1990] AC 109, 283. See also Scott J's judgment at first instance, especially 144–56, 169–72].

Notes

1   The Diceyan tradition holds that the absence of a written constitution in Britain is not a weakness but a source of strength. This is because the protection of the citizen's liberties is not dependent on vaguely-worded constitutional documents but, rather, flow from specific judicial decisions which give the citizen specific remedies for infringement of his or her liberties.[2] Dicey regarded one of the great strengths of the British Constitution as lying in the lack of broad discretionary powers vested in the executive. Citizens could only be criminalised for clear breaches of clearly established laws. Where there was no relevant law they could know with absolute confidence that they could exercise their liberty as they pleased without fear of incurring any sanction. The Dicyean thesis finds support in the recent decision of *Derbyshire v Times Newspapers* (1993)[3] which has been acclaimed as 'a legal landmark'.[4] The House of Lords found, without referring to Art 10 of the European Convention, that the importance the common law attached to free speech was such that defamation could not be available as an action to local (or central) government.

2   Street, in *Freedom, the Individual and the Law* (1982), argues that 'our judges may be relied on to defend strenuously some kinds of freedom. Their emotions will be aroused where personal freedom is menaced by some politically unimportant area of the executive'.[5] The reluctance of judges to intervene in the politically important areas such as national security or deportation is evidenced by the decisions in *Council of Civil Service Unions v Minister for the Civil Service* (1985)[6] and *ex p Hosenball* (1977).[7]

3   Contrary to the Diceyan view, it may be found that where an attempt has been made in a statute (perhaps due to decisions of the European Court of Human Rights or the ECJ) to give the law some coherence with a view to ensuring that a particular freedom is protected, as is the case with freedom of speech in the Contempt of Court Act 1981, it will often be found that the common law begins to take on a role which undermines the statutory provisions.[8] Or the common law provisions may in some respects curtail

---

2   *Op cit*, p190.
3   [1993] AC 534.
4   p67.
5   p318. Reference is to 5th edn.
6   [1985] AC 374.
7   [1977] 1 WLR 766.
8   See Part VI, Chapter 3 at pp951–3.

liberty more than the statutory ones; this has been said of the common law doctrines of breach of the peace,[9] contempt and conspiracy to corrupt public morals. Ewing and Gearty argue that for this reason a Bill of Rights may be undesirable as the people need Parliament to protect them from the judges, not merely the judges to protect them from Parliament.[10]

Judicial review and civil liberties

In one area – judicial review – the judges have shown a general determination to develop the common law with the basic aim of preventing the exercise of arbitrary power. However, at present the doctrine is fundamentally limited in that as long as a minister appears to have followed a correct and fair procedure, to have acted within his or her powers, and to have made a decision which is not clearly unreasonable the decision must stand regardless of its potentially harmful impact on civil liberties. Thus, the fact that basic liberties were curtailed in the GCHQ[11] and Brind[12] cases did not in itself provide a ground for review. In other words, the courts are confined to looking back at the method of arriving at the decision rather than forward to its likely effects. In cases which touch particularly directly on national security, so sensitive are the judges to the executives' duty to uphold the safety of the realm, that they may define their powers even to look back on the decision as almost non-existent.[13] Sir John Laws considers, however, that judicial review may develop in such a way that it provides greater protection for civil liberties.

Sir J Laws, 'Is the High Court the Guardian of Fundamental Constitutional Rights?' (1993) *Public Law* 59, 71–75[13a]

Now there has been much reference in the recent public law learning to [the concept of proportionality], but the courts have in fact only flirted with it. If it is to play the part which I believe it can, it is particularly important to analyse it properly. The first stage is to see why it has not taken root so far.

What has happened is that the courts have only recognised proportionality as a facet or species of *Wednesbury*, often at the invitation or upon the concession of counsel. In *Pegasus Holdings* [[1988] 1 WLR 990 at 1001F], Schiemann J said:

I do not think that Mr Pannick takes issue with the adoption of the principle of proportionality save that he regards it, in his submission, as merely being an aspect of the *Wednesbury* rule.

In *ex p United States Tobacco*, Taylor LJ said:

Mr Beloff argues that the banning of oral snuff was a disproportionate step to guard against the perceived risk. He referred to the principle of proportionality

---

9   See Part VI, Chapter 3 at pp914–16.

10 Ewing and Gearty, *Freedom under Thatcher* (1989), pp270–1.

11 *Council of Civil Service Unions v Minister for Civil Service* [1984] 3 All ER 935 (the Prime Minister's decision struck directly at freedom of association).

12 [1991] 1 All ER 720, HL (political speech was directly curtailed).

13 See *Secretary of State for Home Department, ex p Stitt* (1987) *The Times*, 3 February, 1987.

13a An extract from this article (including some of the material appearing below) appears in Part V, Chapter 2, pp800–3 in relation to general developments in judicial review.

recognised in Community law and mentioned by Lord Diplock in *CCSU* as a possible future criterion for the exercise of judicial review. However, for the purposes of this case, Mr Beloff accepted that proportionality should be considered simply as a facet of irrationality [[1992] 1 QB 353 at 366G].

The difficulty is that if proportionality is merely a facet of irrationality, it adds nothing to *Wednesbury* and lacks all utility as a category of judicial review: indeed it is *not* itself a category of judicial review at all. But if it is to take its place as a distinct concept, then there must be cases where it may succeed as a ground of substantive challenge, where *Wednesbury* would not; and this means that the court must be willing to strike down a decision on substantive and not merely procedural grounds where *ex hypothesi* the decision is not an irrational one. The reason why so far the courts have been unwilling to take this step is surely the received wisdom that to do so would be to turn the public law court into a court of merits, and so to usurp the primary function of the decision-maker under review.

Now, this received wisdom is the very position I have assaulted in proposing that the judges may develop a variable standard of review according to the importance of the rights in question: and an examination of the potential application of proportionality in practice may help reveal the strengths or weaknesses in what I have said. Here there is another important distinction to be drawn; and again I think it is obvious enough when stated, but it has not so far, I believe, played any very significant part in the debates about proportionality so far held in or out of the courts.

The distinction is between two variants, or applications, of the irrationality rule. There is first the case where the decision under review is a finding of fact, and the complaint is that there was no evidence capable of justifying the finding. ... This category of review is to be contrasted with and distinguished from those cases where the subject-matter of the challenge is the exercise of a discretion. In the latter instance, more often than not, there is no dispute about the primary facts. The complaint is as to the way the facts have been perceived by the decision-maker, the order of importance he has attached to them; or it may be against the policy which he has brought to bear on the facts.

The significance of this distinction for my argument is this. In the fact-finding case, irrationality occupies a natural and easily understood position: where the subordinate body's task is to ascertain past facts by the appreciation of evidence, it is self-evidently unreasonable for him to reach a conclusion which the evidence cannot support; he has manifestly failed to bring a rational mind properly to bear on the subject. But this is very rarely an apt model by which to characterise substantive review in a discretion case. ... where the decision is taken by a public body with a sophisticated bureaucracy in support – typically Government – it will be relatively hard to find a case where a relevant consideration has literally been altogether left out of account, and even harder to find one where the decision cannot be supported by any rational process of thought whatever.

The truth is that the most interesting, and important, types of challenge to discretionary decisions – certainly those involving fundamental rights – are not usually about simple irrationality, or a failure to call attention to relevant matters. They are much more likely to be concerned with the way in which the decision-maker has ordered his priorities; the very essence of discretionary decision-making consists, surely, in the attribution of relative importance to the factors in the case. And here is my point: this is precisely what proportionality is about. ... if we are to entertain a form of review in which fundamental rights are to enjoy the court's distinct protection, the very exercise consists in an insistence that the decision-maker is not free to order his priorities as he chooses, ... an insistence that he accord the first priority to the right in question unless he can show a substantial, objective, public justification for overriding it. Proportionality is surely the means of doing this. It is a ready-made tool in our hands.

It will be said that this approach falls foul of one of the received nostrums in our public law, ... the rule that the relative weight to be accorded to the factors in play is always and only for the decision maker to decide. ... In discretion cases, [the negative principle] is obviously and rightly in place where the subject-matter is economic policy, as the charge-capping litigation shows [*Secretary of State for the Environment, ex p Hammersmith and Fulham London Borough Council* (1991) AC 521]; and no doubt in other instances where fundamental rights are not involved. But if the issue is freedom of speech, or person, or the like, the application of this principle would mean that the decision-maker is at liberty to accord a high or low importance to the right in question, as he chooses. This cannot be right.

What is therefore needed is a preparedness to hold that a decision which overrides a fundamental right without sufficient objective justification will, as a matter of law, necessarily be disproportionate to the aim in view. It will be misleading and unhelpful, not to say something of an affront to the decision-maker, to categorise these cases in conventional *Wednesbury* terms. Despite their primacy, fundamental rights may occupy different places in the hearts of different reasonable people. If a Government or a local authority, perhaps too much in love with a particular policy objective, were to take a decision which curtails free speech for no very convincing reason, to excoriate it as having lost its senses looks a little too much like sending people with unacceptable politics to the psychiatric hospital. The deployment of proportionality sets in focus the true nature of the exercise: the elaboration of a rule about permissible priorities.

If the courts do go down this road, many problems will remain and will have to be worked through case by case. In particular, the judges will have to grapple with the need to build principles for the ascertainment of what is to count as a permissible justification for the abrogation of a fundamental right. For the reasons I have given, there is nothing to prevent their looking to the Strasbourg jurisprudence if it is felt to offer assistance. They are likely to take a stricter view, for example, of such issues as the length of time for which entrants to the United Kingdom may be detained pending a decision by immigration officer or Secretary of State; and the new approach is likely to colour their perceptions of problems relating to contempt of court by publication and the right of access to an independent or judicial tribunal for persons detained pending their removal as being conducive to the public good. Instances may readily be multiplied.

Notes

1   Recently the judiciary has shown a determination to use judicial review to protect fundamental rights in a large number of instances. In *Secretary of State for the Home Dept, ex p Pierson* (1995)[14] the Secretary of State had made a determination that a tariff period of 15 years recommended by the trial judge and the Lord Chief Justice in the case of the applicant's mandatory life sentence, should be increased to 20 years. The applicant sought judicial review of the decision of the Secretary of State on the ground that no adverse factor had been found which would justify the increase in the sentence. The main question at issue was whether the Home Secretary's discretion to increase a life sentence was absolute or whether it had to be exercised fairly. It was found that it was not open to the Home Secretary to fix a longer period for the life sentence if no new adverse factors had emerged. The decision of the Secretary of State therefore had to be quashed.

2   In *Secretary of State for the Home Dept and Another, ex p Norney and others* (1995)[15] the Secretary of State had made a determination that he would not refer the cases of the applicants, IRA life sentence prisoners, to the Parole Board until after the expiry of the tariff period of the sentences. Given the timetable of the Parole Board this meant that in effect every tariff period was increased by 23 weeks. The applicants sought judicial review of the decision of the Secretary of State not to refer their cases to the Parole Board until after the expiry of the tariff period. This practice flouted the principles of common law and the European Convention on Human Rights, Art 5(4). A declaration was therefore granted that the Home Secretary should have referred the applicants' cases to the Parole Board at such a time as would have ensured as far as possible that they would be heard immediately after expiry of the tariff period.

3   In *Ministry of Defence, ex p Smith and others* (1996)[16] the argument used by the Master of the Rolls in reaching the decision has some apparent affinity with that advanced by Sir John Laws above. The applicants had sought judicial review of the policy of the Ministry of Defence in maintaining a ban on homosexuals in the armed forces. The applicants had been dismissed due to the existence of the ban. The Divisional Court had dismissed the applications. The applicants appealed from that decision. The court had jurisdiction to grant judicial review of the policy in question since it did not concern national security issues. In conducting such review the court would apply the usual *Wednesbury* principles of reasonableness. This meant that the court could not interfere with the exercise of an administrative discretion on substantive grounds save where it was satisfied that the decision was reasonable in the sense that it was beyond the range of responses open to a reasonable decision maker; but that in judging whether the decision-maker had exceeded that margin of appreciation the human rights context was important; the more substantial the interference with human rights, the

---

14   *The Times*, 29 November 1995.

15   *The Times*, 6 October 1995.

16   1 All ER 257; *The Times*, 6 November 1995. See also *Cambridge Health Authority, ex p B* [1995] TLR 159, CA; (1995) 1 WLR 898 pp804–5.

more the court would require by way of justification before it was satisfied that the decision was reasonable. The Court rejected the argument of the Ministry of Defence that a more exacting test than applying *Wednesbury* principles of reasonableness was required. Applying such principles and taking into account the support of the policy in both Houses of Parliament, it could not be said that the policy crossed the threshold of irrationality. Thus the appeal was dismissed.

Questions

1   How does Laws' thesis fit with the decision in *Brind v Secretary of State for the Home Department*?[17]

2   If judges were prepared to take fundamental rights into account in judicial review proceedings in the manner suggested by Laws, would incorporation of the European Convention on Human Rights be rendered unnecessary?

The influence of Europe

If, contrary to the Diceyan view, further protection for civil liberties is needed, over and above that provided by the traditional constitutional means, the influence of Europe, through the European Convention on Human Rights (ECHR) and the European Union may increasingly provide it.[18] It is clear that membership of the European Community and the influence of the ECHR have had an enormous impact on civil liberties in the United Kingdom in the last two decades. The European Union, which will have an increasing effect whether or not the Social Charter[19] eventually becomes part of British law, has already had an important impact in the areas of sex discrimination,[20] data protection[21] and freedom of movement.[22]

The rulings of the European Court of Human Rights have led to better protection of human rights in such areas as prisoners rights,[23] freedom of expression,[24] and privacy.[25] Its influence as an *external* force is, however, inherently limited. The effect of a ruling of the European Court of Human Rights is dependent on the Government in question making a change in the law.

---

17   (1991) 1 All ER 720. Below, p872.

18   As pointed out in Part II, Chapter 3, the Treaty of European Union Art F2 provides that the EU will respect fundamental rights as recognised by the Convention. For further discussion of the recognition in the Union of fundamental rights as guaranteed under the Convention see pp295–301.

19   The so-called Social Charter lays down minimum rights for workers in the Community countries. The Conservative Government has not ratified it, but in the Agreement annexed to the Protocol on Social Policy in the Treaty of Maastricht the other Member States recorded their agreement to 'continue along the path' laid down in it.

20   See *eg Marshall (No 2)* [1993] 4 All ER 586.

21   The Data Protection Act 1984 derived from the European Convention for the Protection of Individuals with regard to the Automatic Protection of Data, 17 September 1980.

22   Art 48 of the Treaty of Rome, which is directly enforceable.

23   *Golder*, Eur Court HR, Series A, Vol 18 Judgment of 21 February 1975.

24   *Sunday Times case* (1980) 2 EHRR 245.

25   *Gaskin v UK* (1989) 12 EHRR 36.

The British Government may be able to minimise the impact of an adverse judgment by interpreting defeat narrowly,[26] by avoiding implementation of a ruling[27] or by obeying the letter of the Article in question but ignoring its spirit.[28] The impact of the ECHR is also lessened because the process of invoking it is extremely cumbersome, lengthy[29] and expensive.[30] Merger of the European Court and Commission on Human Rights as a means of speeding up the process appears to be imminent, as discussed in Part II, Chapter 3.[31] However, unless merger greatly ameliorates the system of the long trek to Strasbourg (starting with the exhaustion of domestic remedies) it will continue to deter all but the most determined and resourceful litigants.

The ECHR has probably had a more significant influence within domestic law since the judges are increasingly prepared to take it into account in reaching a decision. Each State decides on the status the Convention enjoys in national law; there is no obligation under Art 1 to allow individuals to rely on it in *national* courts. In some States it has the status of constitutional law;[32] in others ordinary law.[33] However, in Britain it has no binding force. Successive UK Governments have considered that it is not necessary for the Convention to be part of British law because they have always maintained that the UK's unwritten constitution is in conformity with it. Thus a UK citizen cannot go before a UK court and simply argue that a Convention right has been violated. Nevertheless the influence of the Convention is rapidly becoming more significant in domestic law through rulings in UK courts.

Brind v Secretary of State for the Home Department (1991) 1 All ER 720, 722–3, 733–5

> **Lord Bridge of Harwich:** ... The obligations of the United Kingdom, as a party to the Convention, are to secure to every one within its jurisdiction the rights which the Convention defines including both the right to freedom of expression under Art 10 and the right under Art 13 to 'an effective remedy before a national authority' for any violation of the other rights secured by the Convention. It is accepted, of course, by the applicants that, like any other treaty obligations which have not been embodied in the law by statute, the Convention is not part of the

---

26   *Golder*, see note 23 above.

27   *Brogan, Coyle, McFadden and Tracey v United Kingdom* (Case No 10/1987/133/184–7) (1988). The Government refused to implement the ruling, entering a derogation under Art 15.

28   *Abdulaziz, Cabales and Balkandali v United Kingdom* (1985) 7 EHRR 471. To implement the ruling, the UK 'equalised down'.

29   The Commission makes over 3,000 provisional files a year. The average petition took five years nine months between 1982/1987 if it went all the way through the system – four years before the Commission, nearly two before the Court (15 EHRR 321 at 327). Petitions can take nine years. See further Part II, Chapter 3, pp286–95.

30   Legal aid is not available until after the complaint has been held admissible by the Commission.

31   In Part II, Chapter 3, pp286–95.

32   Eg Austria.

33   This includes Belgium, France, Italy, Luxembourg and Germany.

domestic law, that the courts accordingly have no power to enforce Convention rights directly and that, if domestic legislation conflicts with the Convention, the courts must nevertheless enforce it. But it is already well settled that, in construing any provision in domestic legislation which is ambiguous in the sense that it is capable of a meaning which either conforms to or conflicts with the Convention, the courts will presume that Parliament intended to legislate in conformity with the Convention, not in conflict with it. Hence, it is submitted, when a statute confers upon an administrative authority a discretion capable of being exercised in a way which infringes any basic human right protected by the Convention, it may similarly be presumed that the legislative intention was that the discretion should be exercised within the limitations which the Convention imposes. I confess that I found considerable persuasive force in this submission. But in the end I have been convinced that the logic of it is flawed. When confronted with a simple choice between two possible interpretations of some specific statutory provision, the presumption whereby the courts prefer that which avoids conflict between our domestic legislation and our international treaty obligations is a mere canon of construction which involves no importation of international law into the domestic field. But where Parliament has conferred on the executive an administrative discretion without indicating the precise limits within which it must be exercised, to presume that it must be exercised within Convention limits would be to go far beyond the resolution of an ambiguity. It would be to impute to Parliament an intention not only that the executive should exercise the discretion in conformity with the Convention, but also that the domestic courts should enforce that conformity by the importation into domestic administrative law of the text of the Convention and the jurisprudence of the European Court of Human Rights in the interpretation and application of it. If such a presumption is to apply to the statutory discretion exercised by the Secretary of State under s29(3) of the Act of 1981 in the instant case, it must also apply to any other statutory discretion exercised by the executive which is capable of involving an infringement of Convention rights. When Parliament has been content for so long to leave those who complain that their Convention rights have been infringed to seek their remedy in Strasbourg, it would be surprising suddenly to find that the judiciary had, without Parliament's aid, the means to incorporate the Convention into such an important area of domestic law and I cannot escape the conclusion that this would be a judicial usurpation of the legislative function.

But I do not accept that this conclusion means that the courts are powerless to prevent the exercise by the executive of administrative discretions, even when conferred, as in the instant case, in terms which are on their face unlimited, in a way which infringes fundamental human rights. Most of the rights spelled out in terms in the Convention, including the right to freedom of expression, are less than absolute and must in some cases yield to the claims of competing public interests. Thus, Art 10(2) of the Convention spells out and categorises the competing public interests by reference to which the right to freedom of expression may have to be curtailed. In exercising the power of judicial review we have neither the advantages nor the disadvantages of any comparable code to which we may refer or by which we are bound. But again, this surely does not mean that in deciding whether the Secretary of State, in the exercise of his discretion, could reasonably impose the restriction he has imposed on the broadcasting organisations, we are not perfectly entitled to start from the premise that any restriction of the right to freedom of expression requires to be justified and that nothing less than an important competing public interest will be sufficient to justify it. The primary judgment as to whether the particular competing public interest justifies the particular restriction imposed falls to be made by the Secretary of State to whom Parliament has entrusted the discretion. But we are entitled to exercise a secondary judgment by asking whether a reasonable Secretary of State, on the material before him, could reasonably make that primary judgment …

Lord Ackner: … The Convention which is contained in an international treaty to which the United Kingdom is a party has not yet been incorporated into English domestic law. The appellants accept that it is a constitutional principle that if Parliament has legislated and the words of the statute are clear, the statute must be applied even if its application is in breach of international law. In *Salomon v Customs and Excise Comrs* [1966] 3 All ER 871 at 875, [1967] 2 QB 116 at 143 Diplock LJ stated:

> If the terms of the legislation are clear and unambiguous they must be – given effect to whether or not they carry out Her Majesty's treaty obligations.

Much reliance was placed upon the observations of Lord Diplock in *Garland v British Rail Engineering Ltd* Case 12/81 [1982] 2 All ER 402 at 4154, [1983] 2 AC 751 at 771 when he said:

> …it is a principle of construction of United Kingdom statutes … that the words of a statute passed after the treaty has been signed and dealing with the subject matter of the international obligation of the United Kingdom, are to be construed, if they are reasonably capable of bearing such a meaning, as intended to carry out the obligation, and not to be inconsistent with it.

I did not take the view that Lord Diplock was intending to detract from or modify what he had said in *Salomon's* case.

It is well settled that the Convention may be deployed for the purpose of the resolution of an ambiguity in English primary or subordinate legislation. *Chief Immigration Officer, Heathrow Airport, ex p Salamat Bibi* [1976] 3 All ER 843, [1976] 1 WLR 979 concerned a lady who arrived at London Airport from Pakistan with two small children saying that she was married to a man who was there and who met her. She was refused leave to enter and an application was made for an order of *certiorari* and also for *mandamus* on the ground that she ought to have been treated as the wife of the man who met her at the airport. During the course of argument a question arose about the impact of the Convention and in particular Art 8 concerning the right to private and family life and the absence of interference by a public authority with that right.

In his judgment Lord Denning MR said ([1976] 3 All ER 843 at 847, [1976] 1 WLR 979 at 984):

> The position, as I understand it, is that if there is any ambiguity in our statutes or uncertainty in our law then these courts can look to the Convention as an aid to clear up the ambiguity and uncertainty … But I would dispute altogether that the Convention is part of our law. Treaties and declarations do not become part of our law until they are made law by Parliament.

In his judgment Geoffrey Lane LJ said ([1976] 3 All ER 843 at 850, [1976] WLR 979 at 988):

> It is perfectly true that the Convention was ratified by this country … Nevertheless the Convention, not having been enacted by Parliament as an

Act, does not have the effect of law in this country; whatever persuasive force it may have in resolving ambiguities it certainly cannot have the effect of overriding the plain provisions of the 1971 Act and the rules made thereunder.

This decision was followed in *Fernandez v Secretary of State for the Home Dept* (1981) Imm AR 1, another case where Art 8 of the Convention was relied upon and where the Court of Appeal held that the Secretary of State in exercising his statutory powers was not obliged to take into account the provisions of the Convention, it not being part of the law of this country. The Convention is a treaty and may be resorted to in order to help resolve some uncertainty or ambiguity in municipal law. These decisions were most recently followed by the Court of Appeal in *Chundawadra v Immigration Appeal Tribunal* (1989) Imm AR 161.

Mr Lester contends that s29(3) *is* ambiguous or uncertain. He submits that although it contains within its wording no fetter upon the extent of the discretion it gives to the Secretary of State, it is accepted that that discretion is not absolute. There is however no ambiguity in s29(3). *It is* not open to two or more different constructions. The limit placed upon the discretion is simply that the power is to be used only for the purposes for which it was granted by the legislation (the so-called *Padfield* doctrine) and that it must be exercised reasonably in the *Wednesbury* sense. No question of the construction of the words of s29(3) arises, as would be the case if it was alleged to be ambiguous, or its meaning uncertain.

There is yet a further answer to Mr Lester's contention. He claims that the Secretary of State before issuing his directives should have considered not only the Convention (it is accepted that he in fact did so) but that he should have properly construed it and correctly taken it into consideration. It was therefore a relevant, indeed a vital, factor to which he was obliged to have proper regard pursuant to the *Wednesbury* doctrine, with the result that his failure to do so rendered his decision unlawful. The fallacy of this submission is however plain. If the Secretary of State was obliged to have proper regard to the Convention, ie to conform with Art 10, this inevitably would result in incorporating the Convention into English domestic law by the back door. It would oblige the courts to police the operation of the Convention and to ask itself in each case, where there was a challenge, whether the restrictions were 'necessary in a democratic society ...' applying the principles enunciated in the decisions of the European Court of Human Rights. The treaty, not having been incorporated in English law, cannot be a source of rights and obligations and the question – did the Secretary of State act in breach of Art 10? – does not therefore arise.

As was recently stated by Lord Oliver in *Maclaine Watson & Co Ltd v Dept of Trade and Industry* (1989) 3 All ER 523 at 544–545, (1990) 2 AC 418 at 500 (the *International Tin Council* case):

> Treaties, as it is sometimes expressed, are not self-executing. Quite simply, a treaty is not part of English law unless and until it has been incorporated into the law by legislation. So far as individuals are concerned, it is *res inter alios acta* from which they cannot derive rights and by which they cannot be deprived of rights or subjected to obligations; and it is outside the purview of the court not only because it is made in the conduct of foreign relations, which are a prerogative of the Crown, but also because, as a source of rights and obligations, it is irrelevant.

...

I would accordingly dismiss this appeal with costs.

Derbyshire County Council v Times Newspapers Ltd [1992] 3 WLR 28, 60–1, CA

Butler-Sloss LJ: In *Attorney General v Guardian Newspapers Ltd (No 2)* [1990] 1 AC 109 Lord Goff of Chieveley said (in relation to breach of confidential information), at p283:

> ...I wish to observe that I can see no inconsistency between English law on this subject and Art 10 of the European Convention on Human Rights. This is scarcely surprising, since we may pride ourselves on the fact that freedom of speech has existed in this country perhaps as long as, if not longer than, it has existed in any other country in the world. The only difference is that, whereas Art 10 of the Convention, in accordance with its avowed purpose, proceeds to state a fundamental right and then to qualify it, we in this country (where everybody is free to do anything, subject only to the provisions of the law) proceed rather upon an assumption of freedom of speech, and turn to our law to discover the established exceptions to it. In any event I conceive it to be my duty, when I am free to do so, to interpret the law in accordance with the obligations of the Crown under this treaty.

Adopting, as I respectfully do, that approach to the Convention, the principles governing the duty of the English court to take account of Art 10 appear to be as follows: where the law is clear and unambiguous, either stated as the common law or enacted by Parliament, recourse to Art 10 is unnecessary and inappropriate. Consequently the law of libel in respect of individuals does not require the court to consider the Convention. But where there is an ambiguity, or the law is otherwise unclear or so far undeclared by an appellate court, the English court is not only entitled but, in my judgment, obliged to consider the implications of Art 10. Ralph Gibson LJ in *Attorney General v Newspaper Publishing plc, The Times*, 28 February 1990: Court of Appeal (Civil Division) Transcript No 171 of 1990, said in respect of contempt of court:

> if it is demonstrated by reference to authority binding on this court, or by reference to clearly established principles of the common law, that the appellants were rightly held to have committed the *actus reus* of contempt of court, this court cannot apply directly the terms of the Convention so as to reach a different conclusion. If, however, it is not clear in what terms the relevant law is to be formulated, and there is no binding authority upon the matter, this court should have regard to the terms of the Convention because it is a safe presumption that the law of contempt of court in this country is in conformity with the requirements of that Convention.

See also Lord Bridge of Harwich and Lord Ackner in *Secretary of State for the Home Department, ex p Brind* [1991] 1 AC 671, 747, 760.

Ralph Gibson LJ's observations seem equally applicable to libel. In the present case there is no binding authority upon this court, and I do not consider the law to be clear. Even if it were, in a decision of the Divisional Court on blasphemy Watkins LJ thought it necessary to consider the Convention, even although the law on blasphemy was clear: *Chief Metropolitan Stipendiary Magistrate, ex p Choudhury* [1991] 1 QB 429, 449. Accordingly, it is for this court to consider the application of Art 10 to the question whether a local authority may sue for libel; and in my judgment Morland J was wrong not to do so.

Notes

1   As this ruling accepts, it is a general principle of construction that statutes will be interpreted if possible so as to conform with International Treaties to which Britain is a party on the basis that the Government is aware of its international obligations and would not intend to legislate contrary to them.

2   The position as regards the Convention was explained in *Re M and H (Minors)* 1988[34] by Lord Brandon of Oakbrook: 'The English courts are under no duty to apply the Convention's provisions directly. Further, while English courts may strive where they can to interpret statutes as conforming with the obligations of Britain under the Convention, they are nevertheless bound to give effect to statutes which are free from ambiguity in accordance with their terms even if those statutes may be in conflict with the Convention'. Thus, if a statute unambiguously violates fundamental rights the courts must apply it, unless the statute implements EU law (see note 7 below).

3   The decision in *Brind* reaffirmed the accepted principle that the Convention should be taken into account where domestic legislation is ambiguous. It also determined that state officials are not bound by the Convention in exercising discretionary power. Lord Bridge, reflecting the view of the majority, accepted nevertheless that the Convention might be relevant in reviewing the exercise of such powers. However, the Government has subsequently accepted that state officials exercising such powers must comply with the Convention.[35]

4   Applying Art 10, the Court of Appeal found in the *Derbyshire* case that a local authority cannot sue for libel. The House of Lords considered that in the particular instance, the common law could determine the issues in favour of freedom of speech,[36] but this does not mean that the guidance offered by the Court of Appeal is not of value in an instance in which the common law is uncertain.

5   The Court of Appeal findings suggest that judges have no choice as to whether to consider the Convention where the law is ambiguous[37] or – and this does appear to be a new development – where it is not yet settled in an appellate court.

6   Lord Scarman in *AG v BBC* (1980)[38] considered the influence of the Convention on the common law. He said that where there was some leeway to do so, a court which must adjudicate on the relative weight to be given to different public interests under the common law should try to strike a balance in a manner consistent with the treaty obligations accepted by the Government. 'If the issue should ultimately be ... a question of legal policy, we must have regard to the country's international obligation to observe the Convention as interpreted by the Court of Human Rights.' Lord Scarman's approach was endorsed by the House of Lords in *AG v Guardian Newspapers (No 2)* (1990),[39] Lord Goff stating: 'I conceive it to be my duty, when I am free to do so, to interpret the law in accordance with the obligations of the Crown under [the Convention]'. In *Chief Metropolitan Magistrates' Court, ex p Choudhury* (1991),[40] Art 10 was taken into account in reviewing the decision of the magistrates' court not to grant summonses against Salman Rushdie and his publishers for the common law offence of blasphemous libel. This was done even though, as Butler-Sloss LJ observes above, the law was clear.

---

34   3 WLR 485, 498.
35   HL Deb 559, WA, 7 December 1994, col 84 and WA, 9 January 1995, vol 560, col 1.
36   [1993] AC 534, esp. at 551.
37   See further on this point [1992] MLR 721.
38   3 WLR 109, 130; [1981] AC 303, 354.
39   1 AC 109, 283.
40   QB 429.

7   Article F2 of the Treaty of Maastricht which created the European Union provides that Member States will respect fundamental rights as guaranteed by the ECHR as general principles of Community law. Thus, in domestic law, implementation of Community measures is clearly subject to respect for the Convention rights. In the *Factortame (No 2)* (1991)[41] and *EOC* (1995)[42] rulings the House of Lords determined that a domestic statute could be disapplied if it conflicted with Community law. Thus, if a British citizen believes that one of his or her Convention rights has been violated by a domestic statute, and the violation arises in an area affected by a European Union measure, it would seem that he or she could seek judicial review of the statutory provision in question (assuming that no private law remedy was available), relying on the incompatibility found between domestic and EU law once the EU measure had been interpreted in accordance with the Convention.[43]

Questions

1   Simon Lee in *Judging Judges* (1989), p160 states: 'We already have a Bill of Rights in the European Convention' as part of an argument that the whole Bill of Rights debate is misguided. Do you agree?

2   Is the decision in the *Smith* case (1996), above, as regards the relevance of the Convention to the exercise of administrative discretion, distinguishable from Lord Bridge's findings on this point in *Brind*?

THE BILL OF RIGHTS ISSUE

If there is a need for some constitutional change to safeguard civil liberties, should that change take the form of a Bill of Rights? In 1968 Anthony Lester QC proposed the incorporation of the European Convention on Human Rights into national law[44] and since then a number of Private Members' Bills have made the same proposal.[45] One of these was Lord Wade's Bill, debated in 1977, which led to appointment of a House of Lords Select Committee to consider the issue. It considered (on a six/five majority) that a Bill of Rights should be introduced and (unanimously) that it should be the ECHR, excluding the Fourth Protocol which has not been ratified. Support for a Bill of Rights appears to have grown among lawyers,[46] academics[47] and politicians during the 1980s and early 1990s; both the present Master of the Rolls and the Lord Chief Justice indicated upon taking office that they shared in this support. During the late 1970s, certain senior Conservatives displayed some support for a Bill of Rights when in

---

41   1 AC 603.

42   1 AC 1.

43   See further Part II, Chapter 3, (section on 'The influence of the Convention in the European Union'), as to rulings of the European Court of Justice taking the Convention into account, in particular Case 13/14 *P v S and Cornwall County Council* (1996), judgment of 30 April 1996.

44   A Lester, 'Democracy and Individual Rights' (1968), pp13–15.

45   Not all Bills proposing the introduction of a Bill of Rights have advocated incorporating the convention. The Charter '88 Group advocates enshrining civil liberties by means of a Bill of Rights but it has not put forward a text. See N Stanger (1990) 8 *Index on Censorship* 14.

46   In particular Lord Scarman: see *English Law – The New Dimension* (1974) Parts II and VII; see also G Robertson, *Freedom, the Individual and the Law*, 7th edn (1993), Chap 12; A Lester, 'Fundamental Rights: The United Kingdom Isolated' (1984) PL 46.

47   See M Zander, *A Bill of Rights?* (1985), p90; E Barendt, *Freedom of Speech* (1987), p329–32.

opposition[48] but made no move to adopt one when they came to power in 1979.[49] Labour opposed a Bill of Rights during the 1980s and up to and beyond the 1992 election, but decided to espouse it as official policy in 1993. On 11 January 1994 the Labour MP Mr Graham Allen introduced a Private Member's Bill, the Human Rights No 3 Bill, which proposed incorporation of the ECHR with the First Protocol and the creation of a Human Rights Commission; it received a first reading in the Commons but did not progress to a second reading. If Labour forms the next government it intends to introduce a Bill along similar lines (see *A New Agenda for Democracy*, Party Conference Document 1993).

The argument from democracy

Some judges[50] and academic writers[51] remain opposed to or uneasy as to the adoption of a Bill of Rights. It has been argued that the whole notion of endowing an unelected group with a considerable area of power removed from the reach of the legislature is incompatible with democratic theory. This issue is discussed by Dworkin and Waldron below.

R Dworkin, *A Bill of Rights for Britain* (1990), pp32–8

Is Incorporation Undemocratic?

The argument for parliamentary supremacy is often thought to rest on a more important and fundamental argument, however, according to which Britain should not have subscribed to the European Convention in the first place. This is the argument: that it is undemocratic for appointed judges rather than an elected Parliament to have the last word about what the law is. People who take that view will resist incorporation, because incorporation enlarges the practical consequences of what they regard as the mistake of accepting the Convention. They will certainly resist the idea that domestic judges should have the power to read the Convention more liberally and so provide more protection than Strasbourg requires.

Their argument misunderstands what democracy is, however. In the first place, it confuses democracy with the power of elected officials. There is no genuine democracy, even though officials have been elected in otherwise fair elections, unless voters have had access to the information they need so that their votes can be knowledgeable choices rather than only manipulated responses to advertising campaigns. Citizens of a democracy must be able to participate in government not just spasmodically, in elections from time to time, but constantly through informed and free debate about their Government's performance between elections. Those evident requirements suggest what other nations have long ago realised: that Parliament *must* be constrained in certain ways in order that democracy be genuine rather than sham. The argument that a Bill of Rights would be undemocratic is therefore not just wrong but the opposite of the truth.

The depressing story of the Thatcher Government's concentrated assault on free speech is more than enough to prove that point. In the *Harman, Ponting* and

---

48 For example, in 1978 Mr Leon Brittan, Opposition Front Bench spokesman on devolution, moved an amendment to the Scotland Bill at committee stage which would have made the European Convention effective in Scotland.

49 The official policy of the Conservative Party is against a Bill of Rights: see *Conservative Research Department Brief: Civil Liberties* (1990).

50 For example, Lord McCluskey in his 1986 Reith Lectures, Lord Browne-Wilkinson (1992) PL 397, 409.

51 See, eg Ewing and Gearty, *Freedom Under Thatcher*, pp273 *et seq*; Waldron (below, pp881–3); M Loughlin *Public Law and Political Theory* (1992), esp pp220–7.

Spycatcher cases, in denying a public interest exception in the new Official Secrets Act, in the broadcasting bans, in the *Death on the Rock* matter, government tried to censor information of the type citizens need in order to vote intelligently or criticise officials effectively. The officials who took these decisions acted out of various motives: out of concern for confidentiality, or to discourage views they thought dangerous, or to improve the morale of the police and security services, or sometimes just to protect themselves from political damage. But none of these reasons is good enough: in a democracy officials have no right to dictate what the voters should know or think. The politicians would very likely have acted differently in every one of these cases if Art 10 of the European Convention had been part of British law, and the prospect of judicial intervention had been immediate and certain rather than delayed and in doubt. British democracy would obviously have been strengthened not weakened as a result.

It is true, however, that the European Convention forbids Governments to adopt or retain some laws that a majority of their citizens do want, and would continue to want even if they had all the information anyone might wish. The European Court struck down Northern Ireland's homosexuality law, for example, not because the Court doubted that a majority of the voters of Northern Ireland wanted that law, but because the Convention prohibits that form of discrimination whether the majority wishes it or not. If the European Convention were incorporated, British judges might strike down Britain's blasphemy law, which prohibits books or art deeply offensive to orthodox Christianity, even if a majority favoured retaining that law. The blasphemy law violates Arts 9 and 10 of the Convention, which protect freedom of conscience and free speech. In my view (although British courts have rejected the suggestion) the blasphemy law also violates Arts 9 and 14, which taken together prohibit religious discrimination, because that law discriminates in favour of Christianity. (Moslems said it was unjust that Salman Rushdie's book, *The Satanic Verses*, could not be prosecuted as blasphemous of their religion.) Of course the blasphemy law should not be extended to other religions, as they argued it should. It should instead be repealed, because it would violate the Convention even if it applied to religion in general.

Would it offend democracy if a British court had the power to strike down the blasphemy law as inconsistent with the Convention? No, because true democracy is not just *statistical* democracy, in which anything a majority or plurality wants is legitimate for that reason, but *communal* democracy, in which majority decision is legitimate only if it is a majority within a community of equals. That means not only that everyone must be allowed to participate in politics as an equal, through the vote and through freedom of speech and protest, but that political decisions must treat everyone with equal concern and respect, that each individual person must be guaranteed fundamental civil and political rights no combination of other citizens can take away, no matter how numerous they are or how much they despise his or her race or morals or way of life.

That view of what democracy means is at the heart of all the charters of human rights, including the European Convention. It is now the settled concept of democracy in Europe, the mature, principled concept that has now triumphed throughout Western Europe as well as in North America. It dominates the powerful movement towards democracy in Eastern Europe and Russia, and it was suppressed only with the most horrible tyranny in China. The rival, pure statistical concept of democracy, according to which democracy is consistent with oppressing minorities, was the concept proclaimed as justification by the Communist tyrannies after the Second World War: they said democracy meant government in the interests of the masses. The civilised world has recoiled from the totalitarian view, and it would be an appalling irony if Britain now embraced it as a reason for denying minorities constitutional rights.

This seems to me a decisive answer to the argument that incorporation would be undemocratic. I hope and believe that a different but equally decisive answer can also be made in Britain now: that the argument is self-defeating because the great majority of British people themselves rejects the crude statistical view of democracy on which the argument is based. Even people who do not think of themselves as belonging to any minority have good reasons for insisting that a majority's power to rule should be limited. Something crucially important to them – their religious freedom or professional independence or liberty of conscience, for example – might one day prove inconvenient to the Government of the day. Even people who cannot imagine being isolated in that way might prefer to live in a genuine political community, in which everyone's dignity as an equal is protected, rather than just in a state they control.

That attractive impulse lies dormant in day-to-day political argument about how to fight terrorism or whether tolerance for homosexuals should be promoted with taxpayers' money or when suspected criminals' telephones should be tapped. But it might well surface during a general constitutional debate, when the nation reflects about its traditions and its image of itself. A public opinion poll in Britain in 1986, taken before a parliamentary debate about incorporation, reported that twice as many of those questioned favoured incorporation as opposed it, and that 71 per cent thought a constitutional Bill of Rights would improve democracy. Such polls are unreliable in various ways, but the dramatic preference for incorporation is nevertheless impressive. Britain will not have a Bill of Rights, even in the relatively weak form we have been discussing, unless it turns out, after an intense period of public debate, that the preference is genuine, that the British people do share a constitutional sense of justice. If so, and if we assume that this sense of justice will be shared by their descendants, then the argument that incorporation is undemocratic will have been defeated on its own terms.

Jeremy Waldron, 'A Right-Based Critique of Constitutional Rights', (1993) 13 Oxford Journal of Legal Studies 18, 46–7, 50–1

Democratic Self-Restraint

If a Bill of Rights is incorporated into British law it will be because Parliament (or perhaps the people in a referendum) will have voted for incorporation. Ronald Dworkin has argued that this fact alone is sufficient to dispose of the democratic objections we have been considering. The objections, in his view, are self-defeating because polls reveal that more than 71 per cent of people believe that British democracy would be improved by the incorporation of a Bill of Rights [Dworkin, *A Bill of Rights for Britain, op cit*, pp36–7].

However, the matter cannot be disposed of so easily. For one thing, the fact that there is popular support, even overwhelming popular support, for an alteration in constitutional procedures does not show that such alteration therefore makes things more democratic. Certainly, my arguments entail that if the people want a regime of constitutional rights, then that is what they should have: democracy requires *that*. But we must not confuse the reason for carrying out a proposal with the character of the proposal itself. If the people wanted to experiment with dictatorship, principles of democracy might give us a reason to allow them to do so. But it would not follow that dictatorship is democratic. Everyone agrees that it is possible for a democracy to vote itself out of existence; that, for the proponents of constitutional reform, is one of their great fears. My worry is that popular support for the constitutional reforms envisaged by Dworkin and other members of Charter 88 amounts to exactly that: voting democracy out of existence, at least so far as a wide range of issues of political principle is concerned.

There *is* a debate going on in Britain about these issues. Citizens are deliberating about whether to limit the powers of Parliament and enhance the powers of the judiciary along the lines we have been discussing. One of the things they are considering in this debate is whether such moves will make Britain more or less democratic. This article is intended as a contribution to that debate: I have offered grounds for thinking that this reform will make Britain less of a democracy. What the participants in that debate do *not* need to be told is that constitutional reform will make Britain more democratic if they think it does. For they are trying to work out *what to think* on precisely that issue.

Dworkin also suggests that the democratic argument against a Bill of Rights is self-defeating in a British context, 'because a majority of British people themselves rejects the crude statistical view of democracy on which the argument is based' [*ibid* p36]. But although democracy connotes the idea of popular voting, it is not part of the concept of democracy that its own content be fixed by popular voting. If a majority of the British people thought a military dictatorship was democratic (because more in tune with the 'true spirit of the people' or whatever), that would not show that it was, nor would it provide grounds for saying that democratic arguments against the dictatorship were 'self-defeating'. If Dworkin wants to make a case against 'the crude statistical view' as a conception of democracy, he must argue for it: that is, he must *show* that a system in which millions of votes cast by ordinary people are actually *counted,* and actually *count* for something when decisions are being made against a background of disagreement, is a worse conception of the values set out in s8 than a model in which votes count only when they accord with a particular theory of what citizens owe one another in the way of equal concern and respect ...

In the end, I think, the matter comes down to this. If a process is democratic and comes up with the correct result, it does no injustice to anyone. But if the process is non-democratic, it inherently and necessarily does an injustice, in its operation, to the participatory aspirations of the ordinary citizen. And it does *this* injustice, tyrannises in *this* way, whether it comes up with the correct result or not.

One of my aims in all this has been to 'dis-aggregate' our concepts of democracy and majority rule. Instead of talking in grey and abstract terms about democracy, we should focus our attention on the individuals – the millions of men and women – who claim a right to a say, on equal terms, in the processes by which they are governed. Instead of talking impersonally about 'the counter-majoritarian difficulty', we should distinguish between a court's deciding things by a majority, and lots and lots of ordinary men and women deciding things by a majority. If we do this, we will see that the question 'Who gets to participate?' always has priority over the question 'How do they decide, when they disagree?'

Above all, when we think about taking certain issues away from the people and entrusting them to the courts, we should adopt the same individualist focus that we use for thinking about any other issue of rights. Someone concerned about rights does not see social issues in impersonal terms: she does not talk about 'the problem of torture' or 'the problem of censorship' but about the predicament of each and every individual who may be tortured or silenced by the State. Similarly, we should think not about 'the people' or 'the majority', as some sort of blurred quantitative mass, but of the individual citizens, considered one by one, who make up the polity in question.

If we are going to defend the idea of an entrenched Bill of Rights put effectively beyond revision by anyone other than the judges, we should try and think what we might say to some public-spirited citizen who wishes to launch a campaign or lobby her MP on some issue of rights about which she feels strongly and on which she has done her best to arrive at a considered and impartial view. She is not asking to be a dictator; she perfectly accepts that her voice should have no more power than that of anyone else who is prepared to participate in politics. But – like her suffragette forebears – she wants a vote; she wants her voice and her activity to count on matters of high political importance.

In defending a Bill of Rights, we have to imagine ourselves saying to her: 'You may write to the newspaper and get up a petition and organise a pressure group to lobby Parliament. But even if you succeed, beyond your wildest dreams, and orchestrate the support of a large number of like-minded men and women, and manage to prevail in the legislature, your measure may be challenged and struck down because your view of what rights we have does not accord with the judges' view. When their votes differ from yours, theirs are the votes that will prevail'. It is my submission that saying this does not comport with the respect and honour normally accorded to ordinary men and women in the context of a theory of rights.

Notes

1   Waldron's position may be criticised on the basis that to characterise a Bill of Rights as setting formulations 'in stone' is to fail to take account of the immense diversity of interpretations which can be extracted from a broadly worded document such as the European Convention,[52] and the way in which such interpretations can develop to reflect changes in popular attitudes.[53] The fact that one document – the American Constitution – has been found at different times to support both black slavery and positive discrimination in favour of black people, is a case in point. A further objection is that Waldron's argument ignores the reasonable degree of consensus that exists around many basic rights. For example, when discussing the possibility of protecting the right to participate in democracy, Waldron argues that democratic procedures themselves cannot be entrenched, because 'People disagree about how participatory rights should be understood ...' (p39). However, he fails to mention the near complete agreement on the fundamental right of universal adult suffrage.

---

52   Waldron's objections *prima facie* do not seem to take account of those adjudicatory theories which explain the vital part that both the judges' moral and political convictions and the mass of shared assumptions and understanding in a particular society play in the interpretation of texts. (For an extremely lucid and accessible exposition of the above point see N Simmonds, 'Between Positivism and Idealism' (1991) CLJ 308). However Waldron considers such theories (eg pp41–43), finding that his objection is not so much that judges should be *able* to interpret and modify peoples' rights but that democratic institutions should be *disabled* from doing so. But once Waldron has conceded the point that judges can radically amend the previously understood meaning of a text, his point about setting rights in stone is lost.

53   It is arguable that judges can more readily respond to marked changes in the moral climate than politicians. For example the judiciary, in response to a growing consensus that the marital rape exemption was indefensible, abolished the immunity of husbands (*R* [1991] 4 All ER 481) at a time when there were no indications that Parliament was imminently prepared to make time for legislation.

2   Dworkin argues that the implications of Waldron's thesis are themselves contrary to true democracy.[54] Further, the refusal to disable the majority by entrenchment of rights includes a refusal to entrench democracy itself. This refusal in effect means that Waldron will not deny the right of the majority of the day to destroy democracy by disenfranchising a group such as all non-whites, or even by voting itself out of existence, thereby denying democracy to future generations. Dworkin argues that a Bill of Rights is ultimately concerned with *preserving* a worthwhile democracy for the future, and therefore that entrenched basic rights show *more* respect for democratic principles than do the advocates of retaining the untrammelled power of the majority of the day.[55]

Questions

1   How much force, if any, would there be in Waldron's argument if the Bill of Rights were protected only by a 'notwithstanding clause'? (See below.)

2   Would the rights of groups who tend to be unpopular with the majority of voters (such as suspected criminals, prisoners, new age travellers, homosexuals) be better protected through the operation of the democratic process or by enacting the European Convention on Human Rights into British law?

Protection for a Bill of Rights

It should be pointed out that the Bill of Rights need not inevitably remove power from the legislature: it could be framed as guidance to legislators, on the lines of the Canadian Bill of Rights 1960 and the New Zealand Bill of Rights 1990. However, the Canadian instrument was less effective than its successor, the Canadian Charter 1982, which does allow for judicial review of legislation, and its example suggests that if Britain is to enact a Bill of Rights it should follow the 1982 instrument in terms of enforcement.

The extent to which democracy might seem to be infringed if unelected judges had to apply the Bill of Rights would partly depend on its authority and the availability of review of legislation. The most contentious possibility would arise if judges were empowered to strike down subsequent legislation in conflict with the Bill of Rights, which was also given a higher authority than other Acts of Parliament by being entrenched, so that no possibility of correction of judicial decisions by subsequent legislation arose except in so far as provided for by the method of entrenchment.

A much less contentious possibility, in democratic terms, arises if the Bill of Rights is allowed to prevail only over prior inconsistent legislation. A 'middle

---

54 A further paradox in Waldron's argument, the existence of which he concedes (at p46), is that if the majority vote in a referendum for an entrenched Bill of Rights they must, on his argument, be allowed to have one. Clearly, the only way to prevent the majority from entrenching a Bill of Rights would be to have an entrenched law forbidding the entrenchment of laws. This would obviously be impossible on its own terms. Since, as Dworkin notes, opinion polls reveal that more than 71% of the population favour an entrenched Bill of Rights, Waldron's argument appears to be self-defeating.

55 See further Dworkin, 'Liberalism' in *A Matter of Principle* (1985). See also Hart, *Law Liberty and Morality* (1963), and Lester, *Democracy and Individual Rights* (1968).

way', which is also the most likely possibility, would be to protect the Bill of Rights by a so-called 'notwithstanding clause' – subsequent legislation would only override the Bill of Rights if the intention to do so was clearly stated in the legislation. This 'middle way' undermines the argument against a Bill of Rights as undemocratic since Parliament, at least in theory, retains the power to amend or repeal part or all of the Bill of Rights.

R Dworkin, *A Bill of Rights for Britain* (1990), pp28–30

How Could the Convention be Incorporated?

Several influential supporters of a Bill of Rights (including Lord Scarman, a former member of the House of Lords, who has been a pioneer in the argument for incorporation) have proposed that in the first instance incorporation should take what is technically a weaker form: the incorporating statute should provide that an inconsistent statute is null and void unless Parliament has expressly stated that it *intends* the statute to override the Convention. In practice this technically weaker version of incorporation would probably provide almost as much protection as the stronger one. If a Government conceded that its statute violated the Convention, it would have no defence before the Commission or Court in Strasbourg. In any case, quite apart from that practical point, no respectable Government would wish to announce that it did not care whether its legislation or decisions violated the country's domestic promises and international obligations. If a Government felt itself able to make such an announcement, except in the most extraordinary circumstances, the spirit of liberty would be dead anyway, beyond the power of any constitution to revive.

At least in the first instance, therefore, proponents should press for the weaker version of incorporation. If they succeed, then unless Parliament has expressly provided to the contrary any citizen will have the right in British courts to challenge a law or an official decision on the ground that it is offensive to the Convention's principles. Some European nations have established special courts to hear constitutional challenges. But it would be better, at least in Britain, to allow any division of the High Court to entertain such a challenge. Constitutional issues are not so arcane or specialised that ordinary judges, assisted by counsel in the normal way, could not master them.

Should Parliament be Supreme?

That is the case for incorporating the European Convention into domestic British law. It is no mystery that powerful politicians are reluctant to accept that case. Ministers and officials are rarely keen to justify themselves before judges, and constitutional rights often make important political objectives more difficult to achieve. These are the costs of a culture of liberty, and politicians, above all, hate to pay them. What is surprising, however, is the ineptness of the arguments politicians have deployed against incorporation. In the rest of this essay, I shall consider all the arguments of which I am aware.

The politicians say that the very idea of a Bill of Rights restricting the power of Parliament is hostile to the British tradition that Parliament and Parliament alone should be sovereign. That supposed tradition seems less appealing now, when a very powerful executive and well-disciplined political parties mean less effective power for back-bench MPs than it did before these developments. The tradition has already been compromised in recent decades, moreover. It was altered by the European Communities Act, for example, under which judges have the power to override parliamentary decisions in order to enforce directly effective Community rules.

In any case, quite apart from these considerations, incorporating the European Convention would not diminish Parliament's present power in any way that could reasonably be thought objectionable. Parliament is *already* bound by international law to observe the terms of that Convention. If the Convention were incorporated in what I have called the strong form, under which a future Parliament would not have the legal power to violate the Convention even if it expressly said it intended to do so, then the power of Parliament might be somewhat more limited than it is now, because British judges might develop a special British interpretation of the Convention that in some cases recognised individual constitutional rights the Strasbourg Court would not.

It is hard to argue that this further limitation would be wrong in principle, however. Britain agreed when it accepted the European Convention and the jurisdiction of the European Court of Human Rights, that it would be bound by the principles laid down in the Convention as these principles were interpreted not by Parliament but by a group of judges. If that limitation on the power of Parliament is acceptable, how can it be unacceptable that the principles be interpreted not by mainly foreign judges but by British judges trained in the common law and in the legal and political traditions of their own country?

The argument for parliamentary supremacy would be irrelevant, moreover, if the Convention were incorporated in the weaker form I suggested should be the initial goal. For then Parliament could override the Convention by mere majority vote, provided it was willing expressly to concede its indifference about doing so. No doubt that condition would, in practice, prevent a Government from introducing legislation it might otherwise enact. That is the point of incorporation, even in the weak form. But forcing Parliament to make the choice between obeying its international obligations and admitting that it is violating them does not limit Parliament's supremacy, but only its capacity for duplicity. Candour is hardly inconsistent with sovereignty.

Notes

1   The proposal to protect a Bill of Rights by means of a 'notwithstanding' clause has also been supported by Dawn Oliver,[56] who notes that such a clause provides effective protection for the Canadian Charter. Oliver offers two reasons why a Government would be unwilling to state clearly that it was legislating in breach of the Bill of Rights with the result that a 'notwithstanding clause' would offer it effective protection. First there would be the general political embarrassment which would be caused to the Government. Secondly, if the ECHR had been adopted as the British Bill of Rights, a declaration of intent to infringe constitutional rights would be tantamount to a declaration of the Government's intention to breach its obligations under international law; this would undoubtedly provoke widespread international condemnation which would be highly embarrassing. The Human Rights No 3 Bill introduced, as noted above, by Allen in January 1994 would have adopted this method of protection for the Bill of Rights. This is the method which the Labour Party would probably adopt if in government.

2   A Bill which had incorporated the ECHR would, as Oliver notes, be further protected by the legal presumption that 'Parliament does not intend to act in breach of international law' (*per* Diplock LJ in *Salomon v Commissioners of*

---

56   See D Oliver 'A Bill of Rights for the UK' in *Government in the UK* (1991), pp158–161.

Customs and Excise[57]), so that a reading of the relevant legislation which did not create a breach of rights would be adopted by the courts if such a reading was possible. Oliver concludes that the above method of protection would provide 'strong protection against legislative encroachment on civil and political rights'.

Questions

Consider the following position: after election of a Labour Government the UK adopts the ECHR as its domestic Bill of Rights, stating (in s1) that all future enactments of Parliament will take effect subject to its terms unless they expressly state that they are to have effect notwithstanding its provisions.

1   Subsequently, statute A is enacted, s9 of which provides that it is to take effect notwithstanding the provisions of Art 8 of the UK Bill of Rights. In the following year, statute B, s3 of which makes further provision in the same area as s9, is enacted, but without a notwithstanding clause. Statute A has impliedly repealed part of Art 8. Assuming that s3 of statute B is incompatible with the impliedly repealed area of Art 8, would the courts give effect to s3? Would the answer to this question differ if statute A was later repealed? Would it matter whether statute A was impliedly or expressly repealed?

2   A statute is passed which contains the following section: 'Section 1 of the Bill of Rights is hereby repealed, notwithstanding the provisions of s1'. How might the courts react to subsequent legislation which was inconsistent with the provisions of the Bill of Rights?

---

57   [1967] 2 QB 116, 143.

CHAPTER 2

FREEDOM OF ASSEMBLY AND PUBLIC ORDER

INTRODUCTION[1]

Freedom of assembly, which is guaranteed under the Universal Declaration of Human Rights, Art 20 and in the European Convention on Human Rights, Art 11, is a fundamental freedom which in part derives its legitimacy from its close association with freedom of speech. Most forms of public protest involve an intertwining of speech and conduct which cannot usually be disentangled,[2] whether support for a group or its views is shown through the medium of pure speech accompanied by conduct (shouting, waving placards, distributing leaflets) or symbolic speech (wearing uniforms or conducting a silent vigil). The European Commission of Human Rights has left open the possibility that Art 10 may protect some forms of symbolic speech.[3] The state has a greater interest in suppressing or restricting conduct, even though incidentally free speech is constrained, than in suppressing pure speech, but in a democratic society public order law should also afford recognition to the freedom to protest. Such freedom allows individuals to make their views known publicly and obtain public support. Free societies recognise the need to allow citizens to express views at variance with Government views, and to allow the public expression of such views. Allowing citizens to engage in public protest is seen as being one of the main distinctions between a totalitarian society and a democracy. Protest is valuable partly as demonstrating to Government that it has strayed too far from the path of acceptability in policy making and partly in deterring it from doing so. The question is where the balance is to be struck; what is the proper middle way between allowing free rein to the riotous mob on the one hand and on the other imposing an absolute prohibition on public meetings?

---

1   On this topic see generally: DGT Williams, *Keeping the Peace* (1967) (excellent historical account); I Brownlie, ed M Supperstone, *Law Relating to Public Order and National Security*, 2nd edn (1981); Geoffrey Marshall, 'Freedom of Speech and Assembly' in *Constitutional Theory* (1971), p154; VT Bevan, 'Protest and Public Disorder' (1979) PL 163; S Uglow, *Policing Liberal Society* (1988); ATH Smith, *Offences Against Public Order* (1987); A Sherr, *Freedom of Protest, Public Order and the Law* (1989); Ewing and Gearty, *Freedom under Thatcher* (1990), Chapter 4; Bailey, Harris and Jones, *Civil Liberties: Cases and Materials,* 4th edn (1995), Chapter 3; Whitty, Murphy and Livingstone, *Civil Liberties Law* (1995), Part V; D Feldman, *Civil Liberties and Human Rights in England and Wales,* (1993) Chapter 17; PAJ Waddington, *Liberty and Order* (1994). For discussion and criticism of the Public Order Act 1986 see D Bonner and R Stone, 'The Public Order Act 1986: Steps in the Wrong Direction?' (1987) PL 202; R Card, *Public Order: the New Law* (1987); ATH Smith, 'The Public Order Act 1986 Part 1' (1987) Crim LR 156.

2   See Lord Denning's comments on this point in *Hubbard v Pitt* [1976] QB 142. However in America it has been determined in the leading 'symbolic speech' case that speech and conduct can be disentangled; the one can be punished so long as the incidental restriction caused to the other goes no further than is necessary for the furtherance of the interest in question (*United States v O'Brien* 391 US (1968); for criticism see: Nimmer (1973) 21 UCLA LR 38–44). See Barendt's discussion of the relationship between freedom of speech and freedom of association: *Freedom of Speech* (1987), pp280–298.

3   *Appl 7215/75 X v UK Yearbook XX1* (1978). The case concerned denial of a right to engage in homosexual practices thereby expressing love for other men. The Commission, having found the application admissible, decided in its report on the merits of the case that the particular facts did not give rise to an issue covered by Art 10.

This Chapter is concerned with the conflict between the legitimate interest of the state in maintaining order and the protection of freedom of assembly. Therefore it will focus on those provisions of the criminal law most applicable in the context of demonstrations, marches or meetings. Many of these restraints are not aimed specifically at assemblies but generally at keeping the peace. However, freedom of assembly is affected by them and, since it has no special constitutional protection, it is in a very vulnerable position due to their number and width. Clearly, some restraint on public protest is needed in order to protect the interests which are at stake due to the possibilities of disorder, of violence to citizens and damage to property.[4] The difficulty is that, in furtherance of the interest in public order (which in itself protects freedom of assembly), the constitutional need to allow freedom of assembly in a democracy may be obscured. The concern of this chapter is to determine how far the legal scheme governing public order manages to reconcile the two interests. The Public Order Act 1986 and the public order provisions of the Criminal Justice and Public Order Act 1994 form a very significant part of the legal framework within which freedom of assembly operates, but it is also important to take into account the part played by a number of wide-ranging and sometimes archaic powers which spring partly from a mix of other statutory provisions, partly from the common law and partly from the royal prerogative.[5]

LEGAL RECOGNITION OF FREEDOM OF ASSEMBLY

UK law affords a degree of positive recognition to freedom of assembly in specific situations.

Burden v Rigler [1911] 1 KB 337, 338, 339–40

The appellant had called together the meeting for the purpose of furthering the cause of tariff reform, he being the chairman of the local branch of the Tariff Reform League. The meeting had been billed and notification of the same had been given to the police who were present at the meeting. At the meeting the appellant attempted to speak, but there was such disturbance that the speech had to be discontinued; the respondents were standing quite close to the van from which the speakers were attempting to speak, and persistently interrupted and led the opposition; the appellant appealed several times to the respondent Rigler to desist from making such a disturbance and to try and induce his followers to permit the meeting to be held; the respondent Rigler said to the appellant, 'You have set us at defiance, we will not allow you to hold a meeting'; and the meeting was broken up. ...

[It was argued for the appellant that] the fact that a public meeting is held on a highway does not necessarily make the meeting unlawful. There must be some interference with police regulations in order to make it unlawful. The justices held that no public meeting on a highway could be lawful. They misinterpreted the *dicta* in *Graham and Burns* (1888) [16 Cox CC 420] and *ex p Lewis* [(1888) 21

---

4   See the leading US case *Hague v Committee for Industrial Organisation* 307 US 496 (1938).

5   For discussion of the various offences see J C Smith *Smith and Hogan Criminal Law*, 8th edn (1996) (standard criminal law text), Chapter 21; P Thornton, *Public Order Law* (1987).

QBD 191]. The meaning of those *dicta* is that there is no 'right' to hold a public meeting on a highway, ie no absolute legal right, but it does not necessarily follow that if a meeting is held it may not be lawful. The *dicta* mean that the convenors of the meeting cannot in all circumstances insist on holding it. There is no limitation in the Public Meeting Act 1908 as to where a political meeting may be held, and the statute implies that it is not unlawful in every case to hold a public meeting on a highway (*Beatty v Gillbanks* (1882) QBD 308). ...

Lord Alverstone CJ: The evidence in support of the charge having been partly given, the justices declined to proceed further with the summons on the ground that the meeting, being held on a highway, was *ipso facto* an unlawful meeting. That ruling goes much too far. ... the justices had no right to assume that, simply because the meeting was held on a highway, it could be interrupted notwithstanding the provisions of the Public Meeting Act 1908. The appeal must be allowed, and the case remitted to the justices to be further dealt with [the other two judges agreed].

Representation of the People Act 1983, ss95–97

Election meetings

95.–(1) Subject to the provisions of this section, a candidate at a parliamentary election is entitled for the purpose of holding public meetings in furtherance of his candidature to the use at reasonable times between the receipt of the writ and the date of the poll of –

   (a) a suitable room in the premises of a school to which this section applies;

   (b) any meeting room to which this section applies.

Schools and rooms for local election meetings

96.–(1) Subject to the provisions of this section, a candidate at a local government election is entitled for the purpose of holding public meetings in furtherance of his candidature to the use free of charge at reasonable times between the notice of election and the day preceding the day of election of –

   (a) in England and Wales, a suitable room in the premises of a county or voluntary school situated in the electoral area for which he is a candidate, or, in a parish or community, as the case may be, in part comprised in that electoral area;

   (b) in Scotland, a suitable room in the premises of any school (not being an independent school within the meaning of the Education (Scotland) Act 1980) situated in the electoral area for which he is a candidate (or, if there is no such school in the area, in any such school in an adjacent electoral area) or any suitable room the expense of maintaining which is payable by the council of an islands area or district.

Disturbances at election meetings

97.–(1) A person who at a lawful public meeting to which this section applies acts, or incites others to act, in a disorderly manner for the purpose of preventing the transaction of the business for which the meeting was called together shall be guilty of an illegal practice.

   (2) This section applies to –

   (a) a political meeting held in any constituency between the date of the issue of a writ for the return of a member of Parliament for the constituency and the date at which a return to the writ is made;

(b) a meeting held with reference to a local government election in the electoral area for that election on, or within three weeks before, the day of election.

(3) If a constable reasonably suspects any person of committing an offence under subsection (1) above, he may be requested so to do by the chairman of the meeting require that person to declare to him immediately his name and address and, if that person refuses or fails so to declare his name and address or gives a false name and address, he shall be liable on summary conviction to a fine not exceeding level 1 on the standard scale, and –

(a) if he refuses or fails so to declare his name and address; or

(b) if the constable reasonably suspects him of giving a false name and address,

the constable may without warrant arrest him.

This subsection does not apply in Northern Ireland.

Education (No 2) Act 1986

Part IV

Freedom of speech in universities, polytechnics and colleges

43.–(1) Every individual and body of persons concerned in the government of any establishment to which this section applies shall take such steps as are reasonably practicable to ensure that freedom of speech within the law is secured for members, students and employees of the establishment and for visiting speakers.

(2) The duty imposed by subsection (1) above includes (in particular) the duty to ensure, so far as is reasonably practicable, that the use of any premises of the establishment is not denied to any individual or body of persons on any ground connected with –

(a) the beliefs or views of that individual or of any member of that body; or

(b) the policy or objectives of that body.

(3) The governing body of every such establishment shall, with a view to facilitating the discharge of the duty imposed by subsection (1) above in relation to that establishment, issue and keep up to date a code of practice setting out –

(a) the procedures to be followed by members, students and employees of the establishment in connection with the organisation:

(i) of meetings which are to be held on premises of the establishment and which fall within any class of meeting specified in the code; and

(ii) of other activities which are to take place on those premises and which fall within any class of activity so specified; and

(b) the conduct required of such persons in connection with any such meeting or activity;

and dealing with such other matters as the governing body consider appropriate.

Notes

1   Under the Representation of the People Act 1983, local authorities are placed under a very limited positive obligation to allow election meetings to take place. No general obligation is placed on state authorities to allow assemblies or the exercise of freedom of speech in public places or buildings.[6] The Education (No 2) Act 1986 s43 provides an exception to this general rule. This provision promotes free speech interests, but it may appear anomalous that a right to meet arises in certain specified buildings but not in others, such as town halls, while it does not arise at all in public places such as town squares or parks. There is a convention that there is a right to meet in certain places such as Trafalgar Square or Hyde Park but it is a fallacy that there is any legal right to do so.[7]

2   The positive obligations placed on the state under these statutory provisions are very limited, but arguably the Public Order Act 1986 ss12 and 14 (see below) impliedly recognises the freedom to meet so long as the statutory requirements are complied with, and this argument may be supported by the existence of certain specific statutory prohibitions on meetings in certain places or at certain times, such as the Seditious Meetings Act 1817 s3 which prohibits meetings of 50 or more in the vicinity of the Westminster during a Parliamentary session. Such restrictions impliedly support the existence of a general negative freedom to meet or march which will exist if not specifically prohibited.[8] The decision in *Burden v Rigler* (1911) also lends support to this view.

3   The Highways Act 1980 s137 provides that a person will be guilty of an offence if he 'without lawful authority or excuse wilfully obstructs the free passage of the highway'. It might appear therefore that the negative freedom to assemble is entirely abrogated so far as the highway is concerned since almost any assembly will create some obstruction. However, according to *Hirst and Agu v Chief Constable of West Yorkshire* (1986)[9] the term 'lawful excuse' refers to activities which are lawful in themselves and which are reasonable, and this was found to cover peaceful demonstrations. This decision supports the view that freedom of assembly is recognised as a common law principle which can only be abrogated by clear statutory words. Where there is leeway to do so the courts will not accept that it has been broadly abrogated.

---

6   See discussion of this point in the European Court of Human Rights in *Platform 'Arzte für das Leben' v Austria* (1988) 13 EHRR 204; it was found that freedom of assembly could not be reduced to a mere duty on the part of the state not to interfere; it did require the state to take some positive steps to be taken although the state was not expected to guarantee that a demonstration was able to proceed.

7   In respect of Trafalgar Square see *ex p Lewis* (1888) 21 QBD 191. By statutory instrument an application must be made to the Department of the Environment to hold a meeting in Trafalgar Square (SI 1952/776). There is no right to hold meetings in the Royal Parks: see *Bailey v Williamson* (1873) LR 8 QB 118).

8   See DG Barnum at (1977) PL 310 and (1981) 29 Am Jo of Comparative Law 59; also L A Stein (1971) PL 115 for discussion of the constitutional status of public protest.

9   85 Cr App R 143. See also *Nagy v Weston* [1966] 2 QB 561; cf *Arrowsmith v Jenkins* [1963] 2 QB 561; 2 All ER 210; for comment see (1987) PL 495.

THE LEGAL CONTROL OF MEETINGS, MARCHES, DEMONSTRATIONS

The 1980s witnessed a series of disturbances beginning with the Brixton riots in 1981[10] and continuing with the disorder associated with the miners' strike 1984–85. Such disorder formed the background to the Public Order Act 1986 but it is unclear that further police powers to control disorder were needed. It did not appear that the police had lacked powers to deal with these disturbances; on the contrary, a number of different common law and statutory powers were invoked, including breach of the peace, obstruction of a constable and watching and besetting under s7 of the Conspiracy and Protection of Property Act 1875.[11] However, the Government took the view that the available powers were confused and fragmented and that there was scope for affording the police additional powers to prevent disorder before it occurred.[12] The 1986 Act itself, however, came to be seen as inadequate as a means of controlling certain forms of protest, and the Criminal Justice and Public Order Act 1994 was passed with a view to creating a further curb on the activities of certain groups such as hunt saboteurs or motorway protesters. However, since the 1994 Act did not remove any of the existing powers, there now exists a web of various overlapping offences.[13]

The offences take the form of both prior and subsequent restraints. Prior restraint on assemblies may mean that an assembly cannot take place at all or that it can take place only under various limitations. Subsequent restraints, usually arrests and prosecutions for public order offences, may be used after the assembly is in being. Although the availability of subsequent restraints may have a 'chilling' effect, they are used publicly and may receive publicity. If an assembly takes place and subsequently some of its members are prosecuted for public order offences, it will have achieved its end in gaining publicity and may in fact have gained greater publicity due to the prosecutions. If the assembly never takes place its object will probably be completely defeated.

DGT Williams, 'Processions, Assemblies and the Freedom of the Individual' (1987) Criminal Law Review 167, 167–8

Rouse Ball Professor of English Law, University of Cambridge

Introduction

Despite Lord Elwyn-Jones's reference in 1986 to 'the right to freedom of speech and of lawful protest, the right of public assembly and of procession, all the

---

10   See the inquiry by Lord Scarman, *The Brixton Disorders*, 1981 Cmnd 8427.

11   See S McCabe and P Wallington, *The Police, Public Order and Civil Liberties: Legacies of the Miners' Strike* (1988), esp appendix 1; P Wallington, 'Policing the Miners' Strike' (1985) 14 ILJ 145. During the miners' strike over 10,000 offences were charged; see P Wallington (1985) 14 ILJ 145.

12   For background to the 1986 Act see: House of Commons, *Fifth Report from the Home Affairs Committee*, Session 1979–80, *The Law Relating to Public Order*, HC 756–1; Lord Scarman, *The Brixton Disorders*, Cmnd 8427, Part VI; ATH Smith, 'Public Order Law 1974–1983; Developments and Proposals' (1984) Crim LR 643; White Paper, *Review of Public Order Law*, Cmnd 9510, 1.7.

13   For background to the 1994 Act, which received the Royal Assent on 3 November 1994, see the introduction in Wasik and Taylor's *Guide to the Act* (1995), p1. For discussion of the public order offences see ATH Smith (1995) Crim LR 19.

hallmarks of a democratic society' [HL Deb, 29 October 1986, vol 481, col 749] there is no formal constitutional or statutory provision in this country for freedom of assembly. Instead the UK has obligations under the European Convention on Human Rights, leading the Government in the White Paper of 1985 to state that the 'rights of peaceful protest and assembly are amongst our fundamental freedoms: they are numbered among the touchstones which distinguish a free society from a totalitarian one'. Touchstones can be surprisingly elusive, however; and the parliamentary proceedings on the 1986 Act are important in revealing different philosophies about freedom of assembly. There is a clash between what, for purposes of simplicity, might be called the 'disruption' view and the 'democratic' view:

(i) the 'disruption' view reflects an emphasis on our changing times. Many things have happened since 1936, claimed the Government in its 1980 Green Paper [Cmnd 7891, *Review of the Public Order Act 1936*]: an increase in the number of major demonstrations; a substantial increase in the amount of disorder; an increase in the cost of policing demonstrations; and the immediacy of contemporary public order problems (particularly enhanced through the presence of television cameras). More broadly, Lord Beloff in the House of Lords debates said that nowadays – with universal suffrage and a whole series of bodies to represent views – we should not put 'quite the accent that has been put on the tradition of assembly, the tradition of marching, the tradition of open-air protest as though the fact that those things were necessary in past ages is a guide to us today' [HL Deb, vol 476, cols 568–69, 13 June 1986]. He added that in his view 'the guaranteeing of the ability of the individual citizen to pursue his lawful avocation, to move freely about the streets of his city and to avoid interruption to the ordinary amenities of daily life, is of infinitely greater importance than guaranteeing the right to hold meetings in public places, to march in processions or to perform any of those other activities' [*ibid* col 569].

(ii) the 'democratic' or 'safety valve' view of the right to demonstrate reflects a different emphasis. In the aftermath of the Trafalgar Square riots of 1886 the *Pall Mall Gazette* spoke against panic legislation on the ground that 'to sit on the safety-valve is not the best means of preventing an explosion'; and in the recent debates Lord Scarman was not alone in maintaining that steam-age metaphor in his views of alternative democracy, when he said [HL Deb, 13 June 1986, vol 476, col 538] that our society has become so complicated and our representative system of government so remote to many fellow citizens, that there has to be an alternative way of expressing dissent other than the constitutional way of doing it through representative institutions'.

Prior restraints

Public Order Act 1986, Part II

Processions and assemblies

Advance notice of public processions

11.–(1) Written notice shall be given in accordance with this section of any proposal to hold a public procession intended–

(a) to demonstrate support for or opposition to the views or actions of any person or body of persons,

(b) to publicise a cause or campaign, or

(c)   to mark or commemorate an event,

unless it is not reasonably practicable to give any advance notice of the procession.

(2)   Subsection (1) does not apply where the procession is one commonly or customarily held in the police area (or areas) in which it is proposed to be held or is a funeral procession organised by a funeral director acting in the normal course of his business.

(3)   The notice must specify the date when it is intended to hold the procession, the time when it is intended to start it, its proposed route, and the name and address of the person (or of one of the persons) proposing to organise it.

(4)   Notice must be delivered to a police station–

(a)   in the police area in which it is proposed the procession will start, or

(b)   where it is proposed the procession will start in Scotland and cross into England, in the first police area in England on the proposed route.

(5)   If delivered not less than six clear days before the date when the procession is intended to be held, the notice may be delivered by post by the recorded delivery service; but section 7 of the Interpretation Act 1978 (under which a document sent by post is deemed to have been served when posted and to have been delivered in the ordinary course of post) does not apply.

(6)   If not delivered in accordance with subsection (5), the notice must be delivered by hand not less than six clear days before the date when the procession is intended to be held or, if that is not reasonably practicable, as soon as delivery is reasonably practicable.

(7)   Where a public procession is held, each of the persons organising it is guilty of an offence if–

(a)   the requirements of this section as to notice have not been satisfied, or

(b)   the date when it is held, the time when it starts, or its route, differs from the date, time or route specified in the notice.

(8)   It is an offence for the accused to prove that he did not know of, and neither suspected nor had reason to suspect, the failure to satisfy the requirements or (as the case may be) the difference of day, time or route.

(9)   To the extent that an alleged offence turns on a difference of date, time or route, it is a defence for the accused to prove that the difference arose from circumstances beyond his control or from something done with the agreement of a police officer or by his direction.

Imposing conditions on public processions

12.–(1)If the senior police officer, having regard to the time or place at which and the circumstances in which any public procession is being held or is intended to be held and to its route or proposed route, reasonably believes that–

(a)it may result in serious public disorder, serious damage to property or serious disruption to the life of the community, or

(b)the purpose of the persons organising it is the intimidation of others with a view to compelling them not to do an act they have a right to do, or to do an act they have a right not to do,

he may give directions imposing on the persons organising or taking part in the procession such conditions as appear to him necessary to prevent such disorder, damage, disruption or intimidation, including conditions as to the route of the procession or prohibit it from entering any public place specified in the directions.

(2) In subsection (1) 'the senior police officer' means–

    (a) in relation to a procession being held, or to a procession intended to be held in a case where persons are assembling with a view to taking part in it, the most senior in rank of the police officers present at the scene, and

    (b) in relation to a procession intended to be held in a case where paragraph (1) does not apply, the chief officer of police.

(3) A direction given by a chief officer of police by virtue of subsection (2)(b) shall be given in writing.

(4) A person who organises a public procession and knowingly fails to comply with a condition imposed under this section is guilty of an offence, but it is a defence for him to prove that the failure arose from circumstances beyond his control.

(5) A person who takes part in a public procession and knowingly fails to comply with a condition imposed under this section is guilty of an offence, but it is a defence for him to prove that the failure arose from circumstances beyond his control.

(6) A person who incites another to commit an offence under subsection (5) is guilty of an offence.

(7) A constable in uniform may arrest without warrant anyone he reasonably suspects is committing an offence under subsection (4), (5) or (6).

Prohibiting public processions

13.–(1) If at any time the chief officer of police reasonably believes that, because of particular circumstances existing in any district or part of a district, the powers under section 12 will not be sufficient to prevent the holding of public processions in that district or part from resulting in serious public disorder, he shall apply to the council of the district for an order prohibiting for such period not exceeding three months as may be specified in the application the holding of all public processions (or of any class of public procession so specified) in the district or part concerned.

    (2) On receiving such an application, a council may with the consent of the Secretary of State make an order either in the terms of the application or with such modifications as may be approved by the Secretary of State.

    (3) Subsection (1) does not apply in the City of London or the metropolitan police district.

    (4) If at any time the Commissioner of Police for the City of London or the Commissioner of Police of the Metropolis reasonably believes that, because of particular circumstances existing in his police area or part of it, the powers under section 12 will not be sufficient to prevent the holding of public processions in that area or part from resulting in serious public disorder, he may with the consent of the Secretary of State make an order prohibiting for such period not exceeding 3 months as may be specified in the order the holding of all public processions (or of any class of public procession so specified) in the area or part concerned.

    (5) An order made under this section may be revoked or varied by a subsequent order made in the same way, that is, in accordance with subsections (1) and (2) or subsection (4), as the case may be.

    (6) Any order under this section shall, if not made in writing, be recorded in writing as soon as practicable after being made.

(7) A person who organises a public procession the holding of which he knows is prohibited by virtue of an order under this section is guilty of an offence.

(8) A person who takes part in a public procession the holding of which he knows is prohibited by virtue of an order under this section is guilty of an offence.

(9) A person who incites another to commit an offence under subsection (8) is guilty of an offence.

(10) A constable in uniform may arrest without warrant anyone he reasonably suspects is committing an offence under subsection (7), (8) or (9).

Imposing conditions on public assemblies

14.–(1) If the senior police officer, having regard to the time or place at which and the circumstances in which any public assembly is being held or is intended to be held, reasonably believes that–

(a) it may result in serious public disorder, serious damage to property or serious disruption to the life of the community, or

(b) the purpose of the persons organising it is the intimidation of others with a view to compelling them not to do an act they have a right to do, or to do an act they have a right not to do,

he may give directions imposing on the persons organising or taking part in the assembly such conditions as to the place at which the assembly may be (or continue to be) held, its maximum duration, or the maximum number of persons who may constitute it, as appear to him necessary to prevent such disorder, damage, disruption or intimidation.

(2) In subsection (1) 'the senior police officer' means–

(a) in relation to an assembly being held, the most senior in rank of the police officers present at the scene, and

(b) in relation to an assembly intended to be held, the chief officer of police.

(3) A direction given by a chief officer of police by virtue of subsection (2)(b) shall be given in writing.

(4) A person who organises a public assembly and knowingly fails to comply with a condition imposed under this section is guilty of an offence, but it is a defence for him to prove that the failure arose from circumstances beyond his control.

(5) A person who takes part in a public assembly and knowingly fails to comply with a condition imposed under this section is guilty of an offence, but it is a defence for him to prove that the failure arose from circumstances beyond his control.

(6) A person who incites another to commit an offence under subsection (5) is guilty of an offence.

(7) A constable in uniform may arrest without warrant anyone he reasonably suspects is committing an offence under subsection (4), (5) or (6).

Criminal Justice and Public Order Act 1994

Trespassory assemblies

70. In Part II of the Public Order Act 1986 (processions and assemblies), after section 14, there shall be inserted the following sections–

'*Prohibiting trespassory assemblies*

14A.–(1) If at any time the chief officer of police reasonably believes that an assembly is intended to be held in any district at a place on land to which the public has no right of access or only a limited right of access and that the assembly–

(a) is likely to be held without the permission of the occupier of the land or to conduct itself in such a way as to exceed the limits of any permission of his or the limits of the public's right of access, and

(b) may result–

   (i) in serious disruption to the life of the community, or

   (ii) where the land, or a building or monument on it, is of historical, architectural, archaeological or scientific importance, in significant damage to the land, building or monument, he may apply to the council of the district for an order prohibiting for a specified period the holding of all trespassory assemblies in the district or a part of it, as specified.

(2) On receiving such an application, a council may–

(a) in England and Wales, with the consent of the Secretary of State make an order either in the terms of the application or with such modifications as may be approved by the Secretary of State; or

(b) in Scotland, make an order in the terms of the application.

(3) Subsection (1) does not apply in the City of London or the metropolitan police district.

(4) If at any time the Commissioner of Police for the City of London or the Commissioner of Police of the Metropolis reasonably believes that an assembly is intended to be held at a place on land to which the public has no right of access or only a limited right of access in his police area and that the assembly–

(a) is likely to be held without the permission of the occupier of the land or to conduct itself in such a way as to exceed the limits of any permission of his or the limits of the public's right of access, and

(b) may result–

   (i) in serious disruption to the life of the community, or

   (ii) where the land, or a building or monument on it, is of historical, architectural, archaeological or scientific importance, in significant damage to the land, building or monument, he may with the consent of the Secretary of State make an order prohibiting for a specified period the holding of all trespassory assemblies in the area or a part of it, as specified.

(5) An order prohibiting the holding of trespassory assemblies operates to prohibit any assembly which–

(a) is held on land to which the public has no right of access or only a limited right of access, and

(b) takes place in the prohibited circumstances, that is to say, without the permission of the occupier of the land or so as to exceed the limits of any permission of his or the limits of the public's right of access.

(6) No order under this section shall prohibit the holding of assemblies for a period exceeding 4 days or in an area exceeding an area represented by a circle with a radius of 5 miles from a specified centre.

(7) An order made under this section may be revoked or varied by a subsequent order made in the same way, that is, in accordance with

subsection (1) and (2) or subsection (4), as the case may be.

(8) Any order under this section shall, if not made in writing, be recorded in writing as soon as practicable after being made.

(9) In this section and ss14B and 14C–

'assembly' means an assembly of 20 or more persons;

'land', means land in the open air;

'limited', in relation to a right of access by the public to land, means that their use of it is restricted to use for a particular purpose (as in the case of a highway or road) or is subject to other restrictions;

'occupier' means–

(a) in England and Wales, the person entitled to possession of the land by virtue of an estate or interest held by him; or

(b) in Scotland, the person lawfully entitled to natural possession of the land,

and in subsections (1) and (4) includes the person reasonably believed by the authority applying for or making the order to be the occupier;

'public' includes a section of the public; and

'specified' means specified in an order under this section.

(10)In relation to Scotland, the references in subsection (1) above to a district and to the council of the district shall be construed–

(a) as respects applications before 1st April 1996, as references to the area of a regional or islands authority and to the authority in question; and

(b) as respects applications on and after that date, as references to a local government area and to the council for that area.

(11)In relation to Wales, the references in subsection (1) above to a district and to the council of the district shall be construed, as respects applications on and after 1st April 1996, as references to a county or county borough and to the council for that county or county borough.

Offences in connection with trespassory assemblies and arrest therefor

14B.–(1) A person who organises an assembly the holding of which he knows is prohibited by an order under section 14A is guilty of an offence.

(2) A person who takes part in an assembly which he knows is prohibited by an order under section 14A is guilty of an offence.

(3) In England and Wales, a person who incites another to commit an offence under subsection (2) is guilty of an offence.

(4) A constable in uniform may arrest without a warrant anyone he reasonably suspects to be committing an offence under this section.

Trespassory assemblies: power to stop persons from proceeding

71.   After the section 14B inserted by section 70 in the Public Order Act 1986 there shall be inserted the following section–

Stopping persons from proceeding to trespassory assemblies

14C.–(1) If a constable in uniform reasonably believes that a person is on his way to an assembly within the area to which an order under section 14A applies which the constable reasonably believes is likely to be an assembly which is prohibited by that order, he may, subject to subsection (2) below–

(a) stop that person, and

(b) direct him not to proceed in the direction of the assembly.

(2) The power conferred by subsection (1) may only be exercised within the area to which the order applies.

(3) A person who fails to comply with a direction under subsection (1) which he knows has been given to him is guilty of an offence.

(4) A constable in uniform may arrest without a warrant anyone he reasonably suspects to be committing an offence under this section.

Notes

1   Sections 12 and 13 of the 1986 Act, which allow banning or limitation of a march, are underpinned by the notice requirement under s11. It should be noted that this provision may not apply to spontaneous marches since it does not apply if it was not reasonably practicable to give any advance notice. This provision was intended to exempt spontaneous demonstrations from the notice requirement but is defective due to the use of the word 'any'. Strictly interpreted, this word would suggest that a phone call made five minutes before the march sets off would fulfil the requirements, thereby exempting very few marches. However, possibly the word 'any' should not be interpreted so strictly as to exclude spontaneous processions where a few minutes was available to give notice, because to do so would defeat the intention behind including the provision. If read in combination with the requirements as to giving notice by hand or in writing it could be interpreted to mean 'any written notice'. If it were not so interpreted it might be argued that s11 breaches the guarantee of freedom of assembly under Art 11 of the European Convention on Human Rights, bearing in mind the principle, affirmed in *Re M and H (Minors)* 1988[14] that where statutes are ambiguous they should be interpreted so as to conform with the UK.'s Convention obligations.

2   Section 11 criminalises what may be trivial administrative errors and, although police officers may use a discretion in bringing prosecutions under it, this leaves the power open to abuse and means that potentially at least it could be more rigidly enforced against marchers espousing unpopular causes. At present prosecutions under s11 are very rarely being brought and therefore its deterrence value to organisers may become minimal.[15] For example, the organisers of a large peace march held on the date the UN Security Council ultimatum against Iraq[16] expired, failed to comply with the notice requirements under s11, but no prosecution was brought. However, organisers of the 'veal calves' protest at Brightlingsea in April 1995 were threatened with prosecution under s11.

3   The power to impose conditions on public assemblies under s14 was an entirely new power, whereas s12 grew out of the power under the Public Order Act 1936 s3 allowing the chief officer of police to impose conditions on a procession if he apprehended serious public disorder. However, the

---

14   3 WLR 485.
15   Dr PAJ Waddington, 'The Dog That Does Not Bark: Law and Public Order Policing' lecture given at St John's College, Cambridge 22 February 1993.
16   Contained in SC resolution 678, 15 January.

power to impose conditions under s12 may be exercised in a much wider range of 'trigger' situations than the old power.

4   The phrase 'serious disruption to the life of the community' used in ss12(1)(a), 14(1)(a) and now 14A(1)(b) is very broad and clearly offers police officers wide scope for interpretation. This 'trigger' has attracted particular criticism from commentators. It has been said that 'some inconvenience is the inevitable consequence of a successful protest. The Act ... threatens to permit only those demonstrations that are so convenient that they become invisible'.[17] Bonner and Stone have warned of 'the dangers that lie in the vague line between serious disruption and a measure of inconvenience'.[18]

5   It has been noted that the term 'the community' used in ss12, 14 and 14A is ambiguous. In the case of London it is unclear whether the term could be applied to Oxford Street or inner London or the whole Metropolitan area.[19] The more narrowly the term is defined the more readily a given march or assembly could be said to cause serious disruption. Serious obstruction of traffic might arguably amount to some disruption of the life of the community. The phrase might be interpreted widely if police officers wished to cut down the cost of the policing requirement for an assembly because the conditions then imposed, such as requiring a limit on the numbers participating, might lead to a reduction in the number of officers who had to be present.

6   The fourth 'trigger' arising under s12(1)(b) and s14(1)(b) requires a reasonable belief in the presence of two elements: intimidation and coercion. Courts tend to take the stance that behaviour of a fairly threatening nature must be present in order to cross the boundary between discomfort and intimidation.[20] This stance was evident in *Reid* (1987).

Police v Lorna Reid [1987] Crim LR 702 (Commentary: Professor D Birch)

The defendant, with about 20 others, demonstrated outside South Africa House in Trafalgar Square on the occasion of a reception there. She shouted slogans through a megaphone and the others joined in. All raised their arms and waved their fingers at the arriving guests as they did so. The slogans included 'Apartheid murderers, get out of Britain' and 'You are a dying breed.' One visitor turned to remonstrate with the demonstrators.

The chief inspector in charge decided that this was intimidatory and purported to impose a condition on the assembly, relying on s14(1) of the Public Order Act 1986. He used a police megaphone to say, 'This is a police message. You are required to go to the mouth of Duncannon Street, north of the tree'. The defendant made a speech over her megaphone, saying that they would not move.

When the group reached the tree, the defendant refused to go further and her arresting officer said that she pushed against him saying 'I am going back to

---

17   Ewing and Gearty, p121.
18   'The Public Order Act 1986: Steps in the Wrong Direction?' (1987) PL 202.
19   Ewing and Gearty, *ibid*.
20   See *News Group Newspapers Ltd v Sogat 1982* [1986] ICR 716.

where I came from'. She was arrested and charged with knowingly failing to comply with a condition imposed on a public assembly, contrary to s14(5) of the 1986 Act.

In cross-examination, the chief inspector said that he defined intimidation as 'putting people in fear or discomfort'.

Held, the question was whether these demonstrators acted with a view to compelling visitors not to go into South Africa House or merely with the intention of causing them discomfort so as to make them look again at what was going on in South Africa. The chief inspector had equated intimidation with discomfort. That was the wrong test. Causing someone to feel uncomfortable would not be intimidation. The officer needed to go further and reasonably believe that the organisers acted with a view to compelling. Since he had not said that he had done so in this case, there was no ground for imposing a condition on the assembly and the defendant had therefore not committed the offence.

Notes

1   The conditions that can be imposed if one of the 'triggers' under ss12(1) or 14(1) is thought be present are limited in scope under s14, but very wide in the case of processions under s12, since any condition may be imposed which appears necessary to the senior police officer in order to prevent the envisaged mischief occurring. It should be noted that the use of such subjective wording does not oust the jurisdiction of the courts to assess the legality of the decision made.[21] Thus, at least in theory, it is not the case that any decision which appears necessary to that officer will in fact be lawful. However, it must be noted that in dealing with police action to maintain public order, the courts have been very unwilling to find police decisions to have been unlawful.[22] Also, unless the conditions were imposed some time before the assembly, a challenge to them by way of judicial review would be pointless.

2   The power to prohibit public processions under s13 reproduced the old power under s3 of the Public Order Act 1936. This power was open to criticism in that once a banning order had been imposed it prevented all marches in the area it covered for its duration. Thus a projected march likely to be of an entirely peaceful character would be caught by a ban aimed at a violent march. The Campaign for Nuclear Disarmament attempted unsuccessfully to challenge such a ban after it had had to cancel a number of its marches: *Kent v Metropolitan Police Commissioner* (1981).[23]

3   The s13 power was being used with increased frequency up to the mid-1980s: there were 11 banning orders in the period 1970 to 1980 and 75 in the period 1981 to 1984[24] (39 in 1981, 13 in 1982, 9 in 1983 and 11 in 1984). However, as Waddington has noted, there have been few bans of marches in

---

21   See eg *Secretary of State for Education and Science v Thameside* [1977] AC 1014.

22   See *Kent v Metropolitan Police Commission* (1981), *The Times*, 15 May 1981.

23   *The Times*, 15 May 1981.

24   White Paper Cmnd 9510, para 4.7.

London since the passing of the 1986 Act.[25] The power may have been used sparingly because police officers preferred to police a march known about for some time as opposed to an assembly formed hastily in response to a ban or a hostile, unpredictable and disorganised march. As Waddington has argued, such considerations may account for the police refusal to ban the third anti-poll-tax march to Trafalgar Square, although such a march had previously led to a riot, and in the face of fierce pressure to ban from Westminster City Council, local MPs and the Home Secretary.[26] However, the power to ban and to impose conditions gives the police bargaining power to use in negotiating with marchers and enables them to adopt a policy of strategic under-enforcement as part of the price of avoiding trouble when a march occurs.

4   It might seem that the s13 banning power would be in breach of Art 11 of the European Convention on Human Rights, in that the banning of a march expected to be peaceful would not appear to be justified under paragraph 2 in respect of the need to prevent disorder. However, in *Christians Against Racism and Fascism v UK* (1984),[27] the applicants' argument that a ban imposed under s3(3) of the Public Order Act 1936 infringed *inter alia* Art 11 was rejected by the Commission as manifestly ill-founded, on the ground that the ban was justified under the exceptions to Art 11 contained in paragraph 2, since there was a real danger of disorder which it was thought could not be 'prevented by other less stringent measures'. Thus it may be irrelevant that a particular march affected by the ban was unlikely in itself to give rise to disorder.

5   The 1986 Act contained no power to ban assemblies, but such a power was provided by s70 of the Criminal Justice and Public Order Act 1994 which inserts s14A into the 1986 Act. An order under the new banning power is subject to certain limitations: it will subsist for four days and operate within a radius of five miles around the area in question. Apart from these restrictions, this is a wider power than that arising under s13 since it is partly based on the very broad and uncertain concept of 'serious disruption to the life of the community'. Section 14A is backed up by s14C which operates before any offence has been committed. Under Williams' 'democracy' model s14A is objectionable since it uses the weakest 'trigger' as the basis for using the most draconian form of prior restraint – a complete ban, albeit in restricted circumstances.

Subsequent restraints

Subsequent restraints arising from a variety of sources can be used as an alternative, or in addition, to the powers arising under the 1986 and 1994 Acts and, as will be seen, many of the powers overlap. It should be noted that the powers arising under ss12 and 14 of the 1986 Act may be used during the assembly, not merely prior to it. The senior police officer present, who may of

25   PAJ Waddington, *Liberty and Order* (1994), pp58–61.
26   Waddington, *op cit.*
27   24 YBECHR 178.

course be a constable, can impose the conditions mentioned if, after the assembly has begun, it is apparent that one of the 'triggers' is in being or is about to come into being.

Violence, threats, abuse, insults

Public Order Act 1986

The Public Order Act 1986 s9 abolishes the common law offences of riot, unlawful assembly and affray and replaces them with similar statutory offences of riot, violent disorder and affray.

Riot

1.–(1)Where 12 or more persons who are present together use or threaten unlawful violence for a common purpose and the conduct of them (taken together) is such as would cause a person reasonable firmness present at the scene to fear for his personal safety, each of the persons using unlawful violence for the common purpose is guilty of riot.

(2) It is immaterial whether or not the 12 or more use or threaten unlawful violence simultaneously.

(3) The common purpose may be inferred from conduct.

(4) No person of reasonable firmness need actually be, or be likely to be, present at the scene.

(5) Riot may be committed in private as well as in public places.

Violent disorder

2.–(1)Where three or more persons who are present together use or threaten unlawful violence and the conduct of them (taken together) is such as would cause a person of reasonable firmness present at the scene to fear for his personal safety each of the persons using or threatening unlawful violence is guilty of violent disorder.

(2) It is immaterial whether or not the three or more use or threaten unlawful violence simultaneously.

(3) No person of reasonable firmness need actually be, or be likely to be, present at the scene.

(4) Violent disorder may be committed in private as well as in public places .

Affray

3.–(1) A person is guilty of affray if he uses or threatens unlawful violence towards another and his conduct is such as would cause a person of reasonable firmness present at the scene to fear for his personal safety.

(2) Where two or more persons use or threaten the unlawful violence, it is the conduct of them taken together that must be considered for the purposes of subsection (1) .

(3) For the purposes of this section a threat cannot be made by the use of words alone.

(4) No person of reasonable firmness need actually be, or be likely to be, present at the scene.

(5) Affray may be committed in private as well as in public places.

(6) A constable may arrest without warrant anyone he reasonably suspects is committing affray.

Fear or provocation of violence

4.–(1) A person is guilty of an offence if he–

(a) uses towards another person threatening, abusive or insulting words or behaviour, or

(b) distributes or displays to another person any writing, sign or other visible representation which is threatening, abusive or insulting,

with intent to cause that person to believe that immediate unlawful violence will be used against him or another by any person, or to provoke the immediate use of unlawful violence by that person or another, or whereby that person is likely to believe that such violence will be used, or it is likely that such violence will be provoked.

(2) An offence under this section may be committed in a public or a private place, except that no offence is committed where the words or behaviour are used, or the writing, sign or other visible representation is distributed or displayed, by a person inside a dwelling and the other person is also inside that or another dwelling.

(3) A constable may arrest without warrant anyone he reasonably suspects is committing an offence under this section.

Harassment, alarm or distress

5.–(1) A person is guilty of an offence if he–

(a) uses threatening, abusive or insulting words or behaviour, or disorderly behaviour, or

(b) displays any writing, sign or other visible representation which is threatening, abusive or insulting within the hearing or sight of a person likely to be caused harassment alarm or distress thereby.

(2) An offence under this section may be committed in a public or a private place, except that no offence is committed where the words or behaviour are used, or the writing, sign or other visible representation is displayed, by a person inside a dwelling and the other person is also inside that or another dwelling.

(3) It is a defence for the accused to prove–

(a) that he had no reason to believe that there was any person within hearing or sight who was likely to be caused harassment, alarm or distress, or

(b) that he was inside a dwelling and had no reason to believe that the words or behaviour used, or the writing, sign or other visible representation displayed, would be heard or seen by a person outside that or any other dwelling, or

(c) that his conduct was reasonable.

(4) A constable may arrest a person without warrant if–

(a) he engages in offensive conduct which the constable warns him to stop, and

(b) he engages in further offensive conduct immediately or shortly after the warning.

(5) In subsection (4) 'offensive conduct' means conduct the constable reasonably suspects to constitute an offence under this section, and the conduct mentioned in paragraph (a) and the further conduct need not be of the same nature.

Mental element: miscellaneous

6.–(1) A person is guilty of riot only if he intends to use violence or is aware that his conduct may be violent.

(2) A person is guilty of violent disorder or affray only if he intends to use or threaten violence or is aware that his conduct may be violent or threaten violence.

(3) A person is guilty of an offence under section 4 only if he intends his words or behaviour, or the writing, sign or other visible representation to be threatening, abusive or insulting, or is aware that it may be threatening, abusive or insulting.

(4) A person is guilty of an offence under section 5 only if he intends his words or behaviour, or the writing, sign or other visible representation to be threatening, abusive or insulting, or is aware that it may be threatening, abusive or insulting or (as the case may be) he intends his behaviour to be or is aware that it may be disorderly.

Criminal Justice and Public Order Act 1994

Offence of causing intentional harassment, alarm or distress

154. In Part I of the Public Order Act 1986 (offences relating to public order), after s4, there shall be inserted the following section–

Intentional harassment, alarm or distress

4A.–(1) A person is guilty of an offence if, with intent to cause a person harassment, alarm or distress, he–

(a) uses threatening, abusive or insulting words or behaviour, or disorderly behaviour, or

(b) displays any writing, sign or other visible representation which is threatening, abusive or insulting,

thereby causing that or another person harassment, alarm or distress.

(2) An offence under this section may be committed in a public or a private place, except that no offence is committed where the words or behaviour are used, or the writing, sign or other visible representation is displayed, by a person inside a dwelling and the person who is harassed, alarmed or distressed is also inside that or another dwelling.

(3) It is a defence for the accused to prove–

(a) that he was inside a dwelling and had no reason to believe that the words or behaviour used, or the writing, sign or other visible representation displayed, would be heard or seen by a person outside that or any other dwelling, or

(b) that his conduct was reasonable.

(4) A constable may arrest without warrant anyone he reasonably suspects is committing an offence under this section.

Note

The words/behaviour must be 'threatening, abusive or insulting'. The term 'insulting' was considered in *Brutus v Cozens* (1973) in respect of disruption of a tennis match involving a South African player by an anti-apartheid demonstrator.

Cozens v Brutus [1973] AC 854, 860–3

Lord Reid: My Lords, the charge against the appellant is that on 28 June 1971, during the annual tournament at the All England Lawn Tennis Club, Wimbledon, he used insulting behaviour whereby a breach of the peace was likely to be occasioned, contrary to s5 of the Public Order Act 1936, as amended.

While a match was in progress on No 2 Court he went on to the court, blew a whistle and threw leaflets around. On the whistle being blown nine or ten others invaded the court with banners and placards. I shall assume that they did this at the instigation of the appellant though that is not made very clear in the case stated by the magistrates. Then the appellant sat down and had to be forcibly removed by the police. The incident lasted for two or three minutes. This is said to have been insulting behaviour.

It appears that the object of this demonstration was to protest against the apartheid policy of the Government of South Africa. But it is not said that that Government was insulted. The insult is said to have been offered to or directed at the spectators.

The spectators at No 2 Court were upset; they made loud shouts, gesticulated and shook their fists and, while the appellant was being removed, some showed hostility and attempted to strike him.

... the question of law in this case must be whether it was unreasonable to hold that the appellant's behaviour was not insulting. To that question there could in my view be only one answer – no.

But as the divisional court [[1972] 1 WLR 484] have expressed their view as to the meaning of 'insulting' I must, I think, consider it. It was said, at p487:

'It is, as I think, quite sufficient for the purpose of this case to say that behaviour which affronts other people, and evidences a disrespect or contempt for their rights, behaviour which reasonable persons would foresee is likely to cause resentment or protest such as was aroused in this case, and I rely particularly on the reaction of the crowd as set out in the case stated, is insulting for the purpose of this section.'

I cannot agree with that. Parliament had to solve the difficult question of how far freedom of speech or behaviour must be limited in the general public interest. It would have been going much too far to prohibit all speech or conduct likely to occasion a breach of the peace because determined opponents may not shrink from organising or at least threatening a breach of the peace in order to silence a speaker whose views they detest. Therefore vigorous and it may be distasteful or unmannerly speech or behaviour is permitted so long as it does not go beyond any one of three limits. It must not be threatening. It must not be abusive. It must not be insulting. I see no reason why any of these should be construed as having a specially wide or a specially narrow meaning. They are all limits easily recognisable by the ordinary man. Free speech is not impaired by ruling them out. But before a man can be convicted it must be clearly shown that one or more of them has been disregarded.

The spectators may have been very angry and justly so. The appellant's conduct was deplorable. Probably it ought to be punishable. But I cannot see how it insulted the spectators.

I would allow the appeal with costs.

Notes

1   The conviction of the defendant under the predecessor of s4 of the 1986 Act was therefore overturned.

2 The test appears to be whether an ordinary sensible person at whom the words in question are directed would find them insulting. The fact that the persons in question who hear the words are particularly likely to find them insulting may not preclude a finding that they are insulting, although whether or not the speaker knows that such persons will hear the words appears to be immaterial as far as this ingredient of s4 is concerned (*Jordan v Burgoyne* (1963)).[28]

3 Section 5 is the lowest level public order offence contained in the 1986 Act and the most contentious, since it brings behaviour within the scope of the criminal law which was previously thought of as too trivial to justify the imposition of criminal liability.[29] In Northern Ireland s5 was used against a poster depicting youths stoning a British Saracen with a caption proclaiming 'Ireland: 20 years of resistance'.[30] As one commentator noted when the Act was passed, 'In the context of pickets shouting or gesturing at those crossing their picket lines, the elements of this offence will usually be established without difficulty.'[31] In the so-called *Madame M* case, four students were prosecuted for putting up a satirical poster depicting Margaret Thatcher as a 'sadistic dominatrix';[32] the students were acquitted but the fact that such a case was brought in a democracy may appear disturbing.

DPP v Clarke, Lewis, O'Connell and O'Keefe [1992] Crim LR 60

It was alleged against the respondents that they 'on 16 December 1989 ... did display writing, a sign or visible representation which was threatening, abusive or insulting, within the hearing or sight of a person likely to be caused harassment, alarm or distress thereby contrary to ss5(1)(b) and 6 of the Public Order Act 1986'.

The events which gave rise to these charges took place outside a licensed abortion clinic. On 16 December the respondents, who were opposed to the procuring of abortions, assembled on the pavement outside the clinic, each carrying a picture of an aborted foetus which they displayed to police officers who were on uniform patrol duty and, in one case, to passers-by. The respondents refused to comply with police requests not to display the pictures. The magistrates concluded that the pictures were abusive and insulting giving the words their ordinary everyday meaning and that they were displayed in the sight of a person likely to be caused harassment alarm or distress, and did in fact cause alarm and distress to the police officer concerned. Applying an objective test to s5(3)(c) they found that, in all the circumstances, the respondents' conduct was not reasonable; applying s6 and using a subjective test they concluded that, on the balance of probabilities, none of the respondents intended the pictures to be threatening, abusive or insulting, nor was any of them aware that they might be. The respondents were therefore acquitted by the magistrates.

28 2 QB 744.
29 For background to s5 see Law Commission Report No 123, *Offences Relating to Public Order* 1983; for comment see D Williams (1984) PL 12.
30 Reported in the *Independent*, 12 September 1988; mentioned in Ewing and Gearty, p123.
31 D Williams (1987) Crim LR 167.
32 P Thornton, *Decade of Decline: Civil Liberties in the Thatcher Years* (1990), p37.

Held, dismissing the appeal.

(i) The two limbs of s5(1) must be distinguished. First, the thing displayed must be threatening, abusive or insulting; secondly, the display must be within the sight of a person likely to be caused harassment, alarm or distress thereby. However, s6(4) provided that a person was only guilty under s5 if he intended the writing, sign or other visible representation to be threatening, abusive or insulting or was aware that it might be. It did not, therefore, avail the appellant to argue that the respondents must have intended the pictures to cause harassment, alarm or distress or been aware that they might do so; a picture might cause harassment, alarm or distress without being threatening, abusive or insulting and vice versa. The magistrates' conclusion that, although the pictures were abusive and insulting and the police officer found them so, the respondents lacked the necessary intention or awareness, was unassailable. The question whether the pictures were abusive or insulting was essentially one for the magistrates; *Brutus v Cozens* (1973) AC 854.

(ii) The magistrates were correct in applying an objective test to the defence of reasonable conduct in s5(3)(c) of the Act.

(iii) The magistrates correctly imputed a subjective awareness to the words 'is aware that it may be threatening, abusive or insulting' in s6(4) of the Act.

Horseferry Road Magistrate, ex p Siadatan [1991] 1 All ER 324, 325–29

Watkins LJ: On 26 September 1988 Viking Penguin Books Ltd (Viking Penguin) published a book entitled *The Satanic Verses,* the author of which is Mr Salman Rushdie. Copies of that book were sent to ten bookshops owned and operated by Viking Penguin; although the book was not displayed in any of these bookshops, it was available in all of them for purchase on request.

It is clear that many devout Muslims have found the book offensive.

[The applicant's] solicitors, acting on the applicant's instructions, laid before the Horseferry Road Magistrates' Court an information in these terms:

> Penguin Books Limited on or before the 19th of June 1989 at 157 Kings Road, Chelsea SW3 and other places unknown distributed books entitled *The Satanic Verses* by Salman Rushdie containing abusive and insulting writing whereby it was likely that unlawful violence would be provoked contrary to s4(1) of the Public Order Act, 1986.

… The issue is whether the words 'such violence', where they appear in that subsection, mean 'unlawful violence' or 'immediate unlawful violence'. …

A consequence of construing the words 'such violence' in s4(1) as meaning 'immediate unlawful violence' will be that leaders of an extremist movement who prepare pamphlets or banners to be distributed or carried in public places by adherents to that movement will not be committing any offence under s4(1) albeit that they intend the words in the pamphlet or on the banners to be threatening, abusive and insulting, and it is likely that unlawful violence will be provoked by the words in the pamphlet or on the banners.

The context in which s4(1) appears in the 1986 Act is the first matter which leads us to our conclusion. Section 4 appears in the first part of the Act together with the creation of new offences, namely riot by s1, violent disorder by s2, affray by s3, harassment, alarm or distress by s5. The provisions of those sections are such that the conduct of the defendants must produce, in an actual or notional person of reasonable firmness, fear in relation to ss1, 2 and 3 which is contemporaneous with the unlawful violence being used by the defendants, or harassment, alarm or distress which is contemporaneous with the threatening, abusive or insulting conduct under s5. We consider it most unlikely that Parliament could have intended to include, among sections which undoubtedly deal with conduct having an immediate impact on bystanders, a section creating an offence for conduct which is likely to lead to violence at some unspecified time in the future.

A ... very compelling reason for our conclusion on the correct construction of this subsection is that here we are construing a penal statute, of which there are, or may be, two possible readings. It is an elementary rule of statutory construction that, in a penal statute where there are two possible readings, the meaning which limits the scope of the offence thus created is that which the court should adopt.

For these reasons we hold that the magistrate was right to refuse to issue a summons.

Finally, we consider it advisable to indicate our provisional view on the meaning of the word 'immediate'.

It seems to us that the word 'immediate' does not mean 'instantaneous', that a relatively short time interval may elapse between the act which is threatening, abusive or insulting and the unlawful violence. 'Immediate' connotes proximity in time and proximity in causation, that it is likely that violence will result within a relatively short period of time and without any other intervening occurrence.

Application dismissed.

Notes

1   In *DPP v Fidler and Moran* (1992)[33] the respondents were part of a group shouting at and talking to persons attending the clinic, displaying plastic models of human foetuses, photographs of dead foetuses and placards. On the basis of these findings it was accepted on appeal that s5 of the Public Order Act 1986 was satisfied.

2   In *DPP v Orum* (1988)[34] the divisional court found that a police officer may be a person who is caused harassment, alarm or distress by the various kinds of words or conduct to which s5(1) applies.

3   The criminalisation of speech which causes the low level of harm connoted by the terms alarm or distress may be contrary to dicta of the European Court of Human Rights in *Müller v Switzerland* (1991),[35] to the effect that the protection of free speech extends equally to ideas which 'offend, shock or disturb'.[36]

4   The number of prosecutions being brought under s5 suggests that the police may not be showing restraint in using this area of the Act. The old s5 offence

---

33   1 WLR 91; for comment see Professor JC Smith (1992) Crim LR 63.

34   3 All ER 449.

35   13 EHRR 212.

36   It should be noted that in *Brutus v Cozens* (1973) AC 854, Lord Reid said that s5 of the previous 1936 Public Order Act was 'not designed to penalise the expressions of opinion that happen to be disagreeable, distasteful or even offensive, annoying or distressing'.

under the 1936 Public Order Act, an offence with a higher harm threshold,[37] accounted for the majority of the 8,194 charges brought in connection with the miner's strike of 1984. In a survey of 470 1988 public order cases, conducted in two police force areas, it was found that 56% of the sample led to charges under s5. Research has also shown that during the period 1986–1988 the number of charges brought for public order offences doubled, and this is thought to be due not to increased unrest, but to the existence of new offences, particularly s5 with its low level of harm.[38]

5   Section 4A of the 1986 Act (as amended) provides a new and wide area of liability which to some extent overlaps with s5. The *actus reus* under s4A is the same as that under s5, with the proviso that the harm in question must actually be caused. The *mens rea* differs somewhat from that under s5 since the defendant must intend the person in question to suffer harassment, alarm or distress.

6   Section 4A provides another possible level of liability with the result that using offensive words is now imprisonable, without any requirement (as under s4) to show that violence was intended or likely to be caused. It may also therefore offend against the protection for freedom of speech under Art 10 of the European Convention on Human Rights, which clearly includes protection for forms of forceful or offensive speech.

7   Section 4 of the Act overlaps with s5 or s4A in terms of the words or behaviour it covers (aside from disorderly behaviour which is not included in s4) but it requires certain additional ingredients in terms of the intention of the defendant or in terms of the consequences which may flow from the words or behaviour used. Its applicability only in the public order context is confirmed by *Horseferry Road Metropolitan Stipendiary Magistrate, ex p Siadatan* (1991).

Questions

1   Had the decision in *Siadatan* found that s4 carries with it no requirement of immediacy, a very wide curb on freedom of speech would have been created. The decision affirms that s4 creates a very clear demarcation between 'pure' speech and speech as an aspect of freedom of assembly. This is also clearly true of ss5 and 4A. Is such demarcation wholly warranted, or can it be argued that forceful and insulting language used as part of a public protest should not be suppressed?

2   Within the context of freedom of assembly (as opposed to the general public order context) is the existence of ss5,4A and 4 both necessary and warranted, bearing in mind the existence of the more serious public order offences under ss1,2 and 3 and the provisions of ss12, 13, 14A, 14B and 14C?

---

37   It was similar to the offence which replaced it, s4 of the 1986 Act.
38   T Newburn *et al*, 'Policing the Streets' (1990) 29 HORB 10 and 'Increasing Public Order' (1991) 7 *Policing* 22; quoted in Bailey, Harris and Jones (1995), *op cit*, pp229–30.

Incitement to racial hatred[39]

Public Order Act 1986, ss17 and 18

Incitement to racial hatred

Meaning of 'racial hatred'

17　In this Part 'racial hatred' means hatred against a group of persons in Great Britain defined by reference to colour, race, nationality (including citizenship) or ethnic or national origins.

Use of words or behaviour or display of written material

18.–(1) A person who uses threatening, abusive or insulting words or behaviour, or displays any written material which is threatening, abusive or insulting, is guilty of an offence if–

(a) he intends thereby to stir up racial hatred, or

(b) having regard to all the circumstances racial hatred is likely to be stirred up thereby.

(2) An offence under this section may be committed in a public or a private place, except that no offence is committed where the words or behaviour are used, or the written material is displayed, by a person inside a dwelling and are not heard or seen except by other persons in that or another dwelling.

(3) A constable may arrest without warrant anyone he reasonably suspects is committing an offence under this section.

(4) In proceedings for an offence under this section it is a defence for the accused to prove that he was inside a dwelling and had no reason to believe that the words or behaviour used, or the written material displayed, would be heard or seen by a person outside that or any other dwelling.

(5) A person who is not shown to have intended to stir up racial hatred is not guilty of an offence under this section if he did not intend his words or behaviour, or the written material, to be, and was not aware that it might be, threatening, abusive or insulting.

(6) This section does not apply to words or behaviour used, or written material displayed, solely for the purpose of being included in a programme broadcast or included in a cable programme service.

Notes

1　This offence is relevant only in relation to racial, not religious groups.

2　There is no need to show disorder or an intent to cause disorder or to stir up racial hatred, and there is no need to show that racial hatred is actually stirred up. It is sufficient to show that hatred might actually be stirred up whether or not the accused realised that it would be. However, the term 'hatred' is a strong one; merely causing offence or bringing into ridicule is not enough, and nor is racial harassment.

3　If the words in question are only used to the group they are aimed at this will not constitute the offence because they are unlikely to be stirred to racial hatred against themselves. However, if members of a particular racial group feel alarmed by a demonstration, ss4, 4A or 5 may be applicable. If a bystander of another racial group is likely to be stirred up to racial hatred

---

39　For discussion see Barendt *Freedom of Speech* (1987), pp161–167; R Cotterell (1982) PL 378; Wolffe (1987) PL 85.

against the group being attacked that would, however, fulfil the terms of the offence.

4   The Commission for Racial Equality has criticised these provisions as ineffective as a means of curbing the activities of racist groups, but the Government has taken the view that uttering words attacking members of a racial group even in scurrilous terms, but without stirring up racial hatred, should not be criminalised as this would represent too severe a curtailment of freedom of expression.

5   The government has declined so far to create a new crime of racial attack or harassment which might sometimes be applicable to racist marches. Section 4A, however, was framed with racial harassment in mind even though it was not limited to such harassment.

Breach of the peace[40]

The common law power to prevent a breach of the peace[41] overlaps with a number of the powers arising under the 1986 Act and is, in one sense, more useful to the police than they are as its definition is so broad and uncertain. This means that it can be used in such a way as to undermine attempts in statutory provisions to carve out more clearly defined areas of liability.

Power to prevent a breach of the peace may be used to disperse or prevent a peaceful protest or meeting which may provoke others to violence or disorder. *Beatty v Gillbanks* 1882[42] established the important principle that organisers of assemblies could not be held responsible for the actions of those opposed to them whose actions in expressing their opposition created a breach of the peace. However, in *Duncan v Jones* it was found that speakers could be held responsible when persons in agreement with them might be induced to breach the peace.

Duncan v Jones [1936] 1 KB 218[43], 221–3

Lord Hewart CJ: There have been moments during the argument in this case when it appeared to be suggested that the Court had to do with a grave case involving what is called the right of public meeting. I say 'called', because English law does not recognise any special right of public meeting for political or other purposes. The right of assembly, as Professor Dicey puts it [Dicey's *Law of the Constitution*, 8th edn, p499], is nothing more than a view taken by the court of the individual liberty of the subject. If I thought that the present case raised a question which has been held in suspense by more than one writer on constitutional law – namely, whether an assembly can properly be held to be unlawful merely because the holding of it is expected to give rise to a breach of the peace on the part of persons opposed to those who are holding the meeting – I should wish to hear much more argument before I expressed an opinion. This case, however, does not even touch that important question.

---

40   For further explanation of what may amount to a breach of the peace see Police Powers, Part VI Chapter 4, p976. For comment see 'Breaching the Peace and Disturbing the Quiet' (1982) PL 212; DGT Williams, *Keeping the Peace: The Police and Public Order* (1967).

41   It should be noted that breach of the peace, although arrestable, is not a criminal offence.

42   9 QBD 308.

43   For comment see Daintith (1966) PL 248.

Our attention has been directed to the somewhat unsatisfactory case of *Beatty v Gillbanks*. The circumstances of that case and the charge must be remembered, as also must the important passage in the judgment of Field J, in which Cave J concurred. Field J said: ' I entirely concede that every one must be taken to intend the natural consequences of his own acts, and it is clear to me that, if this disturbance of the peace was the natural consequence of acts of the appellants, they would be liable, and the justices would have been right in binding them over. But the evidence set forth in the case does not support this contention; on the contrary, it shows that the disturbances were caused by other people antagonistic to the appellants, and that no acts of violence were committed by them'. Our attention has also been directed to other authorities where the judgments in *Beatty v Gillbanks* have been referred to, but they do not carry the matter any further, although they more than once express a doubt about the exact meaning of the decision. In my view, *Beatty v Gillbanks* is apart from the present case. No such question as that which arose there is even mooted here.

The present case reminds one rather of the observations of Bramwell B in *Prebble* [1 F & F 325, 326], where, in holding that a constable, in clearing certain licensed premises of the persons thereon, was not acting in the execution of his duty, he said:

'It would have been otherwise had there been a nuisance or disturbance of the public peace, or any danger of a breach of the peace.'

The case stated which we have before us indicates clearly a causal connection between the meeting of May 1933 and the disturbance which occurred after it – that the disturbance was not only post the meeting but was also prior to the meeting. In my view, the deputy-chairman was entitled to come to the conclusion to which he came on the facts which he found, and to hold that the conviction of the appellant for wilfully obstructing the respondent when in the execution of his duty was right. This appeal should, therefore, be dismissed.

Note

1   The leading case is *Howell* (1981)[44] in which it was determined that breach of the peace will arise if an act is done or threatened to be done which either: harms a person or, in his presence, his property, or is likely to cause such harm, or which puts a person in fear of such harm. Threatening words are not in themselves a breach of the peace but they may lead a police officer to apprehend a breach of the peace. In a later case, *Chief Constable for Devon and Cornwall, ex p CEGB* (1982),[45] Lord Denning offered a rather different definition of the offence. His view was that violence is unnecessary; he considered that 'if anyone unlawfully and physically obstructs a worker – by lying down or chaining himself to a rig or the like – he is guilty of a breach of the peace.'

2   Despite Lord Hewart's comments it is arguable that *Beatty v Gillbanks* (1882)[46] applies to instances in which a peaceful assembly triggers off a violent response, even where such a response was foreseen by members of the peaceful assembly. If the decision in *Beatty v Gillbanks* is interpreted in this way the decision in *Duncan v Jones* is not in accord with it, in that the

---

44   3 All ER 383.
45   QB 458.
46   (1882) 15 Cox CC 138.

freedom of the speaker was infringed, not because of her conduct but because of police fears about the possible response of the audience. Similarly, in *Jordan v Burgoyne*[47] it was found that a public speaker could be guilty of breach of the peace if he spoke words which were likely to cause disorder amongst the particular audience present, even where the audience had come with the express intent of causing trouble.

3 The decision in *Nicol v DPP* (1996),[48] which concerned the behaviour of fishing protesters, has not brought much clarity into this area. The protesters' behaviour in blowing horns and in attempting to dissuade the anglers from fishing provoked the anglers so that they were on the verge of using force to remove the protesters. It was found that the protesters were guilty of conduct whereby a breach of the peace was likely to be caused since their conduct although lawful was unreasonable and was likely to provoke the anglers to violence. This finding places a curb on the use of breach of the peace in this context since it means that behaviour which has as its natural consequence the provoking of others to violence will not amount to a breach of the peace unless it is also unreasonable. However, the decision also affirms that this area of law is subject to a wide and uncertain test of reasonableness. The judiciary may be disinclined to find that the behaviour of groups such as hunt saboteurs or tree protesters, while lawful, was reasonable.

Criminal trespass

Criminal Justice and Public Order Act 1994

Offence of aggravated trespass

68.–(1) A person commits the offence of aggravated trespass if he trespasses on land in the open air and, in relation to any lawful activity which persons are engaging in or are about to engage in on that or adjoining land in the open air, does there anything which is intended by him to have the effect–

(a) of intimidating those persons or any of them so as to deter them or any of them from engaging in that activity,

(b) of obstructing that activity, or

(c) of disrupting that activity.

(2) Activity on any occasion on the part of a person or persons on land is 'lawful' for the purposes of this section if he or they may engage in the activity on the land on that occasion without committing an offence or trespassing on the land.

(3) A person guilty of an offence under this section is liable on summary conviction to imprisonment for a term not exceeding three months or a fine not exceeding level four on the standard scale, or both.

(4) A constable in uniform who reasonably suspects that a person is committing an offence under this section may arrest him without a warrant.

---

47 (1963) 2 QB 744 . It should be noted that the case was concerned with breach of the peace under s5, Public Order Act 1936.

48 1 J Civ Lib 75.

(5) In this section 'land' does not include:

(a) the highways and roads excluded from the application of section 61 by paragraph (b) of the definition of 'land' in subsection (9) of that section; or

(b) a road within the meaning of the Roads (Northern Ireland) Order 1993.

Powers to remove persons committing or participating in aggravated trespass

69.–(1)If the senior police officer present at the scene reasonably believes–

(a) that a person is committing, has committed or intends to commit the offence of aggravated trespass on land in the open air; or

(b) that two or more persons are trespassing on land in the open air and are present there with the common purpose of intimidating persons so as to deter them from engaging in a lawful activity or of obstructing or disrupting a lawful activity,

he may direct that person or (as the case may be) those persons (or any of them) to leave the land.

(2) A direction under subsection (1) above, if not communicated to the persons referred to in subsection (1) by the police officer giving the direction, may be communicated to them by any constable at the scene.

(3) If a person knowing that a direction under subsection (1) above has been given which applies to him–

(a) fails to leave the land as soon as practicable, or

(b) having left again enters the land as a trespasser within the period of three months beginning with the day on which the direction was given, he commits an offence and is liable on summary conviction to imprisonment for a term not exceeding three months or a fine not exceeding level 4 on the standard scale, or both.

(4) In proceedings for an offence under subsection (3) it is a defence for the accused to show:

(a) that he was not trespassing on the land, or

(b) that he had a reasonable excuse for failing to leave the land as soon as practicable or, as the case may be, for again entering the land as a trespasser.

(5) A constable in uniform who reasonably suspects that a person is committing an offence under this section may arrest him without a warrant.

(6) In this section 'lawful activity' and 'land' have the same meaning as in s68.

Notes

1   The new offence of aggravated trespass under s68 appears to be aimed at certain groups such as hunt saboteurs or motorway protesters, animal rights activists and the 'peace convoys' which gather for the summer solstice festival at Stonehenge. No defence is provided and it is not necessary to show that the lawful activity was affected. This is a very broad power since a great many peaceful demonstrations are intended to have some impact of an obstructive nature on lawful activities (eg export of veal calves or closure of schools or hospitals).

2   'Land' is defined in s61(9); it does not include metalled highway or buildings apart from certain agricultural buildings and scheduled monuments; common land and non-metalled roads are included. Thus, s68

does not apply to demonstrations on a metalled highway or in most but not all buildings. It does apply to public paths such as bridleways.

3 Although civil remedies may take too long to invoke where mass trespass such as that by the peace convoy has occurred, and that therefore new powers under the criminal law were necessary, this power is too wide in that it criminalises trespass other than mass trespass. The provisions can also be criticised as adding to the number of offences which can occur due to disobedience to police orders – the point has been made that a person should be obliged to take orders from the police only in the narrowest of circumstances.[49]

4 Where a person is in receipt of the direction under s69, even though it was erroneously given (since in fact the person did not have the purpose of committing the s68 offence), it would seem that he or she will still commit an offence if thereafter he or she re-enters the land in question during the specified time.

Questions

1 In debate on the Criminal Justice and Public Order Bill in the House of Lords it was said that these provisions 'act as an open invitation to the police to interfere in the legitimate activities of people'. Is this more true of the 1994 Act than of the 1986 Act?

2 The Criminal Justice and Public Order Act 1994 has undoubtedly increased the power of the authorities to prevent protest. Do you consider that any of its public order provisions may infringe the European Convention on Human Rights, Arts 10 or 11?

3 'Taking all these provisions together and bearing in mind particularly the decision in *Nicol v DPP* (1996) it may be argued that public protest may now take place only on the basis that it is so anodyne and emasculated that it can hardly be termed protest at all. The far-reachingness of the public order scheme argues strongly for constitutional protection for freedom of assembly.' Is this a fair evaluation of the current scheme or might it be argued that the restrictions placed on the use of some of these provisions, such as the defence of reasonableness under s5(3)(c) of the 1986 Act or under s69(4)(b) of the 1994 Act, provide sufficient protection for peaceful protest?

---

49   See (1987) PL 211.

CHAPTER 3

FREEDOM OF EXPRESSION

INTRODUCTION[1]

Freedom of expression is widely regarded as one of the most important human rights. For example, in the USA the first amendment to the constitution provides: 'Congress shall make no law ... abridging the freedom of speech or of the press'. The justifications for according this particular freedom such significance have been much debated. One of the most significant, which is associated primarily with the American writer Meiklejohn,[2] is that citizens cannot participate fully in a democracy unless they have a reasonable understanding of political issues; therefore open debate on such matters is essential. Directly political speech does not have any general legal guarantee in Britain, but when the British judiciary consider the claims of free speech they sometimes show a particular concern to protect free criticism of the political authorities. Thus, in *Derbyshire County Council v Times Newspapers* (1993),[3] Lord Keith, in holding that neither local nor central government could sustain an action in defamation, said: 'It is of the highest importance that a democratically elected governmental body ... should be open to uninhibited public criticism.' The fact that he based his decision on this justification for free speech and not on, for example, the individual right of journalists to express themselves freely, is evidence of judicial endorsement of the argument from democracy. Barendt considers that this theory is 'probably the most attractive ... of the free speech theories in modern Western democracies', and concludes that 'it has been the most influential theory in the development of 20th century free speech law'.[4]

Barendt also considers the thesis that freedom of speech is necessary to enable individual self-fulfilment.[5] It is argued that individuals will not be able to develop morally and intellectually unless they are free to air views and ideas in debate with each other. This justification is clearly rights-based and as such, in theory at least, is less vulnerable to competing societal claims; however, it does not value speech in itself but rather instrumentally, as a means to individual growth. Therefore, in situations where it seems that allowing free expression of the particular material will be likely to retard or hinder the growth of others, or of the 'speaker', the justification does not offer a strong

---

1   For comment see G Marshall, 'Freedom of Speech and Assembly' in *Constitutional Theory* (1971), p154; E Barendt, *Freedom of Speech* (1987); T Gibbons, *Regulating the Media* (1991); G Robertson and AGL Nichol, *Media Law* (1992); D Feldman, *Civil Liberties and Human Rights* (1993), Part IV; P Carey, *Media Law* (1996); Abel, *Speech and Respect* (1996); A Boyle, 'Freedom of Expression as a Public Interest in English Law' (1982) PL 574; R Singh, 'The Indirect Regulation of Speech' (1988) PL 212; S Kentridge (1996) 45(2) ICLQ 253.

2   See for example his 'The First Amendment is an Absolute' (1961) Sup Ct Rev 245.

3   (1993) AC 534.

4   E Barendt, *Freedom of Speech* (1987), pp20 and 23 respectively.

5   *Op cit*, p15.

defence of speech.[6] Precisely this argument has been used by some feminist commentators to justify the censorship of pornography. Thus, MacKinnon asserts that, far from aiding in the growth of anyone, 'Pornography strips and devastates women of credibility[7] through the image of women it constructs in its readers' minds'. The thesis which forms the basis of the UK law on obscenity – that certain kinds of pornography actually damage the moral development of those who read it by depraving and corrupting them – similarly fastens onto the argument that this kind of material achieves the opposite of the outcome which allowing freedom of expression is designed to ensure.[8] The apparent vulnerability of the argument from self-development when used to justify the protection of material which is arguably degrading leads Barendt to suggest[9] that a sounder formulation of the theory is one which frames it in terms of the individual's right to moral autonomy.

Freedom of expression is not absolute in any jurisdiction; other interests can overcome it including the protection of morals, of national security, and of the administration of justice. Most bills of rights list these interests as exceptions to the primary right of freedom of speech, as does the European Convention on Human Rights, Art 10. This does not mean that the mere invocation of the other interest will lead to displacement of freedom of speech; it is necessary to show that there is a pressing social need to allow the other interest to prevail. In Britain, freedom of speech exists only as a negative freedom; it is necessary to consider the common law and statutory restrictions placed upon it since their width determines how much of an area is left within which freedom of speech can be exercised. The emphasis of this chapter is on the extent to which the judiciary shows a concern to strike a balance between free speech and a variety of other interests.

RESTRAINING FREEDOM OF EXPRESSION TO PROTECT THE STATE OR GOVERNMENT

Introduction

Broadly speaking, speech criticising or attacking the Government or the state will not attract criminal or civil liability.[10] However, there are a number of qualifications to this general rule. Information on which such criticism or attacks might be based may not be available either because, as discussed in Part IV,

---

6   Barendt argues (pp16–17) that justifications for suppressing some forms of speech could be advanced on the basis that human dignity (the value promoted by allowing self-development) would thereby receive protection. He cites the finding of the German Constitutional Court that there was no right to publish a novel defaming a dead person as such publication might violate the 'dignity of man' guaranteed by Art 1 of the German Basic Law (*Mephisto* case (1973)).

7   Mackinnon, *Feminism Unmodified* (1987), p193.

8   It should be noted that many feminists deny that their arguments have anything in common with conservative objections to pornography, eg MacKinnon, *op cit*, p175.

9   *Op cit*, p17.

10 See Lord Keith's comments in the *Derbyshire* case, above.

Chapter 3, it is covered by the Official Secrets Act 1989 or because, although the Act does not apply, it is unavailable under the Government Code on Access to Information.

Some forms of the speech in question may amount to sedition if accompanied by an intention to bring into hatred or contempt or to excite disaffection against the sovereign or the Government, or to attempt otherwise than by lawful means to alter the law or promote feelings of ill will between different classes of subjects.[11] In *Chief Metropolitan Magistrate, ex p Choudhury* (1991),[12] a case which arose out of the publication of Salman Rushdie's *The Satanic Verses*, the applicants argued that the crime of seditious libel would extend to the image of Islam which the book presented. This offence at one time seemed to cover any attack on the institutions of the state, but in modern times it has been interpreted to require an intention to incite to violence, and the words used must have a tendency to incite to violence against such institutions.[13] It was not therefore apt to cover the offence caused to Muslims by the book which could be said to be intended to arouse general hostility and ill will between sections of the community but not against the public authorities. This finding as regards the ambit of seditious libel means that it is likely to be infrequently invoked.

However, there are a number of other disparate means available to the Government in order to suppress speech which may be viewed as undermining the state, emanations of the state or Government. Two such means are discussed in this section.

Breach of confidence

Breach of confidence is a civil wrong affording protection against the disclosure or use of information which is not generally known, and which has been entrusted in circumstances imposing an obligation not to disclose it without authorisation from the person who originally imparted it. This area of law developed as a means of protecting secret information belonging to individuals and organisations. However, it can also be used by Government to prevent disclosure of sensitive information, and it is in that sense complementary to the other measures available to Government, including the Official Secrets Act 1989.[14] The Government has made it clear that actions for breach of confidence will be used against civil servants in instances falling outside the protected categories of the 1989 Act. In some respects, breach of confidence actions may be more valuable than the criminal sanction provided by the 1989 Act. Their use may attract less publicity than a criminal trial, no jury will be involved and they offer the possibility of quickly obtaining an interim injunction. The latter

---

11 *Burns* (1886) 16 Cox 355.

12 1 QB 429; 1 All ER 306, DC; for comment see M Tregilgas-Davey (1991) 54 MLR 294–9.

13 *Burns* (1886) 16 Cox CC 333; *Aldred* (1909) 22 Cox CC 1; cf *Caunt* (1947) unreported but see note 64 LQR 203; for comment see Barendt, pp152–60.

14 See Part IV, Chapter 3. For comment on the role of breach of confidence in this respect see MW Bryan (1976) 92 LQR 180; DGT Williams (1976) CLJ 1; 'Secrets, Media and the Law' (1985) 48 MLR 592.

possibility is very valuable because, in many instances, the other party (usually a newspaper) will not pursue the case to a trial of the permanent injunction since the secret will probably no longer be newsworthy by that time.

However, where the Government as opposed to a private individual is concerned, the courts will not merely accept that it is in the public interest that the information should be kept confidential. The Government will have to show that the public interest in keeping it confidential due to the harm its disclosure would cause is not outweighed by the public interest in disclosure.

Attorney-General v Jonathan Cape [1976] QB 752; [1975] 3 All ER 484, 491, 494, 495, 496

This action concerned publication of the diaries of the Mr Crossman, a cabinet minister in the Wilson Government, which included detailed accounts of Cabinet and Cabinet Committee meetings, including the attribution to members of views which they expressed there.

> **Lord Widgery CJ:** The Attorney-General contends that all cabinet papers and discussions are *prima facie* confidential, and that the court should restrain any disclosure thereof if the public interest in concealment outweighs the public interest in a right to free publication.
>
> ... in *Coco v AN Clarke Ltd* (1969) RPC 41 at 47 Megarry J, reviewing the authorities, set out the requirements necessary for an action based on breach of confidence to succeed:
>
> > In my judgment three elements are normally required if, apart from contract, a case of breach of confidence is to succeed. First, the information itself ... must 'have the necessary quality of confidence about it'. Secondly, that information must have been imparted in circumstances importing an obligation of confidence. Thirdly, there must be an unauthorised use of that information to the detriment of the party communicating it.
>
> It is not until the decision in *Argyll v Argyll* [1963] 3 All ER at 415 that the same principle was applied to domestic secrets such as those passing between husband and wife during the marriage. It was there held by Ungoed-Thomas J that the plaintiff wife could obtain an order to restrain the defendant husband from communicating such secrets, and the principle is well expressed in the headnote in these terms [1965] 1 All ER 611, [1967] Ch 302:
>
> > ... a contract or obligation of confidence need not be express but could be implied, and a breach of contract or trust or of faith could arise independently of any right of property or contract ... and that the court in the exercise of its equitable jurisdiction, would restrain a breach of confidence independently of any right at law.
>
> ... the defendants argue that an extension of the principle of the *Argyll* case to the present dispute involves another large and unjustified leap forward, because in the present case the Attorney-General is seeking to apply the principle to public secrets made confidential in the interests of good government I cannot see why the courts should be powerless to restrain the publication of public secrets, whilst enjoying the *Argyll* powers in regard to domestic secrets. Indeed, as already pointed out, the court must have power to deal with publication which threatens national security, and the difference between such a case and the present case is one of degree rather than kind. ...
>
> 1   In my judgment, the Attorney-General has made out his claim that the expression of individual opinions by Cabinet ministers in the course of

Cabinet discussion are matters of confidence, the publication of which can be restrained by the court when this is clearly necessary in the public interest.

2   The maintenance of the doctrine of joint responsibility within the Cabinet is in the public interest, and the application of that doctrine might be prejudiced by premature disclosure of the views of individual ministers.

3   There must, however, be a limit in time after which the confidential character of the information, and the duty of the court to restrain publication, will lapse. Since the conclusion of the hearing in this case I have had the opportunity to read the whole of volume I of the diaries, and my considered view is that I cannot believe that the publication at this interval of anything in volume I would inhibit free discussion in the Cabinet of today, even though the individuals involved are the same, and the national problems have a distressing similarity with those of a decade ago. It is unnecessary to elaborate the evils which might flow if, at the close of a cabinet meeting, a minister proceeded to give the press an analysis of the voting, but we are dealing in this case with a disclosure of information nearly 10 years later.

It may, of course, be intensely difficult in a particular case, to say at what point the material loses its confidential character, on the ground that publication will no longer undermine the doctrine of joint cabinet responsibility. It is this difficulty which prompts some to argue that cabinet discussions should retain their confidential character for a longer and arbitrary period such as 30 years, or even for all time, but this seems to me to be excessively restrictive. The court should intervene only in the clearest of cases where the continuing confidentiality of the material can be demonstrated. In less clear cases – and this, in my view, is certainly one – reliance must be placed on the good sense and good taste of the minister or ex-minister concerned.

For these reasons I do not think that the court should interfere with the publication of volume I of the diaries and I propose, therefore, to refuse the injunctions sought ...

Attorney-General v Guardian Newspapers Ltd [1987] 3 All ER 316, 319, 321, 322

In 1985 the Attorney-General commenced proceedings in New South Wales[15] in an attempt (which was ultimately unsuccessful)[16] to restrain publication of *Spycatcher* by Peter Wright. The book included allegations of illegal activity engaged in by MI5 and alleged that some MI5 officers had conspired to destabilise the Labour Government under Harold Wilson. In the UK on 22 and 23 June 1986 the *Guardian* and the *Observer* published reports of the forthcoming hearing which included some *Spycatcher* material, and on 27 June the Attorney-General obtained temporary *ex parte* injunctions preventing them from further disclosure of such material. *Inter partes* injunctions were granted against the newspapers on 11 July 1986 by Millet J. On 12 July 1987 the *Sunday Times* began publishing extracts from *Spycatcher* and the Attorney-General obtained an injunction restraining publication on 16 July. On 14 July 1987 the book was published in the United States and many copies were brought into the UK. The *Guardian* and the *Observer* applied to the Vice-Chancellor for discharge of the injunctions.

15   (1987) 8 NSWLR 341.
16   HC of Australia (1988) 165 CLR 30; for comment see FA Mann (1988) 104 LQR 497, M Turnbull (1989) 105 LQR 382.

Sir Nicolas Browne-Wilkinson VC: These are three applications. The first two are made by the *Guardian* and the *Observer* newspapers to discharge interlocutory junctions made against them in two orders made by Millett J on 11 July 1986 and confirmed (subject to minor modifications) by the Court of Appeal on 25 July 1986. The two orders made against the newspapers are in the same terms. As amended, the newspaper is restrained from:

(1) disclosing or publishing or causing or permitting to be disclosed or published to any person any information obtained by Peter Maurice Wright in his capacity as a member of the British security service and which they know, or have reasonable grounds to believe, to have come or been obtained whether directly or indirectly from the said Peter Maurice Wright

(2) attributing, in any disclosure or publication made by them to any person any information concerning the British security service to the said Peter Maurice Wright whether by name or otherwise.

The third application is technically one by the Attorney-General against the *Sunday Times* claiming an injunction restraining the further publication of extracts from Mr Wright's memoirs called *Spycatcher*, the ground of the application in that case being that such publication would constitute a contempt of court in that it would thwart or frustrate the orders of the Court of Appeal made against the *Guardian* and the *Observer*.

It is common ground that if I discharge the orders of 25 July 1986 made against the *Guardian* and the *Observer*, the Attorney-General's claim for relief against the *Sunday Times* on the ground of contempt of court must also fail. I will therefore consider, first, the applications made by the *Guardian* and the *Observer* to vary or discharge the orders made against them. ...

On 14 July Viking Penguin in the United States had copies of the book *Spycatcher* on sale throughout the United States. ...

The book rapidly moved into the best seller category, being on display in bookshops throughout the United States, and in particular on the bookstall at John F Kennedy Airport. The evidence shows that books purchased in the United States were being brought back from the United States to this country. ...

In my judgment, there has been a most substantial change in circumstances. In 1986, as I have said, the publication in the *Guardian* and the *Observer* was, so far as that court was aware and so far as I am aware, the only breach in the security walls. Otherwise the matter had not hit the press in any way, save that the action was pending in Australia. Of the allegations made by Mr Wright in the book there had been no other indication.

Due to the change in circumstances, the Vice-Chancellor discharged the Millet injunctions, but they were restored by the Court of Appeal [1987] 3 All ER 316 in modified form. The newspapers appealed to the House of Lords [1987] 3 All ER 316, 346–7.

Lord Bridge: Having no written constitution, we have no equivalent in our law to the First Amendment to the constitution of the United States of America. Some think that puts freedom of speech on too lofty a pedestal. Perhaps they are right. We have not adopted as part of our law the European Convention on Human Rights (Convention for the Protection of Human Rights and Fundamental Freedoms (Rome, 4 November 1950; TS 71 (1953); Cmnd 8969)) to which this country is a signatory. Many think that we should. I have hitherto not been of that persuasion, in large part because I have had confidence in the capacity of the common law to safeguard the fundamental freedoms essential to a free society including the right to freedom of speech which is specifically safeguarded by Art 10 of the Convention. My confidence is seriously undermined by your Lordships' decision. All the judges in the courts below in this case have been concerned not to impose any unnecessary fetter on freedom of speech. I suspect that what the Court of Appeal would have liked to achieve, and perhaps set out to achieve by its compromise solution, was to inhibit the *Sunday Times* from continuing the serialisation of *Spycatcher*, but to leave the press at large at liberty to discuss and comment on the *Spycatcher* allegations. If there were a method of achieving these results which could be sustained in law, I can see much to be said for it on the merits. But I can see nothing whatever, either in law or on the merits, to be said for the maintenance of a total ban on discussion in the press of this country of matters of undoubted public interest and concern which the rest of the world now knows all about and can discuss freely. Still less can I approve your Lordships' decision to throw in for good measure a restriction on reporting court proceedings in Australia which the Attorney-General had never even asked for.

Freedom of speech is always the first casualty under a totalitarian regime. Such a regime cannot afford to allow the free circulation of information and ideas among its citizens. Censorship is the indispensable tool to regulate what the public may and what they may not know. The present attempt to insulate the public in this country from information which is freely available elsewhere is a significant step down that very dangerous road. The maintenance of the ban, as more and more copies of the book *Spycatcher* enter this country and circulate here, will seem more and more ridiculous. If the Government are determined to fight to maintain the ban to the end, they will face inevitable condemnation and humiliation by the European Court of Human Rights in Strasbourg. Long before that they will have been condemned at the bar of public opinion in the free world.

But there is another alternative. The Government will surely want to reappraise the whole *Spycatcher* situation in the light of the views expressed in the courts below and in this House. I dare to hope that they will bring to that reappraisal qualities of vision and of statesmanship sufficient to recognise that their wafer thin victory in this litigation has been gained at a price which no Government committed to upholding the values of a free society can afford to pay.

I add a postscript to record that I have now had the opportunity to read first drafts of the opinions of my noble and learned friends Lord Templeman and Lord Ackner. I remain in profound disagreement with them.

Lord Brandon of Oakbrook: I was a party to the majority decision of this House given on 30 July 1987 that the injunctions in issue should not be discharged but should be continued until trial. My reasons for being a party to that decision can be summarised in nine propositions as follows.

(1) The action brought by the Attorney-General against the *Guardian* and the *Observer* has as its object the protection of an important public interest, namely the maintenance so far as possible of the secrecy of the British security service.

(2) The injunctions in issue are interlocutory, that is to say temporary injunctions, having effect until the trial of the action only.

(3) Before the publication of *Spycatcher* in America the Attorney-General had a strong arguable case for obtaining at trial final injunctions in terms similar to those of the temporary injunctions.

(4) While the publication of *Spycatcher* in America has much weakened that case, it remains an arguable one.

(5) The only way in which it can justly be decided whether the Attorney-General's case, being still arguable, should succeed or fail is by having the action tried.

(6) On the hypothesis that the Attorney-General's claim, if tried, will succeed, the effect of discharging the temporary injunctions now will be to deprive him, summarily and without a trial, of all opportunity of achieving that success.

(7) On the alternative hypothesis that the Attorney-General's claim, if tried, will fail, the effect of continuing the temporary injunctions until trial will be only to postpone, not to prevent, the exercise by the *Guardian* and the *Observer* of the rights to publish which it will in that event have been established that they have.

(8) Having regard to (6) and (7) above, the discharge of the temporary injunctions now is capable of causing much greater injustice to the Attorney-General than the continuation of them until trial is capable of causing to the *Guardian* and the *Observer*.

(9) Continuation of the injunctions until trial is therefore preferable to their discharge.

By a 3–2 majority the House of Lords upheld the injunctions.

Attorney-General v Guardian (No 2) [1990] 1 AC 109, [1988] 3 All ER 545, 639, 640, 641–6

On 21 December 1987 in the trial of the permanent injunctions, Scott J discharged the interlocutory injunctions. The Court of Appeal upheld this decision. The Attorney-General appealed to the House of Lords.

Lord Keith of Kinkel: The issues raised in the litigation are thus summarised in the judgment of Sir John Donaldson MR in the Court of Appeal [1988] 2 WLR 805, 871:

'(1) Were the *Observer* and the *Guardian* in breach of their duty of confidentiality when, on 22 and 23 June 1986, they respectively published articles on the forthcoming hearing in Australia? If so, would they have been restrained from publishing if the Attorney-General had been able to seek the assistance of the court? ...

(2) Was the *Sunday Times* in breach of its duty of confidentiality when, on 12 July 1987 it published the first extract of an intended serialisation of Spycatcher? ...

(3) Is the Attorney-General now entitled to an injunction (a) in relation to the *Observer* and the *Guardian* and (b) in relation to the *Sunday Times* with special consideration to further serialisation? ...

(4) Is the Attorney-General entitled to an account of the profits accruing to the *Sunday Times* as a result of the serialisation of Spycatcher? ...

(5) Is the Attorney-General entitled to some general injunction restraining future publication of information derived from Mr Wright or other members or ex-members of the security service?'

As regards issue (1), Scott J and the majority of the Court of Appeal (Dillon and Bingham LJJ; Sir John Donaldson MR dissenting) held that the publication of the articles in question was not in breach of an obligation of confidence.

On issue (2), Scott J and the majority of the Court of Appeal (Bingham LJ dissenting) held that the publication of the first extract from *Spycatcher* was in breach of an obligation of confidence.

Upon issue (3), Scott J and the Court of Appeal held that the Attorney-General was not entitled to an injunction against the *Observer* and the *Guardian* nor (Sir

John Donaldson MR dissenting) against further serialisation of *Spycatcher* by the *Sunday Times*.

As to issue (4), Scott J and the majority of the Court of Appeal (Bingham LJ dissenting) decided this in favour of the Attorney-General.

Issue (5) was decided against the Attorney-General both by Scott J and by the Court of Appeal.

The Attorney-General now appeals to your Lordships' House upon all the issues on which he failed below. The *Sunday Times* appeals against the decision on account of profits. ...

In so far as the Crown acts to prevent [disclosure of confidential information] or to seek redress for it on confidentiality grounds, it must necessarily, in my opinion, be in a position to show that the disclosure is likely to damage or has damaged the public interest. How far the Crown has to go in order to show this must depend on the circumstances of each case. In a question with a Crown servant himself, or others acting as his agents, the general public interest in the preservation of confidentiality, and in encouraging other Crown servants to preserve it, may suffice. But where the publication is proposed to be made by third parties unconnected with the particular confidant, the position may be different. The Crown's argument in the present case would go the length that, in all circumstances where the original disclosure has been made by a Crown servant in breach of his obligation of confidence, any person to whose knowledge the information comes and who is aware of the breach comes under an equitable duty binding his conscience not to communicate the information to anyone else irrespective of the circumstances under which he acquired the knowledge. In my opinion that general proposition is untenable and impracticable, in addition to being unsupported by any authority. The general rule is that anyone is entitled to communicate anything he pleases to anyone else, by speech or in writing or in any other way. That rule is limited by the law of defamation and other restrictions similar to these mentioned in Art 10 of the Convention for the Protection of Human Rights and Fundamental Freedoms (1953) (Cmnd 8969). All those restrictions are imposed in the light of considerations of public interest such as to countervail the public interest in freedom of expression. A communication about some aspect of Government activity which does no harm to the interests of the nation cannot, even where the original disclosure has been made in breach of confidence, be restrained on the ground of a nebulous equitable duty of conscience serving no useful practical purpose. [Lord Keith went on to consider *Attorney-General v Jonathan Cape Ltd* (1976) QB 752.]

The second case is *Commonwealth of Australia v John Fairfax and Sons Ltd* (1980) 147 CLR 39. That was a decision of Mason J in the High Court of Australia, dealing with an application by the Commonwealth for an interlocutory injunction to restrain publication of a book containing the texts of Government documents concerned with its relations with other countries, in particular the Government of Indonesia in connection with the 'East Timor crisis'. The documents appeared to have been leaked by a civil servant.

[Mason J found:] 'The equitable principle has been fashioned to protect the personal, private and proprietary interests of the citizen, not to protect the very different interests of the executive Government. It acts, or is supposed to act, not according to standards of private interest, but in the public interest. This is not to say that equity will not protect information in the hands of the Government, but it is to say that when equity protects Government information it will look at the matter through different spectacles.

'It may be a sufficient detriment to the citizen that disclosure of information relating to his affairs will expose his actions to public discussion and criticism. But it can scarcely be a relevant detriment to the Government that publication of material concerning its actions will merely expose it to public discussion and criticism. It is unacceptable in our democratic society that there should be a restraint on the publication of information relating to Government when the only vice of that information is that it enables the public to discuss, review and criticise Government action.

'Accordingly, the court will determine the Government's claim to confidentiality by reference to the public interest. Unless disclosure is likely to injure the public interest, it will not be protected.

'The court will not prevent the publication of information which merely throws light on the past workings of government, even if it be not public property, so long as it does not prejudice the community in other respects. Then disclosure will itself serve the public interest in keeping the community informed and in promoting discussion of public affairs. If, however, it appears that disclosure will be inimical to the public interest because national security, relations with foreign countries or the ordinary business of government will be prejudiced, disclosure will be restrained. There will be cases in which the conflicting considerations will be finely balanced, where it is difficult to decide whether the public's interest in knowing and in expressing its opinion, outweighs the need to protect confidentiality.'

I find myself in broad agreement with this statement by Mason J. In particular I agree that a Government is not in a position to win the assistance of the court in restraining the publication of information imparted in confidence by it or its predecessors unless it can show that publication would be harmful to the public interest.

In relation to Mr Wright, there can be no doubt whatever that, had he sought to bring about the first publication of his book in this country, the Crown would have been entitled to an injunction restraining him. The work of a member of MI5 and the information which he acquires in the course of that work must necessarily be secret and confidential and be kept secret and confidential by him. There is no room for discrimination between secrets of greater or lesser importance, nor any room for close examination of the precise manner in which revelation of any particular matter may prejudice the national interest. Any attempt to do so would lead to further damage. ... The question whether Mr Wright or those acting for him would be at liberty to publish *Spycatcher* in England under existing circumstances does not arise for immediate consideration. These circumstances include the world-wide dissemination of the contents of the book which has been brought about by Mr Wright's wrongdoing. In my opinion general publication in this country would not bring about any significant damage to the public interest beyond what has already been done. It is, however, urged on behalf of the Crown that such publication might prompt Mr Wright into making further disclosures, would expose existing and past members of the British security and intelligence services to harassment by the media, and might result in their disclosing other secret material with a view, perhaps, to refuting Mr Wright's account, and would damage the morale of such members by the spectacle of Mr Wright having got away with his treachery. While giving due weight to the evidence of Sir Robert Armstrong on these matters, I have not been persuaded that the effect of publication in England would be to bring about greater damage in the respects founded upon than has already been caused by the widespread publication elsewhere in the world.

For the reasons which I have indicated in dealing with the position of Mr Wright, I am of the opinion that the reports and comments proposed by the *Guardian* and the *Observer* would not be harmful to the public interest, nor would the continued serialisation by the *Sunday Times*. I would therefore refuse an injunction against any of the newspapers. I would stress that I do not base this upon any balancing of public interest nor upon any considerations of freedom of the press, nor upon any possible defences of prior publication or just cause or excuse, but simply upon the view that all possible damage to the interest of the Crown has already been done by the publication of *Spycatcher* abroad and the ready availability of copies in this country.

The next issue for examination is conveniently the one as to whether the *Sunday Times* was in breach of an obligation of confidentiality when it published the first serialised extract from *Spycatcher* on 12 July 1987. I have no hesitation in holding that it was. Those responsible for the publication well knew that the material was confidential in character and had not as a whole been previously published anywhere. ... Neither the defence of prior publication nor that of just cause or excuse would in my opinion have been available to the *Sunday Times*. As regards the former, the circumstance that certain allegations had been previously made and published was not capable of justifying publication in the newspaper of lengthy extracts from *Spycatcher* which went into details about the working of the security service. As to just cause or excuse it is not sufficient to set up the defence merely to show that allegations of wrongdoing have been made. There must be at least a *prima facie* case that the allegations have substance. The mere fact that it was Mr Wright, a former member of MI5 who, with the assistance of a collaborator, had made the allegations, was not in itself enough to establish such a *prima facie* case.

This leads on to consideration of the question whether the *Sunday Times* should be held liable to account to the Crown for profits made from past and future serialisation of *Spycatcher*. An account of profits made through breach of confidence is a recognised form of remedy available to a claimant: *Peter Pan Manufacturing Corp v Corsets Silhouette Ltd* [1969] 1 WLR 96; cf *Reading v Attorney-General* [1951] AC 507. ... The remedy is, in my opinion, ... to be attributed to the principle that no one should be permitted to gain from his own wrongdoing. Its availability may also, in general, serve a useful purpose in lessening the temptation for recipients of confidential information to misuse it for financial gain. In the present case the *Sunday Times* did misuse confidential information and it would be naive to suppose that the prospect of financial gain was not one of the reasons why it did so. I can perceive no good ground why the remedy should not be made available to the Crown in the circumstances of this case, and I would therefore hold the Crown entitled to an account of profits in respect of the publication on 12 July 1987.

In relation to future serialisation of further parts of the book, however, it must be kept in mind that the proposed subject matter of it has now become generally available and that the *Sunday Times* is not responsible for this having happened. In the circumstances the *Sunday Times* will not be committing any wrong against the Crown by publishing that subject matter and should not therefore be liable to account for any resultant profits.

The next matter for consideration, though the point is not now of any practical importance, is whether the *Observer* and the *Guardian* were in breach of an obligation of confidence by the publication of their articles on 22 and 23 June 1986. The circumstances were that Mr Wright and Heinemann and their solicitors had given to the New South Wales court, pending trial of the action there, undertakings not to disclose any information gained by Mr Wright in the course of his service with MI5. Scott J found, and it has never been disputed by counsel for the two newspapers, that information about the allegations described in the two articles must have been obtained from someone in the office of the publishers or in that of their solicitors. Scott J also inferred that the newspapers must have known of the undertakings that had been given. There can be no question of the articles having been a fair and accurate report of proceedings in the New South Wales court. Such a report could only cover matters which had actually been divulged in open court. The newspapers knew that the information in question was of a confidential nature, deriving as it did from Mr Wright and relating to his experiences in MI5. Some of the allegations, albeit of minor significance, had never previously been published at all. The allegations about Sir Roger Hollis had received quite widespread publicity in various books and newspapers and had been made by Mr Wright himself on a Granada television programme in July 1984. Allegations about the Nasser plot and the Wilson plot and the bugging of embassies and other places had been made in a number of published books, but had been attributed to Mr Wright only in the *Observer* article of 15 March 1985 and another of 9 February 1986, and then only in a somewhat oblique fashion. I do not consider that an injunction would have been granted against publication of the fact that Mr Wright was repeating in his memoirs the allegation about Sir Roger Hollis, because it was quite well known that he had been making that allegation for a considerable time. The specific attribution to Mr Wright of the other allegations is perhaps a different matter. But I would regard it as highly doubtful that the publication of that attribution could reasonably be regarded as damaging to the public interest of the UK in the direct sense that the information might be of value to unfriendly foreign intelligence services, or as calculated to damage that interest indirectly in any of the ways spoken of in evidence by Sir Robert Armstrong. I consider that on balance the prospects are that the Crown would not have been held entitled to a permanent injunction. Scott J and the majority of the Court of Appeal took that view, and I would not be disposed to differ from them.

The final issue is whether the Crown is entitled to a general injunction against all three newspapers, restraining them from publishing any information concerned with the *Spycatcher* allegations obtained by any member or former member of the security service which they know or have reasonable grounds for believing to have come from any such member or former member, including Mr Wright, and also from attributing any such information in any publication to any member or former member of the security service. ... There are a number of problems involved in the general width of the injunction sought. Injunctions are normally aimed at the prevention of some specific wrong, not at the prevention of wrongdoing in general. It would hardly be appropriate to subject a person to an injunction on the ground that he is the sort of person who is likely to commit some kind of wrong, or that he has an interest in doing so. Then the injunction sought would not leave room for the possibility that a defence might be available in a particular case. If Mr Wright were to publish a second book in America or Australia or both and it were to become readily available in this country, as has happened in regard to his first book, newspapers which published its contents would have as good a defence as the respondents in the present case. It would not be satisfactory to have the availability of any defence tested in contempt proceedings. In my opinion an injunction on the lines sought should not be granted.

A few concluding reflections may be appropriate. In the first place I regard this case as having established that members and former members of the security service do have a lifelong obligation of confidence owed to the Crown. Those who breach it, such as Mr Wright, are guilty of treachery just as heinous as that of some of the spies he excoriates in his book. The case has also served a useful purpose in bringing to light the problems which arise when the obligation of confidence is breached by publication abroad. The judgment of the High Court of Australia reveals that even the most sensitive defence secrets of this country may not expect protection in the courts even of friendly foreign countries, although a less extreme view was taken by Sir Robin Cooke P in the New Zealand Court of Appeal (*Attorney-General v Wellington Newspapers Ltd* (unreported), 28 April 1988). The secrets revealed by Mr Wright refer to matters of some antiquity, but there is no reason to expect that secrets concerned with matters of great current importance would receive any different treatment. Consideration should be given to the possibility of some international agreement aimed at reducing the risks to collective security involved in the present state of affairs. The First Amendment clearly poses problems in relation to publication in the USA, but even there there is the prospect of defence and intelligence secrets receiving some protection in the civil courts, as is shown by the decision of the Supreme Court in *Snepp v United States* 444 US 507 (1980). Some degree of comity and reciprocity in this respect would seem desirable in order to promote the common interests of allied nations.

My Lords, upon the whole matter and for the reasons I have expressed, I would dismiss both appeals and also the cross-appeal by the *Sunday Times*.

The majority in the House of Lords concurred.

The Observer and The Guardian v United Kingdom (1991) 14 EHRR 153, 190–5

The *Guardian* and the *Observer* applied to the European Commission on Human Rights alleging, *inter alia*, a breach of Art 10 in respect of the temporary injunctions. The Commission referred the case to the Court, having given its unanimous opinion that the injunctions constituted a breach of Art 10.

56 The Court is satisfied that the injunctions had the direct or primary aim of 'maintaining' the authority of the judiciary,' which phrase includes the protection of the rights of litigants [see *Sunday Times v United Kingdom*, para 56].

It is also incontrovertible that a further purpose of the restrictions complained of was the protection of national security. They were imposed, as has just been seen, with a view to ensuring a fair trial of the Attorney-General's claim for permanent injunctions against the *Observer* and the *Guardian* and the evidential basis for that claim was the two affidavits sworn by Sir Robert Armstrong, in which he deposed to the potential damage which publication of the *Spycatcher* material would cause to the security service [see para 16 above]. Not only was that evidence relied on by Millet J when granting the injunctions initially [see para 18(e) above], but considerations of national security featured prominently in all the judgments delivered by the English courts in this case [see paras 18, 34 and 40 above]. The court would only comment – and it will revert to this point in paragraph 69 below – that the precise nature of the national security considerations involved varied over the course of time.

57 The interference complained of thus had aims that were legitimate under paragraph (2) of Art 10.

Was the interference 'necessary in a democratic society'?

1 *General principles*

59 The Court's judgments relating to Art 10, starting with *Handyside v United Kingdom* (1976) 1 EHRR 737, concluding most recently, with *Oberschlick v Austria*, Series A No 204 ... announce the following major principles.

(a) Freedom of expression constitutes one of the essential foundations of a democratic society; subject to paragraph (2) of Art 10, it is applicable not only to 'information' or 'ideas' that are favourably received or regarded as inoffensive or as a matter of indifference, but also to those that offend, shock or disturb. Freedom of expression, as enshrined in Art 10, is subject to a number of exceptions which, however, must be narrowly interpreted and the necessity for any restrictions must be convincingly established.

(b) These principles are of particular importance as far as the press is concerned. Whilst it must not overstep the bounds set, *inter alia*, in the 'interests of national security' or for 'maintaining the authority of the judiciary', it is nevertheless incumbent on it to impart information and ideas on matters of public interest. Not only does the press have the task of imparting such information and ideas: the public also has a right to receive them. Were it otherwise, the press would be unable to play its vital role of 'public watchdog'. ...

60   For the avoidance of doubt ... the court would only add to the foregoing that Art 10 of the Convention does not in terms prohibit the imposition of prior restraints on publication, as such. This is evidenced not only by the words 'conditions,' 'restrictions', 'preventing' and 'prevention' which appear in that provision, but also by the *Sunday Times* judgment of 26 April 1979 and its *Markt Intern Verlag GmbH and Klaus Beerman* judgment of 20 November 1988 [(1990) 12 EHRR 161]. On the other hand, the dangers inherent in prior restraints are such that they call for the most careful scrutiny on the part of the court. This is especially so as far as the press is concerned, for news is a perishable commodity and to delay its publication, even for a short period, may well deprive it of all its value and interest.

2   *The period from 11 July 1986 to 30 July 1987*

In forming its own opinion, the Court has borne in mind its observations concerning the nature and contents of *Spycatcher* and the interests of national security involved; it has also had regard to the potential prejudice to the Attorney-General's breach of confidence actions, this being a point that has to be seen in the context of the central position occupied by Art 6 of the Convention and its guarantee of the right to a fair trial [see the *Sunday Times v United Kingdom*, para 55]. Particularly in the light of these factors, the court takes the view that, having regard to their margin of appreciation, the English courts were entitled to consider the grant of injunctive relief to be necessary and that their reasons for so concluding were 'sufficient' for the purposes of paragraph (2) of Art 10.

64   It has nevertheless to be examined whether the actual restraints imposed were 'proportionate' to the legitimate aims pursued.

In this connection, it is to be noted that the injunctions did not erect a blanket prohibition. Whilst they forbade the publication of information derived from or attributed to Mr Wright in his capacity as a member of the security service, they did not prevent the *Observer* and the *Guardian* from pursuing their campaign for an independent inquiry into the operation of that service. Moreover, they contained provisos excluding certain material from their scope, notably that which had been previously published in the works of Mr Chapman Pincher and in the Granada Television programmes. Again, it was open to the *Observer* and the *Guardian* at any time to seek – as they in fact did – variation or discharge of the orders.

It is true that, although the injunctions were intended to be no more than temporary measures, they in fact remained in force – as far as the period now under consideration is concerned – for slightly more than a year. And this is a long time where the perishable commodity of news is concerned. As against this, it may be pointed out that the Court of Appeal certified the case as fit for a speedy trial – which the *Observer* and the *Guardian* apparently did not seek – and that the news in question, relating as it did to events that had occurred several years previously, could not really be classified as urgent. Furthermore, the Attorney-General's actions raised difficult issues of both fact and law; time was accordingly required for the preparation of the trial. ...

65   Having regard to the foregoing, the court concludes that, as regards the period from 11 July 1986 to 30 July 1987, the national authorities were entitled to think that the interference complained of was 'necessary in a democratic society'.

3   *The period from 30 July to 13 October 1988*

66   On 14 July 1987 *Spycatcher* was published in the USA [see para 28 above]. This changed the situation that had obtained since 11 July 1986. In the first place, the contents of the book ceased to be a matter of speculation and their confidentiality was destroyed. Furthermore, Mr Wright's memoirs were obtainable from abroad by residents of the UK, the Government having made no attempt to impose a ban on importation.

67   In the submission of the Government the continuation of the interlocutory injunctions during the period from 30 July 1987 to 13 October 1988 nevertheless remained 'necessary', in terms of Art 10, for maintaining the authority of the judiciary and thereby protecting the interests of national security. It relied on the conclusion of the House of Lords in July 1987 that, notwithstanding the US publication:

(a)   the Attorney-General still has an arguable case for permanent injunctions against the *Observer* and the *Guardian*, which case could be fairly determined only if restraints on publication were imposed pending the substantive trial; and

(b)   there was still a national security interest in preventing the general dissemination of the contents of the book through the press and a public interest in discouraging the unauthorised publication of memoirs containing confidential material.

68   The fact that the further publication of *Spycatcher* material could have been prejudicial to the trial of the Attorney-General's claims for permanent injunctions was certainly in terms of the aim of maintaining the authority of the judiciary, a 'relevant' reason for continuing the restraints in question. The court finds, however, that in the circumstances it does not constitute a 'sufficient' reason for the purposes of Art 10.

It is true that the House of Lords had regard to the requirements of the Convention. Even though it is not incorporated into domestic law. It is also true that there is some difference between the casual importation of copies of *Spycatcher* into the UK and mass publication of its contents in the press. On the other hand, even if the Attorney-General had succeeded in obtaining permanent injunctions at the substantive trial, they would have borne on material the confidentiality of which had been destroyed in any event – and irrespective of whether any further disclosures were made by the *Observer* and the *Guardian* – as a result of the publication in the US. Seen in terms of the protection of the Attorney-General's rights as a litigant, the interest in maintaining the confidentiality of that material had, for the purposes of the

Convention, ceased to exist by 30 July 1987 [see, *mutatis mutandis, Weber v Switzerland* (1990) 12 EHRR 508, at para 51].

69   As regards the interests of national security relied on, the Court observes that, in this respect, the Attorney-General's case underwent, to adopt the words of Scott J, 'a curious metamorphosis' [*Attorney-General v Guardian Newspapers Ltd (No 2)* [1990] AC 140F]. As emerges from Sir Robert Armstrong's evidence [see para 16 above], injunctions were sought at the outset, *inter alia,* to preserve the secret character of information that ought to be kept secret. By 30 July 1987, however, the information had lost that character and, as was observed by Lord Brandon of Oakbrook [see para 36(a)(iv) above], the major part of the potential damage adverted to by Sir Robert Armstrong had already been done. By then, the purpose of the injunctions had thus become confined to the promotion of the efficiency and reputation of the security service, notably by: preserving confidence in that service on the part of third parties; making it clear that the unauthorised publication of memoirs by its former members would not be countenanced; and deterring others who might be tempted to follow in Mr Wright's footsteps.

Notes

1   The Court concluded unanimously that the objectives considered were insufficient to justify continuing the restriction after July 1987 since it prevented newspapers exercising their right to purvey information which was already available on a matter of legitimate public interest. Thus a breach of Art 10 was found in respect of the maintenance of the injunctions after, but not before, 30 July 1987.[17] Judge Morenilla's dissenting judgment in relation to the period prior to 30 July is of particular interest. He argued that prior restraint should be imposed only where disclosure would result in immediate, serious and irreparable damage to the public interest.[18] In contrast, the test put forward by the House of Lords at the interlocutory stage allows an injunction to be granted, even where disclosure would not cause clear damage to the public interest on the basis that confidentiality must be preserved until the case can be fully looked into. This may mean that the other party does not pursue the case to the permanent stage and therefore freedom of speech is suppressed on grounds which are not well-founded.

2   While the temporary injunctions were in force the *Independent* and two other papers published material covered by them. It was determined in the Court of Appeal (*A-G v Newspaper Publishing plc* 1990)[19] that such publication constituted the *actus reus* of contempt. The case therefore affirmed the principle that, once an interlocutory injunction has been obtained restraining one organ of the media from publication of allegedly confidential material, the rest of the media may be in contempt if they publish that material, even if their intention in doing so is to bring alleged iniquity to public attention. Such publication must be accompanied by an intention to prejudice the eventual trial of the permanent injunctions.

---

17   *The Sunday Times v United Kingdom (No 2)* (1991) 14 EHRR 229. For comment see I Leigh (1992) PL 200–208.

18   He relied on the ruling to this effect of the US Supreme Court in *Nebraska Press Association v Stuart* 427 US 593 (1976).

19   *The Times,* 28 February (see further below at pp951–3).

3　In 1987 the BBC wished to broadcast a programme to be entitled 'My Country Right or Wrong', which was to examine issues raised by the *Spycatcher* litigation. The Attorney-General obtained an injunction preventing transmission on the ground of breach of confidence (*Attorney-General v BBC* (1987)).[20] According to the Attorney-General, the injunction then affected every organ of the media because of the July ruling of the Court of Appeal in *Attorney-General v Newspaper Publishing plc* (1987) (this was a preliminary ruling on the *actus reus* of common law contempt which was affirmed as noted above).

4　The facts of *Attorney-General v Blake* (1996)[21] bear some resemblance to those in *Attorney-General v Guardian (No 2)*, although the Attorney-General did not claim breach of confidence in the *Blake* case. George Blake, a former member of the Secret Intelligence Service, became a double agent working for the Soviet Union. He was convicted of unlawfully communicating information under s1(1)(c) of the Official Secrets Act 1911. He escaped from prison and went to Moscow where he wrote a book, *No Other Choice*, drawing on information acquired during his term as an intelligence officer. The Crown, suing by the Attorney-General, sought to extract from Blake any financial benefit he might gain from publishing the book on the ground that he had acted in breach of the duty he owed to the Crown as a member of the SIS. The Attorney-General argued that Blake owed the Crown a fiduciary duty not to use his position as a member of the SIS to make a profit for himself and not to use the Crown's property, including originally confidential information, for his own benefit. Sir Richard Scott VC found that this duty was formulated too widely; the relief sought in reliance on it would infringe Blake's rights to freedom of expression under Art 10 of the ECHR and would not fall within para 2 of that Article since the information was not secret or confidential at the time of its disclosure. It could not therefore be necessary in a democratic society in the interests of national security to impose a duty not to disclose it on Blake. The action was therefore dismissed.

This is a significant judgment since it relies directly on Art 10 of the Convention in order to reach its conclusion, rather than identifying an interpretative obligation to do so. It thereby adopts a position not far removed from that which would arise if the Convention were incorporated into UK law. It also prevents the imposition of a continuing duty of secrecy on Crown servants in instances in which the disclosure of confidential information is not in question.

5　The existence of the DA Notice system[22] may tend to deter or dissuade the press and others from the publication of confidential or sensitive

---

20　*The Times*, 18 December 1987.

21　*The Times*, 23 April 1996.

22　On the system generally see J Jaconelli, 'The 'D' Notice System' (1982) PL 39; D Fairley (1990) 10 OJLS 430.

Government information. The 'D' Notice Committee was set up with the object of letting the press know which information could be printed and at what point; it was intended that, if sensitive political information was covered by a 'D' notice, an editor would decide against printing it. The system is entirely voluntary and in theory the fact that a 'D' notice has not been issued does not mean that a prosecution under the Official Secrets Act 1989 is precluded, although in practice it is very unlikely. Press representatives sit on the committee as well as civil servants and officers of the armed forces. The system was reviewed in 1992 (*The Defence Advisory Notices: A Review of the D Notice System*, MOD Open Government Document No 93/06) leading to a reduction in the number of notices to six. They were renamed defence advisory notices to reflect better their voluntary nature.

Questions

1   How far, if at all, do the decisions in the *Spycatcher* case endorse the Diceyan claim that the judges are the guardians of freedom of speech?

2   Does the decision of the European Court of Human Rights in relation to the temporary injunctions in the *Spycatcher* case suggest that the Convention may confidently be relied upon to maintain a high standard of free speech protection?

Government control over broadcasting

Government influence over broadcasting is of enormous significance due to the importance of broadcasting as the main means of informing the public as to matters of public interest.[23] The openly partisan nature of the popular press means that broadcasting provides the only impartial source of information for many people.

The power of the Secretary of State to control broadcasting now arises under s10(3) of the Broadcasting Act 1990 and clause 13(4) of the BBC's licence and agreement. It previously arose under s29(3) of the Broadcasting Act 1981. This power was invoked by the Secretary of State in 1988 in order to issue directives requiring the Independent Broadcasting Authority (IBA) to refrain from broadcasting words spoken by persons representing certain extremist groups or words spoken supporting or inviting support for those groups. The very similar power under clause 13(4) of the 1981 licence and agreement between the Home Secretary and the BBC was invoked in order to apply the same ban to the BBC. The ban covered organisations proscribed under the Northern Ireland (Emergency Provisions) legislation as well as Sinn Fein, Republican Sinn Fein and the Ulster Defence Association. The ban was challenged by the National Union of Journalists and others but not by the broadcasting organisations themselves.

---

23   See generally Gibbons, *Regulating the Media* (1991); Robertson, *Media Law*, Chapter 15.

Brind and others v Secretary of State for the Home Department [1991] 1 All ER 720, 722–4[24]

Lord Bridge of Harwich: My Lords, this appeal has been argued primarily on the basis that the power of the Secretary of State, under s29(3) of the Broadcasting Act 1981 and under clause 13(4) of the licence and agreement which governs the operations of the British Broadcasting Corp (BBC) (Cmnd 8233), to impose restrictions on the matters which the Independent Broadcasting Authority (IBA) and the BBC respectively may broadcast may only be lawfully exercised in accordance with Art 10 of the European Convention on Human Rights. Any exercise by the Secretary of State of the power in question necessarily imposes some restriction on freedom of expression. ... it is already well settled that, in construing any provision in domestic legislation which is ambiguous in the sense that it is capable of a meaning which either conforms to or conflicts with the Convention, the courts will presume that Parliament intended to legislate in conformity with the Convention, not in conflict with it.

Lord Bridge considered, but did not accept the submission that:

... when a statute confers upon an administrative authority a discretion capable of being exercised in a way which infringes any basic human right protected by the Convention, it may similarly be presumed that the legislative intention was that the discretion should be exercised within the limitations which the Convention imposes. ...

See above, p873.

But I do not accept that this conclusion means that the courts are powerless to prevent the exercise by the executive of administrative discretions, even when conferred, as in the instant case, in terms which are on their face unlimited, in a way which infringes fundamental human rights. Most of the rights spelled out in terms in the Convention, including the right to freedom of expression, are less than absolute and must in some cases yield to the claims of competing public interests. Thus, Art 10(2) of the Convention spells out and categorises the competing public interests by reference to which the right to freedom of expression may have to be curtailed. In exercising the power of judicial review we have neither the advantages nor the disadvantages of any comparable code to which we may refer or by which we are bound. But again, this surely does not mean that in deciding whether the Secretary of State, in the exercise of his discretion, could reasonably impose the restriction he has imposed on the broadcasting organisations, we are not perfectly entitled to start from the premise that any restriction of the right to freedom of expression requires to be justified and that nothing less than an important competing public interest will be sufficient to justify it. The primary judgment as to whether the particular competing public interest justifies the particular restriction imposed falls to be made by the Secretary of State to whom Parliament has entrusted the discretion. But we are entitled to exercise a secondary judgment by asking whether a reasonable Secretary of State, on the material before him, could reasonably make that primary judgment.

---

24 For comment see Jowell (1990) PL 149 (on the Court of Appeal ruling).

Applying these principles to the circumstances of the case, of which I gratefully adopt the full account given in the speech of my learned and noble friend Lord Ackner, I find it impossible to say that the Secretary of State exceeded the limits of his discretion. In any civilised and law-abiding society the defeat of the terrorist is a public interest of the first importance. That some restriction on the freedom of the terrorist and his supporters to propagate his cause may well be justified in support of that public interest is a proposition which I apprehend the appellants hardly dispute. Their real case is that they, in the exercise of their editorial judgment, may and must be trusted to ensure that the broadcasting media are not used in such a way as will afford any encouragement or support to terrorism and that any interference with that editorial judgment is necessarily an unjustifiable restriction on the right to freedom of expression. Accepting, as I do, their complete good faith, I nevertheless cannot accept this proposition. The Secretary of State, for the reasons he made so clear in Parliament, decided that it was necessary to deny to the terrorist and his supporters the opportunity to speak directly to the public through the most influential of all the media of communication and that this justified some interference with editorial freedom. I do not see how this judgment can be categorised as unreasonable. What is perhaps surprising is that the restriction imposed is of such limited scope. There is no restriction at all on the matter which may be broadcast, only on the manner of its presentation. The viewer may see the terrorist's face and hear his words provided only that they are not spoken in his own voice. I well understand the broadcast journalist's complaint that to put him to the trouble of dubbing the voice of the speaker he has interviewed before the television camera is an irritant which the difference in effect between the speaker's voice and the actor's voice hardly justifies. I well understand the political complaint that the restriction may be counter-productive in the sense that the adverse criticism it provokes outweighs any benefit it achieves. But these complaints fall very far short of demonstrating that a reasonable Secretary of State could not reasonably conclude that the restriction was justified by the important public interest of combating terrorism.

I would dismiss the appeal.

The House of Lords unanimously dismissed the appeal.

Notes

1 This formal banning power has rarely been used since the early days of broadcasting. The 1988 ban is the most recent example of its use. The ban remained in place until September 1994, when it was lifted after the IRA declared the cessation of violence.

2 In general, BBC censorship operates by a process of 'reference up' the corporation management hierarchy: producers refer to middle management, who may seek direction from departmental heads, who may then consult the managing director or even the director-general. Thus censorship is largely self imposed, but the board of governors of the BBC is appointed by the Government, and although they usually leave editorial matters to the director-general they may occasionally intervene; they did so in 1985 in relation to a programme about an IRA sympathiser in Belfast,

'Real Lives', after condemnation by the Prime Minister of an incident perceived as damaging to the BBC's reputation for independence from the Government.[25]

3   Certain incidents, such as coverage of the US bombing of Libya, have led to expressions of concern from the Conservative party about BBC 'bias' against the Government, although this may have been partly mollified by the banning of a documentary on the Zircon spy satellite project in 1987 and a documentary on the workings of Cabinet government. Both films were eventually shown with modification, the latter by Channel 4 in 1991.[26] Such expressions of concern may have played a part in the inclusion in the 1990 Act of s6, which contains provisions designed to preserve political neutrality in broadcasting; the Independent Television Commission (ITC) must set up a code to ensure impartiality. Politically sensitive programmes can be balanced by means of a series of programmes; it is not necessary that any one programme should be followed by another specific, balancing programme. However, the requirement may mean that some politically controversial programmes are not made; the expense and difficulty of setting up balancing programmes may prove to have a deterrent effect. The ITC code makes it clear that a company cannot be heard to argue that a programme which might be said to have an anti-Government bias may be balanced by programmes broadcast by other companies; the company has to achieve impartiality in its own programming. The impartiality clause only affects non-BBC broadcasting, although the BBC has undertaken to comply generally with the statutory duties placed on the IBA (replaced by the ITC).[27]

RESTRAINING FREEDOM OF EXPRESSION TO PROTECT THE ADMINISTRATION OF JUSTICE

Introduction[28]

This section will be concerned with two conflicting interests: the interest in protecting the administration of justice and in the free speech principle. It should be noted that within UK law protection of the administration of justice is

---

25   Robertson, *Media Law*, p484. See further for recent discussion C Horrie and S Clarke, *Fuzzy Monsters: Fear and Loathing at the BBC* (1994).

26   See further on Government interference with broadcasting: P. Fiddich, 'Broadcasting: a Catalogue of Confrontation' in N Buchan and T Sumner (eds), *Glasnost in Britain: Against Censorship and in Defence of the Word* (1989); C Horrie and S Clarke, *op cit*; Bailey, Harris and Jones (1995), Chapter 5, Part 3.

27   This undertaking is annexed to the corporation's licence agreement. The BBC operates under this agreement and also under the terms of its Royal Charter (see Cmnd 8233 and 8313 respectively).

28   General reading: A Arlidge and D Eady, *Contempt of Court* (1982); B Sufrin and N Lowe, *The Law of Contempt,* 3rd edn (1996); CJ Miller, *Contempt of Court* (1989); E Barendt, *Freedom of Speech* (1987), Chapter 8; G Robertson, *Media Law* (1992), Chapter 6; J Laws 'Problems in the Law of Contempt' (1990) CLP 99; B Naylor (1994) CLJ 492.

viewed as a general societal concern rather than as a means of protecting an individual's right to a fair trial, although it may have that effect. Nevertheless, the fact that many aspects of the law of contempt can be seen as having as their *ultimate* rationale the protection of the right to fair trial leads to the conclusion that in so far as this other individual right is clearly at stake, free speech may be compromised to a certain extent. Such a conclusion would be in accord with the European Convention on Human Rights which guarantees both the right to free speech (Art 10) and the right to a fair trial (Art 6).

Publications prejudicing particular criminal or civil proceedings

Contempt of court at common law curtailed the freedom of the media to discuss and report on issues arising from criminal or civil proceedings on the basis that those proceedings might suffer prejudice. The elements of common law contempt consisted of the creation of a real risk of prejudice (the *actus reus*) and an intention to publish. The period during which the risk in question might arise was known as the *sub judice* period. In *Savundranayagan and Walker* (1968)[29] it was found that the starting point of this period occurred when the proceedings were 'imminent'.

Attorney-General v Times Newspapers Ltd [1973] 3 All ER 54, 65, 73, 74

The decision concerned an article discussing the Thalidomide tragedy, and in particular the legal conflict between Distillers and the parents of the Thalidomide children. The House of Lords considered that the article placed pressure on Distillers to forego their legal rights and settle the dispute by paying full compensation to the children.

> **Lord Reid:** ... There is ample authority for the proposition that issues must not be prejudged in a manner likely to affect the minds of those who may later be witnesses or jurors. But very little has been said about the wider proposition that trial by newspaper is intrinsically objectionable. That may be because, if one can find more limited and familiar grounds adequate for the decision of a case, it is rash to venture on uncharted seas.
>
> I think that anything in the nature of prejudgment of a case or of specific issues in it is objectionable not only because of its possible effect on that particular case but also because of its side effects which may be far reaching. Responsible 'mass media' will do their best to be fair, but there will also be ill-informed, slapdash or prejudiced attempts to influence the public. If people are led to think that it is easy to find the truth, disrespect for the processes of the law could follow and, if mass media are allowed to judge, unpopular people and unpopular causes will fare very badly. Most cases of prejudging of issues fall within the existing authorities on contempt. I do not think that the freedom of the press would suffer, and I think that the law would be clearer and easier to apply in practice if it is made a general rule that it is not permissible to prejudge issues in pending cases. ...

---

29 3 All ER 439.

Contempt of court, except the rare offence of scandalising the court after judgment, is committed before the trial is concluded. Whether in the result the publication will have had any influence on jurors or witnesses is not known when the proceedings for committal for contempt of court are heard. The mischief against which the summary remedy for contempt of court is directed is not merely that justice will not be done, but that it will not be manifestly seen to be done. Contempt of court is punishable because it undermines the confidence not only of the parties to the particular litigation but also of the public as potential suitors, in the due administration of justice by the established courts of law.

My Lords, to hold a party up to public obloquy for exercising his constitutional right to have recourse to a court of law for the ascertainment and enforcement of his legal rights and obligations is calculated to prejudice the first requirement for the due administration of justice: the unhindered access of all citizens to the established courts of law. Similarly, 'trial by newspaper', ie public discussion or comment on the merits of a dispute which has been submitted to a court of law or on the alleged facts of the dispute before they have been found by the court on the evidence adduced before it, is calculated to prejudice the third requirement: that parties to litigation should be able to rely on there being no usurpation by any other person of the function of that court to decide their dispute according to law. If to have recourse to civil litigation were to expose a litigant to the risk of public obloquy or to public and prejudicial discussion of the facts or merits of the case before they have been determined by the court, potential suitors would be inhibited from availing themselves of courts of law for the purpose for which they are established.

... contempt of court in relation to a civil action is not restricted to conduct which is calculated (whether intentionally or not) to prejudice the fair trial of that action by influencing, in favour of one party or against him, either the tribunal by which the action may be tried or witnesses who may give evidence in it; it extends also to conduct that is calculated to inhibit suitors generally from availing themselves of their constitutional right to have their legal rights and obligations ascertained and enforced in courts of law, by holding up any suitor to public obloquy for doing so or by exposing him to public and prejudicial discussion of the merits or the facts of his case before they have been determined by the court or the action has been otherwise disposed of in due course of law.

I agree with all your lordships that the publication of the article proposed to be published by the *Sunday Times* in respect of which an injunction is sought by the Attorney-General would fall within this latter category of conduct. As has already been sufficiently pointed out, it discussed prejudicially the facts and merits of Distillers' defence to the charge of negligence brought against them in the actions before these have been determined by the court or the actions disposed of by settlement.

Notes

1   This ruling created the prejudgment test, which seemed to be wider than the test of real risk of prejudice, in that little risk to proceedings might be shown, but it might still be possible to assert that they had been prejudged. This test had a potentially grave effect on freedom of speech because it was very difficult to draw the line between legitimate discussion in the media of issues of possible relevance in civil or criminal actions and prejudgment.

2   The decision of the House of Lords was found to breach Art 10 of the European Convention on Human Rights.

Sunday Times case (1979) Eur Com HR Series A, vol 30 (1980) 2 EHRR 245, 275–81

The European Court of Human Rights found that the injunction clearly infringed freedom of speech under Art 10(1); the question was whether one of the exceptions within Art 10(2) could be invoked.

[The article in question subjects] Distillers to public and prejudicial discussion of the merits of their case, such exposure being objectionable as it inhibits suitors generally from having recourse to the courts;

- it would subject Distillers to pressure and to the prejudices of prejudgment of the issues in the litigation, and the law of contempt was designed to prevent interference with recourse to the courts;

- prejudgment by the press would have led inevitably in this case to replies by the parties, thereby creating the danger of a 'trial by newspaper' incompatible with the proper administration of justice;

- the courts owe it to the parties to protect them from the prejudices of prejudgment which involves their having to participate in the flurries of pre-trial publicity.

The Court regards all these various reasons as falling within the aim of maintaining the 'authority ... of the judiciary' as interpreted by the court in the second paragraph of Art 10.

Accordingly, the interference with the applicants' freedom of expression had an aim that is legitimate under Art 10(2).

Was the interference 'necessary in a democratic society' for maintaining the authority of the judiciary?

The Court has noted that, whilst the adjective 'necessary', within the meaning of Art 10(2), is not synonymous with 'indispensable', neither has it the flexibility of such expressions as 'admissible', 'ordinary', 'useful', 'reasonable' or 'desirable' and that it implies the existence of a 'pressing social need' [*Handyside case*, Series A, No 24, p22, para 48].

... the Court has underlined that the initial responsibility for securing the rights and freedoms enshrined in the Convention lies with the individual contracting States. Accordingly, 'Art 10(2) leaves to the contracting states a margin of appreciation. This margin is given both to the domestic legislator ... and to the bodies, judicial amongst others, that are called upon to interpret and apply the laws in force' [*ibid*].

'Nevertheless, Art 10(2) does not give the contracting states an unlimited power of appreciation.' 'The Court ... is empowered to give the final ruling on whether a 'restriction' ... is reconcilable with freedom of expression as protected by Art 10. The domestic margin of appreciation thus goes hand in hand with a European supervision' which 'covers not only the basic legislation but also the decision applying it, even one given by an independent court' [*ibid* at p23, para 49].

Again, the scope of the domestic power of appreciation is not identical as regards each of the aims listed in Art 10(2). The *Handyside case* concerned the 'protection of morals'. The view taken by the contracting states of the 'requirements of morals', observed the Court, 'varies from time to time and from place to place, especially in our era', and 'state authorities are in principle in a better position than the international judge to give an opinion on the exact content of these requirements' [*ibid, p22*, para 48]. Precisely the same cannot be said of the far more objective notion of the 'authority' of the judiciary. The domestic law and practice of the contracting states reveal a fairly substantial measure of common ground in this area. This is reflected in a number of provisions of the Convention, including Art 6, which have no equivalent as far as 'morals' are concerned. Accordingly, here a more extensive European supervision corresponds to a less discretionary power of appreciation.

The draft article was nonetheless the principal subject-matter of the injunction. It must therefore be ascertained in the first place whether the domestic courts' views as to the article's potential effects were relevant in terms of the maintenance of the 'authority of the judiciary'.

One of the reasons relied on was the pressure which the article would have brought to bear on Distillers to settle the actions out of court on better terms. However, even in 1972, publication of the article would probably not have added much to the pressure already on Distillers. This applies with greater force to the position obtaining in July 1973, when the House of Lords gave its decision; by that date, the Thalidomide case had been debated in Parliament and had been the subject not only of further press comment but also of a nationwide campaign.

The speeches in the House of Lords emphasised above all the concern that the processes of the law may be brought into disrespect and the functions of the courts usurped either if the public is led to form an opinion on the subject-matter of litigation before adjudication by the courts or if the parties to litigation have to undergo 'trial by newspaper'. Such concern is in itself 'relevant' to the maintenance of the 'authority of the judiciary'. ...

Nevertheless, the proposed *Sunday Times* article was couched in moderate terms and did not present just one side of the evidence or claim that there was only one possible result at which a court could arrive. ... Accordingly, even to the extent that the article might have led some readers to form an opinion on the negligence issue, this would not have had adverse consequences for the 'authority of the judiciary', especially since, as noted above, there had been a nationwide campaign in the meantime.

64   At the time when the injunction was originally granted and at the time of its restoration, the Thalidomide case was at the stage of settlement negotiations. The applicants concur with the Court of Appeal's view that the case was 'dormant' and the majority of the Commission considers it unlikely that there would have been a trial of the issue of negligence.

As the Court remarked in its *Handyside* judgment, freedom of expression constitutes one of the essential foundations of a democratic society; subject to paragraph 2 of Art 10, it is applicable not only to information or ideas that are favourably received or regarded as inoffensive or as a matter of indifference, but also to those that offend, shock or disturb the state or any sector of the population [*ibid* at p23, para 49].

As the Court has already observed, Art 10 guarantees not only the freedom of the press to inform the public but also the right of the public to be properly informed (see para 65 above).

In the present case, the families of numerous victims of the tragedy, who were unaware of the legal difficulties involved, had a vital interest in knowing all the underlying facts and the various possible solutions. They could be deprived of this information, which was crucially important for them, only if it appeared absolutely certain that its diffusion would have presented a threat to the 'authority of the judiciary'.

Notes

1   In the light of these findings, the court ruled that the injunction was not 'necessary'. Thus the exception under Art 10(2) could not apply: Art 10 had been breached.

2   The UK Government responded to this decision in the enactment of the Contempt of Court Act 1981[30] which was supposed to take account of the ruling of the European Court and was also influenced to an extent by the proposals of the Phillimore Committee.[31]

Contempt of Court Act 1981

Strict liability

1.   In this Act 'the strict liability rule' means the Rule of Law whereby conduct may be treated as a contempt of court as tending to interfere with the course of justice in particular legal proceedings regardless of intent to do so.

2.–(1)   The strict liability rule applies only in relation to publications, and for this purpose 'publication' includes any speech, writing, broadcast or other communication in whatever form, which is addressed to the public at large or any section of the public.

(2)   The strict liability rule applies only to a publication which creates a substantial risk that the course of justice in the proceedings in question will be seriously impeded or prejudiced.

(3)   The strict liability rule applies to a publication only if the proceedings in question are active within the meaning of this section at the time of the publication.

(4)   Schedule 1 applies for determining the times at which proceedings are to be treated as active within the meaning of this section.

3.–(1)   A person is not guilty of contempt of court under the strict liability rule as the publisher of any matter to which that rule applies if at the time of publication (having taken all reasonable care) he does not know and has to reason to suspect that relevant proceedings are active.

(2)   A person is not guilty of contempt of court under the strict liability rule as the distributor of a publication containing any such matter if at the time of distribution (having taken all reasonable care) he does not know that it contains such matter and has no reason to suspect that it is likely to do so.

(3)   The burden of proof of any fact tending to establish a defence afforded by this section to any person lies upon that person.

(4)   Section 11 of the Administration of Justice Act 1960 is repealed.

4.–(1)   Subject to this section a person is not guilty of contempt of court under the strict liability rule in respect of a fair and accurate report of legal proceedings held in public, published contemporaneously and in good faith.

(2)   In any such proceedings the court may, where it appears to be necessary for avoiding a substantial risk of prejudice to the administration of justice in those proceedings, or in any other proceedings pending or imminent, order that the publication of any report of the proceedings, or any part of the

---

30   See the Green Paper, Cmnd 7145 of 1978.
31   See Report of the Committee on Contempt of Court 1974, Cmnd 5794.

proceedings, be postponed for such period as the court thinks necessary for that purpose.

...

5. A publication made as or as part of a discussion in good faith of public affairs or other matters of general public interest is not to be treated as a contempt of court under the strict liability rule if the risk of impediment or prejudice to particular legal proceedings is merely incidental to the discussion.

6. Nothing in the foregoing provisions of this Act–

    (a) prejudices any defence available at common law to a charge of contempt of court under the strict liability rule;

    (b) implies that any publication is punishable as contempt of court under that rule which would not be so punishable apart from those provisions;

    (c) restricts liability for contempt of court in respect of conduct intended to impede or prejudice the administration of justice.

Schedule 1

Times when proceedings are active for purposes of section 2

Criminal proceedings

3. Subject to the following provisions of this Schedule, criminal proceedings are active from the relevant initial step specified in paragraph 4 until concluded as described in paragraph 5.

4. The initial steps of criminal proceedings are –

    (a) arrest without warrant;

    (b) the issue, or in Scotland the grant, of a warrant for arrest;

    (c) the issue of a summons to appear, or in Scotland the grant of a warrant to cite;

    (d) the service of an indictment or other document specifying the charge;

    (e) except in Scotland, oral charge.

5. Criminal proceedings are concluded –

    (a) by acquittal or, as the case may be, by sentence;

    (b) by any other verdict, finding, order or decision which puts an end to the proceedings;

    (c) by discontinuance or by operation of law.

7. Proceedings are discontinued within the meaning of paragraph 5(c) –

    (a) in England and Wales or Northern Ireland, if the charge or summons is withdrawn or a *nolle prosequi* entered;

    (b) in Scotland, if the proceedings are expressly abandoned by the prosecutor or are deserted *simpliciter*;

    (c) in the case of proceedings in England and Wales or Northern Ireland commenced by arrest without warrant, if the person arrested is released, otherwise than on bail, without having been charged.

Other proceedings at first instance

12. Proceedings other than criminal proceedings and appellate proceedings are active from the time when arrangements for the hearing 'are made or, if no such arrangements are previously made, from the time the hearing begins, until the proceedings are disposed of or discontinued or withdrawn'; and for the purposes of this paragraph any motion or application made in or for the purposes of any proceedings, and any pre-trial review in the county court, is to be treated as a distinct proceeding.

13. In England and Wales or Northern Ireland arrangements for the hearing of proceedings to which paragraph 12 applies are made within the meaning of that paragraph–

    (a) in the case of proceedings in the High Court for which provision is made by rules of court for setting down for trial, when the case is set down;

    (b) in the case of any proceedings, when a date for the trial or hearing is fixed.

14. In Scotland arrangements for the hearing of proceedings, to which paragraph 12 applies, are made within the meaning of that paragraph–

    (a) in the case of an ordinary action in the Court of Session or in the sheriff court, when the record is closed;

    (b) in the case of a motion or application, when it is enrolled or made;

    (c) in any other case, when the date for a hearing is fixed or a hearing is allowed.

Appellate proceedings

15. Appellate proceedings are active from the time when they are commenced–

    (a) by application for leave to appeal or apply for review, or by notice of such an application;

    (b) by notice of appeal or of application for review;

    (c) by other originating process, until disposed of or abandoned, discontinued or withdrawn.

Attorney-General v English [1983] 1 AC 116; [1982] 2 All ER 903, 914, 919–20, HL

Lord Diplock: My Lords, this is an appeal brought by the editor and publishers of the *Daily Mail* newspaper against a decision of the Divisional Court on 16 December 1981, holding them to be guilty of contempt of court by publishing an article entitled 'The vision of life that wins my vote' on 15 October 1980, which was the morning of the third day of the trial in the Crown Court at Leicester of a well-known paediatrician, Dr Arthur, on a charge of murdering a three-day-old mongoloid baby boy by giving instructions that it should be treated with a drug which had caused it to die from starvation.

... Next for consideration is the concatenation in the subsection [s2(2)] of the adjective 'substantial' and the adverb 'seriously', the former to describe the degree of risk, the latter to describe the degree of impediment or prejudice to the course of justice. 'Substantial' is hardly the most apt word to apply to 'risk' which is a noumenon. In combination I take the two words to be intended to exclude a risk that is only remote.

My Lords, that Mr Malcolm Muggeridge's article was capable of prejudicing the jury against Dr Arthur at the early stage of his trial when it was published seems to me to be clear. It suggested that it was a common practice among paediatricians to do that which Dr Arthur was charged with having done, because they thought that it was justifiable in the interests of humanity even though it was against the law. At this stage of the trial the jury did not know what Dr Arthur's defence was going to be; and whether at that time the risk of the jury's being influenced by their recollection of the article when they came eventually to consider their verdict appeared to be more than a remote one, was a matter which the judge before whom the trial was being conducted was in the best position to evaluate. ... The judge thought at that stage of the trial that the risk was substantial, not remote. So, too, looking at the matter in retrospect, did the Divisional Court despite the fact that the risk had not turned into an actuality since Dr Arthur had by then been acquitted. For my part I am not prepared to dissent from this evaluation. I consider that the publication of the article on the third day of what was to prove a lengthy trial satisfied the criterion for which s 2(2) of the 1981 Act provides.

Having found that s2(2) was satisfied Lord Diplock went on to consider s5.

The article, however, fell also within the category dealt with in s5. It was made, in undisputed good faith, as a discussion in itself of public affairs, *viz* Mrs Carr's candidature as an independent 'pro-life' candidate in the North West Croydon by-election for which the polling day was in one week's time. It was also part of a wider discussion on a matter of general public interest that had been proceeding intermittently over the last three months, on the moral justification of mercy killing and in particular of allowing newly born hopelessly handicapped babies to die. So it was for the Attorney-General to show that the risk of prejudice to the fair trial of Dr Arthur, which I agree was created by the publication of the article at the stage the trial had reached when it was published, was not 'merely incidental' to the discussion of the matter with which the article dealt.

My lords, the article that is the subject of the instant case appears to me to be in nearly all respects the antithesis of the article which this House (*pace* a majority of the judges of the European Court of Human Rights) held to be a contempt of court in *A-G v Times Newspapers Ltd* [1973] 3 All ER 54, [1974] AC 273. There the whole subject of the article was the pending civil actions against the Distillers Co arising out of their having placed on the market the new drug Thalidomide, and the whole purpose of it was to put pressure on that company in the lawful conduct of their defence in those actions. In the instant case, in contrast, there is in the article no mention at all of Dr Arthur's trial. It may well be that many readers of the *Daily Mail* who saw the article and had read also the previous day's report of Dr Arthur's trial, and certainly if they were members of the jury at that trial, would think 'That is the sort of thing that Dr Arthur is being tried for; it appears to be something that quite a lot of doctors do'. But the risk of their thinking that and allowing it to prejudice their minds in favour of finding him guilty on evidence that did not justify such a finding seems to me to be properly described in ordinary English language as 'merely incidental' to any meaningful discussion of Mrs Carr's election policy as a pro-life candidate in the by-election due to be held before Dr Arthur's trial was likely to be concluded, or to any meaningful discussion of the wider matters of general public interest involved in the current controversy as to the justification of mercy killing. To hold otherwise would have prevented Mrs Carr from putting forward and obtaining publicity for what was a main plank in her election programme and would have stifled all discussion in the press on the wider controversy about mercy killing from the time that Dr Arthur was charged in the magistrates' court in February 1981 until the date of his acquittal at the beginning of November of that year; for those are the dates between which under s2(3) and Schedule 1, the legal proceedings against Dr Arthur would be 'active' and so attract the strict liability rule.

Such gagging of bona fide public discussion in the press of controversial matters of general public interest, merely because there are in existence contemporaneous legal proceedings in which some particular instance of those controversial matters may be in issue, is what s5 of the Contempt of Court Act 1981 was in my view intended to prevent. I would allow this appeal.

The other four Law Lords agreed.

Attorney-General v News Group Newspapers [1986] 3 WLR 365, 375, CA

Sir John Donaldson MR: ... [T]here has to be some risk that the proceedings in question will be affected at all. Second, there has to be a prospect that, if affected, the effect will be serious. The two limbs of the test can overlap, but they can be quite separate. I accept Mr Laws' submission that 'substantial' as a qualification of 'risk' does not have the meaning of 'weighty,' but rather means 'not insubstantial' or 'not minimal.' The 'risk' part of the test will usually be of importance in the context of the width of the publication. To declare in a speech at a public meeting in Cornwall that a man about to be tried in Durham is guilty of the offence charged and has many previous convictions for the same offence may well carry no substantial risk of affecting his trial, but, if it occurred, the prejudice would be most serious. By contrast, a nationwide television broadcast at peak viewing time of some far more innocuous statement would certainly involve a substantial risk of having some effect on a trial anywhere in the country and the sole effective question would arise under the 'seriousness' limb of the test. Proximity in time between the publication and the proceedings would probably have a greater bearing on the risk limb than on the seriousness limb, but could go to both.

Notes

1   The 1981 Act modified the common law without bringing about radical change. It introduced various liberalising elements but it was intended, as a number of commentators observed, to maintain the stance of ultimate supremacy of the administration of justice over freedom of speech, while moving the balance further towards freedom of speech.[32] In particular it introduced stricter time limits, a more precise test for the *actus reus*, as proposed by the Phillimore Committee, and under s5 allowed some publications dealing with matters of public interest to escape liability, even though some prejudice to proceedings was created.

2   The test under s2(2) has also been considered in *Attorney-General v Hislop and Pressdram* (1990);[33] and *Attorney-General v Times Newspapers* (1983).[34] In *Attorney-General v Guardian Newspapers* (1992)[35] the publication of the fact that one unidentified defendant out of six in a Manchester trial was also awaiting trial elsewhere was not found to satisfy s2(2) since it was thought that it would not cause a juror of ordinary good sense to be biased against the defendant. In *Attorney-General v Independent TV News and Others* (1995)[36] TV news and certain newspapers published the fact that a defendant in a forthcoming murder trial was a convicted IRA terrorist who had escaped from jail where he was serving a life sentence for murder. It was found that s 2(2) was not satisfied since the trial was not expected to take place for nine months, there had only been one offending news item and there had been limited circulation of only one edition of the offending newspaper items.

---

32   For comment on the 1981 Act see Miller (1982) Crim LR 71; NV Lowe (1982) PL 20; Professor JC Smith (1982) Crim LR 744; G F Zellick (1982) PL 343; M Redmond (1983) CLJ 9.

33   [1991] 1 QB 514; [1991] 1 All ER 911, CA.

34   *The Times*, 12 February 1983, DC.

35   3 All ER 38.

36   2 All ER 370.

The risk of prejudice was found to be too small to be termed substantial. These two recent rulings suggest that courts may not be quick to assume that jurors are incapable of ignoring prejudicial publications.

3   *Attorney-General v English* (1983) is the leading case on s5 and is generally considered to provide a good example of the kind of case for which s5 was framed.[37] Lord Diplock's ruling was seen as giving a liberal interpretation to s5. As he points out, a narrower interpretation of s5 would have meant that all debate in the media on the topic of mercy killing would have been prevented for almost a year – the time during which the proceedings in Dr Arthur's case were active from charge to acquittal. (It may be noted that Dr Arthur was acquitted; therefore the article presumably did not influence the jurors against him. That fact, however, did not preclude a finding that there was a substantial risk of serious prejudice to his trial.) The proper interpretation of s5 has also been considered in the following cases: *Attorney-General v Times Newspaper* (1983); *Attorney-General v Hislop* (1991); *Daily Express* case (1981).[38] In *Attorney-General v TVS Television; Attorney-General v HW Southey and Sons* (1989)[39] it was determined that a TVS programme concerned with the possibility that Rachmanism had arisen in the south of England but focused on landlords in Reading, which coincided with the charging of a Reading landlord with conspiring to defraud the DHSS, could not create a merely incidental risk. Similarly, in *Pickering v Liverpool Daily Post and Echo Newspapers plc* (1991)[40] where the discussion centred on the case itself, it was found that s5 did not apply.

Questions

1   Is the boundary between creation of a risk of prejudice which is merely incidental to a discussion and creation of a risk which is not so incidental (ie it is crucial or fairly crucial to the discussion) reasonably clear? Should a test concerned simply with the public interest in the discussion have been created?

2   Bearing in mind the interpretation of s5 favoured in *A-G v English* (1983), would the article at issue in the *Sunday Times* case fall within s5 if published now (within the active period)?

Restrictions on reporting of court proceedings

Section 11 of the Contempt of Court Act 1981 allows a court which has power to do so to prohibit reporting of certain matters. Thus s11 does not itself confer a power to order such prohibition; it relies on existing statutory or common law powers. Section 4(2) allows a court to order postponement of reporting of certain matters.

---

37   See Zellick (1982) PL 343; Ward (1983) 46 MLR 85; Redmond (1983) CLJ 9; Robertson, *Freedom, the Individual and the Law* (1989), p216.

38   *The Times*, 19 December.

39   *Independent*, 7 July.

40   1 All ER 622.

Attorney-General v Leveller Magazine Ltd [1979] AC 440; 2 WLR 247, 272–3 HL

Three newspapers published the name of a witness who had been allowed to give evidence as Colonel B for security reasons. The newspapers were convicted of contempt but the House of Lords allowed their appeal.

Lord Scarman: Can a court make an order, or give a ruling, which is binding on persons who are neither witnesses nor parties in the proceedings before the court? ... the nature of the criminal offence of contempt ... is interference, with knowledge of the court's proceedings, with the course of administration of justice. ... It was for this reason, no doubt, that Lord Widgery CJ in this case stressed the element of 'flouting' the authority of the court. Though I would not have chosen the word, I think it does reflect the essence of the offence, namely that the conduct complained of, in this case the publication, must be a deliberate frustration of the effort of the court to protect justice from interference.

In the present case the examining justices took a course which was a substitute for sitting in private ... the device is an acceptable extension of the common law power of a court to control its proceedings by sitting in private, where necessary, in the court's judgment, to protect the administration of justice from interference. ...

But since the common law power to sit in private arises only if the administration of justice be threatened, the third question becomes one of fact. What was the reason for the justices' ruling? If it was to avert an interference with the administration of justice, was there material upon which the ruling could reasonably be based? The third question cannot therefore be answered without considering the facts. Here I find myself in a state of doubt.

I do not think that the Attorney-General has discharged the burden of proof upon him. Uncertainly surrounds, and continues to surround, the ruling made by the justices and its object. First, one cannot be sure that they took into account all the matters to which it was their duty to have regard if they were giving notice in open court that to protect the administration of justice the name of the witness was not to be published. The justices clearly had regard to national security, but did they understand that, in exercising their common law power, the national security risk must be shown also to be a risk to the administration of justice and assess the degree of the latter risk? Did they address themselves to that question at all? It cannot be said with any certainty that they did, or that the Crown adduced any material, by way of evidence or otherwise, to show that the national security issue was such that publication of the colonel's name would endanger the due administration of justice.

Notes

1   Section 11 of the 1981 Act allows a departure from the principles of free speech and of open justice since it allows a court which has power to do so to prohibit reporting of certain matters. However, as the *Leveller* decision makes clear, the fundamental importance of open justice will be outweighed only if very clear detriment to the general public interest would be likely to flow from publication of the matters in question.[41]

2   The interest in open justice is recognised under s4(1) of the 1981 Act, although under s4(2) a judge may make an order postponing reporting of the proceedings in order to protect the administration of justice. The

---

41   See also *Dover Justices, ex p Dover District Council and Wells* [1992] Crim LR 371.

following rulings have suggested that s4(2) should be used sparingly: *Horsham Magistrates, ex p Farquharson and Another* (1982);[42] *Clerkenwell Metropolitan Stipendiary Magistrate, ex p the Telegraph and Others* (1993)[43]; *Re Central Independent Television plc and Others* (1991);[44] *ex p the Telegraph plc* (1993).[45]

Intentionally prejudicing proceedings: common law contempt

Section 6(c) of the 1981 Act preserves liability for contempt at common law if intention to prejudice the administration of justice can be shown. 'Prejudice (to) the administration of justice' clearly includes prejudice to particular proceedings. Once the requirement of intent is satisfied it is easier to establish contempt at common law rather than under the Act, as it is only necessary to show at common law 'a real risk of prejudice', proceedings need only be 'imminent', not 'active' and there is no provision protecting free speech equivalent to that under s5.

Attorney-General v Times Newspapers and Another [1992] 1 AC 191; [1991] 2 WLR 994, 1000, 1003, 1004[46]

In 1985 the Attorney-General commenced proceedings in Australia in an attempt to restrain publication of the book *Spycatcher*, by Peter Wright. In 1986, after the *Guardian* and the *Observer* published reports of the forthcoming hearing which included some *Spycatcher* material, the Attorney-General obtained temporary *ex parte* injunctions preventing them from further disclosure of such material.[47] While the temporary injunctions were in force the *Independent* and two other papers published material covered by them. The question arose whether such actions could amount to common law contempt. In *A-G v Newspaper Publishing plc* (1990) the Court of Appeal (1988) Ch 333 found that the respondents' publications could amount to a contempt of court and remitted the case for trial. Just before that ruling the *Sunday Times* had published extracts from *Spycatcher*. The Attorney-General brought proceedings for contempt against the publishers and editors of the *Sunday Times*. At first instance it was found that the publishers and editors of the *Independent* and the *Sunday Times* had been guilty of contempt, and that finding was confirmed by the Court of Appeal. Times Newspapers appealed to the House of Lords. The only matter still at issue was whether the appellants had committed the *actus reus* of common law contempt.

> **Lord Brandon of Oakbrook:** It is, in my opinion, of the utmost importance to formulate with precision the question which falls to be decided in this appeal. For the purpose of such formulation it is necessary to assume a situation in

---

42 [1982] QB 762.

43 [1993] QB 762.

44 [1991] 1 All ER 347.

45 [1993] 2 All ER 971.

46 For comment see J Laws (1990) 43 CLP 99.

47 For discussion of this branch of the litigation see pp923–6, above.

which one person, B, is a party to an action brought against him by another person, A, and the court grants A an injunction restraining B from doing certain acts. Despite the rhetoric employed at times by Mr Lester, the question for decision is not whether such an injunction is binding on a third person, C, who is not a party to the action and is not referred to in the injunction. Clearly such an injunction cannot be binding on C and it has never been contended for the Attorney-General that it could. The question for decision is quite another one. It is whether, in the situation assumed, it is a contempt of court for C, with the intention of impeding or prejudicing the administration of justice by the court in the action between A and B, himself to do the acts which the injunction restrains B from committing. ...

It seems to me, as a matter of principle that, if C's conduct, in knowingly doing acts which would, if done by B, be a breach of the injunction against him, results in impedance to or interference with the administration of justice by the court in the action between A and B, then, so far as the question of C's conduct being a contempt of court is concerned, it cannot make any difference whether such conduct takes the form of aiding and abetting B on the one hand or acting solely of his own volition on the other.

It remains to consider in what circumstances conduct by C, in knowingly doing acts which would, if done by B, be a breach of an injunction against him, is such as to impede or interfere with the administration of justice by the court in the action between A and B.

I do not think that it would be wise, even if it were possible, to try to give an exhaustive answer to that question. A principal example, however, of circumstances which will have that effect is where the subject matter of the action is such that, if it is destroyed in whole or in part before the trial of the action, the purpose of the trial will be wholly or partly nullified.

The present case presents a similar situation. The claims of the Attorney-General in the confidentiality actions were for permanent injunctions restraining the defendants from publishing what may conveniently be called *Spycatcher* material. The purpose of the Millett injunctions was to prevent the publication of any such material pending the trial of the confidentiality actions. The consequence of the publication of *Spycatcher* material by the publishers and editor of the *Sunday Times* before the trial of the confidentiality actions was to nullify, in part at least, the purpose of such trial, because it put into the public domain part of the material which it was claimed by the Attorney-General in the confidentiality actions ought to remain confidential. It follows that the conduct of the publishers and editor of the *Sunday Times* constituted the *actus reus* of impeding or interfering with the administration of justice by the court in the confidentiality actions. *Mens rea* in respect of such conduct having been conceded by Mr Lester, both the necessary ingredients of contempt of court were present. I therefore reject as wrong in law the main contention advanced by Mr Lester on behalf of the publishers and editor of the *Sunday Times*.

In the result I would affirm the judgment of the Court of Appeal and dismiss the appeal [the other four Law Lords concurred].

Notes

1   Liability can be established at common law in instances when it might also be established under the 1981 Act as occurred in *Attorney-General v Hislop* (1991),[48] and in instances in which the Act will not apply because

---

48   [1991] 1 QB 514.

proceedings are inactive. Possibly it might also be established where one of the statutory tests other than the 'active' requirement was not satisfied. The *actus reus* of common law contempt will be satisfied by a publication which creates a real risk of prejudice to the administration of justice (*Thompson Newspapers* (1968)).[49] There may be a number of different methods of fulfilling this test as *Hislop* (1991) demonstrated. In *Attorney-General v Times Newspaper* (1992) the House of Lords found that the test may be fulfilled in certain circumstances if part of the media frustrates a court order against another part. This decision affirmed the principle that, once an interlocutory injunction has been obtained restraining one organ of the media from publication of allegedly confidential material, the rest of the media may be in contempt if they publish that material, even if their intention in doing so is to bring alleged iniquity to public attention. The decision thus created an inroad into the general principle that a court order should only affect the party to which it is directed as only that party will have a chance to argue that the making of the order would be wrong.

2   From the Court of Appeal ruling[50] it is clear that the *mens rea* for common law contempt is specific intent and therefore it cannot include recklessness. The test may be summed up as follows: did the defendant either wish to prejudice proceedings or foresee that such prejudice was a virtually inevitable consequence of publishing the material in question? Thus it is not necessary to show a desire to prejudice proceedings or that where there was such a desire it was the sole desire. This test is based on the meaning of intent arising from two rulings on the *mens rea* for murder from *Hancock and Shankland* (1986)[51] and *Nedrick* (1986).[52]

3   At common law the *sub judice* period began when proceedings could be said to be imminent (*Savundranayagan* (1968)).[53] However, it may not always be necessary to establish imminence. In *Attorney-General v Newsgroup Newspapers plc* (1988)[54] it was held *obiter* that, where it is established that the defendant intended to prejudice proceedings, it is not necessary to show that proceedings are imminent. This was endorsed, *obiter*, in one of the rulings on imminence in *Attorney-General v Sport* (1992).[55]

Refusing to disclose sources

Section 10 of the 1981 Act provides: 'no court may require a person to disclose ... the source of information contained in a publication for which he is responsible, unless it be established to the satisfaction of the court that disclosure is necessary in the interests of justice or national security or for the prevention of

49   1 WLR 1; 1 All ER 268.

50   *Attorney-General v Newspaper Publishing plc* (1990), *The Times*, 28 February.

51   AC 455; 1 All ER 641; 3 WLR 1014.

52   3 All ER 1; 1 WLR 1025.

53   1 WLR 1761; 3 All ER 439.

54   2 All ER 906.

55   1 All ER 503.

disorder or crime'. Section 10 creates a presumption in favour of journalists who wish to protect their sources which is, however, subject to four wide exceptions, of which the widest arises where the 'interests of justice' require that disclosure should be made.[56]

X Ltd v Morgan-Grampian Ltd [1990] 2 All ER 1, 6–10

A confidential plan was stolen from the plaintiffs; information apparently from the plan was given by an unidentified source by telephone to William Goodwin, a journalist. The plaintiffs applied for an order requiring Goodwin to disclose the source and sought discovery of his notes of the phone conversation in order to discover the identity of the source. The House of Lords had to consider the application of s10 to these facts.

> **Lord Bridge:** The courts have always recognised an important public interest in the free flow of information.

> It has been accepted in this case at all levels that [s 10 of the 1981 Act] applies to the circumstances of the instant case ... It is also now clearly established that the section is to be given a wide, rather than a narrow, construction in the sense that the restriction on disclosure applies not only to direct orders to disclose the identity of a source but also to any order for disclosure of material which will indirectly identify the source, and applies, notwithstanding that the enforcement of the restriction may operate to defeat rights of property vested in the party who seeks to obtain that material: see *Secretary of State for Defence v Guardian Newspapers Ltd* [1984] 1 All ER 453 at 459 [1984] Ch 156 at 166–7 *per* Griffiths LJ; [1984] 3 All ER 601 at 607, [1985] AC 339 at 349–50 *per* Lord Diplock. As a statement of the rationale underlying this wide construction I cannot do better than quote from the passage in the judgment of Griffiths LJ to which I have referred, where he said:

> The press have always attached the greatest importance to their ability to protect their sources of information. If they are not able to do so, they believe that many of their sources would dry up and this would seriously interfere with their effectiveness. It is in the interests of us all that we should have a truly effective press, and it seems to me that Parliament by enacting s10 has clearly recognised the importance that attaches to the ability of the press to protect their sources ... I can see no harm in giving a wide construction to the opening words of the section because by the latter part of the section the court is given ample powers to order the source to be revealed where in the circumstances of a particular case the wider public interest makes it necessary to do so.

> It follows then that, whenever disclosure is sought, as here, of a document which will disclose the identity of a source within the ambit of s10, the statutory restriction operates unless the party seeking disclosure can satisfy the court that 'disclosure is necessary' in the interests of one of the four matters of public concern that are listed in the section. ... [A judge] starts with the assumptions, first, that the protection of sources is itself a matter of high public importance, second, that nothing less than necessity will suffice to override it, third, that the necessity can only arise out of concern for another matter of high public importance, being one of the four interests listed in the section. ...

> In discussing the section generally Lord Diplock said in *Secretary of State for Defence v Guardian Newspapers Ltd* [1984] 3 All ER 601 at 607, [1985] AC 339 at 350:

The exceptions include no reference to 'the public interest' generally and I would add that in my view the expression 'justice', the interests of which are entitled to protection, is not used in a general sense as the antonym of 'injustice' but in the technical sense of the administration of justice in the course of legal proceedings in a court of law. ...

I agree entirely with the first half of this dictum. To construe 'justice' as the antonym of 'injustice' in s10 would be far too wide. But to confine it to 'the technical sense of the administration of justice in the course of legal proceedings in a court of law' seems to me, with all respect due to any dictum of Lord Diplock, to be too narrow. It is, in my opinion, 'in the interests of justice', in the sense in which this phrase is used in s10, that persons should be enabled to exercise important legal rights and to protect themselves from serious legal wrongs whether or not resort to legal proceedings in a court of law will be necessary to attain these objectives.

Construing the phrase 'in the interests of justice' in this sense immediately emphasises the importance of the balancing exercise. ... The judge's task will always be to weigh in the scales the importance of enabling the ends of justice to be attained in the circumstances of the particular case on the one hand against the importance of protecting the source on the other hand. In this balancing exercise it is only if the judge is satisfied that disclosure in the interests of justice is of such preponderating importance as to override the statutory privilege against disclosure that the threshold of necessity will be reached. ...

In estimating the importance to be given to the case in favour of disclosure there will be a wide spectrum within which the particular case must be located. If the party seeking disclosure shows, for example, that his very livelihood depends on it, this will put the case near one end of the spectrum. If he shows no more than that what he seeks to protect is a minor interest in property, this will put the case at or near the other end. On the other side the importance of protecting a source from disclosure in pursuance of the policy underlying the statute will also vary within a wide spectrum. One important factor will be the nature of the information obtained from the source. The greater the legitimate public interest in the information which the source has given to the publisher or intended publisher, the greater will be the importance of protecting the source. But another and perhaps more significant factor which will very much affect the importance of protecting the source will be the manner in which the information was itself obtained by the source. If it appears to the court that the information was obtained legitimately this will enhance the importance of protecting the source. Conversely, if it appears that the information was obtained illegally, this will diminish the importance of protecting the source unless, of course, this factor is counterbalanced by a clear public interest in publication of the information, as in the classic case where the source has acted for the purpose of exposing iniquity. ...

In the circumstances of the instant case, I have no doubt that Hoffmann J and the Court of Appeal were right in finding that the necessity for disclosure of Mr Goodwin's notes in the interests of justice was established. The importance to the plaintiffs of obtaining disclosure lies in the threat of severe damage to their business, and consequentially to the livelihood of their employees, which would arise from disclosure of the information contained in their corporate plan while their refinancing negotiations are still continuing. This threat, accurately described by Lord Donaldson MR ([1990] 1 All ER 616 at 630, [1990] 2 WLR 421 at 439) as 'ticking away beneath them like a time bomb', can only be defused if they can identify the source either as himself, the thief of the stolen copy of the plan, or as a means to lead to the identification of the thief and thus put themselves in a position to institute proceedings for the recovery of the missing document. The importance of protecting the source on the other hand is much diminished by the source's complicity, at the very least, in a gross breach of confidentiality which is not counterbalanced by any legitimate interest which publication of the information was calculated to serve. Disclosure in the interests of justice is, on this view of the balance, clearly of preponderating importance so as to override the policy underlying the statutory protection of sources and the test of necessity for disclosure is satisfied.

The appeal was accordingly dismissed.

Notes

1   This decision seems to give the phrase 'necessary in the interests of justice' a broad meaning. However, it also made it clear that the fact that such interests would be served would not always provide a basis for making an order of disclosure. Disclosure will only be deemed to be 'necessary' if the interests of justice are so strong as to override the interest in protecting sources which s10 recognises. Thus it will be harder to establish a basis for obtaining a disclosure order under this exception than under the 'prevention of crime' and 'protection of national security' heads.

2   In *Goodwin v UK* (1994)[57] the European Commission on Human Rights found that the order against Goodwin violated his right to freedom of expression under Art 10 of the European Convention on Human Rights. The judgment of the Court of Human Rights in March 1996 was to the same effect,[58] and therefore s10 should be amended, possibly omitting the head 'the interests of justice'.

RESTRAINING FREEDOM OF EXPRESSION ON MORAL GROUNDS

Introduction

The Williams Committee,[59] convened in 1979 to report on obscenity (see *Pornography and Politics: The Williams Committee in Retrospect* (1983)), found that interference with the free flow of ideas and artistic endeavour was unacceptable since it amounted to ruling out in advance possible modes of human development, before it was known whether or not they would be desirable or necessary. Since they also reached the conclusion that '... no one has invented, or in our opinion could invent, an instrument that would suppress only [worthless pornography] and could not be turned against something ... of [possibly] a more creative kind,[60] they concluded that the risk of suppressing

---

57   No 17488/90 Com Rep, *Guardian*, 26 May 1994.
58   Case no 16/1994/463/544, judgment of 27 March 1996; *The Times*, 28 March 1996.
59   *Report of the Committee on Obscenity and Film Censorship* (Williams Committee) Cmnd 7772 of 1979.

worthwhile creative art ruled out censorship of the written word. (They regarded standard photographic pornography as not expressing anything that could be regarded as an 'idea' and so as susceptible to regulation.) This liberal position is not reflected in UK law or in Art 10 of the European Convention on Human Rights which allows restraint of freedom of speech on the ground of protection of morality. The development of UK law has been based on the suppression of speech to avoid the corruption of persons, particularly the more vulnerable.

Obscenity[61]

Obscene Publications Act 1959, as amended by the Obscene Publications Act 1964

Test of obscenity

1.–(1)For the purposes of this Act an article shall be deemed to be obscene if its effect or (where the article comprises two or more distinct items) the effect of any one of its items is, if taken as a whole, such as to tend to deprave and corrupt persons who are likely, having regard to all relevant circumstances, to read, see or hear the matter contained or embodied in it.

(2)In this Act 'article' means any description of article containing or embodying matter to be read or looked at or both, any sound record, and any film or other record of a picture or pictures.

Prohibition of publication of obscene matter

2.–(1)Subject as hereinafter provided, any person who, whether for gain or not, publishes an obscene article [or who has an obscene article for gain (whether gain to himself or gain to another)] shall be liable –

(a) on summary conviction to a fine not exceeding [£5,000] or to imprisonment for a term not exceeding six months;

(b) on conviction on indictment to a fine or to imprisonment for a term not exceeding three years or both.

...

(4)A person publishing an article shall not be proceeded against for an offence at common law consisting of the publication of any matter contained or embodied in the article where it is of the essence of the offence that the matter is obscene.

(5)A person shall not be convicted of an offence against this section if he proves that he had not examined the article in respect of which he is charged and had no reasonable cause to suspect that it was such that his publication of it would make him liable to be convicted of an offence against this section.

Defence of public good

4.–(1)A person shall not be convicted of an offence against section 2 of this Act, and an order for forfeiture shall not be made under the foregoing section, if it is proved that publication of the article in question is justified as being for the

---

60 *Op cit*, para 5.24.

61 See generally P O'Higgins, *Censorship in Britain* (1972); G Robertson, *Obscenity* (1979) and *Media Law* (with A Nichol) (1992), Chapter 3; P Carey, *Media Law* (1996); PR MacMillan, *Censorship and Public Morality* (1983).

public good on the ground that it is in the interests of science, literature, art or learning, or of other objects of general concern.

(2) It is hereby declared that the opinion of experts as to the literary, artistic, scientific or other merits of an article may be admitted in any proceedings under this Act either to establish or to negative the said ground.

Anderson [1972] 1 QB 304, 313, 314

At first instance it was found that a certain magazine, *Oz School Kids' Issue*, was obscene.

> **Lord Widgery CJ:** In the ordinary run of the mill cases ... the issue 'obscene or no' must be tried by the jury without assistance of expert evidence on that issue, and we draw attention to the failure to observe that rule in this case in order that that failure may not occur again.
>
> We are not oblivious of the fact that some people, perhaps many people, will think a jury, unassisted by experts, a very unsatisfactory tribunal to decide such a matter. Those who feel like that must campaign elsewhere for a change of the law. ...
>
> I turn now to criticisms which have been made ... of the directions given by the judge in this case, ... It is said that in directing the jury as to the meaning of 'obscenity' under the Obscene Publications Act 1959, the judge did not make it clear that for the purpose of that Act 'obscene' means, and means only, a tendency to deprave or corrupt.
>
> ... we feel ... that at least there is grave danger that the jury from that passage in the direction to them, took the view, or might have taken the view, that 'obscene' for all purposes including the purposes of the Obscene Publications Act 1959 included 'repulsive', 'filthy', 'loathsome' or 'lewd'.

The appeal was allowed, partly on this ground.

DPP v Whyte [1973] AC 849, [1972] 3 All ER 12, 23

This decision concerned a book shop which sold pornographic material. The proprietors were prosecuted under s1 of the 1959 Act.

> **Lord Pearson:** ... in my opinion, the words 'deprave and corrupt' in the statutory definition, as in the judgment of Cockburn CJ in *Hicklin* [(1868) LR 3 QB 360], refer to the effect of pornographic articles on the mind, including the emotions, and it is not essential that any physical sexual activity (or any 'overt sexual activity', if that phrase has a different meaning) should result. According to the findings the articles did not leave the regular customers unmoved. On the contrary, they fascinated them and enabled them to engage in fantasies. Fantasies in this context must, I think, mean fantasies of normal or abnormal sexual activities. In the words of Cockburn CJ, the pornographic books in the respondents' shop suggested to the minds of the regular customers 'thoughts of a most impure and libidinous character'.

The majority in the House of Lords found that the respondents should have been convicted.

Knuller (Publishing, etc) Ltd v DPP [1973] AC 435, [1972] 3 WLR 143, 148, 149

In *Shaw v DPP* (1962)[62] the House of Lords found that a common law offence known as conspiracy to corrupt public morals existed. This was reconsidered in *Knuller v DPP* which concerned homosexual contact advertisements.

Lord Reid: Section 1(1) [of the 1959 Act] provides: 'For the purposes of this Act an article shall be deemed to be obscene if its effect ... is, ... such as to tend to deprave and corrupt persons' likely to read it. The obvious purpose of s2(4) is to make available, where the essence of the offence is tending to deprave and corrupt, the defences which are set out in the Act. ...

This matter was raised in the House of Commons on 3 June 1964, when the Solicitor General gave an assurance, repeating an earlier assurance 'that a conspiracy to corrupt public morals would not be charged so as to circumvent the statutory defence in subsection (4)' (*Hansard*, vol 695, col 1212).

That does at least show that Parliament has not been entirely satisfied with *Shaw's* case. It is not for me to comment on the undesirability of seeking to alter the law by undertakings or otherwise than by legislation. ...

Although I would not support reconsidering *Shaw's* case, I think that we ought to clarify one or two matters. In the first place conspiracy to corrupt public morals is something of a misnomer. It really means to corrupt the morals of such members of the public as may be influenced by the matter published by the accused. ...

I think that the meaning of the word 'corrupt' requires some clarification. One of my objections to the *Shaw* decision is that it leaves too much to the jury. I recognise that in the end it must be for the jury to say whether the matter published is likely to lead to corruption. But juries, unlike judges, are not expected to be experts in the use of the English language and I think that they ought to be given some assistance. In *Shaw's* case a direction was upheld in which the trial judge said:

> And really the meaning of debauched and corrupt is again, just as the meaning of the word induce is, essentially a matter for you. After all the arguments, I wonder really whether it means in this case and in this context much more than lead astray morally. [See [1962] AC 220 at 290.]

I cannot agree that that is right. 'Corrupt' is a strong word and the jury ought to be reminded of that, as they were in the present case. The Obscene Publications Act appears to use the words 'deprave' and 'corrupt' as synonymous, as I think they are. We may regret that we live in a permissive society but I doubt whether even the most staunch defender of a better age would maintain that all or even most of those who have at one time or in one way or another been led astray morally have thereby become depraved or corrupt. I think that the jury should be told in one way or another that, although in the end the question whether matter is corrupting is for them, they should keep in mind the current standards of ordinary decent people.

[T]he appellants ... say that homosexual acts between adult males in private are now lawful so it is unreasonable and cannot be the law that other persons are guilty of an offence if they merely put in touch with one another two males who wish to indulge in such acts. But there is a material difference between merely exempting certain conduct from criminal penalties and making it lawful in the full sense. Prostitution and gaming afford examples of this difference. So we

---

62   AC 220; [1961] 2 WLR 897; for comment see 24 MLR 626; (1964) 42 *Canadian Bar Review* 561. See also *Gibson* [1990] 2 QB 619.

must examine the provisions of the Sexual Offences Act 1967 to see just how far it altered the old law. It enacts subject to limitation that a homosexual act in private shall not be an offence but it goes no farther than that. Section 4 shows that procuring is still a serious offence and it would seem that some of the facts in this case might have supported a charge under that section.

I find nothing in the Act to indicate that Parliament thought or intended to lay down that indulgence in these practices is not corrupting. I read the Act as saying that, even though it may be corrupting, if people choose to corrupt themselves in this way that is their affair and the law will not interfere. But no licence is given to others to encourage the practice. So if one accepts *Shaw's* case as rightly decided it must be left to each jury to decide in the circumstances of each case whether people were likely to be corrupted. In this case the jury were properly directed and it is impossible to say that they reached a wrong conclusion. It is not for us to say whether or not we agree with it. So I would dismiss the appeal as regards the first count.

The House of Lords upheld the conviction for conspiracy to corrupt public morals.

Handyside case (1976) Eur Court HR, Series A, vol 24 (1976), 1 EHRR 737, 753–6[63]

A book called *The Little Red Schoolbook,* which contained chapters on masturbation, sexual intercourse and abortion, was prosecuted under the 1959 Act on the basis that it appeared to encourage early sexual intercourse. The publishers applied for a ruling under Art 10 to the European Commission on Human Rights. The Commission referred the case to the Court.

European Court of Human Rights – judgment

The Court points out that the machinery of protection established by the Convention is subsidiary to the national systems safeguarding human rights [*Belgian Linguistic case (No 2)* (1968), 1 EHRR 252, 296, para 10 *in fine*]. The Convention leaves to each contracting state, in the first place, the task of securing the rights and freedoms it enshrines. The institutions created by it make their own contribution to this task, but they become involved only through contentious proceedings and once all domestic remedies have been exhausted (Art 26).

These observations apply, notably, to Art 10(2). In particular, it is not possible to find in the domestic law of the various contracting states a uniform European conception of morals. The view taken by their respective laws of the requirements of morals varies from time to time and from place to place, especially in our era which is characterised by a rapid and far-reaching evolution of opinions on the subject. By reason of their direct and continuous contact with the vital forces of their countries, state authorities are in principle in a better position than the international judge to give an opinion on the exact content of these requirements as well as on the 'necessity' of a 'restriction' or 'penalty' intended to meet them. The Court notes at this juncture that, whilst the adjective 'necessary', within the meaning of Art 10(2), is not synonymous with 'indispensable' [cf in Arts 2(2) and 6(1), the words 'absolutely necessary' and 'strictly necessary'; and in Art 5(1), the phrase 'to the extent strictly required by the exigencies of the situation'], neither has it the flexibility of such expressions

---

63   For case notes see Duffy, 5 H Rts Rev 17; Mann (1979) 95 LQR 348.

as 'admissible', 'ordinary' [cf Art 4(3)] 'useful', 'reasonable' [cf Arts 5(3) and 6(1)] or 'desirable'. Nevertheless, it is for the national authorities to make the initial assessment of the reality of the pressing social need implied by the notion of 'necessity' in this context.

Consequently, Art 10(2) leaves to the contracting states a margin of appreciation. This margin is given both to the domestic legislator ('prescribed by law') and to the bodies, judicial amongst others, that are called upon to interpret and apply the laws in force [*Engel v The Netherlands* (1976) EHRR 684, para 100; *Golder v UK* (1975) 1 EHRR 524 at 539, para 45].

The Court's supervisory functions oblige it to pay the utmost attention to the principles characterising a 'democratic society'. Freedom of expression constitutes one of the essential foundations of such a society, one of the basic conditions for its progress and for the development of every man. Subject to Art 10(2), it is applicable not only to 'information' or 'ideas' that are favourably received or regarded as inoffensive or as a matter of indifference, but also to those that offend, shock or disturb the state or any sector of the population. Such are the demands of that pluralism, tolerance and broadmindedness without which there is no 'democratic society'. This means, amongst other things, that every 'formality', 'condition', 'restriction' or 'penalty' imposed in this sphere must be proportionate to the legitimate aim pursued.

From another standpoint, whoever exercises his freedom of expression undertakes 'duties and responsibilities' the scope of which depends on his situation and the technical means he uses. The Court cannot overlook such a person's 'duties' and 'responsibilities' when it enquires, as in this case; whether 'restrictions' or 'penalties' were conducive to the 'protection of morals' which made them 'necessary' in a 'democratic society'.

50 It follows from this that it is in no way the Court's task to take the place of the competent national courts but rather to review under Art 10 the decisions they delivered in the exercise of their power of appreciation.

52 The Court attaches particular importance to a factor to which the judgment of 29 October 1971 did not fail to draw attention, that is the intended readership of the *Schoolbook*. It was aimed above all at children and adolescents aged from 12 to 18. ... The applicant had made it clear that he planned a widespread circulation. He had sent the book, with a press release, to numerous daily papers and periodicals for review or for advertising purposes. What is more, he had set a modest sale price (30p), arranged for a reprint of 50,000 copies shortly after the first impression of 20,000 and chosen a title suggesting that the work was some kind of handbook for use in schools.

... the book included, above all in the section on sex and in the passage headed 'Be yourself' in the chapter on pupils, sentences or paragraphs that young people at a critical stage of their development could have interpreted as an encouragement to indulge in precocious activities harmful for them or even to commit certain criminal offences. In these circumstances, despite the variety and the constant evolution in the UK of views on ethics and education, the competent English judges were entitled, in the exercise of their discretion, to think at the relevant time that the *Schoolbook* would have pernicious effects on the morals of many of the children and adolescents who would read it.

Paragraph 2 of Art 10 therefore applied; no breach of the Article was found.

Notes

1   The 1959 Act covers books, magazines and other printed material, broadcasts, films or videos.[64] The harm sought to be prevented is a corrupting effect on an individual.

2   The idea of preventing corruption had informed the common law long before the 1959 Act; it sprang from the ruling in *Hicklin* 1868.[65] Determining whether material would 'deprave and corrupt' was problematic, especially as it was unclear to whom the test should be applied. The 1959 Act was passed in an attempt to clear up some of this uncertainty, although it failed to lay down a clear test for the meaning of the term 'deprave and corrupt'. It creates a crime of strict liability; there is no need to show an intention to deprave and corrupt, merely an intention to publish. Once it is shown that an article is obscene within the meaning of the Act, it will be irrelevant, following the ruling of the Court of Appeal in *Calder and Boyars* (1969),[66] that the defendant's motivation could be characterised as pure or noble. It does not cover live performances on stage which fall within the similarly worded Theatres Act 1968.

3   This 'deprave and corrupt' test could be applied to any material which might corrupt; it is clear from the ruling in *Calder, John (Publications) Ltd v Powell* (1965)[67] that it is not confined to descriptions or representations of sexual matters, and it could therefore be applied to a disturbing book on the drug-taking life of a junkie. This ruling was followed in *Skirving* (1985)[68] which concerned a pamphlet on the means of taking cocaine in order to obtain maximum effect. In all instances the test for obscenity should not be applied to the type of behaviour advocated or described in the article in question but to the article itself. Thus in *Skirving* the question to be asked was not whether taking cocaine would deprave and corrupt but whether the pamphlet itself would.

4   The jury has to consider whether the article would be likely to deprave and corrupt a significant proportion of those likely to encounter it. It was determined in *Calder and Boyars Ltd* (1969)[69] that the jury must determine what is meant by a significant proportion, and this was approved in *DPP v Whyte* (1973), Lord Cross explaining that 'a significant proportion of a class means a part which is not numerically negligible but which may be much less than half'. This formulation was adopted in order to prevent sellers of pornographic material claiming that most of their customers would be unlikely to be corrupted by it.

5   The defence of public good, which arises under the 1959 Act s4 and the Theatres Act 1968 s3, was intended to afford recognition to artistic merit and thus may be seen as a significant step in the direction of protecting freedom

---

64   In *Attorney-General's Reference (No 5 of 1980)* [1980] 3 All ER 816 it was found that a video constituted an article for the purposes of the 1959 Act.
65   3 QB 360.
66   1 QB 151; [1968] 3 WLR 974; 3 All ER 644; 52 Cr App R 706.
67   1 QB 159.
68   [1985] QB 819.
69   1 QB 151.

of speech. The 1968 Act provides a narrower defence than the 1959 Act; it covers 'the interests of drama, opera, ballet or any other art, or of literature or learning'. Expert evidence will be admissible under both statutes to prove that the material in question is of merit under one of the heads of s4 or s3; it may include considering other works. In *Penguin Books* (1961)[70] it appeared that the jury found *Lady Chatterley's Lover* to be obscene but considered that the s4 defence applied. The defence will not be available if, as in *Knuller*, conspiracy to corrupt public morals is charged, thus circumventing the statutory protection for free speech.

6   Although the test of public good has afforded protection to freedom of expression in relation to publications of artistic merit, it has been criticised: it requires a jury to embark on the very difficult task of weighing a predicted change for the worse in the minds of the group of persons likely to encounter the article, against literary or other merit. Geoffrey Robertson has written: 'the balancing act is a logical nonsense [because it is not] logically possible to weigh such disparate concepts as "corruption" and "literary merit".'[71]

7   Under s3 of the Act, magazines and other material, such as videos, can be seized in forfeiture proceedings if they are obscene and have been kept for gain. No conviction is obtained; the material is merely destroyed and no other punishment is imposed, and therefore s3 may operate at a low level of visibility. These proceedings may mean that the safeguards provided by the Act can be by-passed; in particular, consideration may not be given to the possible literary merits of such material because the public good defence need not be taken into account when the seizure warrant is issued. However, s3 can be used only in respect of material which may be obscene rather than in relation to any form of pornography; it was held in *Darbo v DPP* (1992)[72] that a warrant issued under s3 allowing officers to search for 'sexually explicit material' was bad on its face as such articles would fall within a much wider category of articles than those which could be called obscene.

8   In the *Handyside* case the European Court of Human Rights found that domestic law on obscenity was in harmony with Art 10 of the ECHR. In finding that paragraph 2 applied, the judgment accepted that domestic legislators would be allowed a wide margin of appreciation in attempting to secure the freedoms guaranteed under the Convention in this area. This stance was again taken in *Müller v Switzerland* (1991)[73] in respect of a conviction arising from the exhibition of explicit paintings; the fact that the paintings had been exhibited in other parts of Switzerland and abroad did not mean that their suppression could not amount to a pressing social need.

---

70   Unreported.
71   *Obscenity*, p164.
72   *The Times*, 4 July; [1992] Crim LR 56.
73   13 EHRR 212.

CHAPTER 4

POLICE POWERS

INTRODUCTION[1]

The exercise of police powers such as arrest and detention represents an invasion of personal liberty which is tolerated in the interests of the prevention and detection of crime. However, in accepting the need to allow such invasion, the interest in personal liberty requires that it should be strictly regulated. The rules governing the exercise of police powers are largely contained in the scheme created under the Police and Criminal Evidence Act 1984 (PACE), which is made up of rules deriving from the Act itself, from the codes of practice made under it and the notes for guidance contained in the codes. It is also influenced by Home Office circulars. The difference in status between these four levels is indicated below.

Before the inception of PACE the police had no general and clear powers of arrest, stop and search or entry to premises. They wanted such powers put on a clear statutory basis so that they could exercise them where they felt it was their duty to do so without laying themselves open to the possibility of a civil action. PACE was introduced in order to provide clear and broad police powers, but these were supposed to be balanced by greater safeguards for suspects. Such safeguards were in part adopted due to the need to ensure that miscarriages of justice such as that which occurred in the *Confait* case,[2] would not recur. The Royal Commission on Criminal Procedure,[3] whose report influenced PACE, was set up largely in response to the inadequacies of safeguards for suspects which were exposed in the *Confait* report.[4] Ironically, a further spate of miscarriages of justice, some post-dating the introduction of PACE,[5] led in 1992 to the setting up of another Royal Commission in order to consider further measures which could be introduced to address the problem.[6] However, the report of that Commission did not suggest any significant safeguards for

---

1   For background reading see: Hewitt, *The Abuse of Power* (1982), Chapter 3; Lustgarten, *The Governance of Police* (1986); Leigh, *Police Powers*, 2nd edn (1985); J Robilliard and J McEwan, *Police Powers and the Individual* (1986); Benyon and Bourn, *The Police: Powers, Procedures and Proprieties* (1986). For early comment on the Police and Criminal Evidence Act see (1985) PL 388; (1985) MLR 679; (1985) Crim LR 535. For current comment on the 1984 Act and on the relevant provisions under the Criminal Justice and Public Order Act 1994 see: D Feldman, *Civil Liberties and Human Rights in England and Wales* (1993), Chapters 5 and 9; H Fenwick, *Civil Liberties* (1994), Chapter 9; Sanders and Young, *Criminal Justice* (1994); Levenson and Fairweather, *Police Powers* (1990); Bailey Harris and Jones, *Civil Liberties: Cases and Materials*, 4th edn, (1995), Chapter 2; Zander, *The Police and Criminal Evidence Act 1984*, 3rd edn (1995); K Lidstone and C Palmer, *The Investigation of Crime*, 2nd edn (1996).

2   See report of the inquiry by the Hon Sir Henry Fisher, HC 90 (1977–78).

3   Royal Commission on Criminal Procedure Report (Cmnd 8092) (RCCP report).

4   Report of an inquiry by Sir Henry Fisher, *ibid*.

5   Including *Paris* (the 'Cardiff Three' case) (1993) 97 Cr App R 99; and the *Silcott* case, *The Times*, 9 December 1991.

6   The Royal Commission on Criminal Procedure chaired by Lord Runciman; it was announced by the Home Secretary on 14 March 1991, HC Deb, vol 187, col 1109. Report: Cm 2263; see 143 NLJ 933–96 for a summary of its recommendations in respect of police investigations, safeguards for suspects, the right to silence and confession evidence.

suspects which could be introduced in order to balance increases in police powers. Since the Commission reported, the Major Government has passed legislation, most notably the Criminal Justice and Public Order Act 1994, which increases police powers significantly while removing a number of safeguards for suspects. In particular, the 1994 Act curtailed the right of silence, although the Runciman Royal Commission had recommended that the right should be retained since its curtailment might lead to further miscarriages of justice. Thus, there have been significant developments in police powers during the Major years and the balance PACE was supposed to create between such powers and due process has, it is suggested, been undermined.

In this Chapter the powers of the police and the safeguards which affect the use of their powers are considered first, and this is followed by a consideration of the means of redress available if the police fail to comply with the rules.

STOP AND SEARCH POWERS

Current statutory stop and search powers are meant to maintain a balance between the interest of society as represented by the police in crime control and the interest of the citizen in personal liberty. The use of such powers may be a necessary part of effective policing and represents less of an infringement of liberty than an arrest, but on the other hand their exercise may create a sense of grievance and of violation of personal privacy. There was no general power at common law to detain without the subject's consent in the absence of specific statutory authority.[7] Instead there were a miscellany of such powers, the majority of which were superseded under PACE.

Police and Criminal Evidence Act 1984 (as amended by the Criminal Justice Act 1988, s140)

Part I – Powers to stop and search

Power of constable to stop and search persons, vehicles etc

1.–(1)A constable may exercise any power conferred in this section –

    (a) in any place to which at the time when he proposes to exercise the power the public or any section of the public has access, on payment or otherwise, as of right or by virtue of express or implied permission; or

    (b) in any other place to which people have ready access at the time when he proposes to exercise the power but which is not a dwelling.

(2)Subject to subsection (3) to (5) below, a constable –

    (a) may search –

        (i) any person or vehicle;

        (ii) anything which is in or on a vehicle, for stolen or prohibited articles [or any article to which subsection 8A below applies]; and

    (b) may detain a person or vehicle for the purpose of such a search.

    ...

(6)If in the course of such a search a constable discovers an article which he has reasonable grounds for suspecting to be a stolen or prohibited article, he may seize it.

---

7   For a full list of the powers arising from 16 statutes see the RCCP report 1981.

(7)An article is prohibited for the purposes of this part of this Act if it is –

   (a) an offensive weapon; or

   (b) an article –

       (i) made or adapted for use in the course of or in connection with an offence to which this sub-paragraph applies; or

       (ii) intended by the person having it with him for such use by him or by some other person.

(8)The offences to which subsection (7)(b)(i) above applies are –

   (a) burglary;

   (b) theft;

   (c) offences under section 12 of the Theft Act 1968 (taking motor vehicle or other conveyance without authority); and

   (d) offences under section 15 of that Act (obtaining property by deception).

[(8A) This subsection applies to any article in relation to which a person has committed, or is committing, or is going to commit an offence under section 139 of the Criminal Justice Act 1988].

(9)In this part of this Act 'offensive weapon' means any article –

   (a) made or adapted for use for causing injury to persons, or

   (b) intended by the person having it with him for such use by him or by some other person; …

Provisions relating to search under s1 and other powers

2.–(2)If a constable contemplates a search, other than a search of an unattended vehicle, in the exercise –

   (a) of the power conferred by section 1 above; or

   (b) of any other power, except the power conferred by section 6 below and the power conferred by section 27(2) of the Aviation Security Act 1982 –

       (i) to search a person without first arresting him; or

       (ii) to search a vehicle without making an arrest,

it shall be his duty, subject to subsection (4) below, to take reasonable steps before he commences the search to bring to the attention of the appropriate person –

       (i) if the constable is not in uniform, documentary evidence that he is a constable; and

       (ii) whether he is in uniform or not, the matters specified in subsection (3) below,

and the constable shall not commence the search until he has performed that duty.

(3)The matters referred to in subsection (2)(ii) above are –

   (a) the constable's name and the name of the police station to which he is attached;

   (b) the object of the proposed search;

   (c) the constable's grounds for proposing to make it; and

   (d) the effect of section 3(7) or (8) below, as may be appropriate.

(4)A constable need not bring the effect of section 3(7) or (8) below to the attention of the appropriate person if it appears to the constable that it will not be practicable to make the record in section 3(1) below.

(5)In this section 'the appropriate person' means –

(a) if the constable proposes to search a person, that person; and

(b) if he proposes to search a vehicle, or anything in or on a vehicle, the person in charge of the vehicle.

Duty to make records concerning searches

3.–(1)Where a constable has carried out a search in the exercise of any such power as is mentioned in section 2(1) above, other than a search –

(a) under section 6 below; or

(b) under section 27(2) of the Aviation Security Act 1982,

he shall make a record of it in writing unless it is not practicable to do so.

(7)If a constable who conducted a search of a person made a record of it, the person who was searched shall be entitled to a copy of the record if he asks for one before the end of the period specified in subsection (9) below.

(8)If –

(a) the owner of a vehicle which has been searched or the person who was in charge of the vehicle at the time when it was searched asks for a copy of the record of the search before the end of the period specified in subsection (9) below; and

(b) the constable who conducted the search made a record of it,

the person who made the request shall be entitled to a copy.

Notes

1 It may be that the suspect appears to be in innocent possession of the goods or articles; this will not affect the power to stop although it would affect the power to arrest, and in this sense the power to stop is broader than the arrest power.

2 The concept of reasonable suspicion as the basis for the exercise of stop and search powers is set out briefly in Code of Practice A on 'stop and search', paragraphs 1.6 and 1.7 (below). It is not enough for a police officer to have a hunch that a person has committed or is about to commit an offence; there must be a concrete basis for this suspicion which relates to the particular person in question and could be evaluated by an objective observer. However, research in the area suggests that there is a tendency to view reasonable suspicion as a flexible concept which may denote quite a low level of suspicion.[8]

Criminal Justice and Public Order Act 1994

Powers to stop and search in anticipation of violence

60.–(1)Where a police officer of or above the rank of superintendent reasonably believes that –

(a) incidents involving serious violence may take place in any locality in his area; and

(b) it is expedient to do so to prevent their occurrence,

he may give all authorisation that the powers to stop and search persons

---

8   D Dixon (1989) 17 Int J Soc Law 185–206.

and vehicles conferred by this section shall be exercisable at any place within that locality for a period not exceeding 24 hours.

(2) The power conferred by subsection (1) above may be exercised by a chief inspector or an inspector if he reasonably believes that incidents involving serious violence are imminent and no superintendent is available.

(3) If it appears to the officer who gave the authorisation or to a superintendent that it is expedient to do so, having regard to offences which have, or are reasonably suspected to have, been committed in connection with any incident falling within the authorisation, he may direct that the authorisation shall continue in being for a further six hours.

(4) This section confers on any constable in uniform power –

    (a) to stop any pedestrian and search him or anything carried by him for offensive weapons or dangerous instruments;

    (b) to stop any vehicle and search the vehicle, its driver and any passenger for offensive weapons or dangerous instruments.

(5) A constable may, in the exercise of those powers, stop any person or vehicle and make any search he thinks fit whether or not he has any grounds for suspecting that the person or vehicle is carrying weapons or articles of that kind.

(6) If in the course of a search under this section a constable discovers a dangerous instrument or an article which he has reasonable grounds for suspecting to be an offensive weapon, he may seize it.

(7) This section applies (with the necessary modifications) to ships, aircraft and hovercraft as it applies to vehicles.

(8) A person who fails to stop or (as the case may be) to stop the vehicle when required to do so by a constable in the exercise of his powers under this section shall be liable on summary conviction to imprisonment for a term not exceeding one month or to a fine not exceeding level 3 on the standard scale or both.

(9) Any authorisation under this section shall be in writing signed by the officer giving it and shall specify the locality in which and the period during which the powers conferred by this section are exercisable and a direction under subsection (3) above shall also be given in writing or, where that is not practicable, recorded in writing as soon as it is practicable to do so.

(10) Where a vehicle is stopped by a constable under this section, the driver shall be entitled to obtain a written statement that the vehicle was stopped under the powers conferred by this section if he applies for such a statement not later than the end of the period of 12 months from the day on which the vehicle was stopped and similarly as respects a pedestrian who is stopped and searched under this section.

Prevention of Terrorism (Temporary Provisions) Act 1989[9]

Powers to stop and search vehicles, etc, and persons[10]

13A.–(1) Where it appears to –

    (a) any officer of police of or above the rank of commander of the

---

9   See C Walker, *The Prevention of Terrorism in British Law*, 2nd edn (1992), pp191–7.

10 Inserted by Criminal Justice and Public Order Act 1994 s81(1) and amended by the Prevention of Terrorism (Additional Powers) Act 1996 s1.

Metropolitan Police, as respects the Metropolitan Police district;

(b) any officer of police of or above the rank of commander of the City of London Police, as respects the City of London, or

(c) any officer of police of or above the rank of assistant chief constable for any other police area,

that it is expedient to do so in order to prevent acts of terrorism to which this section applies he may give an authorisation that the powers to stop and search vehicles and persons conferred by this section shall be exercisable at any place within his area or a specified locality in his area for a specified period not exceeding 28 days.

(2) The acts of terrorism to which this section applies are –

(a) acts of terrorism connected with the affairs of Northern Ireland; and

(b) acts of terrorism of any other description except acts connected solely with the affairs of the UK or any part of the UK other than Northern Ireland.

(3) This section confers on any constable in uniform power –

(a) to stop any vehicle;

(b) to search any vehicle, its driver or any passenger for articles of a kind which could be used for a purpose connected with the commission, preparation or instigation of acts of terrorism to which this section applies;

(4) A constable may exercise his powers under this section whether or not he has any grounds for suspecting the presence of articles of that kind.

(4A) Nothing in this section authorises a constable to require a person to remove any of his clothing in public other than any headgear, footwear, outer coat, jacket or gloves.

(5) This section applies (with the necessary modifications) to ships and aircraft as it applies to vehicles.

(6) A person is guilty of an offence if he –

(a) fails to stop the vehicle when required to do so by a constable in the exercise of his powers under this section; or

(b) wilfully obstructs a constable in the exercise of those powers.

(7) A person guilty of an offence under subsection (6) above shall be liable on summary conviction to imprisonment for a term not exceeding six months or a fine not exceeding level 5 on the standard scale or both.

(8) If it appears to a police officer of the rank mentioned in subsection (1)(a), (b) or (c) (as the case may be) that the exercise of the powers conferred by this section ought to continue beyond the period for which their exercise has been authorised under this section he may, from time to time, authorise the exercise of those powers for a further period, not exceeding 28 days.

(9) Where a vehicle is stopped by a constable under this section, the driver shall be entitled to obtain a written statement that the vehicle was stopped under the powers conferred by this section if he applies for such a statement not later than the end of the period of 12 months from the day on which the vehicle was stopped.

Powers to stop and search pedestrians[11]

13B.–(1)(1)Where it appears to a police officer of the rank mentioned in subsection (1)(a), (b) or (as the case may be) (c) of section 13A above that it is expedient to do so in order to prevent acts of terrorism to which that section applies, he may give an authorisation that the powers to stop and search persons conferred by this section shall be exercisable at any place within his area or a locality in his area which is specified in the authorisation.

(2) This section confers on any constable in uniform power to stop any pedestrian and search him, or anything carried by him, for articles of a kind which could be used for a purpose connected with the commission, preparation or instigation of such acts of terrorism.

(3) A constable may exercise his powers under this section whether or not he has any grounds for suspecting the presence of articles of that kind.

(4) Nothing in this section authorises a constable to require a person to remove any of his clothing in public other than any headgear, footwear, outer coat, jacket or gloves.

(5) A person is guilty of an offence if he –

  (a) fails to stop when required to do so by a constable in the exercise of his powers under this section; or

  (b) wilfully obstructs a constable in the exercise of those powers.

(6) A person guilty of an offence under subsection (5) above shall be liable on summery conviction to imprisonment for a term not exceeding six months or a fine not exceeding level five on the standard scale or both.

(7) An authorisation under this section may be given in writing or orally but if given orally must be confirmed in writing by the person giving it as soon as is reasonably practicable.

(8) A person giving an authorisation under this section must cause the Secretary of State to be informed, as soon as is reasonably practicable, that it was given.

(9) An authorisation under this section –

  (a) may be cancelled by the Secretary of State with effect from such time as he may direct;

  (b) ceases to have effect if it is not confirmed by the Secretary of State before the end of the period of 48 hours beginning with the time when it was given; but

  (c) if confirmed continues in force –

    (i) for such period, not exceeding 28 days beginning with the day on which it was given, as may be specified in the authorisation; or

    (ii) for such shorter period as the Secretary of State may direct.

(10) If a person is stopped by a constable under this section, he shall be entitled to obtain a written statement that he was stopped under the powers conferred by this section is he applies for such a statement not later than the end of the period of 12 months from the day on which he was stopped.

(2) Section 13A of the 1989 Act (powers to stop and search vehicle etc and person carrying things) is amended as follows.

(3) Subsection (3)(c) (power to stop and search pedestrians) is repealed and, in consequence, the following words are also repealed –

  (a) in subsection (6)(a), 'or (as the case may be) to stop'; and

---

11 Inserted by the Prevention of Terrorism (Additional Powers) Act 1996, s1.

(b) in subsection (9), 'and similarly as respects a pedestrian who is stopped under this section for a search of anything carried by him'.

Notes

1   The powers under s60 of the 1994 Act and ss13A and 13B of the Prevention of Terrorism Act (PTA) arise in addition to the general PACE power to stop and search in connection with all offences including, of course, those under the PTA.

2   Section 60 of the 1994 Act provides police officers with a further stop and search power which does not depend on showing reasonable suspicion of particular wrong-doing on the part of an individual.

3   The PTA also provides a power to stop and search under s15(3) which does not depend on the need to show reasonable suspicion that the suspect is carrying the items which may be searched for. However, the officer must have reasonable grounds for suspecting that the suspect is liable to arrest for certain offences under the 1989 Act. There is a further power to search a person who has arrived in or is seeking to leave Britain or Northern Ireland under paragraph 4(2) of Schedule 5 to the 1989 Act, and again this power is not dependent on showing reasonable suspicion.

4   Section 81 of the Criminal Justice and Public Order Act 1994 inserts s13A into the 1989 Act, thereby providing a further broad stop and search power based on 'expediency', not reasonable suspicion. The 1989 Act was also amended by the Prevention of Terrorism (Additional Powers) Act 1996 to include a number of new stop and search powers. These include a power to stop and search citizens in designated areas without reasonable suspicion under s1 which inserts s13B into the PTA. The authorisation to search persons in a designated area must be given where it is 'expedient' to do so to prevent terrorism. The use of the word expedient in ss13A and B was questioned in debate in Parliament on the ground that it seemed to signal something much more uncertain than reasonable suspicion.

5   It is notable that no judicial body is involved in the supervision of the power under s60 of the 1994 Act, above, or those under ss13A or B. All the powers are subject to supervision by the police themselves, except that under s13B which is subject to supervision by the Home Secretary.

6   The Government considered that introduction of the powers under the 1996 Act, including in particular that under s13B, was necessary due to the threat of IRA activity on the British mainland in Spring 1996. However, s13B may be criticised on the basis that it hands the police a power which is clearly open to abuse, since a decision to undertake a stop and search can be taken on very flimsy grounds.

7   It is arguably unclear that s13A or s13B will be effective in preventing terrorist activity. In debate on the Prevention of Terrorism (Additional Powers) Bill, Michael Howard was asked how many arrests and convictions had followed use of the existing s13A power to stop and search. In reply he said that there have been 1,746 stops and 1,695 searches of vehicles, 2,373 searches of persons as occupants of vehicles in the five Metropolitan Police areas, and 8,142 stops and 6,854 searches of vehicles and 40 searches of

persons as occupants of vehicles within the Heathrow perimeter. These had together led to two arrests under the PTA and to 66 other arrests.[12] The point was made that this does not represent the whole picture since would be terrorists may be diverted from their activity and weapons may be found. This point was not backed up by any specific evidence.

These figures suggest that stopping and searching without reasonable suspicion leads to an extremely low level of arrests and therefore may not be the most effective use of police resources. They also suggest that use of such powers leads to a low level of apprehension of persons engaged in non-terrorist offences. This low level of arrests may be compared with the general level of arrests flowing from stop and search with reasonable suspicion, which is around 13%. This figure itself is low (and may not be reliable) but nevertheless suggests that stop and search with reasonable suspicion (even though that concept may be interpreted flexibly) is more productive on the face of it in crime control terms than stop and search without it.

8   Research into past use of blanket police powers suggests that they may tend to arouse resentment rather than lead to a clear reduction in crime. Since the powers under s60 of the 1994 Act and ss13A and B of the 1989 Act, on the face of it, allow for stop and search on subjective grounds, they may tend to be used disproportionately against the black community. In 1995, of 160,000 people stopped under PACE in London, 60% were black. The justification given by the police was that the number of arrests which followed use of this power against black people was the same as the proportion arrested from other stops of whites. In 1995 note 1A of Code A was revised to add the requirement that the selection of those questioned or searched is based upon objective factors and not upon personal prejudice. Thus, as far as ss60, 13A and 13B are concerned, this requirement, contained in a non-legal provision, is the only 'safeguard' against a racially stereotyped use of these powers.

Code of Practice A

1 General

1.3   This code governs the exercise by police officers of statutory powers to search a person without first arresting him or to search a vehicle without making an arrest. ...

1.5   This code applies to stops and searches under powers –

(a)   requiring reasonable grounds for suspicion that articles unlawfully obtained or possessed are being carried;

(b)   authorised under section 60 of the Criminal Justice and Public Order Act 1994 based upon a reasonable belief that an incident involving serious violence may take place within a specific locality;

(c)   authorised under section 13A of the Prevention of Terrorism (Temporary Provisions) Act 1989 as amended by section 81 of the Criminal Justice and Public Order [Act 1994];

---

12   HC Deb 2 April 1996, col 211.

(d) exercised under paragraph 4(2) of Schedule 5 to the Prevention of Terrorism (Temporary Provisions) Act 1989.

(a) Powers requiring reasonable suspicion

1.6 Whether reasonable grounds for suspicion exist will depend on the circumstances in each case, but there must be some objective basis for it. An officer will need to consider the nature of the article suspected of being carried in the context of other factors such as the time and the place, and the behaviour of the person concerned or those with him. Reasonable suspicion may exist, for example, where information has been received such as a description of an article being carried or of a suspected offender; a person is seen acting covertly or warily or attempting to hide something; or a person is carrying a certain type of article at an unusual time or in a place where a number of burglaries or thefts are known to have taken place recently. But the decision to stop and search must be based on all the facts which bear on the likelihood that an article of a certain kind will be found.

1.7 Reasonable suspicion can never be supported on the basis of personal factors alone. For example, a person's colour, age, hairstyle or manner of dress, or the fact that he is known to have a previous conviction for possession of an unlawful article, cannot be used alone or in combination with each other as the sole basis on which to search that person. Nor may it be founded on the basis of stereotyped images of certain persons or groups as more likely to be committing offences.

Notes for guidance

1D Nothing in this code affects –

(a) the routine searching of persons entering sports grounds or other premises with their consent, or as a condition of entry; or

(b) the ability of an officer to search a person in the street on a voluntary basis. In these circumstances, an officer should always make it clear that he is seeking the consent of the person concerned to the search being carried out by telling the person that he need not consent and that without his consent he will not be searched.

1E If an officer acts in an improper manner this will invalidate a voluntary search. Juveniles, persons suffering from a mental handicap or mental disorder and others who appear not to be capable of giving an informed consent should not be subject to a voluntary search.

Notes

1 The procedural requirements of ss2 and 3 and Code A must be met. However, a failure to make a written record of the search will not render it unlawful: *Basher v DPP*, 2 March 1993 (unreported), whereas a failure to give the grounds for it will do so: *Fennelley*.[13]

2 Information giving and record keeping is intended to ensure that officers do not overuse the stop and search power, partly because it means that the citizen can make a complaint later and partly because the police station will have a record of the number of stops being carried out.

3 Code A does not affect ordinary consensual contact between police officer and citizen; officers can ask members of the public to stop and can ask them to consent to a search without exerting any compulsion.

---

13 [1989] Crim LR 142.

4   Voluntary contacts can have a sinister side: some people might 'consent' to a search in the sense of offering no resistance to it due to uncertainty as to the basis or extent of the police power in question.[14] Under the 1995 revision note for guidance 1D(b) requires the officer to tell the person to be searched that he need not consent to the search. However, the notes for guidance are not part of the codes and therefore appear to have no legal status. If a search took place in breach of note for guidance 1D(b) it could then be classified as voluntary, and subsequently it would be difficult, if not impossible, to determine whether such classification was justifiable. Once a search is so classified, none of the statutory or Code A safeguards need be observed.

5   Under note 1E persons belonging to certain vulnerable groups may not be subject to a voluntary search at all. The prohibition also applies to a range of other persons who do not appear capable of giving an informed consent to a search. This group may well include the hearing impaired or persons not proficient in English who are also recognised in the codes as belonging to vulnerable groups,[15] but perhaps they should have been expressly included.

6   The ss60, 13A and 13B powers are (or will soon be) subject to the same procedural requirements under Code A as those relating to the powers under s1 of PACE, apart from the Code A provisions relating to reasonable suspicion (Code A, para 1.5(b)). At present Code A does not apply to the amendments made by the 1996 Act. However, in debate on the Bill, Mr Howard said that Code A will be applied to it and that, until the new provisions are brought formally within the scope of Code A, the police will apply the Code A provisions voluntarily.

Questions

1   What problems are posed if police stop and search on a consensual basis?

2   Are the Code A safeguards for suspects likely to maintain, in practice, a balance between suspects' rights and the increased police powers under the 1984, 1989 and 1994 Acts?

POWERS OF ARREST AND DETENTION

Any arrest represents a serious curtailment of liberty; therefore use of the arrest power requires careful regulation. An arrest is seen as *prima facie* illegal necessitating justification under a specific legal power. If an arrest is effected where no arrest power arises, a civil action for false imprisonment may lie. Despite the need for a clarity and precision such powers were, until relatively recently, granted piecemeal with the result that, prior to PACE, they were contained in a mass of common law and statutory provisions. The powers are now contained largely in PACE but common law powers remain, while some statutes create a specific power of arrest which may overlap with the PACE powers.

---

14   See D Dixon, 'Consent and the Legal Regulation of Policing' (1990) 17 JL and Soc 245–362.

15   See Code C, para 3: Detained Persons – Special Groups.

At common law – power to arrest for breach of peace[16]

PACE has not affected the power to arrest which arises at common law for breach of the peace. Factors present in a situation in which breach of the peace occurs may also give rise to arrest powers under PACE, but may extend further than they do due to the wide definition of breach of the peace. The leading case is *Howell* (1981).[17]

Howell [1981] 3 All ER 383

Watkins LJ: We hold that there is power of arrest for breach of the peace where:

(1) a breach of the peace is committed in the presence of the person making the arrest; or

(2) the arrestor reasonably believes that such a breach will be committed in the immediate future by the person arrested although he has not yet committed any breach; or

(3) where a breach has been committed and it is reasonably believed that a renewal of it is threatened.

The public expects a policeman not only to apprehend the criminal but to do his best to prevent the commission of crime, to keep the peace in other words. To deny him, therefore, the right to arrest a person who he reasonably believes is about to breach the peace would be to disable him from preventing that which might cause serious injury to someone or even to many people or to property. The common law, we believe, whilst recognising that a wrongful arrest is a serious invasion of a person's liberty, provides the police with this power in the public interest. In those instances of the exercise of this power which depend on a belief that a breach of the peace is imminent it must, we think we should emphasise, be established that it is not only an honest, albeit mistaken, belief but a belief which is founded on reasonable grounds.

Arrest under the Police and Criminal Evidence Act 1984

Part III – Arrest

Arrest without warrant for arrestable and other offences

24.–(1) The powers of summary arrest conferred by the following subsections shall apply –

(a) to offences for which the sentence is fixed by law;

(b) to offences for which a person of 21 years of age or over (not previously convicted) may be sentenced to imprisonment for a term of five years (or might be so sentenced but for the restrictions imposed by s33 of the Magistrates' Courts Act 1980); and

(c) to the offences to which subsection (2) below applies, and in this Act 'arrestable offence' means any such offence.

---

16 For commentary on breach of the peace generally see Glanville Williams (1954) Crim LR 578. The view that there is no power to arrest once a breach of the peace is over was put forward in the commentary on *Podger* [1979] Crim LR 524 and endorsed *obiter* in *Howell*. See Part VI, Chapter 3 for full discussion of the use of breach of the peace.

17 3 All ER 383; for comment see Glanville Williams (1982) 146 JPN 199–200, 217–19. Recent decisions include *Percy v DPP* (1994) and *Nicol and Another v DPP* (1995): see (1996) 1 J Civ Lib 73–80.

(2) The offences to which this subsection applies are –

    (a) offences for which a person may be arrested under the customs and excise Acts, as defined in section 1(1) of the Customs and Excise Management Act 1979;

    (b) offences under the Official Secrets Act 1911 and 1920 that are not arrestable offences by virtue of the term of imprisonment for which a person may be sentenced in respect of them;

    (c) offences under section 14 (indecent assault on a woman), 22 (causing prostitution of women) or 23 (procuration of girl under 21) of the Sexual Offences Act 1956;

    (d) offences under section 12(1) (taking motor vehicle or other conveyance without authority, etc) or 25(1) (going equipped for stealing, etc) of the Theft Act 1968; and

    (e) offences under section 1 of the Public Bodies Corrupt Practices Act 1889 (corruption in office) or section 1 of the Prevention of Corruption Act 1906 (corrupt transactions with agents).

(3) Without prejudice to section 2 of the Criminal Attempts Act 1981, the powers of summary arrest conferred by the following subsections shall also apply to the offences of –

    (a) conspiring to commit any of the offences mentioned in subsection (2) above;

    (b) attempting to commit any such offence; and

    (c) inciting, aiding, abetting, counselling or procuring the commission of any such offence,

and such offences are also arrestable offences for the purposes of this Act.

(4) Any person may arrest without a warrant –

    (a) anyone who is in the act of committing an arrestable offence;

    (b) anyone whom he has reasonable grounds for suspecting to be committing such an offence.

(5) Where an arrestable offence has been committed, any person may arrest without a warrant –

    (a) anyone who is guilty of the offence;

    (b) anyone whom he has reasonable grounds for suspecting to be guilty of it.

(6) Where a constable has reasonable grounds for suspecting that an arrestable offence has been committed, he may arrest without a warrant anyone whom he has reasonable grounds for suspecting to be guilty of the offence.

(7) A constable may arrest without a warrant –

    (a) anyone who is about to commit an arrestable offence;

    (b) anyone whom he has reasonable grounds for suspecting to be about to commit an arrestable offence.

General arrest conditions

25.–(1) Where a constable has reasonable grounds for suspecting that any offence which is not an arrestable offence has been committed or attempted, or is being committed or attempted, he may arrest the relevant person if it appears to him that service of a summons is impracticable or inappropriate because any of the general arrest conditions is satisfied.

(2)In this section, 'the relevant person' means any person whom the constable has reasonable grounds to suspect of having committed or having attempted to commit the offence or of being in the course of committing or attempting to commit it.

(3)The general arrest conditions are –

(a) that the name of the relevant person is unknown to, and cannot be readily ascertained by, the constable;

(b) that the constable has reasonable grounds for doubting whether a name furnished by the relevant person as his name is his real name;

(c) that –

(i) the relevant person has failed to furnish a satisfactory address for service; or

(ii) the constable has reasonable grounds for doubting whether an address furnished by the relevant person is a satisfactory address for service;

(d) that the constable has reasonable grounds for believing that arrest is necessary to prevent the relevant person –

(i) causing physical harm to himself or any other person;

(ii) suffering physical injury;

(iii)causing loss of or damage to property;

(iv)committing an offence against public decency; or

(v) causing an unlawful obstruction of the highway;

(e) that the constable has reasonable grounds for believing that arrest is necessary to protect a child or other vulnerable person from the relevant person.

(4)For the purposes of subsection (3) above an address is a satisfactory address for service if it appears to the constable –

(a) that the relevant person will be at it for a sufficiently long period for it to be possible to serve him with a summons; or

(b) that some other person specified by the relevant person will accept service of a summons for the relevant person at it.

(5)Nothing in subsection (3)(d) above authorises the arrest of a person under sub-paragraph (iv) of that paragraph except where members of the public going about their normal business cannot reasonably be expected to avoid the person to be arrested.

(6)This section shall not prejudice any power of arrest conferred apart from this section.

Notes

1   In broad terms s24 provides a power of arrest in respect of more serious offences while s25 covers all offences however trivial (including eg dropping litter) if certain conditions are satisfied apart from suspicion that the offence in question has been committed.

2   The difference between s24 and s25 is significant since, once a person has been arrested under s24, he or she is said to have been arrested for 'an arrestable offence' and this may have an effect on his or her treatment later on. An 'arrestable offence' is therefore one for which a person can be arrested, if the necessary reasonable suspicion is present without need to

show any other ingredients in the situation at the time of arrest. Offences for which a person can be arrested under s24 may also be classified as 'serious arrestable offences' under s116. This does not affect the power of arrest, but does affect various safeguards and powers which may be exercised during detention.

3   In order to arrest under s25 two steps must be taken: first, there must be reasonable suspicion relating to the offence in question; second, one of the arrest conditions must be fulfilled. The need for the officer to have suspicion of the offence in question and the general arrest conditions was emphasised in *Edwards v DPP* (1993).[18]

4   Sections 24 and 25 both depend on the concept of reasonable suspicion; the idea behind it is that an arrest should take place at quite a late stage in the investigation. This limits the number of arrests and makes it less likely that a person will be wrongfully arrested. It seems likely that it will be interpreted in accordance with the provisions as to reasonable suspicion under Code A. It would appear strange if a more rigorous test could be applied to the reasonable suspicion necessary to effect a stop than that necessary to effect an arrest. If this is correct it would seem that certain matters, such as an individual's racial group, could never be factors which could support a finding of reasonable suspicion.

5   The objective nature of suspicion required under Code A is echoed in various decisions on the suspicion needed for an arrest.[19] In *Dallison v Caffrey* (1965)[20] Lord Diplock said the test was whether 'a reasonable man assumed to know the law and possessed of the information which in fact was possessed by the defendant would believe there were [reasonable grounds]'. Thus it is not enough for a police officer to have a hunch that a person has committed or is about to commit an offence; there must be a concrete basis for this suspicion which relates to the particular person in question and could be evaluated by an objective observer.

6   PACE seems to endorse a fairly low level of suspicion due to the distinction it maintains between belief and suspicion, suspicion probably being the lower standard.[21] The decision in *Ward v Chief Constable of Somerset and Avon Constabulary* (1986)[22] suggested that a high level of suspicion was not required, and this might also be said of *Castorina v Chief Constable of Surrey* (1988).[23] Detectives were investigating a burglary of a company's premises

---

18   (1993) 97 Cr App R 301.

19   For example, *Nakkuda Ali v Jayaratne* [1951] AC 66, 77; *Allen v Wright* (1835) 8 C & P 522.

20   [1965] 1 QB 348, 371.

21   Section 17(2)(a) requires belief, not suspicion, that a suspect whom an officer is seeking is on premises; similarly, powers of seizure under s19(2) depend on belief in certain matters. The difference between belief and suspicion and the lesser force of the word 'believe' was accepted as an important distinction by the House of Lords in *Wills v Bowley* (1983) 1 AC 57, 103.

22   *The Times,* 26 June; cf *Monaghan v Corbett* (1983) 147 JP 545, DC (however, although this demonstrated a different approach the restriction it imposed may not be warranted: see *DPP v Wilson* [1991] Crim LR 441, DC).

23   (1988) NLJ 180, transcript from LEXIS.

and on reasonable grounds came to the conclusion that it was an 'inside job'. The managing director told them that a certain employee had recently been dismissed and that the documents taken would be useful to someone with a grudge. However, she also said that she would not have expected the particular employee to commit a burglary. The detectives then arrested the employee, having found that she had no previous criminal record. She was detained for nearly four hours and then released without charge. She claimed damages for false imprisonment and was awarded £4,500. The Court of Appeal overturned the award. The question was whether there was reasonable cause to suspect the plaintiff of burglary. Given that certain factors could be identified, including inside knowledge of the company's affairs and the motive of the plaintiff, it appeared that there was sufficient basis for the detectives to have reasonable grounds for suspicion.

7 Apart from situations in which reasonable suspicion relating to an offence arises, there is nothing to prevent a police officer asking any person to come to the police station to answer questions, although there is no legal power to do so. This creates something of a grey area as the citizen may not realise that he or she does not need to comply with the request.[24] The Government refused to include a provision in PACE requiring the police to inform citizens of the fact that they are not under arrest at the point when the request is made.

Arrest under the Prevention of Terrorism Act 1989

Part IV – Arrest, detention and control of entry

Arrest and detention of suspected persons

14.–(1) Subject to subsection (2) below, a constable may arrest without warrant a person whom he has reasonable grounds for suspecting to be –

(a) a person guilty of an offence under section 2, 8, 9, 10 or 11 above;

(b) a person who is or has been concerned in the commission, preparation or instigation of acts of terrorism to which this section applies; or

(c) a person subject to an exclusion order.

(2)The acts of terrorism to which this section applies are –

(a) acts of terrorism connected with the affairs of Northern Ireland; and

(b) acts of terrorism of any other description except acts connected solely with the affairs of the UK or any part of the UK other than Northern Ireland.

Notes

1 Almost all the indictable offences under the Prevention of Terrorism (Temporary Provisions) Act 1989 (PTA) carry a penalty of at least five years imprisonment and are therefore arrestable offences under s24 PACE.

2 Section 14(1)(a) empowers a constable to arrest for certain specified offences under the PTA. As these offences are arrestable offences in any event this power would seem to overlap with that under s24. However, if an arrest is

---

24 See I McKenzie, R Morgan, R Reiner, 'Helping the Police with their Enquiries' (1990) Crim LR 22.

effected under s14 PTA as opposed to s24 PACE this has an effect on the length of detention, as will be seen below.

3 The second limb of s14 (s 14(2)(b)) provides a completely separate power from the PACE power; it allows arrest without needing to show suspicion relating to a particular offence. Instead the constable needs to have reasonable grounds for suspecting that a person is concerned in the preparation or instigation of acts of terrorism connected with the affairs of Northern Ireland or 'any other act of terrorism except those connected solely with the affairs of the UK or a part of the UK'. This arrest is not for an offence but in practice for investigation, questioning and general intelligence gathering which may be conducted for the purpose of 'isolating and identifying the urban guerrillas and then detaching them from the supportive or ambivalent community'.[25] Thus, this power represents a departure from the principle that liberty should be curtailed only on clear and specific grounds which connect the actions of the suspect with a specific offence under criminal law.[26]

Power of arrest with warrant

Magistrates' Courts Act 1980

Part I

Issue of summons to accused or warrant for his arrest

1.–(1) Upon an information being laid before a justice of the peace for an area to which this section applies that any person has, or is suspected of having, committed an offence, the justice may, in any of the events mentioned in subsection (2) below, but subject to subsections (3) to (5) below –

(a) issue a summons directed to that person requiring him to appear before a magistrates' court for the area to answer to the information, or

(b) issue a warrant to arrest that person and bring him before a magistrates' court for the area or such magistrates' court as is provided in subsection (5) below.

(4) No warrant shall be issued under this section for the arrest of any person who has attained the age of 17 unless –

(a) the offence to which the warrant relates is an indictable offence or is punishable with imprisonment, or

(b) the person's address is not sufficiently established for a summons to be served on him.

---

25 DR Lowry (1976–77) 8–9 Colum Human Rights LR 185, 210.

26 For discussion of this arrest power under the PTA 1984 see C Walker (1984) 47 MLR 704–708; D Bonner, *Emergency Powers in Peace Time* (1985), pp170–81.

Procedural elements of a valid arrest[27]

Police and Criminal Evidence Act 1984

Information to be given on arrest

28.–(1)Subject to subsection (5) below, when a person is arrested otherwise than by being informed that he is under arrest, the arrest is not lawful unless the person arrested is informed that he is under arrest as soon as is practicable after his arrest.

(2)Where a person is arrested by a constable, subsection (1) above applies regardless of whether the fact of the arrest is obvious.

(3)Subject to subsection (5) below, no arrest is lawful unless the person arrested is informed of the ground for the arrest at the time of, or as soon as is practicable after, the arrest.

(4)Where a person is arrested by a constable, subsection (3) above applies regardless of whether the ground for the arrest is obvious.

(5)Nothing in this section is to be taken to require a person to be informed –

(a) that he is under arrest; or

(b) of the ground for the arrest,

if it was not reasonably practicable for him to be so informed by reason of his having escaped from arrest before the information could be given.

Notes

1   For an arrest to be made validly, not only must the power of arrest exist, whatever its source, but the procedural elements must be complied with. The fact that a power of arrest arises will not alone make the arrest lawful.

2   The procedural elements are of crucial importance due to the consequences which may flow from a lawful arrest which will not flow from an unlawful one.[28] Such consequences include the right of the officer to use force in making an arrest if necessary and the loss of liberty inherent in an arrest. If an arrest has not occurred the citizen is free to go wherever she will and any attempt to prevent her doing so will be unlawful.[29] It is therefore important to convey the fact of the arrest to the arrestee and to mark the point at which the arrest comes into being and general liberty ceases.

3   At common law there had to be a physical detention or a touching of the arrestee to convey the fact of detention, unless he or she made this unnecessary by submitting to it;[30] the fact of arrest had to be made clear[31] and the reason for it had to be made known.[32]

---

27   The term 'valid arrest' is open to attack on the ground that there can be no such thing as an invalid arrest. However, a valid arrest may be contrasted with a purported arrest and this is the sense in which it is used in this section.

28   The question as to the difference between a valid and invalid arrest has been much debated; see KW Lidstone [1978] Crim LR 332; D Clark and D Feldman [1979] Crim LR 702; M Zander (1977) NLJ 352; JC Smith [1977] Crim LR 293.

29   *Rice v Connolly* [1966] 2 QB 414; *Kenlin v Gardner* [1967] 2 QB 510.

30   *Hart v Chief Constable of Kent* (1983) RTR 484.

31   *Alderson v Booth* [1969] 3 QB 216.

32   *Christie v Leachinsky* [1947] AC 573.

4   Conveying the fact of the arrest under s28 does not involve using a
particular form of words,[33] but it may be that reasonable detail must be
given so that the arrestee will be in a position to give a convincing denial
and therefore be more speedily released from detention.[34] The reason for the
arrest need only be made known as soon as practicable. The meaning and
implications of this provision were considered in *DPP v Hawkins* (1988).[35]

DPP v Hawkins [1988] 3 All ER 673, 675, 676

A police officer took hold of the defendant to arrest him but did not give the
reason. The youth struggled and was therefore later charged with assaulting an
officer in the execution of his duty. The question which arose was whether the
officer was in the execution of his duty as he had failed to give the reason for
the arrest. If the arrest was thereby rendered invalid he could not be in the
execution of his duty as it could not include effecting an unlawful arrest.

> **Simon Brown J:** ... The question raised on this appeal may therefore be stated
> thus: is a police officer acting in the execution of his duty during the period of
> time between his arresting a person and it first thereafter becoming practicable
> for him to inform that person of the ground of arrest, given that, at this later
> time, he in fact gives the wrong ground or no ground at all? If so, then clearly an
> assault on him by the person arrested during that period of time would
> constitute a criminal offence. Otherwise not.
>
> ... by virtue of s28(3) the arrest ultimately proved to be unlawful. But that is not
> to say that all the earlier steps taken during the course of events leading to that
> ultimate position must themselves be regarded as unlawful. Still less does it
> follow that conduct on the part of the police officer, which at the time was not
> only permitted but positively required of him in the execution of his duty, can
> become retrospectively invalidated by reference to some later failure (a failure
> which, I may add, could well have been that of some officer other than himself).
>
> The answer to the question posed in this appeal is, I have no doubt, this. Section
> 28(3) plainly dictates the circumstances in which an arrest may be found to have
> been unlawful and it determines decisively the consequences following the time
> at which that becomes apparent. In my judgment, however, it says nothing in
> respect of the intermediate period during which it is not practicable to inform the
> person arrested of the ground for his arrest. Least of all does it supply the answer
> to the question, hitherto unconsidered by the authorities, whether a police officer
> is acting in the execution of his duty during that intermediate period. That is a
> question which I regard as logically separate and apart from the eventual
> lawfulness or otherwise of the arrest on which he is engaged. ...

Notes

1   The Court of Appeal found that the arrest became unlawful when the time
came at which it was practicable to inform the defendant of the reason but
he was not so informed. This occurred at the police station or perhaps in the

---

33   The Court of Appeal confirmed this in *Brosch* [1988] Crim LR 743. In *Abassy and Others v
Newman and Others* (1989), *The Times,* 18 August, it was found that there was no need for
precise or technical language in conveying the reason for the arrest; the question whether the
reason had been given was a matter for the jury. See also *Nicholas v Parsonage* (1987) RTR 199.

34   *Murphy v Oxford,* 15 February (1988) unreported, CA. This is out of line with the CA decision
in *Abassy* above in which *Murphy* unfortunately was not considered.

35   1 WLR 1166, 3 All ER 673, DC; see also *Brosch* [1988] Crim LR 743, CA.

police car, but did not occur earlier due to the defendant's behaviour. Thus, the officer in question was acting in the course of his duty during the period until informing of the reason for arrest became practicable, despite the fact that when so informing became practicable the officer failed to do so.

2   The police therefore have a certain leeway as to informing the arrestee; the arrest will not be affected and nor will other acts arising from it, until the time when it would be practicable to inform of the reason for it has come and gone. However, if there was nothing in the behaviour of the arrestee to make informing him or her impracticable, then the arrest will be unlawful from its inception. Following this decision, what can be said as to the status of the suspect before the time came and passed at which the requisite words should have been spoken? Was he or was he or not under arrest at that time?

3   In *Murray v Ministry of Defence* (1988)[36] soldiers occupied a woman's house, thus clearly taking her into detention, but did not inform her of the fact of arrest for half an hour. The question arose whether she was falsely imprisoned during that half hour. The House of Lords found that delay in giving the requisite information was acceptable due to the alarm which the fact of arrest, if known, might have aroused in the particular circumstances – the unsettled situation in Northern Ireland.

Members of Mrs Murray's family applied to the European Commission on Human Rights, alleging a breach of Art 5 which guarantees liberty and security of the person and of Art 8 which protects the right to privacy. Article 5(1) requires *inter alia* that deprivation of liberty can occur only if arising from a lawful arrest founded on reasonable suspicion. The European Court of Human Rights found (*Murray v United Kingdom* (1994))[37] that no breach had occurred even though the relevant legislation (s 14 of the Northern Ireland (Emergency Provisions) Act 1987) required only suspicion, not reasonable suspicion, since there was some evidence which would provide a basis for the suspicion in question. No breach was found of Art 5(2) which provides that a person must be informed promptly of the reason for arrest. Mrs Murray was eventually informed during interrogation of the reason for the arrest, and allowing an interval of a few hours between arrest and informing of the reason for it could still be termed prompt. The violation of privacy fell within the exception under Art 8(2) in respect of the prevention of crime. No violation of the Convention was therefore found.

It seems that, under UK law and under Art 5 of the Convention, an arrest which does not comply with all the procedural requirements will still be an arrest as far as all the consequences arising from it are concerned, for a period of time. It is therefore in a more precarious position than an arrest which from its inception complies with all the requirements, because it will cease to be an arrest at an uncertain point. It is clear that some departure has occurred from the principle that there should be a clear demarcation

---

36   2 All ER 521, HL; for comment see Williams [1991] 54 MLR 408.
37   19 EHRR 193.

between the point at which the citizen is at liberty and the point at which her liberty is restrained.

Questions

1 At what point after the police had detained him, if at all, could a suspect in the position of the suspect in *DPP v Hawkins* attempt lawfully to regain his liberty?

2 Does the decision in *DPP v Hawkins* accept the existence of a concept of lawful detention as distinct from the concept of an arrest?

Use of force[38]

Criminal Law Act 1967

Use of force in making arrest, etc

3.–(1)A person may use such force as is reasonable in the circumstances in the prevention of crime, or in effecting or assisting in the lawful arrest of offenders or suspected offenders or of persons unlawfully at large.

Police and Criminal Evidence Act 1984

Power of constable to use reasonable force

117. Where any provision of this Act –

    (a)   confers a power on a constable, and

    (b)   does not provide that the power may only be exercised with the consent of some person, other than a police officer,

the officer may use reasonable force, if necessary, in the exercise of the power.

Note

Force may include, as a last resort, the use of firearms; such use is governed by Home Office guidelines[39] which provide that firearms should be issued only where there is reason to suppose that a person to be apprehended is so dangerous that he could not be safely restrained otherwise. An oral warning should normally be given unless impracticable before using a firearm.[40]

POWER TO ENTER PREMISES[41]

In America, the Fourth Amendment to the Constitution guarantees freedom from unreasonable search and seizure, thus recognising the invasion of privacy which a search of premises represents. A search without a warrant will

---

38   For comment see: (1982) Crim LR 475; *Report of Commissioner of Police of the Metropolis for 1983*, Cmnd 9268.

39   The guidelines were reviewed in 1987 and reissued: see 109 HC Deb 3 February 1987, cols 562–3; (1987) 151 JPN 146.

40   For comment on the use of firearms see: (1990) Crim LR 695; PAJ Waddington, *The Strong Arm of the Law* (1991).

41   See D Feldman, *The Law Relating to Entry, Search and Seizure* (1986); RTH Stone, *Entry, Search and Seizure* (1989); Lidstone and Bevan, *Search and Seizure under the Police and Criminal Evidence Act 1984* (1992).

normally[42] be unreasonable; therefore an independent check is usually available on the search power.[43] In contrast, the common law in Britain, despite some rulings asserting the importance of protecting the citizen from the invasion of private property,[44] allowed search and seizure on wide grounds, going beyond those authorised by statute.[45] Thus the common law did not provide full protection for the citizen and PACE goes some way towards remedying this by placing powers of entry and seizure on a clearer basis and ensuring that the person whose premises are searched understands the basis of the search and can complain as to its conduct if necessary.

Entry without warrant

Police and Criminal Evidence Act 1984

Entry for purpose of arrest, etc

17.–(1) Subject to the following provisions of this section, and without prejudice to any other enactment, a constable may enter and search any premises, for the purpose –

    (a) of executing –

        (i) a warrant of arrest issued in connection with or arising out of criminal proceedings; or

        (ii) a warrant of commitment issued under section 76 of the Magistrates' Courts Act 1980;

    (b) of arresting a person for an arrestable offence;

    (c) of arresting a person for an offence under –

        (i) section 1 (prohibition of uniforms in connection with political objects), 4 (prohibition of offensive weapons at public meetings and processions) or 5 (prohibition of offensive conduct conducive to breaches of the peace) of the Public Order Act 1936;

        (ii) any enactment contained in sections 6–8 or 10 of the Criminal Law Act 1977 (offences relating to entering and remaining on property);

    (d) of recapturing a person who is unlawfully at large and whom he is pursuing; or

    (e) of saving life or limb or preventing serious damage to property.

(2) Except for the purpose specified in paragraph (e) of subsection (1) above, the powers of entry and search conferred by this section –

    (a) are only exercisable if the constable has reasonable grounds for believing that the person whom he is seeking is on the premises ...

(5) Subject to subsection (6) below, all the rules of common law under which a constable has power to enter premises without a warrant are hereby abolished.

---

42 *Coolidge v New Hampshire* 403 US 443 (1973); exception accepted where evidence might otherwise be destroyed.

43 See W Lafave, *Search and Seizure* (1978).

44 See eg rulings in *Entinck v Carrington* (1765) 19 St Tr 1029; *Morris v Beardmore* [1981] AC 446.

45 The ruling in *Ghani v Jones* [1970] 1 QB 693 authorised seizure of a wide range of material once officers were lawfully on premises. The ruling in *Thomas v Sawkins* [1935] 2 KB 249 allowed a wide power to enter premises to prevent crime.

(6)Nothing in subsection (5) above affects any power of entry to deal with or prevent a breach of the peace.

Entry and search after arrest

18.–(1) Subject to the following provisions of this section, a constable may enter and search any premises occupied or controlled by a person who is under arrest for an arrestable offence, if he has reasonable grounds for suspecting that there is on the premises evidence other than items subject to legal privilege, that relates –

(a) to that offence; or

(b) to some other arrestable offence which is connected with or similar to that offence.

(2)A constable may seize and retain anything for which he may search under subsection (1) above.

(3)The power to search conferred by subsection (1) above is only a power to search to the extent that is reasonably required for the purpose of discovering such evidence.

(4)Subject to subsection (5) below, the powers conferred by this section may not be exercised unless an officer of the rank of inspector or above has authorised them in writing.

(5)A constable may conduct a search under subsection (1) above –

(a) before taking the person to a police station; and

(b) without obtaining an authorisation under subsection (4) above, if the presence of that person at a place other than a police station is necessary for the effective investigation of the offence.

Search upon arrest

32.–(1) A constable may search an arrested person, in any case where the person to be searched has been arrested at a place other than a police station, if the constable has reasonable grounds for believing that the arrested person may present a danger to himself or others.

(2)Subject to subsections (3) to (5) below, a constable shall also have power in any such case –

(a) to search the arrested person for anything –

(i) which he might use to assist him to escape from lawful custody; or

(ii) which might be evidence relating to an offence; and

(b) to enter and search any premises in which he was when arrested or immediately before he was arrested for evidence relating to the offence for which he has been arrested.

(5)A constable may not search a person in the exercise of the power conferred by subsection (2)(a) above unless he has reasonable grounds for believing that the person to be searched may have concealed on him anything for which a search is permitted under that paragraph.

(6)A constable may not search premises in the exercise of the power conferred by subsection (2)(b) above unless he has reasonable grounds for believing that there is evidence for which a search is permitted under that paragraph on the premises.

(8)A constable searching a person in the exercise of the power conferred by subsection (1) above may seize and retain anything he finds, if he has reasonable grounds for believing that the person searched might use it to cause physical injury to himself or to any other person.

(9)A constable searching a person in the exercise of the power conferred by subsection (2)(a) above may seize and retain anything he finds, other than an item subject to legal privilege, if he has reasonable grounds for believing –

(a) that he might use it to assist him to escape from lawful custody; or

(b) that it is evidence of an offence or has been obtained in consequence of the commission of an offence.

Note

The s18 power to enter and search without a warrant is subject to a significant limitation since it does not arise in respect of an arrest under s25 PACE. If a search was considered necessary in respect of a s25 arrest, a search warrant would have to be obtained unless the provisions of s32 applied.

Prevention of Terrorism (Temporary Provisions) Act 1989

Schedule 7

Urgent cases

7.–(1)If a police officer of at least the rank of superintendent has reasonable grounds for believing that the case is one of great emergency and that in the interests of the state immediate action is necessary, he may by a written order signed by him give to any constable the authority which may be given by a search warrant under paragraph 2 or 5 above.

(2)Where an authority is given under this paragraph particulars of the case shall be notified as soon as may be to the Secretary of State.

(3)An order under this paragraph may not authorise a search for items subject to legal privilege.

(4)If such a police officer as is mentioned in subparagraph (1) above has reasonable grounds for believing that the case is such as is there mentioned he may by a notice in writing signed by him require any person specified in the notice to provide an explanation of any material seized in pursuance of an order under this paragraph.

(5)Any person who without reasonable excuse fails to comply with a notice under subparagraph (4) above is guilty of an offence and liable on summary conviction to imprisonment for a term not exceeding six months or a fine not exceeding level 5 on the standard scale or both.

(6)Subparagraphs (2) to (5) of paragraph 6 above shall apply to a requirement imposed under subparagraph (4) above as they apply to a requirement under that paragraph.

Entry to premises under a search warrant

Police and Criminal Evidence Act 1984

Part II – Powers of entry, search and seizure

Search warrants – power of the justice of peace to authorise entry and search of premises

8.–(1)If on an application made by a constable a justice of the peace is satisfied that there are reasonable grounds for believing –

(a) that a serious arrestable offence has been committed; and

(b) that there is material on premises specified in the application which is likely to be of substantial value (whether by itself or together with other material) to the investigation of the offence; and

(c) that the material is likely to be relevant evidence; and

(d) that it does not consist of or include items subject to legal privilege, excluded material or special procedure material; and

(e) that any of the conditions specified in subsection (3) below applies,

he may issue a warrant authorising a constable to enter and search the premises.

(2)A constable may seize and retain anything for which a search has been authorised under subsection (1) above.

(3)The conditions mentioned in subsection (1)(e) above are –

(a) that it is not practicable to communicate with any person entitled to grant entry to the premises;

(b) that it is practicable to communicate with a person entitled to grant entry to the premises but it is not practicable to communicate with any person entitled to grant access to the evidence;

(c) that entry to the premises will not be granted unless a warrant is produced;

(d) that the purpose of a search may be frustrated or seriously prejudiced unless a constable arriving at the premises can secure immediate entry to them.

Search warrants – safeguards

15.–(1) This section and section 16 below have effect in relation to the issue to constables under any enactment, including an enactment contained in an Act passed after this Act, of warrants to enter and search premises and an entry on or search of premises under a warrant is unlawful unless it complies with this section and section 16 below.

(2)Where a constable applies for any such warrant, it shall be his duty –

(a) to state –

(i) the ground on which he makes the application; and

(ii) the enactment under which the warrant would be issued;

(b) to specify the premises which it is desired to enter and search; and

(c) to identify, so far as is practicable, the articles or persons to be sought.

(3)An application for such a warrant shall be made *ex parte* and supported by an information in writing.

(4)The constable shall answer on oath any question that the justice of the peace or judge hearing the application asks him.

(5)A warrant shall authorise an entry on one occasion only.

(6)A warrant –

(a) shall specify –

(i) the name of the person who applies for it;

(ii) the date on which it is issued;

(iii)the enactment under which it is issued; and

(iv)the premises to be searched; and

(b) shall identify, so far as is practicable, the articles or persons to be sought.

Execution of warrants

16.–(1) A warrant to enter and search premises may be executed by any constable.

(2) Such a warrant may authorise persons to accompany any constable who is executing it.

(3) Entry and search under a warrant must be within one month from the date of its issue.

(4) Entry and search under a warrant must be at a reasonable hour unless it appears to the constable executing it that the purpose of a search may be frustrated on an entry at a reasonable hour.

(5) Where the occupier of premises which are to be entered and searched is present at the time when a constable seeks to execute a warrant to enter and search them, the constable –

(a) shall identify himself to the occupier and, if not in uniform shall produce to him documentary evidence that he is a constable;

(b) shall produce the warrant to him; and

(c) shall supply him with a copy of it.

...

(12) If during the period for which a warrant is to be retained the occupier of the premises to which it relates asks to inspect it, he shall be allowed to do so.

Prevention of Terrorism (Temporary Provisions) Act 1989

Schedule 7 – Terrorist investigations

Search for material other than excluded or special procedure material

2.–(1) A justice of the peace may, on an application made by a constable, issue a warrant under this paragraph if satisfied that a terrorist investigation is being carried out and that there are reasonable grounds for believing –

(a) that there is material on premises specified in the application which is likely to be of substantial value (whether by itself or together with other material) to the investigation;

(b) that the material does not consist of or include items subject to legal privilege, excluded material or special procedure material; and

(c) that any of the conditions in subparagraph (2) below are fulfilled.

(2) The conditions referred to in subparagraph (1)(c) above are –

(a) that it is not practicable to communicate with any person entitled to grant entry to the premises;

(b) that it is practicable to communicate with a person entitled to grant entry to the premises but it is not practicable to communicate with any person entitled to grant access to the material;

(c) that entry to the premises will not be granted unless a warrant is produced; and

(d) that the purpose of a search may be frustrated or seriously prejudiced unless a constable arriving at the premises can secure immediate entry to them.

(3) A warrant under this paragraph shall authorise a constable to enter the premises specified in the warrant and to search the premises and any person found there and to seize and retain anything found there or on any such person, other than items subject to legal privilege, if he has reasonable grounds for believing –

(a) that it is likely to be of substantial value (whether by itself or together with other material) to the investigation; and

(b) that it is necessary to seize it in order to prevent it being concealed, lost, damaged, altered or destroyed.

(4)In Northern Ireland an application for a warrant under this paragraph shall be made by a complaint on oath.

Notes

1   The PACE search warrant provisions provide a scheme which is reasonably sound in theory but which is dependent on magistrates observing its requirements. Research suggests that in practice some magistrates make little or no attempt to ascertain whether the information a warrant contains may be relied upon, while magistrates who do take a rigorous approach to the procedure and refuse to grant warrants may not be approached again.[46]

2   A warrant authorising the police to search premises does not of itself authorise officers to search persons on the premises. The Home Office Circular on PACE stated that such persons could be searched only if a specific power to do so arose under the warrant (eg warrants issued under the Misuse of Drugs Act 1971 s23).

3   Searching of premises other than under ss17 and 18 of PACE or under the PTA can, in general, only occur if a search warrant is issued under s8 PACE by a magistrate. However, there are also special provisions arising under the Drug Trafficking Offences Act 1986 s27 and the Criminal Justice Act 1987 s2(4).

The general power of seizure

Police and Criminal Evidence Act 1984

General power of seizure

19.–(1) The powers conferred by subsections (2), (3) and (4) below are exercisable by a constable who is lawfully on any premises.

(2)The constable may seize anything which is on the premises if he has reasonable grounds for believing –

(a) that it has been obtained in consequence of the commission of an offence; and

(b) that it is necessary to seize it in order to prevent it being concealed, lost, damaged, altered or destroyed.

(3)The constable may seize anything which is on the premises if he has reasonable grounds for believing –

(a) that it is evidence in relation to an offence which he is investigating or any other offence; and

(b) that it is necessary to seize it in order to prevent the evidence being concealed, lost, altered or destroyed.

(4)The constable may require any information which is contained in a computer and is accessible from the premises to be produced in a form in which it can be taken away and in which it is visible and legible if he has reasonable grounds for believing –

---

46   See Dixon (1991) 141 NLJ 1586.

(a) that –

(i) it is evidence in relation to an offence which he is investigating or any other offence; or

(ii) it has been obtained in consequence of the commission of an offence; and

(b) that it is necessary to do so in order to prevent it being concealed, lost, tampered with or destroyed.

(5) The powers conferred by this section are in addition to any power otherwise conferred.

(6) No power of seizure conferred on a constable under any enactment (including an enactment contained in an Act passed after this Act) is to be taken to authorise the seizure of an item which the constable exercising the power has reasonable grounds for believing to be subject to legal privilege.

Notes

1   At common law prior to PACE a wide power of seizure had developed where a search was not under warrant. Articles could be seized so long as they either implicated the owner or occupier in any offence, or implicated third parties in the offence for which the search was conducted.[47] The power of seizure is now governed by ss8(2), 18(2), 19 and 22(1).

2   It was made clear in *Chief Constable of Lancashire ex p Parker and McGrath* (1992)[48] that material seized during an unlawful search cannot be retained and, if it is, an action for trespass to goods may arise. It was accepted that the search was unlawful but the chief constable contended that the material seized could nevertheless be retained. This argument was put forward under the provision of s22(2)(a) which allows the retention of 'anything seized for the purposes of a criminal investigation'. The chief constable maintained that these words would be superfluous unless denoting a general power to retain unlawfully seized material. However, it was held that the subsection could not bear the weight sought to be placed upon it: it was merely intended to give examples of matters falling within the general provision of s22(1). Therefore the police were not entitled to retain the material seized.

DETENTION IN POLICE CUSTODY

Detention after arrest under the Police and Criminal Evidence Act 1984

Police and Criminal Evidence Act 1984, Part IV

Limits on period of detention without charge

41.–(1) Subject to the following provisions of this section and to sections 42 and 43 below, a person shall not be kept in police detention for more than 24 hours without being charged.

---

47   *Ghani v Jones* [1970] 1 QB 693; *Garfinkel v MPC* [1972] Crim LR 44.
48   [1993] QB 577; [1993] 2 WLR 428; (1992) 142 NLJ 635.

(2) The time from which the period of detention of a person is to be calculated (in this Act referred to as 'the relevant time') –

    (a) in the case of a person to whom this section applies, shall be –

        (i) the time at which that person arrives at the relevant police station, or

        (ii) the time 24 hours after the time of that person's arrest, whichever is the earlier.

Authorisation of continued detention

42.–(1) Where a police officer of the rank of superintendent or above who is responsible for the police station at which a person is detained has reasonable grounds for believing that –

    (a) the detention of that person without charge is necessary to secure or preserve evidence relating to an offence for which he is under arrest or to obtain such evidence by questioning him;

    (b) an offence for which he is under arrest is a serious arrestable offence; and

    (c) the investigation is being conducted diligently and expeditiously, he may authorise the keeping of that person in police detention for a period expiring at or before 36 hours after the relevant time.

(2) Where an officer such as is mentioned in subsection (1) above has authorised the keeping of a person in police detention for a period expiring less than 36 hours after the relevant time, such an officer may authorise the keeping of that person in police detention for a further period expiring not more than 36 hours after that time if the conditions specified in subsection (1) above are still satisfied when he gives the authorisation.

Warrants of further detention

43.–(1) Where, on an application on oath made by a constable and supported by an information, a magistrates' court is satisfied that there are reasonable grounds for believing that the further detention of the person to whom the application relates is justified, it may issue a warrant of further detention authorising the keeping of that person in police detention.

(2) A court may not hear an application for a warrant of further detention unless the person to whom the application relates –

    (a) has been furnished with a copy of the information; and

    (b) has been brought before the court for the hearing.

(3) The person to whom the application relates shall be entitled to be legally represented at the hearing and, if he is not so represented, but wishes to be so represented –

    (a) the court shall adjourn the hearing to enable him to obtain representation; and

    (b) he may be kept in police detention during the adjournment.

(4) A person's further detention is only justified for the purposes of this section or section 44 below if –

    (a) his detention without charge is necessary to secure or preserve evidence relating to an offence for which he is under arrest or to obtain such evidence by questioning him;

    (b) an offence for which he is under arrest is a serious arrestable offence; and

    (c) the investigation is being conducted diligently and expeditiously.

Extension of warrants of further detention

44.–(1) On an application on oath made by a constable and supported by information, a magistrates' court may extend a warrant of further detention issued under section 43 above if it is satisfied that there are reasonable grounds for believing that the further detention of the person to whom the application relates is justified.

(2) Subject to subsection (3) below, the period for which a warrant of further detention may be extended shall be such period as the court thinks fit, having regard to the evidence before it.

(3) The period shall not –

    (a)   be longer than 36 hours; or

    (b)   end later then 96 hours after the relevant time.

(4) Where a warrant of further detention has been extended under subsection (1) above, or further extended under this subsection, for a period ending before 96 hours after the relevant time, on an application such as is mentioned in that subsection, a magistrates' court may further extend the warrant if it is satisfied as there mentioned; and subsections (2) and (3) above apply to such further extensions as they apply to extensions under subsection (1) above.

...

(7) Where an application under this section is refused, the person to whom the application relates shall forthwith be charged or, subject to subsection (g) below, released, either on bail or without bail.

Notes

1   The position under the law prior to the 1984 Act with regard to detention before charge and committal before a magistrate was vague and the police had no clearly defined power to hold a person for questioning. It was governed by the Magistrates' Courts Act 1980 s43 which allowed the police to detain a person in custody until such time as it was 'practicable' to bring him before a magistrate, in the case of a 'serious' offence. Since a person would be charged before being brought before the magistrate this meant that the police had to move expeditiously in converting suspicion into evidence justifying a charge.[49] However, the common law had developed to the point when it could be said that detention for the purpose of questioning was recognised.[50] The detention scheme governed by Part IV of PACE put the power to hold for questioning on a clear basis and it is made clear under s37(2) that the purpose of the detention is to obtain a confession.

2   The safeguards surrounding the powers to detain under ss41–44 have been called into question. D Dixon in 'Safeguarding the Rights of Suspects in Police Custody' (1990) 1 *Policing and Society* 130–1 suggests that the periodic review of detention and the right of the detainee or his solicitor (if available) to make written or oral representations[51] tend to be treated not as genuine investigations into the grounds for continuing the detention, but as formalities.

---

49   See *Holmes* [1981] 2 All ER 612; [1981] Crim LR 802.

50   *Mohammed-Holgate v Duke* [1984] QB 209, HL.

51   Section 40(12) and (13).

3   The power to detain under PACE is intended to embody the principle that a detained person should normally be charged within 24 hours and then either released or brought before a magistrate. The power is also supposed to be balanced by all the safeguards created by Part V of PACE and by Codes of Practice C and E.

Detention under the Prevention of Terrorism Act 1989

Arrest, detention and control of entry

Arrest and detention of suspected persons

14.–(4) Subject to subsection (5) below, a person arrested under this section shall not be detained in right of the arrest for more than 48 hours after his arrest.

   (5) The Secretary of State may, in any particular case, extend the period of 48 hours mentioned in subsection (4) above by a period or periods specified by him, but any such further period or periods shall not exceed five days in all and if an application for such an extension is made the person detained shall as soon as practicable be given written notice of that fact and of the time when the application was made.

   (6) The exercise of the detention powers conferred by this section shall be subject to supervision in accordance with Schedule 3 to this Act.

Notes

1   Under these provisions the whole detention can be for seven days and, in contrast to the general PACE provision, the courts are not involved in the authorising process; it occurs at a low level of visibility as an administrative decision.

2   The provision for detention under the PTA 1984 was found to be in breach of the European Convention on Human Rights Art 5(3) in *Brogan v UK* (1989),[52] on the ground that holding a person for longer than four days without judicial authorisation was a violation of the requirement that persons should be brought promptly before a judicial officer. The Government made no move to comply with this requirement; instead it entered a derogation under Art 15 to Art 5(3) which was challenged unsuccessfully as broader than it needed to be.[53] The European Court of Human Rights found that the derogation was justified as the state of public emergency in Northern Ireland warranted exceptional measures. As a result, at present, periods of up to six days detention may not breach Art 5.

POLICE INTERVIEWING

This section does not concentrate only on treatment of suspects inside the police station because contact between police and suspect may take place a long time before the police station is reached. This has been recognised in the provisions of Part V of PACE and Code of Practice C which govern treatment of suspects and interviewing, but have some application outside as well as inside the police

---

52   11 EHRR 117.
53   *Brannigan and McBride v UK*, Appeals 14553/89 and 14554/89. The ruling of the ECHR was given on 26 May 1993: *Brannigan and McBride v UK* (1993) 17 EHRR 539.

station. The most crucial event during a person's contact with police will probably be the interview, and therefore this section will concentrate on the safeguards available for the suspect which are intended to ensure that interviews are fair and that admissions made can be relied upon, if necessary, in court.

Under the pre-PACE rules, safeguards for the interview were governed largely by the Judges Rules and Administrative Directions to the Police[54] and s 62 of the Criminal Law Act 1977. The latter provided for access to a solicitor (though it was frequently ignored). The former provided *inter alia* for the issuing of cautions when a person was charged (not necessarily when he was arrested) and for the exclusion in evidence of statements and confessions which were not 'voluntary' (see below). Under PACE, those rules were replaced by provisions contained in the Act itself and in Codes of Practice C or E.

The most significant safeguards available for interviews include contemporaneous recording or tape recording,[55] the ability to read over, verify and sign the notes of the interview as a correct record, notification of legal advice,[56] the right to have advice before questioning and, where appropriate, the presence of an adult.[57] One of the most important issues in relation to these safeguards, and reflected in the 1991 and 1995 revisions of Code C, is the question when they come into play. There may be a number of stages in a particular investigation, beginning with first contact between police and suspect, and perhaps ending with the charge. Two factors can be identified which decide which safeguards should be in place at a particular time. Firstly, it must be asked whether an exchange between police and suspect can be called 'an interview' and secondly whether it took place inside or outside the police station.

Interviews and exchanges with suspects

Code of Practice C (revised 1995)

11. Interviews: general

(a) Action

11.1A An interview is the questioning of a person regarding his involvement or suspected involvement in a criminal offence or offences which, by virtue of paragraph 10.1 of Code C, is required to be carried out under caution.

11.1 Following a decision to arrest a suspect he must not be interviewed about the relevant offence except at a police station or other authorised place of detention unless the consequent delay is be likely –

  (a) to lead to interference with or harm to evidence connected with an offence or interference with or physical harm to other persons; or

  (b) to lead to the alerting of other persons suspected of having committed an offence but not yet arrested for it; or

---

54 eg Home Office Circular 89/1978, Appendices A and B.
55 Under Code E, para 3.
56 Under Code C, para 3.1.
57 Under Code C, para 11.14.

(c) to hinder the recovery of property obtained in consequence of the commission of an offence.

Interviewing in any of these circumstances should cease once the relevant risk has been averted or the necessary questions have been put in order to attempt to avert that risk.

11.2 Immediately prior to the commencement or re-commencement of any interview at a police station or other authorised place of detention, the interviewing officer shall remind the suspect of his entitlement to free legal advice. ... It is the responsibility of the interviewing officer to ensure that all such reminders are noted in the record of interview.

11.2A At the beginning of an interview carried out in a police station, the interviewing officer, after cautioning the suspect, shall put to him any significant statement or silence (ie failure or refusal to answer a question or failure or refusal to answer it satisfactorily) which occurred before the start of the interview, and shall ask him whether he confirms or denies that earlier statement or silence and whether he wishes to add anything. A 'significant' statement or silence means one which appears capable of being used in evidence against the suspect, in particular a direct admission of guilt, or failure or refusal to answer a question or to answer it satisfactorily which might give rise to an inference under Part III of the Criminal Justice and Public Order Act 1994.

11.3 No police officer may try to obtain answers to questions or to elicit a statement by the use of oppression or shall indicate, except in answer to a direct question, what action will be taken on the part of the police if the person being interviewed answers questions, makes a statement or refuses to do either. If the person asks the officer directly what action will be taken in the event of his answering questions, making a statement or refusing to do either, then the officer may inform the person what action the police propose to take in that event provided that that action is itself proper and warranted.

(b) Interview records

11.5 (a) An accurate record must be made of each interview with a person suspected of an offence, whether or not the interview takes place at a police station.

(b) The record must state the place of the interview, the time it begins and ends, the time the record is made (if different), any breaks in the interview and the names of all those present; and must be made on the forms provided for this purpose or in the officer's pocketbook or in accordance with the code of practice for the tape recording of police interviews with suspects.

(c) The record must be made during the course of the interview, unless in the investigating officer's view this would not be practicable or would interfere with conduct of the interview, and must constitute either a verbatim record of what has been said or, failing this, an account of the interview which adequately and accurately summarises

11.7 If an interview record is not made during the course of the interview it must be made as soon as practicable after its completion.

11.8 Written interview records must be timed and signed by the maker.

11.10 Unless it is impracticable the person interviewed shall be given the opportunity to read the interview record and to sign it as correct or to indicate the respects in which he considers it inaccurate. ...

11.13 A written record should also be made of any comments made by a suspected person, including unsolicited comments, which are outside the context of an interview but which might be relevant to the offence. Any such record must be timed and signed by the maker. Where practicable the person shall be given the opportunity to read that record and to sign it as correct or to indicate the respects in which he considers it inaccurate. Any refusal to sign should be recorded.

Notes for guidance

11A [Not used]

11B It is important to bear in mind that, although juveniles or persons who are mentally disordered or mentally handicapped are often capable of providing reliable evidence, they may, without knowing or wishing to do so, be particularly prone in certain circumstances to provide information which is unreliable, misleading or self-discriminating. Special care should therefore always be exercised in questioning such a person, and the appropriate adult should be involved, if there is any doubt about a person's age, mental state or capacity. Because of the risk of unreliable evidence it is also important to obtain corroboration of any facts admitted whenever possible. ...

Annex C

Urgent interviews at police stations

If, and only if, an officer of the rank of superintendent or above considers that delay will lead to the consequences set out in paragraph 11.1(a)–(c):

1   (a)   a person heavily under the influence of drink or drugs may be interviewed in that state; or

(b)   an arrested juvenile or a person who is mentally disordered or mentally handicapped may be interviewed in the absence of the appropriate adult; or

(c)   a person who has difficulty in understanding English or who has a hearing disability may be interviewed in the absence of an interpreter.

2   Questioning in these circumstances may not continue once sufficient information to avert the immediate risk has been obtained.

Notes

1   The term 'interview' has been given a wide interpretation;[58] the definition given to it by the Court of Appeal in *Mathews* (1990)[59] – 'any discussion or talk between suspect and police officer' – brought within its ambit many exchanges far removed from formal interviews. It also covered many interviewees, as it spoke in terms of 'suspects', rather than arrestees. However, it was qualified by the ruling in *Scott* (1991)[60] that unsolicited admissions cannot amount to 'interviews', and by the ruling in *Marsh* (1991)[61] to the same effect as regards 'genuine requests' from the police for information.

---

58   The Court of Appeal in *Absolam* (1988) 88 Cr App R 332 defined it as 'a series of questions directed by the police to a suspect with a view to obtaining admissions'. For criticism of the interpretation of the term 'interview' under the 1991 revision of Code C, see Fenwick (1993) Crim LR 174 and S Field (1993) 13 LS 254.

59   91 Cr App R 43; [1990] Crim LR 190, CA.

60   Crim LR 56, CA. See also *Younis* [1990] Crim LR 425, CA.

61   Crim LR 455.

2   Where the level of suspicion falls within paragraphs 11.1A and 10.1 as, clearly, it will do after arrest, the use of the term 'questioning' impliedly excludes instances where nothing definable as questioning has taken place, such as chats or discussions between suspect and police officer or statements or commands which happen to elicit an incriminating response.[62]

3   Paragraph 11.1 allows for some interviewing outside the police station due to its requirement of a higher level of suspicion than that denoted by paragraph 11.1A. It implies that a police officer should categorise someone either as possibly involved in an offence or as on the verge of arrest; so long as the first category is applicable questioning can continue. The suspect interviewed outside the police station may be unaware of the right to legal advice[63] and it is also at present unlikely that the interview would be tape recorded; Code E does not envisage tape recording taking place anywhere but inside the police station.[64]

4   Once the suspect is inside the police station under arrest or under caution,[65] any interview[66] (using this term to connote an exchange which falls within paragraph 11.1A) should be tape recorded unless an exception under the tape recording code, Code E, applies. Interviews with certain groups of terrorist suspects need not be taped.

7   PACE does not attempt to regulate the conduct of the interview except in so far as such regulation can be implied from the provision of s76 that confessions obtained by oppression or in circumstances likely to render them unreliable will be inadmissible (see also Code C para 11.3). Obviously the provisions governing detention and the physical comfort of the detainee[67] have relevance in this context; they provide the setting for the interrogation and remove from the situation some of the reasons why a suspect might make an unreliable confession. But once their limits have been set they cannot influence what occurs next, and it seems that use of a degree of intimidation, haranguing, and indirect threats is still quite common, especially in interviews with juveniles.[68] The 1993 Royal Commission on Criminal Justice put forward proposals which would affect the conduct of the interview with a view to ensuring that police officers would perceive its purpose to be the discovering the truth rather than obtaining a confession. Such proposals were thought to be particularly relevant after the evidence of use of bullying techniques in interrogations which arose from the post-PACE case of *Paris* (the 'Cardiff Three' case) (1993).[69]

---

62 See *Absolam* (1988) 88 Cr App R 332.

63 Notification of the right to legal advice is governed by Code C, para 3.1 which is expressed to apply only within the police station.

64 Code E, para 3.1. Some police forces have experimented with hand-held tape recorders used outside the police station, but at present this is by no means common practice.

65 Under para 3.4 of Code E, once a volunteer becomes a suspect (ie at the point when he should be cautioned) the rest of the interview should be tape recorded.

66 Under para 3.1(a), an interview with a person suspected of an offence triable only summarily need not be taped.

67 Paras 8, 9 and 12 of Code C.

68 See R Evans, *The Conduct of Police Interviews with Juveniles*, Home Office Research Study No 8, 1993.

69 97 Cr App R 99.

Questions

1 Will the new definition of an interview under paragraph 11.1A cover all exchanges between police and suspect when there are grounds to suspect him or her of an offence? Can an 'interview' be distinguished clearly from 'relevant' comments (para 11.13)?

2 Is the point at which the suspect must be taken to the police station for further questioning clearly demarcated? Why is this a matter of significance?

Legal advice

Police and Criminal Evidence Act 1984

Access to legal advice

58.–(1) A person who is in police detention shall be entitled, if he so requests, to consult a solicitor privately at any time.

(2) Subject to subsection (3) below, a request under subsection (1) above and the time at which it was made shall be recorded in the custody record.

(3) Such a request need not be recorded in the custody record of a person who makes it at a time while he is at a court after being charged with an offence.

(4) If a person makes such a request, he must be permitted to consult a solicitor as soon as is practicable except to the extent that delay is permitted by this section.

(5) In any case he must be permitted to consult a solicitor within 36 hours from the relevant time, as defined in section 41(2) above.

(6) Delay in compliance with a request is only permitted --

    (a) in the case of a person who is in police detention for a serious arrestable offence, and

    (b) if an officer of at least the rank of superintendent authorises it.

(7) An officer may give an authorisation under subsection (6) above orally or in writing but, if he gives it orally, he shall confirm it in writing as soon as is practicable.

(8) An officer may only authorise delay where he has reasonable grounds for believing that the exercise of the right conferred by subsection (1) above at the time when the person in police detention desires to exercise it –

    (a) will lead to interference with or harm to evidence connected with a serious arrestable offence or interference with or physical injury to other persons; or

    (b) will lead to the alerting of other persons suspected of having committed such an offence but not yet arrested for it; or

    (c) will hinder the recovery of any property obtained as a result of such an offence.

(8A) An officer may also authorise delay where the serious arrestable offence is a drug trafficking offence or an offence to which part VI of the Criminal Justice Act 1988 applies and the officer has reasonable grounds for believing –

    (a) where the offence is a drug trafficking offence, that the detained person has benefited from drug trafficking and that the recovery of the value of that person's proceeds of drug trafficking will be hindered by the exercise of the right conferred by subsection (1) above; and

(b) where the offence is one to which Part VI of the Criminal Justice Act 1988 applies, that the detained person has benefited from the offence and that the recovery of the value of the property obtained by that person from or in connection with the offence or of the pecuniary advantage derived by him from or in connection with it will be hindered by the exercise of the right conferred by subsection (1) above.[70]

Code of Practice C

6 Right to legal advice

(a) Action

6.1 Subject to the provisos in Annex B all people in police detention must be informed that they may at any time consult and communicate privately, whether in person, in writing or by telephone with a solicitor [see para 3.1, note 6B and note 6J]. ...

6.4 No attempt should be made to dissuade the suspect from obtaining legal advice .

6.5 The exercise of the right of access to legal advice may be delayed only in accordance with Annex B to this code. Whenever legal advice is requested (and unless Annex B applies) the custody officer must act without delay to secure the provision of such advice to the person concerned. If, on being informed or reminded of the right to legal advice, the person declines to speak to a solicitor in person, the officer shall point out that the right to free legal advice includes the right to speak with a solicitor on the telephone and ask him if he wishes to do so. If the suspect continues to waive his right to legal advice the officer should ask him the reasons for doing so and any reasons shall be recorded on the custody record. ... Reminders of the right to free legal advice must be given in accordance with paragraphs 3.5, 11.2, 15.3, 16.4 and 16.5 of this code and paragraphs 2.15(ii) and 5.2 of Code D.

6.6 A person who wants legal advice may not be interviewed or continue to be interviewed until he has received it unless –

(a) annex B applies; or

(b) an officer of the rank of superintendent or above has reasonable grounds for believing that –

(i) delay will involve an immediate risk of harm to persons or serious loss of, or damage to, property; or

(ii) where a solicitor, including a duty solicitor, has been contacted and has agreed to attend, awaiting his arrival would cause unreasonable delay to the process of investigation; or

(c) The solicitor nominated by the person, or selected by him from a list –

(i) cannot be contacted; or

(ii) has previously indicated that he does not wish to be contacted; or

(iii) having been contacted, has declined to attend;

and the person has been advised of the Duty Solicitor Scheme (where one is in operation) but has declined to ask for the duty solicitor, or the duty solicitor is unavailable. (In these circumstances the interview may be started or continued without further delay provided that an officer of

---

70 Subs (8A) (like s56(5A)) was added by the Drug Trafficking Offences Act 1986, s32 and was amended by the Criminal Justice Act 1988, s99.

the rank of Inspector or above has given agreement for the interview to proceed in those circumstances – see note 6B.)

(d) The person who wanted legal advice changes his mind.

In these circumstances the interview may be started or continued without further delay provided that the person has given his agreement in writing or on tape to being interviewed without receiving legal advice and that an officer of the rank of Inspector or above, having inquired into the suspect's reasons for his change of mind, has given agreement for the interview to proceed in those circumstances. The name of the authorising officer and the reason for the suspect's change of mind should be recorded and repeated on tape at the beginning or re-commencement of interview [see note 61].

6.9   The solicitor may only be required to leave the interview if his conduct is such that the investigating officer is unable properly to put questions to the suspect [see notes 6D and 6E].

6.12 In codes of practice issued under the Police and Criminal Evidence Act 1984, 'solicitor' means a solicitor who holds a current practising certificate, or a trainee solicitor, or an accredited representative. ... If a solicitor wishes to send a non-accredited or probationary representative to provide advice on his behalf, then that person shall be admitted to the police station for this purpose unless an officer of the rank of inspector or above considers that such a visit will hinder the investigation of crime and directs otherwise. ... Once admitted to the police station, the provisions of paras 6.6 to 6.10 apply.

Samuel [1988] 2 All ER 135; 2 WLR 920, 930, 931, 932 CA

The leading case determining the scope of the s58 exceptions is *Samuel*. The appellant was arrested on suspicion of armed robbery and, after questioning at the police station, asked to see a solicitor. The request was refused, apparently on the grounds that other suspects might be warned[71] and that recovery of the outstanding stolen money might thereby be hindered;[72] the appellant subsequently confessed to the robbery and was later convicted. On appeal the defence argued that the refusal of access was not justifiable under s58(8) and that therefore the confession obtained should not have been admitted into evidence as it had been obtained due to impropriety.

Hodgson J: ... The right denied is a right 'to consult a solicitor privately'. The person denied that right is in police detention. In practice, the only way that the person can make any of [s 58(8)] (a) to (c) happen is by some communication from him to the solicitor. For (a) to (c) to be made to happen the solicitor must do something. If he does something knowing that it will result in anything in (a) to (c) happening he will, almost inevitably, commit a serious criminal offence. Therefore, inadvertent or unwitting conduct apart, the officer must believe that a solicitor will, if allowed to consult with a detained person, thereafter commit a criminal offence. Solicitors are officers of the court. We think that the number of times that a police officer could genuinely be in that state of belief will be rare. ...

By 4.45pm on 7 August [when the solicitor was refused access] the police knew the identity of the solicitor, a highly respected and very experienced professional lawyer, unlikely to be hoodwinked by a 24-year-old. In addition the appellant's mother had been told of his arrest that morning. Further, the earliest time at

---

71   See s58(8)(b).
72   See s58(8)(c).

which Mr Warner would be able to do something inadvertent would be well after 6pm that evening, allowing time for his getting to the police station, seeing his client and being present at the interview which the police clearly wanted to have that evening. By 6pm there would only remain some eight hours during which access to a solicitor could be lawfully delayed (s 58(5)), so that, if s 58(8)(a)–(c) were to be brought about by inadvertence there was very little time left for it to happen. Mr Jones was unable to point to any inadvertent conduct by Mr Warner which could have led to any of the results in (a)–(c) save his transmission to someone of some sort of coded message. We do not know who made the decision at 4.45pm but we find it impossible to believe that whoever did had reasonable grounds for the belief required by s58(8).

The more sinister side to the decision is, of course, this. The police had, over a period exceeding 24 hours, interviewed this young man four times without obtaining any confession from him in respect of the robbery. Time was running out for them. It was a Thursday evening. Thirty-six hours from the relevant time would expire in the early hours of the morning; then access to a solicitor would have to be permitted. On the following day the appellant would have to be taken before the magistrates' court: s46. As he had already been interviewed four times and been in police custody for over 24 hours, the expectation would be that a solicitor might well consider that, at least for that evening, enough was enough and that he ought to advise his client not to answer further questions. There were, therefore, very few hours left for the police to interview the appellant without his having legal advice. And, as events showed, that was something the police very much wanted to do; this one knows because, within 37 minutes, he was in fact interviewed. All previous interviews had been conducted by a detective sergeant with a detective constable as note taker. The interview at 5.20pm was conducted by a detective inspector, the sergeant and detective being present, so that the appellant now faced a different questioner and a total of three police officers. At that interview he made the confession to the robbery. Regrettably we have come to the conclusion that whoever made the decision to refuse Mr Warner access at 4.45pm was very probably motivated by a desire to have one last chance of interviewing the appellant in the absence of a solicitor.

... we find that the refusal of access to Mr Warner at 4.45pm was unjustified. That being so the interview, without a solicitor being present, should not have taken place: Code 6.3.

Notes

1   The consequence of finding that s58 had been breached is considered below.

2   Apart from the provisions of Code C, para 6.6, there are a number of less formal means of evading access to legal advice such as subverting the notification of advice and encouraging the suspect to defer it.[73]

The right to silence

The large body of writing on the right to silence generally came down on the side of its retention.[74] The 1993 Royal Commission on Criminal Justice favoured

---

73   See A Sanders, 'Access to Legal Advice and Police Malpractice' (1990) Crim LR 494.

74   See Philips Commission Report (1981), Cmnd 8092; Report of the Home Office Working Group on the Right to Silence 1989 (in favour of modification of the right). For criticism of the report see Zuckermann (1989) Crim LR 855. For review of the debate see S Greer (1990) 53 MLR 709; J Coldrey (1991) 20 Anglo-Am LR 27. In favour of modification of the right see G Williams (1987) 137 NLJ 1107; *Police Review*, editorial, 29 April 1988.

retention[75] but considered that, once the prosecution case was fully disclosed, defendants should be required to offer an answer to the charges made against them at the risk of adverse comment at trial on any new defence they then disclose. This proposal would have dealt with the 'ambush defence', often put forward as one of the reasons for abolishing the right to silence, while leaving the right itself intact in the investigation as a safeguard against undue police pressure to speak. However, despite the proposals of the Royal Commission, the right to silence was curtailed under the Criminal Justice and Public Order Act 1994 and this is reflected in the new cautioning provisions under the 1995 revision of Code C.

Criminal Justice and Public Order Act 1994

Effect of accused's failure to mention facts when questioned or charged

34.–(1) Where, in any proceedings against a person for an offence, evidence is given that the accused –

    (a) at any time before he was charged with the offence, on being questioned under caution by a constable trying to discover whether or by whom the offence had been committed, failed to mention any fact relied on in his defence in those proceedings; or

    (b) on being charged with the offence or officially informed that he might be prosecuted for it, failed to mention any such fact,

being a fact which in the circumstances existing at the time the accused could reasonably have been expected to mention when so questioned, charged or informed, as the case may be, subsection (2) below applies.

(2) Where this subsection applies –

    (a) a magistrates' court, in deciding whether to grant an application for dismissal made by the accused under s6 of the Magistrates' Courts Act 1980 (application for dismissal of charge in course of proceedings with a view to transfer for trial);

    (b) a judge, in deciding whether to grant an application made by the accused under –

        (i) section 6 of the Criminal Justice Act 1987 (application for dismissal of charge of serious fraud in respect of which notice of transfer has been given under section 4 of that Act); or

        (ii) paragraph 5 of Schedule 6 to the Criminal Justice Act 1991 (application for dismissal of charge of violent or sexual offence involving child in respect of which notice of transfer has been given under section 53 of that Act);

    (c) the court, in determining whether there is a case to answer; and

    (d) the court or jury, in determining whether the accused is guilty of the offence charged,

may draw such inferences from the failure as appear proper.

36.–(1) Where –

    (a) a person is arrested by a constable and there is –

        (i) on his person; or

        (ii) in or on his clothing or footwear; or

---

75   Cm 2263, Proposal 82.

(iii)otherwise in his possession; or

(iv)in any place in which he is at the time of his arrest, any object, substance or mark, or there is any mark on any such object; and

(b) that or another constable investigating the case reasonably believes that the presence of the object, substance or mark may be attributable to the participation of the person arrested in the commission of an offence specified by the constable, and

(c) the constable informs the person arrested that he so believes, and requests him to account for the presence of the object, substance or mark; and

(d) the person fails or refuses to do so, then if, in any proceedings against the person for the offence so specified, evidence of those matters is given, subsection (2) below applies.

[Subsection (2) of ss36 and 37 echoes s34(2).]

Effect of accused's failure or refusal to account for presence at a particular place

37.–(1) Where –

(a) a person arrested by a constable was found by him at a place at or about the time the offence for which he was arrested is alleged to have been committed; and

(b) that or another constable investigating the offence reasonably believes that the presence of the person at that place and at that time may be attributable to his participation in the commission of the offence; and

(c) the constable informs the person that he so believes, and requests him to account for that presence; and

(d) the person fails or refuses to do so. then if, in any proceedings against the person for the offence, evidence of those matters is given, subsection (2) below applies.

Code C

(a) When a caution must be given

10.1 A person whom there are grounds to suspect of an offence must be cautioned before any questions about it (or further questions if it is his answers to previous questions that provide grounds for suspicion) are put to him regarding his involvement or suspected involvement in that offence if his answers or his silence (ie failure to answer a question or failure to answer satisfactorily) may be given in evidence to a court in a prosecution. He therefore need not be cautioned if questions are put for other purposes, for example, solely to establish his identity or his ownership of any vehicle or to obtain information in accordance with any relevant statutory requirement (see para 10.5C) or ... the proper and effective conduct of a search ... or to seek verification of a written record in accordance with paragraph 11.13.

10.2 Whenever a person who is not under arrest is initially cautioned before or during an interview he must at the same time be told that he is not under arrest and is not obliged to remain with the officer (see para 3.15).

(b) Action: general

10.4 The caution shall be in the following terms –

'You do not have to say anything. But it may harm your defence if you do not mention when questioned something which you later rely on in court. Anything you do say may be given in evidence.'

Minor deviations do not constitute a breach of this requirement provided that the sense of the caution is preserved [see note 10C].

10.5 When there is a break in questioning under caution the interviewing officer must ensure that the person being questioned is aware that he remains under caution. If there is any doubt the caution should be given again in full when the interview resumes [see note 10A].

Special cautions under ss36 and 37 of the Criminal Justice and Public Order Act 1994

10.5A When a suspect who is interviewed after arrest fails or refuses to answer certain questions after due warning, a court or jury may draw such inferences as appear proper under ss36 and 37 of the Criminal Justice and Public Order Act 1994. This applies when –

(a) a suspect is arrested by a constable and there is found on his person or in or on his clothing or footwear or otherwise in his possession or in the place where he was arrested, any objects, marks or substances, or marks on such objects, and the person fails or refuses to account for the objects, marks or substances found; or

(b) an arrested person was found by a constable at a place at or about the time the offence for which he was arrested, is alleged to have been committed, and the person or fails or refuses to account for his presence at that place.

10.5B For an inference to be drawn from a suspect's failure or refusal to answer a question about one of these matters, or to answer it satisfactorily, the interviewing officer must first tell him in ordinary language –

(a) what offence he is investigating;

(b) what fact he is asking the suspect to account for;

(c) that he believes this fact may be due to the suspect's taking part in the commission of the offence in question;

(d) that a court may draw a proper inference if he fails or refuses to account for the fact about which he is being questioned.

(e) that a record is being made of the interview and that it may be given in evidence if he is brought to trial.

(c) Juveniles, the mentally disordered and the mentally handicapped

10.6 If a juvenile or a person who is mentally disordered or mentally handicapped is cautioned in the absence of the appropriate adult, the caution must be repeated in the adult's presence.

(d) Documentation

10.7 A record shall be made when a caution is given under this section, either in the officer's pocketbook or in the interview record as appropriate.

Notes

1 Curtailment of the right to silence had already been foreshadowed. It was abolished in Northern Ireland in 1988 and curtailed in Britain in cases involving serious fraud.

2 In *Director of the Serious Fraud Office, ex p Smith* (1992)[76] after Mr Smith had been charged with an offence under s458 of the Companies Act 1985, the Director of the Serious Fraud Office (SFO) decided to investigate him and

---

76 3 WLR 66; see also *AT and T Istel Ltd v Tulley* [1992] 3 All ER 523, HL.

served a notice on him under the Criminal Justice Act 1987 s2(2) requiring him to attend for an interview. He was informed that he would not be cautioned but would be obliged to answer questions truthfully, and that his replies could be used in evidence against him if anything he said at his trial was inconsistent with them. He applied for judicial review. The question to be determined was whether the 1987 Act had effected an erosion of the right to silence which had been preserved by Code C made under PACE 1984. If a person fell within s2(2) of the 1987 Act would he lose the protection conferred by the 1984 Act? The answer given by the House of Lords was that the 1987 Act could override the right to silence as enshrined in the caution given on arrest and could also do so once the suspect had been charged. The House of Lords found that the powers under s2 operated even after charge on the basis that Parliament had clearly intended to institute an inquisitorial regime. Thus even though the prosecutor must have thought that there might well already be sufficient evidence to convict, questioning could continue.

3   *Saunders* (1995)[77] also concerned the existence of the right to silence in serious fraud investigations. Inspectors of the Department of Trade and Industry interviewed Saunders, regarding allegations of fraud. They acted under s437 of the Companies Act 1985 which provides for a sanction against the person being investigated if he refuses to answer questions. Thus Saunders lost his privilege against self-incrimination, which he argued was unfair and amounted to an abuse of process. He further argued that the transcript of answers given should have been found inadmissible under s78 of the Police and Criminal Evidence Act 1984. It was found that Parliament had eroded the privilege against self-incrimination in relation to DTI interviews and therefore that ground alone could not provide a basis for finding that an abuse of process had occurred. In relation to exclusion of the interviews the House of Lords considered the relevance of Art 6 of the European Convention in Human Rights which provides *inter alia* that the presumption of innocence must not be eroded. However, domestic law was unambiguous and therefore must be applied regardless of Art 6. However, in exercising discretion under s78 the judge could take into account the question whether the statutory regime in question had created unfairness. In the particular circumstances it was found that admission of the evidence did not render the trial unfair. The appeal was therefore dismissed. This decision will clearly have no impact in terms of curbing the erosion of the privilege against self-incrimination which has been brought about under the particular statutory regime in question.

4   The value of the right to silence and the likely impact of the new provisions are discussed below.

S Greer, 'The Right to Silence: A Review of the Current Debate' (1990) 53 *Modern Law Review* 709, 726–8

Innocent suspects in England and Wales must currently balance two risks which police interviews pose for any subsequent trial: the risk that if they stay silent

---

77   *The Times*, 28 November.

this may be taken as an indication of guilt even if no adverse comment is made about it in court, and the risk that if they talk they may inadvertently make a remark which is misinterpreted at the trial, thus damaging their defence. The abolition of the right to silence would tend to oblige them to take the latter option even if there were good reasons for staying silent. One of the key considerations in balancing these risks is that the suspect is likely to be at least partially ignorant of the police case against him and is thus open to manipulation. The Criminal Law Committee of the Law Society notes in its response to the report of the Home Office Working Group: 'Practitioners have alerted the committee to many incidents in which clients would have been misled if they had taken what was said to them during the interview by the police at face value' [Law Society, January 1990, para 6]. If they would have been misled, they might have made responses which would have unfairly damaged them at trial. This is not necessarily to imply bad faith on the part of the police, although the Guildford Four, Birmingham Six and West Midlands Serious Crime Squad scandals show that it can clearly no longer be ruled out. Police officers acting in good faith are likely to see themselves as being capable of skilfully manoeuvring a guilty offender into giving the game away. The problem is that police assumptions about the guilt or innocence of any given suspect can be fundamentally mistaken. Instead of winkling a crook out of his shell they may instead inadvertently trick an innocent suspect into compromising his position by making remarks which are open to misrepresentation at trial. It is now widely recognised that under pressure people are capable of confessing to offences which it would have been impossible for them to have committed.

The right to silence also provides an incentive for other evidence to be sought by the police and subsequently adduced at trial. Its removal might create a risk of a decline in policing standards. It also ensures that anything which the suspect does say will have added credibility because it was offered without fear of the consequences of staying silent.

Innocent reasons for silence

There are a number of legitimate reasons why an entirely innocent suspect may be well advised not to answer at least certain police questions. They may be in an emotional and highly suggestible state of mind. They may feel guilty when in fact they have not committed an offence. They may be ignorant of some vital fact which explains away otherwise suspicious circumstances. They may be confused and liable to make mistakes which could be interpreted as deliberate lies at the trial. They may forget important details which it would have been to their advantage to have remembered. They may use loose expressions unaware of the possible adverse interpretations which could be placed upon them at trial. They may not have heard or understood what the police interviewer said. They may be concerned that an early disclosure of their defence could be to their disadvantage. They may have already given an explanation in the police car on the way to the police station which was not believed and thus prove reluctant to repeat it in the formal interview. Their silence may be an attempt to protect others or a reluctance to admit to having done something discreditable but not illegal. Some suspects may not want to be tricked into giving information about others because this could result in being stigmatised as an informer with all the dangers which this label carries, particularly in Northern Ireland.

Of particular importance in determining whether or not a suspect stays silent in police custody is his/her general attitude towards the police. According to Dixon: 'Silent suspects are more likely to hold anti-police attitudes. Exercises of the right to silence may therefore be an indicator of public confidence in the police at least in particular police districts. This may or may not be related to the suspect's guilt. The abolition of the right to silence would thus tend to make hostility to the police an offence. The polls indicate that public confidence in the police has been severely damaged by the Guildford Four scandal. To make fear of, or hostility to, the police a ground for conviction is likely to diminish public confidence further and increase the tendency for policing to be conducted by coercion rather than by consent. The police are likely to find the suspect who is uncooperative for this reason particularly irksome since non-cooperation both signifies a refusal to acknowledge police authority and obstructs the eliciting of confessions. Confessions are of importance to the police irrespective of their value as items of evidence in any subsequent trial for two principal reasons: they can act as bargaining counters in the negotiation of guilty pleas; and they open up opportunities for the police to 'solve' other crimes and thus improve the clear-up rate.

The construction of offences in police interviews

A final reason why an innocent suspect may want to remain silent in police interviews deserves separate consideration. Criminal offences are not only capable of being discovered in police interviews. The interview process can itself create them. A crude conception of guilt or innocence, according to which the suspect either 'did it' or 'didn't do it' has tended to underpin the debate about the right to silence. However, legal guilt or innocence can be considerably more complicated. Some offences are defined in ways which separate them by a hairsbreadth from innocent conduct. Police interviews can, therefore, construct offences out of otherwise innocent behaviour. The abolition of the right to silence is likely to increase the opportunities for this to occur.

Ian Dennis, 'The Evidence Provisions' Criminal Law Review (1995) 4, 11–12, 15–16

One of the conditions of use specified by [s 34(1)] is that the fact in question was one which in the circumstances existing at the time *the accused* could reasonably have been expected to mention (my emphasis). This reference suggests a test which is at least partly subjective. It seems to presuppose some inquiry not only into that person's knowledge, but also into his understanding, of the offence which the constable is investigating and of the facts which might be relevant in determining liability for the offence. It would hardly be reasonable to expect a person to mention facts which he did not know or perceive to be relevant. In many cases of course it will be obviously reasonable to expect a person to mention facts such as, for example, that his use of force on another was in self-defence or that he had the consent of the owner to take property. Nevertheless the point about knowledge and understanding may be important, particularly in cases where the accused is of below average intelligence or even mentally handicapped. In such cases it may not be reasonable to expect particular facts to be mentioned unless the accused has actually received legal advice in connection with the offence.

If the conditions of use are satisfied, so that subsection (2) applies, the court or jury may draw such inferences as appear proper from the failure to mention facts relied on subsequently. However, the Act gives no further guidance on what inferences might be proper. It is likely that the courts will say, as they have done in relation to legislation restricting the right to silence at trial [*Haw Tua Tau v Public Prosecutor* [1981] 3 All ER 14 at 21; *Murray v DPP* (1993) 97 Cr App R 151 at 160], that what inferences are proper depends upon the circumstances of the particular case, and is a question to be decided by applying ordinary common sense. The most obvious inference is that the previously undisclosed fact is untrue, a conclusion based on an argument that the accused did not mention the fact to the police because he knew that they would expose its falsity. Whether this inference can form part of a chain of reasoning leading to a conclusion that the accused is guilty rather depends on the issue in the case, the nature of the fact in question and the state of the other evidence. If the 'fact' is in the nature of a 'confession and avoidance' defence, whereby the accused admits the *actus reus* and *mens rea* of the offence but sets up some independent ground of justification or excuse such as self-defence, then the rejection of that defence is almost certain to lead to the conclusion that the accused has no defence at all and is guilty. On the other hand, if the issue is identity, and the other evidence against the accused is circumstantial, the rejection of one fact offered as an innocent explanation of one piece of circumstantial evidence may not necessarily yield a further inference of guilt. This suggests that it would be wrong for a court to conclude simply because an accused fails to mention a fact relied on subsequently that he is therefore guilty. Accordingly trial judges will have to direct juries carefully on the inferences which may fairly be drawn from such failures. I predict that at least one trip to the House of Lords will be necessary to clarify this point.

Notes

1   It might appear that the right to silence would have a significant impact on the conduct of the interview and would ensure that a suspect had a bulwark against giving in to pressure to speak. In fact few suspects refuse to answer questions[78] and silence is not routinely advised by solicitors.

2   Greer suggests that the main reason for retaining the right to silence is that the suspect may be under stress and unable to assess the situation clearly; he or she may have a number of reasons for reluctance to speak including fear of incriminating another and uncertainty as to the significance of various facts. In discussing curtailment of the right to silence a number of commentators have made similar points.[79]

3   The courts are at present coming to grips with ss34, 36 and 37 of the 1994 Act. The decision in *Cowan* (1995)[80] on s35 suggests that, although these provisions are at variance with established principle, the courts will not be prepared to marginalise and reduce them.

4   It is possible that curtailment of the right to silence under ss34, 36 and 37 of the 1994 Act may breach Art 6 of the ECHR on the basis that it infringes the presumption of innocence under Art 6(2) and/or on the basis that it infringes the right to freedom from self-incrimination which the Court has found to be covered by the right to a fair hearing under Art 6(1) (*Funke v France* (1993)).[81] In *Murray (John) v UK* (1996)[82] however, the Commission did not find that Art 6(1) had been breached where inferences had been drawn at trial from the applicant's refusal to give evidence. The Court found no breach of Art 6 in the particular circumstances of the case, taking into account the fact that 'the right to silence' could not be treated as absolute,

---

78   See R Leng, *The Right to Silence in Police Interrogation*, Home Office Research Study No 10 1993. Only 4.5% of suspects exercised their right to silence.

79   See Zander, *The Police and Criminal Evidence Act 1984* (1995), pp303–23; H Fenwick (1995) Crim LR 132–6; D Jackson (1995) Crim LR 587–601; R Pattenden (1995) Crim LR 602–611; D Morgan and G Stephenson, *Suspicion and Silence* (1994).

80   4 All ER 939.

81   16 EHRR 297.

82   *The Times*, 9 February 1996; for comment see R Munday (1996) Crim LR 370.

the degree of compulsion exerted on the applicant and the weight of the evidence against him. In *Saunders v UK* (1994)[83] the Commission found that the applicant's right to freedom from self-incrimination had been infringed in that he had been forced to answer questions put to him by inspectors investigating a company take over or risk the imposition of a criminal sanction. The ruling of the Court is awaited. If it finds that the regime in question is in breach of Art 6, this might appear to call into question the provisions under the Criminal Justice and Public Order Act 1994. However, it is probable, taking the *Murray* decision into account, that the Government response to any such ruling would relate only to the powers of DTI inspectors and would leave the general regime curtailing the right to silence intact.

Questions

1   Do ss36 and 37 of the Criminal Justice and Public Order Act 1994 apply only to suspects being interviewed within the police station?

2   Are there grounds for suggesting that s34 of the 1994 Act will largely be confined, in its application, to questioning in the police station?

3   Should ss34, 36 and 37 have been confined clearly to formal interviews within the police station? Why is this a matter of significance?

4   Are there grounds for fearing that curtailment of the right to silence may lead to further miscarriages of justice?

REDRESS FOR POLICE IMPROPRIETY

Introduction[84]

This Chapter has been concerned so far with the question of the balance to be struck between the exercise of powers by the police in conducting an investigation on the one hand, and safeguards for the suspect against abuse of power on the other. As we have seen, PACE sets out to maintain this balance by declaring certain standards for the conduct of criminal investigations. However, it may be that an investigation does not, at certain points, reach those standards. In such circumstances certain means of redress are available, and these are considered below.

Exclusion of evidence

Under the common law prior to the passing of the Police and Criminal Evidence Act 1984, illegally obtained evidence other than 'involuntary' confessions was admissible in a criminal trial. Involuntary confessions were inadmissible on the ground that, if a defendant was in some way induced to confess during a police interrogation, his confession might be unreliable. A confession would be involuntary if it was obtained by oppression[85] or 'by fear of prejudice or hope of

---

83   No 19187/91 Com Rep, paras 69–75.

84   See generally D Birch [1989] Crim LR 95; D Feldman [1990] Crim LR 452.

85   *Prager* [1972] 1 All ER 1114.

advantage exercised or held out by a person in authority'.[86] According to the Court of Appeal in *Isequilla* (1975)[87] 'oppression' denoted some impropriety on the part of the police, but the House of Lords in *DPP v Ping Lin* (1976)[88] doubted whether such impropriety was necessary if the real issue was the reliability of the confession. Uncertainty as to the need for impropriety on the part of the police, and as to the kind of impropriety which could amount to oppression, may have contributed to allowing miscarriages of justice such as the *Confait* case[89] to occur. In that case, three young boys, one of them mentally handicapped, confessed to involvement in a murder they could not have committed after they had been denied both legal advice and the presence of an adult during the police interrogation. The confessions were admitted in evidence and led to the conviction of all three. They were finally exonerated seven years later.

PACE provides four separate tests which can be applied to a confession to determine whether it is admissible in evidence.[90] In theory, all four tests could be applied to a particular confession, although in practice it may not be necessary to consider all of them. They are the 'oppression' test (s 76(2)(a)), the 'reliability' test (s 76(2)(b)) and the 'fairness' test (s 78). PACE also preserves the residual common law discretion to exclude evidence, under s82(3). The scheme in respect of non-confession evidence is less complex: only ss78 and 82(3) need be considered. Thus PACE preserves the common law distinction between confessions and other evidence. Physical evidence is likely to be reliable (unless it has been 'planted' on the detainee) while a confession may not be. This is not, however, true of all non-confession evidence, including identification evidence or silences, which nevertheless can be considered only under ss78 and 82(3). Physical evidence which is discovered as a result of an inadmissible confession will be admissible under s76(4)(a).

Police and Criminal Evidence Act 1984

Confessions

76.–(1) In any proceedings a confession made by an accused person may be given in evidence against him in so far as it is relevant to any matter in issue in the proceedings and is not excluded by the court in pursuance of this section.

(2) If, in any proceedings where the prosecution proposes to give in evidence a confession made by an accused person, it is represented to the court that the confession was or may have been obtained –

(a) by oppression of the person who made it; or

(b) in consequence of anything said or done which was likely, in the circumstances existing at the time, to render unreliable any confession which might be made by him in consequence thereof,

the court shall not allow the confession to be given in evidence against him except in so far as the prosecution proves to the court beyond reasonable

---

86 *Ibrahim* [1914] AC 599.

87 1 All ER 77.

88 AC 574.

89 See Christopher Price, *The Confait Confessions* (1976).

90 See D Birch, 'Confessions and Confusions under the 1984 Act' [1989] Crim LR 95.

doubt that the confession (notwithstanding that it may be true) was not obtained as aforesaid.

(3) In any proceedings where the prosecution proposes to give in evidence a confession made by an accused person, the court may of its own motion require the prosecution, as a condition of allowing it to do so, to prove that the confession was not obtained as mentioned in subsection (2) above.

(4) The fact that a confession is wholly or partly excluded in pursuance of this section shall not affect the admissibility in evidence –

(a) of any facts discovered as a result of the confession; or

(b) where the confession is relevant as showing that the accused speaks, writes or expresses himself in a particular way, of so much of the confession as is necessary to show that he does so.

(8) In this section 'oppression' includes torture, inhuman or degrading treatment, and the use or threat of violence (whether or not amounting to torture).

Exclusion of unfair evidence

78.–(1) In any proceedings the court may refuse to allow evidence on which the prosecution proposes to rely to be given if it appears to the court that, having regard to all the circumstances, including the circumstances in which the evidence was obtained, the admission of the evidence would have such an adverse effect on the fairness of the proceedings that the court ought not to admit it.

(2) Nothing in this section shall prejudice any Rule of Law requiring a court to exclude evidence.

Fulling [1987] QB 426; [1987] 2 All ER 65, 67, 69, 70, CA

Lord Lane CJ [at first instance the judge found]: 'Bearing in mind that whatever happens to a person who is arrested and questioned is by its very nature oppressive, I am quite satisfied that in s76(2)(a) of the Police and Criminal Evidence Act 984, the word oppression means something above and beyond that which is inherently oppressive in police custody and must import some impropriety, some oppression actively applied in an improper manner by the police. I do not find that what was done in this case can be so defined and, in those circumstances, I am satisfied that oppression cannot be made out on the evidence. ... In those circumstances, her confession (if that is the proper term for it) and the interview in which she confessed, I rule to be admissible.'

'... oppression' in s76(2)(a) should be given its ordinary dictionary meaning. The *Oxford English Dictionary* as its third definition of the word runs as follows: 'Exercise of authority or power in a burdensome, harsh, or wrongful manner; unjust or cruel treatment of subjects, inferiors, etc; the imposition of unreasonable or unjust burdens.' One of the quotations given under that paragraph runs as follows: 'There is not a word in our language which expresses more detestable wickedness than oppression.'

We find it hard to envisage any circumstances in which such oppression would not entail some impropriety on the part of the interrogator. We do not think that the judge was wrong in using that test. What however is abundantly clear is that a confession may be invalidated under s76(2)(b) where there is no suspicion of impropriety

Appeal dismissed.

Beales [1991] Crim LR 118

His Honour Judge Hyam: It was submitted [by the defence, in respect of D's admissions] that the Crown were unable to discharge the burden under s76. The following features were relied upon:

(i)   the officer falsely told B in forceful terms on more than one occasion that in addition to the mother, the child himself was saying that B had swung him by the ankles;

(ii)   the officer told B that a yellow bruise on the child's left shoulder was caused 'last night' although the officer had no information to that effect (a subsequent medical examination determined that the bruise was old);

(iv) in general terms, the demeanour of the officer and the whole tenor of the interview was to compel B to make a confession by distorting the state of the evidence against him.

It was submitted that such conduct was oppressive within the definition approved by the Lord Chief Justice in *Fulling* (1987) 85 Cr App R 136 (CA) and further that the conduct of the officer was analogous to that which led to the exclusion of the confession in *Mason* [1987] 3 All ER 481 (CA).

Held, the interview would be excluded on the grounds that it 'stepped into the realm' of oppression and albeit that the oppression was not so serious as was found in *Mason*, the officer here had deliberately misstated the evidence in order to bring pressure to bear on B.

However, even if the conduct was not oppressive, the interview would also be excluded on the grounds that there was 'no doubt whatsoever' that the confession was unreliable having been obtained during the course of an interview in which B was 'hectored and bullied from first to last'.

Keenan [1990] 2 QB 54

Hodgson J: ... We think that in cases where there have been 'significant and substantial' breaches of the 'verballing' provisions of the code, the evidence so obtained will frequently be excluded. We do not think that any injustice will be caused by this. It is clear that not every breach or combination of breaches of the code will justify the exclusion of interview evidence under s76 or s78: see *Hallett* (7 March 1989, unreported). They must be significant and substantial. If this were not the case, the courts would be undertaking a task which is no part of their duty; as Lord Lane CJ said in *Delaney* (at 341): 'It is no part of the duty of the court to rule a statement inadmissible simply in order to punish the police for failure to observe the codes of practice.'

But if the breaches are 'significant and substantial' we think it makes good sense to exclude them. At the *voir dire* stage a judge can foresee that a number of different situations may arise which the 'verballing' provisions are specifically designed to prevent. If the rest of the evidence is strong, then it may make no difference to the eventual result if he excludes the evidence. In cases when the rest of the evidence is weak or non-existent, that is just the situation where the temptation to do what the provisions are aimed to prevent is greatest, and the protection of the rules most needed.

As we have said before, this case was tried at a time when Bench and Bar were struggling to understand and properly apply new and complicated provisions, and it is entirely understandable if the assistant recorder got it wrong. We think he did. He was wrong to assume that any unfairness could be cured by the appellant going into the witness box. If the appellant intended not to give evidence if the officers' evidence was excluded, then admitting it unfairly robbed him of his right to remain silent: see *Hamand* (1985) 82 Cr App R 65. If the defence case was to be (as it turned out to be in fact) that the evidence was concocted, then it was unfair to admit it, because by doing so the appellant was not only forced to give evidence but also, by attacking the police, to put his character in issue. If the defence was to be that the interview was inaccurately recorded, then it was plainly unfair to admit it, because it placed the appellant at a substantial disadvantage in that he had been given no contemporaneous opportunity to correct any inaccuracies, nor would he have his own contemporaneous note of what he had said.

Without the evidence of the interview the case against the appellant would have been very much weaker, and in those circumstances we are of the opinion that no question of applying the proviso can arise. Accordingly the conviction must be quashed.

Samuel [1988] 2 WLR 920, 933, 934

The Court of Appeal found that the appellant had been unlawfully denied access to a solicitor and that, if the right to such access is denied, this can lead to the exclusion of evidence obtained at unlawful interviews conducted after the denial by the exercise of the judge's power under s78(1).

Hodgson J: [The solicitor in question] gave evidence. He said it was not his policy always to advise a client not to answer questions put to him by the police. In his view, in many cases, it was of advantage to someone in detention to answer proper questions put to him. However on this occasion, knowing that his client had already been interviewed on four occasions and at each had strenuously denied complicity in the robbery and had already been charged with two serious offences, he would probably, after consultation, have advised his client, for the time being at any rate, to refuse to answer further questioning. The probable result of allowing the appellant to exercise his right would therefore, in all probability, have been that, had a further interview taken place (and we think it improbable that the police would, in those circumstances, have thought it worth their while to interview him further) no incriminating replies would have been given.

It is undesirable to attempt any general guidance as to the way in which a judge's discretion under s78 or his inherent powers should be exercised. Circumstances vary infinitely. Mr Jones has made the extreme submission that, in the absence of impropriety, the discretion should never be exercised to exclude admissible evidence. We have no hesitation in rejecting that submission, although the propriety or otherwise of the way in which the evidence was obtained is something which a court is, in terms, enjoined by the section to take into account.

The Court of Appeal is always reluctant to interfere with the exercise of a judge's discretion, but the position is different where there was no discretion to exercise on the judge's ruling and all the court has is an indication of how the judge would have exercised it. This is particularly so in this case where, on the s58(8) point, the judge failed properly to address his mind to the point in time which was most material and did not in terms give consideration to what his decision would have been had he ruled in favour of the defence on this more fundamental issue before him.

In this case this appellant was denied improperly one of the most important and fundamental rights of a citizen. The trial judge fell into error in not so holding. If he had arrived at correct decisions on the two points argued before him he might well have concluded that the refusal of access and consequent unlawful interview compelled him to find that the admission of evidence as to the final interview would have 'such an adverse effect on the fairness of the proceedings' that he ought not to admit it. Such a decision would, of course, have very significantly weakened the prosecution case (the failure to charge earlier ineluctably shows this). In those circumstances this court feels that it has no alternative but to quash the appellant's conviction on count 1 in the indictment, the charge of robbery.

Thomas (1990) Criminal Law Review LR 269

Parker LJ and Tudor Evans J: T was stopped by police officers who suspected that he had consumed alcohol. He was told that he would be required to take a breath test and was asked to wait for the testing kit to be brought. He gave no indication whether he was willing to take the breath test. A police sergeant arrived and arrested T, having misunderstood the situation (as the justices found). He was taken to the police station where he refused to give specimens of breath. He was charged with failing, without reasonable excuse, to provide a specimen of breath (at the roadside) contrary to s7(4) of the Road Traffic Act 1972, as substituted and with failing, without reasonable excuse, to provide two specimens of breath (at the police station) contrary to s8(7) of the 1972 Act as substituted.

Held, dismissing the appeal, ... It followed [from] ... the express finding that there was no police misconduct, that there was no discretion (under s78 of the Police and Criminal Evidence Act 1984) to exclude evidence of the procedure at the police station; such discretion existed only where was *mala fides*, and that had been negatived by the justices' finding *(Sang* [1980] AC 402; *Matto v DPP* (1987) RTR 337 distinguished). The alternative submission that the unlawful arrest vitiated the subsequent procedure was also clearly wrong: *Fox v Chief Constable of Gwent* [1986] AC 281, 291 *per* Lord Fraser of Tullybelton. The justices were entitled to find that:

(i)   notwithstanding the dismissal of the s7(4) charge T had no reasonable excuse for refusing to provide a specimen at the police station; and

(ii) there was no *mala fides* although they had rejected the sergeant's evidence and found that he had arrested T without either administering a roadside test or receiving a refusal to take it.

Notes

1   The principle underlying the oppression test under s76(2)(a), which derives from the rule as it was at common law, is that threats of violence or other oppressive behaviour are so abhorrent that no further question as to the reliability of a confession obtained by such methods should be asked. This rule appears to have the dual function of removing any incentive to the police to behave improperly and of protecting the detainee from the consequences of impropriety if it has occurred. Under this head, once the defence has advanced a reasonable argument (*Liverpool Juvenile Court, ex p R* (1987))[91] that the confession was obtained by oppression, it will not be admitted in evidence unless the prosecution can prove that it was not so obtained. The reliability of a confession obtained by oppression is irrelevant; it matters not whether the effect of the oppression is to frighten the detainee into telling the truth or alternatively into lying in order to get out of the situation.

---

91   2 All ER 688.

2 In *Paris* (1994),[92] the case of the 'Cardiff Three', confessions made by one of the defendants after some 13 hours of high-pressured and hostile questioning were excluded on the ground of oppression. He was a man of limited intelligence but the Court of Appeal thought that the questioning would have been oppressive even with a suspect of normal intelligence. It does not appear that a breach of the Act or codes can constitute oppression unless accompanied by bad faith. The Court of Appeal in *Hughes* (1988)[93] held that a denial of legal advice due, not to bad faith on the part of the police, but to a misunderstanding could not amount to oppression. In *Alladice* (1988)[94] the Court of Appeal also took this view in suggesting, *obiter*, that an improper denial of legal advice, if accompanied by bad faith on the part of the police, would certainly amount to 'unfairness' under s78 and probably also to oppression. The Court of Appeal has not consistently invoked s76(2)(a) rather than s78 when the police have deliberately misused their powers in obtaining a confession; in *Mason* (1987),[95] for example, a trick played deliberately on the appellant's solicitor led to exclusion of the confession under s78. Bad faith appears to be a necessary but not sufficient condition for the operation of s76(2)(a), whereas it will probably automatically render a confession inadmissible under s78. If bad faith is shown it would seem that it should be accompanied by improper behaviour which reaches a certain level of seriousness.[96]

3 The 'reliability' test under s76(2)(b) is concerned with objective reliability; the judge must consider the situation at the time the confession was made and ask whether the confession would be likely to be unreliable, not whether it is unreliable.

4 In many instances the 'something said or done' under s76(2)(b) will consist of some impropriety on the part of the police, and in such instances a court will go on to consider whether any circumstances existed which rendered the impropriety particularly significant. The 'circumstances' could include the particularly vulnerable state of the detainee. The vulnerability may relate to a physical or mental state. In *Trussler* (1988)[97] the defendant, who was a drug addict, had been in custody 18 hours, had been denied legal advice and had not been afforded the rest period guaranteed by Code C 12.3. His confession was excluded as likely to be unreliable. In *Delaney* (1988)[98] the defendant was 17, had an IQ of 80 and, according to an educational psychologist, was subject to emotional arousal which would lead him to wish to bring a police interview to an end as quickly as possible. These were circumstances in which it was important to ensure that the interrogation was conducted with all propriety. In fact, the officers offered some inducement to the defendant to confess by playing down the gravity of the offence and

---

92 Crim LR 361.
93 Crim LR 545.
94 87 Cr App R 380.
95 3 All ER 481.
96 See *L* (1994) Crim LR 839.
97 Crim LR 446.
98 88 Cr App R 339.

by suggesting that if he confessed he would get the psychiatric help he needed. They also failed to make an accurate, contemporaneous record of the interview in breach of Code C 11.3. Failing to make the proper record was of indirect relevance to the question of reliability as it meant that the court could not assess the full extent of the suggestions held out to the defendant. The confession was excluded under s76(2)(b).

5   Under s78 it has been found that a 'substantial and significant' breach of PACE and/or a code provision may affect any admissions made after it, and admission of the confession may render the trial unfair. In *Walsh* (1990)[99] the Court of Appeal held that what was significant and substantial would be determined by reference to the nature of the breach, except in instances where the police had acted in bad faith; 'although bad faith may make substantial or significant that which might not otherwise be so, the contrary does not follow. Breaches which are themselves significant and substantial are not rendered otherwise by the good faith of the officers concerned'.

6   In *Samuel* (1988) the Court of Appeal found that the confession should have been excluded under s78 because it was causally linked to the police impropriety – a failure to allow the appellant access to legal advice. The Court of Appeal in *Alladice* (1988),[100] also faced with a breach of s58, accepted that the key factor in exercising discretion under s78 after a breach of the interrogation procedure was the causal relationship between breach and confession, and, by implication, between breach and fairness at the trial. However, since the appellant stated that he did not need a solicitor to advise on the right to silence but only in order to see fair play, the causal relationship between breach and confession could not be established, and therefore the Court found that admitting the confession had not had an adverse effect on the fairness of the proceedings.

7   If a substantial breach of a recording provision has been identified, a court will be likely to react by excluding the confession on the basis that it is impossible to be sure of its reliability,[101] and therefore its prejudicial quality may outweigh its probative value. In other words a jury may place reliance on an inaccurate record or believe a fabricated confession which clearly has no evidential value at all. An obvious example of such a breach is a failure to make contemporaneous notes of the interview in breach of C 11.5. The defence may then challenge the interview record on the basis that the police have fabricated all or part of it or may allege that something adverse to the detainee happened during the interview which has not been recorded. The court then has no means of knowing which version of what happened is true, precisely the situation which Code C was designed to prevent. In such a situation a judge may well exclude the confession on the basis that it would be unfair to allow evidence of doubtful reliability to go before the jury.

---

99 91 Cr App R 161.

100 87 Cr App R 380. The Court of Appeal appeared to have a similar test in mind in relation to a failure to caution in *Weerdesteyn* [1995] Crim LR 239.

101 See eg *Keenan* [1990] 2 QB 54.

8   Non-confession evidence can be excluded under s78 or s82(3). Identification evidence is seen as particularly vulnerable; if some doubt is raised as to the reliability of the identification due to delay[102] or to a failure to hold an identification parade where one was practicable,[103] the identification evidence is likely to be excluded. Although there is as yet no case law on the point, it would be possible to apply the test from *Samuel* to a silence. For example, if no notification as to the availability of legal advice was given before an interview occurred in which the suspect may have needed advice in order to appreciate the import of the caution, it could be argued that the failure to notify of the right to advice was causally linked to the silence.

9   Illegally obtained physical evidence, such as fingerprints, was admissible at common law unless the evidence had been tricked out of the detainee,[104] in which case there would be a discretion to exclude it. However, this rule did not include instances where the police had acted as agents provocateurs, entrapping the defendant into a crime he would not otherwise have committed (*Sang*).[105] Under s78 the argument from *Samuel* as to the causal relationship between an impropriety and a confession (where bad faith is not shown) could be applied to physical evidence such as a weapon or drugs found on the suspect or his premises; in practice it appears that it may not be. The first instance decision in *Edward Fennelly* (1989),[106] in which a failure to give the reason for a stop and search led to exclusion of the search, appear to be on the wrong track. Furthermore, even if the principles developed under s78 with respect to confession evidence could properly be applied to physical evidence, *Edward Fennelly* would still be a doubtful decision as no causal relationship could exist between the impropriety in question and the evidence obtained. According to *Thomas* (1990)[107] and *Quinn* (1990),[108] physical evidence will be excluded only if obtained with deliberate illegality; the pre-PACE ruling of the House of Lords in *Fox* (1986) would also lend support to this contention. On the other hand, as Zander points out (Zander (1995), pp236–7), citing *inter alia Sharpe v DPP* (1993),[109] that courts have rejected the 'real' evidence of intoxication in certain drink-driving cases under s78 due to the way in which the evidence was obtained, even where bad faith may not have been present.

Questions

1   The confession made in *Samuel* may have been truthful. Why was it excluded from evidence?

2   What was the reason for the decision of the Court of Appeal in *Keenan*?

3   What principles may underlie determinations as to the admissibility of

---

102 *Quinn* [1990] Crim LR 581.
103 *Ladlow* [1989] Crim LR 219.
104 *Callis v Gunn* [1964] 1 QB 495.
105 [1980] AC 402.
106 Crim LR 142.
107 Crim LR 269.
108 Crim LR 581, CA.
109 158 JP 595.

physical evidence?

4   Assume that s34 of the 1994 Act was in force when Samuel was detained and interviewed. What effect, if any, would it have had on the decision of the Court of Appeal that Samuel's confession should have been excluded from evidence?

Tortious remedies[110]

Tort damages will be available in respect of some breaches of PACE. For example, if a police officer arrests a citizen where no reasonable suspicion arises under ss24 or 25 of PACE, an action for false imprisonment will be available. Equally, such a remedy would be available if the Part IV provisions governing time limits on detention were breached.[111] Trespass to land or to goods will occur if the statutory provisions governing search of premises or seizure of goods are not followed. Malicious prosecution will be available where police have abused their powers in recommending prosecution to the Crown Prosecution Service. Also, one of the ancient 'malicious process torts' may be available where a malicious search or arrest has occurred, although in fact these actions are extremely rare and their continued existence is in doubt.[112] Such actions may not be brought because a claim of false imprisonment is preferred, but there is a distinction between malicious process torts and false imprisonment in that in the former case, but not the latter, all the proper procedural formalities will have been carried out. Actions for malicious prosecution are quite common but the plaintiff carries quite a heavy burden in the need to prove that there was no reasonable or probable cause for the prosecution.[113] It may be that if the prosecution is brought on competent legal advice this action will fail, but this is unclear.[114]

Almost the whole of the interviewing scheme which is contained mainly in Codes C and E rather than in PACE itself is unaffected by tortious remedies. Section 67(10) of PACE provides that no civil or criminal liability arises from breaches of the codes of practice. This lack of a remedy also extends to some statutory provisions, in particular the most significant statutory interviewing provision, the entitlement to legal advice. There is no tort of denial of access to legal advice; the only possible tortious action would be for breach of statutory duty. It has been thought that an action for false imprisonment might lie; argument could be advanced that where gross breaches of the questioning provisions had taken place, such as interviewing a person unlawfully held incommunicado, a detention in itself lawful might thereby be rendered

---

110 See generally R Clayton and H Tomlinson, *Civil Actions Against the Police*, 2nd edn (1992); for a list of examples of recent damages awards see *op cit*, pp411–431.

111 eg, *Edwards v Chief Constable of Avon and Somerset*, 9 March 1992 (unreported): the plaintiff was detained for eight hours 47 minutes following a lawful arrest. The detention was wrongful because it was 'unnecessary'; compensation awarded.

112 See Clayton and Tomlinson, p284. For discussion see Winfield, *History of Conspiracy and Abuse of Legal Process* (1921).

113 See *Glinskie v McIver* [1962] AC 726.

114 *Abbott v Refuge Assurance Co Ltd* [1962] 1 QB 632.

unlawful. However, although the ruling in *Middleweek v Chief Constable of Merseyside* (1992)[115] gave some encouragement to such argument, it now seems to be ruled out due to the decision in *Weldon v Home Office* (1991)[116] in the context of lawful detention in a prison. It seems likely therefore that access to legal advice, like the rest of the safeguards for interviewing, will continue to be unaffected by the availability of tortious remedies.

Examples of the use of civil actions are given below:

R Clayton and H Tomlinson, *Civil Actions Against the Police*, 2nd edn (1992), pp413, 420

Ballard, Stewart-Park, Findlay v Metropolitan Police Commissioner (1983) 133 New LJ 1133; *Legal Action*, 10 January 1984.

Westminster County Court, judge.

Facts: P1 and P2 had been hit over the head by police officers with truncheons in the course of a demonstration, P2 carried spread-eagled and dumped on ground from a height of four feet. P3 was lawfully arrested and was prodded in stomach, hit over eye with truncheon and, as a result suffered migrainous attacks.

Damages: P1 – compensatory £400 including small sum for aggravated damages (1992 value: £660). P2 – compensatory L600 including aggravated damages (1992 value: £990). P3 – compensatory £3,000 including aggravated damages (1992 value: £4,950).

Kearley and Redhead v Metropolitan Police Commissioner, June 1989; unreported.

West London County Court, jury.

Facts: P1 and P2 were unlawfully arrested on suspicion of robbery.

Damages: £5,000 for each P (1992 value: £5,906).

Lewis v Chief Constable of South Wales, 5 October 1989; unreported.

Bridgend County Court, jury.

Facts: Ps' arrest unlawful as a result of their not being given reasons. The unlawfulness of these arrests was cured by subsequent giving of reasons, to P1 after 10 minutes and P2 after 23 minutes (Court of Appeal upheld judge's ruling on law (1991) 1 All ER 206).

Damages: £200 for each P (1992 value: £232).

McDonagh v Metropolitan Police Commissioner, Guardian , 19 December 1989.

High Court, Popplewell J and a jury.

Facts: Husband and wife wrongfully arrested and detained for 10 hours. Damages: compensatory P1 – £750 (1992 value: £860; hourly rate: £86). P2 – £1,250 (1992 value: £1,434; hourly rate: £143).

Leigh-Williams v Chief Constable of Essex, Guardian, 18 October 1990.

High Court, Michael Davies J and a jury.

Facts: P, a former vicar, was unlawfully arrested and detained for 40 hours for breach of the peace. He had previously been lawfully arrested for assault on a 13 year old boy and was unlawfully arrested near the boy's home.

Damages: £4,000 (1992 value: £4,184).

---

115 1 AC 179; [1990] 3 WLR 481.
116 3 WLR 340, HL.

Notes

1   One of the highest awards was made in *White v Metropolitan Police Commissioner* (1982).[117] Police officers unlawfully entered a house and, it was alleged, attacked one of the plaintiffs, an elderly man. The police then charged both plaintiffs with various offences in order to cover up their own conduct. The plaintiffs were awarded £20,000 exemplary damages each plus, respectively, £6,500 and £4,500 aggravated damages. One of the highest recent awards was made in *Treadaway v Chief Constable of West Midlands* (1994);[118] £50,000, which included £40,000 exemplary damages, was awarded in respect of a serious assault perpetrated in order to obtain a confession.

In 1996 a number of very high awards were made against the Metropolitan Police. In *Goswell v Commissioner of Metropolitan Police* (1996)[119] Goswell was awarded £120,000 damages for assault, £12,000 for false imprisonment and £170,000 exemplary damages for arbitrary and oppressive behaviour. Mr Goswell, who is black, was waiting in his car for his girlfriend when PC Trigg approached. Goswell complained about the lack of police activity over an arson attack on his home. He was handcuffed to another officer and struck by Trigg; the blow required stitches and left a permanent scar. Goswell was then arrested for assault and threatening behaviour. He was cleared of these charges and then brought the civil action. In *Hsu v Commissioner of Metropolitan Police* (1996)[120] the plaintiff won £220,000 damages for assault and wrongful arrest at his home. In *Kownacki v Commissioner of Metropolitan Police* (1996)[121] actions for false imprisonment and malicious prosecution against the Metropolitan Police were successful; 200 police invaded the plaintiff's pub and charged him with supplying cannabis and allowing the premises to be used for drug dealing. When the case came to trial the prosecution offered no evidence and he was acquitted. As a result he suffered depression and paranoia which affected his work. The jury found that the officers had failed to prove that they had seen cannabis being openly smoked and sold on the premises during the surveillance operation; £108,750, including £45,000 of punitive damages, were awarded to reflect the jury's disapproval. All three cases are to be appealed.

2   If a civil action against a police officer is successful, he or she will not be personally liable; s48 of the Police Act 1964 provides that a chief constable will be vicariously liable in respect of torts committed by constables under his direction or control in the performance or purported performance of their functions.

3   If a civil action is brought against an officer on the basis that he or she has acted *ultra vires* and the officer shows that the statutory conditions for the

---

117 *The Times*, 24 April.
118 *The Times*, 25 October.
119 *Guardian*, 27 April 1996.
120 Unreported.
121 *Guardian*, 30 April 1996.

exercise of power were present, the onus lies on the plaintiff to establish the relevant facts (*Greene v Home Secretary* (1942)).[122]

4   In *Holgate-Mohammed v Duke* (1984)[123] the House of Lords confirmed that, in addition to showing that the relevant statutory conditions are satisfied, the exercise of statutory powers by officers must not offend against *Wednesbury* principles; officers must not take irrelevant factors into account or fail to have regard to relevant ones; an exercise of discretion must not be so unreasonable that no reasonable officer could have exercised it in the manner in question. In applying these principles, the civil liberties dimension of police decisions to arrest, etc, will be relevant in determining when an officer has acted unreasonably, following the decision in *Ministry of Defence, ex p Smith and Others* (1996).[124] The Court of Appeal affirmed that the court could not interfere with the exercise of an administrative discretion on substantive grounds, save where it was satisfied that the decision was unreasonable in the sense that it was beyond the range of responses open to a reasonable decision maker, but that in judging whether the decision-maker had exceeded that margin of appreciation the human rights context was important; the more substantial the interference with human rights, the more the court would require by way of justification before it was satisfied that the decision was reasonable.

Police complaints[125]

Police and Criminal Evidence Act 1984

Establishment of the Police Complaints Authority

84.–(1) Where a complaint is submitted to the chief officer of police for a police area, it shall be his duty to take any steps that appear to him to be desirable for the purpose of obtaining or preserving evidence relating to the conduct complained of.

(2) After performing the duties imposed on him by subsection (1) above, the chief officer shall determine whether he is the appropriate authority in relation to the officer against whom the complaint was made.

(3) If he determines that he is not the appropriate authority, it shall be his duty –

(a)   to send the complaint or, if it was made orally, particulars of it to the appropriate authority, and

(b)   to give notice that he has done so to the person by or on whose behalf the complaint was made.

---

122 AC 284, HL.

123 AC 437, HL.

124 1 All ER 271.

125 See M Maguire, 'Complaints Against the Police: the British Experience' in A Goldsmith (ed), *Complaints Against the Police: A Comparative Study* (1990); J Harrison, *Police Misconduct: Legal Remedies* (1987). Triennial Review of the PCA 1991–94, HC 396 (1994–95); 4th report of the Home Affairs Committee, HC 179 (1991–92); Sanders and Young, *Criminal Justice* (1994), pp400–415.

(4) In this Part of this Act –

'complaint' means any complaint about the conduct of a police officer which is submitted –

(a) by a member of the public; or

(b) on behalf of a member of the public and with his written consent;

'the appropriate authority means –

(a) in relation to an officer of the Metropolitan Police, the Commissioner of Police of the Metropolis; and

(b) in relation to an officer of any other police force –

(i) if he is a senior officer, the police authority for the force's area, and

(ii) if he is not a senior officer, the chief officer of the force;

'senior officer' means an officer holding a rank above the rank of chief superintendent.

Investigation of complaints: standard procedure

85.–(1) If a chief officer determines that he is the appropriate authority in relation to an officer, about whose conduct a complaint has been made and who is not a senior officer, he shall record it.

(2) After doing so he shall consider whether the complaint is suitable for informal resolution and may appoint an officer from his force to assist him.

(3) If it appears to the chief officer that the complaint is not suitable for informal resolution, he shall appoint an officer from his force or some other force to investigate it formally.

(4) If it appears to him that it is suitable for informal resolution, he shall seek to resolve it informally and may appoint an officer from his force to do so on his behalf.

(5) If it appears to the chief officer, after attempts have been made to resolve a complaint informally –

(a) that informal resolution of the complaint is impossible; or

(b) that the complaint is for any other reason not suitable for informal resolution

he shall appoint an officer from his force or some other force to investigate it formally.

(6) An officer may not be appointed to investigate a complaint formally if he has previously been appointed to act in relation to it under subsection (4) above.

(7) If a chief officer requests the chief officer of some other force to provide an officer of his force for appointment under subsection (3) or (5) above, that chief officer shall provide an officer to be so appointed.

(8) No officer may be appointed under this section unless he is –

(a) of at least the rank of chief inspector; and

(b) of at least the rank of the officer against whom the complaint is made.

(9) Unless investigation under this section is supervised by the Authority under section 89 below, the investigating officer shall submit his report on the investigation to the chief officer.

(10) A complaint is not suitable for informal resolution unless –

(a) the member of the public concerned gives his consent; and

(b) the chief officer is satisfied that the conduct complained of even if proved, would not justify a criminal or disciplinary charge.

Investigation of complaints against senior officers

86.–(1) Where a complaint about the conduct of a senior officer –

    (a) is submitted to the appropriate authority; or

    (b) is sent to the appropriate authority under section 84(3) above, it shall be the appropriate authority's duty to record it and, subject to subsection (2) below, to investigate it.

(3) In any other case the appropriate authority shall appoint an officer from the appropriate authority's force or from some other force to investigate the complaint.

References of complaints to Authority

87.–(1) The appropriate authority –

    (a) shall refer to the Authority –

        (i) any complaint alleging that the conduct complained of resulted in the death of or serious injury to some other person; and

        (ii) any complaint of a description specified for the purposes of this section in regulations made by the Secretary of State; and

    (b) may refer to the Authority any complaint which is not required to be referred to them.

(2) The Authority may require the submission to them for consideration of any complaint not referred to them by the appropriate authority, and it shall be the appropriate authority's duty to comply with any such requirement not later than the end of a period specified in regulations made by the Secretary of State.

References of other matters to Authority

88. The appropriate authority may refer to the Authority any matter which –

    (a) appears to the appropriate authority to indicate that an officer may have committed a criminal offence or an offence against discipline; and

    (b) is not the subject of a complaint, if it appears to the appropriate authority that it ought to be referred by reason –

        (i) of its gravity; or

        (ii) of exceptional circumstances.

Supervision of investigations by Authority

89.–(1) The Authority shall supervise the investigation –

    (a) of any complaint alleging that the conduct of a police officer resulted in the death or a serious injury to some other person; and

    (b) of any other description of complaint specified for the purposes of this section in regulations made by the Secretary of State.

(2) The Authority shall supervise the investigation –

    (a) of any complaint the investigation of which they are not required to supervise under subsection (1) above; and

    (b) of any matter referred to them under section 88 above, if they consider that it is desirable in the public interest that they should supervise that investigation.

(6) At the end of an investigation which the Authority have supervised, the investigating officer –

    (a)   shall submit a report on the investigation to the Authority; and

    (b)   shall send a copy to the appropriate authority.

(7) After considering a report submitted to them under subsection (6) above the Authority shall submit an appropriate statement to the appropriate authority.

(8) If it is practicable to do so, the Authority, when submitting the appropriate statement under subsection (7) above, shall send a copy to the officer whose conduct has been investigated.

(9) If –

    (a)   the investigation related to a complaint; and

    (b)   it is practicable to do so, the Authority shall also send a copy of the appropriate statement to the person by or on behalf of whom the complaint was made.

Steps to be taken after investigation – general

90.–(1) It shall be the duty of the appropriate authority, on receiving –

    (a)   a report concerning the conduct of a senior officer which is submitted to them under section 86(6) above; or

    (b)   a copy of a report concerning the conduct of a senior officer which is sent to them under section 89(7) above, to send a copy of the report to the Director of Public Prosecutions unless the report satisfies them that no criminal offence has been committed.

(2) Nothing in the following provisions of this section or in sections 91–93 below has effect in relation to senior officers.

(3) On receiving –

    (a)   a report concerning the conduct of an officer who is not a senior officer which is submitted to him under section 85(9) above; or

    (b)   a copy of a report concerning the conduct of such an officer which is sent to him under section 89(7) above;

It shall be the duty of a chief officer of police –

    (i)   to determine whether the report indicates that a criminal offence may have been committed by a member of the police force for his area; and

    (ii)   if he determines that it does, to determine whether the offence indicated is such that the officer ought to be charged with it.

(4) If the chief officer –

    (a)   determines that the report does indicate that a criminal offence may have been committed by a member of the police force for his area; and

    (b)   considers that the offence indicated is such that the officer ought to be charged with it;

he shall send a copy of the report to the Director of Public Prosecutions.

(5) Subject to section 91(1) below, after the Director has dealt with the question of criminal proceedings, the chief officer shall send the Authority a memorandum, signed by him and stating whether he has preferred disciplinary charges in respect of the conduct which was the subject of the investigation and, if not, his reasons for not doing so.

(6) If the chief officer –

    (a)   determines that the report does indicate that a criminal offence may have been committed by a member of the police force for his area; and

(b) considers that the offence indicated is not such that the officer ought to be charged with it;

he shall send the Authority a memorandum to that effect, signed by him and stating whether he proposes to prefer disciplinary charges in respect of the conduct which was the subject of the investigation and, if not, his reasons for not proposing to do so.

(9) Where the investigation –

(a) related to conduct which was the subject of a complaint; and

(b) was not supervised by the authority,

the chief officer shall send the Authority –

(i) a copy of the complaint or of the record of the complaint; and

(ii) a copy of the report of the investigation at the same time as he sends them the memorandum.

Police and Magistrates' Courts Act 1994

Part I Chapter 2

Repeal of certain provisions about discipline

37. The following provisions of the Police and Criminal Evidence Act 1984 shall cease to have effect –

(a) section 67(8) (failure to comply with a code of practice is a disciplinary offence);

(b) section 92 (powers of Complaints Authority to direct reference of reports, etc, to Director of Public Prosecutions);

(c) section 94 (disciplinary tribunals);

(d) section 97(4) (review of complaints procedure and reports by Complaints Authority);

(e) section 101 (discipline regulations);

(f) in section 104, subsections (1) and (2) (which prevent a police officer convicted or acquitted of a criminal offence being charged with an equivalent disciplinary offence).

Notes

1 Commentators tend to view the police complaints mechanism as ineffective as a means of redress.[126] It does not allow for compensation to the victim or for the victim to attend any disciplinary proceedings. In any event, most complaints do not result in disciplinary proceedings; as many as 30% of complaints are dealt with by informal resolution[127] and commentators have suggested that unreasonable pressure may be put on complainants to adopt the informal resolution process. Clayton and Tomlinson note (p13) that the 16,712 complaints dealt with in 1990 led to 305 criminal or disciplinary charges and advice or admonishment in 573 cases; thus less than 2% of complaints led to any disciplinary action. Maguire and Corbett conducted a review of the operation of the complaints system from 1968–1988 (*A Study of*

---

126 See eg comment from J Harrison and S Cragg (1993) 143 NLJ 591.

127 *PCA Triennial Review* 1985–88 HC 466, para 1.14, p8.

the Police Complaints System, HMSO, 1991) which found that the majority of complainants were dissatisfied and that the public did not have confidence in the system.

The PCA report of 1995 stated that, out of 245 complaints of serious assault by police officers, eight led to disciplinary charges; none led to dismissal of an officer from the service. Out of 6,318 complaints of assaults, in only 64 cases were disciplinary charges preferred; none led to dismissal of the officer concerned. It may be noted that the plaintiff in *Goswell v Commissioner of Metropolitan Police* (1996)[128] also made a complaint prior to bringing the civil action. The complaint led to the sacking of the officer concerned in the assault, PC Trigg, but he appealed against his dismissal and was reinstated by the Home Secretary, Michael Howard.

2   Bringing a complaint may affect any civil action available detrimentally since, until the *Wiley* decision discussed below, statements made in relation to the complaint could not be disclosed in civil proceedings,[129] while by bringing it the plaintiff has to disclose part of his or her case to the police.[130] The positions of the plaintiff and defendant in relation to disclosure of material relating to a complaint have been placed on a more equal basis as a result of *Chief Constable of West Midlands Police, ex p Wiley* (1995), *Chief Constable of Nottinghamshire Police, ex p Sunderland* (1994).[131] All the parties concerned argued that public interest immunity did not attach to documents coming into existence during a police complaints investigation. The House of Lords had to consider whether *Neilson v Laugharne* (1981)[132] and the decisions following it were wrongly decided. In *Neilson* Lord Oliver had determined that a class immunity should attach to police complaints documents on the basis that the police complaints procedure would be placed in jeopardy if that was not the case. However the House of Lords considered that there was insufficient evidence to support Lord Oliver's conclusion as to the need for a new class claim to public interest immunity. Thus it was found that *Neilson* must be regarded as wrongly decided, but that did not mean that public interest immunity would never attach to police complaints documents; whether it did or not would depend on the particular contents of the document. This decision may be welcomed as emphasising that a clear case must be made out for use of a broad class claim to public interest immunity. Moreover, it is to be welcomed in the interests of justice as going some way towards ensuring that, in civil actions against the police, plaintiff and defendant have access to the same information.

This decision left open the possibility of a contents claim. In *Taylor v Anderton* (1995)[133] the Court of Appeal found that the reports prepared by investigating

---

128 *Guardian*, 27 April 1996.
129 *Neilson v Laugharne* [1981] 1 QB 736; cf *Bearmans v Metropolitan Police Receiver* [1961] 1 WLR 634.
130 See Clayton and Tomlinson, pp61–3.
131 1 AC 274. 3 All ER 420.
132 QB 736.
133 2 All ER 420, CA.

officers were entitled to class immunity, but that a litigant might nevertheless obtain disclosure of part or all of a report if the judge could be persuaded that the public interest in disclosure outweighed the interest in immunity.

3 A great deal of criticism has been directed against the whole police disciplinary process including the hearings,[134] and this led the Runciman Royal Commission to propose that the burden of proof in such hearings should no longer be the criminal standard.[135] The Government issued a consultation paper in April 1993 which included various proposals, including abolition of the criminal standard of proof in discipline cases and the double jeopardy rule, which means that criminal proceedings against officers are not followed by disciplinary proceedings.[136] This rule was abolished under s37(f), above, as part of a radical overhaul of the police disciplinary process which is taking place under the Police and Magistrates' Courts Act 1994. It is intended that the civil standard of proof will apply in formal disciplinary procedures. Changes in the system are part of the Government's overhaul of the police service generally which is occurring in response to the RCCJ report.

4 An independent complaints system is not proposed. In its briefing guide in 1984 the Home Office stated that an independent system would be ineffective as it would probably be unable to obtain the confidence of police officers; friction might develop and thus public confidence in the system would be lost. The PCA Triennial Review 1991–94 was opposed to the establishment of a body staffed by independent investigators, considering that it would require a very substantial allocation of resources which on the evidence available would not be justifiable, and that it might fail to win the co-operation of the police. Maguire and Corbett commented in their 1991 review that an independent system might lead to an improvement in public confidence in the system, although they expressed doubts about its effectiveness in other respects. The current overhaul of the complaints procedure has not included introduction of a new, independent element into the process. The Police and Magistrates' Courts Act 1994 made only limited changes to the functions and powers of the PCA. At present, radical change in the complaints procedure, as opposed to the police disciplinary process, is not proposed.

---

134 See A Greaves (1985) Crim LR; A Khan, 129 SJ 455; Williams (1985) Crim LR 115; Lustgarten (1986), pp139–40. The Runciman Commission considered that the existing arrangements probably do not command public confidence: Cm 2263, p46.

135 Proposal 77.

136 See 143 NLJ 591; in its Triennial Review 1988–91, HC 352, 1991 the PCA also made this proposal.

INDEX